Critical values of *t*.

Degrees of Freedom	$t_{.100}$	$t_{.050}$	$t_{.025}$	$t_{.010}$	$t_{.005}$
1	3.078	6.314	12.706	31.821	63.657
2	1.886	2.920	4.303	6.965	9.925
3	1.638	2.353	3.182	4.541	5.841
4	1.533	2.132	2.776	3.747	4.604
5	1.476	2.015	2.571	3.365	4.032
6	1.440	1.943	2.447	3.143	3.707
7	1.415	1.895	2.365	2.998	3.499
8	1.397	1.860	2.306	2.896	3.355
9	1.383	1.833	2.262	2.821	3.250
10	1.372	1.812	2.228	2.764	3.169
11	1.363	1.796	2.201	2.718	3.106
12	1.356	1.782	2.179	2.681	3.055
13	1.350	1.771	2.160	2.650	3.012
14	1.345	1.761	2.145	2.624	2.977
15	1.341	1.753	2.131	2.602	2.947
16	1.337	1.746	2.120	2.583	2.921
17	1.333	1.740	2.110	2.567	2.898
18	1.330	1.734	2.101	2.552	2.878
19	1.328	1.729	2.093	2.539	2.861
20	1.325	1.725	2.086	2.528	2.845
21	1.323	1.721	2.080	2.518	2.831
22	1.321	1.717	2.074	2.508	2.819
23	1.319	1.714	2.069	2.500	2.807
24	1.318	1.711	2.064	2.492	2.797
25	1.316	1.708	2.060	2.485	2.787
26	1.315	1.706	2.056	2.479	2.779
27	1.314	1.703	2.052	2.473	2.771
28	1.313	1.701	2.048	2.467	2.763
29	1.311	1.699	2.045	2.462	2.756
30	1.310	1.697	2.042	2.457	2.750
35	1.306	1.690	2.030	2.438	2.724
40	1.303	1.684	2.021	2.423	2.704
50	1.299	1.676	2.009	2.403	2.678
60	1.296	1.671	2.000	2.390	2.660
120	1.289	1.658	1.980	2.358	2.617
∞	1.282	1.645	1.960	2.326	2.576

ALAN H. KVANLI

Al Kvanli is Associate Professor of Management Science and Statistics at the University of North Texas. Texas is very attractive to a native of Minnesota who has seen enough snow for a lifetime. He received the M.A. degree in mathematics from the University of Kansas and the Ph.D. in mathematical statistics from Southern Methodist University.

For the past 15 years Dr. Kvanli has been the statistical consultant for the Department of Health and Human Services (HHS), Office of Audit. In this role, he created much of the statistical software used by federal auditors and teaches sampling courses for state and federal auditors. He often serves as expert witness in appeals of monetary recovery by HHS and he has written a number of articles related to the application of statistical sampling in an audit environment.

Dr. Kvanli and his wife live in north Dallas and share their lives with a 10-year-old hockey enthusiast. He enjoys traveling, sports, and singing (tenor in an international champion barbershop quartet).

ROBERT J. PAVUR

Dr. Robert Pavur is Professor of Management Science and Statistics at the University of North Texas. He received the Ph.D. in statistics from Texas Tech University. He has held various officer positions, including president, in the Southwest Regional Decision Science Institute and received its distinguished service award in 2000.

He has published a number of articles on alternative approaches to solving the statistical classification problem. His papers have appeared in journals such as the *Annals of Operations Research, IEEE Transactions on Reliability, European Journal of Operational Research, Journal of the Operational Research Society,* and *International Journal of Operations and Quantitative Management.* He uses his statistical skills as a cryptologist in the Naval Reserve.

KELLIE B. KEELING

Kellie B. Keeling is an Assistant Professor of Business Information Technology at Virginia Tech. She received the Ph.D. in Management Science from the University of North Texas and the M.B.A. and B.S. in Mathematics from Wayland Baptist University. She has taught statistics, operations management, and simulation courses. Dr. Keeling has received the R. B. Pamplin College of Business Certificate of Teaching Excellence and the Virginia Tech University Certificate of Teaching Excellence. She plays the oboe in the Blacksburg community band and enjoys reading mysteries and working logic and jigsaw puzzles.

brief contents

contents

Contents

chapter 8   Hypothesis Testing for the Mean and Variance of a Population

chapter 9   Inference Procedures for Two Populations

chapter 10   Estimation and Testing for Population Proportions

chapter 11   Analysis of Variance

chapter 12   Quality Improvement

chapter 13   Applications of the Chi-Square Statistic

chapter 14   Correlation and Simple Linear Regression

chapter 15   Multiple Linear Regression

chapter 16   Time Series Analysis and Index Numbers

chapter 17   Quantitative Business Forecasting

chapter 18   Nonparametric Statistics

preface

As authors and instructors, we feel that a statistics text that *fully* integrates the use of computers with statistics is necessary for today's students. *Introduction to Business Statistics*, 6e retains our non-intimidating approach to describing the concepts and applications of statistics while giving students the opportunity to observe and actually prepare solutions using a computer. The textbook coverage fully integrates Microsoft® Excel (a spreadsheet package), as well as SPSS® for Windows® and MINITAB (easy-to-use and powerful statistical packages). The featured software throughout all of the chapter examples and many of the exercises is Excel. Corresponding SPSS descriptions are contained in appendices at the ends of chapters—a feature unique to this text. The MINITAB appendices are contained on the textbook CD.

The long-standing format of the chapter exercises has been maintained. Students first learn the mechanics of a new technique, see its application, and finally apply this new procedure to several large data sets using a set of computer exercises. However, the text has once again been designed so that professors who want a more traditional calculator-based approach will find an abundance of examples and exercises that can be solved without a computer. Most of the exercises do not require a computer package and contain reasonably sized data sets.

WHAT'S NEW IN THE SIXTH EDITION?

While the basic premise of *Introduction to Business Statistics* has not changed, the new sixth edition brings a number of important improvements.

A New Author

We are very proud to introduce Kellie B. Keeling of Virginia Polytechnic Institute and State University as our new co-author. She was selected because of her expertise with Excel and Visual Basic as well as her fine student ratings in teaching. She recently received Virginia Tech's very competitive University Award for Excellence in Teaching. Her teaching experience includes three respected institutions: Texas Christian University, University of North Texas, and Virginia Tech. She understands the difficulties students face with statistics courses. Kellie Keeling is an active member of several professional organizations, including the Decision Sciences Institute and INFORMS. She has worked in an advisory capacity for nearly ten years with Phi Beta Lambda, an organization dedicated to bringing business and education together in a positive working relationship through leadership and career development programs. Her varied academic background in statistics, information technology, and business brings additional quality to the macro add-ins and the problems in which students learn through simulation, and fresh ideas on chapter-opener case studies and real-world problems.

SPSS

The new edition also introduces SPSS® Student Version for Windows®. SPSS is a major statistical package, ideally suited for integrating and analyzing marketing, customer, and operational data. The company has received a number of awards from the data mining and knowledge discovery industry. We are very pleased to offer coverage of this respected software to professors who wish to include it in their coursework. Each chapter concludes with an SPSS appendix that demonstrates the procedures for using SPSS to carry out the calculations discussed within that chapter.

KPK Macros for Microsoft® Excel

In the fifth edition of this textbook, we integrated Microsoft® Excel into the chapter discussion. We overcame many of the statistical shortcomings of Excel by constructing a number of macros (add-ins) that allowed the user to perform a complex statistical task on a very large set of data with the click of a mouse button. The KPK Excel macros perform *every* analytical technique discussed in the text. Microsoft Excel's built-in toolbox and function set provide many standard statistical functions/procedures and the add-in macros complement and enhance these standard Excel tools.

For this new edition, we have enhanced and fine-tuned our KPK Excel macros. You and your students will find them to be very complete and easy-to-use. The help screens have been modified to make them more consistent throughout all the modules. Be sure to refer to the Add-Ins section of Appendix C (Introduction to Excel) before attempting to install the KPK Excel macros.

Other Materials New to the Sixth Edition

We are very pleased to present a number of additional new features for the sixth edition of *Introduction to Business Statistics:*

- **New simulation exercises** are used to illustrate the concepts of probability, the distribution of a random variable, the Central Limit Theorem, hypothesis testing, and regression lines. Interactive graphical simulations enhance the student's understanding of these concepts by allowing the student to change parameters and observe the output. These exercises are shaded for easy recognition. The simulations are part of the KPK Excel macros, and are contained in Chapters 4, 5, 7, 8, and 14.
- There is **more emphasis on data and graphical interpretation** within the chapter examples, exercises, and case studies.
- **All case studies are new,** designed to develop an international perspective and provide the student with more in-depth applications in the quality improvement area.
- **Chapter 12 on Quality Improvement is updated considerably,** including the 2002 scoring system for the Malcolm Baldrige National Quality Award and a discussion of the ISO 9000, 9001, and 9004 standards.
- **New Table A-2** contains cumulative binomial probabilities.

FEATURES FOR TEACHING AND LEARNING

The text is written for an undergraduate or MBA-level business statistics course. We assume that the student has a good understanding of basic algebra. Reference is made on a few occasions to calculus applications, but no calculus background is required. The text is written in a conversational style to make it less intimidating to the student. Our intent was for the student to read the text, not just use it as a source of homework exercises. We've included a large number of examples to better guide the student to an understanding of statistical concepts and applications. These examples include more realistic illustrations, many taken from the process/quality improvement area.

We have maintained many of the features that appeared in previous editions. Some of the important ones include:

- **Introductory case study opens each chapter.** The case provides an actual situation that explains *what* type of problem the chapter addresses and *why* the chapter is important. The case study questions at the end of each chapter return to the scenario and ask in-depth questions that require an understanding beyond just number crunching. All case studies are new in this edition.
- **Look Back/Introduction at the start of each chapter ties the chapter to the relevant material from the preceding chapters.** Each chapter closes with a summary section containing the key terms introduced in the chapter and a summary of the formulas.
- **More than 1,300 exercises that are based on realistic business situations.** The exercises within each section are split into three categories: *Understanding the Mechanics; Applying the New Concepts,* using actual applications in a business setting; and *Using the Computer,* using data sets from the accompanying CD.
- **Full treatment of the use of *p*-values to make statistical decisions.** These are derived and discussed throughout the entire text.
- **Distributions.** Coverage includes three continuous distributions (normal, uniform, and exponential), along with four discrete distributions (uniform, binomial, hypergeometric, and Poisson).
- **Sampling procedures** (including stratified and cluster sampling), along with corresponding sample estimators and confidence intervals, are presented as separate sections in two of the earlier chapters. In this way, professors are able to cover this often-neglected material without having to spend the time to cover an entire chapter.
- **Four chapters of coverage of inference.** Chapters 7, 8, and 9 are strictly devoted to normal inference, both one population (Chapters 7 and 8) and two populations (Chapter 9). Binomial inference (one and two populations) is covered in Chapter 10.
- **An entire chapter devoted to forecasting using time series data.** Chapter 17 includes several exponential smoothing models and discusses the pros and cons of using multiple regression versus time series modeling techniques for such data. The KPK Excel macros make time series decomposition (Chapter 16) and time series forecasting astonishingly simple while at the same time providing a great deal of numerical and graphical output.
- **An entire chapter on statistical decision theory.** This chapter can be covered at any time, including the first semester, if desired. For ease of use, this chapter is now located on the textbook CD.
- **Two large databases.** The first database (1,140 observations) contains data on family income, family size, total indebtedness, monthly utility expenditures, and other variables. There is also a second database that contains 1,000 observations selected from companies listed in the Moody's Investor Service Industrial Manual. Both databases are contained in the accompanying CD.
- **Appendices that provide introductions to Microsoft® Excel, SPSS, and MINITAB.**

ANCILLARY TEACHING AND LEARNING MATERIALS

This new edition uses a more streamlined presentation, and some topical and appendix materials have been moved to the CD-ROM that accompanies the textbook. The CD contains:

- the revised KPK Excel macros (add-ins) that include new interactive simulation exercises

- more than 200 data sets, for problems and the case studies
- the two large databases (Appendices F and G)
- the Introduction to Excel, Introduction to SPSS, and Introduction to MINITAB appendices
- the end-of-chapter MINITAB appendices
- the Statistical Decision Theory chapter
- some textbook materials that were optional sections in the fifth edition

Discussion of the separate ancillaries that accompany the new edition of our text allows us to introduce three additional new members to the KPK team. P. S. Sundararaghavan of The University of Toledo brought his statistical expertise and teaching experience to the Study Guide. We feel that his new study guide will be a big plus for students. Many thanks also to Constantine Loucopoulos of Northeastern Illinois University for his significant revision and extension of the test bank. Jeff Heyl of Lincoln University in New Zealand brought his skill, creativity and teaching experience to the new Microsoft® PowerPoint slides.

The **Study Guide** (ISBN 0-324-15751-7) will provide the student with important supplemental study and review materials. It contains supplementary problems with solutions, self-test questions, and answers, and will guide the student through applications of the chapter material. If desired, students may purchase the Study Guide directly online at *http://www.swlearning.com.*

The **Instructor's Resource CD-ROM** (ISBN 0-324-15752-5) is available to adopters from the Thomson Learning Academic Resource center at 800-423-0563 or through *http://www.swcollege.com.* The Instructor's Resource CD-ROM includes:

- **Instructor's Manual.** The Instructor's Manual, prepared by the authors, contains solutions to all exercises and case studies presented within the text.
- **PowerPoint Presentation Slides.** The Microsoft PowerPoint slides contain the important concepts introduced within each chapter and are designed to assist instructors in creating colorful visually stimulating lectures.
- **Test Bank and ExamView™ Pro.** The test bank includes true/false and multiple-choice questions, and additional application problems. ExamView is a fully integrated software suite of test creation, delivery, and classroom management tools. Instructors can also create and administer tests online.

The new textbook's **website** will include supplementary materials for students and instructors. The URL for the website is *http://www.kvanli.swcollege.com.*

ACKNOWLEDGMENTS

We would like to thank our academic colleagues who had a multitude of excellent suggestions for this edition. We took every suggestion very seriously and we hope that you can see your contributions in this latest edition. The reviewers include:

Frances F. Barbera, Louisiana State University

Robert F. Brooker, Gannon University

Linda Becerra, University of Houston–Downtown

John E. Charalambakis, Asbury College

Bruce P. Christensen, Weber State University

Concetta DePaolo, Indiana State University

Erin M. Hodgess, University of Houston–Downtown

Ghebre Y. Keleta, Grambling State University

Dimitris J. Kraniou, Point Park College

John K. LeBlanc, Cedarville University

Constantine Loucopoulos, Northeastern Illinois University

Bruce D. McCullough, Drexel University

Tammy Prater, Alabama State University

Luh Yu Ren, University of Houston at Victoria

Stephen H. Russell, Weber State University

Anna R. Simmons, University of Houston–Downtown

We are very much indebted to the people who helped in the production and preparation of this text. Beverly Kenney has once again done a superb job of putting her word processing skills to work on the Instructor's Manual. As noted earlier, Constantine Loucopoulos, P. S. Sundararaghavan, and Jeff Hyle brought a new focus to the ancillaries.

In this edition, we also received exceptional editorial support from the Decision Sciences Team at Thomson/South-Western. Senior Acquisitions Editor Charles McCormick was very instrumental in encouraging and guiding this entire project. Senior Developmental Editor Alice Denny was most helpful in keeping track of the million and one details and lining up top-notch people to assist in our efforts. Production Editor Chris Hudson kept this (at times overwhelming) project on course and helped the authors keep a positive attitude as time and energy were dwindling.

We certainly feel that this text will meet the needs of your course and students. If you care to offer comments or suggestions, we would like to hear from you. Address any correspondence to Al Kvanli, College of Business Administration, University of North Texas, Denton, Texas 76203 (Email: Kvanli@unt.edu).

Alan H. Kvanli
Robert J. Pavur
Kellie B. Keeling

TO THE STUDENT

We believe you will find this text to be a readable and easy-to-understand treatment of business statistics. Our intent is to carefully explain the various statistical concepts and strategies without getting bogged down in unnecessary mathematics. This textbook allows you to learn the application of statistics, and let the computer carry out the heavy number crunching, using either Microsoft® Excel (a popular spreadsheet package) or SPSS or MINITAB (Windows-based and easy-to-use statistical packages). The KPK Excel add-in macros may be easily used with your home or office version of Excel. These click-and-go procedures make using Excel to carry out statistical analyses extremely simple, and maybe even fun! Be sure to refer to the Add-Ins section of Appendix C (Introduction to Excel) before attempting to install the KPK Excel macros.

Many examples and Excel illustrations within each chapter allow you to see how each procedure works. Each chapter opener provides an actual application of the chapter material. The goal here is to illustrate what completion of the chapter will allow you to accomplish. The Look Back/Introduction section will help you tie the current chapter in with the previous chapters. Each chapter concludes with a summary that contains all the key definitions and concepts introduced within the chapter, along with a summary of the formulas. The CD-ROM packaged with the textbook contains the KPK Excel add-in macros, more than 200 data sets, two large databases, and some optional materials your instructor may choose to use.

Successful mastery of statistics is the direct result of practice. To this end, the text contains a large number of exercises. All of the data sets for those exercises requiring a computer are provided on the accompanying CD. Also, you will find the solutions to the odd-numbered exercises at the end of the text. A *Study Guide* (ISBN 0-324-15751-7) that contains additional examples and problems, along with their solutions, is available for individual purchase online at *http://www.swlearning.com*.

Alan H. Kvanli
Robert J. Pavur
Kellie B. Keeling

DEDICATION

Elaine and Justin
(A.H.K.)

Gail, Robert, Michael, and Gregory
(R.J.P.)

Kevin and Ervin
(K.B.K.)

A First Look at Statistics and Data Collection

X

Statistics in Action
Online Surveys: E-xpress Yourself

Online surveys are proliferating on the World Wide Web. In a recent online survey by Direct Marketing Services, results showed that 68 percent of participating consumers have also participated in a telephone, mall, or mail survey. The other 32 percent indicated that they were now responding only to online surveys. This survey consisted of more than 2,000 randomly selected men and women aged 18 or older who were polled by Direct Marketing Services through Opinion Place on America Online. The vice president of research services at Direct Marketing Services proclaims, "Our research concludes that online surveys are reaching the same consumer groups that traditional research methods are targeting, but with more success."

Telephone and mail surveys have traditionally been conducted by corporations and newspapers, such as the *Wall Street Journal*, to obtain quick feedback from the general population. These procedures have benefited business decision makers in a variety of business fields, including marketing, finance, accounting, management, and information systems. However, a challenge for those involved in conducting survey research is to ensure that the quality of surveys on the Internet is at least at the same level as the traditional approaches of collecting data. Only by fully understanding the benefits and drawbacks of this nontraditional method can the potential of online surveys be fully exploited.

Bankers are using online surveys to determine the potential of using the Internet as a

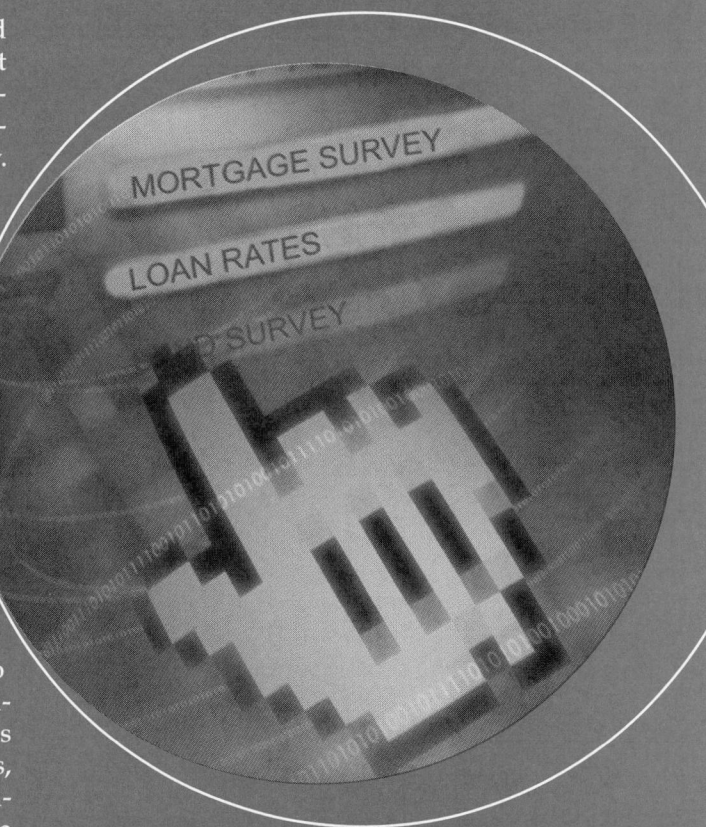

resource for providing expert advice, fast service, and low rates to the consumer while still making a profit. For example, in a recent mortgage survey with 317 respondents, 46 percent indicated that they would select a bank 2,000 miles away if they could receive loan rates that were just 0.125 percent lower. This information assists bankers in committing to investing in a

Web site to tap this market. Bankers realize that offering their services via the Internet is a viable option, provided that loan rates offered through this means are competitive with those of local banks. In general, the use of online surveys allows for faster data collection in a cost-effective manner while providing convenience for the respondents. Surveys are one of the tools that keep companies in the best position to compete in a world where the consumer rules.

When you have completed this chapter, you will be able to examine the results of a poll and discuss such questions as

- What is the *population* of interest?
- Can the respondents of the poll be viewed as a *random sample*?
- What is the *level of measurement* of the data collected?
- What is meant by a *statistic*?

A First Look at Statistics

Many people probably think a statistician is someone who figures batting averages during a baseball game broadcast. You might wonder how we can devote an entire textbook to compiling numbers and making simple calculations. Surely it cannot be that complicated!

Statistics is the science comprising rules and procedures for collecting, describing, analyzing, and interpreting numerical data. The applications of statistics are evident everywhere. Hardly a day goes by in which we are not bombarded by such statements as these:

> Results show that Crest toothpaste helps prevent tooth decay.
>
> The chance of rain tomorrow is 30%.
>
> The state court has ruled that the XYZ Company is guilty of age discrimination in its termination procedure.
>
> Smoking causes lung cancer, heart disease, emphysema, and may complicate pregnancy.

Or how about:

> American companies are continuing to place more emphasis on quality improvement in an attempt to offer better products that can be delivered on time at less cost.

Besides using statistics to inform the public, statisticians help businesses make forecasts for planning and decision making.

The use of statistics began as early as the first century A.D., when governments used a census of people, land, and properties for tax purposes. Census taking was gradually extended to include such local events as births, deaths, and marriages. The *science* of statistics, which uses a sample to predict or estimate some characteristics of a population, began its development during the nineteenth century.

Use of statistical methods has undergone a dramatic change as computers and powerful calculators have entered the research environment. Companies can store and manipulate large collections of data, and once-formidable statistical calculations are reduced to a few keystrokes. Sophisticated computer software allows users merely to specify the type of analysis desired and input the necessary data. This textbook concentrates on three of these software packages: Excel (a spreadsheet package developed by Microsoft), MINITAB (a statistical computer package originally designed at Penn State University specifically for students), and SPSS (a large-scale statistical software package designed to integrate and analyze marketing, customer, and operational data).

Although most statistical functions are performed by professional statisticians, it might be your job to draw a valid conclusion from a statistical report. In addition, you might be asked to perform a statistical analysis. Although you might elect to obtain outside assistance, you will need to know when to consult a statistician and how to tell him or her what you need.

So welcome to the world of uncertainty. Statistical methods offer you a way of evaluating an uncertain future by using limited information to assess the likelihood of future events occurring. But despite the best intent of statistical measurements, it is important to remember that an event with a high chance of occurring might, in fact, not occur at all. Anyone who has changed plans because of a 90% chance of rainy weather only to sit home on a sunny day can attest to this fact.

1.1 USING THE COMPUTER

Use of statistical methods has undergone a dramatic change as computers and powerful calculators have entered the everyday business environment. Companies can store and manipulate large collections of data so that once-formidable statistical calculations are reduced to a few keystrokes. Sophisticated windows software allows users merely to specify the type of analysis required and input the necessary data. This textbook concentrates on three of these software packages: Excel, MINITAB, and SPSS. Excel is a spreadsheet package developed by Microsoft, whereas MINITAB and SPSS are true statistical software systems. We briefly describe these three software products.

Microsoft Excel

Excel is a spreadsheet program that can be used to access, process, analyze, display, and share information for running a business. Excel continues to make the existing functionality easier to use while offering a wide array of tools for making the more advanced tasks less complex and more intuitive. Excel was not designed to be a statistical package; however, it does offer a number of built-in statistical functions and analysis procedures. To overcome Excel's statistical shortcomings, the CD that accompanies this textbook contains a number of Excel macros. These are programs written by the authors that operate within Excel and provide a number of graphical and analytical procedures that are not included in the standard (off-the-shelf) Excel package. For more information on implementing these macros, consult the *Introduction to Excel* file in the textbook CD.

MINITAB

MINITAB is a widely used statistical analysis package, originally developed in 1972 at Penn State University to help professors teach basic statistics. Over the years, MINITAB has grown into a powerful and accurate, yet easy-to-use, set of statistical tools. MINITAB is used by a number of Fortune 500 companies and by more than 4,000 colleges and universities worldwide. In 2001, *Scientific Computing and Instrumentation,* a publication covering computing and analytical instrument technology, named MINITAB as the winner in the Reader's Choice Awards Statistical Software category. For first-time users, an *Introduction to MINITAB* is provided in the textbook CD. This CD also contains a file for each chapter in the textbook, discussing the necessary MINITAB instructions to carry out the graphical, descriptive, or analytical procedures discussed within that particular chapter.

SPSS

SPSS is a large-scale statistical software package designed to integrate and analyze marketing, customer, and operational data. SPSS was recently named "best decision support system for business intelligence" in a RealWare award competition.

The letters *SPSS* originally meant "Statistical Package for the Social Sciences." As the system evolved from its academic roots in the late 1960s into a leading enterprise analytical solutions provider, the company simply began using *SPSS Inc.* for the company name and *SPSS* for the original product. Today, SPSS provides solutions that discover what customers want and predict what they will do. Although this might appear to be intimidating to the first-time user of SPSS, rest assured that, like many Windows-based programs, this statistical package is very easy to use. An *Introduction to SPSS* is included with the textbook CD, which also contains files for each chapter that illustrate the steps to use when using SPSS to carry out the necessary calculations.

1.2   USES OF STATISTICS IN BUSINESS

Modern businesses have more need to predict future operations than did those of the past, when businesses were smaller. Small-business managers often can solve problems simply through personal contact. Managers in large corporations, however, must try to summarize and analyze the various data available to them. They do this by using modern statistical methods.

Here we list six areas of business that rely on statistical information and techniques:

1. *Quality improvement.* Statistical quality-control procedures can help to assure high product quality and enhance productivity.

2. *Product planning.* Statistical methods are used to analyze economic factors and business trends and to prepare detailed sales budgets, inventory-control systems, and realistic sales quotas.

3. *Forecasting.* Statistics are used to predict sales, productivity, and employment trends.

4. *Yearly reports.* Annual reports for stockholders are based on statistical treatment of the many cost and revenue factors analyzed by the business comptroller.

5. *Personnel management.* Statistical procedures are used in such areas as age- and sex-discrimination lawsuits, performance appraisals, and workforce-size planning.

6. *Market research.* Corporations that develop and market products or services use sophisticated statistical procedures to describe and analyze consumer purchasing behavior.

1.3   SOME BASIC DEFINITIONS

Statistics has specialized definitions for terms crucial to statistical reasoning. In **descriptive statistics,** you collect and describe data. If you analyze the data and make decisions or estimates based on information obtained from the data, you are using **inferential statistics.**

Descriptive statistics are used to describe a large set of data. For example, you can reduce the set of data values to one or more single numbers, such as the average of 150 test scores, or you can construct a graph that represents some feature of the data.

You use inferential statistics to form conclusions about a large group—a population—by collecting a portion of it—a sample. Thus, a **population** is the set of all possible measurements (generally pertaining to a group of people or objects) that is of interest. A **sample** is the portion of the population from which information is gathered.

Another way to distinguish between a population and a sample is to view a population as the set of values you would obtain if you observed a particular **variable** indefinitely. For example, this variable could be the total of two dice, and the *population* would consist of the dice totals when the two dice are rolled time and time again. To gain insight into this population, you could observe this variable, say, 100 times; that is, roll the dice 100 times and record the resulting totals. This set of *observations* of the corresponding variable (total of two dice) results in a *sample*. Consequently, you can view a sample as a set of values obtained by observing a variable of interest a finite number of times. Such variables are actually called *random variables* and will be explored further in Chapters 5 and 6.

The analyst decides what the population is. Typically, the population is so large that it would be nearly impossible to obtain information about every item in it. Instead, we obtain information about selected population members and attempt to draw a conclusion about all members. In other words, we attempt to infer something about the population using information about only some of the members of this population.

To make an early prediction of the election results for governor of California, for example, analysts could use a sample of voters leaving the voting booths, as illustrated in Figure 1.1. The population is all the votes cast in the election. To make a valid statistical inference using a sample, it is crucial that the sample *represent* the population; that is, the values in the sample must be representative (typical) of values in the population. One way to make sure the sample is representative is to collect a sample of size n, where each set of n people has the same chance of being selected for the sample. This is a **simple random sample** (Figure 1.1). It is akin to drawing names out of a hat; each name in the hat has the same chance of being pulled out. Thus, if our population is all votes cast on the day of the gubernatorial election, a sample of votes cast in only one city would not be representative, because we would have no guarantee that these votes would represent the votes of the entire state. A random sample obtained across the entire state would better represent this population.

As another illustration, assume that Calcatron, a producer of electronic calculators, orders 50,000 components from GLC. Calcatron instructs GLC that it will accept the shipment if an outside laboratory that randomly selects 100 components from the batch finds that fewer than 3 are defective. Calcatron relies on inferential statistics; it infers that the population of components is of satisfactory quality if the sample is satisfactory. Note that it is possible that the sample could

Population (all votes cast)

Sample (selected votes for observation)

FIGURE

1.1

Population versus a sample.

contain fewer than 3 defective components even if the population contains, say, 80% defective parts. Whenever we attempt to infer something about a population from a sample, there is always a chance of drawing an incorrect conclusion. The only way of being 100% sure is to examine the entire population. Such a sample is called a **census.**

In the Calcatron example, there are two proportions of interest. The first proportion, the proportion of defective components in the *population*, is referred to as a **parameter.** The second proportion, the proportion of defective components in the *sample*, is referred to as a **statistic.** In general, any value describing a population (such as the average or a particular proportion) is a parameter. Parameters typically are unknown and are estimated using the corresponding statistic derived from a statistical sample. In the chapters to follow we will examine a number of sample statistics and their corresponding population parameters.

1.4   DISCRETE AND CONTINUOUS NUMERICAL DATA

Proper use of numerical data can be a great aid in making a critical decision. However, using an improper technique or "bad data" can lead you down the wrong path. Generally, the technique we use to analyze data in statistics depends on the nature of the data. We can distinguish between two types of numerical data.

How do the following two sets of numbers differ?

3, 5, 2, 1, 4, 4, 3, 5, 5, 1, 2, 4
4.31, 11.62, 5.37, 1.55, 3.71, 6.88, 7.23, 9.52, 2.36, 7.42, 6.11, 4.85

The primary difference is that the values in the first data set consist of *counting numbers,* or *integers.* Such data are **discrete.** For example, these data may be the coded responses from 12 people who answered a particular question in a marketing survey where 1 = strongly agree, 2 = agree, 3 = uncertain, 4 = disagree, and 5 = strongly disagree. Note that discrete data may contain a decimal point. Nevertheless, discrete data have *gaps* in their possible values. For example, if you throw a single die twice and record the average of the two throws, the possible values are 1, 1.5, 2, 2.5, 3, 3.5, 4, 4.5, 5, 5.5, and 6. If you repeatedly averaged two throws of the die, you would obtain discrete data.

Examples of discrete data that have integer values are the number of automobiles that arrive at a drive-up window over a 5-minute period, the number of children in your family, and the total of the two numbers appearing on a throw of two dice. Note that although the first two have infinite (theoretically, at least) possible values, the data are discrete. Your family cannot have 2.5 children.

Now consider the second data set. These data might represent the weights of 12 parcels received at a post office. A list of all the possible values of package weights would be long—if our scale were completely accurate, the list would be infinite and any value would be possible. Such data are **continuous:** *any value* over some particular range is possible. There are no gaps in possible values for continuous data. For example, although we may say Sandra is 5.5 feet tall, we mean her height is about 5.5 feet. In fact, it might be 5.50372 feet. Height data are continuous. Or consider the contents of a coffee cup filled by a vending machine. Will the machine release exactly 6 ounces every time? Certainly not. In fact, if you were to observe the machine fill five such cups and measure the contents to the nearest .001 ounce, you might observe values of 6.031, 5.932, 5.871, 6.353, and 5.612 ounces. Here again, any value between, say, 5.5 ounces and 6.5 ounces is possible:

these are continuous data. *Data such as weights, heights, age (actual), and time are generally continuous data and will be used in the examples in the chapters to follow.*

It is important to remember that *discrete data* can be the result of observing a *continuous variable.* For example, actual age is a continuous variable, but if a recorded age is the age at the last birthday, the data will be discrete. Very often, measurements on a continuous variable (such as height in inches) result in discrete data. However, discrete data can also be the result of observing a discrete variable, such as the number of traffic tickets a person has received during the past three years.

To simplify matters, remember that you can use these guidelines in most applications in a business environment:

- Discrete data are the result of *counting* something (such as the number of defective parts or the number of scratches on a newly painted door panel).
- Continuous data are the result of *measuring* something (such as weight or length of time to complete a task).

1.5 LEVEL OF MEASUREMENT FOR NUMERICAL DATA

In addition to classifying numerical data as discrete or continuous, we can also classify these data according to their level of measurement. We will discuss them in order of strength, beginning with the weakest. **Nominal data** are really not numerical at all but are merely labels or assigned values. Examples include gender (1 = male, 2 = female), manufacturer of automobile (1 = General Motors, 2 = Ford, 3 = Toyota), or color of eyes (1 = blue, 2 = green, 3 = brown). Assigning a numerical code to such data is merely a convenience so that, for example, one can store the information in a computer. Therefore, it makes no sense to perform calculations with such numbers, such as finding their average. What would it mean to claim that "the average eye color is 2.73"? This statement is meaningless. Generally, we are interested in the *proportion* of such data in each category. Consider Calcatron's shipment, in which each component is either defective or not defective. We could assign the code 1 = defective, 0 = not defective. The parameter of interest here is p, where p = proportion of defective components in the population of 50,000 components. If Calcatron believes p is too large, it will not accept the shipment. We will consider what is "too large" in Chapter 10.

Ordinal data can be arranged in order such as worst to best or F to A (grades on an exam). A classic example of ordinal data is the result of a cross-country race, where ten people compete and 1 = the fastest (the winner), 2 = the runner-up, and so on, with 10 = the slowest. Here, the *order* of the values is important (3 finished before 4) but the *difference* of the values is not. For example, $2 - 1 = 1$ and $10 - 9 = 1$, but this does not imply that 1 and 2 were just as close in the final results as were 9 and 10.

The difference between values of **interval data** *does* have meaning. It is meaningful to add and average such data. The classic example is *temperature,* where it is true that the difference in heat between 60°F and 61°F is the same as that between 80°F and 81°F. Many of the techniques used to analyze data in statistics require data that are at least of this strength.

Ratio data differ from interval data in that there is a definite *zero point* that indicates that nothing exists for the variable being measured. To decide if your data are interval or ratio, ask yourself whether twice the value is twice the

---

TABLE

1.1

Summary of data levels of measurement.

Property	Level of Measurement			
	Nominal	**Ordinal**	**Interval**	**Ratio**
Order of data is meaningful	N	Y	Y	Y
Difference between data values is meaningful	N	N	Y	Y
Zero point represents total absence	N	N	N	Y

---

strength. For example, is 100°F twice as hot as 50°F? The answer is no, so these data are interval. Is a 4-acre field twice as large as a 2-acre field? The answer is yes, so these are ratio data. Here the zero point is a field of 0 acres. An important distinction between interval and ratio data is that for interval data, a value of zero (such as 0°F) is an arbitrary point and does not reflect an absence of the characteristic of interest (such as temperature). Typically, data consisting of areas, counts, volumes, and weights are ratio data. These four levels of measurement are summarized in Table 1.1.

Comments

1. When deciding whether data are interval or ratio, the good news is that techniques used in statistics generally do not distinguish between these two data types; that is, these techniques can be used on interval *or* ratio data.

2. Interval and ratio data are often referred to as **quantitative data** because such data consist of values that naturally take on numerical (quantitative) values (such as age or weight).

3. Nominal and ordinal data can be grouped together under the heading **qualitative data** because they consist essentially of labels that are either unordered (nominal data) or ordered (ordinal data).

A summary of the various data classifications is shown in Figure 1.2. Notice that discrete data can result from any of the four levels of measurement, whereas continuous data can be only interval or ratio.

X Exercises 1.1–1.6

1.1 Give an example of a population of interest to a business manager. Do you think that a business manager would prefer to select a sample from this population or take a census? Why?

1.2 What differentiates ratio data from data that are only interval?

1.3 To generalize the results of a statistical study, what type of statistics is more useful—descriptive statistics or inferential statistics?

1.4 Nielsen Media Research is a popular TV ratings company. This company estimates the number of viewers tuned in to TV programs during specified rating periods. These estimates are computed from a relatively small random sample of homes selected across the United States. For example, on July 25, 2001, *60 Minutes* was estimated to have 9.7 million viewers with an estimated 13% of the TV sets tuned into this program at 8:00 P.M.

a. To obtain completely accurate figures on the number of viewers and percent share of the homes viewing this program, Nielsen Media Research would need to obtain a census. A disadvantage to using a sample is that only an estimate can be obtained. What are the advantages of obtaining a sample in this case?

b. What level of measurement would you classify the figures provided to Nielsen Media Research?

c. What impact do you think these statistics have on advertisers?

(Source: "Nielsen Ratings," *USA Today*, August 1, 2001, p. 4D.)

1.5 Classify each of the following variables as being either qualitative or quantitative and as having nominal, ordinal, interval, or ratio level of measurements:

a. The time that a chief executive officer spends at work

b. The ordered preference that investors have for different investment funds for retirement purposes

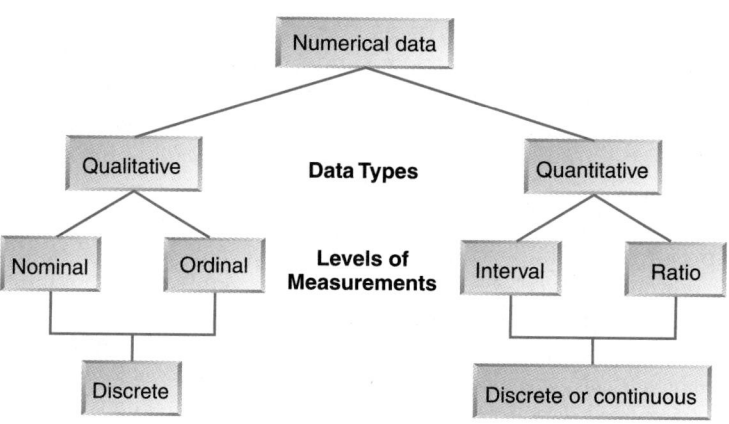

FIGURE

1.2

Classifications of
numerical data.

EXAMPLES OF DISCRETE DATA

1. Nominal: Ownership status of resident dweller
    (1 = own, 2 = rent)

2. Ordinal: Level of customer satisfaction
    (1 = very dissatisfied, 2 = somewhat dissatisfied,
    3 = somewhat satisfied, 4 = very satisfied)

3. Interval: Person's score on IQ test

4. Ratio: Number of defective lightbulbs in a carton

EXAMPLES OF CONTINUOUS DATA

1. Interval: Actual temperature, °F

2. Ratio: Weight of packaged dog food

c. The state where an individual was born

d. The average temperature for the summer months in Chicago

e. The ranking of computer stores with respect to their competitors, based on sales

1.6 An executive within the automotive industry wished to determine the proportion of used import automobiles with odometers that showed less miles than their recorded reading in Japan. A random sample of Japanese imported automobiles revealed that 24% of the odometers had readings that were less than that recorded before being shipped to the United States.

a. What is the population of interest?

b. What is the difference between numerical facts and statistics? What does the value of 24% represent?

c. What type of data is the value of the odometer setting?

d. Why would a sample be used in this study? Explain.

SOURCES OF DATA 1.6

Without the availability of data, the science of statistics would cease to exist. Information obtained from sample data is typically used to gain insight into a much larger population. The reliability of conclusions drawn from sample data depends to a great extent on the *quality* of the data. Are they accurate? Do the data really represent the population of interest? Was the sample obtained properly? Before we can answer such questions, we first examine where to look for such data, that is, the source of the data.

Primary and Secondary Data

Data sources can be categorized as being *primary* or *secondary* sources. **Primary data** come from an original (primary) source and are collected with a specific research question in mind, such as, "Are single women more likely to encounter sexual harassment in the workplace?" Very often, you may wish to design a questionnaire that addresses your research question and then to collect the data yourself by administering the questionnaire to a representative sample (of women, in our example). This would be an example of primary data. In our example, rather than having to prepare a questionnaire, you might elect instead to personally interview a group of women at the company where you are employed. The latter sample, a *convenience sample,* might give you some valuable insight into the harassment question. Another method of collecting primary data that is gaining momentum in manufacturing-based industries is the use of *designed experiments*. This is rather a time-consuming and seemingly expensive method of data collection, but in the long run it can provide information that saves a company a great deal of money and, more importantly, allows it to build a product of better quality.

Secondary data represent previously recorded data collected for another purpose or as part of a regularly scheduled data collection procedure (such as an annual report released by the U.S. Department of Transportation). Such data are considerably easier and cheaper to obtain than primary data, but may not adequately address your research question. Here are some other advantages of secondary data.

- Secondary data can cover many years of operation.
- Secondary data may exist for many geographical regions (including foreign facilities and workers).

There are also other disadvantages of using secondary data:

- The data may be out of date.
- There is no way to verify that the data were obtained properly.

Primary Data Sources. Obtaining primary data generally requires more effort, but has the huge advantage of specifically addressing your particular research question, such as the harassment question mentioned earlier, or determining cause-and-effect relationships in a designed experiment. The usual procedure for obtaining primary data involves designing a questionnaire that addresses this question, pretesting this instrument several times, refining it each time, and finally, administering it to a sample from the population of interest. Then comes the job of coding the responses for computer input, analyzing the results, and coming to a conclusion on the research question. There are many things to consider and to watch out for when designing a questionnaire; these will be explored further in Section 1.8.

The statistical and management worlds of *quality improvement* are getting a great deal of attention these days. As you get further into this area, you will begin to view business operations as a collection of *processes* that can be monitored, measured, and improved. This applies to processes within manufacturing companies, service industries, city and government organizations, and educational institutions. The use of statistics enters in since, if we intend to improve a process, we first need to measure a quality characteristic associated with this process (such as the number of rejected parts in a manufacturing process) so that we are able to determine if, in fact, the quality has been improved.

Consider a situation where the local fire department is attempting to improve the response time to a fire call. They have gone to a great deal of effort and expense to improve this process, including computerizing the dispatch operation and improving the "state of readiness" for workers on duty. Suppose that you were asked to offer your opinion prior to implementation of this quality improvement effort as to whether response time is improved as a result of these changes.

One possibility would be to obtain a sample of times before the changes were made and another sample afterward. This is another example of *primary data,* because you obtain the data first-hand for a specific purpose. The intent would be to determine whether the average response time after the quality improvement effort was less than the average time before the effort—a question we will deal with in Chapter 9.

To recap, primary data are obtained using a "hands-on" procedure, such as designing and administering a questionnaire that addresses a particular research question or observing and measuring a characteristic of interest within a particular business process. Very often this is the only data source available if there are no other published data (secondary data) that address the question or process of interest. As you delve into specific research topics, or hot topics (such as cloning or racial profiling), you will need current data that address these issues; designing a procedure to collect primary data is your only alternative, despite the fact that such a method can be very time-consuming and costly.

Secondary Data Sources.   Once you begin to search out sources of secondary data, you will soon discover that there is an overwhelming amount of data stored up in (1) government reports, (2) industry financial statements, (3) business periodicals (magazines), and (4) sites available through the World Wide Web. Often the difficulty is finding data that meet your needs, appear to be current, and were obtained in a proper manner (*yes:* a random sample of industrywide computer programmers; and *no:* a haphazard sample of programmers within a particular department at Texas Instruments).

It would be impossible in this short space to discuss all sources of secondary data. However, here are several sources that provide a large volume of data on a very wide assortment of variables.

- U.S. Bureau of the Census, *Statistical Abstracts of the United States.* This is published by the U.S. Government Printing Office.* This document (also available on CD-ROM) contains summary statistics on the political, social, industrial, and economic climate in the United States. It contains data from more than 200 authoritative sources summarized in more than 1,500 tables. Often, if specific data are not presented, the source notes for these tables in the attached bibliography are useful guides for further research. The easiest access to this information is through the Web (http://www.census.gov/statab/www), although a subscription is required. You should also check the availability at your local public or university library.
- *Canadian Business and Current Affairs (CBCA) Fulltext Business.* This provides full-text access to nearly 140 Canadian industry and professional periodicals and newspapers. This information is updated every month, and many of the sources appear for the first time as part of an electronic database. *CBCA Fulltext Business* contains more than 175,000 full-text articles and corporate report citations with 60,000 records added annually.
- *United Nations Statistical Yearbook.* This is an annual publication containing data on a variety of topics gathered *worldwide.* There are summary statistics on international trade, industry and construction, demographic and housing, and international price comparisons. This information is available via CD-ROM and hardcopy. The United Nations' Web site is http://www.un.org.
- *Census of the Population.* This is published by the U.S. government every 10 years, the next to appear after the census in the year 2010. This is a powerful data source in which the U.S. population is categorized according to income level, ethnicity, geographical location, and occupation. The easiest access to this information is via the U.S. Census Bureau's home page at http://www.census.gov.

*An easier-to-read version with larger type size is available through Bernan Press, Lanham, Maryland.

- Business periodicals, including the *Wall Street Journal* and *Fortune.* Periodicals offer a good method of retrieving current (perhaps daily) information. Three comprehensive business periodical indexes are the *Reader's Guide Abstracts* (cites articles from more than 240 popular general-interest periodicals, including *Newsweek, Fortune,* and *Business Week*), *Business Abstracts* (references to 345 business and economic periodicals, allowing the researcher to target a particular type of business), and *Periodical Abstracts* (contains indexing and abstracting to significant articles appearing in top general and academic periodicals, as well as full text from more than 600 journals).

- *The ABI/INFORM index.* Many libraries have this business index, available via the Internet. It offers a *very* extensive database of business-related information and articles. You merely specify the company, journal, author, geographical area, or key words (such as *Bankruptcy* and *Delaware*) for which you need information, and ABI/INFORM will identify the corresponding source(s) stored in the database. ABI/INFORM is also available on shared resources networks, which can be accessed in some locations. Check your local public or university library for availability. A similar resource, also available via the Web, is EBSCOhost's Business Source Premier, which provides indexing and full text access to 2,260 scholarly business journals. As with ABI/INFORM, check your local public or university library for availability.

- *The Internet.* The latest (and largest) source of secondary data is the World Wide Web. Using the Web, you have access to many periodical abstracts and newspapers, DIALOG (a collection of more than 600 industry and academic databases), Ingenta (a database of current article information taken from multidisciplinary journals with brief description information for more than 7 million articles), and electronic journals (complete electronic versions of more than 260 journals). Whenever a subscription is required, be sure to check your local public or university library for availability.

Designing an Experiment. In the previous discussion, it was pointed out that one advantage of collecting primary data is that you have direct control over the data collection. In this way, you are able to get data obtained for a specific purpose that will generally be of high quality due to the hands-on nature of this procedure. Designing an industrial experiment is another source of primary data—one that at first glance appears to be a very elaborate and costly method of collecting sample data. But as many industrial testimonials in the literature have made clear, experimental designs provide an extremely effective way of studying an industrial process. Data collected from such an experiment can help design better quality into a product so that, long-range, such a procedure *is* very cost effective.

One of the key advantages to collecting data from a designed experiment is that you are able to study the effect of changes to a process. For example, Acme Brick produces brick for residential construction. One of the key decisions in the production process is the oven firing temperature, since this can affect the strength of the brick. A quality engineer at Acme decides to test the brick strength at oven temperatures of 150°C, 175°C, and 200°C. Fifteen bricks are randomly selected and randomly assigned to one of the three temperatures. Using a test device, the strength of the bricks is measured, with the following results.

150°	175°	200°
110	145	103
106	132	110
118	151	105
122	148	112
114	144	126

At first glance, it would appear that 175°C produces the strongest brick. (The analysis for such a design will be discussed in Chapter 11, where it could be shown that this conclusion is supported.)

This chapter will demonstrate that data collected from designed experiments allow you to determine what variables (such as oven temperature) affect the process and in what manner these variables are related to each other.

Random Sampling versus Nonrandom Sampling

When it comes time to obtain (primary) sample data, a key decision you will need to make is whether to gather data that are obtained in a random manner or are obtained using a more deliberate selection procedure. Samples generated using the latter method are **nonrandom samples** and are often referred to as *nonprobability samples*. There are many situations, such as an exploratory study, where you simply want to gain insight into a population of interest rather than make a statistical decision or estimate.

Nonrandom Sampling. When using nonrandom sampling methods, you can use a variety of procedures for obtaining a sample with little or no attention paid to randomization. For example, you may wish to restrict your sample to hand-picked individuals who satisfy a certain requirement, such as individuals over age 50 who have recently been laid off from their jobs. This section will consider three nonrandom sampling strategies: convenience sampling, judgment sampling, and quota sampling.

- *Convenience sampling.* A **convenience sample** is obtained just as the name implies—in a convenient manner. You may elect to use a group of friends, fellow students in your marketing class, shoppers at a local mall, and so on. Individuals for such a sample are selected based on their presumed resemblance to the population of interest (potential customers of your new product or service) and their ready availability. Such a sample can be extremely valuable in gaining insight into a new idea or the sentiment of a much larger population. If a convenience sample of 20 coworkers indicates that 19 of these 20 people think your idea is not a good one, it's probably time to go back to the drawing board. On the positive side, many a good idea has been born by obtaining information through a convenience sample.

  Consider a situation in which a company's records are being audited. If the audit is merely exploratory, a convenience sample may be in order. Typically, no effort is made to locate missing items, records that are in storage, or records that are at another location. It is important to realize that these missing records may be "missing" because the auditee does not want them to be reviewed. However, if the purpose of the audit is to determine a total amount owed to another party (such as an insurance carrier's improper Medicare charges owed to the federal government), then a simple random sample* is essential. For this situation, you will need to outline your sampling procedure carefully and to use a method that will hold up in court should this result be appealed.

- *Judgment sampling.* For situations where you want to handpick individuals who satisfy certain requirements or who you believe have expertise regarding the population, a **judgment sample** often works very well. The earlier illustration of laid-off workers over age 50 is an example of a judgment sample, and this group of people may provide excellent insight into problems facing middle-aged employees. Other examples of judgment samples would include divorced individuals or voting districts likely to represent the opinions of the entire state or nation. A certain city may be selected to test market a new product since it is believed that potential customers within this city have buying behaviors that are typical of a much larger population.

  When using a judgment sample, you take the risk that your sample is not representative of the associated population. Generally, there is no attempt to

---

*Other types of sampling besides simple random sampling that are also legally defensible, and often preferred, are discussed in Chapter 7. These include *stratified* sampling and *cluster* sampling.

cover the entire spectrum of key population characteristics, such as age and income. The judgment sample may include mostly middle-age and middle-income individuals. But if your interest is to gain insight into the population rather than represent them as a whole, a pilot study conducted using a judgment sample can be very valuable.

- *Quota sampling.* Quota sampling is a form of nonrandom sampling that is a bit more deliberate in an attempt to obtain a sample that is representative of the entire population. To illustrate this technique, if you know that 60% of the registered voters in a particular community are women, you may, in a sample of 100 voters, restrict your sample to 60 women and 40 men. In this way, your sample is a miniature of the population.

  Very often in a *quota sample,* the researcher restricts the sample according to more than one criteria, such as age level, religious affiliation, race, or smoking status. Such criteria are believed by the researcher to have an effect on the response of the person being interviewed. Certainly, one's religious affiliation could have an effect on his or her view of a proposed ordinance forbidding the sale of alcoholic beverages. Consequently, a quota sample would attempt to duplicate the proportions of each religious category present in the community where the ordinance would take effect. Oftentimes, these proportions are estimated (or known) from prior surveys or government census results.

  Once the criteria have been determined, a judgment sampling technique can then be used to make the sample selection. The sample may in fact not represent the population if care is not taken in obtaining a representative cross section of people satisfying the sample criteria. Despite this defect of quota sampling, it remains a very popular technique among opinion pollsters, market researchers, and other researchers since it is usually less expensive than obtaining a random sample and takes less time.

Random Sampling. When using a *simple random sample* (usually referred to as a *random sample*), you will need to make sure that every sample of size n has the same chance of being selected. One method of doing this is to use a computer to generate random numbers between 1 and N, where N is the size of the population. For example, you might want to select a set of six numbers between 1 and 50 for a lottery ticket. Here, n is 6, and N is 50. We will illustrate this procedure in the next section. The main advantage of using a random sample is that the sample results can be extended to estimating something of interest in the population. Furthermore, you can measure and control how reliable this estimate is. *The use of simple random samples will be the primary focus of the chapters to follow.*

The main advantage of random sampling is that you can generalize beyond the sample itself. A result derived from such a sample (such as a recovery amount estimated from an audit) is legally defensible in a court of law. Just the opposite holds for the results of a nonrandom sample—you cannot safely generalize to the entire population, and the results are *not* legally defensible. The main advantages behind the use of nonrandom sampling are that (1) data are more easily obtained, (2) such data may provide you with enough information to make a decision with much less expense, and (3) data from a nonrandom sample can be used as an informal base of knowledge in preparation for a later sample based on random sampling.

Generating a Set of Random Numbers

When obtaining a simple random sample, you will need to generate your sample using a set of random values. One option is to use a table of randomly generated numbers, such as Table A.13 (page A–XX) at the end of this textbook. A much simpler method is to utilize a computer-generated list of random digits to determine your sample elements.

To illustrate the process of generating a set of random numbers, consider a situation in which an auditor is responsible for obtaining a random sample of 50 hospital records from a list of 1,000 records, numbered sequentially from 1 to 1,000. For this procedure to work, it is vital that you be able to list sequentially all of the population elements from 1 to 1,000. Here is one way you could use the table of random numbers (Table A.13).

1. Start in any arbitrary position, such as row 5 of column 3.

2. Select a list of 50 random numbers by reading either across or down the table.

3. For each five-digit number selected, place a decimal between the third and fourth digits and round this value to the nearest counting number (integer); for example, 24127 would become 241.27, which is then rounded to 241. One of the sample elements will be the population element in location 241.

Excel provides a simple method of generating a computerized list of random numbers. A set of random numbers can be obtained using Excel's Analysis Tool-Pack by (1) selecting the **Tools** menu from the menu bar, (2) choosing **Data Analysis,** and (3) clicking on **Random Number Generation** and then on **OK.** The random number generation dialog window will appear, and the values should be filled in as illustrated in Figure 1.3. This set of input values will result in column A of Figure 1.4 and consists of a list of 50 numbers randomly selected from the values 1 through 1,000.

To obtain integer values (no decimal places) in column A, you must (1) highlight column A by clicking on the column A heading (the letter "A" at the top of this column) and (2) click on the **Decrease Decimal** icon ( ) the same number of times as the number of decimal places that appear. For example, if the values in column A have four decimal places (such as 383.2931), then click on this icon four times. Column A now should contain a list of 50 integers between 1 and 1000. The first 10 values from one such execution of this procedure are shown in Figure 1.4.

Column B in Figure 1.4 contains the values in column A arranged in ascending order. To obtain this column (and still retain column A) you must first copy column A into column B by (1) highlighting column A by clicking on the column A heading, (2) placing the mouse pointer on the right-hand boundary of this column until its shape becomes a white arrow, (3) while holding the **Ctrl** key (you should observe a small plus sign alongside the white arrow), pressing and holding the left mouse button while dragging column A onto column B, and finally (4) releasing the mouse button and then releasing the **Ctrl** key. Column B should now contain the same values as column A. To arrange the column B values in

FIGURE

1.3

Excel input screen for generating 50 random numbers between 1 and 1000.

FIGURE

1.4

Excel spreadsheet containing first 10 random numbers arranged in original and ascending order.

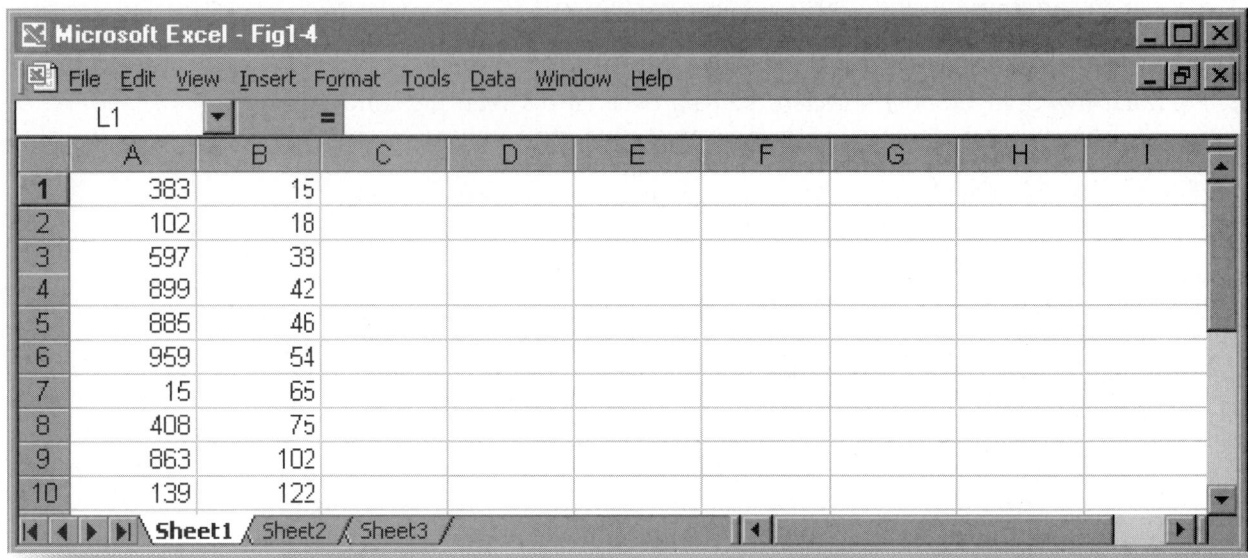

ascending order, highlight column B by clicking on the column B heading and then click on the **Sort Ascending** icon ( ).

The values in column A of Figure 1.4 are arranged in the *original* order. The main advantage of obtaining your sample elements in this order is that the auditor maintains the randomness of the sample. At any interim point, if there is sufficient evidence, the auditor can terminate sampling. When using the sorted values in column B of Figure 1.4, the sample elements can be located in *sequential* order. The advantage of obtaining the sample values in this order is that oftentimes it becomes much easier to locate each value, particularly if the sample elements are selected from a hard-copy format (computer listing, files in a drawer, boxes in a storage area). On the other hand, when selecting the sample using the sequential order, the sample results cannot be generalized to the population unless the entire sample is examined; otherwise you would be ignoring a section of the population.

X   Exercises 1.7–1.11

1.7 All of the following sources are secondary data sources except for one. Which one?

   a. Census data from the United States Census Bureau.

   b. *Fortune* magazine's listing of mutual funds and their annual performance.

   c. Financial data from the Interactive Edition of the *Wall Street Journal*.

   d. Telephone interviews conducted during a class project to obtain data on the satisfaction of college graduates with their first job.

1.8 A sports medicine researcher wants to determine if there was a difference among athletes who were primar-ily runners, swimmers, or cyclists with regard to the amount of muscle discomfort experienced during their activities. Does this researcher need to obtain random samples of athletes from each category? What effect would a convenience sample have on the results of the experiment?

1.9 To obtain information, primary or secondary sources are used. For each of the following statements, indicate the company's most likely source of information.

   a. "The majority of the employees of our company are willing to work in self-directed work teams to achieve a 10% reduction in administrative cost."

b. "Last year, the 4.2 million tons of steel imported by the United States had a significant impact on the earnings of all American steel companies, including our own."

c. "Our company conducted a poll of 1,000 of its employees. The poll indicates that the company's president enjoys increasing popularity among all employees of the company."

d. "The Value Line Survey has recently given our company the highest ranking for price appreciation."

1.10 The sales of luxury-car maker BMW were 220,000 units during the first quarter of 2001 versus 200,000 units during the first quarter of 2000. With the economic slowdown in the United States during 2001, high-level management at BMW was concerned that this upward trend would not continue because demand for mid-price cars of the American auto makers had already slipped. Suppose management selected four dealerships in the New York City and Boston metropolitan areas to sample prospective buyers to determine if they planned to delay purchase of a luxury car due to a slow down in the economy. Would you consider this to be a convenience sample? How do you think management should randomly select dealerships to conduct a survey?

(Source: "BMW's Net Helped by Robust U.S. Sales," *The Wall Street Journal*, August 8, 2001, p. A8.)

1.11 [DATA SET EX1-11] *Variable Description:*

ZipCodes: A list of zip codes from the Memphis Metropolitan area

A property manager in Memphis is interested in the average rental price for a three-bedroom house. The property manager takes note of the latest surveys showing the average housing costs by renters for a three-bedroom house. In 2001, this cost was $549. However, the property manager believes that this cost might be higher in the Memphis metropolitan area. The manager decides to do a survey of homes in selected areas of Memphis to determine the cost of renting a three-bedroom home. From the list of 70 Zip codes in this data set, the manager will first select 20 at random and then select five three-bedroom homes that are being rented.

a. Explain how Table A.13 can be used to choose 20 numbers between 1 and 70.

b. Use computer software to determine a random sample of these Zip codes. In Excel, click on **Tools ➤ Data Analysis ➤ Random Number Generation** and choose the uniform distribution. In MINITAB, click on **Calc ➤ Random Data ➤ Uniform.** In SPSS, click on **Data ➤ Select Cases ➤ Random Sample** and select 20 out of the 70 cases.

(Source: "How Much Renting Costs," *USA Today,* July 11, 2001, p. 1A.)

On the CD . . .

Section 1.7: Business Research Questions in Practice
Section 1.8: Designing and Coding a Questionnaire
Exercises 1.12–1.20

Summary

Decision making using statistical procedures continues to grow in popularity, since calculators and computers make it easy to avoid "seat-of-the-pants" decisions by analyzing sample results in a scientific manner. Contemporary applications (such as, should a particular company accept an outside shipment of components based upon a sample of these components?) can be found in a variety of business disciplines.

The science of statistics comprises a set of rules and procedures used to describe numerical data or to make decisions based on these data. The group of measurements that are of interest define the **population.** The portion of a population selected for observation is a **sample.** A **variable** is an observable descriptor that defines the population—such as height or weight. A characteristic (such as the average) of the population is referred to as a **parameter,** and the corresponding sample characteristic is a **statistic.** For example, the average age of a sample of 100 people passing the most recent CPA exam is a statistic. The average age of *all* people passing this exam is a parameter. A sample that contains the entire population is a **census.**

Descriptive statistics is concerned only with collecting and describing data. **Inferential statistics** is used when tentative conclusions about a population are drawn on the basis of data contained in a representative sample. The question of whether to accept a shipment of components (the population) based on a sample of 100 components is an example of inferential statistics.

Numerical data are either discrete or continuous. **Discrete data** have limited, specific possible values. **Continuous data** can assume any value over some range. A further classification of data is their level of measurement. At the lowest level, **nominal data** are categorical data that are assigned numeric codes. **Ordinal data** are ranked—the order of the data values is meaningful. In **interval data,** both the order of the data and the difference between any two data values have meaning. Finally, **ratio data** have all the properties of interval data and also contain a definite zero point. Nominal and ordinal data make up the category of **qualitative data,** while **quantitative data** consist of interval and ratio data. Most statistical techniques do not distinguish between interval and ratio data but do require that the data have at least an interval level of measurement; that is, the sample consists of quantitative data.

To obtain information (a sample), data can be obtained from primary or secondary sources. **Primary data** come from an original (primary) source, and are meant to gain insight into a specific research question. Sources of primary data include mail-in questionnaires, personal interviews, and designed experiments. **Secondary data** consist of previously recorded data, such as information contained in government reports, industry financial statements, and business periodicals.

Most statistical methods assume that a **simple random sample** of size n has been collected such that each set of n measurements has the same chance of being selected for the sample. Such a sample allows you to generalize information from the sample to the entire population. An easy way of producing random numbers is via a computerized random number generator.

Nonrandom samples are samples selected in a convenient or deliberate manner with little or no attention paid to randomization. The three nonrandom sampling strategies discussed in this chapter were convenience sampling, judgment sampling, and quota sampling. A sample selected on the accessibility of the sample subjects is a **convenience sample.** Such a sample may consist of close friends, a classroom of students, shoppers haphazardly selected at a local mall, and so on. A **judgment sample** is one where sample subjects are deliberately selected because they are believed to have expertise regarding the population of interest. Data collected from a city intentionally selected to test market a new product would also be an example of a judgment sample. A sample that matches proportions for one or more key characteristics of the population is a **quota sample.**

X Review Exercises 1.21–1.30

1.21 An operations manager at a semiconductor company is interested in the satisfaction level of the firms that buy computer chips from the company. Approximately 1,000 firms buy chips from this company. The manager has developed a satisfaction scale from 1 to 100 for the respondents to mark their level of satisfaction with the company's products. This scale is to be included on a survey to a sample of 100 firms that buy from this firm.
   a. What is the population of interest?
   b. How can a random sample be selected?
   c. What is the parameter of the population that is of interest?
   d. What is the statistic corresponding to the parameter requested in part (c)?

1.22 Classify each of the following data sources as primary or secondary.
   a. Data collected during a manufacturing process to determine the proportion of defective items produced
   b. Data published by the U.S. Bureau of Census in *Statistical Abstracts of the United States*
   c. Data collected by management to determine the acceptability of a new policy by its employees
   d. Data published in *Standard & Poor's* on the financial liabilities of energy service companies

1.23 America Online raised the price of its flagship online service by 9% during the summer of 2001, potentially adding hundreds of millions of dollars to its annual revenues. Management was concerned that some of its online users would start to seek out its lower-priced competitors. The chief executive officer was interested in estimating the percentage of users who thought that this increase would cause them to discontinue using its online service. A survey could be conducted to estimate this percentage.
   a. What is the population of interest?
   b. How might a random sample of users be selected for a survey?
   c. Do you think a convenience sample or a random sample would be a better way to obtain an estimate of the percentage of users that would likely discontinue the online service?

(Source: "America Online Boots Price for Flagship Service," *Wall Street Journal*, May 23, 2001, p A3.)

1.24 Financial planning is a dynamic process that starts with the identification of an individual's specific goals. Personal data are gathered to determine the extent to which a person can achieve these goals. In a recent survey, over 50% of working individuals identified extensive travel as a specific goal during their golden years and approximately 60% identified a particular hobby that they want to pursue. List some questions that you believe may help individuals think about goals for retirement. For example, how much do you plan on spending for travel during your retirement? For which of your questions would you consider the response to be descriptive? Which of your responses would allow you to calculate a numerical average?

(Source: "Great Expectations for Aging," *USA Today,* August 7, 2001, p. 1D.)

1.25 Determine whether each of the following groups of people or objects represents a population or a sample.
   a. A list of 500 employees of General Motors (*Hint:* Could this be either a sample or a population? Explain.)
   b. Forty students who were randomly stopped and questioned on a university campus
   c. Two hundred people who were selected randomly from a telephone book to receive a marketing questionnaire
   d. The list of all possible choices of 2 cards from a deck of 52 cards
   e. A batch of electronic parts ready for inspection

1.26 Typically after live presidential candidate debates on network television, there appears a phone number for viewers to call and state which candidate performed the best. Would this be considered a simple random sample? a convenience sample? Why?

1.27 Dr. Ronald Kessler, a researcher at Harvard Medical School, reports that health conditions of workers cost industry 2.5 billion days each year. Besides fighting increases in health care costs, employers are concerned about how health care education can help improve the day-to-day efficiency of their workers. Assume that a health care professional was contracted to collect information from workers at an automotive assembly factory. The following items are examples of questions. What type of data and which level of measurement would you classify each response? Explain how descriptive statistics might be used to summarize the findings.
   a. How many times do you perform physical fitness exercise per week?
   b. Approximately how many times do you see a doctor per year?
   c. Do you fall asleep easily at night and sleep soundly?
   d. Do you enjoy your current work (always, sometimes, usually not, never)?
   e. Do you consume less than 2 glasses of water per day, at least 2 but less than 4, or at least 4?
   f. How many pounds do you think you should lose to be considered healthy?

(Source: "Programs Aim to Keep Staffers Healthy and on the Job," *Dallas Morning News,* June 21, 2001, p. 1D.)

1.28 Upscale retailer Neiman Marcus announced in the summer of 2001 that it hoped to profit from adding a store at the newly constructed 1.3-million-square-foot retail center in San Antonio's North Star mall. Tourists spend an average of $1,083 per trip to San Antonio. Neiman Marcus would like to lure these tourists to its new store after they are finished viewing the sights. Suppose that a random sample of tourists visiting the Alamo were selected to answer the following questions. Classify each of the requested data items as either qualitative or quantitative and give the appropriate level of measurement.
   a. How often do you believe you will visit San Antonio over the next three years?
   b. Is the amount of money that you will spend in San Antonio during your visit less than $500, at least $500 but less than $1000, at least $1000 but less than $1500, at least $1500 but less than $2000, or more than $2000?
   c. How much time will you spend shopping during your visit?
   d. What is the name of the store that you are most likely to go shopping in while visiting San Antonio?
   e. Rank your three most favorite activities during this trip.

(Source: "Elegant Ideas," *Dallas Morning News,* June 14, 2001, p. 1D.)

1.29 At the end of 2000, Apple, the erstwhile leading supplier of computers to schools, realized that it grossly overestimated demand for the pricey Power Macintosh G4 Cube. Revenues slumped by 57% for the year. In 2001, Apple had a new hot product, the Titanium Power-Book laptop, or TiBook. Suppose you are working for the marketing department of

Apple and are asked to conduct a sample survey on how satisfied purchasers are with the new product.

a. What is the population of interest?

b. Describe a procedure to select a random sample.

c. Write three questions for the survey to gather information on demographics and three questions to gather information on how satisfied the customer is with the product.

d. What incentive might be appropriate to encourage customers to complete the survey?

e. What follow-up action might achieve a higher response rate?

(Source: "Steve Jobs: The Graying Price of a Shrinking Kingdom," *Fortune*, May 14, 2001, pp. 118–131.)

1.30 Marketing researchers often use a list for drawing simple random samples of consumers to assess a new product. To illustrate one way of selecting a random sample from a list of members, perform the following procedure. In Excel, type a 1 in A1 and a 2 in A2. Highlight both A1 and A2. Now drag the handle on the highlighted region down to row 100. Think of the 100 numbers as representing 100 consumers on a list. Click on **Tools ➤ Data Analysis ➤ Sampling.** Now select the 100 numbers in the first column for input (A1: A200) and click on Random and type in 10. Select an output cell (say, B1). Then click OK. Note that the 10 numbers displayed represent a random sample from the population of 100 members.

Computer Exercises Using the Databases

Exercise 1—Appendix F

For each of the variables defined in the database of household financial variables, determine if the corresponding data would be classified as discrete or continuous.

Exercise 2—Appendix F

For each of the variables in the database of household financial variables, what is the highest level of measurement for the corresponding data?

Exercise 3—Appendix F

Would you classify the data in this database as primary or secondary?

Exercise 4—Appendix F

For each of the variables defined in the database of household variables, would you classify the corresponding data as qualitative or quantitative?

Exercise 5—Appendix G

Answer exercises 1 through 4 for each variable defined in the database using the financial variables on companies.

Insights from Statistics in Action

Online Surveys: E-xpress Yourself

The introductory case study in Statistics in Action discussed the ever-increasing use of the Internet as a means of obtaining survey information from customers and Web-site visitors. This survey method provides for faster data collection at a much lower cost. Using the concepts introduced in this chapter, answer the following questions.

1. Suppose that the manager at Direct Marketing Services wishes to construct a survey on the experiences that consumers have after the purchase of a Chevrolet suburban. List two questions, one with a qualitative response and one with a quantitative response, for each of the following areas in which a dealership might be interested: (1) financing of the vehicle by purchaser, (2) information about a purchaser's previously owned vehicles, (3) satisfaction with the purchase experience, and (4) satisfaction with the vehicle.

2. Suppose that a health-care administrator wishes to obtain information on the service provided by a children's health center. What do you think the population of interest would be? Give an example of discrete and continuous data that could be obtained from a survey requesting information on the service provided by the health center.

3. Here are some questions that a *Wall Street Journal* poll might use in a survey. Which level of measurement would you classify each response?
   a. Are you a voting citizen?
   b. What is your mortgage payment?
   c. How much money have you saved in a Roth IRA?
   d. How long have you owned your home?
   e. Would you say that your confidence in the current government administration is 1, very high; 2, somewhat high; 3, low; or 4, very low?
   f. List your favorite three TV commercials.
   g. Rank your favorite three TV commercials in the order in which you believe that they are creative.

4. Suppose that a major hotel chain has a Web site that allows visitors to rate the services of its facilities. List examples of questions for this survey that would be useful to the hotel chain's management. What is the level of measurement for the responses to each of these questions?

Source: "How This Poll Was Conducted," The *Wall Street Journal*, June 25, 1998, p. A24. "Study: On-Line Surveys Effective," *Direct Marketing*, vol. 61, no. 7, 1998, p. 8. "Web Surveys: A Review of Issues and Approaches," *Public Opinion Quarterly*, vol. 64, no. 4, 2000, pp. 464–494. "The 2000 Internet Survey," *Mortgage Banking*, vol. 61, no. 1, 2000, p. 42–53.

Appendix **SPSS**®

Chapter 1 Appendix: Data Analysis with SPSS

Opening Excel Files in SPSS

To open an Excel file in SPSS, click on **File ➤ Open ➤ Data.** In the **Files of type** box, select **Excel (*.xls)** as shown below.

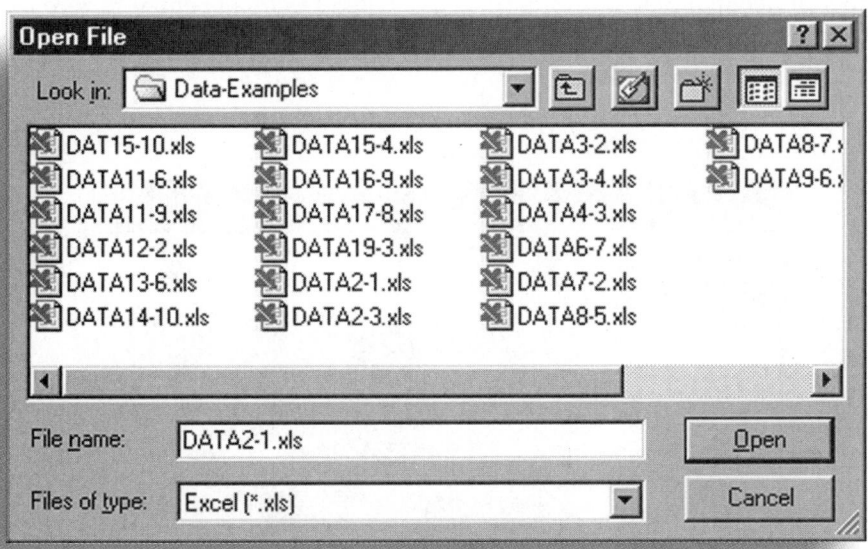

If the first row of this file contains variable names, be sure to click on the **Read variable names** . . . check box.

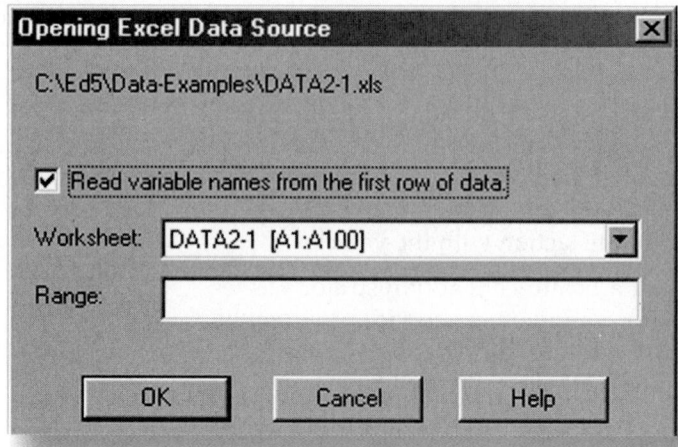

Generating Random Uniform Observations

As an example, suppose that 20 random values between 1 and 1,000 are desired. Begin by entering 1 through 20 in the first column of a fresh data worksheet and name this variable "counter." Click on **Transform ➤ Compute.** In the following **Compute Variable** dialog box, enter the variable name "values" in the **Target Variable** box. From the function list in the right-hand-side, double-click on **RV.UNIFORM(min,max)** and replace the question marks in what appears in the **Numeric Expression** box with 1 and 1,000. Click on **OK.** Your first two columns should resemble those in the data window immediately following the **Compute Variable** dialog box. *Note:* If you desire 20 random *integers* between 1 and 1,000, click on **Transform ➤ Compute.** In the **Compute Variable** dialog box, enter the variable name integers in the **Target Variable** box. From the function list in the right-hand side, double-click on **RND(numexpr)** and replace "numexpr" with the variable name "values" in the **Numeric Expression** box. Click on **OK.** Set the number of decimal places (in the column labeled Decimals) equal to zero for the integers variable.

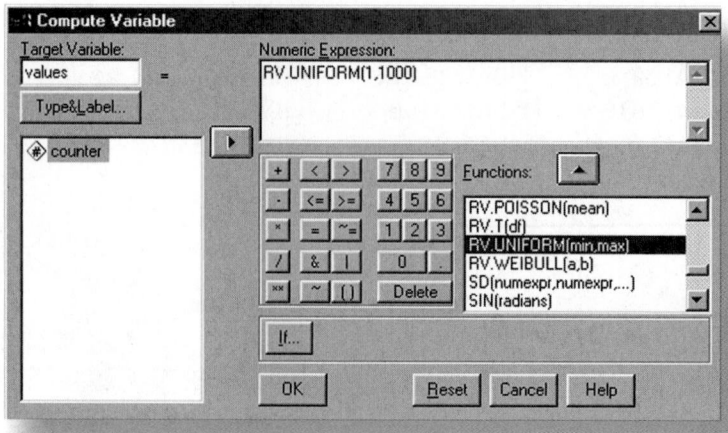

	counter	values	integers
1	1	140.50	141
2	2	431.87	432
3	3	612.57	613
4	4	291.46	291
5	5	156.58	157
6	6	699.80	700
7	7	346.95	347
8	8	446.19	446
9	9	53.36	53
10	10	104.10	104
11	11	142.02	142
12	12	43.90	44
13	13	622.08	622
14	14	154.44	154
15	15	715.50	715
16	16	928.37	928
17	17	578.56	579
18	18	262.60	263
19	19	725.10	725
20	20	38.05	38
21			
22			

◄ ►\ **Data View** ⋀ Variable View /

On the CD . . .
Chapter 1 Appendix: Data Analysis with MINITAB

23

2

Data Presentation Using Descriptive Graphs

X

Statistics in Action
Lean Philosophy Drives Productivity Growth

Productivity growth, usually defined as getting more output from every hour worked, has been identified as key to sustaining the economy and raising living standards. Both service and manufacturing companies are giving managers and workers special incentives in an effort to encourage company output and reward gains in productivity. Companies have realized that output is a team effort. As a consequence, 86% of companies in the service sector have an output award initiative in place for workers, while 68% of the manufacturing companies have similar programs.

Some of the biggest gains in productivity have resulted from management decisions that often seem brilliant in hindsight. For example, AutoNation USA's used car megastores, where haggling and hassling are not allowed and salespeople are trained in communication instead of intimidation, made the difficult decision to overhaul its used-car megastores by coupling them with new-car franchises. That resulted in AutoNation's employment being reduced from 47,100 to 33,000 over a couple of years. The action increased revenue per employee by 82%. When PepsiCo sold its restaurant operations (Taco Bell, Pizza Hut, and KFC restaurants), its employment was reduced by 74% with only a 25% drop in assets. Although its revenue did decrease, its revenue per worker showed an increase in productivity by 33%.

Information technology is also responsible for making businesses more efficient. New

ways of doing business using computers and the Internet have reduced the energy and materials needed for each dollar of output and hence, increased overall productivity. For example, a PepsiCo delivery driver who is making rounds at the convenience stores is now equipped with a handheld computer to key in the inventory of soft drinks and chips.

Computers have even made some companies more productive during periods of economic slowdown. Economists hailed the Bureau of Labor Statistics report during the second quarter of 2001 that showed a 2.5% annual rate of rising productivity during a period of economic contraction. However, economic debates continue as to whether such strong productivity gains can persist, or whether these gains will settle back to slower historical figures. High-tech companies do not always benefit from technology in the same way as many traditional companies. For example, the productivity for telecommunications giant AT&T was negative in 2001 because of flat revenue during the economic slowdown and an increase in employees and assets.

When you have completed this chapter, you will be able to examine the total productivity gains of major corporations and discuss these questions:

- How can productivity figures be presented graphically in a form that is easy to understand?
- What does the *frequency distribution* of productivity figures reveal?
- How can *bar charts* be used to describe the average productivity for various industries?
- What makes certain graphs *deceptive*?

A Look Back/Introduction

Chapter 1 introduced you to some of the basic terms used in statistics. One of the key concepts was the idea of acquiring data using a sample from a population. It also emphasized that the proper use of statistics depends on the nature of the data involved. Are the data discrete or continuous? Are the values nominal, ordinal, interval, or ratio?

Once the data have been gathered, the problem becomes learning whatever we can from them. One method is to describe the data by means of a graph. A graph allows us to discuss intelligently the "shape" of the data.

Everyone has heard the expression that a picture is worth a thousand words (or, more appropriate here, a thousand numbers). This is especially true in statistics, where it may be vital to reduce a large set of numbers to a graph (or picture) that illustrates the structure underlying the data. For example, in a business meeting a quick glance at a graph demonstrates a point much more easily than does a page filled with numbers and words.

Let's illustrate why you may want to describe a data set by using a graph. Suppose that the student affairs director at Bellaire College (a fictitious, small private college in California) has compiled the starting salaries of the 50 graduating business majors. Bellaire offers business degrees in accounting, information systems, and marketing. The salaries, along with the number of campus interviews for each person, are shown in Table 2.1.

How can you summarize and present these data in a form that is easily understood? There are many graphical methods that can be used, depending on the nature of the data and what you are trying to demonstrate about them. When presenting data graphically, the first step usually is to combine the data values into a frequency distribution.

2.1 FREQUENCY DISTRIBUTIONS

We need to reduce a large set of data to a much smaller set of numbers that can be more easily comprehended. If you have recorded the population sizes of 500 randomly selected cities, there is no easy way to examine these 500 numbers visually and learn anything. It would be easier to examine a condensed version of this set of data, such as that presented in Table 2.2.

TABLE

2.1

Starting salaries (thousands of dollars) and number of campus interviews for graduating business majors at Bellaire College.

Major	No. of Graduating Students	Starting Salary/No. of Interviews						
Accounting	26	41.5	39.4	40.9	35.9	37.4	39.5	40.3
		15	19	5	7	14	12	11
		39.3	41.6	36.6	41.1	35.7	43.7	37.0
		6	7	5	12	13	7	6
		41.3	40.6	38.0	42.4	35.7	41.4	39.2
		7	10	16	5	11	21	4
		36.8	39.3	43.8	38.5	43.0		
		19	21	5	16	19		
Information systems	10	36.3	35.6	36.2	38.1	34.8	38.1	35.7
		15	14	10	16	5	16	21
		36.5	39.5	37.9				
		8	14	14				
Marketing	14	34.3	36.8	33.8	35.0	37.8	38.7	37.2
		11	13	7	12	5	17	9
		32.8	38.2	37.0	39.7	38.8	35.2	36.2
		8	20	16	19	8	20	8

TABLE

2.2

Frequency distribution of the population of 500 cities.

Class Number	Size of City	Frequency
1	Under 10,000	4
2	10,000 and under 15,000	51
3	15,000 and under 20,000	77
4	20,000 and under 25,000	105
5	25,000 and under 30,000	84
6	30,000 and under 35,000	60
7	35,000 and under 40,000	45
8	40,000 and under 45,000	38
9	45,000 and under 50,000	31
10	50,000 and over	5
		500

This type of summary, called a **frequency distribution,** consists of *classes* (such as "10,000 and under 15,000") and *frequencies* (the number of data values within each class). What do you gain using this procedure? You reduce 500 numbers to 10 classes and frequencies. You can study the frequency distribution in Table 2.2 and learn a great deal about the shape of this data set. For example, approximately 50% of the cities in your sample have a population between 20,000 and 35,000. Also, only 1% of the cities contain 50,000 people or more.

Frequency Distribution for Continuous Data

A frequency distribution is typically condensed from data having an interval or ratio level of measurement. When you construct a frequency distribution for continuous data, you need to decide how many classes to use (10 in Table 2.2) and the class width (5,000 in Table 2.2).

There is no "correct" number of **classes** (K) to use in a frequency distribution. However, you can best condense a set of data by using between 5 and 20 classes. The usual procedure is to choose what you think would be an adequate number of classes and to construct the resulting frequency distribution. A quick look at this distribution will tell you if you have reduced the data too much (not enough classes; K is too small) or not enough (too many classes; K is too large). One indication that K is too small is that a large portion of your data (say, nearly 50%) lies in one class. If you observe a number of empty classes, or many classes with a frequency of 1 or 2, this may indicate that K is too large. If you have a very large set of data, you can use a larger number of classes than you would for a smaller data set. Whenever you construct frequency distributions using a computer, select several different values of K and look at the effects of the different choices.

Having chosen a value for K, the next step is to examine

$$\frac{\text{range}}{\text{number of classes}} = \frac{H - L}{K}$$

where H = the highest value in your data and L = the lowest value in your data. Round the result to a value that provides an easy-to-interpret frequency distribution. This is the **class width (CW).** The width of each class should be the same. Later we will discuss possible exceptions to this rule for the first and last classes.

DEFINITION

Class width (CW) = the value of $\dfrac{H - L}{K}$ rounded (up or down) to a value that is easy to interpret.

Suppose that, for a particular set of data, you have elected to use $K = 10$ classes in your frequency distribution and that $H = 106$ and $L = 10$. Then

$$\frac{H - L}{K} = \frac{106 - 10}{10} = 9.6$$

The desirable class width to use here is CW = 10.

Here are some additional examples of rounding to determine the class width:

$\dfrac{H - L}{K}$	Rounded Value (the CW)
89.6	100
1.38	1.5
48.2	50
12.4	10

Now let us use the 50 salaries in Table 2.1 to construct a frequency distribution of the salaries, using six classes. Our first step should be to arrange the data from smallest to largest. This arrangement is called an **ordered array.** Both the original data and the ordered data are *raw data,* since they are not grouped into classes. The ordered salaries are listed in Table 2.3. Using the ordered data, $H = 43.8$ and $L = 32.8$. Since $K = 6$, we compute CW:

$$\frac{43.8 - 32.8}{6} = 1.83$$

The best choice for CW is CW = 2.

There are two rules to remember in selecting the first class: this class must contain L, your lowest data value, and it should begin with a value that makes the frequency distribution easy to interpret. Because $L = 32.8$, our first class should begin with 32, that is, \$32,000. The resulting frequency distribution is shown in Table 2.4, which also shows each **relative frequency,** where

$$\text{relative frequency} = \frac{\text{frequency}}{\text{total number of values in data set}}$$

TABLE

2.3

Fifty starting salaries for business majors at Bellaire College, presented as original data and as an ordered array.

Raw Data					Ordered Array				
41.5	39.4	40.9	35.9	37.4	32.8	33.8	34.3	34.8	35.0
39.5	40.3	39.3	41.6	36.6	35.2	35.6	35.7	35.7	35.7
41.1	35.7	43.7	37.0	41.3	35.9	36.2	36.2	36.3	36.5
40.6	38.0	42.4	35.7	41.4	36.6	36.8	36.8	37.0	37.0
39.2	36.8	39.3	43.8	38.5	37.2	37.4	37.8	37.9	38.0
43.0	36.3	35.6	36.2	38.1	38.1	38.1	38.2	38.5	38.7
34.8	38.1	35.7	36.5	39.5	38.8	39.2	39.3	39.3	39.4
37.9	34.3	36.8	33.8	35.0	39.5	39.5	39.7	40.3	40.6
37.8	38.7	37.2	32.8	38.2	40.9	41.1	41.3	41.4	41.5
37.0	39.7	38.8	35.2	36.2	41.6	42.4	43.0	43.7	43.8

TABLE

2.4

Frequency distribution of starting salaries using six classes. This format is used for *continuous* data.

Class Number	Class	Frequency	Relative Frequency
1	32 and under 34	2	.04
2	34 and under 36	9	.18
3	36 and under 38	13	.26
4	38 and under 40	14	.28
5	40 and under 42	8	.16
6	42 and under 44	4	.08
		50	1.00

For example, in class 2 the relative frequency is .18; this class contains 9 of the 50 values. The advantage of using relative frequencies is that the reader can tell immediately what percentage of the data values lies in each class.

Comments

Often a set of data contains one or two very small or very large numbers quite unlike the remaining data values. Such values are called **outliers.** It is generally better to include these values in one or two **open-ended classes.** The distribution in Table 2.2 contains two open-ended classes: class 1 (under 10,000) and class 10 (50,000 and over). *You may need an open-ended class if your data set includes one or more outliers or your current frequency distribution has too many empty classes on the low or high end.*

Another alternative for the salary data is to use CW = 1, to provide more detail in the frequency distribution. This would produce 12 classes, as shown in Table 2.5. We could argue that 12 classes are too many, considering that the data set has only 50 values. Many classes contain only one or two data values. Another alternative would be to use open-ended classes on each end of the distribution, such as "under 34" and "42 and over."

The highest and lowest values describing a class are the **class limits.** For example, in Table 2.4, the lower class limit of class 2 is 34, and the upper class limit is 36. The **class midpoints** are those values in the center of the class.* Each midpoint, in a sense, *represents* its class. These values often are used in a statistical graph, as well as for calculations performed on the information contained within a frequency distribution. The midpoint of class 2 in Table 2.4 is $(34 + 36)/2 = 35$.

*Class midpoints are often referred to as *class marks.*

TABLE

2.5

Frequency
distribution of
starting salaries
using CW = 1.

Class Number	Class	Frequency	Relative Frequency
1	32 and under 33	1	.02
2	33 and under 34	1	.02
3	34 and under 35	2	.04
4	35 and under 36	7	.14
5	36 and under 37	7	.14
6	37 and under 38	6	.12
7	38 and under 39	7	.14
8	39 and under 40	7	.14
9	40 and under 41	3	.06
10	41 and under 42	5	.10
11	42 and under 43	1	.02
12	43 and under 44	3	.06
		50	1.00

CONSTRUCTING A FREQUENCY DISTRIBUTION

1. Gather the sample data.
2. Arrange the data in an ordered array.
3. Select the number of classes to be used.
4. Determine the class width.
5. Determine the class limits for each class; begin by assigning to the first class a lower class limit that will make the frequency distribution easy to interpret.
6. Count the number of data values in each class (the class frequencies).
7. Summarize the class frequencies in a frequency distribution table.

Frequency Distribution for Discrete Data

When your data are discrete, the procedure is almost the same as when they are continuous, except (1) we define the class width CW to be the difference between the lower class limits and not the difference between an upper and lower limit (this also will work for continuous data) and (2) the description of each class is slightly different because we no longer use the "and under" definition of each class. Thus, if CW = 5, and *the data are continuous,* our classes might be 5 and under 10, 10 and under 15, and 15 and under 20. *If the data are discrete,* they might be 5 to 9, 10 to 14, and 15 to 19. Note that for the continuous data, the class midpoints are 7.5, 12.5, and 17.5. For the discrete data, however, the midpoints are 7, 12, and 17.

Using the data in Table 2.1, we can construct a frequency distribution using six classes for the number of campus interviews for each student. First we develop an ordered array:

4	5	5	5	5	5	5	6	6	7	7
7	7	7	8	8	8	8	9	10	10	11
11	11	12	12	12	13	13	14	14	14	14
15	15	16	16	16	16	16	17	19	19	19
19	20	20	21	21	21					

So, $H = 21$ and $L = 4$. Since

$$\frac{H - L}{K} = \frac{21 - 4}{6} = 2.83$$

we use CW = 3. The resulting frequency and relative frequency distributions are shown in Table 2.6.

Class Number	Class	Frequency	Relative Frequency
1	4–6	9	.18
2	7–9	10	.20
3	10–12	8	.16
4	13–15	8	.16
5	16–18	6	.12
6	19–21	9	.18
		50	1.00

TABLE

2.6

Frequency distribution of the number of interviews. This format is used for discrete data.

X Exercises 2.1–2.7

Understanding the Mechanics

2.1 The following frequency table indicates the number of individuals with a minimum balance in their checkbook at a local bank.

Minimum Balance in Dollars	Frequency
0 and under 1,000	1,200
1,000 and under 2,000	1,500
2,000 and under 3,000	2,500
3,000 and under 4,000	2,300
4,000 and under 5,000	500
5,000 and under 6,000	50
6,000 and under 7,000	10
7,000 and under 8,000	2

a. What is the class width?
b. What are the class limits?
c. Calculate the group relative frequencies of each group.

2.2 The number of times that 36 employees used the World Wide Web during the course of their business day are as follows:

```
11   9  12   7   1  17   8  14  18   1  13  11
16  11   6  13  16   7  11  12   2  12  13  17
15   8  23   6  18  24   4  21  11  12  22   6
```

a. Convert the original data into an ordered array.
b. What number of classes would you use?
c. Are the data discrete or continuous?
d. Construct a frequency distribution.
e. What is the shape of the frequency distribution?

2.3 A random sample of two-bedroom condominium apartments at Vera Beach, Florida, revealed that the asking price of units on the market varied from $111,000 to $224,000. A frequency distribution of the asking price of the condominiums is needed.

a. Set up class limits if 5 classes are desired.
b. Set up class limits if 6 classes are desired.
c. Set up class limits if 12 classes are desired.

Applying the New Concepts

2.4 The percentage of increase in the property tax of 26 randomly selected homes in a certain subdivision of Memphis, Tennessee, are as follows.

```
5.10    7.35   13.34   18.19    9.12
9.89   10.45   12.89   17.91     .51
3.42    8.34   11.12   14.51    7.25
12.35   11.89   14.10   29.1    14.91
11.89   17.89   15.30   26.1    19.80
18.45
```

a. Construct a relative frequency distribution with six classes.
b. From the relative frequency distribution, determine what proportion of homes had an increase of more than 15% in property tax.
c. What interpretation can you give to the shape of the distribution?

2.5 The U.S. Office of Employment Projections conducted a population survey to determine the characteristics about the work force. In its survey, a tabulation was performed to state the number of multiple job holders (in thousands) and their respective weekly earnings. The results are presented below.

Weekly Earnings	Number of Multiple Job Holders
$0 and under $211	1,462
$211 and under $334	1,295
$334 and under $493	1,354
$493 and under $730	1,297
$730 and higher	1,288

a. What do you achieve by tabulating the data in the form of a frequency distribution?
b. Form a relative frequency distribution.
c. What proportion of the multiple job holders were making $493 or more per week?

Using the Computer

2.6 [DATA SET EX2-6] *Variable Description:*

Country: Twenty-six industrialized nations

WirelessConnections: Number of wireless connections per 100 people

The wireless revolution has made voice service more affordable and convenient than traditional telephone service for people in many countries. Companies selling wireless phones believe that the potential for mobile phone sales worldwide is phenomenal. The number of wireless connections per 100 people across 26 industrialized nations reveals the potential for wireless sales.

a. Display the number of wireless connections per 100 people for the 26 countries using a relative frequency histogram with nine classes. Describe its shape.

b. Suppose that countries having less than 60 wireless connections per 100 people are considered to have the most potential for future growth in wireless phone sales. What percent of the countries have less than 60 wireless connections per 100 people?

c. Is it easier to make conclusions about the shape of the distribution of data using the raw data or a histogram? Comment.

(Source: "Wireless World," *Dallas Morning News,* June 23, 2001, p. 1F.)

2.7 [DATA SET EX2-7] *Variable Description:*

Company: A company in the portfolio of the Money Index of Stocks

PE: Price-to-earnings ratio

Money magazine tracks the performance of its Money Index of Stocks. In addition to the performance of the stocks in this index, *Money* also keeps track of the price-to-earnings (PE) ratios. By definition, a PE ratio is simply the price of the common stock divided by its earnings per share. Investors use this measure as one gauge of risk. For example, a company with disappointing sales and a PE greater than 100 may experience a substantial downturn because of the high expectations for that stock.

a. Display the data using a frequency histogram. Use a class width of 5 and let 15 be the lower endpoint of the first class.

b. Repeat part a, but use a class width of 7. How has the shape of the histogram changed?

c. What do you hope to accomplish by displaying the data in the form of a histogram?

(Source: "Tyco Sizzles, Enron Fizzles," *Money,* July 2001, p. 30.)

2.2   HISTOGRAMS AND STEM-AND-LEAF DIAGRAMS

Histograms

After you complete a frequency distribution, your next step will be to construct a "picture" of these data values using a histogram. A **histogram** is a graphical representation of a frequency distribution. It describes the shape of the data. You can use it to answer quickly such questions as, are the data symmetric? and where do most of the data values lie? For the frequency distribution in Table 2.4, the corresponding histogram is illustrated in Figure 2.1. The height of each bar represents the frequency of that particular class, and the bars must be adjoining (no gaps).

Avoid constructing a "squashed" histogram by using the vertical axis wisely. The top of this axis (15 in Figure 2.1) should be a value close to your largest class frequency (14). Notice also that, for this example, you obtain a more concise picture by starting the horizontal axis at 32 rather than at zero and putting a scale break ($\sqrt{}$) before the 32 mark.

A histogram can be constructed using the relative frequencies rather than the frequencies. A *relative frequency histogram* of the salary distribution in Table 2.4 is shown in Figure 2.2. Notice that the shape of a frequency histogram (Figure 2.1) and its corresponding relative frequency histogram (Figure 2.2) are the same. One advantage of using a relative frequency histogram is that the units on the vertical axis are always between zero and one, so the reader can tell at a glance what percentage of the data lies in each class.

Most standard statistical packages will construct a histogram from your data. Using the Excel macro provided with this textbook,* or using MINITAB, you can

---

*An Excel macro is a set of instructions that greatly simplifies an Excel graph or statistical procedure. These macros will be invisible to you but are available whenever you click on KPK Data Analysis in the menu bar at the top of your Excel screen.

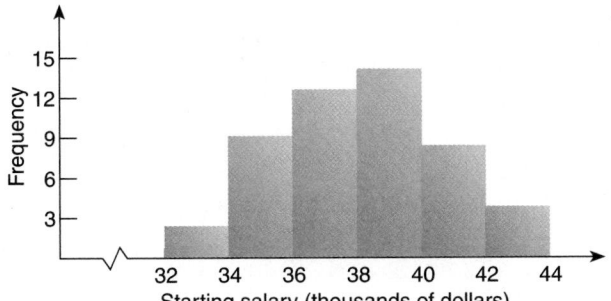

FIGURE

2.1

Frequency histogram for the frequency distribution shown in Table 2.4. Twenty-seven (out of 50) salaries were between $36,000 and $40,000, with 12 people receiving $40,000 or more.

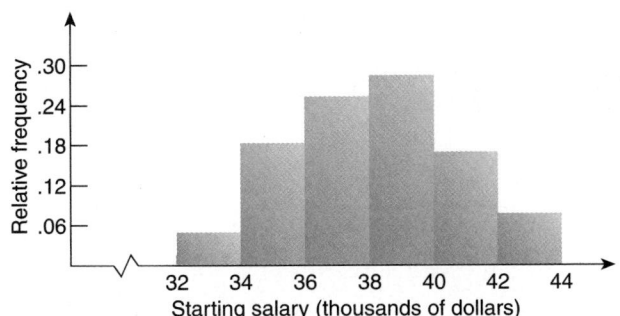

FIGURE

2.2

Relative frequency histogram for the frequency distribution in Table 2.4. This histogram shows that 54% (26% plus 28%) of the salaries were between $36,000 and $40,000. 24% (16% plus 8%) of the people received $40,000 or more.

control the number of classes and the class width in your histogram. Constructing a MINITAB histogram is discussed in the end-of-chapter appendix. We will illustrate the Excel procedure using the salary data in Table 2.3. The data must first be entered into column A of your Excel spreadsheet. The first 13 values (out of 50) are shown in Figure 2.4. To use the Excel macro provided with this textbook, click on **KPK Data Analysis ➤ Quantitative Data Charts/Tables ➤ Histogram/Freq. Charts.** You will then see the input form shown in Figure 2.3. Fill in the input range (A1:A50—that is, cells A1 through A50) and the output range (B1—this is the upper-left cell of the output section). Also click on the checkbox alongside Frequencies in the **Table** section and **Frequency Histogram** in the **Chart Output Options** section and finally click on **OK.** The result of this is the frequency distribution in Figure 2.4 and the histogram in Figure 2.5, obtained by clicking on the **Frequency Histogram** tab at the bottom of your spreadsheet. To obtain the histogram in Figure 2.1, refer to Figure 2.3 and click on **Number of Classes** (enter "6") and **Class Width** (enter "2"), followed by **OK.** You should now see the frequency distribution shown in Figure 2.6, and the histogram will be an Excel version of the histogram in Figure 2.1.*

When constructing a histogram for discrete data, the boxes should be constructed so there are no gaps between them. This can best be accomplished by extending each upper and lower class limit to a value midway between this limit and the adjoining limit (in a sense, *stretching* each class). For example, a histogram

---

*The Excel frequency distribution and histogram provided by the KPK Data Analysis procedure attempts to derive an easy-to-interpret table and graph, as stressed in the chapter discussion. As a result, a lot of rounding to "nice numbers" takes place, and the final frequency distribution and histogram may contain slightly more (or less) classes than you specified. If you specified a class width, it will not be changed.

FIGURE

2.3

Input form for the Excel KPK Data Analysis macro. Click on **KPK Data Analysis ➤ Quantitative Data Charts/Tables ➤ Histogram/Freq. Charts.**

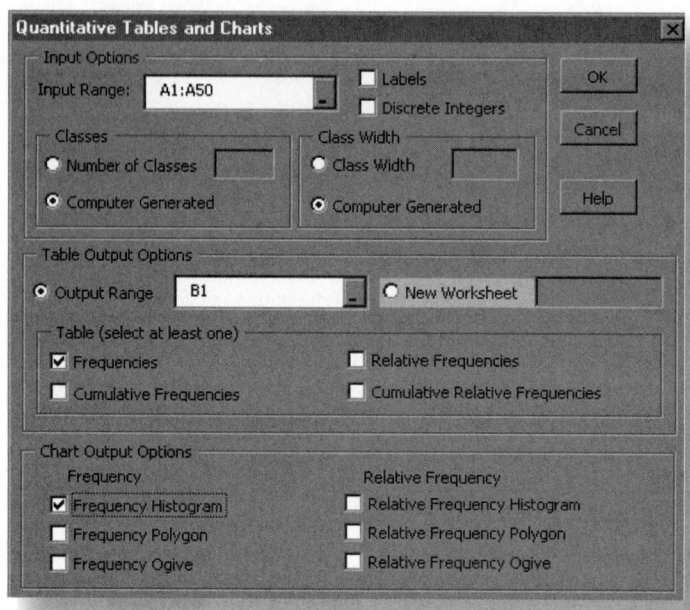

FIGURE

2.4

Excel spreadsheet created by KPK Data Analysis procedure.

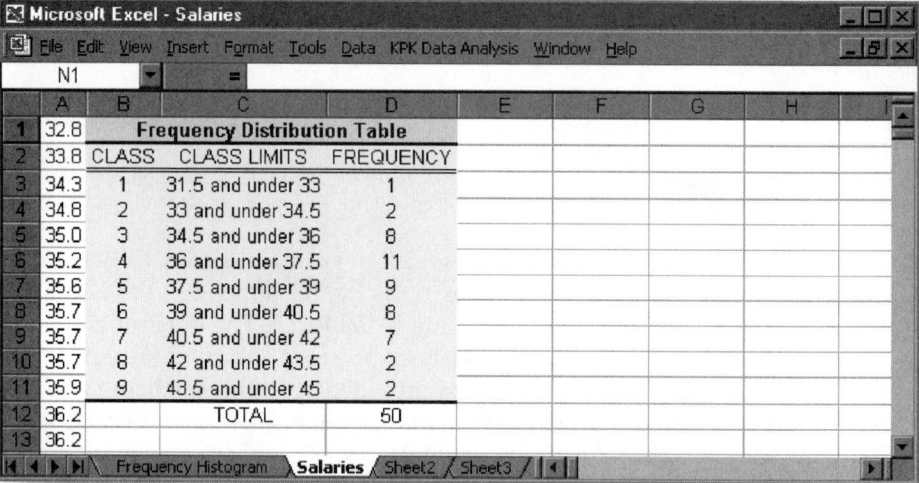

of Table 2.6 will contain a bar between 3.5 and 6.5 (height of 9), the next bar between 6.5 and 9.5 (height of 10), and so forth. The final bar (height of 9) will extend from 18.5 to 21.5. In this way, the histogram takes on the appearance of a continuous-data histogram, with no space between successive boxes. This is illustrated in Figure 2.7.

Stem-and-Leaf Diagrams

Stem-and-leaf diagrams were originally developed by John Tukey (pronounced Too'key) of Princeton University. They are extremely useful in summarizing reasonably sized data sets (under 150 values as a general rule) and, unlike histograms, result in no loss of information. By this we mean that it is possible to retrieve the original data set from a stem-and-leaf diagram, which is not the case

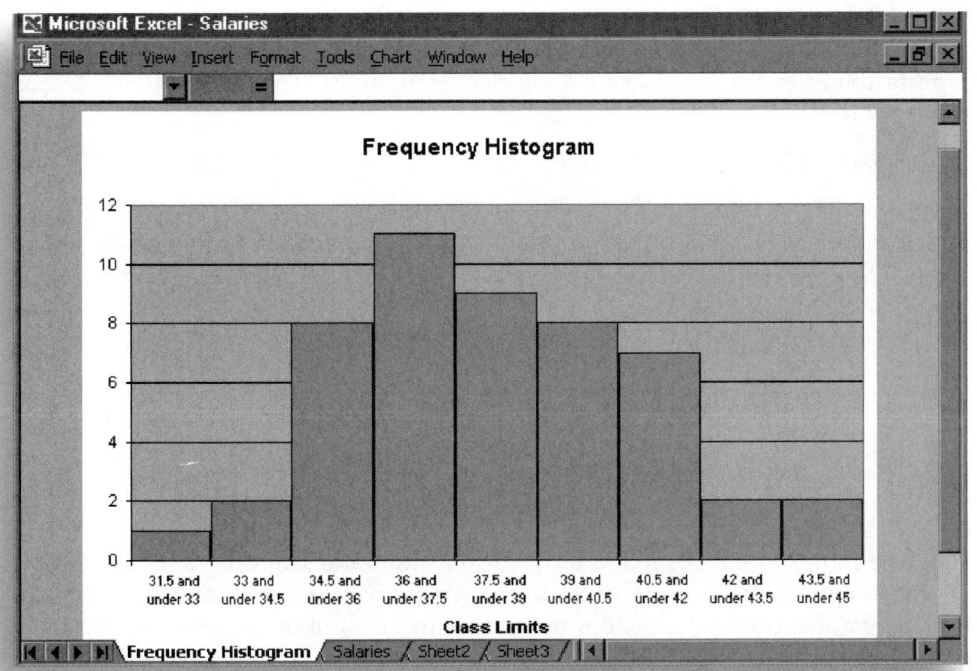

FIGURE

2.5

Histogram created by KPK Data Analysis (frequency distribution in Figure 2.4).

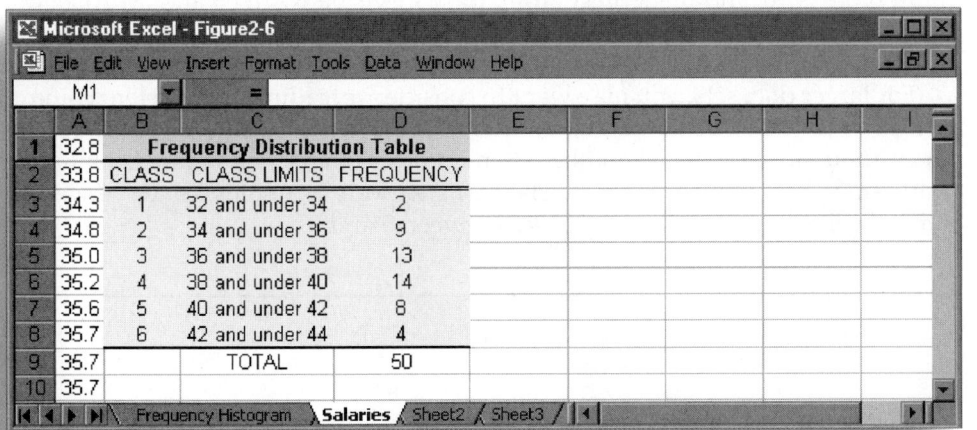

FIGURE

2.6

Excel spreadsheet created by KPK Data Analysis procedure where number of classes is 6 and class width is 2 (refer to Figure 2.3).

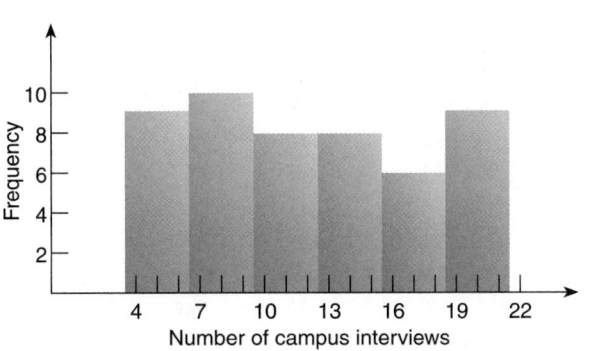

FIGURE

2.7

Histogram for discrete data from Table 2.6.

when using a histogram—some of the information in the original data is lost when a histogram is constructed. Nevertheless, histograms provide the best alternative when attempting to summarize a large set of sample data.

To illustrate the construction of a stem-and-leaf diagram, suppose that a study reports the after-tax profits of 12 selected companies. The profits (recorded as cents per dollar of revenue) are as follows:

$$3.4 \quad 4.5 \quad 2.3 \quad 2.7 \quad 3.8 \quad 5.9 \quad 3.4 \quad 4.7 \quad 2.4 \quad 4.1 \quad 3.6 \quad 5.1$$

The stem-and-leaf diagram for these data is shown in Figure 2.8. Each observation is represented by a *stem* to the left of the vertical line and a *leaf* to the right of the vertical line. For example, the stems and leaves for the first and last observation would be:

Stem	Leaf (unit = .1)		Stem	Leaf (unit = .1)
3	4		5	1

In a stem-and-leaf diagram, the stems are put *in order* to the left of the vertical line. The leaf for each observation is generally the last digit (or possibly the last two digits) of the data value, with the stem consisting of the remaining first digits. The leaf values are generally arranged in ascending order. The value 562 could be represented as 5|62 or as 56|2 in a stem-and-leaf diagram, depending on the range of the sample data. If the diagram is rotated counterclockwise, it has the appearance of a histogram and clearly describes the shape of the sample data.

To illustrate this diagram, suppose that the personnel manager at Texas Industries has administered an aptitude test to 50 applicants. The ordered data are shown in Table 2.7; the corresponding stem-and-leaf diagram is shown in Figure 2.9. From this diagram we observe that the minimum score is 22, the maximum score is 96, and the largest group of scores is between 60 and 69. Also, the 5 leaves in stem row 3 indicate that 5 people scored at least 30 but less than 40. The 3 leaves in stem row 9 tell us at a glance that 3 people scored 90 or better.

For larger data sets, you may want to consider spreading out the stem column by repeating the stem value two or three times. To illustrate, the same 50 test scores are used to construct another stem-and-leaf diagram in Figure 2.10, where each stem value is repeated twice. The first stem value contains leaves between 0 and 4, the second stem contains leaves between 5 and 9.

FIGURE 2.8

Stem-and-leaf diagram for after-tax profits.

Stem	Leaf (unit = .1)
2	3 4 7
3	4 4 6 8
4	1 5 7
5	1 9

TABLE 2.7

Ordered array of aptitude test scores for 50 applicants.

22	44	56	68	78
25	44	57	68	78
28	46	59	69	80
31	48	60	71	82
34	49	61	72	83
35	51	63	72	85
39	53	63	74	88
39	53	63	75	90
40	55	65	75	92
42	55	66	76	96

Although there is no built-in Excel procedure to construct a stem-and-leaf diagram, you can use the stem-and-leaf macro contained under **KPK Data Analysis** to construct such a graph. To illustrate this procedure, first enter the 50 values from Table 2.7 into column A (refer to Figure 2.11). Next, click on **KPK Data Analysis ➤ Quantitative Data Charts/Tables ➤ Stem and Leaf Plot** and enter A1:A50 as the input range and B1 as the output range. The resulting output in columns B, C, E, and F is shown in Figure 2.11. The stem-and-leaf plot in columns B and C is identical to the one in Figure 2.9, again illustrating that the largest group of scores is in the 60 to 69 range.

In many situations, the leaves in your diagram may consist of a *pair* of digits. In Figure 2.12, the tons of chemical produced by Sarhad Industries are illustrated for 20 randomly selected days. The amounts range from 521 pounds to 892 pounds.

Stem	Leaf (unit = 1)
2	2 5 8
3	1 4 5 9 9
4	0 2 4 4 6 8 9
5	1 3 3 5 5 6 7 9
6	0 1 3 3 3 5 6 8 8 9
7	1 2 2 4 5 5 6 8 8
8	0 2 3 5 8
9	0 2 6

FIGURE 2.9

Stem-and-leaf diagram for aptitude test scores.

Stem	Leaf (unit = 1)
2	2
2	5 8
3	1 4
3	5 9 9
4	0 2 4 4
4	6 8 9
5	1 3 3
5	5 5 6 7 9
6	0 1 3 3 3
6	5 6 8 8 9
7	1 2 2 4
7	5 5 6 8 8
8	0 2 3
8	5 8
9	0 2
9	6

FIGURE 2.10

Stem-and-leaf diagram for aptitude test scores using repeated stems.

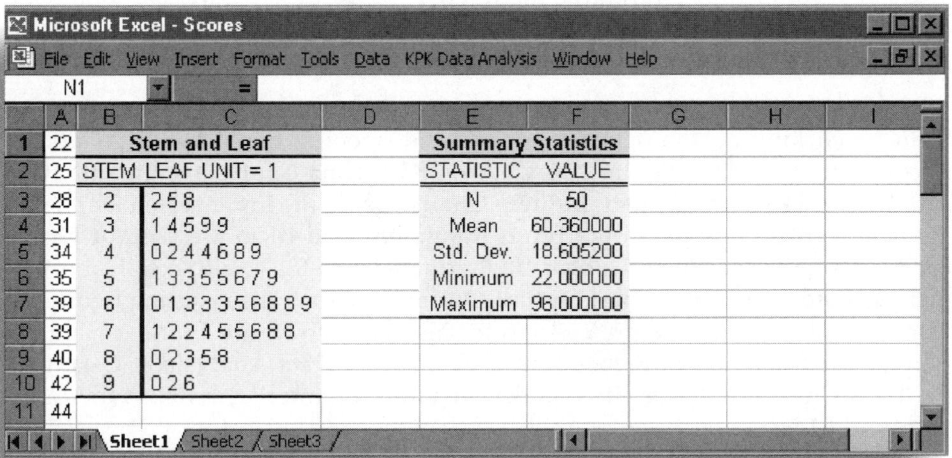

FIGURE 2.11

Excel spreadsheet obtained using **KPK Data Analysis ➤ Quantitative Data Charts/Tables ➤ Stem and Leaf Plot.**

FIGURE

2.12

Stem-and-leaf
diagram for
production
amounts
(leaf unit = 1).

Stem	Leaf (unit = 1)						
5	21	36	50	72			
6	33	47	55	62	71		
7	11	21	31	40	57	62	83
8	16	35	44	92			

FIGURE

2.13

Stem-and-leaf
diagram for
production
amounts
(leaf unit = 10).

Stem	Leaf (unit = 10)						
5	2	3	5	7			
6	3	4	5	6	7		
7	1	2	3	4	5	6	8
8	1	3	4	9			

Here each stem consists of a single digit and each leaf represents the last two digits of the production amount. An alternative would be to use a single digit in each leaf by dropping the right-hand digit in each data value. The leaf unit would then be 10 pounds; the resulting stem-and-leaf diagram is shown in Figure 2.13. Notice that we cannot *exactly* reproduce the sample from this diagram. To illustrate, the first value in this figure is $52 \times 10 = 520$, which means that the actual value is between 520 and 529.

Microsoft® Excel Application Use DATA2-1

EXAMPLE 2.1

Using Excel to Construct a Histogram and a Stem-and-Leaf Diagram

In a production process, certain requirements referred to as *specification limits* are often imposed on the product. For example, the inside diameter of a certain machined part must be between 10.1 millimeters and 10.3 millimeters. The value 10.1 is the lower specification (spec) limit, and 10.3 is the upper spec limit. These spec limits can be written as $10.2 \pm .1$ millimeters. Any part with an inside diameter outside these limits is called *nonconforming* and is considered unacceptable.

By gathering a sample and constructing a histogram and stem-and-leaf diagram, production personnel can learn a great deal about a process, in particular, whether the process is capable of meeting these specifications. The Boston plant of Allied Manufacturing produces these parts. As an Allied employee, you have obtained a sample of 100 machine part diameters, contained in column A. What can you conclude about this production process?

Solution   Begin by clicking on the open icon ( ) and opening file **DATA2-1.** The first 16 values can be seen in Figure 2.14. Click on **KPK Data Analysis ➤ Quantitative Data Charts/Tables ➤ Histogram/Freq. Charts.** Using the input screen (shown in Figure 2.3) enter A1:A100 in the **Input Range** box and B1 in the **Output Range** box. Click on the checkboxes alongside **Frequencies** in the **Table** section and **Frequency Histogram** in the **Chart Output Options** section. The resulting frequency distribution is shown in Figure 2.14 and the histogram in Figure 2.15. To obtain the stem-and-leaf diagram in Figure 2.14, click on **KPK Data Analysis ➤ Quantitative Data Charts/Tables ➤ Stem and Leaf Plot** and enter A1:A100 as the input range and E1 as the output range.

Since any part with a diameter over 10.3 is nonconforming, both the histogram and the stem-and-leaf diagram make it clear that the process is struggling

FIGURE

2.14

Excel frequency distribution and stem-and-leaf diagram for Example 2.1.

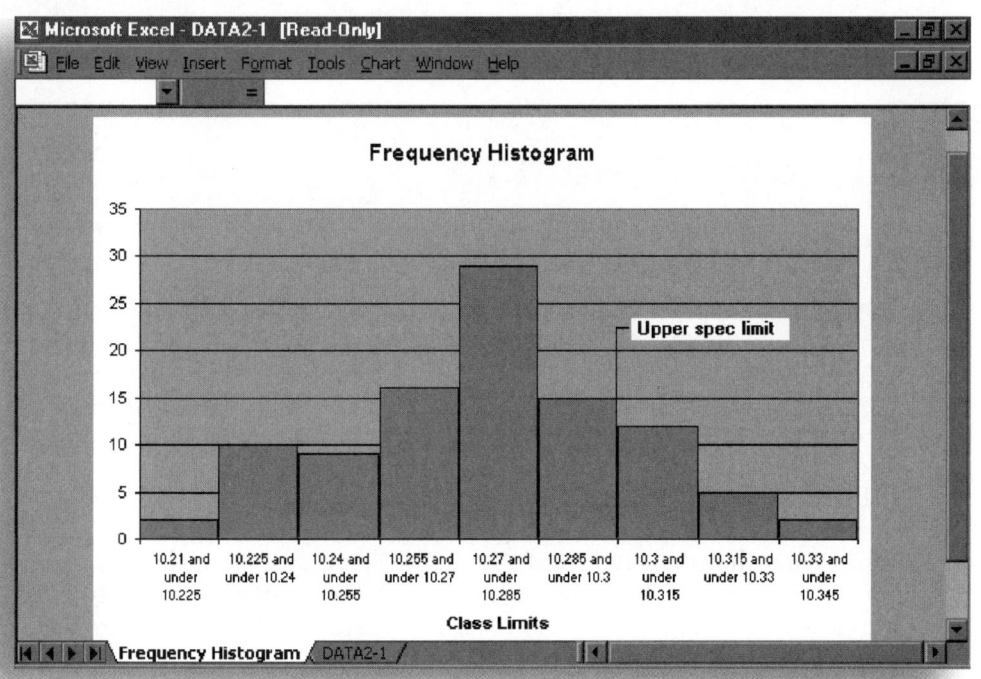

	A	B	C	D	E	F
1	10.22	**Frequency Distribution Table**				**Stem and Leaf**
2	10.22	CLASS	CLASS LIMITS	FREQUENCY	STEM LEAF	UNIT = 0.001
3	10.23	1	10.21 and under 10.225	2	1021	6
4	10.23	2	10.225 and under 10.24	10	1022	1 6 8
5	10.23	3	10.24 and under 10.255	9	1023	0 0 1 1 4 7 9 9
6	10.23	4	10.255 and under 10.27	16	1024	0 0 4 5 9
7	10.23	5	10.27 and under 10.285	29	1025	2 3 4 4 5 5 6 7 8 9
8	10.23	6	10.285 and under 10.3	15	1026	0 2 4 4 6 6 7 7 9 9
9	10.23	7	10.3 and under 10.315	12	1027	0 0 1 1 1 1 1 2 4 4 4 6 6 7 7 8 8 9 9 9
10	10.24	8	10.315 and under 10.33	5	1028	0 0 1 1 1 2 3 4 5 6 9
11	10.24	9	10.33 and under 10.345	2	1029	0 0 1 1 1 3 3 3 3 4 6 8
12	10.24		TOTAL	100	1030	0 0 1 4 9
13	10.24				1031	0 1 1 1 2 2 4 5 5 8
14	10.24				1032	6 8
15	10.24				1033	3 8
16	10.25					

FIGURE

2.15

Excel histogram of 100 inside diameters (Example 2.1).

to meet specifications and is shifted too far to the right. The stem-and-leaf diagram is especially useful here since you actually are able to see the 17 values (underlined) that are exceeding the upper spec limit—not possible using a histogram, where the data are condensed into classes.

A suggestion would be for Allied to try shifting the process to the left by whatever means are available, such as making a machine adjustment or changing raw material. With such a change, the process will be more capable of meeting the required specifications.

Histograms and stem-and-leaf diagrams are simple yet powerful tools for analyzing and improving product quality. (Additional graphical and measurement techniques will be discussed in Chapter 12, "Quality Improvement.")

FIGURE

2.16

Excel frequency polygon using KPK Data Analysis and Table 2.4. Twenty-seven (out of 50) salaries are between $36,000 and $40,000, with 12 people receiving $40,000 or more.

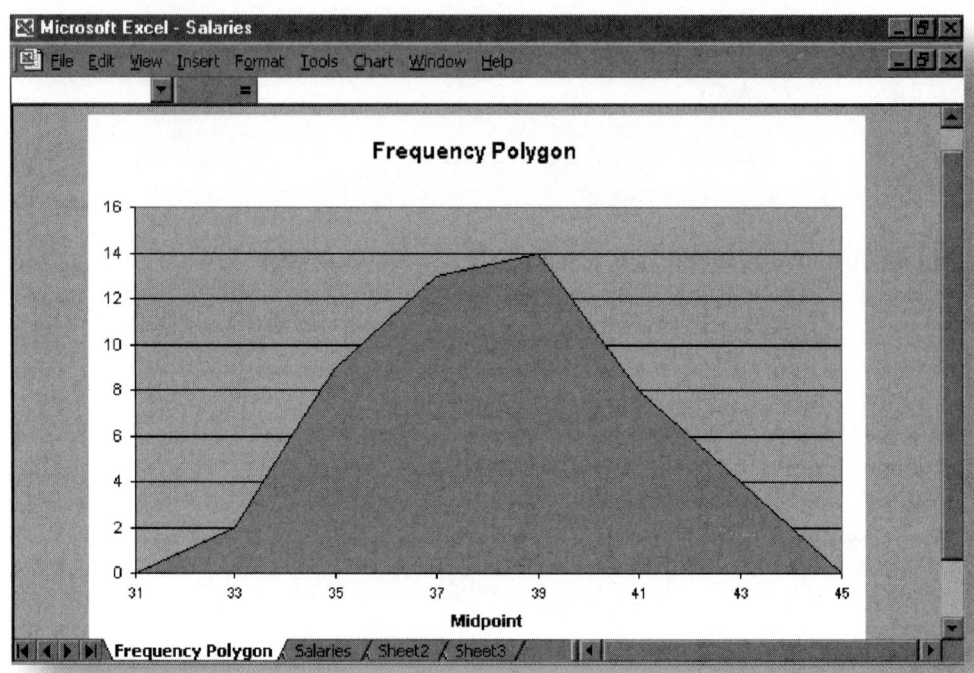

2.3   FREQUENCY POLYGONS

Although a histogram does demonstrate the shape of the data, perhaps the shape can be more clearly illustrated by using a **frequency polygon.** Here, you merely connect the centers of the tops of the histogram bars (located at the class midpoints) with a series of straight lines. The resulting multisided figure is a frequency polygon. Figure 2.16 is an example that uses the frequency distribution of salaries in Table 2.4.

To obtain the Excel-generated frequency polygon in Figure 2.16, begin by entering the 50 salaries into column A of the spreadsheet. Next, click on **KPK Data Analysis ➤ Quantitative Data Charts/Tables ➤ Histogram/Freq. Charts.** Fill in the input screen as shown in Figure 2.3, except set the number of classes equal to 6 and the class width equal to 2 in the **Classes** section. Finally, click on the checkbox alongside **Frequency Polygon.**

Comments

The polygon can also be constructed from the relative frequency histogram. The shape will not change, but the units on the vertical axis will now represent relative frequencies. The polygon must begin and end at zero frequency (as in Figure 2.16). To accomplish this, imagine a class at each end of the corresponding histogram that is empty (contains no data values). Begin and end the polygon with the class midpoints of these imaginary classes. Thus, your vertical axis *must* begin at zero. This need not be true for the horizontal axis.

How do you handle an open-ended class? The easiest way is to construct a frequency polygon of the closed classes and place a footnote at each open-ended class location indicating the frequency of that particular class. Figure 2.17 demonstrates this, using the city size data from Table 2.2.

Frequency polygons are usually better than histograms for comparing the shape of two (or more) different frequency distributions. For example, Figure 2.18 demonstrates at a glance that salaries at Texcom Electronics are higher (for the most part) for management personnel who have a college degree.

FIGURE
2.17

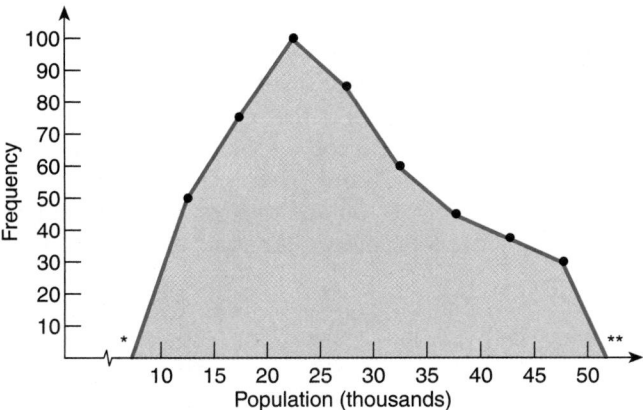

* 4 cities had populations of less than 10,000.
** 5 cities had populations of 50,000 or greater.

FIGURE
2.18

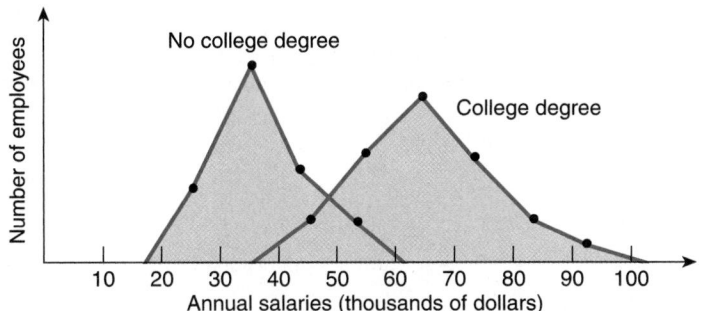

Both histograms and frequency polygons represent the actual number of data values in each class. Suppose that your annual salary is one of the values contained in a sample of 250 salaries. One question of interest might be, what fraction of the people in the sample have a salary *less than* mine? Such information can be displayed using a statistical graph called an *ogive.*

2.4

CUMULATIVE FREQUENCIES (OGIVES)

Another method of examining a frequency distribution is to list the number of observations (data values) that are *less than* each of the class limits rather than how many are *in* each of the classes. You are then determining **cumulative frequencies.** Table 2.8 shows the cumulative frequencies for the frequency distribution in Table 2.4. Notice that you can determine cumulative frequencies (column 4) or cumulative relative frequencies (column 6). The results in Table 2.8 can be summarized more easily in a simple graph called an **ogive** (pronounced oh'-jive). The ogive is useful whenever you want to determine what percentage of your data lies *below* a certain value. Figure 2.19 is constructed by noting that

2 values (2/50 = .04) are less than $34,000

2 + 9 = 11 values (11/50 = .22) are less than $36,000

11 + 13 = 24 values (24/50 = .48) are less than $38,000, and so on.

The ogive allows you to make such statements as, "Twenty-two percent of the salaries were less than $36,000," and, "Fifty percent of the salaries were under $38,100."

You always begin at the lower limit of the first class (32 here). The cumulative relative frequency at that point is always 0, because the number of data values less than this number is 0. You always end at the upper limit of the last class (44 here). The cumulative relative frequency at the upper limit is always 1, because all the data values are less than this upper limit. This ogive value would be n = the number of data values ($n = 50$ here) if you are constructing a frequency ogive rather than a relative frequency ogive. *However, the shape of the ogive is the same for both procedures.*

TABLE 2.8

Summary of starting salaries from Table 2.3, including the cumulative frequencies and cumulative relative frequencies

Class Number	Class	Frequency	Cumulative Frequency	Relative Frequency	Cumulative Relative Frequency
1	32 and under 34	2	2	.04	.04
2	34 and under 36	9	11	.18	.22
3	36 and under 38	13	24	.26	.48
4	38 and under 40	14	38	.28	.76
5	40 and under 42	8	46	.16	.92
6	42 and under 44	4	50	.08	1.00
		50		1.00	

FIGURE 2.19

Excel ogive (cumulative relative frequencies) using KPK Data Analysis and Table 2.8. One half of the graduates received a salary less than $38,100; 22% of the salaries were less than $36,000.

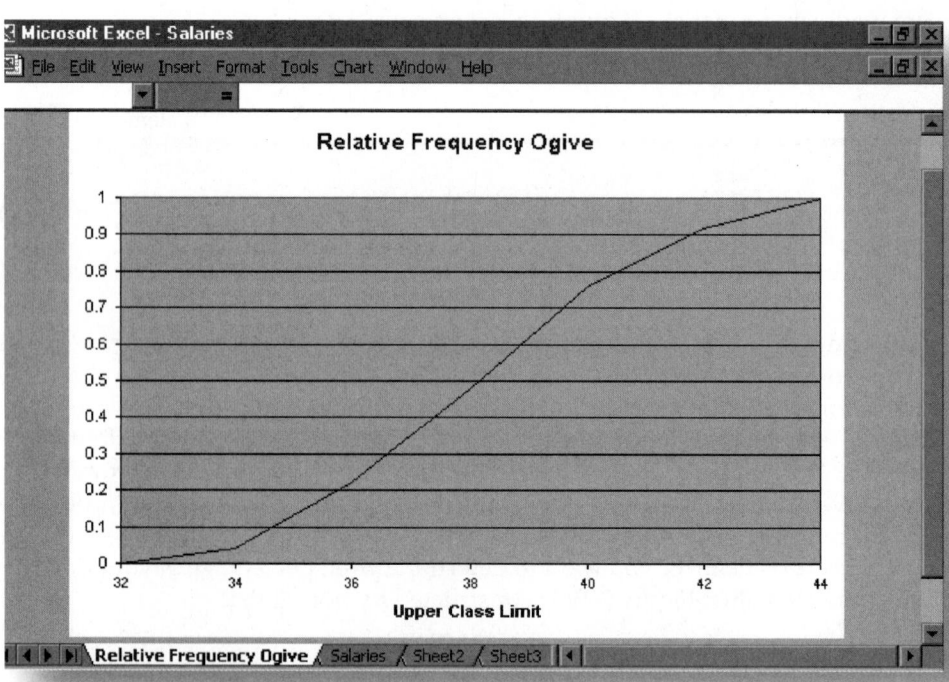

To obtain the Excel generated ogive in Figure 2.19, begin by entering the 50 salaries into column A of the spreadsheet. Next, click on **KPK Data Analysis ➤ Quantitative Data Charts/Tables ➤ Histogram/Freq. Charts.** Fill in the input screen as shown in Figure 2.3, except set the number of classes equal to 6 and the class width equal to 2 in the **Classes** section. Finally, click on the checkbox alongside **Relative Frequency Ogive.**

X Exercises 2.8–2.26

Understanding the Mechanics

2.8 The distribution of the salaries of 100 employees at a small consulting firm are as follows.

Salary	Number of Employees
$30,000 and under $40,000	10
$40,000 and under $50,000	25
$50,000 and under $60,000	30
$60,000 and under $70,000	20
$70,000 and under $80,000	15

  a. Construct a relative frequency distribution.
  b. Construct a relative frequency histogram.
  c. Construct a relative frequency polygon.
  d. Construct a cumulative relative frequency distribution.
  e. Construct a relative frequency ogive.

2.9 The number of vacant seats on a sample of 40 flights is as follows.

Number of Vacant Seats	Number of Flights with Vacant Seats
0–4	15
5–9	10
10–14	8
15–19	5
20–24	2

  a. Construct a frequency histogram.
  b. Describe the shape of the histogram.
  c. Construct a cumulative frequency distribution.
  d. Construct a frequency polygon.
  e. Construct an ogive.

2.10 The monthly repair costs for videocassette recorders (VCR) returned within the past 3 years for malfunction problems are as follows, in dollars.

73.20	99.60	72.80	102.97	87.45	92.45
89.75	63.70	112.60	68.40	96.75	68.70
80.57	93.80	115.90	89.98	77.93	82.50
84.67	99.75	103.65	63.71	74.39	110.90
69.45	88.70	107.40	86.90	82.25	74.80
88.69	113.30	67.50	87.50	92.57	94.45

  a. Convert the data into an ordered array using six classes.
  b. Construct a relative frequency distribution. Start the first class at $60.00.
  c. Construct a relative frequency histogram.
  d. Construct a cumulative frequency distribution.
  e. Draw a stem-and-leaf diagram.

2.11 The response times to emergency maintenance problems at an assembly plant for 27 randomly selected emergency calls are as follows, in hours.

1.21	1.87	2.35	4.16	1.50	1.30	2.78	3.71	2.80
1.80	2.60	3.30	4.30	3.10	1.80	3.07	2.19	1.67
2.89	4.25	1.10	2.25	3.94	4.22	1.73	2.54	3.27

  a. Arrange the observations in increasing order of magnitude.
  b. Present the data in the form of a frequency distribution. Use seven classes.
  c. Construct a cumulative frequency distribution.
  d. Construct an ogive.
  e. Draw a stem-and-leaf diagram.

2.12 Construct the cumulative frequency distribution for the frequency distribution in Exercise 2.1. Draw the corresponding ogive.

2.13 Construct a frequency histogram and a frequency polygon for the number of times that employees accessed the World Wide Web in Exercise 2.2. Describe the shape of the two charts.

2.14 Bonuses for 40 mid-level managers at a manufacturing plant are as follows, in units of $1,000.

4.5	4.8	5.3	5.9	4.6	4.8	4.9	5.2	4.1	5.8
4.6	4.9	5.1	5.3	3.8	3.9	2.8	6.4	4.7	7.1
7.8	7.3	2.9	3.2	4.9	5.2	4.5	6.2	5.7	4.3

  a. List the stem possibilities.
  b. Form a stem-and-leaf display.
  c. Comment on the shape of the distribution of the data.

Applying the New Concepts

2.15 The price of an alternator for a Buick LeSabre was priced at various auto parts outlet stores throughout the Dallas and Ft. Worth Metroplex. The resulting prices are as follows, in dollars.

95	86	89	105	89	99	78	110	113	87
77	96	115	103	86	95	94	106	99	99
83	76	99	94	102	99	104	93	101	94

Use a stem-and-leaf diagram to describe the distribution of the data. What is the most commonly quoted price?

2.16 A quality-control engineer has been gathering a sample of cylinders that have completed the manufacturing process. The cylinders must be manufactured such that the inside diameter is between 10.6 centimeters and 11.0 centimeters. These two limits are called the specification limits. Any cylinder with an inside diameter outside of these limits is called nonconforming and is considered a defective cylinder.

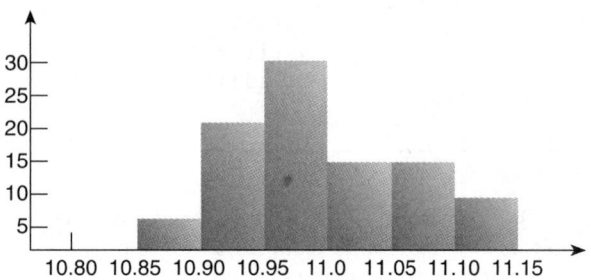

The engineer can make a machine adjustment to shift the process to the right or left. How far and in what direction should the process be shifted to minimize the number of nonconforming cylinders?

2.17 A county library's records show the following information regarding the number of patrons who used the library during the past 30 days.

100, 87, 44, 53, 17, 34, 88, 67, 31, 40, 98, 77, 55, 41, 73, 62, 88, 28, 70, 51, 82, 44, 32, 50, 33, 49, 59, 67, 79, 84

a. Construct a cumulative frequency distribution.

b. Convert the cumulative frequency distribution in part a into an ogive graph.

c. The number of patrons attending the library was less than what value 80% of the time?

2.18 The following is a frequency distribution of the number of daily automobile accidents reported for a month in Newark, New Jersey.

Accidents Per Day	Frequency
0–3	12
4–7	10
8–11	7
12–15	1
16–19	1

a. Construct a cumulative relative frequency distribution for the data.

b. What percentage of the time do eight or more daily accidents occur?

c. Construct a cumulative frequency distribution for the data.

d. Compare the shape of the distributions in parts a and c.

2.19 The number of Web users for March 1998 are listed below for 20 Web search engines. Frequencies are listed in millions of users.

Search Engine	Number of Users
altavista.digital.com	7.5
amazon.com	4.9
angelfire.com	4.5
aol.com	17.7

Search Engine	Number of Users
cnn.com	4.2
hotmail.com	6.6
infoseek.com	13.5
lycos.com	11.5
microsoft.com	17.9
msn.com	8.7
netscape.com	23.4
real.com	5.2
webcrawler.com	6.3
yahoo.com	31.8
zdnet.com	6.4

a. Construct a frequency histogram.

b. Draw a stem-and-leaf diagram.

c. What can you say about the frequency with which a search engine is used?

(Source: "Top Web Domains for March," *USA Today,* April 15, 1998, p. 5D.)

2.20 Wildfires in the western United States have been a continual threat to burgeoning populations who want to live in the woods. Each year, the U.S. Department of the Interior assesses the vulnerability of regions of the country to forest fires and requests funding from Congress to respond to the fire season. The number of areas burned by forest fires yearly is difficult to predict. The following data list the total area burned yearly between 1980 and 2000.

Year	Acres Burned (in Millions)	Year	Acres Burned (in Millions)
1980	5.3	1990	5.5
1981	4.9	1991	2.2
1982	2.5	1992	2.5
1983	5.1	1993	2.3
1984	2.4	1994	4.8
1985	4.5	1995	2.4
1986	3.3	1996	6.8
1987	4.2	1997	3.5
1988	7.4	1998	2.2
1989	4.2	1999	5.0
		2000	8.4

a. Construct a stem-and-leaf diagram of the yearly number of acres burned. Are there any unusually large figures in this data set?

b. Construct a cumulative relative frequency distribution using a class width of 1. What percent of the years had less than 5 million burned acres of forest?

(Source: "Risks for Fire Overgrown in West," *USA Today,* August 1, 2001, p. 3A.)

2.21 Loudspeaker measurements published by many manufacturers and magazines have led audiophiles to lose faith in what they have to reveal about "audible accuracy." Consumer reports selected 23 bookshelf speakers and rated the accuracy with no adjustment of bass or treble controls. These ratings are presented below. No loudspeaker received a perfect score (reflected by a value of 100), but only a few loudspeakers received scores below 80.

83	79	86	86	87	83	84	79	76	82	76	88
76	81	90	87	85	90	85	88	86	89	89	

a. Construct a relative frequency polygon. Describe the shape of the distribution.

b. Construct a relative frequency ogive. Describe the percentage of the loudspeakers that you would consider to have an acceptable score in your judgment.

(Source: "Loudspeaker Ratings," *Consumer Reports*, August 2001, p. 36.)

2.22 A survey of households in a certain metropolitan district revealed the number of consumers that have purchased camping equipment and also the number that have purchased exercise equipment. The following table displays the age groups and number of consumers purchasing these products.

Age Group (in Years)	Camping Equipment	Exercise Equipment
15 and under 20	37	4
20 and under 25	30	10
25 and under 30	29	12
30 and under 35	20	13
35 and under 40	19	20
40 and under 45	20	24
45 and under 50	22	21
50 and under 55	12	30
55 and under 60	8	28
60 and under 65	6	31
65 and under 70	5	35

a. Construct a relative frequency distribution for the consumers purchasing camping equipment.

b. Construct a relative frequency distribution for the consumers purchasing exercise equipment.

c. Comment on the differences in the relative frequency distributions in parts a and b.

2.23 Metro Power manufactures a high-powered copper coil to be used in giant power transformers. Tensile strength (given in thousands of pounds per square inch) is of critical importance in the manufacture of the copper coil. The following data are from a sample of copper coils tested for tensile strength:

5, 8, 12, 10, 15, 18, 21, 24, 7, 26, 7, 18, 10, 6, 4, 11, 15, 9, 22, 10

a. Construct an ogive.

b. Find an appropriate value, X, in units of pounds per square inch, such that more than one-half of the coils sampled have tensile strengths greater than X.

Using the Computer

2.24 [DATA SET EX2-24] *Variable description:*

PhoneTime: Total daily times spent on the telephone by an employee (in hours).

The manager of a marketing firm wished to determine the distribution of the total daily time that the firm's 50 employees spend on the telephone. Data were collected for a randomly selected day.

a. Use the command **KPK ➤ Quantitative ➤ Histogram** to construct a histogram of the data.

b. Select a class width of 1 hour. What happens to the shape of the frequency distribution?

2.25 [DATA SET EX2-25] *Variable Description:*

YearMonth: Year and month that electricity consumption is recorded

ElectricConsump: California's Monthly Electricity Consumption (in millions of MWh)

California lawmakers are assessing whether to expand restraints on the wholesale price of electricity in the state. Currently, controls become effective when California's energy reserves slip below 7% of demand. For lawmakers to decide how frequently controls should go into effect, consumption data are studied to determine the distribution of usage.

a. Using a relative frequency ploygon, describe the distribution of consumption for the data from years 1998 and 1999. Use a class width of two.

b. Repeat part a for the years 1998 to 2001 and compare the shapes of both distributions. Can you conclude that the distribution of usage has shifted during the 1998 to 2001 period?

(Source: "White House Looks Isolated in Its Opposition to Energy Price Caps," *Wall Street Journal*, June 14, 2001, p. A22.)

2.26 [DATA SET EX2-26] *Variable Description:*

HourlyComp91-95: Quarterly percent increases in hourly wage compensation from 1991 through 1995.

HourlyComp96-00: Quarterly percent increases in hourly wage compensation from 1996 through 2000.

Quarterly increases in wage compensation have varied according to the economic climate. The 1990s have seen an upward trend in productivity. During this period, quarterly increases in hourly wages nationwide have varied approximately between 2% and 5%. This decade has seen exceptional economic performance with low inflation.

a. Compare the distribution of quarterly percent increases for the time period 1991 to 1995 and 1996 to 2000 by forming two histograms (if using the KPK macros, click on the Stacked Histogram option).

b. Construct two separate relative frequency polygons for the time periods in part a. Use a class width of one. Do you prefer the relative frequency polygons or the histograms to represent the distribution of the data?

c. Construct an ogive using the combined data from 1991 through 2000. How would you interpret this graph?

(Source: "Fed's Meyer Warns of Inflation, Joblessness," *Wall Street Journal*, June 7, 2001, p. A2.)

2.5

BAR CHARTS

Histograms, frequency polygons, and ogives are used for data having an interval or ratio level of measurement. For data having a *nominal* level, we use a **bar chart.** For situations producing a sample of *ordinal* level data with a reasonable set of possible values (such as 1 = strongly agree, 2 = agree, . . . , 5 = strongly disagree), a bar chart can be used to summarize the sample. A bar chart is similar to a histogram, in that the height of each bar is proportional to the frequency of that class. Such a graph is most helpful when you have many categories to represent.

Consider the data in Table 2.1. If you are interested in the number of business graduates in each of the three disciplines (accounting, information systems, and marketing), a bar chart will do a good job of summarizing this information (Figure 2.20). Notice that a gap is inserted between each of the bars in a bar chart. The data here are nominal, so the length of this gap is arbitrary.

Figure 2.21 is an example of a bar chart in which the bars are constructed horizontally rather than vertically. This form enables you to label each category *within* the bar.

FIGURE

2.20

Bar chart showing the number of this year's graduating business majors at Bellaire College in each of the three disciplines. Twenty-six were accounting majors; the smallest group consisted of the information systems majors (20%).

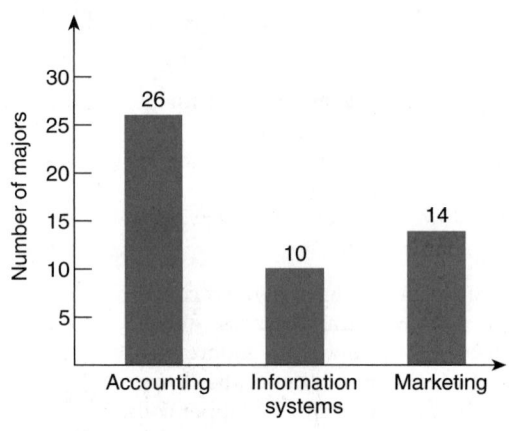

FIGURE

2.21

Bar chart drawn horizontally; note that it is easy to place labels within the boxes.

Q. If the price of natural gas goes down by 25% in the next few years, would you and your family use more or less?

A.

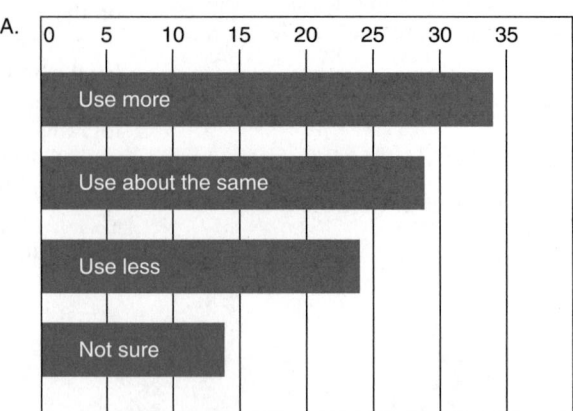

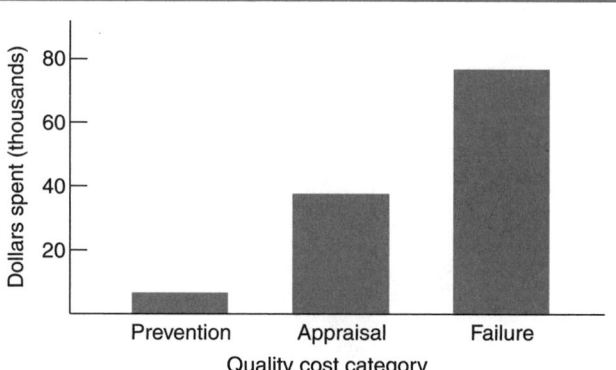

FIGURE

2.22

Bar chart of quality costs for Microtech (Example 2.2).

EXAMPLE
2.2

The head of Quality Assurance at Microtech (a fictional company) has categorized company costs related to quality improvement into three categories: prevention, appraisal, and failure. These three costs for the past fiscal year were:

$$\text{Prevention costs: } \$ 3,600$$
$$\text{Appraisal costs: } \$38,400$$
$$\text{Failure costs: } \$78,000$$

She wants to demonstrate at a glance the small amount spent on prevention measures and the large amount spent on failure costs (largely due to warranty claims but also due to having to rework defective components). Construct a bar chart to illustrate this information.

Solution

The bar chart consists of three boxes (bars), where the height of each box represents the dollar amount for that category. It is shown in Figure 2.22. This bar chart is a rather dramatic illustration that many more dollars are being spent in the failure cost category than in the other two categories—in particular, for prevention costs. Such a chart can have a tremendous impact in a business presentation.

2.6 PIE CHARTS

An alternative to the bar chart for nominal or ordinal data is the **pie chart.** This graph is used to split a particular quantity into its component pieces, typically at some specified point in time or over a specified time span. It is a convenient way of representing percentages or relative frequencies (rather than frequencies). Figure 2.23 shows a pie chart of the major discipline for the 50 graduates in Table 2.1. To construct a pie chart, draw a line from the center of the circle to the outer edge. Then construct the various pieces of the pie chart by drawing the corresponding angles. For example, the accounting majors represent 52% of the total number of business graduates (26 out of 50), so angle A in Figure 2.23 is 52% of 360°, or 187.2°. Angle B is 20% of 360°, or 72°, and angle C represents the remaining portion.

FIGURE

2.23

Pie chart showing the percentage of this year's graduating business majors at Bellaire College in each of the three disciplines. Fifty-two percent were accounting majors, with the smallest percentage being the information systems majors (20%).

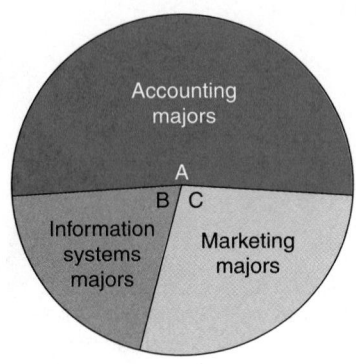

Microsoft® Excel Application Use DATA2-3

EXAMPLE

2.3

Using Excel to Construct a Bar Chart and Pie Chart

The manager of Freedman Furniture Store has compiled a list of the types of written customer complaints during the past three months. The complaints have been categorized as follows:

Type	Coded Value
Error in billing	1
Rudeness by store personnel	2
Late delivery	3
Question not answered during telephone inquiry	4
Other	5

The total complaints for the three months is 75 and the coded values (1s, 2s, . . . , 5s) are contained in a column in DATA2-3. Using Excel, construct the corresponding bar chart and pie chart and discuss the results.

Solution

Click on the **Open** icon ( ) and open the file **DATA2-3.** You should see 75 integers, 1 through 5. You can see the first 8 values in column A of Figure 2.24. Next, click on **KPK Data Analysis ➤ Qualitative Data Charts ➤ Bar Chart.** For the input range enter A1:A75, and for the output range enter B1. You should then see the bar chart table in Figure 2.24 (columns B and C) and the bar chart in Figure 2.25. Repeat this sequence and use **Pie Chart** in place of **Bar Chart,** entering D1 for the output range. This produces the pie chart table in Figure 2.24 (columns D and E) and the corresponding pie chart in Figure 2.25. To make the output easier to interpret, replace the integers 1 through 5 using the labels "Billing," "Rudeness," "Late," "Not Answered," and "Other" in cells B3 through B7 and cells D3 through D7 as shown in Figure 2.24. By doing this, you also change the labels on the graphs to the ones shown in Figure 2.25.*

Both charts make it very clear that the bulk of the customer complaints during this three-month period (42 out of 75) are related to billing errors, with rudeness by store personnel a distant second (14 out of 45). The quality of service at Freedman would be greatly improved if the billing department would make a serious effort to eliminate the billing errors.

---

*When you clicked on **KPK Data Analysis ➤ Qualitative Data Charts,** you might have noticed another option called Pareto Chart. This particular graph modifies the bar chart to distinguish the few important categories (one, in this example) from the categories with low relative frequencies. This chart will be illustrated in the exercises at the end of this section.

FIGURE

2.24

Excel spreadsheet
after running **KPK
Data Analysis ➤
Qualitative Data
Charts ➤ Bar Chart
and Pie Chart.**

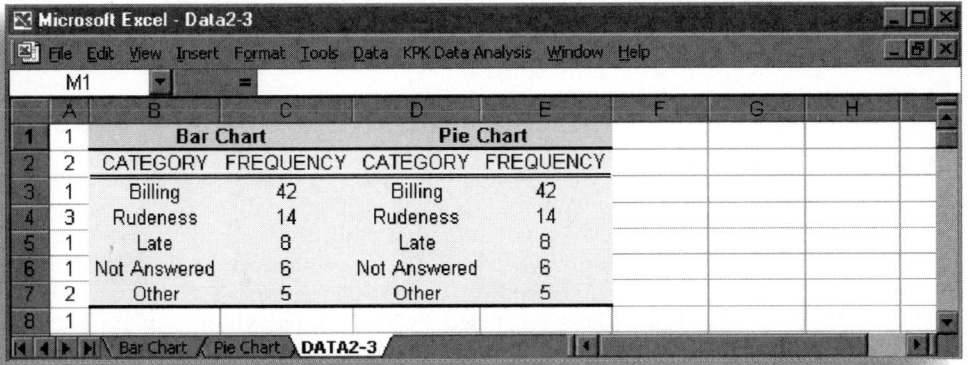

FIGURE

2.25

Excel bar chart and
pie chart created
by KPK Data
Analysis
(Example 2.3).

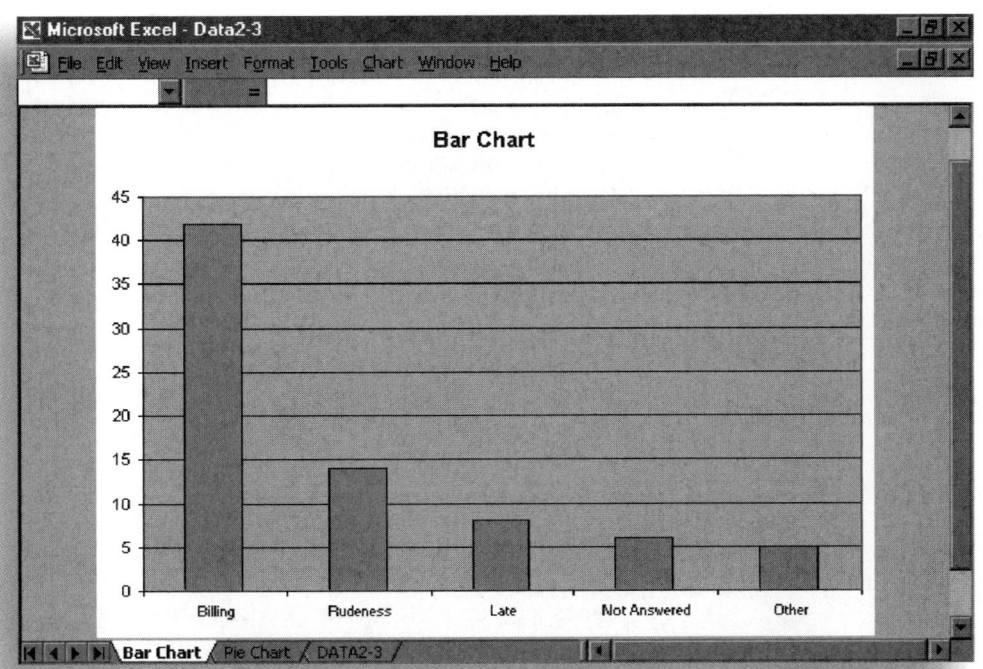

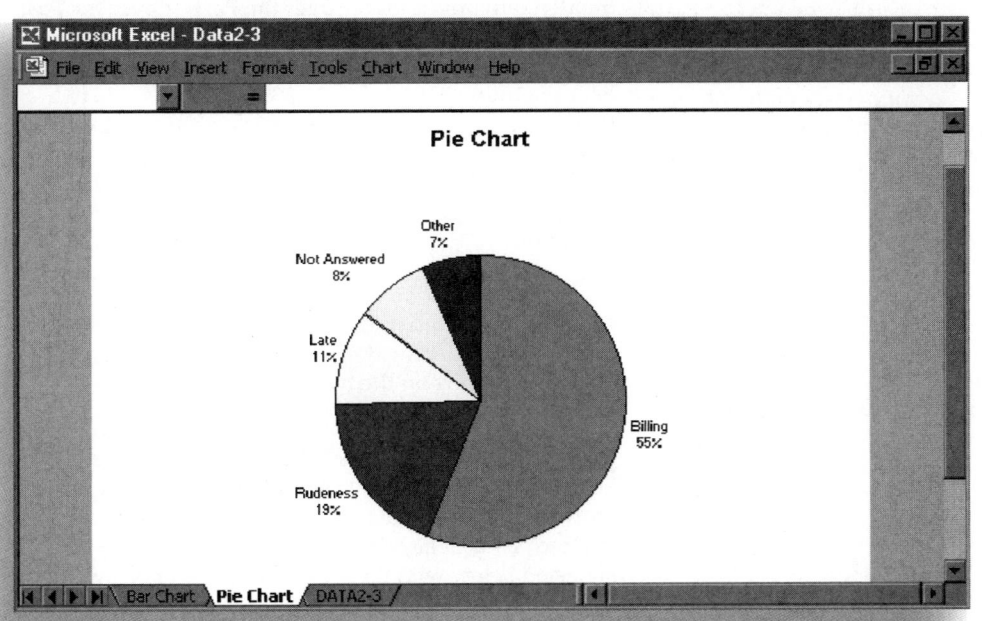

Exercises 2.27–2.50

Understanding the Mechanics

2.27 The ratings of a conference speaker were marked E (excellent), G (good), F (fair), or P (poor). Construct a bar chart and a pie chart to represent the following ratings provided by the audience.

E E F E G P G E G F P E G G F G
G G E P F G G G E G G G E G G

2.28 An electronics firm has the following percentages of its employees with different educational backgrounds. Construct a pie chart to display the data.

Highest Educational Degree	Percentage of Employees
High school degree	5
Associate degree	20
College degree	50
Masters degree	15
Doctorate degree	10

2.29 A survey of 200 households revealed the following results on how residential homeowners feel about a proposed increase in property tax.

Category	Number of Households
Strongly Agree	23
Agree	30
Neutral	10
Disagree	90
Strongly Disagree	27
Not Sure	20

a. Draw a bar graph.
b. Change the numbers to relative percentages and construct a bar graph.
c. Draw a pie chart.

Applying the New Concepts

2.30 The following sport-utility vehicles (SUVs) are listed in rank order according to their performance rating by *Consumer Reports* on handling and driving tests. Construct relative frequency distributions with a class width of 5,000 and a class width of 3,000 to display the distribution of the costs of top ranked SUVs. Which class width do you think should be used to display these prices? Why?

Vehicle	Price
Acura MDX	39,450
Lexus RX300	42,961
Mercedes-Benz ML320	40,270
Ford Explorer XLT	32,600
Nissan Pathfinder LE	34,724
Jeep Grand Cherokee LTD V8	37,950
Toyota 4Runner SR5	33,395
GMC Envoy SLE	33,320
Dodge Durango SLT Plus	34,745
Land Rover Discovery	40,395
Jeep Grand Cherokee Laredo	33,030

(Source: "Luxury-brand SUVs Top List," *USA Today*, August 8, 2001, p. 6B.)

2.31 Office investment sales brokers bring together investors and investment opportunities in office real estate. These brokers provide counseling to all parties in an investment interchange involving office space. Their careful market and financial analysis and negotiations help lead to successful purchasing decisions of office space. The following office investment sales brokers are listed by total dollar volume of transactions during the year 2000.

Broker	Total Amount in Millions of Dollars Transacted
Cushman & Wakefield, Inc.	931.0
CBRichard Ellis	741.5
Insignia/ESG	735.4
Eastdil Realty Company	671.3
NewMark & Company Real Estate, Inc.	395.2
Eastern Consolidated Properties	281.8
Clarion Partners	210.0
Kennedy-Wilson Properties, Ltd.	207.5
Helmsley-Spear, Inc.	174.1
Murray Hill Properties/TCN	59.5

a. Summarize the data in the form of a pie chart.
b. Omit the companies Cushman & Wakefield, Inc and CBRichard Ellis and construct a pie chart.
c. Describe how your findings change from part a to part b.

(Source: "Top 10 Office Investment Sales Brokers," *Wall Street Journal*, August 1, 2001, p. B7.)

2.32 Small-company stocks funds are prone to periodic bursts of hot performance. Consider the five small-company mutual funds and their performance, as listed below.

Small-Company Mutual Fund	Performance over the Past 12 Months	Performance over the Past 5 Years
Babson Enterprises II	31.8%	119%
Eclipse Equity	33.8%	131%
Fasciano	25.3%	133%
Gabelli Small Cap Growth	36.8%	123%
Nicholas Limited Edition	30.0%	119%

(Source: "Hot Small-Company Funds," *USA Today*, February 20, 1998, p. 4B.)

Construct a bar chart for the 12-month performance and another bar chart for the 5-year performance. Comment on the differences in the two charts.

2.33 Many developing countries receive loans or loan guarantees from the U.S. Export-Import Bank. These loans help some of these countries to have economies that are growing faster than that of the United States. Ten important recipients of large loans from the Export-Import Bank are listed below with their current amount borrowed.

Country	Amount (in Billions of Dollars)
Brazil	3.9
Russia	1.5
Indonesia	3.5
Argentina	2.3
Philippines	2.2
Turkey	2.0
Mexico	5.4
China	4.1
India	1.5

(Source: "U.S. Ex-Im Bank Is Beating the Drum in China," *Wall Street Journal,* June 20, 1997, p. A12.)

To analyze this data, a Pareto diagram is used. A Pareto diagram summarizes the findings of categorical responses so that the few important categories are distinguished from the numerous categories with low-relative frequencies. A Pareto diagram is a vertical bar chart with the categories placed in descending rank order of their bar heights. A cumulative graph is plotted with the bar chart. The scale on the right-hand side displays the cumulative percentages. The left-hand axis shows the amount of loans borrowed by a country. The 100% figure on the right-hand axis corresponds to the total amount of loans borrowed by all the countries.

a. What conclusions can be drawn from the Pareto diagram?

b. What information is available through a Pareto diagram that is not available from a bar chart or pie chart?

Pareto Chart

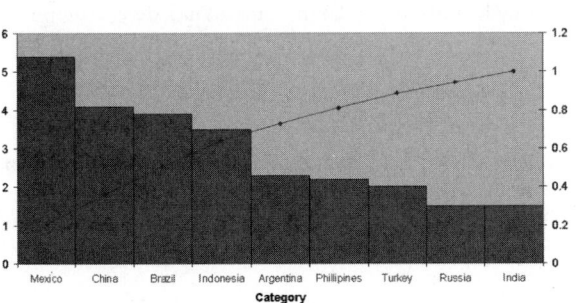

2.34 A senior manager at Four-Mile-Island Utility Company collected various complaints from customers during the past 6 months. The following table shows the types of complaints and the frequency of each.

Type of Complaint	Number of Customers with this Complaint
A. Customer's check was lost	10
B. Customer's bill was mailed late	80
C. The serviceman was rude to the customer	20
D. The meter was read incorrectly	60
E. The electric utility service was mistakenly disconnected	5
F. Other	25

a. Draw a Pareto diagram (see Exercise 2.33) to summarize the data.

b. Draw a pie diagram to summarize the data.

c. What course of action does the Pareto diagram suggest that the senior manager take?

2.35 A successful businessperson receives the following yearly incomes (in dollars) from seven business partnerships.

Business Partnership	Yearly Income
A	23,160
B	30,070
C	32,732
D	35,900
E	37,304
F	43,608
G	60,014
Total	262,788

Express the yearly incomes from each partnership as a percentage of the businessperson's total income, and summarize this information using a pie chart.

2.36 The Backstreet Boys were among the leaders of the wave of pop music boy bands that took America by storm. The popularity of bands is sometimes fickle in the world of pop music. *Airplay Monitor,* a trade publication, estimates the number of listeners who hear a given record. The following song titles by the Backstreet Boys illustrate that not all of their songs have made it to the top of the charts. However, the figures do reveal that a couple of their hits reached an audience of more than 70 million.

Backstreet Boys' Songs	Audience (in Millions)
"All I Have to Give"	38.5
"I Want It That Way"	80.4
"Larger Than Life"	43.7
"Show Me the Meaning of Being Lonely"	75.8
"The One"	35.3
"Shape of My Heart"	48.1
"The Call"	24.6
"More Than That"	33.7

a. Construct a Pareto diagram for the audience size for each song. What songs account for most of the audience listening?

b. Construct a pie chart to display the proportion of the audience size for each song. What conclusions can you make from viewing this chart that are similar to those revealed by the Pareto diagram?

(Source: "Charting the Teen-Pop Audience," *USA Today,* July 20, 2001, p. 1F.)

2.37 Consumer electronic companies are competing to become leaders in marketing home entertainment products. Many of these companies are counting on new life with the introduction of MP3 and DVD players, plasma screen, and high-definition televisions that are Web-ready. The following is a list of consumer electronic companies and their current share of that market.

Brand	Market Share
General Electric	4.6
Orion	3.9
Panasonic	6.4
Philips	11.0
RCA	12.5
Samsung	4.2
Sanyo	15.4

Brand	Market Share
Sharp	3.9
Sony	10.8
Zenith	4.2

a. Display these data using a bar chart. Is it obvious who the big four companies are in consumer electronics?

b. Use a pie chart to display the market share of the consumer electronic companies. Try both the regular pie chart and a three-dimensional pie chart. Which of the two pie charts do you prefer? Explain.

(Source: "Zenith Sees Its Future in Digital TV," *USA Today*, July 20, 2001, p. 7B.)

2.38 Cellphones are perhaps becoming a teen status symbol, the BMW roadster for the under-20 group. Cellphone makers and wireless companies are counting on the under-20 group to drive the growth in the cellphone market. By the year 2006, wireless companies are forecasting that 74% of the under-20 group will have cellphones, as compared to 22% in 1999. The following data illustrate the estimates of the percentage of the under-20 group that will own mobile phones and the estimates of the adult group that will own mobile phones.

Year	Under-20 (percent)	Adults (percent)
1999	22	32
2000	34	38
2001	42	42
2002	51	50
2003	56	53
2004	62	58
2005	68	61
2006	74	63

a. Construct two separate bar charts for the under-20 group and the adult group.

b. Construct a side-by-side single bar chart that has both groups adjacent to each other.

c. Do you prefer viewing the two separate bar charts or the single bar chart? Why?

(Source: "Should Kids Have Cellphones?" *Wall Street Journal*, September 10, 2001, p. R12.)

2.39 Recruiting online has allowed corporations to reach a larger segment of the population. Fortune 500 companies have been very successful at recruiting entry-level and staff-position online, but appear to have less success for higher than entry-level positions. From a survey involving 1,500 individuals recruited online by Fortune 500 companies, the percentages of individuals recruited online as executives, directors, managers, team leaders, entry-level individuals, and staff are 3%, 5%, 17%, 18%, 28%, and 29%, respectively. Suppose that in five years, survey analysts believe that the percentages will shift to 2%, 15%, 10%, 10%, 32%, and 31%, respectively. Construct two pie charts and discuss the shift in percentages based on the pie charts.

(Source: "Recruiting Online Triples," *USA Today*, August 7, 2001, p. 1B.)

2.40 A survey asking how satisfied Americans are with the economy yielded the following results. The cross-classification table presents the frequency of individuals belonging to an age category and a category representing the individual's response.

Survey Results on "Are you satisfied with the economy today?"

Age Group	Very Satisfied	Satisfied	Dissatisfied	Very Dissatisfied	Total
20 and under 30	50	75	20	10	155
30 and under 40	30	40	35	45	150
40 and under 50	20	22	50	34	126
over 50	5	30	65	35	135

a. Construct a bar chart for the age group categories.

b. Construct a bar chart for the four categories representing the responses to the question.

c. Construct a pie chart for the age group categories.

d. Construct a pie chart for the four categories representing the responses to the question.

e. What conclusions can you draw from the bar and pie charts?

2.41 To understand the preferences of its clients, a large brokerage firm surveyed 1,300 clients to determine the investment strategy with which their clients are most comfortable. The following cross-classification table reveals the results.

Survey Results on "What investment mix do you prefer?"

Current Salary	100% Bonds and 0% Stocks	70% Bonds and 30% Stocks	50% Bonds and 50% Stocks	30% Bonds and 70% Stocks	0% Bonds and 100% Stocks	Total
less than $40,000	20	140	130	35	25	350
at least $40,000 but less than $60,000	15	120	100	45	50	330
at least $60,000 but less than $80,000	10	40	55	95	115	315
at least $80,000	0	15	50	160	80	305

a. Construct a bar chart to display the investment preferences. How would you describe the investment preferences after viewing this chart?

b. Construct a bar chart to display the salary categories of the clients that were selected by the brokerage firm. How would you describe the differences in these categories?

c. Omit the category of clients who have a salary of at least $80,000 and repeat part a. How does the bar chart change?

2.42 Various occupational groups are employed by a textile apparel manufacturer. The following table lists the number of employees in each occupation for the years 1990 and 1993.

Occupation	1990	1993
Professional researchers	120	290
Managers	200	130
Technicians	530	740
Salespersons	210	220
Clerical workers	175	120
Unskilled workers	250	350

a. Construct a bar chart for each of the years 1990 and 1993.

b. Construct a pie chart for each of the years 1990 and 1993.

c. Explain what changes have occurred in the company from 1990 to 1993. Which chart do you think provides the easiest means of comparison?

2.43 BEA Systems is one of the world's leading e-business infrastructure software companies. This company paid for an advertisement in the *Wall Street Journal* showing that 80% of the Fortune 500 companies prefer BEA when it comes to e-business platforms. The advertisement used a three-dimensional pie chart to show that the remaining choices are IBM at 6% and "others" at 11%. Construct both a regular pie chart and a three-dimensional pie chart to display this information. Do you think that BEA's use of the three-dimensional chart was a good marketing strategy?

(Source: "The World's #1 E-business Software Platform," *Wall Street Journal,* July 19, 2001, p. B5.)

2.44 A mutual fund has its assets spread over seven sectors of the economy. The following data are the total value (in millions of dollars) of the stocks in which the fund is invested for each sector.

Stock	Value
Electronics and electrical equipment	2.116
Aerospace and defense	10.375
Food and beverage	4.864
Utilities	2.713
Insurance and finance	6.538
Health care	3.675
Oil and gas	1.532

a. Express the amount invested in each sector of the economy as a percent.

b. Summarize the list in a pie chart.

2.45 A survey of 12th graders across Europe and the United States was conducted to assess their mathematical and science aptitude. The results of the International Mathematical and Science Study (TIMSS) are presented below. A score of 500 is considered average.

Country	Score
Austria	519
Czech Republic	476
Denmark	528
France	505
Germany	496
Italy	475
Norway	536
Russian Federation	476
United States	471

(Source: "Global Report Card," *USA Today,* February 25, 1998, p. 2D.)

Present the data collected from TIMSS using a bar chart.

2.46 An independent oil firm recently hired 10 engineers, five geologists, three accountants, one statistician, four computer scientists, and one chemist. Present these data in the form of a pie chart.

2.47 The price for a one-day admission cost at Disney World is presented below for 1993 to 1998.

Year	Cost for an Adult	Cost for a Child
1993	34.00	27.00
1994	36.00	29.00
1995	37.00	30.00
1996	40.81	32.86
1997	42.14	33.92
1998	44.52	36.04

(Source: "The Price of Fun," *USA Today,* April 13, 1998, p. 8B.)

a. Draw a bar chart for an adult's cost.

b. Draw a bar chart for a child's cost.

c. Compare the two bar charts.

2.48 With airports becoming busier, the number of runway incidences has increased over the years. There are stories of how outbound jets have come within 100 feet of striking another plane. The Federal Aviation Administration (FAA) closely examines each incursion. Considering that there are more than 3,000 take-offs daily at many airports, the safety record is considered to be amazingly good. From 1997 through 2000, the following airports and their number of extremely close calls and number of overall incursions are listed.

Airport	Number of Extremely Close Calls	Total Number of Incursions
Dallas/Fort Worth	2	24
Chicago O'Hare	5	13
Los Angeles	5	34
Detroit	1	11
Atlanta	2	13
San Francisco	6	23
New York LaGuardia	3	11
Orlando International	0	2
Washington, D.C. Dulles	0	4
Seattle	1	7

a. Use a Pareto chart (see Exercise 2.33) to display the number of extremely close calls. What can you conclude from viewing this chart?

b. Use a Pareto chart to display the total number of incursions. What can you conclude about which airports the FAA should concentrate on in order to improve airport safety procedures?

(Source: "Runway Close Calls," *The Dallas Morning News,* June 21, 2001, p. 20A.)

2.49 A Pareto diagram (See Exercise 2.33) is useful for showing that only a few categories account for a large percentage of the observed frequencies. Consider the following data, illustrating a breakdown of all federal income taxes paid in 1995.

Income Level	Total Income	Percentage of All Federal Income Taxes Paid
Top 1 percent	Above $209,105 a year	30.2%
Top 5 percent	Above $96,104 a year	48.8%
Top 10 percent	Above $72,092 a year	60.5%
Bottom 50 percent	Below $22,361 a year	4.6%

(Source: "Who Pays What in Taxes?" *The Washington Times,* April 15, 1998, p. A10.)

Explain how income categories can be created so that a Pareto diagram would illustrate that only a few categories contribute to a very large percentage of all federal income taxes paid. The last category listed on the horizontal scale is sometimes listed as an "other" category even if its frequency is not the smallest (see Exercise 2.33).

Using the Computer

2.50 [DATA SET EX2-50] *Variable Description:*

Manufacturer: Automotive Company producing vehicles in Mexico

VehiclesProduced: Number of vehicles produced in year 2000 in Mexico

VehiclesExported: Number of vehicles exported from Mexico in year 2000

The cost of manufacturing vehicles in Mexico is very attractive to automakers. Global carmakers build approximately 1.9 million vehicles in Mexico. Of these, nearly 76% are exported, primarily to the United States. Although General Motors is the largest manufacturer of vehicles in Mexico, DaimlerChrysler exports the most vehicles. Automotive analysts examine both the number of vehicles produced and the number exported to determine the potential market share of each company.

a. For the data on vehicles produced in Mexico, construct a bar chart displaying the amount produced by each company.

b. Repeat part a using a pie chart.

c. Construct a bar chart displaying the number of vehicles exported from Mexico.

d. Repeat part d using a pie chart.

e. Do you prefer the bar charts or the pie charts for displaying the data? Explain.

f. What differences do the charts reveal for the automotive companies with respect to number of vehicles produced and number of vehicles exported?

(Source: "DaimlerChrysler Tops in Mexico Exports," *USA Today,* August 8, 2001, p. 2B.)

2.7   DECEPTIVE GRAPHS

You might be tempted to be creative in your graphical displays by using, for example, a three-dimensional figure. Such originality is commendable, but does your graph accurately represent the situation? Consider Figure 2.26, which someone drew in an attempt to demonstrate that there are twice as many men as women in management positions. The artist constructed a box for the category "men" twice as high—but also twice as deep—as that for the category "women." The result is a rectangular solid for men that is, in fact, four times the volume of the one for women. The illustration is misleading—it appears that there are four times as many men as women in management.

When data values correspond to specific time periods—such as monthly sales or annual expenditures—the resulting data collection is a **time series.** A time series is represented graphically by using the horizontal axis for the time increments. For example, Figure 2.27 contains a return-on-investment time series for two mutual funds, plotted over a six-year period. A glance at this figure might lead you to believe that mutual fund A is performing nearly twice as well as mutual fund B. A closer look, however, reveals that *the vertical axis does not start at zero;* such a construction can seriously distort the information contained in such a graph. The 2001 return for fund A appears to be roughly twice that for fund B. However, the actual returns are 15.8% for fund A and 14.5% for fund B. Granted, fund A is outperforming fund B, but not nearly as dramatically as Figure 2.27 seems to indicate. Also, fund B is not as "unstable" as Figure 2.27 would indicate, since the return only fluctuates between 14% and 15%.

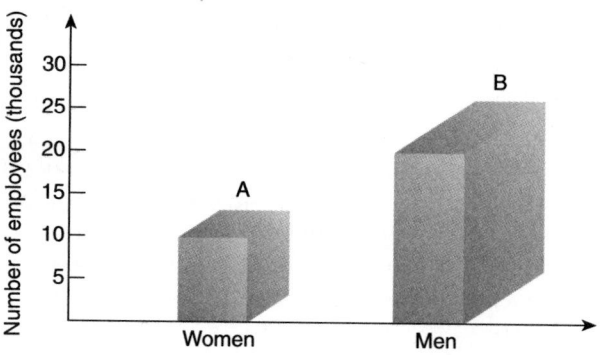

FIGURE

2.26

The illustrator wished to show that there are twice as many men as women in management positions. However, box B is twice the height *and* twice the depth of box A and thus is four times the volume.

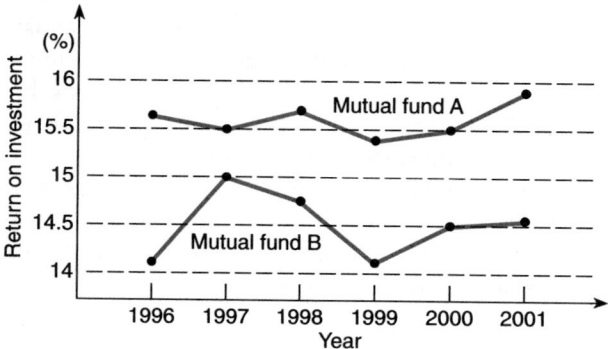

FIGURE

2.27

Time-series graph of the performance of two mutual funds. The graph is misleading because the vertical axis does not start at zero.

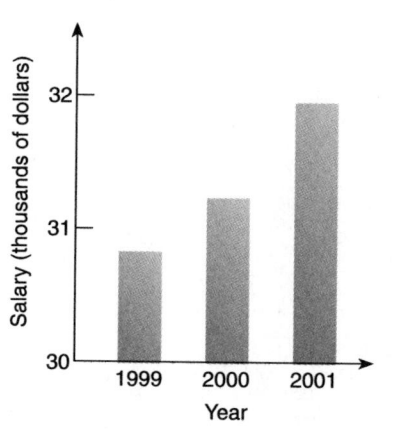
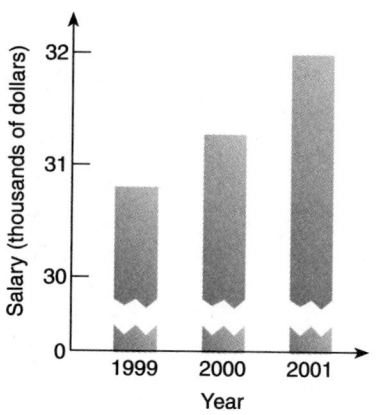

FIGURE

2.28

Two misleading bar charts. The vertical axis of the left-hand chart does not begin at zero, and the bars in the right-hand chart are chopped without a corresponding adjustment in the vertical axis.

Such examples, and many others, are contained in an entertaining and enlightening book by Darrell Huff titled *How to Lie with Statistics.** Other deceptive graphs described by Huff include bar charts similar to those in Figure 2.28. Here, you may be tempted to conclude that there is a significant difference in bar heights, either because the vertical axis does not begin at zero (left side) or because the bars are chopped in the middle without a corresponding adjustment of the vertical axis (right side). *As an observer, beware of such trickery. As an illustrator, do not intentionally mislead your reader by disguising the results through the use of a misleading graph.* This practice tends to give statisticians a bad name!

---

*Darrell Huff, *How to Lie with Statistics* (New York: Norton, 1954 [and 1993 by Darrell Huff with Irving Geis, illustrator]). Other discussions are included in *Statistics: Concepts and Controversies* by David S. Moore, 5th ed. (New York: Freeman, 2000), *Seeing Through Statistics* by Jessica M. Utts, 2nd ed. (Pacific Grove, CA: Duxbury, 1999), and "How to Display Data Badly" by Howard Wainer, *The American Statistician* (May 1984).

2.8

USING COMPUTER GRAPHICS

With the fairly recent introduction of powerful graphics available on the micro-computer, sales of graph paper and protractors have taken a heavy hit! A large number of PC packages allow you to construct a variety of multicolored and multidimensional bar charts, pie charts, and histograms. These are available in most word processing (e.g., Word), spreadsheet (e.g., Excel), and statistical (e.g., SPSS and MINITAB) software.

MINITAB graphics will be illustrated in the end-of-chapter appendix. Excel gives you the option of obtaining three-dimensional graphs. The bar chart in Figure 2.29 is a summary of the majors of the 50 individuals in Table 2.1 and is a three-dimensional representation of the bar chart in Figure 2.20. Excel's three-dimensional pie chart in Figure 2.30 uses the same data and is a more colorful and interesting version of the pie chart in Figure 2.23. When constructing a graph using **KPK Data Analysis ➤ Qualitative Data Charts,** you will have the option of selecting either a two-dimensional or a three-dimensional graph. There are many other graphics packages available that can be used for statistical graphics presentations. The most popular one is MS PowerPoint.

If you think you will have to create graphical summaries, try to gain access to a computer package with easy-to-use graphics capabilities, such as Excel, SPSS, or MINITAB. One thing the authors picked up in their industrial experience is that no presentation or report is complete without at least one of the graphs discussed in this chapter!

FIGURE

2.29

Illustration of Excel's three-dimensional bar chart (see two-dimensional chart in Figure 2.20).

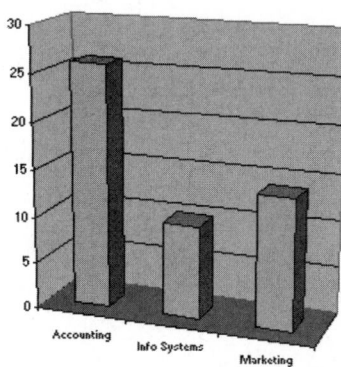

FIGURE

2.30

Illustration of Excel's three-dimensional pie chart.

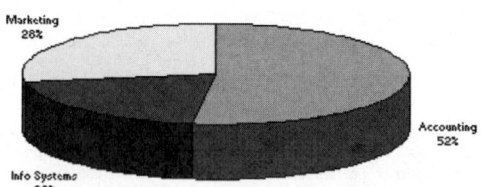

✓ Summary

This chapter examined methods of summarizing and presenting a large set of data using a graph. You begin by placing the sample data in order, from smallest to largest (an **ordered array**). The next step is to summarize the data in a **frequency distribution,** which consists of a number of classes (such as "150 and under 250") and corresponding frequencies.

The data summary can then be displayed using an appropriate graph. We discussed five kinds of graphs.

1. A **histogram** is a graphical view of a frequency distribution that summarizes a sample by placing the values into groups (classes).
2. A **stem-and-leaf diagram** is a graphical representation of an *entire* sample.
3. An **ogive** is a graph that allows you to illustrate **cumulative,** or "less-than" percentages of, **frequencies.**
4. A **bar chart** summarizes categorical (nominal) or ordinal data.
5. A **pie chart** presents a percentage breakdown of a particular quantity.

A frequency distribution provides a summary of the data by placing them into groups called **classes.** The number of values in each class is the **class frequency.** For example, there may be 10 values in the class "150 and under 250." The numbers 150 and 250 here are the **class limits,** and the difference between consecutive lower class limits is the **class width.** The center of this class [(150 + 250)/2 = 200] is the **class midpoint.** All classes should have the same width, except possibly the first and last class, which may be **open-ended classes** if you have a few **outliers.** For comparisons, the same data can be summarized using **relative frequencies,** which indicate the fraction of data values in each class rather than actual counts **(frequencies).**

Histograms and *stem-and-leaf diagrams* are graphical representations of a frequency distribution and are generally used for data having an interval or ratio level of measurement. A *stem-and-leaf diagram* does not condense the sample data into classes, but rather represents *each* value in an easy-to-read graph. An excellent way to indicate the shape of the data values is to use a **frequency polygon,** which is constructed by replacing the bars in the histogram with straight lines connecting the midpoints at the top of each bar. An *ogive* allows you to make such statements as "40% of the data values are less than 500." Like a frequency polygon, an ogive consists of many straight lines; in an ogive, the lines always increase from 0 to 1 on the vertical axis.

When the data are nominal or ordinal, a *bar chart* provides an excellent graphical summary. When constructing a bar chart, gaps are inserted between the bars because of the nature of this data type. A *pie chart* is also useful for nominal or ordinal data. This circular graph can be used to represent percentages (relative frequencies) at some point in time or over a certain time period. When data are collected to correspond to specific time periods, the result is called a **time series.**

What's Next?

A graph such as a frequency polygon is an excellent method of describing a set of data, but it does have its limitations. For example, we might look at Figure 2.16 and ask where the middle (center) of the data is. One person might argue that it is somewhere around $38,000, whereas someone else might decide that it is some value closer to $39,000. The point is that we need to define what the word *middle* means and define some method of calculating this value, so that we all get the *same* result. Such a value is called a *numerical measure.*

The next chapter examines a variety of such numerical measures. Rather than reducing a set of data to a graph, we will reduce the data to one or more *numbers* that give us some information about the data.

X Review Exercises 2.51–2.61

2.51 Buying a portable CD player with a snazzy appearance and sharp sound quality is important to most consumers. However, a buyer should assess the hassle of frequent battery changes before buying a player. Portable CD players consume AA batteries at an amazing rate. Not only is this expensive, but it is a nuisance if the consumer does not have a back-up supply. *Consumer Reports* rated the battery life of the following portable CD models.

Model	Battery Life (Hours)
Sony D-MJ95	26
Sony D-SJ17CK	29
Sony D-SJ01	33

Model	Battery Life (Hours)
Sony D-EJ611	26
Sony D-SJ15	25
Panasonic SL-SX280	23
Aiwa XP-SP911	23
Panasonic SL-SW869V	23
Aiwa XP-V713	20
Panasonic SL-CT470	12
Philips AZ9213	17
RCA RP-2360FM	10
RCA RP-2300	12

a. Construct a stem-and-leaf display. Do you notice any outliers?
b. Construct a frequency distribution using a class width of 5.
c. Interpret the shape of the distribution.

(Source: "Portable CD Players," *Consumer Reports,* July 2001, p. 43.)

2.52 With decreases forecasted in many state budgets due to an economic slowdown in 2001, many state universities increased the cost of full tuition. Suppose that in the Midwest, these increases ranged from $200 to $1,398 for the year 2002. Assume that 60 state schools in the Midwest were randomly sampled.

a. Would you use a frequency distribution for discrete or continuous data to summarize this data set?
b. What class limits would you select to construct a frequency distribution?
c. Suppose that only six classes were desired. What class limits would you choose?

(Source: "College Tuition Swells," *USA Today,* July 19, 2001, p. 1A.)

2.53 Some business leaders and scientists are concerned about the effect that greenhouse gases have on global warming and how sensitive the Earth's climate is to a buildup of greenhouse gases. The most industrialized nations are studying how much each country should reduce carbon dioxide emissions. Construct bar charts for the percentage contribution by that country to global dioxide emissions and for the per capita emissions. Compare the two charts. Interpret the two bar charts.

Country	Percentage Contribution to Global Dioxide Emission	Per Capita Emissions (Metric Tons)
United States	24.8%	5.6
Russia	6.5%	2.7
Japan	5.0%	2.4
Germany	3.7%	2.8
United Kingdom	2.5%	2.6
Canada	2.5%	4.9

(Source: "Who Pollutes the Most," *USA Today,* July 16, 2001, p. 2A.)

2.54 When money is allowed to grow in a tax-deferred retirement account for several decades, the results can be impressive. Consider the following results.

Starting Age	Investment Value at Age 65 When Investing $500 Annually
20	$221,238
30	$ 96,216
40	$ 39,890

Starting Age	Investment Value at Age 65 When Investing $1000 Annually
20	$442,475
30	$192,431
40	$ 79,781

Construct a bar chart for the investment values at age 65 for the case where an investor saves $500 annually and for the case where an investor saves $1,000 annually. Compare the two charts. How will an investor who saves $1,000 annually starting at age 30 fare against an investor who starts at age 20 and saves $500 annually?

(Source: "A Little Can Go a Long Way," *Stages: The Fidelity Investments Magazine of Personal Finance,* Winter 1998, p. 22–23.)

2.55 Many car-rental companies offer special weekly rates on economy cars. A sample of Hertz's weekly economy rate at 18 locations (3 of which are in Canada) is presented below.

City	Weekly Economy Rate (in Dollars)
Miami	137
Orlando	144
Tampa	145
Los Angeles	169
San Francisco	190
Las Vegas	120
Seattle	179
Denver	131
Atlanta	207
Detroit	191
Dallas/Fort Worth	169
Boston	194
Chicago	184
Honolulu	142
Puerto Rico	170
Toronto	190
Calgary	133
Vancouver	137

(Source: "Plan Ahead and Save Rates," *USA Today*, April 14, 1998, p. 9A.)

a. Construct a stem-and-leaf diagram using the last digit as the leaf.

b. Construct a frequency histogram with nine class intervals.

c. Compare the shapes of the stem-and-leaf diagram in part a and the histogram in part b.

2.56 The long-time economic expansion of the 1990s has made the United States dependent on immigrant labor. Congress recognized this need and decided to allow for granting legal status to all illegal immigrants working and paying taxes during 2001. This ruling affected about 8.5 million illegal immigrants. The following table displays the occupations of these immigrants and the percentage in each category.

Occupation	Percentage
Household Work	34
Farming and Fishing	23
Labor and Equipment Handling	18
Professional	11
Sales	10
Other	4

a. Construct a bar chart to display the occupations and the percentage of immigrants in each category.

b. Use a pie chart to display the data.

(Source: "USA Just Wouldn't Work Without Immigrant Labor," *USA Today*, July 23, 2001, p. 1A.)

2.57 In the wake of the September 11, 2001, terrorist attacks, automakers offered incentives to boost sales and invigorate the economy. As a result, 2001 sales almost matched the record levels of 2000. December 2001 sales for U.S. cars and light trucks follow.

Company	December Sales
DaimlerChrysler	198,077
Ford	280,568
General Motors	359,024
Honda	94,882
Isuzu	4,430
Mazda	19,063
Mitsubishi	31,635
Nissan	61,172
Subaru	15,926
Suzuki	3,917
Toyota	144,202
Volkswagen	36,581

a. Draw a Pareto diagram (see Exercise 2.33) to summarize the data.

b. What percentage of the market value do Ford, General Motors, and DaimlerChrysler constitute? What conclusions can you make from viewing the diagram?

(Source: "U.S. Car, Truck Sales Eased in December," *Wall Street Journal,* January 4, 2002, p. A4.)

2.58 [DATA SET EX2-58] *Variable Description:*

LongTermHealthFacility: Name of company providing long-term care

Ownership: Public or private

NetRevenue: Net revenue for year 2000 for long-term health care provider

More than 60% of people age 65 or older will require long-term care during their lifetime. Medicare and Medicaid typically pay only a fraction of the costs of long-term health care. Managers of long-term health facilities must keep costs low at these facilities so that people seeking assisted living can afford the facility. Those companies that manage to keep their costs very low typically generate higher net revenue. Compare histograms of net revenue for 2000 for publicly owned and privately owned long-term providers. What differences do you notice from viewing these two histograms?

(Source: "Post-Acute-Care Companies Ranked by 2000 Net Revenue," *Modern Healthcare,* July 9, 2001, p. 29.)

2.59 [DATA SET EX2-59] *Variable Description:*

Company: Forty randomly selected retail stores

2001April: Percent change in sales over prior year's April time period

2001June: Percent change in sales over prior year's June time period

Retail store sales are an important economic indicator for the financial position of the consumer. Economists watch changes in retail sales from one year to the next to determine the robustness of the economy. Using a sample of retail stores, data were obtained for the percentage increase in sales from the prior year. Compare the percentages of change in retail store sales for the April and June time periods in 2001. Use a relative frequency histogram. Comment on the similarities of the shape of the distribution for these two time periods.

(Source: "April Comps Beat Forecasts, Rise 3.8%," *Chain Store Age,* June 2001, p. 136.)

2.60 [DATA SET EX2-60] *Variable Description:*

Year: Years range from 1938 to 2001

ValueMinWage: Real value of minimum wage reflecting inflation and changes in consumer spending patterns

The real value of the minimum wage changes frequently as economic conditions change and as consumer spending patterns change. The real value of the minimum wage has hovered between $4.50 and $6.70 between 1960 and 2001. The nominal value of the minimum wage has increased gradually over these years. These values increase gradually because economists believe that raising the minimum wage too quickly kills jobs.

a. Using a class width of .50, develop a relative frequency histogram for the value of the minimum wage from 1960 to 2001. Would you say that the distribution is approximately a bell-shaped curve?

b. Construct two histograms—one for the period 1938 to 1969 and the other for 1970 to 2001 (if using the KPK macros, click on the Stacked Histogram option). Compare the distributions and comment on differences.

(Source: "A Bumpy Road for Those at the Bottom," *Wall Street Journal,* July 19, 2001, p. A10.)

2.61 [DATA SET EX2-61] *Variable Description:*

State: 50 states plus Washington, D.C.

MathProficiency: Percentage of eighth graders that were at or above the proficiency level in Mathematics

The National Assessment of Educational Progress (NAEP), also known as "the Nation's Report Card," is the nation's representative in assessing what America's students know in various academic subject areas. This organization reports results for student achievement at grades 4, 8, and 12. States pay close attention to this report card to assess the regional educational systems.

a. Construct a relative frequency polygon using the math proficiency data. How would you describe the shape of this graph?

b. Construct a relative frequency ogive using the math proficiency data. At least 20% of the states have a math proficiency value higher than what value (approximately)?

c. Assign values of A, B, C, and D to states that have a math proficiency value greater than 30, greater than 20 but less than or equal to 30, greater than 10 but less than or equal to 20, and less than or equal to 10, respectively. Construct a pie chart of these categories and comment on the size of the categories.

d. Use a bar chart to describe the categories in part c. Which chart do you prefer? Explain.

(Source: "Math Scores by State," *USA Today*, August 3, 2001, p. 4A.)

Computer Exercises Using the Databases

Exercise 1—Appendix F

Select 50 observations at random from the database. Using a convenient statistical package, construct a frequency histogram and a stem-and-leaf diagram on the variable HPAYRENT (house payment or house/apartment rent). Using this same set of observations, construct separate frequency histograms and stem-and-leaf diagrams on the variable HPAYRENT for those who own their residence and for those who rent their residence. Comment on the shapes of the frequency histograms.

Exercise 2—Appendix F

Choose at random 30 observations from families living in the NE sector and then choose another 30 observations at random from families living in the SW sector. Using a convenient statistical computer package, construct frequency histograms and stem-and-leaf diagrams on the variable INCOME1 (income of principal wage earner) for each group of 30 observations, and comment on the frequency distribution of each.

Exercise 3—Appendix G

Select 100 observations at random from the database. Construct a frequency distribution and a histogram of the values of the variable ASSETS (current assets). Construct a stem-and-leaf diagram. What do you observe from these two graphs?

Exercise 4—Appendix G

Repeat Exercise 3 using the variable LIABIL (current liability).

Insights from Statistics in Action

Lean Philosophy Drives Productivity Growth

The Statistics in Action discussion at the beginning of the chapter emphasized the importance of measuring gains in company productivity and the reasons behind recorded productivity gains for several large companies. To gain more insight into figures describing productivity gains, consider the data from 70 corporations contained in data set StatInActChap2.xls and answer the following questions.

1. You would like to include a descriptive graphic with a report discussing the distribution of the productivity gains for these 70 corporations. Present this graphic. How would you describe the shape of the frequency distribution of the productivity gains?

2. Construct a histogram for only the companies listed as being part of the energy industry. Repeat this for the companies listed as being part of the banking or insurance industry. Compare these two graphs.

3. Find the separate average productivity gain for the corporations in each of the following industries by summing the productivity gains and dividing by the total number of corporations in

that industry: aerospace, banking, energy, insurance, merchandiser, and pharmaceutical. Present a bar graph of these industries showing the average productivity gain for each.

4. Construct a histogram of the productivity gains for all the corporations except those in energy. Compare this to the histogram that you obtained in Question 1.

5. Change the class width on the histogram in Question 1 and determine if the shape of the histogram is sensitive to the value assigned to the class width.

Source: "Companies Pay Out for Productivity Gains," *Information Week*, October 30, 2000. "A Who's Who of Productivity," *USA Today*, August 30, 2001, p. 1B.)

Appendix **SPSS**®

Chapter 2 Appendix: Data Analysis with SPSS

Histograms and Stem-and-Leaf Plots

The SPSS procedure will be illustrated using the salary data in Table 2.3. When using SPSS, the class boundaries are defined with "less than or equal to" limits rather than "under" limits. For example, the first class using six classes of salaries would be "32 and less than or equal to 34" rather than "32 and under 34," as described in this chapter. Missing data are automatically omitted. To construct a histogram using SPSS, click on **Analyze ➤ Descriptive Statistics ➤ Explore.** In the screen below, click on the variable name (salaries) and the top pointer button to move this variable into the **Dependent List** box. In the **Display** frame, select **Statistics** (summary statistics only), **Plots** (plots only), or **Both.** If **Plots** or **Both** is selected in this frame, click on the **Plots** button and select Stem-and-leaf and/or Histogram in the window that appears. Click on **Continue** to return to the screen below. Finally, click on **OK.**

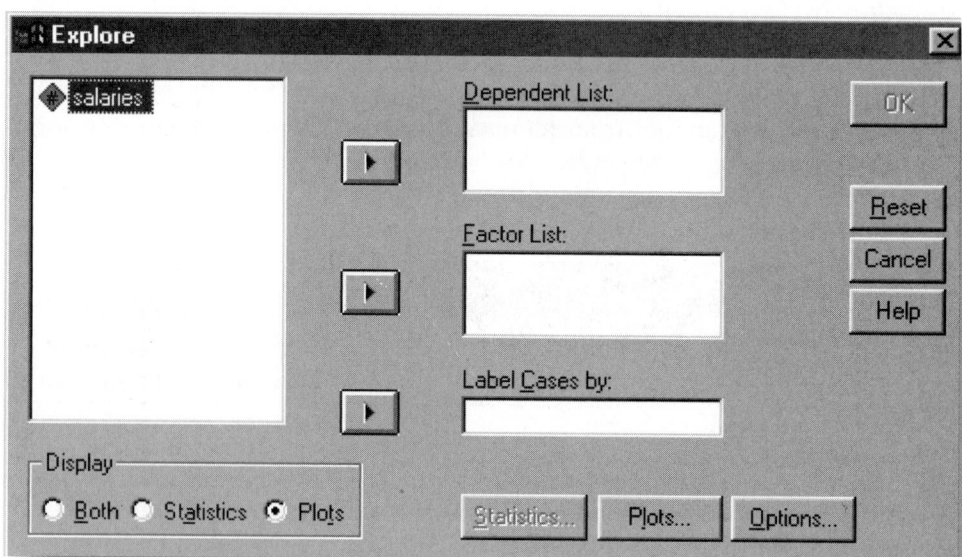

The resulting histogram and stem-and-leaf plot immediately follow. SPSS places decimal places on the stem. As a result, each actual data value is the number appearing in the stem-and-leaf plot times the stem width value. For example, the smallest sample value is (32.8)(1.0) = 32.8. If the sample values had been equal to 328, 338, 348, 350, . . . , the resulting stem-and-leaf plot would look exactly the same, but the stem width value would now be 10.

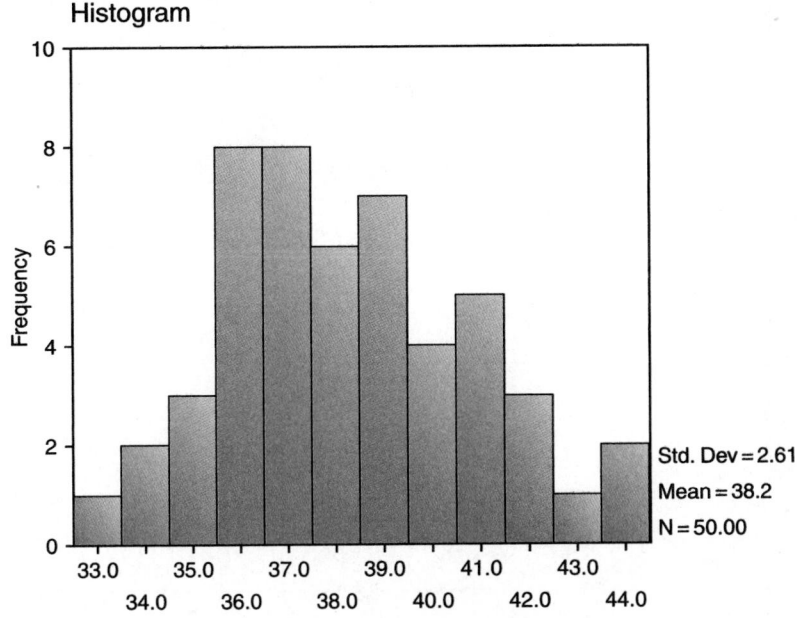

Histogram

Std. Dev = 2.61
Mean = 38.2
N = 50.00

All Stem-and-Leaf Plot

Frequency	Stem & Leaf
1.00	32 . 8
1.00	33 . 8
2.00	34 . 38
7.00	35 . 0267779
7.00	36 . 2235688
6.00	37 . 002489
7.00	38 . 0112578
7.00	39 . 2334557
3.00	40 . 369
5.00	41 . 13456
1.00	42 . 4
3.00	43 . 078

Stem width: 1.0
Each leaf: 1 case(s)

Interactive Histograms

To specify the class width or number of classes for a histogram, click on **Graphs ➤ Interactive ➤ Histogram**. In the following form, click on salaries in the left box and drag it into the indicated box.

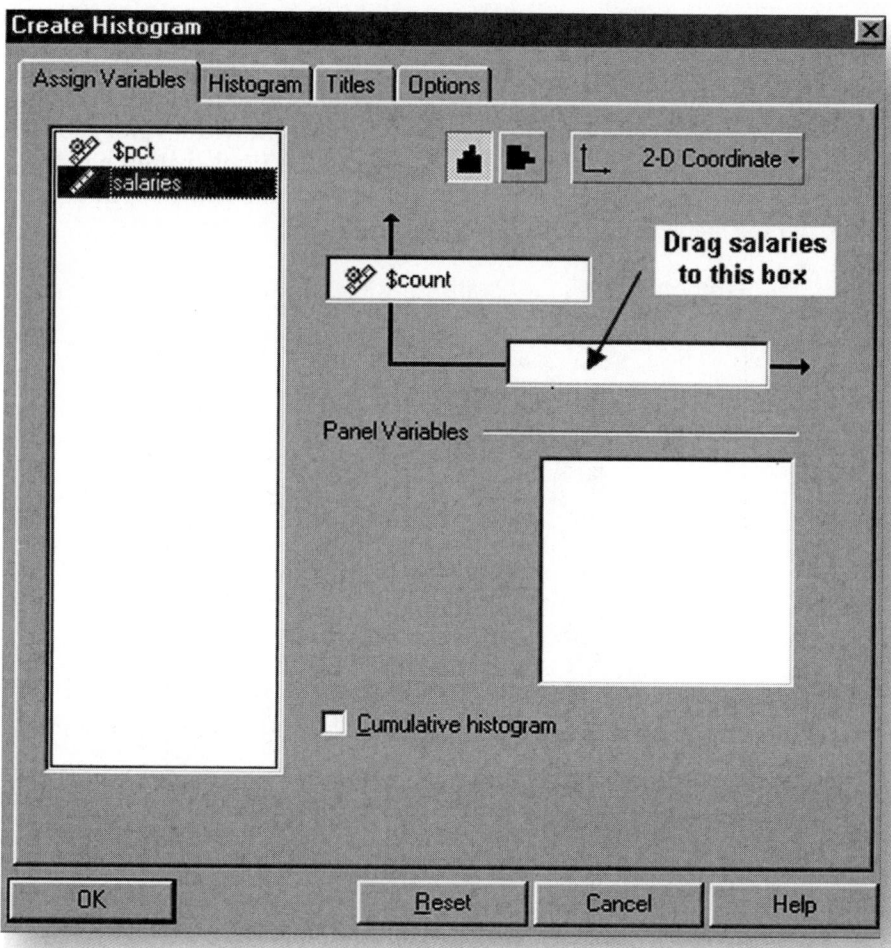

Next, click on the **Histogram** tab. In the **Interval Size** frame, unselect the box that says "Set interval size automatically." Set the **Number of intervals** value (or **Width of intervals** value) equal to the desired value. The resulting histogram using six intervals immediately follows. Notice that this six-interval histogram differs from that in Figure 2.1 because classes are defined using less than or equal to. As a result, the value 38.0 now falls into the third class, rather than the fourth class, as in Figure 2.1 and Table 2.4. *Note:* To obtain a relative frequency histogram, replace "$count" with "$pct" by dragging the "$pct" label into the box now containing "$count."

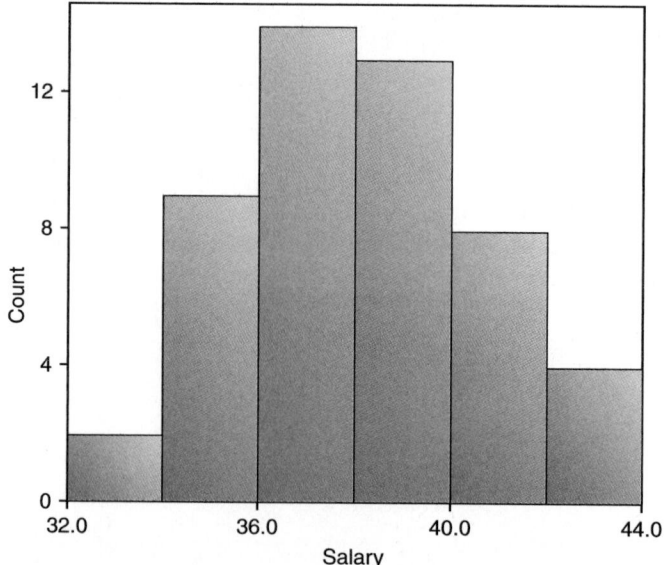

Frequency Polygon

To construct a frequency polygon with SPSS, you must put the class midpoints and frequencies into a data window. Be sure to add a class at each end having a zero frequency. The resulting data window for the salary data using six classes immediately follows.

	midpoint	freq
1	31	0
2	33	2
3	35	9
4	37	14
5	39	13
6	41	8
7	43	4
8	45	0

Click on **Graphs ➤ Interactive ➤ Line** and drag the variable names (midpoint and freq) into the appropriate boxes (refer to the following screen). Click on **OK.** The graph immediately following the **Create Lines** window will appear in the display pane.

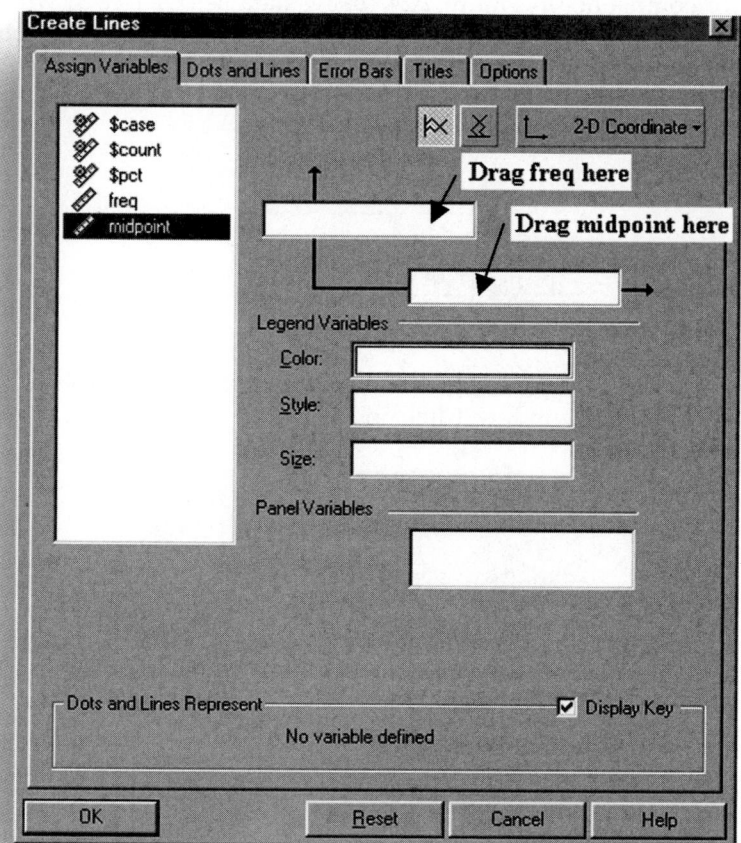

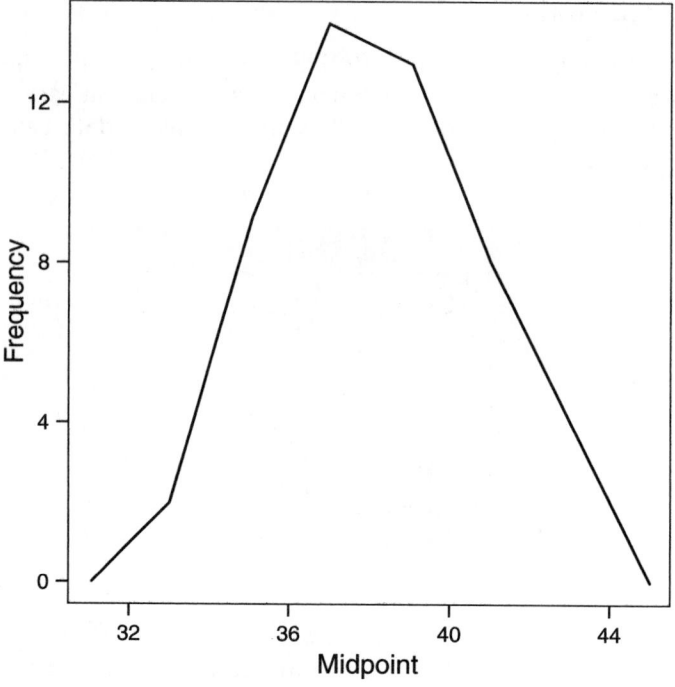

Bar Charts and Pie Charts

To illustrate the construction of bar charts and pie charts, the data consisting of the frequency of complaints in Figure 2.24 (using data set DATA2-3) will be used. Begin by putting the category names and frequencies in the first two columns.

	category	freq
1	Billing	42
2	Rude	14
3	Late	8
4	Not Ans	6
5	Other	5

Click on **Graphs ➤ Bar** and select **Simple** and **Values of individual cases** as shown in the following window. Click on **Define.**

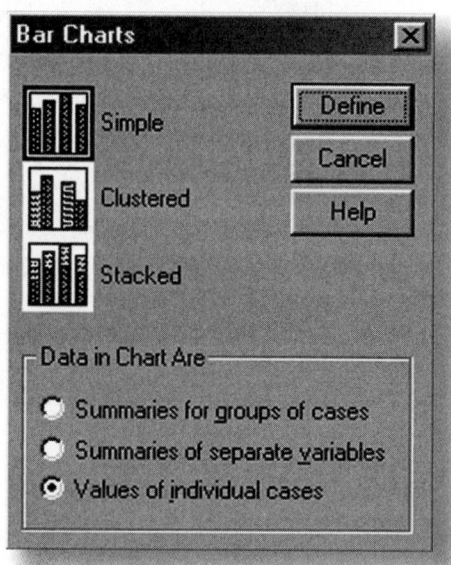

In the following window, select the freq variable and click on the top pointer to move this variable into the **Bars Represent** box. Select the category variable and click on the lower pointer to move this variable into the **Variable** box inside the **Category Labels** frame. The graph title (Bar Chart of Complaints) can be specified by clicking on the **Titles** button. Click on **OK** to obtain the bar chart that follows this window.

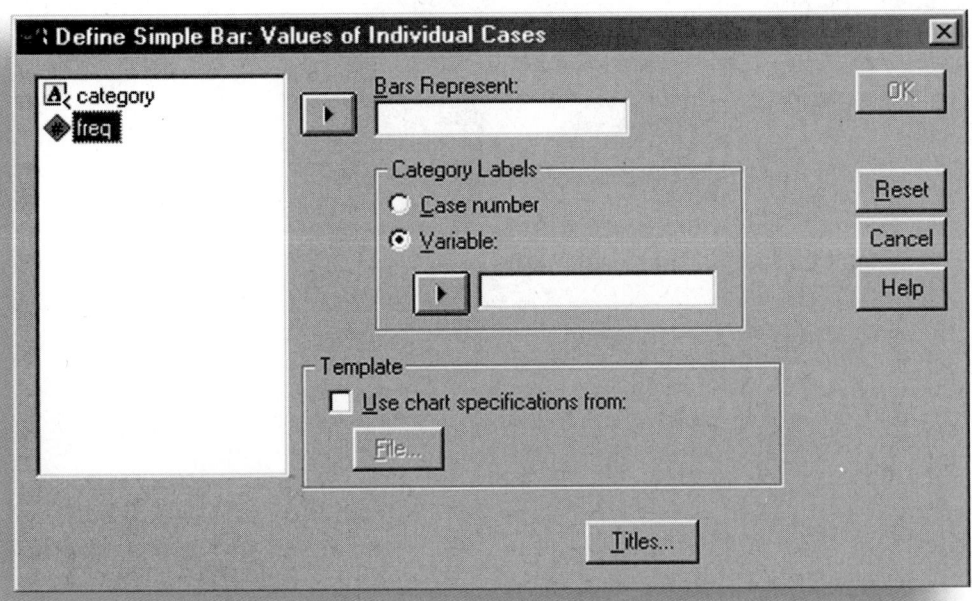

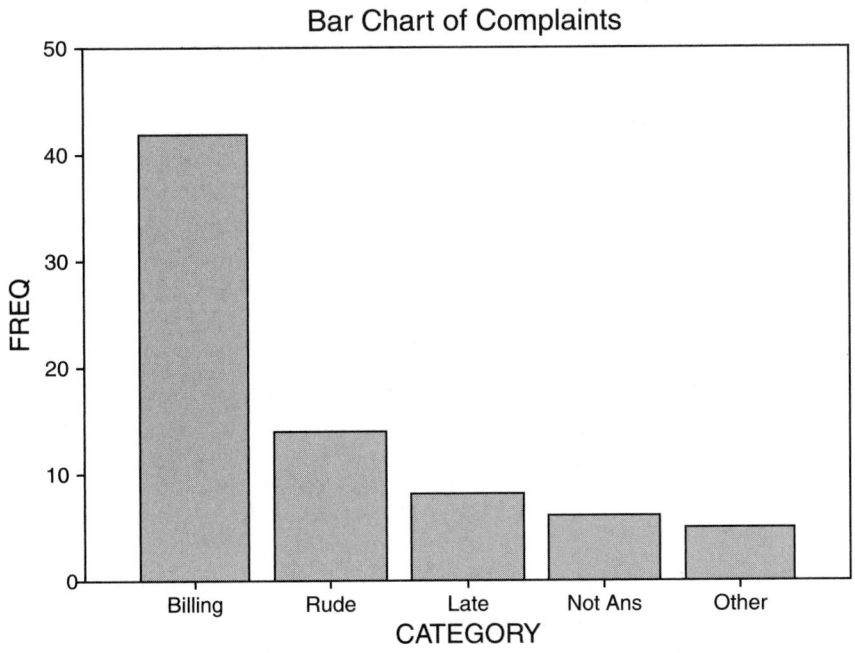

The procedure to construct a pie chart is identical. To construct the pie chart, click on **Graphs ➤ Pie.** The resulting pie chart immediately follows.

Pie Chart of Complaints

Other

Not Ans

Late

Rude

Billing

 On the CD . . .
Chapter 2 Appendix: Data Analysis with MINITAB

3

Data Summary Using Descriptive Measures

X

What do personal computer upgrades, increased automobile production, and Christmas gaming toys have in common? These products are each fueled by the technological wonder called the *semiconductor.* Companies such as Intel and Texas Instruments have been major players in supplying industry with semiconductors to further advance the high-technology revolution. This revolution has resulted in hard-to-be-seen chips making many difficult tasks seem effortless, ranging from operating a coffee maker to controlling the space shuttle. The most sophisticated chip is a microprocessor, whose transistors can execute hundreds of millions of instructions per second.

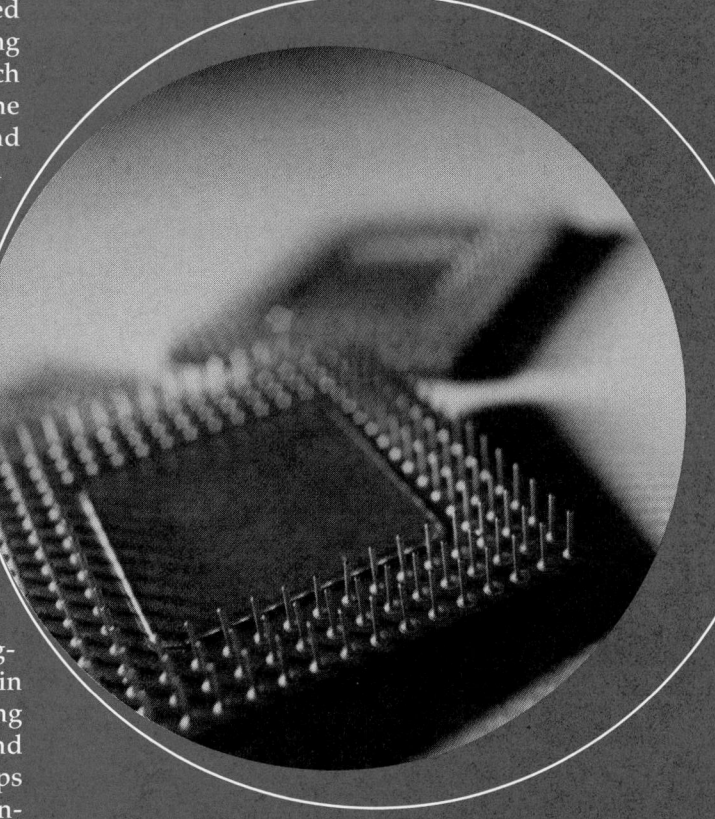

The technology revolution has provided semiconductor solutions to so many domestic and international business decisions that semiconductor funding has become dependent on business cycles. Emerging applications have influenced investments in the semiconductor sector. When fast-moving markets (e.g., digital cameras, wireless and broadband access) cool, inventories of chips increase and prices fall. The silicon wafer manufacturers must cut costs to keep businesses buying their chips.

Chips are essentially a commodity. A case in point was the project proposed by Cypress Semiconductor Corporation of San Jose, California. In early 1996, Cypress had a ground-breaking ceremony at Round Rock, Texas, for its Fab V facility. In fact, then-governor George Bush was in attendance. However, in late 1996

the chip business went into a dramatic decline. Cypress was forced to put the project on indefinite hold. This Fab V facility eventually became known as the "Slab V" facility, as Cypress stopped investing money into the project.

The two largest global players in the semiconductor market are the United States and Japan. In the early 1990s, the United States and

Japan consumed more than 60% of the chips made worldwide. By 2001, that percentage dropped below 50%. Countries such as Taiwan have dramatically increased their consumption of semiconductors. In the past six years the consumption of semiconductors, as a percentage of total world consumption, has doubled for the country of Taiwan. This is in contrast to Japan, which had approximately 30% of the world's consumption of semiconductors in the early 1990s and now has less than 18%. These figures illustrate how business cycles worldwide can make the market for semiconductors dynamic and volatile. Business analysts are obtaining a better understanding of the semiconductor demand cycle by examining semiconductor consumption data worldwide.

When you have completed this chapter, you will be able to examine data illustrating the consumption of semiconductors internationally and discuss such questions as

- What class of *descriptive measures* could be used to compare the percentage of semiconductor consumption by several key global players?
- For each global player, what measure would you use to describe the *middle* of the data collected over a 10-year period?
- For each global player, what measure would you use to describe the *variation* in the data over a 10-year period?
- Are the figures illustrating consumption of semiconductors *skewed?*

A Look Back/Introduction

The first two chapters focused on different types of numerical sample data and methods of summarizing and presenting data. A frequency distribution is used to condense data from a sample into groups (called classes). Different types of statistical graphs can be used to illustrate sample data in different ways. The types of graphs we have discussed so far include the histogram, stem-and-leaf diagram, bar chart, ogive, frequency polygon, and pie chart. The purpose of these graphs is to convey information at a glance about the distribution of the values in your sample.

Every sample data set is a small part of a much larger population. Even if we don't always mention the word *population,* it is always there, since the sample values were selected from this group of interest. Every population has properties (called **parameters**) that describe it. By collecting a set of sample data, we can then estimate these properties by computing statistics and making graphs.

We have seen how to reduce a set of sample data to a graph. It also is helpful to reduce data to one or more numbers (such as an average). Such a number is called a descriptive measure. Because this number is derived from a sample, it also can be called a sample statistic. In this chapter we discuss the commonly used descriptive measures and explain what you can expect to learn from each one. In later chapters, we discuss how you can use many of these sample statistics to estimate the corresponding population parameters.

3.1 VARIOUS TYPES OF DESCRIPTIVE MEASURES

A **descriptive measure** is a *single* number computed from the sample data that provides information about the data. The class of descriptive measures described here consists of four types. Which one you select depends on what you want to measure. These types are:

1. *Measures of central tendency.* These answer the questions, where is the "middle" of my data? and, which data value occurs most often?

2. *Measures of variation.* These answer the questions, how spread out are my data values? and, how much do the data values jump around?

3. *Measures of position.* These answer the questions, how does my value (score on an exam, for example) compare with all the others? and, which data value was exceeded by 75% of the data values? by 50%? by 25%?

4. *Measures of shape.* These answer the questions, are my data values symmetric? and, if not symmetric, just how nonsymmetric (skewed) are the data?

MEASURES OF CENTRAL TENDENCY 3.2

The purpose of a **measure of central tendency** is to determine the "center" of your data values, or possibly the most typical data value. Some measures of central tendency are the *mean, median, midrange,* and *mode*. We will illustrate each of these measures using as data the number of accidents (monthly) reported over a particular five-month period:

accident data: 6, 9, 7, 23, 5

The Mean

The **mean** is the most popular measure of central tendency. It is merely the average of the data. The mean is easy to compute and explain, and it has several mathematical properties that make it more advantageous to use than the other three measures of central tendency.

Business managers often use a mean to represent a set of values. They select one value as typical of the whole set of values, such as average sales, average price, average salary, or average production per hour. In economics, the term *per capita* is a measure of central tendency. The income per capita of a certain district, the number of clothes washers per capita, and the number of televisions per capita are all examples of a mean.

The *sample mean,* $\bar{x}$ (read "x bar"), is equal to the sum of the data values divided by the number of data values. For the accident data set,

$$\bar{x} = \frac{6 + 9 + 7 + 23 + 5}{5} = 10.0$$

In general, let an arbitrary data set be represented as

$$x_1, x_2, x_3, \ldots, x_n$$

where n is the number of data values. (In the accident data set, $x_1 = 6$, $x_2 = 9$, $x_3 = 7$, $x_4 = 23$, $x_5 = 5$, and n is 5.) Then,

$$\bar{x} = \frac{x_1 + x_2 + \cdots + x_n}{n} = \frac{\sum x}{n}$$

3.1

The symbol Σ (sigma) means "the sum of." In this case, the sample mean, $\bar{x}$, is the sum of the x values divided by n.* When dealing with discrete data, the sample mean is often *not* an integer (such as 10, here) and should *not* be rounded to an integer. For example, remove the last value (5) from the accident data set. The sample mean is now

$$\bar{x} = \frac{6 + 9 + 7 + 23}{4} = 11.25$$

In subsequent chapters, we will be concerned with the mean of the *population*. The symbol of the population mean is μ (mu). For a population consisting of N elements, denoted by

$$x_1, x_2, x_3, \ldots, x_N$$

the *population mean* is defined to be

$$\mu = \frac{x_1 + x_2 + \cdots + x_N}{N} = \frac{\Sigma x}{N}$$

3.2

Population: $x_1, x_2, \ldots, x_N$

Population mean $= \mu = \dfrac{x_1 + x_2 + \cdots + x_N}{N} = \dfrac{\Sigma x}{N}$

Sample values (selected from the population): $x_1, x_2, \ldots, x_n$, where $n \leq N$

Sample mean $= \bar{x} = \dfrac{x_1 + x_2 + \cdots + x_n}{n} = \dfrac{\Sigma x}{n}$

The Median

The **median** of a set of data is the value in the center of the data values when they are arranged from smallest to largest. Consequently, it is in the center of the ordered array.

Using the accident data set, the median, **Md**, is found by first constructing an ordered array:

5, 6, **7,** 9, 23

The value that has an equal number of items to the right and the left is the median. Thus, $Md = 7$.

In general, if n is *odd*, Md is the center data value of the ordered set:

$$Md = \left(\frac{n+1}{2}\right) \text{ st ordered value}$$

Here, the median is the $(5 + 1)/2 = 3$rd value in the ordered array. Note that for these data, the *position* of the median is 3, and the *value* of the median is 7. If n is *even, Md* is the average of the two center values of the ordered set. Thus, the median of the array, 3, 8, 12, 14 is $(8 + 12)/2 = 10.0$.

---

*In another application of this symbol, we square each of the sample values and sum these values. For the accident data, this operation would be written as

$$\Sigma x^2 = 5^2 + 6^2 + 7^2 + 9^2 + 23^2$$
$$= 25 + 36 + 49 + 81 + 529$$
$$= 720$$

For these data, then, $\Sigma x = 50$ and $\Sigma x^2 = 720$

In our accident data set, one of the five values (23) is much larger than the remaining values—it is an outlier. Notice that the median ($Md = 7$) was much less affected by this value than was the mean ($\bar{x} = 10$). *When dealing with data that are likely to contain outliers (for example, personal incomes or prices of residential housing), the median usually is preferred to the mean as a measure of central tendency, since the median provides a more "typical" or "representative" value for these situations.*

Finally, note that newspaper and magazine articles often refer to both the mean and the median as an "average" value. Care must be taken not to always interpret this word as representing the sample mean unless this is specified in the discussion.

The Midrange

Although less popular than the mean and median, the **midrange (Mr)** provides an easy-to-grasp measure of central tendency. Notice that it also is severely affected (even more than $\bar{x}$) by the presence of an outlier in the data. In general:

$$Mr = \frac{L + H}{2}$$

3.3

where L = smallest (lowest) value in the sample and H = largest (highest) value in the sample. Using the accident data set, $L = 5$, $H = 23$, and

$$Mr = \frac{5 + 23}{2} = 14.0$$

Compare this to $\bar{x} = 10$ and $Md = 7$.

The Mode

The **mode (Mo)** of a data set is the value that occurs more than once and the most often. The mode is not always a measure of central tendency; this value need not occur in the "center" of your data. One situation in which the mode is the value of interest is the manufacturing of clothing. The *most common* hat size is what you would like to know, not the *average* hat size. Can you think of other applications where the mode would provide useful information? Consider situations where your sample consists of nominal data.

Note that there is no mode for our accident data set because all values occur only once. Instead, consider the data set

4, 8, 7, 6, 9, 8, 10, 5, 8

$Mo = 8$ (occurs three times).

There may be more than one mode if several numbers occur the same (and the largest) number of times. This is the only exception to our earlier statement that a descriptive measure consists of a *single* number.

EXAMPLE 3.1

A sample of 10 was taken to determine the typical completion time (in months) for the construction of a particular model of Brockwood Homes:

4.1, 3.2, 2.8, 2.6, 3.7, 3.1, 9.4, 2.5, 3.5, 3.8

We find the mean completion time as follows:

$$\bar{x} = \frac{4.1 + 3.2 + \cdots + 3.8}{10} = \frac{38.7}{10} = 3.87 \text{ months}$$

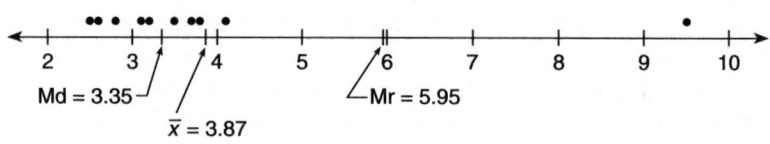

FIGURE

3.1

Dot plot, along with several measures of central tendency for a sample of 10 housing construction times. See text for application.

Construction time (months)

Notice that there is an outlier in the data, namely, 9.4 months. To be safe, you should double-check this figure to make sure that it is, in fact, correct—that is, that there was no mistake in recording or transcribing this value. In the presence of one or two outliers, the median generally provides a more reliable measure of central tendency, so we construct an ordered array:

2.5, 2.6, 2.8, 3.1, **3.2, 3.5,** 3.7, 3.8, 4.1, 9.4

Consequently, since n is even,

$$Md = \frac{3.2 + 3.5}{2} = 3.35 \text{ months}$$

Also, the midrange is given by

$$Mr = \frac{2.5 + 9.4}{2} = 5.95 \text{ months}$$

This value is severely affected by the presence of the outlier; the midrange value of nearly 6 months is a poor measure of central tendency for this application.

Finally, no mode exists because there are no repeats in the data values. These results are summarized in the graph in Figure 3.1, a *dot plot*. Each data value is represented as a dot on the horizontal line. The outlier of 9.4 is very obvious when the data are displayed in this type of plot.

Microsoft® Excel Application   Use DATA3-2

E X A M P L E

3.2

Using Excel to Compute Measures of Central Tendency

In Chapter 2, we examined the starting salaries of the 50 business majors at Bellaire College. The data are presented in Tables 2.1 and 2.3. Dataset DATA3-2 contains these 50 sorted salaries, stored in a single column (column A in Figure 3.3) and also by type of major (columns B, C, and D). After opening this file, you should see columns A through D in Figure 3.3. Determine the mean, median, and midrange for the entire class of graduating business majors and for each of the three disciplines (accounting, information systems, and marketing). What can you conclude about the "typical" starting salaries for these three groups at Bellaire?

Solution

To obtain the various statistics in Figure 3.3, use the Excel Descriptive Statistics command. To obtain this command, click on **Tools ➤ Data Analysis ➤ Descriptive Statistics ➤ OK.** You should see the input screen in Figure 3.2. Fill in the values as shown and be sure to click on the box for **Labels in First Row** and the box for **Summary Statistics.** After clicking on "OK" you obtain the statistics in Figure 3.3 describing all 50 individuals in the sample. You will need to widen column E by placing the cursor on the cell boundary alongside "E" and dragging it to the right

FIGURE

3.2

Excel input screen for **Tools ➤ Data Analysis ➤ Descriptive Statistics.**

FIGURE

3.3

File DATA3-2 and the four measures of central tendency using Excel's descriptive statistics (midrange added).

until all the titles in this column are visible. *You can ignore the shaded cells for now; they'll be covered later in the chapter.* To obtain the midrange, type "Midrange" in cell E16 and enter "=(F12+F13)/2" in cell F16. This uses Excel's formula capability and merely averages the minimum and maximum values in cells F12 and F13.

To derive the same set of statistics for the three disciplines, refer to Figure 3.2; for the input range, enter "B1:D27" and for the output range, type "G1." This results in columns G through L shown in Figure 3.4. The midranges can be obtained by: (1) highlighting cells E16 and F16 by dragging the mouse across these two cells, (2) finding the fill handle in cell F16 (the small square in the lower right corner) and placing the cursor over the fill handle (you should see a black "+"), and (3) dragging the fill handle through L16. You should now see the midrange label and the corresponding value for each of the three majors.

FIGURE

3.4

The four measures of central tendency using descriptive statistics on the three samples (midrange added).

	G	H		I	J	K	L	M
1	**Accounting**			**Info. Systems**		**Marketing**		
2								
3	Mean	39.61154	Mean		36.87	Mean	36.53571	
4	Standard Error	0.479946	Standard Error		0.461652	Standard Error	0.552776	
5	Median	39.45	Median		36.4	Median	36.9	
6	Mode	35.7	Mode		38.1	Mode	#N/A	
7	Standard Deviation	2.447256	Standard Deviation		1.459871	Standard Deviation	2.068298	
8	Sample Variance	5.989062	Sample Variance		2.131222	Sample Variance	4.277857	
9	Kurtosis	-0.96244	Kurtosis		-0.65336	Kurtosis	-0.87532	
10	Skewness	-0.06037	Skewness		0.444149	Skewness	-0.29774	
11	Range	8.1	Range		4.7	Range	6.9	
12	Minimum	35.7	Minimum		34.8	Minimum	32.8	
13	Maximum	43.8	Maximum		39.5	Maximum	39.7	
14	Sum	1029.9	Sum		368.7	Sum	511.5	
15	Count	26	Count		10	Count	14	
16	Midrange	39.75	Midrange		37.15	Midrange	36.25	

TABLE

3.1

Summary of levels of measurement and appropriate measure of central tendency. A "Y" indicates this measure can be used with the corresponding level of measurement.

Measure of Central Tendency	Level of Measurement			
	Nominal	Ordinal	Interval	Ratio
Mean			Y	Y
Median		Y	Y	Y
Midrange			Y	Y
Mode	Y	Y	Y	Y

Since there appear to be no unusual values (outliers)* in each of the three sets of salaries, we will examine the means. The mean average starting salary for these 50 business graduates is $38,202. The accounting graduates had the largest mean starting salary ($39,612), followed by the information systems graduates ($36,870) and the marketing graduates ($36,536). For this graduating class at Bellaire, on the average, accounting graduates received a starting salary approximately $3000 higher than for the other two disciplines.

Often the choice of which measure of central tendency to use is affected by the level of measurement (nominal, ordinal, interval, ratio) of the sample data. For interval/ratio data, you can use any of these four measures. For ordinal data, the difference between data values has no meaning, so only the mode and median are appropriate. For nominal data (such as hair color), the sample mode is the only measure of central tendency that should be used. These comments are summarized in Table 3.1.

---

* The subject of outliers will be discussed in more detail in Section 3.8.

X Exercises 3.1–3.11

Understanding the Mechanics

3.1 The following five numbers were obtained from a random sample: 48, 4, 12, 8, 24.
  a. Find the mean, median, and midrange.
  b. Divide the five numbers by 4. Find the mean, median, and midrange.

3.2 The following are two ordered sets of data each with a sample size of 6:

| Set 1: | 2 | 4 | 6 | 6 | 8 | 10 |
| Set 2: | 2 | 2 | 6 | 8 | 14 | 80 |

  a. By simply observing the ordered figures, would you say that data set one is "symmetric" about the value of 6? Without computing, what do you think the mean, median, mode, and midrange are for data set 1? Compute these measures and compare to the answer you provided.
  b. Would you consider the value of 80 to be unusually large for data set 2? Do you think that this might make the mean and median rather different? Compute the mean, median, mode, and midrange. Do the mean and median differ as much as you expected?

Applying the New Concepts

3.3 Select five different values between 1 and 20 such that
  a. The mean is smaller than the median.
  b. The mean is larger than the median.

3.4 The number of automobiles that are serviced daily by EZ Service Stations are recorded as follows for 30 days.

50	45	50	51	42	49	80	42	52	49
48	50	88	49	42	50	50	48	50	46
50	51	52	49	49	50	51	40	50	42

  a. Calculate the mean, median, mode, and midrange.
  b. Interpret each statistic in part a. Which measure of central tendency appears to be most appropriate? Why?

3.5 Several years ago, the office occupancy costs, which include rents, real estate taxes, and operating expenses, were sky-high in Japan. Recently, the costs have fallen. The average occupancy costs have slid from $130 to $95 in Tokyo. Interpret this information. Does this imply that the median occupancy costs have decreased by this amount?

(Source: "Less of a Gulf in Office Rents," *Business Week,* June 16, 1997, p. 28.)

3.6 A traveling salesperson in Canada records the number of kilometers his Ford Taurus can drive on a full tank of gas. The following data give the kilometers traveled on a full tank of gas until the gas gauge indicated "empty."

| 640 | 620 | 640 | 521 | 655 | 605 | 638 | 678 | 630 | 650 |
| 420 | 595 | 670 | 633 | 628 | 660 | 595 | 670 | 640 | 630 |

  a. Calculate the mean, median, and mode.
  b. Which value appears to be more appropriate as a measure of central tendency?

  c. Recalculate the mean, median, and mode with the value of 420 kilometers omitted. Compare your answers to part a.

3.7 The National Safety Board has investigated ship fires that have occurred on the open seas. In the past 19 years, of 7 the 15 major cruise ship fires in U.S. waters occurred on older ships. A listing of major ship fires and their damage in millions of dollars is presented below.

Ship	Damage (in Millions)
Vistafjord	.68
Universe Explorer	1.50
Celebration	4.00
Regal Empress	.25
Song of America	.29
Britanis	.08
Sovereign of the Seas	.50
Regent Star	.02
Song of America	.35
Scandinavian Star	3.50
Emerald Seas	.30
Scandinavian Sea	16.00
Boheme	2.00
Angelina Lauro	26.30

Compute the mean and median for these data. Which observation affects the value of the mean the most if it is omitted? How is the median affected if this observation is omitted?

(Source: "Poor Fire Protection Sends Ships Cruising into Danger," *USA Today,* May 5, 1998, p. 12A.)

3.8 The number of slight imperfections noted in manufacturing a sheet of aluminum is recorded below for 10 sheets of aluminum manufactured from each of two different processes.

Process 1					Process 2				
13	11	13	15	12	13	19	13	14	13
14	12	15	11	13	20	12	13	15	10

  a. Calculate the mean, median, mode, and midrange for each process.
  b. Explain to the production manager what the statistics in part a mean.

Using the Computer

3.9 [DATA SET EX3-9] *Variable Description:*

Year: Productivity results are recorded over the years 1980 through 2001

IndustrialProd: The percentage of operating capacity used by factories

The percentage of operating capacity used by factories represents a productivity measure that economists use as a leading indicator of economic growth. Rarely do factories operate above 85% of their capacity. These figures fluctuate depending on the outlook for the economy.

a. For the years 1980 through 1989, find the mean, median, and midrange.

b. For the years from 1990 through 2001, find the mean, median, and midrange.

c. Compare these two periods of time using the mean, median, and midrange. Which period of time appears to be more productive?

(Source: "Industrial Production Falls for Ninth Straight Month," *Wall Street Journal,* July 18, 2001, p. A2.)

3.10 [DATA SET EX3-10] *Variable description:*

Waittime: Time that airline completely unloads luggage

Passengers have complained to airport authorities at Baltimore/Washington International (BWI) airport that the waiting time to pick up baggage from a particular flight from Mexico to BWI was excessive. After monitoring the wait time, management implemented a system that should on average take no more than 25 minutes to completely unload the plane. A sample of 50 flights yielded wait times for each flight.

a. Use the histogram command to view the waittime data. Does it appear that management is successful in having the wait time be no more than 25 minutes?

b. What is the mean and median of wait time? (Excel: Use the **Paste Function ➤ Statistical.**) What can you say about the new procedure with respect to the target of having passengers wait no more than 25 minutes?

3.11 [DATA SET EX3-11] *Variable Description:*

Company: Selected Fortune 500 companies

CEOComp: Total compensation for the year 2000 for CEOs

Chief executive officers (CEOs) of Fortune 500 companies typically receive a compensation package worth many millions. Sometimes these packages are so unbelievably large that share holders publicly criticize top management and the company's compensation committee. Of course, most CEOs still seem to believe they are worth every dollar they get.

a. Find the mean, median, and midrange of the total compensation for CEOs of the selected companies.

b. Remove the CEO pay for Citigroup and General Electric and repeat part a. Compare these statistics to those obtained in part a.

c. Suppose that these compensation packages were to be compared to those of Japanese firms. To make a comparison, the amount of compensation could be converted into yen. Assuming that 1 dollar is equal to 120 yen, what do you think the new mean and median would be for the total compensation in units of yen for the CEOs of the selected companies?

d. Transform the compensation figures by multiplying them by 120 to obtain equivalent figures in yen and find the mean and median. Compare the computed values to your values in part c.

(Source: "CEO Pay: Whoosh!" *Fortune,* June 25, 2001, p. 78.)

3.3   MEASURES OF VARIATION

Measures of central tendency, such as the mean, are certainly useful. However, the use of any single statistic to describe a complete distribution fails to reveal important facts.

Homogeneity refers to the degree of similarity within a set of data values. For example, the values in data set 1 (sunrise times for 10 randomly selected days in May) are much more homogeneous than the values in data set 2 (current batting averages for the starting lineup of the Cincinnati Reds.)

Data set 1:   6:20, 6:20, 6:20, 6:21, 6:21, 6:22, 6:22, 6:24, 6:26, 6:27
Data set 2:   .163, .186, .220, .250, .278, .283, .294, .318, .334

The more homogeneous a set of data is, the better the mean will represent a typical value. **Variation** is the tendency of data values to scatter about the mean, $\bar{x}$. If all the data values in a sample are identical, then the mean provides perfect information, the variation is zero, and the data are perfectly homogeneous. This is rarely the case, however, so we need a measure of this variation that will increase as the scatter of the data values about $\bar{x}$ increases.

Knowledge of variation can sometimes be used to control the future variability of your data values. Industrial production operations maintain quality control by observing and measuring the variation of the units produced. If there is too much variation in the production process, the causes are determined and corrected using an inspection control procedure.

Commonly used measures of variation are the *range, variance, standard deviation,* and *coefficient of variation.* Such measures are meaningful only when computed from *interval* or *ratio* data. To illustrate the various variation measures, we will use the accident data from the previous section: 6, 9, 7, 23, 5.

The Range

The simplest measure of variation is the **range** of the data, which is the numerical difference between the largest value (H) and the smallest value (L). For the accident data,

$$\text{range} = H - L = 23 - 5 = 18$$

The range is a rather crude measure of variation, but it is an easy number to calculate and contains valuable information for many situations. Stock reports generally give prices in terms of their ranges, citing the high and low prices of the day. The value of the range is strongly influenced by an outlier in the sample data.

The Variance and Standard Deviation

By far the most commonly used measures of variation are the **variance** and **standard deviation.** Both measures describe the variation of the sample values about the sample mean, $\bar{x}$. Using the accident data, the sample mean is $\bar{x} = 10$. To calculate the sample variance, you begin by finding (1) the distance from each sample value to the mean, (2) the square of these distances, and (3) the sum of the squared distances. The closer the sample values are to $\bar{x} = 10$, the smaller this sum will be. Figure 3.5 illustrates the distance from the second sample value (6) to the mean, $\bar{x}$. The calculations necessary to compute the variance are as follows.

Data Value (x)	($x - \bar{x}$)	($x - \bar{x}$)^2
5	−5	25
6	−4	16
7	−3	9
9	−1	1
23	13	169
	$\sum(x - \bar{x}) = 0$	$\sum(x - \bar{x})^2 = 220$

So, $\sum(x - \bar{x})^2 = 220$.

The obvious thing to do next would be to find the average of these squared deviations:

$$\frac{\sum(x - \bar{x})^2}{n}$$

One use of this particular statistic in subsequent chapters is an *estimator.* In particular, we will need to estimate the variation within an entire population, using sample data collected from the population. However, a better estimator is

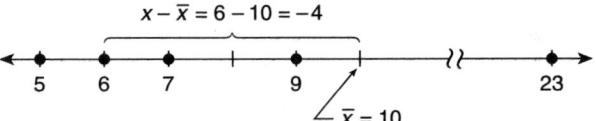

$x - \bar{x} = 6 - 10 = -4$

$\bar{x} = 10$

FIGURE

3.5

This presentation of the accident data shows their variation.

obtained by dividing the sum of the squared deviations by $n-1$ rather than by n. This leads to the **sample variance, s^2**. In general,

---

DEFINITION

$$s^2 = \frac{\Sigma(x - \bar{x})^2}{n-1}$$

3.4

Using the accident data,

$$s^2 = \frac{220}{5-1} = \frac{220}{4} = 55.0$$

The square root of the variance is referred to as the **sample standard deviation, s.** In general,

---

$$s = \sqrt{\frac{\Sigma(x - \bar{x})^2}{n-1}}$$

3.5

Using the accident data,

$$s = \sqrt{55.0} = 7.416$$

As previously mentioned, the sample variance, s^2, is used to estimate the variance of the entire population. The symbol for the population variance is σ^2 (read as sigma squared). For a population consisting of N elements,

$$x_1, x_2, x_3, \ldots, x_N$$

the population variance is defined to be

$$\sigma^2 = \frac{\Sigma(x - \mu)^2}{N}$$

3.6

---

where μ is the population mean, defined in equation 3.2.

As we saw, the *population* variance can be obtained by dividing the sum of the squared deviations about μ by the population size N. The *sample* variance is calculated by dividing the sum of the squared deviations about $\bar{x}$ by the sample size (n) minus one. Had we chosen to divide by n rather than by $n-1$, the resulting estimator would (on the average) underestimate σ^2. For this reason, we use $n-1$ in the denominator of s^2.

- Population: $x_1, x_2, \ldots, x_N$

- Population variance $= \sigma^2 = \dfrac{(x_1 - \mu)^2 + \cdots + (x_N - \mu)^2}{N}$

  $= \dfrac{\Sigma(x - \mu)^2}{N}$

- Population standard deviation $= \sigma = \sqrt{\dfrac{\Sigma(x - \mu)^2}{N}}$

- Sample values (selected from the population): $x_1, x_2, \ldots, x_n$, where $n \leq N$

- Sample variance $= s^2 = \dfrac{(x_1 - \bar{x})^2 + \cdots + (x_n - \bar{x})^2}{n-1} = \dfrac{\Sigma(x - \bar{x})^2}{n-1}$

- Sample standard deviation $= s = \sqrt{\dfrac{\Sigma(x - \bar{x})^2}{n-1}}$

Now consider what the units of measurement are for s and s^2. The units of s are the same as the units on the data. If the data are measured in pounds, the units of s are pounds. Consequently, the units of the variance, s^2, would be (pounds)^2—a rather difficult unit to grasp, at best. For the accident data, $s = 7.416$ accidents and $s^2 = 55$ (accidents)^2.

Comments

The units of measurement for s are the same as the units of measurement on the mean ($\bar{x}$)—namely, the units of measurement for the sample values. As a result, we are able to combine the sample standard deviation and the sample mean and ask questions such as, "How many of the sample values are less than $\bar{x} + s$?" or "How many of the sample values lie between $\bar{x} - s$ and $\bar{x} + s$?" Such questions will be discussed in Section 3.6.

There is another way to compute the sample variance. Using equation 3.4 to compute the value of s^2 may have appeared easy enough, but the computation was helped in part by the fact that the sample mean, $\bar{x}$, was an integer (10). When $\bar{x}$ is not an integer, it is easier to find s^2 using

COMPUTING FORMULA FOR s^2

$$s^2 = \frac{\sum x^2 - (\sum x)^2 / n}{n - 1}$$

3.7

As before, the standard deviation is the square root of the variance. To illustrate the use of equation 3.7, consider the accident data:

x	x^2
5	25
6	36
7	49
9	81
23	529
50	720

So, $n = 5$, $\sum x = 50$, $\sum x^2 = 720$. Consequently, using equation 3.7

$$s^2 = \frac{720 - (50)^2 / 5}{5 - 1}$$

$$= \frac{720 - 500}{4} = 55.0 \qquad \text{(as before)}$$

Also

$$s = \sqrt{55.0} = 7.416 \qquad \text{(as before)}$$

Finally, you may wish to interpret the magnitude of the value of s or s^2—that is, whether your value of s (or s^2) is large. This is difficult to determine because the values of s and s^2 depend on the magnitude of the data values. In other words, large data values generally lead to large values of s. For example, which of the following two data sets exhibits more variation?

Data set 1:   5, 6, 7, 9, 23   (accident reports)
Data set 2:   5,000, 6,000, 7,000, 9,000, 23,000   (seating capacity of five football stadiums)

As we have already seen, for data set 1, $\bar{x} = 10.0$ and $s = 7.416$. For data set 2, the mean and standard deviation are $\bar{x} = 10,000$ and $s = 7,416$.

Do these results mean that data set 2 has a great deal more variation, given that its standard deviation is 1,000 times that of data set 1? Another look at the values reveals that the large value of s for data set 2 is due to the large values within this set. In fact, considering the size of the numbers within each data set, the *relative* variation within each group of values is the same. So comparing the standard deviations or variations of two data sets is not a good idea unless you know that their mean values ($\bar{x}$) are approximately equal. The next section deals with another statistical measure that will allow you to compare the relative variation within two data sets.

The Coefficient of Variation

Consider again our two data sets, which appear to have the same variation (relative to the size of the data values) yet have vastly different standard deviations:

Data set 1: 5, 6, 7, 9, 23   ($\bar{x} = 10, s = 7.416$)
Data set 2: 5,000, 6,000, 7,000, 9,000, 23,000   ($\bar{x} = 10{,}000, s = 7{,}416$)

To compare their variation, we need a measure of variation that will produce the same value for both of them. The solution here is to measure the standard deviation in terms of the mean; that is, what percentage of $\bar{x}$ is s? This measure of variation is the **coefficient of variation, CV.** In general, for samples containing non-negative values,

$$CV = \frac{s}{\bar{x}} \cdot 100$$

3.8

For our example data sets:

Data set 1: $CV = \dfrac{7.416}{10} \cdot 100 = 74.16$

Data set 2: $CV = \dfrac{7{,}416}{10{,}000} \cdot 100 = 74.16$

So our conclusion here is that both data sets exhibit the same relative variation; s is 74.16% of the mean for both sets. As a final word here, we must point out that for data sets with *extreme* variation, it is possible to obtain a coefficient of variation larger than 100%.

EXAMPLE 3.3

To review the various measures of variation, let's use the data on housing construction time in Example 3.1.

Completion time: 4.1, 3.2, 2.8, 2.6, 3.7, 3.1, 9.4, 2.5, 3.5, 3.8 (months)

First, compute the range:

$$H - L = 9.4 - 2.5 = 6.9 \text{ months}$$

To find the variance and the standard deviation, first determine

$$\Sigma x = 4.1 + 3.2 + \cdots + 3.8 = 38.7$$

and

$$\Sigma x^2 = (4.1)^2 + (3.2)^2 + \cdots + (3.8)^2 = 186.25$$

Hence,

$$s^2 = \frac{186.25 - (38.7)^2/10}{10 - 1}$$

$$= \frac{186.25 - 149.77}{9} = 4.05 \text{ (months)}^2$$

and

$$s = \sqrt{4.05} = 2.01 \text{ months}$$

To calculate the coefficient of variation, use the previously obtained values of s and $\bar{x}$, where

$$CV = \frac{2.01}{3.87} \cdot 100 = 51.9$$

The standard deviation is 51.9% of the sample mean.

Microsoft® Excel Application Use DATA3-4

Using Excel to Compute Various Sample Statistics

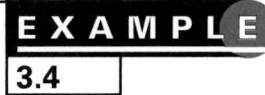

EXAMPLE 3.4

Example 2.1 introduced a sample of inside diameters for 100 machined parts produced at the Boston facility of Allied Manufacturing. This sample is also contained in Excel file DATA3-4. The machined part is supposed to have an inside diameter of 10.2 millimeters, with specification (spec) limits of 10.1 to 10.3 millimeters. Prior to examining this sample, you received word that the Toronto facility of Allied obtained a random sample of their parts, which have the same specs. Their sample produced a mean of 10.191 millimeters and a standard deviation of .0448 millimeter. Determine the sample mean, range, standard deviation, and coefficient of variation of the Boston sample. Comment on this sample. In particular, do these parts appear to be better than the Toronto parts?

Solution

The Excel output using the descriptive statistics command is shown in Figure 3.6. To obtain this output, refer to Figure 3.2 and enter A1:A101 for the input range and B1 for the output range. Be sure to click on the checkboxes for **Labels in First Row** and **Summary Statistics** (as illustrated in Figure 3.2). The coefficient of variation in cells B16 and C16 is not part of the initial output but can be easily obtained by entering "Coeff. of Variation" in cell B16 and "=(C7/C3)*100" in cell C16.

FIGURE 3.6

Descriptive statistics for 100 machined parts (inside diameters) (coefficient of variation added).

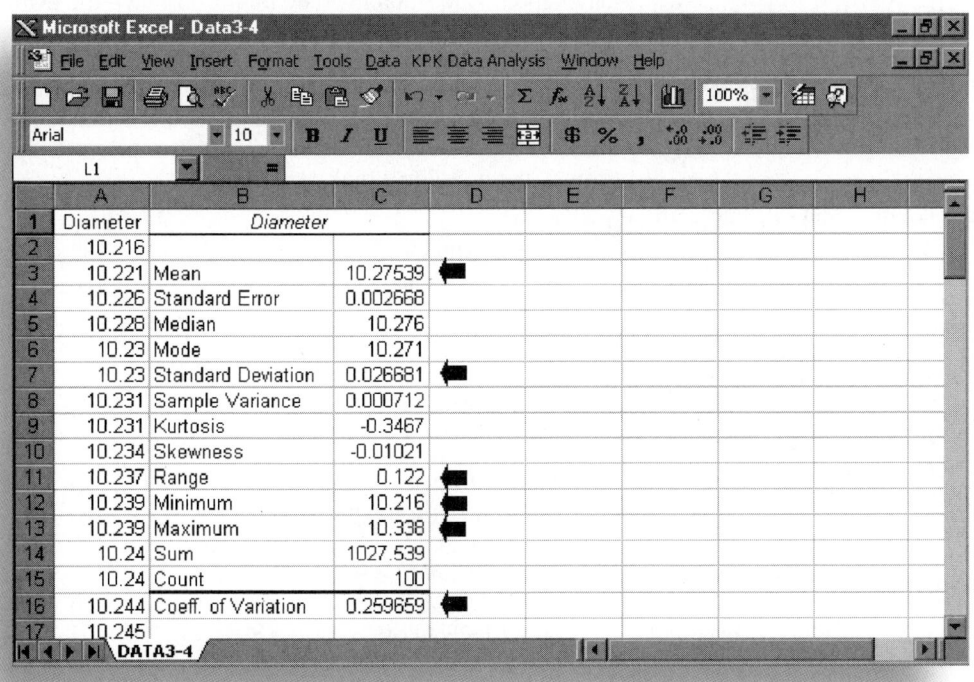

The smallest sample value is 10.216, the largest value is 10.338, and the range is $10.338 - 10.216 = .122$ millimeter. This machined part is supposed to have an inside diameter of 10.2 millimeters. The specification limits were from 10.1 to 10.3 millimeters; that is, these parts are of acceptable quality only if the diameter is between these two values. The sample mean of 10.275 is much larger than 10.2 millimeters, so the conclusion here would be the same as in Example 2.1: The process is off center and needs adjustment. The standard deviation for the Boston sample is .0267, and the coefficient of variation is .260. Consequently, the sample standard deviation is .26% of the sample mean.

To compare the Boston and Toronto samples, consider the following summary information:

	$\bar{x}$	s
Boston	10.275	.0267
Toronto	10.191	.0448

Based on this information, is the Boston process better or worse than the Toronto process? The answer is *both!* The Boston process is worse based on the value of $\bar{x}$, since this indicates that this process is .075 (10.275 − 10.2) millimeter off center, whereas for the Toronto sample, the production process is .009 (10.2 − 10.191) millimeter off center. However, the Boston process is more consistent, since the standard deviation ($s = .0267$ millimeter) is much smaller than for the Toronto sample ($s = .0448$ millimeter). So you have mixed results here—the Boston process has less variation but is producing parts having inside diameters that are too large, on the average.

So far, you can reduce a set of sample data to a number that indicates a typical or average value (a measure of central tendency) or one that describes the amount of variation within the data values (a measure of variation). The next section examines yet another set of statistics—measures of position.

X Exercises 3.12–3.21

Understanding the Mechanics

3.12 From 50 collected data points, the statistics Σx and Σx^2 are calculated to be 20 and 33, respectively. Compute the sample mean, sample variance, sample standard deviation, and coefficient of variation.

3.13 Find the range, standard deviation, and coefficient of variation for each of the following data sets and comment on your results:

    a. 2   4   6   8   10
    b. 20 40 60 80 100
    c. .02 .04 .06 .08 .10

3.14 The values of the difference between the data values and the sample mean are −5, 1, −3, 2, 3, and 2.
    a. Do these values add to 0? Should they?
    b. What is the variance of the data?
    c. What is the standard deviation?

Applying the New Concepts

3.15 There are many factors to consider in deciding which portable CD player to buy. One determining factor is the price. Although less-expensive CD players might

have good sound quality, they might not have the extra features of some of the more expensive models. For example, one feature is the ESP Plus feature, which stands for "electronic shock protection" and provides skip protection. The following 16 models illustrate how variable the price of a portable CD player can be. The prices range from a low of $40 to a high of $200.

Model	Price
Sony D-MJ95	130
Sony D-SJ17CK	160
Sony D-SJ01	200
Sony D-EJ611	80
Sony D-SJ15	130
Panasonic SL-SX280	50
Aiwa XP-SP911	80
Panasonic SL-SW869V	170
Aiwa XP-V713	70
Panasonic SL-CT470	100
Philips AZ9213	80
Philips Expanium EXP103/17	180
GPX C394881	60
RCA RP-2360FM	65
Lenoxx Sound CD-91	55
RCA RP-2300	40

a. What is the mean price for a portable CD player?

b. Without computing the standard deviation, a rough estimate can be obtained by dividing the range by 4. What is this approximation of the standard deviation?

c. Compute the standard deviation and compare it to the answer obtained in part b.

d. Compute the coefficient of variation for portable CD players. Would you use this statistic or the standard deviation to compare the variability of the price of portable CD players to the prices of high-priced consumer electronics, such as television sets?

(Source: "Portable CD Players," *Consumer Reports,* July 2001, p. 43.)

3.16 The prices of two stocks are shown to vary over a 12-month period. Describe the variability of the stocks. Which stock appears to be more stable? Why?

Month	Stock A	Stock B
Jan	10	30
Feb	11	33
Mar	12	36
Apr	11	32
May	15	45
June	18	49
Jul	13	37
Aug	16	48
Sept	11	33
Oct	10	30
Nov	9	33
Dec	13	39

3.17 Show that

$$s^2 = \frac{\Sigma(x - \bar{x})^2}{n - 1}$$

is equivalent to

$$s^2 = \frac{\Sigma x^2 - (\Sigma x)^2/n}{n - 1}$$

3.18 a. Name an advantage and a disadvantage of using either the range or the standard deviation as a measure of variation.

b. What is the smallest value for either the range or the standard deviation?

c. If either the range or standard deviation is equal to zero, what can you say about each value of the sample?

3.19 Apparel sales in summer are difficult for apparel retailers because shoppers are usually looking for summer discounts. The July sales for six large apparel retailers for July 2001 are as follows:

Apparel Retailer	Sales in Millions
Gap	948.0
Limited	612.3
TJX	745.0
Kohl's	466.3
Talbots	106.6
AnnTaylor	84.9

a. From observing the data, what would you guess is the mean and standard deviation?

b. Compute the mean and the standard deviation.

c. Remove the apparel retailers with the largest and smallest sales. How do you believe the mean and standard deviation of the sales will change with the removal of these figures?

d. Compare the calculated mean and standard deviation with the values that you guessed. What characteristics about the data give you a clue as to what the mean and standard deviation might be?

(Source: "Discounts in Demand: Shoppers Sought Bargains in July," *Wall Street Journal,* August 10, 2001, p. B3.)

Using the Computer

3.20 [DATA SET EX3-20] *Variable Description:*

YearMonth: Year and months ranging from January 1982 to August 2001

CPI: The consumer price index

CPILessE&G: The consumer price index excluding energy and food

Economists use the Consumer Price Index (CPI) to obtain insights into the effects of inflation on purchases made by consumers. The CPI is a measure of the average change in prices over time in a market basket of goods and services. This measure is also computed excluding energy and food since these two categories can change dramatically.

a. Compute the mean and standard deviation for the CPI for the time period from January 1982 to August 2001.

b. Repeat part a using the CPI excluding energy and food.

c. Compute the coefficient of variation for the CPI and for CPI excluding energy and food. Discuss your findings when comparing these two measures.

(Source: "Taming Inflation," *Wall Street Journal,* August 17, 2001, p. A2.)

3.21 [DATA SET EX3-21] *Variable description:*

TimeTV: Total daily time in minutes spent watching TV

Marketing managers are interested in TV viewership to attract company advertising. Viewers are customers for many products. To justify the millions of dollars spent on advertising, marketing departments must assess the percentage of the population that TV advertisement will reach as well as the likelihood of a viewer seeing the advertisement. One hundred adult viewers were sampled, and their total daily time in minutes spent watching TV for that day was recorded.

a. Find the mean and standard deviation of TimeTV. (Excel: Use the **Paste Function ➤ Statistical.**) Compute the coefficient of variation and variance from these values.

b. Convert the values of TimeTV to hours by dividing by 60. How do you think the mean, standard deviation, and variance will change?

c. Compute the mean, standard deviation, and variance of the values of TimeTV in units of hours. Compare these results to your answer in part b. Is this what you expected?

3.4

MEASURES OF POSITION

Suppose that you think you are drastically underpaid compared with other people with similar experience and performance. One way to attack the problem is to obtain the salaries of these other employees and demonstrate that *comparatively* you are way down the list. To evaluate your salary compared with the entire group, you would use a measure of position. *Measures of position* are indicators of how a particular value fits in with all the other data values. Two commonly used measures of position are (1) a percentile (and quartile), and (2) a z-score.

To illustrate these measures, we suppose that the personnel manager of Texon Industries has administered an aptitude test to 50 applicants. The ordered data are shown in Table 3.2. The mean of the data is $\bar{x} = 60.36$, and the standard deviation is $s = 18.61$. Ms. Jenson received the score of 83. She wishes to measure her performance in relation to all the applicant scores. We will return to this illustration in Example 3.5.

Percentiles

A **percentile** is the most common measure of position. The value of, for example, the 35th percentile is essentially the value that exceeds 35% of all the data values. More precisely, the 35th percentile is that value (say, P_{35}) such that at most 35% of the data values are less than P_{35} and at most 65% of the data values are greater than P_{35}. We will use the Texon Industries applicant data to determine the 35th percentile. Which data value is located 35% of the way between the first and last locations? Here the number of data values is $n = 50$ and the percentile is $P = 35$. We define the *position* of the 35th percentile as follows:

$$n \cdot \frac{P}{100} = 50 \cdot .35 = 17.5$$

To satisfy the more precise definition of a percentile, whenever $n \cdot P/100$ is *not* a counting number, it should be rounded *up* to the next counting number. So, 17.5 is rounded up to 18, and the 35th percentile is the 18th value *of the ordered values.* Referring to Table 3.2, the 35th percentile is $P_{35} = 53$.

TABLE

3.2

Ordered array of aptitude test scores for 50 applicants ($\bar{x} = 60.36$, $s = 18.61$).

22	44	56	68	78
25	44	57	68	78
28	46	59	69	80
31	48	60	71	82
34	49	61	72	83
35	51	63	72	85
39	53	63	74	88
39	53	63	75	90
40	55	65	75	92
42	55	66	76	96

In general, to find the *location* of the Pth percentile, determine $n \cdot P/100$ and use one of the following two location rules.

Location rule 1. If $n \cdot P/100$ is *not* a counting number, round it *up*, and the Pth percentile will be the value in this position of the ordered data.

Location rule 2. If $n \cdot P/100$ *is* a counting number, the Pth percentile is the average of the number in this location (of the ordered data) and the number in the next largest location.

Now we can use the applicant data to determine the 40th percentile. Here $n \cdot P/100 = (50)(.4) = 20$. Then, using the second rule,

$$P_{40} = 40\text{th percentile} = \frac{(20\text{th value}) + (21\text{st value})}{2}$$

$$= \frac{55 + 56}{2} = 55.5$$

Notice here that the 40th percentile is *not* one of the data values but is an average of two of them. Now work out the 50th percentile yourself. What measure of the central tendency uses the same procedure? From our previous discussion, you should realize that *the 50th percentile is the median.*

EXAMPLE 3.5

Recall that Ms. Jenson received a score of 83. What is her percentile value?

Solution

Her value is the 45th largest value (out of a total of 50). An initial guess of her percentile would be:

$$P = \frac{45}{50} \cdot 100 = 90$$

However, due to the percentile rules used here, this guess may be slightly incorrect. Your next step should be to examine this value of P, along with the next two smaller values. The following calculations of $P = 88$, $P = 89$, and $P = 90$ reveal that Ms. Jenson's score is the 89th percentile.

P	$\dfrac{n \cdot P}{100}$	Pth Percentile
88	$50 \cdot .88 = 44$	$(82 + 83)/2 = 82.5$
89	$50 \cdot .89 = 44.5$	45th value $= 83$
90	$50 \cdot .90 = 45$	$(83 + 85)/2 = 84$

EXAMPLE 3.6

What is the 50th percentile for the applicant data in Table 3.2?

Solution

Here, $n \cdot P/100 = 50 \cdot .5 = 25$. The 50th percentile is an average of the 25th and 26th ordered data values:

$$P_{50} = 50\text{th percentile} = \frac{61 + 63}{2} = 62$$

Quartiles

Quartiles are merely particular percentiles that divide the data into quarters, namely:

$Q_1 = $ 1st quartile $= $ 25th percentile (P_{25})

$Q_2 = $ 2nd quartile $= $ 50th percentile $= $ median (P_{50})

$Q_3 = $ 3rd quartile $= $ 75th percentile (P_{75})

They are used as benchmarks, much like the use of A, B, C, D, and F on examination grades. Using the applicant data in Table 3.2, we can determine the first quartile by first calculating:

$$n \cdot \frac{P}{100} = (50)(.25) = 12.5$$

This result is rounded up to 13, and $Q_1 = $ 13th ordered value $= 46$.

$$Q_2 = \text{median} = 62$$

from Example 3.6. Finally, for Q_3,

$$n \cdot \frac{P}{100} = (50)(.75) = 37.5$$

This is rounded up to 38, and $Q_3 = $ 38th ordered value $= 75$.

Another measure, commonly used in conjunction with quartiles is the **interquartile range (IQR),** defined as

$$IQR = Q_3 - Q_1$$

In the applicant data, the interquartile range is

$$IQR = 75 - 46 = 29$$

Consequently, the middle 50% of the data are between 46 and 75.

Strictly speaking, the interquartile range is a measure of variation, since it can be expected to increase as the data become more spread out. It is not a commonly used measure of variation, although it is certainly easy to compute (much like the range of a sample data set). Its primary disadvantage is that it measures the spread within the middle of the data, not within the entire data set. The interquartile range can be illustrated in a simple graph called a box plot, discussed in Section 3.8.

z-Scores

Another measure of position is a sample z-score, which is based on the mean ($\bar{x}$) and standard deviation of the data set. Like a percentile, a z-score determines the relative position of any particular data value x; it is expressed in terms of the number of standard deviations above or below the mean. The z-score of x is defined as

$$z = \frac{x - \bar{x}}{s} \qquad \text{3.9}$$

Recall from Example 3.5 that Ms. Jenson had a score of 83 on the test. For this data set, $\bar{x} = 60.36$ and $s = 18.61$. Her score of 83 is the 89th percentile. The corresponding z-score is

$$z = \frac{83 - 60.36}{18.61} = 1.22$$

This z-score means that Ms. Jenson's score of 83 is 1.22 standard deviations to the *right* of the mean, or above the group's average. Thus, if z is positive, it indicates how many standard deviations x is to the right of the mean.

A negative z-score implies that x is to the *left* of the mean. Again referring to Table 3.2, what is the z-score for the individual who obtained a total of 35 on the aptitude examination?

$$z = \frac{35 - 60.36}{18.61} = -1.36$$

This individual's score is 1.36 standard deviations to the left of the mean, or below the group's average.

The process of subtracting the mean and dividing by the standard deviation is referred to as *standardizing* the sample data, and the corresponding z-value is the *standardized* value. So Ms. Jensen's raw score is 83, and her standardized score is 1.22 indicating that her raw score is 1.22 standard deviations to the right of the mean. For a "typical" sample, you can expect nearly all of the standardized values to lie between –3 and 3 (the z-scores range from –3 to 3). This will be discussed further in Section 3.6.

EXAMPLE 3.7

Example 3.4 contained data listing 100 measurements for the inside diameter of a certain machined part. The specification limits for this part are 10.1 millimeters (the lower spec limit, or LSL) and 10.3 millimeters (the upper spec limit, or USL). Any part falling outside this range is said to be nonconforming and is not of acceptable quality. Of interest here is the following question: What is the z-score for both the LSL and the USL and which z-score has the smaller absolute value?

Solution

The z-score for each of these limits is found by subtracting the sample mean and dividing by the standard deviation. In Example 3.4, the sample mean was found to be $\bar{x} = 10.275$ and the sample standard deviation was $s = .0267$. The z-score for the USL (10.3) is

$$\frac{10.3 - 10.275}{.0267} = .94$$

and the z-score for the LSL is

$$\frac{10.1 - 10.275}{.0267} = -6.55$$

The absolute values of these two z-scores are .94 and 6.55. The minimum of these two absolute values is .94, indicating that the nearer spec limit is the upper spec limit and that the sample mean is .94 standard deviations away from this limit. *A general rule here is that to consistently produce products of acceptable quality, the minimum absolute value of these two z-scores should be at least 3.* In this case, the product is not capable of meeting these specifications—a result consistent with Examples 2.1 and 3.4.

3.5 MEASURES OF SHAPE

A basic question in many applications is whether your data exhibit a *symmetric* pattern. **Measures of shape** include measures of skewness and kurtosis.

Skewness

The histogram in Figure 3.7 demonstrates a perfectly symmetric distribution. When the data are symmetric, the sample mean, $\bar{x}$, and the sample median, Md, are the same. As the data tend toward a nonsymmetric distribution, referred to as skewed, the mean and median drift apart. The easiest method of determining the

FIGURE

3.7

Histogram
constructed with
symmetric data.
The mean, median,
and mode are
equal.

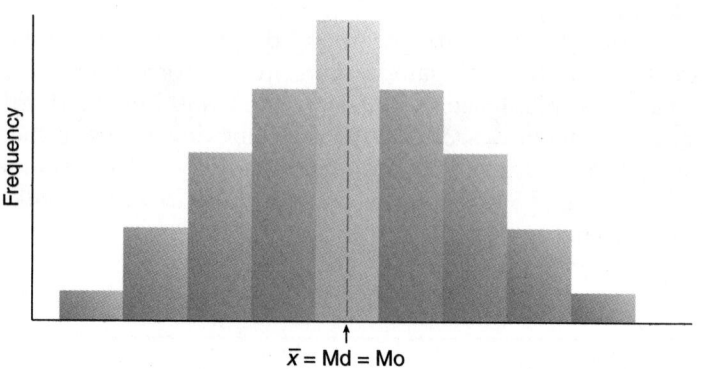

$\bar{x} = Md = Mo$

FIGURE

3.8

Histogram
showing right
(positive) skew.

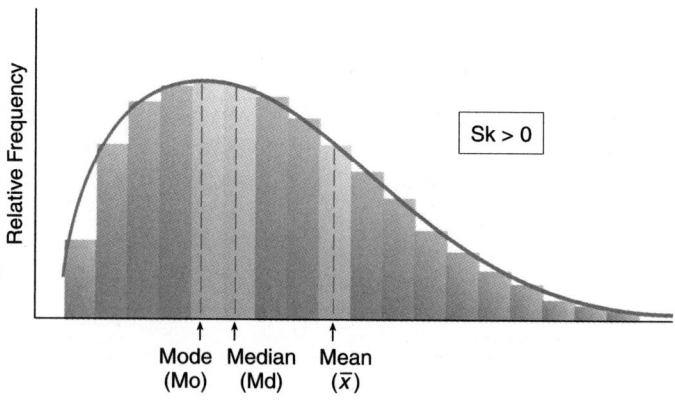

Sk > 0

Mode   Median   Mean
(Mo)   (Md)   ($\bar{x}$)

degree of *skewness* present in your sample data is to calculate a measure referred to as the **Pearson's coefficient of skewness, *Sk*.** Its value is given by:

$$Sk = \frac{3(\bar{x} - Md)}{s}$$

3.10

where *s* is the standard deviation of the sample data.

The value of *Sk* ranges from –3 to 3.* If the data are perfectly symmetric (a rare event), *Sk* = 0, because $\bar{x} = Md$. For Figure 3.7, *Sk* is zero. If the mean is larger than the median, then *Sk* is positive, and we say that the data are *skewed right*. Consequently, for data that are skewed right, *values above the mean occur less frequently than values below the mean.* This merely means the data exhibit a pattern with a right tail, as illustrated in Figure 3.8. We know the mean is affected by extreme values, so we would expect the mean to move toward the right tail, above the median, resulting in a positive value of *Sk*. Similarly, if the mean is smaller than the median, then *Sk* is negative and the data are *skewed left*. As a result, in a negatively skewed sample, *values above the mean occur more frequently than values below the mean.* Figure 3.9 shows a data distribution exhibiting a left tail and negative skew.

*One proof of this statement can be found in Colm Art O'Cinneide, "The Mean is Within One Standard Deviation of Any Median," *The American Statistician* 44, no. 4 (1990), p. 292.

FIGURE

3.9

Histogram
showing left
(negative) skew.

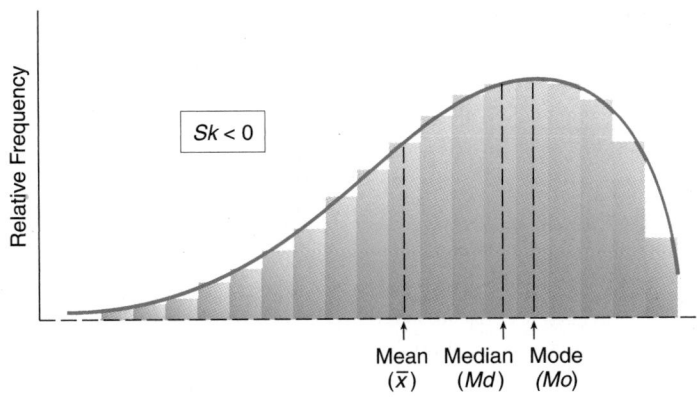

Excel, SPSS, and MINITAB use a slightly more complicated measure of skewness. This involves finding the z-score for each data value, cubing each z-score, and then summing the results (that is, $(z\text{-score})_1^3 + (z\text{-score})_2^3 + (z\text{-score})_3^3 + \ldots$). This measure of skewness will be written as Sk' and uses the formula given below.

$$Sk' = \frac{n}{(n-1)(n-2)}\sum\left(\frac{x-\bar{x}}{s}\right)^3 = \frac{n}{(n-1)(n-2)}\sum(z\text{-score})^3 \qquad 3.11$$

Similar to the Pearson's skewness measure, this measure of skewness will be positive for samples that are skewed right (Figure 3.8) and negative for samples that are skewed left (Figure 3.9).

Examples 3.4 and 3.7 were concerned with the inside diameters of 100 machined parts. To examine the symmetry of the data, we can use the various statistics in Figure 3.6. The Pearson's measure of skewness is

$$Sk = \frac{3(10.27539 - 10.276)}{.02668} = -.069$$

This is nearly zero, and we conclude that the data are nearly symmetric and a histogram of these 100 values would resemble the one in Figure 3.7. According to Figure 3.6, the Excel, SPSS, and MINITAB measure of skewness is $Sk' = -.0102$ (in cell C10). Since this skewness measure is nearly zero, we again conclude that the data are nearly symmetric.

Kurtosis

Sk measures the tendency of a distribution to stretch out in a particular direction. Another measure of shape, referred to as the **kurtosis,** measures the *peakedness* of your distribution. The calculation of this measure is a bit cumbersome, and the kurtosis value is not needed in the remaining text material.* Briefly, this value is large if there is a high frequency of observations near the mean and in the tails of the distribution.

---

*Using Excel, you can click on **Help ➤ Contexts and Index,** and type "kurtosis." The formula used by Excel is in this discussion.

Exercises 3.22–3.33

Understanding the Mechanics

3.22 The number of defects in 10 rolls of carpets are

$$3 \quad 2 \quad 6 \quad 0 \quad 1 \quad 3 \quad 2 \quad 1 \quad 0 \quad 4$$

   a. What are the 75th percentile and the 50th percentile?
   b. What are the mean and standard deviation?
   c. What is the coefficient of skewness?

3.23 Assume that the sum of 10 observations is 10, that the sum of the squares of 10 observations is 20, and that the median is 1.5. What is the coefficient of skewness?

3.24 The percentage of unemployed workers in each of 20 randomly selected cities are as follows.

   3.1   4.5   8.2   1.4   6.3   1.8   2.4   8.8   1.9   2.4
   5.4   3.8   7.2   3.8   4.6   7.2   2.5   4.8   3.7   4.2

   a. Calculate the 20th percentile.
   b. Calculate the 40th percentile.
   c. Calculate the 60th percentile.
   d. Calculate the 80th percentile.
   e. Calculate the interquartile range.

3.25 From a random sample, the mean is 50 and the sample standard deviation is 5.
   a. What is the z-score if an observation's value is 40?
   b. What is the z-score if an observation's value is 65?
   c. What is the value of an observation with a z-score of 1?
   d. What is the value of an observation with a z-score of –2.5?

3.26 The time (in minutes) that it takes 20 people to complete a task follows.

   30   35   51   65   22   35   44   55   30   50
   40   60   64   38   52   68   38   53   62   49

   a. Find the interquartile range.
   b. Find the mean of the data.
   c. Find the standard deviation of the data.
   d. Find the coefficient of skewness.

Applying the New Concepts

3.27 The following data were obtained from a survey requesting 30 different families to list their weekly expenditure on food.

   105   85   72   59   130   120   95   83   78   91
   64   106   86   87   78   108   145   102   86   74
   72   103   94   63   73   89   75   88   107   101

   a. Calculate the 20th percentile.
   b. Calculate the 80th percentile.
   c. Calculate the interquartile range.
   d. Calculate the mean, median, standard deviation, and coefficient of skewness.
   e. Write up a brief description of the survey's results, and interpret each of the values of the statistics.

3.28 Consider the following grades recorded on an aptitude test.

   70   15   42   21   73   45   22   71   20   74
   74   53   74   86   52   19   77   84   73   54
   87   90   71   53   21   71   75   72   12   47

   a. Calculate each of the quartiles and the coefficient of skewness to describe the distribution of the data.
   b. What observations would you consider to be unusually low or high? Why?
   c. How would you evaluate a student who scored 75 on the exam?

3.29 Select five numbers between 0 and 10.
   a. Calculate the standard deviation of these five numbers.
   b. Form the z-scores for these five numbers.
   c. What do you think is the standard deviation of the z-scores? Calculate the standard deviation of the z-scores.

3.30 The prices (in dollars) for unleaded gas at 10 service stations in Boyston and in Farmersville are as follows. Describe the distribution of the price of unleaded gas using the mean, standard deviation, and coefficient of skewness.

Boyston: 1.20 1.17 1.20 1.25 1.24 1.35 1.18 1.20 1.40
            1.18
Farmersville: 1.19 1.25 1.14 1.20 1.30 1.25 1.33 1.25
            1.20 1.24

Using the Computer

3.31 [DATA SET EX3-31] *Variable Description:*

YearandQuarter: Time period ranging from the third quarter of 1996 to the second quarter of 2001

VolStocks: Quarterly trading volume of stocks

VolBonds: Quarterly trading volume of bonds

In 2000, Nasdaq, NYSE, and American Stock Exchange markets processed more than five times the volume as in 1990. Online day trading has become popular and has contributed to the increased trading volume. Fortunately, the technology of automated computer systems has reached a level that easily enables the markets to handle the increased trading volume. The trading volume over the past few years has fluctuated dramatically. Data for quarterly trading volumes of stocks and bonds from 1996 to 2001 are given in billions of shares.
   a. What is the coefficient of variation for the quarterly trading volume of stocks from the third quarter of 1996 to the second quarter of 2001?
   b. Repeat part a for the quarterly volume of bonds.
   c. Compare the two coefficients of variation from parts a and b. Why is the coefficient of variation a better measure than the standard deviation when comparing the variability of the quarterly trading volumes of stocks and bonds?

d. Compute Pearson's coefficient of skewness for the quarterly trading volume of stocks. Interpret this number.

e. Compute the interquartile range for the quarterly trading volume of bonds. Would this measure be affected by a single outlier?

(Source: "Quarterly Volume of New Global Stocks and Bonds," *Wall Street Journal*, July 2, 2001, p. C18.)

3.32 [DATA SET EX3-32] *Variable description:*

Checkfee: Fee that financial institution charges for a checking account with no minimum

Bank and financial institutions have been steadily increasing checking fees for no-minimum checking accounts. A sample of 75 banks and financial institutions that offer checking accounts with no minimum balance required was selected in the Toronto metropolitan area. Data are presented in units of Canadian dollars.

a. What are the mean, median, and standard deviation, coefficient of skewness, and the interquartile range? How would you interpret these statistics?

b. Convert the data to U.S. dollars. Use the conversion 1 Canadian dollar equals .70 U.S. dollars. Calculate the statistics in part a. How do these values change?

3.33 [DATA SET EX3-33] *Variable Description:*

District: Forty school districts in North Texas

Graduates: Number of high school graduates in the year 2000

State funding and salary structure in school districts depend on a formula that takes into account the number of students. Because the number of students varies greatly across the school districts of North Texas, educational administrators face a considerable challenge in providing all school districts with the necessary resources to provide a quality education to their students.

a. Obtain a histogram of the number of high school graduates for the year 2000. Would you conclude that the data are skewed?

b. Use the mean, median, and standard deviation to compute Pearson's coefficient of skewness. Does this number confirm your conclusion in part a?

c. Delete the five districts with the largest values from the list of the number of high school graduates for 2000. Recompute the coefficient of skewness. Did you think that the coefficient of skewness would change by this much?

(Source: "High School Attrition," *The Dallas Morning News*," May 20, 2001, p. 17A.)

3.6 INTERPRETING $\bar{x}$ AND s

Now that you have gone through several pencils determining the sample mean and standard deviation, what can you learn from these values? The type of question that you can answer is, how many of the data values are within two standard deviations of the mean?

Take a look at the aptitude test scores in Table 3.2. Here $\bar{x} = 60.36$ and $s = 18.61$, and so we obtain

$$\begin{aligned}
\bar{x} - s &= 60.36 - 18.61 & \bar{x} + s &= 60.36 + 18.61 \\
&= 41.75 & &= 78.97 \\[6pt]
\bar{x} - 2s &= 60.36 - 37.22 & \bar{x} + 2s &= 60.36 + 37.22 \\
&= 23.14 & &= 97.58 \\[6pt]
\bar{x} - 3s &= 60.36 - 55.83 & \bar{x} + 3s &= 60.36 + 55.83 \\
&= 4.53 & &= 116.19
\end{aligned}$$

Examine these data and observe that (1) 33 out of the 50 values (66%) lie between $\bar{x} - s$ and $\bar{x} + s$; (2) 49 out of the 50 values (98%) lie between $\bar{x} - 2s$ and $\bar{x} + 2s$; and (3) 50 out of the 50 values (100%) lie between $\bar{x} - 3s$ and $\bar{x} + 3s$. Or, put another way: (1) 66% of the data values have a z-score between −1 and 1; (2) 98% have a z-score between −2 and 2, and (3) 100% have a z-score between −3 and 3.

What can we say in general for any data set? First, **Chebyshev's inequality** is usually conservative but makes *no assumption* about the population from which you obtained your data. Following are the components of Chebyshev's inequality.

FIGURE

3.10

A bell-shaped (normal) population.

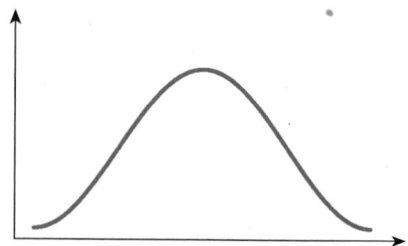

CHEBYSHEV'S INEQUALITY

For any data set:
1. At least 75% of the data values are between $\bar{x} - 2s$ and $\bar{x} + 2s$.
   At least 75% of the data values have a z-score between –2 and 2.
2. At least 89% of the data values are between $\bar{x} - 3s$ and $\bar{x} + 3s$.
   At least 89% of the data values have a z-score between –3 and 3.
3. In general, at least $(1 - 1/k^2) \times 100\%$ of your data values lie between $\bar{x} - ks$ and $\bar{x} + ks$ (have z-scores between $-k$ and k) for any $k > 1$.

Note that if $k = 1$, $1 - 1/k^2 = 0$; so Chebyshev's inequality provides no information on the number of data values to expect between $\bar{x} - s$ and $\bar{x} + s$.

The other type of statement is called the **empirical rule.** We make a key assumption here; namely, that the population from which you obtain your sample has a *bell-shaped distribution;* that is, it is symmetric and tapers off smoothly into each tail. Such a population is called a **normal population** and is illustrated in Figure 3.10. Thus, the data set should have a skewness measure, *Sk*, near zero and a histogram similar to that in Figure 3.7. The empirical rule has three components.

EMPIRICAL RULE

Under the assumption of a bell-shaped population:*
1. Approximately 68% (roughly two-thirds) of the data values lie between $\bar{x} - s$ and $\bar{x} + s$ (have z-scores between –1 and 1).
2. Approximately 95% (19 out of 20) of the data values lie between $\bar{x} - 2s$ and $\bar{x} + 2s$ (have z-scores between –2 and 2).
3. Approximately 99.7% (nearly all) of the data values lie between $\bar{x} - 3s$ and $\bar{x} + 3s$ (have z-scores between –3 and 3).

Returning to Table 3.2, we can summarize our previous results along with the information provided by Chebyshev's inequality and the empirical rule. The actual percentages of the sample values in each interval, as well as the percentages specified using each of the two rules, are shown in Table 3.3.

As you can see, Chebyshev's inequality is very conservative, but it always works. The empirical rule predicted results close to what was observed. For these data, the median is $Md = 62$ (see Example 3.6), and so Pearson's measure of skewness is

$$Sk = \frac{3(60.36 - 62)}{18.61} = -.26$$

---

*Strictly speaking, the empirical rule applies to population values (substituting μ for $\bar{x}$ and σ for s). However, this rule works very well for large samples having an approximate bell-shaped histogram.

TABLE

3.3

Between	Actual Percentage	Chebyshev's Inequality Percentage	Empirical Rule Percentage
$\bar{x} - s$ and $\bar{x} + s$	66% (33 out of 50)	—	≈68%
$\bar{x} - 2s$ and $\bar{x} + 2s$	98% (49 out of 50)	≥75%	≈95%
$\bar{x} - 3s$ and $\bar{x} + 3s$	100% (50 out of 50)	≥89%	≈100%

Summary of percentages of sample values by interval, using data from Table 3.2.

Recalling that this measure ranges from –3 to 3, we could call this skewness measure "close to zero," and so it is not surprising that the empirical rule was quite accurate, since we are dealing with a nearly symmetric set of data.

In a random sample of 200 automobile insurance claims obtained from Landmark Insurance Company, $\bar{x} = \$615$ and $s = \$135$.

1. What statement can you make using Chebyshev's inequality?

2. If you have reason to believe that the population of all insurance claims is bell-shaped (normal), what does the empirical rule say about these 200 values?

Solution 1

Chebyshev's inequality provides information regarding the number of sample values within a specified number of standard deviations of the mean. For $k = 2$, we have:

$$\bar{x} - 2s = 615 - 2(135) = \$345$$

$$\bar{x} + 2s = 615 + 2(135) = \$885$$

We conclude that at least 75% of the sample values lie between $345 and $885 and have z-scores between –2 and 2. Because $.75 \cdot 200 = 150$, this implies that at least 150 of the claims are between $345 and $885.

For $k = 3$,

$$\bar{x} - 3s = 615 - 3(135) = \$210$$

$$\bar{x} + 3s = 615 + 3(135) = \$1,020$$

and we conclude that at least 8/9 (89%) of the data values are between $210 and $1,020. Here, $8/9 \cdot 200 = 177.8$, so at least 178 of the claims are between $210 and $1,020.

Solution 2

If the distribution of automotive claims at Landmark Insurance Company is believed to be bell-shaped, the empirical rule allows us to draw stronger conclusions. In particular, for $k = 1$, we have

$$\bar{x} - s = 615 - 135 = \$480$$

$$\bar{x} + s = 615 + 135 = \$750$$

and we conclude that approximately 68% of the data values ($.68 \cdot 200 = 136$) are between $480 and $750 and have z-scores between –1 and 1.

For $k = 2$,

$$\bar{x} - 2s = \$345$$
$$\bar{x} + 2s = \$885$$

and we conclude that approximately 95% of the data values ($.95 \cdot 200 = 190$) will lie between $345 and $885.

EXAMPLE 3.9

Examples 2.1 and 3.4 examined the 100 inside diameters produced at the Boston plant of Allied Manufacturing. Based on the histogram of these diameters in Figure 2.15 (page xx), do you think the empirical rule is applicable? What does this rule tell you about the number of data values with corresponding z-scores between –2 and 2? Examining the data in Example 3.4, does this appear to be a correct statement?

Solution The histogram in Figure 2.15 has an approximate bell-shaped (normal) appearance. The shape is not perfectly symmetric with tails that taper off smoothly; but in practice, histograms based on sample data from bell-shaped populations rarely are perfectly bell-shaped in appearance. As a result, use of the empirical rule is appropriate here.

The number of sample values with z-scores between –2 and 2 is the same as the number of data values within two standard deviations of the mean, that is, the number of data values between $\bar{x} - 2s$ and $\bar{x} + 2s$. Here, $\bar{x} - 2s = 10.275 - 2(.0267)$ $= 10.2216$ and $\bar{x} + 2s = 10.275 + 2(.0267) = 10.3284$. Referring to the ordered data in Example 3.4, the only values that are *not* between 10.2216 and 10.3284 are 10.216 and 10.221 on the low end and 10.333 and 10.338 on the upper end. As a result, 96 out of 100 (96%) of the data values have z-scores between –2 and 2, a result consistent with the empirical rule, which states that this percentage should be approximately 95%.

X Exercises 3.34–3.45

Understanding the Mechanics

3.34 A random sample of observations has a sample mean of 20 and a standard deviation of 5. Use Chebyshev's inequality to find the following intervals:
  a. An interval that has at least 75% of the data within it
  b. An interval that has at least 89% of the data within it

3.35 A random sample from a bell-shaped population yields a mean of 100 and a standard deviation of 20. Calculate the following intervals:
  a. An interval that has approximately 68% of the data values within it
  b. An interval that has approximately 99.7% of the data values within it

Applying the New Concepts

3.36 A manager notices that the mean weight of a bag of grain from a recent shipment is 50 pounds, with a standard deviation of 3. At least what percentage of values can the manager say will lie within 4 standard deviations of the mean?

3.37 The following random sample of annual salaries was recorded. Units are in thousands of dollars.

  50 52 48 46 32 51 47 20 53 49

  a. Calculate the mean and standard deviation.
  b. Using Chebyshev's inequality, between what two bounds will at least 75% of the data lie?
  c. Using Chebyshev's inequality, between what two bounds will at least 89% of the data values lie?
  d. Are the percentage of values within the bounds in parts b and c from these data consistent with Chebyshev's inequality?

3.38 The sample mean is 120 and the standard deviation is 30 for a random sample of 300 observations.
  a. At least how many observations are expected to lie between 60 and 180?
  b. Under the assumption that the data are from a bell-shaped population, how many observations are expected to lie between 60 and 180?

3.39 Refer to the data in Exercise 3.4 on the number of automobiles serviced daily by EZ Service Station. Calculate the percentage of observations between 1, 2, and 3 standard deviations of the mean. Could these data be considered to have been collected from a normal population?

3.40 An increasing number of foreign carriers are allowing their cockpit crews to take short, planned naps on long-haul flights. These planned naps are intended to counteract the effects of fatigue. Currently, the Federal Aviation Administration does not allow domestic carriers to nap, even on overseas flights. Suppose that it is known that on approximately 95% of the flights between Tokyo and Sydney, pilots nap between 30 minutes and 1 hour, with the average being 45 minutes. Assuming that the empirical rule can be used, what is the standard deviation of the time spent napping by the pilots?

(Source: Adapted from "Nap Time," *Wall Street Journal*, May 8, 1998, p. W6.)

3.41 Refer to the data in the weekly expenditure on food by various families in Exercise 3.27. Between what two values would you expect at least 75% of the data to fall? How many observations actually lie within this interval?

3.42 Approximately how many standard deviations from the mean will at least 55% of the data values lie for any population. Note that this number is not an integer value.

Using the Computer

3.43 [DATA SET EX3-43] *Variable Description:*

State: Name of state located in the mid south and southeastern parts of United States

1980NonAgEmp: Nonagricultural employment in 1980

1998NonAgEmp: Nonagricultural employment in 1998

Most states have seen a substantial increase in nonagricultural employment from 1980 to 1998. Employment gains in the mid south and southeastern U.S. have exceeded the national growth rate by a wide margin. Nonagricultural data are provided for these states in units of thousands for the years 1980 and 1998.

  a. Using Chebyshev's inequality, between what two bounds will at least 75% of the data lie for the 1980 employment data.

  b. Repeat part a using the 1998 data and compare these bounds.

  c. What percentage of the data actually lie within the bounds found in part a? Is this consistent with Chebyshev's inequality?

  d. Repeat part c for the bounds found for the 1998 data in part b.

  e. What percentage of the 1998 nonagricultural employment data lie within one standard deviation of the mean? Would this figure support the empirical rule?

(Source: "The Southern U.S. Economy 1980–1998: Growth Without Prosperity," *Economic Development Review*, vol. 16, 1999, pp. 89–93.)

3.44 [DATA SET EX3-44] *Variable description:*

Servtime: Amount of time that it takes to be served the main course at Anthony's Restaurant

The manager of Anthony's restaurant is interested in examining the total wait time that customers spend in the restaurant before being served their main course. A random sample of 75 parties was observed and their total wait time in minutes was recorded.

  a. Plot a histogram of the data. Would you conclude that the data appear to be bell-shaped?

  b. Use the mean and standard deviation functions to compute intervals such that the mean is in the center of the interval and the distance from the mean to either endpoint is two standard deviations. Use an appropriate rule to approximate the percentage of data values within this interval.

3.45 [DATA SET EX3-45] *Variable description:*

MMbal: Balance in money market fund

A local bank offers a money market fund that pays above average interest rates provided the investor maintains a minimum balance of $10,000. A vice president of the bank has a random sample of 200 accounts examined and their balances were recorded.

  a. Find the mean and standard deviation of MMbal. Compute ranges in which at least 75% and 89% of the data will lie.

  b. Sort the data. (Excel: Use **Data ➤ Sort.**) Determine how many observations actually fall outside the ranges computed in part a. Compare these to the minimum numbers expected by Chebyshev's inequality.

3.7

GROUPED DATA

Sometimes we may have to work with data in the form of a frequency distribution, called **grouped data,** when the raw data are not available. This situation can arise when a magazine or newspaper article displays a histogram or frequency distribution but does not include the actual raw data used to construct the histogram. We do not have the data values used to make up this frequency distribution, so we are forced to approximate the sample statistics, in particular the mean and standard deviation.

TABLE 3.4			
	Class Number	Class (Age in Years)	Frequency
	1	20 and under 30	5
	2	30 and under 40	14
	3	40 and under 50	9
	4	50 and under 60	6
	5	60 and under 70	2
			36

Age of 36 individuals who recently passed a CPA examination.

Approximating the Sample Mean, $\bar{x}$

Assume we obtain the frequency distribution shown in Table 3.4, which contains the ages of 36 individuals who recently passed a CPA examination. The 36 data values are not available, so we cannot add them up. A procedure that works well for estimating $\bar{x}$ is simply to pretend that the 36 data values are equal to their respective class midpoints. Consequently, there are

$$5 \text{ values at } (20 + 30)/2 = 25$$
$$14 \text{ values at } (30 + 40)/2 = 35$$
$$.$$
$$.$$
$$.$$
$$2 \text{ values at } (60 + 70)/2 = 65$$

We can then estimate the value of $\bar{x}$ ($\cong$ means "is approximately equal to"):

$$\bar{x} \cong \frac{(25 + 25 + 25 + 25 + 25) + \cdots + (65 + 65)}{36}$$

$$= \frac{(5)(25) + (14)(35) + (9)(45) + (6)(55) + (2)(65)}{36}$$

$$= \frac{1,480}{36} = 41.1$$

Our estimate of the average age of these 36 individuals is

$$\bar{x} \cong 41.1 \text{ years}$$

In general,

$$\bar{x} \cong \frac{\sum f \cdot m}{n}$$

3.12

where n = sample size, f = frequency of each class, and m = midpoint each class.

Approximating the Sample Standard Deviation, s

Using the same fictitious data set at the various class midpoints, the variance, s^2, can be found in the usual way, using equation 3.7.

$$s^2 = \frac{\sum (\text{each data value})^2 - [\sum (\text{each data value})]^2/n}{n-1}$$

$$\overbrace{\sum (\text{each data value})^2 = (25^2 + 25^2 + \cdots + 25^2)}^{5 \text{ times}}$$

TABLE

3.5

Class Number	Class	f	m	f · m	f · m²
1	20 and under 30	5	25	125	3,125
2	30 and under 40	14	35	490	17,150
3	40 and under 50	9	45	405	18,225
4	50 and under 60	6	55	330	18,150
5	60 and under 70	2	65	130	8,450
		36		$\Sigma f \cdot m = 1{,}480$	$\Sigma f \cdot m^2 = 65{,}100$

Summary of
calculations for
grouped data.

FIGURE

3.11

Using Excel to
determine the
mean and
standard deviation
for grouped data.

$$\overset{14 \text{ times}}{\overbrace{+\ (35^2 + 35^2 + \cdots + 35^2)}} + \cdots + (65^2 + 65^2)$$

$$= (5)(25^2) + (14)(35^2) + (9)(45^2) + (6)(55^2) + (2)(65^2)$$

$$= 65{,}100$$

Also, Σ (each data value) = 1,480, as we determined previously when approximating $\bar{x}$.

$$s^2 \cong \frac{65{,}100 - (1{,}480)^2/36}{35} = \frac{4{,}255.56}{35} = 121.59$$

and

$$s \cong \sqrt{121.59} = 11.03$$

In general,

$$s^2 \cong \frac{\Sigma f \cdot m^2 - (\Sigma f \cdot m)^2/n}{n - 1}$$

3.13

where f, m, and n are as defined in equation 3.12.

The calculations necessary to estimate $\bar{x}$ and s are performed more easily using a table similar to Table 3.5. An even simpler procedure is to use Excel, SPSS, or MINITAB. To use Excel on the Table 2.4 values, refer to Figure 3.11 and begin by placing 25 in cell A1. Click on the fill handle in the lower right corner of cell A1 and drag it down through cell A5. You should now have five values of 25 in cells A1 through A5. Next, enter 35 in cell A6 and drag this cell down through cell A19. At this point, you have five values of 25 and 14 values of 35. Repeat this by entering 45 in cell A20 and dragging through cell A28, entering 55 in cell A29 and dragging through cell A34, and finally entering 65 in cells A35 and A36. Finally, enter

"=AVERAGE(A1:A36)" in cell B1, "=STDEV(A1:A36)" in cell B2, "Mean" in cell C1, and "St. Dev." in cell C2. Referring to Figure 3.11, cell B1 will contain the mean of the grouped data (41.11), and cell B2 will contain the standard deviation (11.03).

Remember that these procedures for approximating the sample statistics are used only when the raw data are not available and your only information is a frequency distribution or corresponding histogram. *If the actual data values are available, these statistics can be determined exactly, and the approximation procedures described in this section should not be used.*

X Exercises 3.46–3.52

Understanding the Mechanics

3.46

Class	Midpoint	Frequency
0 and under 10	5	4
10 and under 20	15	7
20 and under 30	25	5
30 and under 40	35	4

a. Approximate the sample mean.
b. Approximate the sample standard deviation.

3.47 A set of grouped continuous data has five classes. Each class has a frequency of 10. The midpoints are:

$$10 \quad 20 \quad 30 \quad 40 \quad 50$$

a. Approximate the sample mean.
b. Approximate the sample variance.
c. Approximate the sample standard deviation.

Applying the New Concepts

3.48 Advertising expenditures constitute one of the important components of the cost of goods sold. From the following data giving the advertising expenditures (in millions of dollars) of 50 companies, approximate the mean advertising expenditure.

Advertising Expenditure	Number of Companies
25 and under 35	5
35 and under 45	11
45 and under 55	18
55 and under 65	6
65 and under 75	10
	50

3.49 The cost for an overnight stay in the center of one of the major cities across the United States has been rising over the years. Listed below is a frequency table of the total cost of an overnight stay in the center of one of 22 cities. Find the approximate mean and standard deviation of the cost of an overnight stay at these cities.

Frequency Distribution Table
Total Costs of an

Class	Overnight Stay	Frequency
1	100 and under 130	2
2	130 and under 160	12
3	160 and under 190	4
4	190 and under 220	1
5	220 and under 250	2
6	250 and under 280	1
	TOTAL	22

(Source: "The Dow Jones Travel Index," *Wall Street Journal*, May 8, 1998, p. W6.)

3.50 The year-to-date performance of the 15 largest stock funds is presented below for the first four months of 1998.

Stock Mutual Fund	Year-to-Date Performance (in Percentage)
Fidelity Magellan	14.0
Vanguard Index 500 Port	13.4
Washington Mutual	11.1
Investment Co of America	11.8
Fidelity Growth and Income	11.3
Fidelity Contrafund	11.9
Vanguard Windsor II	13.4
Amer. Century 20 Ultra	15.7
Fidelity Puritan	7.8
Fidelity Equity Income	10.4
Vanguard Wellington	8.4
Fidelity Adv. Growth Oppty	9.2
Vanguard Windsor	14.2
Income Fund of America	6.6
Janus Fund	15.7

a. Construct a frequency table, using the class intervals 6 and under 9, 9 and under 12, 12 and under 15, 15 and under 18.

b. Find the approximate mean and standard deviation of the performance of these mutual funds from the frequency table.

c. Calculate the mean and standard deviation from the data and compare your answer to that obtained in part b.

(Source: "15 Largest Stock Funds," *USA Today*, May 8, 1998, p. 3B.)

3.51 A summary of the price paid for dinner at the Green Garden restaurant is as follows, in dollars.

Dinner Cost	Number of Customers
5 and under 10	5
10 and under 15	15
15 and under 20	31
20 and under 25	30
25 and under 30	16
30 and under 35	3

a. Approximate the sample mean.

b. Approximate the sample standard deviation.

c. Is the mean an appropriate summary statistic for these data?

Using the Computer

3.52 [DATA SET EX3-52] *Variable description:*

OilServTime: Service time for oil change

The manager of Express Oil Change is interested in examining the service times for an oil change. A random sam-

ple of 200 oil changes was selected and the time to perform an oil change was recorded in minutes.

a. Form a frequency table of the data. Use intervals of width 5 starting at 10 minutes.

b. Approximate the mean and standard deviation of the data set from the frequency table.

c. To understand how accurate these approximations are, find the mean and standard deviation of the OilServTime data. Compare the computed mean and standard deviation from the data to that obtained in part a.

3.8 BOX PLOTS

Exploratory data analysis (EDA) is a recently developed set of tools for providing easy-to-construct pictures that summarize and describe a sample. Two popular diagrams that fall under this category are *stem-and-leaf diagrams* (introduced in Chapter 2) and *box plots*. Section 2.2 gave several illustrations of stem-and-leaf diagrams. These graphs provide a representation of the *entire* sample and, unlike histograms, do not condense the data into classes. This section discusses box plots that are graphical illustrations of the quartile measures of position discussed in Section 3.4.

A **box plot** is a graphical representation of a set of sample data that illustrates the lowest data value (L), the first quartile (Q_1), the median (Q_2, Md), the third quartile (Q_3), the interquartile range (IQR), and the highest data value (H).

In Section 3.4, the following values were determined for the aptitude test scores in Table 3.2:

$$L = 22 \qquad\qquad Q_3 = 75$$
$$Q_1 = 46 \qquad\qquad IQR = 75 - 46 = 29$$
$$Q_2 = Md = 62 \qquad\qquad H = 96$$

A box plot of these values is shown in Figure 3.12. The ends of the box are located at the first and third quartiles, with a vertical bar inserted at the median. Consequently, the length of the box is the interquartile range. If the data are symmetric, the median bar should be located at the center of the box. *Consequently, the bar location indicates the skewness of the data: If located in the left half of the box, the data are skewed right; and if located in the right half, the data are skewed left.*

Box plots provide a very easy method of detecting outliers in a set of sample data. First, we define the two *inner fences*. The lower inner fence is the first quartile

---

FIGURE

3.12

Box plot for 50 aptitude test scores (data in Table 3.2).

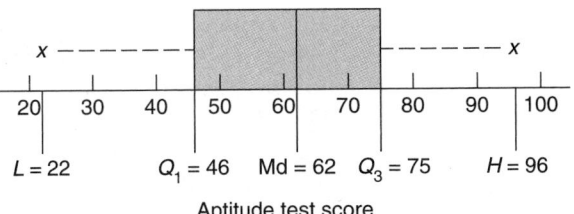

Aptitude test score

minus 1.5 times the interquartile range, and the upper inner fence is the third quartile plus 1.5 times the interquartile range.

$$\text{lower inner fence} = Q_1 - 1.5 \cdot IQR$$

$$\text{upper inner fence} = Q_3 + 1.5 \cdot IQR$$

3.14 3.15

Any value smaller than the lower inner fence or larger than the upper inner fence will be classified as an outlier. Using the aptitude test scores in Table 3.2, we get

$$\text{lower inner fence} = 46 - (1.5)(29) = 2.5$$

$$\text{upper inner fence} = 75 + (1.5)(29) = 118.5$$

Since none of the data values are less than 2.5 or larger than 118.5, we conclude that this sample contains no outliers.

Extreme outliers are identified by defining *outer fences:*

$$\text{lower outer fence} = Q_1 - 3 \cdot IQR$$

$$\text{upper outer fence} = Q_3 + 3 \cdot IQR$$

3.16 3.17

Any value less than the lower outer fence or greater than the upper outer fence are **extreme outliers.** We expect *less than one-hundreth of 1%* of the sample values from a bell-shaped population to lie outside the outer fence. Sample values that lie beyond an inner fence but inside the outer fence are **mild outliers.** For a sample from a bell-shaped population, we expect *less than 1%* of the values to lie outside the inner fences. The sample in Table 3.2 contains no values beyond the inner fences (mild outliers), and, as a result, contains no extreme outliers.

We mentioned earlier that in a box plot, the ends of the box are the first and third quartiles. To be more precise, the left end of the box is defined to be the **lower hinge,** and the right end of the box is the **upper hinge.** For n even, the lower hinge is the same as Q_1, and the upper hinge is the same as Q_3, according to our quartile definitions. This is also true for n odd, where $n - 1$ is evenly divisible by 4 (that is, $n = 5, 9, 13, 17, . . .$). For the remaining odd values of n (that is, $n = 3, 7, 11, 15, . . .$), the lower hinge is defined to be the average of Q_1 and the ordered data value to the *right* of Q_1, and the upper hinge is defined to be the average of Q_3 and the ordered data value to the *left* of Q_3. To illustrate, consider the following ordered sample of seven values:

Sample: 25, 31, 45, 52, 63, 87, 95

Here, Q_1 is the second value (31), the lower hinge is $(31 + 45)/2 = 38$, Q_3 is the sixth value (87), and the upper hinge is $(63 + 87)/2 = 75$. Despite this slight discrepancy, we will continue to refer to the ends of the box as the first quartile (lower hinge) and third quartile (upper hinge).

The dotted lines on a box plot, called the **whiskers,** connect the highest and lowest data values *contained within the inner fences* to the ends of the box. Thus, approximately 25% of the data values will lie in each whisker and in each portion of the box.

Using Excel to Construct a Box Plot

Excel does not have a data analysis tool to construct a box plot, but the set of KPK data analysis macros supplied with this textbook does have this feature. The spreadsheet in Figure 3.13 is a result of (1) entering (loading) the data into column A, and (2) clicking on **KPK Data Analysis ➤ Quantitative Data Charts/Tables ➤ Box Plot.** In Figure 3.13, the data in column A consist of 75 residential appraisals (in thousands of dollars) having a median value of $206,000. After clicking on **Box Plot** you

FIGURE

3.13

Excel spreadsheet
using box plot in
KPK Data Analysis
(data are
75 residential
appraisals).

Microsoft Excel - Appraisals				
	A	B	C	D	E
1	211	**Values of Box Plot Parameters**		
2	205	PARAMETER	VALUE	
3	212	First Quartile	174	
4	205	Median	206	
5	235	Third Quartile	230	
6	182	IQR	56	
7	232	Minimum	151	
8	184	Maximum	410	
9	225	Upper Inner Fence	314	
10	157	Lower Inner Fence	90	
11	155	Upper Outer Fence	398	
12	241	Lower Outer Fence	6	
13	195			

Box Plot Calc / Box Plot \ **Sheet1** / Sheet2 / Sheet3

FIGURE

3.14

Excel box plot
created using KPK
Data Analysis (data
are 75 residential
appraisals).

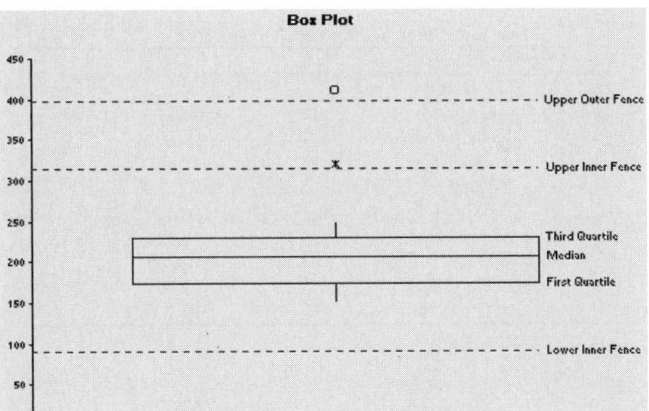

Box Plot

* mild outlier   o extreme outlier

should see a small input screen. Enter "A1:A75" as the input range and enter "B1" in the output range box. The resulting box plot is shown in Figure 3.14 where the median value ($206,000) is represented by the line inside the box. Any mild outlier is represented by the symbol ✳ and extreme outliers are represented using the symbol **O**. The sample of residential appraisals contains one mild outlier and one extreme outlier. A closer look at the data revealed one appraised value of $320,000 (the mild outlier) and one value of $410,000 (the extreme outlier). The extreme outlier is equal to the maximum value in cell C8, Figure 3.13.

For the aptitude test scores, Figure 3.12 indicates that the data appear to have a very slight left skew, since the vertical line is slightly right of center in the box. This same box plot using Excel is shown in Figure 3.15. Since the symbols ✳ and **O** do not appear in the plot, we conclude that the sample contains no outliers.

In Examples 2.1 and 3.4, we examined a sample of 100 inside diameters of a particular machined part produced by the Boston plant of Allied Manufacturing. The conclusion so far has been that the process is off center and too near the upper spec limit of 10.3 mm. A summary of the data from the Excel spreadsheet and the corresponding box plot are shown in Figure 3.16. A large portion of the upper

FIGURE

3.15

Excel box plot created by KPK Data Analysis (data are aptitude test scores in Table 3.2).

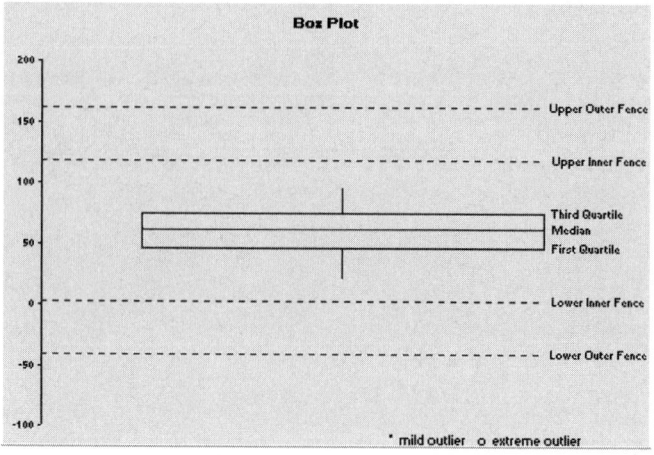

FIGURE

3.16

Excel summary and box plot using KPK Data Analysis (data are 100 machine part diameters from Example 3.4).

Values of Box Plot Parameters	
PARAMETER	VALUE
First Quartile	10.257
Median	10.276
Third Quartile	10.293
IQR	0.036
Minimum	10.216
Maximum	10.338
Upper Inner Fence	10.347
Lower Inner Fence	10.203
Upper Outer Fence	10.401
Lower Outer Fence	10.149

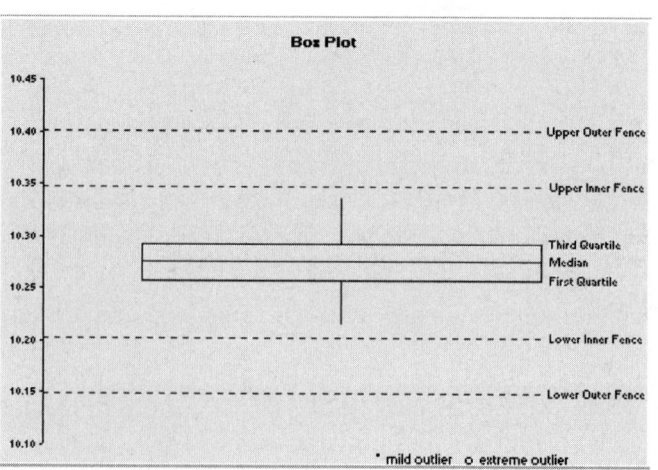

whisker is larger than 10.3, indicating that a large number of sample items have a diameter beyond the upper spec limit. The first quartile (10.257) is the lower end of the box, and the third quartile (10.293) is the upper end of the box. The median of 10.276 is centered inside the box, indicating that the data are nearly symmetric. This observation is supported by the fact that the two whiskers are nearly the same length. Finally, no ✱ or O symbols appear in the plot, indicating the sample contains no outliers.

EXAMPLE

3.10

The personnel manager of Texon Industries is interested in comparing the aptitude scores from the 50 job applicants (Table 3.2) with those of 100 people randomly selected from people currently employed at Texon. Both box plots are shown in Figure 3.17, which illustrates SPSS's ability to put two box plots in the same graph. What conclusions can be drawn? (*Note:* MINITAB can also provide graphs of multiple box plots.)

A number of observations can be made, including:

1. The median of each group is represented by the line within the corresponding box. The median score of the job applicants [sample (1)] is roughly 62 − 50 = 12 points higher than for the sample of 100 current employees [sample (2)].

2. The range for sample (1), using Table 3.2, is 96 − 22 = 74 points. The range for sample (2) is 80 − 30 = 50 points. The middle 50% for sample (1), as indicated by the ends of the box, covers a spread of roughly 30 points. The corresponding spread for sample (2) is 15 points. *Conclusion:* There is much more variation in the job applicant scores.

3. The job applicant scores have a slight left skew (the median line is slightly above center in the box), whereas for sample (2), the scores contain a heavy right skew, since the median line is considerably below center, and the right whisker is quite long. Consequently, the sample of current employees contains a higher concentration of scores at the low end.

4. After examining the box plots, we could conclude that, based on the aptitude test scores, there are some very good and some not-so-good applicants (a lot of variation in scores), but that overall this group outscored the sample of current employees.

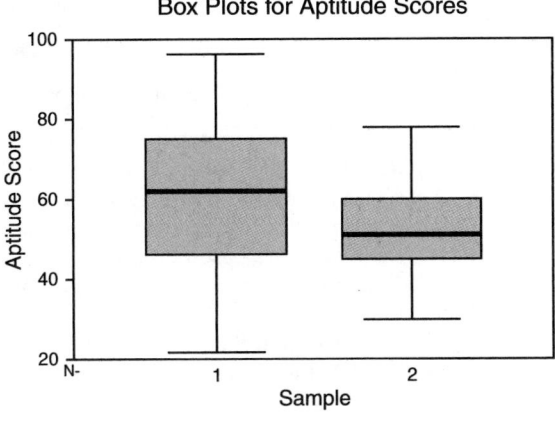

Box Plots for Aptitude Scores

FIGURE

3.17

SPSS box plots of 50 job applicants (sample 1) and 100 current employees (sample 2).

X Exercises 3.53–3.60

Understanding the Mechanics

3.53 Construct a box plot using only the following information about a data set with 30 observations.

$$\begin{aligned}
\text{First Quartile} &= 25 \\
\text{Second Quartile} &= 50 \\
\text{Third Quartile} &= 75 \\
\text{Lowest Value} &= 1 \\
\text{Largest Value} &= 100
\end{aligned}$$

3.54 From the MINITAB box plot displayed below, approximate the following:

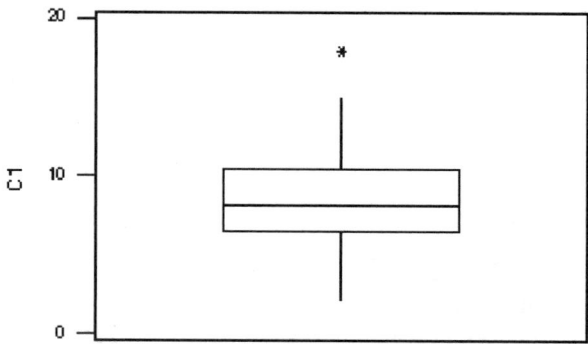

a. Lower hinge
b. Median
c. Upper hinge
d. Any mild outliers
e. Any extreme outliers

3.55 The following is a sample of size 10:

15   20   12   30   25   33   70   24   32   22

a. Find the first, second, and third quartiles.
b. What are the largest and smallest values?
c. Construct a box plot and comment on the shape of the distribution.

Applying the New Concepts

3.56 The manager of a small restaurant wished to determine how long the average customer had to wait to be served during the lunch hour. At the lunch hour on a particular typical day, 20 customers experienced the following waiting times (in minutes):

5.5, 10.3, 7.5, 8.1, 6.8, 11.0, 10.2, 9.0, 7.0, 5.8, 12.5, 7.5, 6.0, 13.7, 5.5, 14.0, 7.0, 6.9, 6.3, 7.4

a. Construct a box plot of the data.
b. Should the manager feel comfortable in advertising that if meals are not served in 10 minutes or less, the customer eats for free?

3.57 The following list of Uniform Resource Locators (URLs) contains some of the most visited sites on the World Wide Web.

URL	Number of Daily Visitors (in Millions)
www.yahoo.com	12.5
www.msn.com	11.8
www.passport.com	6.3
www.hotmail.com	6.2
www.aol.com	5.1
www.netscape.com	3.0
www.iwon.com	2.9
www.excite.com	2.6
www.ebay.com	2.6
www.lycos.com	2.4

a. Construct a box plot of the number of daily visitors to the selected Web sites.
b. Describe the distribution obtained from the box plot. Are there any outliers? Extreme or mild?

(Source: "Internet at a Glance," *Business 2.0*, July 10, 2001, p. 85.)

3.58 Refer to the weekly expenditure on food by 30 different families in Exercise 3.27. Construct a box plot for these data. How many outliers would you expect if these data were from a normal population?

Using the Computer

3.59 **[DATA SET EX3-59]** *Variable Description:*

Show: Television program

Rating: Nielsen rating of selected television programs

The name Nielsen Media Research is synonymous with television ratings and audience estimates. The ratings provide an estimate of audience size and composition for television programmers and commercial advertisers. These ratings are used as a barometer of people's viewing habits. For May 14 and May 15, a sample of television programs and their ratings by Nielsen Media Research are provided. Use a box plot to describe the distribution of the data.

(Source: "Nielsen Ratings," *USA Today*, May 23, 2001, p. 6D.)

3.60 **[DATA SET EX3-60]** *Variable Description:*

OccRateNorth: Occupancy rate of Holiday Hotel North

OccRateSouth: Occupancy rate of Holiday Hotel South

To better manage two hotels in the north and south side of Atlanta, the managers decide to collect 60 days of data representing the occupancy rate in percentage. Staff and resources could be more proportionally divided between the two hotels based on projected occupancy rates.

a. Construct box plots—one for each hotel's occupancy rate.
b. Compare and contrast the distribution of each hotel. Which hotel has fewer outliers?

☒ Summary

The purpose of analyzing or describing sample data is to learn more about the population from which it was obtained. Every population has properties that describe it. These properties are referred to as **parameters.** We can estimate these parameters by obtaining a sample and deriving the corresponding sample statistic, which is a particular **descriptive measure.**

This chapter has introduced you to some of the more popular descriptive measures used to describe a set of sample values. **Measures of central tendency** are used to describe a typical value within the sample: the **mean** (the average of the sample data), the **median** (the value in the center of the ordered data), the **mode** (that data value occurring the most often), and the **midrange** (an average of the lowest and highest data values). To measure the variation within a set of sample data, we use **measures of variation:** the **range** (difference between the highest and lowest data values), the **variance** (sum of the squares of the deviations from the sample mean, divided by $n - 1$), the **standard deviation** (square root of the variance), and the **coefficient of variation** (standard deviation divided by the mean, times 100).

Percentiles and **quartiles** are **measures of position** and indicate the relative position of a particular value. The first quartile (Q_1) and the third quartile (Q_3) are the 25th and 75th percentiles, respectively. The second quartile (Q_2) is the 50th percentile, which is identical to the sample median. The difference between the first and third quartiles is the **interquartile range** (IQR), which is another measure of dispersion, since it measures the spread within the middle 50% of the data values. Another measure of position is the sample **z-score,** which is derived for a particular observation by subtracting the sample mean and dividing by the sample standard deviation.

Finally, the shape of a data set can be described using various **measures of shape.** Two such measures are the sample **skewness** (the degree of symmetry in the data) and **kurtosis** (the tendency of a distribution to stretch out in a particular direction). Skewness is measured by **Pearson's coefficient of skewness.**

The two most commonly used measures are the sample mean and standard deviation. These two statistics can be used together to describe the sample data by applying **Chebyshev's inequality** or the **empirical rule.** The latter procedure draws a stronger conclusion about the concentration of the data values but assumes that the population of interest is bell-shaped, and is thus a **normal population.**

We examined how to approximate the sample mean and standard deviation when the only information available is a frequency distribution, or **grouped data.**

Exploratory data analysis provides easy-to-construct, yet very powerful, graphs that summarize and describe a set of sample data. Chapter 2 introduced one such graph—the *stem-and-leaf diagram.* The **box plot** introduced in this chapter contains (1) the lowest and highest values within the portion of your sample not considered to be outliers, (2) the three quartiles, and (3) any sample values determined to be outliers. A sample value is considered to be an **extreme outlier** if it lies beyond either of the **outer fences,** and is considered a **mild outlier** if it lies beyond either of the **inner fences** but not beyond the corresponding outer fence. The left and right ends of the box are at the first and third quartiles (more accurately, the **lower** and **upper hinges**). The **whiskers** are the dotted lines on a box plot that connect the highest and lowest data values *contained within the inner fences* to the ends of the box. A box plot can be used to detect sample skewness by observing the position of the median line inside the box.

Summary of Formulas

Measures of Central Tendency

1. Sample mean

$$\bar{x} = \frac{\sum x}{n}$$

2. Population mean

$$\mu = \frac{\sum x}{N}$$

3. Midrange

$$Mr = \frac{L + H}{2}$$

Measures of Variation

1. Range

$$\text{range} = H - L$$

2. Sample variance

$$s^2 = \frac{\sum (x - \bar{x})^2}{n - 1}$$
$$= \frac{\sum x^2 - (\sum x)^2/n}{n - 1}$$

3. Population variance

$$\sigma^2 = \frac{\sum (x - \mu)^2}{N}$$

4. Sample standard deviation

$$s = \sqrt{\frac{\sum (x - \bar{x})^2}{n - 1}}$$
$$= \sqrt{\frac{\sum x^2 - (\sum x)^2/n}{n - 1}}$$

5. Population standard deviation

$$\sigma = \sqrt{\frac{\sum (x - \mu)^2}{N}}$$

6. Coefficient of variation

$$CV = \frac{s}{\bar{x}} \cdot 100$$

Measures of Position

1. Sample z-score

$$z = \frac{x - \bar{x}}{s}$$

Measures of Shape

1. Pearson's coefficient of skewness

$$Sk = \frac{3(\bar{x} - Md)}{s}$$

2. Excel, SPSS, and Minitab coefficient of skewness

$$Sk' = \frac{n}{(n-1)(n-2)} \sum \left(\frac{x - \bar{x}}{s} \right)^3$$
$$= \frac{n}{(n-1)(n-2)} \sum (z\text{-}score)^3$$

Grouped Data

1. Sample mean

$$\bar{x} \cong \frac{\sum f \cdot m}{n}$$

2. Sample variance

$$s^2 \cong \frac{\sum f \cdot m^2 - (\sum f \cdot m)^2/n}{n - 1}$$

Box Plots

1. Interquartile range

$$IQR = Q_3 - Q_1$$

2. Lower inner fence

$$Q_1 - 1.5 \cdot IQR$$

3. Upper inner fence

$$Q_3 + 1.5 \cdot IQR$$

4. Lower outer fence

$$Q_1 - 3 \cdot IQR$$

5. Upper outer fence

$$Q_3 + 3 \cdot IQR$$

Review Exercises 3.61–3.80

3.61 Many rough and tough looking sport-utility vehicles (SUVs) have weak bumpers that are costly to repair, even in minor collisions. The following data illustrate the dollar amount of damage in a 5 miles-per-hour bumper crash conducted by the Insurance Institute for Highway Safety.

SUV	Crash Test Damage
2001 Acura MDX	448
2001 Toyota Highlander	747
2002 Chevrolet Trailblazer	810
2001 Pontiac Aztek	856
2002 Isuzu Axiom	1126
2002 Buick Rendezvous	1400
2001 Suzuki Grand Vitara XL-7	1451

a. Compute the mean, median, and midrange of the crash test damage data. Which measure would be most reasonable to use?

b. Interpret the coefficient of skewness for the crash test damage data.

c. Compare the z-scores for Chevrolet Trailblazer and Suzuki Grand Vitara XL-7. What do these figures tell you about these two vehicles?

(Source: "Tests: Some SUV Bumpers Weak," *USA Today*, August 1, 2001, p. 3B.)

3.62 Cities that have the most high-tech jobs appear to also be plagued with the worst traffic conditions. A study involving a sample of 10 such cities is used to estimate the average speed of a daily worker during the peak rush-hour period on the freeways.

City	Speed (mph) on Freeway During Peak Rush Hour Period
Austin	50
San Jose, Calif	45
Boston	43
Chicago	41
Washington, D.C.	38
Dallas	46
Los Angeles	31
Atlanta	44
New York	46
Minneapolis	45

a. Find the first, second, and third quartiles of the speed data.

b. Construct a box plot. Describe the distribution of the data from viewing this graph.

c. Compute the Pearson's coefficient of skewness. Interpret this statistic.

d. Using Chebyshev's inequality, between what two bounds will at least 75% of the data lie?

(Source: "High-Tech Traffic," *Business2.com*, July 10, 2001, p. 82.)

3.63 While software is becoming easier to use, computer users are demanding new features that make programs more complex. To deliver a satisfying experience, a software package must strike a balance between new features and ease of use. The software must also have the support behind it to get customers up and running. Satisfaction scores for telephone technical support with various database, spreadsheet, and word processor applications are presented below.

Databases/Spreadsheets/Word Processors	Satisfaction Score
dBase	7.3
Lotus Approach	7.1
Microsoft Access	6.7
Microsoft FoxPro	6.5
Paradox	7.5
Corel Quattro Pro	7.9

Databases/Spreadsheet/Word Processors	Satisfaction Score
Lotus 1-2-3	7.5
Microsoft Excel	6.9
Ami Pro/Word Pro	7.4
Corel WordPerfect	8.0
Microsoft Word	6.8

a. Find the interval in which at least 75% of the data would be expected to lie.

b. Calculate the interquartile range. Is this value easily affected by an extreme observation? Calculate with 8.0 removed and compare.

(Source: "Telephone Technical Support," *PC Magazine,* July 1997, p. 206.)

3.64 The price of long-distance service has decreased steadily over recent years. Many long-distance carriers are trying to capture more of the international phone market. For example, Net2Phone advertises that its rates are the lowest per minute. The following data illustrate their costs of a phone call to both European and Asian countries from the United States.

Europe		Asia	
Country	Cents per Minute	Country	Cents per Minute
Belgium	7.9	Hong Kong	7.9
Finland	9.9	India	49.0
France	7.9	Japan	7.9
Germany	7.9	Pakistan	49.0
Ireland	7.9	Philippines	21.0
Italy	9.9	Singapore	11.0
United Kingdom	7.9	South Korea	9.9
		Taiwan	9.9

a. Compute the mean, standard deviation, coefficient of variation, and Pearson's coefficient of skewness for the cost of a phone call to the European countries.

b. Repeat part a for the cost of a phone call to the Asian countries.

c. Compare and contrast the statistics in parts a and b.

d. Using the combined data from both European and Asian countries, find the 25th and 75th percentiles.

e. Construct a box plot for the combined data from both European and Asian countries. Interpret this diagram. How many outliers are there?

(Source: "Low Rates to Over 250 Countries Worldwide," *USA Today,* July 30, 2001, p. 13A.)

3.65 The following task completion times were recorded for a task presented to 15 teams of employees. Units are in hours.

1.8	2.7	3.4	2.6	2.7	4.4
6.9	3.4	4.1	3.0	2.1	2.4
3.1	4.7	3.0	3.5	4.2	3.8

a. Calculate the interquartile range and the standard deviation of these data.

b. Remove the observation with a value of 6.9. Recalculate the statistics in part a. Which statistics are affected the most by omitting this observation?

3.66 The number of phone calls received daily by a secretary at a bank is recorded over a 30-day period.

18	30	10	16	34	25	13	21	19	29
24	17	34	40	20	16	18	22	17	28
31	24	26	18	32	23	20	31	21	27

a. Calculate the coefficient of skewness for this data set.

b. Calculate a z-score for each observation.

c. Interpret the statistics in parts a and b. Which observations would you say are unusual?

3.67 To determine the risk of owning a security, some investors might believe that the standard deviation is a good measure of risk. Whereas the standard deviation of a security's performance is a measure of the dispersion of its performance about its average performance, this measure is not adjusted to take into account the security's performance. Investors often use the Sharpe ratio as a risk-adjusted performance measure. This measure can be computed by first subtracting the performance of a riskless treasury bill from the performance of the security and then dividing this difference by the standard deviation of the performance of the security. The following data provide annualized performance returns for two top performing mutual funds over the period 1991 to 2000.

Year	Legg Mason Value	Fidelity Aggressive
2000	–7.14	–27.14
1999	26.71	103.02
1998	48.04	43.28
1997	37.05	19.45
1996	38.43	15.8
1995	40.76	35.94
1994	1.39	–0.18
1993	11.26	19.88
1992	11.44	8.36
1991	34.73	67.1

a. Find the mean and standard deviation for the Legg Mason Value fund and the Fidelity Aggressive fund.

b. Suppose the performance of a riskless treasury bill is 4.0%. Subtract this from the mean performances of these funds. Then divide by the standard deviation of the respective fund to compute the Sharpe ratios.

c. What conclusion can you make based on the Sharpe ratios for these two mutual funds?

d. How is the Sharpe ratio related to the coefficient of variation?

(Source: "An Information Theoretic Indicator for Evaluating Superior Performance," *American Business Review*, vol. 19, no. 2, 2001, pp. 26–31.)

3.68 Consider a sample of observations:

$$10 \quad 15 \quad 30 \quad 25$$

Transform these values into z-scores. What is the mean and standard deviation of the z-scores? Show that the mean of any set of z-scores is always equal to zero.

3.69 Answer the questions below for the following data set:

.7, 1.5, 1.5, 1.8, 1.9, 2.1, 2.4, 2.5, 2.8, 2.9, 2.9, 3.3, 3.7, 3.8, 3.9, 4.0, 4.1, 4.3, 4.9, 5.0, 5.4, 6.1

a. Do the data appear to be bell-shaped?

b. Calculate the coefficient of skewness.

c. Using the empirical rule, estimate the range of values within which about 68% of the data values are expected to lie.

3.70 Each week, a list of the top revenue-producing films appears in *USA Today*. The top revenue-producing films for the first week of August 2001 are as follows. Often the films that have recently been released gross the most revenue at the box office. For a film to have been released 5 or 6 weeks and still appear among the top revenue-producing films demonstrates that the film is truly popular.

Film	Box Office Earnings in Millions	Weeks Out
Rush Hour 2	67.4	1
Planet of the Apes	27.5	2
The Princess Diaries	22.9	1
Jurassic Park 3	12.3	3
America's Sweethearts	8.0	3
Original Sin	6.4	1
Legally Blonde	5.9	4
The Score	4.9	4
Dr. Dolittle 2	2.3	7
Cats & Dogs	2.2	6

a. From viewing the data, would you expect the mean and median to be very different for the box office earnings? Compute the mean and median for the box office earnings.

b. From viewing the data, would you expect the box office earnings to be skewed? Compute the Pearson's coefficient of skewness for the box office earnings. Does this value indicate skewness?

c. Eliminate *Rush Hour 2* and then compute the mean, median, and Pearson's coefficient of skewness. Are the mean and the median closer after eliminating *Rush Hour 2?* How has the coefficient of skewness changed?

d. Compute the mean, median, and mode for the number of weeks out. Is the mode a useful measure for measuring these data?

e. Repeat part d with *Dr. Dolittle 2* and *Cats & Dogs* omitted. Discuss the changes in these measures.

f. Comment on which films you believe are especially popular. What information are you using to base your conclusions?

(Source: "Rush Hour Over Apes," *USA Today,* August 7, 2001, p. 1D.)

3.71 The mean rate charged by the CPAs in a certain city is about $75 per hour, with a standard deviation of $15. Assuming that the data came from a normal population, estimate the range of rates within which about 95% of the CPA's charges are expected to lie.

3.72 The z-score is -1.50, the mean is 45, and $x = 15$. What is the value of the variance?

3.73 A manufacturing plant requires one of its suppliers to provide aluminum sheets that have a special coating that is between 1.5 and 4.5 millimeters in depth. A shipment of 800 coated aluminum sheets was delivered to the plant. The supervisor at the plant was told that the mean depth of the coating was 3.0 millimeters, with a standard deviation of .5. If there are more than 100 aluminum sheets with a coating thickness outside of the range 1.5 to 4.5 millimeters, the plant supervisor will not accept the shipment. What decision should the supervisor make?

3.74 The mean GMAT score of the 65 applicants who were accepted into the MBA program of Xavier Business School was 520 with a standard deviation of 25. About how many applicants scored between 470 and 570 on the GMAT?

3.75 [DATA SET EX3-75] *Variable Description:*

ETF: Name of exchange traded fund

ExpenseRatio: Expense ratio for selected exchange traded funds

Exchange traded funds (ETFs) represent unit investment trusts that hold portfolios of common stocks generally corresponding to the price and yield performance of a financial sector of the stock market. They allow investors to buy a portfolio of securities as easily as buying a single security. For example, the Nasdaq-100 Trust is a popular EFT used by investors wishing to invest in a portfolio that reflects the performance of the Nasdaq-100 Index. A major advantage is the low expense ratio. To buy each security separately in a similar portfolio would cost many times the expense ratio of an ETF.

a. Display the data by using a box plot. Identify any outliers.

b. Find the mean, median, and standard deviation of the expense ratios of the ETFs.

c. Determine Pearson's coefficient of skewness. Interpret this value.

d. Construct a stem-and-leaf diagram to display the expense ratios. Which expense ratios would you identify as outliers?

(Source: "Tracking Exchange-Traded Portfolios," *The Wall Street Journal,* August 6, 2001, p. R12.)

3.76 [DATA SET EX3-76] *Variable Description:*

Year: Years range from 1960 to 2001

ValueMinWage: Real value of minimum wage reflecting inflation and changes in consumer spending patterns

The real value of the minimum wage changes frequently as economic conditions change and as consumer spending patterns change. The real value of the minimum wage has hovered between $4.50 and $6.70 between 1960 and 2001. The nominal value of the minium wage has increased gradually over these years. These values increase gradually because economists believe that raising the minimum wage too quickly kills jobs.

a. Using a class width of .50, develop a relative frequency histogram for the value of the minimum wage from 1960 to 2001. Would you say that the distribution is approximately a bell-shaped curve?

b. Using the empirical rule, estimate the interval in which approximately 68% of the data lie.

c. Obtain summary statistics for the value of the minimum wage.

(Source: "A Bumpy Road for Those at the Bottom," *Wall Street Journal*, July 19, 2001, p. A10.)

3.77 [DATA SET EX3-77] *Variable Description:*

JobArr: Number of job orders arriving at a manufacturing plant

A production facility manufactures air compressors for automobiles. The facility tries to accommodate special orders that arrive on a daily basis. Allowing capacity for the special orders is important to the planning process. For 120 working days, the number of job orders have been recorded.

a. Plot a histogram and a box plot of the data.

b. How would you describe the data?

c. Find the mean and standard deviation of the data. From these values, compute the coefficient of skewness. Does the value of this measure appear to be consistent with your description in part b?

3.78 [DATA SET EX3-78] *Variable Description:*

MarketExp: Travel expenses for the marketing department

R&DExp: Travel expenses for the research and development department

The vice president of a semiconductor company wished to compare the distribution of travel expenses in two departments, the marketing department and the research and development department. The travel expenses of 120 persons from the marketing department and 150 persons from the research and development department are listed under MarketExp and R&DExp, respectively, in dollars.

a. Form a box plot for the expenses of each department.

b. Form a histogram for the expenses of each department.

c. Do the data from either department appear to be bell shaped?

d. Contrast the distributions of the two departments.

3.79 [DATA SET EX3-79] *Variable Description:*

TimePeriod: Quarters for the years 1998 to 2002

QuarterlyPerformance: The percentage change per quarter in the Global Technology Fund

To measure the average rate of change of a variable over time, the geometric mean is more useful than a simple average. To compute the geometric mean for rates of return over n time periods, first add 1 to the rate, then multiply these figures, raise this result to $1/n$, and subtract 1. For example, suppose that the rate of return over two quarters is 100% and −50%. First, add one to these figures to get 2.00 and .50. Then multiply these two numbers to get 1.00. Raise this result to $1/2$ (this is the same as taking the square root). After taking the square root and subtracting 1, the result is 0. If the simple average was used, then the calculation would be $(1.00 + (−.50))/2 = .25$. However, that would not reflect the change in investment value.

a. Compute the geometric mean of the quarterly performances of the Global Technology Fund. (In Excel, use the **Product** function to multiply the figures and use the **Power** function to raise the product of the numbers to the 1/20th power).

b. Compute the mean and the median for the quarterly performance. Would you say that these figures would be misleading in representing the average rate of return?

3.80 A TV cable company in Houston wanted to estimate the hours per week that households watch television. A random sample of 50 households was used to construct the box plot below. Write a brief summary of the characteristics of the data in a report to the management of the TV cable company based on this plot.

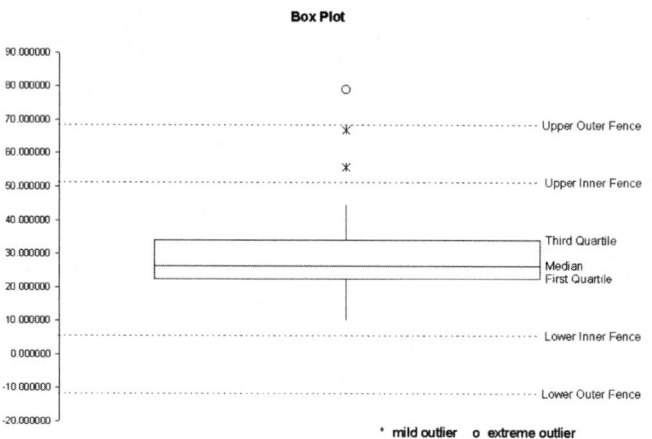

Computer Exercises Using the Databases

Exercise 1—Appendix F

Randomly select 100 observations of variable INCOME1 (income of principal wage earner) from the database.
a. Use a convenient statistical computer package to determine the various descriptive measures that describe the distribution of INCOME1.
b. What are the actual proportions of observations that are between ±2.0 and ±3.0 standard deviations of the mean of the data set? Are these proportions consistent with:
 (i) Chebyshev's inequality?
 (ii) the empirical rule?

c. Construct a box plot of this sample. What do you observe from this graph?

Exercise 2—Appendix G

Randomly select 100 observations of the variable SALES from the database.
a. Use a convenient statistical computer package to find the mean, median, range, variance, coefficient of variation, and coefficient of skewness for this variable.
b. Construct a box plot, and use this graph to describe your sample of SALES values.

Insights from Statistics in Action

Semiconductor Business: When the Chips Are Down

The Statistics in Action section at the beginning of this chapter discussed the cyclical nature of the semiconductor business and the worldwide players in this market (primarily, the United States and Japan). Data for the following questions are listed in StatInActChap3.xls. These data contain the consumption of semiconductors by key global companies as a percentage of world consumption. The percentages are

presented for the 10-year period from 1994 to 2003. The percentages for the years 2001, 2002, and 2003 are projected (estimated) values.

1. For each of the global players, find the mean and the median over the 10-year period for the consumption of semiconductors. For which global player is the difference between the mean and the median the largest?

2. By looking at the data, which global players do you think would exhibit the largest standard deviation for the percentage of semiconductor consumption over this ten-year period? Find the standard deviations. Which global player has the largest standard deviation?

3. Using the formula for Pearson's coefficient of skewness in the text, find the skewness of the data for each global player over this 10-year period. Which global players have a positive coefficient of skewness and which have a negative?

4. Which yearly figure do you think most influenced the coefficient of skewness for the United States? Eliminate this figure and recalculate the mean, median, and standard deviation. By how much does the coefficient of skewness change?

5. Find the coefficient of variation for each of the global players over this 10-year period. Which global player exhibits the least variation using this measure?

(Source: "The Semi Swing," *Red Herring,* June 15, 2001, pp. 142–144. "All Eyes Turn Toward South," *Electronic Business,* July 2000, pp. 104–112.)

Appendix **SPSS**®

Chapter 3 Appendix: Data Analysis with SPSS

Descriptive Statistics

The SPSS procedure to display descriptive statistics will be illustrated using the salary data from Figure 3.2. Click on **Analyze ➤ Descriptive Statistics ➤ Descriptives.** In the **Descriptives** window, select each of the four variables and click on the pointer to move them into the **Variable(s)** box. Click on **Options.** In the window immediately following, click on the boxes corresponding to the desired descriptive statistics. Notice that skewness, kurtosis, and several other options were selected for this illustration. The resulting descriptive statistics immediately follow the **Options** window.

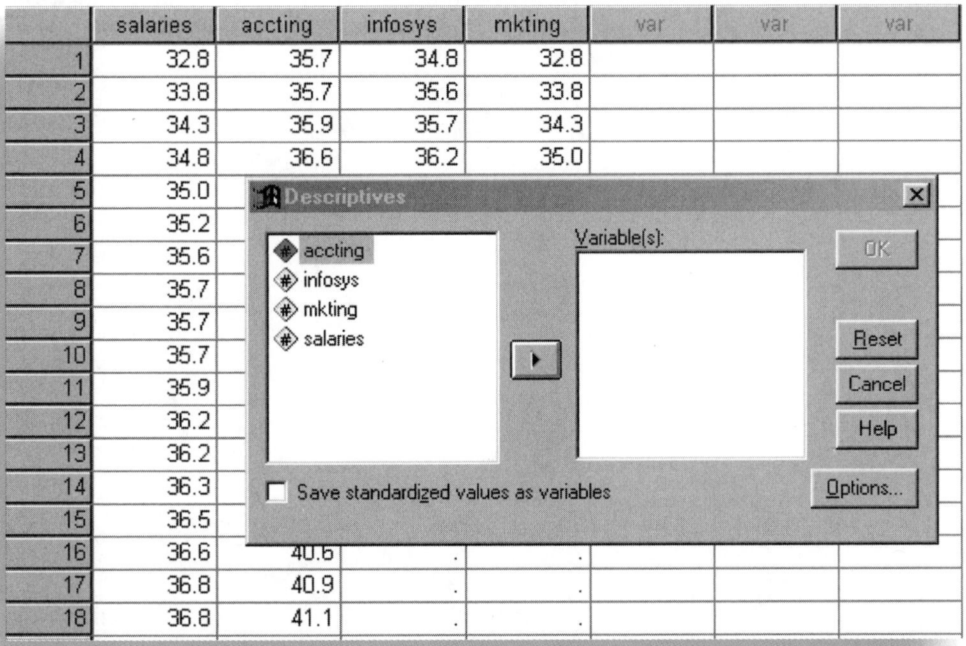

	salaries	accting	infosys	mkting	var	var	var
1	32.8	35.7	34.8	32.8			
2	33.8	35.7	35.6	33.8			
3	34.3	35.9	35.7	34.3			
4	34.8	36.6	36.2	35.0			
5	35.0						
6	35.2						
7	35.6						
8	35.7						
9	35.7						
10	35.7						
11	35.9						
12	36.2						
13	36.2						
14	36.3						
15	36.5						
16	36.6	40.6	.	.			
17	36.8	40.9	.	.			
18	36.8	41.1	.	.			

Descriptives window:

accting
infosys
mkting
salaries

Variable(s):

OK
Reset
Cancel
Help
Options...

☐ Save standardized values as variables

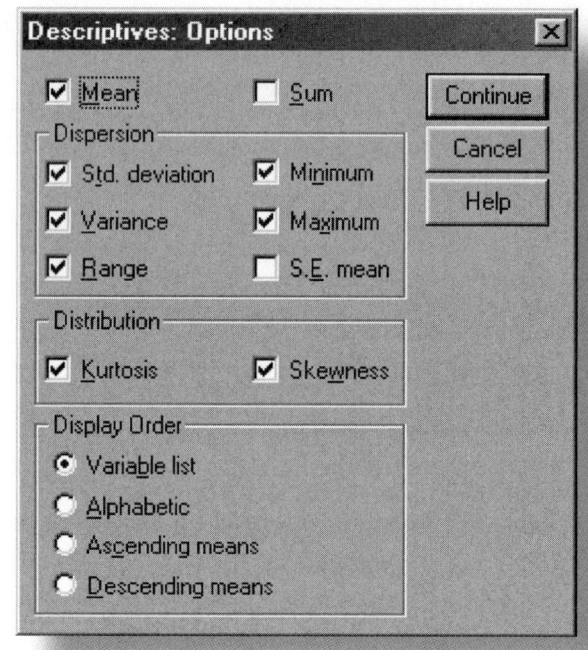

Descriptive Statistics

	N Statistic	Range Statistic	Minimum Statistic	Maximum Statistic	Mean Statistic	Std. Deviation Statistic	Variance Statistic	Skewness Statistic	Kurtosis Statistic
accting	26	8.1	35.7	43.8	39.612	2.447	5.989	−.060	−.962
mkting	14	6.9	32.8	39.7	36.536	2.068	4.278	−.298	−.875
infosys	10	4.7	34.8	39.5	36.870	1.460	2.131	.444	−.653
All	50	11.0	32.8	43.8	38.202	2.606	6.792	.268	−.481

Box Plots

To obtain a box plot from the aptitude test scores of 50 applicants listed in Table 3.2, click on **Graphs ➤ Boxplot**. In the window immediately following, click on **Simple** and **Summaries of separate variables**. Click on **Define**. Select the variable scores and click on the pointer to move this variable into the **Boxes Represent** box. Click on **OK**. The resulting box plot follows this window.

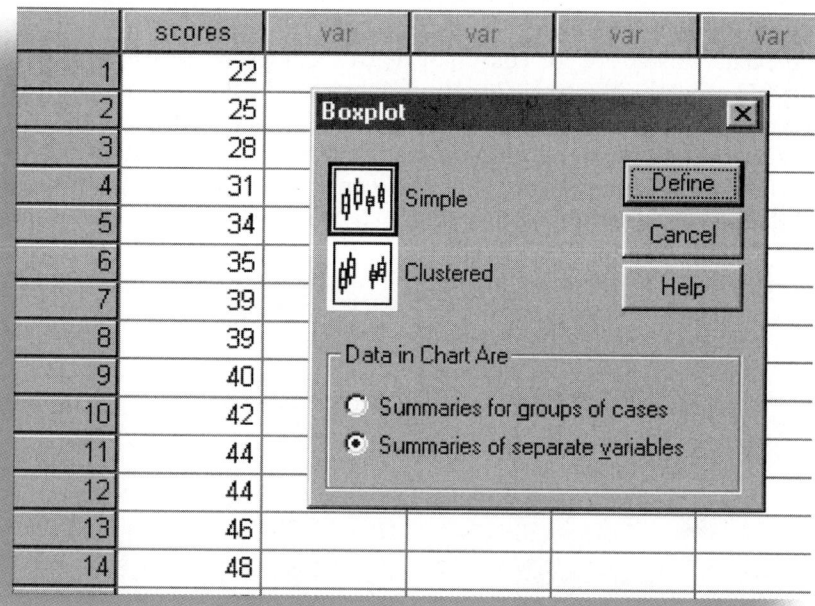

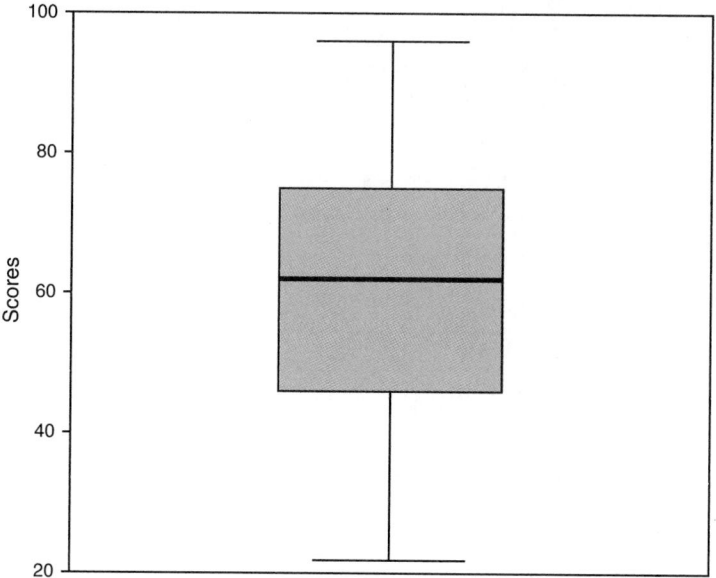

Grouped Data

SPSS can be used to construct the "made-up" data discussed in Section 3.7. To construct this sample of size 36, begin by entering 1 through 36 in the first column of a data sheet. Enter the first class midpoint (25) in the top cell of the second column (see below). Copy this cell using **Edit ➤ Copy** (or by holding down the Control key while entering the letter C). We need five values of 25 so in the next four cells, click on **Edit ➤ Paste** (or hold down the Control key while entering the letter V). In the sixth cell enter the next class midpoint (35). Repeat the preceding copy and paste procedure for cells 7 through 19 since we need 14 values of 35. Continue this procedure until all 36 cells in the second column have been set. Then click on **Analyze ➤ Descriptive Statistics ➤ Descriptive.** Move the value variable into the **Variable(s)** box and click on **OK.** The output immediately following the data window will appear in the display pane. The approximate mean of the grouped data is 41.11 and the approximate standard deviation is 11.03.

	obs	value
1	1	25.00
2	2	25.00
3	3	25.00
4	4	25.00
5	5	25.00
6	6	35.00
7	7	35.00
8	8	35.00
9	9	35.00
10	10	35.00
11	11	35.00
12	12	35.00
13	13	35.00
14	14	35.00
15	15	35.00
16	16	35.00
17	17	35.00
18	18	35.00
19	19	35.00
20	20	45.00
21	21	45.00
22	22	45.00

◄ │ ► │ **Data View** ╱ Variable View ╱

Descriptive Statistics

	N	Minimum	Maximum	Mean	Std. Deviation
VALUE	36	25.00	65.00	41.1111	11.0267

On the CD . . .
Chapter 3 Appendix: Data Analysis with MINITAB

chapter

4

Probability Concepts X

Statistics in Action
Cable and DSL Connections: Wired for Speed

With high-speed Internet connections, users can watch video online or download software and other data-rich files in a matter of seconds. In addition to offering speed, broadband access provides a continuous "always on" connection (no need to dial-up) and a "two-way" capability to both receive (download) and transmit (upload) data at high speeds. One high-speed Internet application that has held considerable promise is video-on-demand services. Five major Hollywood studios—MGM Home Entertainment Group, Paramount Pictures, Sony Pictures Entertainment, Universal Studios and Warner Bros.—announced plans in August 2001 to deliver this service.

The use of the Internet has grown exponentially during the 1990s. According to the Department of Commerce, more than 60% of American households now have access to the Internet, while more than 50% of all Americans have Internet access at home. In 2001, high-speed Internet connections were still a small proportion, at about 8 million or 12% of all ISP subscribers. However, in large metropolitan areas such as Boston, Dallas, Los Angeles, and New York, the percent of Internet subscribers connected to high-speed Internet technology is approximately 25%. It is exciting that there are all kinds of new and amazing Web technologies. However, if the average user doesn't have the connection speeds to use the technology effectively, most of this technology will be ignored. For many of the remaining 88% who have not opted for DSL or cable connec-

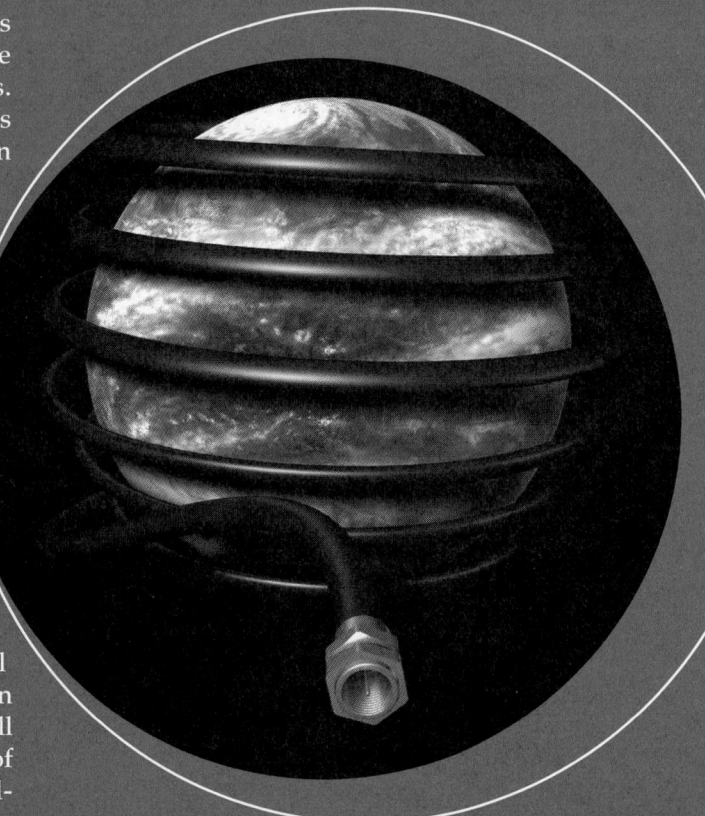

tions, the options include living with a slow dial-up connection or spending $400 to $1,000 for wireless or satellite technology that bypasses the hard-wired world of phones and cable.

Research firms are forecasting that cable modem and Digital Subscriber Line (DSL) use is expected to grow steadily over the next five years. They differ on whether cable or DSL will maintain the greatest share. The growth will be driven largely by a range of widely available technologies, as well as by content and services. High-speed Internet connection providers are betting that once subscribers try DSL or cable connections, they will become addicted to the speed and want to yank out the slowpoke 56K modem (narrow band) from their computer. In fact, AT&T, Verizon, SBC Communications, BellSouth, and EarthLink hiked DSL rates for new customers during the summer of 2001, the first increase since 1998. SBC Communications Inc., the leading provider of DSL service, signed up more than 1 million subscribers to its service by the end of the second quarter of 2001, though the growth rate slowed in 2001. Indeed, companies can't put off high-speed Internet connections for long.

Research firms believe that the future of high-speed Internet access is full of uncertainty, as competing companies and industries try to anticipate technological advances, market conditions, consumer preferences, and even cultural and societal trends. When you have completed this chapter, you will be able to examine the market for broadband Internet and discuss such questions as

- How can market share be understood in terms of probabilities?
- What is the probability that a high-speed Internet consumer will select cable or DSL?
- How can the probability that a high-speed Internet consumer makes a monthly purchase online be revised if the type of connection that the consumer purchased is known?

A Look Back/Introduction

You use descriptive statistics to summarize or present data that consist of observations that have already occurred. If these data are drawn from a population, then you describe your sample in some way. If you wish to infer something about the population using the smaller sample, you must deal with uncertainty. To measure the chance that something will occur, you use its **probability**. The concepts of probability form the foundation of all decision making in statistics. By using probabilities, you are able to deal with uncertainty because you are able, at least, to measure it.

To illustrate this idea, suppose that a recent report contained the results of a random sample of 100 homes within a large metropolitan city and stated that the average electric bill was $185. However, the electric company claims that the average bill for all of its customers is $110. Is something wrong here? Do you believe that the *population* mean is $110 based on the fact that the *sample* mean is $185? Here we need a probability, in particular the probability of observing a sample mean at least this large (that is, $185 or more), assuming that the electric company is correct in their claim. If we decide that this probability is extremely small, we can infer that the *population* claim is incorrect, based on the *sample* results.

As mentioned in Chapter 1, there is always the possibility of arriving at the wrong decision (maybe the electric company *is* correct) when using sample results to infer something concerning a population. This particular type of question will be addressed in Chapter 8. We begin the journey into probability in this chapter by introducing some basic concepts and discussing various ways of determining probabilities.

4.1 EVENTS AND PROBABILITY

An activity for which the outcome is uncertain is an **experiment.** An experiment need not involve mixing chemicals in the laboratory; it could be as simple as throwing two dice and observing the total of the faces turned up. At the completion of an experiment, a measurement of some kind is obtained. An **event** consists of one or more possible outcomes of the experiment; it is usually denoted by a capital letter.* The following are examples of experiments and some corresponding events:

- *Experiment:* Rolling two dice; *events:* A = rolling a total of 7, B = rolling a total greater than 8, C = rolling two 4s.
- *Experiment:* Taking a CPA exam; *events:* A = pass, B = fail.
- *Experiment:* Observing the number of arrivals at a drive-up window over a 5-minute period; *events:* A_0 = no arrivals, A_1 = one arrival, A_2 = two arrivals, and so on.

When you estimate a probability, you are estimating the probability *of an event*. For example, when rolling two dice, the probability that you will roll a total of 7 (event A) is the probability that event A occurs. It is written **P(A)**. The probability of any event is always between 0 and 1, inclusive.

NOTATION

$P(A)$ = probability that event A occurs

Classical Definition of Probability

Suppose a particular experiment has n possible outcomes and event A occurs in m of the n outcomes. The **classical definition** of the probability that event A will occur is

$$P(A) = m/n \qquad \text{4.1}$$

This definition assumes that all n possible outcomes have the same chance for occurring. Such outcomes (events) are said to be **equally likely**, and each has probability $1/n$ of occurring. If this is not the case, the classical definition does not apply.

Consider the experiment of tossing a nickel and a dime into the air and observing how they fall. Event A is observing one head and one tail. The possible outcomes are (H = head, T = tail):

Nickel	Dime
H	H
H	T
T	H
T	T

Thus, there are two ($m = 2$) outcomes that constitute event A of the four possible outcomes ($n = 4$). These four outcomes are equally likely, so each occurs with probability $1/4$. Consequently,

$$P(A) = 2/4 = .5$$

Relative Frequency Approach

Another method of estimating a probability is referred to as the **relative frequency** approach. It is based on observing the experiment n times and counting the number of times an event (say, A) occurs. If event A occurs m times, your estimate of the probability that A will occur in the future is

$$P(A) = m/n \qquad \text{4.2}$$

---

*The set of all possible outcomes of an experiment is often referred to as the *sample space*.

Suppose that a particular production process has been in operation for 250 days; 220 days have been accident-free. Let A = a randomly chosen day in the future is free of accidents. Using the relative frequency definition, then

$$P(A) = 220/250 = .88$$

Subjective Probability

Another type of probability is **subjective probability.** It is a measure (between 0 and 1) of your belief that a particular event will occur. A value of one indicates that you believe this event will occur with complete certainty.

Examples of situations requiring a subjective probability are:

The probability that the Dow Jones closing index will be below 8500 at some time during the next 6 months.

The probability that your newly introduced product will capture at least 10% of the market.

The probability that an audited voucher will contain an error.

The probability that your recently married cousin, divorced five times already, will once again go down alimony lane.

Although no two people may agree on a particular subjective probability, these probabilities are governed by the same rules of probability, which are developed later in the chapter.

4.2 BASIC CONCEPTS

Datacomp recently conducted a survey of 200 selected purchasers of their newly introduced laptop computer to obtain a gender-and-age profile of its new customers. A summary by gender revealed

Class	Frequency
Male	120
Female	80
	200

and a summary by age resulted in the following frequency distribution (note that 30–45 includes the 30 and 45 year olds):

Class	Frequency
Under 30	100
30–45	50
Over 45	50
	200

These two categories (gender and age) can be summarized *together* in a **contingency,** or **cross-tab, table,** shown in Table 4.1. The numbers within the table represent the frequency, or number of individuals, within each pair of subcategories, and so the contingency table allows you to see how these two categories interact.

There are 60 purchasers who are male *and* under 30; 10 purchasers are female *and* over 45. One person from the total group of 200 is to be selected at random to receive a free software package. We can define the following events:

TABLE

4.1

Datacomp survey of microcomputer purchasers.

Sex	Age (Years)			Total
	<30 (U)	30–45 (B)	>45 (O)	
Male (M)	60	20	40	120
Female (F)	40	30	10	80
Total	100	50	50	200

M = a male is selected

F = a female is selected

U = the person selected is under 30

B = the person selected is between 30 and 45

O = the person selected is over 45

Because there are 200 people, there are 200 possible outcomes to this experiment. All 200 outcomes are equally likely (the person is randomly selected), so the classical definition proves an easy way of determining probabilities.

Marginal Probability

The probability of any one single event used to define the contingency table is a **marginal probability.** When you use a contingency table, you can obtain the marginal probabilities by merely counting. For example, of the 200 purchasers, 120 are males. So the probability of selecting a male is

$$P(M) = 120/200 = .6$$

Similarly,

$$P(F) = 80/200 = .4$$
$$P(U) = .5$$
$$P(B) = .25$$
$$P(O) = .25$$

Notice that $P(O) = 50/200 = .25$, which implies that (1) if you repeatedly selected a person at random from this group, 25% of the time the person selected would be over 45 years of age, and (2) 25% of the people in this group are over 45 years old. So a probability here is simply a *proportion.*

The **complement** of an event A is the event that A does *not* occur. This event is denoted by $\bar{A}$. For example, A = it rains tomorrow, $\bar{A}$ = it does not rain tomorrow; or A = stock market rises tomorrow, $\bar{A}$ = stock market does not rise tomorrow.

In our Datacomp survey, $P(M) = .6$, and so

$$P(\bar{M}) = P(F) = .4$$

Notice that $P(M) + P(\bar{M}) = .6 + .4 = 1.0$. In general, for any event A, either A or $\bar{A}$ must occur. Consequently,

$$P(A) + P(\bar{A}) = 1$$

and so

$$P(\bar{A}) = 1 - P(A)$$

Written another way,

$$P(A) = 1 - P(\bar{A})$$

How can we determine what proportion of the purchasers are age 45 or younger?

$$P(\bar{O}) = 1 - P(O) = 1 - .25 = .75$$

Joint Probability

What if we wish to know the probability of selecting a purchaser who is female *and* under age 30? Such a person is selected if events F *and* U occur. This probability is written $P(F \text{ and } U)$ and is referred to as a **joint probability**.* There are 40 purchasers who are female and under 30, so

$$P(F \text{ and } U) = 40/200 = .2$$

What proportion are males between 30 and 45? This is the same as

$$P(M \text{ and } B) = 20/200 = .1$$

because 20 out of 200 satisfy both requirements.

Probability of A or B

In addition to calculating joint probabilities involving two events, we can also determine the probability that *either* of the two events will occur. In our discussion, "either A or B" will refer to the event that A occurred, B occurred, or both occurred. This probability is written as

$$P(A \text{ or } B)$$

for any two events A and B.†

Now we will calculate the probability of selecting someone who is a male *or* under 30 years of age. This is $P(M \text{ or } U)$. How many people qualify? There are 120 males and there are 100 people under 30. Is the answer $(120 + 100)/200 = 1.1$? You should realize that this is not correct, because *a probability is never greater than 1*. What is the mistake here? The problem is that the 60 males under age 30 were counted *twice*. How many purchasers are male or under 30? The answer is the 120 males plus the 40 females under age 30. So

$$P(M \text{ or } U) = (120 + 40)/200 = .8$$

What is $P(F \text{ or } B)$? In Table 4.1, the 80 females and 20 of the males qualify. So,

$$P(F \text{ or } B) = (80 + 20)/200 = .5$$

Conditional Probability

Suppose that someone has some inside information about who has been selected from the group of 200 purchasers. This person informs you that the selected individual is under 30 years of age; that is, event U occurred. Armed with this information, we can calculate the probability that the selected person is a male. Given that event U occurred, we have immediately narrowed the number of possible outcomes from 200 to the 100 people under age 30. Each of these 100 people is equally likely to be chosen, and 60 of them are male. So the answer is $60/100 = .6$.

Whenever you are given information and are asked to find a probability based on this information, the result is a **conditional probability**. This probability is written as

$$P(A \mid B)$$

---

*The joint probability of events A and B is often written as $P(A \cap B)$, read as "the probability of A intersect B."
†The probability $P(A \text{ or } B)$ can be written as $P(A \cup B)$, read as "the probability of A union B."

where B is the event that you know occurred and A is the uncertain event whose probability you need, given that event B has occurred. The vertical line indicates that the occurrence of event B is given, so the expression is read as the "probability of A given B." In the example, $P(M \mid U) = .6$.

Suppose that you were given *no information* about U and were asked to find the probability that a male is selected. This is a marginal probability. We earlier determined that $P(M) = .6$. For our example, note that

$$P(M) = P(M \mid U) = .6$$

This means that being given the information that the person selected is under 30 has *no effect* on the probability that a male is selected. In other words, whether U happens has no effect on whether M occurs. Such events are said to be independent. *Thus, events* A *and* B *are* **independent** *if the probability of event* A *is unaffected by the occurrence or nonoccurrence of event* B.

There are a number of ways to demonstrate that any two events A and B are independent.

DEFINITION

Events A and B are **independent** if and only if:

1. $P(A \mid B) = P(A)$ (assuming $P(B) \neq 0$), or

2. $P(B \mid A) = P(B)$ (assuming $P(A) \neq 0$), or

3. $P(A \text{ and } B) = P(A) \cdot P(B)$.

You need not demonstrate all three conditions. If one of the equations is true, they are all true; if one is false, they are all false (in which case A and B are not independent). Events that are not independent are **dependent** events.

In our example, are events F and O independent? We previously showed that

$$P(O) = 50/200 = .25$$

Since $P(O \mid F) = 10/80 = .125$ then $P(O) \neq P(O \mid F)$ and these events are dependent. Put another way, if someone informs you that event F (a female) has occurred, this *does* have an effect on whether the person selected is over 45 years of age. If you are told that F occurred, the probability that the selected person is over 45 *drops* from .25 to .125. These events do affect each other and so are dependent events.

We could also approach this by showing that $P(F \mid O)$ is not the same as $P(F)$:

$$P(F \mid O) = 10/50 = .2$$
$$P(F) = 80/200 = .4$$

These are not the same values, so events F and O are not independent.

The final option is to show that $P(F \text{ and } O)$ is not the same as $P(F) \cdot P(O)$. This follows since

$$P(F \text{ and } O) = 10/200 = .05$$
$$P(F) \cdot P(O) = (.4)(.25) = .1$$

In our discussion of joint probabilities, we showed that

$$P(F \text{ and } U) = 40/200 = .2$$

Consequently, events F and U *can both occur* because their joint probability is not zero.

How would you calculate $P(F \text{ and } M)$? One cannot be both a male and a female, so $P(F \text{ and } M) = 0$. Because events M and F cannot both occur, these events are said to be mutually exclusive.

DEFINITION

Events A and B are **mutually exclusive** if A and B cannot both occur simultaneously. To demonstrate that two events A and B are mutually exclusive, you must show that their joint probability is zero: $P(A \text{ and } B) = 0$.

The quality-improvement department of Lectron has selected 10 devices for testing purposes. Which of these outcomes are mutually exclusive?

A = exactly one device is defective

B = more than two devices are defective

C = fewer than four devices are defective

Solution   A and B are mutually exclusive events—they cannot both occur.
A and C are *not* mutually exclusive—if A occurs, so does event C.
B and C are *not* mutually exclusive—if three devices are defective, both events B and C will occur.

By *not mutually exclusive*, we do not mean that both of these events *must* occur, only that both *could* occur. Also, be sure to distinguish between the terms *mutually exclusive* and *independent*. Loosely, mutually exclusive means that they cannot both occur and independent means that one event occurring has no effect on the other. For example, when drawing a single card from a deck of 52 playing cards, the events K = drawing a king and H = drawing a heart are *not* mutually exclusive since they can both occur, namely when drawing the king of hearts. However, they *are* independent, since $P(K) = 4/52 = 1/13$ (there are four kings out of 52 cards), and $P(K \mid H) = 1/13$ (there are 13 hearts and one of them is a king). Consequently, knowing that a heart was selected has *no effect* on whether this card was a king, and so these events are independent.

SUMMARY OF PROBABILITY DEFINITIONS

1. *Experiment.* An experiment is any process that yields a measurement (observation).
2. *Outcome.* An outcome is any particular result of an experiment.
3. *Event.* An event consists of one or more possible outcomes of an experiment.
4. *Complement.* The complement of event A is the event that A does not occur. This is written $\bar{A}$.
5. *Mutually exclusive events.* Two events are mutually exclusive if they cannot both occur simultaneously.
6. *Independent events.* Two events are independent if the probability of one event occurring is unaffected by the occurrence or nonoccurrence of the other.
7. *Probability.* A probability is a measure of the likelihood that an event will occur when the experiment is performed.
8. *Marginal probability.* A marginal probability is the probability that any one single event used to define a contingency table will occur.
9. *Joint probability.* The joint probability of events A and B is the probability that both A and B will occur. This is written as $P(A \text{ and } B)$.
10. *Conditional probability.* The conditional probability of A given B is the probability that event A occurs given that event B occurs. This is written $P(A \mid B)$.

 Exercises 4.1–4.15

Understanding the Mechanics

4.1 Assume that there are only four distinct possible outcomes in an experiment: *A*, *B*, *C*, and *D*. Explain what is incorrect about each of the following sets of assigned probabilities.
- **a.** $P(A) = .25$ $P(B) = 1.25$ $P(C) = .50$ $P(D) = .25$
- **b.** $P(A) = .15$ $P(B) = .01$ $P(C) = .01$ $P(D) = .01$
- **c.** $P(A) = .40$ $P(B) = .40$ $P(C) = .40$ $P(D) = .40$

4.2 Consider an experiment of randomly selecting a card from a deck of 52 cards.
- **a.** What is the probability of selecting a queen?
- **b.** What is the probability of not selecting a queen?
- **c.** What is the probability of selecting the queen of hearts?
- **d.** Is the event of selecting a queen mutually exclusive from the event of selecting a heart?

4.3 Let *A* and *B* be two events such that $P(A \text{ or } B) = .60$, $P(A \text{ and } B) = .10$, $P(A \mid B) = .25$, $P(B \mid A) = .333$, $P(\bar{A}) = .70$, and $P(\bar{B}) = .60$.
- **a.** What is the joint probability of events *A* and *B*?
- **b.** What is the probability of event *A* conditioned on the occurrence of event *B*?
- **c.** What is the probability of either event *A* or event *B* occurring?
- **d.** What is the probability that event *A* does *not* occur?

4.4 The probability of *A* occurring is .3 and the probability of *B* occurring is .5.
- **a.** What is the probability of both *A* and *B* occurring if *A* and *B* are mutually exclusive?
- **b.** What is the probability of *A* occurring given that *B* is known to occur if *A* and *B* are independent?
- **c.** What is the probability of *B* occurring given that *A* is known to occur if *A* and *B* are independent?

Applying the New Concepts

4.5 Let *A* represent freshmen and *B* represent both juniors and seniors at a community college with various undergraduate programs. Are *A* and *B* mutually exclusive? What is the complement of *A*? Are the complement of *A* and the complement of *B* mutually exclusive?

4.6 Four hundred randomly sampled automobile owners were asked whether they selected the particular make and model of their present car mainly because of its appearance or because of its performance. The results were as follows:

Owner	Appearance	Performance	Totals
Male	95	55	150
Female	85	165	250

- **a.** What is the probability that an automobile owner buys a car mainly for its appearance?
- **b.** What is the probability that an automobile owner buys a car mainly for its appearance and the automobile owner is a male?

- **c.** What is the probability that a female automobile owner purchases the car mainly because of its appearance?

4.7 A quality-control engineer summarized the frequency of the type of defect with the manufacturing of a certain motor. The following table shows which of three shifts was responsible for the type of defect.

		Type of Defect			
Shift	Misaligned Component	Missing Component	Measurement Outside of Specification Limits	Other	Total
1	23	13	12	14	62
2	15	15	18	12	60
3	5	11	10	2	28

- **a.** What is the probability that a defective motor will have a measurement outside of its specification limits?
- **b.** What is the probability that a defective motor was not produced by Shift 1?
- **c.** What is the probability that a defective motor produced by Shift 3 does not have a misaligned component?
- **d.** What is the probability that a defective motor has a misaligned component or was produced by Shift 1?

4.8 The employment center at a university wanted to know the proportion of students who worked and also the proportion of those who lived in the dorm. The following data were collected:

	Work Situation			
Living Arrangements	Full Time	Part Time	Do not Work	Total
In dorm	19	22	20	61
Not in dorm	25	9	5	39
				100

- **a.** What is the probability of selecting a student at random who works either full or part time?
- **b.** What is the probability that a student who works lives in the dorm?
- **c.** What is the probability that a student either works full time or does not live in the dorm?
- **d.** Is the event that a student lives in the dorm independent of the event that a student works full time? Discuss what your answer means.

4.9 An investment newsletter writer wanted to know in which investment areas her subscribers were most interested. A questionnaire was sent to 331 randomly selected professional clients, with the following results:

			Investment Area			
Business	Stocks	Bonds	Commercial Paper	Commodities	Stock Options	Total
Doctors	30	25	15	2	0	72
Lawyers	29	34	12	0	5	80
Bankers	50	35	29	5	10	129
Others	21	14	10	3	2	50
						331

- **a.** What is the probability that an investment client is neither a doctor nor a lawyer?

b. What is the probability that an investment client is a banker and that the investment client's main investment interest is in commodities?

c. If an investment client's main investment interest is commodities, what is the probability that he or she is a banker?

d. What is the probability that an investment client's main investment interest is not in stock options?

e. Let *A* be the event that an investment client is a lawyer. Let *B* be the event that an investment client's main investment interest is in commodities. Are the events *A* and *B* mutually exclusive?

4.10 If events *A* and *B* are mutually exclusive, is the occurrence of event *A* affected by the occurrence of event *B*? Can one say that if two events are mutually exclusive, they are not independent?

4.11 Computer-controlled cameras are being used experimentally to ticket automobile drivers for speeding and running red lights. These devices are operated by private firms and have an incentive to pull in as many drivers as they can. Although approximately 70% of the motorists stoically accept and pay these tickets, others resent this procedure and fight the tickets. Assume that the actions of 200 motorists who received a ticket from a computer controlled camera produced the following results.

Traffic Violation	Pay Ticket	Fight Ticket
Run Red Light	40	20
Speeding	100	40

a. What is the probability of selecting a person at random who receives a speeding ticket?

b. What is the probability or selecting a person at random who receives a speeding ticket and fights the ticket?

c. What is the probability that a person, selected at random, either receives a speeding ticket or pays for the traffic violation ticket?

d. What is the probability that a person, selected at random, does not run a red light and does not fight the traffic violation ticket?

(Source: "Speeders, Say Cheese," *Time*, vol. 158, no. 11, September 17, 2001, p. 32.)

4.12 Several airlines have online fares that are less than the sale fares obtained from phoning the airline company to make a reservation. The following is a list of the number of flights with seats that were still available 7 days prior to departure for a randomly selected day in July 2001.

Flight	Online Discount Available	Seven Day Discount Available	Full Fare Only Available
New York– Los Angeles	2	7	4
Houston– Denver	4	5	3
Houston– San Francisco	3	5	2

a. Suppose that a flight is selected randomly from the flights between New York and Los Angeles. What is the probability that the flight has only full-fare seats available?

b. What is the probability that a flight selected at random from the flights traveling between Houston and Denver or between Houston and San Francisco has online discount tickets available?

c. What is the probability that a flight selected randomly from the flights traveling from New York to Los Angeles does not have seven-day discount tickets available?

(Source: Adapted from "Get the Lowest Fares When You Book Online," *The Wall Street Journal*, July 31, 2001, p. A11.)

4.13 A recent survey in ownership of home entertainment products shows that Sanyo is the leading brand of television sets sold in America. The following table illustrates how competitive the other brands are among families making less than $60,000 a year and those with incomes of at least $60,000 annually.

Television Brand	Family Income Less than $60,000	Family Income at Least $60,000
Sanyo	25	50
RCA	24	40
Sony	22	36
Panasonic	30	25
General Electric	32	15
Samsung	18	12
Zenith	20	10

a. What is the probability that an individual in the survey owned a Sanyo television?

b. What is the probability that an individual in the survey has a family income of at least $60,000?

c. What is the probability that an individual in the survey owns a Sanyo television and has a family income of at least $60,000?

d. Use parts a, b, and c to establish if television brand is independent of the family income level?

e. What is the probability that an individual has a family income of at least $60,000 or owns a Sanyo television set?

f. What is the probability that an individual who owns either a Samsung or Zenith television has an income of at least $60,000?

(Source: "Zenith Sees Its Future in Digital TV," *USA Today*, July 20, 2001, p. 7B.)

4.14 Lipton aired a commercial showing Loni Anderson and Mr. T spoofing how "real families" behave while enjoying "real cooking." However, a poll indicates that overall, only about a third of the audience enjoyed the ad. The following table presents the number of individuals who liked the ad among males and females.

	Liked the Ad	Did Not Like the Ad
Male	13	25
Female	20	42

a. What is the probability that an individual who saw the Lipton commercial was a male who liked the ad or was a female who did not like the ad?

b. What is the probability that a female liked the ad?

c. What is the probability that an individual who did not like the ad was a female?

(Source: "Unreal Ad Families Tout Real Lipton Fare," *USA Today*, June 11, 2001, p. 4B.)

4.15 Employers have expanded benefits for workers over the past several years to make recruiting easier and to increase morale. Among the benefits have been full or partial school tuition reimbursement and up to three months leave of absence unrelated to the Family Medical and Leave Act. The following table illustrates employee benefit programs provided by 200 randomly selected companies.

	At Least 3 Months of Leave Allowed	Less than 3 Months of Leave Allowed
No Tuition Reimbursement	10	15
Partial Tuition Reimbursement	60	50
Full Tuition Reimbursement	50	15

a. What is the probability that a company will offer partial or full tuition reimbursement?

b. What is the probability that a company will not offer full tuition reimbursement and will offer at least three months of leave?

c. What is the probability that a company that allows at least three months of leave will provide partial or full tuition reimbursement?

d. Are the events of no tuition reimbursement and at least three months of leave allowed mutually exclusive? If not, what would have to occur to make them mutually exclusive?

(Source: "Employers Expand Benefits," *USA Today*, June 28, 2001, p. 1B.)

GOING BEYOND THE CONTINGENCY TABLE 4.3

Our Datacomp survey served as an intuitive introduction to probability definitions. The classical approach was used to derive probabilities by dividing the number of outcomes favorable to an event by the total number of (equally likely) outcomes. Not all probability problems, however, are concerned with randomly selecting an individual from a contingency table.

When dealing with two or more events in general, one approach is to illustrate these events by means of a **Venn diagram.** A Venn diagram representing any two events A and B is shown in Figure 4.1.

In a Venn diagram, the probability of an event occurring is its corresponding area. This might sound complicated, but it really is not. The Venn diagram for $P(A) = .4$ is shown in Figure 4.2. The area of the rectangle is 1; it represents all possible outcomes. The shaded area is the complement of A, namely, $\bar{A}$. Here, $P(\bar{A}) = 1 - P(A) = 1 - .4 = .6$. No effort is made to construct a circle with an area of .4; it is simply labeled .4. The shaded area then represents $\bar{A}$, and the corresponding area must be .6.

Figure 4.3 shows $P(A$ and $B)$, and Figure 4.4 shows $P(A$ or $B)$.

If A and B are mutually exclusive (they cannot both occur), then $P(A$ and $B) = 0$. For example, an auto dealer has data that indicate that 20% of all new cars ordered contain a red interior and 25% have a blue interior. Only one interior color

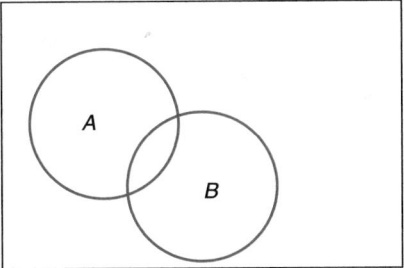

FIGURE 4.1

Venn diagram for events A and B. The rectangle represents all possible outcomes of an experiment.

FIGURE

4.2

Venn diagram for $P(A) = .4$.

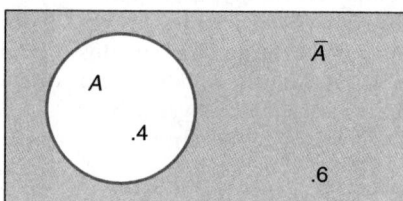

FIGURE

4.3

$P(A \text{ and } B)$. The points in the shaded area are in A and B.

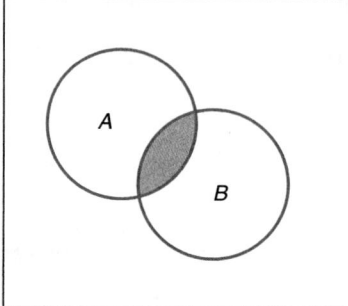

FIGURE

4.4

$P(A \text{ or } B)$. The points in the shaded area are in A or B.

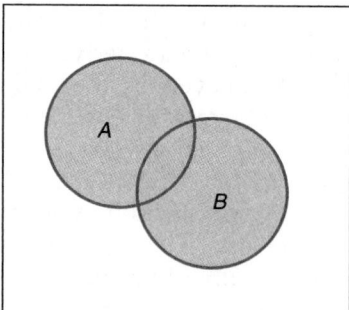

FIGURE

4.5

Venn diagram of mutually exclusive events. $P(A \text{ and } B) = 0$. $P(A \text{ or } B) = P(A) + P(B) = .2 + .25 = .45$.

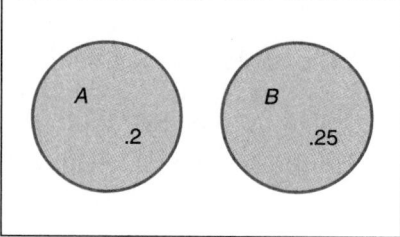

is allowed. Let A be the event that a red interior is selected and B be the event that a blue interior is selected. A Venn diagram for this situation is shown in Figure 4.5.

Each person can select only one color, so events A and B are mutually exclusive, and the resulting circles do not overlap in the Venn diagram. What is the probability that a person selects red *or* blue? This is $P(A \text{ or } B)$ and is represented by the shaded area in the circles in Figure 4.5. The Venn diagram allows us to see clearly that this shaded area is $P(A) + P(B) = .2 + .25 = .45$. In other words, 45% of the people will purchase either red or blue interiors. We thus have the following rule.

FIGURE

4.6

A Venn diagram
illustrating
$P(A$ or $B)$ and
$P(A$ and $B)$.

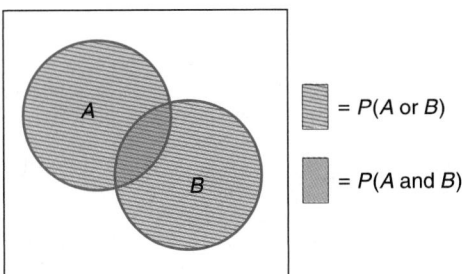

SPECIAL CASE

If events A and B are *mutually exclusive,* then
$$P(A \text{ or } B) = P(A) + P(B)$$

4.6

This rule does *not* work when A and B can both occur, but there is an easy way to devise another solution. Look at the Venn diagram for this situation, shown in Figure 4.6. By adding $P(A) + P(B)$, we do not obtain $P(A$ or $B)$ because we have counted $P(A$ and $B)$ *twice.* So we need to subtract $P(A$ and $B)$ to obtain the actual area corresponding to $P(A$ or $B)$. This is the **additive rule of probability.**

ADDITIVE RULE

For *any* two events, A and B,
$$P(A \text{ or } B) = P(A) + P(B) - P(A \text{ and } B)$$

4.7

Notice that if A and B are mutually exclusive, then $P(A$ and $B) = 0$, and we obtain the previous rule; namely, that $P(A$ or $B) = P(A) + P(B)$.

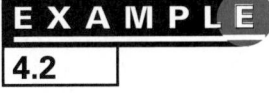

Draw a single card from a deck of 52 playing cards. Let Q be the event that the card is a queen and H be the event that the card is a heart. What is $P(Q$ or $H)$?

Solution

First, determine $P(Q$ and $H)$. $P(Q$ and $H)$ is the probability of selecting a queen of hearts from the deck. There is only one such card, so

$$P(Q \text{ and } H) = 1/52$$

A Venn diagram for this situation is shown in Figure 4.7. Using the additive rule, the proportion of draws (probability) on which a queen *or* a heart will be selected from the deck is

$$P(Q \text{ or } H) = P(Q) + P(H) - P(Q \text{ and } H)$$
$$= 4/52 + 13/52 - 1/52$$
$$= 16/52$$

Refer back to the Datacomp survey data in Table 4.1. Does the additive rule work here also? It does—this rule works for *any* two events—but it certainly is a hard way to solve this problem. Suppose we want to find the probability (from our previous example) that the person selected is a male or is under age 30. By inspection, we previously found that

$$P(M \text{ or } U) = 160/200 = .8$$

FIGURE

4.7

$P(Q) = 4/52;$
$P(H) = 13/52.$

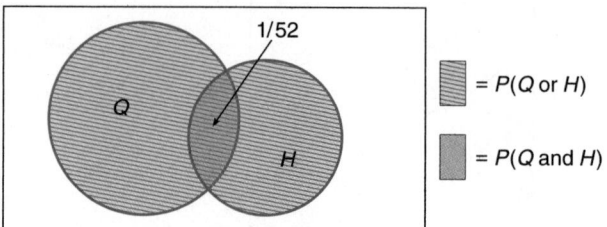

FIGURE

4.8

A Venn diagram illustrating a conditional probability.

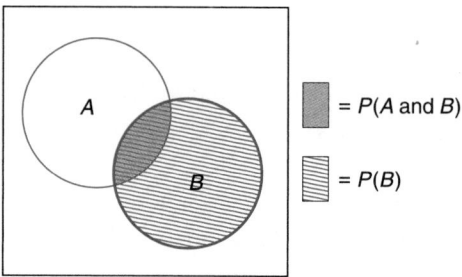

Using the additive rule, we obtain the same result:

$$P(M \text{ or } U) = P(M) + P(U) - P(M \text{ and } U)$$
$$= 120/200 + 100/200 - 60/200$$
$$= 160/200 = .8$$

Rules for Conditional Probabilities

Using the Datacomp survey data, we found that the probability the person selected is a male (M), given the information that the person selected is under 30 (U), was ($M \mid U$) = .6. Our reasoning here was: (1) There are 100 people under 30 years of age, (2) 60 of them are male, (3) each of these 100 people is equally likely to be selected, and so (4) the result is 60/100 = .6. Notice that

$$P(U) = 100/200 = .5$$
$$P(M \text{ and } U) = 60/200 = .3$$
$$P(M \mid U) = P(M \text{ and } U)/P(U) = .3/.5 = .6$$

This procedure for finding a conditional probability applies to *any* two events. Use the Venn diagram in Figure 4.8 to determine $P(A \mid B)$. Given the information that event B occurred, we are immediately restricted to the lined area (B). What is the probability that a point in B is also in A (that is, event A occurs)? A point is also in A if it lies in the shaded area, and

$$P(A \mid B) = \frac{\text{shaded area}}{\text{striped area}}$$
$$= \frac{P(A \text{ and } B)}{P(B)}$$

This is the rule for conditional probabilities.

RULE FOR CONDITIONAL PROBABILITIES

For any two events, A and B,

$$P(A \mid B) = \frac{P(A \text{ and } B)}{P(B)} \qquad (P(B) \neq 0)$$

4.8

and

$$P(B \mid A) = \frac{P(A \text{ and } B)}{P(A)} \qquad (P(A) \neq 0)$$

4.9

Independent Events

In the Datacomp example, equations 4.3, 4.4, and 4.5 provided a summary of how to demonstrate that two events are independent. *One need demonstrate only that one of these equations holds to verify independence.* These three methods of proving independence apply to *any two events,* not just to contingency table applications.

To summarize, events A and B are *independent* if any of the following statements can be verified:

$$P(A \mid B) = P(A)$$
$$P(B \mid A) = P(B)$$
$$P(A \text{ and } B) = P(A) \cdot P(B)$$

In many situations, it is unnecessary (or impossible) to prove independence of two events. However, one can often argue convincingly that two events are independent or dependent without resorting to a mathematical proof. Consider these events:

A = Procter & Gamble's new laundry detergent will capture at least 5% of the market next year

and

B = General Motors will introduce a new line of compact automobiles next year

Whether event B happens should have no effect on whether event A occurs. So $P(A \mid B) = P(A)$, and these events are independent. Next, change event A to: Toyota automobile sales will drop next year. Now whether event B occurs could very well have an effect on whether event A occurs. It is not safe to assume that $P(A \mid B) = P(A)$—it seems reasonable that $P(A \mid B)$ is *larger* than $P(A)$. Notice that we have not discussed the values of $P(A)$ and $P(A \mid B)$. The probability values are not necessary to show that the events are dependent. The important thing is that $P(A \mid B) \neq P(A)$, so these events are clearly dependent events.

Multiplicative Rule

The rule for conditional probabilities in equations 4.8 and 4.9 can be rewritten as

MULTIPLICATIVE RULE

For any two events A and B,

$$P(A \text{ and } B) = P(A \mid B) \cdot P(B)$$

4.10

$$= P(B \mid A) \cdot P(A)$$

4.11

This is the **multiplicative rule of probability.** Using equation 4.5, we also have the following rule for two independent events.

SPECIAL CASE

For any two independent events A and B,

$$P(A \text{ and } B) = P(A) \cdot P(B)$$

You may be wondering how we can use the same equation to define the rule for $P(A \mid B)$ (equation 4.8) and the rule for $P(A \text{ and } B)$ (equation 4.10). This is not a bad question! It appears that we have used the same rule twice to make two different statements—and in fact we have. However, for any application you encounter, either $P(A \mid B)$ or $P(A \text{ and } B)$ must be provided or can be determined without resorting to formulas. We can clarify this using our card-drawing example:

$$Q = \text{select a queen}$$

$$H = \text{select a heart}$$

Here $P(Q \text{ and } H)$ (the probability of selecting a queen of hearts) is 1/52. No formulas were necessary to determine this, only a little head scratching.

Now, what is $P(Q \mid H)$? Using equation 4.8,

$$P(Q \mid H) = P(Q \text{ and } H)/P(H)$$

$$= (1/52)/(13/52)$$

$$= 1/13$$

Replacement in Sampling

Assume that you select a card from a deck, examine it, and then discard it. You then select another card. This procedure is called *sampling without replacement*. Let

$$A = \text{selecting a queen on the first draw}$$

$$B = \text{selecting a queen on the second draw}$$

What is the probability of drawing two queens [$P(A \text{ and } B)$]? If you selected a queen on the first draw, then, of the 51 cards remaining, three are queens. So $P(B \mid A) = 3/51$. Again, we used no formulas.

Next, we use the multiplicative rule, equation 4.11:

$$P(A \text{ and } B) = P(B \mid A) \cdot P(A)$$

$$= \left(\frac{3}{51}\right) \cdot \left(\frac{4}{52}\right) \cong .0045$$

Notice that $P(A) = 4/52$ because there are four queens available on the first draw. So you would expect to draw two queens from a card deck about 45 times out of 10,000, if you are drawing without replacement.

Now suppose you select a card from a deck but replace it before selecting the second card. This procedure is called *sampling with replacement*. What is $P(B \mid A)$? There are still 52 cards in the deck when you select your second card, and four of these are queens. So

$$P(B \mid A) = 4/52 = P(B)$$

If event A occurs, the probability of a queen on the second draw is unaffected. This probability is 4/52 *whether or not A* occurs; these events are now independent. For this situation,

$$P(A \text{ and } B) = P(A \mid B) \cdot P(B)$$

$$= P(A) \cdot P(B) \qquad \text{(since they are independent)}$$

$$= 4/52 \cdot 4/52 = .0059$$

The probability of getting two queens is higher when drawing cards with replacement—not a surprising result.

Microsoft® Excel Application Use DATA4-3

EXAMPLE
4.3

Using Excel to Construct a Contingency Table

A quality engineer at Microtek obtained a random sample of 200 electrical components produced over a one-week period. Each component was inspected and classified as (1) OK, (2) OK after the component was reworked (repaired), or (3) scrap (unusable). The engineer also made note of which of the three Microtek plants produced the component: Memphis, Miami, or Pittsburgh. The sample information was stored in two columns in dataset DATA4-3, where

City = the city producing the component: 1 = Memphis
                                           2 = Miami
                                           3 = Pittsburgh

Quality = the component quality: 1 = OK
                                           2 = OK after rework
                                           3 = scrapped

Using Excel, construct a contingency table. (i) If a component is selected at random, determine the probability that this component is OK and produced in Miami. (ii) What percentage of the reworked components in the sample were produced in Memphis?

Solution

To construct the contingency table using Excel, first open the Excel file DATA4-3 by clicking on the Open file icon and identifying the location of this file. You should then see the first two columns labeled "City" and "Quality" in Figure 4.9. The Excel Tool Pack does not contain a procedure for constructing a contingency table from these two columns; however, the KPK data analysis add-ins do allow you to do this. Click on **KPK Data Analysis ➤ Qualitative Data Charts ➤ Contingency Table.** It is important when using this procedure to make sure that the two columns of data contain labels in the top row ("City" and "Quality" here). Enter "A1:A201" in the top box. This is the input range for the row variable (City), and includes the label. Repeat this for the column variable (Quality) by typing "B1:B201" in the second box. Enter "C1" as the output range and click on **OK.** You will obtain the output shown in Figure 4.9. To make this table easier to interpret, enter the city names in cells C4, C5, and C6 and the quality labels in cells D3, E3, and F3 (as in Figure 4.9).

FIGURE

4.9

Excel contingency table for Example 4.3.

	A	B	C	D	E	F	G	H
1	City	Quality			Contingency Table			
2	2	2			Quality			
3	1	1	City	OK	OK-Rework	Scrapped	Grand Total	
4	2	2	Memphis	60	15	5	80	
5	1	1	Miami	35	20	10	65	
6	2	3	Pittsburgh	25	15	15	55	
7	1	1	Grand Total	120	50	30	200	
8	2	2						
9	1	1						

Microsoft Excel - DATA4-3 [Read-Only]

File Edit View Insert Format Tools Data KPK Data Analysis Window Help

DATA4-3

Solution to (i) Thirty-five of the 200 components (in cell D5) are OK and produced in Miami, and so

$$P(\text{OK and Miami}) = 35/200 = .175$$

That is, 17.5% of the components are OK *and* produced in Miami.

Solution to (ii) There are 50 reworked components in the sample, 15 of which were produced in Memphis. Consequently,

$$P(\text{Memphis} \mid \text{reworked}) = 15/50 = .3$$

That is, 30% of the reworked components were produced in Memphis.

4.4   APPLYING THE CONCEPTS

Thus far, we have described methods of solving probabilities for one or two events using formulas or contingency tables. This section will use the concepts discussed in Sections 4.2 and 4.3 to derive various probabilities. Here we are going to leave our Datacomp example to consider some other probabilities. Some examples will present more than one solution to show how the problem can be solved using either formulas or contingency tables.

These examples are set up as word problems. *The most important step in solving a word probability problem is to set up the problem correctly.* Your first step should always be to define the events clearly, using capital letters. If you do not recall the correct formula to use, refer back to Section 4.2 or 4.3.

EXAMPLE 4.4

In a particular city, 20% of the people subscribe to the morning newspaper, 30% subscribe to the evening newspaper, and 10% subscribe to both. Determine the probability that an individual from this city subscribes to the morning newspaper, the evening newspaper, or both.

Using the Formulas

Solution Your initial step should be to define

$$M = \text{person subscribes to the morning newspaper}$$
$$E = \text{person subscribes to the evening newspaper}$$

We do not need to define another event for a person subscribing to both newspapers, as we shall see.

We now have

$$P(M) = .2$$
$$P(E) = .3$$

The probability that a selected individual subscribes to the morning *and* the evening newspaper is given as .10. This a *joint* probability:

$$P(M \text{ and } E) = .1$$

We want to find the probability of M or E. Using the additive rule,

$$P(M \text{ or } E) = P(M) + P(E) - P(M \text{ and } E)$$
$$= .2 + .3 - .1$$
$$= .4$$

So 40% of the people in this city subscribe to at least one of the two newspapers.

Suppose we also know that 1/3 of the evening newspaper subscribers are also morning newspaper subscribers. How can you translate this statement into a probability? We can restate the preceding sentence as "Given that a randomly selected individual subscribes to the evening newspaper, the probability that this person also subscribes to the morning newspaper is 1/3." In other words, this is a *conditional* probability:

$$P(M \mid E) = 1/3$$

EXAMPLE

4.5

Referring to the subscription data in Example 4.4, what percentage of the evening subscribers do not subscribe to the morning newspaper?

Solution 1

A Venn diagram for this problem is shown in Figure 4.10. Notice that M (the morning subscribers) is made up of two components: (1) those people in E (the evening subscribers) and (2) those not in E. Since $P(M \text{ and } E) = .1$, the area of M that is striped is

$$P(M) - P(M \text{ and } E) = P(M \text{ and } \bar{E})$$
$$= .2 - .1 = .1$$

Similarly, the area of E that is striped is

$$P(E) - P(M \text{ and } E) = P(\bar{M} \text{ and } E)$$
$$= .3 - .1 = .2$$

Our question could be stated, "Given that a person subscribes to the evening newspaper, what is the probability that this person does not subscribe to the morning newspaper?" This is the *conditional* probability

$$P(\bar{M} \mid E)$$

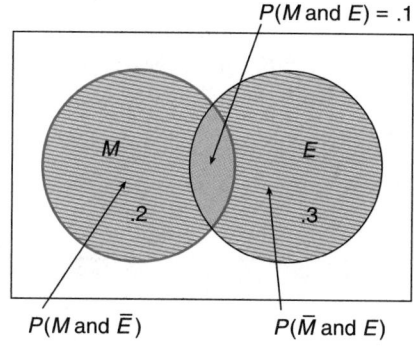

FIGURE

4.10

Venn diagram for Example 4.5.

137

Look at the Venn diagram. You know that E occurred, so the outcome is in the E circle. What is the probability that the outcome is not in M? We know that the total area of E is .3 and that the area that is not in M but is in E is .2. So

$$P(\overline{M} \mid E) = .2/.3 = 2/3$$

Another approach here is to utilize the formulas in the section by noting that given event E has occurred, either event M occurs or it doesn't. Consequently,

$$P(\overline{M} \mid E) = 1 - P(M \mid E)$$
$$= 1 - [P(M \text{ and } E)]/P(E)$$
$$= 1 - (.1/.3) = 2/3$$

Using a Contingency Table

Solution 2   Although Example 4.4 made no mention of a random sample, a useful device here is to imagine that a random sample of, say, $n = 100$ people is obtained (actually, any sample size (n) could be used). Next, construct a contingency table like the one in Section 4.2, by *assuming that the population percentages given in the problem apply to these 100 people.* In Example 4.4, we would assume that 20% of the sample (20 people) subscribe to the morning newspaper and 30% of the sample (30 people) subscribe to the evening newspaper. So far, the contingency table would be

	M	$\overline{M}$	
E			30
$\overline{E}$			
	20		100

Since the sample size is 100, the totals for $\overline{M}$ and $\overline{E}$ are 80 and 70, respectively, producing the following table:

	M	$\overline{M}$	
E			30
$\overline{E}$			70
	20	80	100

The final piece of information is that 10% of the people (10 people) subscribe to *both* newspapers. So 10 people are in the cell in the upper-left corner, corresponding to E and M, and the table is now

	M	$\overline{M}$	
E	10		30
$\overline{E}$			70
	20	80	100

By using the row and column totals, the remaining cells can be filled in.*

	M	$\overline{M}$	
E	10	20	30
$\overline{E}$	10	60	70
	20	80	100

Once the table is filled in, probabilities become very easy to derive via the approach used in Section 4.2. To illustrate, the solution to Example 4.4 is

$$P(M \text{ or } E) = \frac{10 + 10 + 20}{100} = \frac{40}{100} = .4$$

---

*This procedure is easier to apply and explain if the sample size (n) is chosen so that all numbers in the contingency table are counting numbers (integers).

The conditional probability in Example 4.5 is

$$P(\overline{M} \mid E) = \frac{20}{30} = 2/3$$

since there are 30 people who subscribe to the evening newspaper (E), 20 of whom do not subscribe to the morning newspaper ($\overline{M}$).

HELPFUL HINTS FOR PROBABILITY APPLICATIONS

Using the Formulas
1. Define each event using capital letters.
2. Translate each statement into a probability. Does a particular statement tell you $P(A)$? $P(B)$? $P(A$ and $B)$? $P(A$ or $B)$? $P(A \mid B)$? $P(B \mid A)$?
3. Determine the answer by identifying the probability rule that applies and by using a Venn diagram. Using both allows you to check your logic and your arithmetic.

Using a Contingency Table
1. Select *any* sample size, say, $n = 100$ or 1000.
2. Using the information given, fill in the row and column totals.
3. Using the final piece of information given, fill in the appropriate cell and complete the contingency table.
4. Determine the answer by dividing the proper value by the appropriate total.

In a certain northeastern state that is going through financial difficulties, it is believed that 5% of the banks will fail. It is known that the deposits of 90% of the banks in this state are insured by the Federal Depository Insurance Company (FDIC). It is also believed, from past experience, that 3% of the banks protected by FDIC will fail. A bank examiner employed by the federal government would like to know:

EXAMPLE 4.6

1. What is the probability that, for a randomly chosen bank, the bank has deposits protected by FDIC and the bank will fail?

2. What is the probability that, for a randomly chosen bank, the bank has deposits covered by FDIC or the bank will fail?

3. What percentage of the banks that go under have deposits protected by FDIC?

Using the Formulas

The first step is to define appropriate events:

Solution 1

$$A = \text{bank has deposits protected by FDIC}$$
$$B = \text{bank will fail}$$

We now translate each of the statements into a probability. We have the following marginal probabilities:

$$P(A) = .90$$
$$P(B) = .05$$

139

The last statement in the problem can be written as "Given that a bank has accounts protected by FDIC, the probability that the bank will fail is .03." So this is a conditional probability; namely,

$$P(B \mid A) = .03$$

What does question 1 ask for? $P(A \text{ or } B)$? $P(A \mid B)$? $P(A \text{ and } B)$? The examiner wishes to know the probability that a bank is protected by FDIC *and* will fail. This is $P(A \text{ and } B)$. Using the multiplicative rule,

$$P(A \text{ and } B) = P(B \mid A) \cdot P(A)$$

$$= (.03)(.90) = .027$$

Solution 2   For question 2, we wish to know the probability that A or B occurs. By the additive rule,

$$P(A \text{ or } B) = P(A) + P(B) - P(A \text{ and } B)$$

$$= .90 + .05 - .027 = .923$$

Thus, 92.3% of the banks are covered by the FDIC, will fail, or both.

Solution 3   Question 3 can be phrased as, "Given that a bank has failed, what is the probability that this bank has deposits protected by FDIC?" This is $P(A \mid B)$.

$$P(A \mid B) = [P(A \text{ and } B)]/P(B) = .027/.05 = .54$$

Therefore, 54% of those banks that fail have deposits protected by FDIC.

Using a Contingency Table

To obtain a table containing all counting numbers, a sample size of $n = 1,000$ is selected here. Remember that any sample size can be used with this approach. Five percent of the banks failed ($.05 \times 1,000 = 50$ banks) and 90% of the banks are insured by FDIC ($.90 \times 1,000 = 900$ banks). Filling in the remaining row and column totals, we get the following table:

	FDIC	$\overline{\text{FDIC}}$	
FAIL			50
$\overline{\text{FAIL}}$			950
	900	100	1000

Finally, 3% of the banks *protected by FDIC* failed. There are 900 banks protected by FDIC, so we find $.03 \times 900 = 27$ banks.* Thus, 27 of the banks are protected by FDIC and failed. This value goes into the upper left cell and the table is

	FDIC	$\overline{\text{FDIC}}$	
FAIL	27		50
$\overline{\text{FAIL}}$			950
	900	100	1000

Filling in the remaining cells, we get the following completed contingency table:

	FDIC	$\overline{\text{FDIC}}$	
FAIL	27	23	50
$\overline{\text{FAIL}}$	873	77	950
	900	100	1000

---

*A sample size of $n = 100$ would have produced a value of 2.7 here. The problem can still be solved using $n = 100$, but is easier to explain using counting numbers in each cell; hence, $n = 1000$ was selected.

$$P(\text{FDIC and FAIL}) = 27/1{,}000 = .027 \qquad \textbf{Solution 1}$$

$$P(\text{FDIC or FAIL}) = \frac{27 + 873 + 23}{1{,}000} = \frac{923}{1{,}000} = .923 \qquad \textbf{Solution 2}$$

$$P(\text{FDIC} \mid \text{FAIL}) = 27/50 = .54 \qquad \textbf{Solution 3}$$

since 50 of the banks failed, 27 of which are protected by FDIC.

X Exercises 4.16–4.35

Understanding the Mechanics

4.16 The probability of event A is .5 and the probability of event B is .2.

    a. If $P(A \text{ and } B)$ is .1, what is $P(A \text{ or } B)$?

    b. If the probability of A given B is .5, what is the $P(A \text{ and } B)$?

    c. If $P(A \text{ and } B)$ is .2, what is the probability of B given A?

4.17 Let $A = \{1, 3, 5, 7, 9\}$ and $B = \{4, 5, 6\}$. An experiment results in any number between 1 and 10, inclusively, being randomly selected.

    a. Draw a Venn diagram.

    b. Find $P(A \text{ and } B)$.

    c. Find $P(\bar{A} \text{ and } \bar{B})$.

    d. Find $P(\bar{A} \mid B)$.

4.18 The probabilities of the independent events A and B are .3 and .6, respectively.

    a. What is the probability of A or B?

    b. What is the probability of A and B?

    c. What is the probability of A given B?

    d. What is the probability of B given A?

    e. What is the probability of neither A nor B occurring?

4.19 An experiment has the following outcomes and probabilities:

Outcome	Probability
2	.1
4	.2
6	.4
8	.2
10	.1

Let $A = \{2, 6, 8\}$ and $B = \{6, 8, 10\}$.

    a. Find the probability that either A or B occurs.

    b. Find the probability that B occurs if A occurs.

    c. Find the probability that A occurs and B does not occur.

    d. Find the probability that A occurs if B does not occur.

4.20 The probabilities of the independent events A and B are .4 and .5, respectively. Find the following probabilities.

    a. The probability of A and B occurring.

    b. The probability of A but not B occurring.

    c. The probability of A or B occurring.

    d. The probability of A or not B occurring.

    e. The probability of A occurring given that B has occurred.

    f. The probability of A occurring given that B has not occurred.

4.21 Assume that events A, B, C, and D are the only possible events to an experiment. Furthermore, assume that every pair of these events is mutually exclusive. The following probabilities are known:

$$P(A) = .20 \qquad P(B) = .30$$

Find the following probabilities.

    a. $P(A \text{ or } B)$

    b. $P(\bar{A})$

    c. $P(A \mid D)$

    d. $P(C \text{ or } D)$

    e. $P(C \text{ and } D)$

    f. $P(A \mid \bar{B})$

    g. $P(B \mid \bar{A})$

4.22 Let $P(A) = .6$, $P(B) = .2$, and $P(A \mid B) = .1$. Find the following probabilities.

    a. $P(\bar{A} \text{ or } B)$

    b. $P(\bar{A} \text{ or } B)$

    c. $P(B \mid A)$

    d. $P(B \mid \bar{A})$

    e. $P(\bar{A} \text{ and } B)$

    f. $P(\bar{A} \text{ and } \bar{B})$

    g. $P(\overline{A \text{ or } B})$

    h. $P(\overline{A \text{ and } B})$

4.23 Do you have enough information to determine if A and B are mutually exclusive or are independent from the following: The probabilities of A and B are .7 and .5, respectively, and the probability of A or B occurring is .85? Why? (*Hint:* Can you find the probability of A and B?)

4.24 Define event A to consist of the even numbers from 1 to 20. Define B to consist of numbers that are multiples of 3 between 1 and 20. Assume that each number between 1 and 20 is equally likely to occur as the outcome to an experiment.

    a. Draw a Venn diagram representing the events.

    b. Find $P(A \text{ or } B)$.

    c. Find $P(A \mid B)$.

    d. Find $P(B \mid \bar{A})$.

Applying the New Concepts

4.25 Approximately 9 million students are enrolled in colleges across the United States. The electronic entertainment industry estimates that approximately 60% of these students have CD players and 40% have DVD players.

a. Assume that having a CD player is independent of the event of having a DVD player. What is the probability that a student has both a CD player and a DVD player?

b. What is the probability that a student has a CD player or a DVD player?

c. What is the probability that a student has a CD player and does not have a DVD player?

4.26 Two quality-control inspectors need to examine boxes of electrical components at random to determine if certain specifications are being met during the manufacturing process. Assume that the first inspector and the second inspector have a 90% and 60% chance, respectively, of noticing a flawed component if the component is truly flawed. Also, assume that the percentage of defective components in each box is 20%. The inspectors inspect only one component at random from each box.

a. If one of two inspectors is randomly selected to examine a box, what is the probability that a defective component will be noticed in that box?

b. If both inspectors inspect the same box, what is the probability that at least one will notice a defective component?

4.27 When high school teenagers were asked who has taught them the most about managing money, 73% percent said their parents. Suppose that 11% of the teenagers said that a relative other than their parents taught them the most about managing money. What is the probability that a high school teenager learned the most about money from someone other than the teenager's parents or relatives if it is known that the teenager did not learn the most about managing money from his/her parents?

(Source: "Mom's the Money Teacher," *USA Today*, May 8–10, 1998, p. 1A.)

4.28 Brokerage firms receive awards for their analysts' stock-picking abilities. The following security firms are the top eight firms in terms of investment research for the year 2000.

Security Firms	Total Awards
Salomon Smith Barney	39
Merrill Lynch	28
Morgan Stanley	25
Lehman Brothers	24
Goldman Sachs	22
A.G. Edwards	21
Credit Suisse First Boston	21
J.P. Morgan Chase	20

a. What is the probability that an award selected at random from the above list is either to Salomon Smith Barney or to Merrill Lynch?

b. What is the probability of selecting an award at random from the above list that is not to Credit Suisse First Boston and not to J.P. Morgan Chase?

c. What is the probability of selecting an award at random from the above list that is to Credit Suisse First Boston or to J.P. Morgan Chase if it is selected from those not at Salomon Smith Barney and not at Merrill Lynch?

(Source: "Salomon Takes Top Spot Among Firms," *The Wall Street Journal*, June 26, 2001, p. R16.)

4.29 At a semiconductor plant, 60% of the workers are skilled and 80% of the workers are full-time. Ninety percent of the skilled workers are full-time.

a. What is the probability that an employee selected at random is a skilled full-time employee?

b. What is the probability that an employee selected at random is a skilled worker or a full-time worker?

c. What percentage of the full-time workers are skilled?

4.30 Assessment of colleges of business have become increasingly important as the environment is characterized by rising costs and scarce resources. In addition, business schools face the challenge of producing capable graduates who can meet the job-related demands of employers. In a survey of deans of colleges of business, approximately 90% of the deans said they would use the results of the survey to make curriculum changes. Of the deans that said they would make curriculum changes, 40% said that they would make these changes to meet changing requirements of industry.

a. What is the probability that a dean, selected at random from the survey, responds that the assessment results were used for curriculum changes and were used to make changes to meet the changing requirements of industry?

b. What is the probability that a dean, selected at random from the survey, responds that the assessment results were used for curriculum changes and were not used to make changes to meet the changing requirements of industry?

(Source: "A Survey of Assessment Practices in Schools of Business," *Central Business Review*, vol. 19, no. 1, 2000, pp. 13–18.)

4.31 For every person who visits the leasing office of an apartment community near a certain university, there is an 80% chance that the person will lease an apartment if the person is a student and a 50% chance that the person will lease an apartment if the person is not a student. If two people, one of whom is a student and the other of whom is not, enter the office, what are the chances of leasing an apartment to at least one of the two people? What assumption did you have to make here?

Using the Computer

4.32 [DATA SET EX4-32] *Variable Description:*

Year-Quarter: Time period ranging from the first quarter of 1990 to the first quarter of 2001.

Productivity: Each quarter is categorized as having high or low productivity.

HourlyPayIncreases: Each quarter is categorized as having large or small hourly pay increases.

Higher productivity in the economy usually translates into higher increases in hourly compensation to workers. However, management often delays increasing compensation to show profits for the company. For the period 1990 to 2001, productivity is labeled as *high* for each quarter if the annualized economic growth is at least 2%. In addition, the amount of pay increase during that quarter is labeled *large* if the hourly compensation is at least 4% on an annualized basis.

a. Construct a contingency table with the rows showing the categories of high and low productivity and the columns showing the categories of small or large pay increases. (Excel: Use Contingency Table option in KPK Data Analysis Menu.)

b. Suppose that a quarter is randomly selected, what is the probability that this quarter has high productivity growth and has a large pay increase?

c. If a quarter has high productivity, what is the probability that the quarter has a small pay increase?

d. Are the events of productivity and amount of hourly pay increase independent? Explain.

(Source: "Fed's Meyer Warns of Inflation, Joblessness," *The Wall Street Journal*, June 7, 2001, p. A2.)

4.33 [DATA SET EX4–33] *Variable Description:*

Month: January through December

Year: 1998, 1999, and 2000

ElecConsumption: Data are labeled "High" and "Low" for California's Monthly Electricity Consumption (In Millions of MWh)

In recent years, California confronted an unprecedented electricity crisis which threatens to impact its economy. High wholesale market prices of energy, unanticipated reductions in the supply, and increases in the demand for electricity have compounded its energy supply problems. Predicting the consumption of electricity is also difficult. Data collected on California's monthly electricity consumption for the years 1998, 1999, and 2000 illustrate months that have low and high consumption.

a. Construct a contingency table using year as the row variable and *High* and *Low* usage as the column categories for the 36 months of data on electricity consumption.

b. What is the probability that a month selected at random shows high electricity consumption?

c. What is the probability that a month selected at random from the year 2000 shows high electricity consumption?

d. What is the probability that a month selected at random from the years 1998 or 1999 shows high electricity consumption? Compare your response to part c. Would you say that the demand for electricity during 2000 was a greater challenge for utility companies than during 1998 and 1999?

e. What is the probability that a month selected at random from the high consumption months was in the year 2000?

(Source: "White House Looks Isolated in Its Opposition to Energy Price Caps," *The Wall Street Journal*, June 14, 2001, p. A22.)

4.34 People are often amazed when they find someone who was born on the same day as themselves. To keep the solution simple, assume in this problem that leap years can be ignored and that all years have 365 days. Also assume that the probability of being born on any day of the year is the same for all days of the year.

a. If two persons are selected at random, what is the probability that these two persons were born on the same day? (*Hint:* For one person, there are 365 distinct birthdays. For two people, there are 364 different ways that the second could have a birthday without matching the first.)

b. If three persons are selected at random, what is the probability that at least two of the three persons were born on the same day?

c. In general, the probability that at least two of *n* people have the same birthday is given by the formula:

Probability $= 1 - (365/365)(364/365) \ldots ((365 - n + 1)/365)$

Use the formula to determine the probability that at least two people out of a class of 40 people have the same birthday.

d. The following graph displays the probability of having at least two people having the same birthday. For what number of people is the probability of a match at least .20?

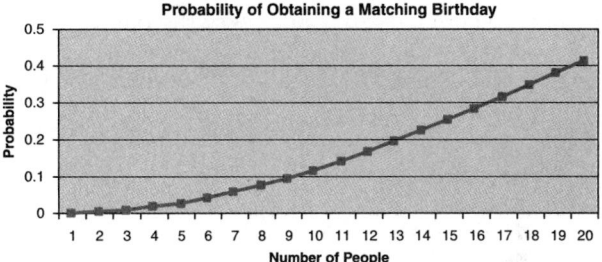

Probability of Obtaining a Matching Birthday

e. Construct a similar graph but extend the graph to 60 people. For what number of people is the probability of obtaining at least one match at least .9?

4.35 [Simulation Exercise] The birthday problem in Ex 4.34 considers the probability of at least two individuals having the same birthday. Additional questions can be asked in the birthday problem. For example, how likely are matches of three, four, or even five? Coincidences fascinate people. Suppose you were in a large class and you found three individuals born on the same day. Would you say that is to be expected, or would you perhaps resort to some sort of cosmic conclusion? A simulation of the birthday problem can help to answer these type of questions. On the KPK menu, select the **Birthday Problem** by clicking on **Simulation Exercises.** Enter the number of people in a group and discover what type of birthday matches can be expected through a simulation of birthday dates.

a. How large of a group of people would you say is necessary to have at least a 50-50 chance that three individuals have the same birthday? Does the simulation support it?

b. How large of a group of people would you say is necessary to have at least a 50-50 chance that four individuals have the same birthday? Does the simulation support it?

c. Enter 100 people for the group size. Perform the simulation 20 times and count how many times there are at least three individuals with the same birthday. Is this estimate of the probability of a three-way match what you might have expected?

d. What type of birthday matches do you think could reasonably occur with a group of 2,000 individuals? What does the simulation say?

4.5

TREE DIAGRAMS

Another useful device for determining probabilities is a **tree diagram.** Notice in Example 4.6 that both marginal probabilities $P(\text{FDIC})$ and $P(\text{Fail})$ were known; that is, the percentage of banks protected by FDIC was known (90%) and the percentage of banks that would fail was known (5%). The contingency table approach illustrated in the previous section works well for this situation.

Suppose instead that one of the marginal probabilities is missing, say, $P(\text{Fail})$, but that we *do* know that

1. 90% of the banks are protected by FDIC (and 10% are not).

2. 3% of the banks protected by FDIC will fail.

3. 23% of the banks not protected by FDIC will fail.

So we can write

$$P(\text{FDIC}) = .90$$

$$P(\overline{\text{FDIC}}) = .10$$

$$P(\text{Fail} \mid \text{FDIC}) = .03$$

$$P(\text{Fail} \mid \overline{\text{FDIC}}) = .23$$

This information can be summarized in the following picture, which we refer to as a tree diagram.

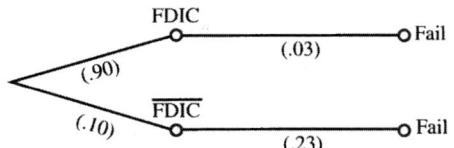

Each number in parentheses is the probability associated with that particular branch. For example, .03 is the probability of a bank failing *given* that it is protected by FDIC, and so this value is placed on the Fail branch corresponding to FDIC.

To find the remaining marginal probability, $P(\text{Fail})$, the following rule is used.

RULE #1 WHEN USING A TREE DIAGRAM

The probability of the event on the right side (say, event *B*) of the tree is equal to the sum of the paths; that is, all probabilities along a path leading to event *B* are multiplied, and then summed over *all* paths leading to *B*.

For the preceding tree diagram, Rule #1 states that

$$P(\text{Fail}) = (.90)(.03) + (.10)(.23)$$

$$= .027 + .023 = .05$$

Consequently, we conclude that 5% of the banks will fail, the same conclusion reached in Example 4.6.

FIGURE

4.11

General form of a
tree diagram.

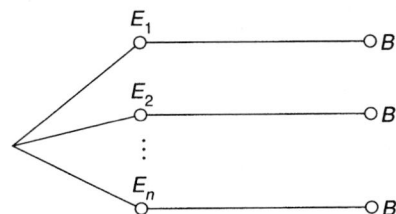

Another question of interest might be, given that a bank fails, what is the probability it is protected by FDIC? Or put another way, what percentage of banks that fail are protected by FDIC? This can be written

$$P(\text{FDIC} \mid \text{Fail})$$

Recall that earlier we were given that $P(\text{FDIC}) = .90$; that is, 90% of the banks are protected by FDIC. For this probability we were given no conditions at all; it is referred to as a **prior probability.** Now we are asked to determine the probability of this event having been given some information, namely that the bank failed. The probability $P(\text{FDIC} \mid \text{Fail})$ is called a **posterior probability** and is always a conditional probability; in particular, we are given that the event on the right side of the tree diagram (Fail) did, in fact, occur. Since FDIC lies on the first branch and $\overline{\text{FDIC}}$ lies on the second branch, we are asked to determine the probability that we got to event Fail along the first path, given that event Fail occurred.

The tree diagram used in this example has two paths. In general, there can be any number of paths, as illustrated in Figure 4.11.

To determine a posterior probability, written as $P(E_i \mid B)$ for some i, we use the following rule, usually referred to as **Bayes' rule** (named after Thomas Bayes, an English Presbyterian minister and mathematician).

RULE #2 FOR TREE DIAGRAMS (BAYES' RULE)

The posterior probability for the ith path is

$$P(E_i \mid B) = \frac{i\text{th path}}{\text{sum of paths}}$$

where the "sum of paths" is found using Rule #1.

To illustrate:

$$P(\text{FDIC} \mid \text{Fail}) = \frac{1\text{st path}}{\text{sum of paths}}$$

since FDIC lies on the first path. By "1st path" we mean the product of all probabilities along this path. So

$$P(\text{FDIC} \mid \text{Fail}) = \frac{(.9)(.03)}{(.9)(.03) + (.1)(.23)}$$

$$= \frac{.027}{.05} = .54$$

Consequently, 54% of the banks that fail are protected by FDIC (the same result obtained in Example 4.6).

4.7

Zetadyne Corporation produces electrical components utilizing three nonoverlapping work shifts. It is known that 50% of the components are produced during shift 1, 20% during shift 2, and 30% during shift 3. A further look at product quality reveals that 6% of the components produced during shift 1 are defective. The corresponding percentage for shift 2 is 8%. Shift 3, the late-night shift, produces a relatively large percentage, 15%, of defective components. Determine

1. What percentage of all components is defective?

2. Given that a defective component is found, what is the probability that it was produced during shift 3?

Solution 1   The tree diagram for this example is

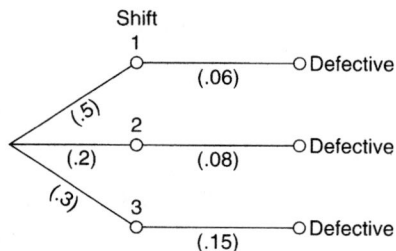

Using Rule #1, we find that

$$P(\text{Defective}) = \text{sum of paths}$$
$$= (.5)(.06) + (.2)(.08) + (.3)(.15)$$
$$= .030 + .016 + .045$$
$$= .091$$

Consequently, 9.1% of the components produced are defective.

Solution 2   We know that $P(\text{shift } 3)$ is .3; that is, 30% of the components produced are produced during shift 3. This is a *prior probability*. To determine the *posterior probability*, $P(\text{shift } 3 \mid \text{defective})$, we use Rule #2.

$$P(\text{shift } 3 \mid \text{defective}) = \frac{\text{3d path}}{\text{sum of paths}}$$
$$= \frac{(.3)(.15)}{.091}$$
$$= \frac{.045}{.091} = .495$$

So approximately half of the defective components produced are produced during shift 3. This means that once a component is identified as defective, the probability that it came from shift 3 increases from .3 (the prior probability) to .495 (the posterior probability).

On the CD   The tree diagram illustrated in Figure 4.11 is actually a simplified version of more elaborate decision trees that can be used for more complicated decision problems. A full treatment of decision trees and how they can be used to structure more complex types of decision analyses is provided in the CD accompanying this textbook. To locate this file using Windows Explorer or My Computer, double click on file Chapter 19. In previous editions of this book, the material in this file consisted of the entire contents of Chapter 18.

X Exercises 4.36–4.43

Understanding the Mechanics

4.36 Construct a tree diagram to find the probability of B.

  a. Assume that the probability of A is .8, the probability of B given that A occurs is .05, and the probability of B given that A does not occur is .25.

  b. Assume that the probability of A is .6, the probability of B given that A occurs is .20, and the probability of B given that A does not occur is .40.

4.37 Using the given probabilities, construct a tree diagram to find $P(B)$.

  a. $P(E_1) = .4$, $P(E_2) = .1$, $P(E_3) = .5$, $P(B \mid E_1) = .2$, $P(B \mid E_2) = .6$, $P(B \mid E_3) = .4$

  b. $P(E_1) = .6$, $P(E_2) = .1$, $P(E_3) = .1$, $P(E_4) = .2$, $P(B \mid E_1) = .3$, $P(B \mid E_2) = .4$, $P(B \mid E_3) = .1$, $P(B \mid E_4) = .1$

4.38 Using the given probabilities, construct a tree diagram to find $P(E_1 \mid B)$.

  a. $P(E_1) = .4$, $P(E_2) = .6$, $P(B \mid E_1) = .5$, $P(B \mid E_2) = .3$

  b. $P(E_1) = .35$, $P(E_2) = .25$, $P(E_3) = .2$, $P(E_4) = .2$, $P(B \mid E_1) = .2$, $P(B \mid E_2) = .4$, $P(B \mid E_3) = .2$, $P(B \mid E_4) = .1$

Applying the New Concepts

4.39 Many organizations, including military and defense-related companies, require their employees to be screened for drugs. Some employees are concerned that a "false positive" may be recorded from the screening; that is, employees who are not drug abusers may incorrectly test positive. Assume that 10% of a certain population are drug abusers. Suppose that the probability of a "false positive" is .5% and that the probability of a correct positive on someone who is under the influence of certain drugs is 99.9%. What is the probability that a person who tests positive is really a drug user?

4.40 Sixty percent of individual investors blamed themselves for stock portfolio losses during the bear market of 2001. Of those investors that blame themselves for their personal losses, 40% had a loss of more than 30%. Of those individual investors who did not blame themselves for their portfolio losses, 60% had a loss of more than 30%.

  a. What is the probability that an individual investor had a loss of more than 30%?

  b. What is the probability that a randomly selected individual investor with a loss of more than 30% takes the blame for his/her portfolio losses?

(Source: "Investors: We Messed Up," *USA Today*, July 17, 2001, p. 1B.)

4.41 A large manufacturing company is in the process of training its personnel in quality-control procedures. At present, 40% of the assembly lines use control charts, 40% use inspection techniques, and 20% do not use any method for controlling quality. The assembly lines that use control charts have a 1% defective rate. The assembly lines that use inspection techniques have a 5% defective rate. The assembly lines that do not use any quality-control techniques have a 12% defective rate. What is the probability that an item produced by this company is defective?

4.42 The Social Security Advisory Council recently considered several plans to keep Social Security healthy. If nothing changes, the Social Security System will run a deficit around 2030 because of the large number of retirees expected then and the relatively lower number of workers paying into the system. Of importance is the percentage of retirement income for which retirees depend on Social Security. For retirees between the ages of 55 and 64, approximately 10% feel dependent on Social Security. For retirees between the ages of 65 and 80, this increases to 35%. And for retirees over 80, it is approximately 50%. Suppose that the retirees between the ages of 55 and 64, between 65 and 80, and over 80 years of age are 30%, 45%, and 25% respectively.

  a. What is the probability that a retiree selected at random feels dependent on Social Security?

  b. What is the probability that a retiree who feels dependent on Social Security is over 80 years old?

4.43 Materials for a food-processing plant are supplied by four companies. The following table lists the percentage of defective items from each company and the percentage of materials supplied by that company to the food-processing plant.

	Percentage of Materials Supplied	Percentage of Defective Materials
Supplier 1	40	2
Supplier 2	5	10
Supplier 3	20	8
Supplier 4	35	3

  a. Determine the percentage of all materials that are defective.

  b. Given that a material supplied to the plant is defective, what is the probability that it came from supplier 3?

4.6 PROBABILITIES FOR MORE THAN TWO EVENTS

We illustrate what happens when you encounter more than two events by considering three events, *A*, *B*, and *C*. The following rules can easily be extended to any finite number of events. In the applications of probability in the chapters that follow, we typically will be dealing with multiple events that are either mutually exclusive or independent.

Mutually Exclusive Events

Events *A*, *B*, and *C* are pairwise mutually exclusive if no two events can occur simultaneously. A Venn diagram of this situation is shown in Figure 4.12. When dealing with mutually exclusive events, we usually will be interested in the probability that *one* of these events will occur, that is, $P(A \text{ or } B \text{ or } C)$. We can use a simple rule here:

> For mutually exclusive events, *A*, *B*, and *C*,
> $$P(A \text{ or } B \text{ or } C) = P(A) + P(B) + P(C)$$

4.13

Thus, to determine "or" probabilities when the events are mutually exclusive, add the respective probabilities.

Independent Events

Events *A*, *B*, and *C* are independent if all the following are true:

$$P(A \text{ and } B) = P(A) \cdot P(B)$$
$$P(A \text{ and } C) = P(A) \cdot P(C)$$
$$P(B \text{ and } C) = P(B) \cdot P(C)$$
$$P(A \text{ and } B \text{ and } C) = P(A) \cdot P(B) \cdot P(C)$$

Thus the events are independent if the "and" probability for *any* subset of the events (including the set containing all the events) is equal to the corresponding product of marginal probabilities. When dealing with independent events, the probability of interest usually is that *all* of the events occur, that is, $P(A \text{ and } B \text{ and } C)$. Using the fourth condition just given, we can make the following statement.

> For independent events, *A*, *B*, and *C*,
> $$P(A \text{ and } B \text{ and } C) = P(A) \cdot P(B) \cdot P(C)$$

4.14

FIGURE

4.12

Three mutually exclusive events.

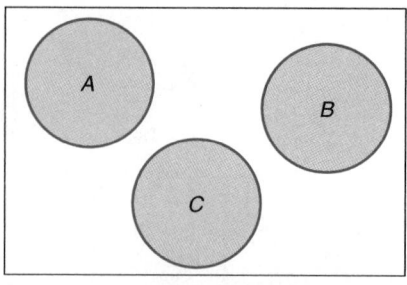

Thus, to determine "and" probabilities when the events are independent, multiply the respective probabilities.

EXAMPLE 4.8

Dellex Industries makes memory units for a microcomputer. Dellex customers have agreed to select three units randomly from a very large shipment and test them. If none of the units is defective, the customer will accept the shipment.

Usually, 2% of all Dellex units are defective. Determine the probability that the shipment will be accepted, that is, that all three units tested will be nondefective.

Solution

Let

$$A = \text{first unit is nondefective}$$

$$B = \text{second unit is nondefective}$$

$$C = \text{third unit is nondefective}$$

We know that 2% of the units produced are defective, so 98% of them are not defective; consequently, $P(A) = P(B) = P(C) = .98$.

We want to find $P(A \text{ and } B \text{ and } C)$. Are the events independent? There is no need to use fancy formulas here. The answer is yes, simply because the units are selected randomly from the very large shipment. Therefore,

$$P(A \text{ and } B \text{ and } C) = P(A) \cdot P(B) \cdot P(C)$$

$$= .98 \cdot .98 \cdot .98 = .94$$

Consequently, there is a 94% chance that the customer will accept the shipment.

X Exercises 4.44–4.51

Understanding the Mechanics

4.44 The probability of events A, B, and C are .2, .4, and .3, respectively.

a. What is the probability of event A or B or C occurring if these events are mutually exclusive?

b. What is the probability of events A, B, and C occurring at the same time if these events are independent?

4.45 The probabilities of A, B, and C are .2, .3, and .5, respectively.

a. If the probability of event A or B or C occurring is 1.0, can you conclude that events A, B, and C are mutually exclusive?

b. If the probability of all of the events A, B, and C occurring at the same time is .06, are events A, B, and C independent?

4.46 The Colony, a thriving city north of Dallas, has a current population of approximately 28,500. The percentage of individuals between the ages of 55 and 64, inclusively, is 4%. The younger population between the ages of 35–54, inclusively, and between the ages of 20–34, inclusively, is 21% and 34%, respectively. Let the events A, B, and C represent individuals between the ages of 20–34, 35–54, and 55–64 respectively.

a. Are the events A, B, and C mutually exclusive?

b. What is the probability that an individual selected at random from The Colony belongs to A, B, or C?

c. If three individuals were selected at random from The Colony, what is the probability that all three belong to A?

d. If three individuals were selected at random from The Colony, what is the probability that all three belong to A or B?

(Source: "The Colony Age Distribution," *The Dallas Morning News*, June 6, 2001, p. 1M.)

4.47 An engineer has a very large batch of electronic components that were produced when the machinery was malfunctioning. The engineer knows that half are defective and half are nondefective. The engineer suggests taking a sample of the components to place in certain test equipment. Assume that one component is randomly selected and then a second component is randomly selected. The events A, B, and C are defined as follows:

A is the event that the pair of sampled components is either (first component is nondefective, second component is nondefective) or (first component is nondefective, second component is defective).

B is the event that the pair of sampled components is either (first component is defective, second component is nondefective) or (first component is nondefective, second component is nondefective).

C is the event that the pair of sampled components is either (first component is defective, second component is nondefective) or (first component is nondefective, second component is defective).

a. Find $P(A)$, $P(B)$, and $P(C)$.

b. Find $P(A \text{ and } B)$, $P(A \text{ and } C)$, and $P(B \text{ and } C)$.

c. Find $P(A \text{ and } B \text{ and } C)$.

d. What can the engineer conclude about the independence of the events *A*, *B*, and *C*?

4.48 For NBC, the last series of *Seinfeld* was a big blowout, drawing viewers from 41.6% of U.S. TV households. Suppose that three TV households are randomly selected.

a. What is the probability that all three households have viewed the last series of *Seinfeld*?

b. What is the probability that none of the three households have viewed the last series of *Seinfeld*?

(Source: "Even Show's Producer Embarrassed by the Hype," *USA Today*, May 14, 1998, p. 2A.)

4.49 The cable industry estimates that there are approximately 70 million subscribers. Of these, 24% use AT & T, 20% use Time Warner, and 11% use Comcast Cable Communications. Suppose that three subscribers were randomly selected.

a. What is the probability that the first one uses AT & T and the other two use Comcast Cable Communications?

b. What is the probability that the first one does not use AT & T and the other two use Time Warner?

c. What assumptions are you making about the subscribers to answer this question?

(Source: "Sizing Up an Industry and AOL Time Warner's Place in It," *The New York Times*, June 11, 2001, p. C4.)

4.50 A special Newspoll revealed that South Australia's election would go down to the wire. The Newspoll surveyed a sample of 1,700 voters from South Australia. The results are presented below for the three political parties. What is the probability that a person either prefers ALP, the Democrats, or Others? Are these events mutually exclusive?

Political Party	Voters Preference (in Percentage)
Coalition	39
ALP	34
Democrats	18
Others	9

(Adapted from "Margin Slashed in Surprise Poll Swing," *The Weekend Australian*, October 11, 1997, p. 1.)

4.51 Many technology initiatives fail. Upper management often needs to decide which projects to continue funding and which ones to kill. The probability of a project being successfully completed is determined from the probability that the project will be completed on time, the probability that the cost of the project will not escalate, the probability that the project will be of strategic value, and the probability that the project will increase market share for the company.

a. Suppose that project *A* is identified as having probabilities of .8, .93, .98, and .92, respectively and that project *B* is identified as having probabilities of .92, .76, .99, and .98, respectively for the criteria used to determine the probability of success. Which project has a higher probability of success?

b. What are you assuming in computing the probabilities in part a?

(Source: "Determining a Project's Probability of Success," *Research Technology Management*, vol. 44, issue 3, May/June 2001, pp. 51–57.)

4.7 COUNTING RULES

Counting rules determine the number of possible outcomes that exist for a certain broad range of experiments. They can be extremely useful in determining probabilities. For instance, consider an experiment that has 200 possible outcomes, all of which are equally likely to occur. The probability of any one such outcome is $1/200 = .005$.

The question we wish to answer here is, for a particular experiment, how many possible outcomes are there? No set of rules applies to all situations, but we will consider three very popular counting procedures: (1) filling slots, (2) permutations (a special case of filling slots), and (3) combinations.

Filling Slots

We use **counting rule 1** to fill *k* different slots. Let

n_1 = the number of ways of filling the first slot

n_2 = the number of ways of filling the second slot *after* the first slot is filled

n_3 = the number of ways of filling the third slot *after* the first two slots are filled

.
.
.

n_k = the number of ways of filling the *k*th slot *after* filling slots 1 through $k-1$

The number of ways of filling all the *k* slots is

$$n_1 \cdot n_2 \cdot n_3 \cdot \;\cdots\; \cdot n_k$$

EXAMPLE 4.9

When ordering a new car, you have a choice of eight interior colors, ten exterior colors, and four roof colors. How many possible color schemes are there?

Solution

There are three slots to fill here, (eight) interior color, (ten) exterior color, and (four) roof color. To answer the question, you simply *multiply* the number of ways of filling each slot. So the answer is $8 \cdot 10 \cdot 4 = 320$ different color schemes.

The order in which you fill the slots is unimportant. So $n_2 = 10$, regardless of whether you have filled the first slot. For some applications, this is not the case. Consider the following example.

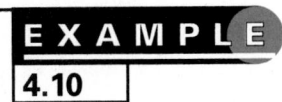

EXAMPLE 4.10

A local PTA group is selecting their officers for the current year. There are 15 individuals in the group, whom we label as $I_1, I_2, \ldots, I_{15}$. They need to select a president, vice president, secretary, and treasurer. How many possible groups of officers are there?

Solution

We have four slots to fill here, president (n_1), vice president (n_2), secretary (n_3), and treasurer (n_4). We know that n_1 is 15. After a president is elected, only 14 people remain, so $n_2 = 14$. By a similar argument, $n_3 = 13$ and $n_4 = 12$. The answer is $15 \cdot 14 \cdot 13 \cdot 12 = 32{,}760$ different slates of officers.

Permutations

Example 4.10 is a counting situation in which you select people *without replacement* because duplication is not allowed; that is, 4 different people must be selected. If a particular individual, say, I_3, is elected president, then I_3 is not available to fill the remaining slots. Another way of stating the result is that there are 32,760 ways of selecting 4 distinct people out of 15, where the **order of selection** is important. For example,

$$I_2 = \text{president}$$
$$I_6 = \text{vice president}$$
$$I_{12} = \text{secretary}$$
$$I_7 = \text{treasurer}$$

is not the same slate of officers as

$$I_7 = \text{president}$$

$$I_{12} = \text{vice president}$$

$$I_2 = \text{secretary}$$

$$I_6 = \text{treasurer}$$

even though the same four people are involved.

The number of ways of selecting k distinct objects (or people) from a group of n distinct objects, where the order of selection is important, is referred to as the number of permutations of n objects using k at a time. This is written

$$_nP_k$$

In Example 4.10, $_{15}P_4 = 32{,}760$. Determining the number of permutations is just a special case of counting rule 1; this is also a slot-filling application.

The symbol $n!$ is read as "n factorial." Its value is determined by multiplying n by all the positive integers smaller than n.

$$n! = (n)(n-1)(n-2)\cdots(2)(1)$$

4.15

For example,

$$5! = (5)(4)(3)(2)(1) = 120$$

$$1! = 1$$

$$0! = 1 \text{ (by definition)}$$

Notice that $n!$ is the number of ways of filling n slots using n objects. There are n ways of filling the first slot, $(n-1)$ ways of filling the second slot, $(n-2)$ ways for the third slot, and so on.

In Example 4.10 the result was obtained by finding $15 \cdot 14 \cdot 13 \cdot 12 = 32{,}760$. This also can be written as

$$\frac{15 \cdot 14 \cdot 13 \cdot 12 \cdot \cancel{11} \cdot \cancel{10} \cdot \cancel{9} \cdot \cancel{8} \cdot \cancel{7} \cdot \cancel{6} \cdot \cancel{5} \cdot \cancel{4} \cdot \cancel{3} \cdot \cancel{2} \cdot \cancel{1}}{\cancel{11} \cdot \cancel{10} \cdot \cancel{9} \cdot \cancel{8} \cdot \cancel{7} \cdot \cancel{6} \cdot \cancel{5} \cdot \cancel{4} \cdot \cancel{3} \cdot \cancel{2} \cdot \cancel{1}} = 32{,}760$$

This is an application of **counting rule 2** where the order of selection *does* produce different arrangements (permutations). The number of **permutations** of n objects using k objects at a time is

$$_nP_k = \frac{n!}{(n-k)!} = (n)(n-1)\cdots(n-k+1)$$

4.16

EXAMPLE 4.11

How many two-digit numbers can you construct using the digits, 1, 2, 3, and 4, without repeating any digit?

Solution The order of selection is certainly important here—the number 42 is not the same as 24. The answer is $_4P_2$, where

$$_4P_2 = \frac{4!}{(4-2)!} = \frac{(4)(3)(\cancel{2!})}{\cancel{2!}} = 12$$

These 12 permutations are

$$
\begin{array}{cccc}
12 & 21 & 31 & 41 \\
13 & 23 & 32 & 42 \\
14 & 24 & 34 & 43
\end{array}
$$

Combinations

Take another look at Example 4.10, where we selected 4 people from a group of 15. This time, however, choose a committee of 4 people from a group of 15 where the order of selection does not matter. Each such committee is one **combination** of the 15 people, using four at a time. For example,

$$I_2 \quad I_6 \quad I_{12} \quad I_7 \qquad \text{and} \qquad I_7 \quad I_{12} \quad I_2 \quad I_6$$

are different permutations but the same combination. These two arrangements are made up of the same individuals; hence they form the same committee or combination.

Clearly, there are not as many combinations (using I_2, I_6, I_{12}, I_7) as there are permutations. The two preceding permutations form the same combination. There are now 24 possible permutations of this combination ($4 \cdot 3 \cdot 2 \cdot 1 = 24$).

Now we wish to determine how many possible committees (combinations) of 4 there are for the group of 15. This is written as

$$_{15}C_4$$

Each combination has 24 permutations, so

$$_{15}C_4 = \frac{_{15}P_4}{24} = \frac{32,760}{24} = 1,365$$

There are 1365 possible committee combinations. Notice that 24 is the number of *permutations* of these four numbers (2, 6, 7, and 12); that is, $24 = {_4}P_4 = 4!$

Counting rule 3 is used to count the number of possible combinations where the order of selection *does not* produce different arrangements (combinations). The number of **combinations** of n objects using k at a time is

$$_nC_k = \frac{_nP_k}{k!} = \frac{n!}{k!(n-k)!}$$

4.17

E X A M P L E

4.12

A company must select 5 employees from a department of 40 people to attend a national conference. How many possible delegations are there?

Solution

The order of selection is not a factor here, so this is a combination problem rather than a permutation problem. The answer is

$$_{40}C_5 = \frac{40!}{5!\,35!}$$

$$= \frac{(40)(39)(38)(37)(36)(\cancel{35!})}{(5!)(\cancel{35!})} = \frac{\overset{8}{\cancel{(40)}}\overset{13}{\cancel{(39)}}\overset{19}{\cancel{(38)}}(37)\overset{9}{\cancel{(36)}}}{(\cancel{5})(\cancel{4})(\cancel{3})(\cancel{2})(\cancel{1})} = 658,008$$

X Exercises 4.52–4.67

Understanding the Mechanics

4.52 Calculate each of the following.
   a. 5!
   b. $_3P_2$
   c. $_7P_6$
   d. $_5C_3$
   e. $_{10}C_8$

4.53 Suppose there is a pool of 10 applicants.
   a. What is the number of ways of selecting two applicants from this pool of applicants?
   b. What is the number of ways of ranking the applicants?
   c. What is the number of permutations of four applicants from this pool of applicants?

Applying the New Concepts

4.54 Identify whether it is permutations or combinations that need to be calculated in each of the following statements.
   a. The number of ways 1st, 2nd, and 3rd place can be selected by a judge in an art contest.
   b. The number of ways 3 cities can be selected from a group of cities used to test a new product.
   c. The number of ways of selecting 5 managers from the list of managers in a company to attend a conference being held in Hawaii.
   d. The number of ways of ordering 4 different pairs of shoes in a display window.

4.55 How many ways can a random sample (sampling without replacement) of size 5 be taken from a box of eight electronic switches?

4.56 How many ways can a quality-control inspector select 4 components from a batch of 20 components if the inspector samples without replacement?

4.57 How many ways can an investor pick five mutual funds from 15 top-performing growth funds?

4.58 How many different phone numbers are possible at a university with all 7-digit phone numbers starting with 565?

4.59 How many ways can the positions of president and vice president be filled for a student organization that has 20 members?

4.60 A builder has five different house styles and three lots on which to build. If each lot has a different style of house on it, how many sets of the five house styles are possible on these three lots?

4.61 A firm has 100 laborers, 20 salespersons, and 10 executives. If an employee is chosen from each of these categories, how many different sets of three employees are possible?

4.62 A company is automating the outsourcing of several of its logistics functions involving inventory transportation. If the company wishes to reduce its logistics staff from 25 to 20 personnel, how many ways can this be achieved?

4.63 An investor chooses five stocks for her portfolio. How many different arrangements are possible in which at least three stocks increase and the rest do not increase in value?

4.64 A company is trying to encourage women to fill executive positions. For the latest batch of executive trainees, it wishes to fill seven vacancies with five women and two men. The company has seven women and eight men, making a total of 15 finalists for these seven vacancies.
   a. In how many ways can the vacancies be filled if sex is disregarded?
   b. In how many ways can the vacancies be filled if the company insists on five women and two men?
   c. What is the probability that the company gets the combination it wants if positions are filled randomly?

4.65 The Monetary Authority of Singapore has been busy examining bank mergers. Six of its largest banks in Singapore are Overseas Union Bank, OCBC Bank, United Overseas Bank, DBS Bank, Keppel Bank, and Tat Lee Bank. A merger typically achieves significant cost savings through elimination of duplicated functions and operations as well as through optimizing the deployment of human and capital resources.
   a. How many ways can a merger occur among the six banks? List all combinations.
   b. Suppose that Keppel Bank and Tat Lee Bank merge. How many ways can a merger occur among the remaining four banks?

(Adapted from "OUB to Merge with Wholly-Owned Unit IBS," *The Straits Time* (Singapore), March 21, 1998, p. 70.)

4.66 Mr. Pirate, a well-known computer programmer and a not-so-well-known user of copyrighted software that he did not purchase, has 20 software programs installed on his personal computer. He has 4 programs on his personal computer that are not authorized. An auditor will randomly check 5 programs for legitimate use of software.
   a. How many ways can the auditor choose 5 programs at random and not select one of the unauthorized programs.
   b. How many ways can the auditor choose 5 programs at random from the 20 installed programs?
   c. What is the probability that the auditor will not select one of the unauthorized programs from the installed programs on Mr. Pirate's personal computer?

4.67 List all the ways in which three different numbers can be selected without replacement from the set {1, 3, 5, 7, 8, 9}? What is the probability of selecting the numbers 7, 8, and 9?

SIMPLE RANDOM SAMPLES

In later chapters, practically all the applications that use probabilities derived from sample results to make a decision concerning the population are based on the assumption of a simple random sample, or, more simply, a random sample.

We introduced this concept in Chapter 1. A sample of size n, selected from a population of size N, constitutes a *simple random sample* if every possible sample of size n has the same probability of being selected.

To obtain a representative sample when N is extremely large or unknown requires good judgment. Stopping the first 10 people you meet on the street is a very poor way of sampling your population.

You sometimes may be forced to select items for the sample in a nonrandom manner, realizing that a poorly gathered sample can easily lead to an incorrect decision having serious consequences. Accountants often encounter this problem when performing a statistical audit. However, when such a sample is *not* a random sample, it is not correct to use probability theory in your analysis.

In Example 4.12, we determined that there were 658,008 possible delegations when selecting 5 people from a group of 40. If we view this group as the population of interest, then $n = 5$ and $N = 40$. Our concern here is to determine the probability that any specified group of 5 individuals will be the designated delegation if simple random sampling is used.

Notice here that we do not allow any one person to be selected more than once (that is, all five members of the delegation are different people). In effect, we randomly select the first individual from the group of 40, randomly select the second individual from the remaining group of 39, randomly select the third individual from the remaining group of 38, and so on. Consequently, at each step we do *not* replace the people previously selected for the sample when selecting the next individual. In Section 4.3, this sampling procedure was referred to as *sampling without replacement.* This procedure can be simplified in practice by randomly selecting 5 different individuals *at one time* from the group of 40.

When the sample data are obtained one at a time by returning a person or object to the population prior to selection of the next sample value, this procedure is *sampling with replacement.* Using this scheme, a particular person (or object) can be selected *more than once* in the sample. These sampling procedures will be discussed further in Chapter 7.

For this illustration there are $_{40}C_5 = 658,008$ possible delegations when selecting without replacement, and each has the same probability of being selected. Therefore, the probability that any one combination of people will be picked is $1/658,008 = .000002$.

In general, when employing a simple random sample of size n, selected without replacement from a population of size N, the total number of possible random samples is

$$_NC_n$$

Also, each of these samples has a probability of being selected equal to

$$\frac{1}{_NC_n}$$

EXAMPLE 4.13

Your task is to obtain a random sample of two individuals selected without replacement from a group of five employees (E_1, E_2, E_3, E_4, and E_5). What is the probability that you select E_2 and E_5 as your sample?

Solution There are

$$_5C_2 = \frac{5!}{2!\,3!} = 10$$

possible random samples:

Sample Number	Sample	Sample Number	Sample	
1	E_1, E_2	6	E_2, E_4	
2	E_1, E_3	7	E_2, E_5	← contains E_2 and E_5
3	E_1, E_4	8	E_3, E_4	
4	E_1, E_5	9	E_3, E_5	
5	E_2, E_3	10	E_4, E_5	

Each random sample (including the one containing E_2 and E_5) has a probability of being selected of $1/10 = .1$.

EXAMPLE 4.14

In the Texas lottery, you select six *different* numbers between 1 and 54. To win the lottery, you must select all six numbers in any order. You buy one lottery ticket and select six numbers. What are the chances that your ticket is a winner?

Solution The order of the numbers does not matter, and all six numbers must be different; that is, the six numbers are selected *without replacement*. The question can then be stated, "How many combinations are there when selecting six numbers from a set of 54?" This is

$$_{54}C_6 = \frac{(54)(53)(52)(51)(50)(49)}{(6)(5)(4)(3)(2)(1)} = 25,827,165$$

Consequently, your chances of winning the lottery with one ticket are 1 in 25,827,165; that is, $\dfrac{1}{_{54}C_6} = .000000039$—not exactly astronomical odds.

X Exercises 4.68–4.71

Understanding the Mechanics

4.68 Calculate the following probabilities.

a. The probability of selecting two particular objects from five objects when sampling two objects without replacement

b. The probability of selecting eight particular objects from ten objects when sampling eight objects without replacement

c. The probability of selecting 15 particular objects from 20 objects when sampling 15 objects without replacement

Applying the New Concepts

4.69 An automotive company is considering 10 different locations for possible sites as distribution centers. Two of these sites are in Texas. What is the probability that these two sites will be chosen if the two sites are selected at random?

4.70 Explain how to select a simple random sample for a population of 100,000 using the computer-generated random numbers in Table A.13.

4.71 The school-newspaper photographer takes 10 different pictures of the homecoming queen at the school's football game. All 10 pictures are excellent, so the photographer chooses two at random to place in the school newspaper. What is the probability that the first two pictures taken will be selected?

✓ Summary

This chapter has examined methods of dealing with uncertainty by applying the concept of **probability.** An activity that results in an uncertain outcome is called an **experiment;** the possible outcomes are **events.** The **complement** of an event consists of all outcomes not in this event. Uncertainty is measured in terms of the probabilities of events. To determine the value of a particular probability, we used the classical approach, the relative frequency method, and the subjective probability approach. The **classical definition** for the probability of event A occurring assumes that the experiment has n **equally likely** outcomes and event A occurs in m of the n outcomes with a resulting probability of occurring equal to m/n. When using the **relative frequency** approach, the experiment is observed n times. Letting m represent the number of times event A occurs out of the n times, then the resulting probability of event A occurring in the future is m/n. A **subjective probability** is a measure of your belief that a particular event will occur, and like all probabilities, ranges from zero to one, inclusive.

Events can be summarized together in a **contingency (cross-tab) table.** The numbers in the table represent frequencies within each pair of subcategories, so comparisons can be made. When examining more than one event, say A and B, several types of probabilities can be derived. The probability of A and B occurring is a **joint probability** and is written $P(A$ and $B)$. The **multiplicative rule** is a method of determining a joint probability. The probability of A or B (or both) occurring is written $P(A$ or $B)$ and can be obtained using the **additive rule.** When asked to find a probability given particular information about events, you determine a **conditional probability.** For example, the probability that B occurs given that A has occurred is a conditional probability, written $P(B \mid A)$. A variation of the multiplicative rule provides a method of determining a conditional probability. The probability of a single event, such as P(the person selected is a female) or P(an individual subscribes to the *Wall Street Journal*), is a **marginal probability.**

Two events are said to be **independent** if the occurrence of the one event has no effect on the probability that the other event occurs. Events that are not independent are **dependent** events. Do not confuse "has no effect" with "will never occur simultaneously." If two events can never occur simultaneously, they are **mutually exclusive.** For example, these two events are certainly independent but are not mutually exclusive (since both events could occur): A, the stock market drops more than two points during a particular week, and B, your company's copying machine breaks down during the same week.

An effective method of determining a probability in complicated situations is to use a **Venn diagram.** When you represent the various events visually, you can often obtain a seemingly complex probability easily. Another useful device for structuring a decision problem is a **tree diagram.** Using this approach, one or more **prior probabilities** are provided; they state the probability of these events occurring when no additional information is available. If such information is available, these probabilities can be revised, producing **posterior probabilities.** By using **Bayes' rule,** these posterior probabilities are easily derived, once the tree diagram is constructed.

We discussed various **counting rules,** including **permutations** and **combinations.** These rules are used to count the number of possible outcomes for experiments that select a certain number of people or objects (k) from a large group of n such objects. When determining the corresponding number of permutations (written $_nP_k$), the **order of selection** is considered. The number of combinations for this situation (written $_nC_k$) ignores the order of selection and counts only the number of groups that can be obtained.

We also discussed the number of random samples that exists when the population size is known, and we examined methods of obtaining such a sample. *In the chapters to follow, any results using a statistical sample assume that the sample is obtained randomly.*

✓ Summary of Formulas

1. Additive rule

$$P(A \text{ or } B) = P(A) + P(B) - P(A \text{ and } B)$$

Special case: If A and B are *mutually exclusive,*

$$P(A \text{ or } B) = P(A) + P(B)$$

2. Multiplicative rule

$$P(A \text{ and } B) = P(A \mid B) \cdot P(B)$$
$$= P(B \mid A) \cdot P(A)$$

Special case: If A and B are independent,

$$P(A \text{ and } B) = P(A) \cdot P(B)$$

3. Conditional probability

$$P(A \mid B) = \frac{P(A \text{ and } B)}{P(B)}$$

4. Independence Two events A and B are independent if one of the following can be shown:

$$P(A \mid B) = P(A)$$
$$P(B \mid A) = P(B)$$
$$P(A \text{ and } B) = P(A) \cdot P(B)$$

5. Mutually exclusive Two events A and B are mutually exclusive if $P(A \text{ and } B)$ is zero.

6. Posterior probability (Bayes' Rule) For any event E_i, the posterior probability of event E_i, given that the final event B occurred is

$$P(E_i \mid B) = \frac{i \text{th path}}{\text{sum of paths}}$$

where the sum of paths is obtained by multiplying all probabilities along a path leading to event B and summing the results over all paths leading to event B.

7. Permutations and combinations The number of permutations of n objects taking k objects at a time is

$$_nP_k = \frac{n!}{(n-k)!}$$

The number of combinations of n objects taking k objects at a time is

$$_nC_k = \frac{n!}{k!(n-k)!}$$

X Review Exercises 4.72–4.92

4.72 Let the events A, B, and C consist of the integers from 1 to 10, 5 to 15, and 10 to 20, respectively. Suppose that the integers from 1 to 20 are equally likely to occur.
  a. Draw a Venn diagram.
  b. What is the probability that A occurs?
  c. What is the probability that A or B occurs?
  d. What is the probability that B and C occurs?
  e. If A occurs, what is the probability that B occurs?

4.73 Define the events A, B, and C to have the probabilities $P(A) = .4$, $P(B) = .3$, $P(C) = .1$.
  a. Find $P(A \text{ and } B)$ if A and B are independent.
  b. Find $P(A \text{ or } B)$ if A and B are independent.
  c. Find $P(\bar{A} \text{ and } B)$ if A and B are mutually exclusive.
  d. Find $P(A \mid B)$ if A and B are mutually exclusive.
  e. Find $P(A \text{ and } B \text{ and } C)$ if A, B, and C are mutually exclusive.
  f. Find $P(\bar{A} \text{ or } \bar{C})$ if A and C are mutually exclusive.
  g. Find $P(A \text{ and } B \text{ and } C)$ if A, B, and C are independent.
  h. Find $P(A \text{ or } B \text{ or } C)$ if A, B, and C are mutually exclusive.

4.74 A study by Clayton/Curtis/Cottrell found significant numbers of consumers in the mood for breakfast foods at dinner. This may be because many adults are sufficiently awake to enjoy the eggs and bacon if they are eating them at 7:00 P.M. rather than at 7:00 A.M. Assume that the following table shows the results of a survey of teenagers, working adults, and retired adults and their likelihood of ordering breakfast-type meals at a restaurant for dinner.

	Very Likely	Somewhat Likely	Somewhat Unlikely	Not at All Likely
Teenager	12	20	15	53
Working Adults	10	25	20	45
Retired Adults	5	15	20	60

Consider the following events.
A: {A person is a working adult or a retired adult}
B: {A person is very likely or somewhat likely to order a breakfast-type meal at dinner time}

C: {A person is not a retired adult}
D: {A person is not at all likely to order a breakfast-type meal at dinner time}
   a. Find the probability of each event.
   b. Find $P(A$ and $B)$, $P(A \mid B)$, and $P(B \mid A)$.
   c. What is $P(A$ or $D)$ and $P(A$ and $D)$?
   d. Which events are mutually exclusive?

(Adapted from "A Toast to Consumers Who Want a Change of Pace," *Adweek*, March 24, 1997, p. 21.)

4.75 A marketing-research group conducted a survey to find out where people did their holiday shopping. Out of a group of 110 randomly selected shoppers, 70 said that they shopped exclusively at the local mall, 30 said that they shopped exclusively in the downtown area, and 10 said that they shopped both at the local mall and in the downtown area.
   a. What is the probability that a customer shops both at the local mall and in the downtown area?
   b. What proportion of customers who shop at the local mall also shop in the downtown area?
   c. What is the probability that a customer shops downtown but not at the local mall?

4.76 An electronics firm decides to market three different software packages for its personal computers. The marketing analyst gives each of the three packages an 80% chance of success. The outcomes for each of the software packages are independent.
   a. What is the probability that all three will be a success?
   b. What is the probability that only two of the packages will be a success?
   c. What is the probability that none will be successful?

4.77 A payroll record with an error in it is placed in a filing cabinet with six error-free payroll records. Two payroll records are randomly selected, without replacement, by an auditor.
   a. What is the probability of drawing the payroll record with the error on the first draw?
   b. What is the probability of drawing the payroll record with the error on the second draw?
   c. What is the probability of drawing the payroll record with the error on the first or second draw?
   d. What is the probability of drawing an error-free payroll record on the first or second draw?

4.78 Thousands of counterfeit software manufacturing sites exist worldwide. Law enforcement officials believe that approximately 40% of all software used in business is counterfeit. Suppose that an auditor selects three software packages from small business companies in Europe, say companies A, B, and C.
   a. What is the probability that either company A or company B has a counterfeit copy?
   b. What is the probability that company A has a counterfeit copy and that company C does not have a counterfeit copy?
   c. What is the probability that none of the three companies has a counterfeit copy?
   d. What is the probability that at least one of the three companies has a counterfeit copy?
   e. What is the probability that either all three companies have a counterfeit copy or none of them have a counterfeit copy?

(Source: "Piracy on Rise," *USA Today*, August 1, 2001, p. 2B.)

4.79 The Internet, as a marketing medium, offers many challenges to marketers. Knowing the Internet population's demographic profile is critical to advertisers. From a survey, the following information on the age of Internet users and how often they viewed Internet advertising was compiled.

Age	No More than Once a Month	Several Times a Month	Once a Week	Several Times a Week	Every Day
18–24	24	7	20	19	10
25–34	33	18	23	27	20
35–44	33	9	14	29	19
45–54	19	5	14	12	10
55–64	17	1	3	7	3

   a. What is the probability that an Internet user is between 18 and 24 years of age and reads Internet advertising at least once a week?

b. What is the probability that an Internet user reads Internet advertising no more than once a month or is between 45 and 64 years of age?

c. What is the probability that an Internet user reads Internet advertising at least several times a week if that person is between 18 and 34 years of age?

d. Are age and frequency of viewing Internet advertising independent? Explain.

(Source: "Survey of Internet Users' Attitudes toward Internet Advertising," *Journal of Interactive Marketing,* vol. 13, no. 3, 2001, pp. 34–54.)

4.80 "We've noticed a big increase in the number of Americans coming into our store," said Richard Montgomery, manager of Eaton's at Yorkdale Mall in Toronto. But the biggest change is the number of Canadian shoppers looking for deals at home instead of south of the border. "It's the Canadian consumer that's making the difference." Since the beginning of October 1997 to April 1998, the Canadian dollar has fallen from 73 cents per U.S. dollar to below 70 cents per U.S. dollar. Assume that the table below is from a sample of Americans and Canadians that shopped at Yorkdale Mall in Toronto.

	Shopping at Mall Because of Weak Canadian Dollar	Shopping at Mall Because of Reasons Other Than the Weak Canadian Dollar
American	55	45
Canadian	60	140

a. What is the probability that a person selected at random from the sample is an American who is shopping at the mall for reasons other than the weak Canadian dollar?

b. What is the probability that a Canadian person selected at random from the sample is shopping at the mall because of the weak Canadian dollar?

(Adapted from "Lower C$ Prompts U.S. Bargain Hunting," *The Financial Post,* January 2, 1998, p. 6.)

4.81 A small company has 20% white-collar workers and 80% blue-collar workers. Of the white-collar workers, 50% believe that they would be financially secure for at least six months if they lost their job. Of the blue-collar workers, 30% believe that they would be financially secure for at least six months if they lost their job.

a. What is the probability that a company employee believes that he/she would be financially secure if he/she lost his/her job?

b. If a company employee believes that he/she would be financially secure for at least six months if he/she lost his/her job, what is the probability that the employee is a white-collar worker?

4.82 A busy executive has to meet with five production managers during the day. The executive needs to decide in which order to see the managers. How many different orderings can the executive choose? What is the probability of the executive's choosing any one ordering, if the choice is random?

4.83 A defective tape recorder is inspected by two service representatives. If one representative has a 50% chance of finding the defect, and the other has a 60% chance, what is the probability that at least one will find the defect if both check the tape recorder independently? What is the probability that neither will spot the defect?

4.84 A student forgot the combination for his bike lock. The combination consists of a sequence of three numbers and each number can range from 0 to 9. How many different sequences are possible?

4.85 Sun Microsystems dominates the Unix market. To compete in this market, IBM recently unveiled a new Unix machine, named Regatta, at half the cost. However, Sun Microsystems claims that their Unix machine still provides the best system performance. The current market share of Unix machines shows Sun Microsystems at approximately 50%, followed by IBM at 20%, and Hewlett-Packard at 10%. Suppose that a university purchases two Unix computer servers—one for the administrative functions of the university and one for research activity.

a. What is the probability that a Unix computer server for the administrative functions of the university is either a Sun Microsystems, an IBM, or a Hewlett-Packard machine?

b. Assuming that the decisions for purchasing the two Unix computer servers are made independently, what is the probability that the one used for administrative functions is either a Sun Microsystems, an IBM, or a Hewlett-Packard machine and that the one for research activity on campus is either an IBM or a Hewlett-Packard machine?

(Source: "IBM Unveils High-End Computer Server," *The Wall Street Journal,* October 4, 2001, p. B7.)

4.86 Many of Fidelity's Select mutual funds have yielded remarkable returns in the five-year period ending March 31, 1998, with the highest return being 330% from Fidelity Select Electronics. The Standard & Poor's 500 Index yielded 174.71% during this period. A breakdown of the performance is presented below.

Performance Level for Five-Year Period	Number of Select Mutual Funds
Less than 100%	11
At least 100% and less than 174.71%	12
At least 174.71%	14

   a. Are the mutual fund performance categories mutually exclusive?

   b. What is the probability that a Fidelity Select mutual fund does not perform better than the Standard & Poor's 500 Index?

   c. Suppose that two Fidelity Select mutual funds are selected at random. What is the probability that at least one performs better than the Standard & Poor's 500 Index?

   d. Suppose that three Fidelity Select mutual funds are selected at random. What is the probability that none of the funds yields a return less than 100%?

(Source: *Fidelity Focus,* Summer 1998, pp. 33–34.)

4.87 During June 2001, most airlines experienced an improvement in the number of flight delays. This improvement was due in part to smarter flight scheduling and a reduction in the number of passengers. The percentages of late arrivals for American, Delta, and Northwest airlines were approximately 25%, 30%, and 20%, respectively.

   a. Suppose that the probability of either a Delta or Northwest airline flight being delayed is .46. Would this indicate that the event of a Delta airline flight being delayed is independent of a Northwest airline flight being delayed?

   b. Assuming independence of flight delays among the airlines, what is the probability that for three randomly selected flights, one from American, Delta, and Northwest airlines, that none of the three flights experienced delays?

(Source: "Air Travel Improves Compared with Last Summer," *USA Today,* August 9, 2001, p. 3B.)

4.88 Much controversy was stirred by Marilyn VosSavant's response to whether contestants on a game show should switch their random selection of a door with a possible prize behind it when the host gives additional information. The following is a basic description of the game as described in *Ask Marilyn:* "Suppose you're on a game show and you're given a choice of three doors. Behind one door is a car; behind the others are goats. You pick a door—say, Number 1—and the host, who knows what's behind each door, opens another door—say, Number 3—which has a goat behind it. He then says to you, 'Do you want to keep door Number 1 or switch doors?' Is it to your advantage to switch your choice?" Marilyn's response is, "Yes, you should switch. The first door has a ⅓ chance of winning, but the second has a ⅔ chance." Marilyn received letters from numerous mathematicians that described her response as being absurd. In particular, one comment was: "I am in shock that after being corrected by at least three mathematicians, you still do not admit your mistake."

   a. Pair up with another student and label three paper cups Number 1, Number 2, and Number 3. While one student (the contestant) is not looking, the other student (the host) generates a number between 1 and 3 using the following Excel commands:

Put the numbers 1, 2, and 3 in cells A1, A2, and A3.

Type = 1/3 in cells B1, B2, and B3.

Click on **Tools ➤ Data Analysis ➤Random Number Generator.**

Type into the user form:

    1 for the number of variables;

    1 for the number of random numbers;

    Discrete for distribution;

    A1:B3 for value and probability input range; and

    C1 for output range.

The host puts a key under the cup corresponding to the random integer generated. The contestant then randomly selects a cup using the same Excel commands. The host then lifts a losing cup. Let's say that the contestant never switches. Then the contestant lifts his or her cup. Keep a tally of the contestant's wins. Repeat this game 100 times.

b. Perform the game in part a, except have the contestant switch cups each time.

c. Compare the number of wins in parts a and b. Do you believe Marilyn's response is correct?

d. Give a convincing argument that either supports Marilyn's response or supports the contention that there is no advantage in switching doors.

(Adapted from "Ask Marilyn," *The Dallas Morning News,* by Marilyn VosSavant, February 17, 1991.)

4.89 Political contributions from the Washington Education Association (WEA) dropped by 77%, even though the dues-paying membership of the teachers union actually grew by 7,000. Why? Because since 1992, under the state of Washington's law, prior written permission is required before a union can devote part of an employee's dues to political causes. This is known as Initiative 134. Now 30 states, through referendums and legislative efforts, either have or are considering enacting laws similar to Washington's.

a. What is the probability that a state in the United States, picked at random, is not considering and does not have laws similar to Initiative 134?

b. What is the probability that two states in the United States, picked at random, are considering or already have laws similar to Initiative 134? (Note that one state is picked first, and then the second state is picked. The probability for the second state considering laws similar to Initiative 134 is different since there are only 50 states in the nation, with 30 states considering Initiative 134.)

(Source: "Last Gasp for Unions' Political Clout," *Legal Times,* May 18, 1998, p. S34.)

4.90 The schematic diagram presented below denotes three components that operate in series. That is, if one component fails, the system does not work. Suppose that the probabilities of C1, C2, and C3 failing are .4, .1, and .1, respectively. What is the probability that the system operates without failure?

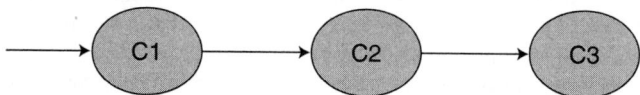

4.91 The schematic diagram presented below denotes four components such that C1 and C2 operate in parallel to C3 and C4. The system will not fail unless the system C1 and C2 fails and the system C3 and C4 fails. Note that C1 and C2 operate in series, and C3 and C4 operate in series. Suppose that the probabilities of C1, C2, C3, and C4 failing are .4, .1, .1, and .2, respectively. What is the probability that the system operates without failure?

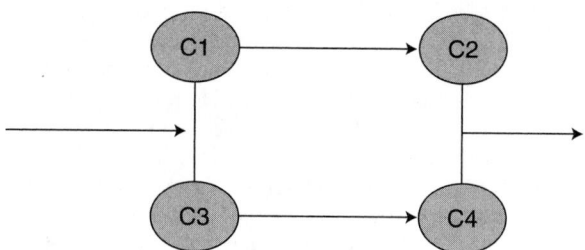

4.92 **[DATA SET EX4-92]** *Variable Description:*

SecurityFirm: A listing of 39 stock brokerage firms

StockPicking: Each brokerage firm is classified as being either excellent, good, or fair in stock picking for the year 2000.

EarningsForecast: Each brokerage firm is classified as being either excellent, good, or fair in forecasting stock earnings for the year 2000.

Stock brokerage firms receive awards for stock picking and for forecasting the earnings of stocks. A list of 39 firms that provide research and recommendations on stocks have been classified as being excellent, good, or fair in the stocking picking recommendations and also in being able to accurately forecast the earnings of companies.

a. Form a contingency table with the rows being the classification of a company for its stock picking ability and the columns being the classification of a company for its accuracy in forecasting earnings.

b. Suppose that one of these 39 brokerage firms is selected at random. What is the probability that its ability to pick stocks is at least good or its ability to accurately forecast earnings is at least good?

c. If a brokerage firm is classified as fair in picking stocks, what is the probability that it is classified as fair in accurately forecasting earnings?

d. What is the probability that a brokerage firm is not classified as fair in picking stocks and not classified as fair in accurately forecasting earnings?

(Source: "Salomon Takes Top Spot Among Firms," *The Wall Street Journal*, June 26, 2001, p. R16.)

Computer Exercises Using the Databases

Exercise 1—Appendix F

Select a random sample of 100 observations from the database. Using the relative frequency approach of finding a probability value, find the probability that a family owns its home.

Exercise 2—Appendix G

Generate 200 random numbers from a uniform distribution and use them to select 200 observations from the database. Using the relative frequency approach, find the probability that a company has an A bond rating. Also find the probability that a company has a B bond rating.

Insights from Statistics in Action

Cable and DSL Connections: Wired for Speed

The Statistics in Action case study presented at the beginning of this chapter introduced the concept of viewing a market share as a probability. For example, if the cable industry has a 50% market share of the consumers of high-speed Internet access, then the following probability can be used to express this:

P(Select cable modem for Internet connection | a consumer decides to have high speed Internet access) = .50

So market share can be thought of as a conditional probability. Suppose that the market share for cable, DSL, and other (satellite and wireless) are as follows. Since advertisers are highly interested in the proportion of individuals that purchase online, probabilities of making an online purchase are given. The proportion of individuals that purchase online are presented conditioned on the type of high-speed Internet connection they have.

	Proportion of High-Speed Internet Users
Using cable for Internet connection	50%
Using DSL for Internet connection	40%
Using Other (satellite & wireless) for Internet connection	10%
Make a purchase online once a month given that user has a cable connection	20%
Make a purchase online once a month given that user has a DSL connection	40%
Make a purchase online once a month given that user has a satellite or wireless connection	25%

1. Should the proportions of the market share for high-speed Internet consumers using cable, DSL, or "other" sum to one? Should the proportions of those consumers who make a monthly purchase online given their type of high-speed connection also sum to one? Why?

2. What is the probability that a high-speed Internet consumer has a cable connection and also makes a monthly purchase online? What is the probability that the consumer has a DSL connection and makes a monthly purchase online? What is the probability that the consumer has a satellite or wireless connection and makes a monthly purchase online?

3. What is the probability that a high-speed Internet consumer will make a monthly purchase online?

4. Suppose that it is known that a high-speed Internet consumer makes a monthly purchase online. What is the probability that the consumer has a cable connection? A DSL connection? A satellite or wireless connection?

(Source: "The Coming DSL Debacle," *Business Communications Review,* vol. 31, no. 6, June 2001, p. 6; "Speed Junkies," *American Demographics,* June 2001, p. 27; "Broadband Internet Access," *Red Herring,* October 1, 2001, p. 34.)

Appendix SPSS®

Chapter 4 Appendix: Data Analysis with SPSS

Contingency Table

To illustrate the construction of a two-way contingency table in SPSS, the data in file DATA4-3 for Example 4.3 will be used. A portion of this data file is shown in the data window below.

	city	quality
1	2	2
2	1	1
3	2	2
4	1	1
5	2	3
6	1	1
7	2	2
8	1	1
9	2	1
10	2	2
11	3	1
12	2	2
13	3	2
14	2	2
15	1	2
16	1	1
17	1	2
18	3	3
19	1	2
20	2	1
21	2	1
22	2	1

◀ ▶ **Data View** ⟍ Variable View ╱

Click on **Analyze ➤ Descriptive Statistics ➤ Crosstabs**. Move the city variable into the **Row(s)** box and the quality variable into the **Column(s)** box. Click on **OK.** The output immediately following will appear in the display pane.

CITY * QUALITY Crosstabulation Count

		QUALITY			Total
		1	2	3	
CITY	1	60	15	5	80
	2	35	20	10	65
	3	25	15	15	55
Total		120	50	30	200

While in the display pane, double-click somewhere inside the contingency table. By next double-clicking on the 1 under City, the city name (Memphis) can be entered to replace this number. Repeat for the other two cities (Miami and Pittsburgh). Similarly, by double-clicking on the 1 under Quality, the word "OK" can be substituted for this number. This can be repeated for the other two Quality categories ("OK-Rework" and "Scrapped"). The revised contingency table follows.

CITY * QUALITY Crosstabulation Count

		QUALITY			Total
		OK	OK-Rework	Scrapped	
CITY	Memphis	60	15	5	80
	Miami	35	20	10	65
	Pittsburgh	25	15	15	55
Total		120	50	30	200

On the CD . . .
Chapter 4 Appendix: Data Analysis with MINITAB

chapter

5

Discrete Probability Distributions X

Statistics in Action
AACSB Accreditation: A Commitment to Excellence in Business Education

The Association to Advance Collegiate Schools of Business (AACSB) is a not-for-profit corporation of approximately 900 members representing colleges, universities, and business and professional organizations committed to excellence in business education. Business schools nationwide strive to obtain AACSB accreditation, considered to be the premier accreditation for colleges of business. More than 400 business schools have affirmed their commitment to academic excellence and to continuous improvement by receiving accreditation.

The accreditation process uses the tools of quality management that emphasize examining and improving the *process*. Colleges of business must perform a self assessment that involves defining customers, improving the processes used to deliver services to customers, and reviewing their school's strengths, limitations, and opportunities, with the ultimate purpose of improving educational effectiveness. Participation in the accreditation process affirms the school's responsibility for the quality of education offered and demonstrates its commitment to continuous improvement. In this accreditation process, deans and faculty members have to ask themselves: Is the business school doing its job? Is research in the ivory tower relevant or simply "fuzzy and pretentious"?

Each college of business participating in the accreditation process can define its school's mission and can identify competencies that it views as important to its mission. Typical competencies include communication skills, professional knowledge, critical thinking, problem solving, technology/computer usage, interpersonal skills, knowledge and comprehension, global issues, professional integrity/ethics, and lifelong learning. Approximately 90% of the schools participating in this process use the assessment process to monitor the effectiveness of their programs. At least 75% of the schools participating in this accreditation believe that the stakeholders are the faculty, employers, current students, and the business community. The cost of this assessment process varies with the size of the college. Nearly 20% of the business schools have indicated that the annual cost exceeds $10,000.

Assessment by deans may be performed using a variety of procedures. Some schools of business use exit surveys, while others obtain feedback from faculty surveys or alumni surveys. Another form of assessment is to use focus groups. These groups of faculty and/or students meet to examine a particular aspect of their college of business's operations or performance. This process contributes to the harmony of the business administration disciplines by bringing together all constituents in continuous improvement.

With each college of business being able to establish its own mission, the accreditation process is sometimes full of uncertainties. Deans often obtain information from other universities to better understand how their schools stack up. When you have completed this chapter, you will be able to

- Examine the mean and standard deviation for measurements of the importance of competencies considered necessary for a quality business education.
- Understand how to obtain a probability that a certain number of randomly selected schools of business will use the results of the assessment process to make changes in their curriculum.
- Understand what is meant by a discrete probability distribution when viewing the proportions of importance ratings rendered by deans on competencies deemed to be part of a quality business education.

A Look Back/Introduction

The early chapters were concerned with describing sample data that had been gathered from a previous experiment, a printed report, or some other source. The data were summarized using one or more numerical measures (for example, a sample mean, variance, or correlation) or using a statistical graph (such as a histogram, bar chart, or scatter diagram).

Chapter 4 introduced you to methods of dealing with uncertainty by using a probability to measure the chance of a particular event occurring. Rules were defined that enabled you to compute various probabilities of interest, such as a conditional or a joint probability. However, so far we have defined only the probability of a certain event happening.

Whenever an experiment results in a numerical outcome, such as the total value of two dice, we can represent the various possible outcomes and their corresponding probabilities much more conveniently by using a *random variable,* the topic of this chapter. Suppose that your company manufactures a product that is sometimes defective and is returned for repair during the warranty period in 10% of the cases. An excellent way of describing the chance that 3 of 20 products will be returned before the warranty runs out is to use the concept of a random variable.

Random variables can be classified into two categories: discrete and continuous. This chapter introduces both but concentrates on the discrete type. Several commonly used discrete random variables will be discussed, as will methods of describing and applying them.

DEFINITION

A **random variable** is a function that assigns a numerical value to each outcome of an experiment.

In Chapter 3 we used various statistics (numerical measures) to describe a set of sample data. For example, the sample mean and standard deviation provide measures of a "typical" value and variation within the sample, respectively.

Similarly, we will use a random variable and its corresponding distribution of probabilities to describe a *population.* Just as a sample has a mean and standard deviation, so does the population from which the sample was obtained. We will use the basic concepts from Chapter 4 to derive probabilities related to a random variable.

RANDOM VARIABLES 5.1

Discrete Random Variables

The probability laws developed in the previous chapter provide a framework for the discussion of random variables. We will still be concerned about the probability of a particular event; often, however, some aspect of the experiment can be easily represented using a random variable. The result of a simple experiment can sometimes be summarized concisely by defining a discrete random variable to describe the possible outcomes.

Flip a coin three times. The possible outcomes for each flip are heads (H) and tails (T). According to counting rule 1 from Chapter 4, there are $2 \cdot 2 \cdot 2 = 8$ possible results. These are TTT, TTH, THT, HTT, HHT, HTH, THH, and HHH. Let

A = event of observing 0 heads in 3 flips (TTT)

B = event of observing 1 head in 3 flips (TTH, THT, HTT)

C = event of observing 2 heads in 3 flips (HHT, HTH, THH)

D = event of observing 3 heads in 3 flips (HHH)

We wish to find $P(A)$, $P(B)$, $P(C)$, and $P(D)$.

Consider one outcome, say, HTH. The coin flips are independent, so we use equation 4.14:

$P(\text{HTH})$ = (probability of H on 1st flip) · (probability of T on 2nd flip) ·
(probability of H on 3rd flip)

$= (1/2) \cdot (1/2) \cdot (1/2) = 1/8$

This same argument applies to all eight outcomes. These outcomes are all equally likely, and each occurs with probability 1/8.

Event A occurs only if you observe TTT. It has the probability of occurring one time out of eight:

$$P(A) = 1/8$$

Event B will occur if you observe HTT, TTH, or THT. It would be impossible for HTT and TTH *both* to occur, so $P(HTT \text{ and } TTH) = 0$. *This is true for any combination of these three outcomes so these three events are all mutually exclusive. Consequently, according to equation 4.13,*

$$P(B) = P(\text{HTT or TTH or THT})$$

$$= P(\text{HTT}) + P(\text{TTH}) + P(\text{THT})$$

$$= 1/8 + 1/8 + 1/8 = 3/8$$

By a similar argument,

$P(C) = 3/8$ (using HHT, HTH, THH)

$P(D) = 1/8$ (using HHH)

The variable of interest in this example is X, defined as

$$X = \text{number of heads out of three flips}$$

We defined all the possible outcomes of X by defining the four events A, B, C, and D. This method works but is cumbersome. Consider having to do this for 100 flips of a coin! A more convenient way to represent probabilities is to examine the value of X for each possible outcome.

Outcome	Value of X	
TTT	0	1 outcome
THT	1	
TTH	1	3 outcomes
HTT	1	
HHT	2	
HTH	2	3 outcomes
THH	2	
HHH	3	1 outcome

Each outcome has probability 1/8, so the probability that X will be 0 is 1/8, written:

$$P(X = 0) = P(0) = 1/8$$

The probability that X will be 1 is 3/8, written:

$$P(X = 1) = P(1) = 3/8$$

The probability that X will be 2 is 3/8, written:

$$P(X = 2) = P(2) = 3/8$$

The probability that X will be 3 is 1/8, written:

$$P(X = 3) = P(3) = 1/8$$

Notice that

$$P(X = 0) + P(X = 1) + P(X = 2) + P(X = 3) = 1/8 + 3/8 + 3/8 + 1/8 = 1$$

because 0, 1, 2, and 3 represent *all the possible values of X.*

The values and probabilities for this random variable can be summarized by listing each value and its probability of occurring.

$$X = \begin{cases} 0 & \text{with probability } 1/8 \\ 1 & \text{with probability } 3/8 \\ 2 & \text{with probability } 3/8 \\ 3 & \text{with probability } 1/8 \end{cases}$$

This list of possible values of X and the corresponding probabilities is a **probability distribution.**

In any such formulation of a problem, the variable X is a *random variable.* Its value is not known in advance, but there is a probability associated with each possible value of X. Whenever you have a random variable of the form

$$X = \begin{cases} x_1 & \text{with probability } p_1 \\ x_2 & \text{with probability } p_2 \\ x_3 & \text{with probability } p_3 \\ \vdots \\ x_n & \text{with probability } p_n \end{cases}$$

where $x_1, \ldots, x_n$ is the set of possible values of X, then X is a **discrete random variable.** In the coin-flipping example, $x_1 = 0$ and $p_1 = 1/8$; $x_2 = 1$ and $p_2 = 3/8$, $x_3 = 2$ and $p_3 = 3/8$, and $x_4 = 3$ and $p_4 = 1/8$.

Other examples of a discrete random variable include:

X = the number of cars that drive up to a bank within a 5-minute period ($X = 0, 1, 2, 3, \ldots$).

X = the number of people out of a group of 50 who will suffer a fatal accident within the next 10 years ($X = 0, 1, 2, \ldots, 50$).

X = the number of people out of 200 who make an airline reservation and then fail to show up ($X = 0, 1, 2, \ldots, 200$).

X = the number of calls arriving at a telephone switchboard over a two-minute period ($X = 0, 1, 2, 3, \ldots$).

Notice that, for each example, the discrete random variable is a count *of the number of people, calls, accidents, and so on that can occur.*

You roll two dice, a red die and a blue die. What is a possible random variable X for this situation? What are its possible values and corresponding probabilities? (*Hint:* Roll the dice and observe a particular number. This number is your value of the random variable, X. What observations are possible from the roll of two dice?)

Solution

There are many possibilities here, including

X = total of the two dice

X = average of the two dice

X = the higher of the two numbers that appear (possible values: 1, 2, 3, 4, 5, 6)

X = the number of dice with 3 appearing (possible values: 0, 1, 2)

Suppose that the random variable X equals the total of the two dice. The next step is to determine the possible values of X and the corresponding probabilities. When you roll the two colored dice, there are $6 \cdot 6 = 36$ possible outcomes, using counting rule 1 from Chapter 4.

Outcome	Red Die	Blue Die	Value of X	
1	1	1	2	
2	1	2	3	
3	1	3	4	
4	1	4	5	
5	1	5	6	$P(X = 3)$ is 2/36
6	1	6	7	
7	2	1	3	
8	2	2	4	
9	2	3	5	
⋮	⋮	⋮	⋮	
34	6	4	10	
35	6	5	11	
36	6	6	12	

The 36 outcomes are equally likely because the number appearing on each die (1, 2, 3, 4, 5, or 6) has the same chance of appearing. Notice that we are *not* saying that each value of X is equally likely, as the following discussion will make clear. Each of the above 36 outcomes has probability 1/36 of occurring. If you write down all 36 outcomes and note what can happen to X, your random variable, you will observe:

Value of X	Number of Possible Outcomes	
2	1	(rolling a 1, 1)
3	2	(rolling a 1, 2, or 2, 1)
4	3	(rolling a 1, 3 or 3, 1 or 2, 2)
5	4	(and so on)
6	5	
7	6	
8	5	
9	4	
10	3	
11	2	
12	1	

Consequently,

$$X = \begin{cases} 2 \text{ with probability } 1/36 \\ 3 \text{ with probability } 2/36 \\ 4 \text{ with probability } 3/36 \\ 5 \text{ with probability } 4/36 \\ 6 \text{ with probability } 5/36 \\ 7 \text{ with probability } 6/36 \\ 8 \text{ with probability } 5/36 \\ 9 \text{ with probability } 4/36 \\ 10 \text{ with probability } 3/36 \\ 11 \text{ with probability } 2/36 \\ 12 \text{ with probability } 1/36 \end{cases}$$

Total 1.0

Because 2 through 12 represent all possible values of X, the total of all probabilities is equal to 1.

Suppose instead X is defined to be the *average* of the two dice, rather than the total. Now the possible values of X are 1 (with probability 1/36), 1.5 (with probability 2/36), . . . , 5.5 (with probability 2/36), and 6 (with probability 1/36). Notice that X is still a discrete random variable, since there are gaps in the possible values (a value of 4.2 is not possible, for example). However, the possible values of X are *not* all counting numbers. In general, the possible values of a discrete random variable need not be positive integers but generally are since the discrete random variable typically counts the number of occurrences of a particular event.

Continuous Random Variables

The previous section introduced you to the discrete random variable, where the possible values of X can be listed along with corresponding probabilities. Characteristic of this type of random variable is the presence of *gaps* in the list of possible values. For example, when throwing two dice, a total of 8.5 cannot occur.

The other type of random variable is the **continuous random variable,** for which *any* value is possible over some continuous range of values. For a random variable of this type, there are no gaps in the set of possible values. As a simple example, consider two random variables: X is the number of days that it rained in Boston during any particular month, and Y is the amount of rainfall during this month. X is a *discrete* random variable, because it counts the number of days, and consequently there are gaps in the possible values (7.4, for example, is not possible). Y, on the other hand, is a *continuous* random variable because (at least in principle) the amount of rainfall could be any nonnegative value.

FIGURE

5.1

Any value is possible in this range.

Example of a continuous random variable. X = height, in feet, of a randomly selected adult male in the United States.

Suppose the heights of all adult males in the United States range from 3.0 feet to 7.5 feet. Your task is to describe these heights using such statements as:

15% of the heights are under 5.5 ft.

88% of the heights are between 5.0 ft and 6.0 ft.

We first define the random variable

X = height of a randomly selected adult male in the United States

Figure 5.1 shows the range of X.

We are unable to list all possible values of X, since *any* height is possible over this range. However, we can still discuss probabilities associated with X. For example, the two preceding statements can be described by using the probability statements

$$P(X < 5.5) = .15$$

$$P(X \text{ is between 5 ft and 6 ft}) = P(5 < X < 6) = .88$$

For this situation, X is a continuous random variable. Probabilities for continuous random variables can be found only for *intervals*. (Probabilities of exact values are meaningful only for discrete random variables.) *Determining probabilities for a continuous random variable is discussed in Chapter 6.*

The discussion in Chapter 1 on discrete and continuous data is directly related to our present topic. *When you observe a discrete random variable, you obtain discrete data. When you observe a continuous random variable (such as 100 heights), you obtain continuous data.*

X Exercises 5.1–5.8

Understanding the Mechanics

5.1 In a batch of circuit boards there are two boards that need to be returned to the factory, three boards that need repair but do not need to be sent back to the factory, and three boards that are in good working condition.
   a. What is the probability that a circuit board selected at random needs to be returned to the factory?
   b. What is the probability that a circuit board is in good working condition?

5.2 A manager can either hire or not hire an applicant after an interview. Let H represent "hire" and N represent "not hire." Suppose that both outcomes are equally likely. Let X equal the number of of Ns after two interviews.
   a. List all possible outcomes from two interviews. List these as pairs. Are each of these pairs of outcomes equally likely?
   b. What is $P(X = 0)$? $P(X = 1)$? $P(X = 2)$?

5.3 Consider a deck of 52 cards with 13 hearts, 13 spades, 13 clubs, and 13 diamonds and assume that a card is drawn at random. Define a random variable X to be 1 if a heart is drawn, 2 if a spade is drawn, and 3 if either a club or a diamond is drawn.
   a. List the values of X and their probabilities.
   b. What is the probability that X is greater than 1?
   c. What is the probability that X is either 1 or 3?

5.4 State the values that the following random variables can assume. Classify each random variable as either discrete or continuous.
   a. The percentage change in the S&P 500.
   b. The number of small businesses that fail each month in Chicago.
   c. The number of cases heard daily in a Common Pleas Court.
   d. The time that it takes a family to decide on purchasing a new home.

e. The number of times that a manufacturing process needs readjustment during a week.

5.5 Consider an experiment in which a coin is tossed and a die is rolled. Let X be the number observed from rolling the die. Let Y be the value 1 if a head appears and 0 if a tail appears. List the values that the random variables X and Y can have, along with the corresponding probabilities.

Applying the New Concepts

5.6 Several companies have hired information systems personnel to be the company's Internet cop. Thanks to inexpensive software that can track what employees are doing online, when they are online, and for how long, these Internet cops submit reports to the company's directors about their employees' usage of the Internet. If personnel are shopping for jobs on their competitors' Web site, management wants to know. Companies are careful not to overreact, as management typically does not want to hurt morale.

a. List examples of discrete variables that would be of interest to management in the report submitted by the Internet cops.

b. Can you think of any continuous variables that would be of interest to management?

(Source: "Worker Watchers," *Fortune*, vol. 143, no. 13, 2001, pp. 70–80.)

5.7 An IRS auditor only has time to audit two of three tax returns. Suppose two of the tax returns show a refund due to the taxpayer and one tax return shows that the taxpayer owes the IRS. Assume that the IRS auditor is to randomly select two of the returns. Define X to equal the number of tax returns among the two selected that show a refund due the taxpayer.

a. List all possible outcomes of this experiment.

b. Show the values that the random variable X can assume.

c. List the probabilities associated with the values in part a.

5.8 The distribution of the sum of two random variables is not always obvious. Follow the steps below to find the distribution of the sum of two discrete random variables, each of which takes on a value of 0 or 1 with equal probability.

a. Generate two columns of 300 numbers consisting of 0's and 1's such that each value is equally likely. (In Excel, click on **Tools** > **Data Analysis** ➤ **Random Number Generation** and use the Discrete option with the values 0 and 1 in one column and the values .5 and .5 in another column for input to the dialog box. In SPSS, create uniform data for var1 by clicking on **Transform** ➤ **Compute** ➤ **RV.UNIFORM(min, max)** inserting 0 for the min and 2 for the max. Then click on **Transform** ➤ **Compute** ➤ **TRUNC(numexpr)** and insert var1 for numexpr. In MINITAB click on **Calc** ➤ **Random Data** ➤ **Discrete** and put 0 and 1 in a column and the values .5 and .5 in another column.)

b. Create a new column of values that is equal to the sum of the two columns generated in part a. What do you think is the shape of the distribution of these two numbers?

c. Form a histogram of the data values obtained in part b. Describe the distribution of the sum of two random variables each of which takes on the value of 0 or 1 with equal probability.

5.2

REPRESENTING PROBABILITY DISTRIBUTIONS FOR DISCRETE RANDOM VARIABLES

There are three popular methods of describing the probabilities associated with a discrete random variable X. They are:

List each value of X and its corresponding probability.

Use a histogram to convey the probabilities corresponding to the various values of X.

Use a function that assigns a probability to each value of X.

Remember our coin-flipping example, in which X = number of heads in three flips of a coin. We can list each value and probability:

$$X = \begin{cases} 0 \text{ with probability } 1/8 \\ 1 \text{ with probability } 3/8 \\ 2 \text{ with probability } 3/8 \\ 3 \text{ with probability } 1/8 \end{cases}$$

This works well when there is only a small number of possible values for X; it would not work well for 100 flips of a coin.

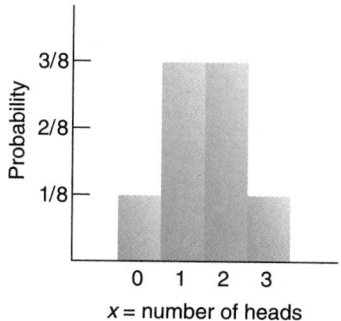

FIGURE

5.2

A histogram representation of a discrete random variable, where X = number of heads in three coin flips.

Using a histogram also is a convenient way to represent the shape of a discrete distribution having a small number of possible values. For this situation, you construct a histogram in which the height of each bar is the probability of observing that value of X (Figure 5.2). It is easier to determine the shape of the probability distribution by using such a chart. The distribution in Figure 5.2 is clearly symmetric and concentrated in the middle values.

Using a function (that is, an algebraic formula) to assign probabilities is the most convenient method of describing the probability distribution for a discrete random variable. For any given application of such a random variable, however, this function may or may not be known. Later in the chapter we identify certain useful discrete random variables, each of which has a corresponding function that assigns these probabilities.

The function that assigns a probability to each value of X is called a **probability mass function (PMF)**. Denoting a particular value of X as x, this function is of the form

$$P(X = x) = \text{some expression (usually containing } x\text{)}$$
$$\text{that produces the probability of observing } x$$

$$= P(x)$$

Not every function can serve as a PMF. The requirements for a PMF function are:

1. $P(x)$ is between 0 and 1 (inclusively) for each x

2. $\sum P(x) = 1$

Consider a random variable X having possible values of 1, 2, or 3. The corresponding probability for each value is:

$$X = \begin{cases} 1 \text{ with probability } 1/6 \\ 2 \text{ with probability } 1/3 \\ 3 \text{ with probability } 1/2 \end{cases}$$

Determine an expression for the PMF.

Consider the function

Solution

$$P(X = x) = P(x) = x/6 \quad \text{for } x = 1, 2, 3$$

This function provides the probabilities

$$P(X = 1) = P(1) = 1/6 \quad \text{(OK)}$$

$$P(X = 2) = P(2) = 2/6 = 1/3 \quad \text{(OK)}$$

$$P(X = 3) = P(3) = 3/6 = 1/2 \quad \text{(OK)}$$

This function satisfies the requirements for a PMF: each probability is between 0 and 1, and $P(1) + P(2) + P(3) = 1/6 + 1/3 + 1/2 = 1$. Consequently, the function

$$P(x) = x/6 \qquad \text{for } x = 1, 2, 3 \qquad \text{(and zero elsewhere)}$$

is the PMF for this discrete random variable.

EXAMPLE 5.3

Consider Example 5.1, where X is the total of two dice. Determine the PMF for this discrete random variable.

Solution   Consider the expression

$$P(x) = \frac{x - 1}{36} \qquad \text{for } x = 2, 3, 4, \ldots, 12 \qquad \text{(and zero elsewhere)}$$

If this is the proper PMF, then, for example,

$$P(2) = P(X = 2) = \frac{2 - 1}{36} = 1/36$$

This does appear to be correct, so far. Also,

$$P(5) = P(X = 5) = \frac{5 - 1}{36} = 4/36$$

This also is correct. But now consider

$$P(10) = P(X = 10) = \frac{10 - 1}{36} = 9/36$$

According to our previous solution, we know that $P(10) = 3/36$, not $9/36$. So this particular function is not the PMF for this random variable; the PMF must work for *all* values of X.

Consider the expression

$$P(x) = \frac{6 - |x - 7|}{36} \qquad \text{for } x = 2, 3, \ldots, 12 \qquad \text{(and zero elsewhere)}$$

where $|\ |$ represents the absolute value of a number. See if you can demonstrate that this function is a bona fide PMF for this example (it is). Do not worry about where this expression came from, but do verify that it works. The truth of the matter is that often PMFs are derived by trial and error.

Notice that a probability mass function provides a theoretical "model" of the population by describing the chance of observing any particular value of the random variable. *You can view the population as what you would obtain if you observed the corresponding random variable indefinitely.*

X Exercises 5.9–5.19

Understanding the Mechanics

5.9 Which of the following probability mass functions are valid? Why?

a.
x	P(x)
−2	.4
−3	.4
4	.2

b.
x	P(x)
10	−.1
20	.9
30	.2

c.
x	P(x)
1	.1
2	.2
3	.3
4	.4

d.
x	P(x)
0	.1
5	.6
7	.1
9	.1

e.
x	P(x)
100	.3
120	.3
300	.3
500	.3

5.10 Let $P(X = x)$ be equal to .125 for x equal to 10, 20, 30, 40, 50, 60, 70, or 80 and zero elsewhere. Why is this function a probability mass function?

5.11 Is the following function a probability mass function? Why?

$P(X = x) = x/30$ for $x = 0, 10,$ and 20 (and zero elsewhere)

5.12 Is the following function a probability mass function? Why?

$$P(X = x) = \frac{3}{4(3 - x)! \, x!} \text{ for } x = 0, 1, 2, 3$$

5.13 Is the following function a probability mass function? Why?

$$P(X = x) = \frac{\sqrt{x}}{9} \text{ for } x = 4, 9, 16 \quad \text{(and zero elsewhere)}$$

Applying the New Concepts

5.14 There are 3 electrical components that a quality-control inspector needs to inspect. One of the components does not function. Suppose that the inspector only chooses two randomly and that the random variable X represents the number of components not working.
    a. List all possible outcomes.
    b. Find the probability mass function for X.

5.15 A quality manager receives shipments of probe cards from three suppliers—say, suppliers A, B, and C. Probe cards are complex, multilayer printed circuit boards with some electrical points of contact smaller than a human hair. Suppose that the manager receives two boxes of probe cards from supplier A, which are believed to be of substandard quality. The manager receives 4 boxes of probe cards from supplier B, which are considered to be of good quality. From supplier C, the manager receives 6 boxes of very high quality probe cards. Suppose that a probe card is selected at random from this shipment. Define the random variable X to be 1, 2, or 3 if the probe card was manufactured by supplier A, B, or C, respectively. Verify that the following function is the probability mass function of X.

$P(X = x) = x/6 \quad$ if $x = 1, 2, 3 \quad$ (and zero elsewhere)

5.16 A real estate broker needs to advertise two townhouses, two duplexes, and two single-family homes. However, the broker decides to choose at random only one of the six properties for open house on a certain weekend. Let the random variable X take on the value 1 if a townhouse is chosen, 2 if a duplex is chosen, and 3 if a single-family home is chosen. Write the probability mass function of X.

5.17 Suppose that in Exercise 5.16, the random variable X is assigned the value of 2 if a townhouse is chosen, 4 if a duplex is chosen, and 6 if a single-family home is chosen. Write the probability mass function of X.

5.18 An investor has two investments, A and B. The investor believes that investment A is equally likely to increase by $1000 or to decrease by $1000 by the end of the year. The investor also believes that investment B is equally likely to increase by $2000 or decrease by $2000 by the end of the year. Let X represent the total amount of change in investments A and B. Assume that these investments perform independent of each other. Find the probability mass function of X.

5.19 [Simulation Exercise] What happens if you roll two dice many times? How can you analyze this situation? To find the distribution of the sum of the values appearing on each dice roll a computer simulation can be created. On the KPK menu, select the **Sum of Dice Problem** by clicking on **Simulation Exercises.**
    a. Enter the number of times you think that you need to roll a pair of dice to determine the distribution. Continue to increase the number selected until the shape of the graph appears to stabilize.
    b. What is the probability of the most frequently occurring value for the sum of two dice? Does this agree with the solution to Example 5.1?
    c. Using the values from the simulation, what is the probability that the sum of dice will be between 5 and 8, inclusively? Does this agree with the solution to Example 5.1?

5.3

MEAN AND VARIANCE OF DISCRETE RANDOM VARIABLES

Mean of Discrete Random Variables

Chapter 3 introduced you to the mean and variance of a set of sample data consisting of n values. Suppose that these values were obtained by observing a particular random variable n times. The sample mean, $\overline{X}$, represents the *average* value of the sample data. In this section, we determine a similar value, the **mean of a discrete random variable,** written as **μ.** The value of μ represents the average value of the random variable if you were to observe this variable over an indefinite period of time.

Reconsider our coin-flipping example, where X is the number of heads in three flips of a coin. Suppose you flip the coin three times, record the value of X, flip the coin three times again, record the value of X, and repeat this process 10 times. Now you have 10 observations of X. Suppose they are

2, 1, 1, 0, 2, 3, 2, 1, 1, 3

The mean of these data is the *statistic* $\overline{X}$, where

$$\overline{x} = \frac{2+1+1+\cdots+1+3}{10}$$

$$= 1.6 \text{ heads}$$

If you observed X *indefinitely*, what would X be on the average?

$$X = \begin{cases} 0 \text{ with probability } 1/8 \\ 1 \text{ with probability } 3/8 \\ 2 \text{ with probability } 3/8 \\ 3 \text{ with probability } 1/8 \end{cases}$$

So 1/8 of the time you should observe the value 0; 3/8 of the time, the value 1; 3/8 of the time, the value 2; and 1/8 of the time, the value 3. In a sense, each probability represents the *relative frequency* for that particular value of X. So the average value of X is

$$(0)(1/8) + (1)(3/8) + (2)(3/8) + (3)(1/8) = 1.5 \text{ heads}$$

Notice that X cannot be 1.5; this is merely the value of X on the average.

DEFINITION

The average value of the discrete random variable X (if observed indefinitely) is the mean of X. The symbol for this parameter is μ.

We found that $\mu = 1.5$ by multiplying each value of X by its corresponding probability and summing the results:

$$\mu = 1.5 = 0 \cdot P(0) + 1 \cdot P(1) + 2 \cdot P(2) + 3 \cdot P(3)$$

This procedure applies to any discrete random variable, and so we define*

$$\mu = \sum xP(x)$$

5.1

5.4

A personnel manager in a large production facility is investigating the number of reported on-the-job accidents over a period of one month. We define the random variable

$$X = \text{number of reported accidents per month}$$

Based on past records, she has derived the following probability distribution for X:

$$X = \begin{cases} 0 \text{ with probability } .50 \\ 1 \text{ with probability } .25 \\ 2 \text{ with probability } .10 \\ 3 \text{ with probability } .10 \\ 4 \text{ with probability } \underline{.05} \\ \phantom{4 \text{ with probability }} 1.00 \end{cases}$$

*μ is often referred to as the *expected* value of the random variable, X, and is written $\mu = E(X)$.

During 50% of the months there were no reported accidents, 25% of the months had one accident, and so on. (Notice that deriving an algebraic expression for the PMF for this distribution would be extremely difficult. This poses no problem, however.)

What is the mean (average value) of X?

Solution

Using equation 5.1,

$$\mu = (0)(.5) + (1)(.25) + (2)(.1) + (3)(.1) + (4)(.05)$$
$$= .95$$

There is .95 (nearly 1) accident reported on the average per month.

Variance of Discrete Random Variables

We previously considered 10 observations of the random variable that counted the number of heads in three flips of a coin. These data were 2, 1, 1, 0, 2, 3, 2, 1, 1, 3. We used the notation from Chapter 3 to define the mean of these data, and we obtained $\bar{x} = 1.6$. The variance of these data, using equation 3.8, is $s^2 = .933$. Since s^2 describes a sample, it is a statistic.

Once again, consider observing X indefinitely. For this situation, the average value of X is defined as the mean of X, μ. When we observe X indefinitely, this particular variance is defined to be the variance of the random variable, X, and is written σ^2 (read as "sigma squared").

$$\sigma^2 = \text{variance of the discrete random variable, } X$$

The **variance of a discrete random variable,** X, is a parameter describing the variation of the corresponding population. It is the average (expected) value of $(X - \mu)^2$ if X were observed indefinitely, and it can be obtained by using one of the following expressions, which are mathematically equivalent:*

$$\sigma^2 = \sum (x - \mu)^2 \cdot P(x)$$ 5.2
$$\sigma^2 = \sum x^2 P(x) - \mu^2$$ 5.3

Equation 5.3 generally provides an easier method of determining the variance and will be used in all of the examples to follow. For the coin-flipping example,

$$\sigma^2 = \sum x^2 P(x) - \mu^2$$
$$= [(0)^2 \cdot (1/8) + (1)^2 \cdot (3/8) + (2)^2 \cdot (3/8) + (3)^2 \cdot (1/8)] - (1.5)^2$$
$$= 3 - 2.25 = .75$$

So our final results would be:

Using the Sample of 10 Observations		For the Random Variable, X (Indefinite Number of Observations)	
$\bar{x} = 1.6$	$s^2 = .933$	$\mu = 1.5$	$\sigma^2 = .75$
mean	variance	mean	variance
statistics		parameters	

---

*Using the expectation notation, σ^2 is the expected value of $(X - \mu)^2$ and can be written $\sigma^2 = E(X - \mu)^2$ or $\sigma^2 = E(X^2) - [E(X)]^2$.

In Chapter 3, the square root of the variance, s, was defined to be the standard deviation of the data. The same definition applies to a random variable. The **standard deviation of a discrete random variable**, X, is denoted σ, where:

$$\sigma = \sqrt{\sum (x - \mu)^2 \cdot P(x)}$$

$$\sigma = \sqrt{\sum x^2 P(x) - \mu^2}$$

5.4 5.5

EXAMPLE 5.5

Determine the variance and standard deviation of the random variable concerning on-the-job accidents in Example 5.4.

Solution   A convenient method of determining both the mean and variance of a discrete random variable is to summarize the calculations in tabular form:

x	$P(x)$	$x \cdot P(x)$	$x^2 \cdot P(x)$
0	.5	0	0
1	.25	.25	.25
2	.1	.2	.4
3	.1	.3	.9
4	.05	.2	.8
	1.00	.95	2.35

So,

$$\mu = \sum xP(x) = .95 \text{ accident}$$

and

$$\sigma^2 = \sum x^2 P(x) - \mu^2 = 2.35 - (.95)^2$$

$$= 1.45$$

Also

$$\sigma = \sqrt{1.45} = 1.20 \text{ accidents}$$

EXAMPLE 5.6

Suppose that a computerized procedure generates integer values between 1 and 5 (that is, 1, 2, 3, 4, and 5) in such a way that each value has the same chance of selection. Let X represent a generated value. (i) Describe the probability distribution of X. (ii) What is the mean and variance of this random variable?

Solution to (i)   Since each value of X has the same chance of selection, namely, 1 chance in 5, the probability distribution of X is

$$X = \begin{cases} 1 \text{ with probability } 1/5 \\ 2 \text{ with probability } 1/5 \\ 3 \text{ with probability } 1/5 \\ 4 \text{ with probability } 1/5 \\ 5 \text{ with probability } 1/5 \end{cases}$$

The corresponding probability mass function is

$$P(X = x) = 1/5 \quad \text{for } x = 1, 2, 3, 4, 5 \quad \text{(and zero elsewhere)}$$

Solution to (ii)   The mean of X is

$$\mu = 1 \cdot \frac{1}{5} + 2 \cdot \frac{1}{5} + 3 \cdot \frac{1}{5} + 4 \cdot \frac{1}{5} + 5 \cdot \frac{1}{5} = \frac{15}{5} = 3$$

and the variance of X is

$$\sigma^2 = \sum x^2 P(x) - \mu^2$$

$$= \left[1 \cdot \frac{1}{5} + 4 \cdot \frac{1}{5} + 9 \cdot \frac{1}{5} + 16 \cdot \frac{1}{5} + 25 \cdot \frac{1}{5} \right] - (3)^2$$

$$= \frac{55}{5} - 9 = 2$$

Also, the standard deviation of X is $\sqrt{2} = 1.414$.

A discrete random variable X having the property that each value of X has the same probability of occurring is called a **discrete uniform random variable.** In general, for such a random variable, the possible values of X are all values between, say, a and b, that is, $a, a + 1, a + 2, \ldots , b$. In Example 5.6, $a = 1$ and $b = 5$. Since each of the $(b - a) + 1$ values of X has the same probability of occurring, the probability mass function for the discrete uniform random variable is

$$P(X = x) = \frac{1}{(b - a) + 1} \text{ for } x = a,\ a + 1,\ a + 2,\ \ldots,\ b$$

(and zero elsewhere)

5.6

A nice feature of this type of random variable is that there is a shortcut method of determining the mean and variance of X. It can be shown that for the discrete uniform random variable,

$$\mu = \frac{a + b}{2}$$

5.7

$$\sigma^2 = \frac{(b - a)(b - a + 2)}{12}$$

5.8

In Example 5.6, $a = 1$ and $b = 5$, so

$$\mu = \frac{1 + 5}{2} = 3 \qquad \text{(same as before)}$$

$$\sigma^2 = \frac{(5 - 1)(5 - 1 + 2)}{12} = \frac{24}{12} = 2 \qquad \text{(same as before)}$$

In the sections to follow, we will examine three other "special" discrete random variables. Each of these random variables will also have a shortcut formula for calculating the mean and variance.

EXAMPLE 5.7

Refer to Example 5.6. Generate 100 random integer values between 1 and 5, inclusively. What are the mean and variance of these values? Do they agree with the results of Example 5.6? If not, why not?

Solution

To generate these values using Excel, follow the following sequence: (1) click on the **Paste Function** icon (f_*), (2) click on **Math & Trig** in the **Function** category list, (3) click on **RANDBETWEEN** in the **Function** name list, (4) set the bottom value equal to 1 and the top value equal to 5, and (5) click on **OK**. Assuming the spreadsheet is empty, this random value will appear in cell A1. Next, place the cursor on the small square in the lower right corner of this cell and drag it down through cell A100. You should now see 100 integers between one and five in column A. The first 16 values for one such run are shown in Figure 5.3.

FIGURE

5.3

Random sequence generated by Excel and descriptive statistics.

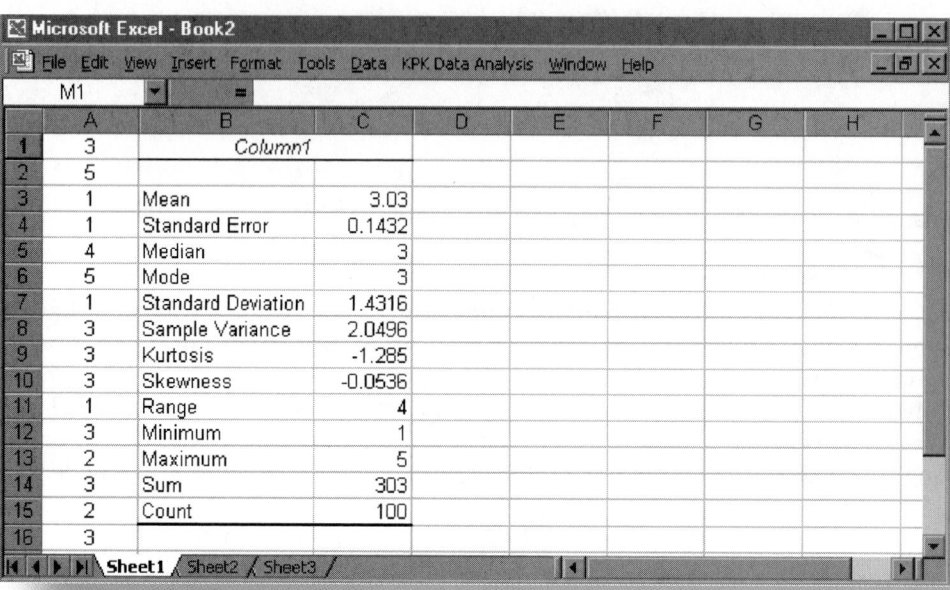

To obtain the descriptive statistics, click on **Tools ➤ Data Analysis ➤ Descriptive Statistics.** For the input range, enter "A1:A100," and for the output range, enter "B1." Finally, click on the white square alongside **Summary Statistics.** These results are also shown in Figure 5.3.

The mean of the 100 values in the sample is $\bar{x} = 3.03$, and the sample variance is $s^2 = 2.05$. According to Exercise 5.6, the mean of the random variable is 3, and the variance is 2. What we have in the solution is 100 *observations* of the random variable—that is, a sample. The population here consists of the observations we would obtain if we were to observe this random variable *indefinitely.* The mean of this population is the mean of the random variable—that is, 3. Since we only observed the variable 100 times, it is not surprising that the sample mean of 3.03 is unequal to 3—although it is quite close. A similar argument applies to the variance since the *population* variance here is 2, and the *sample* variance obtained from the sample of 100 observations is 2.05.

This example illustrates once again the difference between a *population* (indefinite number of observations of a random variable) and a *sample* (a finite number of actual observations of this random variable).

X   Exercises 5.20–5.27

Understanding the Mechanics

5.20 Find the mean and standard deviation for the random variable X with the following distributions.

a. x	P(x)		b. x	P(x)		c. x	P(x)
0	.2		−3	.1		1	.1
1	.6		0	.3		2	.1
2	.2		3	.6		3	.4
						4	.3
						5	.1

5.21 For each of the following probability mass functions, determine the mean and standard deviation.
  a. $P(X = x) = x/60$ for $x = 20$ and 40 (and zero elsewhere)
  b. $P(X = x) = \sqrt{x}/11$ for $x = 4$, 16, and 25 (and zero elsewhere)

5.22 A random variable has a discrete uniform distribution with possible values of 20, 21, 22, 23, and 24.
  a. What is the probability that the random variable is less than 23?

b. What is the mean of the random variable?

c. What is the standard deviation of the random variable?

Applying the New Concepts

5.23 Suppose that a coin is flipped three times. Define the random variable X to be equal to twice the number of heads that appear. Determine the mean and variance of X.

5.24 The discrete uniform random variable X has a positive probability for the values 5, 6, 7, 8, 9, and 10. Verify that the mean and variance of this random variable can be calculated using formulas 5.1 and 5.3 or formulas 5.7 and 5.8.

5.25 A Times Orange County poll sampled voters from Orange County, California, whether a commercial airport at El Toro should be built. Although voters countywide believed an airport would benefit the local economy, Orange County respondents remained deeply divided over building a county airport. The results of the poll were as follows:

	Percentage (%)
Favor building the airport	43
Undecided	13
Disfavor building the airport	44

a. Let the random variable X represent the following values:

X	Category
1	Favor building the airport
0	Undecided
−1	Disfavor building the airport

What is the mean and the standard deviation of X?

b. Let the random variable X represent the following values:

X	Category
3	Favor building the airport
2	Undecided
1	Disfavor building the airport

What is the mean and the standard deviation of X?

c. Compare the answers in part a to those in part b. Do they appear to be what you would expect?

(Source: "EL TORO: Will It Fly?" *Los Angeles Times*, May 24, 1998, p. 1A.)

5.26 The accessibility that business professionals have to information technology creates the potential for misuse of this technology. Business professionals were asked to give their perceived importance of two ethical issues. Scenario 1 says that a programmer uses company equipment for personal use. Scenario 2 says that an employee uses proprietary software without paying the fee.

Importance of the Issue	Scenario 1	Scenario 2
Very important	.16	.61
Undecided	.18	.21
Not very important	.66	.18

a. Code very important, undecided, and not very important as having the values 1, 2, and 3. Find the mean and standard deviation for Scenario 1.

b. Repeat part a for Scenario 2.

c. Compare and interpret the statistics found in parts a and b.

(Source: "Making Ethical Decisions," *Communications of the ACM*, vol. 43, no. 12, December 2000, p. 66.)

Using the Computer

5.27 A discrete uniform random variable has the following probability mass function:

$$P(X = x) = 1/4 \text{ if } x = 1, 2, 3, \text{ and } 4 \text{ (and zero elsewhere)}$$

a. Generate 400 numbers from this distribution. (In Excel, click on **Tools ➤ Data Analysis ➤ Random Number Generation** and use the Discrete option with the values 1, 2, 3, and 4 in one column and the values .25, .25, .25, and .25 in another column for input to the dialog box. In SPSS, create uniform data for var1 by clicking on **Transform ➤ Compute ➤ RV.UNIFORM(min, max)** inserting 1 for the min and 5 for the max. Then click on **Transform ➤ Compute ➤ TRUNC(numexpr)** and insert var1 for numexpr. In MINITAB click on **Calc ➤ Random Data ➤ Discrete** and put the numbers 1, 2, 3, and 4 in a column and the values .25, .25, .25 and .25 in another column.)

b. Use the sample mean and sample standard deviation formulas from Chapter 3 on the values created in part a to estimate the population mean and standard deviation.

c. Determine the population mean and standard deviation using the formulas in this chapter.

d. Compare your answers to parts b and c.

5.4

BINOMIAL RANDOM VARIABLES

The random variable X representing the number of heads in three flips of a coin is a special type of discrete random variable, a **binomial random variable.**

We next list the conditions for a binomial random variable in general and as applied to our coin-flipping example:

A Binomial Situation	**For Example 5.1**
1. Your experiment consists of n repetitions, called **trials.**	**1.** $n = 3$ (flips of a coin)
2. Each trial has two mutually exclusive possible outcomes (or can be considered as having two outcomes) referred to as **success** and **failure.**	**2.** Success = head, failure = tail (this is arbitrary)
3. The n trials are *independent.*	**3.** The results on one coin flip do not affect the results on another flip.
4. The probability of a success for each trial is denoted p; the value of p remains the same for each trial.	**4.** p = the probability of flipping a head on a particular trial $= 1/2$
5. The random variable X is the number of *successes* out of n trials.	**5.** X = the number of heads out of three flips

You encounter a binomial random variable when a certain experiment is repeated many times (n trials), the trials are independent, and each experiment results in one of two mutually exclusive outcomes. For example, a randomly selected individual is either male or female, is on welfare or is not, will vote Republican or will not, and so on.

The two outcomes for each experiment are labeled as *success* or *failure.* A success need not be considered "good" or "desirable." Instead, it depends on what you are counting at the completion of the n trials. If, for example, the object of the experiment is to determine the probability that 3 people out of 20 randomly selected individuals *are* on welfare, then a success on each of the $n = 20$ trials is the event that the person selected on each trial *is* on welfare.

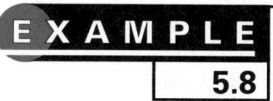

EXAMPLE 5.8

In Example 4.4, it was noted that 30% of the people in a particular city read the evening newspaper. Select four people at random from this city. Consider how many of these four people read the evening paper. Does this situation satisfy the requirements of a binomial situation? What is your random variable here?

Solution Refer to conditions 1 through 5 in our list for a binomial situation.

1. There are $n = 4$ trials, where each trial consists of selecting one individual from this city.

2. There are two outcomes for each trial. We are interested in counting the number of people, out of the four selected, who *do* read the evening paper, so define

success = read the evening newspaper

failure = do not read the evening newspaper

3. The trials are independent since the people are selected randomly.

4. p = probability of a success on each trial = .3.

5. The random variable here is X, where

X = number of successes in n trials

X = number of people (out of four) who read the evening newspaper

All the requirements are satisfied. Thus, X is a binomial random variable (it is also discrete).

Counting Successes for a Binomial Situation

How many ways are there of getting two heads out of four flips of a coin? There are six: HHTT, HTHT, HTTH, THHT, THTH, and TTHH. How many ways can you select two people from a group of four people, where the order of selection is unimportant (say, you are selecting a two-person committee)? Label the individuals as I_1, I_2, I_3, and I_4. You want to find the number of combinations of four people using two at a time:

$$_4C_2 = \frac{4!}{2!\,2!} = 6$$

Put these results side by side. The scheme for matching the two results is to select I_1 if H appears on the first flip, select I_2 if H appears on the second flip, and so on.

Two Heads Out of Four Flips	Two People from a Group of Four
HHTT	I_1, I_2
HTHT	I_1, I_3
HTTH	I_1, I_4
THHT	I_2, I_3
THTH	I_2, I_4
TTHH	I_3, I_4

You should see a direct correspondence between the two solutions. Our conclusion is that the number of ways of getting two heads out of four flips of a coin is $_4C_2$. Extending this to any number of flips of a coin, the number of ways of getting k heads out of n flips of a coin is $_nC_k$. Finally, for any binomial situation, the number of ways of getting k successes out of n trials is $_nC_k$. We are thus able to determine the *probability mass function* (PMF) for any binomial random variable.

Once again, let X equal the number of heads out of three flips. Here X is a binomial random variable, with $p = .5$. Consider any value of X, say, $X = 1$. Then the probability of any one outcome where $X = 1$, such as HTT, is $1/8$ and the number of ways of getting one head (success) out of three flips (trials) is $_3C_1 = 3$. Consequently, the probability that X will be 1 is:

$$P(1) = {}_3C_1(1/8) = 3/8$$

The resulting PMF for this situation can be written as

$$P(x) = {}_3C_x \cdot (1/8) \quad \text{for } x = 0, 1, 2, 3 \quad \text{(and zero elsewhere)}$$

Using this function, we obtain the same results as before:

$$P(0) = {}_3C_0(1/8) = 1 \cdot (1/8) = 1/8$$
$$P(1) = {}_3C_1(1/8) = 3 \cdot (1/8) = 3/8$$
$$P(2) = {}_3C_2(1/8) = 3 \cdot (1/8) = 3/8$$
$$P(3) = {}_3C_3(1/8) = 1 \cdot (1/8) = \underline{1/8}$$
$$1$$

EXAMPLE 5.9

In Example 5.8, the binomial random variable X is the number of people (out of four) who read the evening newspaper. Also, there are $n = 4$ trials (people) with $p = .3$ (30% of the people read the evening newspaper). Let S denote a success and F a failure. Then define:

$S =$ a person reads the evening newspaper

$F =$ a person does not read the evening newspaper

What is the probability that exactly two people (out of four) will read the evening paper?

Solution   This is $P(X = 2)$, or $P(2)$. Consider any one result where $X = 2$, such as SFSF. The probability of this result, using equation 4.14, is

(probability of S on first trial) · (probability of F on second trial)
· (probability of S on third trial) · (probability of F on fourth trial)

which is

$$(.3)(.7)(.3)(.7) = (.3)^2(.7)^2$$

Also note that the probability of *each* result with two S's and two F's ($X = 2$) also is $(.3)^2(.7)^2 = p^2(1 - p)^2$. How many ways can we get two successes out of four trials? This is:

$$_4C_2 = \frac{4!}{2!2!} = 6$$

So the final result here is

$$P(2) = \text{(number of ways of getting } X = 2\text{)(probability of each one)}$$
$$= {_4C_2}(.3)^2(.7)^2$$
$$= (6)(.09)(.49) = .265$$

So 26.5% of the time, exactly two people out of four will read the evening newspaper.

We can extend the results of Example 5.9 to obtain the PMF for a binomial random variable:

$$P(x) = {_nC_x}\,p^x(1 - p)^{n-x} \quad \text{for } x = 0, 1, 2, \dots, n$$
$$\text{(and zero elsewhere)}$$

5.9

where n is the number of trials and p is the probability of a success for each trial.

For the newspaper example, $x = 2$, $n = 4$, and $p = .3$. The complete list of probabilities for this example is:

$$X = \begin{cases} 0 \text{ with probability } {_4C_0}\,(.3)^0\,(.7)^4 = & .240 \\ 1 \text{ with probability } {_4C_1}\,(.3)^1\,(.7)^3 = & .412 \\ 2 \text{ with probability } {_4C_2}\,(.3)^2\,(.7)^2 = & .265 \\ 3 \text{ with probability } {_4C_3}\,(.3)^3\,(.7)^1 = & .076 \\ 4 \text{ with probability } {_4C_4}\,(.3)^4\,(.7)^0 = & .008 \\ \hline & 1.001 \end{cases}$$

Note that the total value may be slightly greater or less than 1.0, because of rounding. A graphical representation of this PMF is shown in Figure 5.4.

Using Binomial Table A.1

The binomial PMFs have been tabulated in Table A.1 for various values of n and p. The maximum number of trials in this table is $n = 20$. For binomial situations where $n > 20$, we suggest the use of a computer package, such as Excel, SPSS, or MINITAB.

For the evening newspaper illustration in Example 5.9, $n = 4$ and $p = .3$. To find $P(2)$, locate $n = 4$ and $x = 2$. Go across the table to $p = .3$ and you will find the corresponding probability. This probability is .265. Similarly, $P(0) = .240$, $P(1) = .412$, $P(3) = .076$, and $P(4) = .008$, as before.

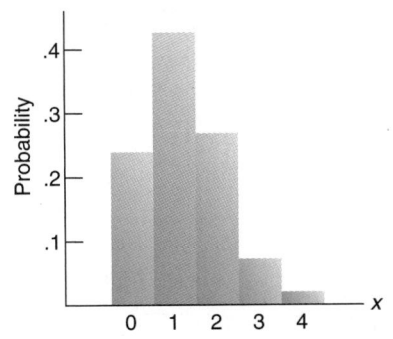

FIGURE

5.4

Probability mass function for $n = 4$, $p = .3$.

x = number of evening newspaper subscribers

The probability that no more than two people will read the evening paper is written $P(X \leq 2)$, where

$$P(X \leq 2) = P(X = 0) + P(X = 1) + P(X = 2)$$
$$= P(0) + P(1) + P(2)$$
$$= .240 + .412 + .265$$
$$= .917$$

This is a *cumulative probability* and is obtained by summing $P(x)$ over the appropriate values of X.

Using Binomial Table A.2

Cumulative binomial probabilities are tabulated in Table A.2 for the same values of n and p used in Table A.1. The value in this table corresponding to $n = 4$, $x = 2$, and $p = .3$ is .916. Since this is a *cumulative* probability, then $P(X \leq 2) = .916$. Note that this value agrees with the previous result, except in the third decimal place. In general, using this table for cumulative probabilities will provide slightly more accurate results than summing the values in Table A.1.

Shape of the Binomial Distribution

Figure 5.5 contains a graphical representation of four binomial distributions. In particular, notice these three relationships hold:

1. When $p = .5$, the shape is perfectly *symmetrical* and resembles a bell-shaped (normal) curve.

2. When $p = .2$, the distribution is *skewed right*. This skewness increases as p decreases.

3. For $p = .8$, the distribution is *skewed left*. As p approaches 1, the amount of skewness increases.

Compare Figure 5.5(c) and (d). Notice that, in both cases, p is .2; however, the number of trials increased from $n = 10$ in (c) to $n = 20$ in (d). For the larger value of n, the shape of this distribution is nearly bell-shaped, *despite the small value of* p. *This suggests that, regardless of the value of* p, *the shape of a binomial distribution approaches a bell-shaped distribution as the number of trials* (n) *increases.* We will use this fact in the next chapter, when we demonstrate an approximation to the binomial distribution using a bell-shaped (normal) curve for large samples.

FIGURE

5.5

Shape of the binomial distribution.

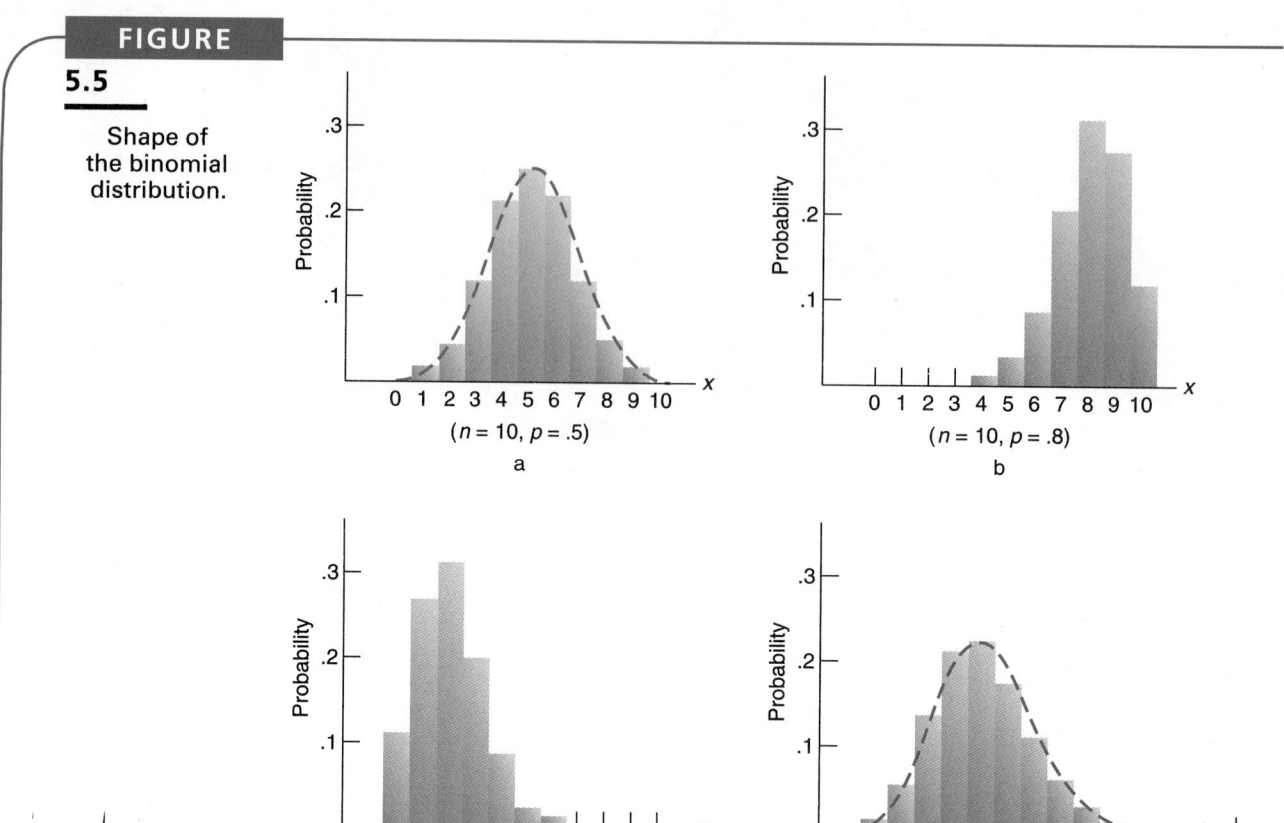

In summary, the shape of a binomial distribution is

- Skewed left for $p > 1/2$ and small n
- Skewed right for $p < 1/2$ and small n
- Approximately bell-shaped (symmetric) if p is near $1/2$ or if the number of trials is large

Mean and Variance of Binomial Random Variables

In Example 5.9, we examined the binomial random variable X representing the number of people (out of four) who read the evening newspaper. If you select four people, observe X, select four more people, observe X, and repeat this procedure indefinitely, what will X be on the average? This is the mean of X, where, using equation 5.1,

$$\mu = \sum xP(x)$$

$$= (0)(.240) + (1)(.412) + (2)(.265) + (3)(.076) + (4)(.008)$$

$$= 1.2 \text{ people}$$

Also, using equation 5.3, the variance of X is

$$\sigma^2 = \sum x^2 P(x) - \mu^2$$

$$= [(0)^2(.240) + (1)^2(.412) + (2)^2(.265) + (3)^2(.076) + (4)^2(.008)] - (1.2)^2$$

$$= 2.28 - 1.44 = .84$$

and so σ = standard deviation of $X = \sqrt{.84} = .92$ people. (Watch the units.)

The good news is that there is a convenient shortcut for finding the mean and variance of a binomial random variable. For this situation, you need not use equations 5.1 and 5.3. Instead, for any binomial random variable,

$$\mu = np$$

$$\sigma^2 = np(1 - p)$$

How these expressions were derived is certainly not obvious, but let us verify that they work for Example 5.9. Here $n = 4$ and $p = .3$, so

$$\mu = (4)(.3) = 1.2 \quad \text{(OK)}$$

$$\sigma^2 = (4)(.3)(.7) = .84 \quad \text{(OK)}$$

EXAMPLE 5.10

If you repeat Example 5.9 using $n = 50$ people (rather than $n = 4$ people), how many evening newspaper readers will you observe on the average?

Solution

Now, X is the number of people (out of 50) who read the evening paper. Consequently,

$$\mu = np = (50)(.3) = 15$$

So, on the average, X will be 15 people. For this situation, the variance of X is

$$\sigma^2 = np(1 - p) = (50)(.3)(.7) = 10.5$$

Also,

$$\sigma = \sqrt{10.5} = 3.24 \text{ people}$$

EXAMPLE 5.11

Airline overbooking is a common practice. Many people make reservations on several flights due to uncertain plans and then cancel at the last minute or simply fail to show up. Eagle Air is a small commuter airline. Its planes hold only 15 people. Past records indicate that 20% of the people making a reservation do not show up for the flight. We will assume that all reservations are independent; that is, each reservation is for one person and these reservations are made independent of one another.

Suppose that Eagle Air decides to book 18 people for each flight.

1. Determine the probability that on any given flight, at least one passenger holding a reservation will not have a seat.

2. What is the probability that there will be one or more empty seats for any one flight?

3. Determine the mean and standard deviation for this random variable.

Solution 1

The binomial random variable for this situation is X = the number of people (out of 18) who book a flight and actually do appear. For this binomial situation, $n = 18$ (18 reservations are made) and $p = 1 - .2 = .8$ (the probability that any one person will show up). At least one passenger will have no place to sit if X is 16 or more. Using Table A.1,

$$P(X \geq 16) = P(X = 16) + P(X = 17) + P(X = 18)$$

$$= .172 + .081 + .018 = .271$$

We see that if the airline follows this policy, 27% of the time one or more passengers will be deprived of a seat—not a good situation.

This result could also be obtained using Table A.2:

$$P(X \geq 16) = 1 - P(X < 16) = 1 - P(X \leq 15)$$
$$= 1 - .729 = .271.$$

Solution 2   We want to find the probability that the number of people who actually arrive (X) is 14 or less. Using Table A.2 (where $n = 18$, $p = .8$),

$$P(X \leq 14) = .499$$

With this booking policy, the airline will have flights with one or more empty seats approximately one-half of the time.

Solution 3   The mean of X is

$$\mu = np = (18)(.8) = 14.4 \text{ people}$$

which implies that the average number of people who book a flight and do appear is 14.4.

The standard deviation of X is

$$\sigma = \sqrt{np(1-p)} = \sqrt{(18)(.8)(.2)} = 1.70 \text{ people}$$

EXAMPLE 5.12

It is estimated that one out of 10 vouchers examined by the audit staff employed by a branch of the Department of Health and Human Services will contain an error. Define X to be the number of vouchers in error out of 20 randomly selected vouchers.

1. What is the probability that at least three vouchers will contain an error?

2. What is the probability that no more than one contains an error?

3. Determine the mean and standard deviation of X.

Solution 1   The random variable X satisfies the requirements for a binomial random variable with $n = 20$ and $p = .1$. For this situation, a "success" is defined to be that a voucher contains an error. The probability that at least three vouchers will contain an error is the probability that X is *3 or more*, which is

$$P(X \geq 3) = 1 - P(X < 3)$$
$$= 1 - P(X \leq 2)$$
$$= 1 - .677 \text{ (using Table A.2)}$$
$$= .323$$

Consequently, the probability that at least three vouchers will contain an error is .323.

Solution 2   The chance that no more than one voucher is in error is the probability that X is *1 or less*, which is

$$P(X \leq 1) = P(0) + P(1) = .392 \text{ (using Table A.2)}$$

So this event will occur with probability .392.

The mean of the random variable X is

$$\mu = np = (20)(.1) = 2 \text{ vouchers}$$

Solution 3

and the standard deviation of X is

$$\sigma = \sqrt{np(1-p)} = \sqrt{(20)(.1)(.9)} = 1.34 \text{ vouchers}$$

This implies that, on the average, the audit staff will encounter two vouchers containing an error (out of 20 randomly selected vouchers).

One situation that requires the use of a binomial random variable is **lot acceptance sampling,** in which you decide whether to accept or send back a lot (batch) of many electrical components, machine parts, or whatever.

Using Excel to Determine Binomial Probabilities

In an earlier section titled Using the Binomial Table, we mentioned that this table only contains values of $n \le 20$. Excel offers a simple way of finding binomial probabilities for any sample size (n)—in particular, for values of n greater than 20. Excel can be used to calculate an individual probability [such as $P(X = 3)$] or a cumulative probability [such as $P(X \le 3)$]. This will be illustrated in the next example.

E X A M P L E
5.13

A shipment of 2,500 calculator chips arrives at Cassidy Electronics. The contract specifies that Cassidy will accept this lot if a sample size of 100 from the shipment has no more than one defective chip. What is the probability of accepting the lot if, in fact, 5% of the lot (125 chips) are defective?

Solution

This is approximately a binomial situation where:

1. There are $n = 100$ trials.

2. Each trial has two outcomes:

success = chip is defective

failure = chip is not defective

(*Note:* Since the object is to count the number of *defective* chips in the shipment, a success on each trial (chip) will be that the chip is defective. As mentioned earlier, a success need not be a desirable event.)

3. p = probability of a success = .05*

4. The random variable here is X = number of successes out of n trials = number of defective chips out of 100. Cassidy accepts the lot of chips if X is 0 or 1. The corresponding probability is a cumulative probability:

$$P(\text{accept}) = P(X \le 1)$$
$$= P(0) + P(1)$$

---

*If the lot size is large (2,500 here) and the sample size is relatively small (100 here), then the value of p is nearly, although not completely, unaffected by the previous trials. For example, if 5% of the chips are defective, then on the first trial, p is 125/2,500 = .05. On the second trial, p is either 125/2,499 = .05002 (if the first chip was nondefective) or 124/2,499 = .04962 (if the first chip was defective). We typically ignore this minor problem in lot sampling from large populations, but this is why at the start of the solution we mentioned that this is "approximately a binomial situation." Situations in which the value of p is severely affected by what occurred on previous trials will be dealt with in the next section, where we discuss the hypergeometric distribution. Refer to Example 5.16.

FIGURE

5.6

Using Excel to find individual probabilities (panels A and B) or cumulative probabilities (panel C).

A.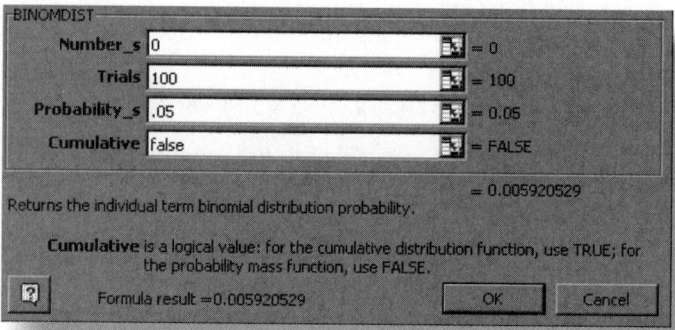

B.

C.

To determine binomial probabilities using Excel, click on the **Paste Function** icon (f_x), click on **Statistical** under **Function Category,** and click on **BINOMDIST** under **Function Name.** You should then see the input screen shown in Figure 5.6. Panel A of Figure 5.6 is what you would enter to determine $P(X = 0)$, and Panel B provides $P(X = 1)$. Notice that "false" was entered in the box labeled **Cumulative** since individual probabilities were desired. From Panels A and B, we also learn that $P(X \leq 1) = P(X = 0) + P(X = 1) = .0059 + .0312 = .0371$. Consequently, there is about a 4% chance that a sample of size 100 from this population will contain zero or one defective chip (the lot will be accepted).

The easiest way to find $P(X \leq 1)$ is to use Panel C in Figure 5.6 where "true" was entered in the **Cumulative** box and the result .0371 (rounded) appears. To summarize: enter "false" in the **Cumulative** box for individual probabilities and "true" for cumulative probabilities.

The concept of lot acceptance sampling was originally presented in Chapter 1 to illustrate the distinction between a population and a sample. It also serves as a brief introduction to the area of inferential statistics, discussed at length in Chapter 7. In Example 5.13, we inferred something about a population (the lot of 2,500 chips) using a sample (the 100 chips selected for testing). The sample does not include all elements of the population, so there is a risk of making an incorrect decision, such as (1) accepting the lot of chips when in fact it should be rejected or (2) rejecting the lot of chips when in fact it was satisfactory. *Such possibilities for error always exist when a statistical sample is used as a basis for an assertion about a population.*

X Exercises 5.28–5.41

Understanding the Mechanics

5.28 Using the binomial probabilities in Table A.1, find the following probabilities for a binomial random variable X.

   a. $P(X = 2)$, $n = 4$, $p = .2$
   b. $P(X = 7)$, $n = 9$, $p = .8$
   c. $P(X = 4)$, $n = 10$, $p = .5$
   d. $P(X = 0)$, $n = 20$, $p = .1$

5.29 Find the probabilities of the following events for a binomial random variable with $n = 10$ and $p = .5$.

   a. exactly 2 successes
   b. more than 2 successes
   c. no more than 2 successes
   d. less than 2 successes
   e. at least 2 successes

5.30 For a binomial random variable with $n = 5$ and $p = .25$, compute the following.

   a. $P(X = 1)$
   b. $P(X \geq 1)$
   c. $P(X \leq 3)$
   d. $P(1 \leq X \leq 3)$

5.31 What is the probability that a binomial random variable with $n = 21$ and $p = .1$ does not exceed 1?

Applying the New Concepts

5.32 A lawyer estimates that 40% of the cases in which she represented the defendant were won. If the lawyer is presently representing 10 defendants in different cases, what is the probability that at least 5 of the cases will be won? What are you assuming here?

5.33 A market-research firm has discovered that 30% of the people who earn between $25,000 and $50,000 per year have bought a new car within the past two years. In a sample of 12 people earning between $25,000 and $50,000 per year, what is the probability that between 4 and 10 people, inclusive, have bought a new car within the past two years?

5.34 Web site visitors are often loath to disclose personal information when making a purchase on the Internet. Despite safeguards that have been in place, approximately 60% of all consumers who make purchases on the Internet do not feel comfortable giving their credit card number. Suppose that X is a random variable that represents the number of Web site purchasers that do not feel comfortable typing their credit card number online from a sample of 20 purchasers.

   a. Why is X a binomial random variable?
   b. What is the probability that X is less than six?
   c. Would you consider the event of X less than six to be unusual?
   d. What value would you expect X to be on average? What is the standard deviation of X?

(Source: "Why Do You Ask," *The Wall Street Journal*, June 25, 2001, p. R17.)

5.35 According to the Consumer Aerosol Products Council, when adults were asked if it is true or false that aerosol cans may use CFC propellants (which eat the earth's ozone), approximately three in 10 adults knew that it was false. CFCs were banned in almost all sprays 20 years ago. However, 37% of the adults still believed the answer to be true.

   a. For a random sample of 10 adults, what do you think the probability is that fewer than three adults know that the answer is false? Compute it.
   b. For a random sample of 10 adults, what do you think the probability is that fewer than three believe that the answer is true (the incorrect answer)? Compute it.
   c. What is the mean number of sampled adults that you would expect to say that the answer is false [part a] and to say that the answer is true [part b]?

(Source: "Do Spray Cans Use CFCs?" *USA Today*, April 22, 1998, p. 1A.)

5.36 Sun Microsystems has approximately 50% of the high-end Unix machines, with its closest competitor being IBM. Suppose that 15 corporations were in the market to purchase a high-end Unix machine. Assume that these corporations listened to sales pitches by all the major players selling high-end Unix machines.

   a. What is the mean and standard deviation of the number of corporations that purchase a Unix machine from Sun Microsystems?
   b. What is the probability that exactly eight corporations purchase a Unix machine from Sun Microsystems?
   c. What is the probability that between five and 10 corporations, inclusively, purchase a Unix machine from Sun Microsystems?

(Source: "IBM Unveils High-End Computer Server," *The Wall Street Journal*, October 4, 2001, p. B7.)

5.37 Let the random variable X represent the number of correct responses on a multiple choice test that has 15 questions. Each question has five multiple choice answers.

  a. What is the probability that the random variable X is greater than 8 if the person taking the test randomly guesses?

  b. What is the mean value of X if the person randomly guesses?

  c. What is the standard deviation of X if the person randomly guesses?

  d. Estimate the probability that X will fall within the limits $\mu \pm 2\sigma$.

5.38 The *Professional Technician* recommends stocks each month. If 40% of the stocks recommended advance at least 20%, what is the probability that of the five stocks most recently recommended, at least three will advance at least 20%?

5.39 The manager of a retail store knows that 10% of all checks written are "hot" checks. Of the next 25 checks written at the retail store, what is the probability that no more than three checks are hot?

5.40 Mergers and slow periods in the economy often spell layoffs at many companies. Many employees count on two or three months of severance pay to carry them over to the next job. However, job searches can sometimes take longer than 6 months. A survey of workers who have been with companies for more than a year revealed that only 30% of the workers would be financially secure if they lost their job for 6 months to a year. Let X represent the number of employees out of a sample of 80 who would feel financially secure if they lost their job for 6 months to a year.

  a. What is the probability that at least 30 employees out of 80 would be financially secure if they lost their job for 6 months to a year? (In Excel, click on **Paste Function** ➤ **Statistical** ➤ **Binomdist**. In SPSS, click on **Transform** ➤ **Compute** ➤ **CDF.BINOM(q,n,p)**. In MINITAB, click on **Calc** ➤ **Probability Distributions** ➤ **Binomial**.)

  b. Do a "what if" analysis by changing the probability to .4 and to .5 and rework part a.

(Source: "How Long Workers Believe That They Would Be Financially Secure If They Lost Their Jobs," *USA Today*, June 5, 2001, p. 1B.)

5.41 Home ownership in the United States soared to its highest level in the late 1990s. The average percentage of the population owning a home is 66.2%. However, that rate varies from state to state. For example, in New York, approximately 50% of the population own their home and in Indiana, the home ownership rate is about 70%.

  a. Supposing that 100 families were randomly selected from New York, what is the probability that at least 50 families own their home. Use a statistical computer package.

  b. Supposing that the 100 families in part a were from Indiana, what would the probability be?

  c. If the 100 families in part a were from across the United States, what would the probability be?

  d. What is the expected number of families that are owners from New York, Indiana, and across the United States in a random sample of 100 families?

  e. Which sample (from New York, Indiana, or across the USA) would you expect to have the highest standard deviation? Compute the standard deviations and compare.

(Source: "Homeownership Gets Sweeter, Hits Record," *USA Today*, May 23, 2001, p. 2B.)

5.5 THE HYPERGEOMETRIC DISTRIBUTION

Another type of discrete random variable that fits many sampling situations is the **hypergeometric random variable.** It bears a strong resemblance to the binomial random variable since the experiment once again consists of n trials, with each trial having two possible outcomes (success or failure).

There are three conditions for a hypergeometric random variable:

1. Population size = N. In this population, k members are S (successes) and $N - k$ are F (failures).

2. Sample size = n trials, obtained *without replacement*.

3. $X =$ the number of successes out of n trials (a hypergeometric random variable).

The main distinction between a hypergeometric and a binomial situation is that the trials in the former *are not independent*. As a result, the probability of a success on each trial is affected by the results of the previous trials. This situation occurs when sampling *without replacement* from a *finite* population.

The situation surrounding a hypergeometric random variable is similar to the binomial situation in that you count "successes" in both cases. However, for the hypergeometric situation, you have a *finite* population (of size N) and you know the number of successes (k) and failures ($N - k$) that make up this population. For example, you might select a random sample of $n = 8$ from a group of $N = 30$ unionized workers, of which $k = 20$ are in favor of a strike and $N - k = 10$ are not. For this situation, the hypergeometric random variable is $X =$ the number of workers (of the 8) who favor the strike.

We can repeat Example 5.13 using 50 chips (instead of 2,500), 10 of which are selected for testing. Suppose that 10% of these chips (five chips) are defective. As before, define

$$S = \text{success} = \text{chip is defective}$$

$$F = \text{failure} = \text{chip is not defective}$$

Here, out of the 50 chips, five are defective. So

$$P(S \text{ on first trial}) = 5/50 = .10$$

The conditional probability of S on the second trial is:

$5/49 = .102$ if the first chip was not defective

$4/49 = .082$ if the first chip was defective

The probability of a success on the second trial is affected by what occurred on the first trial; this is a hypergeometric situation.

The PMF for the hypergeometric random variable is:

$$P(x) = \frac{{}_kC_x \cdot {}_{N-k}C_{n-x}}{{}_NC_n}$$

5.12

for $x = a, a + 1, a + 2, \ldots , b,$ where a is the maximum of 0 and $n + k - N$ and b is the minimum of k and n. The value of $P(x)$ is zero for all other values of X. Also, n is the sample size and N is the population size, k of which are successes.

EXAMPLE 5.14

Determine the probability of observing exactly one defective chip in a sample of size 10.

Solution

Imagine two containers (the population). One contains five S's and the other has 45 F's. The sample consists of 10 chips, randomly selected from these two containers. If x chips are selected from the success container, then $10 - x$ chips are selected from the failure container. For this situation, $N = 50$, $k = 5$, and $n = 10$. The possible values for X are from $a =$ maximum of 0 and -35 (0) to $b =$ minimum of 5 and 10 (5). The probability of obtaining one S and nine F's in your sample is

$$P(X = 1) = P(1) = \frac{{}_5C_1 \cdot {}_{45}C_9}{{}_{50}C_{10}}$$

As you will quickly see, the term ${}_NC_n$ gets very large—in fact, it becomes too large for many calculators. The only practical way to evaluate a hypergeometric probability, short of relying on a computer, is to cancel as many terms as possible in the expression.

The final result here is $P(1) = .431$; 43% of the time, you will obtain exactly one defective chip in your sample of size 10.

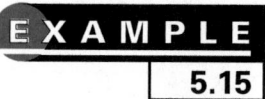

A local group of 30 unionized workers contains 20 people who are in favor of a strike and 10 who are not. Determine the probability that a random sample of eight workers contains 5 individuals who favor the strike and 3 who are opposed.

Solution   This situation fits the requirements for a hypergeometric random variable, where X is the number of workers (out of 8) who favor a strike, $n = 8$, $N = 30$, and $k = 20$. Consequently,

$$P(X = 5) = P(5) = \frac{_{20}C_5 \cdot _{10}C_3}{_{30}C_8}$$

$$= \frac{\frac{20!}{5!15!} \cdot \frac{10!}{3!7!}}{\frac{30!}{8!22!}}$$

$$= \frac{(15,504)(120)}{5,852,925} = .318$$

Approximately 32% of the time, in a sample of size eight from this group, five people would favor a strike.

Mean and Variance of a Hypergeometric Random Variable

As we did with the binomial random variable, we could use the definition of the mean and variance of a discrete random variable contained in equations 5.1 and 5.3. For example,

$$\mu = \sum xP(x)$$

where $P(x)$ is the PMF given in equation 5.12.

As in the binomial situation, simpler expressions exist for both the mean and the variance of the hypergeometric random variable. These are:

$$\mu = \sum xP(x) = \frac{nk}{N}$$

5.13

and

$$\sigma^2 = \sum x^2 P(x) - \mu^2$$

$$= \frac{k(N-k)n(N-n)}{N^2(N-1)} = \left[n\left(\frac{k}{N}\right)\left(1 - \frac{k}{N}\right)\right]\left(\frac{N-n}{N-1}\right)$$

5.14

For Example 5.14, $N = 50$, $k = 5$, $n = 10$. Consequently,

$$\mu = \frac{(10)(5)}{50} = 1 \text{ chip}$$

$$\sigma^2 = \frac{(5)(45)(10)(40)}{(50)^2(49)} = .735$$

and so

$$\sigma = \sqrt{.735} = .857 \text{ chip}$$

This means that if we observed this process of sampling 10 chips out of a batch of 50 indefinitely, we would obtain one $(= \mu)$ defective chip on the average. Also, $\sigma = .857$ (or $\sigma^2 = .735$) is our measure of the variation in the observations of this random variable if we observe it over an indefinite period.

FIGURE

5.7

Determining a
hypergeometric
probability using
Excel.

HYPGEOMDIST

Sample_s	5	= 5
Number_sample	8	= 8
Population_s	20	= 20
Number_pop	30	= 30

= 0.317871833

Returns the hypergeometric distribution.

Number_pop is the population size.

Formula result = 0.317871833   OK   Cancel

Using Excel to Determine Hypergeometric Probabilities and the Binomial Approximation

As the earlier examples illustrate, calculating hypergeometric probabilities with paper and pencil gives new meaning to the expression *gruesome calculation.* Excel offers a very simple method of determining these probabilities—nearly identical to the procedure used for finding binomial probabilities. To find a hypergeometric probability: click on the **Paste Function** icon (f_x), click on **Statistical** under **Function Category,** and click on **HYPGEOMDIST** under **Function Name.** The input screen in Figure 5.7 contains the solution to Example 5.15. Notice that: (1) the first box contains the particular value of X (5, here), (2) the second box contains the sample size, n, (3) the third box contains the number of successes in the population, k, and (4) the fourth box contains the population size, N. The formula result is .318 and agrees with the solution in Example 5.15. This formula result also appears in your spreadsheet in the current active cell.

Comment

Excel does not offer a cumulative probability option for hypergeometric probabilities as was available for binomial probabilities. To determine accumulative probability, sum the corresponding individual probabilities. This can be done easily using Excel's **Sum** function, found by clicking on the **Paste Function** icon, **Math & Trig, Sum.**

EXAMPLE
5.16

In Example 5.13 a sample of 100 chips was randomly selected from a lot of 2,500 chips. It was assumed that 5% of the chips in the lot were defective—that is, the lot contained $k = 125$ defective chips and $N - k = 2,375$ nondefective chips. The footnote in this example mentioned that this was an "approximate" binomial situation because the chances of selecting a defective chip on each draw was nearly the same, but not exactly. In fact, this example satisfies the requirements of a hypergeometric situation, and the important thing to remember is that whenever you select a random sample *without replacement* from a finite population, you are dealing with a hypergeometric situation.

The footnote in Example 5.13 explained that whenever the sample size (n) is small compared to the population size (N), treating the situation as binomial will work quite well. *A general rule is that you can treat such a situation as binomial, provided* n/N *is < .05.* For that example, $n/N = 100/2,500 = .04$, and so we would expect the final answer to be quite accurate. However, using Excel's ability to determine hypergeometric probabilities, we can easily determine the exact answer.

The problem is to find the chances of a sample of 100 chips containing one or fewer defective chips when sampling from a population of size 2,500 containing 125 defective

FIGURE

5.8

Determining
hypergeometric
probabilities for
Example 5.16.

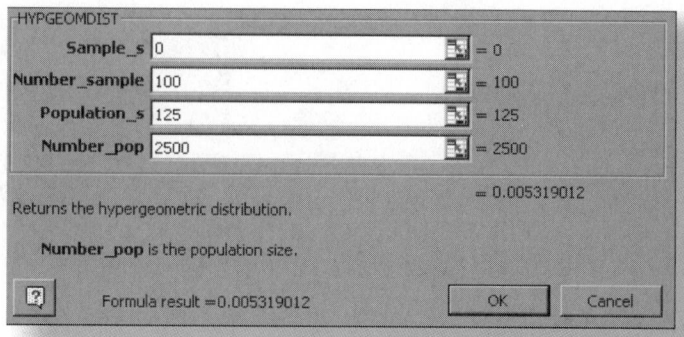

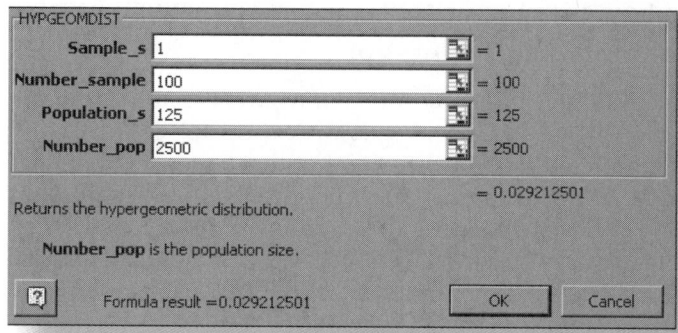

chips. In this case, the shipment of 2,500 chips is accepted. Refer to Figure 5.8. The top panel is used to find $P(X = 0)$ for this situation, and the bottom panel contains $P(X = 1)$. Summing the results, we see that $P(X \leq 1) = P(X = 0) + P(X = 1) = .0053 + .0292 = .0345$, which is quite close to the binomial solution of .0371 in Example 5.13. To recap: the hypergeometric value of .0345 is the exact probability of accepting this shipment, and the binomial probability of .0371 offers an excellent approximation since n/N is less than .05.

5.6 THE POISSON DISTRIBUTION

The Poisson distribution, named after the French mathematician Simeon Poisson, is useful for counting the number of times a particular event occurs over a specified period of time. It also can be used for counting the number of times an event (such as a manufacturing defect) occurs over a specified area (such as a square yard of sheet metal) or in a specified volume. *We will restrict our discussion to counting over time, although any unit of measurement is permissible.*

The random variable X for this situation is the number of occurrences of a particular event over a specified period of time. The possible values are 0, 1, 2, 3, ... For X to be a **Poisson random variable** over a given interval of time, the occurrences of this event need to occur *randomly*, as summarized by the following three conditions:

1. *The number of occurrences in one interval of time is unaffected by the number of occurrences in any other nonoverlapping time interval.* That is, the variables are statistically independent. For example, what took place between 3:00 and 3:20 P.M. is unaffected by what took place between 9:00 and 10:00 A.M.

2. *The expected (or average) number of occurrences over any time period is proportional to the size of this time interval.* For example, we would expect half as many occurrences between 3:00 and 3:30 P.M. as between 3:00 and 4:00 P.M.

   This condition also implies that the probability of an occurrence must be constant over any intervals of the same length. A situation in which this is usually *not* true is at a restaurant from 12:00 noon to 12:10 P.M. and 2:00 to 2:10 P.M. Due to the differences in traffic flow for these two intervals, we would not expect the arrivals between, say, 11:30 A.M. and 2:30 P.M. to satisfy the requirements of a Poisson situation.

3. *Events cannot occur exactly at the same time.* More precisely, there is a unit of time sufficiently small (such as one second) that no more than one occurrence of an event is possible during this time.

Four situations that usually meet these conditions are:

   The number of arrivals at a local bank over a five-minute interval.
   The number of telephone calls arriving at a switchboard over a one-minute interval.
   The number of daily accidents reported along a 20-mile stretch of an intercity toll road.
   The number of trucks in a fleet that break down over a one-month period.

For each situation, the (discrete) random variable X is the number of occurrences over the time period T. If all the assumptions are satisfied, then X is a Poisson random variable. Define μ to be the expected (or average) number of occurrences over this period of time.* For any application, the value of μ must be specified or estimated in some manner. The Poisson PMF for X follows.

POISSON PROBABILITY MASS FUNCTION

X = number of occurrences over time period T.

$$P(x) = \frac{\mu^x e^{-\mu}}{x!} \qquad \text{for } x = 0, 1, 2, 3, \ldots$$

5.15

where μ = expected number of occurrences over T.

Equation 5.15 contains the number e, which is an interesting and useful number in mathematics and statistics. To get an idea how this number is derived, consider the following sequence:

$$(1 + 1/2)^2 = 2.25$$
$$(1 + 1/3)^3 = 2.37$$
$$(1 + 1/4)^4 = 2.44$$
$$(1 + 1/5)^5 = 2.49$$
$$\vdots$$
$$(1 + 1/100)^{100} = 2.705$$
$$\vdots$$
$$(1 + 1/1000)^{1000} = 2.717$$
$$\vdots$$

This sequence of numbers is approaching e. The actual value of e is

$$e = 2.71828 \ldots$$

---

*The symbol λ (lambda) often is used to denote this parameter.

One interesting application of the number e occurs when calculating compound interest. For example, if you invest $100 at 12% compounded annually, then at the end of the year you will have $112. However, if your interest is compounded not monthly, not daily, but continuously, the amount in your account will be $(100)(e^{.12}) = (100)(1.1275) = \$112.75$. The difference in these amounts is not as large as you might expect!

We will use e again in Chapter 6.

Mean and Variance of a Poisson Random Variable

Once again, we could use the definition of the mean and variance of a discrete random variable in equations 5.1 and 5.3. However, this is not necessary. It is fairly easy to show, using equation 5.15, that

$$\text{mean of } X = \sum xP(x)$$

$$= \mu$$

This is hardly a surprising result, given how μ was originally defined. Also,

$$\text{variance of } X = \sigma^2$$

$$= \sum x^2P(x) - \mu^2$$

$$= \mu$$

So, *both the mean and the variance of the Poisson random variable X are equal to μ.* Recall that the Poisson random variable is the number of occurrences of a particular event (such as a traffic accident) over a given time period (such as an hour). If the time period is doubled to two hours, then the mean of the "new" Poisson random variable is twice the original mean; if the time period is halved to 30 minutes, the corresponding mean is halved, and so on. This is illustrated in the next two examples.

Applications of a Poisson Random Variable

5.17

Handy Home Center specializes in building materials for home improvements. They recently constructed an information booth in the center of the store. Define X to be the number of customers who arrive at the booth over a 5-minute period. Assume that the conditions for a Poisson situation are satisfied with

$$\mu = 4 \text{ customers over a 5-minute period}$$

A graph of the Poisson probabilities for $\mu = 4$ is contained in Figure 5.9.

1. What is the probability that over any 5-minute interval, exactly four people arrive at the information booth?

2. What is the probability that more than one person will arrive?

3. What is the probability that exactly six people arrive over a 10-minute period?

Solution 1   First, this probability is not 1, because $\mu = 4$ is the *average* number of arrivals over this time period. The actual number of arrivals over some 5-minute period may be fewer than four, more than four, or exactly four. The fraction of time that you observe exactly four people is, using Table A.3,

$$P(4) = \frac{4^4 e^{-4}}{4!} = .1954$$

FIGURE

5.9

Poisson
probabilities for
$\mu = 4$.

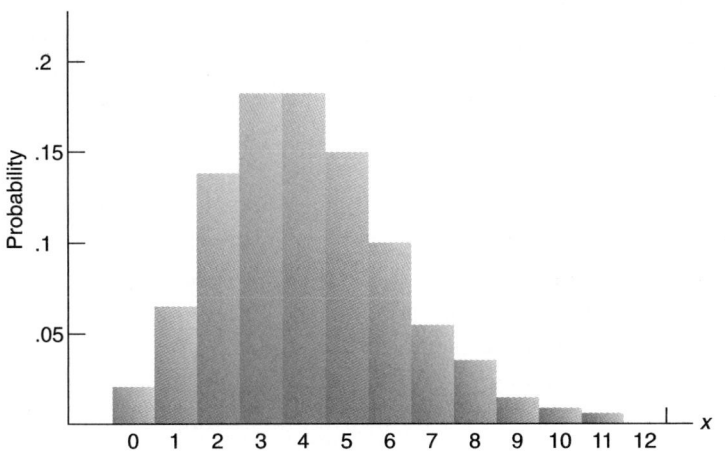

If you stand in the booth for many 5-minute periods, 19.5% of the time you will observe four people arrive.

Solution 2

This is $P(X > 1) = P(X \geq 2)$. We could try

$$P(X \geq 2) = P(X = 2) + P(X = 3) + \cdots$$
$$= P(2) + P(3) + \cdots$$
$$= .1465 + .1954 + \cdots$$

There is an infinite number of terms here, however, so this is *not* the way to find this probability. A much better way is to use the fact that these probabilities sum to 1. Consequently,

$$P(X \geq 2) = 1 - P(X < 2)$$
$$= 1 - P(X \leq 1)$$
$$= 1 - [P(0) + P(1)]$$
$$= 1 - \left[\frac{4^0 e^{-4}}{0!} + \frac{4^1 e^{-4}}{1!} \right]$$
$$= 1 - [.0183 + .0733] = .9084$$

Solution 3

For this time interval,

μ = expected (average) number of people over a 10-minute time period

$\mu = 8$ (we expect four people over a 5-minute period)

Therefore, the probability of observing six people over a 10-minute period is

$$\frac{8^6 e^{-8}}{6!} = .1221$$

using Table A.3.

The Poisson distribution is widely used in the area of quality control for describing the number of nonconformities observed in a sampling unit. A *nonconformity* is defined as a failure to conform to a particular specification, such as "no scratches on a strip of sheet metal" or "no leaks in an automobile radiator." If a sampling unit is a square yard of sheet metal, then the number of nonconformities might be the number of observed scratches. Or if the sampling unit is a radiator, the number of nonconformities is the number of observed leaks. If the occurrences of a nonconformity are relatively rare (compared to the number that could occur if everything went wrong), then the Poisson distribution typically works well to describe the random variable X = number of nonconformities per sampling unit, as illustrated in the following example.

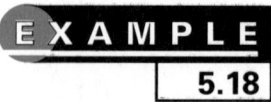

5.18

A certain process produces 100-foot-long sheets of vinyl composed of a simulated wood grain top layer and a black bottom layer. A blemish (nonconformity) occurs when the black layer shows through or the wood grain pattern is not distinct. A 10-foot sample is obtained by trimming the end of a roll, at which point the number of blemishes is observed and recorded. It is believed that the number of blemishes per sample follows a Poisson distribution with an average of two blemishes per 10-foot sample. Determine the probability that:

1. There will be no blemishes observed in a 10-foot sample.

2. There will be more than eight blemishes observed if a 30-foot sample is used.

Solution 1   The Poisson variable X for this situation is the number of observed blemishes. The average number of observed blemishes in a 10-foot sample is two, so

$$P(X = 0) = \frac{2^0 e^{-2}}{0!} = .1353$$

using Table A.3. This result means that 13.5% of the 10-foot samples will contain no blemishes.

Solution 2   The average number of blemishes in a 30-foot sample is six, given that the average is two for a 10-foot sample. Therefore, using Table A.3 with $\mu = 6$,

$$P(X > 8) = 1 - P(X \le 8)$$

$$= 1 - \left[\frac{6^0 e^{-6}}{0!} + \frac{6^1 e^{-6}}{1!} + \cdots + \frac{6^7 e^{-6}}{7!} + \frac{6^8 e^{-6}}{8!} \right]$$

$$= 1 - (.0025 + .0149 + \cdots + .1377 + .1033) = .153$$

We can expect more than eight blemishes in a 30-foot sample about 15% of the time.

Using Excel to Determine Poisson Probabilities

To find a Poisson probability using Excel: (1) click on the **Paste Function** icon (f_x), (2) click on **Statistical** under **Function Category,** and (3) click on **POISSON** under **Function Name.** The Poisson probabilities in Example 5.18 are calculated using Excel in Figure 5.10. The top panel is used to find $P(X = 0)$, where the mean of X is 2. Notice that "false" is entered in the **Cumulative** box since an individual probability is desired. The formula result of .1353 will appear in the current active cell in the Excel spreadsheet and agrees with Solution 1 in Example 5.18.

The bottom panel of Figure 5.10 is used to determine $P(X > 8)$ for the situation posed in the second part of Example 5.18, where the mean of X is now 6. To find $P(X > 8)$, remember that $P(X > 8)$ is the same as $1 - P(X \le 8)$. According to the Excel

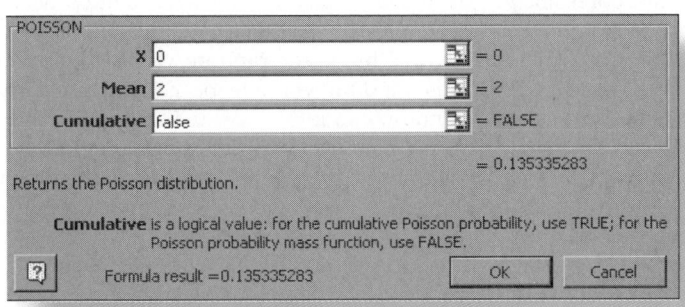

FIGURE

5.10

Using Excel to determine Poisson probabilities for Example 5.18.

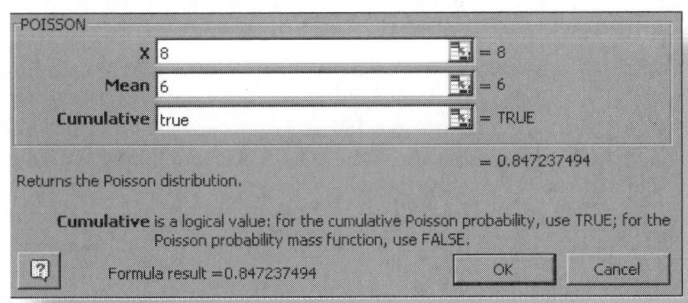

output, $P(X \leq 8)$ is .847, and so $P(X > 8)$ is $1 - .847 = .153$, which agrees with Solution 2 in Example 5.18. To find the cumulative probability $P(X \leq 8)$, enter "true" in the **Cumulative** box.

X Exercises 5.42–5.56

Understanding the Mechanics

5.42 Let X be a random variable with a hypergeometric distribution. Assume that $N = 10$ and $n = 5$.
   a. Find $P(X = 3)$ if $k = 3$.
   b. Find $P(X = 3)$ if $k = 6$.

5.43 A Poisson random variable has a mean of 8. What is the probability of each of the following events?
   a. The random variable is exactly equal to 8.
   b. The random variable is less than 8.
   c. The random variable is no more than 8.
   d. The random variable exceeds 8.
   e. The random variable is between 8 and 10, inclusively.

5.44 Find the mean and standard deviation of each of the following random variables.
   a. X is a hypergeometric random variable with $N = 6$, $k = 2$, $n = 3$.
   b. X is a hypergeometric random variable with $N = 100$, $k = 20$, $n = 40$.

   c. X is a Poisson random variable with expected number of occurrences equal to 9.

Applying the New Concepts

5.45 A batch of 350 resistors is to be shipped if a random sample of 15 resistors has two or fewer defective resistors. If it is known that there are 50 defective resistors in the batch, what is the probability that two or fewer of the sample of 15 resistors will be defective?

5.46 The Good Olde Boys used-car lot has 20 cars for sale. It is known that eight of the cars get over 28 miles per gallon on the highway and 12 do not. Let X be the random variable equal to the number of cars out of the next five cars sold that get over 28 miles per gallon. Assume that each car is equally likely to sell.
   a. What is $P(X \leq 2)$?
   b. What is $P(1 \leq X \leq 3)$?
   c. Find the mean and variance of X.

5.47 Only about a third of all employees have a will, whereas approximately three-quarters of all retirees have a will. Employers have sometimes encouraged employees to visit with an attorney to write a will. Suppose that a department head has 10 employees and three have a will.

a. If the department head were to randomly select four individuals from this group of 10, what is the probability that the number of employees with a will is 2?

b. Do a "what if" analysis by finding the solution to part a by changing the number of randomly selected individuals to 5, 6, and 7. Use a statistical computer package to find these probabilities. (In Excel, click on **Paste Function ➤ Statistical ➤ Hypgeomdist.** In SPSS, click on **Transform ➤ Compute ➤ CDF.HYPER(q, total, sample, hit).** In MINITAB, click on **Calc ➤ Probability Distributions ➤ Hypergeometric.**)

(Source: "Retirees Most Likely to Have Wills," *USA Today,* September 11, 2001, p. 1B.)

5.48 Each year, stock brokerage firms receive awards for the stock picking expertise of their research analysts. Bear Stearns was in the top 10 stock brokerage firms to receive awards. This company had 44 analysts and received 19 awards. Assume that the 19 awards were to different analysts. If an investor were to randomly select three analysts to follow for investment advice, what is the probability that at least two of these analysts have received awards for their stock recommendations?

(Source: "Salomon Takes Top Spot Among Firms," *The Wall Street Journal,* June 26, 2001, p. R16.)

5.49 Since most of the lucrative customers of cell phone companies already have cellphones, these companies are luring the under-20 segment of the population. These companies are offering inexpensive phones that young people can personalize with ring tones and games. Assume that an average number of cell phones sold weekly by The Cellphone Store for use by individuals less than 20 years of age is 10. The owner believes that the Poisson distribution can be used to approximate the probability of the number of cellphones sold weekly to this segment of the population.

a. What is the probability that at least eight phones are sold weekly to the under-20 population?

b. What is the probability that no more than 12 phones are sold weekly to the under-20 population?

c. What is the mean and standard deviation of the number of cellphones sold to the under-20 group?

d. Does it make sense to use the Poisson distribution to approximate the probability of the sales to the under-20 group?

(Source: "Should Kids Have Cellphones?" *The Wall Street Journal,* September 10, 2001, p. R12.)

5.50 Approximately 30% of all online airline travel is for family trips. Suppose that a car rental agency has a database of 10,000 people who purchased airline tickets online with 3,000 purchasing travel tickets for family trips. This agency's marketing department has decided to randomly select 125 individuals from this database for free vacation upgrades if a car is rented from the company during the next 3 months. The manager of the marketing department is interested in knowing what is the probability of at least 40 of these individuals making a purchase for family trips.

a. What is the random variable of interest? Why can this random variable be considered a hypergeometric random variable?

b. Can the binomial approximation to the hypergeometric distribution be used to find the probability that the sample includes at least 40 individuals who make online purchases for family trips?

c. Using a computer statistics package, compute the probability in part b using a hypergeometric distribution.

d. Repeat part c using the binomial approximation. Compare this probability to that obtained in part c.

(Source: "Buying Breakdown," *The Wall Street Journal,* September 24, 2001, p. R4.)

5.51 Some analysts believe that the number of Internet surfers clicking on a Web site has a Poisson distribution. Suppose that the number of times that the University of North Texas's (UNT) home page is accessed over the noon hour has an average rate of 10 times per hour. The Web master of this home page wants to determine various probabilities. Assuming that the number of times this Web page is accessed during the noon hour is Poisson distributed, find the following probabilities.

a. What is the probability that no more than 10 Internet users will access the UNT home page during the noon hour?

b. What is the probability that the number of Internet users accessing the UNT home page will exceed 15 during the noon hour?

5.52 California has the highest compliance of use of shoulder belts by the vehicle's front-seat occupants. On a 10 mile stretch of I-10 near Los Angeles, traffic officers estimate that approximately 1,000 cars pass every 15 minutes during the evening rush hour. Suppose that the average number of vehicles not complying with seat-belt laws is 10 during this period of time.

a. Does it appear reasonable to assume that the number of vehicles not complying with seat-belt laws during the evening traffic follows a Poisson distribution?

b. What is the likelihood during a particular 15-minute period that at least eight vehicles do not comply with the seat-belt laws?

(Source: "Seat Belt Use Highest in California," *USA Today,* June 28, 2001, p. 1A.)

5.53 The auto parts department of an automotive dealership sends out an average of eight special orders daily. The number of special orders is assumed to follow a Poisson distribution.

a. What is the probability that for any day, the number of special orders sent out will be more than four?

b. What is the standard deviation of the number of special orders sent out daily?

5.54 Seattle coffee-retailer Starbucks currently has 56 Starbucks-style retail stores in Britain. One problem that Starbucks stores in Britain face is persuading Europeans, who generally regard American coffee as watery, that a U.S. company can brew a good cup. Suppose that at 45 of these stores, the coffee is brewed to taste more European than that served in the United States. If two of the Starbucks-style retail stores in Britain are selected at random, what is the probability that one will serve coffee brewed to taste more European than that served in the United States? Compare the binomial approximation to the actual value obtained using the hypergeometric distribution.

(Adapted from "Starbucks Wafts Toward Europe," *The Wall Street Journal*, April 30, 1998, p. A12.)

5.55 A certain manufacturer sells a machine that has numerous moving parts. A quality-control inspector counts the number of moving parts that are misaligned as the number of nonconformities for a particular machine. It is believed that the number of nonconformities per machine follows a Poisson distribution, with an average of three nonconformities per machine.

a. Determine the probability that the quality-control inspector finds no more than one nonconformity on a particular machine selected at random.

b. What is the standard deviation of the number of nonconformities per machine.

5.56 The URLs of the three most visited Web sites in the first quarter of 2001 were *www.yahoo.com*, *www.msn.com*, and *www.passport.com*. These three Web sites have averaged 30 million visitors per day. Assume that the conditions of a Poisson distribution are satisfied.

a. What is the probability that less than 35 million visitors per day visit these three Web sites? (In Excel, click on **Paste Function ➤ Statistical ➤ Poisson.** In SPSS, click on **Transform ➤ Compute ➤ CDF.POISSON(q,mean).** In MINITAB, **click on Calc ➤ Probability Distributions ➤ Poisson.**)

b. What is the probability that more than 50 million visitors per day visit these three Web sites?

c. Would the event of more than 50 million visitors per day at these three Web sites be considered unusual?

d. What is the standard deviation of the number of visitors per day that visit these three Web sites?

(Source: "Most Visitors," *Business 2.0*, July 10, 2001, p. 85.)

✓ Summary

When an experiment results in a numerical outcome, a convenient way of representing the possible values and corresponding probabilities is to use a random variable. A **random variable** takes on a numerical value for each outcome of an experiment. If the possible values of this variable can be listed along with the probability for each value, this variable is said to be a **discrete random variable.** Conversely, if any value of this variable can occur over a specific range, then it is a **continuous random variable.** This chapter concentrated on the discrete type, whereas Chapter 6 discusses the continuous random variable.

For a discrete random variable, the set of possible values and corresponding probabilities is a **probability distribution.** There are several ways of representing such a distribution, including a list of each value and its probability, a histogram, or an expression called a **probability mass function (PMF),** which is a numerical function that assigns a probability to each value of the random variable.

If you could observe a random variable indefinitely, you would obtain the corresponding *population.* A *sample* then consists of a finite number of random variable observations. In Chapter 3, we introduced ways of describing a set of sample data using various statistics, including the sample mean and variance. Similarly, we can describe a random variable using its mean and variance. Since they describe the population, they are parameters. The **mean of a discrete random variable,** μ, is the average value of this variable if observed over an indefinite period. The mean is found by summing the product of each value and its probability of occurring. The **variance of a discrete random variable,** σ^2, is a measure of the variation for this variable. The **standard deviation,** σ, also measures this variation and is the square root of the variance.

Four popular discrete random variables used in a business setting are the discrete uniform, binomial, hypergeometric, and Poisson random variables. A **discrete uniform** random variable has possible values between two integers (say, *a* and *b*), where each integer in this interval has the same chance of occurring. A **binomial random variable** counts the number of successes out of *n* independent trials. When the trials are dependent and the population size (*N*) as well as the number of successes in the population (*k*) are known, the **hypergeometric random variable** can be used to describe the number of successes out of the *n* trials. The **Poisson random variable** is used for situations in which you observe the number of occurrences of a particular event over a specified period of time or space. The Poisson distribution is also used in the area of quality improvement to describe the number of nonconformities observed in a sampling unit, such as the number of surface flaws in a square yard of finished sheet metal.

Summary of Formulas

Any Discrete Random Variable, X

1. Mean $= \mu = \sum xP(x)$

2. Variance $= \sigma^2 = \sum (x - \mu)^2 P(x) = \sum x^2 P(x) - \mu^2$

3. Standard deviation $= \sigma = \sqrt{\sum (x - \mu)^2 P(x)} = \sqrt{\sum x^2 P(x) - \mu^2}$

Binomial Distribution

1. X = the number of successes out of n independent trials. Each trial results in a success (with probability p) or a failure (with probability $1 - p$).

2. PMF is $P(X = x) = P(x) = {}_nC_x p^x (1 - p)^{n-x}$ for $x = 0, 1, \ldots, n$

3. Mean $= \mu = np$

4. Variance $= \sigma^2 = np(1 - p)$ and standard deviation $= \sigma = \sqrt{np(1-p)}$

5. Probabilities for the binomial random variable are provided in Table A.1 and Table A.2.

Hypergeometric Distribution

1. X = the number of successes in a sample of size n when selecting from a population of size N containing k successes and $N - k$ failures

2. PMF is $P(x) = ({}_kC_x \cdot {}_{N-k}C_{n-x})/{}_NC_n$ for $x = a$, $a + 1, \ldots, b$, where a = maximum $\{0, n + k - N\}$ and b = minimum $\{k, n\}$

3. Mean $= \mu = n(k/N)$

4. Variance $= \sigma^2 = [n(k/N)(1 - k/N)] [(N - n)/(N - 1)]$

Poisson Distribution

1. X = the number of occurrences of a particular event over a certain unit of time, length, area, or volume

2. PMF is $P(x) = (\mu^x e^{-\mu})/(x!)$ for $x = 0, 1, 2, \ldots$

3. Mean $= \mu$

4. Variance $= \mu$

5. Probabilities for the Poisson random variable are provided in Table A.3.

X Review Exercises 5.57–5.78

5.57 Which of the following is a property of a discrete probability distribution?
  a. The probability for every value of a random variable is positive and not greater than .9.
  b. The sum of the probabilities for the values of a random variable is 1.
  c. The probabilities for any two different values of a random variable are different.
  d. At least one of the values of a random variable has a probability equal to .5.

5.58 Which of the following situations would be best described by a Poisson distribution, and which would be best described by a hypergeometric distribution? What assumptions do you have to make in each case?
  a. The number of students in your class that voted in a campus election.
  b. The number of accidents on interstate I-10 each month.
  c. The number of defects in a new automobile.
  d. The number of tires on your car that are underinflated.

5.59 A manager has four employees with 0, 1, 3, and 4 years of job experience. The manager will assign two of the employees at random to a team. Define X to be equal to the total number of years of job experience for the two selected employees.
  a. What values can X assume?
  b. What is the probability mass function of X?
  c. What is the mean of X?
  d. What is the standard deviation of X?

5.60 A realtor conducts a survey of 300 homeowners and finds that 30 have no mortgage on their homes.
  a. If a random sample of 10 homes from those surveyed is selected, what is the approximate probability that exactly one home has no mortgage.
  b. In part a, what is the probability that more than one home has no mortgage?

5.61 A supervisor believes that a new worker installs the wrong electrical component 30% of the time. The supervisor randomly selects 20 components installed by the new worker. The supervisor finds one incorrectly installed component. Is this a likely occurrence if the supervisor's belief is correct? What assumptions are necessary?

5.62 Let the variable X be equal to -1 if stock XYZ declines, 0 if stock XYZ remains unchanged, and 1 if stock XYZ increases in price. If $P(X = x)$ is equal to $(x + 2)/6$, what are the mean and standard deviation of X?

5.63 A manager has 10 research projects to assign to either engineer 1 or engineer 2. If each research project is randomly assigned to either one of the two engineers, what is the probability that engineer 1 will be assigned no more than 5 research projects?

5.64 An average of five books per week are returned to a bookstore. Assume that the number of returned books is Poisson distributed.
  a. What is the probability that less than four books will be returned in one week?
  b. What is the standard deviation of the distribution of the number of books returned in one week?

5.65 A Gallup Poll of 1,025 adults revealed that 20% of Americans do not own a credit card. However, the majority of adults own at least two credit cards. Define a random variable X to be equal to the number of credit cards owned by an adult. The probability mass function is as follows:

X: Number of Credit Cards Owned	P(x)
0	.20
1	.20
2	.15
3	.13
4	.10
5	.06
6	.07
7	.05
8	.04

  a. From viewing the probability mass function, what do you think the mean and standard deviation are for the number of credit cards owned by Americans?
  b. Find the mean and standard deviation and compare to your answer in part a.

(Source: "Most Americans Have One or Two Credit Cards," *USA Today*, June 1, 2001, p. 1A.)

5.66 Ten employees are being reviewed for promotion. Four of the employees are females. If each employee is equally likely to get promoted, what is the probability that two females and three males will be promoted, if a total of five promotions are given?

5.67 There are 90 drill bits in a box at a machine shop. Fifty of the drill bits are 3/8-inch diameter, and 40 are 7/16-inch diameter. If four drill bits are selected at random, what is the probability that two drill bits of 3/8-inch diameter and two drill bits of 7/16-inch diameter will be chosen?

5.68 A population consists of 15 employees, six of whom have less than two years experience. Let X equal the number of employees with less than two years experience from a sample of eight employees randomly drawn from this population.
  a. Find $P(X = 3)$.
  b. Find $P(X \leq 2)$.
  c. Find the average value of X.
  d. Find the standard deviation of X.

5.69 Blair's Moving Company loads an average of three boxes of damaged merchandise daily. What is the probability that exactly three boxes of damaged merchandise are shipped daily? What is the standard deviation of the number of boxes of damaged merchandise that are shipped daily? Assume a Poisson distribution.

5.70 For most investors, the only practical way to invest in China is through mutual funds. However, most mutual funds don't publicize the percentage that are based in China and, indeed, this percent can change over time. As of April 10, 1998, the following list displays mutual funds that have a concentration of their assets in China. If an investor chooses two of the following 13 mutual funds, what is the probability of the following:

Mutual Fund	Percent of Assets in China (in Percentage)
Greater China	59
Lexington Crosby Small Cap Asia Growth	31
Jardine Fleming China Region	30
U.S. Global Investors China Reg Opportunity	24
Guinness Flight Asia Small Cap	23
Matthews Pacific Tiger I	23
Robertson Stephens Global Low-Priced	21
Matthews Asian Convertible Securities	17
Templeton China World	16
Merrill Lynch Emerging Tigers	16
Govett Asia	15
China Fund	12
Templeton Dragon	11

    a. Exactly one mutual fund having at least 20% of its assets invested in China.

    b. None of the mutual funds having at least 20% of their assets invested in China.

    c. Both of the mutual funds having at least 20% of their assets invested in China.

(Adapted from "Getting in the Door," *The Wall Street Journal*, April 30, 1998, p. R16.)

5.71 What binomial expression would you use to approximately evaluate the following expression?

$$(_{200}C_3 \cdot {}_{300}C_7)/{}_{500}C_{10}$$

5.72 According to Consumer Reports Travel Letter, which asked 840 travel agents about airline fares for 12 of the most popular routes for leisure travel, not all travel agents are providing their customers with the cheapest fare. For the airline route from Chicago to Santa Ana, only 50% of the agencies provided the cheapest fare.

    a. If a traveler contacted eight travel agencies, how many would you expect to provide the cheapest airfare for the Chicago to Santa Ana route?

    b. What is the standard deviation of the number of agencies that provide the cheapest airfare for this route assuming that eight travel agencies were contacted?

    c. What is the probability that none of the travel agencies from the eight randomly selected provide the cheapest airfare for this route? Would this be unusual?

    d. What assumptions are you making in answering parts a, b, and c?

(Source: "Playing 'Fare'," *Consumer Reports*, July 2001, p. 8.)

5.73 The most accurate golfing clubs reported to be sold by retailers are manufactured by Olimar, Callaway, Taylor Made, and Adams. Independent tests by golfing facilities demonstrated that Olimar manufactured the most accurate club. If a golfing professional were to randomly choose two of the four brands to recommend to golfers, what is the probability that at least one of the two recommended brands is an Olimar?

(Adapted from "Oversize Is Overrated," *USA Today*, June 12, 1998, p. 2B.)

5.74 In spring of 2001, a University of Virginia professor fed 1,800 student term papers into a computer program and found 122 that appeared to have been plagiarized. Many universities, including the University of Virginia, have strict honor codes. In fact, at this university violating the code means expulsion. Suppose that in a class section of 100 students, the teacher suspects that there are 10 papers that are plagiarized.

    a. If the professor were to randomly check 15 papers for plagiarism, what is the probability that the professor would catch exactly three papers that were plagiarized?

    b. Do a "what if" analysis by changing the number of papers that the professor randomly checked to 30 and rework part b. Compare this new probability to that obtained with only 15 papers randomly selected.

    c. What is the number of plagiarized papers that the professor would expect to find in parts a and b?

(Source: "Cheating Thrives on Campus, As Officials Turn Their Heads," *USA Today*, May 21, 2001, p. 13A.)

5.75 According to CAP Ventures, Inc., a leading consulting and market research firm, approximately 26% of all documents printed for business purposes, from in-house employee manuals to glossy marketing brochures, are thrown away without ever seeing the light of day. For example, in a run of 5,000 sales brochures, roughly 1,300 are expected to be lost due to damage or neglect or perhaps discarded because they are considered outdated.

a. Using a statistical computer package, find the probability that for 1,000 copies of a brochure, that no more than 250 are never read. (In Excel, click on **Paste Function ➤ Statistical > Binomdist**. In SPSS, click on **Transform ➤ Compute ➤ CDF.BINOM(q,n,p)**. In MINITAB, click on **Calc ➤ Probability Distributions ➤ Binomial**.)

b. Do a "what if" analysis in part (a) by using the proportion of copies never read to be .28, .30, and .32. Is the probability changing as much as you would have expected?

c. Do a "what if" analysis in part a by using the proportion of copies never read to be .24, .22, and .20. Do these probabilities seem reasonable to you?

(Source: "From Copies to Customized Business Solutions," *Forbes*, September 3, 2001, pp. 81–83.)

5.76 Many e-commerce sites find that the percentage of Web site visitors who actually make a final purchase is disappointingly small. The average percentage of all e-tailing sites is only about 5%. However, J.C. Penney's Web site has been averaging close to 10%. One problem that visitors to e-tailing sites often encounter is finding the product that they wish to purchase. One estimate of the number of clicks that it takes visitors to find their product is 10. However, after finding their product, Web site visitors frequently do not make the purchase.

a. What is the probability that at least 5 of 50 Web site visitors to J.C. Penney's Web site will actually make a purchase?

b. Do a "what if" analysis in part a by changing the probability that any one person will make a final purchase to be .13, .15, .20.

c. What is the probability that a Web site visitor takes more than 8 clicks to find the product that they wish to find? Assume that the average is 10 clicks. What distribution are you using to solve for this probability? Explain.

d. What is the standard deviation of the number of clicks it takes to find the product on the Web site in part c?

(Source: "Making the Sale," *The Wall Street Journal*, September 24, 2001, p. R6.)

5.77 To obtain a better idea of what plots of binomial probabilities look like, consider two binomial distributions, both with $n = 20$ and one with $p = .2$, and the other with $p = .8$. In Excel, fill column A with numbers from 0 to 20. In B1, put "=Binomdist(A1,20,.2,0)" to obtain the probability of a binomial random variable being equal to 0 when $n = 20$ and $p = .2$. Now fill column B (down through B21) with the probabilities. Repeat this process in column C to obtain the probabilities for a binomial random variable with $n = 20$ and $p = .8$. Now select the scatter plot from chart wizard to obtain the plot below.

a. Comment on the shape of each binomial distribution. If the probabilities for a binomial distribution with $p = .2$ are known, how can the probabilities for a binomial distribution with $p = .8$ be easily found.

b. Plot other binomial distributions with the probability of a success being p and also being $1 - p$. Comment on the shape of the graphs.

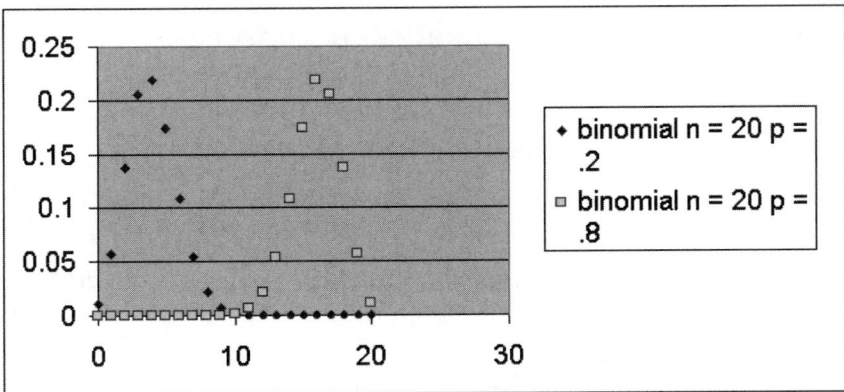

5.78 To obtain insight into how the shape of the Poisson distribution changes by varying the mean, consider four values for the mean of a Poisson distribution: 1, 4, 8, and 15. Starting in A2, fill column A with the numbers 0 through 25. Now in B1 put the value 1 (for the mean of the Poisson). In cell B2, put "=Poisson(A2,B$1,0)" and fill down to B26. Now put 4, 8, and 15 in cells C1, D1, and E1, respectively. Fill down through C26, D26, and E26, with the Poisson distribution just as for column B. Use the scatter plot from the chart wizard to obtain the graphs on the next page.

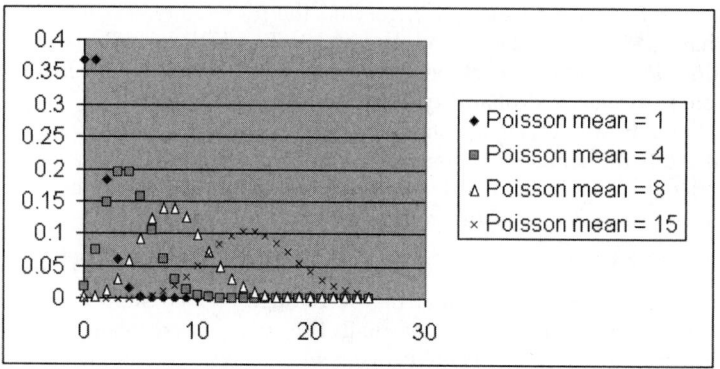

Comment on the shape of the Poisson distribution as the value of the mean changes. For which value of the mean would you say that the Poisson distribution appears to be most bell shaped? Repeat the plot of the graphs by assigning other values of the mean between 1 and 20. Simply change the values in B1, C1, D1, and E1, and watch the plots change shape.

Computer Exercises Using the Databases

Exercise 1—Appendix F

Generate 100 random numbers, and select a sample of 100 observations from the database. Consider the variable FAMLSIZE (family size). Let p represent the proportion of observations in your set of 100 observations in which the family size is no greater than 2. If you randomly select 10 observations (with replacement) from the 100 possible, what is $P[X \le 5]$, where X is the number of observations (out of 10) in which the family size is no greater than 2? What type of random variable is X?

Note: The MINITAB procedure here is

MTB > SAMPLE 10 FROM Cxx, PUT INTO Cyy;
SUBC > REPLACE.

where the 100 values of FAMLSIZE are in column Cxx and the 10 selected values are in column Cyy.

Exercise 2—Appendix F

Repeat Exercise 1, where 10 observations are selected without replacement.

Note: The MINITAB procedure here is the same as in Exercise 1, except the subcommand is omitted.

Exercise 3—Appendix F

Referring to Exercise 2, if you were to obtain samples of size 10 indefinitely, what would X be on the average? What is the standard deviation of this random variable?

Exercise 4—Appendix F

Estimate the proportion of homeowners in a randomly selected set of 100 observations. From this set of 100 observations, select with replacement a random set of 10 observations. Can this be considered a binomial experiment with $n = 10$ and p equal to the proportion of homeowners in the set of 100 observations? Estimate the probability that the number of homeowners in the set of 10 observations is greater than or equal to 5.

Exercise 5—Appendix F

Randomly select 200 observations from the database. From this set, estimate the proportion of observations in which the location of residence is in one of the northern sectors. From this set of observations, randomly select without replacement 8 observations. Find the probability that, in this sample of size 8, the residences of 4 or fewer observations are in the northern sectors. Can the binomial approximation be used? Why?

Exercise 6—Appendix G

Select 200 observations at random from the database. Let p be the proportion of companies with a positive net income. If you were randomly to select (with replacement) 15 observations from the 200 possible, what would be the probability of selecting at least nine companies with a positive net income?

Exercise 7—Appendix G

For the 200 observations in Exercise 6, let p equal the proportion of companies in which the number of employees exceeds 10,000. If you were randomly to select 15 observations (with replacement) from the 200 possible, what would be the probability of selecting at least seven companies in which the number of employees exceeds 10,000?

Insights from Statistics in Action

AACSB Accreditation: A Commitment to Excellence in Business Education

From surveys, assume that the following table represents the proportion of ratings by deans on their view of the importance of each of eight top competencies. That is, the proportions represent probabilities that a dean will respond on a scale of 1 = Strongly Agree to 5 = Strongly Disagree in response to the statement: Improvement in this competency is crucial to receiving AACSB accreditation.

Competency/Response	Strongly Agree	Agree	Neither Agree Nor Disagree	Disagree	Strongly Disagree
Communication skills	.40	.40	.16	.04	.00
Professional knowledge	.35	.30	.20	.12	.03
Critical thinking	.40	.30	.25	.03	.02
Problem solving	.30	.32	.23	.10	.05
Technology computer usage	.45	.25	.10	.16	.04
Knowledge and comprehension	.33	.28	.19	.15	.05
Global issues	.25	.35	.15	.10	.15
Professional integrity/ethics	.26	.22	.12	.30	.10

1. For the eight competencies listed above, what are the means and standard deviations? What two competencies have the highest means? What two competencies have the highest standard deviations? Are these what you would expect from viewing the probabilities presented in the table?

2. If 10 business schools were selected at random, what is the probability that at least five of the business school deans agree or strongly agree that improvement in technology and computer usage is crucial to their school receiving accreditation?

3. Suppose that 20 business schools were selected at random. What is the probability that at least 15 of these schools have deans that agree or strongly agree that improvement in communications skills is crucial to their school receiving accreditation?

4. From question 3, how many business schools would you expect to have deans that agree or strongly agree that improvement in communication skills is crucial to receiving accreditation at their school? What is the standard deviation?

5. For 20 business schools selected from Michigan, suppose it is known that 15 agree or strongly agree that improvement in the global issues competency is crucial to their business school receiving accreditation. If eight of these 20 business schools were selected at random, what is the probability that all eight schools agree or strongly agree that improvement in the global issues competency is crucial to their accreditation?

(Source: "The Relationship Between Student Evaluations of Teaching and Faculty Evaluations," *Journal of Education for Business*, vol. 76, issue 4, March/April 2001, pp. 4, 189; "Forces Driving Organizational Change: A Business School Perspective," *Journal of Education for Business*, vol. 75, issue 3, 2000, pp. 5, 133; "A Survey of Assessment Practices in Schools of Business," *Central Business Review*, vol. 19, no. 1, 2000, pp. 13–17.)

Appendix SPSS®

Chapter 5 Appendix: Data Analysis with SPSS

Determining Discrete Probabilities

Probabilities and cumulative probabilities can be calculated for binomial, hypergeometric, and Poisson distributions using SPSS. The following discussion will demonstrate how to construct the columns in the data window immediately following.

	x	cumbin	probbin	cumhyp	probhyp	cumpois	probpois
1	0	.000977	.000977	.095116	.095116	.135335	.135335
2	1	.010742	.009766	.363049	.267933	.406006	.270671
3	2	.054687	.043945	.681220	.318171	.676676	.270671
4	3	.171875	.117188	.890428	.209208	.857123	.180447
5	4	.376953	.205078	.974535	.084107	.947347	.090224
6	5	.623047	.246094	.996067	.021531	.983436	.036089
7	6	.828125	.205078	.999608	.003541	.995466	.012030
8	7	.945312	.117187	.999976	.000368	.998903	.003437
9	8	.989258	.043945	.999999	.000023	.999763	.000859
10	9	.999023	.009766	1.000000	.000001	.999954	.000191
11	10	1.000000	.000977	1.000000	.000000	.999992	.000038

Binomial Probabilities. Consider a binomial situation with $n = 10$ and $p = .5$. Begin by entering 0 through 10 in the first column of the data worksheet (shown above). After clicking on the **Variable View** tab, change the name of this variable to "x" and set the number of decimal places equal to zero. SPSS does not allow the direct calculation of "equal to" binomial probabilities (contained in Table A.1), only cumulative probabilities (contained in Table A.2). However, by first determining the cumulative probabilities, SPSS can easily calculate the "equal to" probabilities.

Click on **Transform ➤ Compute.** Enter the variable name "cumbin" in the **Target Variable** box. Find the function name CDF.BINOM(q,n,p) inside the function list box and double-click on it. Replace the question marks inside the **Numeric Expression** box as shown in the next window. Here, "q" refers to the name of the variable in the first column, "n" is the sample size, and "p" is the probability of a success on each trial. By clicking on **OK,** the column containing the cumulative binomial probabilities (cumbin) appears in the data window. Click on the **Variable View** tab and set the number of decimal places for this variable equal to six.

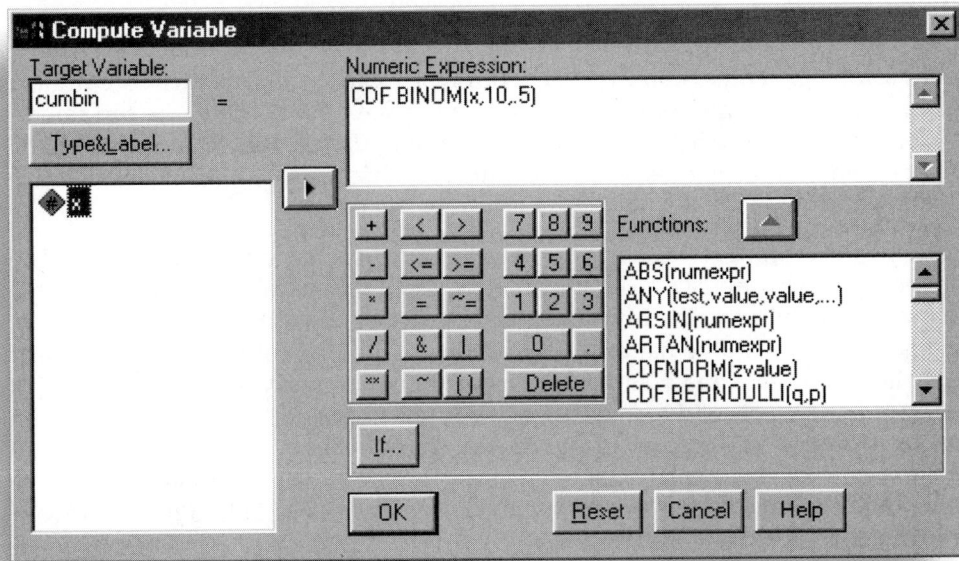

To create the "equal to" probabilities, click on **Transform ➤ Compute.** In the **Target Variable** box, enter "probbin" and inside the **Numeric Expression** box, enter "cumbin - lag(cumbin)." Click on **OK.** After entering the value from the top row of the cumbin column (i.e., .000977) into the top row of the probbin column, the third column containing the "equal to" binomial probabilities is now complete. Set the number of decimal places for the probbin variable equal to six.

Hypergeometric Probabilities. Consider a hypergeometric situation with $N = 100$, $n = 10$, and $k = 20$. Click on **Transform ➤ Compute.** Enter the variable name "cumhyp" in the **Target Variable** box. Find the function name CDF.HYPER (q,total,sample,hits) inside the function list box and double-click on it. Replace the question marks inside the **Numeric Expression** box as shown below. Here, "q" refers to the name of the variable in the first column, "total" is the population size (N), "sample" is the sample size (n), and "hits" refers to the number of successes in the population (k). By clicking on **OK,** the column containing the cumulative hypergeometric probabilities (cumhyp) appears in the data window. Click on the **Variable View** tab and set the number of decimal places for this variable equal to six.

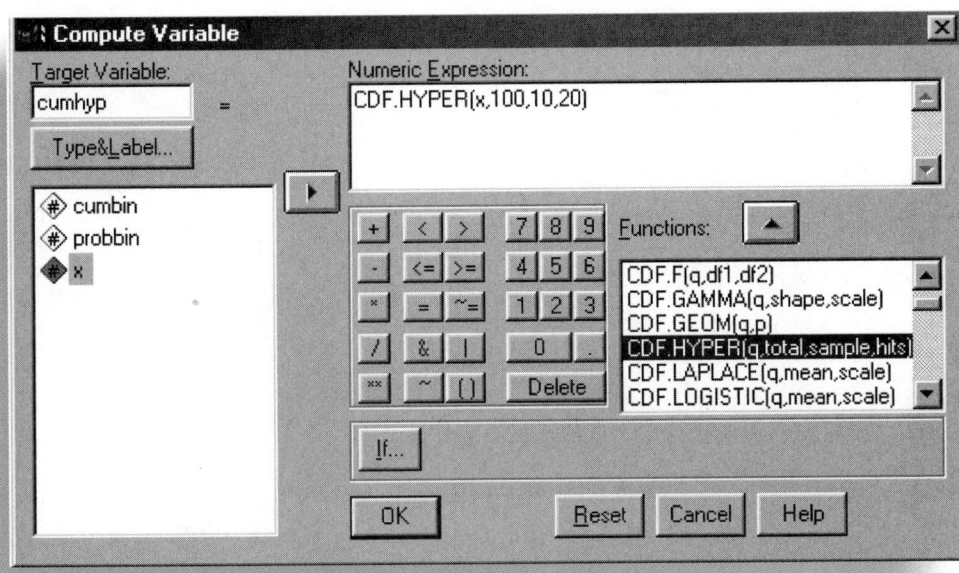

To create the "equal to" hypergeometric probabilities, click on **Transform ➤ Compute.** In the **Target Variable** box, enter "probhyp" and inside the **Numeric Expression** box, enter "cumhyp - lag(cumhyp)." Click on **OK.** After entering the value from the top row of the cumhyp column (i.e., .095116) into the top row of the probhyp column, the fifth column containing the "equal to" hypergeometric probabilities is now complete. Set the number of decimal places for this variable equal to six.

Poisson Probabilities. Consider a Poisson situation having a mean of 2.0. The preceding procedure can be used to determine both cumulative and "equal to" Poisson probabilities. The function to use here is CDF.POISSON(q,mean) where "q" is replaced with the name of the variable in the first column (x) and "mean" is replaced by the value 2. Enter "cumpois" in the **Target Variable** box and click on **OK.** The "equal to" Poisson probabilities are obtained (as before) by clicking on **Transform ➤ Compute.** In the **Target Variable** box, enter "probpois" and inside the **Numeric Expression** box, enter "cumpois - lag(cumpois)." Enter the value from the top row of the cumpois column (i.e., .135335) into the top row of the probpois column and set the number of decimal places for both columns equal to six. These two columns should agree with the corresponding two columns in the data window inside the first paragraph of this appendix.

On the CD . . .
Chapter 5 Appendix: Data Analysis with MINITAB

Continuous Probability Distributions X

Statistics in Action
Examining Unethical Behavior: More Fun Than Decent People Think Should Be Legal

Many assume the pursuit of profit is the reason for being in business. Some even assume it is a right. Upper-level managers are often faced with decisions that involve ethical considerations. For example, should a company purchase supplies at a discount price or pay full price for more environmentally responsible supplies? Company representatives have a responsibility to their customers to provide them with accurate information concerning, for example, pricing. At the same time, they have a responsibility to meet the profit goals of their organization. Suppose that in an effort to meet their organization's profit goals they quote less-competitive prices to buyers who use their firm as a sole source of supply than for buyers who have multiple supply sources. Is this an ethical problem? Balancing duties and responsibilities can be a challenge for aggressive managers. The scandal surrounding the mass shredding of Enron documents by Arthur Andersen, auditors for the bankrupt U.S. energy giant, revealed that senior executives cannot balance company duties with ethical responsibilities.

Surveys of U.S. business employees reveal that at least one in three workers observed behavior that violated the organization's ethics standards. One in eight business workers have, in fact, felt pressure to compromise their organization's ethics standards. Withholding needed information, using intimidating behavior toward other employees, and willfully misrepresenting information in reports are some of the

behaviors that ethical people would consider unacceptable. The vast amount of statistical data available to businesses creates the potential for misuse of statistics. An unethical person might use only selective data to make a point. A manager might want to ignore the validity of certain assumptions necessary for the proper use of a statistical procedure. Business personnel need to be aware of the ethical pitfalls that can occur even in the field of statistics.

Research examining ethical behavior indicates that business decisions vary by type of ethical situation. When an ethical issue is perceived as being very important, business professionals are more inclined to follow the business code of ethics. To measure ethical behavior, researchers have developed vignettes describing a situation in which a business decision is made. Respondents, who first read these vignettes, rate the scenario on an acceptable–unacceptable scale. For example, a simple vignette could explain a scenario in which a salesperson has a customer who is almost ready to sign a contract. To avoid further delays with the customer making a final decision, the salesperson falsely explains to the customer that someone else is interested in this same deal and, therefore, this opportunity will not last long. Although this case is clearly deceptive, it appears to be a common business practice.

Chapter 5 introduced you to discrete random variables. Such variables, when observed, produce a countable number of distinct values. In this chapter, continuous random variables will be studied. These random variables are often used in measurements and can assume any value across a range of numbers. In examining the ethical behavior of business professionals, variables, such as the proportion of vignettes considered ethically acceptable and scores used to rate an individual's ethical perception, are considered *continuous variables*. When you have completed this chapter, you will be able to

- Recognize the distribution of normally distributed data as well as uniformly and exponentially distributed data.
- Standardize data by forming the corresponding z values.
- Determine the probability of a continuous random variable being between two specified values.

A Look Back/Introduction

After we discussed the use of descriptive statistics, we introduced you to the area of uncertainty by using probability concepts and random variables. Random variables offer you a convenient method of describing the various outcomes of an experiment and their corresponding probabilities.

When each value of the random variable as well as its probability of occurring can be listed, the random variable is discrete. The other type of random variable, a continuous random variable, can assume any value over a particular range. Continuous random variables include such variables as $X =$ height, $X =$ weight, and $X =$ time. For such variables it is impossible to list all values of X, yet you can still make probability statements regarding X if you can make certain assumptions about the type of population.

In statistics, making decisions from sample information is called **statistical inference**. In subsequent chapters, we will develop a formal set of rules to offer you as a guide in making statistical decisions. Making such a decision typically involves one or more assumptions about the population from which the sample was obtained. One such assumption, widely used in statistics, is that the data came from a normal population, which means that you are dealing with a normal random variable.

6.1

CONTINUOUS RANDOM VARIABLES

The concept of a continuous random variable was introduced in Chapter 5. What distinguishes a discrete random variable from one that is continuous is the presence of *gaps* in the possible values for a discrete random variable. To illustrate, $X =$ total of two dice is a discrete random variable; there are many gaps over the

FIGURE

6.1

Finding a
probability for a
continuous
random variable.

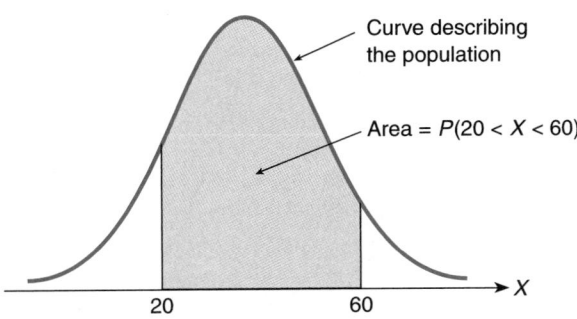

Curve describing
the population

Area = $P(20 < X < 60)$

20   60 X

range of possible values, and a value of 10.4, for example, is not possible. One can list the possible values of a discrete variable, along with the probability that each value will occur.

Determining probabilities for a continuous random variable is quite different. For such a variable, any value over a specific range is possible. Therefore we are unable to list all the possible values of this variable. Probability statements for a continuous random variable (such as X) are not concerned with specific values of X (such as the probability that X will equal 50) but rather deal with probabilities over a range of values, such as the probability that X is *between* 40 and 50, *greater than* 65, or *less than* 20, for example.

Such probabilities can be determined by first making an assumption regarding the nature of the population involved. We assume that the population can be described by a curve having a particular shape—such as normal, uniform, or exponential. Once this curve is specified, a probability can be determined by finding the corresponding area under this curve. As an illustration, Figure 6.1 shows a particular curve (called the normal curve) for which the probability of observing a value of X between 20 and 60 is the area under this curve between these two values. *The entire range of probability is covered using such a curve, since, for any continuous random variable, the total area under the curve is equal to 1.*

The following sections examine the normal, uniform, and exponential distributions, since these are the most widely encountered random variables in practice. The graphs and descriptive statistics discussed in the previous chapters can help determine if one of these random variables might be appropriate for a particular situation. If a histogram of the sample data appears nearly flat, the population might be represented by a uniform random variable. If the histogram is symmetric with decreasing tails at each end, a normal random variable may be in order. If the sample histogram steadily decreases from left to right, the population of all possible values perhaps can be described using an exponential random variable. In the first two cases, the mean and median should be nearly equal (the population is symmetric), providing a skewness measure near zero. For the exponential case, the median should be less than the mean with a corresponding positive measure of skewness.

6.2   NORMAL RANDOM VARIABLES

The normal distribution is the most important of all the continuous distributions. You will find that this distribution plays a key role in the application of many statistical techniques. When attempting to make an assertion about a population,

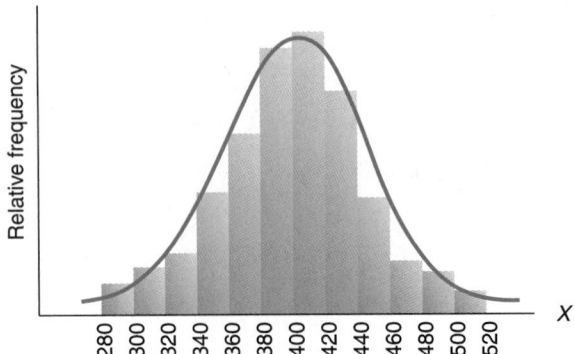

FIGURE

6.2

Histogram of 200 Everglo light bulb lifetimes (in hours). The curve represents all possible values (population). The histogram represents the sample (200 values).

oftentimes a major assumption (based on sample evidence) is that the population has a normal distribution.

When discussing measurements such as height, weight, thickness, or time, the resulting population of all measurements often can be assumed to have a probability distribution that is normal if evidence obtained from the sample supports this assumption.

A histogram constructed from a large *sample* of such measurements can help determine whether this assumption is realistic. Assume, for example, that data were collected on the length of life of 200 high-intensity Everglo light bulbs. Let X represent the length of life (in hours) of an Everglo bulb. One thing we are interested in is the *shape* of the distribution of the 200 lifetimes. Where are they centered? Are they symmetric? The easiest way to approach such questions is to construct a histogram of the 200 values, as illustrated in Figure 6.2. This histogram indicates that the data are nearly symmetric and are centered at approximately 400.

The curve in Figure 6.2 is said to be a **normal curve** because of its shape. A normal curve is characterized by a *symmetric, bell-shaped appearance*, with tails that "die out" rather quickly. We use such curves to represent the *assumed population* of all possible values. This example contained 200 values observed in a *sample*. Consequently:

1. A histogram represents the shape of the sample data.

2. A smooth curve represents the assumed shape (distribution) of the population.

If all possible values of a variable X follow an assumed normal curve, then X is said to be a **normal random variable,** and the population is **normally distributed.**

When you assume that a particular population follows a normal distribution, you assume that X, an observation randomly obtained from this population, is a normal random variable. Based on the histogram in Figure 6.2, it appears to be a reasonable assumption that the smooth curve describing the population of *all* Everglo bulbs can be approximated using a normal curve centered at 400 hours. Therefore, we will assume that X is a normal random variable, centered at 400 hours.

There are two numbers used to describe a normal curve (distribution); they tell where the curve is centered and how wide it is. The center of a normal curve is called the *mean* and is represented by the symbol μ (mu). The width of a normal curve can be described using the *standard deviation*, which is represented by the symbol σ (sigma). These descriptions are illustrated in Figure 6.3, which shows the normal curve representing the lifetime of Everglo light bulbs. Another way of stating this situation is: X is a normal random variable with $\mu = 400$ hours and $\sigma = 50$ hours. Notice that the units of μ and σ are the same as the units of the data (hours).

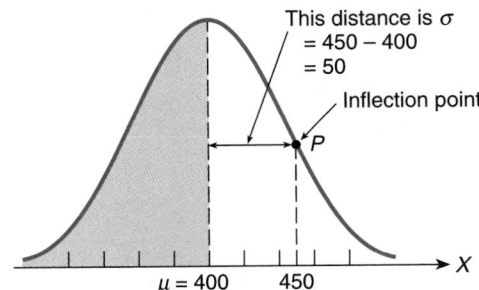

FIGURE

6.3

Distribution of the lifetime of Everglo bulbs showing the mean ($\mu = 400$), the standard deviation ($\sigma = 50$), and the inflection point (P).

In Figure 6.3, there is a point P on the normal curve. Above this point P, the curve resembles a bowl that is upside down, and below P the curve is "right side up." In calculus, this point is referred to as an *inflection point*. The distance between vertical lines through μ and P is the value of σ.

Because μ and σ represent the location and spread of the normal distribution, they are called *parameters*. The parameters are used to define the distribution completely. The values of μ and σ of a normal population are all you need to distinguish it from all other normal populations that have the same bell shape but different location and/or variability. The values of the parameters must be specified in order to make probability statements regarding X. As a result, there are infinitely many normal curves (populations), one for each pair of values of μ and σ.

In Chapter 5, we discussed the mean of (say) 10 observations of the random variable X, written as $\bar{X}$. If you were to observe X indefinitely, then you could obtain the mean of the population, μ. The same concept applies to continuous random variables; for the Everglo example, $\bar{X}$ represents the mean of the 200 bulbs (the sample) and μ is the mean of all Everglo bulbs (the population).

Mean		Standard Deviation	
Sample	**Population**	**Sample**	**Population**
$\bar{X}$	μ	s	σ
the average of the sample	the average of the population	the standard deviation of the sample	the standard deviation of the population

In our Everglo example, the average lifetime of all bulbs is *assumed* to be $\mu = 400$ hours. The standard deviation of the population, σ, just like s, is a measure of *variability*. The larger σ is, the more variation (jumping around) we would see if X were observed indefinitely. For both the sample and the population, the square of the standard deviation is referred to as the variance. It is another measure of the variability of X. The *variance* of a random variable, X, is represented by σ^2.

Consider whether the sample average ($\bar{X}$) of the 200 values in our example is the *same* as μ. It is not. Do not confuse the average lifetime of all light bulbs (μ) with the average lifetime of just 200 bulbs ($\bar{X}$). This is an important distinction in statistics. However, if our assumed normal distribution (with $\mu = 400$ and $\sigma = 50$) is correct, then $\bar{X}$ most often will be "close to" μ. We examine this again in Chapter 7.

The curve in Figure 6.3 is an illustration of a normal random variable with a mean of 400 hours and a standard deviation of 50 hours. We can compare normal curves that may differ in mean, standard deviation, or both. The normal curves in Figure 6.4 indicate that, on the average, males are taller than females. The mean of the male curve is to the right of the mean of the female curve. The male heights "jump around" about as much as female heights. In other words, there is about the same amount of *variation* in male and female heights because the standard deviation of each curve is the same; that is, each curve is equally wide.

6.4

Two normal curves
with unequal
means and equal
standard
deviations.

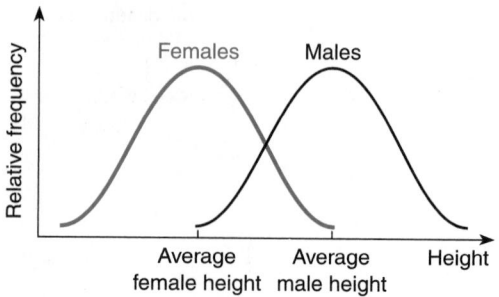

6.5

Two normal curves
with equal means
and unequal
standard
deviations.

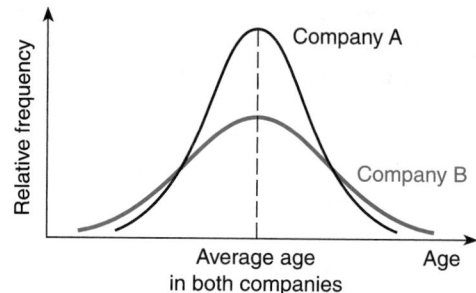

In Figure 6.5, the two normal curves represent the ages of the employees at two large companies. It appears that:

1. The average age of employees for the two companies is the same.

2. The ages in Company B have more variability. This simply means that there are more old people and more young people in Company B than in Company A.

6.3   DETERMINING A PROBABILITY FOR A NORMAL RANDOM VARIABLE

So you have assumed that the lifetime of an Everglo light bulb is a normal random variable with $\mu = 400$ and $\sigma = 50$. Now what? This brings us back to the subject of probability. Before we describe probabilities for a normal random variable, consider one important property of *any* normal curve (or of any curve representing a continuous random variable, for that matter), namely, that the total area under the curve is 1 (see Figure 6.6). When we described the normal curve as bell-shaped, we also determined that it was symmetrical. If the halves are identical, then the probability above the mean (μ) is equal to .5 and is the same as the probability below the mean. Thus, in Figure 6.3 the shaded area is equal to the nonshaded area under the curve.

Returning to the Everglo bulb example, what percentage of the time will the burnout time, X, be less than 360? This probability is written as

$$P(X < 360)$$

We discuss how to determine this area (a simple procedure) later in the chapter, but for now, just remember that when dealing with a normal random variable,

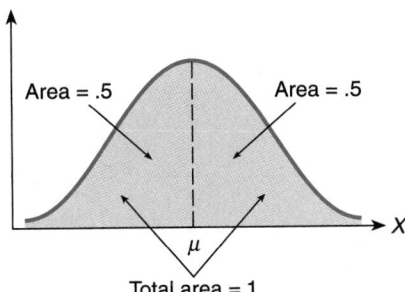

FIGURE

6.6

Area under a
normal curve.

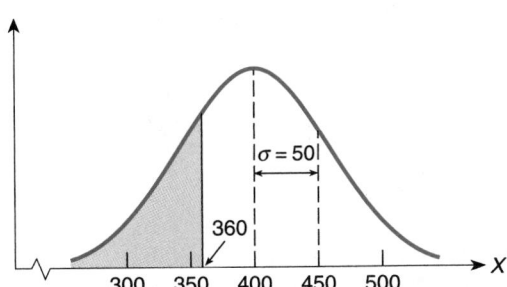

FIGURE

6.7

Normal curve for
Everglo light bulbs
showing
$P(X < 360)$. The
shaded area is the
percentage of time
that X will be less
than 360.
(X = lifetime of
Everglo bulb.)

a *probability* is represented by an *area* under the corresponding normal curve. The value of $P(X < 360)$ is illustrated in Figure 6.7. It appears that roughly 20% of the total area has been shaded, so we can conclude that (1) roughly 20% of the Everglo bulbs will burn out in less than 360 hours, and (2) the probability that X is less than 360 is approximately .2.

6.4

FINDING AREAS UNDER THE STANDARD NORMAL CURVE

We begin our discussion by finding the area under a special normal curve—namely, one that is centered at 0 ($\mu = 0$) and has a standard deviation of 1 ($\sigma = 1$). This random variable is typically represented by the letter Z and is referred to as the **standard normal random variable.** As Figure 6.8 demonstrates, Z is as likely to be negative as positive; that is, $P(Z \le 0) = P(Z \ge 0) = .5$. Although you probably never will observe a random variable like Z in practice, it is a useful normal random variable. In fact, an area under *any* normal curve (as in Figure 6.7) can be determined by finding the corresponding area under the standard normal curve.

To derive the area under the standard normal curve requires the use of integral calculus. Unfortunately, the integral of the function describing the standard normal curve does not have a simple (closed form) expression. By using excellent approximations of this integral, however, we can tabulate these areas—see Table A.4 and Figure 6.9.

For example, suppose we want to determine the probability that a standard normal random variable will be between 0 and 1.62. This is written as

$$P(0 < Z < 1.62)$$

FIGURE

6.8

Standard normal curve.

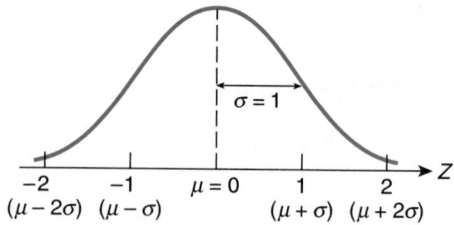

FIGURE

6.9

Shaded area = .4474, from Table A.4.

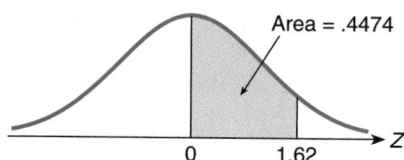

The value of this probability is obtained from Table A.4, which contains the area under the curve between the mean of zero and the particular value of Z. The far left column of Table A.4 identifies the first decimal place for Z, and you read across the table to obtain the second decimal place.

In our example, we find the intersection between 1.6 on the left and .02 on the top, because Z = 1.62. Look at Table A.4; the value .4474 is the *area* between 0 and 1.62. In other words, the probability that Z will lie between 0 and 1.62 is .4474.

You can begin to see why it is a good idea to sketch the curve and shade in the area when dealing with normal random variables. It gives you a clear picture of what the question is asking and cuts down on mistakes.

EXAMPLE

6.1

What is the probability that Z will be greater than 1.62?

Solution We wish to find $P(Z > 1.62)$. Examine Figure 6.10. The area under the right half of the Z curve is .5, so, using our value from Table A.4, the desired area here is

$$.5 - .4474 = .0526$$

So the probability that Z will exceed 1.62 is .0526.

What if we wish to know the probability that Z is equal to a particular value, such as $P(Z = 1.62)$? There is no area under the curve corresponding to Z = 1.62, so

$$P(Z = 1.62) = 0$$

In fact,

$$P(Z = \text{any value}) = 0$$

One nice thing about this fact is that $P(Z \geq 1.62)$ is the *same* as $P(Z > 1.62)$ (that is, .0526). So putting the equal sign on the inequality ($\geq$ or $\leq$) has *no* effect on the resulting probability.

By looking at the Z curve in Figure 6.11, you can see that

$$P(Z < 1.62) = .5 + .4474 = .9474$$

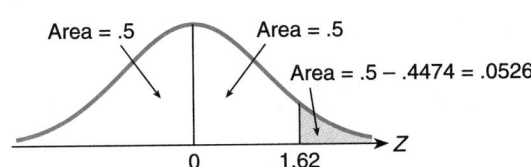

FIGURE

6.10

The shaded area represents the probability that Z will be greater than 1.62 [$P(Z > 1.62)$].

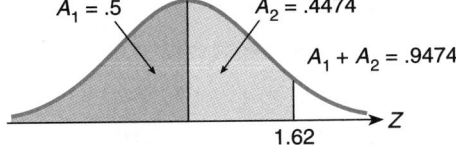

FIGURE

6.11

Area under the Z curve for $P(Z < 1.62)$.

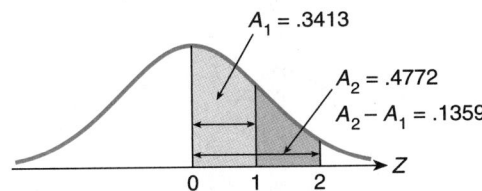

FIGURE

6.12

Area under the Z curve for $P(1.0 < Z < 2.0)$.

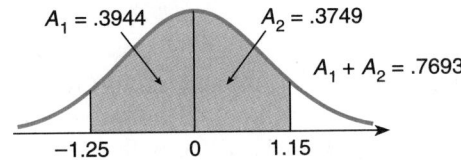

FIGURE

6.13

Area under the Z curve for $P(-1.25 < Z < 1.15)$.

As before, this also is $P(Z \leq 1.62)$.

Figure 6.12 shows $P(1.0 < Z < 2.0)$ (areas from Table A.4). We see that

$$P(1.0 < Z < 2.0) = P(0 < Z < 2.0) - P(0 < Z \leq 1.0)$$

$$= .4772 - .3413$$

$$= .1359$$

By subtracting the two areas, we find that the probability that Z will lie between 1.0 and 2.0 is .1359.

We use Figure 6.13 and Table A.4 to determine $P(-1.25 < Z < 1.15)$:

$$P(-1.25 < Z < 1.15) = P(-1.25 < Z < 0) + P(0 < Z < 1.15)$$

$$= A_1 + A_2$$

Using the symmetry of the Z curve and Figure 6.14, the area of A_1 is the same as $P(0 < Z < 1.25)$ and thus is .3944. The area of A_2, from Table A.4, is .3749. So we add A_1 and A_2:

$$.3944 + .3749 = .7693$$

FIGURE

6.14

Z curve for
$P(0 < Z < 1.25) =$
$P(-1.25 < Z < 0)$.

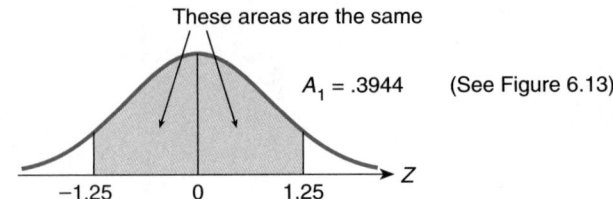

FIGURE

6.15

Area under the
Z curve for
$P(Z < -1.45)$.

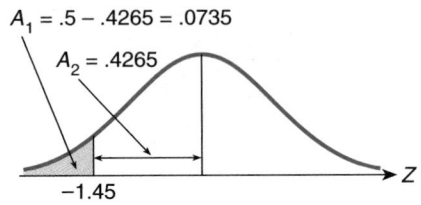

FIGURE

6.16

Value of Z having
a right-tailed area
of .03.

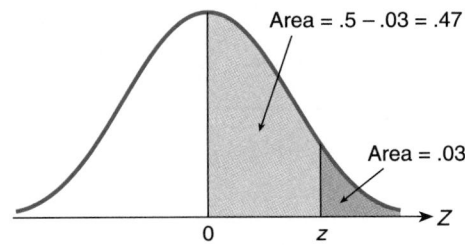

Finally, we can determine $P(Z < -1.45)$ using Figure 6.15. This can be written as $P(Z < 0) - P(-1.45 < Z < 0)$, that is, $.5 - A_2$. Using the symmetry of the Z curve, the area between 0 and -1.45 is $A_2 = .4265$ (from Table A.4). As a result, Z will be less than (or equal to) -1.45 approximately 7.35% of the time.

Finding the Z Value for a Specified Area. This is the reverse of what we have discussed so far. Here, you will be given the area and asked to determine the value of Z having this specified area. For example, for what value of Z (say, z) is the following statement true?

$$P(Z \geq z) = .03$$

The value of z is the one having a right-tailed area (due to the $\geq$ in this statement) of .03. This is illustrated in Figure 6.16. The value of z having a right tail of .03 is the value of z having a shaded area in Table A.4 of $.5 - .03 = .47$. By examining this table, we see that the value closest to .47 is .4699 (belonging to 1.88). Consequently, $z = 1.88$.

Another example: For what value of Z (say, z) is the following statement true?

$$P(Z \leq z) = .2$$

This is a left-tailed area of .2 due to the $\leq$ (see Figure 6.17). The z having this left-tailed area is the negative of the z having a shaded area in Table A.4 of $.5 - .2 = .3$. Examining this table, we see that the value closest to .3 is .2995, belonging to .84. We know that z is negative because it is to the left of zero, and so $z = -.84$.

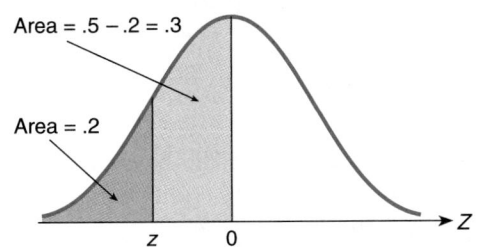

FIGURE

6.17

Value of Z having
a left-tailed area
of .2.

☒ Exercises 6.1–6.10

Understanding the Mechanics

6.1 Draw a normal curve with the following values for μ and σ.
  a. $\mu = 0, \sigma = 1$
  b. $\mu = 4, \sigma = 1$
  c. $\mu = 4, \sigma = 3$
  d. $\mu = -4, \sigma = 3$

6.2 Find the area under the standard normal distribution between the following Z values.
  a. $Z = 0$ and $Z = 1$
  b. $Z = 0$ and $Z = 2$
  c. $Z = 0$ and $Z = .55$
  d. $Z = 0$ and $Z = -1.52$

6.3 For a random variable that has a standard normal distribution, find the following probabilities.
  a. The probability that the random variable is between -2 and 0.
  b. The probability that the random variable is between -1.66 and -1.00.
  c. The probability that the random variable is between -1.15 and 2.15.

6.4 Find the following probabilities. Sketch the corresponding area.
  a. $P(0 \leq Z \leq .5)$
  b. $P(Z \leq .5)$
  c. $P(Z \leq -.5)$
  d. $P(Z \geq .5)$
  e. $P(-.5 \leq Z \leq .5)$

6.5 For a standard normal random variable Z, what is the probability that:
  a. Z is less than 1.23.
  b. Z is less than or equal to 1.23.
  c. Z is at least -1.23.
  d. Z is between the mean and 1.96.
  e. Z is less than -1.5 or greater than .62.

6.6 Find the value of z for the following probability statements, and sketch the corresponding area.
  a. $P(0 \leq Z \leq z) = .4901$
  b. $P(z \leq Z \leq 0) = .2324$
  c. $P(Z \leq z) = .8888$
  d. $P(Z \geq z) = .2090$
  e. $P(Z \geq z) = .7910$

6.7 Find the value of z for the following probability statements, and sketch the corresponding area.
  a. $P(-1.0 \leq Z \leq z) = .6898$
  b. $P(1.0 \leq Z \leq z) = .0072$
  c. $P(-2.0 \leq Z \leq z) = .0164$
  d. $P(-2.0 \leq Z \leq z) = .9544$
  e. $P(z \leq Z \leq 2.0) = .9544$

Applying the New Concepts

6.8 An educational testing service administers a national test to measure the reading comprehension of third-grade students. Only standardized scores are reported. The scores are approximately normally distributed. The testing service classifies scores above the 90th percentile as outstanding, between the 70th and 90th percentile as above average, between the 30th percentile and 70th percentile as average, between the 10th percentile and the 30th percentile as below average, and below the 10th percentile as poor. Find the z-scores corresponding to the 90th, 70th, 30th, and 10th percentiles.

6.9 A production manager uses z values to identify observations that appear to be unusually large or small. The manager identifies a z value as being unusually large if the $P(Z > z) < .01$. A z value is considered to be unusually small if $P(Z < z) < .01$. (To use the cumulative probability function in Excel, click on **Paste Function,** then click on **Statistical ➤ NORMSDIST(z).** In SPSS, click on **Transform ➤ Compute ➤ CDF.NORMAL(q,mean, stddev)** and in MINITAB, click on **Calc ➤ Probability Distributions ➤ Normal** and select cumulative distribution.)
  a. Is a value of z equal to 2.0 considered unusually large?
  b. Is a value of z equal to 3.4 considered unusually large?
  c. Is a value of z equal to -1.8 considered unusually small?
  d. Is a value of z equal to -3.8 considered unusually small?

6.10 A researcher represents outcomes from an experiment using z values. The researcher is interested in the z values that correspond to the 50th, 75th, and 90th percentiles. Find these z values. (In Excel, click on **Paste Function,** then click on **Statistical ➤ NORMINV.** In SPSS, click on **Transform ➤ Compute ➤ IDF.NORMAL(p,mean,stddev)** and in MINITAB, click on **Calc ➤ Probability Distributions ➤ Normal** and then select inverse cumulative probability.)

6.5

AREAS UNDER ANY NORMAL CURVE

Take another look at the histogram of the 200 Everglo light bulb lifetimes in Figure 6.2. A normal curve with $\mu = 400$ hours and $\sigma = 50$ hours was used to describe the population of *all* Everglo lifetimes. So $X =$ Everglo lifetime is a normal random variable with $\mu = 400$ and $\sigma = 50$.

What happens to the shape of the data if we take each of the 200 lifetimes in this example and subtract 400 (that is, subtract μ)? As you can see in Figure 6.18, the histogram (and corresponding normal curve) is merely "shifted" to the left by 400. It resembles the normal curve for X, except the "new" mean is 0. The random variable defined by $Y = X - 400$ has these characteristics:

- It is a normal random variable.
- It has a mean equal to zero.
- It has a standard deviation equal to that of X, that is, 50.

Figure 6.19 shows what happens to the shape of 200 Y values if each of them is *divided* by 50 (that is, by σ). Notice the horizontal axis in the histogram and the corresponding normal curve. The resulting normal curve resembles a normal curve with a mean of 0 and a standard deviation equal to 1.

Thus, if X is a normal random variable with mean 400 and standard deviation 50, then the random variable defined by

$$Z = \frac{X - 400}{50}$$

FIGURE

6.18

Histogram
obtained by
subtracting $\mu = 400$
(compare with
Figure 6.2).

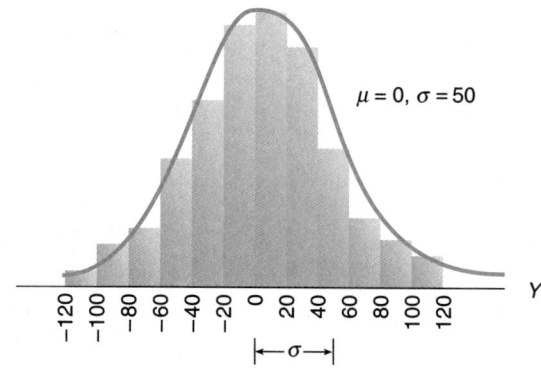

FIGURE

6.19

Histogram
obtained by
subtracting μ and
dividing by σ
(compare with
Figures 6.2
and 6.18).

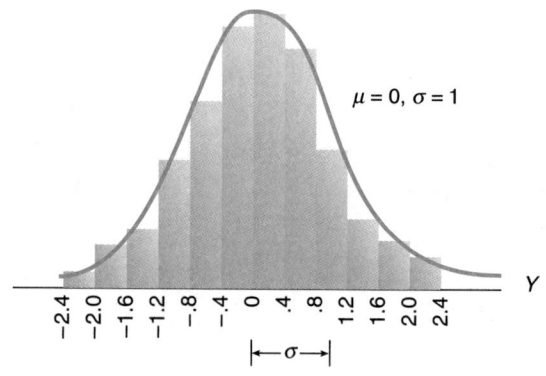

has these characteristics:

- It is a normal random variable.
- It has a mean equal to zero.
- It has a standard deviation equal to 1.

In general, for *any normal* random variable X,

$$Z = \frac{X - \mu}{\sigma}$$

is a **standard normal random variable.** This procedure of subtracting μ and dividing by σ is referred to as **standardizing** the normal random variable X. *It allows us to determine probabilities for any normal random variable by first standardizing it and then using Table A.4. So the standard normal distribution turns out to be much more important than you might have expected!*

E X A M P L E

6.2

The normal curve in Figure 6.7 represented the lifetime of all Everglo bulbs, with $\mu = 400$ hours and $\sigma = 50$ hours. What percentage of the bulbs will burn out in less than 360 hours? Or, put another way, what is the probability that any particular bulb will last less than 360 hours?

Solution

This probability is written as

$$P(X < 360)$$

This random variable is continuous, so $P(X < 360) = P(X \le 360)$. To determine the probability, you need to standardize this variable:*

$$P(X < 360) = P\left(\frac{X - 400}{50} < \frac{360 - 400}{50} \right)$$
$$= P(Z < -.8)$$

where $Z = (X - 400)/50$ (Figure 6.20).

Earlier, by examining Figure 6.7, we estimated this area to be roughly 20%. The actual area, from Figure 6.20, is .2119; that is, it is 21.19% of the total area. The conclusion here is that

$$P(X < 360) = .2119$$

and so 21% of all Everglo bulbs will have a lifetime of less than 360 hours.

Interpreting Z

What does a Z value of $-.8$ imply in Example 6.2? It simply means that 360 is .8 standard deviations to the left of the mean (Z is negative). So

$$\mu - .8(\sigma) = 400 - .8(50) = 360$$

Recall that a z-score was defined in exactly the same way in Chapter 3 using a sample mean ($\overline{X}$) and standard deviation (s). In this chapter, we use the population mean (μ) and standard deviation (σ). In general:

1. A *positive* value of Z designates how many standard deviations (σ) X is to the *right* of the mean (μ).

2. A *negative* value of Z designates how many standard deviations X is to the *left* of the mean.

---

*Since 400 is subtracted from *both* sides of the inequality and *both* sides are divided by 50, the events described by the original inequality $P(X < 360)$ and the standardized inequality $P(Z < -.8)$ are the same.

FIGURE
6.20

Compare the areas for (a) the *X* and (b) the *Z* normal curves to find *P*(*X* < 360).

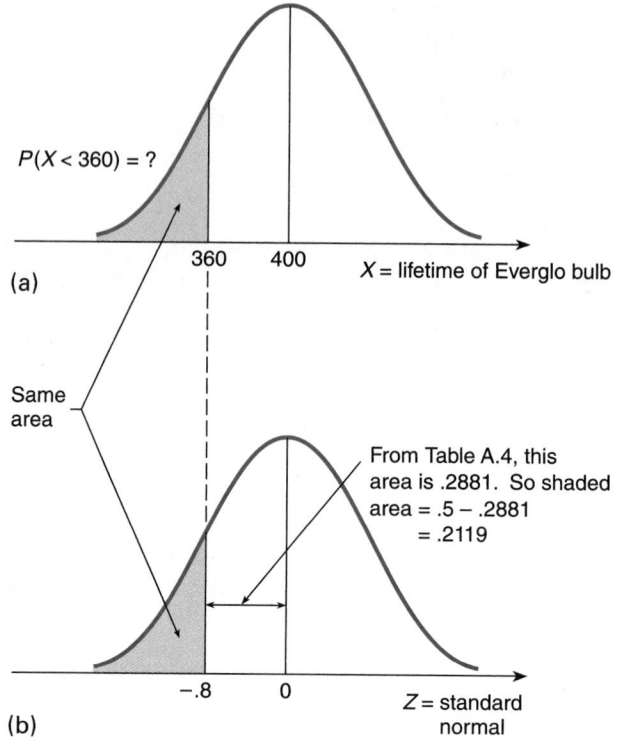

$P(X < 360) = ?$

360   400   *X* = lifetime of Everglo bulb

(a)

Same area

From Table A.4, this area is .2881. So shaded area = .5 − .2881 = .2119

−.8   0   *Z* = standard normal

(b)

EXAMPLE
6.3

The funds dispensed daily by an automatic teller machine (ATM) in a Denver grocery store are believed to be normally distributed with a mean of $3,700 and a standard deviation of $625. The machine is programmed to notify the store manager if the daily dollar volume is very low (less than or equal to $2,000) or unusually high (greater than or equal to $5,000). What percentage of the time will the daily dollar volume *not* be in either of these two conditions?

Solution   This probability can be written as

$$P(2000 < X < 5000)$$

Using the standardization procedure:

$$P(2000 < X < 5000) = P\left(\frac{2000 - 3700}{625} < \frac{X - 3700}{625} < \frac{5000 - 3700}{625} \right)$$

$$= P(-2.72 < Z < 2.08)$$

where Z once again represents the *standardized* normal random variable, which for this example is defined by

$$Z = \frac{X - 3700}{625}$$

Refer to Table A.4 and Figure 6.21 and note that the shaded areas in Figure 6.21(a) and (b) are both equal to .4967 + .4812 = .9779. As a result, the manager can expect no notification of unusual activity approximately 98% of the time.
  Also note two other values:

1. The value of $5,000 is 2.08 standard deviations to the right of the mean, since Z = 2.08 and 5000 = 3700 + (2.08)(625).

2. The value of $2,000 is 2.72 standard deviations to the left of the mean, since Z = −2.72 and 2000 = 3700 − (2.72)(625).

FIGURE

6.21

(a) The probability that X is between $2000 and $5000.
(b) The probability that Z is between −2.72 and 2.08.

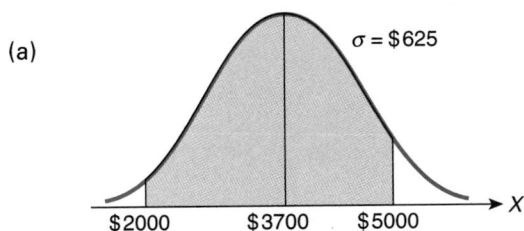

(a)

$\sigma = \$625$

$2000 \quad \$3700 \quad \$5000 \qquad X$

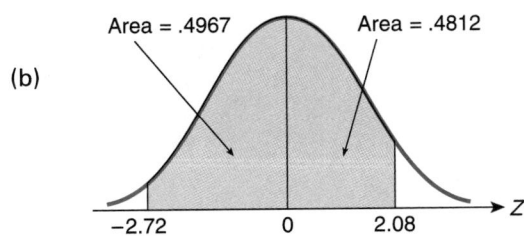

(b)

Area = .4967   Area = .4812

−2.72   0   2.08 Z

EXAMPLE

6.4

Actuarial scientists in an insurance company formulate insurance policies that will be both profitable and marketable. For a particular policy, the lifetimes of the policyholders follow a normal distribution with $\mu = 66.2$ years and $\sigma = 4.4$ years. One of the options with this policy is to receive a payment following the 65th birthday and a payment every five years thereafter.

1. What percentage of policyholders will receive at least one payment using this option?

2. What percentage will receive two or more payments?

3. What percentage will receive exactly two payments?

Solution 1

The normal curve for the policyholder lifetimes is shown in Figure 6.22. To receive at least one payment, the policyholder must live beyond 65 years of age. So we need to determine (see Figure 6.23):

$$P(X > 65) = P[(X - 66.2)/4.4 > (65 - 66.2)/4.4]$$
$$= P(Z > -.27) = .1064 + .5$$
$$= .6064$$

So nearly 61% of the policyholders will receive at least one payment.

Solution 2

Because the policyholder receives a payment every five years, he or she will receive two or more payments provided he or she lives to be older than 70 years of age. Thus the probability of two or more payments is determined by (see Figure 6.24):

$$P(X > 70) = P[(X - 66.2)/4.4 > (70 - 66.2)/4.4]$$
$$= P(Z > .86) = .5 - .3051$$
$$= .1949$$

Thus, 19.5% of the policyholders will survive long enough to collect two payments.

Solution 3

To receive exactly two payments, the policyholder must live longer than 70 years and less than 75 years. This probability is

$$P(70 < X < 75)$$

229

Using the same standardization procedure (see Figure 6.25):

$$P(70 < X < 75) = P[(70 - 66.2)/4.4 < (X - 66.2)/4.4 < (75 - 66.2)/4.4]$$

$$= P(.86 < Z < 2.00)$$

$$= .4772 - .3051 = .1721$$

So 17.21% of the policyholders will receive exactly two payments.

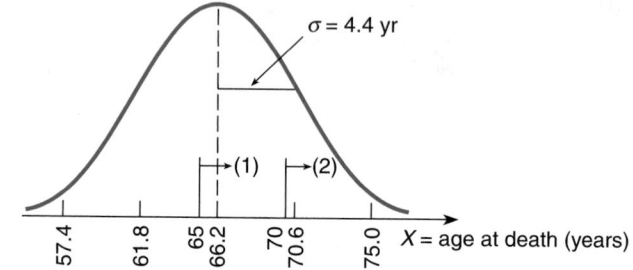

FIGURE

6.22

The normal curve for policyholder lifetimes. X = age at death (in years).

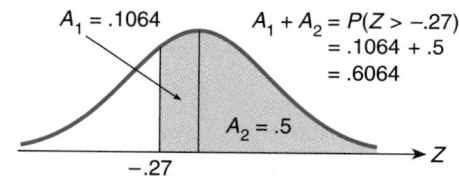

FIGURE

6.23

Z curve for $P(Z > -.27)$.

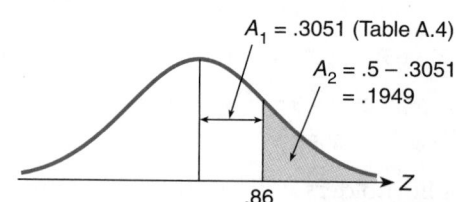

FIGURE

6.24

Z curve for $P(Z > .86)$.

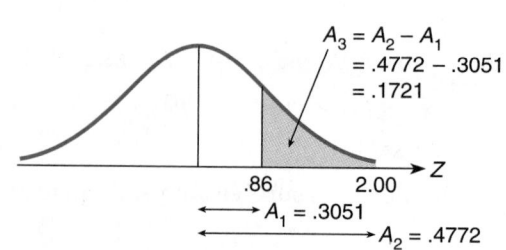

FIGURE

6.25

Z curve for $P(.86 < Z < 2.00)$.

Applications Where the Area Under a Normal Curve Is Provided

Another twist to dealing with normal random variables is a situation where you are given the area under the normal curve and asked to determine the corresponding value of the variable. This is a common application of a normal random variable. For example, the manufacturer of a product may want to determine a warranty period during which the product will be replaced if it becomes defective, so that at most 5% of the items are returned during this period. Or, in a grocery store on any given day, the demand for a freshly made food item may or may not exceed the supply. The owner may want to determine how much to supply each day, such that the demand (a normal random variable) will exceed this value 10% of the time (in other words, the customers will be disappointed no more than 10% of the time).

EXAMPLE 6.5

Referring to Example 6.2, after how many hours will 80% of the Everglo bulbs burn out? Recall that $\mu = 400$ and $\sigma = 50$.

Solution

The first step here is to sketch this curve [Figure 6.26(a)] and estimate the value of X (say x_0) so that

$$P(X < x_0) = .8$$

Because .8 is larger than .5, x_0 must lie to the *right* of 400.

Next, find the point on a standard normal (Z) curve such that the area to the left is also .8 [Figure 6.26(b)]. Using Table A.4, the area between 0 and .84 is .2995. This means that

$$P(Z < .84) = .5 + .2995$$

$$= .7995$$

$$= .8 \quad \text{(approximately)}$$

FIGURE 6.26

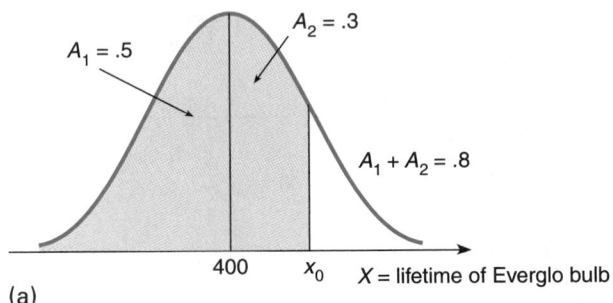

(a)

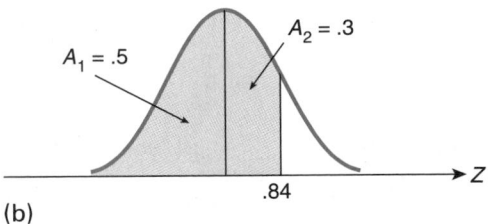

(b)

(a) $P(X < x_0) = .8$.

(b) $P(Z < .84) = .8$.

By standardizing X, we conclude that

$$\frac{x_0 - 400}{50} = .84$$

$$x_0 - 400 = (50)(.84) = 42$$

$$x_0 = 400 + 42 = 442$$

So 80% of the Everglo bulbs will burn out within 442 hours.

EXAMPLE 6.6

A bakery shop sells loaves of freshly made French bread. Any unsold loaves at the end of the day are either discarded or sold elsewhere at a loss. The demand for this bread has followed a normal distribution with $\mu = 35$ loaves and $\sigma = 8$ loaves.

How many loaves should the bakery make each day so that they can meet the demand 90% of the time?

Solution   The normal random variable X here is the demand for French bread (measured in loaves) [Figure 6.27(a)]. To meet the demand 90% of the time, the bakery must determine an amount, say x_0 loaves, such that:

$$P(X \le x_0) = .90$$

Proceeding as before, examine a Z curve and find the value having an area to the left equal to .90 [Figure 6.27(b)]. Using Table A.4:

$$P(0 \le Z \le 1.28) = .4 \qquad \text{(more accurately, .3997)}$$

which means that

$$P(Z \le 1.28) = .4 + .5 = .9$$

So

$$\frac{x_0 - 35}{8} = 1.28$$

and

$$x_0 = 35 + (1.28)(8) = 45.24$$

To be conservative, round this value up to 46 loaves. By stocking 46 loaves each day, the bakery will meet the demand for this product 90% of the time.

FIGURE 6.27

(a) $P(X \le x_0) = .90$.

(b) $P(Z \le 1.28) = .90$.

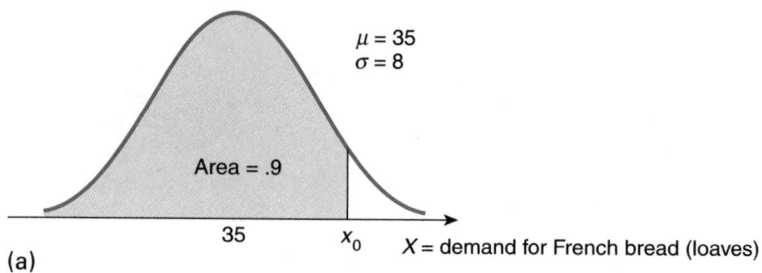

$\mu = 35$
$\sigma = 8$

Area = .9

35   x_0 X = demand for French bread (loaves)

(a)

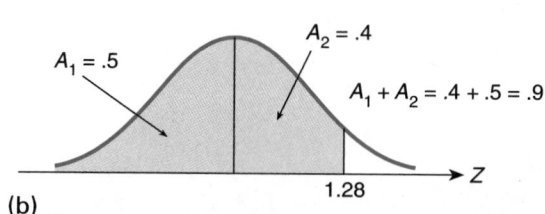

$A_1 = .5$

$A_2 = .4$

$A_1 + A_2 = .4 + .5 = .9$

1.28 Z

(b)

FIGURE

6.28

Z curve for
$P(-1 \leq Z \leq 1) \cong .68.$

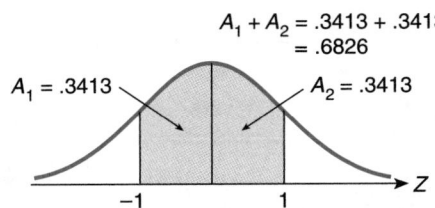

$$A_1 + A_2 = .3413 + .3413$$
$$= .6826$$

$A_1 = .3413$ $A_2 = .3413$

-1 1 Z

6.6

ANOTHER LOOK AT THE EMPIRICAL RULE

In Chapter 3, the empirical rule specified that when sampling from a bell-shaped distribution (which means a normal distribution), three guidelines apply:

1. Approximately 68% of the data values should lie between $\overline{X} - s$ and $\overline{X} + s$.

2. Approximately 95% of them should lie between $\overline{X} - 2s$ and $\overline{X} + 2s$.

3. Approximately 99.7% of them should lie between $\overline{X} - 3s$ and $\overline{X} + 3s$.

Nothing was said at that time about the origin of these numbers. They actually came directly from Table A.4. To see this, consider Figure 6.28, in which

$$P(-1 < Z < 1) = .68$$

This implies that, for any normal random variable X,

$$P[-1 < (X - \mu)/\sigma < 1] = .68$$

That is,

$$P[(\mu - \sigma) < X < (\mu + \sigma)] = .68$$

As a result, for a set of data from a normal population where $\overline{X}$ is the sample mean and s is the sample standard deviation, we would expect approximately 68% of the data to lie between $\overline{X} - s$ and $\overline{X} + s$.

Similarly, $P(-2 < Z < 2) = .4772 + .4772 = .9544$, so you can expect (approximately) 95% of the data points from a normal (bell-shaped) population to lie between $\overline{X} - 2s$ and $\overline{X} + 2s$.

Finally, $P(-3 < Z < 3) = .4987 + .4987 = .9974$, which leads to the third conclusion of the empirical rule.

6.7

USING EXCEL TO DETERMINE AREAS AND VALUES HAVING A SPECIFIED AREA FOR NORMAL POPULATIONS

The calculations demonstrated in Sections 6.4 and 6.5 to determine areas under a normal curve or determine a value of a normal random variable having a specified area can be done very easily using Excel, SPSS, and MINITAB. In Example 6.2, the area to the left of 360 was determined for a normal curve with a mean of 400 and a standard deviation of 50. To find this area (probability) using Excel, click on

FIGURE

6.29

Illustration of Excel functions NORMDIST (Example 6.2) and NORMINV (Example 6.5).

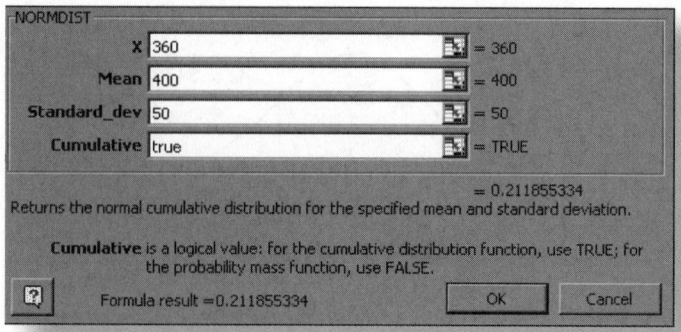

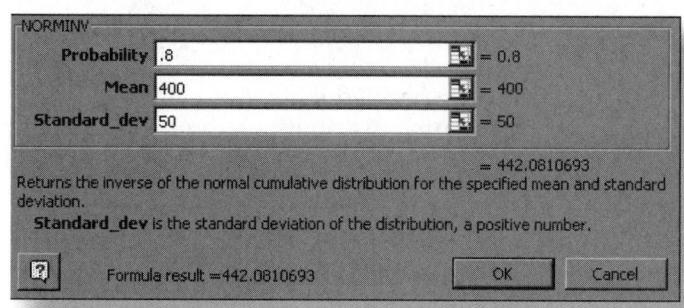

the **Paste Function** icon (*fx*), click on **Statistical** under **Function Category** and click on **NORMDIST** under **Function Name.** Fill in the entries as in the top panel of Figure 6.29. Entering "true" in the last box indicates that you want the area to the *left* of 360, and you will always enter "true" in this box for all the applications in this textbook. The formula result is .2119 and agrees with Example 6.2.

Comment

Whenever you need to find $P(X > \text{some value})$, use Excel's **NORMDIST** function as described here and subtract the result from one. For example, the probability that the bulb lifetime (X) in Example 6.2 exceeds 360 hours is $1 - .2119 = .7881$. Remember, Excel always determines the area to the left of the specified value of X.

The bottom panel of Figure 6.29 illustrates Excel's **NORMINV** function and repeats the solution to Example 6.5. The **NORMINV** function finds the value of X having a specified area to the *left* of this value. Using the Excel solution in Figure 6.29, 80% of the Everglo bulbs will burn out within 442 hours—that is, $P(X \le 442) = .8$, where X is normally distributed with a mean of 400 hours and a standard deviation of 50 hours.

Microsoft® Excel Application Use DATA6-7

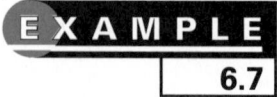

Using Excel to Find Areas Under a Normal Curve

In Chapter 3 (Examples 3.4 and 3.9), we examined a sample of 100 inside diameters of a machined part produced at the Boston facility of Allied Manufacturing. It was concluded in Example 3.9 that the sample histogram was approximately bell shaped (normal). Consequently, an assumption of a normal population was rea-

FIGURE

6.30

Partial listing of
DATA6-7 and
results of
descriptive
statistics.

	A	B	C	D	E	F	G	H
1	10.216	*Column1*						
2	10.221							
3	10.226	Mean	10.27539	←				
4	10.228	Standard Error	0.002668					
5	10.230	Median	10.276					
6	10.230	Mode	10.271					
7	10.231	Standard Deviation	0.026681	←				
8	10.231	Sample Variance	0.000712					
9	10.234	Kurtosis	-0.3467					
10	10.237	Skewness	-0.01021					
11	10.239	Range	0.122					
12	10.239	Minimum	10.216					
13	10.240	Maximum	10.338					
14	10.240	Sum	1027.539					
15	10.244	Count	100					
16	10.245							

sonable, and the empirical rule was applied. Earlier discussion of this sample in Chapter 2 (Example 2.1) mentioned that for this part to be acceptable, the diameter must be between 10.1 mm (the lower spec limit) and 10.3 mm (the upper spec limit). Any part outside these spec limits is said to be nonconforming. The targeted diameter is 10.2 mm.

This same data set is contained in DATA6-7. Determine the mean and standard deviation of this sample and compute the sample Z scores for the two spec limits. Assuming the population is normal, with mean $\bar{x}$ and standard deviation s, what proportion of the population will lie outside the spec limits—that is, be nonconforming? What can you say about this process?

Solution

In Figure 6.30 you can see the first 16 of the 100 values in DATA6-7. By clicking on **Tools ➤ Data Analysis ➤ Descriptive Statistics** and (1) entering "A1:A100" for the input range, (2) entering "B1" for the output range, and (3) clicking on the small box to the left of **Summary Statistics,** you will obtain the remaining portion of Figure 6.30. Notice that $\bar{x} = 10.27539$, and $s = .026681$.

Using Figure 6.31 and Excel's NORMDIST function, the area to the left of the lower spec limit of 10.1 mm is 2.46843E-11—that is, 2.46843 with the decimal point moved 11 places to the left. This number is nearly zero, so we will treat it as zero. The area to the left of the upper spec limit of 10.3 mm is .8218, and so the area to the right of this spec limit is $1 - .8218 = .1782$.

Conclusion

The total tail area outside the spec limits is $0 + .1782 = .1782$. For this population, we can expect 17.82% of the parts to be nonconforming. As a reminder, this percentage is approximate, since we have estimated the population parameters (μ and σ) using the corresponding sample statistics ($\bar{x}$ and s). It is interesting to note that in Example 2.1, it was determined that 17% of the 100 values in this sample were outside the spec limits. Our observations regarding this process remain the same as in earlier examples that examined the process: The z-score for the upper spec limit is $(10.3 - 10.27539)/.026681 = .922$, which indicates that this process is shifted too far to the right (both z-scores should be at least 3 in absolute value) and is producing parts that are too large in diameter. An adjustment to the process that shifts the mean toward the stated target of 10.2 mm will reduce the percentage of parts exceeding the upper spec limit (now an estimated 17.82%).

FIGURE

6.31

Areas to the left of
the spec limits.

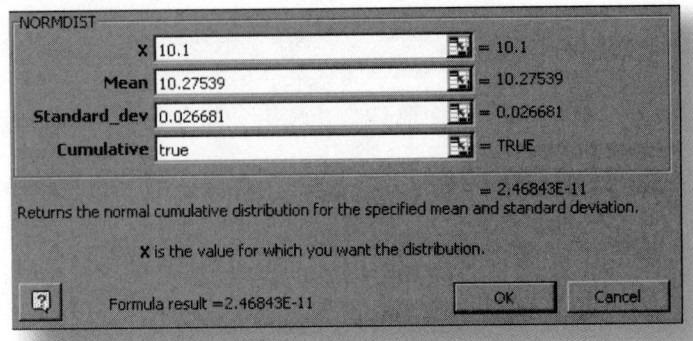

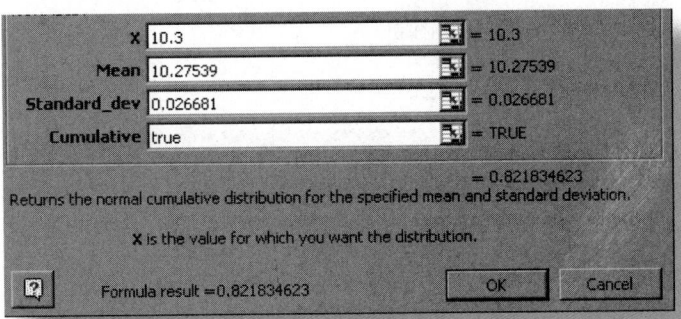

X   Exercises 6.11–6.25

Understanding the Mechanics

6.11 Let X be a random variable with a normal distribution having a mean of 30 and a standard deviation of 20.
   a. What is the probability that X is less than 10?
   b. What is the probability that X is greater than 70?
   c. What is the probability that X is between 20 and 40?

6.12 Find the value of x if the random variable X is normally distributed with mean 50 and standard deviation 6.
   a. $P(X \geq x) = .0655$
   b. $P(X \leq x) = .8686$
   c. $P(40 \leq X \leq x) = .6715$
   d. $P(x \leq X \leq 50) = .3531$

Applying the New Concepts

6.13 High-Tech, Inc., produces an electronic component, GX-7, that has an average life span of 4,500 hours. The life span is normally distributed with a standard deviation of 500 hours. The company is considering a 3,800 hours' warranty on GX-7. If this warranty policy is adopted, what proportion of GX-7 components should High-Tech expect to replace under warranty?

6.14 The estimated miles-per-gallon (on the highway) ratings of a class of trucks are normally distributed with a mean of 12.8 and a standard deviation of 3.2. What is the probability that one of these trucks selected at random would get
   a. between 13 and 15 miles per gallon?
   b. between 10 and 12 miles per gallon?

6.15 The yearly cost of dental claims for the employees of D. S. Inc. is normally distributed with a mean of $75 and a standard deviation of $30. At least what yearly cost would be expected for 40% of the employees?

6.16 Housing has become more affordable over the past couple of decades, thanks to low inflation and low interest rates. Soon-to-be buyers participating in the National Association of Home Builders' 2001 buyer-preference survey indicated that they typically spent between six months and a year to buy a home. Suppose that the distribution of the time that it takes to buy a home can be approximated by a normal distribution with a mean of 9 months and a standard deviation of 3 months.
   a. What is the probability that a home buyer selected a random spends less than a year to buy a home?
   b. At least what amount of time would 60% of the home buyers be expected to spend looking for a home to buy?

(Source: "Most Shoppers Take Six Months to a Year to Find a New Home," *Los Angeles Times*, October 14, 2001.)

6.17 Credit cards with low APRs might not offer low international charges to credit-card providers making a transaction abroad. The average international charge is 2.46% on standard credit cards, 2.55% on gold cards, and rising to 2.65% on platinum cards. Few credit-card users compare credit cards based on their international charges. Suppose that the standard deviation of the percent charge when using a credit card overseas is .6%. Assume that the international charges by credit-card companies can be approximated by a normal distribution.

a. What is the probability that a credit-card company charges more than 3% for international transactions with a standard credit card?

b. Repeat part a for a gold credit card.

c. Repeat part a for a platinum credit card.

d. Compare your findings in parts a, b, and c.

(Source: "Credit Cards," *The Times* (London, England), August 11, 2001, p. 2.)

6.18 The thickness of a manufactured sheet of metal is believed to follow a normal distribution with a mean of .30 inches and a standard deviation of .02 inches. The lower spec limit is 2.5 standard deviations to the left of the mean. The upper spec limit is 3.0 standard deviations to the right of the mean. Nonconforming sheets of metal have thicknesses outside of these two spec limits. What proportion of the sheets of metal are nonconforming?

6.19 The vice president of a computer networking equipment company named Force10 Networks travels upwards of 100,000 miles a year visiting clients who purchase his networking equipment. To save time, he started booking business jets with charter brokers. He claims that he can make five stops across the country in just two days and that this same trip on a commercial airline would take at least a week with delays and connecting flights. However, companies that charter the use of a small jet can average around $1,800 per flight hour. Assume that the distribution of the cost of a flight hour by companies that charter small jets is approximately normally distributed with a mean of $1,800 and a standard deviation of $200.

a. What is the probability that a randomly selected jet broker charges less than $2,000?

b. What is the probability that a randomly selected jet broker charges less than $1,200? Would you consider this to be an unusual occurrence?

(Source: "A Jet You Can Call Your Own," *Business Week*, October 8, 2001, p. 120.)

6.20 The vice president of Offshore Oil and Gas, a consulting firm, notices that the average length of time that a consultant spends on the telephone with a client at any one time is 40 minutes with a standard deviation of 18 minutes. Assuming that the length of such conversations is normally distributed, what percent of the consultant's phone calls would take longer than 50 minutes?

6.21 A production manager is analyzing quality data from a manufacturing process. Sometimes the manager knows certain probabilities but is missing information on the mean or standard deviation. Assume that the manager knows that the proportion of values less than 19.8 is .975.

a. What is the mean of the process if the standard deviation is known to be 5?

b. What is the standard deviation of the process if the mean is known to be 15.88?

6.22 Hotels at Walt Disney World Village in Orlando, Florida, charge considerably more than the hotel room prices in the local area. The cost of a hotel room is seasonal and depends on demand. The average rate for a room at the Courtyard by Marriott at Walt Disney World Village is $130. Assume that the distribution of the cost of a room at the Courtyard over a year can be approximated by a normal distribution with a mean of $130 and a standard deviation of $20.

a. What is the probability that the cost of a room on a randomly selected day is at least $115?

b. What is the probability that the cost of a room on a randomly selected day is between $110 and $150?

c. Between what two numbers, centered at $130, will the cost of a room be 80% of the time?

(Source: "For the Record," *Time*, vol. 158, no. 17, October 15, 2001, p. 29.)

Using the Computer

6.23 **[DATA SET EX6-23]** *Variable description:*

Refunddamage: Amount of refund to customers who return damaged merchandise.

A store manager recorded the refund to customers on 100 returned items that were sold to the customer and found to be damaged. The manager knows that historically the average refund is $70 with a standard deviation of $20 on such merchandise.

a. The manager would like to know the probability of randomly receiving a refund that is at least as large as the amount in **Refunddamage.** For very small probabilities, the manager may suspect that customers have damaged very expensive goods and returned them. The manager treats these refunds as unusual. Find these probabilities. In Excel, put the values of **Refunddamage** in column A, starting in A1. Then type into cell B1 "=1-NORMDIST (A1,70,20,1)." Drag this cell down to B100.

b. How many of the probabilities obtained in part a are less than .01? Do you think that the manager should consider these refunds as unusual?

6.24 **[DATA SET EX6-24]** *Variable description:*

RentResident: Amount of monthly profit from residential rent homes

RentCommercial: Amount of monthly profit from rent paid on commercial buildings

A realtor owns numerous residential and commercial buildings and collects rent on these properties. The realtor selects 100 months over the past several years and lists the monthly profit in thousands of dollars for these properties. These values are listed in the variables **RentResident** and **RentCommercial,** in thousands of dollars.

a. Plot a histogram of the data in **RentResident** and also of the data in **RentCommercial.** Would you say that the data are approximately normally distributed? Find the mean and the variance for each of the variables.

b. What type of distribution do you believe the sum of **RentResident** and **RentCommercial** would have? What do you think the resulting mean and variance would be?

c. Plot a histogram of the sum of **RentResident** and **RentCommercial**. Does the distribution appear to be approximately normally distributed? Find the mean and variance. Compare these results to your answers in part b. Is the variance of the sum equal to the sum of the variances?

6.25 To gain insight into how the standard deviation changes the shape of a normal distribution, first generate 200 observations from a normal distribution with a mean of 0 and standard deviation of 1. Then, generate two more sets of 200 observations changing the standard deviation to 3 and to 5. Construct three frequency histograms and compare the heights and widths of the histograms and comment on how the standard deviation changes the shape of a normal distribution. (In Excel, click on **Tools ➤ Data Analysis ➤ Random Number Generation** and select the Normal distribution to generate the random values. Use the Stacked Histogram option in the KPK menu to form a stacked histogram for the data sets. In SPSS, click on **Transform ➤ Compute ➤ RV.NORM(q, mean, stddev)** to generate the random values. In MINITAB, click on **Calc ➤ Random Data ➤ Normal** to generate the random values.)

6.8 NORMAL APPROXIMATION TO THE BINOMIAL

The binomial random variable was introduced in Chapter 5. It is a discrete random variable used to count the number of successes in a binomial situation.

CHARACTERISTICS OF A BINOMIAL SITUATION

1. You have n independent identical trials.
2. Each trial is a success (with probability p) or a failure (with probability $1 - p$).
3. The binomial random variable X is the number of successes out of n trials.
4. The mean of X is $\mu = np$, and the standard deviation of X is $\sigma = \sqrt{np(1-p)}$.

Examples included:

X = the number of heads (successes) out of three flips (trials) of a coin

X = the number of people who read the evening newspaper (successes) out of a sample of 50 people (trials)

X = the number of defectives (successes) out of a sample of 10 electrical components (trials)

Table A.1 contains values of n (the number of trials) up to only $n = 20$. One option here is to use the Poisson approximation to determine binomial probabilities for values of $n > 20$. In other words, we pretend that X is a Poisson random variable *having the same mean* as the actual binomial random variable. This is a good approximation, provided n is large (> 20), p is small, and $np \leq 7$.

Despite the fact that Table A.1 only contains values of $n \leq 20$, many statistical and spreadsheet packages (including SPSS, MINITAB, and Excel) provide binomial probabilities for extremely large sample sizes (n). Using Excel to determine binomial probabilities was illustrated in Figure 5.6, and the SPSS procedure was discussed in the end-of-chapter appendix for Chapter 5. A less-preferred alternative here is to use the *normal approximation* to the binomial random variable. Here we pretend that X is a normal random variable *having the same mean and standard deviation as the actual binomial random variable*. This approximation works well when p is near .5 and in general offers a good estimate when both $np > 5$ and $n(1 - p) > 5$.

APPROXIMATIONS TO THE BINOMIAL

- Poisson approximation: Use when $n > 20$ and $np \leq 7$.
- Normal approximation: Use when $np > 5$ and $n(1 - p) > 5$.

Consider 12 flips of a coin. We want to determine (1) the probability of observing no more than 4 heads, and (2) the probability of observing more than 5 heads. First, notice that a normal approximation is not necessary here. This is a binomial situation with $n = 12$ and $p = .5$, and Table A.1 does contain probabilities for this set of values. We chose this illustration to compare the actual binomial probability to the approximated probability using the normal distribution. Look at Figure 6.32, which demonstrates how we estimate binomial probabilities using a normal curve.

To solve question 1, let X = the number of heads in 12 flips, so X is a binomial random variable. We want to determine $P(X \leq 4)$. We can obtain an exact solution using Table A.1:

$$P(X \leq 4) = P(0) + P(1) + P(2) + P(3) + P(4)$$
$$= 0 + .003 + .016 + .054 + .121$$
$$= .194$$

In Figure 6.32, this value is the sum of the areas of the boxes corresponding to $X = 0, 1, 2, 3,$ and 4. Note that the width of each box is 1, and so the height of the box (the probability) is the same as the area of the box. As a result, the total area of all the boxes is 1.

We can also obtain an approximate solution. For this binomial random variable,

$$\mu = np = (12)(.5) = 6$$

and

$$\sigma = \sqrt{np(1 - p)}$$
$$= \sqrt{3} = 1.732$$

To obtain an approximation, treat X as a normal random variable with $\mu = 6$ and $\sigma = 1.732$, illustrated in Figure 6.32. Note that both the total area of the boxes and the total area under the normal curve are 1. The area under the normal curve that approximates $P(X \leq 4)$ is the area to the left of 4.5. So we obtain a better approximation here if we find the area under the normal curve to the left of 4.5, not 4.0. This .5 adjustment is referred to as an *adjustment for continuity*. This adjustment is necessary whenever you approximate a *discrete* random variable (such as a binomial random variable) using a *continuous* distribution (such as the normal distribution). Remember that the discrete distribution has gaps, whereas the continuous does not, so we must assign a portion of the space (probability) between 4

FIGURE

6.32

Approximating binomial probabilities using a normal curve.

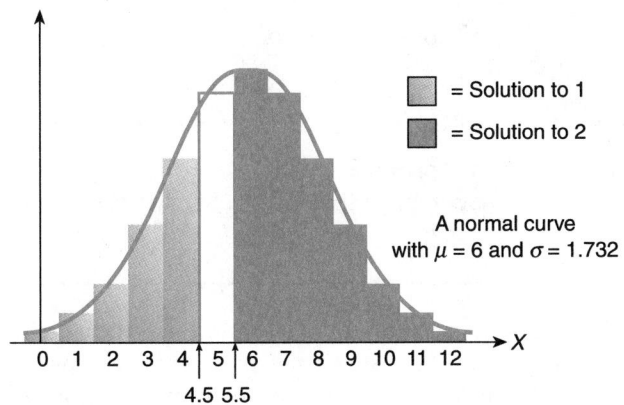

= Solution to 1

= Solution to 2

A normal curve with $\mu = 6$ and $\sigma = 1.732$

and 5 when we use a continuous distribution to approximate a discrete one. Using Table A.4:

Binomial **Normal**

$(n = 12,\ p = .5)$ $(\mu = 6,\ \sigma = 1.732)$

$P(X \le 4) \cong P(X \le 4.5)$

$$= P\left[Z \le \frac{4.5 - 6}{1.732}\right]$$

$$= P(Z \le -.87) = .1922$$

Notice that the approximate solution of .1922 is very close to the actual probability of .194. This is helped in part by the fact that $p = .5$ for this situation, which means that the binomial distribution is perfectly symmetric. *As the value of* p *moves away from .5, larger values of* n *are necessary to achieve an approximation this good.*

Now consider question 2, the probability of observing more than five heads in 12 flips, or $P(X > 5) = P(X \ge 6)$. Using Table A.1, we can obtain an *exact* solution:

$$P(X \ge 6) = P(6) + P(7) + \cdots + P(11) + P(12)$$

$$= .226 + .193 + \cdots + .003 + 0 = .613$$

We can also obtain an approximate solution. Using Figure 6.32, the area under the normal curve that corresponds to the dark shaded area representing the exact solution is the area to the right of 5.5. So, using Table A.4:

Binomial **Normal**

$(n = 12,\ p = .5)$ $(\mu = 6,\ \sigma = 1.732)$

$P(X \ge 6) \cong P(X \ge 5.5)$

$$= P\left(Z \ge \frac{5.5 - 6}{1.732}\right)$$

$$= P(Z \ge -.29) = .6141$$

Again, we obtain a very good approximation, helped by the fact that we are using a perfectly symmetrical binomial distribution.

HOW TO ADJUST FOR CONTINUITY

If X is a binomial random variable with n trials and probability of success $= p$, then:

1. $P(X \le b) \cong P\left(Z \le \dfrac{b + .5 - \mu}{\sigma}\right)$

2. $P(X \ge a) \cong P\left(Z \ge \dfrac{a - .5 - \mu}{\sigma}\right)$

3. $P(a \le X \le b) \cong P\left(\dfrac{a - .5 - \mu}{\sigma} \le Z \le \dfrac{b + .5 - \mu}{\sigma}\right)$ where $\mu = np$,

   $\sigma = \sqrt{np(1 - p)}$, and Z is a standard normal random variable.

4. Be sure to convert a $<$ probability to a $\le$, and to convert a $>$ probability to a $\ge$ before switching to the normal approximation.

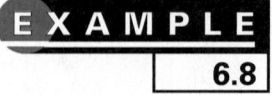

In Example 5.11, we discussed a binomial situation in which Eagle Air was intentionally overbooking flights. On a particular flight from Dallas to El Paso, it uses a much larger aircraft that holds 200 people. As in our previous example, 20% of the people who make reservations do not show up. Assume that all reservations are for one individual and are made independent of each other. If Eagle Air accepts 235 reservations, what is the probability that at least one passenger will end up without a seat on this flight?

Solution

The binomial random variable X here is the number of people (out of 235) who show up for the flight. For this situation, $n = 235$, and $p = .8$ represents the probability that any one passenger *will* show up. The mean of this random variable is

$$\mu = (235)(.8) = 188$$

and the standard deviation is

$$\sigma = \sqrt{(235)(.8)(.2)} = 6.13$$

At least one person holding a reservation will be deprived of a seat if $X \geq 201$ because the plane holds only 200 people. Once again, we use the normal approximation (Table A.4) to obtain the following probability:

Binomial	**Normal**
$(n = 235,\ p = .8)$	$(\mu = 188,\ \sigma = 6.13)$

$$P(X \geq 201) \cong P(X \geq 200.5)$$

$$= P\left[Z \geq \frac{200.5 - 188}{6.13}\right]$$

$$= P(Z \geq 2.04)$$

$$= .5 - .4793$$

$$= .0207$$

So on approximately two flights out of 100, at least one person will be unable to secure a seat.*

---

*Using Excel (see Figure 5.6c), SPSS, or MINITAB, the exact value of $P(X \leq 200)$ is .9821, and so the exact answer here is $P(X \geq 201) = 1 - P(X \leq 200) = .0179$. This value is quite close to the normal approximation (.0207), and so we again conclude that approximately 2% of the flights will end up with at least one passenger without a seat.

X Exercises 6.26–6.33

Understanding the Mechanics

6.26 Let the random variable X have a binomial distribution. For which of the following cases would it be reasonable to approximate the binomial distribution with the normal distribution?
  a. $n = 50, p = .12$
  b. $n = 100, p = .1$
  c. $n = 11, p = .6$
  d. $n = 100, p = .99$

6.27 Suppose that X is a binomial random variable with $n = 50$ and $p = .2$.
  a. Are these values of n and p sufficient to have a reasonably good approximation to the binomial distribution using a normal distribution?
  b. Use the normal approximation to find the probability that X is larger than 8.
  c. Use the normal approximation to find the probability that X is at least 7 but less than 11.

6.28 Let X be a binomial random variable with $n = 20$ and $p = .5$. Find the following probabilities by using the normal approximation and also by using the binomial distribution.
  a. $P(X \leq 12)$
  b. $P(X > 5)$
  c. $P(6 \leq X < 15)$

Applying the New Concepts

6.29 A travel agency promotes vacation packages by phoning households at random in the evening hours. Historically, only 65% of heads of households are at home when the agency phones. If 30 households are phoned on a given evening, what is the probability that the agency will find between 15 and 25 households, inclusive, with the head of the household at home?

6.30 How life in the college dorm has changed! In the late 1970s or the early 1980s, you weren't likely to see anything more high-tech than an LP turntable, a color TV, or perhaps, a computer-science student communicating with a far-off mainframe computer using a slow-poke modem. Now the essentials for college dorm life include a personal computer, a CD player, and perhaps a DVD player. Some students even hook DVD players directly to their computers, which essentially become television sets. Approximately 40% of college students living in college dorms have access to a DVD player.

a. Suppose that 100 students were selected at random. What is the probability that between 35 and 45, inclusively, have access to a DVD player?

b. From a sample of 100 students, how many students would you expect to have access to a DVD player?

c. What is the probability that exactly 40 students in a sample of 100 students have access to a DVD player?

(Source: "College Kids Plug in for Fun," *USA Today*, September 11, 2001, p. 1D.)

6.31 The U.S. department of transportation believes that the number of flight delays during the year 2000 was a warning that the national airspace system is "operating at the fringes of capacity." Across 11 national carriers, approximately 20% of all flights failed to arrive on time.

a. Suppose that 40 flights were randomly selected. What is the probability that no more than eight flights failed to arrive on time?

b. In part a, would no more than two flights failing to arrive on time be considered unusual? Why?

(Source: "Airlines Log More Late Flights," *The Dallas Morning News*, December 12, 2000, p. 2D.)

Using the Computer

6.32 For the binomial distribution with $n = 12$ and $p = .6$, find the normal approximation to the probability that the random variable is equal to 0, 1, 2, . . . , 12. Compare these to the exact probabilities from the binomial distribution. Use the cumulative normal distribution function in either Excel, SPSS, or MINITAB to obtain the normal approximation to the probability. For which values of this binomial distribution is the normal approximation the most accurate?

6.33 For a normally distributed population, we would expect approximately 68% of the sample data to lie between $\mu - \sigma$ and $\mu + \sigma$ for normally distributed data. Using Excel, SPSS, or MINITAB, generate 100 observations from a binomial distribution with $n = 12$ and $p = .3$. For this distribution the interval $\mu - \sigma$ and $\mu + \sigma$ is 2.0 to 5.2 or approximately 2 to 5, inclusively. Calculate the proportion of values between 2 and 5, inclusively. Repeat five times. How do these proportions compare to 68%? Would you say that the normal approximation should not be recommended for this binomial distribution?

6.9

OTHER CONTINUOUS DISTRIBUTIONS

The normal distribution is one example of a continuous distribution. A normal random variable X is a continuous random variable; that is, over some specific range, *any* value of X is possible. We used X to represent the lifetime of an Everglo bulb to illustrate a continuous random variable because any value between 280 hours and 520 hours (see Figure 6.2) is possible. In fact, any value less than 280 or more than 520 is also possible, although not likely to occur.

In the Everglo example, a normal distribution seemed appropriate because the histogram of 200 sample bulbs in Figure 6.2 revealed a concentration of burnout times in the "middle" and not nearly as many burnout times around 300 or 500. These features give the normal curve its "mound" in the center and "tails" on each end.

There are many continuous distributions that do not resemble a normal curve in appearance. For example, consider the following two situations, in which a random variable, X, ranges from 1 to 10.

Situation 1. The chance that X is between 1.0 and 1.5

$$= \text{the chance that } X \text{ is between 1.5 and 2.0}$$

$$= \text{the chance that } X \text{ is between 2.0 and 2.5}$$

$$\vdots$$

$$= \text{the chance that } X \text{ is between 9.0 and 9.5}$$

$$= \text{the chance that } X \text{ is between 9.5 and 10.0}$$

Situation 2. The larger X is, the less likely it is to occur. Thus, the chance that X is between 1.0 and 1.5

> the chance that X is between 1.5 and 2.0

> the chance that X is between 2.0 and 2.5

$\vdots$

> the chance that X is between 9.0 and 9.5

> the chance that X is between 9.5 and 10.0

These two cases can be represented by two other frequently occurring continuous distributions. Situation 1 can be represented by a uniform random variable; situation 2 could be described using an exponential random variable.

Although there are other random variables that apply to these two situations, the uniform and exponential distributions fit many of the applications encountered in business.

The Uniform Distribution

Consider spinning the minute hand on a clock face. Define a random variable X to be the stopping point of the minute hand. It seems reasonable to assume, for example, that the probability that X is between 2 and 4 is *twice* the probability of observing a value of X between 8 and 9. In other words, the probability that X is in any particular interval is *proportional* to the width of that interval.

A random variable of this nature is a **uniform random variable.** The values of such a variable are evenly distributed over some interval because the random variable occurs *randomly* over this interval. Unlike the normal random variable, values of the uniform random variable do not tend to be concentrated about the mean.

Assume that the manager of Dixie Beverage Service is concerned about the amount of soda that is released by the dispensing machine that the company is now using. He is considering the purchase of a new machine that electronically controls the cutoff time and is supposed to be very accurate. The present machine cuts off mechanically, and he suspects that the device shuts off the fluid flow *randomly* anywhere between 6 and 8 ounces. To test the present system, a sample of 150 cups is taken from the machine, and the amount of soda released into each cup is recorded. The relative frequency histogram made from these 150 observations is shown in Figure 6.33.

Would you be tempted to describe the population of *all* cup contents using a normal curve? We hope not, because there is no evidence of a declining number of observations in the tails. A word of warning here: though we often have a tendency to think of all continuous random variables as being normally distributed, as this application demonstrates this is certainly not the case. Instead, this distribution is a flat or uniform distribution. The random variable $X =$ cup contents is a

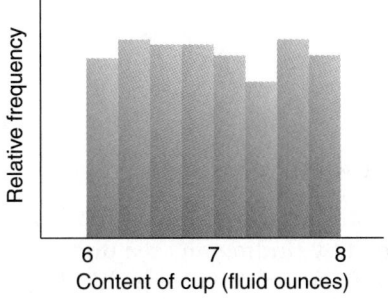

FIGURE

6.33

Relative frequency histogram of a sample of 150 cups of soda.

FIGURE

6.34

Uniform
distribution for
X = soda content
(compare with
Figure 6.33).

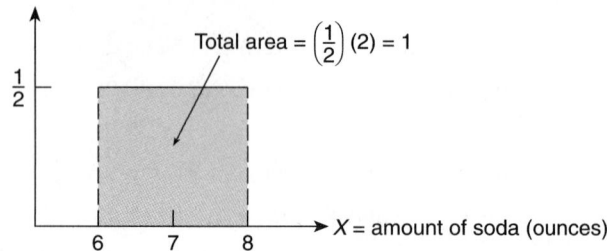

FIGURE

6.35

Total area of a
uniform
distribution.

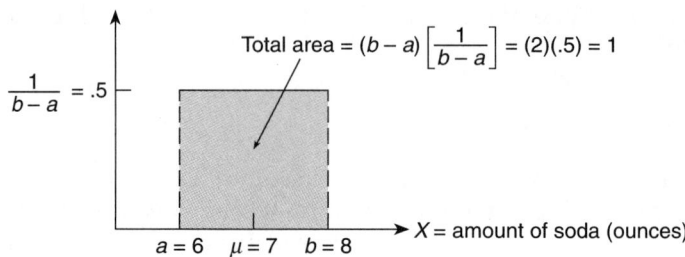

uniform random variable. The corresponding smooth curve describing the population is shown in Figure 6.34. Notice that the total area here is given by a rectangle, and, as is true of all continuous random variables, this total area must be 1. The area of a rectangle is given by (width) · (height). By making the height of this curve (a straight line, actually) equal to .5, the total area is

$$(8 - 6)\ (.5) = 1.0$$

In general, the curve defining the probability distribution for a uniform random variable is as shown in Figure 6.35. The total area is

$$(b - a)\left[\frac{1}{b - a}\right] = 1.0$$

Mean and Standard Deviation

Refer to Figure 6.35. The mean (μ) of X is the value midway between a and b, namely,

$$\mu = \frac{a + b}{2}$$

The standard deviation (σ) of X is, as before, a measure of how much variation there would be in X if you were to observe it indefinitely. Unlike the standard deviation of a normal distribution, σ for a uniform distribution is hard to represent graphically as a particular distance on the probability curve. Its value, however, is given by

$$\sigma = \frac{b - a}{\sqrt{12}}$$

Determining Probabilities

As it is for all continuous random variables, a probability based on a uniform random variable is determined by finding an area under a curve. Suppose, for example, the manager of Dixie Beverage Service would like to know what percentage

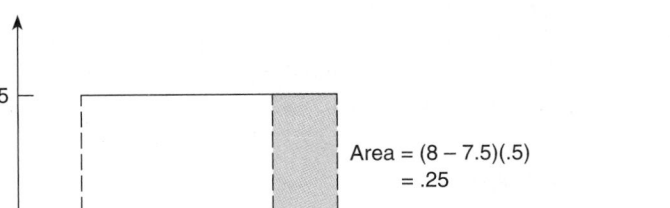

FIGURE 6.36

The probability that X exceeds 7.5. The shaded area represents the percentage of cups containing more than 7.5 ounces.

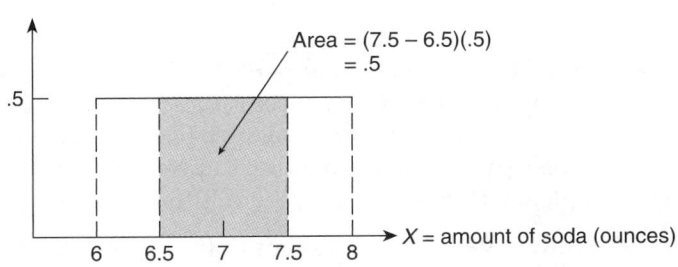

FIGURE 6.37

The probability that X is between 6.5 and 7.5.

of the cups will contain more than 7.5 ounces, using the present machines. In Figure 6.36, the shaded area is a rectangle, so its area is easy to find:

$$area = (width) \cdot (height) = (8 - 7.5) \cdot .5 = .25$$

So 25% of the cups will contain more than 7.5 ounces.

EXAMPLE 6.9

What is the probability that a cup will contain between 6.5 and 7.5 ounces? What is the average content?

Solution

The first result is the same as the percentage of cups containing between 6.5 and 7.5 ounces. Based on Figure 6.37, we conclude that

$$P(6.5 < X < 7.5) = .5$$

The average cup content (mean of X) is

$$\mu = \frac{6 + 8}{2} = 7 \text{ ounces}$$

The standard deviation of X is

$$\sigma = \frac{8 - 6}{\sqrt{12}} = 0.58 \text{ ounce}$$

Notice that, as with the normal random variable, the probability that X is equal to any particular value is zero. So,

$$P(X = 6.5) = P(X = 7.5) = 0$$

As a result,

$$P(6.5 \leq X \leq 7.5) = P(6.5 < X < 7.5) = .5$$

Simulation is an area of statistics that relies heavily on the uniform distribution. In fact, the uniform distribution is the underlying mechanism for this often-complex procedure. So, although not as many "real-world" populations have uniform distributions as have normal ones, the uniform distribution is extremely important in the application of statistics.

The Exponential Distribution

The final continuous distribution we will discuss is the *exponential distribution*. Similar to the uniform random variable, the **exponential random variable** is used in a variety of applications in statistics. One application is observing the time between arrivals at, for example, a drive-up bank window. Another situation that often fits the exponential distribution is observing the lifetime of certain components in a machine.

Chapter 5 discussed the Poisson random variable, which often is used to describe the *number* of arrivals over a specified time period. If the random variable Y, representing the number of arrivals over period T, follows a Poisson distribution, then X, representing the *time between* successive arrivals, will be an *exponential random variable*. The exponential random variable has many applications when describing any situation in which people or objects have to wait in line. Such a line is called a *queue*. People, machines, or telephone calls may wait in a queue.

The Exponential Random Variable. The shape of the exponential distribution is represented by a curve that steadily decreases as the value of the random variable, X, increases. Thus, the larger X is, the probability of observing a value of X at least this large decreases exponentially. This type of curve is illustrated in Figure 6.38.

Determining Probabilities. Determining areas for exponential random variables is not as simple as for uniform ones, but it is easier than for normal random variables because exponential probabilities can be derived on a calculator. Table A.2 also can be used to determine the probability for an exponential random variable.

As Figure 6.39 illustrates, for an exponential random variable, X, the probability that X exceeds or is equal to a specific value, x_0, is

$$P(X \geq x_0) = e^{-Ax_0}$$

FIGURE

6.38

Curve showing the distribution of an exponential random variable.

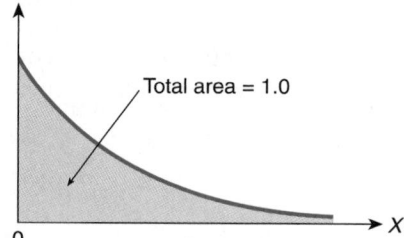

FIGURE

6.39

Curve used for determining a probability for an exponential random variable.

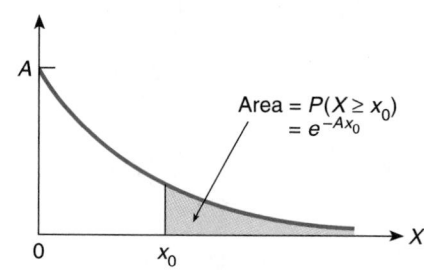

The parameter A is related to the Poisson random variable we used when discussing arrivals. In fact, the Poisson distribution for arrivals per unit time and the exponential distribution for time *between* arrivals provide two alternative ways of describing the same thing. For example, if the number of arrivals per unit time follows a Poisson distribution with an average of $A = 6$ per hour, then an alternate way of describing this situation is to say that the time between arrivals is exponentially distributed with mean time between arrivals equal to $1/A = 1/6$ hour (10 minutes).

In general, $1/A$ is the average (mean) value of the exponential random variable, X. It is also equal to the standard deviation of X. So,

$$\mu = 1/A$$

$$\sigma = 1/A$$

In applications using this distribution, the value of A either will be given or can be estimated in some way.

EXAMPLE 6.10

The owner of the Downtown Haircut Emporium believes the best way to run his barbershop is to rely on walk-in customers and not to schedule appointments. From past experience, the arrival of customers follows a Poisson distribution with an average arrival rate of $A = 4$ customers per hour.

1. If the owner just witnessed the arrival of a customer, what is the probability that there will be a new arrival within 30 minutes?

2. If X represents the time between successive arrivals, what are the mean and standard deviation of X?

Solution 1

To determine this probability, we must first convert 30 minutes to .5 hour, since the arrival rate is 4 *per hour*. The desired probability then is $P(X \leq .5)$. Referring to Figure 6.40, the probability that X *exceeds* .5 is

$$P(X > .5) = P(X \geq .5)$$
$$= e^{-(4)(.5)}$$
$$= e^{-2}$$
$$= .135$$

Consequently, $P(X \leq .5) = 1 - .135 = .865$, and so 86.5% of the time, the time between successive arrivals will not exceed 30 minutes.

Solution 2

Both the mean and standard deviation of X (the time between successive arrivals) are $1/A = 1/4$ hour (15 minutes).

FIGURE 6.40

Curve showing the probability that X exceeds .5 $[P(X > .5)]$.

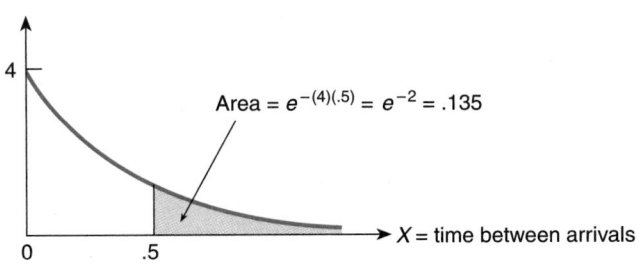

247

EXAMPLE

15.3

The exponential distribution is widely used in the area of *reliability engineering* to describe the time to failure of a component or system. The parameter μ is called the *mean time to failure* and $A = 1/\mu$ is the *failure rate of the system*. Suppose that an automobile battery has a useful life described by the exponential distribution with a mean of 1,000 days.

1. What is the probability that a battery will fail before its expected lifetime of 1,000 days?

2. If the battery has a 12-month (365-day) warranty, what fraction of the batteries fail during the warranty period?

Solution 1   The battery lifetime (X) follows an exponential distribution with $\mu = 1{,}000$ and $A = 1/1{,}000 = .001$. Referring to Figure 6.41, we wish to find the probability that X is less than 1,000:

$$P(X < 1000) = 1 - e^{-(.001)(1000)} = 1 - e^{-1} = .632$$

Consequently, there is a 63% chance that the battery will fail prior to its mean lifetime of 1,000 days. This value is larger than 50% since this distribution is not symmetric and is positively skewed.

Solution 2   According to Figure 6.42, the probability that the battery fails before the warranty expires is

$$P(X \le 365) = 1 - e^{-(.001)(365)} = 1 - e^{-.365} = .306$$

The manufacturer will be forced to replace 30.6% of the batteries during the one-year warranty period. This large percentage is encountered despite the fact that the average lifetime of the battery is nearly three years because of the positive skewness and the heavy concentration of probability on the "low end" of the distribution.

FIGURE

6.41

Curve showing the probability that X is less than 1,000 days.

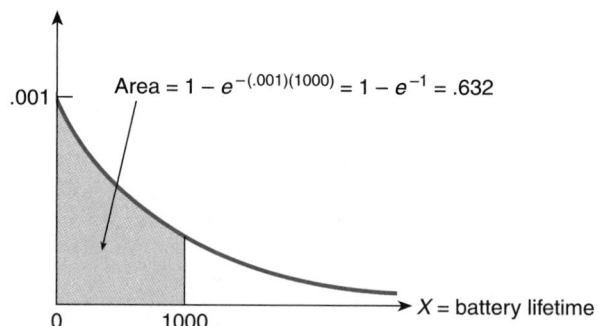

FIGURE

6.42

Curve showing the probability that X is less than 365 days.

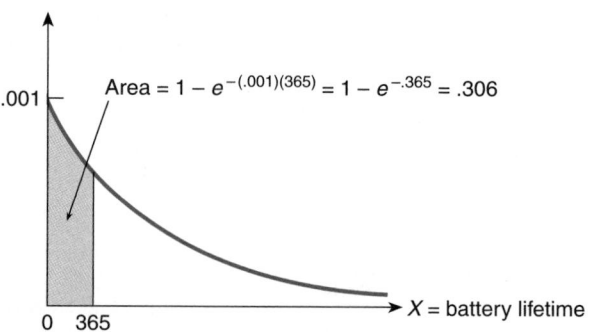

X Exercises 6.34–6.45

Understanding the Mechanics

6.34 For a random variable that is uniformly distributed between 5 and 10, find the probability that the random variable is:
  a. between 6 and 8.
  b. greater than 7.
  c. less than 9.

6.35 Let X be a random variable with a uniform distribution between 55 and 70.
  a. What is the probability that X is between $\mu - \sigma$ and $\mu + \sigma$?
  b. Find the value of x such that the $P(X \leq x) = .80$.

6.36 Suppose that the distribution of a random variable X is approximately exponential with a mean of 10.
  a. What is $P(X \geq 8)$?
  b. What is $P(X \leq 11)$?
  c. What is $P(6 \leq X \leq 10)$?
  d. What is the standard deviation of X?

Applying the New Concepts

6.37 The rate at which a swimming pool is filled is uniformly distributed between 20 and 26.3 gallons per minute.
  a. What is the probability that the filling rate at any one time is between 21.3 and 24.6 gallons per minute?
  b. What is the mean rate at which the swimming pool is filled?
  c. What is the standard deviation of the rate at which the swimming pool is filled?

6.38 Suppose that customers arrive at a bank to either deposit money or withdraw money. Assume that the interarrival time (time between arrivals) is exponentially distributed with a mean of four minutes.
  a. What is the probability that the interarrival time is greater than five minutes?
  b. What is the probability that the interarrival time is between one minute and four minutes?
  c. What is the standard deviation of the interarrival time?

6.39 The time intervals (in operating hours) between successive failures of air conditioning equipment in certain aircraft is believed to follow an exponential distribution. Assume that the mean time between failures is 300 hours. What is the probability that air conditioning equipment in a particular aircraft will fail after 200 operating hours?

6.40 From surveys, Holiday Inn knew that guests found the bathrooms at its hotels to be dirty. If the company shifted from tubs to shower stalls, it would mean much less dingy grout and an end to dark showers and discolored shower curtains. Moreover, consultants estimate that the cleaning time required for each guest room would fall to 13 minutes on average from the current 23 minutes required for guest rooms with tubs. That translates into a savings of $150 per room per year in maintenance costs.

  a. Assume that the time to clean a guest room is uniformly distributed between 15 and 31 minutes for guest rooms with bathtubs. What is the standard deviation of the time that it takes to clean a guest room which has a tub?
  b. What is the probability that a guest room with a tub is cleaned in less than 25 minutes?

(Adapted from "Shower or Bath? It's a Hotel's Tough Call," *The Wall Street Journal*, May 14, 1998, p. B1.)

6.41 Yellow Rose taxi company estimates that it makes an average of $415 in profits per day. Assuming that the daily profit follows an exponential distribution, what is the probability that on a given day at least $500 in profits will be made?

6.42 The president of Bright-Light Candles estimates that the average burning time of their "medium-K" candles is 40 hours. Assuming that burning time follows an exponential distribution, calculate the probability that a given medium-K candle will burn for at least 50 hours?

6.43 AT&T recently offered an exclusive rebate program with Nokia, a Finnish telecommunications equipment company, on the Nokia 8260 wireless phone. These phones sold for $39.99 after rebate, weigh only 3.4 oz each, and have standard extended-life batteries with a mean life of 200 hours of standby time. Assuming that the extended-life batteries have a life that is exponentially distributed with a mean of 200 hours, what is the probability that an extended-life battery will last longer than 200 hours?

(Source: http://store.yahoo.com/1800mobiles/nokia8260.html.)

Using the Computer

6.44 A production manager believes that the insulating effectiveness of a certain padding has a life span that is exponentially distributed with a mean equal to three years. The manager would like to know the reliability of this material. The reliability of a product is often measured by the formula 1 minus the cumulative exponential distribution evaluated at a specified time period. (To use the cumulative exponential distribution in Excel, click on the paste function, then click on **Statistical ➤ EXPONDIST** and enter $1/\mu$ for the Lambda value where μ is the population mean. In SPSS, click on **Transform ➤ Compute ➤ CDF.EXP(q, scale)** and enter $1/\mu$ for the value of the scale. In MINITAB, click on **Calc ➤ Probability Distributions ➤ Exponential** and then select cumulative probability.)
  a. What is the reliability of the padding after 4 years?
  b. What is the reliability of the padding after 5 years? Compare this reliability to that in part a.
  c. After how many years would the reliability be .1?

6.45 [DATA SET EX6-45] *Variable description:*

BotErr : Error in manufacturing bottom half of rod

TopErr : Error in manufacturing top half of rod

A quality-control engineer is monitoring the production of a metal rod that is made in two parts. The bottom (steel) part is manufactured to a length of 1 meter. The top (aluminum) part is also manufactured to a length of 1 meter. The errors in manufacturing these rods are recorded for 400 observations in variables **BotErr** and **TopErr**.

a. Plot a histogram of **BotErr** and a histogram of **TopErr**. Which of the following distributions most closely fits this data: normal, exponential, or uniform?

b. Define the variable **TotalErr** to be equal to **BotErr** + **TopErr**. Plot a histogram of the data for this variable. What is the approximate shape of the distribution?

 # Summary

A random variable that can assume any value over a specific range is a **continuous random variable.** Many business applications have continuous probability distributions that can be approximated using a *normal, uniform,* or *exponential random variable.* Each of these distributions has a unique curve that can be used to determine probabilities by finding the corresponding area under this curve. The **normal distribution** is characterized by a bell-shaped curve with values concentrated about the mean. The **uniform distribution** (curve) is flat; values of this random variable are evenly distributed over a specified range. The **exponential distribution** has a shape that steadily decreases as the value of the random variable increases. Any calculator with an e^x key can be used to derive probabilities for the exponential distribution.

We discussed examples illustrating the shape of each distribution. The exact curve for a particular random variable is specified using one or two *parameters* that describe the corresponding population. As in the case of a discrete random variable, the population consists of what you would obtain if the random variable was observed indefinitely. The resulting average value and standard deviation represent the *mean* and *standard deviation* of the random variable and corresponding population.

There are infinitely many normal random variables, one for each mean (μ) and positive standard deviation (σ). If $\mu = 0$ and $\sigma = 1$, this normal random variable is the **standard normal random variable,** Z. Consequently, there is only *one* normal random variable of this type. Table A.4 gives the probabilities (areas) under the standard normal curve. You can also use this table to determine a probability for any normal random variable if you first **standardize** the variable by defining $Z = (X - \mu)/\sigma$. For this situation, Z represents the number of standard deviations that X is to the right (Z is positive) or left (Z is negative) of the mean.

A **uniform random variable** is one in which the values of such a variable are evenly distributed over some interval because the random variable occurs *randomly* over this interval. **Simulation** is an area of statistics that relies heavily on the uniform distribution. An **exponential random variable** is useful for situations that have a time component, such as when people or objects are waiting in a line (*queue*).

 # Summary of Formulas

1. Standardizing a normal random variable (X)

$$Z = \frac{X - \mu}{\sigma}$$

2. Approximating a binomial random variable (X) using a standard normal random variable (Z)

$$P(X \leq b) = P\left(Z \leq \frac{b + .5 - \mu}{\sigma}\right)$$

$$P(X \geq a) = P\left(Z \geq \frac{a - .5 - \mu}{\sigma}\right)$$

$$P(a \leq X \leq b) = P\left(\frac{a - .5 - \mu}{\sigma} \leq Z \leq \frac{b + .5 - \mu}{\sigma}\right)$$

where $\mu = np$ and $\sigma = \sqrt{np(1-p)}$.

3. Uniform distribution

$$\mu = \frac{a + b}{2} \quad \text{and} \quad \sigma = \frac{b - a}{\sqrt{12}}$$

$$P(X \leq x_0) = \frac{x_0 - a}{b - a} \quad \text{for } a \leq x_0 \leq b$$

4. Exponential distribution

$$P(X \leq x_0) = 1 - e^{-Ax_0} \quad \text{for } x_0 \geq 0$$

where $A = 1/\mu$, $\mu = \frac{1}{A}$, and $\sigma = \frac{1}{A}$.

X Review Exercises 6.46–6.75

6.46 Assume that the expenditure of a family of four at Six Flags over Texas for food, souvenirs, and parking is approximately normally distributed with a mean of $150 and a standard deviation of $25. What percentage of four-member families will have an expenditure:
  a. greater than $200?
  b. less than $125?
  c. between $100 and $200?

6.47. Refer to Exercise 6.46. Determine the expenditure by a family of four, say x, such that
  a. 50% of the time the expenditure is less than x.
  b. 20% of the time the expenditure is greater than x.
  c. 80% of the time the expenditure is less than x.

6.48 Which distribution, the normal or exponential distribution, would be most suitable for approximating the distributions of the following quantities.
  a. The time between arrivals at a bank drive-up window.
  b. The heights of seniors in a high school class.
  c. The time between placement and execution of a market order on the New York Stock Exchange.

6.49 A quality-control engineer of a high-tech company noted that 4% of all parts provided by the company's main supplier were of inferior quality (nonconforming items). Out of a sample of 300 parts provided by the company's main supplier, what is the probability that more than 10 parts are of inferior quality?

6.50 Wireless service is much more reliable than it was several years ago. However, blocked calls remain a fact of life for wireless carriers and users. Figures from various industry sources put the average percentage of blocked calls at nearly 2% per carrier on a per-market basis. Blocked calls are defined technically as calls where users fail to access the network due to network congestion or other capacity shortcomings. Assume that the percentage of blocked calls per user is approximately normally distributed with a mean of 2% and a standard deviation of a half percent. What percentage of the users of wireless service experience blocked calls that are in excess of 2.5% of their calls?

(Source: "Blocked Out," *Wireless Review*, vol. 18, September 16, 2001, pp. 36–37.)

6.51 Automotive analysts contend that a weak Japanese yen enables Japanese automakers to keep a lid on the price of vehicles sold in the United States because it is cheaper for them to develop and build autos at home. U.S. automakers must cut costs when the yen reaches a very high level. Suppose that an analyst believes that for 2002, the value of the yen to the dollar will follow approximately a normal distribution with a mean of 130 yen to the dollar and a standard deviation of 5 yen to the dollar. Find the values, symmetrical about the mean of 130, between which the price of yen to the dollar should lie 60% of the time.

(Adapted from "Another Strike Against GM," *USA Today*, June 16, 1998, p. 4B, and U.S. dollar table, *The Wall Street Journal*, January 14, 2002, p. C1.)

6.52 Marketing professionals say that coupons are very important to consumers. In 2000, U.S. businesses distributed 330 billion coupons with an average face value of 71 cents, up from 307 billion coupons with an average face value of 66 cents in 1999. Approximately 70% of adult men use coupons at least once a year, compared with 85% of adult women. Assume that the value of coupons in local newspapers can be approximated by a normal distribution with a mean of 71 cents and a standard deviation of 25 cents.
  a. What is the probability that a coupon randomly selected from a local newspaper is worth at least 50 cents?
  b. What is the probability that a randomly selected coupon is worth more than $1.50? Would you consider this occurrence to be unusual?
  c. What is the probability that in a random sample of 100 adult men at least 80 use coupons at least once a year?
  d. Repeat part c for women and compare the probabilities.

(Source: "Redeeming Value," *American Demographics*, vol. 23, October 2001, p. 25.)

6.53 The examination committee of the Institute of Chartered Accountants passes only 20% of those who take the examination. If the scores follow a normal distribution with an average of 72 and a standard deviation of 18, what is the passing score?

6.54 The shelf life of cookies made by a small bakery is considered to be exponentially distributed with a mean equal to three days. What percentage of the boxes of cookies placed on the shelf today would still be considered marketable after 2.75 days?

6.55 The time that a certain drug has an effect on a normal human being is considered to be exponentially distributed when a standard dose is taken. If the average length of time that the drug has an effect is 30 hours, what is the probability that any given normal person will be affected by the drug for at least 32 hours? What is the standard deviation for the length of time that the drug affects a person?

6.56 Becoming an entrepreneur can be a radical career change. Last year U.S. credit-card companies wrote off at least $2 billion attributable to failed businesses, estimates Frederick, Maryland-based RAM Research Group. Fully half of all new businesses fail in their first six years. Close to 5% go belly-up, owing money to creditors each year.
   a. If 100 entrepreneurial enterprises were randomly selected, what is the probability that more than 45 of these enterprises failed in their first six years?
   b. If 100 entrepreneurial enterprises were randomly selected, what is the probability that at least six enterprises will go belly-up, owing money to creditors? Is it advisable to approximate this probability using the normal approximation to the binomial distribution?

(Adapted from "Go Ahead: Buy the Dream," *Forbes*, June 15, 1998, p. 146.)

6.57 Clearvision Company manufactures picture tubes for color television sets and claims that the life spans of its tubes are exponentially distributed with a mean of 1,800 hours. What percentage of the picture tubes will last no more than 1,600 hours?

6.58 The amount of time each day that the copying machine is used at a certain business is approximately exponentially distributed with a mean of 3.5 hours. What is the probability that the copying machine will be used at least two hours a day?

6.59 The diameter of a special aluminum pipe made by Everything Aluminum Inc. is normally distributed with a mean of 3.00 centimeters and a standard deviation of .1 centimeter. Calculate the proportion of pipes whose diameters are more than 3.15 centimeters.

6.60 Bacterial meningitis is not a common disease in the United States, striking about one person in 100,000 each year. However, it causes alarm far out of proportion to the number of people affected. College students appear to get very concerned about this disease, perhaps because it attracts a lot of public attention.
   a. Assume that the probability that an individual will get bacterial meningitis is .00001. In a population of 500,000 college students, what is the probability that exactly five students develop this disease?
   b. What is the probability that at least five students in a population of 500,000 develop this disease?
   c. Is it advisable to use the normal approximation to the binomial distribution in answering parts a and b?

(Source: "Lowering the Risk of Bacterial Meningitis," *The New York Times*, September 4, 2001, p. F8.)

6.61 A manufacturer of heating elements for water heaters ships boxes that contain 100 elements. A quality-control inspector randomly selects a box in each shipment and accepts the shipment if there are five or fewer defective heating elements in the box. Assuming that the manufacturer has had a rate of 6% defective items, what is the probability that a shipment of heating elements will pass the inspection?

6.62 A majority of households own mutual funds for their retirement. Outside of retirement, an estimated 40% of households own mutual funds in taxable accounts. During the bull market days of the 1990s, many households moved money from money-market accounts to equity mutual funds to get into the action.
   a. If 50 households were randomly selected, what is the probability that no more than 20 households own mutual funds in taxable accounts?
   b. If 50 households were randomly selected, what is the probability that less than 15 or more than 25 households own mutual funds in taxable accounts?

(Source: "Majority of U.S. Households Investing in Mutual Funds," *Los Angeles Times*, October 4, 2001, p. C4.)

6.63 Skiers can visit Vail, Colorado, for a fraction of peak-season prices by scheduling their trips in November and December. For example, four people can share a two-bedroom condo for $50 to $80 during November and December, whereas from January to March the prices vary from $100 to $150. Assume that the distribution of these rates is uniformly distributed over these time periods.

a. What is the mean and standard deviation of the price of a condo for four people during November and December?

b. During November and December, 30% of the condos for four people would be priced higher than what value?

c. What is the mean and standard deviation of the price of a condo for four people during the January to March time frame?

d. During January and March, 30% of the condos for four people would be priced higher than what value?

(Source: "Deal of the Week: Early Skiing in Vail," *Los Angeles Times*, October 14, 2001, p. L3.)

6.64 The rate at which a sack of soybeans is filled varies uniformly from 50 to 65 pounds per hour. What percentage of the time is the rate greater than 55 pounds per hour?

6.65 If X is a uniform random variable that represents the percentage of time each day that a machine does not work, what is the probability that X is greater than the mean percentage of time that the machine does not work?

6.66 If the random variable X has a uniform distribution between -10 and 10, find the value of x such that $P[X \geq x] = .25$.

6.67 In a 1965 issue of *Electronics Magazine*, Mr. Moore published an article articulating the concept that underpins what has become known as Moore's Law: The power of a silicon chip will double every 18 to 24 months, accelerating the pace of technological change. One consequence of the pace of technological change is that consumers sometimes feel that the moment they buy a computer it is no longer a cutting-edge product. Financial analysts estimate that during the 1990s the lifespan of a personal computer has been approximately two years before a consumer gets an upgrade.

a. If the lifespan of a personal computer bought during the 1990s is exponentially distributed with a mean of two years, what is the probability that a consumer will keep a personal computer beyond three years?

b. If the lifespan of a personal computer bought during the 1990s is approximately normally distributed with a mean of two years and a standard deviation of .5 years, what is the probability that a consumer will keep a personal computer beyond three years?

(Source: "Technology Intensifies the Law of Change," *The New York Times*, May 27, 2001, p. 4I.)

6.68 The random variable X is normally distributed with mean μ and variance σ^2. Find k if $P(\mu - k\sigma \leq X \leq \mu + k\sigma) = .67$.

6.69 If the random variable X is normally distributed with mean 25, find the variance if $P(X \geq 29) = .27$.

6.70 The random variable X is normally distributed such that $P(X \leq 10) = .12$ and $P(X \geq 15) = .4$. Find the mean and variance of the random variable X.

6.71 After a $2 billion investment, Sprint is offering businesses the Integrated On-Demand Network (ION). This digital service allows customers to simultaneously hold a phone conversation, send faxes, watch video, and log onto the Internet over a single line. Sprint is pricing the ION access so that 90% of the sales are priced between $110 and $150. If the sales of the ION access can be considered to be approximately normally distributed with a mean of $130, what is the standard deviation of the sales prices?

(Adapted from "Sprint Starts Up Single-Line Service," *USA Today*, June 3, 1998, p. 1B.)

6.72 The Automobile Club of Southern California monitors the price of gasoline in southern California. The following data are prices of regular self-serve gasoline during September 2001 at randomly selected locations in southern California. Historically, the distribution of the price of gasoline at locations across southern California has followed an approximate normal distribution.

Location	Price of Gas	Location	Price of Gas
Bakersfield	1.52	Riverside	1.61
Burbank	1.62	San Bernardino	1.62
Fullerton	1.76	San Diego	1.74
Huntington Beach	1.59	Santa Barbara	1.74
La Jolla	1.58	Santa Monica	1.69
Long Beach	1.66	Ventura	1.68
Los Angeles	1.66	Woodland Hills	1.63

a. Construct a histogram using class widths of .05 and using the lower endpoint of the first class to be $1.50. Assuming that these data are representative of the entire southern California region, would you agree that the distribution of the price of gas in southern California can be approximated by a normal distribution?

b. Using a mean of $1.65 and a standard deviation of 7 cents, between what two values (centered at $1.65) would you say that 80% of the locations in southern California charge for the regular self-serve gasoline?

c. Using the information in part b, 30% of the locations charge higher than what price?

(Source: "At the Pump," *Los Angeles Times,* September 19, 2001, p. G1.)

6.73 A study by the University of Toronto found that drivers in the Toronto metropolitan area who use a cell phone are four times more likely to get in an accident than drivers without cell phones and that their accident rate is equal to that of a driver who is legally intoxicated. The study doesn't suggest that cell phones cause accidents but that cell phone users need to be very careful when driving and using a cell phone.

a. Suppose that a Canadian driver in Toronto has a accident rate of .25 per year, assuming that the driver does not use a car cell phone. Assume that those drivers who use a car cell phone have an accident rate four times this rate. If the length of time between car accidents is exponentially distributed, what is the probability that an accident will occur within two years for a driver in Toronto who does not use a car cell phone?

b. In part a, what is the probability that a driver in Toronto who uses a car cell phone will be involved in an accident within the next two years?

(Adapted from "Driven to Distraction," *Chicago Tribune,* June 14, 1998, p. 20L.)

6.74 Sometimes discrete distributions can have a shape that approximates the shape of the normal distribution. Consider the Poisson distribution. For a mean of 1, 3, and 6, the probability of a Poisson random variable being equal to the integer values 0 through 15 is illustrated in the following graph.

a. Would you say that the shape of the Poisson distribution is looking more like the shape of a normal distribution as the mean increases?

b. Plot the probabilities of a Poisson distribution with a mean of 9. Describe the shape of the distribution. (In Excel, put 0 through 15 in the first 16 rows of column A. In cell B1, type in "=Poisson(A1, 9, 0)." Drag this cell to B16. Highlight B1 through B16. Click on **Chart Wizard ➤ Line.** Select the chart sub-type that says "line with markers displayed at each data value." In SPSS, first put 0 through 15 in a column, then click on **Transform ➤ Compute ➤ CDF.POISSON(q, mean)** to obtain the cumulative probabilities. Use the variable value minus its lagged value (lag function) to obtain the discrete probabilities. Click on **Graphs ➤ Line ➤ Define** (after selecting the icon **Simple** in the **Line Chart** dialog box) to form the graphs. In Minitab, first put the numbers 0 through 15 in a column. Then click on **Calc ➤ Probability Distributions ➤ Poisson** and enter an input and output column in the dialog box. Click on **Graph ➤ Plot,** input the variables to graph and select "connect" in the display box.)

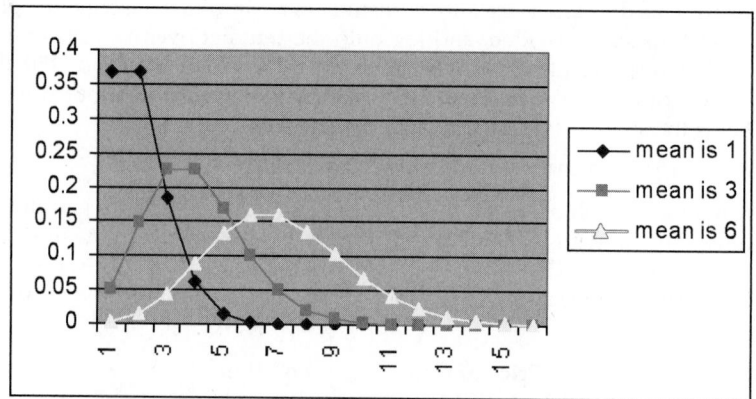

6.75 Data were collected from two computer service divisions of a large semiconductor company. In division A, the salaries were approximately normally distributed with a mean of $5,000 per month and a standard deviation of $1,000 per month. In division B, the salaries were approximately normally distributed with a mean of $7,000 and a standard deviation of $1,500 per month. In Excel, type in the two rows displayed below, with the upperleft most cell starting in cell A1.

	A	B	C	D	E	F	G
1	0	=NORMDIST(A1,D2,E2,0)	=NORMDIST(A1,F2,G2,0)	mean1	std1	mean2	std2
2	0.25	=NORMDIST(A2,D2,E2,0)	=NORMDIST(A2,F2,G2,0)	5	1	7	1.5

Now highlight the first two rows of columns A, B, and C. Drag these rows down through the 41st row. Highlight columns A and B from row 1 to row 41. Click on **Chart Wizard ➤ Scatter Plot with Data Values Connected by Smooth Lines ➤ Next ➤ Series.** Add series two by first clicking on the **Add** button and then entering the range of values in column A into **X Values** and the range of values in column C into **Y Values.** The resulting graph presented below will be displayed.

a. The units in the plot are in thousands of dollars. What range of salaries appears to be at least somewhat likely to occur in both groups?

b. If an employee is selected at random from division A, what is the probability that the employee's salary falls within the range in part a?

c. Do a "what if" analysis by changing the mean values in cells D2 and F2. What mean salaries for divisions A and B would allow almost no overlap in salaries?

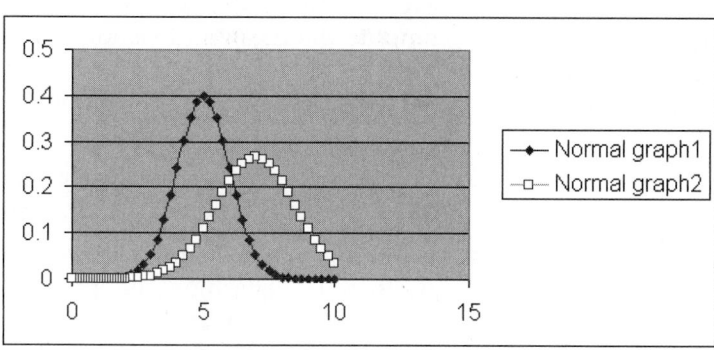

Computer Exercises Using the Databases

Exercise 1—Appendix F

Select 100 observations at random from the database and use a convenient statistical computer package to estimate the mean and standard deviation of the variable HPAYRENT (house payments or apartment/house rents). Find the percentage of the observations between $\bar{x} \pm s$, $\bar{x} \pm 2s$, and $\bar{x} \pm 3s$. Comment on whether these percentages support the conclusion that the data come from a normally distributed population.

Exercise 2—Appendix F

Select 150 observations at random from the database and, with reference to the variable OWNORENT, calculate the proportion of those observations that indicate the house is owned rather than rented. If a random sample of 20 observations were chosen from this set of 150 observations with replacement, what is the probability that more than half of the homes in the sample of 20 are owned by their occupants? Is the normal approximation appropriate for this situation?

Exercise 3—Appendix G

Select 100 observations at random from the database on the variable EMPLOYEES (number of employees). Use a convenient statistical computer package to construct a histogram. What type of distribution does the histogram approximate? normal? uniform? exponential? none of these?

Exercise 4—Appendix G

Repeat Exercise 3 using the variable SALES.

Insights from Statistics in Action

Examining Unethical Behavior: More Fun Than Decent People Think Should Be Legal

In the Statistics in Action discussion at the beginning of this chapter, we examined the question of measuring the ethical behavior of business professionals. Often, vignettes are used to determine if an individual would act in a professional way. Some examples of these vignettes are the following:

- *Vignette 1.* A programmer who works for a bank decides to modify a bank's accounting system to hide his overdrawn account and thus avoid an overdraft charge. After making a deposit, the programmer corrects his modification.
- *Vignette 2.* A business manager receives software ordered from a mail-order company but also finds another software package sent in error. The extra software is not listed on the invoice. The manager decides to keep the extra software without paying for it.
- *Vignette 3.* An employee uses the company's copier to make copies for a friend of hers who does not work for the company.

Suppose that a researcher investigating ethical behavior surveys 100 business professionals from each of three groups: the under-30-years-of-age group, the at-least-30-years-old-but-less-than-50-years-old group, and the at-least-50-years-of-age group. The researcher uses 50 vignettes and records the proportion of vignettes that each respondent says he/she would not act in the same way because the behavior is ethically unacceptable. Use this data, contained in StatInActChap6.xls, to answer the following questions.

1. Plot a histogram of the data for each age group. In practice, the distribution of data never conforms exactly to a particular distribution. However, approximate distributions are often used to conveniently describe the distributions and to find probabilities. What continuous distribution approximates the distribution of each of these data sets?

2. Find the sample mean and sample standard deviation of each of the distributions and compare. If a distribution is approximately uniform, compute the mean and standard deviation provided by the formulas for the uniform distribution and compare these to the sample mean and sample standard deviation.

3. For the under-30-years-of-age group, calculate the z score for a value of .98. Interpret this value.

4. Using the approximate distribution found in question 1, determine the probability that a respondent found at least 40 percent of the vignettes ethically unacceptable for the at-least-30-years-old-but-less-than-50-years-old group.

5. Repeat question 4 using the at-least-50-years-of-age group and compare the probabilities.

(Sources: "Thoughtful Book Tackles Business Ethics," *Toronto Star*, July 25, 2001, p. BU02; "An Empirical Examination of Marketing Professionals' Ethical Behavior in Differing Situations," *Journal of Business Ethics*, vol. 23, 2001, pp. 331–342; "New Survey Shows Greater Concern for Ethical Behavior," *Strategic Finance*, September 2001, pp. 22–24; "Making Ethical Decisions," *Communications of the ACM*, vol. 43, no. 12, 2000, pp. 66–71.)

Appendix SPSS®

Chapter 6 Appendix: Data Analysis with SPSS

Normal Probabilities

Cumulative probabilities can be calculated for a number of continuous distributions in SPSS. The following examples will illustrate how to find cumulative probabilities for a specified value of (1) the standard normal random variable (Z) and (2) any normal random variable (X). A *cumulative probability* is defined as $P(X \le x)$; that is, the area to the left of x under the continuous curve (normal here) describing the random variable, X.

The following discussion will demonstrate how to obtain the probabilities in the data window.

	z	cumz	x	cumx
1	1.75	.9599	487.50	.9599
2				

To obtain a cumulative probability for the standard normal random variable (Z), enter the value of Z (say, 1.75) as shown above. Click on the **Variable View** tab and name this variable z. Click on **Transform ➤ Compute.** Enter the variable name "cumz" in the **Target Variable** box. Find the function name **CDFNORM(zvalue)** inside the function list box and double-click on it. Replace the question mark inside the **Numeric Expression** box with z. Click on **OK.** In the data window, click on the **Variable View** tab and set the number of decimal places for variable cumz to four. *Note:* The z column can contain more than one value of Z. The corresponding number of cumulative probabilities will be determined in the "cumz" column.

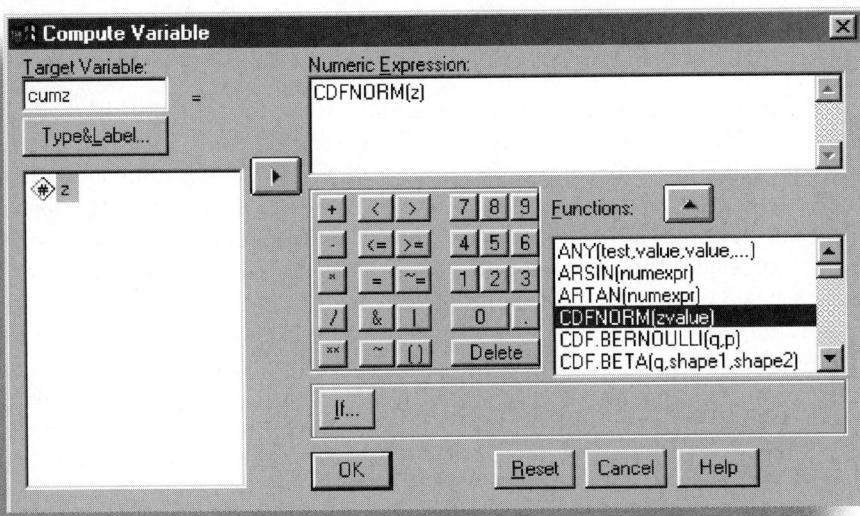

To obtain a cumulative probability for any normal random variable (X), enter the value of X (say, 487.5) in one of the cells. Click on the **Variable View** tab and name this variable x. Click on **Transform ➤ Compute.** Enter the variable name "cumx" in the **Target Variable** box. Find the function name **CDF.NORMAL(q,mean,stddev)** inside the function list box and double-click on it. Replace the question marks inside the **Numeric Expression** box as shown below. This assumes the normal random variable X has a mean of 400 hours and a standard deviation of 50. Click on **OK.** In the data window, click on the **Variable View** tab and set the number of decimal places for variable "cumx" to four. *Note:* The x column can contain more than one value of X. The corresponding number of cumulative probabilities will be determined in the "cumx" column.

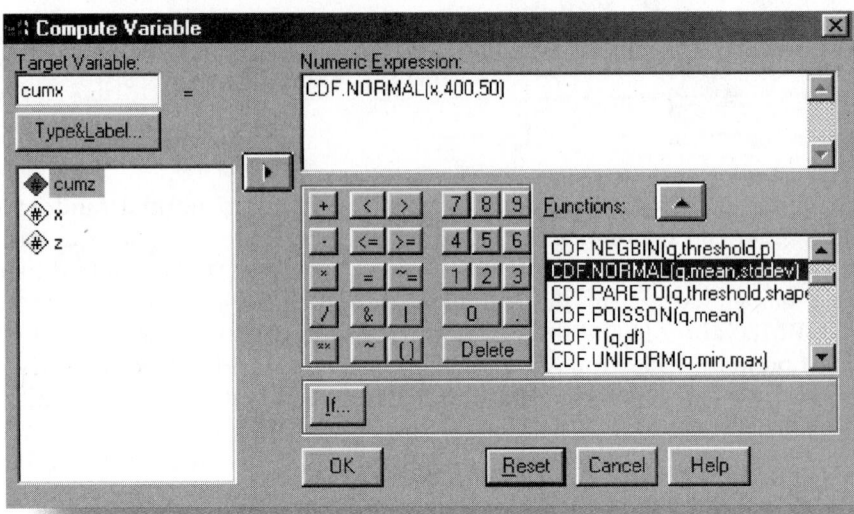

Exponential Probabilities

To obtain one or more cumulative exponential probabilities, enter the value(s) of X (say, 2.0) starting in the upper-left cell. Click on the **Variable View** tab and name this variable x. Click on **Transform ➤ Compute.** Enter the variable name "cumx" in the **Target Variable** box. Find the function name **CDF.EXP(q,scale)** inside the function list box and double click on it. Replace the question marks inside the **Numeric Expression** box as shown below. This assumes the exponential random variable X has a mean of 1.0. Click on **OK.** In the data window, click on the **Variable View** tab and set the number of decimal places for variable cumx to four. *Note:* The x column can contain more than one value of X. The corresponding number of cumulative probabilities will be determined in the "cumx" column. The output immediately following the **Compute Variable** window should appear in the data window. This output indicates that $P(X \leq 2.0)$ is 0.8647 where X is an exponential random variable having a mean of 1.0.

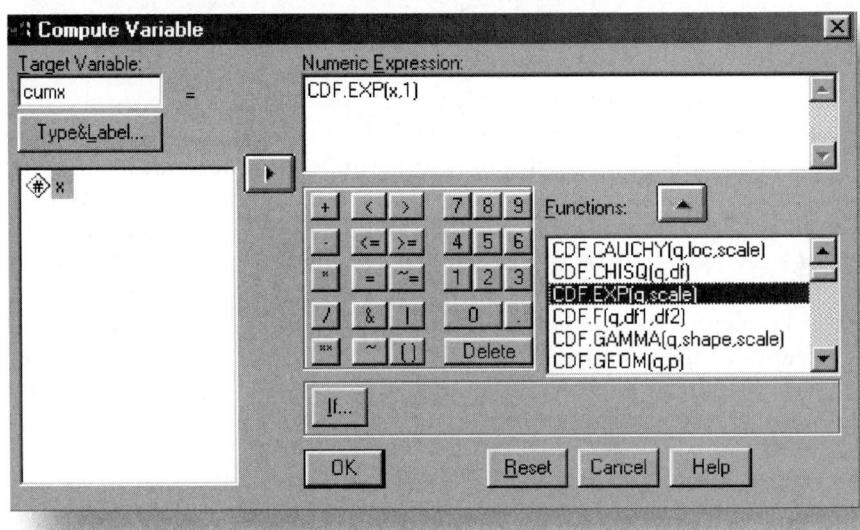

	x	cumx
1	2.00	.8647
2		

On the CD . . .
Chapter 6 Appendix: Data Analysis with MINITAB

Statistical Inference and Sampling

X

Statistics in Action
Traffic Congestion Takes Its Toll

It's not your imagination. According to a national study of 18 years of traffic data from 68 urban areas, traffic congestion is getting worse, and it is costing us billions in lost time and excess fuel costs. In fact, the amount of time drivers spend stuck in traffic has tripled since 1982, climbing from an average per driver of 11 hours a year to 36 hours in 1999. Of course, in certain cities, the amount of time stuck in traffic greatly exceeds these figures. A thriving economy can compound a city's traffic problems, causing productivity to decline as people spend more time on the roads. Los Angeles's traffic is a major cost to its economy. An estimated $12.5 billion in congestion costs puts Los Angeles at the top of the list of cities with the worst traffic congestion. The top ten congested cities, in order, are Los Angeles, Seattle–Everett, Atlanta, Houston, Dallas, Washington, D.C., Austin, Denver, St. Louis, and San-Francisco–Oakland.

The department of transportation in various states is collaborating with universities and consulting firms to find solutions to the traffic problems of various urban cities. Supercomputers are being used to run simulation models to understand the behavior of traffic in cities such as Dallas and Los Angeles. In some research studies, survey data are collected to obtain a better understanding of the behavior of drivers. These data contain information on where the drivers live, work, and drop off their kids.

These studies assist traffic planners in deciding whether to construct more freeways, to implement HOV (high occupancy vehicle) lanes, or to be more creative in coming up with solutions. In addition, these studies show that the behavior of drivers during rush hour can be unpredictable.

If one car slows and moves on, it forces the next car to overreact, and the next, and the next, in a giant ripple effect, which can last long after the first car went merrily on its way. That is why one often spends an hour in a traffic jam, and then returns to normal speed, without ever seeing any sign of what caused the problem.

One solution to relieving traffic congestion has been mass transit. For example, Dallas Area Rapid Transit has operated light rail and commuter rail trains for about five years. Although traffic has become worse, mass transit's ability to improve conditions in niche markets, such as downtown Dallas, is substantial. Mass transit is only one part of the solution to traffic congestion. Another solution to relieving traffic gridlock is an instant traffic monitoring system. This system gives updates to the public on the radio and updates a Web site illustrating bottlenecks.

Texas, which has the largest state highway system in the nation, is now only spending 8% of its budget on new construction. This is in contrast to the days when it spent 30% of its budget on new construction. Data collected in surveys from drivers on their driving patterns, frequency of delays, and costs of various options are helping states such as Texas to spend transportation dollars more wisely. When you have completed this chapter, you will be able to

- Use the average time spent by a random sample of motorists on freeways as an estimate of the average time spent by all motorists on freeways.
- Discuss the reliability of the estimate of the average time spent in traffic and construct and interpret an interval in which the average time spent in traffic by the population of interest might reasonably lie.
- Discuss how many motorists should be included in a random sample so that the estimated time spent in traffic is within a certain margin of error.

A Look Back/Introduction

The previous three chapters laid the foundation for using statistical methods in decision making. Any such decision will have uncertainty associated with it, but we can attempt to measure this uncertain outcome using a probability. Random variables (both discrete and continuous) allow you to represent certain outcomes of an experiment and their corresponding probabilities conveniently. If the experiment involves a particular discrete situation (such as a binomial random variable), you can easily determine the probability of certain events or determine the mean (average) value of the related distribution.

If the random variable of interest is continuous, you can make probability statements after assuming the probability distribution involved (such as normal, exponential, uniform, or others we have not discussed). Both discrete and continuous random variables come into play in all areas of decision making. They allow us to make decisions concerning a large population using the information contained in a much smaller sample.

Such decision making lies in the area of **statistical inference,** which this chapter introduces by demonstrating how to estimate something about a population (such as its average value, μ) by using the corresponding value from a sample (such as the sample average $\bar{X}$). Recall that μ (belonging to the population) is a *parameter* and $\bar{X}$ (belonging to the sample) is a *statistic.* When dealing with a normal population, for example, what does one do if the population mean, μ, is unknown? So far in the text, this value has been specified for you. In this chapter, we discuss methods of estimating population parameters using sample statistics, along with several methods of gathering sample data.

In sections 7.1 and 7.2, we continue to pretend that the population mean is known. Beginning with section 7.3, we discuss the more realistic situation where this parameter is unknown and must be estimated using the sample mean. Estimating an unknown population mean is the real purpose behind this chapter.

RANDOM SAMPLING AND THE DISTRIBUTION OF THE SAMPLE MEAN

In Chapter 3, you learned how to calculate the mean of a sample, $\overline{X}$. This sample is drawn from a population having a particular distribution, such as normal, exponential, or uniform. If you were to obtain another sample (you probably will not, as most decisions are made from just one sample), would you get the same value of $\overline{X}$? Assuming that the new sample was made up of different individuals than was the first sample, then almost certainly the two $\overline{X}$'s would not be the same. So, $\overline{X}$ itself is a random variable. We will demonstrate that if a sample is large enough, $\overline{X}$ is very nearly *normally* distributed regardless of the shape of the sampled population. That is, if you were to obtain many large samples, calculate the resulting $\overline{X}$'s, and then make a histogram of these $\overline{X}$'s, *this histogram would always approximately resemble a bell-shaped (normal) curve.*

Simple Random Samples

In Chapters 1 and 4, the concept of a simple random sample was introduced. The mechanics of obtaining a random sample range from drawing names out of a hat to using a computer to generate lists of random numbers. For extremely large populations, one is often forced to select individuals (elements) from the population in a *nearly* random manner.

The underlying assumption behind a random sample of size n is that any sample of size n has the same chance (probability) of being selected. To be completely assured of obtaining a random sample from a *finite* population, you should number the members of the population from 1 to N (the population size) and, using a set of n random numbers, select the corresponding sample of n population elements for your sample.

This procedure was described in Chapter 4 and is often used in practice, particularly when you have a sampling situation that needs to be legally defensible, as is the case in many statistical audits. However, for situations in which the population is extremely large, this strategy may be impractical, and instead you can use a sampling plan that is nearly random. Several other sampling procedures are discussed in the last section of this chapter.

The main point of all this lengthy discussion is that practically all the procedures presented in subsequent chapters relating to decision making and estimation assume that you are using a random sample. In the chapters that follow, the word *sample* will mean *simple random sample.*

Estimation

The idea behind statistical inference has two components:

1. The *population* consists of everyone of interest. By "everyone" we mean measurements taken from all people, machine parts, daily sales, or whatever else you are interested in measuring or observing. The mean value (for example, average height, average income) of everyone in this population is μ and generally is not known.

2. The *sample* is randomly drawn from this population. Elements of the sample thus are part of the population—but certainly not all of it. The exception to this is a *census*, a sample that consists of the entire population.

The sample values should be selected randomly, one at a time, from the entire population. Figure 7.1 emphasizes our central point—namely, an unknown

FIGURE

7.1

The sample mean, $\overline{X}$, is used to estimate the population mean, μ. In general, sample statistics are used to estimate population parameters.

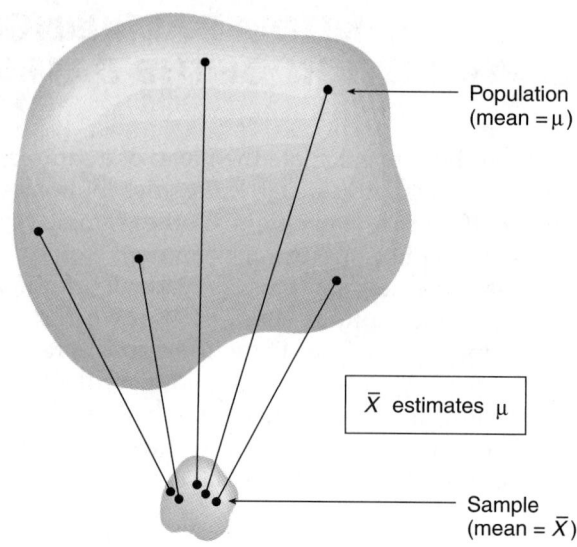

Population (mean = μ)

$\overline{X}$ estimates μ

Sample (mean = $\overline{X}$)

population **parameter** (such as μ = the mean value for the entire population) can be **estimated** using the corresponding sample statistic (such as $\overline{X}$ = the mean of your sample).

It makes sense, doesn't it? It would be most desirable to know the average value for everyone in the population, but in practice this is nearly always impossible. It may take too much time or money, we may not be able to obtain values for them all even if we want to, or the process of measuring the individual items may destroy them (such as measuring the lifetime of a light bulb). In many instances, estimating the population value using a sample estimate is the best we can do.

EXAMPLE

7.1

In Example 6.3, the funds dispensed daily by an automatic teller machine (ATM) were believed to follow a normal distribution with a mean of μ = $3,700 and a standard deviation of σ = $625. There is no way of *knowing* that μ is $3,700 unless the population of all daily dispersements is examined. Assume that

$$X = \text{daily funds released by this ATM}$$

is a normal random variable, but do not assume anything about the mean and standard deviation. Ignoring the standard deviation, estimating the mean, μ, involves obtaining a random sample of daily dispersements. Suppose you obtain a random sample of size $n = 10$, with the following results (in dollars):

| 3,880 | 3,460 | 3,530 | 4,240 | 3,470 | 3,770 | 3,990 | 4,550 | 3,310 | 2,300 |

What is the estimate of μ, based on these values?

Solution   The sample mean is $\overline{x} = \$3,650.00$. Thus, based on these 10 sample values, our best estimate of μ is $\overline{x} = \$3,650.00$.*

Distribution of $\overline{X}$

Referring to Example 7.1, the value of $\overline{X}$ would almost certainly change if you were to obtain another sample. The question of interest here is, if we *were* to obtain

---

*The notation $\hat{\mu}$ is commonly used in place of $\overline{x}$ to denote an *estimate* of μ. For this example, the estimate of μ is $\hat{\mu} = \$3,650.00$.

many values of $\bar{X}$, how would they behave? If we observed values of $\bar{X}$ indefinitely, where would they center; that is, what is the **mean** of the distribution for the random variable, $\bar{X}$? Is the variation of the $\bar{X}$ values more, less, or the same as the variation of individual observations? This variation is measured by the **standard deviation** of the distribution for $\bar{X}$.

In Example 6.2, it was assumed that the average lifetime of an Everglo light bulb was $\mu = 400$ hours, with a population standard deviation of $\sigma = 50$ hours. This result does not imply that if you obtain a random sample of these bulbs, the resulting sample mean, $\bar{X}$, always will be 400. Rather, a little head scratching should convince you that $\bar{X}$ will not be exactly 400, but $\bar{X}$ should be *approximately* 400.

Microsoft® Excel Application Use DATA7-2

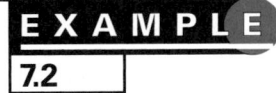

EXAMPLE 7.2

Determining the Distribution of the Sample Mean

Twenty samples of 10 Everglo bulbs each and the calculated $\bar{X}$'s for each sample are shown in Table 7.1. The data are contained in columns 1 to 20 in dataset DATA7-2. For now we will assume that the population parameters are $\mu = 400$ hours and $\sigma = 50$ hours (Figure 7.2). (1) Using Excel, determine the mean and standard deviation of the means of these 20 samples. What do you observe here? (2) Construct a histogram of these 20 means. What can you say about the "shape" of the $\bar{X}$ values?

Solution 1

Rather than using Excel to determine the 20 means one at a time, use the Excel KPK Data Analysis. First you must open file DATA7-2. Then click on **KPK Data Analysis ➤ Means and CIs for Multiple Samples.** Enter "A1:T10" as the **Input Range,** "50" as the **Population Std. Dev.,** and "U1" as the **Output Range.** Make sure the button alongside **Means** at the bottom of the form is selected. The output from this macro is shown in Figure 7.3 and does not include the frequency distribution in cells W1:Y11. Examining cell V24, we conclude that the average of the 20 sample means is 402.89 hours, and so the $\bar{X}$ values appear to be centered approximately at $\mu = 400$ hours. Look at the 20 standard deviations in Table 7.1. These values are in the neighborhood of $\sigma = 50$, as they should be. However, the standard deviation of the 20 $\bar{X}$ values (contained in cell V25) is 12.78, so we conclude that the $\bar{X}$ values have much less variation than the individual observations in each of the samples.

Solution 2

To obtain the frequency distribution of the twenty sample means in Figure 7.3 and corresponding histogram, click on **KPK Data Analysis ➤ Quantitative Data Charts/Tables ➤ Histogram/Freq. Charts.** You will then see the input form for this macro (see Figure 2.3 on page 00). For the **Input Range,** enter "V3:V22," and for the **Output Range,** enter "W1." Also, click on the circle to the left of **Number of Classes** and enter "7" in the text box. Finally, click on the check box for **Frequencies** in the **Table** list and the check box for **Frequency Histogram** in the **Chart Output Options** list. This will result in the frequency distribution table shown in Figure 7.3 and the histogram in Figure 7.4 (obtained by clicking on the **Frequency Histogram** tab at the bottom of your spreadsheet). Notice that the procedure produced eight classes, rather than the requested seven. As mentioned in earlier chapters, this Excel macro creates a frequency distribution containing an easy-to-interpret class width and classes, and very often will modify the intended number of classes to achieve this.

Based on the histogram in Figure 7.4 and the solution to (1), it seems reasonable to assume that the values of $\bar{X}$ follow a normal distribution centered at $\mu = 400$ hours but one that is much narrower than the population of individual lifetimes described in Figure 7.2.

TABLE

7.1

Twenty samples of 10 Everglo bulbs.

	Sample 1	Sample 2	Sample 3	Sample 4	Sample 5
	308	431	416	373	354
	419	448	361	451	385
	389	380	389	329	449
	432	371	497	460	419
	362	387	400	481	483
	302	410	489	350	396
	440	400	406	431	317
	430	426	333	356	457
	375	381	307	410	404
	383	361	375	353	480
$\bar{x} =$	384.0	399.5	397.3	399.4	414.4
$s =$	49.30	28.54	60.51	53.99	54.25

	Sample 6	Sample 7	Sample 8	Sample 9	Sample 10
	404	372	449	403	354
	390	404	389	350	446
	390	493	397	565	343
	454	344	428	354	458
	386	396	374	358	404
	385	441	502	412	468
	384	373	365	441	416
	351	438	402	340	340
	392	360	416	359	409
	396	367	316	446	408
$\bar{x} =$	393.2	398.8	403.8	402.8	404.6
$s =$	25.45	46.10	50.32	68.93	46.28

	Sample 11	Sample 12	Sample 13	Sample 14	Sample 15
	329	429	461	448	457
	473	286	399	386	432
	336	382	416	375	425
	356	380	378	488	391
	385	423	359	447	429
	365	388	408	429	448
	419	329	393	377	416
	448	438	374	380	429
	459	423	440	372	414
	449	378	454	408	315
$\bar{x} =$	401.9	385.6	408.2	411.0	415.6
$s =$	54.12	47.91	34.60	40.12	39.73

	Sample 16	Sample 17	Sample 18	Sample 19	Sample 20
	491	439	331	418	428
	353	336	427	422	368
	375	425	445	341	445
	536	419	420	485	429
	447	346	401	442	475
	415	408	389	470	437
	322	392	363	404	475
	350	409	439	370	458
	453	313	352	539	308
	343	334	346	435	408
$\bar{x} =$	408.5	382.1	391.3	432.6	423.1
$s =$	71.46	45.28	41.35	56.78	51.48

FIGURE

7.2

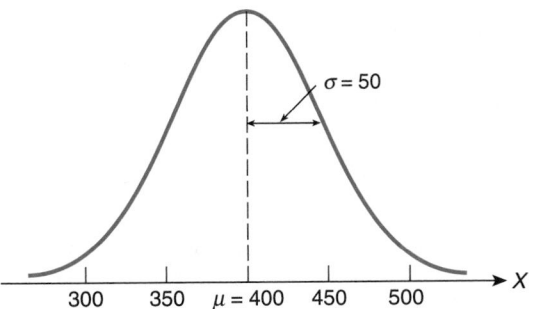

Assumed
distribution of
Everglo bulb
lifetimes.

FIGURE

7.3

Sample means
created using **KPK
Data Analysis ➤
Means and CIs for
Multiple Samples.**

File	Edit	View	Insert	Format	Tools	Data	KPK Data Analysis	Window	Help			
	Q	R	S	T	U		V	W	X		Y	
1	439	331	418	428	**Multiple Samples**			**Frequency Distribution Table**				
2	336	427	422	368	SAMPLE		MEANS	CLASS	CLASS LIMITS		FREQUENCY	
3	425	445	341	445	1		384.00	1	377 and under 384		1	
4	419	420	485	429	2		399.50	2	384 and under 391		2	
5	346	401	442	475	3		397.30	3	391 and under 398		3	
6	408	389	470	437	4		399.40	4	398 and under 405		7	
7	392	363	404	475	5		414.40	5	405 and under 412		3	
8	409	439	370	458	6		393.20	6	412 and under 419		2	
9	313	352	539	308	7		398.80	7	419 and under 426		1	
10	334	346	435	408	8		403.80	8	426 and under 433		1	
11					9		402.80		TOTAL		20	
12					10		404.60					
13					11		401.90					
14					12		385.60					
15					13		408.20					
16					14		411.00					
17					15		415.60					
18					16		408.50					
19					17		382.10					
20					18		391.30					
21					19		432.60					
22					20		423.10					
23					SUMMARY FOR X-BARs							
24					Mean		402.89					
25					St. Dev.		12.78					
26												
	Frequency Histogram	DATA7-2										

FIGURE

7.4

Excel histogram of
20 sample means.

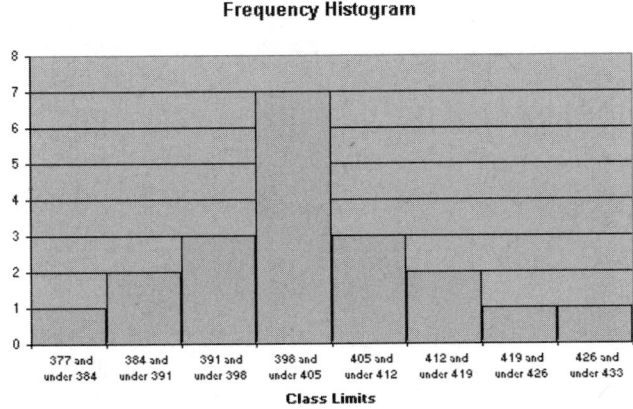

In the previous example, we observed that the values of $\bar{X}$ were centered about the mean of the population, μ. In addition, the standard deviation of the $\bar{X}$ values was considerably less than the standard deviation of the population, σ. In general, what can you say about the mean and standard deviation of the random variable $\bar{X}$? This is summarized as follows:

Mean of the random variable $\bar{X}$ is

$$\mu_{\bar{X}} = \mu$$

7.1

Standard deviation of the random variable $\bar{X}$ is

$$\sigma_{\bar{X}} = \frac{\sigma}{\sqrt{n}}$$

7.2

For the previous example, $\mu = 400$, $\sigma = 50$, and $n = 10$. As a result, the mean and standard deviation of the $\bar{X}$ values, if samples of size 10 were obtained *indefinitely*, are

$$\mu_{\bar{X}} = 400 \qquad \text{and} \qquad \sigma_{\bar{X}} = \frac{50}{\sqrt{10}} = 15.81$$

Recall that the mean and standard deviation of the 20 observed $\bar{X}$ values was 402.89 and 12.78, respectively. These values will tend toward 400 and 15.81 if we were to take additional samples of size 10. These results are summarized in Figure 7.5, where $\mu_{\bar{X}} = 400$ and $\sigma_{\bar{X}} = 15.81$.

FIGURE

7.5

Normal curves for population and sample mean.

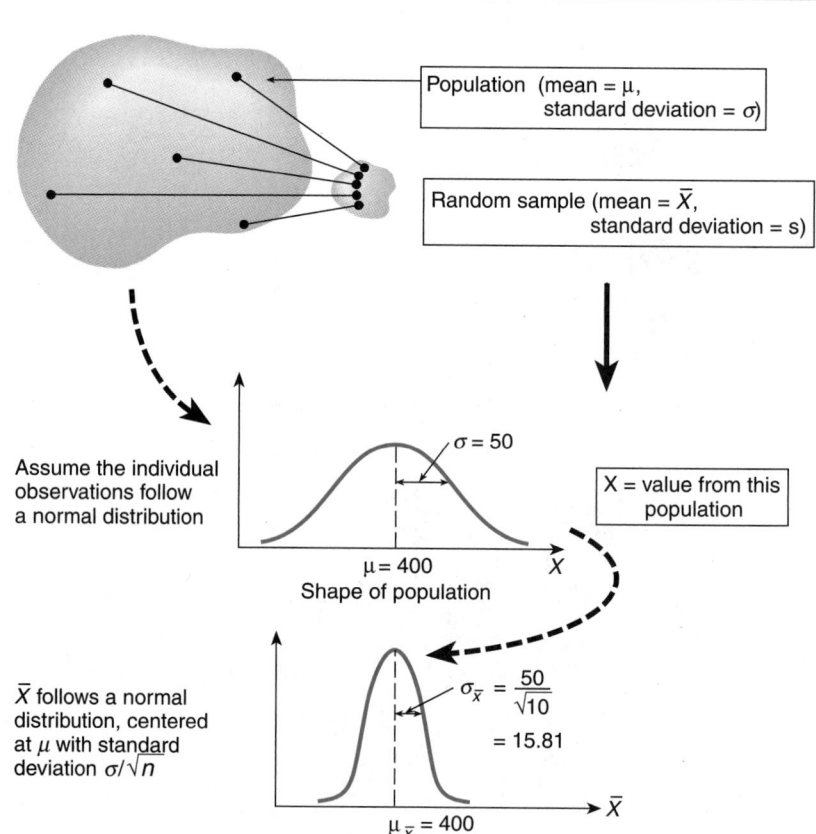

THE CENTRAL LIMIT THEOREM

In the previous example, we observed that the shape of the $\overline{X}$ curve was approximately normal. This is not a surprising result, considering that the population from which the samples were obtained followed an assumed normal curve; that is, the random variable X = lifetime of Everglo bulb is a normal random variable. What may surprise you is that the random variable $\overline{X}$ follows an approximate normal curve *regardless* of the shape of the population curve, *provided large samples are obtained*. This is summarized in the **Central Limit Theorem.**

CENTRAL LIMIT THEOREM

When obtaining large samples (generally $n > 30$) from any population, the sample mean $\overline{X}$ will follow an approximate normal distribution.

Based on the Central Limit Theorem and equations 7.1 and 7.2, whenever large samples are obtained from *any* population, the sample mean, $\overline{X}$, will follow an approximate normal distribution with mean μ and standard deviation $\sigma/\sqrt{n}$. In practice, you are likely to obtain your one and only sample of size n. However, these results allow you to make probability statements regarding $\overline{X}$, as illustrated in the examples to follow.

Comments

1. Not having to know the shape of the sampled population for large samples makes the Central Limit Theorem a very strong tool in statistics. For example, if you repeatedly took large samples from a population with an exponential distribution (look ahead to Figure 7.11), the resulting $\overline{X}$'s would follow a *normal* (not an exponential) curve.

2. Based on equations 7.1 and 7.2, the mean of $\overline{X}$ is μ and the standard deviation of $\overline{X}$ is $\sigma/\sqrt{n}$ for *any* sample size n. However, for $\overline{X}$ to be approximately normally distributed, a large value of n is necessary if the population is not assumed to be normally distributed.

3. If the population from which you are sampling is a normal population, the Central Limit Theorem isn't necessary. For this situation, the random variable $\overline{X}$ is *exactly* normally distributed, with mean μ and standard deviation $\sigma/\sqrt{n}$. For Example 7.2, we can say that the random variable $\overline{X}$ follows an exact normal distribution with mean = 400 and standard deviation $50/\sqrt{10} = 15.81$.

Basically, equations 7.1 and 7.2 along with the Central Limit Theorem state that the normal curve (distribution) for $\overline{X}$ is centered at the same value as the population distribution but has a much smaller standard deviation. Notice that as the sample size, n, increases, $\sigma/\sqrt{n}$ decreases, and so the spread relative to the mean of the $\overline{X}$ curve (that is, the variation in the $\overline{X}$ values) decreases. In the Everglo bulb example, if we repeatedly obtained samples of size 100 (rather than 10), the corresponding $\overline{X}$ values would lie even closer to $\mu_{\overline{X}} = 400$ because now $\sigma_{\overline{X}}$ would equal $50/\sqrt{100} = 5$ (see Figure 7.6).

For the 20 values of $\overline{X}$ in Table 7.1, it was assumed that the population mean was *known* to be $\mu = 400$, so each of the $\overline{X}$ values estimates μ with a certain amount of error. The more variation in the $\overline{X}$ values, the more error we encounter using $\overline{X}$ as an estimate of μ. Consequently, the standard deviation of $\overline{X}$ also serves as a measure of the error that will be encountered using a sample mean to estimate a population mean. The standard deviation of the $\overline{X}$ distribution is often referred to as the **standard error** of $\overline{X}$.

FIGURE

7.6

Normal curves for the sample mean ($n = 10, 20, 50, 100$).

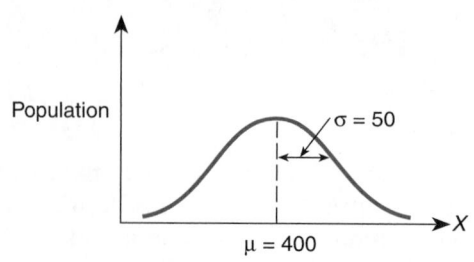

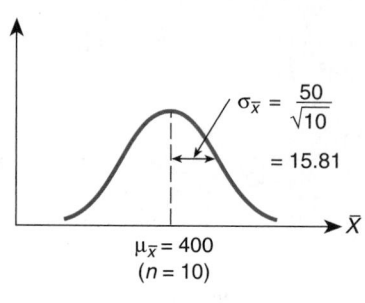

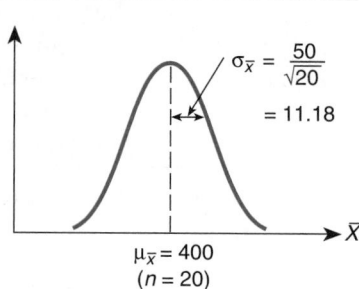

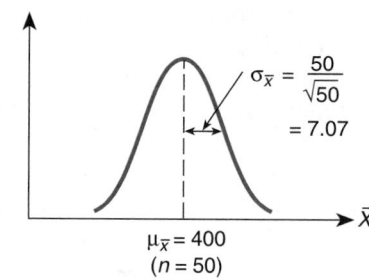

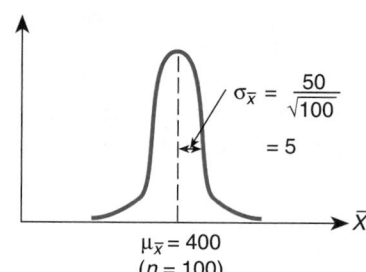

Standard error of $\bar{X}$ = standard deviation of the probability distribution for $\bar{X}$

$$= \frac{\sigma}{\sqrt{n}}$$

The previous discussion has described the probability distribution of the sample mean, $\bar{X}$. This distribution is referred to as the *sampling distribution* of $\bar{X}$.

DEFINITION

The probability distribution of a sample statistic is its **sampling distribution.**

To summarize this section: For large samples, the sampling distribution of $\bar{X}$ is approximately normal, centered at μ, with a standard deviation (standard error) of $\sigma/\sqrt{n}$, regardless of the shape of the sampled population.

EXAMPLE

7.3

Electricalc has determined that the assembly time for a particular electrical component is normally distributed with a mean of 20 minutes and a standard deviation of 3 minutes.

1. What is the probability that an employee in the assembly division takes longer than 22 minutes to assemble one of these components?

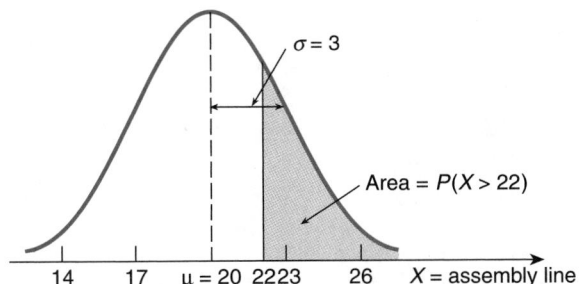

FIGURE

7.7

Assembly time for the population of electrical components. (See Example 7.3.)

FIGURE

7.8

Curve for $\overline{X}$ = average of 15 employees' assembly times. Shaded area shows $P(\overline{X} > 22)$.

2. What is the probability that the average assembly time for 15 such employees exceeds 22 minutes?

3. What is the probability that the average assembly time for 15 employees is between 19 and 21 minutes?

Solution 1

The random variable X here is the assembly time for a component. It is assumed to be a normal random variable, with $\mu = 20$ minutes and $\sigma = 3$ minutes (Figure 7.7). We wish to determine $P(X > 22)$. Standardizing this variable and using Table A.4, we obtain

$$P(X > 22) = P\left[\frac{X - 20}{3} > \frac{22 - 20}{3}\right]$$
$$= P(Z > .67)$$
$$= .5 - .2486 = .2514$$

Therefore, a randomly chosen employee will require longer than 22 minutes to assemble the component with probability .25.

Solution 2

Figure 7.7 does *not* apply to this question, because we are concerned with the *average* time for 15 employees, not an individual employee. Using comment 3 on page 267, we know that the curve describing $\overline{X}$ (an average of 15 employees) is normal with

$$\text{mean} = \mu_{\overline{X}} = \mu = 20 \text{ minutes}$$

$$\text{standard deviation (standard error)} = \sigma_{\overline{X}} = \frac{\sigma}{\sqrt{n}}$$

$$= \frac{3}{\sqrt{15}} = .77 \text{ minutes}$$

(See Figure 7.8.)

FIGURE

7.9

Curve for average
assembly time of
15 employees.
Shaded area
shows
$P(19 < \overline{X} < 21)$.

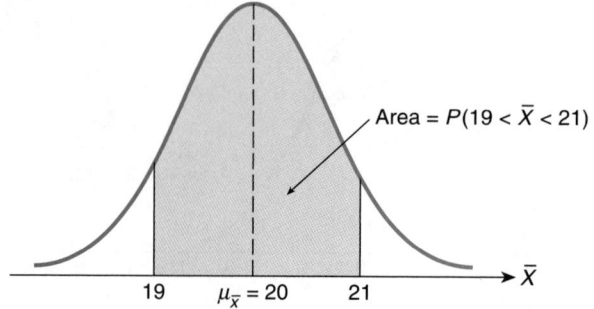

Area = $P(19 < \overline{X} < 21)$

19   $\mu_{\overline{x}} = 20$ 21 $\overline{X}$

This procedure is the same as in solution 1, except now the standard deviation of this curve is .77 rather than 3:

$$P(\overline{X} > 22) = P\left[\frac{\overline{X} - 20}{.77} > \frac{22 - 20}{.77}\right]$$

$$= P(Z > 2.60)$$

$$= .5 - .4953 = .0047$$

So an average assembly time for a sample of 15 employees will be more than 22 minutes with less than 1% probability; that is, it is very unlikely that an average of 15 assembly times will exceed 22 minutes.

Solution 3   The curve for this solution is shown in Figure 7.9. We wish to find $P(19 > \overline{X} > 21)$.

$$P(19 < \overline{X} < 21) = P\left[\frac{19 - 20}{.77} < \frac{\overline{X} - 20}{.77} < \frac{21 - 20}{.77}\right]$$

$$= P(-1.30 < Z < 1.30)$$

$$= .4032 + .4032 = .8064$$

Thus, a sample of 15 employees will produce an average assembly time between 19 and 21 minutes with probability about .81.

In Example 7.3, it was assumed that the individual assembly times followed a normal distribution. *However, remember that the strength of the Central Limit Theorem is that this assumption is not necessary for large samples.* We can answer questions 2 and 3 for *any* population whose mean is 20 minutes and standard deviation is 3 minutes, provided we take a *large* sample ($n > 30$). In this case, the normal distribution of $\overline{X}$ may not be exact, but it provides a very good approximation.

EXAMPLE

7.4

The price–earnings (P/E) ratio of a stock is usually considered by analysts who put together financial portfolios. Suppose a population of all P/E ratios has a mean of 10.5 and a standard deviation of 4.5.

1. What is the probability that a sample of 40 stocks will have an average P/E ratio less than 9?

2. What assumptions about the population of all P/E ratios are necessary in your answer to question 1?

By the Central Limit Theorem and equations 7.1 and 7.2, $\bar{X}$ is approximately a normal random variable with mean $= \mu = 10.5$ and standard deviation $= \sigma/\sqrt{n} = 4.5/\sqrt{40} = .71$. So

Solution 1

$$Z = \frac{\bar{X} - 10.5}{.71}$$

is approximately a standard normal random variable, and consequently

$$P(\bar{X} < 9) = P\left[\frac{\bar{X} - 10.5}{.71} < \frac{9 - 10.5}{.71}\right]$$

$$= P(Z < -2.11) = .0174$$

No assumptions regarding the shape of the P/E ratio population are necessary. This population might be normal or it might not be—it simply does not matter because we are using a fairly large sample ($n = 40$). The distribution of $\bar{X}$ is approximately normal, regardless of the shape of the population of all P/E ratios. Our only assumptions in solution 1 were that $\mu = 10.5$ and $\sigma = 4.5$.

Solution 2

X Exercises 7.1–7.8

Understanding the Mechanics

7.1 A sample of $n = 100$ observations from a normal population is drawn. The population mean is 500 and the population standard deviation is 200. Find the following.
    a. $P(\bar{X} > 480)$
    b. $P(460 < \bar{X} < 480)$
    c. $P(\bar{X} < 530)$

7.2 A population has a mean of 200 and a standard deviation of 50. Let $\bar{X}$ be used to estimate the mean of the population from a random sample of size 100. Find the following probabilities.
    a. $P(\bar{X} \le 205)$
    b. $P(\bar{X} \ge 190)$
    c. $P(195 \le \bar{X} \le 210)$
    d. $P(188 \le \bar{X} \le 198)$

Applying the New Concepts

7.3 Surveys indicate that an adult between the ages of 20 and 30 years of age spends a mean of four hours per day either watching TV or listening to the radio. The standard deviation of the amount of time spent doing these activities is one hour.
    a. If a sample of 50 adults between the ages of 20 and 30 years of age was drawn, what does the Central Limit Theorem tell us about the distribution of the sample mean of the time spent by the adults either watching TV or listening to the radio?
    b. If the sample size were to increase to 100, how would this change the distribution of the sample mean of the time spent by the adults either watching TV or listening to the radio?

7.4 Five machines produce electronic components. The number of components produced per hour is normally distributed with a mean of 25 and a standard deviation of 4.
    a. What percentage of the time does a machine produce more than 27 components per hour?
    b. What percentage of the time is the average rate of output of the five machines more than 27 components per hour?

7.5 A quality engineer knows from past data that in a shipment lot, the number of wire cables that have tensile strengths below the lower specification limit follows a Poisson distribution with a mean of 50. For a sample of 45 shipment lots, what is the probability that the sample mean for the number of wire cables with tensile strengths below the lower specification limit exceeds 53?

7.6 The average length of actual running time (excluding advertisements) for television feature films is 1 hour and 40 minutes, with a standard deviation of 15 minutes. If a sample of 49 TV feature films is taken at random, what is the probability that the average running time for this group is 1 hour and 45 minutes or more?

7.7 The Labor Department measures the changes in a set list of food, clothing, housing, energy, and medical costs to calculate the consumer price index. The government uses the time span from October to September each year to figure increases in Social Security benefits based on this index. For 2002, the estimated average Social Security check is $850 due to an increase in this index. Assume that the population standard deviation is $240.
    a. A random sample of 64 Social Security recipients is selected. What is the probability that the average Social Security check for this sample is between $820 and $880?

b. Suppose that in part a the sample size is increased to 100. Do you think the probability would increase or decrease? Find the probability and compare.

(Source: "Social Security Checks to Rise 2.6%," *The New York Times*, October 20, 2001, p. C1.)

7.8 California's olive-oil industry may never match the glorious success of the wine industry. However, California olive-oil producers have expanded to approximately 120 producers statewide. This compares to tens of thousands of olive-oil producers in Europe, mostly concentrated in Spain and Italy. Olive-oil analysts say that the California producers are able to compete with European olive-oil producers by marketing their product as a per-

ishable commodity that is ideally made, bought, and consumed locally, and that California olive oil has its own distinctive taste. These analysts estimate that the average price that California consumers pay for a 350-milliliter bottle of olive oil is $21, with a standard deviation of $2.40.

a. What is the probability that the average price paid by a random sample of 36 olive-oil-buying consumers in California is less than $22?

b. Do a "what if" analysis by changing the standard deviation to $3.00 and answering part a. Do you think that the probability will increase or decrease? Why?

(Source: "California Dreaming," *Los Angeles Times*, October 17, 2001, p. H1.)

A Look at the Sampling Distribution of $\overline{X}$ for Normal Populations

The Central Limit Theorem tells us that $\overline{X}$ tends toward a normal distribution as the sample size increases. If you are dealing with a population that has an assumed normal distribution (as in Example 7.3), then $\overline{X}$ is normal regardless of the sample size. However, as the sample size increases, the variability of $\overline{X}$ decreases, as is illustrated in Figure 7.6. This means that for large sample sizes, if you were to get many samples and corresponding values of $\overline{X}$, these values of $\overline{X}$ would be more concentrated around the middle, with very few extremely large or extremely small values.

Look at Figure 7.6, which illustrates the assumed normal distribution of all Everglo bulbs. We know (using Table A.4) that 95% of a normal curve is contained within 1.96 standard deviations of the mean. For a sample size of $n = 10$ from a normal population with $\mu = 400$ and $\sigma = 50$, $\sigma_{\overline{X}} = 15.81$. Now,

$$\mu_{\overline{X}} - 1.96\sigma_{\overline{X}} = 400 - 1.96(15.81) = 369.0$$

and

$$\mu_{\overline{X}} + 1.96\sigma_{\overline{X}} = 400 + 1.96(15.81) = 431.0$$

Thus, if we repeatedly obtain samples of size 10, 95% of the resulting $\overline{X}$ values will lie between 369.0 and 431.0.

This result and the corresponding results using $n = 20$, 50, and 100 are contained in Table 7.2, which reemphasizes that for larger samples, you are much more likely to get a value of $\overline{X}$ that is close to $\mu = 400$. In practice, you typically do not know the value of μ. However, by using a larger sample size, you are more apt to obtain an $\overline{X}$ that is a good estimate of the unknown μ.

	TABLE 7.2

Sample from a normal population with $\mu = 400$ and $\sigma = 50$; 95% of the time, the value of $\overline{X}$ will be between $\mu_{\overline{X}} - 1.96\sigma_{\overline{X}}$ and $\mu_{\overline{X}} + 1.96\sigma_{\overline{X}}$. Refer to Figure 7.6 for the values of $\sigma_{\overline{X}}$.

Sample Size	$\sigma_{\overline{X}}$	$\mu_{\overline{X}} - 1.96\sigma_{\overline{X}}$	$\mu_{\overline{X}} + 1.96\sigma_{\overline{X}}$	Conclusion
$n = 10$	15.81	369.0	431.0	95% of the time, the value of $\overline{X}$ will be between 369.0 and 431.0
$n = 20$	11.18	378.1	421.9	95% of the time, the value of $\overline{X}$ will be between 378.1 and 421.9
$n = 50$	7.07	386.1	413.9	95% of the time, the value of $\overline{X}$ will be between 386.1 and 413.9
$n = 100$	5	390.2	409.8	95% of the time, the value of $\overline{X}$ will be between 390.2 and 409.8

Applying the Central Limit Theorem to Nonnormal Populations

The real strength of the Central Limit Theorem is that $\overline{X}$ will tend toward a normal random variable regardless of the shape of your population. You need a large sample ($n > 30$) to obtain a nearly normal distribution for $\overline{X}$. The Central Limit Theorem also holds when sampling from a discrete population.

Figures 7.10, 7.11, and 7.12 illustrate the distribution of $\overline{X}$ for three nonnormal populations. Notice that the uniform population (Figure 7.10) is at least symmetric about the mean, so the distribution of the sample mean, $\overline{X}$, tends toward a

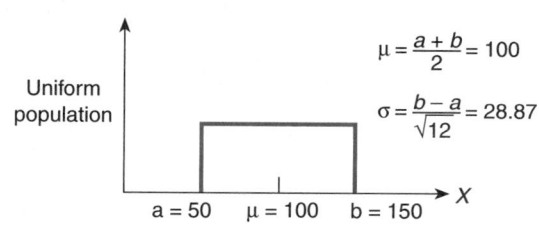

$$\mu = \frac{a+b}{2} = 100$$

$$\sigma = \frac{b-a}{\sqrt{12}} = 28.87$$

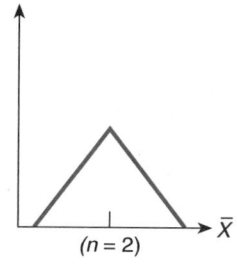 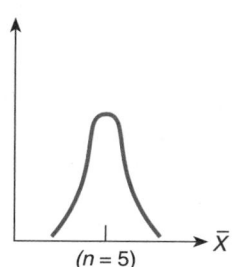 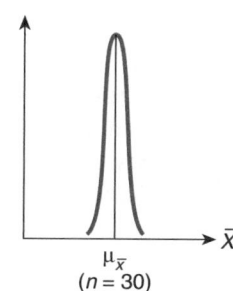

For $n = 30$, $\mu_{\overline{x}} = \mu = 100$

$$\sigma_{\overline{x}} = \frac{\sigma}{\sqrt{n}} = \frac{28.87}{\sqrt{30}} = 5.27$$

FIGURE

7.10

Distribution of $\overline{X}$ for a uniform population.

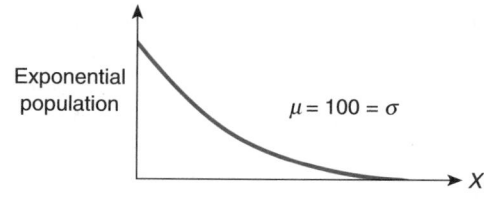

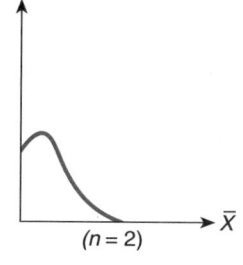 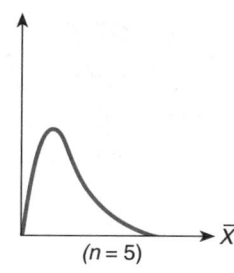 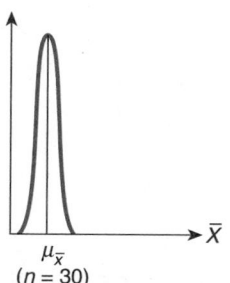

For $n = 30$, $\mu_{\overline{x}} = \mu = 100$

$$\sigma_{\overline{x}} = \frac{\sigma}{\sqrt{n}} = \frac{100}{\sqrt{30}}$$

$$= 18.26$$

FIGURE

7.11

Distribution of $\overline{X}$ for an exponential population.

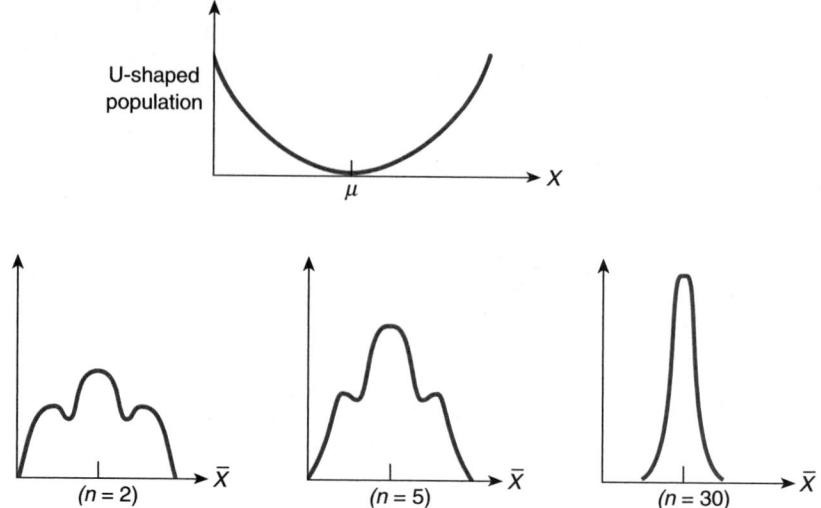

FIGURE 7.12

Distribution of $\bar{X}$ for a U-shaped population.

normal distribution for much smaller sample sizes. The U-shaped distribution (Figure 7.12) is another continuous distribution. It is characterized by many small and large values, with few values in the middle. This distribution is symmetric about the mean, but its shape is opposite to that of a normal distribution. Here, $\bar{X}$ requires a large sample ($n \geq 30$) to attain an approximate normal distribution.

Sampling from a Finite Population

In the previous discussion, we assumed that the population was large enough that the sample was extremely small by comparison. We will now consider whether our results, including the Central Limit Theorem, apply when the exact size of the population is known and the sample is a large portion of the population.

Sampling with Replacement. When you return each element of the sample to the population before taking the next sample element, you are sampling *with replacement*. This sampling procedure is not common; people generally obtain their sample all at once, making it impossible to sample with replacement. When sampling with replacement, it is possible to obtain the same element more than once. For example, the same person could be chosen all three times in a sample of size $n = 3$. When sampling with replacement, the previous results apply exactly as before, without any adjustments necessary.

> ### SAMPLING WITH REPLACEMENT FROM A FINITE POPULATION
>
> When sampling with replacement from a finite population with mean μ and standard deviation σ, the sample mean $\bar{X}$ tends toward a normal distribution with
>
> $$\text{mean} = \mu_{\bar{X}} = \mu$$
>
> $$\text{standard deviation (standard error)} = \sigma_{\bar{X}} = \frac{\sigma}{\sqrt{n}}$$
>
> where n = sample size.

7.3
7.4

Sampling without Replacement. We first encountered the problem of sampling without replacement from a finite population in Chapter 5, where the hypergeometric distribution considered the population size (N) and the binomial distribution did not. It is easy to show that, for this situation,

$$\begin{bmatrix} \text{variance of hypergeometric} \\ \text{random variable} \end{bmatrix} = \begin{bmatrix} \text{variance of corresponding} \\ \text{binomial random variable} \end{bmatrix} \cdot \begin{bmatrix} \dfrac{N-n}{N-1} \end{bmatrix}$$

because

$$\frac{k(N-k)n(N-n)}{N^2(N-1)} = n\frac{k}{N}\left[1-\frac{k}{N}\right] \cdot \left[\frac{N-n}{N-1}\right]$$

$$= np(1-p) \cdot \left[\frac{N-n}{N-1}\right]$$

where $p = k/N$. Here, $(N-n)/(N-1)$ is called the **finite population correction (fpc) factor.** When the sample size, n, is very small compared with the population size, N, the fpc factor is nearly 1 and can be ignored. In fact, as discussed in Chapter 5, the binomial distribution serves as a good approximation to the hypergeometric whenever $n/N < .05$. The same result applies to sampling situations as well. We can express this as a rule: The fpc can be ignored whenever $n/N < .05$.

For this situation, the standard error of $\overline{X}$ includes the finite population correction.

SAMPLING WITHOUT REPLACEMENT FROM A LARGE, FINITE POPULATION

When sampling without replacement from a large finite population (of size N), with mean μ and standard deviation σ, the sample mean $\overline{X}$ tends toward a normal distribution with

$$\text{mean} = \mu_{\overline{X}} = \mu$$

$$\text{standard deviation (standard error)} = \sigma_{\overline{X}} = \frac{\sigma}{\sqrt{n}} \cdot \sqrt{\frac{N-n}{N-1}}$$

where n = sample size.*

7.5 7.6

The fpc recognizes that our estimate is better for a finite population than for an infinite population and shrinks the size of the standard error. In fact, when the sample size (n) and the population size (N) are the same, the fpc is 0, making the standard error equal to 0. This value is correct, since repeated samples of size $n = N$ would produce the same sample, namely the entire population, and consequently, the same value of $\overline{X}$. Since there is no variation in the $\overline{X}$ values, the standard deviation of $\overline{X}$ (standard error) *should* be zero. *As a final note, remember that although the effect of the fpc is negligible when* $n/N < .05$, *it can (and some will argue "should") always be used to derive a more accurate standard error.*

EXAMPLE 7.5

A group of women managers at Compumart is considering filing a sex-discrimination suit. A recent report stated that the average annual income of all employees in middle management positions at Compumart is \$48,000 and the standard deviation is \$8,500. A random sample of 45 women taken from a population of 350 female middle managers at Compumart had an average income of $\overline{x} = \$43,900$. If the population of all female incomes at this level is assumed to have

---

*The standard error in equations 7.2, 7.4, and 7.6 assumes that the population standard deviation σ is known. If this parameter is estimated from the sample and the sample standard deviation (s) is substituted for σ, the resulting standard error is referred to as the "estimated standard error." For this situation, the fpc in equation 7.6 becomes $(N-n)/N$ rather than $(N-n)/(N-1)$. Section 7.6 contains additional discussion on this topic.

FIGURE

7.13

Distribution of
sample mean of
annual salaries
(assuming
$\mu = \$48,000$,
$\sigma = \$8,500$). The
shaded area
represents the
solution to
Example 7.5,
$P(\overline{X} \le 43,900)$.

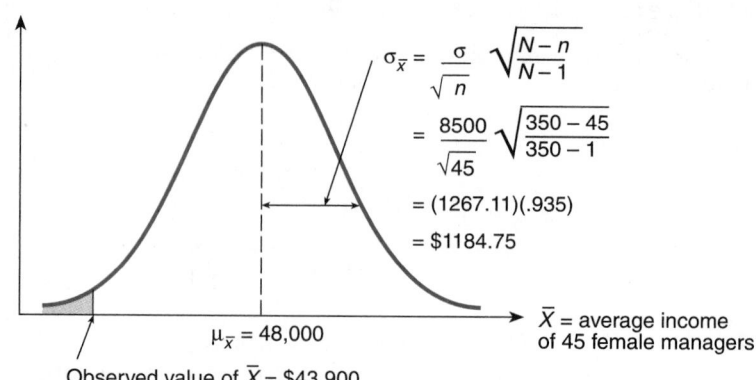

$$\sigma_{\overline{x}} = \frac{\sigma}{\sqrt{n}} \sqrt{\frac{N-n}{N-1}}$$

$$= \frac{8500}{\sqrt{45}} \sqrt{\frac{350-45}{350-1}}$$

$$= (1267.11)(.935)$$

$$= \$1184.75$$

$\overline{X}$ = average income
of 45 female managers

$\mu_{\overline{x}} = 48,000$

Observed value of $\overline{X} = \$43,900$

the same mean ($48,000) and standard deviation ($8,500) as the distribution of incomes for all employees, what is the probability of observing a value of $\overline{X}$ this low?

Solution Because we have a large sample, we can assume (using the Central Limit Theorem) that the curve describing $\overline{X}$ is normal, as shown in Figure 7.13. Here, $n = 45$ and $N = 350$. We need to find $P(\overline{X} \le 43,900)$. Standardizing and using Table A.4, we find that

$$P(\overline{X} \le 43,900) = P\left[Z \le \frac{43,900 - 48,000}{1184.75} \right]$$

$$= P(Z \le -3.46) = .0003$$

So, if the female population has an average salary of $48,000 (and standard deviation of $8,500), then the chance of obtaining an $\overline{X}$ as low as $43,900 is extremely small. If we assume that the standard deviation is correct, then, based strictly on this set of data, our conclusion would be that the average salary for women at this level is not $48,000 but is less than $48,000.

With the type of question asked in Example 7.5, there is always the chance that we will reach an incorrect decision using the sample data; there is always the chance of error due to sampling. This possible error will be a concern whenever you test a hypothesis. For now, remember that when dealing with sample data, statistics never *prove* anything. They do, however, *support or fail to support* a claim (such as $\mu < \$48,000$).

X **Exercises 7.9–7.18**

Understanding the Mechanics

7.9 A finite population is approximately normally distributed with a mean of 20 and a standard deviation of 6. Let $\overline{X}$ be used to estimate the mean of this population from sampling 40 observations without replacement.

  a. Find $P(\overline{X} \le 21)$ if the finite population is of size 100.
  b. Find $P(\overline{X} \le 21)$ if the finite population is of size 300.
  c. Find $P(\overline{X} \le 21)$ if the finite population is of size 1,000.

7.10 Consider a finite population whose distribution can be approximated by a normal distribution. Assume that the population is of size 400 with a mean of 100 and a standard deviation of 25. Let $\overline{X}$ be used to estimate the mean of the population from a sample of size 30.

  a. Find $P(95 \le \overline{X} \le 105)$ if sampling is performed without replacement.
  b. Find $P(95 \le \overline{X} \le 105)$ if sampling is performed with replacement.

Applying the New Concepts

7.11 The electric bill for 250 households in a small midwestern town was found to have a mean of $120 with a standard deviation of $25 for the month of November. If 10 households are selected at random from the 250 households, what is the probability that the sample mean will be between $110 and $130? What are you assuming about the population?

7.12 General Appliances has 70 microwave ovens that need repair. The mean cost of repair for the 70 microwaves is $80. The standard deviation of the cost is $35. The cost can be considered to be approximately normally distributed.

    a. If a sample of 10 of the 70 microwaves is selected without replacement, what is the probability that the mean cost for the sample is greater than $100?

    b. If a sample of 10 of the 70 microwaves is selected with replacement, what is the probability that the mean cost of the sample is greater than $100?

7.13 The mean daily time spent on the telephone by the 60 personnel managers of Retail Products is 1.25 hours; the standard deviation is .62 hours. Assuming that the time spent on the telephone is approximately normally distributed, what is the probability that the mean daily time spent on the telephone by 10 different personnel managers selected at random is greater than 1.5 hours?

7.14 Explain how the finite population correction factor is affected as the finite population size gets large for a fixed sample size.

7.15 A shipment of 200 treated-lumber boards arrives at a construction site. The lengths of the lumber boards are approximately normally distributed with a mean of 10 feet and a standard deviation of .14 feet. Would it be considered unusual for a quality inspector to find a sample of 20 lumber boards with a mean of 9.92 feet or less?

7.16 Game Boy is counting on its Barbie Pet Rescue game to be a hit with children ages 5 to 8. The company believes that this is an ideal game to help children increase their reading skills and to have fun with animals as the player gets to work with Barbie and her sister Stacie at a pet rescue center that nurtures and cares for more than 20 different pets. Across 400 retail stores in Texas and Oklahoma that sell the game, the average retail price is $25, with a standard deviation of $2.50.

    a. If a random sample of 50 retail stores across Texas and Oklahoma are randomly selected, what is the probability that the average price for the Barbie Pet Rescue game is more than $25.50?

    b. Suppose that the number of retail stores that sold the Barbie Pet Rescue was 200 instead of 400. By how much would the probability in part a decrease?

(Source: "Electronic Adventures: Video and Computer Game Reviews," *Dallas Morning News*, October 11, 2001, p. 4D.)

Using the Computer

7.17 The finite population correction factor reduces the standard deviation of the sample mean. If n/N is less than .05, this factor does not seriously affect the probability that the sample mean is less than a particular number. Assume that $N = 200$, $\sigma = 100$, and $\mu = 100$. Using the cumulative normal distribution function in either Excel, SPSS, or MINITAB, find the probability that the sample mean is less than 80 with and without the finite population correction factor for the following values of n. Comment on the differences between these two calculations.

    a. $n = 10$
    b. $n = 20$
    c. $n = 40$
    d. $n = 80$

7.18 **[Simulation Exercise]** The Central Limit Theorem is important to statistical analysis because it says that the sample mean will tend toward a normal random variable regardless of the shape of the population. To demonstrate this theorem using Excel, click on **KPK menu ➤ Simulation Exercises ➤ Central Limit Theorem.**

    a. Select values of .1 for the probability of each of the numbers from 1 through 10. Click on the button to start the simulation. Comment on the histogram shapes for sample sizes of 2, 5, 10, 20, and 50. Would you say that the sample mean tends toward a normal random variable quickly as the sample size increases for this population?

    b. Select values of .4, .1, .1, and .4 for the values 1, 2, 9, and 10 and zeros for the remaining values. Repeat part a using this very nonnormal population.

    c. Try other population shapes and discover for which shapes the sample mean tends quickly toward a normal random variable as the sample size increases.

7.3
CONFIDENCE INTERVALS FOR THE MEAN OF A NORMAL POPULATION (σ KNOWN)

Return to the situation where we have obtained a sample from a normal population with unknown mean, μ. We first consider a case in which we know σ, the standard deviation of the normal random variable (Figure 7.14). (The situation where both μ and σ are unknown is dealt with in the next section.)

FIGURE

7.14

An example where the standard deviation σ is known but the mean μ is unknown.

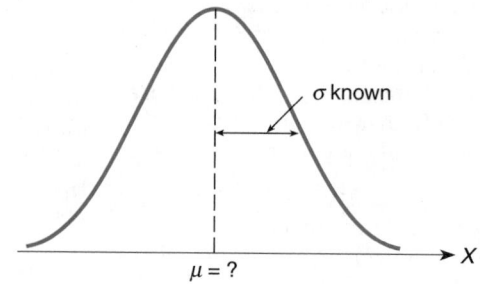

FIGURE

7.15

Distribution of $\bar{X}$ if μ = 20 minutes.

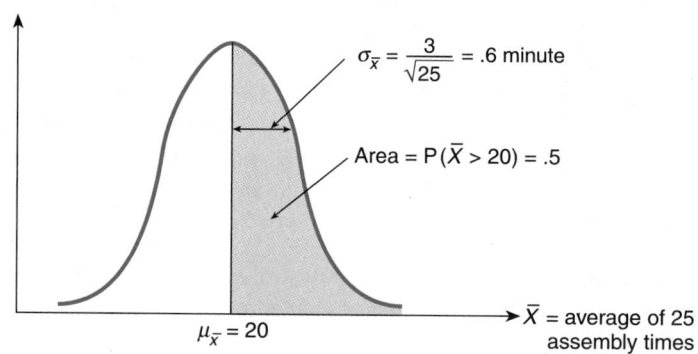

We know that to estimate μ, the average of the entire population, we obtain a sample from this population and calculate $\bar{X}$, the average of the sample. The sample mean, $\bar{X}$, is the estimate of μ and is also called a **point estimate**, because it consists of a single number.

In Example 7.3, it was assumed that the assembly time for a particular electrical component followed a normal distribution, with μ = 20 minutes and σ = 3 minutes. What if μ is not known for *all* workers? A random sample of 25 workers' assembly times was obtained with the following results (in minutes):

22.8, 29.3, 27.2, 30.2, 24.0, 23.2, 22.9, 30.3, 27.1, 31.2, 27.0, 32.0, 28.6, 24.1, 28.9, 26.8, 26.6, 23.4, 25.1, 26.6, 25.7, 28.1, 31.5, 24.8, 25.2

Based on these data,

$$\text{estimate of } \mu = \text{sample mean, } \bar{X}$$

$$= \frac{22.8 + 29.3 + \cdots + 25.2}{25} = 26.9 \text{ minutes}$$

Is this large value of $\bar{X}$ (= 26.9) due to random chance? We know that 50% of the samples drawn will have $\bar{X}$ larger than 20, even if μ = 20 (Figure 7.15). Or is this value large because μ is a value larger than 20? In other words, does this value of $\bar{X}$ provide just cause for concluding that μ is larger than 20? We tackle this type of question in Chapter 8.

How accurate is a derived estimate of the population mean, μ? The accuracy depends, for one thing, on the sample size. We can measure the precision of this estimate by constructing a **confidence interval.** By providing the confidence interval, one can make such statements as "I am 95% confident that the average assembly time, μ, is between 25.7 minutes and 28.1 minutes." For this illustration, (25.7, 28.1) is called a 95% confidence interval for μ. The following discussion demonstrates how to construct such a confidence interval.

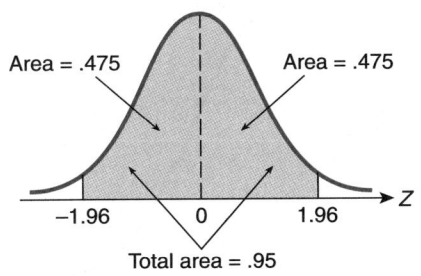

FIGURE

7.16

$P(-1.96 \leq Z \leq 1.96)$
$= .95.$

Using comment 3 on page 267, we know that $\overline{X}$ is a normal random variable with

$$\mu_{\overline{X}} = \mu$$

$$\sigma_{\overline{X}} = \frac{\sigma}{\sqrt{n}}$$

where μ and σ represent the mean and standard deviation of the population.* To standardize $\overline{X}$, you subtract the mean (μ) of $\overline{X}$ and divide by the standard deviation ($\sigma/\sqrt{n}$) of $\overline{X}$. Consequently,

$$Z = \frac{\overline{X} - \mu}{\sigma/\sqrt{n}}$$

is a standard normal random variable. Consider the following statement and refer to Figure 7.16:

$$P(-1.96 \leq Z \leq 1.96) = .95$$

so

$$P\left(-1.96 \leq \frac{\overline{X} - \mu}{\sigma/\sqrt{n}} \leq 1.96\right) = .95$$

After some algebra and rearrangement of terms, we get

$$P\left(\overline{X} - 1.96\frac{\sigma}{\sqrt{n}} \leq \mu \leq \overline{X} + 1.96\frac{\sigma}{\sqrt{n}}\right) = .95$$

How does the last statement apply to a *particular* sample mean, $\overline{x}$? Consider the interval

$$\left(\overline{x} - 1.96\frac{\sigma}{\sqrt{n}}, \ \overline{x} + 1.96\frac{\sigma}{\sqrt{n}}\right) \qquad 7.7$$

Using the values from our assembly-time example, we have $\overline{x} = 26.9$, $\sigma = 3$, and $n = 25$. The resulting 95% confidence interval is

$$\left(26.9 - 1.96 \cdot \frac{3}{\sqrt{25}}, \ 26.9 + 1.96 \cdot \frac{3}{\sqrt{25}}\right)$$

or

$$(25.72, 28.08)$$

---

*This discussion ignores the finite population correction (fpc) factor defined in the previous section. For the case of sampling without replacement, where the population size (N) is known, see the discussion of simple random sampling in Section 7.6.

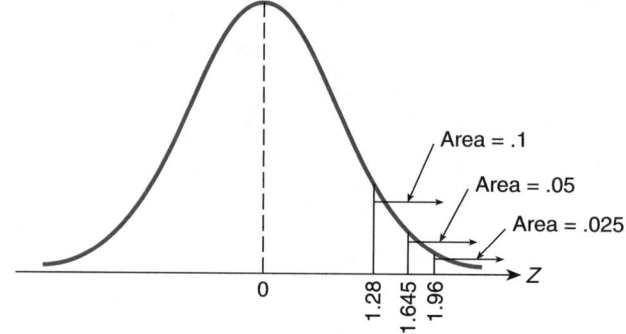

FIGURE

7.17

$1.28 = Z_{.1}$,
$1.645 = Z_{.05}$, and
$1.96 = Z_{.025}$.

Area = .1

Area = .05

Area = .025

0   1.28 1.645 1.96   Z

Since μ is unknown, we do not know whether μ lies between 25.72 and 28.08 minutes. However, if you were to obtain random samples repeatedly, calculate $\bar{x}$, and determine the intervals defined by formula 7.7, then 95% of these intervals would contain μ and 5% would not. For this reason, formula 7.7 is called a **95% confidence interval** for μ. Using our assembly-time illustration, we are 95% confident that the average assembly time, μ, lies between 25.72 and 28.08 minutes.

Notation. Let Z_a denote the value of Z such that the area *to the right* of this value is equal to a. How can we determine $Z_{.025}$, $Z_{.05}$, and $Z_{.1}$ (Figure 7.17)? Using Table A.4, $Z_{.025} = 1.96$, $Z_{.05} = 1.645$, and $Z_{.1} = 1.28$.

When defining a confidence interval for μ, we can define a 99% confidence interval, a 95% confidence interval, a 90% confidence interval, or whatever. The specific percentage represents the **confidence level**. The *higher* the confidence level, the *wider* the confidence interval. The confidence level is written as $(1 - \alpha) \cdot 100\%$, where $\alpha = .01$ for a 99% confidence interval, $\alpha = .05$ for a 95% confidence interval, and so on. Thus, a $(1 - \alpha) \cdot 100\%$ confidence interval for the mean of a normal population, μ, is

$$\left[\bar{x} - Z_{\alpha/2}\left(\frac{\sigma}{\sqrt{n}} \right), \ \bar{x} + Z_{\alpha/2}\left(\frac{\sigma}{\sqrt{n}} \right) \right]$$

7.8

According to the Central Limit Theorem, formula 7.8 provides an approximate confidence interval for the mean of any population, provided the sample size, n, is large (n > 30).

E X A M P L E

7.6

Determine a 90% and a 99% confidence interval for the average assembly time of all workers using the 25 observations given on page 278.

Solution   The sample mean here was $\bar{x} = 26.9$. The population standard deviation is assumed to be 3 minutes. The resulting 90% confidence interval for the population mean μ is

$$26.9 - Z_{.05}\left(\frac{3}{\sqrt{25}} \right) \quad \text{to} \quad 26.9 + Z_{.05}\left(\frac{3}{\sqrt{25}} \right)$$

$$= 26.9 - 1.645\left(\frac{3}{\sqrt{25}} \right) \quad \text{to} \quad 26.9 + 1.645\left(\frac{3}{\sqrt{25}} \right)$$

$$= 26.9 - .99 \quad \text{to} \quad 26.9 + .99$$

$$= 25.91 \text{ minutes} \quad \text{to} \quad 27.89 \text{ minutes}$$

The 99% confidence interval for μ is

$$26.9 - Z_{.005}\left(\frac{3}{\sqrt{25}}\right) \quad \text{to} \quad 26.9 + Z_{.005}\left(\frac{3}{\sqrt{25}}\right)$$

$$= 26.9 - 2.575\left(\frac{3}{\sqrt{25}}\right) \quad \text{to} \quad 26.9 + 2.575\left(\frac{3}{\sqrt{25}}\right)$$

$$= 26.9 - 1.54 \quad \text{to} \quad 26.9 + 1.54$$

$$= 25.36 \text{ minutes} \quad \text{to} \quad 28.44 \text{ minutes}$$

Consequently, we are 90% confident that the mean assembly time for all workers is between 25.91 and 27.89 minutes. We are also 99% confident that this parameter is between 25.36 and 28.44 minutes, based on the results of this sample. Notice that the width of the interval increases as the confidence level increases when using the same sample data.

Discussing a Confidence Interval

The narrower your confidence interval, the better, for the same level of confidence. Suppose Electricalc spent $50,000 investigating the average time necessary to assemble their electrical components. Part of this study included obtaining a confidence interval for the average assembly time, μ. Which statement would Electricalc prefer to see?

1. I am 95% confident that the average assembly time is between 2 minutes and 50 minutes.

2. I am 95% confident that the average assembly time is between 25 minutes and 27 minutes.

The information contained in the first statement is practically worthless, and that's $50,000 down the drain. The second statement contains useful information; μ is narrowed down to a much smaller range.

Given the second statement, can you tell what the corresponding value of $\overline{X}$ was that produced this confidence interval? For any confidence interval for μ, $\overline{X}$ (the estimate of μ) is always *in the center*. So $\overline{X}$ must have been 26 minutes.

For the 90% confidence interval in Example 7.6, the following conclusions are valid:

1. I am 90% confident that the average assembly time for the population (μ) lies between 25.91 and 27.89 minutes.

2. If I repeatedly obtained samples of size 25, then 90% of the resulting confidence intervals would contain μ and 10% would not. (Question from the audience: Does this confidence interval [25.91, 27.89] contain μ? Your response: I don't know. All I can say is that this procedure leads to an interval containing μ 90% of the time.)

3. I am 90% confident that my estimate of μ (namely, $\overline{x} = 26.9$) is within .99 minute of the actual value of μ.

Here .99 is equal to $1.645 \cdot (\sigma/\sqrt{n})$. This quantity is referred to as the **margin of error, E.**

$$E = \text{margin of error} = Z_{\alpha/2}\left(\frac{\sigma}{\sqrt{n}}\right)$$

7.9

Be careful! The following statement is *not* correct: The probability that μ lies between 25.91 and 27.89 is .90. What is the probability that the number 27 lies in this confidence interval? How about 24? The answer to the first question is 1, and to the second, 0, because 27 lies in the confidence interval and 24 does not. So what is the probability that μ lies in the confidence interval? Remember that μ is a fixed number; we just do not know what its value is. It is *not* a random variable, unlike its estimator, $\bar{X}$. As a result, this probability is either 0 or 1, not .90. Therefore, remember that once you have inserted your sample results into formula 7.8 to obtain your confidence interval, the word *probability* can no longer be used to describe the resulting confidence interval.

EXAMPLE 7.7

Refer to the 20 samples of Everglo bulbs in Table 7.1. Using sample 1, what is the resulting 95% confidence interval for the population mean, μ? Assume that σ is 50 hours.

Solution   Here, $n = 10$ and $\bar{x} = 384.0$. The confidence level is 95%, so $Z_{\alpha/2} = Z_{.025} = 1.96$ (from Table A.4). Therefore, the resulting 95% confidence interval for μ is

$$384.0 - 1.96\left(\frac{50}{\sqrt{10}}\right) \quad \text{to} \quad 384.0 + 1.96\left(\frac{50}{\sqrt{10}}\right)$$

$$= 384.0 - 31.0 \quad \text{to} \quad 384.0 + 31.0$$

$$= 353.0 \quad \text{to} \quad 415.0$$

So we are 95% confident that μ lies between 353 and 415 hours. Also, we are 95% confident that our estimate of μ ($\bar{x} = 384.0$) is within 31.0 hours of the actual value.

Using Excel to Determine a Confidence Interval for a Population Mean (σ Known)

You can determine this type of confidence interval very easily using Excel. The two commands that are necessary are AVERAGE and CONFIDENCE, as illustrated in Figure 7.18. To see how this works, enter the 10 values from Example 7.7 into column A. In cell B1, click on the **Paste Function** icon (f_x) and **Statistical** under **Function Category** and AVERAGE under **Function Name.** Enter "A1:A10" in the **Number1** box, as shown in the top panel of Figure 7.18, and then click on **OK.** To obtain the margin of error, **E,** click on cell B2. Then click on the **Paste Function** icon and **Statistical** under **Function Category** and CONFIDENCE under **Function Name.** Fill in the values as shown in the bottom panel of Figure 7.18, and click on **OK.** The number in cell B2 is the value of **E.**

To determine the confidence interval, you must add and subtract the values in cells B1 and B2. So, (1) in cell B3, enter "=B1–B2"; (2) in cell B4, enter "=B1+B2"; (3) in cell C3, enter "LL" (for Lower Limit); and (4) in cell C4, enter "UL" (Upper Limit). The results of all this are shown in Figure 7.19, which agree with the solution found in Example 7.7.

Microsoft® Excel Application Use DATA7-2

EXAMPLE 7.8

How Many Confidence Intervals Contain the Population Mean?

Referring to Example 7.7, if the procedure of obtaining samples of size 10 were repeated indefinitely, we would expect 95% of the resulting confidence intervals to contain the population mean (known to be $\mu = 400$ here), and 5% would not. To illustrate this, repeat Example 7.7 using all 20 samples contained in DATA7-2.

FIGURE

7.18

Excel screens for commands AVERAGE and CONFIDENCE.

AVERAGE
Number1 | A1:A10 | = {308;419;389;432;3
Number2 | | = number

= 384

Returns the average (arithmetic mean) of its arguments, which can be numbers or names, arrays, or references that contain numbers.

Number1: number1,number2,... are 1 to 30 numeric arguments for which you want the average.

Formula result =384   OK   Cancel

CONFIDENCE
Alpha | .05 | = 0.05
Standard_dev | 50 | = 50
Size | 10 | = 10

= 30.98970573

Returns the confidence interval for a population mean. See Help for the equation used.

Size is the sample size.

Formula result =30.98970573   OK   Cancel

FIGURE

7.19

Excel spreadsheet containing a 95% confidence interval in cells B3 and B4.

	A	B	C	D	E	F	G	H	I
1	308	384							
2	419	30.98971							
3	389	353.0103	LL						
4	432	414.9897	UL						
5	362								
6	302								
7	440								
8	430								
9	375								
10	383								

Microsoft Excel - Book2
File Edit View Insert Format Tools Data KPK Data Analysis Window Help
Sheet1 / Sheet2 / Sheet3 /

Solution

To make your life a bit easier, we have written an Excel macro inside KPK Data Analysis that will construct these 20 intervals. First, open file DATA7-2. Then click on **KPK Data Analysis ➤ Means and CIs for Multiple Samples.** Click on **Means and CIs** at the bottom of the input form and enter "A1:T10" as the **Input Range,** "50" as the **Population Std. Dev.,** "95" as the **Confidence Level,** and "U1" as the **Output Range.** The output from this macro is shown in Figure 7.20. Notice that all the samples contain the known mean (μ = 400) except sample 19 (highlighted). In practice, however, the population mean is *unknown,* so all we can say is that this procedure will produce a confidence interval containing the population mean 95% of the time.

FIGURE

7.20

Confidence
intervals created
using **KPK Data
Analysis ➤ Means
and CIs for
Multiple Samples.**

	Q	R	S	T	U	V	W	X	Y	Z
						Multiple Samples				
1	439	331	418	428		**Multiple Samples**				
2	336	427	422	368	SAMPLE	MEANS	E	Lower 95%	Upper 95%	
3	425	445	341	445	1	384.00	30.99	353.01	414.99	
4	419	420	485	429	2	399.50	30.99	368.51	430.49	
5	346	401	442	475	3	397.30	30.99	366.31	428.29	
6	408	389	470	437	4	399.40	30.99	368.41	430.39	
7	392	363	404	475	5	414.40	30.99	383.41	445.39	
8	409	439	370	458	6	393.20	30.99	362.21	424.19	
9	313	352	539	308	7	398.80	30.99	367.81	429.79	
10	334	346	435	408	8	403.80	30.99	372.81	434.79	
11					9	402.80	30.99	371.81	433.79	
12					10	404.60	30.99	373.61	435.59	
13					11	401.90	30.99	370.91	432.89	
14					12	385.60	30.99	354.61	416.59	
15					13	408.20	30.99	377.21	439.19	
16					14	411.00	30.99	380.01	441.99	
17					15	415.60	30.99	384.61	446.59	
18					16	408.50	30.99	377.51	439.49	
19					17	382.10	30.99	351.11	413.09	
20					18	391.30	30.99	360.31	422.29	
21					19	432.60	30.99	401.61	463.59	
22					20	423.10	30.99	392.11	454.09	
23					SUMMARY FOR X-BARs					
24					Mean	402.89				
25					St. Dev.	12.78				
26										

DATA7-2

X Exercises 7.19–7.30

Understanding the Mechanics

7.19 A random sample of 100 observations is obtained from a normally distributed population with a standard deviation of 10. What is a 95% confidence interval for the mean of the population if the sample mean is 40?

7.20 Find the 90% confidence interval for the mean of a normally distributed population using the following data. Assume a standard deviation of 5.

50 43 65 52 45 60 38 62 53 49

7.21 Fifty observations are randomly selected from a normally distributed population with a population standard deviation of 25. The sample mean is 175.
  a. Find a 90% confidence interval for the mean.
  b. Find a 95% confidence interval for the mean.
  c. Find a 99% confidence interval for the mean.

Applying the New Concepts

7.22 The monthly advertising expenditure of Discount Hardware Store is normally distributed with a standard deviation of $100. If a sample of 10 randomly selected months yields a mean advertising expenditure of $380

monthly, what is a 90% confidence interval for the mean of the store's monthly advertising expenditure?

7.23 In analyzing the operating cost for a huge fleet of delivery trucks, a manager takes a sample of 25 cars and calculates the sample mean and sample standard deviation. Then he finds a 95% confidence interval for the mean cost to be $253 to $320. He reasons that this interval contains the mean operating cost for the fleet of delivery trucks since the sample mean is contained in the interval. Do you agree? How would you interpret this confidence interval?

7.24 The perfectionist owner of Kwik Kar Kare has reduced an oil-change job to a science and wants to keep it that way. The owner constantly monitors the performance of the staff. This week, 15 oil-change jobs were sampled with a sample mean of 9.8 minutes per job. Experience has shown that the times follow a normal distribution, and the standard deviation of the population is known to be 1.2 minutes. Based on this week's sample, construct a 90% confidence interval for the population mean (average time for an oil-change job).

7.25 Brazil was Latin America's leading economic power by the 1970s. In the past, this country has also had one of the highest inflation rates in Latin America. In an attempt to regain investor confidence, the Brazilian government has increased interest rates and has worked to establish a sound fiscal policy to keep inflation under control. In 2001, a random sample of locations across the country revealed that the average year-to-year increase in food prices was 6%. Assume that the standard deviation of the increase in food prices is known to be 1.75%. Construct a 99% confidence interval for the population mean using

   a. a sample size of 30.
   b. a sample size of 60.
   c. a sample size of 120.

(Source: "Brazil Inflation Slows Sharply," *The Financial Times,* October 5, 2001, p. 13.)

7.26 A quality-control engineer is concerned about the breaking strength of a metal wire manufactured to stringent specifications. A sample of size 25 is randomly obtained, and the breaking strengths are recorded. The breaking strength of the wire is considered to be normally distributed with a standard deviation of 3. Find a 95% confidence interval for the mean breaking strength of the wire.

> 26, 27, 18, 23, 24, 20, 21, 24, 19, 27, 25, 20, 24, 21, 26, 19, 21, 20, 25, 20, 23, 25, 21, 20, 21

7.27 Federal law requires GTE to allow competing long-distance carriers to use its infrastructure, and it regulates how much GTE can charge for the service. To compensate for the lost revenue from new federal regulations related to long-distance access charges, GTE has asked the Idaho Public Utilities Commission for permission to approve hikes in basic monthly rates. Commission members will schedule public meetings and seek written comments from customers before making a decision. Suppose that the standard deviation of charges to business customers by GTE in Idaho is $10. A concerned business association surveyed 20 business members to collect data on the monthly charges paid to GTE to reveal how high current charges were. Construct a 90% confidence interval on the average business customer's monthly bill to GTE using the data below. What assumption is necessary for this to be a reliable confidence interval?

> | 35 | 45 | 57 | 21 | 46 | 78 | 52 | 32 | 24 | 81 |
> |----|----|----|----|----|----|----|----|----|----|
> | 34 | 29 | 45 | 51 | 33 | 26 | 46 | 37 | 40 | 34 |

(Adapted from "GTE Requests Rate Increase in North Idaho," *Spokane Spokesman-Review,* May 30, 1998, p. B2.)

7.28 As the sample size increases, would a confidence interval given by equation 7.8 get smaller or larger? For a given random sample, would the confidence interval given by equation 7.8 for a 90% confidence interval be wider or narrower than that obtained using an 80% confidence level?

Using the Computer

7.29 [DATA SET EX7-29] *Variable description:*

LuggageCharge: Fee for shipping suitcases owned by domestic travelers

Virtual Bellhop, based in Volo, Illinois, picks up, ships, and delivers packages for any domestic traveler. With the increase in baggage restrictions and security at airports, this company is experiencing a substantial increase in business for shipping air travelers' suitcases. Assume that the standard deviation for the fee charged for suitcases is $11.60.

   a. Find a 95% confidence interval for the mean fee charged for shipping suitcases owned by domestic travelers. (In Excel, click on **KPK Data Analysis ➤ One Population Inference,** select Population Mean (z statistic), and use 5 for the alpha level (this value is the percentage value for one minus the confidence level) and enter 11.60 for the standard deviation. In MINITAB, click on **Stat ➤ Basic Statistics ➤ 1-Sample Z,** select confidence interval, and type in 95 for the confidence level. SPSS does not have an option to directly compute a mean confidence interval using the normal distribution. However, the menu obtained from clicking on **Transform ➤ Compute** features the mean function and the cumulative normal distribution function that can be used to calculate the confidence interval.)

   b. Change the standard deviation to $16.00 in part b. How much has the length of the confidence interval changed?

(Source: "Don't Check That Bag. Ship It," *The New York Times,* October 21, 2001, p. 8I.)

7.30 [DATA SET EX7-30] *Variable description:*

SATscoresNorthTexas: SAT scores for randomly selected high school seniors across north Texas

The SAT scores for Texas have been lagging behind the national average. The state education commissioner of Texas believes that one of the factors that affects the average SAT score for the state is the increase in the number of high school students taking this test. More students who have not taken college preparatory course work are taking the SAT. In Texas, about 52 percent of graduating seniors took the SAT, compared with 44 percent nationally. An education administrator decided to take a random sample across five high schools in north Texas. This sample consisted of 100 seniors who have opted for college preparatory courses. The education administer believes that the scores for seniors who have taken college preparatory courses are usually higher than the average. Assume a population standard deviation of 150.

   a. Find a 90% confidence interval for the mean SAT score for the high schools across north Texas. Give an interpretation for this interval.

   b. Find a 99% confidence interval for the mean SAT score for the high schools across north Texas. Compare the length of this interval with the 90% confidence interval in part a.

(Source: "Texas Loses Ground on SAT Scores," *Dallas Morning News,* August 30, 2000, p. 27A.)

7.4

CONFIDENCE INTERVALS FOR THE MEAN OF A NORMAL POPULATION (σ UNKNOWN)

If σ is unknown, it is impossible to determine a confidence interval for μ using formula 7.8 because we are unable to evaluate the standard error $\sigma/\sqrt{n}$. Let us take another look at how we estimate the parameters of a normal population.

When a population mean is unknown, we can estimate it using the sample mean. The logical thing to do if σ is unknown is to replace it by its estimate, the standard deviation of the sample, s. But consider what happens when

$$\frac{\overline{X} - \mu}{\sigma/\sqrt{n}}$$

is replaced by

$$\frac{\overline{X} - \mu}{s/\sqrt{n}}$$

This is no longer a standard normal random variable, Z. However, it does follow another identifiable distribution, the **t distribution.** Its complete name is *Student's t distribution,* named after W. S. Gosset, a statistician in a Guinness brewery who used the pen name Student. The distribution of

$$\frac{\overline{X} - \mu}{s/\sqrt{n}}$$

will follow a t distribution, *provided* the population from which you are obtaining the sample is normally distributed.

The t Distribution

The t distribution is similar in appearance to the standard normal (Z) distribution in that it is symmetric about zero. Unlike the Z distribution, however, its shape depends on the sample size, n. Consequently, when you use the t distribution, you must take into account the sample size. This is accomplished by using **degrees of freedom.** For this application using the t distribution,

$$\text{degrees of freedom} = \text{df} = n - 1$$

The value of df $= n - 1$ can be explained by observing that for a given value of $\overline{X}$, only $n - 1$ of the sample values are free to vary. For example, in a sample of size $n = 3$, if $\overline{x} = 5.0$, $x_1 = 2$, and $x_2 = 7$, then x_3 must be 6 because this is the only value providing a sample mean equal to 5.0.

Two t distributions are illustrated in Figure 7.21. Notice that the t distributions are symmetrically distributed about zero but have wider tails than does the stan-

FIGURE

7.21

The t distribution.

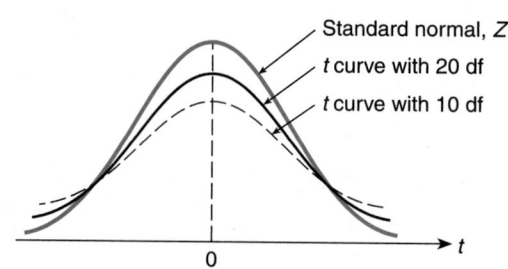

dard normal, Z. Observe that as n increases, the t distribution tends toward the standard normal, Z. In fact, for $n > 30$, there is little difference between these two distributions. Values having a specified tail area under a t curve are provided in Table A.5 for various df. So, for large samples ($n > 30$), it does not matter whether σ is known (Z distribution, Table A.4) or σ is unknown (t distribution, Table A.5) because the t and Z curves are practically the same. For this reason, the t distribution often is referred to as the *small-sample distribution* for $\overline{X}$. The Z table can be used as an approximation even if σ is unknown, provided n is larger than 30. *Remember, however, that a more accurate confidence interval is always obtained using the t table when the sample standard deviation (s) is used in the construction of this interval.*

Using the t distribution, then, a $(1 - \alpha) \cdot 100\%$ confidence interval for μ is

$$\overline{x} - t_{\alpha/2,n-1}\left(\frac{s}{\sqrt{n}}\right) \qquad \text{to} \qquad \overline{x} + t_{\alpha/2,n-1}\left(\frac{s}{\sqrt{n}}\right)$$ 7.10

where $t_{\alpha/2,n-1}$ denotes the t value from Table A.5 using a t curve with $n - 1$ df and a right-tail area of $\alpha/2$.

Do you remember our sample of 25 assembly times that produced a point estimate for μ having a value of $\overline{x} = 26.9$ minutes? This estimate was used in Example 7.6, where it was assumed that the population standard deviation was σ = 3, in constructing a confidence interval for μ. Furthermore, the assembly times were assumed to follow a *normal* distribution.

Suppose that we do not know σ, either. Then the point estimate of the population standard deviation is

$$s = \sqrt{\frac{(22.8^2 + 29.3^2 + \cdots + 25.2^2) - (22.8 + 29.3 + \cdots + 25.2)^2/25}{24}}$$

$$= \sqrt{\frac{18,285.14 - (672.6)^2/25}{24}}$$

$$= \sqrt{7.896} = 2.81 \text{ minutes}$$

Using Table A.5 to find a 90% confidence interval for μ, you first determine that

$$t_{\alpha/2,n-1} = t_{.05,24} = 1.711$$

The resulting 90% confidence interval is

$$26.9 - 1.711\left(\frac{2.81}{\sqrt{25}}\right) \qquad \text{to} \qquad 26.9 + 1.711\left(\frac{2.81}{\sqrt{25}}\right)$$

$$= 26.9 - .96 \qquad \text{to} \qquad 26.9 + .96$$

$$= 25.94 \qquad \text{to} \qquad 27.86$$

Using these data, we are 90% confident that the estimate for the mean of this normal population ($\overline{x} = 26.9$) is within .96 minute of the actual value. Comparing this result with Example 7.6, we notice little difference in the two 90% confidence intervals. Their agreement is due mostly to the fact that the estimate of σ ($s = 2.81$) is very close to the assumed value of σ = 3.

EXAMPLE 7.9

The output voltage of power supplies manufactured by Clark Products is believed to follow a normal distribution. Of primary concern to the company is the average output voltage of a particular power supply unit, believed to be 10 volts. Eighteen observations taken at random from this unit are

10.85, 11.40, 10.81, 10.24, 10.23, 9.49, 9.89, 10.11, 10.57, 11.21, 10.10, 11.22, 10.31, 11.24, 9.51, 10.52, 9.92, 8.33

What is the 95% confidence interval for the average output voltage for this power supply unit?

Solution   Your point estimate of σ is $s = .7667$ volt. Also, your point estimate of μ is $\bar{x} = 10.3306$ volts. A 95% confidence interval for the average output voltage (μ) is

$$10.3306 - t_{.025,17}\left(\frac{.7667}{\sqrt{18}}\right) \qquad \text{to} \qquad 10.3306 + t_{.025,17}\left(\frac{.7667}{\sqrt{18}}\right)$$

$$= 10.3306 - 2.11\left(\frac{.7667}{\sqrt{18}}\right) \qquad \text{to} \qquad 10.3306 + 2.11\left(\frac{.7667}{\sqrt{18}}\right)$$

$$= 10.3306 - .3813 \qquad \text{to} \qquad 10.3306 + .3813$$

$$= 9.949 \qquad \text{to} \qquad 10.712$$

We are 95% confident that the average output voltage of this power supply unit is between 9.949 and 10.712 volts. Notice here that the margin of error is

$$E = 2.11\left(\frac{.7667}{\sqrt{18}}\right) = .3813 \text{ volt}$$

which implies that we are 95% confident that $\bar{X}$ is within .3813 volt of the actual average voltage.

Using Excel to Determine a Confidence Interval for a Population Mean (σ Unknown)

Excel provides this type of confidence interval as an option in its **Descriptive Statistics** command. To illustrate this procedure using Example 7.9, enter the 18 voltage values in column A. Then click on **Tools ➤ Data Analysis ➤ Descriptive Statistics** and fill in the boxes as illustrated in Figure 7.22. Be sure to click on the small boxes alongside **Summary Statistics** and **Confidence Level for Mean.** This produces columns B and C in Figure 7.23.

Referring to Figure 7.23, to obtain the confidence interval, we need to subtract and add cells C3 (the sample mean) and C16 (the margin of error, E). To do this, (1) click on cell D1 and enter "=c3-c16," (2) click on cell D2 and enter "=c3+c16," (3) enter "LL" in cell E1, and (4) enter "UL" in cell E2. The resulting confidence interval is shown in Figure 7.23, and this interval agrees with the solution to Example 7.9.

FIGURE

7.22

Input screen for using Excel's DESCRIPTIVE STATISTICS to determine a confidence interval for a population mean (σ unknown).

FIGURE
7.23

The Excel spreadsheet containing the 95% confidence interval in cells D1 and D2.

	A	B	C	D	E	F	G	H
1	10.85	*Column1*		9.949276	**LL**			
2	11.40			10.71183	**UL**			
3	10.81	Mean	10.33056					
4	10.24	Standard Error	0.180717					
5	10.23	Median	10.275					
6	9.49	Mode	#N/A					
7	9.89	Standard Deviation	0.766715					
8	10.11	Sample Variance	0.587853					
9	10.57	Kurtosis	1.332968					
10	11.21	Skewness	-0.83726					
11	10.10	Range	3.07					
12	11.22	Minimum	8.33					
13	10.31	Maximum	11.4					
14	11.24	Sum	185.95					
15	9.51	Count	18					
16	10.52	Confidence Level (95.0%)	0.381279					
17	9.92							
18	8.33							

X Exercises 7.31–7.42

Understanding the Mechanics

7.31 For a t distribution with 20 degrees of freedom, what is the t value such that the following are true?

a. 90% of the area under the t distribution is to the right of the t value.

b. 10% of the area under the t distribution is to the right of the t value.

c. 5% of the area under the t distribution is to the left of the t value.

7.32 A t distribution has 30 degrees of freedom.

a. Find the area to the right of 2.750.

b. Find the area to the left of 1.697.

c. Find the area to the left of −1.310.

d. Find the area between −2.042 and 2.042.

7.33 A random sample of size 20 is selected from a normally distributed population. The sample mean is 50 and the sample standard deviation is 10.

a. Find a 90% confidence interval for the population mean.

b. Find a 95% confidence interval for the population mean.

c. Find a 99% confidence interval for the population mean.

Applying the New Concepts

7.34 The manager of a gift shop would like to estimate the average retail price of a particular greeting card by its competitors. A random sample of 20 retail stores in a 100-mile radius of the store were selected. The sample mean and standard deviation were $2.05 and $0.40, respectively. Find a 99% confidence interval for the mean price of the greeting card.

7.35 The mean monthly expenditure on gasoline per household in Middletown is determined by selecting a random sample of 36 households. The sample mean is $68, with a sample standard deviation of $17.

a. What is a 95% confidence interval for the mean monthly expenditure on gasoline per household in Middletown?

b. What is a 90% confidence interval for the mean monthly expenditure on gasoline per household in Middletown?

7.36 Second Federal Savings and Loan would like to estimate the mean number of years in which 30-year mortgages are paid off. Eighteen paid-off 30-year mortgages are randomly selected, and the numbers of years in which the loans were paid in full are

19.6, 20.8, 29.6, 6.3, 3.1, 10.6, 30.0, 21.7, 10.5, 26.3, 10.7, 6.1, 7.3, 12.6, 9.8, 27.4, 20.1, 10.8

Assuming that the number of years in which 30-year mortgages are paid off is normally distributed, construct an 80% confidence interval for the mean number of years in which the mortgages are paid off.

7.37 An apartment-finder service would like to estimate the average cost of a one-bedroom apartment in Kansas City. A random sample of 41 apartment complexes yielded a mean of $310 with a standard deviation of $29. Construct a 90% confidence interval for the mean cost of one-bedroom apartments in Kansas City.

7.38 People are conscious of fuel economy, global warming, and safety rollovers, but they still seem to love their sport-utility vehicles (SUVs). In fact, despite the problems with recalled Firestone tires, the Ford Explorer remains the best selling SUV. Automobile analysts are curious as to how much consumers are willing to pay for an SUV. A random sample of 10 recently sold SUVs was obtained for this purpose and the results are as follows:

SUV	Selling Price
Acura MDX	$39,450
Mercedes-Benz ML320	$40,270
Ford Explorer XLT	$32,600
Nissan Pathfinder LE	$34,724
Jeep Grand Cherokee LTD V8	$37,950
Toyota 4Runner SR5	$33,395
GMC Envoy SLE	$33,320
Dodge Durango SLT	$34,745
Land Rover Discovery	$40,395
Jeep Grand Cherokee Laredo 6	$33,030

a. Find a 99% confidence interval for the mean price that consumers are willing to pay for a new SUV.

b. Repeat part a using a 90% confidence interval. Compare and interpret the 90% and 99% confidence intervals.

(Source: "New Explorer Passes Magazine's Test," *USA Today*, August 8, 2001, p. 6B.)

7.39 An investment advisor believes that the return on interest-sensitive stocks is approximately normally distributed. A sample of 24 interest-sensitive stocks was selected, and their yearly return (including dividends and capital appreciation) was as follows (in percentages):

11.1, 12.5, 13.6, 9.1, 8.7, 10.6, 12.5, 15.6, 13.8, 8.0, 10.9, 7.6, 5.2, 1.2, 12.8, 16.7, 13.9, 10.1, 9.6, 10.8, 11.6, 12.3, 12.9, 11.6

Find a 90% confidence interval for the mean yearly return on interest-sensitive stocks.

7.40 Monthly fees by Internet service providers are competitive. The following 15 Internet service providers and their monthly fees in dollars were randomly sampled from an extensive list of Internet providers in *Computer Currents*. Find a 90% confidence interval on the mean monthly fee by Internet providers.

Provider	Monthly Fee
Fast Lane	20
FlashNet	14
Industrial Strength Internet	12
IDT	30
Internet Global	25
Internet Texas	21
Mesh Net	17
Mind Spring	27
Netcom	20
Netgazer Solutions	15
NorthStar Technologies	16
SouthNet Telecom	18
Vnet Internet Access	25

Provider	Monthly Fee
WebUSA	20
WhyWeb	16

(Source: "Internet Service Providers," *Computer Currents*, October 1998, p. 90.)

Using the Computer

7.41 **[DATA SET EX7-41]** *Variable description:*

MoneyMarketFund: Name of taxable money market fund

Yield: annualized yield of taxable money market fund

Money market funds, which investors can quickly buy into and sell out of without penalty or much risk, are among the safest investments. When the stock market starts to falter, the low yields on money market funds start to look attractive to investors. Peter Crane, the managing editor of iMoneyNet, says that he expects the average money market fund yield to break the record low of 2.6 percent set in May 1993. A random sample of 50 taxable money market funds and their yields are selected.

a. What is a 90% confidence interval on the mean yield based on the sample of 50 taxable money market funds. (In Excel, click on **KPK Data Analysis ➤ One Population Inference,** select **Population Mean (*t* statistic),** and use 10 for the alpha level (this value is the percentage value for one minus the confidence level). In SPSS, click on **Analyze ➤ Compare Means ➤ One-Sample T Test.** Click on the pointer button to move variable yield into the **Test Variable(s)** box. To set the confidence level, click on **Options** and enter "90" in the **Confidence Interval** box. In MINITAB, click on **Stat ➤ Basic Statistics ➤ 1-Sample t,** select confidence interval, and type in 90 for the confidence level.)

b. Repeat part a with only the first 25 taxable money market funds.

c. Compare the lengths of the confidence intervals in parts a and b and interpret.

(Sources: "Even Yielding 3%, Money Market Funds Appeal to Many," *The New York Times*, September 25, 2001, p. C11, and "Money Market Mutual Funds," *The Wall Street Journal*, October 25, 2001, p. C18.)

7.42 **[DATA SET EX7-42]** *Variable description:*

BookshelfSpeakers: Brand model of bookshelf loudspeaker

Accuracy: Score by Consumer Reports on the reproduction of sound by the speaker

What distinguishes the best speakers is the accuracy with which they reproduce the original signals fed into them, from the thump of the bass to the tinkle of the triangle. Ideally, speakers should reproduce every sound exactly as recorded. *Consumer Reports* rates speakers on this feature. Consider the 23 speakers scored to be a random sample of bookshelf loudspeakers.

a. Find a 99% confidence interval for the average accuracy of bookshelf loudspeakers. Interpret this interval.

b. Repeat part a for a 90% confidence interval and a 95% confidence interval.

c. Comment on the change in the length of the confidence intervals as the confidence level changes.

(Source: "Loudspeakers," *Consumer Reports*, August 2001, p. 36.)

7.5

SELECTING THE NECESSARY SAMPLE SIZE

Sample Size for Known σ

How large a sample do you need? This is often difficult to determine, although a carefully chosen *large* sample generally provides a better representation of the population than does a smaller sample. Acquiring large samples can be costly and time-consuming. Why obtain a sample of size $n = 1000$ if a sample size of $n = 500$ will provide sufficient accuracy for estimating a population mean? This section will show you how to determine what sample size is necessary when the margin of error, E, is specified in advance.

In Example 7.7, we assumed that the lifetime of Everglo bulbs is normally distributed with standard deviation $\sigma = 50$ hours but unknown mean μ. Based on the results of sample 1 from Table 7.1, we concluded that we were 95% confident that the estimate of μ ($\bar{x} = 384.0$) was within 31.0 hours of the actual value of μ for $n = 10$. How large a sample is necessary if we want our point estimator ($\bar{x}$) to be within 15 hours of the actual value of μ, with 95% confidence? The value 15 here is the margin of error, E, defined in equation 7.9. We would like the estimate of μ (that is, $\bar{x}$) to be within 15 of the actual value, so

$$E = 15 = Z_{\alpha/2} \left(\frac{50}{\sqrt{n}} \right)$$

Because the confidence level is 95%, $Z_{\alpha/2} = Z_{.025} = 1.96$. Consequently,

$$15 = (1.96) \frac{50}{\sqrt{n}}$$

$$\sqrt{n} = \frac{(1.96)(50)}{15} = 6.53$$

Squaring both sides of this statement produces

$$n = (6.53)^2 = 42.68$$

To be a bit conservative, this number should always be rounded *up*. So a sample size of $n = 43$ will produce a confidence interval with $E \leq 15$ hours. Your point estimate of μ $\bar{x}$, will then be within 15 hours of the actual value, with 95% confidence.

This sequence of steps can be summarized by the following expression:

$$n = \left[\frac{Z_{\alpha/2} \cdot \sigma}{E} \right]^2$$

7.11

Sample Size for Unknown σ

Equation 7.11 works if σ is known, but it doess not apply to situations where both μ and σ are unknown. There are two approaches to the latter situation.

A Preliminary Sampling

If you have already obtained a small sample, you have an estimate of σ, namely, the sample standard deviation, s. Replacing σ by s in equation 7.11 gives you the desired sample size, n. Assuming that the resulting value of n is greater than 30, the $Z_{\alpha/2}$ notation in equation 7.11 is still valid because the actual t distribution here will be closely approximated by the standard normal distribution.

When you do obtain the confidence interval using the larger sample, the resulting margin of error, E, may not be exactly what you originally specified, because the new sample standard deviation will not be the same as that belonging to the smaller original sample.

EXAMPLE 7.10

In Example 7.9, Clark Products obtained 18 observations of the output voltages for a particular power supply unit. For these data,

$$\bar{x} = 10.3306 \text{ volts}$$

$$s = .7667 \text{ volt}$$

How large a sample would they need for $\overline{X}$ to be within .2 volts of the actual average output voltage with 95% confidence?

Solution   Based on the results of the original sample, $s = .767$, so

$$n = \left[\frac{z_{\alpha/2} \cdot s}{E} \right]^2 = \left[\frac{(1.96)(.7667)}{.2} \right]^2 = 56.5$$

We round this number up to 57. Consequently, they would need 57 observations to make a statement with this much precision, that is, within .2 volt. Of course, they already have 18 observations that can be included in the larger sample.

Obtaining a Rough Approximation of σ

We know from the empirical rule and Table A.4 that 95.4% of the population will lie between $\mu - 2\sigma$ and $\mu + 2\sigma$. Because $(\mu + 2\sigma) - (\mu - 2\sigma) = 4\sigma$, this is a span of 4 standard deviations. One method of obtaining an estimate of σ is to ask a person who is familiar with the data to be collected these questions:

1. What do you think will be the highest value in the sample (H)?

2. What will be the lowest value (L)?

The approximation of σ is then obtained by assuming that $\mu + 2\sigma = H$ and $\mu - 2\sigma = L$, so

$$H - L = (\mu + 2\sigma) - (\mu - 2\sigma) = 4\sigma$$

Consequently,

$$\sigma \cong \frac{H - L}{4}$$

7.12

In other words, a rough approximation of σ is the *anticipated range* (H–L) divided by 4. This (somewhat conservative) estimate of σ can be used in equation 7.11 to determine the necessary sample size, n.

EXAMPLE 7.11

The manager of quality assurance for a division that produces hair dryers is interested in the average number of switches that can be tested by the division's employees. Assuming that the number of switches that are tested each hour by an employee follows a normal distribution (centered at μ), the manager wants to estimate μ with 90% confidence. Also, this estimate must be within one unit (switch) of μ. The manager estimates that H is 45 switches and L is 25 switches. How large a sample will be necessary?

Based on $H = 45$ switches and $L = 25$ switches,

$$\sigma \cong \frac{45 - 25}{4} = 5 \text{ switches}$$

The sample size necessary to obtain a margin of error of $E = 1$ is

$$n = \left[\frac{(1.645)(5)}{1} \right]^2 = 67.7$$

Thus, a sample size of 68 should produce a value of E close to one switch. The value will not be exactly one because the sample standard deviation, s, probably will not be exactly 5. Estimating σ in this manner, however, produces a value that is in the neighborhood of σ.

Solution

X Exercises 7.43–7.53

Understanding the Mechanics

7.43 Assume that a 90% confidence interval on the mean is to be constructed with a maximum error of E. The population standard deviation is equal to 50. How large a sample is required if:
   a. $\bar{X}$ is to be within 10 units of the population mean.
   b. $\bar{X}$ is to be within 15 units of the population mean.
   c. $\bar{X}$ is to be within 5 units of the population mean.

7.44 A pilot study yielded the following random sample of 15 observations from a normally distributed population.

69 50 74 40 24 50 49 60 52 44 49 52 39 47 48

   a. Using the sample standard deviation as an estimate for the population standard deviation, what is the necessary sample size for the sample mean to be within 3 units of the population mean with 95% confidence?
   b. Repeat part a using the highest and lowest values of the observations to estimate the population standard deviation.

Applying the New Concepts

7.45 The Chamber of Commerce of Tampa, Florida, would like to estimate the mean amount of money spent by a tourist to within $100 with 95% confidence. If the amount of money spent by tourists is considered to be normally distributed with a standard deviation of $200, what sample size would be necessary for the Chamber of Commerce to meet its objective in estimating this mean amount?

7.46 Security Savings and Loan Association's manager would like to estimate the mean deposit by a customer into a savings account to within $500. If the deposits into savings accounts are considered to be normally distributed with a standard deviation of $1,250, what sample size would be necessary to be 90% confident?

7.47 If a sample size of 70 was necessary to estimate the mean of a normal population to within 1.2 with 90% confidence, what is the approximate value of the standard deviation of the population?

7.48 The marketing agency for computer software of Personal Micro Systems would like to estimate with 95% confidence the mean time that it takes for a beginner to learn to use a standard software package. Past data indicate that the learning time can be approximated by a normal distribution with a standard deviation of 20 minutes. How large a sample size should the marketing agency choose if the mean time to learn to use the software package is to be estimated within 8 minutes with 90% confidence?

7.49 In an effort to lure vacationers to exotic locations, several vacation packages to world-class golf destinations, such as Scotland, New Zealand, and Maui, are offered by the major airlines and vacation agencies. The prices range from $1,200 to $4,000. Suppose that a travel agency wished to obtain a 90% confidence interval on the mean price of an exotic golf vacation offered by numerous vacation agencies throughout the United States. What sample size would be necessary to estimate the mean price to within $250?

(Source: "Charting a Course for World-Class Tee Times," *USA Today*, April 17, 1998, p. D1.)

7.50 A chemist at International Chemical would like to measure the adhesiveness of a new wood glue. From past experiments, a measure used to indicate adhesiveness has ranged from 7.3 to 11.1 units. To be 98% confident, how large a sample would be necessary to estimate the mean adhesiveness to within .5 units?

7.51 For the Canadian government and casino operators, gambling has provided the basis for a very profitable marriage. There are now 55 casinos in Canada, earning $2.5 billion a year, of which the government pockets $1.2 billion. The lion's share of that action is in Central Canada, which has five glitzy casinos—Niagara Falls, Windsor, and Casino Rama near Orillia in Ontario and Hull and Montreal in Quebec. A survey at one of these casinos revealed that the Canadian households that gamble spend between $100 and $3,200 annually in gambling. What sample size would be necessary to estimate the average amount spent by Canadian households that visit the casinos so that the estimate of the average is within $150 with 95% confidence.

(Source: "The Curse of Casinos," *Maclean Hunter Limited*, May 11, 1998, p. 44.)

Using the Computer

7.52 An approximation to the standard deviation of a population is the range (high minus low) divided by 4. To assess the accuracy of this approximation, this exercise considers a simulation of observations from a normal distribution from which the range divided by 4 is calculated.

a. Using Excel, SPSS, or MINITAB, randomly generate 20 observations from a normally distributed population having a mean of 100 and a standard deviation of 15. Compute the range divided by 4. (In Excel, click on **Paste Function ➤ Statistical** to use the max and min functions. In SPSS, click on **Transform ➤ Compute** to use the max and min functions. In MINITAB, click on **Calc ➤ Calculator** to use the max and min functions.)

b. Repeat part a 10 times. Would you say that most of the estimates are rough approximations of the standard deviation of 15? What is the average of the 10 estimates? Is this average close to the standard deviation of 15?

7.53 To understand how the sample size increases as the confidence level increases to maintain a specified margin of error, calculate the required sample for $\sigma = 10$, $E = 1$, and for confidence levels of 86%, 88%, 90%, 92%, 94%, 96%, 98%, and 99%. Compare the size of n as the confidence level increases. To find the z value used in the formula for n, use one of the statistical computer packages. (In Excel, use the **NORMSINV** function after clicking on the **Paste Function ➤ Statistical** to find the z value. In SPSS, use the **IDF.NORMAL** function after clicking on **Transform ➤ Compute**. In MINITAB, select cumulative inverse probability after clicking on **Calc ➤ Probability Distributions.** Note that since it is necessary to divide the alpha level by 2, a confidence level of 97.5%, for example, needs to be used in the cumulative inverse normal probability functions when the confidence level is 95%.)

On the CD . . .

Section 7.6: Bootstrap Confidence Intervals
Exercises 7.54–7.63
Section 7.7: Other Sampling Procedures
Exercises 7.64–7.69

 # Summary

This chapter introduced you to **statistical inference,** an extremely important area of statistics. Inference procedures were used to **estimate** a certain unknown *parameter* (such as the mean, μ, or the standard deviation, σ) of a population by using the corresponding sample *statistic* (such as the sample mean, $\overline{X}$, or the sample standard deviation, s).

The **Central Limit Theorem** states that for large samples, the sample mean $\overline{X}$ always follows an approximate normal distribution. If, in addition, you assume that the population is normally distributed, then $\overline{X}$ will follow an exact normal distribution. The strength of the Central Limit Theorem is that no assumptions need be made concerning the shape of the population, provided the sample is large ($n > 30$). The Central Limit Theorem allows you to make probability statements concerning $\overline{X}$, such as $P(\overline{X} < 150)$. When sampling without replacement from a finite population, the standard deviation of the normal distribution for $\overline{X}$ (the **standard error**) is obtained by including a **finite population correction factor (fpc),** which adjusts the standard error by including the effect of the known population size, N.

The probability distribution of a sample statistic is its **sampling distribution.** Consequently, according to the Central Limit Theorem, the sampling distribution of $\overline{X}$ is approximately normal, regardless of the shape of the sampled population.

The sample mean, $\overline{X}$, provides a **point estimate** of μ because it estimates this parameter using a single number. A **confidence interval** for μ measures the precision of the point estimate. If the population standard deviation σ is known, the standard normal table (Table A.4) is used to derive the confidence interval. Confidence intervals are expressed in percentages, such as a **95% confidence interval.** The specific percentage represents the **confidence level.** If σ is unknown, it can be replaced by its estimate—the sample standard deviation, s. This provided an introduction to the t **distribution.** The shape of the t distribution depends on the sample size and is specified using the corresponding **degrees of freedom (df).** The corresponding confidence interval for μ is constructed using the t table (Table A.5) and assumes that the sampled population is normally distributed (that is, μ is the mean of a normal population). For sample sizes (n) greater than 30, the standard normal table can be used to construct an approximate confidence interval for the population mean when σ is unknown. A summary of this procedure is contained in Figure 7.25.

For many applications, the precision of the point estimate, $\overline{X}$, is specified using the **margin of error, E.** When constructing a confidence interval, E is the amount that is added to and subtracted from the point estimate to obtain the endpoints of the desired interval. The sample size n necessary to achieve a desired accuracy can be obtained using a specified value of E. The population standard deviation can be estimated from a preliminary sample, or a rough approximation procedure can be used.

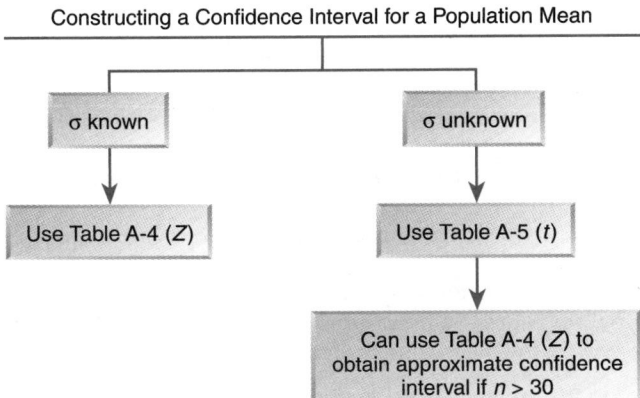

FIGURE

7.25

The correct table to use for constructing a confidence interval for a population mean. *Note:* In all cases, if the population size (N) is known, the fpc can be used to derive a more precise standard error. This adjustment is negligible if $n/N < .05$.

✓ Summary of Formulas

1. Standard error of $\bar{X}$ (simple random sample):

$$\frac{\sigma}{\sqrt{n}} \quad (N \text{ unknown or infinite})$$

$$\frac{\sigma}{\sqrt{n}} \sqrt{\frac{N-n}{N-1}} \quad (N \text{ known})$$

where $(N-n)/(N-1)$ is the finite population correction (fpc).

2. Estimated standard error of $\bar{X}$ (simple random sample):

$$\frac{s}{\sqrt{n}} \quad (N \text{ unknown or infinite})$$

$$\frac{s}{\sqrt{n}} \sqrt{\frac{N-n}{N}} \quad (N \text{ known})$$

where $(N-n)/N$ is the finite population correction (fpc).

3. Confidence interval for a population mean (large simple random sample, σ known):

$$\bar{X} \pm Z_{\alpha/2} \frac{\sigma}{\sqrt{n}}$$

Note: Include the fpc in Formula 1 if N is known.

4. Confidence interval for the mean of a normal population (simple random sample, σ unknown):

$$\bar{X} \pm t_{\alpha/2, n-1} \frac{s}{\sqrt{n}}$$

Note: Include the fpc in Formula 2 if N is known.

5. Necessary sample size (simple random sample):

$$n = \left[\frac{Z_{\alpha/2} \cdot \sigma}{E} \right]^2$$

where E is the specified margin of error.

Additional Bootstrap Readings

1. Biddle, G. C., C. M. Bruton, and A. F. Siegel, "Computer-Intensive Methods in Auditing: Bootstrap Difference and Ratio Estimation," *Auditing: A Journal of Practice & Theory,* vol. 3, no. 3, Fall 1990, pp. 92–114.

2. Davison, A. C., and D. V. Hinkley, *Bootstrap Methods and Their Application,* Cambridge, UK: Cambridge University Press, 1997.

3. Efron, B., "Nonparametric Estimates of Standard Error: The Jackknife, the Bootstrap, and Other Resampling Methods," *Biometrika,* 1981, pp. 589–99.

4. Efron, B., and R. J. Tibshirani, *An Introduction to the Bootstrap,* New York: Chapman & Hall, 1993.

⊠ Review Exercises 7.70–7.87

7.70 After taking a random sample of 40 customers and asking them the amount of time they spend shopping at a particular store, a 95% confidence interval is computed to be 10 to 32 for the average time spent shopping. An analyst can correctly make which of the following statements:

a. I am 95% confident that the average time that a customer spends shopping is between 10 and 32 minutes.

b. The probability is .95 that the midpoint of the interval is equal to the population mean.

c. The mean of the population is between 10 and 32.

d. If I repeatedly obtained samples of size 40, then 95% of the resulting confidence intervals would contain the mean time that customers spend shopping.

7.71 In a survey on the quality of customer service at Car Toys, customers were asked to rate the service on a scale from 1 to 10 with 10 being that a customer was completely satisfied with the service. Assume that the distribution of the responses can be approximated by a normal distribution with a mean of 7 and a standard deviation of 1.

a. What is the probability that an individual customer gives a rating of at least 8?

b. In a random sample of 10, what is the probability that the average rating is at least 8?

7.72 In August 2000, new car prices were on average 11% lower than they were the year before. In August 2001, the price of new cars was again lower, but not by as much. The prices were approximately 5.6% lower in 2001. Suppose that an automobile analyst wished to obtain information on how much lower a new medium-sized car was selling for in Richmond, Virginia. The following data are the results of a random sample of 20 new cars that were sold in August 2001. These figures represent the decrease in the 2001 selling price (in percentage) compared to the 2000 ceiling price.

4.1	5.3	5.8	6.7	4.8	7.3	6.5	5.1	7.2	5.2
6.7	8.1	3.5	5.2	6.1	4.2	3.2	6.8	3.8	7.1

a. Compute a 90% confidence interval for the mean decrease in the price of a new medium sized car selling in Richmond, Virginia. Interpret the confidence interval.

b. What could you do to obtain a narrower confidence interval?

c. What sample size is necessary to estimate the sample mean with 90% confidence such that it is within .2 of the actual decrease in selling price on a year-to-year basis?

(Source: "News Digest," *The Financial Times,* September 27, 2001, p. 10.)

7.73 A quality-assurance manager uses a random sample of size 25 to construct a 95% confidence interval on the average weight of a bag of dry feed. This interval is found to be 49.9174 to 50.0826.

a. What is the point estimate of the average weight of a bag of dry feed?

b. What is the sample standard deviation of the weight of a bag of dry feed?

7.74 Although high school teachers in some states, such as Connecticut, New Jersey, and New York, earn average salaries topping $50,000 for a nine-month year, teachers' salaries in states such as North Dakota and Oklahoma hover around $30,000. To estimate the mean salary of a high school teacher in Connecticut to within $1,000 with 99% confidence, what sample size is necessary? Assume that the range of high school teachers' salaries in Connecticut is $30,000 to $60,000.

(Source: "Schools Discount the Need to Boost Teachers' Salaries," *USA Today,* August 8, 2001, p. 12A.)

7.75 A random variable is found to range from a high of 50 to a low of 25 from past data. The distribution of the random variable can be approximated by a normal distribution. To estimate the mean of the random variable to within 2.1, what sample size would be necessary in selecting a random sample to achieve a 99% confidence level?

7.76 Direct marketing efforts—including catalogs, direct mail and e-mail—refer more potential customers to Web sites and result in higher average order sizes, according to market research company Binary Compass Enterprises, Los Angeles. This marketing research company revealed that 5,153 online buyers have placed orders over the Internet, with the average order size being $213 with a standard deviation of $50. Find the probability that

500 randomly selected online buyers selected from the 5,153 buyers who have placed orders over the Internet have an average order size between $210 and $215?

(Adapted from "DM Drives More Traffic, Higher Average Orders," *Direct Marketing News,* Web marketing news section, p. 21.)

7.77 The research and development department of a large oil company employs 253 engineers who have an average of 6.2 years of practical experience with a standard deviation of 2.1 years.

a. If a sample of 35 engineers is selected randomly without replacement, what is the probability that the average number of years of experience of the sample will be greater than 6.8 years?

b. If a sample of 35 engineers is selected randomly with replacement, what is the probability that the average number of years of experience will be greater than 6.8 years?

7.78 A confidence interval for the mean of a normally distributed population is found to range from 70.1 to 80.2. What is the level of confidence for the confidence interval if the sample size is 36 and the population standard deviation is 13.2?

7.79 The tensile strength of a high-powered copper coil used in giant power transformers is believed to follow a normal distribution. A sample of 14 high-powered copper coils yields the following tensile strength (in units of thousands of pounds per square inch). Construct a 90% confidence interval for the mean tensile strength of copper coils.

6.1, 2.6, 3.5, 4.3, 3.1, 5.2, 3.6, 3.5, 5.4, 4.2, 3.2, 2.8, 4.0, 3.7

7.80 Excluding room, board, and fees, the average tuition at a four-year private college is $65,328 nationwide. Suppose that a financial planner believes that the average cost is higher in the northeast. The following data are the results of a random sample of the tuition expense at 20 four-year private colleges:

65,400	75,500	75,350	58,340
55,320	84,500	100,450	61,250
52,500	65,000	95,500	75,340
88,400	95,000	71,300	65,300
38,500	55,800	66,000	54,320

a. Find a 90% confidence interval for the average tuition expense of a four-year college in the northeast.

b. Would you expect a 99% confidence level to produce a wider or narrower interval in part a? Repeat part a using a 99% confidence level and compare the lengths of the intervals.

(Source: "College Funding: A Class Act," *USAA Magazine,* September 2001, p. 38.)

7.81 Kansas City-based AMC Entertainment Inc. plans to experiment with offering a monthly pass to moviegoers for about $18. This pass would allow the purchaser to see unlimited movies each month. AMC is hoping that the increase in popcorn and soda sales will offset the discount since people will be going more often to the movies. This pass is being tested in several local markets. The entertainment company would like to estimate the amount spent monthly by active moviegoers in a local market to within $2 with 95% confidence. What sample size is necessary if the standard deviation is estimated to be $10.

(Source: "A Buffet for Movie Buffs," *Dallas Morning News,* June 16, 2001, p. 2F.)

7.82 A personnel administrator for Teltronix would like to estimate the amount of term life insurance that an employee carries. Three strata are used for finding a stratified random sample of all employees. From the data, construct a 95% confidence interval for the mean amount of term life insurance that an employee carries (given in units of thousands of dollars).

Stratum	N_i (Total Number in Company)	n_i	$\bar{X}_i$	s_i
Employees paid by the hour	350	67	28.5	5.7
Engineers and technicians	112	22	80.6	10.3
Management	57	11	125.2	13.6
	519	100		

7.83 A machine at a manufacturing plant fills sacks with 10 pounds of oats. Each case contains 10 sacks of oats. The quality-control engineer would like to find a 99% confidence interval for the mean weight per sack of oats. Using cases as clusters, construct the confidence interval if eight cases are chosen at random. Assume that there is a total of 50 cases from which to choose.

Cases	Sacks Per Case	Weight of Case	Cases	Sacks Per Case	Weight of Case
1	10	96.7	5	10	110.8
2	10	99.8	6	10	104.6
3	10	103.5	7	10	93.5
4	10	92.7	8	10	112.3

7.84 The manager of a cafe would like to estimate the proportion of days that the cafe sells out of their daily baked breads. If a 1 is recorded for a day when the baked breads are sold out and a 0 when the baked breads are not sold out, a proportion of days when the breads are sold out can be computed by summing the 1's and 0's and dividing by the total number of days. What is the approximate distribution of the estimate of the proportion of days when the daily baked breads are sold out? (*Hint:* What does the Central Limit Theorem say?)

7.85 **[DATA SET EX7-85]** *Variable description:*

AdjustableMortgageRates: Mortgage rates for one-year adjustable mortgages

In 2001, for one-year adjustable-rate mortgages, lenders were asking an average rate of 5.25 percent. This rate is the lowest since February 16, 1994, for one-year adjustable mortgage rates and is quite a savings compared to 30–year mortgages rates of 6.65%. A random sample of 100 new home owners who financed their homes with one-year adjustable-rate mortgages is selected and their mortgage rates recorded.

a. Find a 99% confidence interval for the mean mortgage rate on one-year adjustable mortgages.

b. Remove the two largest and two smallest rates and repeat part a. How does length of the confidence interval in part a compare to the confidence interval with the two largest and two smallest observations removed?

(Source: "30-Year Mortgage Rates Edge Higher," *The New York Times,* October 26, 2001, p. C6.)

7.86 To understand how the required sample size changes with a change in the maximum error for a confidence interval, plot *n* against the values of $E = 8, 9, 10, \ldots, 20$, when the population standard deviation is equal to 100, and the confidence level is 95%. The plot should look like the one displayed below. Comment on the relationship between *n* and *E*. In Excel, type in "8", "9", "10", . . . , "20" in cells A1 through A13. In cell B1 type in "=(1.96*100/A1)^2". Drag B1 through B13. Then click on the **Chart Wizard** to form a line graph.

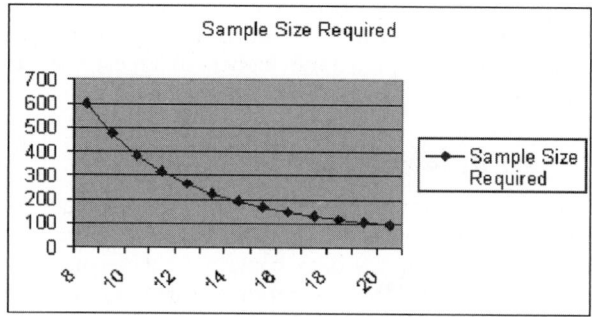

7.87 **[DATA SET EX7-87]** *Variable description:*

LaptopBatteryLife: The number of hours that a laptop computer will function

Most computer laptops use a rechargeable lithium-ion battery, which is lighter and holds a charge longer than the common nickel-metal hydride battery. However, with brighter computer displays and more powerful chips, batteries are not lasting any longer than they did on older computer laptop models. DVD players are particularly tough on batteries. To determine the average number of hours of use that a college student gets on a laptop before the batteries fail, 51 students were randomly selected and values of the variable Laptop-BatteryLife were recorded.

a. Find a 90% confidence interval for the life of a computer laptop battery used by college students. Use the t distribution.

b. Repeat part a using the normal distribution to compute the confidence interval.

c. Compare the confidence intervals in parts a and b. Would you say that the normal approximation is reasonably good?

d. Give two interpretations to the confidence interval computed in part a.

(Source: "Is This Your Next Computer?" *Consumer Reports,* June 2001, pp. 20–23.)

Computer Exercise Using the Databases

Exercise 1—Appendix F

Select the first 500 observations of the database as the population of interest. Estimate the mean of HPAYRENT (house payment or house/apartment rent) for this population by taking a simple random sample of size 40. Also estimate the mean by taking a stratified sample proportional to the size of the two strata. Let stratum 1 be the group of observations in which a secondary wage earner (variable INCOME2) has a positive income, and let stratum 2 be the group of observations in which there is no secondary wage earner. Compare the confidence intervals on mean house payment/rent (HPAYRENT) for both the simple random sample and the stratified random sample.

Note: The necessary steps to select the first 500 rows when using SPSS are:

Data ➤ Select Cases ➤ Based on time or case range ➤ Range ➤ First case = 1, Last case = 500

To obtain the simple random sample of size 40, the steps are:

Data ➤ Select Cases ➤ Select variable HPAYRENT ➤ Random sample of cases (Unselected Cases are Deleted) ➤ Sample ➤ Exactly 40 cases from the first 500 cases ➤ Continue ➤ OK

The MINITAB procedure to select the first 500 rows is

MTB ➤ COPY C1-C9 INTO C11-C19;
SUB ➤ USE ROWS 1:500.

To obtain the simple random sample of size 40, use

MTB ➤ RANDOM 40 FROM C17, PUT INTO C20

Exercise 2—Appendix F

Select a simple random sample of 32 observations from the database. Calculate a 95% confidence interval on the mean income of the principal wage earner (variable INCOME1). Select another simple random sample of size 60 from this database. Calculate a 95% confidence interval on the mean income of the principal wage earner. Comment on the widths of these two confidence intervals.

Exercise 3—Appendix G

Generate 20 random samples of size 10 using the data for the variable ASSETS (current assets). For each sample determine the sample mean. Construct a histogram of these 20 sample means. Also find the mean and the variance of these 20 values. Repeat this procedure for samples of size 25 and 40. Does the Central Limit Theorem appear to be operating correctly here? Discuss.

Insights from Statistics in Action

Traffic Congestion Takes Its Toll

The Statistics in Action introductory case study discussed the problem of excessive time spent on the freeways at major U.S. cities. To estimate the average time spent by motorists on the freeways in the morning and evening rush hours in Dallas, Texas, a random sample of 200 motorists is selected. Use the data set listed in StatInActChap7.xls to answer the following questions. This data set consists of responses to two questions: (1) What is the typical amount of time you spend traveling to downtown Dallas each morning? (2) What is the typical amount of time you spend traveling home each evening? Units are given in minutes.

1. Should a census be taken instead of a random sample to obtain the average time spent by motorists driving in the morning and in the evening rush hours? For what reasons would the researcher want to use a random sample instead of a census? Construct a histogram of the sampled data. Comment on the shape of the distribution of the sampled data.

2. Find two 99% confidence intervals—one for the average time that motorists spend driving in the morning and one for the average time motorists spend driving in the evening.

3. Interpret the confidence intervals in question 2. If you repeatedly obtained samples of 200 and constructed 99% confidence intervals, what general statement can you make about the true average time that motorists in Dallas spend driving in the morning and the evening?

4. What sample size would be necessary for the sample mean time spent driving in the morning to be within 2 minutes of the population average time that motorists in Dallas spend driving in the morning? What sample size would be necessary for the sample size to be within 1 minute of the population average?

5. Repeat question 4 for the time spent driving in the evening and compare sample sizes.

(Sources: "DART: Rail Is Proving the Easiest Way to Go," *Dallas Morning News*, July 3, 2000, p. 18A; "Plans to Raise Road Funds on the Table," *Dallas Morning News*, February 5, 2001, p. 17A; "46 Hours Spent Stuck in Traffic," *Dallas Morning News*, May 8, 2001, p. 2A.)

Appendix SPSS®

Chapter 7 Appendix: Data Analysis with SPSS

Confidence Intervals on the Mean Using the *t* Distribution

To illustrate the construction of a confidence interval for a population mean, consider the output voltage of the 18 power supplies in Example 7.9. Enter these values in the first column of the data window. Click on the Variable View tab and name this variable "voltage."

	voltage	var
1	10.85	
2	11.40	
3	10.81	
4	10.24	
5	10.23	
6	9.49	
7	9.89	
8	10.11	
9	10.57	
10	11.21	
11	10.10	
12	11.22	
13	10.31	
14	11.24	
15	9.51	
16	10.52	
17	9.92	
18	8.33	
19		
20		
21		
22		

Data View / Variable View

To obtain the confidence interval, click on **Analyze ➤ Compare Means ➤ One-Sample T Test.** Click on the pointer button to move variable voltage into the Test Variable(s) box. To set the confidence level, click on **Options** and enter "95" in the **Confidence Interval** box (this is the default value). The output immediately following will appear in the display pane. The only portion of this output that is of interest here is the highlighted portion in the right-hand side. The 95% confidence interval for the mean output voltage of all power supplies is 9.949 to 10.712, which agrees with the solution in Example 7.9.

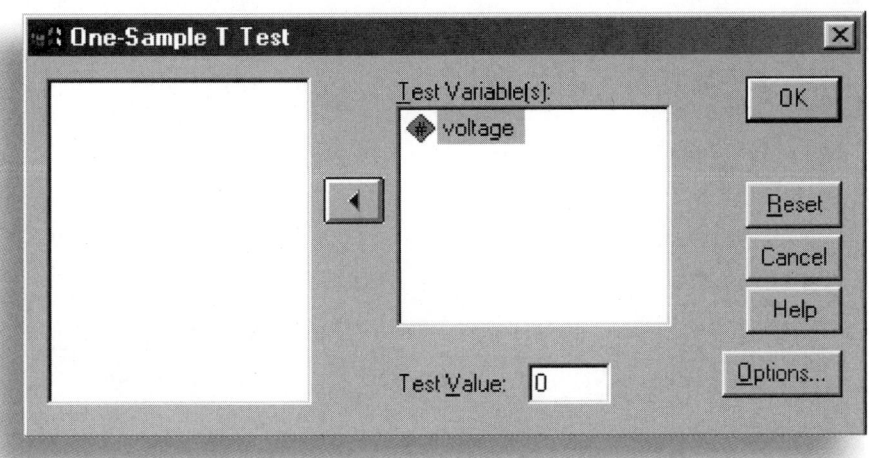

One-Sample Test

					95% Confidence Interval of the Difference	
					Test Value = 0	
	t	df	Sig. (2-tailed)	Mean Difference	Lower	Upper
VOLTAGE	57.164	17	.000	10.3306	9.9493	10.7118

On the CD . . .
Chapter 7 Appendix: Data Analysis with MINITAB

Hypothesis Testing for the Mean and Variance of a Population

X

Statistics in Action
Hillerich & Bradsby Company: Hitting the Quality Mark

The crack of the bat as a home run leaves the park. The sound of a hockey stick meeting the puck on a slap shot. The ping as an iron makes contact with a golf ball to create the perfect shot. These sounds are music to the ears of Hillerich & Bradsby (H & B) executives. The Louisville, Kentucky–based manufacturer, best known for producing Louisville Slugger baseball bats, provides a variety of baseball, hockey, and golf equipment to amateur and professional athletes worldwide.

In the pro bat business, quality means wood craftsmanship and personal service. H & B's Louisville Slugger Division sells around 1 million wooden bats and has approximately 70% of the professional bat market. The first thing the company does when it receives a pro's order is to check the vault for a similar bat. Chances are, H & B can turn a bat that is very close to the player's request. If a player's request involves making an altogether new model, H & B often names it for the player.

H & B has discovered that athletes can be very demanding when choosing equipment. Producing a bat requires many decisions by operators and managers. Billets, from which bats are manufactured, arrive at the Louisville plant weighing 80 to 100 ounces. If a shipment has billets with an average weight outside of this range, the shipment is typically returned. When finished, the bats weigh 30 to 35 ounces.

Quality control is important in the production of wooden bats. There is a chance that the billets have defects hidden inside the wood; high-tech imaging of billet interiors is not considered cost-effective. Computer monitors are able to tell whether a bat is out of spec or if it is drifting away from centerline. But the operator must move through the turning, branding, and sanding process quickly because billets and turned bats lose moisture quickly. Moisture control is critical to meeting weight specifications. Some pros have asked that their bats be measured in quarter ounces. Lighter bats are more apt to be damaged on impact, especially if the batter connects with the ball somewhere other than the center of percussion. But because it is possible to hit better with a thin, lighter bat, most batters are willing to trade durability for performance.

H & B's top managers have learned to use statistical analysis in their decision making. After a certain number of bats are manufactured, operators randomly sample bats to check for weight and length specifications. If the average weight of a sample is more than the target weight, is it safe to assume that the average weight has increased for all bats recently turned? The answer is, not necessarily. Now, if it can be shown that this average weight is *significantly* more than the target weight, the operator should be very concerned about whether bats are being produced outside of specs and should recheck the setup of the machinery.

Producing bats that provide the look and feel that customers want is what has allowed H & B to capture such a large portion of the professional bat market. The use of statistical analysis in their operations keeps the company competitive. When you have completed this chapter, you will be able to

- Determine what is meant by "significantly greater" or "significantly different."
- Understand the types of error that can result when trying to infer something about a population when using a sample.
- Determine the role that sample size plays on the probability that one of the types of error will occur.

A Look Back/Introduction

We have seen that statistical inference is used to estimate a population parameter using a sample statistic. For the rest of this book, the mean (μ) and standard deviation (σ) of the parent population will be unknown and will have to be estimated from the sample. Do not forget that even though you have estimated μ or σ, these values still are unknown and will forever remain unknown.

As a measure of how reliable your point estimate of the population mean μ really is, you can determine a confidence interval for this parameter. For a given confidence level, the narrower your resulting confidence interval is, the more faith you can have in the ability of your sample mean, $\bar{X}$, to provide an accurate estimate of the population mean. Also, when the Central Limit Theorem is applicable, you need not worry about the shape of the parent population (normal, exponential, and so on) when making probability statements regarding $\bar{X}$, provided you have a large sample (generally, $n > 30$). When you do have a large sample, the distribution of $\bar{X}$ closely approximates the normal. You can thus construct confidence intervals for population means without worrying about the nature of the parent population, simply because it doesn't matter.

Next, we turn to the situation in which someone makes a claim regarding the value of the population mean, μ. For example, when dealing with the lifetime of Everglo light bulbs in Chapter 6, we assumed that the population average of *all* bulbs was $\mu = 400$ hours. Where did this value come from? Suppose that Everglo advertisements claim that the average lifetime of the bulbs is 400 hours. By testing a sample of bulbs, can we prove this statement? The answer is an emphatic no; the only way to know the value of μ exactly is to obtain data for *all* Everglo bulbs; that is, obtain the entire population.

The sample, however, may allow us to reject the claim that μ is 400 hours, but since the sample is only a portion of the population, this conclusion may be incorrect. Such is the nature of hypothesis testing.

HYPOTHESIS TESTING ON THE MEAN OF A POPULATION: LARGE SAMPLE

A newspaper article claims that the average height of adult males in the United States is not the same as it was 50 years ago; it claims the average height is now 5.9 feet (approximately 5'11"). Your firm manufactures clothing, so the value of this population mean is of vital interest to you. To investigate the article's claim, you randomly select 75 males and measure their heights.* Your results for $n = 75$ are $\bar{x} = 5.76$ feet and $s = .48$ feet.

Let μ represent the population average (mean) of all U.S. male heights. We do have a point estimate of μ; $\bar{x} = 5.76$ feet is an estimate of μ. Keep in mind that the actual value of μ is unknown (although it *does exist*) and will remain that way. What we can do is estimate μ using the sample data. This situation can be summarized by considering the following pair of hypotheses:

Null Hypothesis	Alternative Hypothesis
$H_0: \mu = 5.9$	$H_a: \mu \neq 5.9$

H_0 asserts that the value of μ that has been claimed to be correct is in fact correct. H_a asserts that μ is some value other than 5.9 feet. The alternative hypothesis typically contains the conclusion that the researcher is attempting to demonstrate using the sample data. In our height example, if you do not believe that the average height is 5.9 feet and you expect the data to demonstrate that μ has some other value, H_a is $\mu \neq 5.9$.

DEFINITION

1. *Null hypothesis* (H_0). A statement (equality or inequality) concerning a population parameter; the researcher wishes to discredit this statement.
2. *Alternative hypothesis* (H_a). A statement in contradiction to the null hypothesis; the researcher wishes to support this statement.

The task of all hypothesis testing is to either **reject** H_0 or **fail to reject** H_0. Notice that we do not say "reject H_0 or accept H_0." This is an important distinction.

In our study of male heights, the (point) estimate of μ is $\bar{x} = 5.76$ feet. Should we reject H_0, given that it claims that μ is 5.9? First, we need not worry about the shape of the underlying population of male heights because, by the Central Limit Theorem, $\bar{X}$ is approximately normally distributed for large samples, regardless of the shape of this population. So, $\bar{X}$ is approximately a normal (and thus continuous) random variable. What is the probability that *any* continuous random variable is equal to a certain value? In particular, what is the probability that $\bar{X}$ is exactly equal to 5.9 feet? The answer to both questions is zero. Thus, we see that we cannot reject H_0 simply because $\bar{X}$ is not equal to 5.9 feet. What we do is allow H_0 to stand, provided $\bar{X}$ is "close to" 5.9 feet, and reject H_0 otherwise. To define what "close" means, we need to take an in-depth look at what happens when you test hypotheses.

---

*The size of this sample is unrealistically small (yet large, statistically).

Type I and Type II Errors

Because the sample does not consist of the entire population, there always is the possibility of drawing an incorrect conclusion when inferring the value of a population parameter using a sample statistic. When testing hypotheses, there are two types of possible errors:

Type I Error. A **Type I error** occurs if you rejected H_0 when in fact it is true. For example, a Type I error would occur if you were to reject the claim (hypothesis) that the population mean is 5.9 feet when in fact it really is true.

Type II Error. A **Type II error** occurs if you fail to reject H_0 when in fact H_0 is not true. For example, a Type II error occurs if you fail to reject the hypothesis that the population mean is 5.9 feet when in fact the mean is *not* 5.9 feet.

	Actual Situation	
Conclusion	H_0 **True**	H_0 **False**
Fail to reject H_0	Correct decision	Type II error
Reject H_0	Type I error	Correct decision

For any test of hypothesis, define

$$\alpha = \text{probability of rejecting } H_0 \text{ when } H_0 \text{ is true}$$

$$= P(\text{Type I error})$$

$$\beta = \text{probability of failing to reject } H_0 \text{ when } H_0 \text{ is false}$$

$$= P(\text{Type II error})$$

For any test of hypothesis, you would like to have control over n (the sample size), α (the probability of a Type I error), and β (the probability of a Type II error). However, in reality, you can control only two of these: n and α, n and β, or α and β. *In other words, for a fixed sample size, you cannot predetermine both α and β.*

Suppose you decide to set $\alpha = .02$. Then the procedure you use to test H_0 versus H_a will reject H_0 when it is true with a probability of .02. You may wonder why we do not set $\alpha = 0$, so that we would never have a Type I error. The thought of never rejecting a correct H_0 sounds appealing, but the bad news is that β (the probability of a Type II error) is then equal to 1; that is, you will *always* fail to reject H_0 when it is false. If we set $\alpha = 0$, then the resulting test of H_0 versus H_a will automatically fail to reject H_0: $\mu = 5.9$ whenever μ is, in fact, any value other than 5.9 feet. If, for example, μ is 7.5 feet (hardly the case, but interesting), we would still fail to reject H_0—not a good situation at all. We therefore need a value of α that offers a better compromise between the two types of error probabilities.

The value of α you select depends on the relative importance of the two types of error. For example, consider the following hypotheses and decide if the Type I error or the Type II error is the more serious: You have just been examined by a physician using a sophisticated medical device, where the hypotheses under consideration are:

H_0: you do not have a particular serious disease

H_a: you do have the disease

$$\alpha = P(\text{rejecting } H_0 \text{ when it is true})$$

$$= P(\text{device indicates that you have the disease when you do not have it})$$

$$\beta = P(\text{fail to reject } H_0 \text{ when in fact it is false})$$

$$= P(\text{device indicates that you do not have the disease when you do have it})$$

For this situation, the Type I error (measured by α) is not nearly as serious as the Type II error (measured by β). Provided the treatment for the disease does you no serious harm if you are well, the Type I error is not serious. But the Type II error means you fail to receive the treatment even though you are ill.

We never set β in advance, only α. This will allow us to carry out a test of H_0 versus H_a. *The smaller α is, the larger β is. Consequently, if you want β to be small, you choose a large value of α.* For most situations, the range of acceptable α values is .01 to .1.

Acceptable
values of α

.01   .1

For the medical-device problem, you could choose a value of α near .1 or possibly larger, due to the seriousness of a Type II error. On the other hand, if you are more worried about Type I errors for a particular test (such as rejecting an expensive manufactured part that really is good), a small value of α is in order. What if there is no basic difference in the effect of these two errors? If there is no significant difference between the effects of a Type I error versus a Type II error, researchers often choose $\alpha = .05$.

Performing a Statistical Test

The claim that the average adult male height is 5.9 feet resulted in the following pair of hypotheses:

$$H_0: \mu = 5.9$$

$$H_a: \mu \neq 5.9$$

We decide to use a test that carries a 5% risk of rejecting H_0 when it is correct; that is, $\alpha = .05$. In hypothesis testing, α is referred to as the **significance level** of your test. Using $n = 75$, $\bar{x} = 5.76$ ft, and $s = .48$ ft, we wish to carry out the resulting statistical test of H_0 versus H_a. We decided to let H_0 stand (not reject it) if $\bar{X}$ was "close to" 5.9 feet. In other words, we will reject H_0 if $\bar{X}$ is "too far away" from 5.9 feet. We write this as follows:

reject H_0 if $|\bar{X} - 5.9|$ is "too large"

or, by standardizing $\bar{X}$, we can

reject H_0 if $\left|\dfrac{\bar{X} - 5.9}{\sigma/\sqrt{n}}\right|$ is "too large"

We rewrite the last statement as

reject H_0 if $\left|\dfrac{\bar{X} - 5.9}{\sigma/\sqrt{n}}\right| > k$, for some k

What is the value of k? Here is where the value of α has an effect. If H_0 is true and the sample size is large, then using the results of section 7.2, $\bar{X}$ is approximately a normal random variable with

mean $= \mu = 5.9$ and   standard deviation $= \dfrac{\sigma}{\sqrt{n}}$

So, if H_0 is true, $(\bar{X} - 5.9)/(\sigma/\sqrt{n})$ is approximately a standard normal random variable, Z, for large samples. In this case, we reject H_0 if $|Z| > k$, for some k. Suppose $\alpha = .05$. Then,

$$.05 = \alpha = P(\text{rejecting } H_0 \text{ when it is true})$$

$$= P\left(\left|\dfrac{\bar{X} - 5.9}{\sigma/\sqrt{n}}\right| > k, \text{ when } \mu = 5.9\right)$$

$$= P(|Z| > k)$$

To find the value of k that satisfies this statement, consider Figure 8.1. When $|Z| > k$, either $Z > k$, or $Z < -k$, as illustrated. Since $P(|Z| > k) = .05$, the total shaded

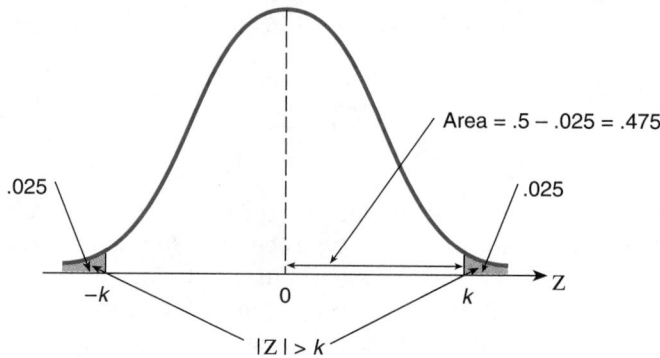

FIGURE

8.1

The shaded area represents the significance level, α.

area is .05, with .025 in each tail due to the symmetry of this curve. Consequently, the area between 0 and k is .475, and, using Table A.4, $k = 1.96$. So our test of H_0 versus H_a is

$$\text{reject } H_0 \text{ if } \left| \frac{\overline{X} - 5.9}{\sigma/\sqrt{n}} \right| > 1.96$$

and fail to reject H_0 otherwise. So,

$$\text{reject } H_0 \text{ if } \frac{\overline{X} - 5.9}{\sigma/\sqrt{n}} > 1.96$$

or

$$\text{reject } H_0 \text{ if } \frac{\overline{X} - 5.9}{\sigma/\sqrt{n}} < -1.96$$

This test will reject H_0 when it is true 5% of the time. This means that there is a 5% risk of making a Type I error.

Using the sample data, we obtained $n = 75$, with $\bar{x} = 5.76$ feet and $s = .48$ feet. Is $\bar{x} = 5.76$ feet far enough away from 5.9 feet for us to reject H_0? This was not at all obvious at first glance; it may have seemed that this value of $\overline{X}$ is "close enough to" 5.9 for us not to reject H_0. Such is not the case, however, because

$$Z = \frac{\overline{X} - 5.9}{\sigma/\sqrt{n}} \approx \frac{\overline{X} - 5.9}{s/\sqrt{n}} = \frac{5.76 - 5.9}{.48/\sqrt{75}} = -2.53 = Z^*$$

where Z^* is the *computed value* of Z. Notice that for the large-sample case, you can substitute for $\sigma/\sqrt{n}$ (typically unknown) its sample estimate $s/\sqrt{n}$.

Conclusion. Because $-2.53 < -1.96$, we reject H_0. Based on the sample results and a value of $\alpha = .05$, the average population male height (μ) is not equal to 5.9 feet.

Another way of phrasing this result is to say that if H_0 is true (that is, if $\mu = 5.9$ feet), the value of $\overline{X}$ obtained from the sample (5.76 feet) is 2.53 standard deviations to the left of the mean using the normal curve for $\overline{X}$ (Figure 8.2). Because a value of $\overline{X}$ this far away from the mean is very unlikely (that is, with probability less than $\alpha = .05$), our conclusion is that H_0 is not true, and so we reject it.

Comments

1. In the preceding procedure, the sample standard deviation (s) was used in place of the population standard deviation (σ). In Chapter 7, we mentioned that $(\overline{X} - 5.9)/(s/\sqrt{n})$ actually follows a t distribution when sampling from a *normal* population, but that for large sample sizes, it can be approximated well using the standard normal (Z) distribution. This section deals with large samples from *any* population, and so $(\overline{X} - 5.9)/(s/\sqrt{n})$ will follow approximately a standard normal distribution for this situation.

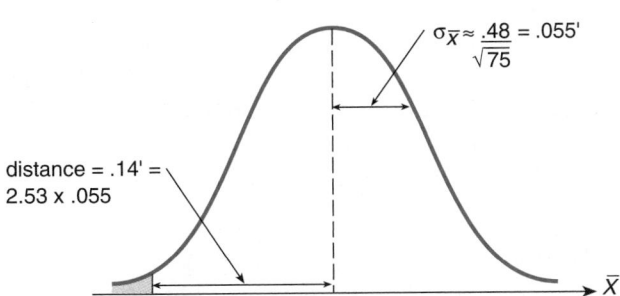

FIGURE

8.2

Distribution of $\bar{X}$ if H_0 is true (H_0: $\mu = 5.9'$).

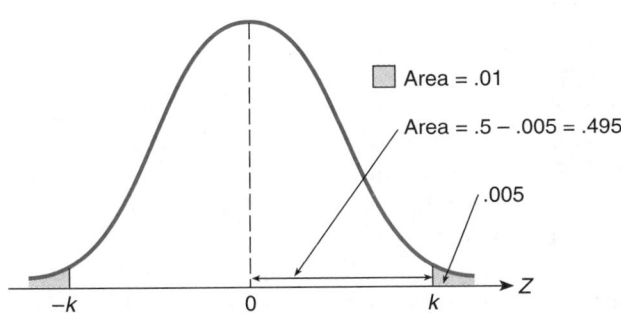

FIGURE

8.3

The shaded area is $\alpha = .01$.

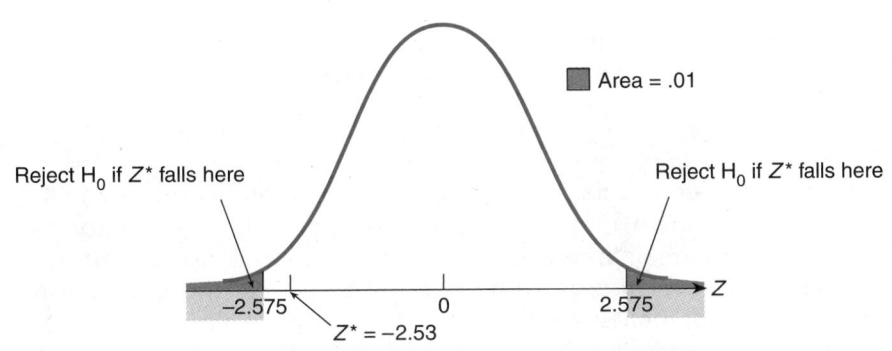

FIGURE

8.4

We reject H_0 if Z^* falls within either tail—the rejection region for $\alpha = .01$.

2. When testing μ = (some value) versus $\mu \neq$ (some value), the null hypothesis, H_0, always contains the =, and the alternative hypothesis, H_a, always contains the $\neq$. In our example, this resulted in splitting the significance level, α, in half and including one-half in each tail of the test statistic, Z. Consequently, a test of H_0: μ = (some value) versus H_a: $\mu \neq$ (some value) is referred to as a **two-tailed test**.

EXAMPLE

8.1

Using the data from our example of male heights, what would be the conclusion using a significance level α of .01?

Solution

The only thing that we need to change from our previous solution is the value of k. Now,

$$P(|Z| > k) = \alpha = .01$$

as shown in Figure 8.3. Using Table A.4, $k = 2.575$, and the test is (see Figure 8.4):

reject H_0 if $Z > 2.575$ or $Z < -2.575$

What is the computed value of Z? Our data values have not changed, so the value of this expression is the same: $Z^* = -2.53$.

The region defined by values of Z to the right of 2.575 and to the left of -2.575 in Figure 8.4 is the **rejection region**. The value of k (2.575) defining this region is the **critical value**. Z^* fails to fall in this region, so we fail to reject H_0. In other words, for $\alpha = .01$, the value of $\overline{X}$ is "close enough" to 5.9 to let H_0 stand; there is insufficient evidence to conclude that μ is different from 5.9 feet.

Clearly then, the choice of the significance level, α, is a delicate matter. It is important to remember that a value of α must be selected prior to obtaining the sample and should reflect the impact of a Type I versus a Type II error.

Accepting H_0 or Failing to Reject H_0

It may appear that there is no difference between "accepting" and "failing to reject" a null hypothesis, but there *is* a difference between these two statements. When you test a hypothesis, H_0 is *presumed innocent* until it is demonstrated to be guilty. In Example 8.1, using $\alpha = .01$ we failed to reject H_0. Now, how certain are we that μ is *exactly* 5.9 feet? After all, our estimate of μ is 5.76 feet. Clearly, we do not believe that μ is precisely 5.9 feet. There simply was not enough evidence to *reject* the claim that $\mu = 5.9$ feet.

For any hypothesis-testing application, the only hypothesis that can be *accepted* is the alternative hypothesis, H_a. Either there is sufficient evidence to *support* H_a (we reject H_0) or there is not (we fail to reject H_0). The focus of our attention is whether there is sufficient evidence within the sample data to conclude that H_a is correct. By failing to reject H_0, we are simply saying that the data do not allow us to support the claim made in H_a (such as $\mu \neq 5.9$ feet) and not that we accept the statement made in H_0 (such as $\mu = 5.9$ feet).

THE FIVE-STEP PROCEDURE FOR HYPOTHESIS TESTING

The discussion up to this point has concentrated on hypothesis testing on the unknown mean of a particular population. We want to emphasize that the shape of the parent population is not important, provided you have a large sample. In other words, the population may be a normal (bell-shaped) one or it may not—it simply does not matter for large samples. Once the level of significance (α) has been determined, there are five steps when attempting to reject or failing to reject a claim regarding the population mean μ:

Step 1. *Set up the null hypothesis, H_0, and the alternative hypothesis, H_a.* If the purpose of the hypothesis test is to test whether the population mean is equal to a particular value (say, μ_0), the "equal hypothesis" always is stated in H_0 and the "unequal hypothesis" always is stated in H_a.

Step 2. *Define the test statistic.* The test statistic will be evaluated, using the sample data, to determine if the data are compatible with the null hypothesis. For tests regarding the mean of a population using a *large sample* (generally, $n > 30$), the test statistic is approximately a standard normal random variable given by the equation

$$Z = \frac{\overline{X} - \mu_0}{\sigma/\sqrt{n}} \approx \frac{\overline{X} - \mu_0}{s/\sqrt{n}}$$

where μ_0 is the value of μ specified in H_0.

Step 3. *Define a rejection region,* having determined a value for α, the significance level. In this region the value of the test statistic will result in rejecting H_0.

8.1

Step 4. *Calculate the value of the test statistic, and carry out the test.* State your decision: to reject H_0 or to fail to reject H_0.

Step 5. *Give a conclusion,* in the terms of the original problem or question. This statement should be free of statistical jargon and should merely summarize the results of the analysis.

Steps 1 through 5 apply to all tests of hypothesis in this and subsequent chapters. The form of the test statistic and rejection region change for different applications, but the sequence of steps always is the same.

EXAMPLE
8.2

Remember that Everglo light bulbs are advertised as lasting 400 hours on the average. As manager of the quality assurance department, you need to examine this claim closely. If the average lifetime is, in fact, less than 400 hours, you can expect at least a half-dozen government watchdog agencies knocking on your door. If the light bulbs last longer than the 400 hours (on the average) claimed, you want to revise your advertising accordingly. To check this claim, you have tested the lifetimes of 100 bulbs, each under the same circumstances (power load, room temperature, and so on). The results of this sample are $n = 100$, $\bar{x} = 411$ hours, and $s = 42.5$ hours. What conclusion would you reach using a significance level of .1?

Solution

Step 1. *Define the hypotheses.* We will test H_0: $\mu = 400$ H_a: $\mu \neq 400$.

Step 2. *Define the test statistic.* The proper test statistic for this problem is

$$Z = \frac{\overline{X} - 400}{\sigma/\sqrt{n}} \approx \frac{\overline{X} - 400}{s/\sqrt{n}}$$

Step 3. *Define the rejection region.* The steps for finding the rejection region are shown in Figure 8.5. We conclude:

reject H_0 if $Z > 1.645$ or $Z < -1.645$

Step 4. *Calculate the value of the test statistic and carry out the test.* The computed value of Z is

$$Z^* \approx \frac{411 - 400}{42.5/\sqrt{100}} = \frac{11}{4.25} = 2.59$$

Since $2.59 > 1.645$, our decision is to reject H_0. In Figure 8.5, Z^* falls in the rejection region.

Step 5. *State a conclusion.* Based on the sample data, there is sufficient evidence to conclude that the average lifetime of Everglo bulbs is not 400 hours.

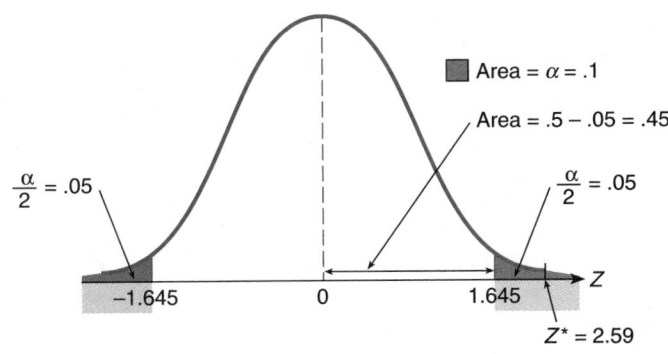

FIGURE
8.5

See Example 8.2; the rejection region is $|Z| > 1.645$.

Comments

In Example 8.2, $\overline{X}$ was "far enough away from" 400 for us to reject the claim that the average lifetime is 400 hours (H_0). However, remember that you cannot decide what is "far enough away from" without also considering the value of the standard deviation ($s = 42.5$ hours in Example 8.2). This is why the value of s (or σ, if it is known) is a vital part of the test statistic. Essentially, when the sample contains much variation (s is large), the sample mean ($\overline{X}$) is a less reliable estimator of the population mean and it is more difficult for $\overline{X}$ to be significantly different than the hypothesized value (400, in the previous value).

Examine the test statistic in Example 8.2. Observe that for *small s*, it is "easier" to reject H_0. As s becomes smaller, the absolute value of the test statistic, Z, becomes larger, and the test statistic is more likely to be in the rejection region for a given value of α.

Confidence Intervals and Hypothesis Testing

What is the relationship, if any, between a 95% confidence interval and performing a *two-tailed* test using $\alpha = .05$? There is a very simple relationship here: When testing $H_0: \mu = \mu_0$ versus $H_a: \mu \neq \mu_0$ using the five-step procedure and a significance level, α, H_0 will be rejected if and only if μ_0 lies outside the $(1 - \alpha) \cdot 100\%$ confidence interval for μ.

The five-step procedure and the confidence interval procedure always lead to the same result. In fact, you can think of a confidence interval as that set of values of μ_0 that would not be rejected by a *two-tailed test* of hypothesis.

In our example involving heights of U.S. males, a sample of 75 heights produced $\overline{x} = 5.76$ feet and $s = .48$ feet. The resulting 95% confidence interval for μ is

$$\overline{X} - k\left[\frac{\sigma}{\sqrt{n}}\right] \quad \text{to} \quad \overline{X} + k\left[\frac{\sigma}{\sqrt{n}}\right]$$

What is the value of k? For large sample sizes, the standard normal table (Table A.4) gives us the probability points we need. The value of k that provides a 95% confidence interval here is the *same* value of k that provides a two-tailed area under the Z curve equal to $1 - .95 = .05$. In other words, we use the same k value that we used in a two-tailed test of H_0 versus H_a—namely, $k = 1.96$. Since we are dealing with large samples, $\sigma/\sqrt{n}$ can be approximated by $s/\sqrt{n}$, and the resulting 95% confidence interval for μ is

$$\overline{X} - 1.96\left(\frac{\sigma}{\sqrt{n}}\right) \quad \text{to} \quad \overline{X} + 1.96\left(\frac{\sigma}{\sqrt{n}}\right)$$

$$\approx \overline{X} - 1.96\frac{s}{\sqrt{n}} \quad \text{to} \quad \overline{X} + 1.96\frac{s}{\sqrt{n}}$$

$$= 5.76 - 1.96\left(\frac{.48}{\sqrt{75}}\right) \quad \text{to} \quad 5.76 + 1.96\left(\frac{.48}{\sqrt{75}}\right)$$

$$= 5.76 - .11 \quad \text{to} \quad 5.76 + .11$$

$$= 5.65 \quad \text{to} \quad 5.87$$

The value of μ we are investigating here is $\mu = 5.9$ feet, and the corresponding hypotheses are $H_0: \mu = 5.9$ and $H_a: \mu \neq 5.9$. For $\alpha = .05$, our result using the two-tailed test was to reject H_0. Using the confidence interval procedure, we obtain the same result because 5.9 does not lie in the 95% confidence interval.

Thus, if you already have computed a confidence interval for μ, you can tell at a glance whether to reject H_0 for a two-tailed test, provided the significance level, α, for the hypothesis test and the confidence level, $(1 - \alpha) \cdot 100\%$, match up.

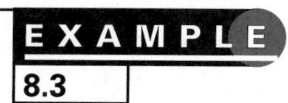

Repeat the example involving the heights of U.S. males, but using a 99% confidence interval. Is the result the same as in Example 8.1, where we failed to reject $H_0: \mu = 5.9$ using $\alpha = .01$?

Solution

Using $\alpha = .01$, we failed to reject H_0 because the absolute value of the test statistic did not exceed the critical value of $k = 2.575$. The corresponding 99% confidence interval for μ is

$$\overline{X} - 2.575\left(\frac{\sigma}{\sqrt{n}}\right) \qquad \text{to} \qquad \overline{X} + 2.575\left(\frac{\sigma}{\sqrt{n}}\right)$$

$$\approx 5.76 - 2.575\left(\frac{.48}{\sqrt{75}}\right) \qquad \text{to} \qquad 5.76 + 2.575\left(\frac{.48}{\sqrt{75}}\right)$$

$$= 5.76 - .143 \qquad \text{to} \qquad 5.76 + .143$$

$$= 5.617 \qquad \text{to} \qquad 5.903$$

Because 5.9 does (barely) lie in this confidence interval, our decision is to fail to reject H_0—the same conclusion reached in Example 8.1.

The Power of a Statistical Test

Up to this point, the probability of a Type II error, β, has remained a phantom—we know it is there, but we don't know what it is. One thing we can say is that a *wide* confidence interval for μ means that the corresponding two-tailed test of H_0 versus H_a has a *large* chance of failing to reject a false H_0; that is, β is large. Now,

$$\beta = P(\text{fail to reject } H_0 \text{ when } H_0 \text{ is false})$$

which means that

$$1 - \beta = P(\text{rejecting } H_0 \text{ when } H_0 \text{ is false})$$

The value of $1 - \beta$ is referred to as the **power** of the test. Since we like β to be small, we prefer the power of the test to be large. Notice that $1 - \beta$ represents the probability of making a *correct* decision in the event that H_0 is false, because in this case we *should* reject it. The more powerful your test is, the better.

Determining the power of your test (hence, β) is not difficult. We will illustrate this procedure for the previous two-tailed test of $H_0: \mu = \mu_0$ versus $H_a: \mu \neq \mu_0$, for some μ_0. We will first consider the case where σ is known and then discuss the situation where σ is unknown.

Power of the Test: σ Known. In Example 8.2 we looked at the data on Everglo light bulbs, where the hypotheses were $H_0: \mu = 400$ hours and $H_a: \mu \neq 400$ hours. Assume that the actual population standard deviation is known to be $\sigma = 50$ hours. For this situation, our test statistic is (using a sample size of $n = 100$):

$$Z = \frac{\overline{X} - 400}{\sigma/\sqrt{n}} = \frac{\overline{X} - 400}{50/\sqrt{100}}$$

$$= \frac{\overline{X} - 400}{5}$$

Proceeding as in Example 8.2, using $\alpha = .10$, we reject H_0 if $Z > 1.645$ or $Z < -1.645$, that is, if $|Z| > 1.645$. So reject H_0 if $(\overline{X} - 400)/5 > 1.645$ [same as $\overline{X} > 400 + (1.645)(5) = 408.225$] or if $(\overline{X} - 400)/5 < -1.645$ [same as $\overline{X} < 400 - (1.645)(5) = 391.775$]. This way of representing the rejection region is illustrated in Figure 8.6, using the shaded area under curve A. The power of this test is

$$1 - \beta = P(\text{rejecting } H_0 \text{ if } H_0 \text{ is false})$$

$$= P(\text{rejecting } H_0 \text{ if } \mu \neq 400)$$

FIGURE

8.6

The shaded area is the probability of rejecting H_0 if $\mu = 400$ (that is, $\alpha = .10$), and the striped area is the probability of rejecting H_0 if $\mu = 403$ (that is, the power of the test $1 - \beta$ when $\mu = 403$).

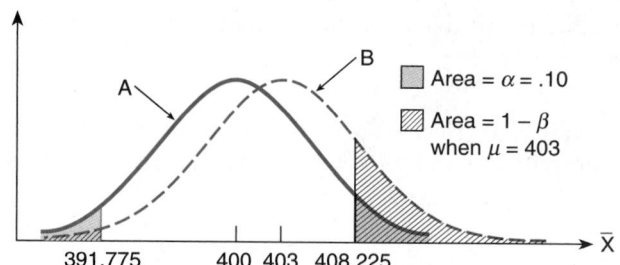

What is the power of this test if μ is not 400 but is 403? What you have here is a value of $1 - \beta$ for *each* value of $\mu \neq 400$.

Recall that we reject H_0 if $\overline{X} > 408.225$ or $\overline{X} < 391.775$. The probability of this occurring if $\mu = 403$ is illustrated as the lined area under curve B in Figure 8.6. Now, if $\mu = 403$ and $\sigma = 50$ (assumed), then

$$Z = \frac{\overline{X} - 403}{50/\sqrt{n}} = \frac{\overline{X} - 403}{5}$$

is a standard normal random variable. So, in Figure 8.6, the striped area to the right of 408.225 is

$$P(\overline{X} > 408.225) = P\left[\frac{\overline{X} - 403}{5} > \frac{408.225 - 403}{5}\right]$$

$$= P\left[Z > \frac{5.225}{5}\right]$$

$$= P(Z > 1.04)$$

$$= .5 - .3508$$

$$= .1492$$

Also, the striped area to the left of 391.775 is

$$P(\overline{X} < 391.775) = P\left[\frac{\overline{X} - 403}{5} < \frac{391.775 - 403}{5}\right]$$

$$= P(Z < -2.24)$$

$$= .5 - .4875$$

$$= .0125$$

Adding these two areas, we find that, if $\mu = 403$, the power of the test of H_0: $\mu = 400$ versus H_a: $\mu \neq 400$ is

$$1 - \beta = .1492 + .0125 = .1617$$

This means that if $\mu = 403$, the probability of making a Type II error (not rejecting H_0) is $\beta = 1 - .1617 = .8383$ (rather high).

This procedure is summarized in the following box. Notice that in the previous discussion, $Z_{\alpha/2} = Z_{.05} = 1.645$, $z_1 = 1.645 - (403 - 400)/(50/\sqrt{100}) = 1.04$, and $z_2 = -1.645 - (403 - 400)/(50/\sqrt{100}) = -2.24$.

FIGURE

8.7

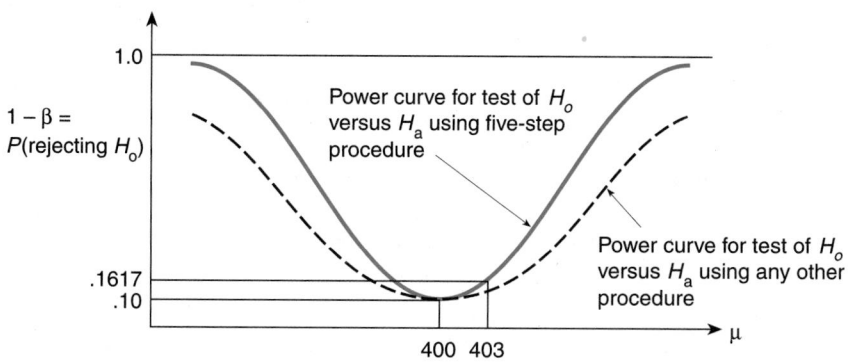

Power curve for
H_0: $\mu = 400$ versus
H_a: $\mu \neq 400$.

POWER OF TEST FOR H_0: $\mu = \mu_0$ VERSUS H_a: $\mu \neq \mu_0$

1. Determine

$$z_1 = Z_{\alpha/2} - \frac{\mu - \mu_0}{\sigma/\sqrt{n}}$$

and

$$z_2 = -Z_{\alpha/2} - \frac{\mu - \mu_0}{\sigma/\sqrt{n}}$$

where $Z_{\alpha/2}$ is the value of Z from Table A.4 having a right-tailed area of $\alpha/2$ and μ is the specific value of the population mean (403 in Figure 8.6).

2. Power of test = $P(Z > z_1) + P(Z < z_2)$.

The power of your test increases (β decreases) as μ moves away from 400, as illustrated in Figure 8.7. Using the five-step procedure, which uses the test statistic $Z = (\overline{X} - 400)/(\sigma/\sqrt{n})$, the resulting **power curve** is the solid-line curve in Figure 8.7. It is symmetric, and its lowest point is located at $\mu = 400$. For this value of μ, H_0 is actually true, so that a Type II error was not committed. Nevertheless, the value on the power curve corresponding to $\mu = 400$ is always

$$P(\text{rejecting } H_0 \text{ if } \mu = 400) = \alpha = .10 \text{ (for this example)}$$

The *steeper* your power curve is, the better. You are more apt to reject H_0 as μ moves away from 400—certainly a nice property. If we assume that the sampled population is normally distributed, Figure 8.7 illustrates that the power curve using the five-step procedure lies above (is steeper than) the power curve for any other testing procedure. To illustrate briefly another testing procedure, rather than basing the test statistic on the sample mean $\overline{X}$, we could derive a test statistic using the sample *median*. The resulting power curve for this procedure would lie *below* the one using $\overline{X}$, indicating that the test using the sample median is less powerful and thus inferior. So, in this sense, the five-step procedure defines the best (most powerful) test of H_0: $\mu = \mu_0$ versus H_a: $\mu \neq \mu_0$.

Power of the Test: σ Unknown. When σ is unknown, we are forced to *approximate* the power of the test by replacing σ with the sample estimate, s. We are dealing with large samples, so we can use Table A.4 (the Z table).

In our discussion of the power of our test for Everglo bulb lifetimes, we treated the population standard deviation, σ, as known. If we make no assumptions about this parameter, we need to approximate the power of the test for $\mu = 403$. We assume $s = 42.5$ hours (as before) and use $\alpha = .10$.

We now reject H_0 if

$$\overline{X} > 400 + 1.645\left[\frac{s}{\sqrt{n}}\right] \qquad \text{or} \qquad \overline{X} < 400 - 1.645\left[\frac{s}{\sqrt{n}}\right]$$

So, H_0 is rejected, provided

$$\overline{X} > 400 + 1.645\left[\frac{42.5}{\sqrt{100}}\right] = 406.99$$

or

$$\overline{X} < 400 - 1.645\left[\frac{42.5}{\sqrt{100}}\right] = 393.01$$

The resulting power of the test for $\mu = 403$ is approximately equal to

$$P(\overline{X} > 406.99 \text{ if } \mu = 403) + P(\overline{X} < 393.01 \text{ if } \mu = 403)$$

$$= P\left[Z > \frac{406.99 - 403}{42.5/\sqrt{100}}\right] + P\left[Z < \frac{393.01 - 403}{42.5/\sqrt{100}}\right]$$

$$= P(Z > .94) + P(Z < -2.35)$$

$$= (.5 - .3264) + (.5 - .4906) = .1736 + .0094$$

$$= .183$$

So there is an 18% chance of rejecting the null hypothesis if the population mean is, in fact, equal to 403.

X Exercises 8.1–8.16

Understanding the Mechanics

8.1 A manager randomly samples 50 containers of juice. The manager is concerned that the containers may be filled to an amount different from 24 ounces.
   a. Develop a suitable null and alternative hypothesis.
   b. How can the manager make a Type I error?
   c. How can the manager make a Type II error?
   d. Will the hypothesis test procedure prove that the containers are filled to an amount different from 24 ounces?

8.2 State if an error is made in the following situations and, if so, what type of error.
   a. The null hypothesis is true and the calculated value of the test statistic falls in the rejection region.
   b. The null hypothesis is true and the calculated value of the test statistic does not fall in the rejection region.
   c. The alternative hypothesis is true and the calculated value of the test statistic falls in the rejection region.
   d. The alternative hypothesis is true and the calculated value of the test statistic does not fall in the rejection region.

8.3 Are the following statements true or false? Explain.
   a. As the significance level increases, the probability of a Type I error increases.
   b. As the power increases, the probability of a Type II error decreases.

   c. As the significance level increases, the size of the rejection region increases.
   d. The probability of a Type I error and the probability of a Type II error always sum to 1.

Applying the New Concepts

8.4 State the null and alternative hypotheses for the following situations.
   a. A federal auditor believes that a health care company has overcharged its patients.
   b. The editor of a magazine believes that the mean income of subscribers to its magazine is $75,000.
   c. An operations manager must maintain machines that produce 50 pound bags of fertilizer.
   d. A manufacturer believes that the average life of its competitor's battery is less than 10 hours.

8.5 The mean of a normally distributed population is believed to be equal to 50.1. A sample of 36 observations is taken, and the sample mean is found to be 53.2. The alternative hypothesis is that the population mean is not equal to 50.1. Complete the hypothesis test, assuming that the population standard deviation is equal to 4. Use a .05 significance level.

8.6 More people are choosing to get married in the Caribbean as the cost of a traditional wedding increases.

In fact, weddings in the Caribbean, with the cost of travel, can cost the bride's father between $5,000 and $10,000. As an additional benefit, the wedding can roll right into the honeymoon. While the disadvantage of such far-away weddings is difficult for many relatives and close friends, the savings over a $25,000 to $30,000 traditional wedding can make the decision easy. Suppose that a Caribbean resort wished to promote its location as a low-cost alternative to the traditional wedding and advertised that the average wedding with travel expenses is $7,500. To confirm this figure, 50 previously held weddings on the Caribbean island are randomly sampled. The data are presented below in dollars. Using a .05 significance level, is there sufficient evidence to indicate that the average cost of a wedding in the Caribbean differs from $7,500?

6,300	8,400	9,000	7,400	7,000	8,100	6,500	8,400
7,700	7,300	5,800	9,700	6,800	6,400	8,300	7,700
5,100	5,800	8,700	9,500	7,800	8,000	7,200	7,500
6,500	9,700	7,400	7,800	6,700	8,900	7,500	8,700
7,700	6,900	7,100	8,200	6,400	7,600	8,700	7,800
9,600	9,200	7,700	5,700	7,900	8,800	9,000	7,300
8,300	8,100						

(Source: "Here Come the Isles: Exotic Ways to Wed," *USA Today,* June 19, 1998, p. 4D.)

8.7 "Most things in the movie business are disappointments," said Ben Feingold, president of the Columbia TriStar Motion Picture Group. "DVD isn't one of them." Industry figures show that the average price of DVD players, expected to be in 25 million homes by the end of the year, is about $180, down from about $500 when the format was introduced in 1997. Suppose that a retail analyst randomly samples 25 retail stores in a certain geographical area and records a sample mean of $193. The retail analyst would like to test whether the average price of DVD players in this region differs from $180.

a. What is the null and alternative hypotheses?

b. Assume that the population standard deviation of the cost of DVD players is $30. Is there evidence that the average price for a DVD player in this region differs from $180? Use a 1% significance level.

c. What would your answer be in part b if the sample size were 50?

d. What assumption are you making about the distribution of the data for the hypothesis test procedure to be valid?

(Source: "Choosing Bells or Whistles," *The New York Times,* October 26, 2001, p. E27.)

8.8 A crime reporter was told that, on the average, 3,000 burglaries per month occurred in his city. The reporter examined past data, which were used to compute a 95% confidence interval for the number of burglaries per month. The confidence interval was from 2,176 to 2,784. At a 5% level of significance, do these data tend to support the alternative hypothesis, $H_a: \mu \neq 3,000$?

8.9 The greatest variation in real estate prices is in California, where recently there was a difference of more than $1 million between a home in Palo Alto and one in Bakersfield. In Palo Alto, the typical four-bedroom, 2,200-square-foot house was appraised at about $1.2 million in 2001, whereas a similar home in Bakersfield was appraised at $200,000. Suppose that a realtor randomly sampled 50 homes in Palo Alto in 2002 and found a 95% confidence interval for the average appraised value of a home in Palo Alto to be .91 to 1.08 million. Assume that the appraised values of homes in Palo Alto are normally distributed. Is there sufficient evidence to indicate that the average price of a home in Palo Alto is different from $1.2 million in 2002? Use a 5% significance level.

(Source: "Palo Alto Tops Realtor List of Most Expensive Markets," *Los Angeles Times,* August 19, 2001, p. K13.)

8.10 The life span of an electronic chip used in a high-powered microcomputer is estimated to be 625.35 hours from a random sample of 40 chips. The life of an electronic chip is considered to be normally distributed with a population variance of 400 hours.

a. Find a 90% confidence interval for the mean life of the electronic chips.

b. Is the true mean life of the electronic chips different from 633 hours? Use a 10% significance level.

8.11 The $450 million Stade de France, built specifically for the 1998 World Cup soccer championship, has 80,000 seats with no pillars or obstructed views. Soccer is so popular that the global television audience will outdraw that of the Olympics. Tickets sold through travel agencies were priced up to $600 for early matches before the World Cup championship. Suppose that a travel agency wished to know the mean selling price of the early matches and a random sample revealed a mean of $430 with a standard deviation of $130.

a. Find an interval with a 90% confidence level for estimating the true mean selling price for the early matches. Assume a sample size of 100.

b. Is there sufficient evidence to indicate that the true mean selling price for the early matches differs from $500? Use a 10% significance level.

(Source: "Frank Talk About State-of-the-Art Stadium," *USA Today,* May 12, 1988, p. 8C.)

8.12 The hypotheses for a situation are

$$H_0: \mu = 20$$

$$H_a: \mu \neq 20$$

If the population of interest is normally distributed, what is the power of the test for the mean if μ is actually equal to 22? Assume that a sample of size 49 is used and the sample standard deviation is 4.2. Use a significance level of .05.

8.13 Windows 98, which was released in June 1998, offers support for technologies that have not caught on to the mass market. One such technology is WebTV for Windows. This technology allows suitably equipped computers to be used as TV receivers so that a user can watch TV while cruising the Web or crunching numbers. A TV tuner card is needed, and costs vary with an ATI card being the more expensive option. Assume that the mean price for a card to connect the PC to a TV is $215 for the population of sales prices for this card. Furthermore, assume the price of these cards can be approximated by a normal distribution with a population standard deviation of $40. Suppose that a marketing analyst randomly samples

25 stores and wishes to test a hypothesis about the mean of this population using a .10 significance level. What would be the power of the statistical test if the hypotheses are as presented below? Compare and comment on the power for the two hypotheses.

    a. $H_0: \mu = 200$, $H_a: \mu \neq 200$
    b. $H_0: \mu = 160$, $H_a: \mu \neq 160$

(Source: "Windows 98 Is an Upgrade That Bears Scrutiny," *USA Today*, June 25, 1998, p. 5D.)

8.14 An electro-optical firm currently uses a laser component in producing sophisticated graphic designs. The time it takes to produce a certain design with the current laser component is 70 seconds, with a standard deviation of 8 seconds. A new laser component is bought by the firm because it is believed that the time it takes this laser to produce the same design is not equal to 70 seconds; the new component also has a standard deviation of 8 seconds. The research-and-development department is interested in constructing the power curve for testing the claim that the time it takes to produce the same design by the new laser component is not equal to 70 seconds. Graph the power function for a sample of size 25 and a significance level of .05.

Using the Computer

8.15 **[DATA SET EX8-15]** *Variable Description:*

ATMwithdrawal: Amount of euro currency withdrawn

For 300 million people in 12 Eurozone countries, the use of ATM machines is making it easier to use the new euro currency. ATM machines are handling up to 90% of the 14.5 billion euro notes issued. Financial analysts have warned that if people have a bad experience with their ATM, that could undermine their belief in the currency. Suppose that a particular bank is interested in how much cash to keep in a local ATM machine. The bank manager believes that the average withdrawal from the local ATM machine on the weekend is 150 euros. A random sample of 60 transactions was recorded. Assume a standard deviation of 50 euros.

    a. Plot a histogram of the amount of euros withdrawn using the local ATM machine. Describe the shape of this distribution.

    b. Is there sufficient evidence to indicate that the average withdrawal differs from 150 euros? Use a 5% significance level. Would your conclusion change if you used a significance level of 10%?

    c. Construct a 95% confidence interval for the average withdrawal. Is the confidence interval consistent with the conclusion in part b?

(Source: "New Notes and Coins Create Problems for Cash Machine Makers," *The Financial Times*, August 28, 2001, p. 2.)

8.16 **[DATA SET EX8-16]** *Variable Description:*

Decibels: The number of decibels produced by power tools used by employees in a manufacturing plant

According to the National Institute for Occupational Safety and Health, or NIOSH, noise-induced hearing loss is the second-most common work-related illness or injury in the United States. Experts say that prolonged exposure to noise louder than 85 decibels can impair hearing. The more decibels, the less time it takes to do damage. Suppose that the power tools at a manufacturing plant are designed to work at 85 decibels. A plant manager performs a random check on 50 power tools to determine if the average number of decibels produced by these tools differs from 85.

    a. Construct a histogram of the data. Would you conclude that the data are approximately normally distributed?

    b. At the 1% significance level and assuming a standard deviation of 2.5 decibels, is there evidence to indicate that the average number of decibels differs from 85?

    c. Suppose that the standard deviation was only 2 decibels instead of 2.5 in part b. Would that change the conclusion to part b?

(Source: "The Healthy Man; Now Hear This, While You Can," *Los Angeles Times*, October 8, 2001, p. 1S.)

8.2   ONE-TAILED TEST FOR THE MEAN OF A POPULATION: LARGE SAMPLE

There are many situations in which you are interested in demonstrating that the mean of a population is *larger* or *smaller* than some specified value. For example, as a member of a consumer-advocate group, you may be attempting to demonstrate that the average weight of a bag of sugar for a particular brand is not 10 pounds (as specified on the bag) but is in fact less than 10 pounds. Because the situation that you (the researcher) are attempting to demonstrate goes into the alternative hypothesis, the resulting hypotheses would be $H_0: \mu \geq 10$ and $H_a: \mu < 10$. *Remember that we said it is standard practice always to put the equals sign in the null hypothesis.* In the testing procedure only the *boundary value* is important, and so the hypotheses may be written as

$$H_0: \mu = 10$$

$$H_a: \mu < 10$$

In this way, we can identify the distribution of $\overline{X}$ when H_0 is true—namely, $\overline{X}$ is approximately a normal random variable centered at 10 with standard deviation $\sigma/\sqrt{n}$ (or $s/\sqrt{n}$ if σ is unknown). Because the focus of our attention is on H_a (can we support it or not?), which of the two ways you use to write H_0 is not an important issue. The procedure for testing H_0 versus H_a is the same regardless of how you state H_0.

The resulting test is referred to as a **one-tailed test,** and it uses the same five-step procedure as the two-tailed test. The only change we make is to modify the rejection region: All the error is in a single tail.

EXAMPLE 8.4

A foreign car manufacturer advertises that its newest model, the Bullet, rarely stops at gas stations. In fact, it claims its EPA rating for highway driving is at least 32.5 mpg. However, the results of a recent independent study determined the miles per gallon (mpg) for 50 identical models of the Bullet, with these results: $n = 50$, $\bar{x} = 30.4$ mpg, and $s = 5.3$ mpg. This report failed to offer any conclusion, and you have been asked to interpret these results by someone who has always felt that the 32.5 figure is too high. What would be your conclusion using a significance level of $\alpha = .05$?

Solution

Step 1. *An important point to be made here is that H_0 and H_a (as well as α) must be defined before you observe any data.* In other words, *do not let the data dictate your hypotheses;* this approach would introduce a serious bias into your final outcome. For this application, we want to demonstrate that the population mean, μ, is less than 32.5 mpg, and so this goes into H_a. The appropriate hypotheses then are H_0: $\mu \geq 32.5$ and H_a: $\mu < 32.5$.

Step 2. The test statistic for a large-sample one-tailed test is the same as that for a large-sample two-tailed test, namely,

$$Z = \frac{\overline{X} - \mu_0}{\sigma/\sqrt{n}} \approx \frac{\overline{X} - \mu_0}{s/\sqrt{n}}$$

Here,

$$Z \approx \frac{\overline{X} - 32.5}{s/\sqrt{n}}$$

Step 3. What happens to Z when H_a is true? Here we would expect $\overline{X}$ to be less than 32.5 (because μ is), so the value of Z should be negative. Consequently, our procedure will be to reject H_0 if Z lies "too far to the left" of 0; that is,

$$\text{reject } H_0 \text{ if } Z \approx \frac{\overline{X} - 32.5}{s/\sqrt{n}} < k \quad \text{for some } k < 0$$

Since $\alpha = .05$, we will choose a value of k (the critical value) such that the resulting test will reject H_0 (shoot down the mpg claim) when it is true, with a 5% risk of an incorrect decision. This amounts to defining a rejection region in the *left tail* of the Z curve, the shaded area in Figure 8.8. Using Table A.4, we see that the critical value is $k = -1.645$, and the resulting test of H_0 versus H_a is

$$\text{reject } H_0 \text{ if } Z \approx \frac{\overline{X} - 32.5}{s/\sqrt{n}} < -1.645$$

Step 4. Using the sample results, the value of the test statistic is

$$Z^* \approx \frac{30.4 - 32.5}{5.3/\sqrt{50}} = -2.80$$

Because $-2.80 < -1.645$, the decision is to reject H_0.

FIGURE

8.8

The one-tailed rejection region is $Z < -1.645$. We reject H_0 if $Z = (\bar{X} - 32.5)/(\sigma/\sqrt{n}) < -1.645$.

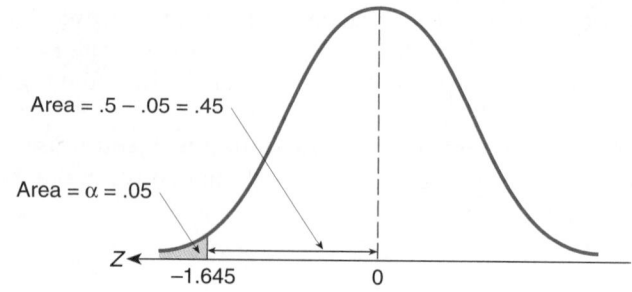

Area = .5 − .05 = .45

Area = α = .05

Step 5. The results of this study support the claim that the average mileage for the Bullet is *less than* 32.5 mpg. This result would provide just cause for claiming false advertising by the auto manufacturer.

One-Tailed Test or Two-Tailed Test?

The decision to use a one-tailed test or a two-tailed test depends on what you are attempting to demonstrate. For example, when the quality-control department of a manufacturing facility receives a shipment from one of its vendors and wants to determine if the product meets minimal specifications, a one-tailed test is appropriate. If the product does not meet specifications, it will be rejected. This type of problem was first encountered in Chapter 5, where we examined lot acceptance sampling. Here, the product is *not* checked to see whether it *exceeds* specifications, because any product that exceeds specifications is acceptable.

On the other hand, the vendors who supply the products would generally run two-tailed tests to determine two things. First, they must know if the product meets the minimal specifications of their customers before they ship it. Second, they must determine whether the product greatly exceeds specifications because this can be very costly in production (making a product that uses too much raw material costs them extra money).

The testing of electric fuses is a classic example of a two-tailed test. A fuse must break when it reaches the prescribed temperature or a fire will result. However, the fuse must not break before it reaches the prescribed temperature or it will shut off the electricity when there is no need to do so. Therefore, the quality-control procedures for testing fuses must be two-tailed.

Microsoft Excel Application   Use DATA8-5

Using Excel to Calculate the Large-Sample Test Statistic for Testing a Population Mean

The mean consumption of electricity for the month of June at the Southern States Power Company (SSPC) historically has been 918 kilowatt-hours per residential customer. As part of its request for a rate increase, SSPC is arguing that the power consumption for June of the current year is substantially higher. To demonstrate this, they hired an independent consulting firm to examine a random sample of 60 customer accounts. The sample results, contained in data set DATA8-5, consist of the 60 kilowatt-hours for June of the current year. Can you conclude that the average consumption for all users during June of this year (denoted by μ) is larger than 918? Use $\alpha = .01$.

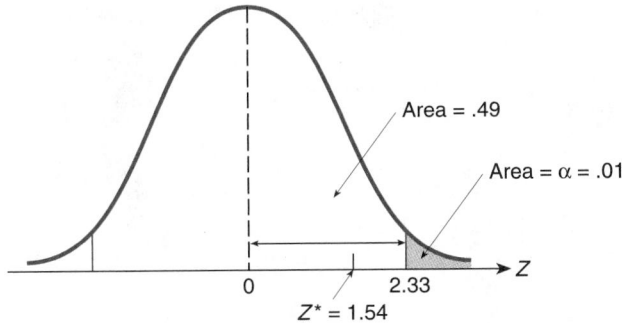

FIGURE

8.9

One-tailed
rejection region;
reject H_0 if $Z > 2.33$.

Solution

Step 1. The hypotheses here are H_0: $\mu \leq 918$ and H_a: $\mu > 918$.

Step 2. The correct test statistic is

$$Z = \frac{\overline{X} - 918}{\sigma/\sqrt{n}} \approx \frac{\overline{X} - 918}{s/\sqrt{n}}$$

Approximating $\sigma/\sqrt{n}$ using $s/\sqrt{n}$ is valid since we are dealing with a large sample here.

Step 3. For this situation, what happens to Z if H_a is true? The value of $\overline{X}$ should then be *larger* than 918 (on the average), resulting in a positive value of Z. So we

$$\text{reject } H_0 \text{ if } Z \approx \frac{\overline{X} - 918}{s/\sqrt{n}} > k \quad \text{for some } k > 0$$

Examine the standard normal curve in Figure 8.9, where the area corresponding to α is the shaded part of the *right tail;* using Table A.4, the critical value is $k = 2.33$. The test of H_0 versus H_a will be

$$\text{reject } H_0 \text{ if } Z > 2.33$$

Step 4. To carry out the test of hypothesis using Excel, begin by opening file DATA8-5. The first step is to determine the standard deviation of the 60 sample values. Referring to Figure 8.11, type "Stand. Dev." in cell B1 and "=STDEV(A2:A61)" in cell B2. The value of 173.92 should appear in cell B2. Although 173.92 is the sample standard deviation, the *Z test procedure will treat this value as the standard deviation of the population.* Next, click on **KPK Data Analysis ➤ One Population Inference** and fill in the various boxes as illustrated in Figure 8.10. The input range is A1:A61, since there are 60 data values and cell A1 contains the label "KW-Hours" (be sure to click on the box alongside **Labels**). By specifying the output range as C1 (upper-left corner), you obtain the output shown in Figure 8.11. The computed value of the test statistic is

$$Z^* = \frac{952.58 - 918}{173.92/\sqrt{60}} = 1.540$$

Because $1.540 < 2.33$ (the rounded value in cell D9), the decision is to fail to reject H_0. A valuable piece of information is contained in cell D8. It is called the *p-value* for the test of hypothesis and will be discussed in Section 8.3.

Step 5. At the .01 significance level, there is insufficient evidence to support the power company's claim that the power consumption for June has increased.

FIGURE

8.10

Excel input screen for testing a population mean using **KPK Data Analysis ➤ One Population Inference.**

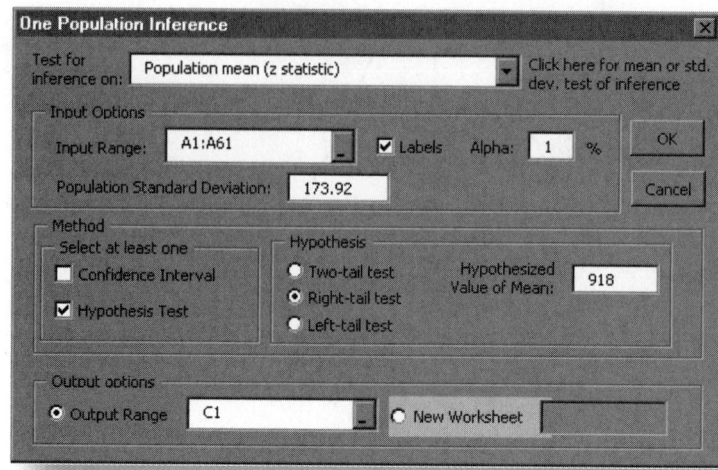

FIGURE

8.11

Excel spreadsheet and output using **KPK Data Analysis ➤ One Population Inference** (refer to Figure 8.10 for input screen; Sample standard deviation is in cell B2).

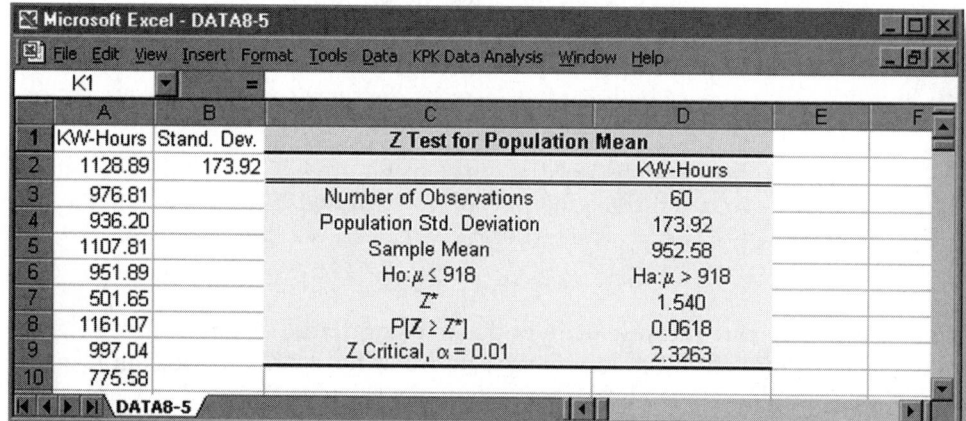

Comments

1. This result is very much tied to the value of α. Using $\alpha = .10$ in Example 8.5, we would obtain the *opposite* conclusion—which you may find somewhat disturbing. You often hear the expression that "statistics lie." This is not true—statistics are merely mistreated, either intentionally or accidentally. One can often obtain the desired conclusion by choosing the value of α that produces the desired conclusion. We therefore reemphasize that you must choose α by weighing the serious-

ness of a Type I versus a Type II error *before* seeing the data. A partial remedy for this dilemma is discussed in Section 8.3.

2. To calculate the power of a one-sided test, refer to the box on page 315. We modify this procedure for a one-sided test as outlined in the following boxes.

3. A summary of the procedure for carrying out a large-sample test on a population mean is contained in the third box.

POWER OF TEST FOR H_0: $\mu \leq \mu_0$ VERSUS H_a: $\mu > \mu_0$

1. Determine

$$z_1 = Z_\alpha - \frac{\mu - \mu_0}{\sigma/\sqrt{n}}$$

where Z_α is the value of Z from Table A.4 having a right-tailed area of α and μ is the specific value of the population mean.

2. Power of the test is $P(Z > z_1)$

POWER OF TEST FOR H_0: $\mu \geq \mu_0$ VERSUS H_a: $\mu < \mu_0$

1. Determine

$$z_2 = -Z_\alpha - \frac{\mu - \mu_0}{\sigma/\sqrt{n}}$$

where Z_α is the value of Z from Table A.4 having a right-tailed area of α and μ is the specific value of the population mean.

2. Power of the test is $P(Z < z_2)$

LARGE-SAMPLE TESTS ON A POPULATION MEAN

Two-Tailed Test

$$H_0: \mu = \mu_0$$
$$H_a: \mu \neq \mu_0$$
$$\text{reject } H_0 \text{ if } |Z^*| > Z_{\alpha/2}$$

where Z^* is the computed value of $Z \approx \dfrac{\overline{X} - \mu_0}{s/\sqrt{n}}$ ($Z_{\alpha/2} = 1.96$ for $\alpha = .05$).

One-Tailed Test

$H_0: \mu \leq \mu_0$	$H_0: \mu \geq \mu_0$
$H_a: \mu > \mu_0$	$H_a: \mu < \mu_0$
reject H_0 if $Z^* > Z_\alpha$	reject H_0 if $Z^* < -Z_\alpha$
($Z_\alpha = 1.645$ for $\alpha = .05$)	($-Z_\alpha = -1.645$ for $\alpha = .05$)

X   Exercises 8.17–8.26

Understanding the Mechanics

8.17 Set up the null hypothesis and the alternative hypothesis for each of the following situations.

a. An automotive analyst believes that the miles per gallon on a new model is less than what the company is advertising. A random sample of data is taken to support the analyst's belief.

b. A phone company claims that the average customer pays less than $30 a month. A random sample of data is taken to verify this claim.

c. A marketing research firm believes that the average number of hours per week that Americans watch television differs from 15 hours a week. A sample of data is taken to support this belief.

8.18 A random sample of 64 observations was selected. Test that the mean of the population is less than 106 using a significance level of .05. The following statistics were calculated from the random sample:

$$\sum(x_i - \overline{x})^2 = 2016 \qquad \sum x = 6592$$

8.19 A random sample of 49 observations from a normal population yields a sample mean of 85 with a standard deviation of 14.

a. Test the claim that the population mean differs from 81. Use a .05 significance level.

b. Test the claim that the population mean is greater than 85. Use a .05 significance level.

Applying the New Concepts

8.20 The Federal Reserve board made eight interest-rate cuts on its benchmark short-term rates during 2001. However, credit cards have averaged around 14%, with the lowest credit cards charging around 8%. A financial analyst believes that the average rate on credit cards that charge monthly fees is lower than the national average of all credit cards. A random sample of 49 different credit cards that charged monthly fees revealed a sample mean of 13.5% and a standard deviation of 1.4%. Test the financial analyst's belief that the average rate charged by credit cards with monthly fees is less than 14%. Use a 5% significance level.

(Source: "Credit Card Fees," *Kiplinger's Personal Finance Magazine,* vol. 55, no. 11, November 2001, p. 101.)

8.21 The idea of a smart mower has been on drawing boards for years. In 1988, the Lawn Ranger, a lawn mower guided by remote control, was introduced to the public, but few of them sold. In 1994 the Turtle was patented and sold for about $2,000. Its computer guides it to cut grass. However, tall grass and a cloudy day can stall out the lawn mower. Michael Gaffney of the Professional Lawn Care Association of America believes that walk-behind lawn mowers will be popular for some time, with the average lawn mower costing $275. Suppose that a venture capitalist, who is interested in putting a new remote-control lawn mower on the market, is advised that this novel lawn mower will be a profitable investment in the Richmond, Virginia, area if the average cost of a push lawn mower sold in that area exceeds $350. A random sample of 100 lawn mower owners was obtained. The sample mean was $375 with a standard deviation of $150. Should the venture capitalist invest in marketing the new lawn mower? Use a significance level of .05.

(Source: "It's Like George Jetson's Lawn Mower," *USA Today,* May 12, 1998, p. 2D.)

8.22 Loews Cineplex Entertainment, the leading movie theater chain in New York City, was the first movie theater to increase its movie ticket prices to $10. Mr. King at AMC, a competing movie theater, said that while a $10 ticket was uncommon in the New York City region, prices had climbed above that level in Canada because of the devalued Canadian dollar. But those increases have not hurt the box office. Entertainment analysts believe that the price of a movie ticket in New York City ranges from $5 to $10 with a mean of $7.50. However, several theater managers claim that the average price is higher than $7.50.

a. Assume that a random sample of 36 theaters revealed a mean of $7.80 with a standard deviation of $1.00. What conclusion can be made using a 10% significance level regarding the claim that the average movie price exceeds $7.50?

b. If the significance level were 5% instead of 10% in part a, would that change the conclusion?

(Source: "Ticket Price for a Movie Goes to $10 at Loews," *The New York Times,* February 24, 2001, p. B3.)

8.23 In an attempt to get AIDS drugs to thousands of HIV-infected people in Africa, Asia, and South America, several major pharmaceutical companies slashed their prices, in some cases by 50% to 75%. The manager of a medical center working under the United Nations' AIDS program is interested in the average cost of widely used anti-HIV drugs in the South African region. The manager believes that the cost is less than $280 per month. Assume that the costs of these anti-HIV drugs are approximately normally distributed with a standard deviation of $100. What is the power of the statistical test to test the manager's belief if the sample size is 35 and the true mean cost is $240 for the anti-HIV drugs in South Africa? Use a significance level of .05.

(Source: "AIDS Medicine Will Cost Less in Poor Nations," *The Wall Street Journal,* June 23, 1998, p. B1.)

8.24 Following the September 11, 2001, terrorist attack, U.S. flags of all sorts were glued, clipped, and taped to American vehicles as a sign of patriotism. Several months later, these flags had been badly beaten by the elements. One man, Tom Fucigna, has made it his mission to pick up flags that lay alongside the interstate. Suppose that Tom claims that the average number of flags that he picks up is greater than 15. The population standard deviation of the number of flags that he picks up is known to be 2.5. Assume that an observer wished to test Tom's claim using a sample size of 35 days and a significance level of 5%. What is the power of the hypothesis test to test this claim if the true average number of flags that Tom picks up is 16?

(Source: "Oh, Say, Can You See That Your Car Flag Is Now a Bit Ragged?" *The Wall Street Journal,* January 21, 2002, p. A1.)

Using the Computer

8.25 [DATA SET EX8-25] *Variable description:*

CartridgLife: Number of pages that a cartridge can be used to print

An office supply company would like to advertise that its new and improved ink jet cartridges last longer than the previous ones. From past tests, the old cartridges had a life of 2,375 pages with a standard deviation of 250 pages. The company believes that the life of the new ink jet cartridges will be longer than the old cartridges and that the standard deviation of the life of the new cartridges is the same. A random sample of 100 new cartridges were used in a study and their life is recorded in variable CartridgLife in units of pages.

a. Using a significance level of .10, is there sufficient evidence that the new cartridges last longer?

b. Explain how practical and statistical significance are important in determining whether the company should advertise the new cartridges as lasting longer?

c. Should the standard deviation also have decreased to really have an improved cartridge? Explain.

8.26 [Simulation Exercise] A rejection of a null hypothesis is affected by four factors: (1) the value of the mean when the alternative hypothesis is true; (2) the sample size; (3) the population standard deviation; (4) the significance level. In Excel, click on **KPK Data Analysis ➤ Simulation Exercises ➤ Hypothesis Testing** to discover through a simulation game how these factors affect rejecting the null hypothesis. This game assumes that $H_0: \mu \leq 50$. Fifty simulations using randomly generated data are performed and a visual display of the value of the test statistic and whether it falls in the rejection or nonrejection region is presented.

a. In the dialog box, enter 50 for the true value of the population mean under the alternative hypothesis. This situation is the case where the null hypothesis is true. Now enter 25 for the sample size, 20 for the σ, and 5 for the alpha level. What is the percent rejected? Repeat this five times. On average, there should be approximately 5% rejections.

b. In part a, change the value of μ under the alternative to 53, 55, 58, and 60. How do the number of rejections change?

c. Select 53 for the value of μ under the alternative. Enter 25 for the sample size and 5 for the alpha level. Change σ to 10, 15, 20, 25, and 30. How does the percentage of rejections change as the value of the population standard deviation increases?

d. Select 53 for the value of μ under the alternative. Enter 20 for the value of σ and 5 for the alpha level. Change the sample size to 25, 50, 75, and 100. How does the percentage of rejections change as the value of the sample size increases?

e. Select 53 for the value of μ under the alternative. Enter 20 for the value of σ and 25 for the sample size. Change the alpha level to 1, 5, 10, and 20. How does the percentage of rejections change as the significance level increases?

8.3 REPORTING TESTING RESULTS USING A *p*-VALUE

In Example 8.1, we noted that for one value of α we rejected H_0, and for another (seemingly reasonable) value of α we failed to reject H_0. Is there a way of summarizing the results of a test of hypothesis that allows you to determine whether these results are barely significant (or insignificant) or overwhelmingly significant (or insignificant)? Did we barely reject H_0, or did H_0 go down in flames?

A convenient way to summarize your results is to use a *p*-value, often called the *observed* α or *observed significance level*.

> The ***p*-value** is the value of α at which the hypothesis test procedure changes conclusions based on a given set of data. It is the largest value of α for which you will fail to reject H_0.

Consequently, the *p*-value is the point at which the five-step procedure leads us to switch from rejecting H_0 to failing to reject H_0 for a given set of data.

Determining the *p*-Value

The *p*-value for *any* test is determined by replacing the area corresponding to α by the area corresponding to the *computed* value of the test statistic. In our discussion and Example 8.1, using $\alpha = .05$ you reject H_0 and using $\alpha = .01$ you fail to reject H_0. We know that the *p*-value here is between .01 and .05. For this example, the computed value of the test statistic was $Z^* = -2.53$, where the hypotheses are $H_0: \mu = 5.9$ feet and $H_a: \mu \neq 5.9$ feet. The Z curve for this situation is shown in Figure 8.12.

For which value of α does the testing procedure change the conclusions here? In Figure 8.12, if you were using a predetermined significance level α, you would split α in half and put $\alpha/2$ into each tail. So the total tail area represents α. Using Figure 8.13, we reverse this procedure by finding the *total* tail area corresponding to a two-tailed test with $Z^* = -2.53$; we add the area to the left of -2.53 (.0057) to that to the right of 2.53 (also .0057). This total area is .0114, which is the *p*-value for this application. Thus, if you choose a value of $\alpha > .0114$ (such as .05), you will reject H_0. If you choose a value of $\alpha < .0114$ (such as .01), you will fail to reject H_0.

FIGURE

8.12

Rejection regions for $\alpha = .01, .05$.

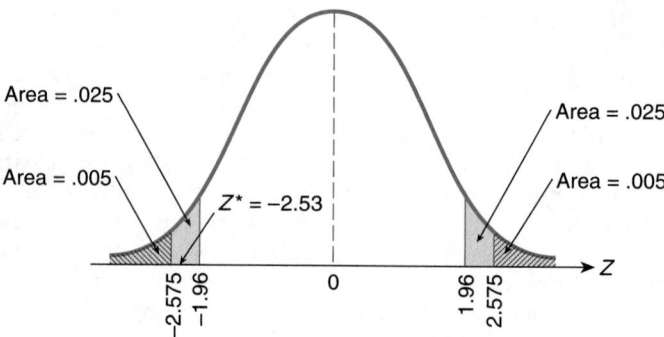

FIGURE

8.13

p-value is determined by replacing the area corresponding to α (see Figure 8.12) by the area corresponding to Z^*. Here $Z^* = -2.53$, and the p-value $= 2 \cdot 0057$ $= .0114$ (total shaded area).

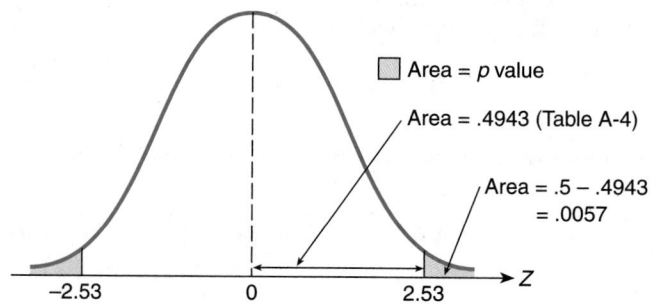

PROCEDURE FOR FINDING THE p-VALUE

1. For H_a: $\mu \neq \mu_0$

$$p = 2 \cdot (\text{area outside of } Z^*)$$

Reason: When using a significance level α, the value of α represents a *two*-tailed area.

2. For H_a: $\mu > \mu_0$

$$p = \text{area to the right of } Z^*$$

Reason: When using a significance level α, the value of α represents a *right*-tailed area.

3. For H_a: $\mu < \mu_0$

$$p = \text{area to the left of } Z^*$$

Reason: When using a significance level α, the value of α represents a *left*-tailed area.

EXAMPLE 8.6

What is the p-value for Example 8.5?

Solution The results of the sample were $n = 60$, $\bar{x} = 952.58$ kilowatt-hours, and $s = 173.92$ kilowatt-hours. The corresponding value of the test statistic was

$$Z^* \approx \frac{952.58 - 918}{173.92/\sqrt{60}} = 1.54$$

The alternative hypothesis is H_a: $\mu > 918$, so the p-value will be the area to the *right* of the computed value, 1.54, as illustrated in Figure 8.14. Notice that the inequal-

FIGURE

8.14

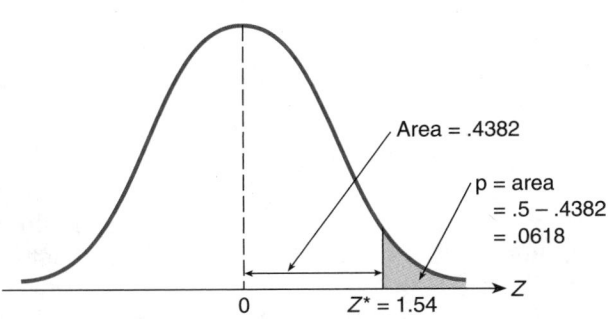

p-value for $Z^* = 1.54$.

ity in H_a determines the *direction* of the tail area to be found. The *p*-value here is .0618, which is consistent with the results of Example 8.5, where we concluded that for $\alpha = .01$, you fail to reject H_0 and for $\alpha = .10$, you reject H_0. That is, the *p*-value is between .01 and .10.

Interpreting the *p*-value

We will consider two ways of using the *p*-value to arrive at a conclusion. The first is the *classical approach* that we have used up to this point: We choose a value for α and base our decision on this value. When using a *p*-value in this manner, the procedure is:

> reject H_0 if *p*-value $< \alpha$
>
> fail to reject H_0 if *p*-value $\geq \alpha$

The second approach is a *general rule of thumb* that applies to most business applications of hypothesis testing on μ. We previously stated that typical values of α range from .01 to .10, implying that for most applications we will not see values of α smaller than .01 or larger than .1. With this in mind, the following rule can be defined:

> reject H_0 if the *p*-value is small ($p < .01$)
>
> fail to reject H_0 if the *p*-value is large ($p > .1$)

Consequently, if $.01 \leq$ *p*-value $\leq .1$, the data are *inconclusive*.

The advantage of this approach is that you avoid having to choose a value of α; the disadvantage is that you may arrive at an inconclusive result.

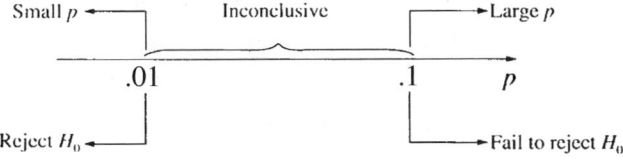

Now for a brief disclaimer: This rule does not apply to all situations. If a Type I error would be extremely serious and you prefer a very small value of α using the classical approach, then you can lower the .01 limit. Similarly, you might raise the .1 limit if the Type II error is extremely critical and you prefer a large value for α. However, this rule gives a working procedure for most applications in business.

What can you conclude if the *p*-value is $p = .0001$? This value is extremely small compared with *any* reasonable value of α. So we would strongly reject H_0. Consequently, if you are making an investment decision based on these results, for example, you can breathe a little easier. This data set supports H_a overwhelmingly. On the other hand, if $p = .65$, this value is large compared with any reasonable value of α. Without question, we would fail to reject H_0.

There is yet one other interpretation of the *p*-value, summarized in the following box.

ANOTHER INTERPRETATION OF THE *p*-VALUE

1. For a two-tailed test where H_a: $\mu \neq \mu_0$ the *p*-value is the probability that the value of the test statistic, Z^*, will be at least as large (in absolute value) as the observed Z^*, if μ is in fact equal to μ_0.
2. For a one-tailed test where H_a: $\mu > \mu_0$, the *p*-value is the probability that the value of the test statistic, Z^*, will be at least as large as the observed Z^*, if μ is in fact equal to μ_0.
3. For a one-tailed test where H_a: $\mu < \mu_0$, the *p*-value is the probability that the value of the test statistic, Z^*, will be at least as small as the observed Z^*, if μ is in fact equal to μ_0.

In Example 8.6, we determined the *p*-value to be .0618; the computed value of the test statistic was $Z^* = 1.54$; the hypotheses were H_0: $\mu \leq 918$ and H_a: $\mu > 918$. So the probability of observing a value of Z^* as large as 1.54 (that is, $Z^* \geq 1.54$) if μ is 918 is $p = .0618$.

Based on this description of the *p*-value, if *p* is small, conclude that H_0 is not true and reject it. We obtain precisely the same result using the classical and rule-of-thumb options of the *p*-value. *Small values of p favor* H_a, *and large values favor* H_0.

Microsoft Excel Application   Use DATA8-7

Using Excel to Calculate the Z Statistic and Corresponding *p*-Value

In Examples 2.1, 3.4, and 6.8 we examined the inside diameter of a certain machined part produced by Allied Manufacturing having specification (spec) limits of 10.1 millimeters (the lower limit) and 10.3 millimeters (the upper limit). Your advice to Allied was that, based on the sample of 100 diameters, the process was producing parts that were, on the average, too large, with a large percentage of the parts exceeding the upper spec limit. The quality-improvement team at Allied took your advice and attempted to modify the manufacturing process to produce parts that were closer to the target diameter of 10.2 millimeters. After this modification, another sample of 100 parts was obtained (stored in data set DATA8-7). They would like to know whether there is sufficient evidence to indicate that the average diameter (μ) differs from 10.2 millimeters. In particular:

1. What is your conclusion based on the corresponding *p*-value, using $\alpha = .05$?

2. Without specifying a value of α, what would be your conclusion based on the calculated *p*-value?

3. Interpret the *p*-value for this application.

4. What can you advise Allied about the present manufacturing process?

Solution 1

Begin by opening dataset DATA8-7. The first 16 values are visible in column A of Figure 8.15, a rather busy Excel spreadsheet. The first step is to determine the standard deviation of the 100 sample values. Referring to Figure 8.15, type "Standard Deviation" in cell B1 and "=STDEV(A2:A101)" in cell B2. The value of .0334 should appear in cell B2. To carry out the test of hypothesis, click on **KPK Data Analysis ➤ One Population Inference.** Referring to Figure 8.10, enter (1) "A1:A101" for the **Input Range,** (2) "5" in the **Alpha** box, (3) ".0334" in the **Population Standard Deviation** box, (4) "two-tail test" in the **Hypothesis** section, (5) "10.2" for the **Hypothesized Value of Mean,** and (6) "B4" for the Output Range. Be sure to click on the box alongside **Labels.** The resulting output is contained in Figure 8.15 (cells B4:C12).

FIGURE

8.15

Excel spreadsheet for Example 8.7.

	A	B	C	D	E		F
1	Diameter	Standard Deviation			**Diameter**		
2	10.158	0.0334			**Frequency Distribution Table**		
3	10.244			CLASS	CLASS LIMITS		FREQUENCY
4	10.202	**Z Test for Population Mean**		1	10.12 and under 10.14		3
5	10.206		Diameter	2	10.14 and under 10.16		5
6	10.257	Number of Observations	100	3	10.16 and under 10.18		10
7	10.149	Population Std. Deviation	0.0334	4	10.18 and under 10.20		14
8	10.202	Sample Mean	10.2102	5	10.20 and under 10.22		29
9	10.237	Ho:μ = 10.2	Ha:$\mu \neq$ 10.2	6	10.22 and under 10.24		25
10	10.220	Z*	3.0629	7	10.24 and under 10.26		8
11	10.223	2 * P[Z ≥ |Z*|] two tail	0.0022	8	10.26 and under 10.28		2
12	10.165	| Z Critical |, α = 0.05	1.960	9	10.28 and under 10.30		3
13	10.166			10	10.30 and under 10.32		1
14	10.210	Spec Limits	Area to Left		TOTAL		100
15	10.229	10.1	0.0005				
16	10.300	10.3	0.9964				
17	10.183						

Frequency Histogram   DATA8-7

FIGURE

8.16

Illustration of the *p*-value for Example 8.7.

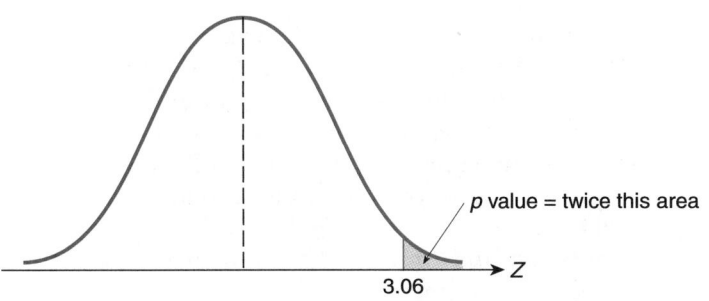

p value = twice this area

Z

3.06

The calculated value of the test statistic is $Z^* = 3.06$, with a corresponding *p*-value of $p = .0022$, illustrated in Figure 8.16. Because *p* is less than $\alpha = .05$, we reject H_0 and conclude that the mean diameter is not 10.2 millimeters. Put another way, the sample mean $\bar{x} = 10.2102$ is *significantly different* from 10.2—certainly not obvious at first glance.

Solution 2

We use the general rule of thumb for interpreting the *p*-value. Since $p = .0022$, this value is small (<.01) and so we reject H_0. Although this is the same conclusion reached in Solution 1, this is not always the case.

Solution 3

We can make the following statements:

1. The significance level at which the conclusion indicated by the testing procedure changes is $\alpha = .0022$.

2. The largest significance level for which we fail to reject the null hypothesis is $\alpha = .0022$.

3. The probability of observing a value of the test statistic as large (in absolute value) as the one obtained (that is, ≥3.06), is .0022 if, in fact, the population mean is 10.2 millimeters.

8.17

Excel-generated histogram of 100 inside diameters (Example 8.7).

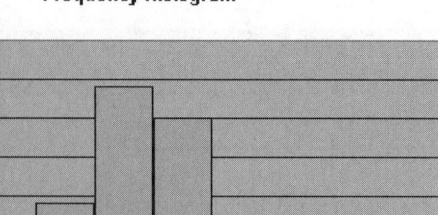

Frequency Histogram

Class Limits

Solution 4   Take a look at the sorted sample data and the sample histogram. Next, determine what percentage of the produced parts in the population can be expected to lie outside the spec limits, using Excel's NORMDIST function.

To obtain the histogram in Figure 8.17, click on **KPK Data Analysis ➤ Quantitative Data Charts/Tables ➤ Histogram/Freq. Charts.** Fill in the input range (A1:A101) and the output range (D1). Be sure to click on the box alongside **Labels.** Also, click on the white square alongside **Frequencies** in the **Table** section and **Frequency Histogram** in the **Chart Output Options** section. You will then obtain the output in cells D1:F13 (Figure 8.15) and the Figure 8.17 histogram. Based on this histogram, it appears safe to assume that the sample was selected from a normal population.

To determine the percentage of produced parts in the population that can be expected outside the spec limits, examine cells B14:C16 in Figure 8.15. Type in the contents of cells B14, B15, B16, and C14. The areas under the normal curve in cells C15 and C16 are obtained by clicking on the **Paste Function** icon (f_*) and clicking on **Statistical** under **Function Category** and **NORMDIST** under **Function Name.** The resulting input screen was first introduced in Figure 6.29. To obtain the Value of .0005 in cell C15, enter 10.1 for the **Value of X,** 10.2102 for the **Mean,** .0334 for the **Standard Deviation,** and "true" in the **Cumulative** box. The value of .9964 in cell C16 is obtained by replacing 10.1 with 10.3 in the previous sentence. The value in cell C15 implies that we can expect .05% of the parts to be less than the lower spec limit of 10.1. The value of .9964 in cell C16 is the area to the *left* of 10.3 under the normal curve, since the **NORMDIST** function always returns the value to the left of the specified *X* value. Consequently, we can expect .36% (that is, 100 – 99.64) of the parts to exceed the upper spec limit of 10.3 and so .05 + .36 = .41% of the population will be outside the spec limits.

Recommendation. Prior to the quality-improvement effort, the mean diameter was 10.275 millimeters and 17% of the sample exceeded the upper spec limit. In one sense, the quality of the process has been improved, since the estimated mean of the new process (10.2102) is much closer to 10.2 than before, and none of the sample values lie outside the spec limits of 10.1 millimeters and 10.3 millimeters. Despite this good news, we can still expect .41% of the population to lie outside the spec limits, which translates to 4,100 nonconforming parts per million.

We also observe additional variation in this sample, since the sample standard deviation has increased from .0267 (before the quality-improvement effort) to .0334 (refer to Solution 1).* Overall, the team should be commended for improving the process. But based on Solution 1, efforts should be made to move the process even closer to 10.2 millimeters and to reduce the process variation.

---

*Section 9.4 will allow you to determine if there is a *significant* change in the variation for the "before" and "after" processes (populations).

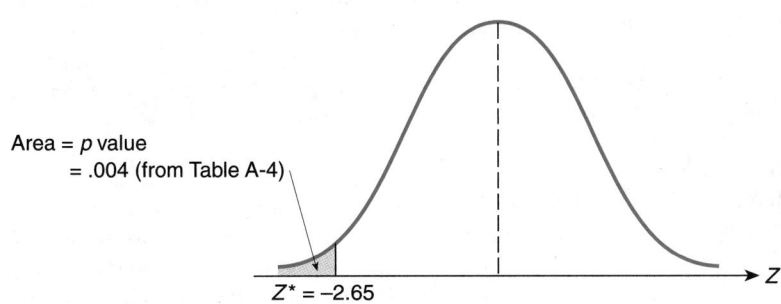

FIGURE

8.18

p-value for
$Z^* = -2.65$.

Practical Versus Statistical Significance

Researchers often calculate what appears to be a conclusive result without considering the practical significance of their findings. For example, consider a situation similar to the one described in Example 8.4; this time, a sample of 1,000 Bullets, tested under normal highway conditions, results in a sample average of $\bar{x} = 32.32$ mpg, with a standard deviation of $s = 2.15$ mpg. Advertising for this car claims that the mpg under test conditions is at least 32.5 mpg. Is there sufficient evidence to reject this claim?

The hypotheses are $H_0: \mu \geq 32.5$ and $H_a: \mu < 32.5$. The value of the test statistic is

$$Z^* \approx \frac{\bar{X} - 32.5}{s/\sqrt{n}} = \frac{32.32 - 32.5}{2.15/\sqrt{1000}} = -2.65$$

The *p*-value here is the area to the left of −2.65 under the Z curve, as illustrated in Figure 8.18. This value (from Table A.4) is .004. Based on this small *p*-value, we reject H_0 and conclude (as we did in Example 8.4) that the mpg for these cars under normal highway conditions is less than 32.5. Statistically speaking, this is correct, and the data do provide sufficient evidence to support the statement that their mpg claim is overstated. As a consumer, however, how concerned would you be that the sample average ($\bar{x} = 32.32$) is (only) .18 mpg under the advertised level? In other words, in a practical sense, how misleading is the Bullet advertising?

What we have seen is that $\bar{X}$ is far enough away from 32.5 (in a statistical sense) to conclude that μ is less than 32.5 mpg. However, perhaps in the eyes of a consumer about to invest $25,000 in a new car, this value of $\bar{X}$ is really "close enough" to 32.5.

Moral: It is possible for a statistically significant result to be of no particular practical significance, depending on the context of the analysis.

X Exercises 8.27–8.36

Understanding the Mechanics

8.27 State the conclusion to testing the null hypothesis assuming each of the following situations.
  a. *p*-value = .10 and significance level is .05
  b. *p*-value = .02 and significance level is .05
  c. *p*-value = .40 and significance level is .10
  d. *p*-value = .001 and significance level is .01

8.28 State the conclusion to testing the null hypothesis assuming each of the following situations. Use the general rule of thumb in using the *p*-value to arrive at a conclusion.

  a. *p*-value = .80
  b. *p*-value = .001
  c. *p*-value = .05
  d. *p*-value = .12

8.29 Find the *p*-values for the following situations, with calculated test statistics given by Z^*.
  a. $H_0: \mu = 50$, $H_a: \mu \neq 50$, $Z^* = 2.53$
  b. $H_0: \mu \leq 50$, $H_a: \mu > 50$, $Z^* = 2.53$
  c. $H_0: \mu = 10$, $H_a: \mu \neq 10$, $Z^* = 1.87$
  d. $H_0: \mu \leq 10$, $H_a: \mu > 10$, $Z^* = 1.87$

Applying the New Concepts

8.30 A pharmaceutical firm found from a random sample of 100 volunteers that the average time it takes a new drug to take effect is 3.5 minutes. It is well known that the mean time for the old drug was 3.7 minutes. The mean time for the new drug was found to be significantly less than the mean time for the old drug, via a statistical analysis of the data. Explain the difference between "significance" in a statistical sense and "significance" in a practical sense for this situation.

8.31 When growth in Tommy Hilfiger Corp.'s casual-menswear business slowed, the company introduced pricey women's apparel under its "Red" and "White" labels, with suits that ranged from $450 to $1,500. A women's retail specialist would like to test that the mean price for Tommy Hilfiger's women's suits differs from $(450 + 1500)/2 = 975$. Suppose that a random sample of 60 stores revealed a sample mean of $925 with a standard deviation of $200. Test the retail specialist's belief.

    a. Find the observed significance level and interpret it.

    b. What conclusion would follow if the significance level was specified as 5%?

(Adapted from "Hilfiger's Fashion Empire Starts to Show Some Wear," *The Wall Street Journal*, June 12, 1998, p. B4.)

8.32 The producer of Take-a-Bite, a snack food, claims that each package weighs 175 grams. A representative of a consumer advocate group selected a random sample of 70 packages. From this sample, the mean and standard deviation were found to be 172 grams and 8 grams, respectively.

    a. Find the p-value for testing the claim that the mean weight of Take-a-Bite is less than 175 grams.

    b. Interpret the p-value in part a.

8.33 A marketing-research analyst is interested in examining the statement made by the makers that brand A cigarettes contain less than three milligrams of tar. The marketing-research analyst randomly selected 60 cigarettes and found the mean amount of tar to be 2.75 milligrams with a standard deviation of 1.5 milligrams. Do the data support the claim? Find the p-value.

8.34 Alice Chang and her husband Jau Huang are the co-founders of a multimedia software start-up company named CyberLink, based in Taiwan. These founders are interested in the average number of hours that engineers would be willing to work for the company if they were given a small salary but a large quantity of stock with the anticipation that an initial public offering would yield a nice return. A consultant advised the founders

that engineers would be willing to work an average of 70 hours per week under those terms. The idea that they could get rich in a short period of time is very enticing to many engineers in Taiwan. Suppose that a sample of 50 start-up companies was randomly selected and the number of hours that the typical engineer worked was recorded.

    a. Does a sample mean of 62 hours and a standard deviation of 20 hours indicate that the average work time that an engineer would be willing to work for a start-up company differs from 70 hours a week? Interpret the p-value.

    b. From the p-value in part a, would you expect a 99% confidence interval for the mean number of weekly hours that an engineer would be willing to work for a start-up company to include 70? Find a 99% confidence interval for this mean.

(Source: "Taiwan Doesn't Shield Firms: Only Strong Survive," *The Wall Street Journal*, June 23, 1998, p. 2B.)

Using the Computer

8.35 **[DATA SET EX8-35]** *Variable description:*

CostGoods: Cost of goods by shoplifters

A manager of a New York retail store believes that the average cost of goods shoplifted by those customers that have shoplifted is greater than $75. A random sample of 60 customers that have shoplifted is selected, and the selling price of the goods shoplifted was recorded.

    a. Test that the average cost of goods shoplifted among the population of shoplifters at the retail store is greater than $75. Use the general rule of thumb concerning the p-value to arrive at a conclusion.

    b. How would you interpret the results of the hypothesis test in part a for the manager?

8.36 **[DATA SET EX8–36]** *Variable description:*

StressIndex: Stress index for managers

An industrial psychologist has a stress test that is used to determine the amount of stress that managers are under. A value of 80 or higher indicates "high stress." The industrial psychologist believes that the managers at a large, profitable pharmaceutical firm are not under "high stress" and that the average stress index is less than 80 for managers of the company. A random sample of 50 managers is selected, and their stress index was recorded.

    a. Test that the data support the industrial psychologist's belief.

    b. What conclusion would you reach if the significance level was .10? .05? .01?

8.4

HYPOTHESIS TESTING ON THE MEAN OF A NORMAL POPULATION: SMALL SAMPLE

Our approach to hypothesis testing with small samples when the standard deviation, σ, is unknown uses the same technique we used for dealing with confidence intervals on the mean of a population: we switch from the standard normal dis-

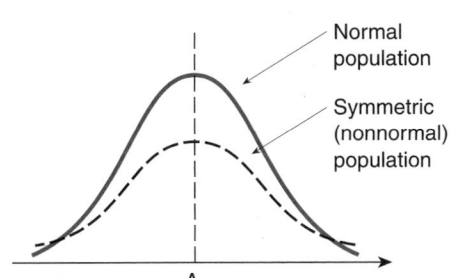
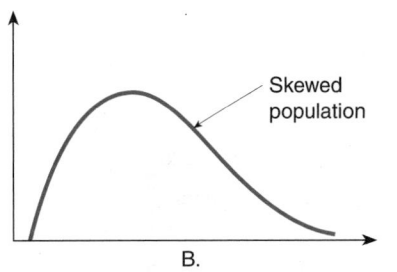

FIGURE

8.19

A. Small-sample test is valid.
B. Small-sample test is not valid.

tribution, Z, to the t distribution. However, we need to examine the distribution of the population when the sample is small—the population distribution determines the procedure that we use. In this section, we have reason to believe that the population has a *normal distribution*. When it does not, we use a nonparametric procedure, which is discussed in Chapter 18.

Certain variations from a normal population *are* permissible with the small-sample test. If a test of hypothesis is still reliable when slight departures from the assumptions are encountered, the test is said to be *robust*. If you believe the parent population to be reasonably symmetric, the level of your confidence interval and Type I error (α) will be quite accurate, even if the population has heavy tails (unlike the normal distribution), as shown in Figure 8.19A. However, when using small samples, the small-sample test is *not* robust for populations that are heavily skewed (see Figure 8.19B.). A nonparametric procedure offers a much better solution for this situation. For larger sample sizes, a histogram of your data often can detect whether a population is heavily skewed in one direction.

To reemphasize, the discussion in this section assumes a normal population. In other words, if X is an observation from this population, then X is a normal random variable with unknown mean μ. Also, we assume that σ is unknown. (If σ is known, the resulting test statistic is $Z = (\overline{X} - \mu_0)/(\sigma/\sqrt{n})$, and the five-step procedure of Section 8.1 allows you to do hypothesis testing on μ.)

The only distinction between using a small and a large sample is the identification of the test statistic. Using the discussion from Chapter 7, if we define the test statistic as

$$t = \frac{\overline{X} - \mu_0}{s/\sqrt{n}}$$

8.2

we now have a t distribution with $n - 1$ degrees of freedom (df). The procedure to use for testing H_0: $\mu = \mu_0$ and H_a: $\mu \neq \mu_0$ is the same five-step procedure, except that the rejection region is defined using the t table (Table A.5) rather than the Z table (Table A.4). This procedure also applies to a one-tailed test.

EXAMPLE

8.8

You may recall from Example 7.9 that Clark Products manufactures a power supply with an output voltage that is believed to be normally distributed with a mean of 10 volts. During the design stage, the quality-engineering staff recorded 18 observations of the output voltage of a particular power supply unit. They decide to use a significance level of .05, since the implications of making a Type I error (rejecting a correct H_0) and a Type II error (failing to reject an incorrect H_0) appear to be the same. Is there evidence to indicate that the average output voltage is not 10 volts?

FIGURE

8.20

t distribution; the rejection region is the lightly shaded area to the right of 2.11 and to the left of –2.11, for Example 8.8.

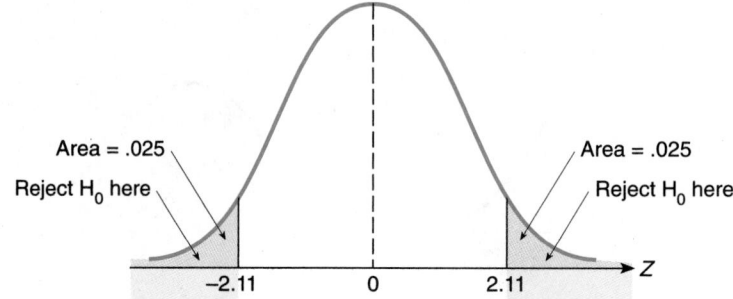

FIGURE

8.21

t curve with 17 df. The *p*-value is twice the area to the right of $t^* = 1.83$, so we can say only that it is between .05 and .10.

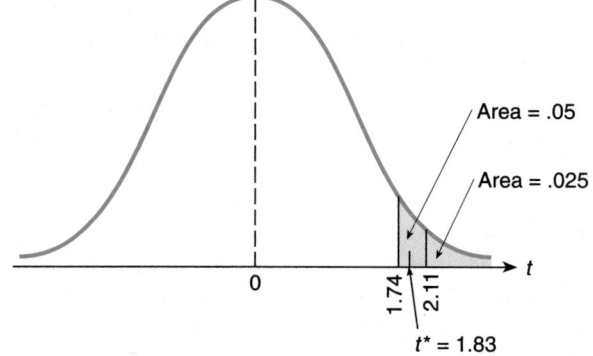

Solution

Step 1. When a question is phrased "Is there evidence to indicate that . . . ," what follows is the *alternative hypothesis*. For this application then, the alternative hypothesis is that the mean is unequal to 10 volts, and the resulting hypotheses are $H_0: \mu = 10$ and $H_a: \mu \neq 10$.

Step 2. The test statistic here is

$$t = \frac{\overline{X} - 10}{s/\sqrt{n}}$$

Step 3. Using a significance level of .05 and Figure 8.20, the corresponding two-tailed procedure is to

$$\text{reject } H_0 \text{ if } |t| > t_{.025,17} = 2.11$$

because df $= n - 1 = 17$.

Step 4. For these data, $n = 18$, $\overline{x} = 10.331$ volts and $s = .767$ volts. The value of the test statistic is

$$t^* = \frac{10.331 - 10}{.767/\sqrt{18}} = 1.83$$

Because $1.83 < 2.11$, we fail to reject H_0.

Step 5. There is insufficient evidence to indicate that the average output voltage is different from 10 volts.

What is the *p*-value in Example 8.8, and what can we conclude based on this value? We run into a slight snag when dealing with the *t* distribution, because we are not able to determine precisely the *p*-value. You can see this in Figure 8.21, using Table A.5 (17 df). The p-value is twice the area to the right of $t^* = 1.83$. The best we can do here is to say that p is *between* (2)(.025) and (2)(.05), that is, between .05 and .10. (*Note:* A reliable computer package or sophisticated calculator will provide the exact p-value. Using Excel, SPSS, or MINITAB, this value is $p = .0847$.)

Using the classical approach and $\alpha = .05$ we *can* say that p is greater than .05, despite not knowing p exactly. Consequently, we fail to reject H_0. *This procedure always produces the same result as the five-step procedure.*

Suppose we choose not to select a significant level (α) but prefer to base our conclusion strictly on the calculated p-value. We use the rule of thumb and decide whether p is small ($<.01$), large ($>.1$), or in between. Despite not having an exact value of p, we can say that this p-value falls in the inconclusive range. These data values do not provide us with any strong conclusion. One approach available to Clark Products is to obtain some additional data.

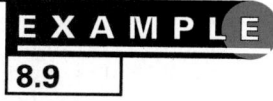

EXAMPLE 8.9

An auditing firm was hired to determine if a particular defense plant was overstating the value of their inventory items. It was decided that 15 items would be randomly selected. For each item, the recorded amount, the audited (exact) amount, and the difference between these two amounts (recorded – audited) were determined. Of particular interest was whether it could be demonstrated that the average difference exceeds \$25, in which case the defense plant would be subject to a loss of contract and financial penalties. The following 15 differences were obtained (in dollars):

$$17, 35, 31, 22, 50, 42, 56, 23, 27, 38, 20, 25, 43, 45, 21$$

So $n = 15$, $\bar{x} = \$33.00$, and $s = \$12.15$. Set up the appropriate hypotheses and test them using a significance level of $\alpha = .05$. The population of differences is believed to be normally distributed.

Solution

Step 1. The hypotheses are H_0: $\mu \leq 25$ and H_a: $\mu > 25$, where μ is the average difference between the recorded and audited amounts for *all* the inventory items.

Steps 2, 3.

$$\text{reject } H_0 \text{ if } t = \frac{\bar{X} - 25}{s/\sqrt{n}} > t_{.05,14} = 1.761$$

where the df = $n - 1 = 14$.

Step 4. The calculated t is

$$t^* = \frac{33 - 25}{12.15/\sqrt{15}} = 2.55$$

Because 2.55 exceeds the tabulated value of 1.761, we reject H_0. Also, the p-value (using Table A.5 and 14 df) is the area to the right of 2.55. It is between .01 and .025, so it is less than $\alpha = .05$, and so (as before) we reject H_0.

Step 5. These data indicate that the defense plant is overstating the value of their inventory items by more than \$25.

To obtain the Excel solution shown in Figure 8.22, enter the 15 values in cells A1:A15. Next, click on **KPK Data Analysis ➤ One Population Inference.** Referring to Figure 8.10, use the down arrow in the top box to select **Population Mean**

FIGURE

8.22

Portion of Excel spreadsheet containing the sample values and output for Example 8.9.

	t Test for Population Mean	
17		
35		
31	Number of Observations	15
22	Sample Standard Deviation	12.148
50	Sample Mean	33.000
42	Ho: $\mu \leq 25$	Ha: $\mu > 25$
56	T*	2.551
23	P[T ≥ T*]	0.012
27	T Critical, $\alpha = 0.05$	1.761
38		
20		
25		
43		
45		
21		

with Est. Std. Dev. (*t* statistic). The resulting input screen is very similar to that in Figure 8.10. Enter "A1:A15" for the **Input Range,** but don't click on the **Labels** box (unless you inserted a label in cell A1). Enter 5 in the **Alpha** box (this is the default value), click on **Hypothesis Test** and **Right-Tail Test,** and enter "25" for the **Hypothesized Value of Mean** and "B1" for the **Output Range.** The *p*-value here is .012 and is in agreement with the solution to Example 8.9—namely that the *p*-value is between .01 and .025.

SMALL-SAMPLE TESTS ON A NORMAL POPULATION MEAN

Two-Tailed Test

$$H_0: \mu = \mu_0$$

$$H_a: \mu \neq \mu_0$$

reject H_0 if $|t^*| > t_{\alpha/2, n-1}$

where n = sample size and t^* is the computed value of

$$t = \frac{\overline{X} - \mu_0}{s/\sqrt{n}}$$

One-Tailed Test

$H_0: \mu \leq \mu_0$	$H_0: \mu \geq \mu_0$
$H_a: \mu > \mu_0$	$H_a: \mu < \mu_0$
reject H_0 if $t^* > t_{\alpha, n-1}$	reject H_0 if $t^* < -t_{\alpha, n-1}$

X Exercises 8.37–8.46

Understanding the Mechanics

8.37 Find the *t* statistic and carry out the statistical test for the following situations in sampling data from a normally distributed population. Use a significance level of .05.

    a. $H_0: \mu = 50$, $H_a: \mu \neq 50$, $\overline{x} = 56$, $s = 24$, $n = 15$

    b. $H_0: \mu \leq 50$, $H_a: \mu > 50$, $\overline{x} = 56$, $s = 24$, $n = 15$

    c. $H_0: \mu \geq 113.7$, $H_a: \mu < 113.7$, $\overline{x} = 111.6$, $s = 2.5$, $n = 30$

    d. $H_0: \mu = 85$, $H_a: \mu \neq 85$, $\overline{x} = 78$, $s = 25$, $n = 25$

8.38 Find the *p*-value for the following situations, with calculated test statistics given by t^*.

    a. $H_0: \mu = 72.5$, $H_a: \mu \neq 72.5$, $t^* = 2.72$, $n = 12$

    b. $H_0: \mu \leq 72.5$, $H_a: \mu > 72.5$, $t^* = 2.72$, $n = 12$

    c. $H_0: \mu = 180.7$, $H_a: \mu \neq 180.7$, $t^* = 1.3$, $n = 41$

    d. $H_0: \mu \leq 180.7$, $H_a: \mu > 180.7$, $t^* = 1.3$, $n = 41$

8.39 The following data were sampled from a normally distributed population. At the 10% significance level, is there evidence to indicate that the mean of the population differs from 16?

$$12 \quad 15 \quad 14 \quad 19 \quad 15 \quad 20 \quad 16$$

Applying the New Concepts

8.40 Easy-Fly Airline took a random sample of 25 flights to determine if the mean time it takes for luggage to reach the travelers departing from a flight is less than 15 minutes. The sample mean was found to be 13.8 minutes with a standard deviation of four minutes.

a. Using a significance level of .05, what conclusion can be reached based on the random sample?

b. What assumption about the data is necessary for the hypothesis test to be valid in this situation?

8.41 The Hungarian-born executive Zsolt Rummy, chairman of Zoltek Company, claims that his company is the world's largest producer of carbon fiber, the strong yet lightweight material used in everything from aircraft to golf clubs. To maintain profitability, the cost of producing carbon fiber is very important. Zoltek has production lines in both Texas and Hungary. A financial analyst interested in estimating the earnings of the company wants to test that the cost of producing a pound of carbon differs from its average cost of $6 per pound last year. Twenty days are randomly selected from the first six months of 1998, and the cost per pound of carbon is recorded. The data are presented below. Using a .05 significance level, what conclusion can the financial analyst make? Assume that the distribution of the cost per pound of carbon can be approximated by a normal distribution.

6.3	6.8	7.5	6.0	5.3	6.2	5.4	7.3	6.1	6.4
6.1	6.5	5.7	6.3	7.2	6.9	6.2	7.0	5.9	6.1

(Source: "Zoltek Touts Potential for Carbon Fiber; Its Shares Reflect Immediate Concerns," *The Wall Street Journal*, June 12, 1998, p. B11.)

8.42 The National Retail Federation in Washington conducted a telephone survey of 1,000 adults in early October 2001 and found that approximately 55% of the respondents planned to do some type of Halloween decorating. The Federation claims that households spend an average of $45 on Halloween candy, costumes, and decorations. The Federation says that the Halloween market generates almost $7 billion in sales. Suppose that a local retail manager wished to determine if the average household in the local area planned to spend more than $45. A random sample of 25 households yielded a mean of $52 with a standard deviation of $18. Do the data support the belief that the average household in the local area spends more than $45 in preparation for Halloween at a significance level of .01?

(Source: "Many Households Plan a Traditional Halloween," *The New York Times*, October 14, 2001, p. 8L.)

8.43 Web accessibility is drawing more people to "virtual" trainers as an alternative to training alone or working with a personal fitness trainer. Personal trainers charge $30 to $150 an hour, while online services charge similar fees per month or per year. Web training is also more flexible since the person being trained does not have to meet at a certain time and place. For example, FITADVISOR.COM charges $71 per year but provides advice from its exercise experts by e-mail and phone. Suppose that a fitness-center manager wished to determine if the average price that "virtual" trainers charged per year was more than $50 per year. The manager randomly selected 16 individuals who paid yearly fees. The sample mean was found to be $62 with a standard deviation of $15. Using the *p*-value, do these data support the fitness center manager's belief? Assume that the distribution of yearly charges for "virtual" training are approximately normally distributed..

(Source: "Get Fit on the Web," *Business Week*, October 15, 2001, p. 128.)

8.44 In an effort to control cost, a quality-control inspector is interested in whether the mean number of ounces of sauce dispensed by bottle-filling machines differs from 16 ounces. From the bottling process, the inspector collects the following measurements.

16.3, 16.2, 15.8, 15.4, 16.0, 15.6, 15.5, 16.1, 15.9, 16.1

Test at a .05 significance level that the bottle-filling machines need adjusting.

Using the Computer

8.45 **[DATA SET EX8-45]** *Variable description:*

Expend: Expenditure per night by guests sharing the same room

The manager at the Ocean Breeze Hotel believes the average expenditure per night for guests sharing the same room is greater than $200. A random sample of 25 rooms was selected, and the expenditure by the guests per night was recorded.

a. Test the manager's belief that the average expenditure for guests sharing the same room is greater than $200. At what significance level can the null hypothesis be rejected?

b. What assumption are you making about the sampled population?

8.46 **[DATA SET EX8-46]** *Variable description:*

Time: Time, in minutes, to correct a defective aluminum sheet

A quality inspector is interested in the average time it takes to correct defective sheets of aluminum manufactured at the plant. A random sample of 25 sheets of defective aluminum sheets was selected, and the time to correct the defect was recorded.

a. Suppose that the quality inspector believes the average time to correct a defective sheet of aluminum is different from 20 minutes, a time given in a recent report on the operations of the company. Test the quality inspector's belief. Use the general rule of thumb for interpreting the *p*-value.

b. Construct a histogram and determine if the data can be assumed to come from an approximately normal population.

8.5

INFERENCE FOR THE VARIANCE AND STANDARD DEVIATION OF A NORMAL POPULATION

Our discussion in Chapters 7 and 8 has been concerned with the mean of a particular random variable or population. In other words, we are trying to decide or estimate what is occurring *on the average.* Suppose someone involved with a production process that manufactures two-inch bolts has just been informed that, without a doubt, these bolts are two inches long, on the average. Is there anything else this person might like to know about the production process? Suppose that half of the bolts produced are one inch long and the other half are three inches. The report was accurate—on the average, they *are* two inches long.* However, such a production process certainly will not satisfy the customers, and this company soon will be out of the bolt business.

What was missing in the report was the amount of *variation* in this production process. If the variation were zero, every bolt would be exactly two inches long—an ideal situation. In practice, there always will be a certain amount of variation in any mechanical or production process. So we are concerned about not only the mean length μ of the population of bolts but also the variance σ^2 or standard deviation σ of the lengths of these bolts. If the variance is *too large*, the process is not operating correctly and needs adjustment. *Consequently, a key element of statistical quality improvement (Chapter 12) is the act of monitoring and attempting to reduce process variation. A process that is "in control" is one that is consistent and contains only random variation.*

The variance of a population also is of vital interest to someone making investment decisions. Here the *risk* of a venture (or portfolio) often is measured by the variance of the return paid by the venture in the past. Often, financial analysts prefer a financial package with a relatively small average return (based on past history) that appears to be low risk on the basis of only small fluctuations in its past performance.

In the inference procedures for a population variance (and standard deviation) to follow, we will assume that the population of interest is normally distributed. Unlike the *t* test, the hypothesis-testing procedures and confidence intervals for the variance are very sensitive to departures from the normal population—notably, heavy tails in the distribution or heavy skewness will have a large effect. In other words, the following tests of hypothesis are less robust than are those we discussed earlier.

Confidence Interval for the Variance and Standard Deviation

The point estimate of a population variance is the obvious one—namely, the sample variance, which was discussed in Chapter 7, where we used the variance, s^2, of a sample to estimate the variance, σ^2, of the much larger population.[†]

When constructing a confidence interval for μ using a small sample, we used the *t* distribution. Such a distribution is referred to as a *derived distribution* because it was derived to describe the behavior of a particular test statistic. This type of distribution is not used to describe a population, as is the normal distribution in many applications. For example, you will *not* hear a statement such as, "Assume that these data follow a *t* distribution"—normal, exponential, uniform, maybe, but not a *t* distribution. The *t* random variable merely offers us a method of testing and constructing confidence intervals for the mean of a *normal* population when the standard deviation is unknown and is replaced by its estimate.

---

*A statistician often is described as someone who thinks that if half of you is in an oven and the other half is in a deep freeze, on the average you are very comfortable.
[†]The notation $\hat{\sigma}^2$ is often used to represent an estimate of σ^2. Consequently, $s^2 = \hat{\sigma}^2$.

FIGURE

8.23

Shape of a chi-square distribution.

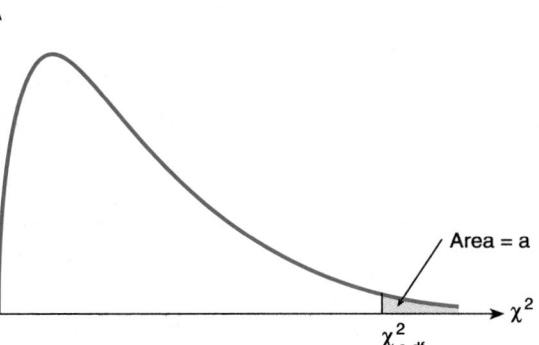

FIGURE

8.24

χ^2 curve with 12 df. The shaded area represents $P(\chi^2 > 18.5493)$.

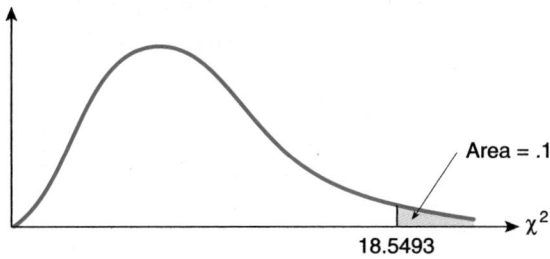

Another such continuous derived distribution, the **chi-square** (pronounced "ky square") distribution, written as χ^2, allows us to determine confidence intervals and perform tests of hypothesis on the variance and standard deviation of a normal population. The shape of this distribution is illustrated in Figure 8.23. Notice that unlike the Z and t curves, the χ^2 distribution is not symmetric and is definitely skewed right.

For chi-square, as for all continuous distributions, a probability corresponds to an area under a curve. Also, the shape of the chi-square curve, like that of its cousin the t distribution, depends on the sample size n. As before, this will be specified by the corresponding degrees of freedom (df).

When using the χ^2 distribution to construct a confidence interval or perform a test of hypothesis on a population variance or standard deviation, the degrees of freedom are given by

$$df = n - 1$$

Let $\chi^2_{a,df}$ be the χ^2 value whose area to the right is a, using the proper df.

EXAMPLE

8.10

Using a chi-square curve with 12 df, determine $P(\chi^2 > 18.5493)$ and $P(\chi^2 < 6.3038)$.

Solution

Tabulated values for the χ^2 distribution are contained in Table A.6. This table contains *right-tailed* areas (probabilities). Based on this table (see Figure 8.24),

$$P(\chi^2 > 18.5493) = .1$$

This can be written as

$$\chi^2_{.1,12} = 18.5493$$

339

For $\chi^2 = 6.3038$, Table A.6 informs us that the area to the right of 6.3038 is .900. Because the total area is 1, the area to the left of 6.3038 is $1 - .900 = .1$, and so $P(\chi^2 < 6.3038) = .1$. As a result, we can say that

$$P(6.3038 \le \chi^2 \le 18.5493) = 1 - .1 - .1 = .8$$

That is, 80% of the time a χ^2 value (with 12 df) will be between 6.3038 and 18.5493.

E X A M P L E

8.11

Using Example 8.10, determine a and b that satisfy

$$P(a < \chi^2 < b) = .95, \qquad \text{with df} = 12$$

Choose a and b so that an equal area occurs in each tail.

Solution   Figure 8.25 shows the areas for a and b. Using Table A.6,

$$a = \chi^2 \text{ value whose left-tailed area is .025}$$
$$= \chi^2 \text{ value whose area to the right is .975}$$
$$= 4.40$$

and

$$b = \chi^2 \text{ value whose right-tailed area is .025}$$
$$= 23.34$$

To derive a confidence interval for σ^2, we need to examine the sampling distribution of s^2. If we repeatedly obtained a random sample from a normal population with mean μ and variance σ^2, calculated the sample variance s^2, and made a histogram of these s^2 values, what would be the shape of this histogram? It can be shown that the shape will depend on the sample size n and the value of σ^2 but *not* on the value of the population mean μ. In fact, the values of n and σ^2, along with the random variable s^2, can be combined to define a chi-square random variable, given by

$$\chi^2 = \frac{(n-1)s^2}{\sigma^2} \qquad \text{8.3}$$

having a chi-square distribution with $n - 1$ df. Therefore, the sampling distribution for s^2 can be defined using the chi-square distribution in equation 8.3.

For example, a sample size of $n = 13$ results in 12 df. From Example 8.11, it follows that

$$P(4.40 < \chi^2 < 23.34) = .95$$

FIGURE

8.25

χ^2 curve with 12 df.

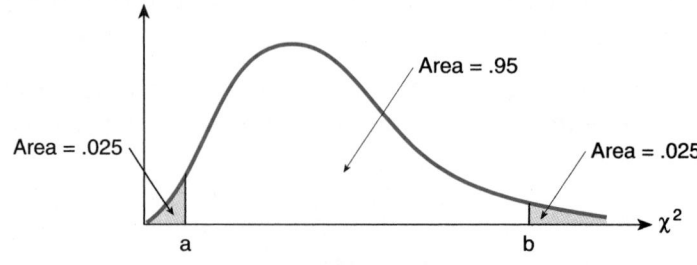

So,

$$P\left[4.40 < \frac{12s^2}{\sigma^2} < 23.34\right] = .95 \qquad \text{using equation 8.3}$$

or

$$P\left[\frac{12s^2}{23.34} < \sigma^2 < \frac{12s^2}{4.40}\right] = .95$$

As in all confidence interval constructions, the parameter (σ^2) is bounded between two limits defined by a random variable (s^2). This means that a 95% confidence interval for σ^2 is

$$\frac{12s^2}{23.34} \qquad \text{to} \qquad \frac{12s^2}{4.40}$$

In general, the following procedure can be used to construct a confidence interval for σ^2 or σ. A $(1 - \alpha) \cdot 100\%$ confidence interval for σ^2 is

$$\frac{(n-1)s^2}{\chi^2_{\alpha/2,n-1}} \qquad \text{to} \qquad \frac{(n-1)s^2}{\chi^2_{1-\alpha/2,n-1}} \qquad \text{8.4}$$

The corresponding confidence interval for σ is

$$\sqrt{\frac{(n-1)s^2}{\chi^2_{\alpha/2,n-1}}} \qquad \text{to} \qquad \sqrt{\frac{(n-1)s^2}{\chi^2_{1-\alpha/2,n-1}}} \qquad \text{8.5}$$

EXAMPLE 8.12

Vitamix Dog Chow comes in 10-, 25-, and 50-pound bags. The owners are concerned about the variation in the weight of the 50-pound bags because they have recently acquired a new mechanical packaging device. A random sample of the weights of 15 bags (in pounds) was obtained, with the following results:

51.2, 47.5, 50.8, 51.5, 49.5, 51.1, 51.3, 50.7, 46.7, 49.2, 52.1, 48.3, 51.6, 49.2, 51.5

For these data, $\bar{x} = 50.15$ pounds and $s = 1.651$ pounds. Determine a 90% confidence interval for σ^2 and for σ. The bag weights are believed to come from a normal population.

Solution

The corresponding 90% confidence interval for σ^2 is

$$\frac{(15-1)(1.651)^2}{\chi^2_{.05,14}} \quad \text{to} \quad \frac{(15-1)(1.651)^2}{\chi^2_{.95,14}} = \frac{(14)(1.651)^2}{23.68} \quad \text{to} \quad \frac{(14)(1.651)^2}{6.57}$$

$$= 1.61 \quad \text{to} \quad 5.81$$

The 90% confidence interval for σ would be

$$\sqrt{1.61} \quad \text{to} \quad \sqrt{5.81}$$

that is, 1.27 pounds to 2.41 pounds.

Hypothesis Testing for the Variance and Standard Deviation

For many applications, we are concerned that the standard deviation or variance of our population may be exceeding some specified value. If this claim is supported, then, for example, we may wish to shut down a production process and make adjustments that will reduce this excessive variation. As you could with the tests of hypothesis examined so far, you can (although this is not the usual case) perform a two-tailed test where either too much variation or too little variation is the topic of concern.

HYPOTHESIS TESTING ON σ^2

Two-Tailed Test

$$H_0: \sigma^2 = \sigma_0^2$$

$$H_a: \sigma^2 \neq \sigma_0^2$$

$$\text{test statistic: } \chi^2 = \frac{(n-1)s^2}{\sigma_0^2}$$

reject H_0 if $\chi^{2*} > \chi_{\alpha/2, n-1}^2$ or $\chi^{2*} < \chi_{1-\alpha/2, n-1}^2$

One-Tailed Test

$$H_0: \sigma^2 \leq \sigma_0^2 \qquad\qquad\qquad H_0: \sigma^2 \geq \sigma_0^2$$

$$H_a: \sigma^2 > \sigma_0^2 \qquad\qquad\qquad H_a: \sigma^2 < \sigma_0^2$$

reject H_0 if $\chi^{2*} > \chi_{\alpha, n-1}^2$ reject H_0 if $\chi^{2*} < \chi_{1-\alpha, n-1}^2$

EXAMPLE

8.13

Example 8.12 was concerned with the variation of the actual weight of a (supposedly) 50-pound bag of Vitamix Dog Chow. Based on earlier production tests, management is convinced that the average weight of all bags being produced is, in fact, 50 pounds. However, the production supervisor has been informed that at least 95% of the bags produced *must* be within one pound of the specified weight (50 pounds). Using a significance level of $\alpha = .1$, what can we conclude? Assume a normal distribution for the bag weights.

What is the supervisor being told about σ? Remember that for a normal population, 95% of the observations will lie within two standard deviations of the mean (empirical rule, Chapter 3). So, if two standard deviations are equivalent to one pound, then the supervisor is being told that σ must be no more than .5 pound. Is there any evidence to conclude that this is not the case—that is, that σ is larger than .5 pound? Let's investigate.

Solution   **Step 1.** The appropriate hypotheses are $H_0: \sigma \leq .5$ and $H_a: \sigma > .5$ (production is not meeting required standards).

(Note that these hypotheses are precisely the same as $H_0: \sigma^2 \leq .25$ and $H_a: \sigma^2 > .25$. Whether you write H_0 and H_a in terms of σ or σ^2 does not matter; the testing procedure is the same in either case.)

Step 2. The test statistic is

$$\chi^2 = \frac{(15-1)s^2}{(.5)^2} = \frac{14s^2}{.25}$$

which has a chi-square distribution with 14 df.

Step 3. Using $\alpha = .1$ and Table A.6, the rejection region for this test is

reject H_0 if $\chi^2 > 21.06$

Step 4. The computed value using the sample data is

$$\chi^2 = \frac{(15-1)(1.651)^2}{(.5)^2} = 152.6$$

Since $152.6 > 21.06$, we reject H_0. This is hardly a surprising result; the point estimate of σ is $s = 1.651$, quite a bit larger than .5.

Step 5. We conclude rather convincingly that σ is larger than .5 pound. The bagging procedure has far too much variation in the weight of the bags produced.

Note that the *p*-value for the test of hypothesis in Example 8.13 is the area to the right of 152.6 under the χ^2 curve with 14 df (illustrated in Figure 8.26). All we are able to determine about this value using Table A.6 is that it is much smaller than .005 (the smallest tabulated value). Using this information, we arrive at the same decision—namely, reject H_0—because (1) using the classical approach, *p* is less than $\alpha = .10$, or (2) the *p*-value is extremely small (<.01) by the general rule of thumb described in Section 8.3.

The Excel macros in KPK Data Analysis allow you to construct a confidence interval and carry out a test of hypothesis for a population variance. The Excel solution to Examples 8.12 and 8.13 is shown in Figure 8.27. To use this procedure, enter the 15 sample values in cells A1:A15. Click on **KPK Data Analysis ➤ One Population Inference.** Referring to Figure 8.10, use the down arrow in the top box to select **Population Standard Deviation (Chi-Square Statistic).** The resulting input screen is very similar to that in Figure 8.10. Enter "A1:A15" for the **Input Range,** but don't click on the **Labels** box (unless you inserted a label in cell A1). Enter "10" in the **Alpha** box, click on **Confidence Interval,** click on **Hypothesis Test (Right-Tail Test),** and enter ".5" for the **Hypothesized Value of Standard Deviation** and "B1" for the **Output Range.** Referring to Figure 8.27, the confidence

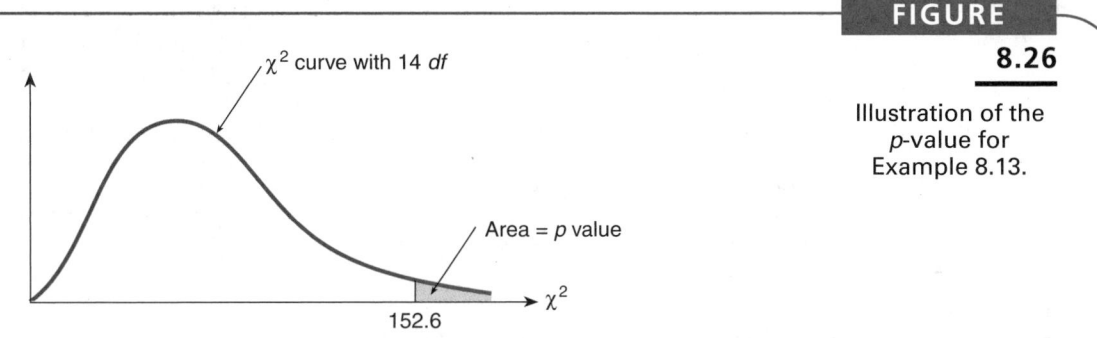

FIGURE

8.26

Illustration of the *p*-value for Example 8.13.

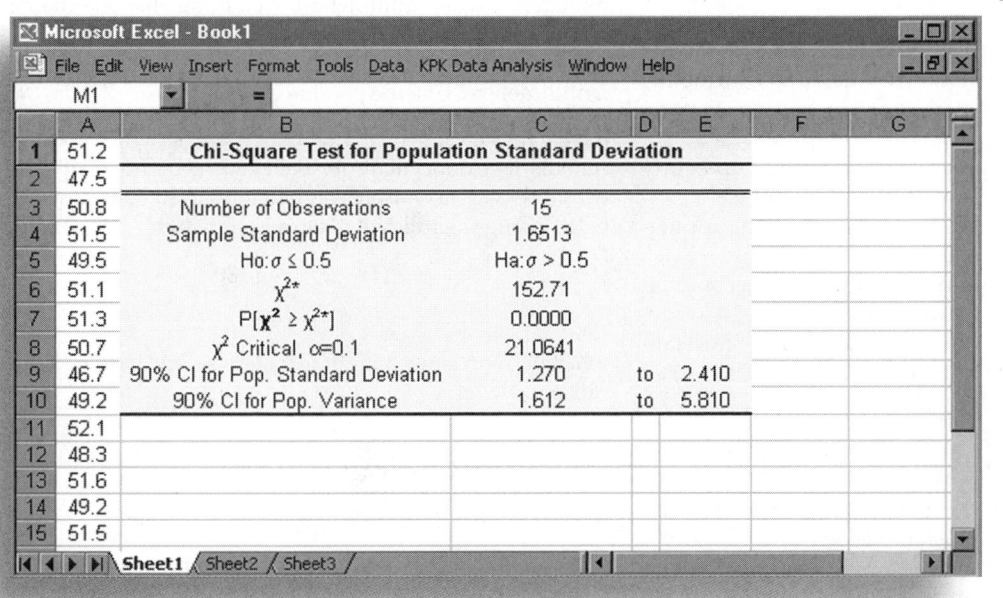

FIGURE

8.27

Excel spreadsheet for solution to Examples 8.12 and 8.13.

interval in row 9 agrees with the solution to Example 8.12. The calculated chi-square statistic is 152.71 (slightly more accurate than the solution to Example 8.13), and the p-value in cell C7 is zero to four decimal places. This solution supports the earlier conclusion that the bagging procedure contains excessive variation in the bag weights.

X Exercises 8.47–8.56

Understanding the Mechanics

8.47 Find the rejection region for testing H_0: $\sigma^2 = 100$ and H_a: $\sigma^2 \neq 100$ using the chi-square statistic for the following values of n and α.

    a. $n = 11$, $\alpha = .10$
    b. $n = 31$, $\alpha = .05$
    c. $n = 8$, $\alpha = .01$
    d. $n = 81$, $\alpha = .05$

8.48 A sample of size 25 from a normally distributed population yields a sample standard deviation of 12.8. At the 10% significance level, determine if there is sufficient evidence to indicate that the population standard deviation is greater than 11.3.

8.49 A random sample of 12 observations from an approximately normally distributed population is as follows.

$$5, 8, 13, 7, 14, 10, 6, 12, 9, 11, 8, 4$$

    a. Construct a 90% confidence interval for the population variance.
    b. Construct a 90% confidence interval for the population standard deviation.
    c. Test that the population standard deviation is less than 5. Use a .10 significance level.

Applying the New Concepts

8.50 According to Sanford C. Bernstein, a New York money management firm, the standard deviation of the daily closing prices of stocks on the New York Stock Exchange was 13% in the 1990s. Suppose that the chairperson of a family of mutual funds wishes to determine if the standard deviation of equity mutual funds during the 1990s differs from 13%. The chairperson believes that the return by equity mutual funds can be approximated by a normal distribution. Assume that a sample of 25 equity mutual funds revealed a standard deviation of 9.8%.

    a. Construct a 95% confidence interval for the population variance of equity mutual funds.
    b. Construct a 95% confidence interval for the population standard deviation of equity mutual funds.
    c. Is there sufficient evidence to indicate that the standard deviation of equity mutual funds differs from 13%? Use a .05 significance level.

(Source: Susan E. Kuyn, "The New Perilous Stock Market," *Fortune*, December 27, 1993, p. 48.)

8.51 As the stock market surged upward amid low inflation in the late 1990s, consumers needed to sock away a smaller portion of their income to achieve their saving goals, leaving them with more to spend. The University of Michigan's consumer-sentiment index is an indicator of consumers' contentment with the economy. In 1998, it remained quite high, and consumers' spending continued to increase. Suppose that financial advisors are concerned with the variability of the index. To be able to predict future changes in consumer sentiment, a low variance for the consumer-sentiment index is desirable. Assume that a financial advisor randomly selected 15 values of the consumer-sentiment index over the past two years and found a standard deviation of 1.7.

    a. Find a 90% confidence interval for the standard deviation of the consumer-sentiment index.
    b. What conclusion would result from the financial advisor testing that the population standard deviation of the consumer-sentiment index was less than three using a significance level of .05?
    c. What assumptions must hold about the data for the statistical inference procedures in parts a and b to be valid?

(Source: "Consumer Spending Rose Faster in April Than Income, and the Savings Rate Fell," *The Wall Street Journal*, June 1, 1998, p. A4.)

8.52 For a random variable χ^2, which has chi-square distribution with 18 df, determine the values of a and b such that $P(a \leq \chi^2 \leq b) = .90$ and such that the areas in each tail are equal, that is, $P(0 \leq \chi^2 < a) = P(b < \chi^2)$.

8.53 A production manager in charge of manufacturing plastic discs must maintain a standard deviation of less than 2 millimeters for the diameter of the disc. A sample of 26 plastic discs randomly selected reveals a standard deviation of 1.85 millimeters. Assuming that the diameters of the disc are normally distributed, do the data indicate that the standard deviation of the disc is less than 2 millimeters? Use the p-value criteria.

8.54 The salaries for mathematics teachers in secondary schools in Connecticut are believed to be normally distributed with a variance greater than $3,000. Test this belief using the following sample statistics:

$$\Sigma(x - \bar{x})^2 = 45{,}130$$

$$n = 14$$

where X represents a math teacher's salary. Use a 1% significance level.

Using the Computer

8.55 [DATA SET EX8-55] *Variable Description:*

Channel 5: Nielsen rating for local evening newscast on Channel 5

Channel 8: Nielsen rating for local evening newscast on Channel 8

Channel 11: Nielsen rating for local evening newscast on Channel 11

Television stations use their Nielsen ratings as audience measurements to adjust the prices charged for commercials. Suppose that random samples of 50 Nielsen ratings for the local evening news on KXAS-TV (Channel 5), WFAA-TV (Channel 8), and KTVT-TV (Channel 11) were selected. Each rating point equals 20,000 homes in the Dallas-Fort Worth viewing area.

a. Construct three histograms for the variables. Describe the differences that you see between the distributions.

b. Test that the mean rating for each of the channels exceeds 10. Use a 1% significance level. What are your conclusions?

c. Test that the standard deviation of these three channels exceeds .7. Use a significance level of 1%.

(Source: "Channel 8 Strengthens Hold in Ratings," *Dallas Morning News,* March 2, 2001, p. 37A.)

8.56 [DATA SET EX8-56] *Variable description:*

CostTuneUp: The cost of tuning up a 2001 Dodge Durango

To understand how prices vary, a news reporter took a 2001 Dodge Durango with 25,000 miles on it for a tune-up at 30 different automotive locations in the Chicago area. The reporter did not explain to the automotive managers that he was checking out the automotive prices of a tune-up at various automotive garages. The reporter simply asked the automotive manager to look at the car and give an estimate on the price of a tune-up. No work was done. The reporter has learned that the standard deviation of the price of a tune-up in the Cleveland metroplex is equal to $5. The reporter believes that the standard deviation of a tune-up is greater in the Chicago metroplex area.

a. Test the hypothesis that the standard deviation of the variable CostTuneUp is greater than $5. Use a 5% significance level.

b. Suppose that the reporter notices that the third value in the random sample (the value of $104.50) is unusually large and decides to delete this value from the sample. What would be your conclusion in part a with this value removed?

Summary

In Chapter 7 you were introduced to the topic of **statistical inference** through discussion of the concept of estimating a population parameter (such as μ or σ) from the corresponding sample estimate. The reliability of using the sample mean to estimate μ was measured via a confidence interval. This chapter presented the other side of statistical inference—**hypothesis testing** regarding these two population parameters, along with a method of deriving a confidence interval for the population standard deviation or variance.

For testing against a hypothetical value of the population mean (μ), we introduced a procedure that used the standard normal *(Z)* distribution for large samples ($n > 30$) and the *t* distribution for small samples. For small samples, the hypotheses are concerned with the mean of a normal population. However, the Central Limit Theorem allows us to discuss the mean of any continuous population when we have a large sample.

The two hypotheses under investigation are the **null hypothesis,** H_0, and the **alternative hypothesis,** H_a. Typically, a claim that one is attempting to demonstrate goes into the alternative hypothesis.

Since any test of hypothesis uses a sample to infer something about a population, errors can result. Two specific errors are of great concern when you use the hypothesis-testing procedure. A **Type I error** occurs in the event you **reject** a null hypothesis when in fact it is true; a **Type II error** occurs when you **fail to reject** a null hypothesis when in fact it is not true.

The probability of a Type I error is the **significance level** of the test and is written as α. The probability of a Type II error is β; large values of β are associated with small values of α, and vice versa. To define a test of hypothesis, you *select a value of* α that considers the cost of rejecting a correct H_0 and failing to reject an incorrect H_0. Typical values of α range from .01 to .1.

The **power** of a statistical test is defined as $1 - \beta$ and is equal to the probability of rejecting H_0 when it is in fact false. The value of β (and so $1 - \beta$) depends on the actual value of the parameter under investigation, and so the power of the test can be obtained for each possible value of this parameter. The resulting set of power values defines a **power curve** for this test of hypothesis.

A five-step procedure was defined for any test of hypothesis:

Step 1. Set up H_0 and H_a.

Step 2. Define the **test statistic,** which is evaluated using the sample data.

Step 3. Define a **rejection region,** using the value of α, by selecting a **critical value** from the appropriate table.

Step 4. Calculate the value of the test statistic from the sample data and carry out the test. This will result in rejecting H_0 or failing to reject H_0.

Step 5. Give a conclusion in the language of the problem.

A test such as H_0: $\mu = 50$ versus H_a: $\mu \neq 50$ is called a **two-tailed test,** because we reject H_0 whenever the sample estimate of μ ($\overline{X}$) is either too large (test statistic is in the right tail) or too small (test statistic is in the left tail). Similarly, a test on the population variance (or standard deviation) such as H_0: $\sigma^2 = .2$ versus H_a: $\sigma^2 \neq .2$ also is a two-tailed test.

H_0: $\mu \leq 50$ vs H_a: $\mu > 50$ or H_0: $\mu \geq 50$ vs H_a: $\mu < 50$

and

H_0: $\sigma^2 \leq .2$ vs H_a: $\sigma^2 > .2$ or H_0: $\sigma^2 \geq .2$ vs H_a: $\sigma^2 < .2$

are all examples of **one-tailed tests** of hypothesis, since the rejection region lies in either the left tail *or* the right tail.

The tests on a population variance introduce the **chi-square distribution,** χ^2. This distribution was used to construct confidence intervals for σ^2 and σ as well as to define a distribution for the test statistic when performing a test of hypothesis on the variance or standard deviation.

Finally, we discussed why you should always include a ***p*-value** in the results of any hypothesis test. This value measures the strength of your point estimate (such as $\overline{X}$ or s^2). When using a predetermined significance level, α, you reject H_0 whenever the *p*-value is less than α and fail to reject H_0 otherwise. Another option is not to select the somewhat arbitrary value of α but simply to reject H_0 whenever the *p*-value is "small" (say, $< .01$), to fail to reject H_0 if it is "large" (say, $> .1$), or to decide that the data are inconclusive if the *p*-value lies between these two values. You can also use the *p*-value to measure the enthusiasm (*p*-value very small) with which you reject H_0 or the authority (*p*-value quite large) with which you fail to reject H_0.

✓ Summary of Formulas

1. Test statistic for hypothesis testing on a population mean:

$$\frac{\overline{X} - \mu_0}{s/\sqrt{n}}$$

This statistic has approximately a standard normal distribution (Z) for *large samples* from any population, and a t distribution with $n - 1$ df for *small samples* from a normal population.

2. Power of a test for H_0: $\mu = \mu_0$ versus H_a: $\mu \neq \mu_0$ (large sample):

$$\text{Power} = P(Z > z_1) + P(Z < z_2)$$

where Z is the standard normal random variable,

$$z_1 = Z_{\alpha/2} - \frac{\mu - \mu_0}{\sigma/\sqrt{n}}$$

$$z_2 = -Z_{\alpha/2} - \frac{\mu - \mu_0}{\sigma/\sqrt{n}}$$

and μ is the specified value of the population mean.

3. Power of a test for H_0: $\mu \leq \mu_0$ versus H_a: $\mu > \mu_0$ (large sample):

$$\text{Power} = P(Z > z_1)$$

where Z is the standard normal random variable and

$$z_1 = Z_\alpha - \frac{\mu - \mu_0}{\sigma/\sqrt{n}}$$

4. Power of a test for H_0: $\mu \geq \mu_0$ versus H_a: $\mu < \mu_0$ (large sample):

$$\text{Power} = P(Z < z_2)$$

where Z is the standard normal random variable and

$$z_2 = -Z_\alpha - \frac{\mu - \mu_0}{\sigma/\sqrt{n}}$$

5. Confidence interval for a normal population variance (σ^2):

$$\frac{(n-1)s^2}{\chi^2_{\alpha/2,n-1}} \quad \text{to} \quad \frac{(n-1)s^2}{\chi^2_{1-\alpha/2,n-1}}$$

6. Confidence interval for a normal population standard deviation (σ):

$$\sqrt{\frac{(n-1)s^2}{\chi^2_{\alpha/2,n-1}}} \quad \text{to} \quad \sqrt{\frac{(n-1)s^2}{\chi^2_{1-\alpha/2,n-1}}}$$

7. Test statistic for hypothesis testing on a normal population variance or standard deviation:

$$\chi^2 = \frac{(n-1)s^2}{\sigma_0^2}$$

where σ_0^2 is the hypothesized variance.

Review Exercises 8.57–8.82

8.57 Which of the following can be an acceptable alternative hypothesis? Why?
  a. H_a: $\mu = 10$
  b. H_a: $\mu \neq 10$
  c. H_a: $\mu \leq 10$
  d. H_a: $\mu > 10$

8.58 A production manager will shut down her production line if the bags of dry feed are overfilled or underfilled. The production operation is designed to produce bags weighing 25 pounds. The manager periodically takes a random sample of 20 bags to decide whether the production line should be shut down so that adjustments can be made to the machinery.
  a. What null and alternative hypotheses should the production manager use?
  b. What conclusion would the manager make if she failed to reject the null hypothesis?
  c. What conclusion would the manager make if she rejected the null hypothesis?

8.59 Which of the following statements are true about a hypothesis test? Explain.
  a. A smaller significance level decreases the probability of a Type I error.
  b. If the p-value is less than the significance level, then the null hypothesis is rejected.
  c. A Type II error can be more serious than a Type I error.
  d. The power of a test decreases as the sample size increases.
  e. A Type I error and a Type II error are the only ways that a wrong conclusion can occur.

8.60 The manager of Lone Star Restaurant believes that the average wait time for the Saturday evening meal is 30 minutes. To test this belief, the manager selects 50 customers at random and determines that the average wait time is 34 minutes with a standard deviation of 12 minutes.
  a. Find a 99% confidence interval for the mean wait time of a customer.
  b. Do the data indicate that the mean wait time differs from 30 minutes at the 1% significance level?

8.61 Calculate the power of the test for the mean of a normally distributed population with known population variance for the following situations, assuming that the true population mean is 10 and the known population standard deviation is 3.1. Use a significance level of .05.
  a. H_0: $\mu = 11$, H_a: $\mu \neq 11$, $n = 14$.
  b. H_0: $\mu = 9.5$, H_a: $\mu \neq 9.5$, $n = 25$.
  c. H_0: $\mu = 8$, H_a: $\mu \neq 8$, $n = 40$.

8.62 A supervisor is interested in whether a new machine will produce a batch of cylinders more quickly than the current machines do. A trial test of 23 batches of cylinders on the new machine yielded a sample mean of 8.5 minutes with a sample standard deviation of 1.2 minutes. The old machine is known to have a mean time of 9 minutes. Assume that the time required to produce a batch of cylinders follows a normal distribution.
  a. Assuming a significance level of .10, what managerial conclusion can be given in testing that the mean time for the new machine is less than 9 minutes?
  b. Explain how statistical significance and practical significance play a role in determining decisions made by the supervisor with regard to the new machine.

8.63 A manufacturer of drugs and medical products claims that a new antiinflammatory drug will be effective for four hours after the drug is administered in the prescribed dosage. A random sample of 50 volunteers demonstrated that the average effective time is 3.70 hours with a sample standard deviation of .606 hours. Use the p-value criteria to determine if there is sufficient evidence to support the hypothesis that the mean effective time of the drug differs from four hours.

8.64 Indicate what the p-values are for the following situations, in which the mean of a normally distributed population is being tested.
  a. H_0: $\mu = 31.6$, H_a: $\mu \neq 31.6$ (population variance is known), $Z^* = 2.16$
  b. H_0: $\mu = 4.07$, H_a: $\mu \neq 4.07$ (population variance is known), $Z^* = -1.35$
  c. H_0: $\mu = 87.6$, H_a: $\mu \neq 87.6$ (population variance is unknown), $t^* = 2.51$, $n = 15$
  d. H_0: $\mu = 195.3$, H_a: $\mu \neq 195.3$ (population variance is unknown), $t^* = -1.71$, $n = 25$

8.65 The economic crisis that Japan faced in 1998 forced many Japanese banks to examine their policies in making loans. Under the tutelage of the International Monetary Fund, many of the banks were forced to abandon the "crony capitalism" that led to Japan's economic woes and adopt financial systems more akin to that in the United States, where bank loans are granted not on who you know but on how much money the borrower is making. Many of the loans made in prior years were primarily based on tight links between banks, businesses, and bureaucrats. Assume that 61 vice presidents of lending institutions in Japan were randomly selected and asked to respond on a 5-point Likert scale, with 5 being strongly agree and 1 being strongly disagree to the statement: The primary basis in qualifying a customer for a loan is his or her potential to repay the loan. The sample mean was found to be 4.2 with a standard deviation of .8. Suppose that financial consultants to the IMF are interested in whether the mean score to this question differs from 4.

a. Use the Z test to test whether the data indicate that the mean score differs from 4. Use a significance level of .05.

b. Use the t test instead of the Z test in part a. How much does the rejection region change?

(Source: "All Eyes on Japan as Crisis Turns a Year Old," *USA Today,* July 2, 1998, p. 3B.)

8.66 The vice president of academic affairs at a small private college believes that the average full-time student who lives off campus spends about $300 per month for housing. A random sample of 200 full-time students living off campus spent an average of $305 per month with a standard deviation of $70 a month.

a. Find the p-value to determine whether there is sufficient evidence to indicate that a full-time student spends more than $300 per month on housing.

b. Would you reject the null hypothesis for the test in part a if $\alpha = .01$? if $\alpha = .05$? if $\alpha = .10$?

8.67 According to a survey of American adults by the Travel Industry Association, 98 million people have enjoyed a "high adventure" trip in the past five years. For example, high adventurers are willing to spend several thousands of dollars to explore Minnesota's Northwoods by dogsled, on snowshoes, and skis over a five-day period. Other high adventurers prefer a 12-day ski and mountaineering expedition to the Torngat Mountains, the tallest mountain range in northeastern Canada. Suppose that a marketing analyst is interested in the average travel expenses of these high adventurers and believes that their average expense is approximately $4,000. A random sample of 100 households taken by the marketing analysts yielded a sample mean of $4,500 with a standard deviation of $1,600.

a. Find a 99% confidence interval for the mean expense by high adventurers. Give an interpretation of this interval.

b. Use the confidence interval in part a to determine if there is sufficient evidence to indicate that the average expense by high adventurers differs from $4,000.

(Source: "Adventure Vacations Can Be Heart-Pounding and Cold," *The Houston Chronicle,* October 21, 2001, p. 7A.)

8.68 International students having little financial support from home can apply for a loan through Citigroup's Student Loan Corp. unit. If the student attends Harvard, no upfront fees and no co-signer are required. What's in it for Citigroup? It hopes that a relationship can be established that will carry forward with the student's career. The president of the Student Loan Corp. is interested in the mean loan value. The president figures that a $50,000 loan would cover a student's primary expenses.

a. To test at the .10 significance level if the mean loan that a student would need over a two-year period differs from this amount, a random sample of students who have graduated and made loans was sampled. The resulting mean was $46,700 with a standard deviation of $14,500. The sample size was 50. What conclusion can the president make?

b. Discuss potential problems in sampling from students who have already graduated when making conclusions about expenses for future students.

(Source: "Harvard and Citigroup Team Up on Low-Rate Loans for MBA Students," *The Wall Street Journal,* July 2, 1998, p. 1.)

8.69 In 1998, 30% of all travelers used e-tickets for airline travel. Electronic ticketing allows passengers to not have to worry about a paper ticket, and it costs the airline companies less to handle an e-ticket than a paper ticket. However, the American Society of Travel Agents (ASTA) has received reports of passengers having problems with their e-tickets, particularly with connecting flights. Suppose that the ASTA randomly sampled 20 airports and collected the number of complaints that the airport had with e-tickets for the month of July.

The data are presented below. Test the hypothesis that the mean number of e-ticketing complaints per airport for the month of July is less than 15. Use a 10% significance level. What managerial decision should the ASTA make based on the results of this test?

$$18 \quad 12 \quad 17 \quad 13 \quad 11 \quad 10 \quad 17 \quad 16 \quad 9 \quad 17$$
$$14 \quad 13 \quad 15 \quad 18 \quad 14 \quad 8 \quad 19 \quad 18 \quad 10 \quad 15$$

(Source: "E-tickets Not Error-free," *USA Today*, June 23, 1998, p. 5B.)

8.70 The owners of a shopping center are contemplating increasing the parking space in front of the shopping center. The owners would like to demonstrate that the average driver parks for more than .75 hours. The length of time parked is considered to be normally distributed. A random sample of 45 parked cars is observed; the average time parked was .80 hours with a standard deviation of .12. Do the data support the idea that the average driver parks for more than .75 hours? Use a 10% significance level.

8.71 Dow Jones & Co. made plans to cut 4.9% of its Ottaway Newspapers, Inc., staff. The publisher said that it would take a third quarter charge in 1998 of $5 million to pay severance and related costs. Suppose that the company decided to poll 20 of its employees to ask the likelihood of accepting a buyout. The employees responded on a scale from 1 to 10, with 10 indicating that the employee would accept any reasonable buyout and 1 indicating that the employee would be totally unwilling to accept any type of buyout. The poll revealed a mean likelihood value of 6.5.

a. To reach its goal of eliminating 4.9% of Ottaway Newspapers staff, a consultant believes that the likelihood value should be greater than 6. Is there sufficient evidence that the company's goal will be reached with respect to eliminating jobs? Assume that the sample standard deviation is 1.3 and that the significance level is .05.

b. If you were a consultant being paid to advise Ottaway Newspapers on how to reach their goal of eliminating 4.9% of their staff, would you want to use a small significance level or a large significance level in part a? Explain.

(*Source:* "Dow Jones Proposes to Trim 125 Jobs at Its Ottaway Unit," *The Wall Street Journal,* June 30, 1998, p. B8.)

8.72 From a normally distributed population, a random sample of size 22 yields the following statistic:

$$\Sigma(x - \bar{x})^2 = 1.67$$

a. Find a 95% confidence interval for the population variance.

b. Find a 95% confidence interval for the population standard deviation.

c. Test the null hypothesis that the population variance is equal to .07. Use a two-tailed test and a .05 significance level.

8.73 Using a significance level of .05, perform the hypothesis test for the standard deviation of a normally distributed population, given the following information:

$$H_0: \sigma \geq 20.6 \qquad \Sigma(x - \bar{x})^2 = 6100$$
$$H_a: \sigma < 20.6 \qquad \qquad n = 18$$

8.74 Eastern State Bank currently operates five drive-in teller windows. Management is concerned about the variability of the time spent waiting by a customer using the windows. A sample of 24 customers was taken, and the sample standard deviation was found to be 4.7 minutes. Management would like to keep the standard deviation below 4 minutes and may consider adding another drive-in teller window.

a. Test the null hypothesis that the standard deviation of a customer's waiting time is less than or equal to 4 minutes. Use a 10% significance level.

b. What assumption should be made about the distribution of the waiting time of customers who use the drive-in teller windows?

8.75 An investment counselor would like to know how much variability there is in the yield of money market funds. The yields of these funds can be considered to be approximately normally distributed for the time frame of interest. A sample of 21 money market funds yields a sample standard deviation of .7%. At the .05 significance level, is there sufficient evidence to indicate that the standard deviation of the yields of money market funds is greater than .6%?

8.76 A large university had recently converted to a computerized registration system for enrollment. After the first semester, administrators found that the average time spent registering per student was quite satisfactory, yet there still continued to be substantial complaints and dissatisfaction among students. Further study indicated that although the *average* time might seem satisfactory, there might be too much *variation* in the registration times. It was decided to study the situation during the next semester's registration period. If the standard deviation was greater than 20 minutes, six additional computer terminals would be installed; otherwise, two new computer terminals would be installed. From a random sample, the following data were obtained:

$$\Sigma(x - \bar{x})^2 = 6900 \qquad n = 18$$

Assume the population is normally distributed.

a. Is there sufficient evidence to indicate that the population standard deviation exceeds 20 minutes? Use a 5% significance level.

b. What is the decision indicated by the test: install six new terminals or two new terminals?

c. State the *p*-value for the test.

8.77 The U.S. Treasury Department uses an e-check program to pay bills and to accept payment. With this system, a check is sent by e-mail. The company or the government makes out a digital check using special software, signs it with a secure digital "signature," and e-mails it to the creditor. Suppose that a banking analyst believes that for this program to become viable, the banking community needs to be very supportive. Assume that a poll of 75 bankers rated the acceptance of this payment system on a scale from 1 to 10, with 10 indicating complete acceptance and 1 indicating that the payment system would never be acceptable. Use a computer package to analyze the data below. Construct a 90%, 95%, and 99% confidence interval on the mean acceptance of this new payment system by the banking community.

8	5	8	4	9	3	7	5	10	2	7	6	3	5	8
7	8	9	5	7	8	5	9	4	10	3	7	4	8	9
3	8	5	8	9	8	7	10	1	3	8	9	7	8	9
5	8	3	7	5	9	3	9	3	7	4	8	9	10	2
4	8	5	8	4	3	8	4	9	4	9	5	9	5	9

(Source: "Treasury Department to Inaugurate Internet-Payment Plan Called 'Echeck'," *The Wall Street Journal*, June 30, 1998, p. B12.)

8.78 [DATA SET EX8-78] *Variable Description:*

FraudulentBill: Amount of fraudulent Medicare bill submitted by health care employees at Amitan

The FBI spent three years investigating Amitan, a Medicare-certified home health care agency, for fraudulent Medicare bills. The FBI claims the agency created false medical records that were signed by nurses and doctors to make them look legitimate. After the investigation, Amitan went out of business. The investigators were interested in the average amount for which the health care employees would make fraudulent bills. A random sample of 100 fraudulent bills was selected for analysis purposes.

a. Test whether there is evidence to indicate that the amount of the fraudulent bills was greater than $600. What is your conclusion at the 5% significance level? At the 10% significance level?

b. Construct a 95% confidence interval for the standard deviation and interpret this interval.

c. Construct a histogram of the data. Do you notice any unusually large fraudulent bills?

d. Remove the two largest bills and repeat part a. Do you think these bills were overly influential?

e. With the two largest bills removed, repeat part b and compare.

(Source: "Health Workers Charged with Fraud," *Los Angeles Times*, October 22, 1998, p. 1A.)

8.79 [DATA SET EX8-79] *Variable Description:*

Contribution: Amount pledged by households during telethon

Appeals by Hollywood actors and musicians during an unprecedented telethon during October of 2001 generated more than $150 million in pledges to benefit families of the World Trade Center and Pentagon attack victims. Pledges were for as little as $10 from households across the nation. The money was then distributed through the United Way. Suppose that the manager of the United Way Fund believes that the average household contributed more than $30. A random sample of 200 contributions is provided to test this belief.

    a. What are the results of a hypothesis test for the manager's belief? Use a 5% significance level.

    b. Construct a histogram of the data. Should the manager be concerned that the distribution of the data may not be normally distributed? What does the Central Limit Theorem say about the sample mean?

    c. Assume that the manager would like to use a bootstrap approach to find a 95% confidence interval on the mean contribution by households. Use 100 bootstrapped samples of size 200. Interpret this interval.

(Source: "Briefs," *Dallas Morning News,* September 25, 2001, p. 25A.)

8.80 [DATA SET EX8-80] *Variable Description:*

DrivingDistance: Increase in golf driving distance using new composite material. Units are in yards

In golf, both the clubs and the balls are big science. Frank Thomas, technical director at the U.S. Golf Association, has been plotting driving distances on PGA tours for some time. He found that players using golf clubs made from a new composite material called Hyper Carbon increased their drive by 7 yards. To confirm this claim, a random sample of 50 players was selected, and their improvement in using the new composite material was recorded.

    a. Test that the improvement in driving distance by golf players differs from 7 yards. Use a 1% confidence level. Do the data support that the improvement in driving distance differs from 7 yards?

    b. Construct a 99% confidence interval for the improvement in golf driving distance using the new composite material. Interpret this interval. Is it possible to use this interval to perform the test in part a? Explain.

    c. Test that the standard deviation is greater than 2.0 yards. Use the *p*-value to make your conclusion.

(Source: "Kit Makers Score," *Professional Engineering,* vol. 12, no. 13, July 7, 1999, pp. 20–21.)

8.81 The chi-square distribution is an important distribution in statistical analysis. The shape of this distribution depends on its degrees of freedom. To gain an understanding of the relationship between the shape of this distribution and its degrees of freedom, randomly generate 200 observations from a chi-square distribution with 3, 12, and 50 degrees of freedom. Form separate histograms for the chi-square distribution for each of these degrees of freedom. Comment on the shapes of each distribution. Which distribution appears to be the most symmetrical? (In Excel, first generate 200 observations from a uniform distribution over the interval 0 to 1. Then click on the **Paste Function ➤ CHIINV** and use the values from the uniform distribution for the probabilities. In SPSS, first type some number in row 200 of one of the columns—this is necessary in order to generate 200 observations in another column. Then click on **Transform ➤ Compute** and select RV.CHISQ(df) and generate random numbers in one of the columns. In MINITAB, click on **Calc ➤ Random Data ➤ Chi-square** to generate 200 observations.)

8.82 Graph the power function for testing the null hypothesis of $\mu = 100$ against the alternative hypothesis of $\mu \neq 100$ when the true value of the mean ranges from 80 to 120. Do this for $n = 40$ and $n = 70$ when the population standard deviation is known to be 25. For which values of the mean does the power function change very little? To obtain a graph of the power function in Excel, put the values 80, 81, . . . , 120 in cells A2 to A42. Then in cells A1 through G1, put the titles presented below. In cells B2 through G2, put in the formulas presented below.

A	B	C	D	E	F	G
True Mean	Term needed in z1 and z2	z1	z2	P(Z > z1)	P(Z < z2)	Power
80	=(A2-100)*SQRT(40)/25	=1.96 - B2	=-1.96-B2	=1-NORMSDIST(C2)	=NORMSDIST(D2)	=E2 + F2

Now highlight the region: cells B1 through G1 and B2 through G2. Click on **Copy.** Now highlight rows 3 through 42 for columns B through G. Click on **Paste.** Use the line chart subtype option of the **Chart Wizard** to plot the power function. A graph of the power function for $n = 40$ is presented on the next page.

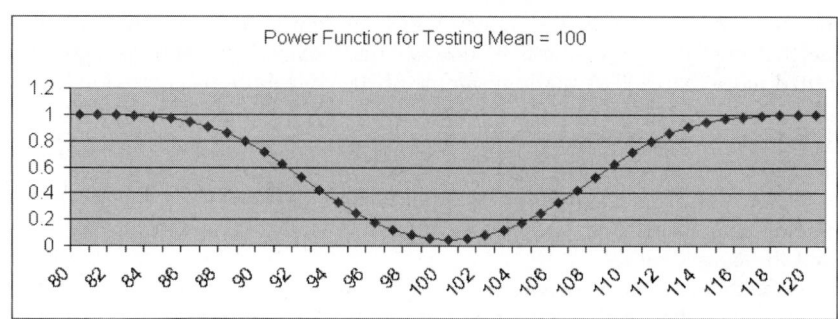

Power Function for Testing Mean = 100

Computer Exercises Using the Databases

Exercise 1—Appendix F

Randomly select 100 observations from the database. Use a convenient statistical computer package to determine whether the sample evidence indicates that the mean of the variable **TOTLDEBT** (total indebtedness) exceeds $14,000 at the .05 significance level. Also determine whether the sample evidence indicates that the standard deviation of the variable **TOTLDEBT** exceeds $4,000 at the .05 significance level.

Exercise 2—Appendix F

Randomly select from the database 30 observations in which the location of residence is in the NE sector, and also randomly select another 30 observa-

tions in which the location of residence is in the NW sector. Find separate 90% confidence intervals on the mean of the variable **INCOME1** (income of principal wage earner) from each of these two sets of data. Comment on the difference in the confidence intervals.

Exercise 3—Appendix G

Randomly select from the database 30 observations from companies with a bond rating of A and 30 observations from companies with a bond rating of C. Find separate 95% confidence intervals on the mean of sales minus cost of sales for each of these two random samples. Compare and comment on the differences.

Insights from Statistics in Action

Hillerich & Bradsby Company: Hitting the Quality Mark

The Statistics in Action introductory case study mentioned that H & B's top managers have learned to use statistical analysis in their decision making. In their operations, random samples of bats are frequently selected to determine if the operator's machinery needs adjusting. Even small deviations from the specs could be enough for a professional baseball player to refuse purchasing a bat. Consider two samples of 15 randomly selected turned bats given in StatInActChap8.xls to answer the following questions. These samples contain the weights in ounces of newly turned bats.

1. Construct 95% confidence intervals for the means of each of the two samples. Interpret these intervals.

2. Construct 95% confidence intervals for the standard deviations of each of the two samples. Interpret these intervals.

3. The newly turned bats being sampled are produced with a target weight of 33 ounces. For each of the two samples, determine if the mean weight of newly turned bats differs from 33 ounces. Use a significance level of .05. What conclusion

would you tell the manager? Are the results of these tests consistent with the confidence intervals in question 1?

4. If the standard deviation of the weights of the bats exceeds .15 ounces, operators readjust their machinery. For each of the two samples, determine if the standard deviation of newly turned bats is greater than .15. Use a significance level of .05. What conclusion would you tell the manager? Are the results of these tests consistent with the confidence intervals in question 2?

5. The manager is considering changing the significance level in testing the mean weights of the bats. What advice would you give to the manager? What error, Type I or Type II, would you think is more important with respect to satisfying the customer?

(Sources: "Louisville Slugger Maker Cuts Errors with Shipping System Upgrade," *Frontline Solutions*, vol. 2, no. 10, September 2001, pp. 16–18; and "Big League Quality," *Quality Progress*, vol. 34, no. 8, August 2001, pp. 27–34.)

Appendix **SPSS**®

Chapter 8 Appendix: Data Analysis with SPSS

Hypothesis Test for a One-Population Mean Using the t Distribution

To illustrate testing the mean of a single population, consider the output voltage of the 18 power supplies in Example 8.8. The hypotheses for this example were H_0: $\mu = 10$ versus H_a: $\mu \neq 10$. Enter these values in the first column of the data window. Click on the **Variable View** tab and name this variable "voltage."

	voltage	var
1	10.85	
2	11.40	
3	10.81	
4	10.24	
5	10.23	
6	9.49	
7	9.89	
8	10.11	
9	10.57	
10	11.21	
11	10.10	
12	11.22	
13	10.31	
14	11.24	
15	9.51	
16	10.52	
17	9.92	
18	8.33	
19		
20		
21		
22		

Data View / Variable View

To carry out the test of hypothesis, click on **Analyze ➤ Compare Means ➤ One-Sample T Test.** Click on the pointer button to move variable voltage into the **Test Variable(s)** box. In the **Test Value** box, enter "10" since this is the hypothesized value of the population mean. The output immediately following will appear in the display pane. The calculated t value is 1.829. The corresponding p-value is .085. Since the p-value is greater than .05 (the specified significance level in Example 8.8), we fail to reject the null hypothesis, and the conclusion is that there is insufficient evidence to indicate that the mean output voltage differs from 10 volts. *Note:* For a one-tailed test, the *p*-value is obtained by dividing the SPSS *p*-value by two. This assumes that the sample mean agrees with the alternative hypothesis. For example, if the alternative hypothesis is H_a: $\mu > 10$, then the sample mean agrees with the alternative hypothesis provided the sample mean ($\bar{x}$) is greater than 10. If the sample mean does not agree with the alternative hypothesis (e.g., $\bar{x}$ is less than or equal to 10), the actual *p*-value is one minus one half of the SPSS two-tail *p*-value; that is, divide the SPSS *p*-value by two and subtract from one.

The column labeled Mean Difference is the sample average minus 10 (the hypothesized value of μ). Consequently, the sample mean is 10 + .3306 = 10.3306. The confidence interval on the right-hand side is the 95% confidence interval for $\mu - 10$. Consequently, the 95% confidence interval for μ is 10 − .0507 to 10 + .7118; that is, 9.949 to 10.712.

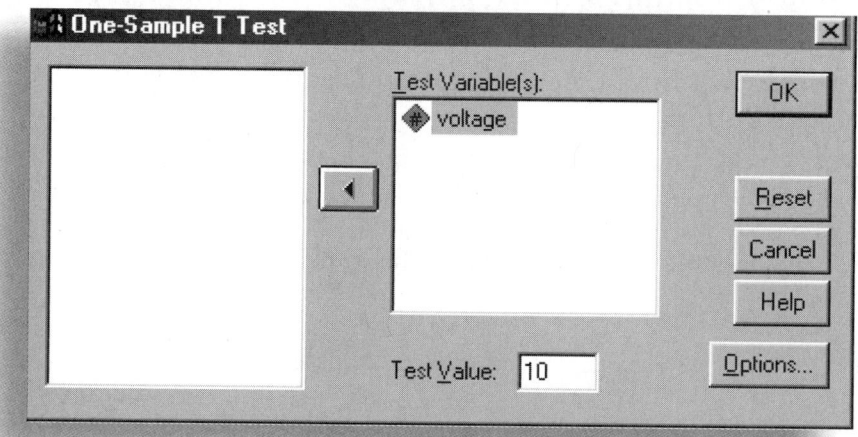

One-Sample Test

| | Test Value = 10 | | | | | |
| | | | | | 95% Confidence Interval of the Difference | |
	t	df	Sig. (2-tailed)	Mean Difference	Lower	Upper
VOLTAGE	1.829	17	.085	.3306	-5.07E-02	.7118

On the CD . . .
Chapter 8 Appendix: Data Analysis with MINITAB

Inference Procedures for Two Populations   X

Statistics in Action
Rollovers with Sport-Utility Vehicles: Assessing the Impact

Once considered farm, work, or off-road vehicles, sport-utility vehicles (SUVs) have become increasingly popular on America's highways and are now made by nearly every automaker. Buyers of SUVs argue that these vehicles appeal to their sense of adventure, expression of personality, feeling of safety (since heavier vehicles typically fare better in accidents), and feeling of power with a higher seating position for a better view of the road. Although an SUV's size might make a driver feel safer, automakers are struggling with the publicity about the risk of rollovers. In 1999, many SUVs began to include an illustrated mandatory label that visually stated that SUVs are more prone to rollovers than standard automobiles. The illustration is of an SUV tipping on its right-side wheels. Because of the extra clearance needed by these off-road vehicles, drivers are being warned that SUVs have a high center of gravity and thus are more prone to rollovers than cars.

The National Highway Traffic Safety Administration (NHTSA) uses the *static stability factor* (SSF) to assign rollover ratings to SUVs. The SSF is determined by dividing half a vehicle's track measurement by the height of its center of gravity. For example, an SSF of 1.13 to 1.24 qualifies for a three-star rating. This rating suggests a rollover risk between 20% and 30%. NHTSA is quick to point out that a low rating does not mean that a vehicle will spontaneously roll over. The popular Ford 2002 Explorer will qualify—but just barely—for an acceptable three-star rollover rating with an SSF of 1.13, and so will the Chevrolet 2002 TrailBlazer with an SSF of 1.15. Only one SUV has a four-star rating, and that is the Pontiac Aztek.

Automakers do not believe the SSF is a reliable predictor of rollover, but they have given in to pressure from safety proponents. Some automotive analysts believe a safety rating should be computed by putting SUVs through numerous real-world tests that involve swerving, turning, and stopping abruptly at fairly high speeds. For example, imagine the common accident scenario, where you've encountered a stopped semi truck 142 feet in front of you while going around a blind curve. If you are in a Porsche Boxster, a Dodge Caravan, a Pontiac Transport, a Ford Explorer, or a Chevrolet Suburban, the braking distance in feet is: 120 (yawn), 135 (Arrgh!), 141 (Whew!), 150 (SMASH!), and 155 (CRUNCH!!), respectively. These types of situations are difficult to incorporate into one safety score.

Automakers are not the only ones struggling with the rollover ratings. Insurance companies are interested in knowing if SUVs with less than a three-star rating have significantly more damage in collisions than SUVs with a three-star rating. When you have completed this chapter, you will be able to

- Determine what is meant by "significantly more damage" by SUVs with less than a three-star rating.
- Understand how to use independent and dependent samples to test hypotheses involving two populations such as SUVs *with less than* a three-star rating and those *with* a three-star rating.
- Construct and interpret a confidence interval for the difference in the amount of damage in a collision involving an SUV with three stars versus an SUV with less than three stars.

A Look Back/Introduction

We have learned to describe and summarize data from a single population using a statistic (such as the sample mean, $\bar{X}$) or a graph (such as a histogram). Chapters 7 and 8 introduced you to statistical inference, where we (1) attempted to estimate a parameter (such as the mean, μ) from this population by using the corresponding sample statistic and (2) arrived at a conclusion about this parameter (such as $\mu > 5.9$ ft) by performing a test of hypothesis. The concept behind hypothesis testing was described, and we paid special attention to the errors (Type I and Type II) that can occur when we use a sample to infer something about a population.

Next we learn how to compare two populations. Questions of interest here include

- Are the values in population 1 larger, on the average, than those in population 2? (For example, are men taller, on the average, than women?)
- Do the values in population 1 exhibit more variation than those in population 2? (For example, do male heights vary more than female heights?)

The two populations under observation may or may not be normally distributed. When we compare two population means using large samples, once again using the Central Limit Theorem, the type of distribution simply does not matter. For small samples, we need to examine the distributions of the populations so that we can use the proper procedure to construct confidence intervals and perform tests of hypothesis.

This chapter discusses two different sampling situations. In the first, random samples from two populations are obtained *independently* of each other; in the second, corresponding data values from the two samples are matched up, or paired. Paired samples are *dependent*.

9.1 INDEPENDENT VERSUS DEPENDENT SAMPLES

When making comparisons between the means of two populations, we need to pay particular attention to how we intend to collect sample data. For example, how would you determine if tire brand A lasts longer than brand B? You might decide to put one of each brand on the rear wheels of ten cars and measure the tires' wear. Or you might randomly select ten brand A and ten brand B tires, attach them to a machine that wears them down for a certain time, and then measure the resulting tire wear. If you use the first procedure (putting both brands of tire on the same car), you obtain *dependent* samples; in the latter situation, you obtain *independent* samples.

Consider another situation. Suppose you are interested in male heights as compared with female heights. You obtain a sample of $n_1 = 50$ male heights and $n_2 = 50$ female heights. You obtain these data:

Observation	Male Heights	Observation	Female Heights
1	5.92 ft	1	5.36 ft
2	6.13 ft	2	5.64 ft
3	5.78 ft	3	5.44 ft
⋮	⋮	⋮	⋮
50	5.81 ft	50	5.52 ft

Is there any need to match up 5.92 with 5.36, 6.13 with 5.64, 5.78 with 5.44, and so on? The male heights were randomly selected and the female heights were obtained independently, so there is no reason to match up the first male height with the first female height, the second male height with the second female height, and so on. Nothing relates male 1 with female 1 other than the accident of their being selected first—these are **independent samples.**

What if you wish to know whether husbands are taller than their wives? To collect data, you select 50 married couples. Suppose you obtain the 100 observations from the previous male and female height example. Now, is there a reason to compare the first male height with the first female height, the second with the second, and so on? The answer is a definite yes, since each pair of heights belongs to a married couple. The resulting two samples are **dependent, or paired, samples.**

In summary,

1. If there is a definite reason for pairing (matching) corresponding data values, the two samples are *dependent* samples.

2. If the two samples were obtained independently and there is no reason for pairing the data values, the resulting samples are *independent* samples.

Why does this distinction matter? *If you are trying to decide whether male heights are, on the average, greater than female heights, the procedure that you use for testing this depends on whether the samples are obtained independently.*

Applications of dependent samples in a business setting include data from the following situations.

- *Comparisons of before versus after.* Sample 1: person's weight before a diet plan is begun. Sample 2: person's weight six months after starting the diet. Why do we pair the data? We pair them because each pair of observations belongs to the same person.
- *Comparisons of people with matching characteristics.* Sample 1: salary for a male employee at Company ABC. Sample 2: salary for a female employee at Company ABC, where the woman's education and job experience are equal to the man's. Why do we pair the data? We pair them because the two paired employees are identical in their job qualifications.
- *Comparisons of observations matched by location.* Sample 1: sales of brand A tires for a group of *n* stores. Sample 2: sales of brand B tires for the same group of stores. Why do we pair the data? We pair them because both observations were obtained from the same store. Your data consist of sales (weekly, monthly, and so on) from a sample of stores selling these two brands.
- *Comparisons of observations matched by time.* Sample 1: sales of restaurant A during a particular week. Sample 2: sales of restaurant B during this week. Why do we pair the data? We pair them because each pair of observations corresponds to the same week of the year.

X Exercises 9.1–9.8

Applying the New Concepts

9.1 For each of the following situations, state whether the samples are independent or dependent.

a. A marketing analyst would like consumers to rate a new potato chip. Two bags of potato chips are given to randomly selected consumers. Each consumer rates the original flavor potato chip and then rates the mesquite bar-b-que flavored potato chip.

b. A manager is interested in the time that it takes a worker to complete each of two tasks. The manager selects two separate groups of 25 workers. One group is assigned the first task and the other group is assigned the second task. The time to complete each task is recorded for workers in both groups.

c. Mortgage rates by institutional lenders on the East Coast and on the West Coast were studied. Random samples of 20 lenders on the East Coast and 20 lenders on the West Coast were selected. Each lender's 30-year mortgage rate was recorded.

9.2 A random sample of CPA accountants and another random sample of non–CPA accountants were used in a study to determine their job satisfaction. Do the data represent dependent or independent samples?

9.3 An industrial psychologist is interested in the changes in a worker's personality when stress is increased. A random sample of 50 employees of a manufacturing firm is selected. Each employee is put under a no-stress situation and a very stressful situation. Data are recorded on the employee's personality under each of these two conditions.

a. Why would the sample of data collected under the no-stress situation and the sample of data collected under the very stressful situation be considered dependent samples?

b. How could this experiment be conducted such that the samples were independent?

9.4 A pharmaceutical firm is interested in the efficacy of a new drug and of a standard drug. The research division of the firm randomly selects two groups of volunteers. One group is given the new drug and the other group is given the standard drug. Data are recorded on the effects of each drug. Is the research division using dependent or independent samples? Why?

9.5 The career placement center at Safire University conducts a survey of beginning salaries for MBAs with no on-the-job experience. Ten pairs of men and women are chosen randomly such that each pair of one man and one woman has nearly identical qualifications. Can the sample of observations from men be independent of the sample of observations from women?

9.6 A retail store would like to compare sales from two different arrangements of displaying its merchandise. Sales are recorded for a 30-day period with one arrangement and then sales are recorded for another 30-day period for the alternative arrangement. Would the data for each of the two 30-day periods be independent or dependent?

9.7 A marketing analyst would like to have two brands of sausage rated by consumers.

a. Explain how the marketing analyst can use dependent samples to collect the data.

b. Explain how the marketing analyst can use independent samples to collect the data.

9.8 An automobile manager would like to know the extent of wear for brand A and brand B tires. Four tires are placed on a car. One brand of tires is placed on one side of the car and the other brand is placed on the other side of the car. The side that receives brand A is randomly selected. The manager uses 10 cars in the study and checks the wear on the tires after 5,000 miles. Two sets of data are recorded—one for the wear on brand A tires and one for the wear on brand B tires. Is the manager using dependent or independent samples?

9.2

COMPARING TWO MEANS USING TWO LARGE, INDEPENDENT SAMPLES

When comparing the means of two independent samples from different populations, we can use Figure 9.1 to help visualize the situation. The two populations are shown to be normally distributed, but, because we will be using large samples (generally, $n_1 > 30$ and $n_2 > 30$) from these populations, this is *not* a necessary assumption. For these populations,

$$\mu_1 = \text{mean of population 1}$$

$$\mu_2 = \text{mean of population 2}$$

$$\sigma_1 = \text{standard deviation of population 1}$$

$$\sigma_2 = \text{standard deviation of population 2}$$

FIGURE

9.1

Example of two populations. Does $\mu_1 = \mu_2$?

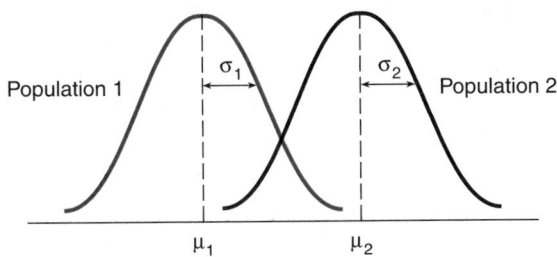

For example, if we wished to compare U.S. adult male and female heights:

$\mu_1 =$ average of all female heights

$\mu_2 =$ average of all male heights

$\sigma_1 =$ standard deviation of all female heights

$\sigma_2 =$ standard deviation of all male heights

The point estimates discussed in earlier chapters apply here as well—we simply have two of everything because we are dealing with two populations.

The procedure we follow is to obtain a random sample of size n_1 from population 1 and then obtain another sample of size n_2, completely independent of the first sample, from population 2. So, $\overline{X}_1$ is our best (point) estimate of μ_1. Likewise, $\overline{X}_2$ estimates μ_2. The sample standard deviations (s_1 and s_2) provide the best estimates of the population standard deviations (σ_1 and σ_2).

Constructing a Confidence Interval for $\mu_1 - \mu_2$

Ace Delivery Service operates a fleet of delivery vans in the Houston area. They prefer to have all their drivers charge their gasoline using the same brand of credit card. Currently, they all use a Texgas credit card. Ace management has decided that perhaps Quik-Chek, a chain of convenience stores that also sells gasoline but does not accept credit cards, is worth investigating. A random sample of gas prices at 35 Texgas stations and 40 Quik-Chek stores in the Houston area is obtained. The cost of 1 gallon of regular gasoline is recorded; the data are summarized:

Sample 1 (Texgas)	Sample 2 (Quik-Chek)
$n_1 = 35$	$n_2 = 40$
$\overline{x}_1 = \$1.48$	$\overline{x}_2 = \$1.39$
$s_1 = \$.12$	$s_2 = \$.10$

Let μ_1 be the average price of regular gasoline at *all* Texgas stations in the Houston area, and let μ_2 be the average price of regular gasoline at all Quik-Chek stores in the Houston area.

When dealing with these two populations, the parameter of interest is $\mu_1 - \mu_2$, rather than the individual values of μ_1 and μ_2. Here, $\mu_1 - \mu_2$ represents the difference between the average gasoline prices at the Texgas stations and Quik-Chek stores. If we conclude that $\mu_1 - \mu_2 > 0$, then $\mu_1 > \mu_2$. In this case, the gasoline *is* more expensive at the Texgas stations.

The point estimator of $\mu_1 - \mu_2$ is the obvious one: $\overline{X}_1 - \overline{X}_2$. For our data, the (point) estimate of $\mu_1 - \mu_2$ is $\overline{x}_1 - \overline{x}_2 = 1.48 - 1.39 = .09$. How much more expensive is the gasoline from all of the Texgas stations, on the average? We do not know because this is $\mu_1 - \mu_2$, but we *do* have an estimate of this value—namely, 9¢.

What kind of random variable is $\overline{X}_1 - \overline{X}_2$? First, because the samples are moderately large, we know by using the Central Limit Theorem that $\overline{X}_1$ is approximately a normal random variable with mean μ_1 and variance σ_1^2/n_1 and that $\overline{X}_2$ is approximately a normal random variable with mean μ_2 and variance σ_2^2/n_2.

Because these are two independent samples, it follows that $\overline{X}_1 - \overline{X}_2$ is also approximately a normal random variable with mean $\mu_1 - \mu_2$ and variance $(\sigma_1^2/n_1) + (\sigma_2^2/n_2)$. Note that the variance of $\overline{X}_1 - \overline{X}_2$ is obtained by *adding* the variances for $\overline{X}_1$ and $\overline{X}_2$.

By standardizing this normal distribution, we obtain an approximate standard normal random variable defined by

$$Z = \frac{(\overline{X}_1 - \overline{X}_2) - (\mu_1 - \mu_2)}{\sqrt{\dfrac{\sigma_1^2}{n_1} + \dfrac{\sigma_2^2}{n_2}}}$$

9.1

We do not need normal populations. The results of equation 9.1 are approximately valid *regardless* of the shape of the two populations, provided both samples are large (from the Central Limit Theorem). We pointed out that the two populations illustrated in Figure 9.1 need not follow a normal distribution. In fact, they can have any shape, such as exponential, uniform, or possibly a discrete distribution of some sort.

We can now derive a confidence interval for $\mu_1 - \mu_2$. From Table A.4, we know that for the standard normal random variable Z,

$$P(-1.96 < Z < 1.96) = .95$$

Using equation 9.1 (and rearranging the inequalities), we can make the following statement about a random interval prior to obtaining the sample data:

$$P\left[(\overline{X}_1 - \overline{X}_2) - 1.96\sqrt{\frac{\sigma_1^2}{n_1} + \frac{\sigma_2^2}{n_2}} < \mu_1 - \mu_2 < (\overline{X}_1 - \overline{X}_2) + 1.96\sqrt{\frac{\sigma_1^2}{n_1} + \frac{\sigma_2^2}{n_2}}\right] = .95$$

This produces the following $(1 - \alpha) \cdot 100\%$ confidence interval for $\mu_1 - \mu_2$ (large samples, where σ_1 and σ_2 are known):

$$(\overline{X}_1 - \overline{X}_2) - Z_{\alpha/2}\sqrt{\frac{\sigma_1^2}{n_1} + \frac{\sigma_2^2}{n_2}} \quad \text{to} \quad (\overline{X}_1 - \overline{X}_2) + Z_{\alpha/2}\sqrt{\frac{\sigma_1^2}{n_1} + \frac{\sigma_2^2}{n_2}}$$

9.2

If σ_1 and σ_2 are *unknown*, we have:

$$(\overline{X}_1 - \overline{X}_2) - Z_{\alpha/2}\sqrt{\frac{s_1^2}{n_1} + \frac{s_2^2}{n_2}} \quad \text{to} \quad (\overline{X}_1 - \overline{X}_2) + Z_{\alpha/2}\sqrt{\frac{s_1^2}{n_1} + \frac{s_2^2}{n_2}}$$

9.3

Notice that this interval is very similar to the confidence interval for a single population mean using a large sample, namely,

(point estimate) $\pm Z_{\alpha/2} \cdot$ (standard deviation of the point estimator)

To construct the confidence interval if σ_1 and σ_2 are unknown (the usual case), you simply substitute the sample estimates in their place *provided* you have large samples ($n_1 > 30$ and $n_2 > 30$). Consequently, the confidence interval in equation 9.2 is exact (σ_1, σ_2 known) and the confidence interval in equation 9.3 is approximate (σ_1, σ_2 unknown).

EXAMPLE 9.1

Using the data from the two gas-price samples, construct a 90% confidence interval for $\mu_1 - \mu_2$.

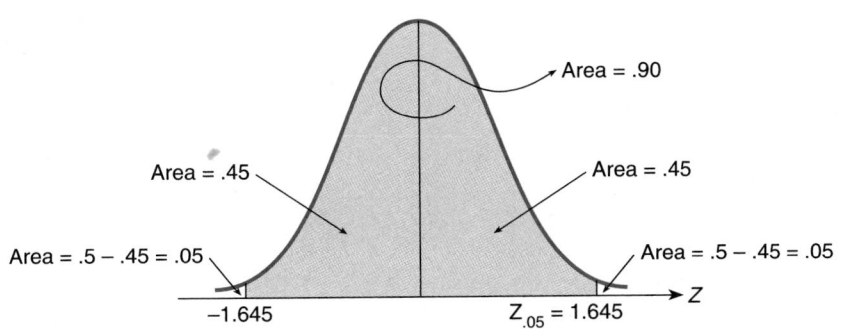

FIGURE

9.2

Finding the pair of
Z values
containing 90% of
the area under the
curve. The values
are −1.645 and
1.645.

Solution

To begin with, the estimate of μ_1 is $\bar{x}_1 = \$1.48$, and the estimate of μ_2 is $\bar{x}_2 = \$1.39$. We are constructing a 90% confidence interval, so (using Table A.4) we find that $Z_{.05} = 1.645$ (Figure 9.2). The resulting 90% confidence interval for $\mu_1 - \mu_2$ is

$$(\overline{X}_1 - \overline{X}_2) - 1.645 \sqrt{\frac{s_1^2}{n_1} + \frac{s_2^2}{n_2}} \quad \text{to} \quad (\overline{X}_1 - \overline{X}_2) + 1.645 \sqrt{\frac{s_1^2}{n_1} + \frac{s_2^2}{n_2}}$$

$$= (1.48 - 1.39) - 1.645 \sqrt{\frac{(.12)^2}{35} + \frac{(.10)^2}{40}} \text{ to } (1.48 - 1.39) + 1.645 \sqrt{\frac{(.12)^2}{35} + \frac{(.10)^2}{40}}$$

$$= .09 - (1.645)(.0257) \quad \text{to} \quad .09 + (1.645)(.0257)$$

$$= .09 - .042 \quad \text{to} \quad .09 + .042$$

$$= .048 \quad \text{to} \quad .132$$

We can summarize this result in several ways:

1. We are 90% confident that $\mu_1 - \mu_2$ lies between .048 and .132.

2. We are 90% confident that the average price of Texgas regular gasoline is between 4.8¢ and 13.2¢ higher than the regular gasoline at Quik-Chek.

3. We are 90% confident that our estimate of $\mu_1 - \mu_2$ ($\overline{X}_1 - \overline{X}_2 = .09$) is within 4.2¢ of the actual value.

The confidence intervals defined in equations 9.2 and 9.3 will contain $\mu_1 - \mu_2$ 90% of the time. In other words, if you repeatedly obtained independent samples and repeated the procedure in Example 9.1, 90% of the corresponding confidence intervals would contain the unknown value of $\mu_1 - \mu_2$, and 10% of them would not.

Sample Sizes

The amount that you add to and subtract from your point estimate to obtain the confidence interval is the *margin of error, E*. For Example 9.1, this value is $E = .042$ (4.2¢). If you think that E is too large and you would like it to be smaller, one recourse is to *obtain larger samples* from your two populations. To determine how large a sample you need, one procedure is to select equal sample sizes. Consider the illustration in Example 9.1, and suppose that you want large enough sample means so that the difference in sample means is within 2¢ (rather than the 4.2¢ in Example 9.1) of the difference in population means, with 90% confidence. So $E = .02$. By insisting on equal sample sizes, where $n_1 = n_2 = n$ (say), then

$$.02 = 1.645 \sqrt{\frac{(.12)^2}{n} + \frac{(.10)^2}{n}}$$

After some algebraic manipulation, we have

$$n = \frac{(1.645)^2 \left[(.12)^2 + (.10)^2 \right]}{(.02)^2} \approx 166 \qquad \text{(by rounding up)}$$

In general, this value is

$$n = \frac{Z_{\alpha/2}^2 (s_1^2 + s_2^2)}{E^2} \qquad \qquad \textbf{9.4}$$

In this illustration, the total sample size is $n_1 + n_2 = 166 + 166 = 332$. A better way to proceed here is to find the values of n_1 and n_2 that *minimize the total sample size.* The values of n_1 and n_2 that accomplish this are

$$n_1 = \frac{Z_{\alpha/2}^2 s_1 (s_1 + s_2)}{E^2} \qquad \qquad \textbf{9.5}$$

$$n_2 = \frac{Z_{\alpha/2}^2 s_2 (s_1 + s_2)}{E^2} \qquad \qquad \textbf{9.6}$$

For this illustration, $Z_{\alpha/2} = Z_{.05} = 1.645$, $s_1 = .12$, $s_2 = .10$, and $E = .02$. Consequently,

$$n_1 = \frac{(1.645)^2 (.12)(.22)}{(.02)^2} \approx 179$$

$$n_2 = \frac{(1.645)^2 (.10)(.22)}{(.02)^2} \approx 149$$

and the total sample size is $179 + 149 = 328$.

A derivation of this result is contained in Appendix H. Keep in mind that when you use these values of n_1 and n_2, the resulting value of E may not be exactly what you previously specified—because the values of s_1 and s_2 in the new samples will change. If no prior estimates of σ_1 and σ_2 are available, each can be roughly estimated using the high/low procedure discussed in Section 7.5.

Using equations 9.5 and 9.6, observe that if $s_1 = s_2$, your total sample size $(n_1 + n_2)$ will be the smallest when $n_1 = n_2$. If $s_1 > s_2$, you will select $n_1 > n_2$, and if $s_1 < s_2$, you will select $n_1 < n_2$. Finally, note that the ratio of the sample sizes (n_1/n_2) is the same as the ratio of the estimated standard deviations (s_1/s_2).

Hypothesis Testing for μ_1 and μ_2 (Large Samples)

Are men on the average taller than women? How do you answer such a question? We know that we can start by getting a sample of male heights and independently obtaining a sample of female heights. Figure 9.3 illustrates the two corresponding populations.

We proceed as before and put the claim that we are trying to demonstrate into the *alternative* hypothesis. The resulting hypotheses are

$$H_0\colon \mu_1 \geq \mu_2 \qquad \text{(men are not taller, on the average)}$$

$$H_a\colon \mu_1 < \mu_2 \qquad \text{(men are taller, on the average)}$$

We have estimators of μ_1 and μ_2, namely, $\overline{X}_1$ and $\overline{X}_2$. A sensible thing to do would be to reject H_0 if $\overline{X}_1$ is "significantly smaller" than $\overline{X}_2$. In this case, the obvious conclusion is that μ_1 (the average of all female heights in your population) is smaller than μ_2 (for male heights).

To define "significantly larger," we need to know what chance we are willing to take of rejecting H_0 when in fact it is true. This chance is α (the significance level) and, as before, it is determined prior to seeing any data. Typical values range from .01 to .1, with $\alpha = .05$ generally providing a good trade-off between Type I and Type II errors. The test statistic here is the same as the one used to

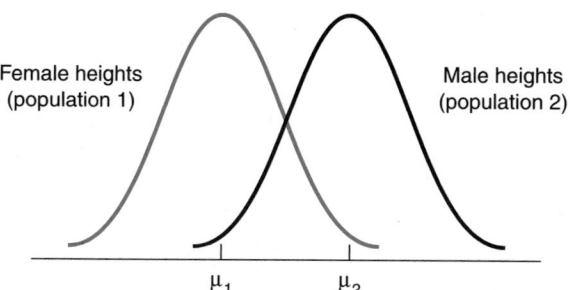

FIGURE

9.3

Hypothesis testing for two populations. Sample 1: size, n_1, mean, $\bar{X}_1$, and standard deviation, s_1. Sample 2: size, n_2, mean, $\bar{X}_2$, and standard deviation, s_2. Is $\mu_1 < \mu_2$?

derive a confidence interval for $\mu_1 - \mu_2$. We are dealing with large samples ($n_1 > 30$ and $n_2 > 30$), so the test statistic is approximately a standard normal random variable, defined by

$$Z = \frac{\bar{X}_1 - \bar{X}_2}{\sqrt{\dfrac{\sigma_1^2}{n_1} + \dfrac{\sigma_2^2}{n_2}}}$$

9.7

EXAMPLE

9.2

The Ace Delivery people suspected that the gasoline at the Quik-Chek stores was less expensive than that at Texgas before they obtained any data. (*Note:* This is important! Do not let the data dictate your hypotheses for you. If you do, you introduce a serious bias into your testing procedure, and the "true" significance level may no longer be the predetermined α.) Here, μ_1 represents the average price at all of the Texgas stations and μ_2 is the average price at the Quik-Chek stores in the area. Is $\mu_2 < \mu_1$? Or, put another way, is $\mu_1 > \mu_2$? Use a significance level of .05.

Step 1. *Define the hypotheses.* The question is whether the data support the claim that $\mu_1 > \mu_2$, so we put this statement in the alternative hypothesis.

Solution

H_0: $\mu_1 \le \mu_2$ (Texgas is less expensive or the same.)

H_a: $\mu_1 > \mu_2$ (Quik-Chek is less expensive.)

As in Chapter 8, the equals sign goes into H_0 for a one-tailed test. In other words, the case where $\mu_1 = \mu_2$ is contained in the null hypothesis.

Step 2. *Define the test statistic.* This is the statistic that you evaluate using the sample data. Its value will either support the alternative hypothesis or it will not. The test statistic for this situation is given by equation 9.7:

$$Z = \frac{\bar{X}_1 - \bar{X}_2}{\sqrt{\dfrac{\sigma_1^2}{n_1} + \dfrac{\sigma_2^2}{n_2}}}$$

Step 3. *Define the rejection region.* In Figure 9.4, where should the null hypothesis H_0 be rejected? We simply ask, what happens to Z when H_a is true? In this case ($\mu_1 > \mu_2$), we *should* see $\bar{X}_1 > \bar{X}_2$. In other words, Z will be positive. So we reject H_0 if Z is "too large," that is,

reject H_0 if $Z > k$ for some $k > 0$

Using $\alpha = .05$, we use Table A.4 to find the corresponding value of Z (that is, k). In Figure 9.4, $k = 1.645$. This is the same value and rejection region

FIGURE

9.4

Z curve showing rejection region for Example 9.2.

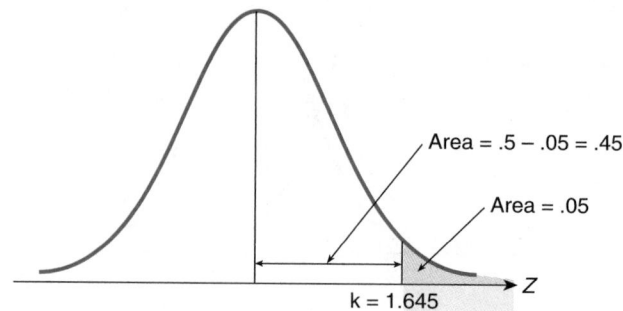

Area = .5 − .05 = .45

Area = .05

k = 1.645

we obtained in Chapter 8 when using *Z* for a one-tailed test in the right tail. The test is

$$\text{reject } H_0 \text{ if } Z > 1.645$$

Step 4. *Evaluate the test statistic and carry out the test.* The data collected showed $n_1 = 35$, $\bar{x}_1 = 1.48$, $s_1 = .12$ (from the Texgas sample) and $n_2 = 40$, $\bar{x}_2 = 1.39$, $s_2 = .10$ (from the Quik-Chek sample). Based on these sample results, can we conclude that $\bar{x}_1 = 1.48$ is *significantly larger* than $\bar{x}_2 = 1.39$? If we can, the decision will be to reject H_0. The following value of the test statistic will answer our question.

$$Z = \frac{\overline{X}_1 - \overline{X}_2}{\sqrt{\dfrac{\sigma_1^2}{n_1} + \dfrac{\sigma_2^2}{n_2}}} \approx \frac{\overline{X}_1 - \overline{X}_2}{\sqrt{\dfrac{s_1^2}{n_1} + \dfrac{s_2^2}{n_2}}} = \frac{1.48 - 1.39}{\sqrt{\dfrac{(.12)^2}{35} + \dfrac{(.10)^2}{40}}}$$

$$= \frac{.09}{.0257} = 3.50 = Z^*$$

Because $3.50 > 1.645$, we reject H_0; $\bar{x}_1$ is significantly larger than $\bar{x}_2$. Therefore, we claim that $\mu_1 > \mu_2$.

Step 5. *State a conclusion.* We conclude that the Quik-Chek stores *do* charge less for gasoline (on the average) than do the Texgas stations. If the locations of these stores are equally convenient to Ace Delivery Service, buying gas from Quik-Chek appears to be a money-saving alternative.

Comment

In Step 4, we replaced the unknown population variances (σ_1^2 and σ_2^2) with their sample estimates (s_1^2 and s_2^2). This is appropriate whenever the sample sizes are large, generally, $n_1 > 30$ and $n_2 > 30$. When one or both sample sizes are less than or equal to 30, this substitution is not appropriate, since the test statistic no longer follows an approximate standard normal distribution. This situation will be discussed in Section 9.3.

Using the corresponding *p*-value for the data in Example 9.2, what would you conclude using the classical approach (with $\alpha = .05$)? For this example, the *p*-value will be the area under the *Z* curve (*Z* is our test statistic) to the right (we reject H_0 in the right tail for this example) of the calculated test statistic, $Z^* = 3.50$. In general,

$$p = p\text{-value} = \begin{cases} \text{area to the right of } Z^* & \text{for } H_a: \mu_1 > \mu_2 \\ \text{area to the left of } Z^* & \text{for } H_a: \mu_1 < \mu_2 \\ 2 \cdot (\text{tail area of } Z^*) & \text{for } H_a: \mu_1 \neq \mu_2 \end{cases}$$

9.8

FIGURE

9.5

Z curve showing
p-value for
$Z^* = 3.50$.

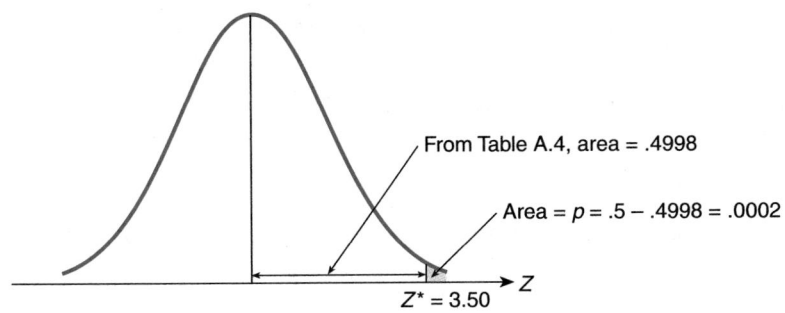

From Table A.4, area = .4998

Area = p = .5 − .4998 = .0002

$Z^* = 3.50$

These three alternative hypotheses are your choices for this situation. Once again, H_0: $\mu_1 = \mu_2$ versus H_a: $\mu_1 \neq \mu_2$ is a two-tailed test, and the first two alternative hypotheses represent one-tailed tests.

Returning to our example, we can see from Figure 9.5 that the resulting p-value is $p = .0002$ (very small). Using the classical approach, because p is smaller than the significance level of .05, we reject H_0—the same conclusion as before. In fact, this procedure *always* leads to the same conclusion as the five step-solution, as we saw in Chapter 8.

If we elect not to select a significance level α and instead use only the p-value to make a decision, we proceed as before:

Reject H_0 if p is small ($p < .01$).

Fail to reject H_0 if p is large ($p > .1$).

Data are inconclusive if p is neither small nor large ($.01 \leq p \leq .1$).

For this example, $p = .0002$ is clearly small, and so we again reject H_0. The Quik-Chek gasoline definitely appears to be less expensive than the Texgas gasoline. As was pointed out in the previous chapter, you often encounter a result that is *statistically* significant but not significant in a *practical sense*. To illustrate, suppose that the p-value of .0002 was the result of two very large samples and that the difference in gasoline price for the two samples was $\bar{x}_1 - \bar{x}_2 = .008$. You might not view this difference (less than 1¢) as being worth the inconvenience of having to pay cash for all gasoline purchases.

Comments

There may well be situations where the severity of the Type I error requires a significance level smaller than .01 on the low end, or the impact of a Type II error dictates a significance level larger than .1 on the upper end. This rule is thus only a general yardstick that applies to most, but certainly not all, business applications.

LARGE-SAMPLE TESTS FOR μ_1 AND μ_2

Two-Tailed Test

$$H_0: \mu_1 = \mu_2$$
$$H_a: \mu_1 \neq \mu_2$$
$$\text{reject } H_0 \text{ if } |Z| > Z_{\alpha/2}$$

where

$$Z = \frac{\bar{X}_1 - \bar{X}_2}{\sqrt{\dfrac{\sigma_1^2}{n_1} + \dfrac{\sigma_2^2}{n_2}}}$$

One-Tailed Test

$$H_0: \mu_1 \le \mu_2 \qquad\qquad H_0: \mu_1 \ge \mu_2$$
$$H_a: \mu_1 > \mu_2 \qquad\qquad H_a: \mu_1 < \mu_2$$
$$\text{reject } H_0 \text{ if } Z > Z_\alpha \qquad \text{reject } H_0 \text{ if } Z < -Z_\alpha$$

Two-Sample Procedure for Any Specified Value of $\mu_1 - \mu_2$

The two-tailed hypotheses for large sample tests for μ_1 and μ_2 can be written as

$$H_0: \mu_1 - \mu_2 = 0$$
$$H_a: \mu_1 - \mu_2 \ne 0$$

The right-sided one-tailed hypotheses are

$$H_0: \mu_1 - \mu_2 \le 0$$
$$H_a: \mu_1 - \mu_2 > 0$$

The left-tailed hypotheses can be written in a similar manner. The point is that H_0 (so far) claims that $\mu_1 - \mu_2$ is equal to 0 or lies to one side of 0 (the one-tailed tests).

Suppose the claim is that $\mu_1 - \mu_2$ is more than ten. To demonstrate that this is true, we must make our alternative hypothesis $H_a: \mu_1 - \mu_2 > 10$; the corresponding null hypothesis is $H_0: \mu_1 - \mu_2 \le 10$.

In general, to test that $\mu_1 - \mu_2 = $ (some specified value, say D_0), the five-step procedure still applies, but the test statistic is now

$$Z = \frac{(\overline{X}_1 - \overline{X}_2) - D_0}{\sqrt{\dfrac{\sigma_1^2}{n_1} + \dfrac{\sigma_2^2}{n_2}}}$$

9.9

Equation 9.9 applies to both one-tailed and two-tailed tests. It can be used to compare two means directly (for example, $H_0: \mu_1 = \mu_2$ versus $H_a: \mu_1 \ne \mu_2$) by setting $D_0 = 0$, as in Example 9.2.

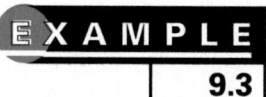

9.3

In Example 9.2, we decided that Ace Delivery Service would save money if they purchased their gasoline from Quik-Chek because that store's average gasoline price appeared to be less than that of the Texgas stations. Because Quik-Chek does not accept credit cards, the owner of Ace is willing to purchase their gasoline only if their average price is more than 6¢ per gallon less than Texgas's. Do the data indicate that it is? (α is still .05.)

Solution The question now is whether the data support the claim that the difference between the two means (Texgas and Quik-Chek) is larger than 6¢. So the hypotheses are $H_0: \mu_1 - \mu_2 \le .06$ and $H_a: \mu_1 - \mu_2 > .06$, where μ_1 is Texgas's mean and μ_2 is Quik-Check's mean. The test statistic is

$$Z = \frac{(\overline{X}_1 - \overline{X}_2) - .06}{\sqrt{\dfrac{\sigma_1^2}{n_1} + \dfrac{\sigma_2^2}{n_2}}} \approx \frac{(\overline{X}_1 - \overline{X}_2) - .06}{\sqrt{\dfrac{s_1^2}{n_1} + \dfrac{s_2^2}{n_2}}}$$

The computed value of Z is

$$Z^* \approx \frac{(1.48 - 1.39) - .06}{\sqrt{\dfrac{(.12)^2}{35} + \dfrac{(.10)^2}{40}}} = \frac{.03}{.0257} = 1.17$$

The testing procedure is exactly as it was previously—reject H_0 if $Z^* > 1.645$. Because $1.17 < 1.645$, we fail to reject H_0. The difference between the two sample means (9¢) was *not* significantly larger than the hypothesized value of 6¢.

These data provide insufficient evidence to conclude that Quik-Chek is more than 6¢ less expensive (on the average) than Texgas. If Ace's owner thinks that not using credit cards would be too much trouble for a savings of less than 6¢ per gallon, Ace should use the Texgas gasoline.

Using Excel to Carry Out a Two-Sample Z Test

Excel has a built-in function to carry out the two-sample Z test. This procedure will ask for the two population variances and assumes they are known. If in fact these two variances are estimated from the two samples, then a better way to go is to use an Excel two-sample t test procedure discussed in the next section. This comment applies to any situation where the sample variances are used in the test statistic but, as we have emphasized in this section, the Z statistics in equations 9.7 and 9.9 are quite reliable, provided both sample sizes are large.

To use Excel on Example 9.3, click on **Tools ➤ Data Analysis ➤ z-Test: Two-Sample for Means,** and you should see the input form in Figure 9.6. The first 12 values for the two samples are visible in Figure 9.7, and these two columns

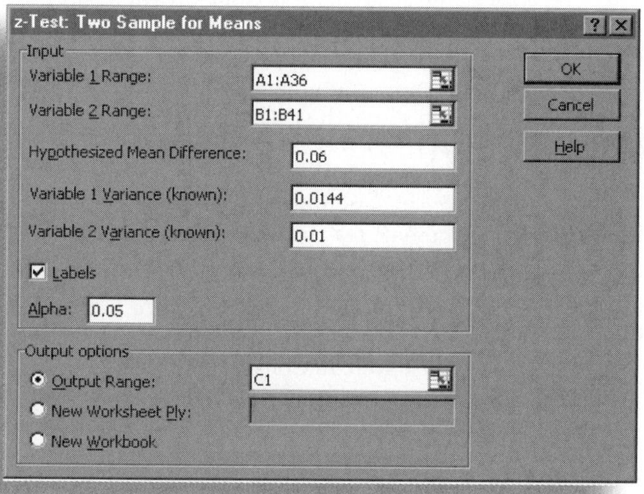

FIGURE 9.6

Input Screen for Excel's **Tools ➤ Data Analysis ➤ z Test: Two-Sample for Means.**

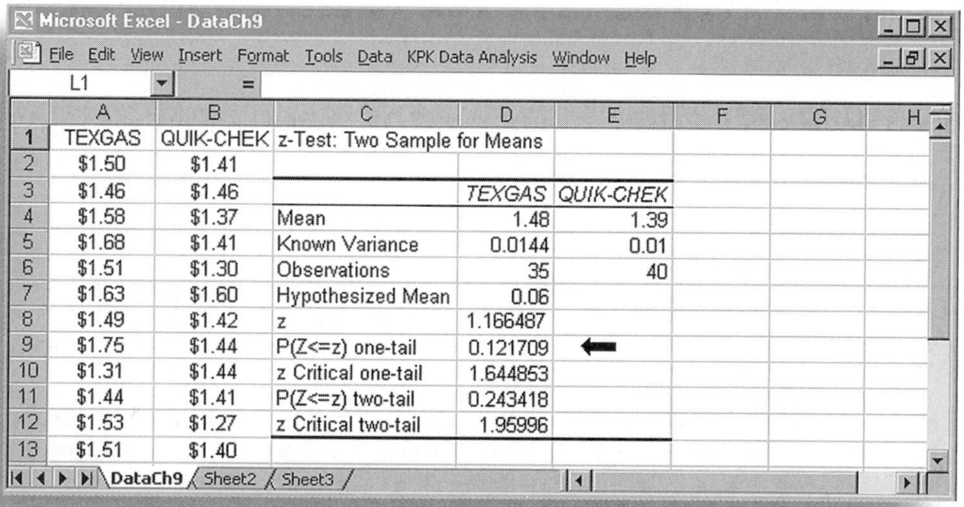

	A	B	C	D	E
1	TEXGAS	QUIK-CHEK	z-Test: Two Sample for Means		
2	$1.50	$1.41			
3	$1.46	$1.46		TEXGAS	QUIK-CHEK
4	$1.58	$1.37	Mean	1.48	1.39
5	$1.68	$1.41	Known Variance	0.0144	0.01
6	$1.51	$1.30	Observations	35	40
7	$1.63	$1.60	Hypothesized Mean	0.06	
8	$1.49	$1.42	z	1.166487	
9	$1.75	$1.44	P(Z<=z) one-tail	0.121709	
10	$1.31	$1.44	z Critical one-tail	1.644853	
11	$1.44	$1.41	P(Z<=z) two-tail	0.243418	
12	$1.53	$1.27	z Critical two-tail	1.95996	
13	$1.51	$1.40			

FIGURE 9.7

Excel spreadsheet using **Tools ➤ Data Analysis ➤ z Test: Two-Sample for Means.**

contain the labels **TEXGAS** and **QUIK-CHEK.** Fill in the various boxes as shown in Figure 9.6 and be sure to click on the box marked **Labels.** Notice that you specify the two variances that, for now, are assumed to be known and equal to $(.12)^2 = .0144$ and $(.10)^2 = .01$. The **Hypothesized Mean Difference** value is .06. If you were using Excel on Example 9.2, this value would be zero. After clicking on **OK,** you should obtain the output in cells C1:E12 in Figure 9.7.

In Figure 9.7, the calculated value of Z is 1.166487 and agrees with Example 9.3, where we obtained $Z^* = 1.17$. The arrow inserted into Figure 9.7 highlights the p-value, which is now .1217.* Since this is larger that .05, we fail to reject H_0 and arrive at the same conclusion reached in the solution to Example 9.3.

---

*In this chapter, Excel's one-tailed p-values are correct *provided* a true statement is obtained when the population means in the *alternative* hypothesis are replaced by the sample means. For this example, you would examine $\bar{x}_1 - \bar{x}_2 > .06$. Using $\bar{x}_1 = 1.48$ and $\bar{x}_2 = 1.39$, you obtain a true statement since $.09 > .06$. Consequently, the Excel p-value of .1217 is correct. If you had obtained a false statement, the correct p-value is 1 minus Excel's p-value (.8783 here).

X Exercises 9.9–9.24

Understanding the Mechanics

9.9 An industrial engineer randomly samples 40 observations from each of two processes. The random sample from the first process yields a sample mean and sample standard deviation of 50 and 12, respectively. The random sample from the second process yields a sample mean and sample standard deviation of 56 and 14, respectively.

a. Compute the 90% confidence interval on the difference in the means of the two processes.

b. Is there evidence to indicate that the mean of the first process is less than the mean of the second process? Use a significance level of 10%.

9.10 Two independent random samples, each of size 80, were selected. Sample means were $\bar{X}_1 = 110$ and $\bar{X}_2 = 105$. Sample variances were $s_1^2 = 49$ and $s_2^2 = 25$.

a. Find a 99% confidence interval for the difference of the population means.

b. Test that the difference in the population means is not equal to 3. Use a .05 significance level. Find the p-value.

9.11 A pilot study estimated the standard deviations of two populations to be 3 and 6. What sample sizes would be necessary to minimize the total sample size when estimating the mean difference of the two populations to within a value of 1 with 95% confidence?

Applying the New Concepts

9.12 First National Bank and City National Bank are competing for customers who would like to open IRAs (individual retirement accounts). Thirty-two weeks are randomly selected for First National Bank and another 32 weeks are randomly selected for City National. The total amount deposited into IRAs is noted for each week. A summary of data (deposits in thousands of dollars) from the survey is as follows. First National: $\bar{x} = 4.1, s = 1.2$. City National: $\bar{x} = 3.5, s = 0.9$. Use a 98% confidence interval to estimate the difference in the mean weekly deposits into IRAs for each bank.

9.13 Two discount stores in a popular shopping mall have their merchandise laid out differently. Both stores claim that the arrangement of goods in their store makes the customer buy more on impulse. A survey of 100 customers from each store is taken. Each customer is asked how much money he or she spent on merchandise he or she did not originally intend to buy before walking into the store. The results are as follows. Discount store 1, $\bar{x} = \$15.50, s = \$3.20$. Discount store 2: $\bar{x} = \$19.40, s = \$4.80$. Find a 90% confidence interval for the difference in the mean amount of cash spent per customer on impulse buying for the two different stores. Is layout affecting impulse buying? How do you know?

9.14 Military managers have had to learn to make the military operations more economical by using the just-in-time system. Consider the following data measuring the time (in days) to deliver tank parts to NATO bases in Europe from the factory in 1992 and in 1999. Assume that the population variances for the two time frames are known to be 28 and 14 for time periods 1992 and 1999, respectively.

1992	1999
20	13
16	15
12	14
19	18
25	12
14	13
21	16
17	17
16	19
22	13

a. Is the mean time for 1999 less than that for 1992? Use a 10% significance level.

b. What assumptions do you need for the validity of the test in part a?

9.15 The manager of an information systems support group would like to test the hypothesis that easy listening music increases the productivity of programmers. Samples of two separate groups of 50 programmers were randomly selected from programmers across the company. The same computer programming task was given to each group and a rating on a scale from 1 to 100 was recorded for each individual programmer. The first group was given the task with easy listening music playing, whereas the second group did the task without music. The results revealed that the easy listening music group had a mean rating of 71 with a sample variance of 30.2. The second group had a mean rating of 67 with a sample variance of 28.1. Use a significance level of 10% to test for the manager's belief.

9.16 Refer to Exercise 9.15.

a. Find a 90% confidence interval for the difference in the mean ratings of the two groups.

b. Can the information in part a be used to test the hypothesis in Exercise 9.15? Why or why not?

c. If the same programmers were used in each group in Exercise 9.15, would the assumptions for the validity of the test change?

9.17 A marketing analyst at a wireless phone company wished to estimate the gross income of adults that choose plan A and those that choose plan B when they subscribe to the company's wireless service. A preliminary survey showed that the standard deviations of the gross income of adults choosing plan A and plan B are $5,200 and $9,600, respectively. The analyst wishes to compute a 95% confidence interval for the difference in the mean gross income of these two groups of adults with a margin of error of $2,000. What sample sizes should the analyst select?

9.18 A production manager wishes to determine if there is a difference in the number of production units produced by the night shift and the day shift. A random sample of night and day shifts is selected, and the number of production units for each shift is recorded. The following statistics resulted.

	$\bar{x}$	s	n
Day shift	27.4	6.4	60
Night shift	18.3	5.9	60

a. Find a 90% confidence interval on the difference in the mean number of production units for the two shifts.

b. Calculate a 99% confidence interval for part a.

c. Compare the two confidence intervals in parts a and b, and comment on the length of the intervals.

9.19 Eurostat, a statistical office of the European Union, reports that on average a person in Ireland bought one more movie ticket per year than a person in Britain. To confirm this report, a marketing entertainment researcher sampled 100 Irish and 150 British citizens. The researcher wished to test the belief that the difference in the average number of movie tickets purchased per year by British and Irish citizens was not equal to one. The results of the sample survey were as follows:

	$\bar{x}$	s_i	n_i
Ireland	3.4	1.5	100
Britain	2.1	1.7	150

At the .10 significance level, do the data support the researchers belief that the difference in the average number of movie tickets purchased per year by British and Irish citizens was not equal to one. Report the p-value and interpret it.

(Source: "Irish Eyes Watching Movies," *USA Today,* May 26, 1998, p. 1D.)

9.20 Mad property tax disease is starting to grip business and homeowners in many provinces in Canada as properties get evaluated using market value assessment (MVA). Tenants in commercial buildings expected to see an approximate 10% to 30% jump in rents at the end of 1998. Suppose that an economist wished to show that the average percent increase in Toronto exceeds that in Quebec by more than 3 percent. A random sample of 100 properties in Quebec and 100 properties in Toronto affected by MVA revealed the average percent increase in rent.

City	$\bar{x}$	s
Quebec	17	5
Toronto	24	10

Report the p-value for testing the economist's belief. Should the economist be concerned with the actual distribution of the data?

(Source: "Tax Revolt Sweeps Province Business Owners across Ontario," *Toronto Sun,* June 28, 1998, p. 69.)

9.21 The financial analyst of Hogan Securities believes there is no difference in the annual average returns for steel industry stocks and mineral industry stocks. Using the following information, test the hypothesis that there is no significant difference in the average returns for these two types of stocks. Steel industry stocks: $\bar{x} = 9\%$, $n = 33$, $s = 2.4\%$. Mineral industry stocks: $\bar{x} = 11\%$, $n = 41$, $s = 4\%$. Use a 10% significance level.

9.22 Because of the scarcity of construction, rising home prices, and robust job growth in Orange County, California, rents have risen 8% on average in 2001. Actually, rents have jumped nearly 50% since 1996 in this county. Within the county, average rents varied widely among larger cities, from $938 in Anaheim to $1,561 in Newport Beach. Suppose that a researcher wished to conduct a survey in 2003 to compute a 95% confidence interval on the difference in average rents for these two cities with a margin of error of $50. Find the sample size for each city that will minimize the total sample size. Assume that the standard deviation of the rents for Anaheim and Newport Beach are $100 and $200, respectively.

(Source: "Apartment Rents in O.C. Climb Nearly 8%," *Los Angeles Times,* July 10, 2001, p. C2.)

Using the Computer

9.23 **[DATA SET EX9-23]** *Variable description:*

Loss1994: Loss from reselling leased car in 1994

Loss1997: Loss from reselling leased car in 1997

Automotive leasing companies usually resell returned leased cars at a loss from their national resale value when the lease terms expired. Automobile analysts believe that the loss from reselling these returned vehicles was at least $200 more in 1997 than in 1994. Suppose that a sample of 40 lease cars resold in 1994 and a sample of 40 lease cars resold in 1997 were randomly selected and their loss was recorded in dollars.

a. Find the mean and standard deviation of both samples. Use the stacked histogram option on the KPK menu to view the two sets of data. What differences do you observe?

b. Use the Z test for testing the hypothesis that the mean loss for 1997 is at least $200 more than in 1994. Use a significance level of .10.

c. Explain how practical significance of the results may differ from the statistical significance of the results for this problem.

(Source: "Lease Losses," *USA Today*, May 6, 1998, p. B1.)

9.24 [DATA SET EX9-24] *Variable description:*

SalesCareer: Monthly sales by salespersons who say that they want to make a career out of sales

SalesNonCareer: Monthly sales by salespersons who say that they will eventually change to a profession that does not involve sales.

A sales manager believes that salespersons who wish to remain in sales as a career will sell at least $400 more than those who have decided that they will eventually change to a profession that does not involve sales. Across the company, 50 of each type of salesperson is selected, and each person's average monthly sales for the past six months is recorded in either the variables SalesCareer or SalesNonCareer. The units are in thousands of dollars. Test the sales manager's belief using a 5% significance level. What managerial conclusion can you give for this situation?

9.3 COMPARING TWO NORMAL POPULATION MEANS USING TWO SMALL, INDEPENDENT SAMPLES

When dealing with *small* samples from two populations, we need to consider the assumed distribution of the populations because the Central Limit Theorem no longer applies. This section is concerned with comparing two population means when two small, independent random samples are used. It differs from the previous section in two respects:

1. We are dealing with *small samples.**

2. We have reason to believe that the two populations of interest are *normal* populations. In Figures 9.1 and 9.3, where we had large sample sizes, this assumption was not necessary. When you use small samples from two populations, one or both of which appear to be *not* normally distributed, a nonparametric procedure is the proper method for analyzing such data. (This procedure is discussed in Chapter 18.)

In Chapter 8, we showed that when going from large samples to small samples from normal populations, the confidence interval and hypothesis-testing procedures both remained exactly the same, except that we used the *t* distribution rather than the Z distribution to describe the test statistic. We will use the same approach for small samples from two populations.

Confidence Interval for $\mu_1 - \mu_2$ (Small, Independent Samples)

When using large samples from two populations to compare μ_1 and μ_2, we used the approximate Z-statistic defined by

$$Z \approx \frac{\overline{X}_1 - \overline{X}_2}{\sqrt{\dfrac{s_1^2}{n_1} + \dfrac{s_2^2}{n_2}}}$$

---

*Strictly speaking, this section applies to any situation where the population standard deviations (σ_1 and σ_2) are unknown and the sample standard deviations (s_1 and s_2) are used in the test statistic. This statement is applicable for *any* sample sizes, n_1 and n_2, but it is especially critical when dealing with small samples, where the Z test from Section 9.2 is no longer reliable.

When using small samples ($n_1 < 30$ or $n_2 < 30$), this statistic no longer approximates the standard normal. To make matters more complicated, it is not a t random variable, either. However, this expression is *approximately* a t random variable if a somewhat complicated expression is used to derive the degrees of freedom (df). So we define

$$t' = \frac{\overline{X}_1 - \overline{X}_2}{\sqrt{\dfrac{s_1^2}{n_1} + \dfrac{s_2^2}{n_2}}}$$

9.10

This statistic approximately follows a t distribution with df given by

$$\text{df for } t' = \frac{\left[\dfrac{s_1^2}{n_1} + \dfrac{s_2^2}{n_2}\right]^2}{\dfrac{\left(\dfrac{s_1^2}{n_1}\right)^2}{n_1 - 1} + \dfrac{\left(\dfrac{s_2^2}{n_2}\right)^2}{n_2 - 1}}$$

9.11

Admittedly, equation 9.11 is a bit messy, but a good calculator or computer package makes this calculation relatively painless. If df as calculated is not an integer (1, 2, 3, . . .), it should be rounded to the nearest integer (procedure used by Excel). MINITAB always rounds *down* to the nearest integer (the conservative procedure) and SPSS does *not* round this value at all. As a check of your calculations, the df should be between A and B, where A is the smaller of $(n_1 - 1)$ and $(n_2 - 1)$ and B is $(n_1 - 1) + (n_2 - 1)$.

When finding the df, you can scale *both* s_1 and s_2 any way you wish, provided you scale them both the same way. By scaling, we mean that you can use s_1 and s_2 as is, or you can move the decimal point to the right or left. The resulting df will be the same *regardless* of the scaling used. However, when you evaluate the test statistic, t', or later perform a test of hypothesis, you must return to the *original* values of s_1 and s_2.

To derive an approximate confidence interval for $\mu_1 - \mu_2$, we use the same logic as in the previous (large samples) procedure. Thus, a $(1 - \alpha) \cdot 100\%$ confidence interval for $\mu_1 - \mu_2$ (small samples) is:

$$(\overline{X}_1 - \overline{X}_2) - t_{\alpha/2,\text{df}}\sqrt{\dfrac{s_1^2}{n_1} + \dfrac{s_2^2}{n_2}} \quad \text{to} \quad (\overline{X}_1 - \overline{X}_2) + t_{\alpha/2,\text{df}}\sqrt{\dfrac{s_1^2}{n_1} + \dfrac{s_2^2}{n_2}}$$

9.12

where df is specified in equation 9.11. If df is not an integer, round this value to the nearest integer.

EXAMPLE 9.4

Checkers Cab Company is trying to decide which brand of tires to use for the coming year. Based on current price and prior experience, they have narrowed their choice to two brands, Beltex and Roadmaster. A recent study examined the durability of these tires by using a machine with a metallic device that wore down the tires. The time it took (in hours) for the tire to blow out was recorded.

Because the test for each tire took a great deal of time and the tire itself was ruined by the test, small samples (15 of each brand) were used. Notice that these are *independent* samples; there is no reason to match up the first Beltex tire with the first Roadmaster tire in the sample, the second Beltex with the second Roadmaster, and so on. (As discussed in Section 9.1, they would be dependent samples if the tires were tested by putting one of each brand on the rear wheels of 15 different cars.) To compensate for any machine fatigue, the order of selection for the 30 tires was determined randomly.

The blowout times (hours) were as follows:

Beltex	Roadmaster	Beltex	Roadmaster
3.82	4.16	2.84	3.65
3.11	3.92	3.26	3.82
4.21	3.94	3.74	4.55
2.64	4.22	3.04	3.82
4.16	4.15	2.56	3.85
3.91	3.62	2.58	3.62
2.44	4.11	3.15	4.88
4.52	3.45		

Construct a 90% confidence interval for $\mu_1 - \mu_2$, letting μ_1 be the average blowout time for *all* Beltex tires and μ_2 be the average blowout time for *all* Roadmaster tires.

Solution   Here is a summary of the data from these two samples.

Sample 1 (Beltex)	Sample 2 (Roadmaster)
$n_1 = 15$	$n_2 = 15$
$\bar{x}_1 = 3.33$ hr	$\bar{x}_2 = 3.98$ hr
$s_1 = .68$ hr	$s_2 = .38$ hr

Your next step is to get a *t*-value from Table A.5. To do this, you first must calculate the correct df using equation 9.11:

$$df = \frac{\left[\dfrac{(.68)^2}{15} + \dfrac{(.38)^2}{15}\right]^2}{\dfrac{\left[\dfrac{(.68)^2}{15}\right]^2}{14} + \dfrac{\left[\dfrac{(.38)^2}{15}\right]^2}{14}}$$

$$= \frac{(.0404)^2}{.0000679 + .00000662} = 21.9$$

Rounding to the nearest integer, we use df = 22. Using Table A.5:

$$t_{.10/2,22} = t_{.05,22} = 1.717$$

The resulting 90% confidence interval for $\mu_1 - \mu_2$ is

$$(\bar{X}_1 - \bar{X}_2) - t_{.05,22}\sqrt{\frac{s_1^2}{n_1} + \frac{s_2^2}{n_2}} \text{ to } (\bar{X}_1 - \bar{X}_2) + t_{.05,22}\sqrt{\frac{s_1^2}{n_1} + \frac{s_2^2}{n_2}}$$

$$= (3.33 - 3.98) - 1.717\sqrt{\frac{(.68)^2}{15} + \frac{(.38)^2}{15}} \text{ to } (3.33 - 3.98) + 1.717\sqrt{\frac{(.68)^2}{15} + \frac{(.38)^2}{15}}$$

$$= -.65 - .35 \text{ to } -.65 + .35$$

$$= -1.00 \text{ hr to } -.30 \text{ hr}$$

So we are 90% confident that the average blowout time for the Beltex tires is between 18 minutes (.3 hours) and 1 hour *less* than the average for the Roadmaster tires. Based on these results, Roadmaster appears to be the better (longer-wearing) tire.

Hypothesis Testing for μ_1 and μ_2 (Small, Independent Samples)

The five-step procedure for testing hypotheses concerning μ_1 and μ_2 with large samples also applies to the small-sample situation. The only difference is that Table A.5 is used (rather than Table A.4) to define the rejection region.

In Example 9.4 a confidence interval was constructed for the difference in average blowout times for Beltex and Roadmaster tires. Can we conclude that these average blowout times are in fact not the same? Use a significance level of .10.

Solution

Step 1. We are testing for a difference between the two means (not that Roadmaster is longer-wearing than Beltex or vice versa). The corresponding appropriate hypotheses are $H_0: \mu_1 = \mu_2$ and $H_a: \mu_1 \neq \mu_2$.

Step 2. The test statistic is

$$t' = \frac{\overline{X}_1 - \overline{X}_2}{\sqrt{\dfrac{s_1^2}{n_1} + \dfrac{s_2^2}{n_2}}}$$

which approximately follows a t distribution with df given by equation 9.11.

Step 3. You next need the df in order to determine your rejection region. In Example 9.4 we found that df = 22. Because $H_a: \mu_1 \neq \mu_2$, we will reject H_0 if t' is too large ($\overline{X}_1$ is significantly *larger* than $\overline{X}_2$) or if t' is too small ($\overline{X}_1$ is significantly *smaller* than $\overline{X}_2$). As in previous two-tailed tests using the Z or t statistic, H_0 is rejected if the absolute value of t exceeds the value from the table corresponding to $\alpha/2$. Using Table A.5, the rejection region for this situation will be

$$\text{reject } H_0 \text{ if } |t'| > t_{\alpha/2, df} = t_{.05, 22} = 1.717$$

Step 4. The value of the test statistic is

$$t'^* = \frac{3.33 - 3.98}{\sqrt{\dfrac{(.68)^2}{15} + \dfrac{(.38)^2}{15}}} = \frac{-.65}{.20} = -3.25$$

Because $|t'^*| = 3.25 > 1.717$, we reject H_0. Consequently, the difference between the sample means (−.65) *is* significantly large (in absolute value), which leads to a rejection of the null hypothesis.

Step 5. There *is* a significant difference in the average blowout times for the two brands.

Comments

The hypotheses in Example 9.5 could be written as $H_0: \mu_1 - \mu_2 = 0$ and $H_a: \mu_1 - \mu_2 \neq 0$. Having already determined a 90% confidence interval for $\mu_1 - \mu_2$, a much simpler way to perform this two-tailed test (using $\alpha = .10$) would be to reject H_0 if 0 does not lie in the confidence interval for $\mu_1 - \mu_2$ and fail to reject H_0 otherwise. The confidence interval according to Example 9.4 is (−1.00, −.30), which does not contain zero, and so we reject H_0 (as before).

This alternative method of testing H_0 versus H_a holds only for a two-tailed test in which the significance level of the test, α, and the confidence level $[(1 - \alpha) \cdot 100\%]$ of the confidence interval "match up." For example, a significance level of $\alpha = .05$ would correspond to a 95% confidence interval, a value of $\alpha = .10$ would correspond to a 90% confidence interval, and so on.

Notice that the procedure in this section for testing μ_1 versus μ_2 and constructing confidence intervals for $\mu_1 - \mu_2$ made no mention as to whether the population variances (or standard deviations) were equal or not. In fact, we can say that this procedure did not assume that $\sigma_1 = \sigma_2$; it also did *not* assume that $\sigma_1 \neq \sigma_2$. Next, we will examine a special case where we have reason to believe that the standard deviations *are* equal. For this situation, we will define another t test to detect any difference between the population means.

Using Excel to Carry Out a Two-Sample t Test

The Excel procedure to use here is the **Two-Sample t Test Assuming Unequal Variances.** The name of this procedure will make more sense after you read the Special Case of Equal Variances discussion to follow. Actually, a better title for the

FIGURE

9.8

Excel input screen
for **Tools ➤ Data
Analysis ➤ t Test:
Two-Sample
Assuming Unequal
Variances.**

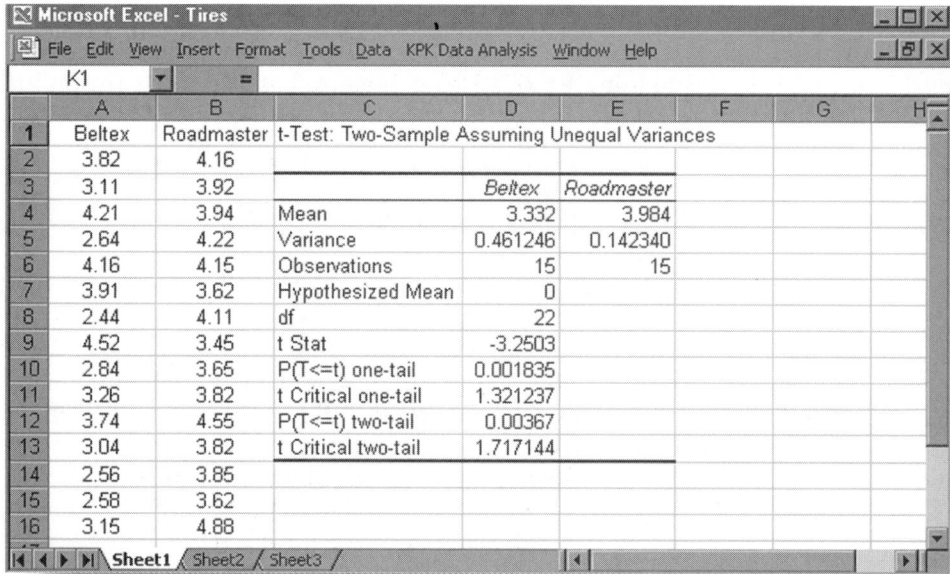

FIGURE

9.9

Excel spreadsheet
using **Tools ➤ Data
Analysis ➤ t Test:
Two-Sample
Assuming Unequal
Variances.**

	A	B	C	D	E
1	Beltex	Roadmaster	t-Test: Two-Sample Assuming Unequal Variances		
2	3.82	4.16			
3	3.11	3.92		*Beltex*	*Roadmaster*
4	4.21	3.94	Mean	3.332	3.984
5	2.64	4.22	Variance	0.461246	0.142340
6	4.16	4.15	Observations	15	15
7	3.91	3.62	Hypothesized Mean	0	
8	2.44	4.11	df	22	
9	4.52	3.45	t Stat	-3.2503	
10	2.84	3.65	P(T<=t) one-tail	0.001835	
11	3.26	3.82	t Critical one-tail	1.321237	
12	3.74	4.55	P(T<=t) two-tail	0.00367	
13	3.04	3.82	t Critical two-tail	1.717144	
14	2.56	3.85			
15	2.58	3.62			
16	3.15	4.88			

Excel procedure would have been "Two-Sample *t* Test Not Assuming Equal Variances," since using this procedure simply makes no assumptions about whether the population variances are the same.

Applying the Excel function to Example 9.5, click on **Tools ➤ Data Analysis ➤ Two-Sample t Test Assuming Unequal Variances** and fill in the input screen as indicated in Figure 9.8. Since we are only comparing the two population means, the value in the **Hypothesized Mean Difference** box is zero. Enter a value of .10 in the **Alpha** box, and be sure to enter a check next to **Labels** since the data contain labels in the first row. The resulting output is shown in Figure 9.9, where the value of the test statistic is again –3.25 (cell D9) and the calculated *p*-value is .00367 (cell D12). Based on this extremely small *p*-value, we once again reject H_0.

Special Case of Equal Variances

There are some situations in which we are willing to assume that the population variances (σ_1^2 and σ_2^2) are equal. This situation is common in many long-running production processes for which, based on past experience, you are convinced that the variation within population 1 is the same as the variation within population 2.

Another situation in which we may assume σ_1 and σ_2 are equal arises when we obtain two *additional* samples from the two populations, which we use strictly to determine if the population standard deviations are equal. If there is not sufficient evidence to indicate that $\sigma_1 \neq \sigma_2$, then there is no harm in assuming that $\sigma_1 = \sigma_2$. (A procedure for comparing the population standard deviations is discussed in Section 9.4.)

Why make the assumption that $\sigma_1 = \sigma_2$? Remember, we are still interested in the means, μ_1 and μ_2. As before, we would like to obtain a confidence interval for $\mu_1 - \mu_2$ and to perform a test of hypothesis. If, in fact, σ_1 is equal to σ_2, we can construct a slightly stronger test of μ_1 versus μ_2. By stronger, we mean that we are *more likely* to reject H_0 when it is actually false. This test is said to be more *powerful*.

For this case, because we believe that $\sigma_1^2 = \sigma_2^2 = \sigma^2$ (say), it makes sense to combine—or **pool**—our estimate of σ_1^2 (s_1^2) with the estimate of σ_2^2 (s_2^2) into one estimate of this common variance (σ^2). The resulting estimate of σ^2 is called the **pooled sample variance** and is written s_p^2. This estimate is merely a *weighted average* of s_1^2 and s_2^2, defined by

$$s_p^2 = \frac{(n_1 - 1)s_1^2 + (n_2 - 1)s_2^2}{n_1 + n_2 - 2} \qquad \text{9.13}$$

Notice that s_p^2 gives more weight to the sample variance from the larger sample. Also, if the sample sizes are the same, then s_p^2 is simply the average of s_1^2 and s_2^2.

Constructing Confidence Intervals for $\mu_1 - \mu_2$

To construct the confidence interval, we make two changes in the previous procedure. First, t' is replaced by

$$t = \frac{\overline{X}_1 - \overline{X}_2}{\sqrt{\dfrac{s_p^2}{n_1} + \dfrac{s_p^2}{n_2}}} \qquad \text{9.14}$$

$$= \frac{\overline{X}_1 - \overline{X}_2}{s_p \sqrt{\dfrac{1}{n_1} + \dfrac{1}{n_2}}} \qquad \text{9.15}$$

Here (unlike the previous test statistic), t exactly follows a t distribution (assuming the two populations follow normal distributions).

Second, the df for t are much easier to derive:

$$df = n_1 + n_2 - 2$$

So you avoid the difficult df calculation in equation 9.11, but you need to derive the pooled variance, s_p^2, using the individual sample variances, s_1^2 and s_2^2.

As a check, your resulting pooled value for s_p^2 should be between s_1^2 and s_2^2, since it is a weighted average of these two values. It may be easier to check that s_p is between s_1 and s_2.

Hypothesis Testing for μ_1 and μ_2

In hypothesis testing for $\mu_1 - \mu_2$, the previous procedure applies, except that t' is replaced by t and the df used in Table A.5 is df $= n_1 + n_2 - 2$ rather than the df value from equation 9.11.

In Examples 9.4 and 9.5, we examined the blowout times for two brands of tires as measured by a machine performing a stress test of the sampled tires.

Assume we have determined from previous tests that the *variation* of the blowout times is not affected by the tire brand. Assuming that σ_1^2 (Beltex) = σ_2^2 (Roadmaster), how can we construct a 90% confidence interval for $\mu_1 - \mu_2$ and determine whether there is a difference in the mean blowout times?

Sample 1 (Beltex)	Sample 2 (Roadmaster)
$n_1 = 15$	$n_2 = 15$
$\bar{x}_1 = 3.33$ hr	$\bar{x}_2 = 3.98$ hr
$s_1 = .68$ hr	$s_2 = .38$ hr

Our first step is to pool the sample variances:

$$s_p^2 = \frac{(15-1)(.68)^2 + (15-1)(.38)^2}{15+15-2} = \frac{(14)(.4624) + (14)(.1444)}{28}$$

$$= \frac{8.495}{28} = .303$$

$$s_p = \sqrt{.303} = .55 \text{ hr}$$

As a check, is .55 between .38 and .68? Yes. Consequently, $s_p^2 = .303$ is our estimate of the common variance (σ^2) of the two tire populations. To find the 90% confidence interval for $\mu_1 - \mu_2$, we use

$$(\bar{X}_1 - \bar{X}_2) - t_{\alpha/2,\text{df}}\sqrt{\frac{s_p^2}{n_1} + \frac{s_p^2}{n_2}} \quad \text{to} \quad (\bar{X}_1 - \bar{X}_2) + t_{\alpha/2,\text{df}}\sqrt{\frac{s_p^2}{n_1} + \frac{s_p^2}{n_2}} \tag{9.16}$$

where df = $n_1 + n_2 - 2$ and $\alpha = .10$.

Because $n_1 + n_2 - 2 = 28$, we find (from Table A.5) that $t_{.05,28} = 1.701$. Next,

$$\sqrt{\frac{s_p^2}{n_1} + \frac{s_p^2}{n_2}} = s_p\sqrt{\frac{1}{n_1} + \frac{1}{n_2}} = .55\sqrt{\frac{1}{15} + \frac{1}{15}} = .20$$

The resulting confidence interval is

$$(3.33 - 3.98) - (1.701)(.20) \quad \text{to} \quad (3.33 - 3.98) + (1.701)(.20)$$

$$= -.65 - .34 \quad \text{to} \quad -.65 + .34$$

$$= -.99 \quad \text{to} \quad -.31$$

Comparing this result to the confidence interval in Example 9.4, you see little difference in the two confidence intervals, although the interval using the pooled variance is a bit narrower. Oftentimes these intervals can differ considerably, depending on the relative sizes of n_1 and n_2 as well as the relative values of s_1^2 and s_2^2.

Now we wish to test H_0: $\mu_1 = \mu_2$ versus H_a: $\mu_1 \neq \mu_2$. For this particular example, we can, as noted earlier, reject H_0 (using $\alpha = .10$) because zero does not lie in the previously derived confidence interval for $\mu_1 - \mu_2$. In the five-step procedure, there are only two changes we need to make when using the pooled sample variances. First, when defining our rejection region, we use $n_1 + n_2 - 2 = 28$ df. From Table A.5, the test procedure is to

$$\text{reject } H_0 \text{ if } |t| > t_{\alpha/2,\text{df}}$$

where $t_{.05,28} = 1.701$.

Second, the form of the test statistic is now

$$t = \frac{\bar{X}_1 - \bar{X}_2}{s_p\sqrt{\frac{1}{n_1} + \frac{1}{n_2}}} \tag{9.17}$$

FIGURE

9.10

Excel output using
**Tools ➤ Data
Analysis ➤ t Test:
Two-Sample
Assuming Equal
Variances.**

t-Test: Two-Sample Assuming Equal Variances		
	Beltex	Roadmaster
Mean	3.332	3.984
Variance	0.461246	0.142340
Observations	15	15
Pooled Variance	0.301793	
Hypothesized Mean Difference	0	
df	28	
t Stat	-3.2503	
P(T<=t) one-tail	0.001499	
t Critical one-tail	1.312526	
P(T<=t) two-tail	0.002997	
t Critical two-tail	1.70113	

Here,

$$t = \frac{3.33 - 3.98}{.55\sqrt{\dfrac{1}{15} + \dfrac{1}{15}}} = \frac{-.65}{.20} = -3.25$$

Because $|-3.25| = 3.25 > 1.701$, we reject H_0; once again the two sample means are significantly different. We conclude that there is a difference in the population mean blowout times for the two brands of tires.

Using Excel to Carry Out a Two-Sample t Test Assuming Equal Variances

An Excel solution for the preceding example can be carried out by clicking on **Tools ➤ Data Analysis ➤ t Test: Two-Sample Assuming Equal Variances.** The input screen for this procedure is identical to that shown in Figure 9.8 (except for the title) and so fill in the same values as in this figure. The output is shown in Figure 9.10 where (1) the calculated t value is -3.25, (2) the corresponding two-tailed p-value is .002997, and (3) the pooled standard deviation is the square root of the pooled variance—that is, $\sqrt{.301793} = .55$. As in Example 9.5 (Figure 9.9), we obtain a very small p-value when pooling the sample variances. For this particular example, we observe little difference in the two solutions.

Microsoft Excel Application Use DATA9-6

Using Excel to Compare Two Population Means

**EXAMPLE
9.6**

In Examples 3.4 and 8.7, we examined the inside diameters of a certain machined part produced by Allied Manufacturing. Data set DATA9-6 contains the samples from Example 3.4 (100 measurements obtained *before* a quality-improvement effort) and Example 8.7 (100 measurements *after* this effort).

Column A contains the 100 measurements from Example 8.7.

Column B contains the 100 measurements from Example 3.4.

Prior to obtaining the second set of data, Allied wanted to know if there was sufficient evidence using a significance level of .05 to say that the mean of the process after the adjustment (data in column A) is less than the mean before the adjustment (data in column B).

What would you tell Allied? Did their adjustment to improve the quality of these parts produce a process having a smaller mean? They are not willing to assume the two population variances are equal. If you *were* to pool the sample variances (and assume equal population variances), would this change your conclusion?

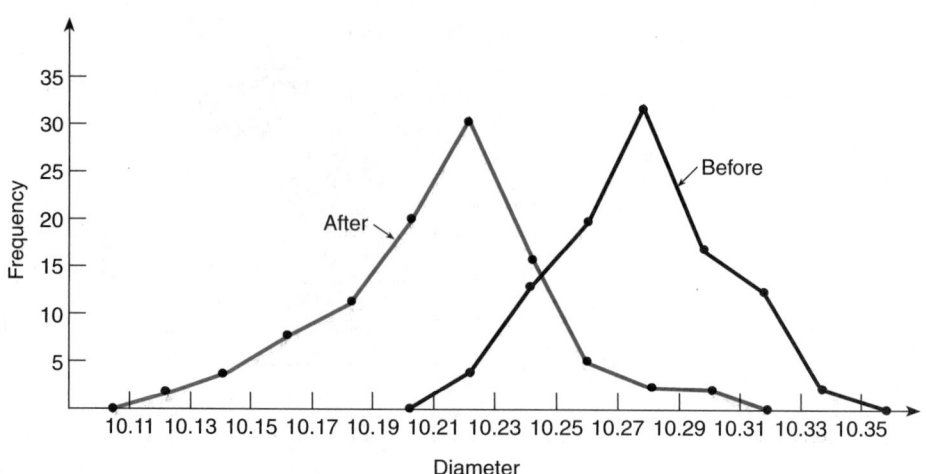

FIGURE

9.11

Frequency polygons of the two samples obtained before and after the process adjustment.

Solution

A nice way to compare the two samples is to use the sample results to construct a pair of frequency polygons, plotted in the same graph (Figure 9.11). From this graph, it is readily apparent that there was a shift in the means after the adjustment. Also, the polygon for the *after* sample is wider than the *before* polygon, indicating more variation in the process after the adjustment. To determine if the *after* sample mean is *significantly* less than the *before* sample mean, the next step is to test the hypothesis.

Letting population 1 represent the process measurements *after* the adjustment and population 2 represent the measurements *before* the adjustment, the hypotheses under investigation are

$$H_0: \mu_1 \geq \mu_2$$

$$H_a: \mu_1 < \mu_2$$

An Excel solution not assuming equal variances is shown in Figure 9.12 (cells C1:E13). The calculated t statistic in cell D9 is -15.2393 and the p-value (in cell D10) is nearly zero.* The output using the equal variances procedure is contained in cells F1:G14 and is very similar to the previous solution—namely the calculated test statistic is -15.2393, and the p-value (in cell G11) is nearly zero.

Conclusion. Due to the extremely large sample sizes, both test statistics could be very closely approximated by the standard normal (Z) statistic used in Section 9.2. As a result, whether or not you pool is not a critical issue for very large sample sizes. The p-value is nearly zero (and less than $\alpha = .05$), and so we reject H_0. There is strong evidence to indicate that the process mean after the quality-improvement adjustment is less than the mean before the adjustment.

To Pool or Not to Pool? You might think, based on the previous examples, that it really does not matter whether you assume $\sigma_1 = \sigma_2$. The two confidence intervals were nearly the same and the tests of hypothesis results were very close, dif-

---

*The value 4.98E-35 is written using *exponential notation*, which is very useful for representing very small or very large numbers. This particular value is actually 4.98, with the decimal place moved 35 places to the left—that is, a decimal point, followed by 34 zeros, followed by 498. This is a very small number (nearly zero). Also, be sure to refer to the footnote at the end of the previous section when interpreting Excel's one-tailed p-values.

FIGURE 9.12

Excel spreadsheet for solutions to Example 9.6.

Microsoft Excel - DATA9-6

After	Before	t-Test: Two-Sample Assuming Unequal Variances			t-Test: Two-Sample Assuming Equal Variances		
10.158	10.216						
10.244	10.221		After	Before		After	Before
10.202	10.226	Mean	10.21023	10.27539	Mean	10.21023	10.27539
10.206	10.228	Variance	0.001116	0.000712	Variance	0.001116	0.000712
10.257	10.230	Observations	100	100	Observations	100	100
10.149	10.230	Hypothesized Mean Difference	0		Pooled Variance	0.000914	
10.202	10.231	df	189		Hypothesized Mean Difference	0	
10.237	10.231	t Stat	-15.2393		df	198	
10.220	10.234	P(T<=t) one-tail	4.98E-35		t Stat	-15.2393	
10.223	10.237	t Critical one-tail	1.652957		P(T<=t) one-tail	1.65E-35	
10.165	10.239	P(T<=t) two-tail	9.97E-35		t Critical one-tail	1.652586	
10.166	10.239	t Critical two-tail	1.972594		P(T<=t) two-tail	3.30E-35	
10.210	10.240				t Critical two-tail	1.972016	
10.229	10.240						

DATA9-6

fering only in their df for the test statistic. However, this is not always the case. *Unless you have strong evidence that the variances are the same,* we suggest you not pool the sample variances *and use the test statistic defined in equation 9.10.* If you assume that $\sigma_1 = \sigma_2$ and use the t test statistic in equation 9.17 but in fact $\sigma_1 \neq \sigma_2$, your results can be unreliable. This test is quite sensitive to this particular assumption if the sample sizes (n_1 and n_2) are unequal. Also, if σ_1 and σ_2 *are* the same, we would expect s_1 and s_2 to be nearly the same. If, in addition, $n_1 = n_2$ (or nearly so), then the computed values of t' and t will be practically identical (including the df). What this means is that you have little to gain by pooling the variances (and using t) but a great deal to lose if your assumption is incorrect.

We will show you in the next section how to use two samples to test the hypothesis that $\sigma_1 = \sigma_2$. With those results in hand, one possible procedure to use when testing the *means* would be (1) if you reject H_0: $\sigma_1 = \sigma_2$, then use t' to test H_0: $\mu_1 = \mu_2$, and (2) if you fail to reject H_0: $\sigma_1 = \sigma_2$, then use t to test H_0: $\mu_1 = \mu_2$.

At first glance this might appear to be statistically sound, but it has some problems. The main one is that these two tests use the same data, and so the tests are not performed independently of one another. Also, your actual significance level may not be the α that you had previously chosen before you saw any data. This *can* be a valid procedure if you obtain separate samples—one to test the σ values and the other to test the μ values. Again, however, caution is in order, since the test of H_0: $\sigma_1 = \sigma_2$ is very sensitive to the assumption of normal populations, and so using small samples to carry out this test can be unreliable. Consequently, if there is reason to believe that the standard deviations might not be equal, a safe procedure is to proceed as if they were not; that is, use the t' statistic to test the means.

The next section provides a procedure for testing the standard deviations from two normal populations using independent samples. By comparing the standard deviations using separate data from the two populations, one can decide whether the pooling procedure should be used when using additional data to test μ_1 versus μ_2. If you reject H_0: $\sigma_1 = \sigma_2$, then the t' statistic in equation 9.10 is the proper test statistic to use on a test for the means because it does *not* assume that the population standard deviations are equal. On the other hand, if you fail to reject H_0, then the t statistic in equation 9.17, which *does* assume that $\sigma_1 = \sigma_2$, is the recommended test statistic for testing μ_1 versus μ_2.

SMALL-SAMPLE TESTS FOR μ_1 AND μ_2

Two-Tailed Test

$$H_0: \mu_1 - \mu_2 = D_0$$

$$H_a: \mu_1 - \mu_2 \neq D_0$$

$$(D_0 = 0 \text{ for } H_0: \mu_1 = \mu_2)$$

$$\text{reject } H_0 \text{ if } |T| > t_{\alpha/2, df}$$

where, not assuming $\sigma_1 = \sigma_2$:

$$T = t' = \frac{(\bar{X}_1 - \bar{X}_2) - D_0}{\sqrt{\dfrac{s_1^2}{n_1} + \dfrac{s_2^2}{n_2}}}$$

$$df = \frac{\left[\dfrac{s_1^2}{n_1} + \dfrac{s_2^2}{n_2}\right]^2}{\dfrac{\left(\dfrac{s_1^2}{n_1}\right)^2}{n_1 - 1} + \dfrac{\left(\dfrac{s_2^2}{n_2}\right)^2}{n_2 - 1}}$$

Or, assuming $\sigma_1 = \sigma_2$:

$$T = t = \frac{(\bar{X}_1 - \bar{X}_2) - D_0}{s_p \sqrt{\dfrac{1}{n_1} + \dfrac{1}{n_2}}}$$

$$df = n_1 + n_2 - 2$$

where

$$s_p = \sqrt{\frac{(n_1 - 1)s_1^2 + (n_2 - 1)s_2^2}{n_1 + n_2 - 2}}$$

One-Tailed Test

$H_0: \mu_1 - \mu_2 \leq D_0$	$H_0: \mu_1 - \mu_2 \geq D_0$
$H_a: \mu_1 - \mu_2 > D_0$	$H_a: \mu_1 - \mu_2 < D_0$
$(D_0 = 0 \text{ for } H_0: \mu_1 \leq \mu_2)$	$(D_0 = 0 \text{ for } H_0: \mu_1 \geq \mu_2)$
reject H_0 if $T > t_{\alpha, df}$	reject H_0 if $T < -t_{\alpha, df}$

X Exercises 9.25–9.36

Understanding the Mechanics

9.25 Independent random samples were selected from two normal populations. The following statistics were calculated.

Sample 1	Sample 2
$n_1 = 12$	$n_2 = 15$
$\bar{x}_1 = 10.0$	$\bar{x}_2 = 12.00$
$s_1 = 2.04$	$s_2 = 1.4$

a. Calculate the pooled estimate of the variance for the populations.

b. Find a 90% confidence interval for $\mu_1 - \mu_2$ using the pooled estimate of the variance for the populations.

c. Find a 90% confidence interval for $\mu_1 - \mu_2$ not assuming that the population variances are equal.

9.26 The observations below resulted from independent random samples selected from approximate normal populations.

Sample 1	Sample 2
4.5	6.5
7.0	5.4
3.1	7.8
6.2	8.1
5.8	7.9
6.1	

a. Conduct a test of hypothesis to determine if the mean of the second population is greater than the mean of the first population. Assume that the population variances are equal. Use a .05 significance level.

b. Perform the statistical test in part a, but don't assume that the population variances are equal.

Applying the New Concepts

9.27 The president of a personnel agency is interested in examining the annual mean salary differences between vice presidents of banks and vice presidents of savings and loan institutions. A random sample of eight of each kind of vice president was selected. Their annual salaries (in dollars) were as follows:

n	Banks	Savings and Loan Institutions	n	Banks	Savings and Loan Institutions
1	84,320	73,420	5	48,940	88,670
2	67,440	49,580	6	56,790	59,640
3	98,590	58,750	7	77,610	65,590
4	111,780	101,400	8	62,000	74,810

Conduct a test of hypothesis to determine if there is a significant difference in the average salary for the two vice president groups. The salaries for both groups are considered to be approximately normally distributed. Use a significance level of .05. Do not assume that the population variances are equal.

9.28 Construct a 90% confidence interval for the difference in the means of the salaries for vice presidents in the banking industry and for vice presidents of savings and loan institutions for Exercise 9.27. Do not assume that the population variances are equal.

9.29 Using the data in Exercise 9.27, test the same hypothesis, but assume that the population variances *are* equal.

9.30 The production supervisor of Dow Plast is conducting a test of the tensile strengths of two types of copper coils. The relevant data are as follows. Coil A: $\bar{x} = 118$, $s = 17$, $n = 9$. Coil B: $\bar{x} = 143$, $s = 24$, $n = 16$. The tensile strengths for the two types of copper coils are approximately normally distributed. Based on the p-value, do the data support the conclusion that the mean tensile strengths of the two coils are different at a significance level of 7%? Do not assume that the population variances are equal.

9.31 Construct a 99% confidence interval for $\mu_A - \mu_B$ in Exercise 9.30. Do not assume that the population variances are equal.

9.32 Using a pooled estimate of the variance, perform the test of hypothesis in Exercise 9.30. Compare the two answers.

9.33 Master-McNeil, Inc., a corporate product and naming firm in Berkeley, California, believes that technology companies that have words such as *cyber, link,* and *Web* in their names have had greater growth over the past year than technology companies that do not. To test this belief,

a random sample of technology companies with and without these words in their company title are sampled and their percentage growth rates in 1998 are recorded. Is there sufficient evidence to support Master-McNeil's belief using a significance level of .10? Assume equal population variances.

Growth Rate of Technology Companies with Cyber Term in the Company Name	Growth Rate of Technology Companies without Cyber Term in the Company Name
30	15
21	20
8	12
7	40
12	27
29	13
41	6
15	17
22	7
25	24

(Source: "Tired of 'Wired'," *The Wall Street Journal*, July 2, 1998, p. 1.)

Using the Computer

9.34 **[DATA SET EX9-34]** *Variable Description:*

SalaryIndustry: Annual salary in 2000 for a network planning manager working for private industry

SalaryGov: Annual salary in 2000 for a network planning manager working for the federal government

Computer network planning managers have been in hot demand for the past few years and received an average pay increase of 16% in 2000. Salaries for network planning managers average around $81,000. The income gap between information technology employees in private industry and in the government is believed to have narrowed recently. Suppose that 20 network planning managers were randomly selected from private industry and 20 were selected from the federal government. Assume that the population variances are equal.

a. Construct a 95% confidence interval for the difference in salaries for network planning managers working for private industry and for the government.

b. Use the confidence interval in part a to test that the average salary for network planning managers differs in jobs within private industry and within the government.

(Source: "Standard Raises," *Dallas Morning News*, March 25, 2001, p. 16I.)

9.35 When assuming that population variances may not be equal, the degrees of freedom for the t' statistic decrease as one of the population variances becomes much larger than the other. To understand this relationship, put a value of 10 in the first 15 rows of column A and the values 10 through 150 in increments of 10 in the first 15 rows of column B. Type the formulas presented at the top of the next page into the cells C1 through F1 and drag these down to row 15. Then plot the degrees of freedom that appear in column F with the variances that appear in column B. The graph should look like that given below. Comment on how quickly the degrees of freedom change as the variance of one group increases while the other group's variance remains constant.

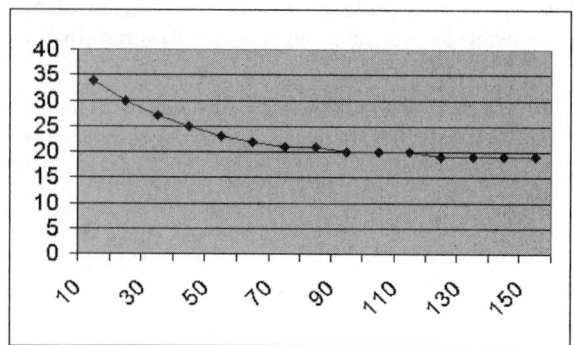

9.36 [DATA SET EX9-36] *Variable Description:*

PrivateUniv: Yearly tuition for a four-year private university in the South

PublicUniv: Yearly tuition for a four-year public university in the South

The American Council on Education claims that nationwide the average difference in tuition between four-year public universities and private universities is $11,500 per year. Suppose that a university administrator believes that the difference is less than this for universities in the South. A random sample of 15 public and 15 private four-year universities in the South is selected.

a. Construct two histograms for the yearly tuition at the selected universities in the South—one for private universities and one for public universities. Do the variances of the two data sets appear to be much different?

b. Using an appropriate t test, test that the tuition difference between private and public four-year universities in the South is less than $11,500. Use a 5% significance level.

(Source: "Why College Costs So Much," *The New York Times,* April 8, 2001, p 47L.)

9.4

COMPARING THE VARIANCES OF TWO NORMAL POPULATIONS USING INDEPENDENT SAMPLES

Once again we concentrate on independent samples from two normal populations, only this time we focus our attention on the *variation* of these populations rather than on their averages (see Figure 9.13). When estimating and testing σ_1 versus σ_2, we will not be concerned about μ_1 and μ_2. They might be equal, or they might not—it simply does not matter for this test procedure.

In business applications, you may want to compare the variation of two different production processes or compare the risk involved with two proposed investment portfolios. As mentioned previously, when testing for population *means* using small, independent samples, you must pay attention to the population standard deviations (variances). Based on your belief that σ_1 does or does not equal σ_2, you select your corresponding test statistic for testing the means, μ_1 and μ_2. As a reminder, it is *not* a safe procedure to use the *same data set* to test both $\sigma_1 = \sigma_2$ and $\mu_1 = \mu_2$. A proper procedure would be to test σ_1 and σ_2 using one set of samples (as outlined in this section) and to obtain another set of samples *independently* of the first to test the means.

In the previous section, when trying to decide if $\mu_1 = \mu_2$, we examined the *difference* between the point estimators, $\overline{X}_1 - \overline{X}_2$. If $\overline{X}_1 - \overline{X}_2$ was large enough (in absolute value), we rejected H_0: $\mu_1 = \mu_2$. When looking at the variances, we use the *ratio of the sample variances*, s_1^2 and s_2^2, to derive a test of hypothesis and construct confidence intervals. We do this because the distribution of $s_1^2 - s_2^2$ is difficult to describe mathematically, but s_1^2/s_2^2 does have a recognizable distribution when in fact σ_1^2 and σ_2^2 are equal. So we define

$$F = \frac{s_1^2}{s_2^2}$$

9.18

If you were to obtain sets of two samples repeatedly, calculate s_1^2/s_2^2 for each set, and make a histogram of these ratios, the shape of this histogram would

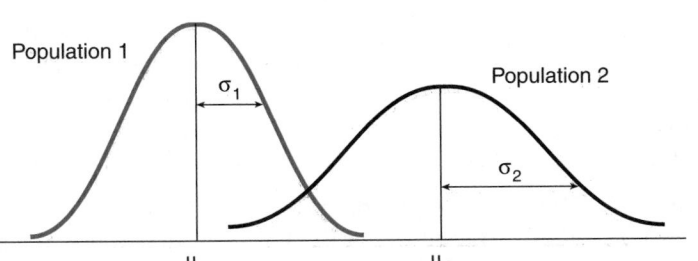

FIGURE 9.13

Compare two standard deviations. Does $\sigma_1 = \sigma_2$?

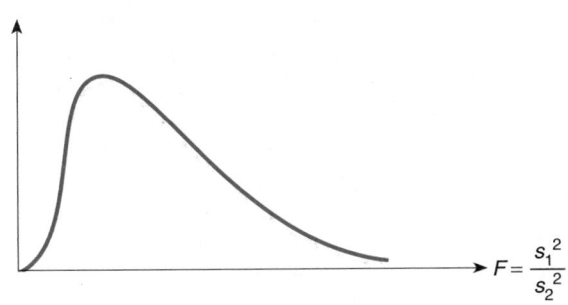

FIGURE 9.14

Shape of the F distribution.

resemble the curve in Figure 9.14, the **F distribution.** Its shape resembles the chi-square curve—it is nonsymmetric, skewed right (right-tailed), and the corresponding random variable is never negative. There are many F curves, depending on the sample sizes, n_1 and n_2. The shape of the F curve becomes more symmetric as the sample sizes, n_1 and n_2, increase. As later chapters will demonstrate, the F distribution has a large variety of applications in statistics. Right-tail areas for this random variable have been tabulated in Table A.7. As a final note here, *the F-statistic in equation 9.18 is highly sensitive to the assumption of normal populations. For larger data sets, it is recommended that you examine the shape of the sample data when using this particular F-statistic.*

When using the t and χ^2 statistics, we needed a way to specify the sample size(s) because the shapes of these curves change as the sample size changes. The same applies to the F distribution. There are two samples here, one from each population, and we need to specify *both* sample sizes. As before, we use the degrees of freedom (df) to accomplish this:

$$v_1 = \text{df for numerator} = n_1 - 1$$

$$v_2 = \text{df for denominator} = n_2 - 1$$

So, the F statistic shown in Figure 9.14 follows an F distribution with v_1 and v_2 df provided $\sigma_1^2 = \sigma_2^2$ ($\sigma_1 = \sigma_2$). What happens to F when $\sigma_1 \neq \sigma_2$? Suppose that $\sigma_1 > \sigma_2$? Then we would expect s_1 (the estimate of σ_1) to be larger than s_2 (the estimate of σ_2). We should see

$$s_1^2 > s_2^2$$

or

$$F = \frac{s_1^2}{s_2^2} > 1$$

Similarly, if $\sigma_1 < \sigma_2$, then we expect an F value < 1. We will use this reasoning to define a test of hypothesis for σ_1 versus σ_2.

Hypothesis Testing for $\sigma_1 = \sigma_2$

Does $\sigma_1 = \sigma_2$? We use the usual five-step procedure for testing a hypothesis concerning the two variances. Your choice of hypotheses is (as usual) a two-tailed test or a one-tailed test. For the two-tailed test the hypotheses are H_0: $\sigma_1 = \sigma_2$ ($\sigma_1^2 = \sigma_2^2$) and H_a: $\sigma_1 \neq \sigma_2$ ($\sigma_1^2 \neq \sigma_2^2$). For the one-tailed test the hypotheses are H_0: $\sigma_1 \leq \sigma_2$ and H_a: $\sigma_1 > \sigma_2$ [Figure 9.15a] or H_0: $\sigma_1 \geq \sigma_2$ and H_a: $\sigma_1 < \sigma_2$ [Figure 9.15b].

Finding Right-Tail F Values. Notice that the hypotheses can be written in terms of the standard deviations (σ_1 and σ_2) or the variances (σ_1^2 and σ_2^2); if $\sigma_1 > \sigma_2$, then $\sigma_1^2 > \sigma_2^2$.

Right-tail areas under an F curve are provided in Table A.7. Notice that we have a table for areas of .1 [Table A.7(a)], .05 [Table A.7(b)], .025 [Table A.7(c)], and .01 [Table A.7(d)]. These are the most commonly used values. For each table, the df for the numerator (v_1) run across the top, and the df for the denominator (v_2) run down the left margin. A portion of Table A.7(a) is shown in Table 9.1.

Suppose we want to know which F value has a right-tail area of .10 using 6 and 8 df. Let the F value whose right-tail area is a, where the df are v_1 and v_2, be

$$F_{a,v_1,v_2}$$

For example, using Table 9.1, $F_{.10,6,8} = 2.67$ (Figure 9.16).

FIGURE

9.15

Unequal population variances.

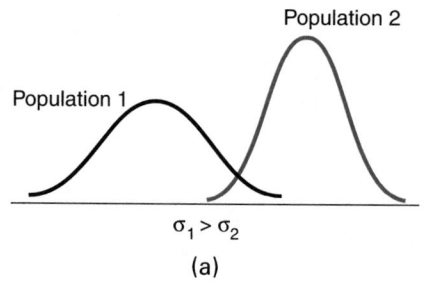
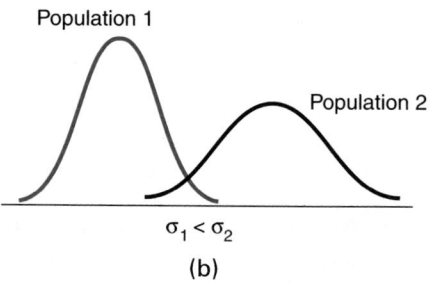

$\sigma_1 > \sigma_2$

(a)

$\sigma_1 < \sigma_2$

(b)

TABLE

9.1

Portion of F distribution table containing values with tail areas of .10 [Table A-7(a)].

V_2 \ V_1	1	2	3	4	5	6	7	8	9
1	39.86	49.50	53.59	55.83	57.24	58.20	58.91	59.44	59.86
2	8.53	9.00	9.16	9.24	9.29	9.33	9.35	9.37	9.38
3	5.54	5.46	5.39	5.34	5.31	5.28	5.27	5.25	5.24
4	4.54	4.32	4.19	4.11	4.05	4.01	3.98	3.95	3.94
5	4.06	3.78	3.62	3.52	3.45	3.40	3.37	3.34	3.32
6	3.78	3.46	3.29	3.18	3.11	3.05	3.01	2.98	2.96
7	3.59	3.26	3.07	2.96	2.88	2.83	2.78	2.75	2.72
→8	3.46	3.11	2.92	2.81	2.73	2.67	2.62	2.59	2.56
9	3.36	3.01	2.81	2.69	2.61	2.55	2.51	2.47	2.44
10	3.29	2.92	2.73	2.61	2.52	2.46	2.41	2.38	2.35

FIGURE
9.16

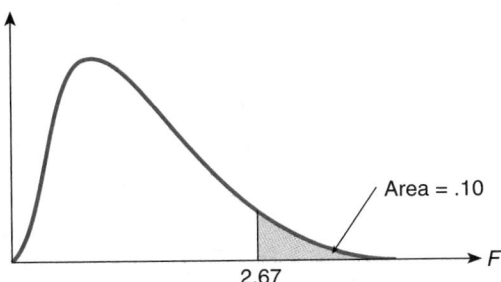

F curve with 6 and 8 df. Shaded area is the probability that F exceeds 2.67 [2.67 is from Table A.7(a)].

FIGURE
9.17

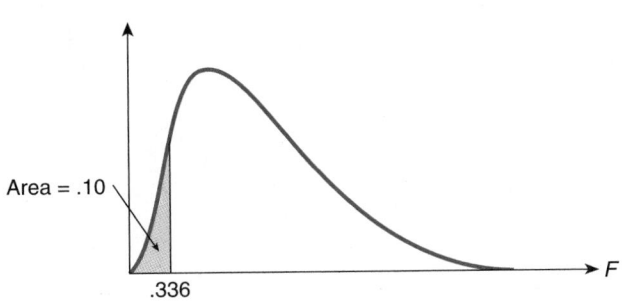

F curve with 6 and 8 df for probability that F is less than .336.

Finding Left-Tail F Values. Notice that Table A.7 contains *right-tail* values only. However, we can use the following rule to determine left-tail values:

F value (df $= v_1, v_2$) having a left-tail area of a

$$= \frac{1}{F \text{ value (df} = v_2, v_1 \text{) having a right-tail area of } a}$$

Take a look at Figure 9.17. From Figure 9.16, we know that the F value having a right-tail area of .10 is 2.67, where the df are 6 and 8. For this curve, what F value has a left-tail area equal to .10? First, you switch the df to 8 and 6. Using Table 9.1 [or Table A.7(a)], find the F value having a right-tail area = .10, where now the df are $v_1 = 8$ and $v_2 = 6$. This value is 2.98. Consequently, for the F curve with 6 and 8 df, the value having a *left*-tail area of .10 is $1/2.98 = .336$.

Since the area to the left of .336 is .10, the area to the right of this value is .90, and using the previously introduced notation we can say that

$$.336 = F_{1-.10,6,8} = F_{.9,6,8}$$

In general, we have

$$F_{1-a,v_1,v_2} = \frac{1}{F_{a,v_2,v_1}}$$

9.19

To test H_0 versus H_a, we use equation 9.18 as the test statistic. This procedure is summarized in the accompanying box.

HYPOTHESIS TESTS FOR σ_1 AND σ_2

Two-Tailed Test

$$H_0: \sigma_1 = \sigma_2$$

$$H_a: \sigma_1 \neq \sigma_2$$

$$F = \frac{s_1^2}{s_2^2}$$

Reject H_0 if $F > F_{\alpha/2, v_1, v_2}$ (right tail)

or if $F < F_{1-\alpha/2, v_1, v_2}$ (left tail)

where $v_1 = n_1 - 1$ and $v_2 = n_2 - 1$.

One-Tailed Test

$H_0: \sigma_1 \leq \sigma_2$	$H_0: \sigma_1 \geq \sigma_2$
$H_a: \sigma_1 > \sigma_2$	$H_a: \sigma_1 < \sigma_2$
$F = \dfrac{s_1^2}{s_2^2}$	$F = \dfrac{s_1^2}{s_2^2}$
Reject H_0 if $F > F_{\alpha, v_1, v_2}$	Reject H_0 if $F < F_{1-\alpha, v_1, v_2}$
where $v_1 = n_1 - 1$	where $v_1 = n_1 - 1$
and $v_2 = n_2 - 1$.	and $v_2 = n_2 - 1$.

EXAMPLE 9.7

Managers at Case Automotive Products are considering the purchase of some new equipment that will fill 1-quart containers with a recently introduced radiator additive. They have narrowed their choices of brand of filling machine to brand 1 and brand 2. Although brand 1 is considerably less expensive than brand 2, they suspect that the contents delivered by the brand 1 machine will have more variation than would be obtained using brand 2. In other words, brand 1 is more apt to slightly (or severely) overfill or underfill containers. The Case people realize that they must use a container slightly larger than 1 quart in any event, to allow for heat expansion and overfill of their product.

The Case production department was able to obtain data on the performance of both brands for a sample of 25 containers using brand 1 and 20 containers using brand 2. Using their summary information, can you confirm Case's suspicions? Use $\alpha = .05$. All mean and standard deviation measurements are in fluid ounces.

Brand 1	Brand 2
$n_1 = 25$	$n_2 = 20$
$\bar{x}_1 = 31.8$	$\bar{x}_2 = 32.1$
$s_1 = 1.21$	$s_2 = .72$

Solution **Step 1.** The purpose of the test is to determine if one standard deviation (or variance) is *larger* than the other; this calls for a one-tailed test. The suspicion is that σ_1 is larger than σ_2, so this statement is put in the alternative hypothesis. The resulting hypotheses are

$$H_0: \sigma_1 \leq \sigma_2 \qquad H_a: \sigma_1 > \sigma_2$$

Step 2. The test statistic is

$$F = \frac{s_1^2}{s_2^2}$$

Step 3. Because the df are $v_1 = 25 - 1 = 24$ and $v_2 = 20 - 1 = 19$, we find $F_{.05,24,19} = 2.11$. The test of H_0 versus H_a will be to

$$\text{reject } H_0 \text{ if } F > 2.11$$

Step 4. The computed F-value is

$$F^* = \frac{(1.21)^2}{(.72)^2} = 2.82$$

Because $2.82 > 2.11$, we reject H_0.

Step 5. On the basis of these data and this significance level, Case is correct in its belief that the variation in the containers filled by brand 1 exceeds that of the containers filled by brand 2.

Microsoft Excel Application Use DATA9-6

Using Excel to Compare Two Population Variances

E X A M P L E

9.8

In Example 9.6, we compared the means of two processes—before and after a quality improvement adjustment to reduce the process mean. Allied Manufacturing would like to use these samples strictly to compare the two population variances to determine if they differ (assuming a significance level of .10). Column A in dataset DATA9-6 contains 100 sample values obtained *after* the adjustment, and column B contains 100 sample values obtained *before* the adjustment. To obtain an Excel solution, click on **Tools ➤ Data Analysis ➤ F Test: Two-Sample for Variances.** The input screen is similar to that shown in Figure 9.8.

The resulting output is contained in Figure 9.18. The one-tailed *p*-value is .013094 and is in cell D9. Since this is a two-tailed test (H_a states that the two standard deviations differ), you will need to double this value. To do this, type "*p*-value (2-tailed)" in cell C11 and "=2*D9" in cell D11. This produces the two-tailed *p*-value of .026188 in Figure 9.18. Since the *p*-value of .026188 is less than .10, we reject H_0 and conclude that the two population (process) variances *are* different. In fact, we see a noticeable increase in the process variation after the adjustment—a concern for the quality-improvement team at Allied.

Solution

FIGURE

9.18

Excel spreadsheet for **Tools ➤ Data Analysis ➤ F Test: Two-Sample for Variances** [*p*-value (2 tailed) added].

Microsoft Excel - DATA9-6

File Edit View Insert Format Tools Data KPK Data Analysis Window Help

L1

	A	B	C	D	E	F	G	H
1	After	Before	F-Test Two-Sample for Variances					
2	10.158	10.216						
3	10.244	10.221		After	Before			
4	10.202	10.226	Mean	10.21023	10.27539			
5	10.206	10.228	Variance	0.0011164	0.0007119			
6	10.257	10.230	Observations	100	100			
7	10.149	10.230	df	99	99			
8	10.202	10.231	F	1.568194				
9	10.237	10.231	P(F<=f) one-tail	0.013094				
10	10.220	10.234	F Critical one-tail	1.29513				
11	10.223	10.237	p-value (2-tailed)	0.026188				
12	10.165	10.239						

DATA9-6

Comment

If this had been the first step in our investigation of these two processes, and additional *small* samples were to be obtained to compare the two process means, the correct procedure would be to use the t' statistic described earlier, which does not assume that σ_1 and σ_2 are equal, provided both populations are believed to be normally distributed.*

Confidence Interval for $\dfrac{\sigma_1^2}{\sigma_2^2}$

Consider an F curve with v_1 and v_2 df. To construct a 95% confidence interval for σ_1^2/σ_2^2, you proceed as you did when performing a two-tailed test of σ_1 versus σ_2, by finding both left-tailed and right-tailed F values. Let F_L and F_R denote the left- and right-tailed F values, respectively. Using equation 9.19 and Figure 9.19,

$$F_R = F_{.025,v_1,v_2} \quad \text{and} \quad F_L = \frac{1}{F_{.025,v_2,v_1}}$$

where $F_{.025,\,v_1,\,v_2}$ and $F_{.025,\,v_2,\,v_1}$ are obtained from Table A.7(c). *Remember:* Be sure to switch the df when finding the left-tailed value, F_L. The confidence interval for σ_1^2/σ_2^2 is then

$$\frac{s_1^2/s_2^2}{F_R} \quad \text{to} \quad \frac{s_1^2/s_2^2}{F_L}$$

In general, we have a $(1 - \alpha) \cdot 100\%$ confidence interval for σ_1^2/σ_2^2 (independent samples):

$$\frac{s_1^2/s_2^2}{F_R} \quad \text{to} \quad \frac{s_1^2/s_2^2}{F_L} \tag{9.20}$$

where

$$F_R = F_{\alpha/2,v_1,v_2}$$

$$F_L = \frac{1}{F_{\alpha/2,v_2,v_1}}$$

$$v_1 = n_1 - 1$$

$$v_2 = n_2 - 1$$

FIGURE

9.19

F curve with v_1 and v_2 df showing *F* values used for a 95% confidence interval.

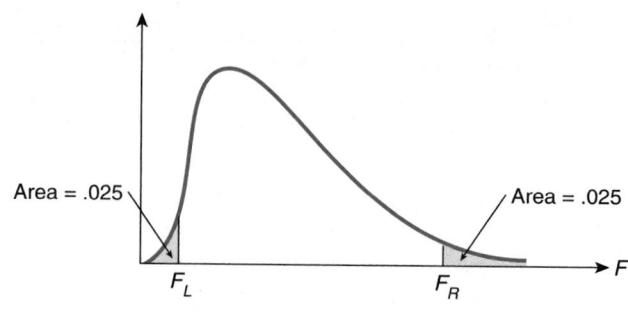

---

*Recently, attention has been given to whether this F test is an effective "screening procedure" for determining which t test is appropriate for subsequent tests of the population means. (See the article by Markowski and Markowski in *The American Statistician*, November 1990, p. 322.) In particular, when the two sample sizes are unequal, the F test tends incorrectly to fail to reject H_0: $\sigma_1 = \sigma_2$ for situations where use of the t statistic in equation 9.14 (which assumes $\sigma_1 = \sigma_2$) is *not* appropriate.

EXAMPLE 9.9

Using the Case Automotive Products data in Example 9.7, determine a 95% confidence interval for σ_1^2/σ_2^2.

Solution

Here, $n_1 = 25$, $s_1 = 1.21$, and $n_2 = 20$, $s_2 = .72$. So we need

$$F_R = F_{.025,24,19} = 2.45$$

$$F_L = \frac{1}{F_{.025,19,24}}$$

$$\approx \frac{1}{2.33} \quad (\text{using } F_{.025,20,24})$$

$$= .43$$

The 95% confidence interval for σ_1^2/σ_2^2 is

$$\frac{(1.21)^2/(.72)^2}{2.45} \quad \text{to} \quad \frac{(1.21)^2/(.72)^2}{.43} = 1.15 \quad \text{to} \quad 6.57$$

As a result, we are 95% confident that σ_1^2/σ_2^2 is between 1.15 and 6.57. This means that we are 95% confident that σ_1^2 is between 1.15 and 6.57 times as large as σ_2^2.

EXAMPLE 9.10

For the Case Automotive Products data in Example 9.7, determine a 95% confidence interval for σ_1/σ_2. Use the results of Example 9.9.

Solution

This is obtained simply by finding the *square root* of each endpoint of the confidence interval for σ_1^2/σ_2^2. Your 95% confidence interval for σ_1/σ_2 will be

$$\sqrt{1.15} \quad \text{to} \quad \sqrt{6.57} = 1.07 \quad \text{to} \quad 2.56 \text{ (fluid ounces)}$$

X   Exercises 9.37–9.46

Understanding the Mechanics

9.37 Find the rejection region for each of the following situations.
   a. $H_0: \sigma_1^2 = \sigma_2^2$ versus $H_a: \sigma_1^2 \neq \sigma_2^2$, $n_1 = 20$, $n_2 = 15$, $\alpha = .05$
   b. $H_0: \sigma_1^2 \geq \sigma_2^2$ versus $H_a: \sigma_1^2 < \sigma_2^2$, $n_1 = 5$, $n_2 = 15$, $\alpha = .10$
   c. $H_0: \sigma_1 \leq \sigma_2$ versus $H_a: \sigma_1 > \sigma_2$, $n_1 = 19$, $n_2 = 11$, $\alpha = .01$

9.38 A random sample of size 10 from population A yielded a mean and standard deviation of 45 and 2.0, respectively. A random sample of size 25 from population B yielded a mean and standard deviation of 44 and 3.0, respectively.
   a. Test that the population standard deviations differ. Use a 5% significance level.
   b. Compute a 95% confidence interval for the ratio σ_A/σ_B. Is this confidence interval consistent with the conclusion in part a?

9.39 The following data were collected from normally distributed populations. Is there evidence that the standard deviation of the second population is less than that of the first? Use a 5% significance level.

Sample 1	Sample 2
7	7
9	6
8	9
2	6
3	7

Applying the New Concepts

9.40 The Water Pollution Prevention Council (WPPC) had recommended that the discharge of industrial waste and effluents into rivers in the district should be done at a slow and steady rate of 100 pound/hour (i.e., 2,400 pound/day). Industrial plants tended to concentrate their effluent discharge activity in the night shift. The WPPC found that although companies might technically achieve an average discharge rate of 2,400 pound/day, the rivers could not cope with the erratic rate of discharge. The effluents needed to be released throughout the day, rather than all at night. It was recommended that the true variance of the discharge rate should not exceed 600. The following results were obtained from samples of 21 observations each.

Factory A: variance 585

Factory B: variance 618

At a 5% significance level, is there sufficient evidence to conclude that the variance for factory A is less than that for factory B?

9.41 A lot of investors have been reading about something called the "new-fund effect." That's the tendency of new funds to outperform their older peers because of any one of a number of factors: better access to initial public offerings, more motivated managers, or better spreads on trades. However, despite the potential growth benefits of new funds, their volatility makes many investors uncomfortable. Consider a sample of 10 newly created mid-cap mutual funds and a sample of 10 newly created small-cap mutual funds randomly selected from all mutual funds that are less than 18 months old. Is there sufficient evidence to conclude that there is a significant difference in the variance of newly created mid-cap and small-cap mutual funds? Use a .10 significance level.

Annualized Performance of New Mid-Cap Funds	Annualized Performance of New Small-Cap Funds
13.7	15.3
7.9	9.8
13.6	13.5
11.4	8.6
14.6	15.2
9.5	14.9
10.8	11.5
11.3	25.2
12.0	6.3
12.7	12.4

(Source: "Early Birds Sometimes Can Fly Higher," *Chicago Tribune,* July 3, 1998, p. 3.)

9.42 The quality-improvement department of a company that manufactures wall clocks is studying the variability of two recently developed types of wall clocks. Using the following information, test the hypothesis that $H_0: \sigma_1 = \sigma_2$, using a significance level of .05. Assume that the samples are taken from populations that are approximately normally distributed. Clock 1: $n = 25$, $s = 1.8$. Clock 2: $n = 21$, $s = 1.39$.

9.43 The Honda Insight and Toyota Prius are the only mass-built hybrid cars available in the United States. These cars are able to get 50 to 60 miles per gallon (mpg) while emitting exhaust that is 90% cleaner than traditional low-emission vehicles, and neither has to be plugged in at night to recharge its battery. Suppose that an automotive analyst believes that the standard deviation in the mpg for the Prius is greater than the standard deviation in the mpg for the Insight. Test drives on a random sample of 25 Insights and 25 Prius yielded standard deviations of 2.30 and 3.25, respectively.

a. At the 5% significance level, do the data support the analyst's belief?

b. What assumptions are necessary for the test in part a to be valid?

(Source: "CHARGING UP: When Gas Prices Rise, So Do Sales of Hybrids," *Dallas Morning News,* July 5, 2001, p. 1D.)

9.44 The following is a summary of the mean annual return ($\overline{X}$) and variance (s^2) of the annual return for common stocks in three different industries. Computer industry: $n = 16$, $\overline{x} = 14.3\%$, $s^2 = 5.6$. Steel industry: $n = 9$, $\overline{x} = 8.5\%$, $s^2 = 11.2$. Oil-and-gas industry: $n = 13$, $\overline{x} = 11.8\%$, $s^2 = 16.4$. Using these data, can we conclude that computer stocks are less risky than oil and gas stocks? Use a significance level of .05. Assume that the mean annual returns for these industries are approximately normally distributed.

Using the Computer

9.45 [DATA SET EX9-45] *Variable description:*

TraditStu: Grades in capstone MBA course for traditional students

NonTraditStu: Grades in capstone MBA course for non-traditional students

An associate dean at the University of North Texas was interested in whether the variation in scores for nontraditional students in the capstone MBA course is greater than that of the traditional student. A nontraditional student is one that has been out of school for more than 10 years. Fifty final grade scores were recorded for each of the types of students.

a. Using a 5% significance level, can the associate dean conclude that the variation in scores is greater for nontraditional students. When using Excel's **F Test: Two-Sample for Variances** procedure, make sure that the group with the larger variance is designated as the first group.

b. Subtract five points from each grade of the nontraditional student. Do you think that these new grades would affect the *F* test in part a? Try it.

9.46 [DATA SET EX9-46] *Variable description:*

FluidMach1: Amount of fluid dispensed by vending machine 1

FluidMach2: Amount of fluid dispensed by vending machine 2

The manager of a vending-machine company decided to purchase one of two types of dispensers to put in her vending machines. Both dispensers are supposed to dispense, on average, 6 ounces of fluid into a plastic cup. The amount dispensed is approximately normally distributed. However, to test this claim, the manager would first like to know whether the variability in the amount of fluid dispensed is the same for both dispensers. Random samples of 16 cups with fluid dispensed by machine 1 and 16 cups with fluid dispensed by machine 2 are selected. The number of ounces of fluid in each cup is recorded in variables FluidMach1 and FluidMach2.

a. Find a 95% confidence interval for the ratio of the variances of the amount of fluid coming from machines 1 and 2.

b. Test for a difference in the variances of the amount of fluid from machines 1 and 2 at the .05 significance level.

c. Can part a be used to test for a difference in the variances of the two machines? If so, how?

COMPARING THE MEANS OF TWO NORMAL POPULATIONS USING PAIRED SAMPLES

The final section of this chapter examines the situation in which the two samples are *not* obtained independently. All discussion up to this point has assumed that the two samples *are* independent. By not independent, we mean that the corresponding elements from the two samples are *paired*. Perhaps each pair of observations corresponds to the same city, the same week, the same married couple, or even the same person. Our discussion focuses on comparing the two population means for the situation in which two *dependent* samples are obtained from the two populations.

When attempting to estimate or test for the difference between two population means, your first question always should be, is there any natural reason to pair the first observation from sample 1 with the first observation from sample 2, the second with the second, and so on? If there is no reason to pair these data and the samples were obtained independently, the previous methods for finding confidence intervals and testing μ_1 versus μ_2 apply. If the data were gathered such that pairing the values is necessary, then it is *extremely* important that you recognize this and treat the data in a different manner. We can still determine confidence intervals and perform a test of hypothesis, but the procedure is different.

As an illustration, Metalloy manufactures metal hinges. The hardness of these hinges is tested by pressing a rod with a pointed tip into the hinge with a specified force and measuring the depth of the depression caused by the tip. Two tips are available for the hardness tester, and it is suspected that tip #1 produces higher hardness readings, on the average. To control for variation in the hardness of the hinges, it was decided to use paired samples in which *both* tips were used to test the hardness of the *same* metal hinge. The following coded data were obtained using 12 randomly selected hinges. The letter d represents the *difference* of each pair of hardness values (tip #1–tip #2).

Hinge	1	2	3	4	5	6	7	8	9	10	11	12
Tip #1	39	32	42	49	45	47	45	48	38	48	41	47
Tip #2	35	34	38	48	47	43	41	47	35	46	37	44
d	4	–2	4	1	–2	4	4	1	3	2	4	3
d^2	16	4	16	1	4	16	16	1	9	4	16	9

$$\Sigma d = 4 - 2 + 4 + \cdots + 3 = 26$$
$$\Sigma d^2 = 16 + 4 + 16 + \cdots + 9 = 112$$

Each pair of values was obtained from the same metal hinge, so these data values clearly need to be paired—they are dependent samples. It seems reasonable to examine the difference of the two values for each hinge, so these differences (d), along with the d^2 values, are also shown. We have thus reduced the problem from two sets of values to a single set. The parameter of interest here is the *difference* of the population means, μ_d. Put another way, μ_d is the **mean of the population differences.**

Since we have a single set of sample values (the 12 differences) and a single parameter (μ_d), the results of Sections 7.4 and 8.4 can be used to construct a confidence interval and perform a test of hypothesis, *provided we have reason to believe that the population differences are normally distributed.* As a result, we need not worry about large versus small samples, because we will use the t distribution for our confidence intervals and tests of hypothesis, regardless of the sample sizes. Of course, if the number of differences is large (generally, >30), this distribution is closely approximated by the standard normal distribution.

If you have reason to suspect that the population of differences is *not* normally distributed, then one alternative is to use a nonparametric procedure, in particular, the Wilcoxon signed rank test (discussed in Chapter 18).

Confidence Interval for μ_d Using Paired Samples

The statistic used to derive a confidence interval for μ_d and perform a test of hypothesis using *dependent* samples is

$$t_D = \frac{\overline{X}_1 - \overline{X}_2}{s_d/\sqrt{n}} = \frac{\overline{d}}{s_d/\sqrt{n}}$$

9.21

where

$$n = \text{the number of pairs of observations}$$

$$s_d = \text{the standard deviation of the } n \text{ differences}$$

$$= \sqrt{\frac{\sum d^2 - (\sum d)^2/n}{n-1}}$$

$$\text{df for } t_D = n-1$$

This is a *t random variable with $n-1$ df.* Notice that the numerator of t_D is the same as before, namely, $\overline{X}_1 - \overline{X}_2$, which is also represented by $\overline{d} = \sum d/n$, the mean of the differences. The mean of the differences $\overline{d}$ always is equal to $\overline{X}_1 - \overline{X}_2$ (this can help you in checking your arithmetic when computing the d's).

Based on the discussion in Section 7.4, we obtain a $(1 - \alpha) \cdot 100\%$ confidence interval for μ_d:

$$\overline{d} - t_{\alpha/2,n-1}\frac{s_d}{\sqrt{n}} \quad \text{to} \quad \overline{d} + t_{\alpha/2,n-1}\frac{s_d}{\sqrt{n}}$$

9.22

E X A M P L E

9.11

Using the hardness data, derive a 95% confidence interval for μ_d, where

$$\mu_d = \text{average difference in hardness}$$

Solution   We have

$$\overline{d} = \frac{\sum d}{n} = \frac{26}{12} = 2.167$$

Notice that

$$\overline{x}_1 = \frac{39 + 32 + \cdots + 47}{12} = 43.417$$

and

$$\overline{x}_2 = \frac{35 + 34 + \cdots + 44}{12} = 41.25$$

so $\overline{d} = \overline{x}_1 - \overline{x}_2 = 2.167$. It checks! Also,

$$s_d = \sqrt{\frac{\sum d^2 - (\sum d)^2/n}{n-1}} = \sqrt{\frac{112 - (26)^2/12}{11}}$$

$$= \sqrt{\frac{55.667}{11}} = \sqrt{5.061} = 2.250$$

The resulting 95% confidence interval for μ_d is

$$\bar{d} - t_{.025,11}\frac{s_d}{\sqrt{n}} \quad \text{to} \quad \bar{d} + t_{.025,11}\frac{s_d}{\sqrt{n}}$$

$$= 2.167 - 2.201\frac{2.250}{\sqrt{12}} \quad \text{to} \quad 2.167 + 2.201\frac{2.250}{\sqrt{12}}$$

$$= 2.167 - 1.430 \quad \text{to} \quad 2.167 + 1.430$$

$$= .737 \quad \text{to} \quad 3.597$$

Based on these data, we are 95% confident that the hardness reading using tip #1 is between .737 and 3.597 *more* than the tip #2 reading. Notice that this is quite a wide confidence interval, due to the small sample sizes.

Hypothesis Testing Using Paired Samples

The test statistic for testing the means is the same as that in Section 8.4, except that we use the sample differences.

$$t_D = \frac{\bar{d} - D_0}{s_d/\sqrt{n}}$$

9.23

where D_0 is the hypothesized value of μ_d. When testing H_0: $\mu_d = D_0$ versus H_a: $\mu_d \neq D_0$, reject H_0 if $|t_D| > t_{\alpha/2,n-1}$. Here, $t_{\alpha/2,n-1}$ is obtained from Table A.5 using $n - 1$ df. One-tailed tests are performed in a similar manner by placing α in either the right tail (H_a: $\mu_d > D_0$) or in the left tail (H_a: $\mu_d < D_0$). A summary is provided in the box on paired sample tests for μ_d and D_0 on page 396.

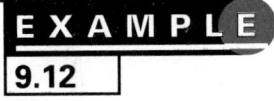

EXAMPLE

9.12

Consider the previous hardness data collected by Metalloy. Can you confirm the suspicion that the average difference in hardness readings (Tip #1–Tip #2) is positive? Use a significance level of $\alpha = .05$.

Solution

Step 1. We are attempting to demonstrate that the average difference in hardness readings is positive; this claim goes into the alternative hypothesis. The resulting hypotheses are

$$H_0: \mu_d \leq 0$$
$$H_a: \mu_d > 0$$

Step 2. We are dealing with paired data, so the correct test statistic is

$$t_D = \frac{\bar{d}}{s_d/\sqrt{n}}$$

Step 3. What happens to t_D when H_a is true? If $\mu_d > 0$, then we would expect $\bar{d}$ to be *positive*. So, the test procedure is to

reject H_0 if $t_D > k$, for some $k > 0$

What is k? As before, this depends on α, and in the usual manner, we have

reject H_0 if $t_D > t_{\alpha,n-1}$

where $t_{\alpha,n-1}$ is obtained from Table A.5. For this situation, $t_{.05,11} = 1.796$, and so we

$$\text{reject } H_0 \text{ if } t_D > 1.796$$

Step 4. Using the sample data,

$$t_D^* = \frac{2.167}{2.250/\sqrt{12}} = 3.34$$

Because $3.34 > 1.796$, we reject H_0.

Step 5. The average hardness reading using tip #1 is higher than that using tip #2.

Using Excel to Compare Means Using Paired Samples

An Excel solution to Example 9.12 is provided in Figure 9.20 (cells C1:E14). First, you must enter the 12 values for Tip #1 in cells A2:A13 and the 12 values for Tip #2 in cells B2:B13. Type "Tip #1" in cell A1 and "Tip #2" in cell B1. To obtain the output in Figure 9.20, click on **Tools ➤ Data Analysis ➤ t Test: Paired Two-Sample for Means.** The input screen is similar to that in Figure 9.8. Enter "A1:A13" for the variable 1 range and "B1:B13" for the variable 2 range. Be sure to click on the box to the left of **Labels** (since these two columns contain a label in the first row) and the (default) value of alpha should be .05. The resulting p-value (highlighted with an arrow) in cell D11 is .003318, which, using $\alpha = .05$, again results in rejecting H_0 since the p-value is less than α.

What happens if you fail to pair these observations and perform a regular two-sample t test, as we did in Section 9.3 for small, *independent* samples? The results are summarized in cells F1:H13 in Figure 9.20, where we observe an interesting result. The t value (using the test statistic from equation 9.10) now is 1.02, with a corresponding p-value of $p = .159$ (highlighted with an arrow). This means that, using this test, we now *fail to reject* H_0. We are unable to demonstrate a difference between the average hardness readings, which, according to the paired sample test, is *not* a correct conclusion. The incorrect solution in cells F1:H13 shows convincingly that failing to pair the observations when you should can cause you to obtain an incorrect result. More importantly, there is nothing to warn you that this has occurred.

FIGURE

9.20

Excel spreadsheet for **Tools ➤ Data Analysis ➤ t Test: Paired Two-Sample for Means** and **Tools ➤ Data Analysis ➤ t Test: Two-Sample Assuming Unequal Variances.**

The market research staff at Allied Foods is considering two different packaging designs for an instant breakfast cereal that Allied is about to introduce. The first type of container under consideration is a rectangular box, whereas the second container type has a cylindrical shape.

The staff decides to conduct a pilot study by placing the product in both containers and locating the two types at opposite ends of the breakfast cereal section in ten different supermarkets. All the containers are placed at eye level to remove any effect due to the height of the display. The main question under consideration is whether there is any difference in the sales of the two types of container. From the following data, can you conclude that there is a difference in sales for the rectangular and cylindrical containers? Use $\alpha = .05$ to define your test.

Supermarket	1	2	3	4	5	6	7	8	9	10
Rectangular	194	152	160	172	118	110	137	126	176	145
Cylindrical	184	161	153	184	105	123	155	111	156	129

Solution

The data were gathered by collecting a pair of observations from each supermarket, so this is a clear-cut case of dependent sampling. Your next step should be to determine the paired differences. Define d to be the rectangular box sales minus the cylindrical box sales.

Supermarket	1	2	3	4	5	6	7	8	9	10	Total
d	10	−9	7	−12	13	−13	−18	15	20	16	29
d^2	100	81	49	144	169	169	324	225	400	256	1917

Step 1. We are attempting to detect a difference in the two means: a two-tailed test is in order. Let

$$\mu_d = \text{average difference in sales for the two container types}$$

The correct hypotheses are

$$H_0: \mu_d = 0$$

$$H_a: \mu_d \neq 0$$

Steps 2, 3. Using the t_D test statistic, the test will be to

$$\text{reject } H_0 \text{ if } |t_D| > t_{\alpha/2, n-1}$$

where $t_{\alpha/2, n-1} = t_{.025,9} = 2.262$.

Step 4. Using the sample data,

$$\bar{d} = \frac{\Sigma d}{n} = \frac{29}{10} = 2.9$$

$$s_d = \sqrt{\frac{\Sigma d^2 - (\Sigma d)^2/n}{n-1}}$$

$$= \sqrt{\frac{1917 - (29)^2/10}{9}}$$

$$= \sqrt{\frac{1832.9}{9}} = 14.271$$

From these values we obtain

$$t_D^* = \frac{\bar{d}}{s_d/\sqrt{n}} = \frac{2.9}{14.271/\sqrt{10}} = .643$$

Because $.643 < 2.262$, we fail to reject H_0.

Step 5. Based on these data, there is *insufficient evidence* to conclude that the container type has an effect on sales.

PAIRED SAMPLE TESTS FOR μ_d

Two-Tailed Test

$$H_0: \mu_d = D_0$$
$$H_a: \mu_d \neq D_0$$
$$\text{reject } H_0 \text{ if } |t_D^*| > t_{\alpha/2, n-1}$$

where

1. Each difference, d, is (sample 1 value – sample 2 value)

2. $t_D = \dfrac{\bar{d} - D_0}{s_d / \sqrt{n}}$

3. $\bar{d} = \bar{X}_1 - \bar{X}_2 = \dfrac{\Sigma d}{n}$

4. $s_d = \sqrt{\dfrac{\Sigma d^2 - (\Sigma d)^2 / n}{n - 1}}$

5. df for $t_D = n - 1$

One-Tailed Test

$$H_0: \mu_d \leq D_0 \qquad\qquad H_0: \mu_d \geq D_0$$
$$H_a: \mu_d > D_0 \qquad\qquad H_a: \mu_d < D_0$$
$$\text{reject } H_0 \text{ if } t_D^* > t_{\alpha, n-1} \qquad \text{reject } H_0 \text{ if } t_D^* < -t_{\alpha, n-1}$$

X Exercises 9.47–9.56

Understanding the Mechanics

9.47 From each of two normally distributed populations, random samples were selected. The observations in the first sample are paired with the observations in the second sample. The following statistics were calculated: $\bar{x}_1 = 5.17$, $\bar{x}_2 = 3.16$, $s_d = 2.4$, $n = 13$.

a. Do the data provide sufficient evidence that the mean of population 1 is greater than the mean of population 2? Use a .05 significance level.

b. Find the p-value for the test statistic in part a.

9.48 The following data are the differences ($d = X_1 - X_2$) of pairs of observations from two normally distributed populations. Is there sufficient evidence to conclude that the mean of the first population is greater than the mean of the second population? Use a 5% significance level.

Pairs	1	2	3	4	5	6	7	8	9	10
d	10	–7	7	–10	13	–9	–18	15	20	16

9.49 Ten individuals were timed on two separate tasks. The times are as follows.

Person	Time for Task 1	Time for Task 2
1	10	6
2	12	14
3	15	10
4	13	11
5	14	16
6	15	11

Person	Time for Task 1	Time for Task 2
7	16	12
8	12	11
9	18	15
10	13	11

a. Construct a 90% confidence interval for the difference in the means of the times for the two tasks.

b. Do the data support the conclusion that the means of the times for the two tasks differ? Use a 10% significance level.

Applying the New Concepts

9.50 The controller of a fast-food chain is interested in determining whether there is any difference in the weekly sales of restaurant 1 and restaurant 2. The weekly sales are approximately normally distributed. The sales, in dollars, for seven randomly selected weeks are:

Week	Restaurant 1	Restaurant 2
1	4100	3800
2	1800	4600
3	2200	5100
4	3400	3050
5	3100	2800
6	1100	1950
7	2200	3400

a. Should this problem be analyzed using an independent or dependent sample t statistic?

b. Using a significance level of .01, is there evidence to support the conclusion that there is a significant difference in the weekly sales of the two restaurants?

9.51 China's one-child policy, which limits most families to one baby to restrict population growth, seems to be making parents and grandparents in China willing to spend a larger portion of their disposable income on their children. Walt Disney Co. has been selling the Disney Babies line of T-shirts since 1993 in China. Suppose that a market analyst believes that these T-shirts sell for $7.00 (dollar equivalent to the Chinese yuan) more than a local children's T-shirt. Suppose that 25 retail stores were randomly sampled in Shanghai and at each store, the price of a Disney T-shirt and the price of a local children's T-shirt were recorded. If the mean difference was $9.50 with a standard deviation of the differences, s_d, equal to $2.80, is there sufficient evidence to support the marketing analyst's belief? Use a significance level of .01.

(Source: "Chinese Babies Are Coveted Consumers," *The Wall Street Journal*, May 15, 1998, p. B1.)

9.52 A *Washington Post* survey of the 100 largest publicly traded companies in the D.C. area showed that the average salary of chief executives was $405,900 in 2000, up 13% from 1999. However, the average bonus increased 22.4% to $200,087. In 2001, the average bonus was believed not to have increased. Suppose that 10 chief executives were randomly selected and the following bonuses were recorded.

Chief Executive Officer	Bonus in 2000 (in thousands)	Bonus in 2001 (in thousands)
1	195	196
2	183	160
3	208	220
4	190	195
5	220	200
6	235	250
7	175	180
8	150	145
9	245	240
10	210	230

a. Construct a 90% confidence interval on the average difference in the bonuses for the years 2000 and 2001. Interpret this interval.

b. Use part a to test that there is a difference in the average bonuses for the years 2000 and 2001. Use a 10% significance level.

(Source: "How Washington's Corporate Elite Stack Up," *The Washington Post*, July 16, 2001, p. E1.)

9.53 Some stock market analysts have speculated that parts of a large Fortune 500 communications company might be worth more than the whole. For example, the company's communication systems serving dense business centers (such as Minneapolis and Seattle) could be sold to other communications companies. However, regulatory hurdles make these transactions difficult to assess financially. Suppose that a stock market analyst randomly sampled 10 acquisition experts and asked each to predict the return (in percent) on an investment in this communications company held to the year 2003 if (1) it does business as usual and keeps all its assets, and (2) if it breaks up its communication systems and sells all its parts.

Acquisition Expert	Return on Investment If Company Does Not Break Up	Return on Investment If Company Breaks Up
1	12.5	18.6
2	15.7	13.0
3	16.8	17.5
4	20.1	23.0
5	16.0	18.5
6	20.0	17.0
7	17.0	18.0
8	21.0	21.0
9	22.0	23.0
10	18.0	20.0

	Company Does Not Break Up	Company Breaks Up
Mean	17.91	18.96
Variance	8.37	8.96
Observations	10	10
Pearson's correlation	0.59	
Hypothesized mean difference	0.00	
df	9	
t Stat	−1.25	
$P(T<=t)$ one-tail	0.12	
t Critical one-tail	1.83	
$P(T<=t)$ two-tail	0.24	
t Critical two-tail	2.26	

a. Is there sufficient evidence to conclude that acquisition analysts believe that the return on investment in this communications company is greater if the company breaks up? Use a .10 significance level.

b. What assumptions are necessary to justify the use of the test procedure in part a?

c. How would the data have to be sampled to test the hypothesis in part a using a t test with independent samples?

Using the Computer

9.54 **[DATA SET EX9-54]** *Variable Description:*

District: Forty school districts in North Texas

Graduates2001: Number of high school graduates in the year 2001

Graduates2000: Number of high school graduates in the year 2000

The number of high school graduates in North Texas has shown an increase in the year 2001, thanks to efforts by educational counselors to keep high school students in school. Suppose educational researchers believe that, on average, the school districts have 30 more high school graduates in the year 2001 than in 2000.

a. Using a random sample of 40 school districts in North Texas, do the data indicate that the increase in the number of high school graduates differs from 30? What is the *p*-value? Would you reject the null hypothesis at the 10% significance level? At the 5% level? At the 1% level?

b. A *t* test for independent samples would not be valid to use in testing the hypothesis in part a. Why? Perform the hypothesis test using a *t* test for independent samples, assuming unequal variances to test this hypothesis. Compare the *p*-value for this test with the *p*-value obtained in part a.

(Source: "High School Attrition," *Dallas Morning News*, May 20, 2001, p. 17A.)

9.55 [DATA SET EX9-55] *Variable description:*

PercentReworkPrior: Percent of materials that need rework prior to using quality control charts

PercentReworkPost: Percent of materials that need rework after use of quality control charts is implemented

The vice president of a manufacturing firm wishs to determine if the implementation of quality control charts at assembly lines will decrease the amount of rework required at each of the assembly lines. There are 35 assembly lines that the vice president selects randomly from plants at various locations. The percent of rework during the month prior to requiring workers to use control charts and the percent of rework afterward is recorded as a percent for variables PercentReworkPrior and PercentReworkPost, respectively.

a. Put PercentReworkPost–PercentReworkPrior in a separate column. Using a one population *t* statistic, test that the mean difference is less than zero. Use a 1% significance level.

b. Use the *t* statistic for paired samples to test that PercentReworkPost is less than PercentReworkPrior. Use a 1% significance level.

c. What similarities do you notice in the analyses in parts a and b?

d. What assumptions are necessary for the analysis in part b to be valid?

e. Do a "what if" analysis by eliminating any pair that has a percentage of rework above 10%. How do the conclusions to part b change?

9.56 [DATA SET EX9-56] *Variable description:*

ThisyearSales: Annual sales of retail stores with advertising on cable channels

LastyearSales: Annual sales of retail stores without advertising on cable channels

Cable television has allowed local retail stores to advertise on certain cable channels. A random sample of 40 retail stores that advertised this year but did not advertise last year was selected. The annual sales were recorded in units of thousands of dollars under the variable names ThisyearSales and LastyearSales.

a. Is there enough evidence to infer at the 5% significance level that the mean sales from this year is greater than the mean sales for last year for retail stores that started advertising on cable this year?

b. Can you say that advertising on cable channels increased the sales of the local retail stores? Could anything else possibly cause this increase? What assumptions need to hold to say that the effect of advertising on cable had a significant positive effect on sales?

c. Do a "what if" analysis by subtracting $15 thousand from the sales of each of the sales in ThisyearSales. Repeat part a. What conclusion do you get?

Summary

This chapter has presented an introduction to **statistical inference for two populations.** We examined tests of hypothesis and confidence intervals for the means and variances (for example, whether they are equal) of two populations, using both **independent** and **dependent samples.**

When we used large *independent samples* to test the population means, we defined a test statistic having approximately a standard normal distribution, and we also used this test statistic to define a confidence interval for $\mu_1 - \mu_2$. For small independent samples ($n_1 < 30$ or $n_2 < 30$), hypothesis testing on μ_1 versus μ_2 is concerned with means from two normal populations. For this situation, although we are concerned with the means, we must pay special attention to whether we also have reason to believe that the population standard deviations (σ_1 and σ_2) are equal.

If we do not assume that the σ values are equal, we use a test statistic for μ_1 versus μ_2 having an *approximate t* distribution. This statistic also results in an approximate confidence interval for $\mu_1 - \mu_2$. If we assume that the σ values are equal, we use a procedure that **pools the sample variances** and results

in a test statistic having an *exact t* distribution. We also derived a confidence interval for $\mu_1 - \mu_2$ for this situation.

To determine whether two population variances (or standard deviations) are the same, we introduced the **F distribution.** This distribution is nonsymmetric (right skew) and assumes that two independent samples were obtained from normal populations. Probabilities (areas under the curve) for the *F* random variable are contained in Table A.7. Using this distribution, we can perform two-tailed tests (such as H_a: $\sigma_1 \neq \sigma_2$) or one-tailed tests (such as H_a: $\sigma_1 > \sigma_2$) on the two standard deviations. We also use it to construct a confidence interval for σ_1^2/σ_2^2 or σ_1/σ_2.

When two samples are obtained such that corresponding observations are paired (matched), the resulting samples are **dependent,** or **paired.** When using two such samples, we defined a *t* statistic to test the **mean of the population differences,** μ_d, and to construct a confidence interval for μ_d. We need not be concerned about whether the population standard deviations are equal for this situation because the test statistic uses the differences between the paired observations, a new variable.

Summary of Formulas

Large Independent Samples

1. Confidence interval for $\mu_1 - \mu_2$ (σ_1, σ_2 known):

$$(\overline{X}_1 - \overline{X}_2) \pm Z_{\alpha/2} \sqrt{\frac{\sigma_1^2}{n_1} + \frac{\sigma_2^2}{n_2}}$$

2. Confidence interval for $\mu_1 - \mu_2$ (σ_1, σ_2 unknown):

$$(\overline{X}_1 - \overline{X}_2) \pm Z_{\alpha/2} \sqrt{\frac{s_1^2}{n_1} + \frac{s_2^2}{n_2}}$$

3. Hypothesis testing for μ_1 and μ_2: Test statistic is

$$Z = \frac{(\overline{X}_1 - \overline{X}_2) - D_0}{\sqrt{\frac{\sigma_1^2}{n_1} + \frac{\sigma_2^2}{n_2}}} \approx \frac{(\overline{X}_1 - \overline{X}_2) - D_0}{\sqrt{\frac{s_1^2}{n_1} + \frac{s_2^2}{n_2}}}$$

where D_0 is the hypothesized value of $\mu_1 - \mu_2$.

Sample Sizes (Minimizing $n = n_1 + n_2$)

$$n_1 = \frac{Z_{\alpha/2}^2 s_1 (s_1 + s_2)}{E^2}$$

$$n_2 = \frac{Z_{\alpha/2}^2 s_2 (s_1 + s_2)}{E^2}$$

Small, Independent Samples

1. Confidence interval for $\mu_1 - \mu_2$ (not assuming $\sigma_1 = \sigma_2$):

$$(\overline{X}_1 - \overline{X}_2) \pm t_{\alpha/2,df} \sqrt{\frac{s_1^2}{n_1} + \frac{s_2^2}{n_2}}$$

where

$$df = \frac{\left[\frac{s_1^2}{n_1} + \frac{s_2^2}{n_2}\right]^2}{\frac{\left(\frac{s_1^2}{n_1}\right)^2}{n_1 - 1} + \frac{\left(\frac{s_2^2}{n_2}\right)^2}{n_2 - 1}}$$

2. Confidence interval for $\mu_1 - \mu_2$ (assuming $\sigma_1 = \sigma_2$):

$$(\overline{X}_1 - \overline{X}_2) \pm t_{\alpha/2,df} \sqrt{\frac{s_p^2}{n_1} + \frac{s_p^2}{n_2}}$$

where

$$df = n_1 + n_2 - 2$$

and

$$s_p^2 = \frac{(n_1 - 1)s_1^2 + (n_2 - 1)s_2^2}{n_1 + n_2 - 2}$$

3. Hypothesis testing for μ_1 and μ_2 (not assuming $\sigma_1 = \sigma_2$): Test statistic is

$$t' = \frac{(\overline{X}_1 - \overline{X}_2) - D_0}{\sqrt{\frac{s_1^2}{n_1} + \frac{s_2^2}{n_2}}}$$

where D_0 is the hypothesized value of $\mu_1 - \mu_2$ and

$$df = \frac{\left[\frac{s_1^2}{n_1} + \frac{s_2^2}{n_2}\right]^2}{\frac{\left(\frac{s_1^2}{n_1}\right)^2}{n_1 - 1} + \frac{\left(\frac{s_2^2}{n_2}\right)^2}{n_2 - 1}}$$

4. Hypothesis testing for μ_1 and μ_2 (assuming $\sigma_1 = \sigma_2$): Test statistic is

$$t = \frac{(\overline{X}_1 - \overline{X}_2) - D_0}{s_p \sqrt{\frac{1}{n_1} + \frac{1}{n_2}}}$$

where

$$df = n_1 + n_2 - 2$$

and

$$s_p = \sqrt{\frac{(n_1 - 1)s_1^2 + (n_2 - 1)s_2^2}{n_1 + n_2 - 2}}$$

Comparing Variances (or Standard Deviations)

1. Confidence interval for σ_1^2 / σ_2^2:

$$\frac{s_1^2 / s_2^2}{F_R} \quad \text{to} \quad \frac{s_1^2 / s_2^2}{F_L}$$

where $F_R = F_{\alpha/2, v_1, v_2}$, $F_L = 1/F_{\alpha/2, v_2, v_1}$, $v_1 = n_1 - 1$, and $v_2 = n_2 - 1$.

2. Hypothesis testing for σ_1^2 / σ_2^2: Test statistic is

$$F = \frac{s_1^2}{s_2^2}$$

Dependent (Paired) Samples

1. Confidence interval for μ_d:

$$\overline{d} \pm t_{\alpha/2, n-1} \frac{s_d}{\sqrt{n}}$$

(continued)

where

n = number of paired observations

$\bar{d}$ = average of n differences

s_d = standard deviation of n differences

2. Hypothesis testing for μ_d: Test statistic is

$$t_D = \frac{\bar{d} - D_0}{s_d/\sqrt{n}} \quad (\text{df} = n - 1)$$

where D_0 is the hypothesized value of μ_d.

[X] Review Exercises 9.57–9.72

9.57 Independent random samples are selected from two normally distributed populations. Determine the value of the test statistic and the p-value from the hypothesis test in each of the following cases.

    a. $H_0: \mu_1 - \mu_2 = 0$, $H_a: \mu_1 - \mu_2 \neq 0$, $n_1 = 64$, $n_2 = 38$, $\bar{x}_1 = 5.6$, $\bar{x}_2 = 6.9$, $s_1 = 48$, $s_2 = 17$

    b. $H_0: \mu_1 - \mu_2 \leq 90$, $H_a: \mu_1 - \mu_2 > 90$, $n_1 = 24$, $n_2 = 26$, $\bar{x}_1 = 180$, $\bar{x}_2 = 80$, $s_1 = 24$, $s_2 = 20$

    c. $H_0: \mu_1 - \mu_2 \geq 203$, $H_a: \mu_1 - \mu_2 < 203$, $n_1 = 100$, $n_2 = 100$, $\bar{x}_1 = 525$, $\bar{x}_2 = 325$, $s_1 = 450$, $s_2 = 165$

9.58 A sandwich shop wishes to test the effectiveness of its coupons. The manager believes that the business brought in by the responses to the coupon in the *Highland Village Daily* is equal to the business brought in by the responses to the coupon placed in the *Green Sheet*. The amount spent by each customer using a coupon is recorded (in dollars) and can be considered to be normally distributed. Test the manager's belief with a significance level of .01. *Highland Village Daily*: $n = 32$, $\bar{x} = 9.50$, $s = 26.3$. *Green Sheet*: $n = 39$, $\bar{x} = 11.80$ $s = 29.4$.

9.59 Dairy Castle wanted to boost the sales of their "Country Baskets." They thought that it might be helpful to hang posters that picture the item. They recorded the number of Country Baskets sold during lunchtime for one week at their various stores. They repeated the sampling for another week when the poster advertising was used. Assume that weekly sales are normally distributed. Is there sufficient evidence to say that hanging the posters improved sales of the Country Baskets? Use a .05 significance level.

Store	Before	After	Store	Before	After
1218	215	240	1270	201	220
1224	180	220	1282	207	215
1236	150	190	1292	195	219
1252	180	175	1304	180	195

9.60 For the 12 months ending July 1, 1998, many mutual funds that invested overseas performed very well. Suppose that a financial analyst would like to determine if the performance by global funds (funds investing anywhere in the world) and international funds (funds investing outside of the United States) differed during this period of time. Consider 10 mutual funds randomly selected from the global funds and eight mutual funds randomly selected from the international funds. The financial analyst would like to test that global funds have outperformed international funds during this period.

Global Funds	Performance	International Funds	Performance
Janus Worldwide	26.36	GAM Intl.	26.51
GAM:Global	32.18	First Amer: Intl	26.95
Gabelli Couch Potato	47.79	Driehaus: Intl Gro.	31.56
Warb Pincus GI	26.38	Waddel&Reed:Intl	37.03
Montgomery:GI Opp	27.15	United Intl Growth	34.50
Phoenix Worldwide	31.45	Amer Cent: TC Intl	25.75
Forum:Austin GLBL	28.75	BJB:Intl Equity	25.99
Dreyfus Prem WW	27.31	BEA Intl Equity	26.12
IDDA GL Val.	41.2		
Righttime Gr.	69.7		

t Test: Two-Sample Assuming Equal Variances

	Global	International
Mean	35.827	29.30125
Variance	192.0672011	19.83972679

*t*Test: Two-Sample Assuming Equal Variances (*continued*)

	Global	International
Observations	10	8
Pooled variance	116.7176811	
Hypothesized mean difference	0	
df	16	
t Stat	1.273417599	
P(*T*<=*t*) one-tail	0.110530042	
t Critical one-tail	1.745884219	
P(*T*<=*t*) two-tail	0.221060084	
Critical two-tail	2.119904821	

a. What conclusion can the financial analyst state from the statistical analysis using a two-sample *t* test assuming equal variances if the significance level is .10?

b. Do you think that the conclusion would change if you used the two-sample *t* test not assuming equal population variances? Try it.

(Source: "Top-Performing Funds in Selected Sectors," *The Wall Street Journal,* July 6, 1998, p. R18.)

9.61. Advertisers examine the average age of viewers of TV programs. For example, *60 Minutes* reportedly has one of the highest average ages at 57. Suppose that a marketing analyst believes that the age gap between *60 Minutes* and *Star Trek: Voyager* has narrowed to less than the historical 15 years. A random sample of 100 viewers from each of the TV programs was selected and the results are as follows.

	60 Minutes	**Star Trek: Voyager**
Sample mean	55.6	41.8
Sample standard deviation	10.8	7.9
Sample size	100	100

a. Construct a 99% confidence interval on the difference of the average ages for the viewers of the two TV programs. How can you interpret this interval?

b. Test the hypothesis that the difference in the average age of viewers for these two programs is less than 15 years. Use a significance level of 1%.

c. Why can you not use the confidence interval in part a to test the hypothesis in part b?

(Source: "Too Old for Your Favorite Show? Viewer Median Age of Prime-Time," *The Washington Post,* January 3, 2000, p. 07.)

9.62 In 1998, companies in South Korea struggled to survive the contracting economy. Many of these companies fell further behind in meeting their payrolls, adding to labor unrest. South Korea's Ministry of Labor said that total unpaid wages more than tripled in the first six months of 1998. Policy makers worried that rising labor unrest could derail economic overhaul in Korea. A labor dispute in Korea is defined as labor unrest that interrupts work for a day or more at a time. Suppose that a labor commission would like to test the hypothesis that the average number of labor disputes per company exceeds the number of labor disputes from a year ago by at least four. A random sample of 19 companies and their number of labor disputes in 1997 and in 1998 are recorded below. At the .05 significance level, what conclusion can the labor commission state from the analysis presented below.

*t*Test: Paired Two Sample for Means

	Number of Disputes in 1998	**Number of Disputes in 1997**
Mean	9.842	3.632
Variance	12.918	4.579
Observations	19	19
Pearson correlation	−0.073	
Hypothesized mean difference	4.000	
df	18	
t Stat	2.233	
P(*T*<=*t*) one-tail	0.019	
t Critical one-tail	1.734	
P(*T*<=*t*) two-tail	0.038	
t Critical two-tail	2.101	

(Source: "South Korean Paychecks, Patience Vanish," *The Wall Street Journal,* July 6, 1998, p. A12.)

9.63 Analysis of real estate volatility, both in the United States and the United Kingdom, suggests that it is indeed less volatile than stocks or bonds. But in both markets, it under-performs. Robin Goodchild, research director of a European pension fund, randomly sampled 21 funds from each of three types of portfolios: one for real estate ventures, one for strictly bonds, and one with large-cap stocks. The standard deviation was recorded for each: .2 percent for real estate, .6 percent for bonds, and .8 percent for large-cap stocks.

 a. What is a 95% confidence interval for the ratio of the standard deviation of the large-cap stock portfolio to the standard deviation of the real estate portfolio?

 b. What is a 95% confidence interval for the ratio of the standard deviation of the bond portfolio to that of the real estate portfolio?

 c. Compare and interpret the confidence intervals in parts a and b.

(Source: "An Asset Apart," *London Financial Times,* May 29, 1998, p. 13.)

9.64 The U.S. Bureau of Labor Statistics completed a wage study and found that in Houston, union-represented employees earn significantly more than nonunion employees. Overall in 1999, union employees earned an average hourly wage of $19.55, compared with nonunion employees, who received an average of $17.22. Suppose that the U.S. Bureau of Labor Statistics wanted to update its study in 2002 and select a random sample of nonunion and union employees from the Houston area to compute a 99% confidence interval for the average difference in salaries for union and nonunion workers with a margin of error of one dollar. Assume that the standard deviations for salaries for union and nonunion employees are $3.00 and $2.75, respectively. What sample sizes should the U.S. Bureau of Labor Statistics use in updating their study?

(Source: "Fact of Work Life: Unions Pay Higher," *The Houston Chronicle,* December 3, 1999, p. 1A.)

9.65 A new packaging method that is proposed has an average output yield of finished units approximately the same as the existing packaging method. This new packaging method will be adopted if the variability in the number of finished units is less, thus providing greater process control. At a .05 significance level, is there sufficient evidence to conclude that the variance of the number of finished units is less for the new packaging method.

	Existing Packaging Method	**New Packaging Method**
Days sampled	9	9
s^2	1190	465

9.66 Determine which of the following sets of hypotheses are equivalent.

 a. $H_0: \sigma_1^2/\sigma_2^2 \leq 1$ and $H_a: \sigma_1^2/\sigma_2^2 > 1$

 b. $H_0: \sigma_2^2/\sigma_1^2 \geq 1$ and $H_a: \sigma_2^2/\sigma_1^2 < 1$

 c. $H_0: \sigma_2^2 \geq \sigma_1^2$ and $H_a: \sigma_2^2 < \sigma_1^2$

 d. $H_0: \sigma_1 \leq \sigma_2$ and $H_a: \sigma_1 > \sigma_2$

9.67 A study is designed to determine the effect of an office-training course on typing productivity. Ten typists are randomly selected and are asked to type 15 pages of equally difficult text before and after completing the training course. Their productivity is measured by the total number of errors made.

Typist	Before	After	Typist	Before	After
1	30	27	6	33	31
2	19	14	7	28	22
3	36	31	8	30	25
4	42	37	9	27	30
5	35	29	10	34	33

Assume that the total number of errors can be approximated by a normal distribution. Test the claim that taking the office-training course leads to a reduction in the average number of errors made by a typist. Use a significance level of .05.

9.68 Suppose that a sample of size 16 is chosen from population 1 and a sample of size 26 is drawn from population 2. Assume that both populations are normally distributed. If a 90% confidence interval for the ratio of the variance of population 1 to the variance of population 2 is .367 to 1.753, what is the point estimate of the ratio of the two population variances?

9.69 Government auditors say that up to 15% of Medicare's $22.7 billion in annual payments to the nursing home industry is wasted or fraudulent. About 1.5 million Americans live in nursing homes. Spending on long-term elderly care approaches $100 billion a year. In addition to Medicare, many patients receive state Medicaid benefits, which can finance as much as a third of the expense. To trim the cost of Medicare, effective July 1998, Medicare payments to the nursing home industry have a cap. Suppose that a social worker is interested in the percentage of nursing home expense paid by the individuals in nursing homes and the percentage paid by Medicare. A random sample of 20 patients living in nursing homes was obtained and the percentages paid by the patient and by Medicare are recorded. The results are presented below. Data are presented in units of percent.

Patient	Percentage Paid by Patient	Percentage Paid by Medicare
1	40	45
2	33	35
3	32	43
4	45	42
5	43	34
6	38	45
7	43	32
8	41	46
9	40	33
10	46	32
11	34	40
12	35	38
13	45	32
14	43	31
15	43	40
16	41	36
17	31	41
18	42	32
19	48	30
20	40	39

t Test: Paired Two Sample for Means

	Paid by Patient	Paid by Medicare
Mean	40.15	37.3
Variance	23.71315789	27.48421053
Observations	20	20
Pearson correlation	−0.476029648	
Hypothesized mean difference	0	
df	19	
t Stat	1.466826723	
$P(T<=t)$ one-tail	0.079390254	
t Critical one-tail	1.729131327	
$P(T<=t)$ two-tail	0.158780509	
t Critical two-tail	2.093024705	

a. Is there sufficient evidence to support that the amount paid by the patient on a nursing home is more than that paid by Medicare? Use a .10 significance level.

b. If patient 10 is removed from the data, how will the analysis change? Rerun the paired *t* test with this observation omitted.

(Adapted from "Medicare Cap Set for Nursing Homes," *USA Today*, July 1, 1998, p. B1.)

9.70 **[DATA SET EX9-70]** *Variable Description:*

Connecticut: Location of home in Connecticut

ConnPrice: Price of advertised home

Florida: Location of home in Florida

FlaPrice: Price of advertised home

Real estate along Connecticut's gold coast is at an all-time high, primarily due to new media, telecom, and financial services industries that have fueled a lot of growth. Many retirees from the Connecticut region move to Florida to enjoy their retirement years away from the hustle and bustle of the northeast. A real estate broker in Connecticut is interested in examining the difference in the price of homes advertised in *The Wall Street Journal*. The broker believes that Connecticut homes advertised in the journal exceed the price of Florida homes by more than $500,000. A random sample of 17 advertised homes from Connecticut and 17 from Florida were selected from *The Wall Street Journal.*

a. Test the broker's belief that the advertised homes from Connecticut exceed the price of the advertised homes from Florida by more than $500,000. Use a significance level of 10% and assume that the populations have equal variances.

b. Construct a 90% confidence interval for the difference of the price of advertised homes in Connecticut and in Florida. Can you use this confidence interval to answer part a? Why?

(Source: "Distinctive Properties & Estates," *The Wall Street Journal,* June 22, 2001, p. W15B.)

9.71 [DATA SET EX9–71] *Variable Description:*

Person: Number representing the person responding

BeforeDemonstration: Rating before viewing demonstration on paying bills online

AfterDemonstration: Rating after viewing demonstration on paying bills online

Josephine Muzzuca, a research analyst at Gallup's Toronto office, said that a Gallup poll of Canadian adults revealed that a quarter of those surveyed currently pay bills online, but that 41% would be more likely to use e-billing if their privacy could be assured. She noted that automated teller machines (ATMs) are now very close to face-to-face interaction with a teller in terms of privacy assurance, and that few people would even stop to consider their privacy before doing their banking at an ATM. Suppose she believes that bank customers would be more willing to pay online if they were given a demonstration at a bank that explains what happens to the information they provide. To test this belief, she randomly samples 30 individuals who are scheduled to attend a demonstration. She asks that they respond on a scale from 1 to 10 on how comfortable they feel about paying bills online (with 10 representing a completely comfortable feeling about paying online). From each participant, she collected a rating on this scale before and after the demonstration. She believes that an individual's rating after the demonstration will be more than two points higher than the individual's rating before viewing the demonstration.

    a. Test the research analyst's belief using a 5% significance level. Would the results of your conclusion change at the 1% significance level?

    b. Construct a 95% confidence interval on the difference of the ratings before and after the demonstration. Also, construct a 99% confidence interval. Can you use these confidence intervals to answer part a? Why?

(Source: "Gallup Poll Reveals Privacy Biggest Problem for E-billing," *Computer Dealer News,* vol. 17, no. 3, p. 12.)

9.72 [DATA SET EX9-72] *Variable Description:*

DallasGasDecrease: The amount in cents that gas prices in Dallas decreased from spring to autumn of 2001

WacoGasDecrease: The amount in cents that gas prices in Waco decreased from spring to autumn of 2001

Nationally, the average price for a gallon of unleaded gasoline was $1.476 at the end of September 2001, compared to a high of $1.718 set in the spring. In Texas, gas averaged $1.381 at the end of September 2001, compared with a high of $1.611 in the spring. In Dallas, the price of gasoline tends to be more variable than in the smaller cities outside of Dallas. Random samples of 50 gas stations in Dallas and 15 gas stations in Waco were selected, and the decrease in gasoline prices from spring to autumn was recorded.

    a. Test that the standard deviation of the decrease in the price of gasoline in Dallas differs from that in Waco. Use a 5% significance level.

    b. Test whether the decrease in the price of gasoline in Dallas differs from the decrease in the price of gasoline at gas pumps in Waco. Use a 5% significance level.

    c. Did you assume equal variances for the populations in part b? Why?

    d. Would the conclusion change if you changed your answer to part c?

(Source: "As Autumn Breaks, Gas Prices Set to Fall $1 a Gallon Possible for Some Markets, Analyst Predicts," *Dallas Morning News,* September 29, 2001, p. 1A.)

Computer Exercises Using the Databases

Exercise 1—Appendix F

Choose at random 10 observations from the database in which the family owns their home and 10 observations in which the family rents their home. (Refer to the variable OWNORENT.) Do the data support the conclusion that the home payment for homeowners is larger than the home payment for renters? Use a .05 significance level. What assumptions are necessary to ensure that the test procedure is valid? Do not assume equal population variances.

Exercise 2—Appendix F

Choose at random 10 observations from the database from a family of size 2 and 10 observations from a family of size 4. Do the data support the conclusion that the monthly utility expenditure (variable UTILITY) is larger for a family of size 4? Use a .05 significance level. Do not assume equal population variances.

Exercise 3—Appendix G

From the database, choose a random sample of 12 companies with an A bond rating and another random sample of 12 companies with a C bond rating. Do the data support the conclusion that the net income of companies with a C bond rating is less than the net income of companies with an A rating? Use a .05 significance level. Do not assume equal population variances.

Exercise 4—Appendix G

From the database, choose a random sample of 15 companies with a B bond rating and another random sample of 15 companies with a C bond rating. Do the data support the conclusion that the variances of the current assets of the companies with B bond ratings and C bond ratings differ significantly at the .05 level?

Insights from Statistics in Action

Rollovers with Sport-Utility Vehicles: Assessing the Impact

The Statistics in Action introductory case discussed the increased attention being given to rollovers by SUVs. Insurance companies are asking themselves, Are the average repair costs for SUVs with less than a three-star rating larger than the repair costs for SUVs with a three-star rating for real-world collisions? This question can be answered by using statistical techniques designed to test for differences in the means of two populations.

1. If an automotive analyst wished to show that damage to SUVs with less than a three-star rating cost over $2,000 more than SUVs with a three-star rating, how would you set up the null and alternative hypotheses?

2. If a random sample of 25 SUVs with a three-star rating that were involved in collisions showed an average damage amount of $5,810 and a random sample of 25 SUVs with less than a three-star rating also involved in collisions showed an average damage amount of $8,000, would these data support the alternative hypothesis in question 1? Use a significance level of 5%. Assume that the data are from normally distributed populations with

known population standard deviations of $1,450 for the SUVs with three-star ratings and $1,625 for the SUVs with less than three-star ratings.

3. Suppose that in question 2, the standard deviations of $1,450 and $1,625 were computed from the sample. Using a *t* test, would the results of the test change?

4. Construct a 95% confidence interval for the difference in the average damage amount for the two types of SUVs in question 2. Interpret this interval.

5. Suppose that an automotive analyst wished to compute a 95% confidence interval for the difference in the average damage amount of the two types of SUVs such that the margin of error is $500. Assume that the standard deviation of the amount of damage in real world collisions is $1,500 for each of the two types of SUVs. What sample size would be required to minimize the total sample size?

(Sources: "Ford, GM Predict Better Rollover Ratings for '02 SUVs," *Ward's Auto World*, vol. 37, issue 5, May 2001, p. 28; "SPORT Utility Vehicles—Safety Measures," *Consumer Reports*, vol. 66, issue 9, September 2001, p. 7.)

Appendix SPSS®

Chapter 9 Appendix: Data Analysis with SPSS

Inference Procedure for Independent Samples from Two Populations

To illustrate the inference procedure for testing the means of two populations with independent samples, consider the tire data in Example 9.4. The blowout times for both brands are entered in the first column and the brand types (1 = Beltex, 2 = Roadmaster) are entered in the second column. By clicking on the **Variable View** tab, the columns can be named as shown below. *Note:* The grouping variable (brand) must be created in order to use this SPSS procedure. If your data to be analyzed (e.g., time) are arranged in two columns (e.g., one for Beltex and one for Roadmaster), they must be stacked in one column and a grouping variable created, as illustrated below.

	time	brand
1	3.82	1
2	3.11	1
3	4.21	1
4	2.64	1
5	4.16	1
6	3.91	1
7	2.44	1
8	4.52	1
9	2.84	1
10	3.26	1
11	3.74	1
12	3.04	1
13	2.56	1
14	2.58	1
15	3.15	1
16	4.16	2
17	3.92	2
18	3.94	2
19	4.22	2
20	4.15	2
21	3.62	2
22	4.11	2

Data View / Variable View

In Example 9.4, the significance level was .10 and the confidence level was 90%. To obtain the 90% confidence interval for the difference of the two means and to carry out the test of hypothesis, click on **Analyze ➤ Compare Means ➤ Independent-Samples T Test.** To obtain the following window, move the time variable from the left box to the **Test Variable(s)** box by clicking on the pointer. Move the brand variable to the **Grouping Variable** box by clicking on the second pointer. Click on **Define Groups,** and enter "1" in the **Group1** box and "2" in the **Group2** box. Click on **Options** and enter "90" in the **Confidence Interval** box. By clicking on **OK,** the output immediately following the Independent-Samples T Test window will appear in the display pane.

SPSS first provides output of the sample means and standard deviations. The final portion of the output contains the confidence interval and the results of the hypothesis test for the case where the variances are assumed to be equal (top) and for the case where the variances are not assumed to be equal (bottom). The resulting confidence intervals and hypothesis tests agree with the examples using these data in Section 9.3. *Notes:* (1) SPSS does not round the df calculation in equation (9.11) but, rather, uses an interpolated value to determine the corresponding t value. (2) The output in the display pane will also contain a test for equal variances (omitted in the output below). However, this test (called the Levene test) is not the one discussed in Section 9.4 and is less dependent on the assumption of normal populations.

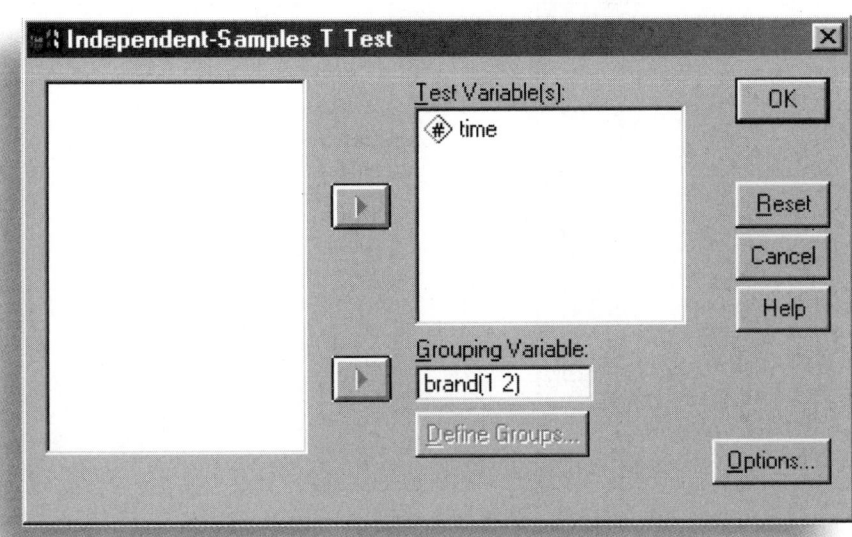

Group Statistics

	BRAND	N	Mean	Std. Deviation	Std. Error Mean
TIME	1	15	3.332	.6792	.1754
	2	15	3.984	.3773	.0974

Independent Samples Test

		t-test for Equality of Means						
							90% Confidence Interval of the Difference	
		t	df	Sig. (2-tailed)	Mean Difference	Std. Error Difference	Lower	Upper
TIME	Equal variances assumed	-3.250	28	.0030	-.6520	.2006	-.9932	-.3108
	Equal variances not assumed	-3.250	21.889	.0037	-.6520	.2006	-.9965	-.3075

Inference Procedure for Dependent Samples from Two Populations

The hardness data in Example 9.11 will be used to illustrate the procedure for constructing a confidence interval or testing a hypothesis when dealing with paired samples from two populations. Enter the data for tip #1 in the first column and for tip #2 in the second column. Click on the **Variable View** tab and name the variables as shown.

	tip1	tip2
1	39	35
2	32	34
3	42	38
4	49	48
5	45	47
6	47	43
7	45	41
8	48	47
9	38	35
10	48	46
11	41	37
12	47	44
13		
14		
15		
16		
17		
18		
19		
20		
21		
22		

Data View / Variable View

In Examples 9.11 and 9.12, the significance level was .05 and the confidence level was 95%. To obtain the 95% confidence interval for the mean of the population differences and to carry out the test of hypothesis, click on **Analyze ➤ Compare Means ➤ Paired-Samples T Test.** To obtain the following window, click on *both* **tip1** and **tip2** in the left-hand box and then click on the pointer to move them into the **Paired Variables** box. By clicking on **OK,** the output immediately following the **Paired-Samples T Test** window will appear in the display pane.

The program output agrees with Examples 9.11 and 9.12. Since the hypothesis test in Example 9.12 was a right-tailed test, the resulting p-value is half the value under **Sig. (2-tailed);** that is, .0066/2 = .0033. Because this p-value is less than .05, the conclusion would be that the average hardness reading using tip #1 is higher than that using tip #2.

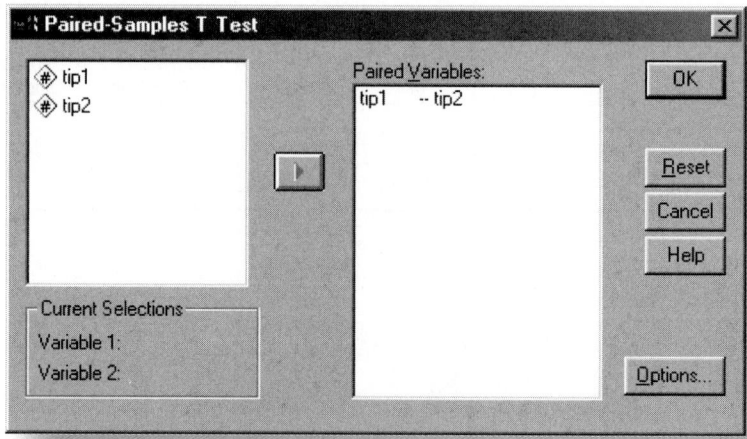

Paired Samples Test

| | | Paired Differences | | | | | | | |
| | | Mean | Std. Deviation | Std. Error Mean | 95% Confidence Interval of the Difference | | t | df | Sig. (2-tailed) |
					Lower	Upper			
Pair 1	TIP1 - TIP2	2.167	2.250	.65	.737	3.596	3.34	11	.0066

Paired Samples Statistics

		Mean	N	Std. Deviation	Std. Error Mean
Pair 1	TIP1	43.417	12	5.143	1.48
	TIP2	41.250	12	5.259	1.52

On the CD . . .
Chapter 9 Appendix: Data Analysis with MINITAB

chapter 10

Estimation and Testing for Population Proportions

X

Statistics in Action
Streaming Meemies: The Most Valuable Consumer Group on the Internet

Streamies, in marketing parlance, is an emerging group of highly interactive consumers who listen or view streaming media on the Internet. They engage in online radio listening and Webcast viewing. Many streamies use their office PCs to tune in to their favorite stations. Some use Web radio as a way to keep up with hometown news from a distance. In particular, sporting event broadcasts are very popular with streamies. Marketing analysts have noticed that the proportion of Internet users who are streamies is increasing.

Why are more Internet users dipping their toes in the stream? Radio is a great driver of online commerce. When consumers switch to broadband, their time spent online and with streaming media, especially video, surges. Internet radio is being compared to the arrival of FM in the 1960s. Many once-skeptical traditional radio stations are realizing that online access to one's favorite radio station is what the consumer wants. Interestingly, stations that play rock are in high demand on the Internet. Arbitron, an international media and marketing research firm serving radio broadcasters, cable companies, and advertisers, keeps track of what Internet users are watching or listening to. Americana music site Texas Rebel Radio (www.texasrebelradio.com), owned by KFAN, Fredericksburg, Texas, and the online arm of KPIG, Freedom, California, which plays alternative rock, were numbers 1 and 2 in the first two monthly audience surveys by Arbitron.

Advertisers are thinking of creative ways to target the streamies. *Ad insertion*, a concept with its roots in the cable television industry, is being used to reach very active streamies. With ad insertion, a station can send its traditional broadcast over the Internet, with advertising that specifically targets a Web user. For example, streamies are targeted to buy music over the Internet immediately after hearing it. This makes Web radio a perfect platform to generate CD sales. Advertisers estimate that approximately 44% of Internet users are streamies, and they want to target this consumer group because they are more highly educated and have higher incomes than nonstreamies.

Executives of various companies are making decisions on buying ads on Webcasts. They must assess if this tech-savvy, affluent group will purchase more of their product than the Internet surfers that are not streaming. Management must rely on surveys to determine the proportion of Internet users that will purchase their product online. When you have completed this chapter, you will be able to

- Construct a confidence interval for a single population proportion (e.g., the proportion of streamies who purchase a particular product).
- Construct a confidence interval for the difference in two population proportions (e.g., difference in the proportion of streamies and nonstreamies who purchase a particular product).
- Use hypothesis testing to determine if the proportion of a population differs from a hypothesized value.
- Use hypothesis testing to determine if the difference in two population proportions supports a claim that the population proportions differ.

A Look Back/Introduction

By now you should be comfortable with the concepts of estimation and hypothesis testing. If, for example, you have reason to believe that the population is normally distributed, you can then estimate the necessary population parameters (such as the mean and standard deviation) using the corresponding sample statistics. You should be well aware that there always is the risk of arriving at an incorrect conclusion when using sample information to infer something about an entire population. We can use the Central Limit Theorem to relax the assumptions regarding normality when making inferences about population means if large samples are used.

Chapters 7, 8, and 9 concentrated primarily on normal populations. We provided you with confidence intervals for the mean and the variance of a single normal population. We examined how to check a statement regarding one of these parameters (such as $\mu < 100$ or $\sigma > .5$) using a test of hypothesis. Then this concept was extended to comparing the means or variances of two normal populations.

Now we return to the *binomial* situation, in which we are interested in the *proportion* of your population that has a certain attribute. Attributes can include personal attributes, such as willingness to buy a product or being in favor of a proposed labor contract. We can also examine proportions as they relate to a particular physical attribute, such as the proportion of defective components in a batch.

We are interested in a single parameter, referred to as *p,* which is the *proportion* of the population having this attribute. For example, suppose that a recent report claims that only 10% of all registered voters in a certain area are in favor of forced busing for school children ($p = .10$). Or suppose it has been reported that a lower proportion of families with children favor busing than do those without children. How can we estimate the actual proportions here and test these claims?

Examining a population proportion plays a *vital* role in describing and monitoring the quality of a production process. Here, the parameter of interest is the proportion (p) of nonconforming units being produced by the process. Based on the results of a statistical sample, we can decide if the parameter p is too large (process is out of control) or acceptable (process is in control). This topic will be discussed further in Chapter 12.

ESTIMATION AND CONFIDENCE INTERVALS FOR A POPULATION PROPORTION

A test for a **population proportion** is a binomial situation. Using the definitions from Chapter 5, each member of your population is either a *success* or a *failure.* These words can be misleading; it is necessary only that each person (or object) in your population either have a certain attribute (a success) or not have it (a failure). So we define p to be the proportion of successes in the population—that is, the proportion that have a certain attribute.

Do not confuse the notation p = a population proportion with the previously used notation for a p-value. They do not mean the same thing. We hope that the context will make it clear which of the two p's is being described.

In Chapter 5 we assumed that p is known. For any binomial situation, perhaps p is known, or more likely it was estimated in some way. This chapter examines how you can estimate p by using a sample from the population. Also, you can support (or fail to support) claims concerning the value of p. The final section in this chapter compares two samples from two separate populations.

Point Estimate for a Population Proportion

Auditors often deal with sample results concerned with a population proportion. This type of sampling is called *attribute sampling,* since the parameter of interest is the proportion of the population having a certain attribute. Suppose that Cassidy Electronics is under an audit investigation (perhaps, routine) to determine the proportion of payroll checks in the current fiscal year containing calculation errors. The proportion of interest is the proportion of payroll checks containing such an error. A random sample of 250 payroll checks turned up 14 containing calculation errors. What can you say about the proportion (p) of all payroll checks in this fiscal year that contain errors in calculation?

We view this as a binomial situation and define a "success" as a payroll check containing an error and a "failure" as a check containing no error. Consequently, p is the proportion of successes in the population (proportion of all payroll checks containing an error). Remember that p, like μ and σ previously, will remain *unknown* forever unless a complete 100% audit is conducted. To *estimate p,* we obtain a random sample and observe the proportion of successes in the sample. We use $\hat{p}$ (read as "p hat") to denote the estimate of p. Consequently, $\hat{p}$ (the proportion of successes in the sample) estimates p (the proportion of successes in the population). Here, $\hat{p}$ = proportion of payroll checks containing calculation errors = $14/250 = .056$.

In general,

$$\hat{p} = \text{estimate of } p$$
$$= \text{proportion of sample having a specified attribute}$$
$$= \frac{x}{n}$$

where n = sample size and x = the number of sample observations having this attribute.

The symbol ˆ is used to denote an *estimate.* Distinguish between $\hat{p}$ obtained from sample information and p, the population proportion being estimated by $\hat{p}$. This is the same type of difference that we previously recognized between a sample mean, $\overline{X}$ (often referred to as $\hat{\mu}$), and a population mean, μ.

The mean of the random variable $\hat{p}$ is the (unknown) value of p. In other words, the average value of $\hat{p}$ is the parameter it is estimating. Such an estimator is said to be **unbiased.** If we obtained random samples indefinitely, the resulting $\hat{p}$'s—on average—will equal p. This is a desirable property for a sample estimator to have. We have actually discussed two other unbiased estimators previously; $\overline{X}$ is an unbiased estimator of a population mean (μ) and s^2 is an unbiased estimator of a population variance (σ^2).

Confidence Intervals for a Population Proportion (Using a Small Sample)

The calculations involved in determining a confidence interval for p using a small sample are fairly complex. To make them easier, we have listed 90% and 95% confidence intervals for sample sizes of $n = 5, 6, \ldots , 20$ in Table A.8. For sample sizes other than these, you can (1) use the large-sample confidence interval (described next) or (2) extend Table A.8 by consulting your local statistician.

Using Table A.8 is much like using Table A.1, the table of binomial probabilities. Let n = sample size and x = the observed number of successes in your sample. Based on these values, the confidence interval (p_L, p_U) can be obtained directly from the table.

EXAMPLE 10.1

A private company is considering the purchase of 200 Beagle microcomputers to monitor seismic activity. These computers will be placed in outdoor stations where they must be able to operate in extremely cold weather. If the computers will operate in temperatures as low as $-10°F$, the company will purchase them. Beagle, anxious to demonstrate the reliability of its system, has agreed to subject 15 computers to a "cold test." Let p = proportion of *all* Beagle computers that will function at $-10°F$.

Of the 15 sample computers, three of them stopped operating at or above $-10°F$. What can you say about p? Construct a 95% confidence interval for p.

Solution   Let a success be that a computer *survives* the cold test (still functions at $-10°F$). We observe 12 successes out of 15 in the sample. So,

$$\hat{p} = \frac{12}{15} = .8$$

Using Table A.8 for $n = 15$, $x = 12$, and $\alpha = .05$, we find $p_L = .519$ and $p_U = .957$. The corresponding 95% confidence interval for p is

$$p_L \quad \text{to} \quad p_U = .519 \quad \text{to} \quad .957$$

So we are 95% confident that the actual (population) percentage of Beagle computers that can function at $-10°F$ is between 51.9% and 95.7%.

Comments

One of the purposes of this section (omitted in many textbooks) is to demonstrate that confidence intervals for a population proportion (p) are typically very wide when using a small sample. In Example 10.1, the company considering the purchase of the Beagle microcomputers still is pretty much in the dark regarding the proportion of computers that will survive the cold test. It is 95% confident that this proportion is between 52% and 96%—a very wide range. The moral of this section is: *To obtain a useful (narrow) confidence interval for* p, *obtain a large sample.*

Confidence Intervals for a Population Proportion (Using a Large Sample)

When dealing with large samples, the Central Limit Theorem once again provides us with a reliable method of determining approximate confidence intervals for a population proportion. For each element in your sample, assign a value of 1 if this observation is a success (has the attribute) or 0 if this observation is a failure (does not have the attribute). Using the audit results at Cassidy Electronics to illustrate, for *each* payroll check in the sample we assign 1 if this check contains an error and 0 otherwise. So what is $\hat{p}$? We can write it as

$$\hat{p} = \frac{\overbrace{1+1+\cdots+1}^{14 \text{ times}} + \overbrace{0+0+\cdots+0}^{236 \text{ times}}}{250} = \frac{14}{250} = .056$$

In this sense, then, $\hat{p}$ is a *sample average:* it is an average of 0s and 1s. *As a result, we can apply the Central Limit Theorem to* $\hat{p}$ *and conclude that* $\hat{p}$ *is (approximately) a* normal random variable *for large samples.* This works reasonably well provided np and $n(1-p)$ are both greater than 5. So the distribution of $\hat{p}$ [large sample; $np > 5$ and $n(1-p) > 5$] can be summarized: $\hat{p}$ is (approximately) a normal random variable with

$$\text{mean} = p$$

$$\text{standard deviation (standard error)} = \sqrt{\frac{p(1-p)}{n}}$$

By standardizing this result, we have

$$Z = \frac{\hat{p} - p}{\sqrt{\dfrac{p(1-p)}{n}}}$$

10.2

which is approximately a standard normal random variable. This variable allows us to use Table A.4 to construct a confidence interval for p. This confidence interval is obtained in the identical manner used to construct previous confidence intervals with the standard normal distribution, namely,

$$(\text{point estimate}) \pm Z_{\alpha/2} \cdot (\text{standard deviation of point estimator})$$

10.3

The standard deviation of $\hat{p}$ (that is, the **standard error** of $\hat{p}$) in the denominator of equation 10.2 contains the unknown parameter, p. To estimate this standard error, it would seem logical to replace $p(1-p)/n$ with $\hat{p}(1-\hat{p})/n$. However, it can be shown that if we were to sample indefinitely, $\hat{p}(1-\hat{p})/n$ on the average *underestimates* $p(1-p)/n$. In fact, an unbiased estimator of $p(1-p)/n$ is obtained by using

$$\frac{\hat{p}(1-\hat{p})}{n-1}$$

and so the *estimated standard error* of $\hat{p}$ is

$$s_{\hat{p}} = \sqrt{\frac{\hat{p}(1-\hat{p})}{n-1}}$$

10.4

Using the estimated standard error, a $(1-\alpha) \cdot 100\%$ confidence interval for p (large sample; $n\hat{p}$ and $n(1-\hat{p})$ both > 5) is

$$\hat{p} - Z_{\alpha/2}\sqrt{\frac{\hat{p}(1-\hat{p})}{n-1}} \qquad \text{to} \qquad \hat{p} + Z_{\alpha/2}\sqrt{\frac{\hat{p}(1-\hat{p})}{n-1}}$$

10.5

EXAMPLE

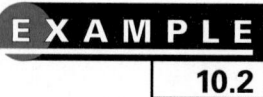

10.2

Using the audit results (14 errors in 250 payroll checks), what is a 90% confidence interval for the proportion of all payroll checks in this fiscal year that contain calculation errors?

Solution   Using Table A.4, $Z_{\alpha/2} = Z_{.05} = 1.645$. Also, $\hat{p} = 14/250 = .056$. So the 90% confidence interval for p is

$$.056 - 1.645\sqrt{\frac{(.056)(.944)}{249}} \quad \text{to} \quad .056 + 1.645\sqrt{\frac{(.056)(.944)}{249}}$$

$$= .056 - .024 \quad \text{to} \quad .056 + .024$$

$$= .032 \quad \text{to} \quad .080$$

Based on the sample results, we are 90% confident that the percentage of payroll checks containing calculation errors is between 3.2% and 8.0%.

EXAMPLE

10.3

Remember that in lot acceptance sampling, we either accept or reject a batch (lot) of components, parts, or assembled products based on tests using a random sample drawn from the lot.

Suppose we draw a sample of size 150 from a lot of calculators. We test each of the sampled calculators and find 13 defectives. Determine a 95% confidence interval for the proportion of defectives in the entire batch.

Solution   Let p = proportion of defective calculators in the batch. Based on the sample of 150 calculators, we have

$$\hat{p} = \frac{13}{150} = .0867$$

Because $Z_{.025} = 1.96$, the 95% confidence interval for p is

$$.0867 - 1.96\sqrt{\frac{(.0867)(.9133)}{149}} \quad \text{to} \quad .0867 + 1.96\sqrt{\frac{(.0867)(.9133)}{149}}$$

$$= .0867 - .045 \quad \text{to} \quad .0867 + .045$$

$$= .042 \quad \text{to} \quad .132$$

Consequently, we are 95% confident that our estimate $\hat{p} = .0867$ is within .045 of the actual value of p. In other words, this sample estimates the actual percentage of defective calculators to within 4.5%, with 95% confidence.

Choosing the Sample Size (One Population)

Suppose that you want your point estimate, $\hat{p}$, to be within a certain amount of the actual proportion, p. In Example 10.3 the *margin of error, E,* was $E = .045$, that is, 4.5%. In general, larger samples will yield lower values of E. What if the buyer's specifications necessitate that we estimate the parameter p to within 2% with 95% confidence? Now,

$$E = 1.96\sqrt{\frac{\hat{p}(1-\hat{p})}{n-1}} \qquad \textbf{10.6}$$

We have an earlier estimate of $p(\hat{p} = .0867)$ using the sample of size 150; this value can be used in equation 10.6. The purpose is to extend this sample in order to obtain this specific margin of error, E. The specified value of E is .02, so

$$E = .02 = 1.96\sqrt{\frac{(.0867)(.9133)}{n-1}}$$

Therefore,

$$\sqrt{\frac{(.0867)(.9133)}{n-1}} = \frac{.02}{1.96}$$

Squaring both sides and rearranging leads to

$$n = \frac{(1.96)^2\,(.0867)(.9133)}{(.02)^2} + 1 = 761.5$$

Rounding up (*always*), we come to the conclusion that a sample of size $n = 762$ calculators will be necessary to estimate p to within 2%.

By solving equation 10.6 for n, we arrive at the following equation, which provides the necessary sample size to estimate p with a specified margin of error, E, and confidence level $(1 - \alpha) \cdot 100\%$.

$$n = \frac{Z^2_{\alpha/2}\hat{p}(1-\hat{p})}{E^2} + 1 \qquad \textbf{10.7}$$

In this illustration, we used an estimate of p from a prior sample to determine the necessary sample size using equation 10.7. If the sample of size n based on this equation is our first and only sample, then *we have no estimate of p*. There is a conservative procedure we can follow here that will guarantee the accuracy (E) that we require. Look at the curve of different values of $\hat{p}(1-\hat{p})$ in Figure 10.1. Consider these values:

$\hat{p}$	$\hat{p}(1-\hat{p})$
.2	.16
.4	.24
.5	.25
.7	.21
.9	.09

Note that the largest value of $\hat{p}(1-\hat{p})$ is .25.

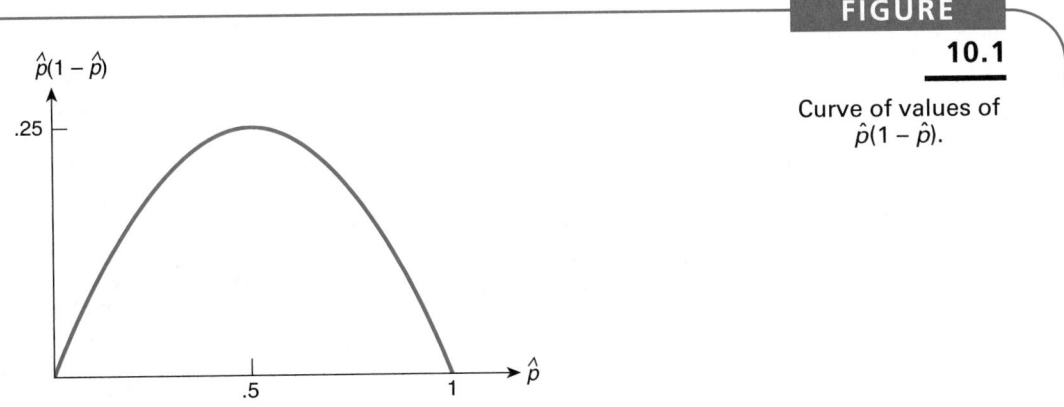

FIGURE

10.1

Curve of values of $\hat{p}(1-\hat{p})$.

If we make $\hat{p}(1 - \hat{p})$ in equation 10.7 *as large as possible,* we will obtain a value of n that will result in a margin of error that is sure to be less than the specified value. So we can formulate this rule: If no prior estimate of p is available, a conservative procedure to determine the necessary sample size from equation 10.7 is to use $\hat{p} = .5$.

EXAMPLE 10.4

The insurance company underwriting the dental plan for Cassidy Electronics wishes to obtain a single sample that will estimate, to within 2% with 90% confidence, the proportion (p) of employees who would purchase the dental insurance. It has *no* prior knowledge of this proportion. Its intent is to obtain a large enough sample the first time so that the company can estimate the population proportion with this much accuracy. How large a sample is required?

Solution   We have no prior knowledge of p, so we use $\hat{p} = .5$ in equation 10.7 to obtain a sample size of

$$n = \frac{(1.645)^2 \, (.5)(.5)}{(.02)^2} + 1 = 1692.3$$

To obtain an estimate of p with a maximum error of $E = .02$, we will need a sample size of $n = 1693$ employees. With a sample of this size, we can safely say that the point estimate, $\hat{p}$, will be within 2% of the actual value of p, with 90% confidence (however, this is a very large sample).

X Exercises 10.1–10.15

Understanding the Mechanics

10.1 Construct 95% confidence intervals on the proportion for the following values of n and x, where n is the number of observations and x is the number of people having a specified attribute.
   a. $n = 15$ and $x = 7$
   b. $n = 20$ and $x = 11$
   c. $n = 30$ and $x = 15$
   d. $n = 50$ and $x = 25$

10.2 In each situation, determine whether the sample size is large enough to conclude that the Z statistic is appropriate to use in a confidence interval.
   a. $n = 12, \hat{p} = .6$
   b. $n = 20, \hat{p} = .45$
   c. $n = 100, \hat{p} = .98$
   d. $n = 200, \hat{p} = .98$
   e. $n = 500, \hat{p} = .98$
   f. $n = 15, \hat{p} = .50$

10.3 Find the necessary sample size so that a 95% confidence interval will have the following margin of error. Assume that a prior estimate of the proportion is .4.
   a. .10
   b. .05
   c. .03

Applying the New Concepts

10.4 According to a poll by Crowne Plaza Hotels and Resorts, 11.1% of the men that travel on business and 33.3% of the women that travel on business usually bring a friend or spouse.
   a. Construct a 90% confidence interval for the percent of men that bring a friend or spouse assuming that the sample size was 9. Use Table A.8. (Hint: Obtain the value of x in Table A.8 by multiplying the percentage by the sample size and rounding to the nearest integer.)
   b. Construct a 90% confidence interval for the percent of women that bring a friend or spouse, assuming that the sample size was 9. Use Table A.8.
   c. Find the confidence interval in part a, assuming a sample size of 90. Compare the length of the confidence interval to that obtained in part a.
   d. Find the confidence interval in part b, assuming a sample size of 90. Compare the length of the confidence interval to that obtained in part b.

(Source: "Men vs. Women: Business Travel Difference," *USA Today,* October 27, 1998, p. 1B.)

10.5 An investment firm surveyed 18 randomly selected economists. The survey found that 13 of them felt that the economy of the United States would not slip into a recession for at least a year. Use Table A.8 to construct 90% and 95% confidence intervals for the percentage of economists who believe that a recession will not occur in the United States for at least a year.

10.6 George W. Bush might be the first president with an MBA degree, but U.S. business is run by CEOs with varying backgrounds, most of which is not business related. Suppose that a researcher believes that approximately 15% of all CEOs have liberal arts degrees. What is the required sample size to estimate with 90% confidence the proportion of CEOs who have liberal arts degrees with a 3% margin of error?

(Source: "Offbeat Majors Help CEOs Think Outside of the Box," *USA Today*, July 24, 2001, p. 1B.)

10.7 Distance learning has attracted the attention of many working people who do not want to lose time at work to go back to school. Approximately 70% of DSL (Digital Subscriber Line) subscribers who are full-time business employees say that they are interested in using their home computer DSL connection to take courses using the distance learning approach. Suppose that the dean of a college of business is interested in obtaining a 90% confidence interval for the proportion of local business professionals who would be interested in taking college courses using the distance learning approach.

a. What sample size is required to obtain a margin of error of 4%?

b. Suppose that the dean had no prior knowledge of the percentage of business professionals who would be interested in taking college courses using the distance learning approach. What would be the necessary sample size in part a?

(Source: "Can't Get Enough," *American Demographics*, June 2001, p. 27.)

10.8 Winthrop Boat Lines is exploring the possibility of offering a ferry service between the cities of Patna and Madura, provided there is sufficient demand to make it feasible. The firm randomly interviewed 210 commuters from the two cities, and 146 of them indicated they would patronize the ferry service instead of the present bus service. Estimate the population proportion p of commuters from the two cities who would prefer the ferry service. Construct a 95% confidence interval for p.

10.9 Employers maintain that drug testing in their company should be performed to lower injury rates and absenteeism costs. In 1987, only 22% of all U.S. companies performed any type of drug testing on their employees. Today, that figure is estimated to be above 60%.

a. What sample size would be required to obtain a 99% confidence interval on the percentage of companies that require some type of drug testing for their employees? Assume that the margin of error is .021.

b. Suppose that the confidence level is decreased to 90% in part a. How much lower is the required sample size?

(Source: "Accused Workers Challenge Drug-Test Results in Court," *USA Today*, July 16, 2001, p. 1B.)

10.10 About 2.8 million people are paid from the public purse at all levels of government across Canada. That was the average for the first quarter of 1998, according to data from Statistics Canada's Public Institutions Division show. The total includes all federal, provincial, and municipal workers, from mandarins to office cleaners, the

military, crown corporation, and government business enterprise staffers, nurses, local police and fire personnel, teachers, public transit workers and on to drivers who chauffeur politicians around. It comes to about 18% of the labor force. Suppose that an economist wished to estimate the proportion of public employees in the Toronto area.

a. What is an estimate of the sample size required to estimate the proportion of public employees in the Toronto area to within .01 with 99% confidence?

b. How would the required sample size change if the estimate of the proportion in part a is to be within .005?

(Source: "2.8 Million Jobs Paid Out of Taxes," *The Toronto Star*, July 3, 1998, News section, p. 1.)

10.11 A manufacturer of microcomputers purchases electronic chips from a supplier that claims its chips are defective only 5% of the time. Determine the sample size that would be required to estimate the true proportion of defective chips if we wanted our estimate, $\hat{p}$, to be within 1.25% of the true proportion, with 99% confidence.

10.12 Congressional elections, mid-term between presidential elections, are considered to be important by both parties to maintain control of the House and Senate. The party in the White House during the mid-term elections usually loses House seats. A 1998 October Gallup poll revealed that among likely voters, 49% would vote Republican. The margin of error was reported to be 4%. Assuming that the confidence level is 95%, approximate the number of voters that were sampled in the Gallup poll.

(Source: "Poll Finds Parties Are in Dead Heat," *USA Today*, October 27, 1998, p. 1A.)

10.13 Computer reservation systems used by many travel agencies do not display Southwest Airlines' fares. Only Sabre, the largest system, displays them. About half of all of Southwest Airlines' travel-agency bookings are through Sabre agencies. Southwest Airlines is trying to get its customers to use its Internet site for making reservations, and it offers lower rates on the Internet site to encourage travelers to book their flights online.

a. Suppose that a random sample of 200 of Southwest Airlines' customers was collected, and 65 customers were found to have booked their flights through the Internet. What is a 90% confidence interval on the proportion of Southwest Airlines' customers that book their flights over the Internet?

b. To obtain a margin of error of 2% for the confidence interval in part a, what sample size would be required?

(Source: "Southwest Limits Most Travel Data to Own Web Site," *USA Today*, July 6, 2001, p. 3B.)

Using the Computer

10.14 To gain insight into how the sample size changes as the margin of error decreases, first calculate the sample size, for a 95% confidence interval, using the following margin of error values: .02, .025, .03, .035, .04, .045, .05, .055, .06, .065, and .07. Assume no prior knowledge of the population proportion; that is, use .5 as the estimate of the proportion. Then graph the sample size versus the margin of error. The plot should look similar to the following graph. (In Excel, put the values of the margin of error in column A of a spreadsheet. Put the value of 1.96 in cell C1. In cell B1, type in "=(C1^2)*(0.5)*(1-0.5)/(A1^2)" and drag down to cell B11. These values are the required sample size.)

a. Do a "what-if" analysis and see how the graph changes when 90% and 99% confidence levels are used.

b. Do a "what-if" analysis by using a 95% confidence level and changing the estimate of the proportion to .3 and .1.

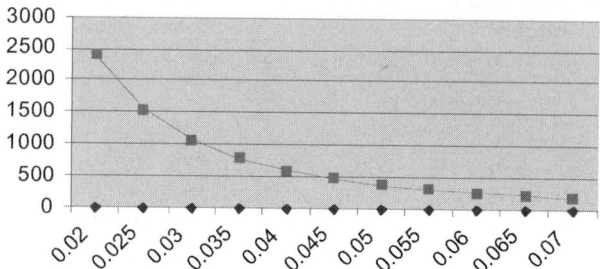

10.15 **[DATA SET EX10-15]** *Variable description:*

Underfill_Overfill: A 1 is recorded if a machine overfills a container and a 0 is recorded if a container is underfilled

A production manager monitors a machine that tends to either slightly overfill or slightly underfill a container. The manager believes that the proportion of time that the machine overfills a bag is is the same as the proportion of time that the machine underfills a bag. The manager collects 100 samples from this machine.

a. Compute a 90% confidence interval on the proportion of time that the machine overfills containers.

b. Change the confidence level to 99% in part a and compute the confidence interval. Contrast the margin of errors for the two confidence levels.

10.2

HYPOTHESIS TESTING FOR A POPULATION PROPORTION

How can you statistically reject a statement such as, at least 60% of all heavy smokers will contract a serious lung or heart ailment before age 65? Perhaps someone merely took a wild guess at the value of 60%, and it is your job to gather evidence that will either shoot down this claim or let it stand if there is insufficient evidence to conclude that this percentage actually is less than 60%. We set up hypotheses and test them much as we did before, only now we are concerned about a population proportion, p, rather than the mean or standard deviation of a particular population.

Hypothesis Testing Using a Small Sample

Because confidence intervals can be used to perform a test of hypothesis, we will use Table A.8 to conduct such a test. Table A.8 contains sample sizes of $n = 5$ to 20 and $\alpha = .05$ and .10. If the sample size exceeds 20 and np and $n(1 - p)$ are both greater than 5, the large-sample approximation will provide an accurate test. For sample sizes contained in Table A.8, use the procedure outlined in the accompanying box.

HYPOTHESIS TESTING
(SMALL SAMPLE; n BETWEEN 5 AND 20)

Two-Tailed Test

$$H_0: p = p_0$$
$$H_a: p \neq p_0$$

1. Obtain the $(1 - \alpha) \cdot 100\%$ confidence interval from Table A.8; that is, (p_L, p_U), using $x =$ the observed number of successes.
2. Reject H_0 if p_0 does not lie between p_L and p_U.
3. Fail to reject H_0 if $p_L \leq p_0 \leq p_U$.

One-Tailed Test

$H_0: p \le p_0$

$H_a: p > p_0$

1. Obtain the $(1 - 2\alpha) \cdot 100\%$ confidence interval from Table A.8; that is, (p_L, p_U), using $x =$ the observed number of successes.
2. Reject H_0 if $p_0 < p_L$.
3. Fail to reject H_0 if $p_0 \ge p_L$.

$H_0: p \ge p_0$

$H_a: p < p_0$

1. Obtain the $(1 - 2\alpha) \cdot 100\%$ confidence interval from Table A.8; that is, (p_L, p_U), using $x =$ the observed number of successes.
2. Reject H_0 if $p_0 > p_U$.
3. Fail to reject H_0 if $p_0 \le p_U$.

Notice that for a one-tailed test, we *double* α when finding the confidence interval for p from Table A.8. For example, if $\alpha = .05$, then $2\alpha = .10$, and so we retrieve a 90% confidence interval from the table. As a result, this particular binomial table can be used only when $\alpha = .025$ or $.05$ for a one-tailed test.

E X A M P L E

10.5

In Example 10.1, suppose that the company interested in the Beagle microcomputers will purchase them if Beagle's claim that the proportion, p, of all Beagle computers that can survive these cold temperatures is greater than .75 (75%) can be shown to be true. Do the data support this claim using $\alpha = .05$?

Solution

The claim under investigation goes into the alternative hypothesis. The appropriate hypotheses are

$$H_0: p \le .75 \quad \text{and} \quad H_a: p > .75$$

We observed, in the sample of 15 computers, $x = 12$ successes (computers that survived). Because $\alpha = .05$, we double this ($2\alpha = .10$) and refer to Table A.8 for a 90% confidence interval for p when $n = 15$, $x = 12$. This confidence interval is:

$$(p_L, p_U) = (.560, .943)$$

We will reject H_0 provided $p_0 = .75$ lies to the left of p_L. Because .75 is greater than $p_L = .560$, we fail to reject H_0.

Based on the evidence gathered from this sample, we cannot demonstrate that p is greater than the required 75%. Notice that we are not *accepting* H_0—we simply *fail to reject* it. This means that the point estimate $\hat{p} = 12/15 = .8$ is not enough larger than .75 to justify the claim made in H_a. The fact that $\hat{p}$ exceeds .75 may be due to the sampling error that is possible when using a sample statistic ($\hat{p}$) to infer something about a population parameter (p).

Comments

In the same sense that confidence intervals for a proportion, p, are typically very wide, it is usually very difficult to obtain a significant result (reject H_0) when using a small sample. The moral mentioned in the confidence interval section applies here as well: *To obtain a reasonably powerful test on a population proportion, use a large sample.*

Hypothesis Testing Using a Large Sample

The standard five-step procedure is used for testing H_0 versus H_a when attempting to support a claim regarding a binomial parameter, p, using a large sample. The approximate standard normal random variable given by equation 10.2 is used as a test statistic for this situation.

The rejection region for this test is defined by determining the distribution of the test statistic, given that H_0 is true. This means that the unknown value of p in equation 10.2 is replaced by the value of p specified in H_0 (say, p_0). For a one-tailed test, the boundary value of p in H_0 is used. This procedure is summarized in the following box.

HYPOTHESIS TESTING (LARGE SAMPLE; np_0 AND $n(1 - p_0)$ BOTH GREATER THAN 5)

Two-Tailed Test

$$H_0: p = p_0$$
$$H_a: p \neq p_0$$
$$\text{reject } H_0 \text{ if } |Z| > Z_{\alpha/2}$$

where

$$Z = \frac{\hat{p} - p_0}{\sqrt{\dfrac{p_0(1 - p_0)}{n}}}$$

One-Tailed Test

$H_0: p \leq p_0$	$H_0: p \geq p_0$
$H_a: p > p_0$	$H_a: p < p_0$
reject H_0 if $Z > Z_\alpha$	reject H_0 if $Z < -Z_\alpha$

Notice that the form of the test statistic is that used in many of the previous large sample test statistics, namely,

$$Z = \frac{\text{(point estimate)} - \text{(hypothesized value)}}{\text{(standard deviation of point estimator)}} \qquad \text{10.8}$$

EXAMPLE 10.6

In Example 10.2, we estimated the proportion of payroll checks containing a calculation error. The audit plan also specifies that a more detailed inspection of the Cassidy Electronics payroll checks be conducted if there is evidence to indicate that this proportion* exceeds .03. Using a significance level of 10%, can you conclude that the percentage of checks in error exceeds 3%?

Solution   **Step 1.** Your hypotheses should be

$$H_0: p \leq .03$$
$$H_a: p > .03$$

Step 2. Since $np_0 = (250)(.03) = 7.5$ and $n(1 - p_0) = (250)(.97) = 242.5$ are both greater than 5, the large-sample test statistic can be used, namely,

$$Z = \frac{\hat{p} - p_0}{\sqrt{\dfrac{p_0(1 - p_0)}{n}}} = \frac{\hat{p} - .03}{\sqrt{\dfrac{(.03)(.97)}{250}}}$$

Step 3. The testing procedure, using $\alpha = .10$, will be to

$$\text{reject } H_0 \text{ if } Z > Z_{.10} = 1.28$$

---

*Auditing textbooks often refer to this value as the *maximum tolerable error rate* (MTER).

FIGURE

10.2

Z curve showing
p-value for
Example 10.6.

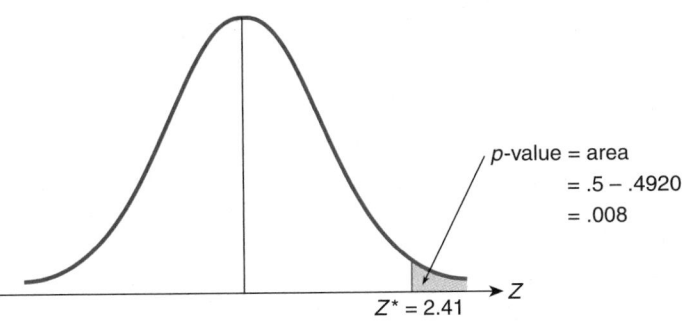

p-value = area

= .5 − .4920

= .008

$Z^* = 2.41$

Step 4. Using the sample data, $\hat{p} = 14/250 = .056$, so

$$Z^* = \frac{.056 - .03}{\sqrt{\dfrac{(.03)(.97)}{250}}} = \frac{.026}{.0108} = 2.41$$

Because $2.41 > 1.28$, we reject H_0 in favor of H_a.

Step 5. This sample indicates that the percentage of payroll checks in error *does* exceed 3%. In other words, at a significance level of $\alpha = .10$, the sample percentage containing an error (5.6%) *is* significantly greater than 3%, and, as a result, the alternative hypothesis is supported.

In Example 10.6, the computed test statistic was $Z^* = 2.41$. Figure 10.2 shows the Z curve and the calculated p-value, which is .008. Using the classical approach, because .008 is less than $\alpha = .10$, we reject H_0. If we choose to base our conclusion strictly on the p-value (without choosing a significance level, α), this value would be classified as "small"—it is less than .01. This means that using the classical approach, we would reject H_0 for both $\alpha = .10$ and $\alpha = .01$.

EXAMPLE

10.7

In Example 10.3, we estimated the proportion of calculators that were defective in a batch (lot). The company has determined that a good target for this defective percentage is 4%. The sample of 150 had 13 defectives. Can we conclude that the actual proportion of defective calculators is different from 4%? Use $\alpha = .05$.

Solution

Step 1. We wish to see if p is *different* from 4%, so we should use a two-tailed test with hypotheses

$$H_0: p = .04$$

$$H_a: p \neq .04$$

Step 2. Here $np_0 = (150)(.04) = 6$ and $n(1 - p_0) = (150)(.96) = 144$. Both are greater than 5, so the appropriate test statistic is

$$Z = \frac{\hat{p} - p_0}{\sqrt{\dfrac{p_0(1 - p_0)}{n}}} = \frac{\hat{p} - .04}{\sqrt{\dfrac{(.04)(.96)}{150}}}$$

Step 3. With $\alpha = .05$, the test procedure of H_0 versus H_a will be to

reject H_0 if $|Z| > 1.96$

Step 4. Using $\hat{p} = 13/150 = .0867$,

$$Z^* = \frac{.0867 - .04}{\sqrt{\dfrac{(.04)(.96)}{150}}} = \frac{.0467}{.016} = 2.92$$

Because $2.92 > 1.96$, we reject H_0.

Step 5. The company is *not* meeting its target percentage of defectives. As a reminder, because $\alpha = .05$, 5% of the time this particular test will reject H_0 when in fact it is true.

In Example 10.7, $Z^* = 2.92$. What is the *p*-value? This is a two-tailed test, so we need to *double* the right-tail area, as illustrated in Figure 10.3. So $p = 2 \cdot .0018 = .0036$. Thus, using either the classical procedure (comparing the *p*-value to $\alpha = .05$) or basing our decision strictly on the *p*-value, we reject H_0 because of this extremely small *p*-value.

An Excel solution to Example 10.7 using the macro from KPK Data Analysis is shown in Figure 10.4. To obtain this solution, click on **KPK Data Analysis ➤ Inference on Proportions ➤ One Population Proportion.** Next, (1) enter 13 in the **Number of Successes** box; (2) enter 150 in the **Sample Size** box; (3) enter 5 in the **Alpha** box; (4) click on the box alongside **Hypothesis Test,** then on **Two-Tail Test,** and enter .04 in the **Hypothesized Value of Proportion** box; and (5) enter "A1" in the **Output Range** box. The resulting output in Figure 10.4 agrees with the previous solution. The Excel *p*-value in cell B7 (namely, .00354) is slightly more accurate than the one illustrated in Figure 10.3. Based on this small *p*-value, we conclude that the percentage of defective calculators is *not* 4%.

FIGURE 10.3

Z curve showing *p*-value (twice the shaded area) for Example 10.7.

p-value $= 2$(area)
$= 2(.5 - .4982)$
$= 2(.0018)$
$= .0036$

$Z^* = 2.92$

FIGURE 10.4

Excel solution to Example 10.7 using **KPK Data Analysis ➤ Inference on Proportions ➤ One Population Proportion.**

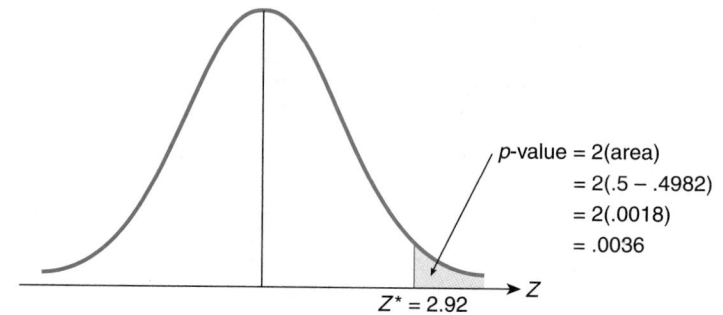

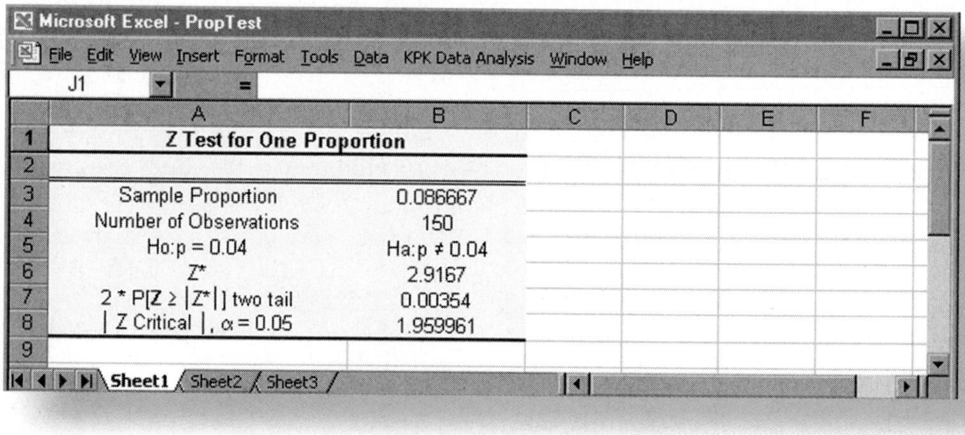

X Exercises 10.16–10.30

Understanding the Mechanics

10.16 In each case, test the hypothesis H_0: $p = p_0$ against H_a: $p \neq p_0$ for a random sample of size n.

    a. $n = 12$, $\hat{p} = 33$, $p_0 = .25$, $\alpha = .05$
    b. $n = 20$, $\hat{p} = .40$, $p_0 = .20$, $\alpha = .10$
    c. $n = 40$, $\hat{p} = .925$, $p_0 = .75$, $\alpha = .01$
    d. $n = 100$, $\hat{p} = .08$, $p_0 = .13$, $\alpha = .05$
    e. $n = 280$, $\hat{p} = .85$, $p_0 = .87$, $\alpha = .10$

10.17 A random sample of 25 observations yielded a value of $\hat{p} = .60$. Test each of the following hypotheses and find the p-values.

    a. H_0: $p = .71$ versus H_a: $p \neq .71$
    b. H_0: $p \geq .71$ versus H_a: $p < .71$
    c. H_0: $p \leq .51$ versus H_a: $p > .51$

Applying the New Concepts

10.18 An official for a computer firm was told by an independent source that 20% of the employees of the computer firm perceived that there was sex discrimination in the salary structure of the company. A quick random survey by the official of 18 employees found that three of the employees thought there was sex discrimination in the salary structure of the company. Is there sufficient evidence in the official's survey to indicate that the figure of 20% given by the independent source is in error? Conduct a hypothesis test using a significance level of .10 and using Table A.8.

10.19 Chief financial officers (CFOs) are usually under pressure from both management and the public to answer for the profitability of the company. An RHI Management Resources survey of 1,400 CFOs revealed that the greatest challenge for CFOs was time management, followed by keeping up with the latest technology. To test if this was also true for CFOs of health care organizations, a quick random sample of 18 CFOs of health care organizations was selected. The survey found that 13 of them felt that their greatest challenge was time management, followed by keeping up with the latest technology. Test the hypothesis that more than 50% of CFOs of health care organizations find that their greatest challenge is in agreement with that found in the RHI Management Resources survey. Use Table A.8 with a significance level of 5%.

(Source: "Time Is Not on Their Side," *USA Today*, November 6, 2001, p. 1B.)

10.20 There are about 87 million households in the United States. In 1970, about 71% of the households were occupied by married couples. In the last 30 years, the trend toward living alone has accelerated. One market researcher believes that at present the proportion of households occupied by married couples is 58%. A random sample of 20 households reveals that 12 are occupied by married couples. At a significance level of 10%, are you in a position to contradict the market researcher and say that this person is probably wrong?

10.21 In order for $np > 5$ and $n(1 - p) > 5$, how large must n be if $p = .03$?

10.22 A random sample of 40 coffee drinkers was asked to taste-test a new coffee brand. The responses follow, with 1 representing "like the brand," 2 representing "indifferent to the brand," and 3 representing "do not like the brand." Do the data support the conclusion that more than half of the coffee drinkers like the new coffee brand? Use a .10 significance level.

1	3	1	3	3	1	2	1	1	1	
1	1	1	2	1	1	3	1	2	1	
1	2	1	1	1	2	1	1	3	2	
1	1	2	1	3	1	3	1	2	1	

10.23 In January 1998, American Airlines created the AAdvantage Executive Platinum program for its frequent-flier passengers. Membership requires that a customer fly 100,000 miles a year. American's move is an example of airlines focusing on their best and highest paying customers. This elite level will allow members to reserve an upgrade to first class 100 hours before their flights versus 72 hours previously allowed for AAdvantage members. Frequent Flyer magazine previously found that 71% of its surveyed readers had difficulty getting upgrades when requested. Suppose that Frequent Flyer takes another survey after the Executive Platinum program has been in effect for a year and from a sample of 200 readers, 125 readers said that they had difficulty getting upgrades when requested.

    a. Do the data from the new survey support the belief that the percentage of readers who have had difficulty in upgrading to first class is less than 71%? Use a .10 significance level.

    b. List any assumptions that you made about the data in testing the hypothesis in part a.

(Source: "American Adds Perks to Frequent Flying," *The Wall Street Journal*, January 21, 1998, p. 2B.)

10.24 More than 80% of retired Americans say that spending time with family and friends is their primary activity. However, approximately 50% say that they do extensive traveling. Suppose a researcher studying the habits of retired Americans believes that the percentage of retired Americans under the age of 80 who do extensive traveling is greater than 50%. The researcher finds that 40 out of 75 randomly sampled retired Americans under the age of 80 do extensive traveling. Test the researcher's belief using a significance level of 5%.

(Source: "Great Expectations for Aging," *USA Today*, August 7, 2001, p. 1B.)

10.25 A consumer group would like to determine the proportion of dealers who charge more than $450 monthly for a 36-month lease on a BMW 323i. The consumer group found a 90% confidence interval for the proportion of dealers in the midwest United States to be 24% to 38%. Suppose that the consumer group wished to find a 90% confidence interval to estimate the proportion to within 4% with 90% confidence. What sample size is necessary?

(Source: "Drive Buys," *The Wall Street Journal*, October 25, 1998, p. W7.)

10.26 In 2001, when gasoline prices were near the two-dollar mark in many parts of the United States, a nationwide survey revealed that only 28% of the population traveled less because of the high prices. Suppose that a survey in southern California was taken at the end of 2001, when gasoline prices returned to more normal levels. The survey revealed that 50 of 200 respondents were traveling less because of gasoline prices. Do these data support the hypothesis that less than 28% of the population traveled less because of gasoline prices? Use a 10% significance level.

(Source: "Few Drivers Yielding to Gas Costs," *USA Today*, May 24, 2001, p. 1B.)

10.27 Today, there are credit cards designed specifically for high school students: the Cobaltcard from American Express, Capital One's High School Student Card, and the Visa Buxx card. According to a *USA Today* survey, 22% of high-school seniors have credit cards. Suppose that a survey was taken in 2002 in Houston to determine if the percentage of high school seniors with credit cards differs from 22%. A random sample of 150 high school students in the Houston area found 34 students with credit cards. Is there sufficient evidence to say that the percentage of high school seniors in Houston differs from 22%? Base your conclusion on the *p*-value.

(Source: "Teen Credit Cards Actually Teach Responsibility," *USA Today*, July 31, 2001, p. 15A.)

10.28 Wal-Mart developed a strategy to attract Christmas shoppers. It broadcasted a live concert by country superstar Garth Brooks in its 2,390 stores during December 1998. Nationwide, Wal-Mart's directors believe that 40% of its shoppers are mothers with children. Suppose that managers for stores in the Houston area believe that this figure is different for the Houston area. A random sample of 300 shoppers in the Houston area revealed 135 shoppers were mothers with children.

  a. Find a 95% confidence interval for estimating the proportion of shoppers that are mothers with children.

  b. Test at the .05 significance level that the percentage of shoppers that are mothers with children differs from the national proportion. How can the confidence interval in part a be used to test this?

(Source: "Wal-Mart's Garth-Quake May Spur Sales," *The Wall Street Journal*, November 2, 1998, p. B1.)

Using the Computer

10.29 [DATA SET EX10-29] *Variable description:*

WatchHomShp: A *Yes* indicates that a family watches a televised home shopping program, and a *No* indicates that they do not

A marketing agency wishes to determine if more than 50% of the families in the Chicago metropolitan area have ever watched a televised home shopping program. A random sample of 100 adults was selected through telephone interviews. A *Yes* reply indicated that the family has watched the program, and a *No* reply indicated that the family has never watched the program. These are the values for the variable WatchHomShp. Test to determine whether there is sufficient evidence to conclude that the true proportion is greater than 50%. Use the *p*-value to support your conclusion.

10.30 [DATA SET EX10-30] *Variable description:*

ReadReport: A 1 indicates that a shareholder reads the annual report, and a 0 indicates that the shareholder does not

The vice president of a public utilities company believes that less than 60% of the shareholders of the company read the annual report. From a random sample of 200 shareholders, a 1 or a 0 is listed for the variable ReadReport. Test the vice president's belief. Use a .01 significance level.

10.3

COMPARING TWO POPULATION PROPORTIONS (LARGE, INDEPENDENT SAMPLES)

Consider the following questions:

> *Is the divorce rate higher in California than it is in New York?*
>
> *Is there a higher rate of lung cancer among cigarette smokers than there is among nonsmokers?*
>
> *Is there any difference in the proportion of engines rebuilt by Engine Masters that fail during the one-year warranty period and the proportion of engines rebuilt by Freed Motors that fail during the warranty period?*

These questions are concerned with proportions from *two* populations. Our method of estimating these proportions will be exactly as it was for one population. We simply have two of everything—two populations, two samples, two estimates, and so on. In this section, it is assumed that the two samples are obtained *independently*.

For example, consider the question concerning the proportion of engines that fail during the warranty period. Population 1 is all engines rebuilt by Engine Masters, with p_1 = proportion of all engines rebuilt by Engine Masters that fail during the warranty period, n_1 = sample size for the Engine Masters engines, and x_1 = number of engines in the Engine Masters sample that fail. Population 2 is all engines rebuilt by Freed Motors, where p_2, n_2, and x_2 are the corresponding values for this population.

Define a "success" to be that an engine fails during the warranty period. (Keep in mind that "success" is merely a label for the trait you are interested in. It need not be a desirable trait.) Our unbiased point estimator of p_1 will be as before:

$$\hat{p}_1 = \frac{\text{observed number of successes in the sample}}{\text{sample size}}$$

$$= \frac{\text{number of engines in the Engine Masters sample}}{\text{that fail during the warranty period}} \Big/ n_1$$

That is, the unbiased point estimator of p_1 is

$$\hat{p}_1 = \frac{x_1}{n_1}$$

10.9

Similarly, the unbiased point estimator of p_2, obtained from the second sample, is

$$\hat{p}_2 = \frac{x_2}{n_2}$$

10.10

For the two-population case, the parameter of interest will be the *difference* between the two population proportions, $p_1 - p_2$. The next section discusses a method of estimating $p_1 - p_2$ by using a point estimate along with a corresponding confidence interval.

Confidence Interval for $p_1 - p_2$ (Large, Independent Samples)

The logical estimator of $p_1 - p_2$ is $\hat{p}_1 - \hat{p}_2$, the difference between the sample estimators. What kind of random variable is $\hat{p}_1 - \hat{p}_2$? We are dealing with large, independent samples (where $n_1\hat{p}_1$, $n_1(1 - \hat{p}_1)$, $n_2\hat{p}_2$, and $n_2(1 - \hat{p}_2)$ are each larger than 5), so it follows that $\hat{p}_1 - \hat{p}_2$ is (approximately) a normal random variable with

$$\text{mean} = p_1 - p_2$$

and

$$\text{standard deviation} = \sqrt{\frac{p_1(1 - p_1)}{n_1} + \frac{p_2(1 - p_2)}{n_2}}$$

In Section 10.1, we observed that $\hat{p}_1$ is a sample mean, where the sample consists of observations that are either a 1 (a particular event occurred) or a 0 (this event did not occur). Because the two samples are obtained independently, the results extend to this situation, leading to the approximate normal distribution for $\hat{p}_1 - \hat{p}_2$. Since and $\hat{p}_1$ and $\hat{p}_2$ are unbiased estimators of p_1 and p_2, respectively, the mean of the estimator $\hat{p}_1 - \hat{p}_2$ is $p_1 - p_2$; that is, $\hat{p}_1 - \hat{p}_2$ is an unbiased estimator of $p_1 - p_2$. Notice that the variance of $\hat{p}_1 - \hat{p}_2$ is obtained by *adding* the variance of $\hat{p}_1$, or $p_1(1 - p_1)/n_1$, to the variance of $\hat{p}_2$, or $p_2(1 - p_2)/n_2$.

To derive a confidence interval for $p_1 - p_2$, we must estimate the unknown population parameters, p_1 and p_2, using the corresponding sample estimates, $\hat{p}_1$ and $\hat{p}_2$. The same argument used to derive the one-population estimated standard error in equation 10.4 can be used here to derive the estimated standard deviation of $\hat{p}_1 - \hat{p}_2$ (that is, the **standard error of $\hat{p}_1 - \hat{p}_2$).** This estimated standard error is

$$s_{\hat{p}_1-\hat{p}_2} = \sqrt{\frac{\hat{p}_1(1-\hat{p}_1)}{n_1 - 1} + \frac{\hat{p}_2(1-\hat{p}_2)}{n_2 - 1}}$$

10.11

The resulting confidence interval for $p_1 - p_2$ using large samples [$n_1\hat{p}_1$, $n_1(1-\hat{p}_1)$, $n_2\hat{p}_2$, and $n_2(1-\hat{p}_2)$ each greater than 5] is

$$(\hat{p}_1 - \hat{p}_2) - Z_{\alpha/2}\sqrt{\frac{\hat{p}_1(1-\hat{p}_1)}{n_1 - 1} + \frac{\hat{p}_2(1-\hat{p}_2)}{n_2 - 1}}$$

$$\text{to} \quad (\hat{p}_1 - \hat{p}_2) + Z_{\alpha/2}\sqrt{\frac{\hat{p}_1(1-\hat{p}_1)}{n_1 - 1} + \frac{\hat{p}_2(1-\hat{p}_2)}{n_2 - 1}}$$

10.12

where $\hat{p}_1 = x_1/n_1$ and $\hat{p}_2 = x_2/n_2$ are the sample proportions. Observe that the construction of this confidence interval was the "usual" procedure employing Table A.4 and described in equation 10.3.

EXAMPLE 10.8

Of a random sample of 100 rebuilt engines from Engine Masters (population 1), 28 failed within the 12-month warranty period. A second sample, obtained independent of the first, consisted of 150 engines rebuilt by Freed Motors (population 2), 48 of which failed during the 12-month warranty period. Both sets of engines were subjected to the same weather conditions, engine stress, and maintenance program. Construct a 90% confidence interval for $p_1 - p_2$.

Solution We have $\hat{p}_1 = 28/100 = .28$ and $\hat{p}_2 = 48/150 = .32$. Also, $Z_{\alpha/2} = Z_{.05} = 1.645$, using Table A.4. The resulting confidence interval for $p_1 - p_2$ is

$$(.28 - .32) - 1.645\sqrt{\frac{(.28)(.72)}{99} + \frac{(.32)(.68)}{149}}$$

$$\text{to} \quad (.28 - .32) + 1.645\sqrt{\frac{(.28)(.72)}{99} + \frac{(.32)(.68)}{149}}$$

$$= -.04 - .097 \quad \text{to} \quad -.04 + .097$$

$$= -.137 \quad \text{to} \quad .057$$

This confidence interval leaves us unable to conclude that either manufacturer produces a better engine. We are 90% confident that the percentage of Engine Masters engines failing during the warranty period is between 13.7% *lower* and 5.7% *higher* than for the Freed Motors engines.

EXAMPLE 10.9

The Redican Corporation manufactures one-quart metal cans to hold canned vegetable juice. A can is *nonconforming* if it is out of round or has a leak in the side weld. The cans are produced during two shifts, shift 1 (the day shift) and shift 2 (the night shift). The quality supervisor suspects that the proportion of nonconforming cans produced during the day shift (p_1) is *lower* than that for the night shift (p_2), since the day shift has better qualified workers. To investigate this, random samples of 500 cans were obtained from each shift. The results were as follows. Of the $n_1 = 500$ cans from the day shift, $x_1 = 70$ were nonconforming, and of the $n_2 = 500$ cans from the night shift, $x_2 = 110$ were nonconforming. Determine a 95% confidence interval for $p_1 - p_2$.

The proportion estimates are

$$\hat{p}_1 = \frac{70}{500} = .14 \qquad \hat{p}_2 = \frac{110}{500} = .22$$

The 95% confidence interval for $p_1 - p_2$ is

$$(.14 - .22) - 1.96\sqrt{\frac{(.14)(.86)}{499} + \frac{(.22)(.78)}{499}}$$

$$\text{to} \quad (.14 - .22) + 1.96\sqrt{\frac{(.14)(.86)}{499} + \frac{(.22)(.78)}{499}}$$

$$= -.08 - .047 \quad \text{to} \quad -.08 + .047$$

$$= -.127 \quad \text{to} \quad -.033$$

So we are 95% confident that (1) our estimate of the difference in proportions (shift 1 minus shift 2), namely, $\hat{p}_1 - \hat{p}_2 = -.08$, is within 4.7% of the actual value, and (2) the proportion of nonconforming cans during shift 1 is between 3.3% and 12.7% *lower* than for shift 2.

Choosing the Samples Sizes (Two Populations)

In Chapter 9, we discussed how to select samples from two populations when the desired accuracy of the point estimate of the difference between two population means is specified—this is the margin of error, E. If E is 10 pounds, for instance, then what sample sizes (n_1 and n_2) are necessary for the point estimate of $\mu_1 - \mu_2$ (namely, $\overline{X}_1 - \overline{X}_2$) to be within 10 pounds of the actual value, with 95% (of whatever) confidence? Using the results in Appendix B contained in the textbook CD, values of n_1 and n_2 were provided in Chapter 9 to minimize the total sample size, $n_1 + n_2$, for this specific value of E.

We encounter a similar situation when dealing with two population proportions, p_1 and p_2. If a margin of error of $E = .10$, for instance, is specified, then the question of interest is, what sample sizes (n_1 and n_2) are necessary for the point estimate of $p_1 - p_2$ (namely, $\hat{p}_1 - \hat{p}_2$) to be within .10 of the actual value, with 95% (or whatever) confidence?

The margin of error, E, always is the amount that you *add to* and *subtract from* the point estimate when determining a confidence interval. When dealing with two proportions, E is

$$E = Z_{\alpha/2}\sqrt{\frac{\hat{p}_1(1 - \hat{p}_1)}{n_1 - 1} + \frac{\hat{p}_2(1 - \hat{p}_2)}{n_2 - 1}}$$

10.13

To evaluate this expression, you will need estimates of p_1 and p_2. You have two options. If you have previously obtained small samples from these two populations, you can use the resulting sample estimates $\hat{p}_1$ and $\hat{p}_2$. The purpose then will be to extend these samples to obtain better accuracy in the point estimate, $\hat{p}_1 - \hat{p}_2$. If no information regarding p_1 and p_2 is available, then you can use the conservative approach discussed in Section 10.1 by letting $\hat{p}_1 = \hat{p}_2 = .5$.

By applying the results of Appendix H to this situation, the sample sizes n_1 and n_2 that minimize the total sample size $n_1 + n_2$ are given by

$$n_1 = \frac{Z_{\alpha/2}^2(A + B)}{E^2} + 1$$

10.14

$$n_2 = \frac{Z_{\alpha/2}^2(C + B)}{E^2} + 1$$

10.15

where

$$A = \hat{p}_1(1 - \hat{p}_1)$$
$$B = \sqrt{\hat{p}_1 \hat{p}_2(1 - \hat{p}_1)(1 - \hat{p}_2)}$$
$$C = \hat{p}_2(1 - \hat{p}_2)$$

To determine A, B, and C, the estimates $\hat{p}_1$ and $\hat{p}_2$ can be obtained by using one of the two options described in the previous paragraph.

EXAMPLE 10.10

Using the situation described in Example 10.9, determine what sample sizes are necessary for the estimate of the difference between the two proportions to be within .03 of the actual difference, with 99% confidence, if (1) the results from Example 10.9 are available, and (2) no sample information is available.

Solution 1 The specified margin of error is $E = .03$. Sample data have been collected regarding these proportions, so we use the corresponding estimates to determine the sample sizes necessary to obtain this degree of accuracy. Using Table A.4, $Z_{\alpha/2} = Z_{.005} = 2.575$. Here, $\hat{p}_1 = .14$ and $\hat{p}_2 = .22$. Consequently,

$$A = \hat{p}_1(1 - \hat{p}_1)$$
$$= .1204$$

$$B = \sqrt{\hat{p}_1 \hat{p}_2(1 - \hat{p}_1)(1 - \hat{p}_2)}$$
$$= .1437$$

$$C = \hat{p}_2(1 - \hat{p}_2)$$
$$= .1716$$

To obtain the *smallest possible* total sample size for the required accuracy, the two sample sizes should be

$$n_1 = \frac{(2.575)^2 (.1204 + .1437)}{(.03)^2} + 1 \approx 1947$$

(remember—always round up) and

$$n_2 = \frac{(2.575)^2 (.1716 + .1437)}{(.03)^2} + 1 \approx 2324$$

providing a total sample size of $n_1 + n_2 = 4271$ cans.

Solution 2 If no prior estimates of p_1 and p_2 are available, using $\hat{p}_1 = \hat{p}_2 = .5$ will result in sample sizes n_1 and n_2 that will provide a margin of error *no larger than* the specified value of $E = .03$. Here, $A = (.5)(.5) = .25$. Similarly, $B = C = .25$, so

$$n_1 = n_2 = \frac{(2.575)^2 (.25 + .25)}{(.03)^2} + 1 \approx 3685$$

Consequently, a total sample size of $n_1 + n_2 = 7370$ cans will be necessary for $\hat{p}_1 - \hat{p}_2$ to be within .03 of the actual value of $p_1 - p_2$, with 99% confidence.

Hypothesis Testing for p_1 and p_2 (Large, Independent Samples)

Suppose that a recent report stated that, based on a sample of 500 people, 35% of all cigarette smokers had at some time in their lives developed a particular fatal disease. On the other hand, 25% of the nonsmokers in the sample acquired the disease. Can we conclude from this sample that, because $\hat{p}_1 = .35 > \hat{p}_2 = .25$, the proportion ($p_1$) of all smokers who will acquire the disease exceeds the proportion (p_2) for nonsmokers? In other words, is $\hat{p}_1$ *significantly* larger than $\hat{p}_2$? After all, even if $p_1 = p_2$, there is a 50–50 chance that $\hat{p}_1$ will be larger than $\hat{p}_2$, because for large samples, the distribution of $\hat{p}_1 - \hat{p}_2$ is approximately a bell-shaped (normal) curve centered at $p_1 - p_2$, which, if $p_1 = p_2$, would be zero.

Are the results of the sample significant, or are they due simply to the sampling error that is always present when estimating from a sample? Your alternative hypothesis can be that two proportions are *different* (a two-tailed test) or that one *exceeds* the other (a one-tailed test). As before, we will assume that the two random samples are obtained *independently*. The possible hypotheses are these:

FOR A TWO-TAILED TEST

H_0: $p_1 = p_2$

H_a: $p_1 \neq p_2$

FOR A ONE-TAILED TEST

H_0: $p_1 \leq p_2$ $\qquad$ H_0: $p_1 \geq p_2$

or

H_a: $p_1 > p_2$ $\qquad$ H_a: $p_1 < p_2$

One possible test statistic to use here would be the standard normal (Z) statistic that was used to derive a confidence interval for $p_1 - p_2$, namely,

$$Z = \frac{\hat{p}_1 - \hat{p}_2}{\sqrt{\dfrac{\hat{p}_1(1 - \hat{p}_1)}{n_1 - 1} + \dfrac{\hat{p}_2(1 - \hat{p}_2)}{n_2 - 1}}}$$

10.16

In previous tests of hypothesis, we always examined the distribution of the test statistic when H_0 was *true*. For a one-tailed test, we assumed the boundary condition of H_0, which in this case is $p_1 = p_2$. Because of this, whenever we obtained a value of the test statistic in one of the tails, our decision was to reject H_0 because this value would be very unusual if H_0 were true. This reasoning was used for test statistics that followed a Z, t, χ^2, or F distribution.

We use the same approach here. If $p_1 = p_2 = p$ (for example), we can improve the test statistic in equation 10.16. For this situation, p is the proportion of successes in the combined population. Our best estimate of p is the proportion of successes in the *combined sample*. So define

$$\bar{p} = \frac{x_1 + x_2}{n_1 + n_2}$$

Thus, assuming $p_1 = p_2$, $\hat{p}_1 - \hat{p}_2$ is approximately a normal random variable with

$$\text{mean} = p_1 - p_2 = 0$$

and

$$\text{standard deviation} = \sqrt{\frac{p_1(1 - p_1)}{n_1} + \frac{p_2(1 - p_2)}{n_2}}$$

$$\approx \sqrt{\frac{\bar{p}(1 - \bar{p})}{n_1} + \frac{\bar{p}(1 - \bar{p})}{n_2}}$$

The resulting test statistic for p_1 versus p_2 (large, independent samples; $n_1\hat{p}_1$, $n_1(1-\hat{p}_1)$, $n_2\hat{p}_2$ and $n_2(1-\hat{p}_2)$ are each greater than 5) is

$$Z = \frac{\hat{p}_1 - \hat{p}_2}{\sqrt{\dfrac{\overline{p}(1-\overline{p})}{n_1} + \dfrac{\overline{p}(1-\overline{p})}{n_2}}} \qquad 10.17$$

where

$$\hat{p}_1 = \frac{x_1}{n_1} \qquad \hat{p}_2 = \frac{x_2}{n_2} \qquad \overline{p} = \frac{x_1 + x_2}{n_1 + n_2}$$

Observe that the form of this test statistic is the same as for the single-population case described in equation 10.8. The test procedure is the standard routine when using the Z distribution.*

FOR A TWO-TAILED TEST

$$H_0: p_1 = p_2$$
$$H_a: p_1 \neq p_2$$
reject H_0 if $|Z| > Z_{\alpha/2}$

---

where Z is defined in equation 10.17.

FOR A ONE-TAILED TEST

$$H_0: p_1 \leq p_2 \qquad\qquad H_0: p_1 \geq p_2$$
$$H_a: p_1 > p_2 \quad \text{or} \quad H_a: p_1 < p_2$$
reject H_0 if $Z > Z_\alpha$ $\qquad$ reject H_0 if $Z < -Z_\alpha$

EXAMPLE 10.11

Using the engine failure data from Example 10.8, determine whether there is any difference between the proportion of Engine Masters engines (population 1) and the proportion of Freed Motors engines (population 2) that failed in the one-year warranty period. Let $\alpha = .10$.

Solution   The five-step procedure is the correct one. The confidence interval derived in Example 10.8 would produce the same result as the five-step procedure *if* the test statistic were the one defined in equation 10.16. *The correct procedure here is to use the Z-statistic in equation 10.17 as your test statistic.*

Step 1. Since we are looking for a difference between p_1 and p_2, define

$$H_0: p_1 = p_2$$
$$H_a: p_1 \neq p_2$$

Step 2. The test statistic is

$$Z = \frac{\hat{p}_1 - \hat{p}_2}{\sqrt{\dfrac{\overline{p}(1-\overline{p})}{n_1} + \dfrac{\overline{p}(1-\overline{p})}{n_2}}}$$

---

*As a final word here, always use the Z statistic in equation 10.17 to test two proportions. Equation 10.16 is included for discussion purposes only in this section and should never be used as the test statistic.

FIGURE

10.5

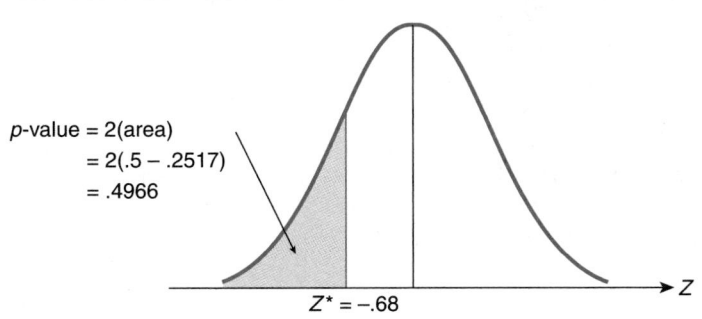

p-value = 2(area)

= 2(.5 − .2517)

= .4966

$Z^* = -.68$

Z curve showing
p-value (twice the
shaded area) for
Example 10.11.

Step 3. Using $\alpha = .10$, then $Z_{\alpha/2} = Z_{.05} = 1.645$. The test procedure will be to

$$\text{reject } H_0 \text{ if } |Z| > 1.645$$

Step 4. Since $n_1 = 100$, $x_1 = 28$, and $n_2 = 150$, $x_2 = 48$, then

$$\bar{p} = \frac{x_1 + x_2}{n_1 + n_2} = \frac{76}{250} = .304$$

Therefore, our estimate of the proportion of engines failing within the warranty period for the combined population (if $p_1 = p_2$) is $\bar{p} = .304$ (30.4%). Also, $\hat{p}_1 = 28/100 = .28$ and $\hat{p}_2 = 48/150 = .32$. The value of the test statistic is

$$Z^* = \frac{.28 - .32}{\sqrt{\dfrac{(.304)(.696)}{100} + \dfrac{(.304)(.696)}{150}}} = \frac{-.04}{.059} = -.68$$

Because $|Z^*| = .68 < 1.645$, we fail to reject H_0.

Step 5. There is *insufficient evidence* to conclude that a difference exists between the two brands of engines as far as engine durability during the warranty period is concerned.

The Z curve and calculated p-value for Example 10.11 are shown in Figure 10.5. The p-value is twice the shaded area (this was a two-tailed test) and is .4966, which is extremely large. Using the classical approach, because .4966 > $\alpha = .10$, we fail to reject H_0—there is insufficient evidence to indicate a difference in engine durability. As a reminder, this reasoning *always* leads to the same conclusion as the five-step procedure. Because .4966 exceeds *any* reasonable value of α, we fail to reject H_0 quite strongly for this application.

EXAMPLE

10.12

In Example 10.9, we examined the proportions of nonconforming metal cans produced by Redican during the day shift (p_1) and the night shift (p_2). Based on these data, can you conclude that the proportion of nonconforming cans during the day shift is lower than during the night shift? Use the p-value and a significance level of .05.

Step 1. We wish to know whether the data warrant the conclusion that p_1 is **Solution**
smaller than p_2. Placing this in the alternative hypothesis leads to

$$H_0: p_1 \geq p_2$$

$$H_a: p_1 < p_2$$

FIGURE

10.6

Z curve showing the calculated *p*-value for Example 10.12.

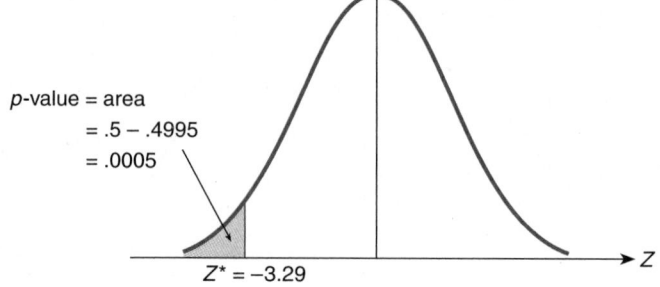

p-value = area
= .5 − .4995
= .0005

$Z^* = -3.29$

Steps 2, 3. Using the test statistic in equation 10.17, the resulting one-tailed test procedure would be to

reject H_0 if $Z < -Z_{.05} = -1.645$

This is the same as rejecting H_0 if the resulting *p*-value < .05.

Step 4. We have

$$\hat{p}_1 = \frac{70}{500} = .14 \qquad \text{and} \qquad \hat{p}_2 = \frac{110}{500} = .22$$

Also,

$$\bar{p} = \frac{(70 + 110)}{(500 + 500)} = \frac{180}{1000} = .18$$

Consequently,

$$Z^* = \frac{.14 - .22}{\sqrt{\dfrac{(.18)(.82)}{500} + \dfrac{(.18)(.82)}{500}}} = \frac{-.08}{.0243} = -3.29$$

The *Z* curve and calculated *p*-value of .0005 are shown in Figure 10.6. H_0 is rejected since (1) −3.29 is less than −1.645 and, as a result, (2) the *p*-value of .0005 is less than $\alpha = .05$. Condition (2) is actually a restatement of condition (1), since .0005 is the area to the left of −3.29 and .05 is the area to the left of −1.645.

Step 5. There *is* evidence that the proportion of nonconforming cans is smaller during the day shift.

An Excel solution to Example 10.12 using the macro from KPK Data Analysis is shown in Figure 10.7. To obtain this solution, click on **KPK Data Analysis ➤ Inference on Proportions ➤ Two Population Proportions.** Under Sample 1, enter "70" in the **Number of Successes** box and "500" in the **Sample Size** box. In the Sample 2 boxes, enter "110" and "500." Next, enter 5 in the **Alpha** box and click on the box alongside **Hypothesis Test.** Finally, click on **Left-Tail Test** and enter "A1" in the **Output Range** box. The resulting output agrees with the previous solution. In particular, the small *p*-value of .0005 (in cell B7, Figure 10.7) supports the alternative hypothesis that the proportion of defective cans *is* smaller during the day shift.

FIGURE

10.7

Excel solution to Example 10.12 using **KPK Data Analysis ➤ Inference on Proportions ➤ Two Population Proportions.**

X Exercises 10.31–10.39

Understanding the Mechanics

10.31 Using random samples from population 1 and population 2, the following sample sizes and number of successes were observed:

$$n_1 = 50, \quad x_1 = 40, \quad n_2 = 80, \quad x_2 = 70$$

a. Construct a 90% confidence interval for the difference in the proportions of successes for the two populations.

b. Test the hypothesis that the proportions of successes for the two populations differ. Use a .05 significance level.

c. Find the p-value for the test in part b.

10.32 Determine what sample sizes are necessary for the estimate of the difference between two proportions to be within .03 of the actual difference with 95% confidence if:

a. Previous estimates of p_1 and p_2 are known to be .18 and .26.

b. No prior estimates of p_1 and p_2 are available.

Applying the New Concepts

10.33 How does the value of the test statistic given in equation 10.17 change if $\hat{p}_1$, the proportion of successes for sample 1, is replaced by the proportion of failures for sample 1 and if $\hat{p}_2$, the proportion of successes for sample 2, is replaced by the proportion of failures for sample 2?

10.34 Nearly three out of four online teenagers, 13 million, use instant messages (IMs), according to a study of children 12 to 17 years of age in a Pew Internet and American Life project. Suppose that a researcher believes that the percentage of females using IMs is higher than the percentage of males using IMs. A random sample of 500 males and 500 females was selected and 390 males and 430 females were found to have used IMs within the past week. Based on these data, can the researcher conclude that the percentage of females using IMs is higher than the percentage of males using IMs during the past week? Use a 10% significance level.

(Source: "Online Teens Are Instantly in Touch," *USA Today*, June 21, 2001, p. 1D.)

10.35 Baby boomers, those born from 1946 through 1964, tend to concentrate in regions of fast job growth. States like Washington and Virginia, each having approximately 31% of its population as boomers, attract baby boomers because of their robust economies. Suppose that a demographer wished to obtain a 95% confidence interval for the difference in the proportions of baby boomers in Washington and Idaho, with a margin of error of 3%.

a. Assume that previous estimates of the proportion of baby boomers in Washington and Idaho were 31% and 27%. What sample sizes would the demographer need?

b. Assume that the demographer had no previous estimates of the proportion of baby boomers in Washington and Idaho. What sample sizes would the demographer need?

(Source: "Baby Boomers Start to Bunch Up," *USA Today*, May 29, 2001, p. 4A.)

10.36 Very few metropolitan areas in the United States have more than 25% of the adult population possessing a passport. New York City and San Francisco have the highest percentages of adults possessing a current U.S. passport. Suppose that a survey by a travel agency was conducted to determine if there is a significant difference in the proportion of adults in these two cities that possess a current passport. If a random sample of 300 adults from each city revealed that 105 and 90 adults from San Francisco and New York City, respectively, hold a current passport, what conclusion can the travel agency make? Use a 5% significance level.

(Adapted from "Passports at the Ready," *USA Today*, September 25–27, 1998, p. 1A.)

10.37 A quality engineer wishes to determine if there is a difference in the number of nonconforming bottle-top seals produced by two different assembly-line processes. A bottle-top seal is nonconforming if the seal is not airtight. To investigate this, the engineer samples 300 bottle-top seals from each assembly-line process. The samples reveal that one process produced eight nonconforming items and the other produced 12 nonconforming items. Based on these data, can the engineer conclude that there is a significant difference in the number of nonconforming bottle-top seals produced by the two assembly-line processes? Use the *p*-value to support your conclusion.

Using the Computer

10.38 **[DATA SET EX10-38]** *Variable description:*

MalesInterested: A *Yes* indicates that a male is interested in a sales manager position, and a *No* indicates no interest

FemalesInterested: A *Yes* indicates that a female is interested in a sales manager position, and a *No* indicates no interest

The vice president at Global Life Insurance Company is interested in the proportion of male college business students and female college business students that would be willing to interview for a sales manager position at the company. Random samples of 170 males and 115 females from college business students were selected. Responses were recorded as *Yes* or *No* and are listed in variables MalesInterested and FemalesInterested. Test that the proportion of male students exceeds the proportion of female students interested in this position. Use the *p*-value of test statistic as the basis for your conclusion.

10.39 **[DATA SET EX10-39]** *Variable description:*

ManufactA: A 1 indicates a defective motor and a 0 indicates that the motor is not defective from manufacturer A

ManufactB: A 1 indicates a defective motor and a 0 indicates that the motor is not defective from manufacturer B

Two manufacturers supply rebuilt motors to an air conditioning repair company. The manager at the air conditioning repair company believes that the proportion of defective motors from the two manufacturers differs. A random sample of 150 rebuilt motors from manufacturer A and 150 rebuilt motors from manufacturer B were selected. Variables ManufactA and ManufactB contain a 1 or a 0 to indicate a defective or nondefective motor.

a. Use the two-sample proportions test to test that there is sufficient evidence to indicate a difference. Use a 5% significance level.

b. What is the estimate of the pooled proportion, $\bar{p}$?

c. Use the Z statistic to test for a difference in the means of the two variables. Assign σ the value of $\sqrt{2\bar{p}(1-\bar{p})}$. What resemblance is there to the test in part a?

 Summary

You will often encounter a situation in which you are concerned with a **population proportion** rather than the mean or variance. For example, the parameter of interest might be the proportion (*p*) of executives earning more than $100,000 annually, rather than the average salary (μ) or the standard deviation (σ) of the salaries. The usual procedure of estimating a population parameter using the sample estimator, $\hat{p}$, allows us to derive a point estimate and construct a confidence interval for *p*. The average value of $\hat{p}$ (if samples were obtained indefinitely) is equal to *p*; hence $\hat{p}$ is said to be an **unbiased** estimator of *p*. The estimated standard deviation of $\hat{p}$ is called the estimated **standard error** of $\hat{p}$. When the sample is small, Table A.8 provides an exact confidence interval for *p*. For large samples, the Central Limit Theorem can be applied to determine an approximate confidence interval, provided that *both* $n\hat{p}$ and $n(1-\hat{p})$ are greater than 5.

When the desired accuracy of the point estimator, $\hat{p}$, is specified in advance, you can determine the sample size necessary to obtain this degree of accuracy for a certain confidence level. To derive this sample size, an estimate of *p* is necessary. You can calculate this value using a previous sample estimate or, if no information is available, using a conservative procedure and making $\hat{p} = .5$.

When you investigate a statement concerning a population proportion, you can use a statistical test of hypothesis. For small samples, the confidence interval from Table A.8 provides an exact procedure for either a one- or two-tailed test. For tests of a hypothesis when a large sample is used, a test statistic having an approximate standard normal distribution can be used.

To compare *two population proportions* (p_1 and p_2), two *independent* random samples are obtained, one from each population. Procedures for large, independent samples generally provide an accurate confidence interval or test of hypothesis whenever $n_1\hat{p}_1$, $n_1(1-\hat{p}_1)$, $n_2\hat{p}_2$, and $n_2(1-\hat{p}_2)$ each exceed 5. Using a standard normal approximation, we can construct a confidence interval for $p_1 - p_2$. If the accuracy of this estimate is specified, the sample sizes necessary to obtain this level of accuracy as well as to minimize the total sample size $n_1 + n_2$ can be obtained.

Two population proportions can be compared by using two large, independent samples to evaluate a test statistic having an approximate standard normal distribution. We examined procedures for a one-tailed test (for example, $H_a: p_1 > p_2$) or a two-tailed test ($H_a: p_1 \neq p_2$). The rejection regions for these tests are defined using the areas from Table A.4.

Summary of Formulas

Single Population

1. Point estimate of population proportion (p):

$$\hat{p} = \frac{x}{n}$$

where

x = number of sample items having the selected attribute

n = sample size

2. Confidence interval for p (large sample):

$$\hat{p} \pm Z_{\alpha/2} \sqrt{\frac{\hat{p}(1-\hat{p})}{n-1}}$$

3. Sample size necessary to obtain margin of error (E) with $(1-\alpha) \cdot 100\%$ confidence:

$$n = \frac{Z_{\alpha/2}^2 \hat{p}(1-\hat{p})}{E^2} + 1$$

4. Test statistic for hypothesis testing on p (large sample):

$$Z = \frac{\hat{p} - p_0}{\sqrt{\frac{p_0(1-p_0)}{n}}}$$

where p_0 is the hypothesized value of p.

Two Populations (Large, Independent Samples)

1. Confidence interval for $p_1 - p_2$:

$$(\hat{p}_1 - \hat{p}_2) \pm Z_{\alpha/2} \sqrt{\frac{\hat{p}_1(1-\hat{p}_1)}{n_1 - 1} + \frac{\hat{p}_2(1-\hat{p}_2)}{n_2 - 1}}$$

2. Samples sizes necessary to obtain margin of error (E) with $(1-\alpha) \cdot 100\%$ confidence (total sample size minimized):

$$n_1 = \frac{Z_{\alpha/2}^2 (A+B)}{E^2} + 1$$

$$n_2 = \frac{Z_{\alpha/2}^2 (C+B)}{E^2} + 1$$

where

$$A = \hat{p}_1(1-\hat{p}_1)$$

$$B = \sqrt{\hat{p}_1 \hat{p}_2 (1-\hat{p}_1)(1-\hat{p}_2)}$$

$$C = \hat{p}_2(1-\hat{p}_2)$$

3. Test statistic for hypothesis testing on p_1 and p_2:

$$Z = \frac{\hat{p}_1 - \hat{p}_2}{\sqrt{\frac{\bar{p}(1-\bar{p})}{n_1} + \frac{\bar{p}(1-\bar{p})}{n_2}}}$$

where

$$\bar{p} = \frac{x_1 + x_2}{n_1 + n_2}$$

X Review Exercises 10.40–10.63

10.40 Conduct the test indicated in each of the following cases for a random sample of size n with an estimate of the population proportion given by $\hat{p}$.
  a. $H_0: p = p_0$ versus $H_a: p \neq p_0$, $n = 10$, $\hat{p} = .60$, $p_0 = .30$, $\alpha = .10$
  b. $H_0: p = p_0$ versus $H_a: p \neq p_0$, $n = 20$, $\hat{p} = .40$, $p_0 = .15$, $\alpha = .05$
  c. $H_0: p = p_0$ versus $H_a: p \neq p_0$, $n = 100$, $\hat{p} = .10$, $p_0 = .16$, $\alpha = .01$
  d. $H_0: p \leq p_0$ versus $H_a: p > p_0$, $n = 150$, $\hat{p} = .88$, $p_0 = .83$, $\alpha = .05$

10.41 An advertising agent for Computerized Telephone Systems claims that the proportion of installed telephone systems that have maintenance problems during the first three years is less than 10%. A random sample of 19 computerized telephone systems that were installed within the last three years was taken, and one of the telephone systems was found to have needed repairs.
  a. Test the advertising agent's claim at the .05 significance level. Use Table A.8.
  b. Find a 90% confidence interval for the true proportion of installed telephone systems that have maintenance problems.

10.42 Seventy-three percent of all retired Americans have a will. However, the percentage of full-time employees that have a will is only 35%. Suppose that an employer randomly asked 15 of the company employees if they had a will. Assume that 6 of them had a will.

a. At the 5% significance level, can it be concluded that the proportion of company employees that have a will is less than 50%?

b. Find a 95% confidence interval for the proportion of employees who have a will. Use Table A.8.

c. Assume you have no prior knowledge of the proportion of company employees that have a will. Estimate the sample size that is required to estimate this proportion with 90% confidence if the margin of error is specified as 8%.

(Source: "Retirees Most Likely to Have Wills," *USA Today,* September 11, 2001, p. 1B.)

10.43 Web site visitors are often loath to disclose personal information when making a purchase on the Internet. Despite safeguards, approximately 60% of all consumers who make purchases on the Internet do not feel comfortable giving their credit card number. Suppose that a random sample of 15 individuals who have made purchases over the Internet were selected at a shopping center and asked if they felt comfortable giving their credit card over the Internet. Assume that nine of the participants of this survey did not feel comfortable with this.

a. At the 5% significance level, can it be concluded that more consumers who make purchases on the Internet do not feel comfortable giving their credit card number than those that do?

b. Find a 95% confidence interval for the proportion of consumers who make purchases on the Internet that do not feel comfortable giving their credit card number.

c. Assume that you have no prior knowledge of p (proportion of consumers who make purchases on the Internet that do not feel comfortable giving their credit card number). Estimate the sample size that is required to estimate p with 95% confidence, assuming a margin of error of 8%.

(Source: "Why Do You Ask?" *The Wall Street Journal,* June 25, 2001, p. R17.)

10.44 A Gallup Poll of 1,025 adults revealed that 205 of these Americans do not own a credit card. Estimate the proportion of all Americans that do not own a credit card. Compute a 90% confidence interval for this proportion. What is the margin of error?

(Source: "Most Americans Have One or Two Credit Cards," *USA Today,* June 1, 2001, p. 1A.)

10.45 California has an unusually large number of small companies. Only 3% of all businesses in California are considered to have over 100 employees. These businesses are especially vulnerable to California's rising electric utility costs. Suppose that a politician believes that the percent of businesses with more than 100 employees is higher in Southern California than the state average of 3%. What sample size is required to estimate the proportion of businesses in Southern California with more than 100 employees with a margin of error of 1% using a confidence level of 95%?

(Source: "California's Many Small Businesses," *USA Today,* July 5, 2001, p. 1B.)

10.46 Holiday Inn ran a TV ad that showed ordinary people achieving extraordinary things like preventing a nuclear power plant accident, exploring a virus, studying the habits of the great white shark, or performing in a rock group. The heroes are not the people that they pretend to be, but when the truth is discovered, they all say that they got their smarts because they stayed at a Holiday Inn Express. Marketing analysts were surprised that only about 20% of the population really liked the ad. Suppose a marketing analyst believes that males think more highly of the ad than females. From a random sample of 500 males and 500 females, the analyst found that 114 males and 74 females really liked the ad a lot. Do the data support the market analyst's belief? Base your conclusion on the p-value.

(Source: "Stay Smart, Save the Day," *USA Today,* July 16, 2001, p. 4B.)

10.47 *People's Choice,* a monthly magazine, claimed that more than 40% of its subscribers had an annual income of $50,000 or more. In a random sample of 62 subscribers, 30 had incomes of $50,000 or more. Does this information substantiate the magazine's claim? Use a significance level of .10.

10.48 Marketing researchers like to contrast cities to gain insight into how consumers will react to different marketing strategies. One example is the difference between New York City and San Diego. The median age in San Diego is 43.8 versus 48.0 in New York City. Also

New York City has about 15% of its population making over $100,000 annually versus 10% for San Diego. Suppose that a marketing researcher is interested in the percentage of adults that watch TV sports. A random sample of 250 for each city yielded 98 and 108 for New York City and San Diego, respectively. Can the marketing researcher conclude that the proportion of adults in San Diego that watch TV sports is greater than that in New York City? Use a 5% significance level.

(Source: "Tale of Two Cities," *USA Today*, October 20, 1998, p. 1A.)

10.49 Microsoft had 10% of the handheld operating systems in 1998. This percentage grew to 20% in 2001. Suppose that a researcher randomly sampled handheld operating systems during 2002 and computed a 95% confidence interval on the percent of handheld operating systems made by Microsoft to be 10% to 36%.

a. What is the researcher's estimate of Microsoft's share of the market for handheld operating systems?

b. What is the margin of error for the researcher's confidence interval?

c. Approximately what sample size did the researcher use?

(Source: "Microsoft Keeps Growing," *USA Today*, June 1, 2001, p. 2B.)

10.50 The rise in the number of TV viewers watching cable TV is directly proportionate to investments in TV programming. TV viewers will watch the channel where the hot program is. Cable TV has been successful at offering many hot programs, thus giving the network programs a smaller viewership. In 1997, 36% of prime-time viewing was done on cable. Suppose that Nielsen Media Research found a confidence interval on the current proportion of viewers who watch cable during prime time to be 30.35% to 49.65% from a random sample of 100 TV viewers.

a. What is the estimate of the proportion of TV viewers who watch cable during prime time?

b. What is the confidence level?

(Source: "Cable Keeps Coming on Strong," *USA Today*, July 17, 1998, p. 2E.)

10.51 Must a confidence interval for a proportion contain the true proportion of the population? Explain what the "level of confidence" means for a confidence interval.

10.52 A market-research firm believed that the proportion of households with more than four family members in county 1 was greater than the probability of households with more than four family members in county 2. The firm gathered random samples of size 180 and 155 from counties 1 and 2, respectively. The number of households with more than four members were 74 from county 1 and 61 from county 2. From these data, can we conclude that the proportion of households with more than four members is higher in county 1 than in county 2? Use a significance level of .01.

10.53 Calculate the *p*-value for Exercise 10.52. Using the *p*-value, would you reject the null hypothesis at the .05 level?

10.54 The percentage of food bought at supermarkets for home-cooked meals has been declining since 1993 as Americans turn more to other grocery sources, such as specialty food stores and warehouse clubs. In 2000, the percentage of households buying their groceries only from supermarkets was 55.8%. Suppose that a supermarket consultant randomly sampled 200 residents from Atlanta, Georgia, to determine if this percentage still held for this locality. Assume that 118 individuals were found to buy their groceries only from supermarkets.

a. What is the estimate of the proportion of residents in Atlanta that buy their groceries only from supermarkets?

b. Using the *p*-value, is there evidence to support the hypothesis that the proportion of Atlanta's residents that buy their groceries only from supermarkets differs from .558?

c. Do you believe that a 95% confidence interval for the proportion of Atlanta's residents that buy their groceries only from supermarkets would include the value .558? Why?

(Source: "Supermarket Purchases Declining," *USA Today*, July 18, 2001, p. 1A.)

10.55 A market-research firm is interested in testing the hypothesis that the proportion of students who own a car is the same for the local state university campus and a local private college. They interviewed 240 students from the state university and 270 from the private college. The number of students who did not own a car was 78 at the state university and 82 at the private college. Using a .02 significance level, test the hypothesis.

10.56 For Exercise 10.55, construct a 95% confidence interval for the difference of the true proportions of students who own cars at the two campuses.

10.57 Two machines are used in a production process to cut metal circles from thin sheets of steel. If the circumference of the steel circles are larger than 9.01 inches or smaller than 9.00 inches, the steel circles are considered to be *nonconforming*. The quality supervisor suspected that the number of nonconforming steel circles produced by the older machine was larger than that for the newer machine. The supervisor randomly selected 400 steel circles from each machine. The data revealed that of the 400 steel circles from the older machine, 86 were nonconforming, and of the 400 steel circles from the newer machine, 56 were nonconforming.

   a. Determine a 95% confidence interval for the difference in the proportion of nonconforming steel circles produced by the machines.

   b. How much larger would the sample size need to be for the difference between the two proportions in part a to be within .05 of the actual difference with 95% confidence?

10.58 Los Angeles and San Francisco are very different in their attraction to the younger population. In 2000, only 14.5% of the population in San Francisco was younger than 18 whereas 26.6% of the population of Los Angeles was younger than 18. Suppose that an urban expert wished to obtain a 95% confidence interval for the difference in the proportions of the population younger than 18 that live in San Francisco and Los Angeles during 2002.

   a. What sample sizes are necessary to obtain a margin of error of 3%?

   b. Use a margin of error of 2% in part a. Contrast the samples sizes needed for a margin of error of 2% and 3%.

(Source: "Percentage of Those Younger than 18 in Most Populous Cities," *USA Today*, June 13, 2001, p. 3A.)

10.59 Hewlett-Packard's CEO Carleton Fiorina points out that Hewlett-Packard has gained market share in each of its product lines. The competition for the disk storage market is particularly challenging with EMC being its main competitor. To determine the difference in the proportion of the market obtained by these two hi-tech companies, suppose that the CEO wishes to obtain a 95% confidence interval for the difference in the proportions of the market for these two companies.

   a. What sample sizes are necessary to obtain a margin of error of 3%? Assume that previous estimates of the proportions for market share of the disk storage market were 18% and 17% for Hewlett-Packard and EMC, respectively.

   b. Suppose that the previous estimates of the proportions of market share were not available. What sample sizes would be necessary in part a?

(Source: "Hewlett-Packard's Diversification," *USA Today*, June 5, 2001, p. 3B.)

10.60 Home ownership in the United States has increased every decade except during the 1980s, when it slipped less than 1%. Today home ownership stands at its highest level in the history of the United States—66.2% of the adult population own their home. However, the two states with the lowest proportion of home ownership are the two most populated states—New York and California. Suppose that 1,000 residents of New York and 1,000 residents of California were randomly sampled. Assume that the sample proportions were 57% for California and 53% for New York.

   a. Construct a 99% confidence interval for the difference of proportions of home ownership in the two states.

   b. If a 99% confidence interval for the difference of proportions of home ownership in the two states is required to have a margin of error of 2%, what sample sizes are required from each city?

   c. Repeat part b using a 90% confidence level. Comment on the difference in the sample sizes.

(Source: "Home Ownership, State by State," *USA Today*, May 23, 2001, p. 2B.)

10.61 Switching to alternate utility providers has not allowed residents to save as much money on their utility bills as they had hoped. In Pennsylvania, the alternate utility provider hired Kenny Loggins, the singer of "Footloose" and "Danger Zone," as its spokesman and awarded prizes to those who switched. Pennsylvania has the highest percentage of residents that have switched to alternate providers. This percentage stood at

12.5% in 2001. The state with the next highest percentage is New York, with 5.3%. Suppose that an energy analyst wished to sample the residents of these two states to estimate the difference in the proportions of residents from these two states who have switched to alternate providers of energy.

a. Determine the necessary sample sizes to estimate the difference between the proportions for these two states to be within .04 of the actual difference with 95% confidence.

b. Find the sample sizes in part a using a 90% confidence level. Compare the sample sizes for both confidence levels.

c. Are the requirements of $n_1\hat{p}_1 > 5$, $n_1(1 - \hat{p}_1) > 5$, $n_2\hat{p}_2 > 5$, and $n_2(1 - \hat{p}_2) > 5$ satisfied for the validity of a confidence interval on $p_1 - p_2$?

(Source: "What Happened?" *The Wall Street Journal,* September 17, 2001, p. R12.)

10.62 Almost 30% of undergraduates in college have taken out a student loan. This percentage is up from 19% ten years ago. The Education Department of the United States has noted that lenders have displayed more flexibility in allowing borrowers to pay off student loans. As a result, the default rate is declining. Suppose that the Education Department believes that the default rate is lower for students graduating from private schools. A random sample of 500 students from each sector yielded default rates of 8.0% and 8.8% from students having attended private and public schools, respectively.

a. Test the Education Department's belief. What is the *p*-value?

b. Suppose that the same proportions were found with sample sizes of 1,000 from each sector. How does the *p*-value change?

(Source: "College Bills: Student Loans Make the Grade," *Kiplinger's Personal Finance Magazine,* vol. 55, issue 10, October 2001, p. 24.)

10.63 Sample proportions can be randomly generated by first randomly generating an observation from a binomial distribution and then dividing that number by the number of trials (*n*) used in the binomial distribution.

a. Generate 40 proportions using a binomial distribution with $n = 20$ and $p = .5$.

b. Calculate the upper and lower bounds of a 90% confidence interval for a proportion using each of the generated proportions in part a.

c. Obtain a graph of the lower and upper bounds in part b similar to the following graph.

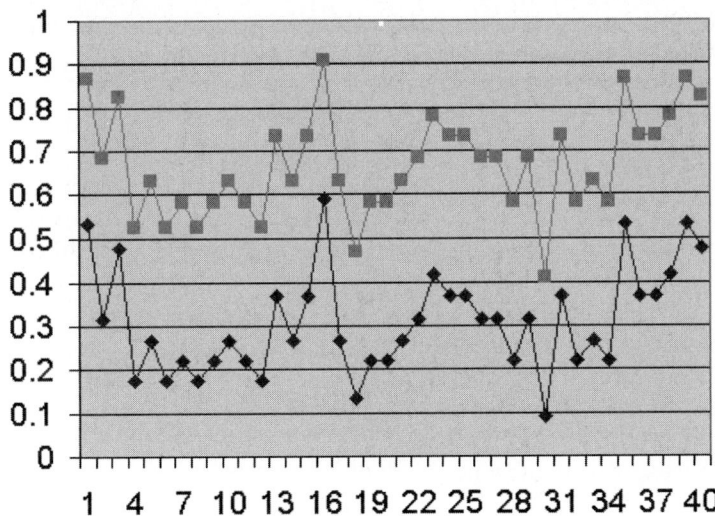

d. The true proportion $p = .5$ is considered to be inside the interval if the line marked .5 on the graph is between the two endpoints. How many intervals contain .5? How many would you expect to contain $p = .5$? Why?

On the CD . . .
Chapter 10 Appendix: Data Analysis with MINITAB

Computer Exercises Using the Databases

Exercise 1—Appendix F

Randomly select 100 observations from the database. Find a 95% confidence interval on the proportion of households that own their homes. (Refer to the variable OWNORENT.)

Exercise 2—Appendix F

Randomly select 100 observations from the database. Estimate the proportion of observations from the NE sector in which the households own their homes. (Refer to the variables LOCATION and OWNORENT.) Also estimate the proportion of observations from the NW sector in which the households own their homes. Find a 95% confidence interval on the difference of the proportions of house owners for the two sectors.

Exercise 3—Appendix G

Randomly select 100 observations from the database. Find a 95% confidence interval on the proportion of companies with a positive net income. (Refer to the variable NETINC.)

Exercise 4—Appendix G

Randomly select 100 observations from the database. Estimate the proportion of observations from companies with an A bond rating that have a positive net income. (Refer to the variables BONDRATE and NETINC.) Also estimate the proportion of observations from companies with a B bond rating that have a positive net income. Find a 95% confidence interval on the difference of the proportions of companies with positive net income between those with A bond ratings and those with B bond ratings.

Insights from Statistics in Action

Streaming Meemies: The Most Valuable Consumer Group on the Internet

The Statistics in Action introductory case discussed how company executives must make decisions on buying ads on Webcasts. They must assess whether streamies are more responsive to their product than nonstreamies. Surveys have illustrated that, in general, streamies are more likely to make online purchases. However, companies must feel assured before making an investment in advertising that the proportion of streamies making purchases of their company's product is significantly more than the Internet surfers that are not focusing on Internet audio or video. A company's decision makers can greatly benefit from using statistical techniques designed to make inferences about a population proportion.

Suppose that a survey of 200 Internet users determined whether the user was a streamie or a nonstreamie and whether the user was very likely to purchase a particular product online. The data are in StatInActChap10.xls. The data in the first column are labeled S for streamie or Non-S for nonstreamie and the data in the second column are labeled Yes, the user is likely to purchase the product online, or No, the user is not likely to purchase the product online. Use these data in answering the following questions.

Form a contingency table with the rows representing the categories of *streamie* or *nonstreamie* and the columns representing the categories of *Yes* or *No* as responses by users to their likelihood of purchasing the product online.

1. Find a 95% confidence interval on the proportion of Internet users that are likely to purchase the product online. Interpret this interval.

2. What sample size would be necessary to obtain a margin of error of 2% in estimating the proportion of Internet users that would purchase the product online?

3. Test that the proportion of Internet users that are streamies differs from the estimate of .44 obtained in a previous survey. Use a 5% significance level.

4. Test that the proportion of streamies who were likely to purchase the product online is greater than the proportion of non-streamies who were likely to purchase the product online. Use a 5% significance level.

(Source: "Marketers Find Lucrative Audience in 'Streamies'," *Advertising Age*, vol. 71, issue 8, 2000, p. 48; "Online Stations Are Still Making Only Small Internet Waves," *The Financial Times*, April 4, 2001, p. 7.).

Analysis of Variance X

Statistics in Action
MBA Programs: Making an Executive Decision to Master Your Career

The MBA degree has evolved over time. An increasing number of business professionals are earning an MBA degree, thinking that their careers will be propelled up the corporate ladder. These professionals know that companies regard these degrees as evidence both of a wider business knowledge beyond one's current functional specialization and of a commitment to furthering one's career. Most employed professionals do not want to forfeit the momentum or the money that their current career provides. So those who decide to pursue an MBA while continuing to work must choose among three hard roads: a traditional Master of Business Administration (MBA) degree, which may be taken part-time generally over three to four years, an executive MBA (EMBA), which can be achieved by giving up weekends during two grueling years, or a global EMBA, which may entail extensive travel.

During the mid-1980s, corporate America was not enamored with MBA degrees. Under pressure from dissatisfied businesses, the American Assembly of Collegiate Schools of Business (AACSB), the accrediting agency for U.S. business schools, commissioned an in-depth study of graduate management programs. When the report came out in 1988, its conclusions were scathing: MBA programs across the country were overly academic and theoretical, needlessly rigid in their requirements, and generally out of touch with the needs of the business world. Many schools—

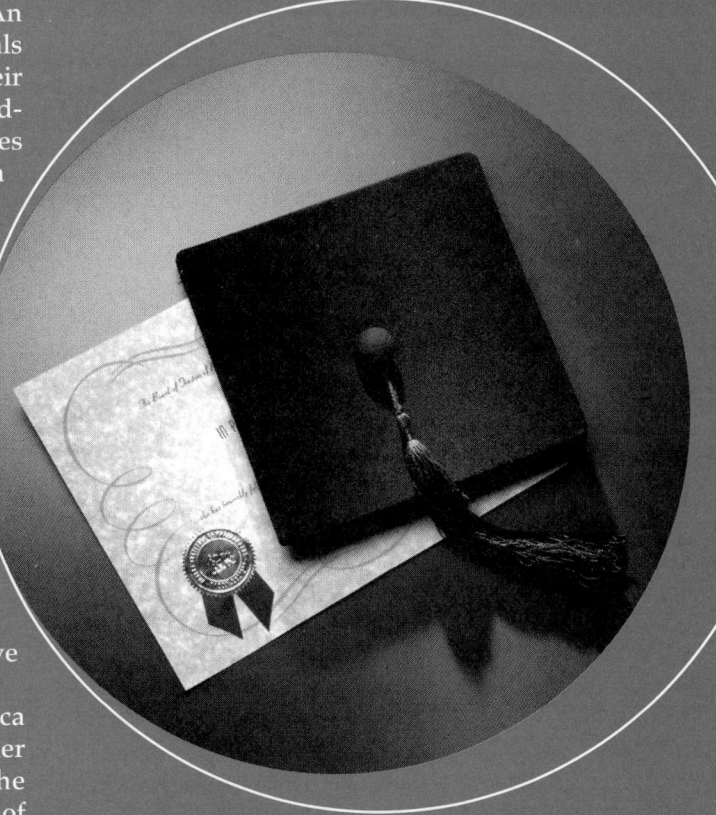

Harvard, Wharton, Maryland, and Georgetown among them—now require students to have worked for at least two years, in some cases, five years. In the Washington, D.C., area, institutions such as Virginia Tech, American University, and George Washington University, all of which candidly admit they are not Stanford, have opted to focus on teaching rather than research and to market themselves as strong regional schools targeting the local job market.

In the past decade, executive MBA programs and global executive MBA programs have emerged as solutions to business's need to invest in the development of their executives. These programs differ from the traditional MBA program in that participants possess substantial corporate experience and remain together for the entire program. The combined experience, expertise, and drive of these executives create an environment that gives them a leg up in understanding how to make businesses thrive. Global EMBA programs take students to "centers of business excellence" around the world, such as Shanghai and Silicon Valley. Global EMBA programs often have partnerships with universities overseas. For example, London Business School and Columbia in New York have modules taught alternately in London and New York.

With the cost of many of the EMBA and global EMBA programs being anywhere from $50,000 to $100,000, corporate leaders are studying the percent change in the salaries of business professionals who have been through either a traditional MBA, an EMBA, or a global EMBA. One question that arises is, "Does the marketability of a business professional differ significantly across these three programs?" When you have completed this chapter, you will be able to

- Test if the mean salary changes for executives participating in a traditional MBA, EMBA, or global EMBA program differ during the years after having completed these programs.
- Obtain a confidence interval on the mean salary change for executives completing any one of the three types of MBA programs.
- Obtain a confidence interval on the *difference* in the mean salary changes for any two of the three types of MBA programs.
- Understand when to use independent and dependent (blocked) samples in testing for differences in group means.

A Look Back/Introduction

In Chapter 9, we considered a question of *type*, do men have the same heights as women? By this we mean, is the *average* height of males equal to the average height of females? We were interested in the means of two populations and performed a test of hypothesis, using, for example, H_0: $\mu_M = \mu_F$ and H_a: $\mu_M \neq \mu_F$. Such tests work well when dealing with two populations, but how can we compare the means of more than two populations? For example, we might wish to examine the average sales of salespeople trained using five different training programs to see whether they are the same. Our hypotheses become

$$H_0: \mu_1 = \mu_2 = \mu_3 = \mu_4 = \mu_5$$

$$H_a: \text{not all } \mu\text{'s are equal}$$

We test such a hypothesis by first collecting five samples, one from each of the training programs (populations). We will see that to compare these five means one pair at a time is *not* the correct approach: This procedure results in 10 different pairwise tests, and what was intended to be a testing procedure with, say, a .05 significance level results in a much higher significance level. In other words, the overall significance level, α, is *larger* than the predetermined value. The correct procedure for this situation is to examine the *variation* of the sales values, both (1) within each of the samples (examining the variability of each sample alone) and (2) among the five samples (for example, are the values in sample 1 larger or smaller, on the average, than the values in the other samples?).

In Chapter 9, we saw that when trying to decide if $\bar{X}_1$ is "significantly different" from $\bar{X}_2$, a key part of the answer rested on the values of s_1 and s_2, the variation *within* the two samples. Both s_1 and s_2 affect the width of the confidence interval for $\mu_1 - \mu_2$. Consequently, we infer something about the *means* of several populations by utilizing the *variation* of the resulting samples. Hence the term *analysis of variance*—our next topic.

COMPARING TWO MEANS: ANOTHER LOOK

We begin with an example. The manufacturer of a small battery-powered tape recorder decides to include four alkaline batteries with its product. Two battery suppliers are being considered; each has its own brand (brand 1 and brand 2). The supervising inspector of incoming quality wants to know if the average lifetimes of the two brands are the same. Based on past experience, she believes that the battery lifetimes follow a *normal* distribution. A simple experiment is conducted: each of 10 batteries (5 of each brand) is connected to a test device that places a small drain on the battery power and records the battery lifetime. The following results (in hours) are obtained:

Brand 1	Brand 2
43	30
48	26
38	37
41	31
51	34

Let μ_1 be the average lifetime (if observed indefinitely) for brand 1 and μ_2 be the average for brand 2. We wish to determine whether the data allow us to conclude that $\mu_1 \neq \mu_2$, using $\alpha = .10$.

We examined the same type of question in Chapter 9; we are dealing with two small, independent samples. In Chapter 9 we advised against assuming that σ_1 was equal to σ_2. As a result, we generally used a t test that did *not* pool the sample variances. However, when examining more than two normal populations (the main concern of this chapter), the following testing procedure for detecting a difference in the population means requires that the populations have the *same* distribution if, in fact, the population means are equal. Consequently, it can be used only when we are willing to assume that the *population variances are equal* (or approximately equal). The analysis of variance procedure is *not* extremely sensitive to departures from this assumption, especially if equal-sized samples are obtained from each population. A procedure for verifying this assumption (similar to the F test used to compare two variances in Chapter 9) is discussed in this chapter.

As a result, we will assume that we have reason to believe that the variation of the brand 1 lifetimes is the same as for brand 2, that is, $\sigma_1 = \sigma_2$. Using the approach discussed in Chapter 9, we first find

$$s_p^2 = \text{pooled variance} = \frac{(n_1 - 1)s_1^2 + (n_2 - 1)s_2^2}{n_1 + n_2 - 2}$$

where n_1, n_2 = sample sizes for brand 1, brand 2 and s_1^2, s_2^2 = sample variances for brand 1, brand 2. Using the sample data,

Brand 1	Brand 2
$n_1 = 5$	$n_2 = 5$
$\bar{x}_1 = 44.2$ hr	$\bar{x}_2 = 31.6$ hr
$s_1 = 5.263$ hr	$s_2 = 4.159$ hr

Consequently,

$$s_p^2 = \frac{(4)(5.263)^2 + (4)(4.159)^2}{8} = \frac{180.0}{8} = 22.5$$

and so

$$s_p = \sqrt{22.5} = 4.74 \text{ hr}$$

The appropriate hypotheses are $H_0: \mu_1 = \mu_2$ and $H_a: \mu_1 \neq \mu_2$. The resulting test statistic is

$$t = \frac{\overline{X}_1 - \overline{X}_2}{s_p \sqrt{\dfrac{1}{n_1} + \dfrac{1}{n_2}}}$$

$$= \frac{44.2 - 31.6}{4.74 \sqrt{\dfrac{1}{5} + \dfrac{1}{5}}} = \frac{12.6}{2.998} = 4.20$$

That is, $t^* = 4.20$.

We are dealing with a two-tailed test using a t statistic with $(n_1 - 1) + (n_2 - 1)$ $= 4 + 4 = 8$ df, so the test procedure is to

$$\text{reject } H_0 \text{ if } |t^*| > t_{\alpha/2,\text{df}} = t_{.05,8} = 1.86$$

Comparing $t^* = 4.20$ to 1.86, we reject H_0 and conclude that the mean lifetimes for the two brands are not the same. Looking at the sample data, we can say that $\overline{x}_1 = 44.2$ is significantly different from $\overline{x}_2 = 31.6$.

The Analysis of Variance Approach

We need to introduce two new terms. The previous example examined the effect of one **factor** (brand), consisting of two **levels** (brand 1 and brand 2). If you want to extend this to four brands (say, brands 1, 2, 3, and 4), then you still have *one* factor but you now have *four* levels.

The purpose of **analysis of variance (ANOVA)** is to determine whether this factor has a *significant effect* on the variable being measured (battery lifetime, in our example). If, for instance, the brand factor *is* significant, the mean lifetimes for the different brands will not be equal. Consequently, testing for equal means among the various brands is the same as attempting to answer the question, is there a significant effect on battery lifetime due to this factor?

This section examines the effect of a single factor on the variable being measured, *one-factor ANOVA*. Extensions of this technique include ANOVA procedures that determine the effect of two or more factors operating simultaneously. These factors may be *qualitative* (such as brand in the previous illustration) or *quantitative* (such as several levels of advertising expenditure).

All 10 values in the battery lifetimes example are different, and we observe a variation in these values. We will look at two *sources of variation:* (1) variation *within* the samples (levels) and (2) variation *between* the samples.

Within-Sample Variation

When you obtain a sample, you usually obtain different values for each observation. The five sample values for brand 1 vary about the mean $\overline{x}_1 = 44.2$ hours, as measured by $s_1 = 5.26$ hours. Likewise, the five values in the second sample also exhibit some variation ($s_2 = 4.16$) about $\overline{x}_2 = 31.6$ hours. These are the **within-sample variations.** They are used when estimating the common population variance, say σ^2. This procedure tends to provide an accurate estimate of σ^2, whether or not the sample means are equal.

Between-Sample Variation

When you compare the two samples, you observe that the values for brand 1 are *larger*, on the average, than those for brand 2. This is summarized in the sample means, where $\overline{x}_1 = 44.2$ appears to be considerably larger than $\overline{x}_2 = 31.6$. So there is a variation in the ten values due to the *brand*; that is, due to the factor. This is **between-sample variation.** In general, if this variation is large, we expect considerable variation among the sample means. The between-sample variation is also used in another estimate of the common variance, σ^2, *provided the population means are equal. In other words, if the means are equal, the between-sample and within-sample estimates of σ^2 should be nearly the same.* As we will see later in this section, we can derive a test of hypothesis procedure for determining whether the means are equal by comparing these two estimates.

Measuring Variation

When using the ANOVA approach, we measure these two sources of variation by calculating various **sums of squares, SS.** We determine

SS(factor), which measures between-sample variation [also called SS(between)]

SS(error), which measures within-sample variation [also called SS(within)]

SS(total) = SS(between) + SS(within) = SS(factor) + SS(error)

Each of the first two sums of squares will have corresponding degrees of freedom, df, which are determined from the number of terms that make up this particular SS. The df for our example are given by

$$df \text{ for factor} = (\text{number of levels}) - 1$$
$$= (\text{number of brands}) - 1$$
$$= 2 - 1 = 1$$
$$df \text{ for error} = (n_1 - 1) + (n_2 - 1)$$
$$= n_1 + n_2 - 2 = 5 + 5 - 2 = 8$$

We will show how to determine these sums of squares and how we combine them and their df into another test statistic for testing $H_0: \mu_1 = \mu_2$ against $H_a: \mu_1 \neq \mu_2$. The beauty of this approach is that it extends nicely to the situation in which you wish to compare more than two means using a *single* test.

Determining SS(Factor). SS(factor) is the sum of squares that determines whether the values in one sample are larger or smaller on the average than the values in the second sample:

$$SS(\text{factor}) = n_1(\bar{x}_1 - \bar{x})^2 + n_2(\bar{x}_2 - \bar{x})^2 \qquad \text{11.1}$$

where, $\bar{x}_1, \bar{x}_2$ are the two sample means and

$$\bar{x} = \frac{\sum(\text{all data values})}{n} = \frac{n_1\bar{x}_1 + n_2\bar{x}_2}{n_1 + n_2}$$

and $n = n_1 + n_2 = $ total sample size.

Another method of determining this sum of squares is much easier if you use a calculator.

$$SS(\text{factor}) = \left[\frac{T_1^2}{n_1} + \frac{T_2^2}{n_2}\right] - \frac{T^2}{n} \qquad \text{11.2}$$

where $T_1 = $ total of the sample 1 observations, $T_2 = $ total of the sample 2 observations, and $T = $ grand total $ = T_1 + T_2$.

Determining SS(Total). SS(total) is a measure of the variation in all $n = n_1 + n_2$ data values. You obtain its value as though you were finding the *variance* of these n values, except that you do not divide by $n - 1$:

$$SS(\text{total}) = \sum(x - \bar{x})^2 \qquad \text{11.3}$$

or (after some algebra similar to that used in Chapter 3),

$$SS(\text{total}) = \sum x^2 - \frac{(\sum x)^2}{n} = \sum x^2 - \frac{T^2}{n}$$

11.4

Determining SS(Error). SS(error) is the measure of the variation *within* each of the samples. Its value simply is the *numerator of the pooled variance, s_p^2,* obtained using the previous *t* test. Thus,

$$SS(\text{error}) = \underbrace{\sum(x - \bar{x}_1)^2}_{\text{first sample}} + \underbrace{\sum(x - \bar{x}_2)^2}_{\text{second sample}}$$

11.5

and therefore,

$$SS(\text{error}) = \sum x^2 - \left[\frac{T_1^2}{n_1} + \frac{T_2^2}{n_2}\right]$$

11.6

Given that

$$SS(\text{total}) = SS(\text{factor}) + SS(\text{error}),$$

a much easier way to find this value is

$$SS(\text{error}) = SS(\text{total}) - SS(\text{factor})$$

11.7

Let us return to the battery lifetimes example. To find the SS(factor) here, we first determine

$$T_1 = 43 + 48 + 38 + 41 + 51 = 221$$
$$T_2 = 30 + 26 + 37 + 31 + 34 = 158$$
$$T = T_1 + T_2 = 221 + 158 = 379$$

So, using equation 11.2,

$$SS(\text{factor}) = \frac{221^2}{5} + \frac{158^2}{5} - \frac{379^2}{10}$$
$$= 14{,}761 - 14{,}361.4 = 396.9$$

To find SS(total), the only new term we need to evaluate is

$$\sum x^2 = \text{sum of each data value squared}$$
$$= 43^2 + 48^2 + \cdots + 31^2 + 34^2 = 14{,}941$$

So, using equation 11.4 [the value 14,364.1 was obtained in SS(factor)],

$$SS(\text{total}) = \sum x^2 - \frac{T^2}{n}$$
$$= 14{,}941 - 14{,}364.1 = 576.9$$

Finally, we find SS(error) by subtraction:

$$SS(\text{error}) = SS(\text{total}) - SS(\text{factor})$$
$$= 576.9 - 396.9 = 180.0$$

ANOVA Test for H_0: $\mu_1 = \mu_2$ versus H_a: $\mu_1 \neq \mu_2$

To begin with, the procedure we are about to define is valid for a *two-tailed test only*. In other words, the alternative hypothesis must be that the two means differ, not that one is larger than the other (a one-tailed test). (When examining more than two means, the alternative hypothesis will be that *at least* two of the means are unequal and H_0 will be that all the means are equal.) The next step when using the ANOVA procedure is to determine something resembling an "average" sum of squares, referred to as a **mean square.** We compute a mean square for only SS(factor) and SS(error), not for SS(total).

$$\text{MS(factor)} = \frac{\text{SS(factor)}}{\text{df for factor}} = \frac{\text{SS(factor)}}{1} \qquad \text{11.8}$$

Note that the df for this term always is (number of levels) − 1. In this section, we are dealing with two levels (populations), and so here df is 1.

$$\text{MS(error)} = \frac{\text{SS(error)}}{\text{df for error}} = \frac{\text{SS(error)}}{n_1 + n_2 - 2} \qquad \text{11.9}$$

We denote the common variance of the two normal populations as σ^2. So $\sigma^2 = \sigma_1^2 = \sigma_2^2$. If the null hypothesis (H_0: the means are equal) is true, then, because the populations have identical means and variances, this implies that under H_0 we are dealing with a *single population.* The ANOVA procedure is based on a comparison between two separate estimates of the variance, σ^2. The first estimate is derived using the variation among the sample means (only two in the previous example). The other estimate is determined using the variation *within* each of the samples.

The ANOVA procedure is based on a comparison of these two estimates of σ^2 because they should be approximately equal *provided H_0 is true.* We have derived these two estimates:

MS(factor) = estimate of σ^2 based on the variation among the sample means

MS(error) = estimate of σ^2 based on the variation within each of the samples

Our new test statistic for testing H_0: $\mu_1 = \mu_2$ versus H_a: $\mu_1 \neq \mu_2$ is the *ratio* of these two estimates:

$$F = \frac{\left(\begin{array}{c}\text{estimated population variance based on}\\ \text{the variation among the sample means}\end{array}\right)}{\left(\begin{array}{c}\text{estimated population variance based on}\\ \text{the variation within each of the samples}\end{array}\right)} = \frac{\text{MS(factor)}}{\text{MS(error)}} \qquad \text{11.10}$$

This test statistic follows an F distribution, which was first introduced in Chapter 9 as a ratio of two variance estimates. The degrees of freedom (df) for the F statistic in equation 11.10 are the df for factor and the df for error; that is, in our present example, the df for F are 1 and $(n_1 + n_2 - 2)$. *Because the* F *statistic is based on a comparison of two variance estimates, this technique is called analysis of variance.*

This is our second encounter with the F distribution. In Chapter 9, we used this distribution to compare two population variances (σ_1^2 and σ_2^2). The shape of this distribution is illustrated in Figure 11.1 and is tabulated in Table A.7. Remember that the shape of the F curve is affected by both the df for the numerator (1 here) and the df for the denominator (here, $n_1 + n_2 - 2$).

Defining the Rejection Region

What happens to the F statistic when H_a is true, that is, when $\mu_1 \neq \mu_2$? In this case, we would expect $\overline{X}_1$ and $\overline{X}_2$ to be "far apart." As a result, the estimate of the variance σ^2 using the *between-sample* variation (measured by MS(factor)) will be *larger*

FIGURE

11.1

Shape of the
F distribution
shown by F curve
with 1 and
$n_1 + n_2 - 2$ df.

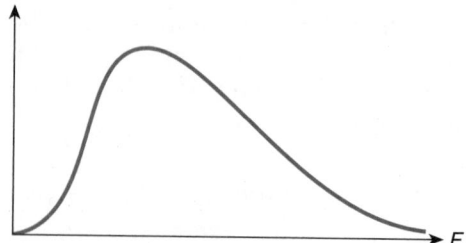

than the estimate of σ^2 based on the *within-sample* variation (measured by MS(error)). This implies that we should reject H_0 in favor of H_a whenever the ratio of these two estimates is large—in which case the computed F value is in the right tail. Consequently, the test procedure will be to

$$\text{reject } H_0 \text{ if } F^* > F_{\alpha, v_1, v_2}$$

where $v_1 = $ df for numerator $= $ (number of levels) $- 1 = 1$, $v_2 = $ df for denominator $= n_1 + n_2 - 2$, and F_{α, v_1, v_2} is obtained from Table A.7 with a right-tail area $= \alpha$.

EXAMPLE

11.1

Using the data from the battery lifetimes example and the previously calculated sums of squares, test $H_0: \mu_1 = \mu_2$ versus $H_a: \mu_1 \neq \mu_2$, where $\mu_1 = $ average lifetime for brand 1, if observed indefinitely, and $\mu_2 = $ average for brand 2. Use a significance level of $\alpha = .10$.

Solution   **Step 1.** The hypotheses are as defined—$H_0: \mu_1 = \mu_2$ and $H_a: \mu_1 \neq \mu_2$.

Step 2. The test statistic is

$$F = \frac{\text{MS(factor)}}{\text{MS(error)}}$$

Step 3. The rejection region [using Table A.7(a)] is

$$\text{reject } H_0 \text{ if } F > F_{.10,1,8} = 3.46$$

Step 4. From the previous calculations, SS(factor) = 396.9 and SS(error) = 180. So,

$$\text{MS(factor)} = \frac{\text{SS(factor)}}{1} = \frac{396.9}{1} = 396.0$$

and

$$\text{MS(error)} = \frac{\text{SS(error)}}{n_1 + n_2 - 2} = \frac{180.0}{8} = 22.5$$

The resulting value of the test statistic is

$$F^* = \frac{396.9}{22.5} = 17.64$$

Because $17.64 > 3.46$, we reject H_0.

Step 5. These data indicate that the mean lifetimes for brand 1 and brand 2 are *not* the same.

Comments

Compare our first treatment of the battery lifetimes problem with Example 11.1. Both solutions led to the same conclusion, namely, that the two average lifetimes are not the same. In fact, the two solutions *always* lead to the same conclusion when comparing *two* means. Furthermore, the *p*-values for the two

FIGURE
11.2

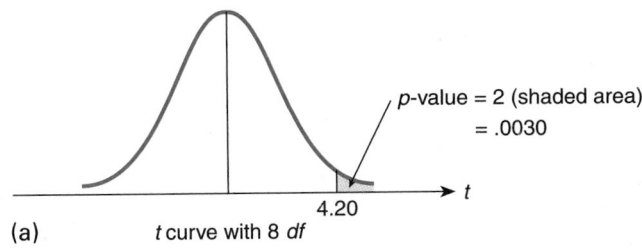

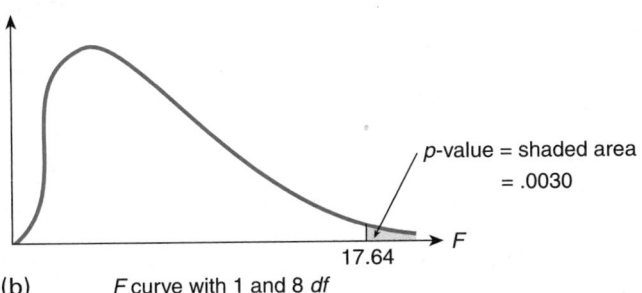

p-values for the solution to the battery lifetimes example.
(a) Solution using pooled variance *t* test. (b) Solution using ANOVA (see Example 11.1).

solutions *are the same*, as illustrated in Figure 11.2. The values were obtained using a computer program (available in Excel and many statistical packages) that provides an exact *p*-value for a *t* or *F*-statistic, given the computed value and corresponding degrees of freedom.

The computed value of the *F*-statistic is equal to the square of the computed value of the *t* statistic because $17.64 = (4.20)^2$. This is true whenever you have an *F*-statistic or table value with 1 df in the numerator. So

$$F^* = (t^*)^2$$

Furthermore, the table values satisfy the same relationship, for example,

$$F_{.10,1,8} = 3.46 = (1.86)^2 = [t_{.05,8}]^2$$

We see that the two tests are *identical*; they produce the same conclusion and *p*-value. Furthermore, the computed value and the table value for the *F*-statistic are the squares of the corresponding values using the *t* statistic. This comparison applies *only* when the *F*-statistic has 1 df in the numerator—that is, when there are two factor levels (as in this illustration). As mentioned previously, the advantage of the ANOVA approach is that it extends very easily to the situation of comparing means for more than two populations (covered in the next section).

The ANOVA Table

Rather than carrying out the five-step procedure using the *F* statistic, an easier method is to use an **ANOVA table** of the various sums of squares. The format of this table is as follows:*

Source	df	SS	MS	F
Factor	1	SS(factor)	$MS(factor) = \dfrac{SS(factor)}{1}$	$\dfrac{MS(factor)}{MS(error)}$
Error	$n-2$	SS(error)	$MS(error) = \dfrac{SS(error)}{n-2}$	
Total	$n-1$	SS(total)		

*The headings under the "Source" column will vary, depending on the computer package. SS(factor) often is labeled "between groups" (Excel and SPSS), "treatment," or "among groups"; SS(error) often is labeled "within groups" (Excel and SPSS), "residual" or "error" (MINITAB).

To fill in this table, you compute the necessary sums of squares along with the mean squares and insert them. Notice that $n = n_1 + n_2 =$ total sample size and that column 3 (MS) = column 2 (SS) divided by column 1 (df).

The ANOVA table for Example 11.1 follows.

Source	df	SS	MS	F
Factor	1	396.9	396.9	17.64
Error	8	180.0	22.5	
Total	9	576.9		

Summary of the ANOVA Approach for One-Factor Tests

In Example 11.1 we concluded that a difference existed between the two *means* because the variation *between* the two samples (measured by MS(factor)) was much greater than the variation *within* the samples (measured by MS(error)). Thus, the ratio of these values was very large and F^* fell in the rejection region. Consequently, we rejected H_0: $\mu_1 = \mu_2$. What this means in the language of ANOVA is that there *is* a significant effect on battery lifetime due to the brand factor.

To carry out the F test, we first randomly obtain observations, called **replicates,** from each population. Example 11.1 used five replicates from each of the two battery brand populations. It is *not necessary* to obtain the same number of replicates from each population.

Figure 11.3 is a dot-array diagram of the data in Example 11.1, where the symbol A represents a value from brand 1, and B represents brand 2. You do not need to be an expert statistician to observe that a clear difference exists between the lifetimes of the two brands of batteries. The variation within the As alone and the Bs alone is the within-sample variation. Because the distances from the A values to the B values are much larger than the distances among the A values alone, the between-sample variation is quite large, as we have already observed.

Suppose instead that your dot-array diagram looks like Figure 11.4. Now the two sources of variation appear to be nearly the same, and there is no obvious difference between the two brands. The resulting F statistic here would not lie within the rejection region, and we would not be able to demonstrate, using the ANOVA approach, a difference between the two mean lifetimes.

FIGURE

11.3

Dot-array diagram
of replicates in
Example 11.1.

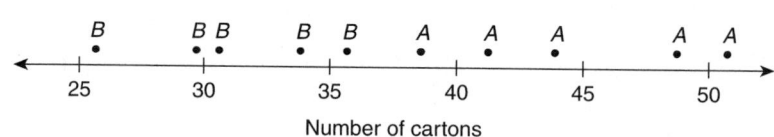

FIGURE

11.4

Dot-array diagram
where between-
sample and within-
sample variations
are nearly the
same. The
F statistic would
not lie in the
rejection region.

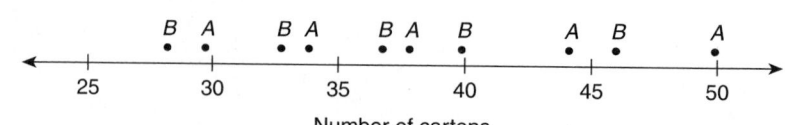

ONE-FACTOR ANOVA COMPARING MORE THAN TWO MEANS

In the previous section, we examined a single *factor* with two *levels*. Our concern was whether there was any difference between the two levels of this factor. We performed a test of hypothesis on the means of two populations. Because we were dealing with the effect of a single factor, this was a one-factor (or one-way) ANOVA.

In general, one-factor ANOVA techniques can be used to study the effect of any single factor on performance, sales, and the like. This factor can consist of any number of levels—say, k levels. To determine if the levels of this factor affect our measured observations, we examine the hypotheses

$$H_0: \mu_1 = \mu_2 = \cdots = \mu_k$$

$$H_a: \text{not all } \mu\text{'s are equal}$$

Suppose we are interested in the average lifetimes of not two but five brands of batteries. Is there any difference in these five mean lifetimes? To answer this question, we test

$$H_0: \mu_1 = \mu_2 = \mu_3 = \mu_4 = \mu_5$$

$$H_a: \text{not all } \mu\text{'s are equal}$$

Note that the complement of H_0 is *not* $H_a: \mu_1 \neq \mu_2 \neq \mu_3 \neq \mu_4 \neq \mu_5$. This alternative hypothesis is "too strong," and the correct form of H_a is that at least two of the means differ or, as stated here, not all of the means are equal.

We have a single factor (brand) consisting of five levels (brand 1, brand 2, . . . , brand 5). One possibility is to examine these samples one pair at a time using the t statistic discussed in the previous section. This appears to be a safe way to proceed here, although there are $_5C_2 = 10$ such pairs of tests to perform this way. The main problem with performing many tests of this nature is determining the probability of making an incorrect decision. In particular, what value does α have, where α is the probability of rejecting H_0: all μ's are equal, when in fact it is true? You set α in advance but, after performing 10 of these pairwise tests ($\mu_1 = \mu_2$, $\mu_1 = \mu_3$, . . .), for instance, what is your *overall* probability of concluding that at least one pair of means are not equal when they actually are? This is a difficult question. The overall probability is not the significance level, α, with which you selected for just one pair. *So we need an approach that will test for the equality of these five means using a single test.* This is what the ANOVA approach does.

Assumptions behind the ANOVA Analysis

When using the ANOVA procedure, there are three key assumptions that must be satisfied. They are basically the same requirements that were necessary when testing two means using small, independent samples and the pooled variance approach:

1. The replicates (observations) are obtained *independently* and *randomly* from each of the populations. The value of one observation has no effect on any other replicates within the same sample or within the other samples.

2. The replicates from each population follow (approximately) a *normal* distribution.

3. The normal populations all have a *common variance*, σ^2. We expect the values in each sample to vary about the same amount. The ANOVA procedure will be much less sensitive to violations of this requirement when we obtain samples of equal size from each population.

Deriving the Sum of Squares

When examining k populations, for example, the data will be configured somewhat like this:

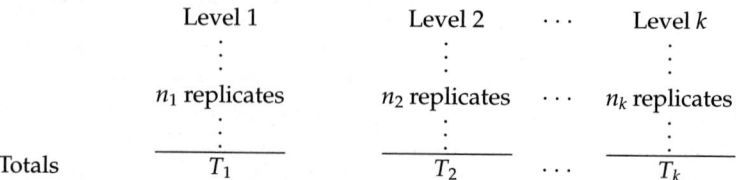

	Level 1	Level 2	$\cdots$	Level k
	$\vdots$	$\vdots$		$\vdots$
	n_1 replicates	n_2 replicates	$\cdots$	n_k replicates
	$\vdots$	$\vdots$		$\vdots$
Totals	T_1	T_2	$\cdots$	T_k

These resemble the data from Example 11.1, where $k = 2$ and $n_1 = n_2 = 5$ replicates. To derive the sum of squares for this situation, we extend the results in equations 11.2, 11.4, and 11.6 to

$$SS(\text{factor}) = \left[\frac{T_1^2}{n_1} + \frac{T_2^2}{n_2} + \cdots + \frac{T_k^2}{n_k} \right] - \frac{T^2}{n} \qquad 11.11$$

$$SS(\text{total}) = \sum x^2 - \frac{T^2}{n} \qquad 11.12$$

$$SS(\text{error}) = \sum x^2 - \left[\frac{T_1^2}{n_1} + \frac{T_2^2}{n_2} + \cdots + \frac{T_k^2}{n_k} \right] \qquad 11.13$$

$$= SS(\text{total}) - SS(\text{factor}) \qquad 11.14$$

Here, n = the total number of observations = $n_1 + n_2 + \cdots + n_k$, and $T = \sum x =$ the sum of all n observations = $T_1 + T_2 + \cdots + T_k$. Also, to find $\sum x^2$, we square each of the n observations and sum the results.

The ANOVA Table

The good news is that the format of the ANOVA table is the same regardless of the number of populations (levels), k. The only change from the two-population case is that

$$\text{df for factor} = k - 1$$

$$\text{df for error} = n - k$$

As before, the total df are $n - 1$. The resulting ANOVA table follows.

Source	df	SS	MS	F
Factor	$k - 1$	SS(factor)	$MS(\text{factor}) = \dfrac{SS(\text{factor})}{k - 1}$	$\dfrac{MS(\text{factor})}{MS(\text{error})}$
Error	$n - k$	SS(error)	$MS(\text{error}) = \dfrac{SS(\text{error})}{n - k}$	
Total	$n - 1$	SS(total)		

Note that

$$MS(\text{factor}) = \frac{SS(\text{factor})}{\text{df for factor}} \qquad 11.15$$

$$= \frac{SS(\text{factor})}{k - 1}$$

$$MS(\text{error}) = \frac{SS(\text{error})}{\text{df for error}} \qquad 11.16$$

$$= \frac{SS(\text{error})}{n - k}$$

The test statistic for testing $H_0: \mu_1 = \mu_2 = \cdots = \mu_k$ versus H_a: not all μ's are equal is

$$F = \frac{\text{MS(factor)}}{\text{MS(error)}}$$

which has an F distribution with $k - 1$ and $n - k$ df.

As in the two-sample case, the procedure is to reject H_0 when the variation among the sample means (measured by MS(factor)) is *large* compared to the variation within the samples (measured by MS(error)). Consequently, the test will be to reject H_0 whenever F lies in the *right-tailed* rejection region defined by the significance level, α.

EXAMPLE 11.2

The manufacturer of the small, battery-powered tape recorder (discussed at the start of this chapter) also manufactures battery-powered AM/FM radio sets that include the required batteries. This unit uses a smaller battery, and four suppliers (brands) of this battery are being considered. Past experience has indicated that the battery lifetimes are normally distributed. The supervising inspector of incoming quality again wants to know whether there is any difference among the average lifetimes of the four battery brands. Twenty-four batteries (six of each brand) are placed on a test device that slowly drains the battery power and records the battery lifetime. The following data (in hours) were obtained:

	Brand 1	Brand 2	Brand 3	Brand 4
	41	32	35	33
	35	37	30	27
	48	46	24	36
	40	53	26	35
	45	41	28	27
	52	43	31	25
Total (T)	261	252	174	183
Average ($\overline{X}$)	43.5	42.0	29.0	30.5
Variance (s^2)	37.1	52.8	15.2	22.3

The four sample averages are $\overline{x}_1 = 43.5$, $\overline{x}_2 = 42.0$, $\overline{x}_3 = 29.0$, and $\overline{x}_4 = 30.5$. Brands 1 and 2 appear to be outlasting brands 3 and 4. In other words, it appears that there is a significant *between-group variation*. But do these sample means provide sufficient evidence to reject $H_0: \mu_1 = \mu_2 = \mu_3 = \mu_4$, where each μ_i represents the average of *all* lifetimes for brand i? Use the ANOVA procedure to answer this question with $\alpha = .05$.

Solution

The requirements for this analysis are (1) the samples were obtained randomly and independently from each of the four populations, and (2) the battery lifetimes for each brand follow a *normal* distribution with a *common variance*, say, σ^2.

$$\text{SS(factor)} = \left[\frac{T_1^2}{n_1} + \frac{T_2^2}{n_2} + \frac{T_3^2}{n_3} + \frac{T_4^2}{n_4} \right] - \frac{T^2}{n}$$

So $n = n_1 + n_2 + n_3 + n_4 = 24$, and

$$T = \Sigma x = T_1 + T_2 + T_3 + T_4$$
$$= 261 + 252 + 174 + 183 = 870$$

Therefore,

$$\text{SS(factor)} = \frac{261^2}{6} + \frac{252^2}{6} + \frac{174^2}{6} + \frac{183^2}{6} - \frac{870^2}{24}$$
$$= 32,565 - 31,537.5 = 1027.5$$

$$SS(\text{total}) = \Sigma x^2 - \frac{T^2}{n}$$

$$= [41^2 + 35^2 + \cdots + 27^2 + 25^2] - \frac{870^2}{24}$$

$$= 33,202 - 31,537.5 = 1664.5$$

$$SS(\text{error}) = SS(\text{total}) - SS(\text{factor})$$

$$= 1664.5 - 1027.5 = 637$$

The ANOVA table for this analysis follows.

Source	df	SS	MS	F
Factor	$k-1=3$	1027.5	$1027.5/3 = 342.5$	$342.5/31.85 = 10.75$
Error	$n-k=20$	637	$637/20 = 31.85$	
Total	23	1664.5		

The computed F value from the ANOVA table is $F^* = 10.75$. Since $\alpha = .05$, we use Table A.7 to find that $F_{.05,3,20} = 3.10$. Comparing these two values, $F^* = 10.75 > 3.10$, so we reject H_0.

We conclude that the average lifetimes for the four brands are not the same. This confirms our earlier suspicion based on the variation among the four sample means. Our results indicate that the brand factor *does* have a significant effect on battery lifetime.

Using a Calculator

If you compare the formulas used to find SS(total) and SS(factor) with the formula used to find a sample variance (equation 3.7 on page 81), you should see a strong similarity. Since most calculators have a key that provides a sample standard deviation (which you should have mastered in Chapter 3), the following steps can be used to determine these two sums of squares.

SS(total)
1. Key in all n observations (41, 35, . . . , 27, 25 in the previous illustration) as though you were determining the standard deviation of these n values.
2. Press the sample standard deviation key on your calculator.
3. Square this value (press the x^2 key) to get the variance of these n observations.
4. Multiply by $n-1$ (23, here). This is SS(total).

SS(factor)   Provided the numbers of replicates within each factor level are the same ($n_1 = n_2 = \cdots n_k$), the following shortcut procedure can be used to find SS(factor).
1. Key in the k factor totals (261, 252, 174, 183 for this illustration) as though you were finding the standard deviation of these k values.
2. Press the sample standard deviation key on your calculator.
3. Square this value by pressing the x^2 key.
4. Multiply by $k-1$ (3, here).
5. Divide this result by the number of replicates within each factor level (6, here). This is SS(factor).

SS(error)   By subtraction, SS(error) = SS(total) − SS(factor)

The Assumptions behind ANOVA and a Test for Equal Variances

Using *independent random samples* is of extreme importance with the ANOVA procedure. The F test used for comparing the population means in the ANOVA table is sensitive to departures from this assumption, so the safest way to guard against incorrect conclusions is to use random sampling techniques. In many situations, however, such as when using the same set of people for before-and-after experiments, this might be difficult or impossible. One solution to this problem is to modify your study design, for example, by using a randomized block design, discussed later in this chapter.

Lack of *normality* within the populations is not a critical matter, provided the departure is not too extreme. The *F* test used to test the means is not severely affected by populations that are somewhat nonnormal in nature. One way of making the ANOVA procedure even less sensitive to this requirement is to use *large samples*.

If the variances of the populations are not equal, the *F*-test used in the ANOVA procedure for testing the means is only slightly affected, provided the *sample sizes are equal* (or nearly so). However, for this case, there is a very simple test of hypothesis for verifying this requirement.

In Chapter 9 an *F* test was defined for determining whether two normal population variances (or standard deviations) are equal. A similar test is used when you are comparing more than two normal population variances, provided the sample sizes are equal.* Here the hypotheses are

$H_0: \sigma_1^2 = \sigma_2^2 = \cdots = \sigma_k^2$

H_a: at least two variances are unequal (the *k* variances are not the same)

We warned you in Chapter 9 about the dangers of using the same data to test both the variances *and* the means. This warning also applies to tests of more than two populations. A better procedure is to use a different data set for testing H_0: the variances are equal. This requires a much larger data set than is necessary if you use the same data for both tests. The test for equal variances is the Hartley test; the test statistic is defined to be

$$H = \frac{\text{maximum } s^2}{\text{minimum } s^2}$$

11.17

which is simply the ratio of the largest sample variance divided by the smallest of these *k* variances.

If H_0 is false, the test statistic will be "large," so the testing procedure is to reject H_0 if the computed value of *H* lies in the right tail. The rejection region for a 5% level of significance can be obtained from Table A.14. This region depends on the number (*k*) of populations or levels and the number of observations in *each* sample.

Suppose we use the battery lifetime data from Example 11.2, only for testing the hypotheses

$H_0: \sigma_1^2 = \sigma_2^2 = \sigma_3^2 = \sigma_4^2$

H_a: at least two variances are unequal

Using $\alpha = .05$ and Table A.14, because $k = 4$ and there are six observations in each sample, the test is to

reject H_0 if $H > 13.7$

Using the data summary in Example 11.2, the minimum s^2 is 15.2 and the maximum s^2 is 52.8. Consequently,

$$H = \frac{52.8}{15.2} = 3.47$$

which is less than 13.7, and so the conclusion is that we have no reason to suspect unequal variances for this situation.

---

*When the sample sizes are unequal, a computationally more difficult test for equal variances can be performed, derived by M. S. Bartlett. For details, see M. Kutner, C. Nachtschiem, W. Wasserman, and J. Neter, *Applied Linear Statistical Models*, 4th ed. (Homewood, Ill.: Richard D. Irwin, 1996).

If other data are available for testing the means, the requirement of equal variances behind the ANOVA procedure appears to be met.

Confidence Intervals in One-Factor ANOVA

When we deal with normal populations, as we do here, we can supply two point estimates:

1. A point estimate of each mean, μ_i; for example, an estimate of μ_2 is $\overline{X}_2$.

2. A point estimate of each mean difference, $\mu_i - \mu_j$; for example, an estimate of $\mu_1 - \mu_3$ is $\overline{X}_1 - \overline{X}_3$.

When using the ANOVA procedure, the populations are believed to have a common variance, say σ^2. To estimate this variance, we use an estimate of σ^2 that does not depend on whether the population means are equal—the *within*-sample variation, measured by MS(error). The point estimate of σ^2 is

$$s_p^2 = \text{pooled variance}$$
$$= \text{MS(error)}$$

where MS(error) is defined in equation 11.16.

In previous chapters, we always supplied a confidence interval along with a point estimate to provide a measure of how reliable this estimate really is. The narrower the confidence interval, the more faith you have in your point estimate. A $(1 - \alpha) \cdot 100\%$ confidence interval for μ_i is

$$\overline{X}_i - t_{\alpha/2, n-k} s_p \sqrt{\frac{1}{n_i}} \quad \text{to} \quad \overline{X}_i + t_{\alpha/2, n-k} s_p \sqrt{\frac{1}{n_i}} \qquad \text{11.18}$$

where

$$k = \text{number of populations (levels)}$$
$$n_i = \text{number of replicates in the } i\text{th sample}$$
$$n = \text{total number of observations}$$
$$s_p = \sqrt{\text{MS(error)}}$$

$t_{\alpha/2, \text{df}}$ is the value from Table A.5 with df = df for error = $n - k$, and right-tail area = $\alpha/2$.

A $(1 - \alpha) \cdot 100\%$ confidence interval for $\mu_i - \mu_j$ is

$$(\overline{X}_i - \overline{X}_j) - t_{\alpha/2, n-k} s_p \sqrt{\frac{1}{n_i} + \frac{1}{n_j}} \quad \text{to} \quad (\overline{X}_i - \overline{X}_j) + t_{\alpha/2, n-k} s_p \sqrt{\frac{1}{n_i} + \frac{1}{n_j}} \qquad \text{11.19}$$

E X A M P L E   11.3

Using the battery lifetime data from Example 11.2, construct a 95% confidence interval for the average lifetime of brand 1. Also determine a 95% confidence interval for the difference between the average lifetimes of brands 1 and 3.

Solution   First, your point estimate of μ_1 is $\overline{x}_1 = 43.5$. Using the ANOVA table from Example 11.2,

$$s_p^2 = \text{MS(error)} = 31.85$$

and so

$$s_p = \sqrt{31.85} = 5.64$$

Because $n = 24$ and $k = 4$, the resulting 95% confidence interval for μ_1 is

$$43.5 - t_{.025,20}(5.64)\sqrt{\frac{1}{6}} \quad \text{to} \quad 43.5 + t_{.025,20}(5.64)\sqrt{\frac{1}{6}}$$

$$= 43.5 - (2.086)(5.64)(.408) \quad \text{to} \quad 43.5 + (2.086)(5.64)(.408)$$

$$= 43.5 - 4.80 \quad \text{to} \quad 43.5 + 4.80$$

$$= 38.7 \quad \text{to} \quad 48.3$$

As a result, we are 95% confident that the average lifetime of the brand 1 battery is between 38.7 and 48.3 hours.

The 95% confidence interval for $\mu_1 - \mu_3$ is

$$(\overline{X}_1 - \overline{X}_3) - t_{.025,20}s_p\sqrt{\frac{1}{n_1} + \frac{1}{n_3}} \quad \text{to} \quad (\overline{X}_1 - \overline{X}_3) + t_{.025,20}s_p\sqrt{\frac{1}{n_1} + \frac{1}{n_3}}$$

$$= (43.5 - 29.0) - (2.086)(5.64)\sqrt{\frac{1}{6} + \frac{1}{6}} \quad \text{to} \quad (43.5 - 29.0) + (2.086)(5.64)\sqrt{\frac{1}{6} + \frac{1}{6}}$$

$$= 14.5 - (2.086)(5.64)(.577) \quad \text{to} \quad 14.5 + (2.086)(5.64)(.577)$$

$$= 14.5 - 6.79 \quad \text{to} \quad 14.5 + 6.79$$

$$= 7.71 \quad \text{to} \quad 21.29$$

Based on this confidence interval, we are 95% confident that the average lifetime for brand 1 is between 7.71 and 21.29 hours *higher* than the average lifetime for brand 3.

A Word of Warning

The procedure we used in Example 11.3 for determining confidence intervals is reliable, providing you decide which intervals you want computed *before* you observe your data. For example, constructing a confidence interval for the difference of two population means having the corresponding largest and smallest sample means is not an accurate procedure. If you do this, you let the data dictate which confidence interval you determine.

When using the procedure in Example 11.3 to construct confidence intervals for the difference of two population means, it is important to keep the number of such intervals as small as possible, because the probability of any one interval containing the true population difference is $1 - \alpha$, but the probability that *all* the intervals contain their respective population differences is not $1 - \alpha$. In other words, if $\alpha = .05$, the overall confidence level of this procedure is not 95%; it is something much less than 95%. *To compare all possible pairs of means effectively, you need to use a technique that will allow you to make all possible comparisons between population means while maintaining the Type I error rate at α. This is called a* **multiple comparisons procedure;** *one such procedure is discussed following Example 11.5.*

EXAMPLE 11.4

The manager of Autoplex, a local car dealership, is interested in examining the average dollar amount of "extras" (such as air conditioning, automatic transmission, exterior trim) for new-car buyers during the past year. In particular, she wants to compare average purchases for three groups: single male purchasers, single female purchasers, and married purchasers. Data from a sample of 20 purchasers contained 5 in each of the first two groups and 10 in the married group.* The sample results (in dollars) are:

	Single Male Purchasers	Single Female Purchasers	Married Purchasers
	5,375	4,802	8,314
	6,913	4,123	5,906
	6,283	3,567	6,025
	5,809	4,355	7,577
	5,346	4,982	6,071
			8,000
			6,489
			7,720
			6,968
			7,538
Total (T)	29,726	21,829	70,608
$\overline{X}_i$	5,945.20	4,365.80	7,060.80

What would be the conclusion using a significance level of .10?

Solution   Examining the sample means, it appears at first glance that there is considerable variation in the sample means; that is, the three population means are not all equal. But is there a significant difference among these three sample means? An ANOVA analysis will clarify this.

The necessary requirements here are:

1. The dollar amounts were obtained randomly and independently from each of the three populations (groups).

2. The dollar amounts for each of the three populations follow a normal distribution, with means μ_1, μ_2, μ_3. The amounts in each of the three populations are required to have the same variation.

Because the sample sizes are not the same, the Hartley test for equal variances cannot be used here. As discussed earlier, we prefer not to use the same data for testing both the means and the variances, and so a better procedure would be to obtain additional data (with equal sample sizes) for testing the equality of these three variances. Despite the lack of a Hartley test, we'll proceed by first calculating the necessary sum of squares:

$$\text{SS(factor)} = \left[\frac{T_1^2}{n_1} + \frac{T_2^2}{n_2} + \frac{T_3^2}{n_3} \right] - \frac{T^2}{n}$$

where

$$T = \Sigma x = T_1 + T_2 + T_3$$

$$= 29{,}726 + 21{,}829 + 70{,}608 = 122{,}163$$

$$n = n_1 + n_2 + n_3$$

$$= 5 + 5 + 10 = 20$$

So

$$\text{SS(factor)} = \frac{29{,}726^2}{5} + \frac{21{,}829^2}{5} + \frac{70{,}608^2}{10} - \frac{122{,}163^2}{20}$$

$$= 770{,}577{,}029.8 - 746{,}189{,}928.4 = 24{,}387{,}101.4$$

---

*A similar data set was presented in Chapter 7 in the discussion on stratified sampling. Knowledge of this sampling procedure is not necessary for the discussion here. However, it is worth mentioning that stratified sampling is more effective if there *is* large variation between the groups (strata)—that is, H_0: $\mu_1 = \mu_2 = \mu_3$ is rejected.

$$SS(total) = \sum x^2 - \frac{T^2}{n}$$

$$= (5{,}375^2 + 6{,}913^2 + \cdots + 6{,}968^2 + 7{,}538^2) - \frac{122{,}163^2}{20}$$

$$= 780{,}700{,}667 - 746{,}189{,}928.4 = 34{,}510{,}738.6$$

$$SS(error) = SS(total) - SS(factor)$$

$$= 34{,}510{,}738.6 - 24{,}387{,}101.4 = 10{,}123{,}637.2$$

Finally, because $k = 3$ and $n = 20$,

$$\text{df for factor} = k - 1 = 2$$

$$\text{df for error} = n - k = 17$$

$$\text{df for total} = n - 1 = 19$$

The resulting ANOVA table is

Source	df	SS	MS	F
Factor	2	24,387,101.4	12,193,550.7	20.48
Error	17	10,123,637.2	595,508.1	
Total	19	34,510,738.6		

The hypotheses are

$$H_0: \mu_1 = \mu_2 = \mu_3$$

$$H_a: \text{not all } \mu\text{'s are equal}$$

where each μ_i represents the average dollar amount of extras for each of the three purchase groups.

We will reject H_0 if

$$F^* > F_{.10,2,17} = 2.64$$

Because $20.48 > 2.64$, H_0 is rejected. There is strong evidence to indicate a difference in the buying behavior for these three groups.

The factor in Example 11.4 was the type of purchaser, and it had three levels. The results indicate that this factor had a significant effect on the amount of extras purchased.

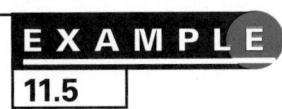

EXAMPLE 11.5

In Example 11.4, before the data were obtained, the manager at Autoplex decided to construct a 95% confidence interval for the average dollar amount of the married purchasers and the difference between the average dollar amounts for the married purchasers and the single male purchasers. What are the confidence intervals?

Solution

The point estimates are

$$\text{for } \mu_3: \quad \bar{x}_3 = \$7{,}060.80$$

$$\text{for } \mu_3 - \mu_1: \quad \bar{x}_3 - \bar{x}_1 = \$7{,}060.80 - \$5{,}945.20 = \$1{,}115.60$$

To construct the confidence intervals, you first need an estimate of the common variance of these three populations. Based on the results of Example 11.4, this is

$$s_p^2 = MS(error) = 595{,}508.1$$

So

$$s_p = \sqrt{595{,}508.1} = 771.69$$

Because $n = 20$, $k = 3$, and $n_3 = 10$, the 95% confidence interval for μ_3 (the mean for the married purchasers) is

$$\bar{x}_3 - t_{.025,17}\, s_p \sqrt{\frac{1}{n_3}} \quad \text{to} \quad \bar{x}_3 + t_{.025,17}\, s_p \sqrt{\frac{1}{n_3}}$$

$$= 7{,}060.80 - (2.110)(771.69)(.316) \quad \text{to} \quad 7{,}060.80 + (2.110)(771.69)(.316)$$

$$= 7{,}060.80 - 514.53 \quad \text{to} \quad 7{,}060.80 + 514.53$$

$$= \$6{,}546.27 \quad \text{to} \quad \$7{,}575.33$$

The 95% confidence interval for $\mu_3 - \mu_1$ is

$$(\bar{x}_3 - \bar{x}_1) - t_{.025,17}\, s_p \sqrt{\frac{1}{n_3} + \frac{1}{n_1}} \quad \text{to} \quad (\bar{x}_3 - \bar{x}_1) + t_{.025,17}\, s_p \sqrt{\frac{1}{n_3} + \frac{1}{n_1}}$$

$$= (7{,}060.80 - 5{,}945.20) - (2.110)(771.69)(.548) \quad \text{to}$$

$$(7{,}060.80 - 5{,}945.20) + (2.110)(771.69)(.548)$$

$$= 1{,}115.60 - 892.29 \quad \text{to} \quad 1{,}115.60 + 892.29$$

$$= \$223.31 \quad \text{to} \quad \$2{,}007.89$$

Consequently, we are 95% confident that the average dollar amount of the purchased extras for the married group is between $223.31 and $2,007.89 *higher* than for the single male group.

Multiple Comparisons: A Follow-Up to the One-Factor ANOVA Procedure

If the one-factor ANOVA procedure leads to a rejection of H_0: all populations means are equal, a logical question would be, which means do differ? In other words, rejecting the ANOVA null hypothesis informs us that the means are not all the same but provides no clue as to which of the population means are different. As we discussed prior to Example 11.4, performing a series of t tests to compare all possible pairs of means is not a good idea, since the chances of making at least one Type I error (concluding that a difference exists between two population means when in fact they are the same) using such a procedure is much larger than the predetermined α used for each of the t tests.

What is needed is a technique that compares all possible pairs of means in such a way that the probability of making one or more Type I errors is α. This is a multiple comparisons procedure. There are several methods available for making multiple comparisons; the one presented here is **Tukey's** test for multiple comparisons (Tukey is pronounced too'-key).

Tukey's procedure is based on a statistical test that uses the largest and smallest sample means. The form of this statistic is

$$Q = \frac{\text{maximum } (\bar{X}_i) - \text{minimum } (\bar{X}_i)}{\sqrt{\text{MS(error)}/n_r}}$$

11.20

where

1. Maximum $(\bar{X}_i)$ and minimum $(\bar{X}_i)$ are the largest and smallest sample means, respectively.

2. MS(error) is the pooled sample variance.

3. n_r is the number of replicates in each sample.

Notice that Tukey's procedure assumes that each sample contains the same number (n_r) of replicates. Critical values of the Q statistic are contained in Table A.16. Define

$Q_{\alpha,k,v}$ = critical value of the Q statistic from Table A.16, using a significance level of α; k is the number of sample means (groups), and v is the df associated with MS(error).

MULTIPLE COMPARISONS PROCEDURE: ONE-FACTOR ANOVA

1. Find $Q_{\alpha,k,v}$ using Table A.16.
2. Determine

$$D = Q_{\alpha,k,v} \cdot \sqrt{\frac{MS(\text{error})}{n_r}}$$

   where MS(error) is the pooled sample variance and n_r is the number of replicates in each sample. For one-factor ANOVA, MS(error) is the same as s_p^2.
3. Place the sample means in order, from smallest to largest.
4. If two sample means differ by more than D, the conclusion is that the corresponding population means are unequal. In other words, if $|\bar{X}_i - \bar{X}_j| > D$, this implies that $\mu_i \neq \mu_j$.

To illustrate this procedure, reconsider Example 11.2. There we concluded that the average lifetime on a test device was not the same for the four brands of batteries. The four sample means were

$$\text{Brand 1: } \bar{x}_1 = 43.5$$
$$\text{Brand 2: } \bar{x}_2 = 42.0$$
$$\text{Brand 3: } \bar{x}_3 = 29.0$$
$$\text{Brand 4: } \bar{x}_4 = 30.5$$

For this study, there were $n_r = 6$ replicates in each sample, with a resulting pooled variance of $s_p^2 = MS(\text{error}) = 31.85$. The study contained $k = 4$ groups and the df for the error sum of squares was $v = n - k = 24 - 4 = 20$. Using a significance level of .05, we begin by finding $Q_{.05,4,20}$ in Table A.16. This value is 3.96. Next we determine

$$D = Q_{.05,4,20} \cdot \sqrt{\frac{MS(\text{error})}{n_r}}$$

$$= 3.96\sqrt{\frac{31.85}{6}} = 9.12$$

The sample means, in order, are

$$\overline{29.0, 30.5}, \quad \overline{42.0, 43.5}$$

Any two sample means are significantly different using the Tukey procedure if they differ by an amount greater than $D = 9.12$. Here there are four significant differences, namely,

$$\bar{x}_1 - \bar{x}_3 = 43.5 - 29.0 = 14.5 > 9.12$$
$$\bar{x}_2 - \bar{x}_3 = 42.0 - 29.0 = 13.0 > 9.12$$
$$\bar{x}_1 - \bar{x}_4 = 43.5 - 30.5 = 13.0 > 9.12$$
$$\bar{x}_2 - \bar{x}_4 = 42.0 - 30.5 = 11.5 > 9.12$$

The conclusion from the multiple comparisons analysis is that $\mu_1 \neq \mu_3$, $\mu_1 \neq \mu_4$, $\mu_2 \neq \mu_3$, and $\mu_2 \neq \mu_4$. There is no evidence of a difference between the brand 1 and the brand 2 populations or between the brand 3 and the brand 4 populations. This is indicated by the two overbars connecting these two pairs of sample means. In general, there is no evidence to indicate a difference in the population means for any group of sample means under such a bar.

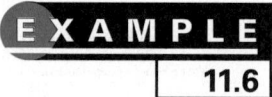

EXAMPLE 11.6

Using Excel for One-Factor ANOVA

LensPro manufactures corrective eyeglasses. Many of its "rimless" frames use a light nylon line (similar to fishing line) to secure the lenses to the frame. LensPro is evaluating the line produced by five different vendors (suppliers). Using a testing device, it determined the breaking strength of 25 different lines obtained independently from each supplier. These breaking strengths are contained in column A for vendor 1, B for vendor 2, . . . , and E for vendor 5.

Using a significance level of .05, do you believe there is sufficient evidence to indicate a difference in average breaking strength for these five suppliers? If so, which of the suppliers would you recommend to LensPro?

In addition, (1) carry out the Hartley test for equal variances using a significance level of .05, (2) determine a 95% confidence interval for the mean breaking strength for vendor 4, and (3) determine a 95% confidence interval for the difference of the mean breaking strengths for vendors 2 and 4 (vendor 4 minus vendor 2).

Solution

A plot of the five group means in Figure 11.5 (generated using SPSS) provides an excellent visual examination of the data.* A glance at this graph suggests that the breaking strengths for vendors 1 and 4 are larger than for the other three vendors. Can we in fact demonstrate this? Let's continue.

Begin by opening the dataset DATA11-6. You should see five columns of 25 values each, with labels in the first row. Click on **KPK Data Analysis ➤ ANOVA.** When using this procedure, you *must* include labels in the first row identifying

FIGURE 11.5

Plot of mean nylon line breaking strength for five vendors.

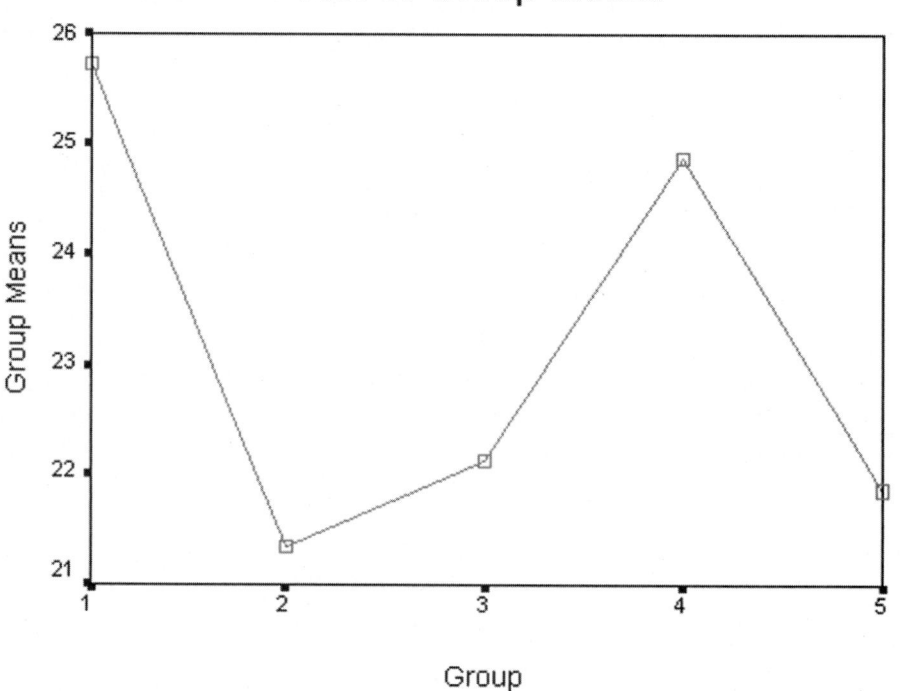

Plot of Group Means

*To obtain the graph in Figure 11.5, read the data into the first five columns. Name the columns "vendor 1", . . . , "vendor 5". Click on **Analyze ➤ Compare Means ➤ One-Way ANOVA ➤ Options ➤ Means plot.** Another interesting representation here is obtained by also clicking on **Graphs ➤ Boxplot.** In this way, you get five box plots arranged side-by-side.

each of the groups. The resulting input screen is shown in Figure 11.6 and should be filled in as shown. The next section will discuss use of the term *experimental design* and mentions that a *completely randomized design* means the same as *one-factor ANOVA*. The resulting Excel-generated ANOVA table is shown in Figure 11.7. Notice that Excel uses "Between Groups" rather than "Factor" in cell F14 and "Within Groups" rather than "Error" in cell F15.

Since the extremely small *p*-value (zero to four decimal places) is less than the 5% significance level, we conclude that the five average breaking strengths are

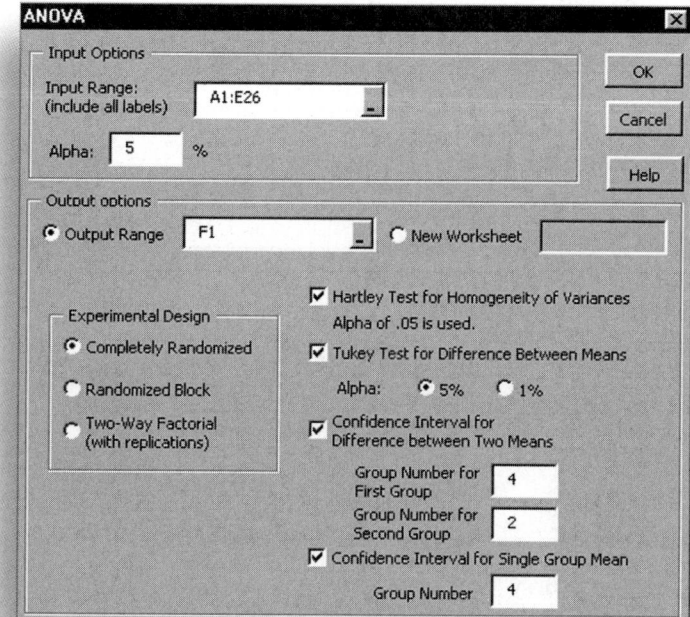

FIGURE

11.6

Excel input screen using **KPK Data Analysis ➤ ANOVA.**

FIGURE

11.7

Portion of Excel spreadsheet containing the one-factor ANOVA output.

	F	G	H	I	J	K	L	M
1	Anova: Single Factor							
2								
3	SUMMARY							
4	Groups	Count	Sum	Average	Variance			
5	Vendor1	25	643.2427	25.7297	1.9931			
6	Vendor2	25	533.5649	21.3426	2.6659			
7	Vendor3	25	553.0550	22.1222	3.5389			
8	Vendor4	25	621.4250	24.8570	2.3495			
9	Vendor5	25	546.6252	21.8650	1.8868			
10								
11								
12	ANOVA							
13	Source of Variation	SS	df	MS	F	P-value	F crit	
14	Between Groups	388.4371	4	97.1093	39.0492	0.0000	2.4472	
15	Within Groups	298.4211	120	2.4868				
16								
17	Total	686.8582	124					

FIGURE
11.8

Remainder of
Excel solution to
Example 11.6.

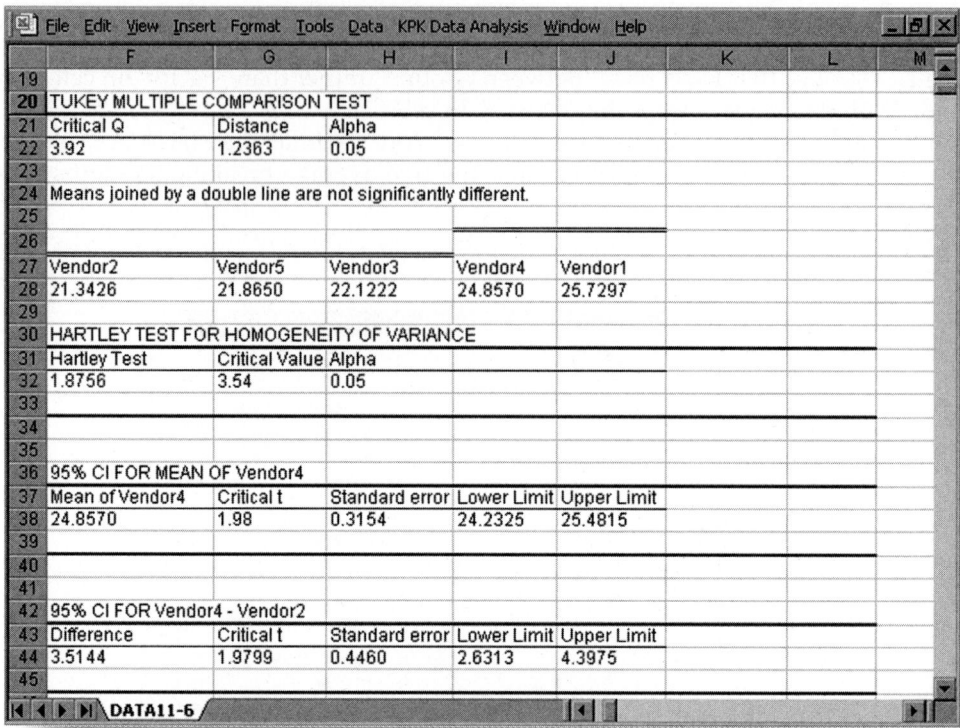

not all the same. To carry out a multiple comparisons procedure (obtained by checking the **Tukey Test for Difference Between Means** box in Figure 11.6), refer to cells F20:J28 in Figure 11.8. The value of D is in the cell labeled **Distance** and is equal to D = 1.236. What pairs of sample means differ by more than 1.236? These are means 1 and 2, 1 and 3, 1 and 5, as well as 4 and 2, 4 and 3, 4 and 5. This is illustrated in cells F26:J28 in Figure 11.8, where the two overbars connect the sample means in row 28 for vendors 2, 3, and 5 and also for vendors 1 and 4. Your recommendation to LensPro would be to use either vendor 1 or vendor 4, based on the breaking strength alone. Other considerations here might consist of cost, supplier dependability, or other "quality" factors (such as durability and breaking strength variability).

The bottom portion of Figure 11.8 indicates that the test statistic value for the Hartley test is H = 1.8756. This is less than the critical value of 3.54, and so the assumption of equal variances appears to be satisfied. The 95% confidence interval for the mean breaking strength for vendor 4 is from 24.2325 to 25.4815, and the 95% confidence interval for $\mu_4 - \mu_2$ is from 2.6313 to 4.3975. This implies that we are 95% confident that the average breaking strength for vendor 4 is between 2.6 and 4.4 *higher* than for vendor 2.

ONE-FACTOR ANOVA PROCEDURE

Requirements

1. The replicates are obtained *independently* and *randomly* from each of the populations. The value of one observation has no effect on any other replicates within the same sample or within the other samples.
2. The observations (replicates) from each population follow (approximately) a *normal* distribution.

3. The normal populations all have a *common variance, σ^2*. We expect the values in each sample to vary about the same amount. The ANOVA procedure will be much less sensitive to this requirement when we obtain samples of equal size from each population.

Hypotheses

$$H_0: \mu_1 = \mu_2 = \cdots = \mu_k$$
$$H_a: \text{not all } \mu\text{'s are equal}$$

Note that H_a is not the same as H_a': all μ's are unequal; H_a states that *at least two* of the μ's are different.

Sum of Squares

$$\text{SS(factor)} = \left[\frac{T_1^2}{n_1} + \frac{T_2^2}{n_2} + \cdots + \frac{T_k^2}{n_k}\right] - \frac{T^2}{n}$$

where $n = n_1 + n_2 + \cdots + n_k$ and $T = \sum x = T_1 + T_2 + \cdots + T_k$.

$$\text{SS(total)} = \sum x^2 - \frac{T^2}{n}$$

$$\text{SS(error)} = \text{SS(total)} - \text{SS(factor)}$$

$$= \sum x^2 - \left[\frac{T_1^2}{n_1} + \frac{T_2^2}{n_2} + \cdots + \frac{T_k^2}{n_k}\right]$$

Degrees of Freedom

$$\text{df for factor} = k - 1$$
$$\text{df for error} = n - k$$
$$\text{df for total} = n - 1$$

Note that $(k - 1) + (n - k) = n - 1$.

ANOVA Table

Source	df	SS	MS	F
Factor	$k - 1$	SS(factor)	$\text{MS(factor)} = \dfrac{\text{SS(factor)}}{k - 1}$	$\dfrac{\text{MS(factor)}}{\text{MS(error)}}$
Error	$n - k$	SS(error)	$\text{MS(error)} = \dfrac{\text{SS(error)}}{n - k}$	
Total	$n - 1$	SS(total)		

where MS = mean square = SS/df.

Testing Procedure

$$\text{reject } H_0 \text{ if } F^* > F_{\alpha, k-1, n-k}$$

where $F_{\alpha, k-1, n-k}$ is obtained from Table A.7.

X Exercises 11.1–11.18

Understanding the Mechanics

11.1 The following two random samples were collected from two populations.

Sample 1:	2	5	3	5	7
Sample 2:	4	3	3	2	1

a. Compute the two-sample t statistic to test if the means of the two populations differ.

b. Compute the ANOVA table to test if the means of the two populations differ.

c. Compare the value of MSE in part b to the pooled variance in part a.

d. Is the square of the t statistic in part a equal to the F statistic in part b?

11.2 Use the following ANOVA table to answer the succeeding questions.

Source	df	SS	MS	F
Factor		180		
Error	36			
Total	39	241		

a. Complete the ANOVA table, and determine the value of the F statistic for testing the null hypothesis that the means of the populations are equal.

b. Do the data provide sufficient evidence to indicate that a difference exists in the means of the populations? Use a .01 significance level.

c. If the number of observations from the random samples of each population are equal, what is the number of observations selected from each population?

d. If $T_1 = 95$, $T_2 = 67$, $T_3 = 70$, and $T_4 = 64$, what pairs of population means are significantly different according to Tukey's multiple comparisons procedure? Use a .01 significance level.

11.3 Four independent samples are collected from four normally distributed populations. The data are as follows:

Group 1	Group 2	Group 3	Group 4
12	14	17	10
11	12	18	9
14	16	20	13
10	15	22	12
12		23	
10			

a. Construct an ANOVA table. The SST is equal to 309.158. The sums for groups 1, 2, 3, and 4 are 69, 57, 100, and 44, respectively.

b. Conduct a test of the null hypothesis that the group means are equal. Use a 5% significance level.

c. Find a 95% confidence level for the mean of Group 1. Find a 95% confidence level for the mean of Group 3.

d. Find a 95% confidence interval for the difference between Group 1 and Group 3.

e. Using a 5% significance level, determine if there is a difference in the variance of the four groups. Assume equal sample sizes of $n_r = 5$.

f. Would you recommend that the same data be used to test both the variances and the means for a completely randomized design?

Applying the New Concepts

11.4 A 1993 survey indicated that for a majority of Canadians, price is more important than brand loyalty when it comes to buying groceries. Research on the buying patterns of the consumer is important to large manufacturing companies. "Consumers have adopted a much more aggressive approach to shopping," says Gord James, vice president of strategic planning for the Quaker Oats Company of Canada, Ltd. A survey by the Grocery Products Manufacturers of Canada found that on the average, in Canada, men spend $44 a week on groceries, compared to $36 a week for women.

a. Suppose that the survey included 200 men and 200 women in the random sample and that the $\sum x^2$, where x is weekly expenditure on groceries, is 600,000 for men and 450,000 for women. Construct the ANOVA table for this completely randomized design.

b. Do the data support the conclusion that the weekly expenditures of men and women in Canada differ? Use a .05 significance level.

c. Use the two-sample t test to test for any differences in the mean weekly grocery expenditure for Canadian men and Canadian women. Use a .05 significance level. Assume equal population variances.

d. What is the relationship between the t test in part c and the F test in part a?

(Source: Lynne Ainsworth, "Men Spend More on Food, Survey Finds," *Toronto Star*, September 16, 1993, p. A4.)

11.5 The science of ergonomics studies the influence of "human factors" in technology (i.e., how human beings relate to and work with machines). With the widespread use of computers for data processing, computer scientists and psychologists are getting together to study human factors. One typical study investigated the productivity of secretaries with different word processing programs. An identical task was given to 18 secretaries, randomly allocated to three groups. Group 1 used a primarily menu-driven program. Group 2 used a command-driven program, and Group 3 used a mixture of both approaches. The secretaries all had about the same level of experience, typing speed, and computer skills. The time (in minutes) taken to complete the task was observed. The results were as follows:

Group 1 (Menu-Driven)	Group 2 (Command-Driven)	Group 3 (Mixed)
12	14	10
15	11	8
11	13	9
12	12	10
10	11	7
13	14	8

a. Do the necessary calculations to construct an ANOVA table, and test the hypothesis that there is no difference between the three types of word processing programs (i.e., on the average, the time taken to complete the task is about the same). Use $\alpha = .05$.

b. State the p-value for the test.

c. Does the type of word processing software used affect the performance of the secretaries?

d. If the secretaries had different levels of experience, typing speed, and computer skills, how would it affect the data? (Would it be an extraneous source of variation, or *noise*? Would it tend to increase the *within-sample* variation, the *between-sample* variation, both, or neither?)

e. Using a significance level of .05, perform a multiple comparisons procedure (if appropriate).

11.6 A small engine-repair shop can special-order parts from any one of the three different warehouses and receive a substantial discount on the price. The manager of the shop is concerned with the length of time that it takes to special-order a part from one of the warehouses. The number of days it takes to special-order a part is recorded for 15 randomly selected orders from each of the three warehouses, as shown in the following table. Do the data indicate that there is a difference in the mean times that it takes to special-order a part from a warehouse? Use a .05 significance level. State the p-value.

Warehouse

A	13	17	14	10	9	15	18	11	13	18	16	13	15	12	16
B	7	12	8	15	6	10	12	10	8	14	10	6	9	13	11
C	10	12	18	19	9	15	20	11	15	13	17	13	10	14	16

11.7 A sales manager wanted to know whether there was a significant difference in the monthly sales of three sales representatives. John is strictly on commission. Randy is on commission and a small salary, and Ted is on a small commission and a salary. Eight months were chosen at random. The data represent monthly sales.

John	969	905	801	850	910	1030	780	810
Randy	738	773	738	805	850	800	690	720
Ted	751	764	701	810	840	790	720	735

a. Using a significance level of .05, test the hypothesis that there is no difference in the mean monthly sales. (Coding the data may make the computations easier.)

b. What is the p-value?

c. Using a significance level of .05, perform a multiple comparisons procedure, if appropriate.

11.8 The Web site www.abia.org lets travelers use cyberspace to peek at the same arrival and departure screens seen by people at the airport and is updated every 30 seconds. This one Web site allows passengers to view the status of flights from several airlines. The mean time to locate information should be less than two minutes. Suppose that four random samples of 20 people each were selected to determine if the mean times that it takes to find the status of flights from American, Northwest, Delta, and Southwest Airlines are the same. How many t tests would have to be performed? What is the advantage of using an ANOVA procedure instead?

(Source: "Thanksgiving Travel Tips," *The Austin American-Statesman*, November 21, 2000, p. B2.)

11.9 The mean age of viewers of the major TV networks is very important to marketing strategists. CBS typically attracts the 50 year olds, NBC attracts the 40 year olds, and Fox attracts the 30 year olds. Suppose that a marketing strategist wanted to determine if the mean age of the following three programs differed: *The Simpsons, That '70s Show,* and *Time of Your Life*. Assume that a random sample of 100 viewers was selected for each of these three programs and that the sample means for *The Simpsons, That '70s Show,* and *Time of Your Life* were 31.38, 31.16, and 30.46 years of age. If the SSE was 3,247.40, construct the ANOVA table. What conclusion can the marketing strategist make? Use a 10% significance level.

(Source: "Too Old for Your Favorite Show? Viewer Median Age of Prime-Time," *The Washington Post*, January 3, 2000, p. 7.)

11.10 The revved-up economy of 1998 produced record profits for many of the partner law firms, with the average profit per partner of approximately $600,000. However, the inflation-adjusted profits per partner—the key measure of law-firm wealth—just matched the booming levels of the early 1980s. Suppose that a corporate partner is interested in whether there was a significant difference in the average partner's annual profit for three different geographical regions in the eastern United States. The results of the survey by this partner are presented below.

Geographical Region	Sample Size	Average Annual Profit (in thousands of dollars)
Northeastern states	12	802
Mid-Atlantic states	12	690
Southeastern states	10	557

a. Assume that the SSE for the data is 1,811,685. Do the data suggest that a significant difference exists in the average annual profit for partner firms across the three geographical regions of the United States? Use a .10 significance level.

b. Find a 90% confidence interval for the difference in the average annual profit for the Northeastern states and the Southeastern states. Would you expect 0 to be between the upper and lower endpoints of this interval? Why?

c. What assumption must be made to assure the validity of the F test in part a?

(Adapted from "Big Law Firms' Profits Evoke 1980s Boom Times," *The Wall Street Journal*, June 30, 1998, p. B1.)

11.11 Although private and public high schools teach an endless assortment of school-specific programs that can often be very challenging, the Advanced Placement (AP) programs at high schools give college admissions administrators a national standard by which to judge the quality of students' college preparation. Educators use the following AP measure to determine those high schools that provide their students the best college preparation: the number of students taking AP exams divided by the total junior and senior enrollment. This AP measure, expressed as a percentage, was collected from five high schools selected at random from the Dallas, Fort Worth, and Arlington areas of the Dallas/Fort Worth metroplex. The samples means are as follows:

High School District	Sample Mean for AP Measure
Dallas	21.4
Fort Worth	20.6
Arlington	13.4

a. What is the error degrees of freedom for an ANOVA procedure?

b. Use a multiple comparisons procedure to determine which population means differ at a 5% significance level. Assume that the value of the MSE is 10.

(Source: "The Best Public High Schools in Dallas–Fort Worth," *D*, vol. 28, no. 11, November 28, 2001, pp. 74–77.)

11.12 The workers at a calculator assembly plant wish to bargain for more breaks during the work day. The manager believes that increasing the number of 15-minute breaks will affect productivity. The workers currently receive three breaks during the 8-hour work day. The manager decides to run a test by choosing four groups of five workers each and giving one group three breaks, the next group four breaks, and so on. The number of calculators assembled per day is recorded for five days. Test the manager's claim using an ANOVA procedure with a .10 significance level. Find the p-value. Using a significance level of .05, perform a multiple comparisons procedure, if appropriate.

3 breaks	200	205	197	210	205
4 breaks	210	203	201	197	199
5 breaks	198	190	185	188	180
6 breaks	197	180	190	192	175

11.13 Some 4,000 teams participate in the CNBC/MCI tournament of buying and selling stocks in a make-believe portfolio initially worth $10,000 in cash over 61 trading days. Team players look for news on the stocks and statistics on the Internet using online services such as Infospace and Datek Online for news and real-time stock quotes. A finance professor was interested in whether there is a significant difference among aggressive trading (high turnover), moderate trading, and a buy-and-hold approach (low turnover). Assume that from a random sample of 25 teams from each of the three categories that the factor sum of squares was equal to 12 and that the total sum of squares was equal to 616.

a. What conclusion can the finance professor make in testing whether there is a difference based on trading strategy? Use the p-value to base your conclusions.

b. Should a multiple comparisons procedure be used for further analysis? Why?

c. What requirements on the data must be met to ensure that the analysis is valid?

(Adapted from "He Was a Teenage Day-Trader," *The Wall Street Journal,* April 22, 1998, p. C1.)

11.14 A shoe manufacturer wanted to test whether there is a difference in the amount of wear on four different designs of rubber soles for a particular jogging shoe. Before collecting a lot of data on the effect of the designs on the wear, a small pilot study was performed to determine whether the population variances for the different groups were the same. The manufacturer used six joggers for each design in the pilot study. After running 200 miles, the joggers turned in their shoes. The manufacturer used an index to indicate the amount of rubber left on the sole. The pilot study yielded the following standard deviations: $s_1 = 3.12$, $s_2 = 11.61$, $s_3 = 12.48$, $s_4 = 7.31$.

a. Do the data provide sufficient evidence that a difference exists in the population standard deviations for the four designs? Use a .05 significance level.

b. If an ANOVA procedure is used for a larger set of data to determine whether there is a difference in the average amount of wear on the four different designs of rubber soles, are you safe in assuming that the population variances are equal?

c. What requirements on the data are necessary for the validity of the statistical test procedure in part a?

Using the Computer

11.15 [DATA EX11-15], *Variable description:*

RevOver2B: Number of employees for private companies with more than $2 billion in revenue

RevOver1B_Under2B: Number of employees for private companies with more than $1 billion in revenue and under $2 billion

RevUnder1B: Number of employees for private companies with under $1 billion in revenue

The basic laws of business—worrying about profit margins, fighting for market share, and staying ahead of the competition—apply equally to private companies as they do to public ones, but private companies are under little or no obligation to divulge detailed information about their operations or financial performance. Some financial analysts believe that private companies are less apt to lay off employees during slow business cycles and that private companies with higher revenue tend to have a larger number of employees. Suppose that a random sample of 10 private companies from each of the following three categories is selected and the number of employees recorded: Private companies with more than $2 billion in revenue, private companies with revenue between $1 billion and $2 billion, and private companies with revenue under $1 billion.

a. Do the data support the belief that the average number of employees for private companies with either more than $2 billion, between $1 billion and $2 billion, and under $1 billion in revenue differ? Use a 5% significance level.

b. Conduct a test for equality of variance for the three groups in part a. What can you conclude at the 5% significance level?

(Source: "500 Largest Private Companies," *Forbes*, November 26, 2001, pp. 162–90.)

11.16 [DATA EX11-16] *Variable description:*

Connecticut: Location of home in Connecticut

ConnPrice: Price of advertised home

Florida: Location of home in Florida

FlaPrice: Price of advertised home

Colorado: Location of home in Colorado

ColoPrice: Price of advertised home

Real estate from across the nation is advertised in *The Wall Street Journal*'s Distinctive Properties & Estate section. Suppose that a real estate broker is interested in determining whether the variance of prices of real estate in Connecticut, Florida, and Colorado differ. To test this hypothesis, the broker sampled six advertised homes from each state. Do the data support this hypothesis? Use a 5% significance level.

(Source: "Distinctive Properties & Estates," *The Wall Street Journal*, June 22, 2001, p. W15B.)

11.17 [DATA SET EX11-17] *Variable description:*

Closing1: Willingness to develop a long-term buying relationship from salesperson using closing technique 1

Closing2: Willingness to develop a long-term buying relationship from salesperson using closing technique 2

Closing3: Willingness to develop a long-term buying relationship from salesperson using closing technique 3

The effectiveness of closing techniques has been debated among sales strategists. Closing technique 1 is the most aggressive technique with closing technique 2 being moderately aggressive and closing technique 3 being a no-pressure technique. To determine the impact that each of the techniques has on developing a long-term buying relationship, 60 purchasing executives, 20 per technique, were subjected to each of the closing techniques and then asked to rate their willingness to develop a long-term buying relationship with the salesperson. The rating scales ranges from 1 (not willing at all) to 9 (extremely willing).

a. Examine the three means in the printout. Which pairs of sample means appear to be significantly different?

b. Do the data provide sufficient evidence to conclude that the mean rating differs across the three closing techniques? Use a 5% significance level.

c. Examine the printout showing Tukey's multiple comparisons procedure using a 5% significance level. Does this agree with your response to part a?

d. Do a "what if" analysis by adding 10 to all the ratings. What parts of the analysis does this change?

e. Do a "what if" analysis by multiplying all the ratings by 10. What parts of the ANOVA table and multiple comparisons procedure change?

Anova: Single Factor

Summary

Groups	Count	Sum	Average	Variance
Closing1	20	115.000	5.750	2.724
Closing2	20	97.000	4.850	2.134
Closing3	20	137.000	6.850	4.450

ANOVA

Source of Variation	SS	df	MS	F	P-value	F crit
Between Groups	40.133	2	20.067	6.468	0.0029	3.159
Within Groups	176.850	57	3.103			
Total	216.983	59				

Tukey Multiple Comparisons Test

Critical Q	Distance	Alpha
3.4	1.339	0.05

Means joined by a double line are not significantly different.

Closing2	Closing1	Closing3
4.850	5.750	6.850

Hartley Test for Homogeneity of Variance

Hartley Test	Critical Value	Alpha
2.085	2.95	0.05

11.18 [DATA EX11-18] *Variable description:*

InvestVentureCapital: Number of years of retirement support from a venture capital portfolio

InvestPersonalFunds: Number of years of retirement support from a portfolio of mutual funds

InvestCompanyStock: Number of years of retirement support from a portfolio investing in company stock

InvestDiversifiedPension: Number of years of retirement support from a diversified pension portfolio

Financial planners are assessing alternative retirement strategies for executives. Some executives tend to become very conservative toward the end of their career and switch to low-risk bonds. Ray Mignone, a Little Neck, New York, financial planner, warns against becoming too conservative too soon. With life expectancies growing, planners now suggest a fairly aggressive investment approach even for those in their fifties. To make the most of your peak earning years as well as your "last chance" to invest for retirement, Mignone suggests "a well-diversified strategy." That means keeping the bulk in stocks, despite the volatile market. Suppose that Ray were to evaluate the retirement funds for 200 executives and determine the number of years that their retirement money could support themselves if their retirement money were moved completely into bonds. These 200 executives were selected so that 50 had most of their retirement money either in venture capital, personal mutual funds, their company's stock, or a diversified pension fund. Data were recorded as to the number of years that the executives could live using the money from their retirement plan assuming that they needed 80% of their current salary to maintain their lifestyle.

a. Form a histogram of the data for each of the four variables (InvestVentureCapital, InvestPersonalFunds, InvestCompanyStock, InvestDiversifiedPension). How would you describe the differences? (In Excel, use the stacked histogram option in the KPK macros.)

b. At the 5% significance level, do the data indicate a difference in the number of years that the retirement strategies would support an executive?

c. Use a multiple comparisons procedure with a 5% significance level to examine the differences in the retirement strategies.

d. What recommendations should the financial planner make to young executives deciding on a retirement strategy?

(Source: "Steps to Retirement," *Business Week*, November 19, 2001, p. 34.)

11.3

DESIGNING AN EXPERIMENT

The previous section introduced you to one-factor (or one-way) ANOVA. In this type of analysis, you randomly obtain samples from each of the k populations (levels) describing a single factor. The variable that is being measured (such as battery lifetime) is referred to as the **dependent** variable. Since replicates (repeat observations) are obtained in a completely random manner from each population, this type of sampling plan is called a **completely randomized design.** This section discusses other experimental designs, including the randomized block design and the two-way factorial design.

Suppose that the human resource director at Blackburn Industries is interested in examining the cost of dental claims filed by Blackburn employees. Let us consider using the amounts of these claims to examine various group differences; we will need to determine what type of design would be appropriate for each situation.

Situation 1: The Completely Randomized Design

One question of interest to the human resource director is whether the average annual amount claimed on the dental insurance plan differs among the four employee classifications. These classifications range from category 1 (consisting of production-line workers) to category 4 (consisting of upper-level management). Replicates are obtained randomly within each population (category), and the four samples are not related in any way. This illustration consists of one factor (employee classification) comprising four levels. The question of interest here is, is there a difference in the average annual dental claims among the four types of employees? The corresponding null hypothesis is

$$H_0: \mu_1 = \mu_2 = \mu_3 = \mu_4$$

Essentially, this type of analysis (called one-way ANOVA) will fail to reject H_0 if the sample means are "close together" and reject this hypothesis otherwise.

Situation 2: The Randomized Block Design

Suppose instead that the human resource director at Blackburn Industries wished to investigate family dental claims. In particular, she wished to know if there was a difference in the amounts claimed (1) by the husband, (2) by the wife, and (3) per child in the family. For the study she randomly selected 15 (or however many) families having at least one child and recorded these three amounts for each family. This is an example of a **randomized block design.** The configuration of the sample results would resemble the following scheme, where each x represents a dollar amount.

Family	Husband	Wife	Per Child	
1	x	x	x	(1st block)
2	x	x	x	(2nd block)
⋮				
15	x	x	x	(15th block)

This design consists of one *factor* (say, family member) with three levels (husband/wife/per child). Unlike the completely randomized design, the three samples *are not independent,* since the data are grouped (blocked) by family. For example, the first husband value is not independent of the first wife value, since they both belong to the same family. We encountered this very same design in Chapter 9, where we compared two population means using paired (that is, blocked) samples. When using the randomized block design, you can compare the means of more than two populations using a blocking strategy to gather your data.

The question of interest here is, is there a difference in the husband, wife, and per-child claims? In a situation similar to that of the completely randomized design, the question of interest is whether the factor of interest (family member type, here) has a significant effect on the value of the dependent variable (amount of the annual claim, here). *The difference between the randomized block design and the completely randomized situation is that here we use a blocking strategy rather than independent samples to obtain a more precise test for examining differences in the factor level means.* The null hypothesis for this illustration is that the group (factor level) means are identical, that is,

$$H_0: \mu_H = \mu_W = \mu_C$$

where μ_H is the average annual amount claimed by the husband, μ_W is the average amount for the wife, and μ_C is the average amount claimed per child.

The analysis for the randomized block design is discussed in the next section, but essentially this procedure removes the effects of the blocks (families, here) before testing for a difference between the factor level means. Consequently, this design removes the block effect from the error sum of squares in the completely randomized design. Several examples in the next section illustrate this technique.

Situation 3: The Two-Way Factorial Design

The **two-way factorial design** is similar to situation 1, the one-way analysis of variance, except now *two* factors are of interest to the individual conducting the study. Suppose that the human resource director at Blackburn Industries decides to examine the dental claims for all the unmarried employees. She wants to investigate the effect of gender (factor A) and employee classification (factor B) on the amount of the annual claims. As before, employee classification ranges from category 1 (production-line workers) to category 4 (upper-level management). The previous one-way ANOVA illustration examined only the effect of employee classification on the amount of dental claims.

The two-way factorial design allows for an **interaction effect;** not only can you examine the effect of each factor individually, but you can also study the combined effect of both factors. For example, the inclusion of the gender factor accomplishes two things: first, you can determine if the gender of the employee has an effect on the amount of the annual claim, and second, you can investigate whether the relationship between employee classification and the amount of the annual claim is different for male and female employees. In other words, whether factor B relates to the dependent variable (amount of annual dental claim) depends on the level of factor A. *The interaction effect between factors A and B differs from the randomized block design, where it is assumed that no interaction exists between the factor of interest and the blocks.*

Consequently, three sets of hypotheses can be tested using the two-way factorial design:

$H_{0,A}$: factor A (gender) is not significant

$H_{0,B}$: factor B (employee classification) is not significant

$H_{0,AB}$: there is no interaction between factor A and factor B

The first two hypotheses are similar to those tested in one-way ANOVA, but the third hypothesis is unique to the two-way (or higher) factorial design.

To collect data for this design, the human resource director would obtain an amount for *every* combination of a factor A level and a factor B level. This particular illustration consists of two levels for factor A (male/female) and four levels

11.9

Illustration of a
2 × 4 factorial
design using three
replicates.

Factor B

		Category 1	Category 2	Category 3	Category 4
Factor A	Male	x, x, x	x, x, x	x, x, x	x, x, x
	Female	x, x, x	x, x, x	x, x, x	x, x, x

for factor B (category 1/ . . . / category 4) and is called a 2 × 4 *factorial design*. Consequently, data are collected for eight possible factor level combinations, referred to as **treatments.** Data values within the same treatment are termed *replicates.* Furthermore, it is necessary when using this type of design to obtain more than one replicate for each treatment. An illustration using three replicates (two would be sufficient) is shown in Figure 11.9. Each *x* represents the amount of the annual dental claim. The actual two-way analysis of variance for this illustration is demonstrated in Section 11.5.

X Exercises 11.19–11.22

Understanding the Mechanics

11.19

a. Name the three types of experimental design discussed in the preceding section.

b. Which design or designs do not involve the necessity of having replicates?

c. What is interaction between factors? Which design permits testing for interaction?

d. In each of the three designs, how many dependent variables are there?

e. If a one-way (one-factor) ANOVA design has four levels of the factor and six replicates at each level, how many treatments are being considered and how many total observations are there?

f. If a 4 × 6 two-way factorial design is chosen for an ANOVA-based experiment, what are the number of treatments being considered and the *minimum* number of total observations necessary?

g. What is the advantage of blocking, and when is it necessary?

h. What potential problems can arise with the randomized block design?

Applying the New Concepts

11.20 Quality managers believe that involving suppliers in fundamental design, production, and logistical decisions of a manufacturing firm can have an impact on productivity. In fact, researchers are investigating the effects of supply chain management on manufacturing performance. Suppose that a researcher wishes to determine if there is a significant difference in manufacturing performance as measured by time to complete an order in manufacturing organizations with high, medium, and low levels of importance placed on supplier selection criteria.

The manufacturing performance is recorded using a self-reporting rating from 1 to 10.

a. What design is appropriate to test whether there is a difference in the levels of importance placed on supplier selection criteria?

b. Suppose that another factor is also considered: firm size (small, medium, and large). What design is appropriate to test whether there is a difference based on the two factors? Should the interaction effect be tested?

c. Is it necessary for the researcher to obtain more than one replicate for each of the combinations of factor levels in part b? What is the minimum number of observations for this design?

(Source: Adapted from "Building Supply Chains: A Key to Enhanced Manufacturing Performance," *Decision Sciences Institute 1998 Proceedings,* pp. 1184–86.)

11.21 Restaurants are recommended by many brokerage firms. These firms often warn investors that these stocks often look appetizing, but timing is essential and buying these stocks after they become too pricey can cause a horrible case of indigestion. Investors also tend to buy restaurant stocks by focusing on just one or two criteria. Analysts take into account many criteria in evaluating a restaurant stock, including (1) How good is the food? (2) How long are the lines? (3) How fast is the restaurant expanding? (4) How sound is the economy in the locations that the restaurant is expanding? (5) How good is the management? and (6) What is the value of the restaurant relative to its competitors? Suppose that a brokerage firm wanted to evaluate three restaurants: Garden Fresh Restaurant, Cheesecake Factory, and RE Chang's. The brokerage firm's manager has available 15 analysts to rate restaurants.

a. What design would you use to analyze the restaurant ratings if five different analysts are used to evaluate each of the three restaurants?

b. What design would you use to analyze the restaurant ratings if all 15 analysts are used to evaluate each of the three restaurants?

c. If you use a randomized block design, how can you randomize the observations within each block?

(Source: "Restaurant Stocks: Not as Tasty as They Look," *Fortune*, November 12, 2001, p. 206.)

11.22 Gillette first produced a razor especially for women in 1915, and since then many of the versions have been "just prettier versions of a man's razor." Schick makes a disposable Slim Twin razor that is gender neutral. Bic's disposable razors differ by gender, although a company spokesperson admits that the distinction is subtle. The blades are set at different angles, and the women's shaver contains a moisturizing strip. Suppose that a marketing analyst at Gillette wished to have women rate three razors: a male razor, a gender neutral razor, and a female razor on a scale from 1 to 10.

a. Explain how a completely randomized design can be used to test whether a difference exists among these three types of razors.

b. Explain how a randomized block design can be used to test whether a difference exists among these three types of razors.

(Source: "Great Questions of Our Age: Do Gender-Specific Razors Differ?" *Fortune*, November 12, 2001, p. 48.)

RANDOMIZED BLOCK DESIGN

The previous section described the difference between the randomized block and completely randomized designs. Rather than obtaining independent samples from the k populations, the data for a randomized block design are organized into homogeneous units referred to as **blocks**. *Within* each block, any predictable difference in the observations is due to the effect of the factor of interest, such as gender or employee classification.

Consider the situation discussed in Section 9.5. Metalloy manufactures metal hinges, and as part of the quality inspection these hinges are subjected to a hardness test in which a rod with a pointed tip is pressed into a hinge and the depth of the depression caused by the tip is measured. Two tips are available for the hardness tester. Twelve hinges were randomly selected, and both tips were used to test the hardness of each metal hinge. The coded data from this hardness test are as follows.

Hinge	Tip #1	Tip #2	Hinge	Tip #1	Tip #2
1	39	35	7	45	41
2	32	34	8	48	47
3	42	38	9	38	35
4	49	48	10	48	46
5	45	47	11	41	37
6	47	43	12	47	44

Once again, there is a single factor of interest, namely, the tip used for the test. But are the 24 sample observations in fact replicates? Replicates (by definition) are obtained under (nearly) identical circumstances, so that any variation in the values within any one sample is due strictly to chance. In this situation, the hinge used in the test heavily influences each sample value. Also, each pair of values is obtained from the same hinge, and so these samples are *not independent*, violating a key assumption of the completely randomized design.

This situation fits the *paired sample* design discussed in Section 9.5, provided we assume that the population of differences (tip #1 minus tip #2) is normally distributed. We will now extend our discussion of Section 9.5 to consider more than two populations.

To determine whether there is a factor (tip) effect in these 24 observations, we must first account for the block (hinge) effect. If we ignore this effect, we could easily come to an incorrect conclusion regarding a difference in the effect of the two tips. This same point was made in Section 9.5, where a crucial question was whether to pair (block) the data. Figure 9.20 illustrated how one can arrive at an incorrect conclusion by failing to block the data.

Metalloy also makes a larger, softer hinge that requires a hardness test as part of the quality inspection. For this test, there are three tips available for inserting into the rod that is then pressed into the hinge with a specified force. The question of interest, as before, is whether there is a difference in the average reading for the three tips. Using 10 hinges, an experiment was conducted in which all three tips were applied to each of the metal hinges. The results were as follows.

Hinge	Tip #1	Tip #2	Tip #3	Hinge	Tip #1	Tip #2	Tip #3
1	68	72	65	6	80	91	86
2	40	43	42	7	47	58	50
3	82	89	84	8	55	68	52
4	56	60	50	9	78	77	75
5	70	75	68	10	53	65	60

The data from this situation constitute a randomized block design with a single factor (tip used in the rod) containing three levels (tip #1, tip #2, tip #3) as well as 10 blocks (hinge 1, . . . , hinge 10). The general appearance of such a design is shown in Table 11.1.

When using the randomized block design, the various levels should be applied in a *random* manner within each block. In the hardness testing, the test should *not* always use tip #1 first, tip #2 second, and tip #3 last. Instead, the three tips should be applied in a randomized order for each hinge—hence the name *randomized block design*.

The requirements for the randomized block design are:

1. The populations within each factor level/block combination (hinge-and-tip combination in our example) are normally distributed, and the sample observation within each factor level/block combination is randomly selected.

2. These normal populations have a common variance, σ^2.

Furthermore, we assume that the factor effects are the same within each block; that is, there is no interaction effect between the factor and the blocks.

The analysis using the randomized block design is similar to that for the one-factor ANOVA, except that the total sum of squares (SS(total)) has an additional component. Now,

$$SS(total) = SS(factor) + SS(blocks) + SS(error)$$

where SS(blocks) measures the variation due to the blocks. Consequently, this design extracts the block effect, as measured by SS(blocks), from the error of sum of squares in the completely randomized design.

If you use the randomized block design when blocking is not necessary, SS(blocks) will be very small in comparison to the other sums of squares. Refer-

TABLE 11.1

The randomized block design.

Block	1	2	3	$\cdots$	k	Total
	FACTOR LEVEL (POPULATION)					
1	x	x	x	$\cdots$	x	S_1
2	x	x	x	$\cdots$	x	S_2
3	x	x	x	$\cdots$	x	S_3
$\vdots$						$\vdots$
b	x	x	x	$\cdots$	x	S_b
Total	T_1	T_2	T_3	$\cdots$	T_k	T
Sample Mean	$\bar{X}_1$	$\bar{X}_2$	$\bar{X}_3$	$\cdots$	$\bar{X}_k$	

ring to Table 11.1, this will occur when $S_1, S_2, \ldots, S_b$ are nearly the same. If all the S_i's are equal, then SS(blocks) = 0. The effect of the blocks will be significant whenever you observe a lot of variation in these block totals.

The sum of squares for the randomized block design is thus

$$\text{SS(factor)} = \frac{1}{b}[T_1^2 + T_2^2 + \cdots + T_k^2] - \frac{T^2}{bk}$$

11.21

where

k = number of factor levels in the design

b = number of blocks in the design

n = number of observations = bk

$T_1, T_2, \ldots, T_k$ represent the totals for the k factor levels

$S_1, S_2, \ldots, S_b$ are the totals for the b blocks

$T = T_1 + T_2 + \cdots + T_k$

$\quad = S_1 + S_2 + \cdots + S_b$ = total of all observations

$$\text{SS(blocks)} = \frac{1}{k}[S_1^2 + S_2^2 + \cdots + S_b^2] - \frac{T^2}{bk}$$

11.22

$$\text{SS(total)} = \sum x^2 - \frac{T^2}{bk}$$

11.23

where $\sum x^2$ = sum of the squares for each of the n (= bk) observations.

$$\text{SS(error)} = \text{SS(total)} - \text{SS(factor)} - \text{SS(blocks)}$$

11.24

The degrees of freedom are

df for factor = $k - 1$

df for blocks = $b - 1$

df for error = $(k - 1)(b - 1)$

df for total = $bk - 1$

The ANOVA table for a blocked design is very similar to the one-factor ANOVA table. There is one additional row because you now include the effect of the various blocks in your design:

Source	df	SS	MS	F
Factor	$k - 1$	SS(factor)	$\text{MS(factor)} = \dfrac{\text{SS(factor)}}{k - 1}$	$F_1 = \dfrac{\text{MS(factor)}}{\text{MS(error)}}$
Blocks	$b - 1$	SS(blocks)	$\text{MS(blocks)} = \dfrac{\text{SS(blocks)}}{b - 1}$	$F_2 = \dfrac{\text{MS(blocks)}}{\text{MS(error)}}$
Error	$(k - 1)(b - 1)$	SS(error)	$\text{MS(error)} = \dfrac{\text{SS(error)}}{(k - 1)(b - 1)}$	
Total	$bk - 1$	SS(total)		

where

$$\text{MS(factor)} = \frac{\text{SS(factor)}}{k - 1}$$

$$\text{MS(blocks)} = \frac{\text{SS(blocks)}}{b - 1}$$

$$\text{MS(error)} = \frac{\text{SS(error)}}{(k - 1)(b - 1)}$$

Hypothesis Testing

Is there a difference in the average reading for the three tips in the previous illustration? In other words, does the tip used have a significant effect on the hardness reading? The hypotheses for this situation are $H_0: \mu_1 = \mu_2 = \mu_3$ and H_a: not all the means are equal. We determine the test statistic exactly as we did for the one-factor ANOVA:

$$F_1 = \frac{MS(factor)}{MS(error)} \qquad 11.25$$

where the mean square values are obtained from the ANOVA table. Notice that the MS(factor) value is the *same*, regardless of whether you block. However, when you use the block effect in the design, the SS(error) is smaller than the SS(error) value obtained using the completely randomized design. The df in the error term are different for the two designs, so it does not necessarily follow that the MS(error) is smaller in the randomized block design. If there is considerable variation among the block totals, then quite likely MS(error) *will* be smaller in the randomized block design. You are thus more likely to detect a difference in these k means when a difference does exist. Had you not included the block effect, the block variation would have been included in SS(error), resulting in a smaller F value. This value often becomes small enough not to fall in the rejection region, leading you to conclude that no difference exists. *But perhaps there is a difference among these means (the factor does have a significant effect) that will go undetected if an incorrect experimental design is used.*

For the randomized block design, the test will be to

$$\text{reject } H_0 \text{ if } F_1 > F_{\alpha, v_1, v_2}$$

where $v_1 = k - 1$ and $v_2 = (k - 1)(b - 1)$. So, once again, we reject H_0 if the F statistic falls in the right-tail rejection region, this time using Table A.7 with $v_1 = k - 1$, the df for factor, and $v_2 = (k - 1)(b - 1)$, the df for error.

Now suppose we wish to determine whether the effect of the hinge used for the hardness test is significant. We are attempting to determine whether there is a block effect, so the hypotheses are

H_0': there is no effect due to the hinges (blocks) (the block means are equal)

H_a': there is an effect due to the hinges (the block means are not all equal)

The corresponding test uses the "other" F statistic from the randomized block ANOVA table, namely,

$$F_2 = \frac{MS(blocks)}{MS(error)} \qquad 11.26$$

and the test procedure is to

$$\text{reject } H_0' \text{ if } F_2 > F_{\alpha, v_1', v_2'}$$

where $v_1' = b - 1$ and $v_2' = (k - 1)(b - 1)$.

Let us reexamine our data. We will use $\alpha = .05$. Here, $k = 3$ levels (tips), $b = 10$ blocks (hinges), and $n = bk = 30$ observations.

Hinge	Tip #1	Tip #2	Tip #3	Totals
1	68	72	65	205
2	40	43	42	125
3	82	89	84	255
4	56	60	50	166
5	70	75	68	213
6	80	91	86	257

Hinge	Tip #1	Tip #2	Tip #3	Totals
7	47	58	50	155
8	55	68	52	175
9	78	77	75	230
10	53	65	60	178
Total	629	698	632	1,959
$\overline{X}$	62.9	69.8	63.2	

$$SS(factor) = \frac{1}{10}[629^2 + 698^2 + 632^2] - \frac{1,959^2}{30}$$
$$= 128,226.9 - 127,922.7 = 304.2$$

$$SS(blocks) = \frac{1}{3}[205^2 + 125^2 + \cdots + 178^2] - \frac{1,959^2}{30}$$
$$= 133,627.7 - 127,922.7 = 5,705.0$$

$$SS(total) = [68^2 + 40^2 + \cdots + 75^2 + 60^2] - \frac{1,959^2}{30}$$
$$= 134,107 - 127,922.7 = 6,184.3$$

$$SS(error) = SS(total) - SS(factor) - SS(blocks)$$
$$= 6,184.3 - 304.2 - 5,705.0 = 175.1$$

So

$$MS(factor) = \frac{SS(factor)}{k-1}$$
$$= \frac{304.2}{2} = 152.1$$

$$MS(blocks) = \frac{SS(blocks)}{b-1}$$
$$= \frac{5,705.0}{9} = 633.9$$

$$MS(error) = \frac{SS(error)}{(k-1)(b-1)}$$
$$= \frac{175.1}{18} = 9.73$$

The resulting ANOVA table is

Source	df	SS	MS	F
Factor	2	304.2	152.1	$152.1/9.73 = 15.63$ (F_1)
Blocks	9	5,705.0	633.9	$633.9/9.73 = 65.15$ (F_2)
Error	18	175.1	9.73	
Total	29	6,184.3		

We first consider the hypotheses

$$H_0: \mu_1 = \mu_2 = \mu_3$$

$$H_a: \text{not all } \mu\text{'s are equal}$$

where

μ_1 = average reading using tip #1 (estimate is $\overline{x}_1 = 62.9$)

μ_2 = average reading using tip #2 (estimate is $\overline{x}_2 = 69.8$)

μ_3 = average reading using tip #3 (estimate is $\overline{x}_3 = 63.2$)

Because $F_1 = 15.63 > F_{.05,2,18} = 3.55$, we reject H_0 and conclude that there *is* a difference in the hardness readings for the three tips. This is not a surprising result, because it appears that the tip #2 readings were much higher than for tips #1 and #3. This means that the factor (tip used) *does* have a significant effect on the hardness reading.

We also wish to test

H_0': there is no block effect

H_a': there is a block effect

$S_1, S_2, \ldots, S_{10}$ appear to contain considerable variation, so our initial guess is that there is a block effect. Carrying out the statistical test, we see that

$$F_2 = 65.15 > F_{.05,9,18} = 2.46$$

Consequently, we strongly reject H_0' in favor of H_a'. The effect of the hinge used for the hardness test *is* significant.

An Excel solution for this problem is shown in Figure 11.11. To obtain this solution, first enter the thirty data values in cells B2:D11 and the corresponding labels as shown in Figure 11.10. Then click on **KPK Data Analysis ➤ ANOVA**. In the resulting input screen (see Figure 11.6), enter "A1:D11" in the **Input Range** box, and enter "E1" in the **Output Range** box. In the **Experimental Design** frame,

---

FIGURE

11.10

Excel spreadsheet containing the hardness data with labels for the rows and columns.

	A	B	C	D
1	Hinge	Tip #1	Tip #2	Tip #3
2	1	68	72	65
3	2	40	43	42
4	3	82	89	84
5	4	56	60	50
6	5	70	75	68
7	6	80	91	86
8	7	47	58	50
9	8	55	68	52
10	9	78	77	75
11	10	53	65	60

FIGURE

11.11

Portion of Excel spreadsheet containing the solution for the hardness testing data.

File Edit View Insert Format Tools Data KPK Data Analysis Window Help

	E	F	G	H	I	J	K	L	M
1	Anova: Two-Factor Without Replication								
2									
3	SUMMARY	Count	Sum	Average	Variance				
4	1	3	205.0000	68.3333	12.3333				
5	2	3	125.0000	41.6667	2.3333				
6	3	3	255.0000	85.0000	13.0000				
7	4	3	166.0000	55.3333	25.3333				
8	5	3	213.0000	71.0000	13.0000				
9	6	3	257.0000	85.6667	30.3333				
10	7	3	155.0000	51.6667	32.3333				
11	8	3	175.0000	58.3333	72.3333				
12	9	3	230.0000	76.6667	2.3333				
13	10	3	178.0000	59.3333	36.3333				
14									
15	Tip #1	10	629.0000	62.9000	216.3222				
16	Tip #2	10	698.0000	69.8000	209.0667				
17	Tip #3	10	632.0000	63.2000	227.9556				
18									
19									
20	ANOVA								
21	Source of Variation	SS	df	MS	F	P-value	F crit		
22	Factor	304.2000	2	152.1000	15.6327	0.0001	3.5546		
23	Blocks	5704.9667	9	633.8852	65.1500	0.0000	2.4563		
24	Error	175.1333	18	9.7296					
25									
26	Total	6184.3000	29						
27									
28									

Sheet1 / Sheet2 / Sheet3 /

click on **Randomized Block.** The alpha value should be 5%. Your resulting output will be that shown in Figure 11.11, except rows 22 and 23 will be interchanged and will have different labels (**Rows** and **Columns**). Excel's ANOVA table will have the block row (labeled **Rows**) first, followed by the factor row (labeled **Columns**).

To swap these two rows (as in Figure 11.11), highlight the cells in E22:K22. Move the cursor up from the bottom toward this row and stop when it becomes a white arrow. Drag this row down one row *while holding down the shift key.* Release the mouse button, then the shift key. You have now swapped these two rows in the ANOVA table. Finally, type "Factor" in cell E22 and "Blocks" in cell E23. Notice that the output contains the (very small) p-values in cells J22 and J23, along with the critical F values for $\alpha = .05$ in cells K22 and K23. Since both p-values are less than .05, this supports the earlier conclusion that there is a difference in the three tips, and there is a significant block effect.

Comments

Notice that the block (hinge) effect is highly significant here, indicating much variation in the totals for each row (hinge). This indicates that there is very little uniformity in the hardness of the hinges being produced, regardless of what tip is used for measurement. Consequently, Metalloy has a serious problem in the quality of the hinges being produced. As Chapter 12 ("Quality Improvement") will point out, one indicator of poor quality is too much variation in the quality characteristic being measured (hardness, here).

What would the result have been had we treated these 30 observations as replicates, 10 from each of the three tips? In other words, what would happen if we failed to recognize that blocking was necessary and we incorrectly used the one-factor ANOVA? Because both SS(factor) and SS(total) do not change, the only difference is a new SS(error). Therefore,

$$SS(error) = SS(total) - SS(factor)$$

$$= 6,184.3 - 304.2$$

$$= 5,880.1$$

Also, in the one-factor ANOVA design,

$$df \text{ for total} = (df \text{ for factor}) + (df \text{ for error})$$

So,

$$df \text{ for error} = (df \text{ for total}) - (df \text{ for factor})$$

$$= 29 - 2 = 27$$

The resulting F value will be

$$F = \frac{MS(factor)}{MS(error)} = \frac{304.2/2}{5,880.1/27} = .70$$

Because $F^* = .70$ is *much less* than $F_{.05,2,27} = 3.35$, *we fail to detect a difference in the three means*, μ_1, μ_2, and μ_3. This is the effect of assuming independence among the samples when it does not exist. This example emphasizes that failing to recognize the need for a randomized block design can have serious consequences!

Using a Calculator

In section 11.2 (Using a Calculator), we provided a shortcut method of determining SS(total) and SS(factor) when using a calculator to carry out the calculations. For the randomized block design, you can use a similar procedure to calculate the three sums of squares used in this design.

SS(total)   1. Key in all n (= bk) observations (68, 40, . . . , 75, 60 in the previous illustration) as though you were determining the standard deviation of these n (= 30, here) values.
2. Press the sample standard deviation key on your calculator.
3. Square this value (press the x^2 key) to get the variance of these n observations.
4. Multiply by $n - 1$ (29, here). This is SS(total).

SS(factor)   Since there are always b (= 10, here) observations within each factor level, the following shortcut procedure can always be used to find SS(factor) for a randomized block design.
1. Key in the k factor totals (629, 698, 632 for this illustration) as though you were finding the standard deviation of these k values.
2. Press the sample standard deviation key on your calculator.
3. Square this value by pressing the x^2 key.
4. Multiply by $k - 1$ (2, here).
5. Divide this result by the number of blocks ($b = 10$, here). This is SS(factor).

SS(blocks)   1. Key in the b block totals (205, 125, . . . , 178 for this illustration) as though you were finding the standard deviation of these b values.
2. Press the sample standard deviation key on your calculator.
3. Square this value by pressing the x^2 key.
4. Multiply by $b - 1$ (9, here).
5. Divide this result by the number of factor levels ($k = 3$, here). This is SS(factor).

SS(error)   By subtraction, SS(error) = SS(total) − SS(factor) − SS(blocks)

EXAMPLE
11.7

The human resource director at Blackburn Industries is investigating dental claims submitted by married employees having at least one child. Of interest is whether the average annual dollar amounts of dental work claimed by the husband, by the wife, and per child are the same. Data were collected by randomly selecting 16 families and recording these three dollar amounts (total claims for the year by the husband, by the wife, and per child). The results of the sample are shown below. Can the human resource director conclude that there is a difference in the three population means using a significance level of .05?

Family	Husband	Wife	Per Child	Total
1	78	84	112	274
2	105	80	274	459
3	95	184	305	584
4	85	158	280	523
5	148	180	263	591
6	284	208	145	637
7	124	145	340	609
8	118	75	130	323
9	153	112	239	504
10	143	204	262	609
11	84	110	182	376
12	106	172	248	526
13	218	185	320	723
14	145	90	226	461
15	175	304	152	631
16	128	161	217	506
Total	2,189	2,452	3,695	8,336
$\overline{X}$	$ 136.81	$ 153.25	$ 230.94	

The hypotheses for this situation are

Solution

$$H_0: \mu_H = \mu_W = \mu_C$$

$$H_a: \text{not all three means are equal}$$

where μ_H is the average annual amount claimed by the husband, μ_W is the average for the wife, and μ_C is the average amount per child.

The various block and factor totals shown are obtained by summing across and down the array of data.

$$SS(\text{factor}) = \frac{1}{16}[2{,}189^2 + 2{,}452^2 + 3{,}695^2] - \frac{8{,}336^2}{48}$$

$$= 1{,}528{,}565.625 - 1{,}447{,}685.33 = 80{,}880.29$$

$$SS(\text{blocks}) = \frac{1}{3}[274^2 + 459^2 + \cdots + 506^2] - \frac{8{,}336^2}{48}$$

$$= 1{,}520{,}999.33 - 1{,}447{,}685.33 = 73{,}314$$

$$SS(\text{total}) = (78^2 + 105^2 + \cdots + 152^2 + 217^2) - \frac{8{,}336^2}{48}$$

$$= 1{,}699{,}824 - 1{,}447{,}685.33 = 252{,}138.67$$

$$SS(\text{error}) = SS(\text{total}) - SS(\text{factor}) - SS(\text{blocks})$$

$$= 97{,}944.38$$

The corresponding ANOVA table follows. Note that the df for the factor are $3 - 1 = 2$, for blocks are $16 - 1 = 15$, and for total are $48 - 1 = 47$, leaving $47 - 2 - 15 = 30$ df for error.

Source	df	SS	MS	F
Factor	2	80,880.29	40,440.14	$40{,}440.14/3{,}264.81 = 12.39$
Blocks	15	73,314	4,887.60	$4{,}887.60/3{,}264.81 = 1.50$
Error	30	97,944.38	3,264.81	
Total	47	252,138.67		

To test $H_0: \mu_H = \mu_W = \mu_C$, we use $F_1 = 12.39$. Since $12.39 > F_{.05,2,30} = 3.32$, we reject H_0 and conclude that the three average claim amounts are not equal. By observing the sample means, we notice that the claims per child are considerably higher than those for the husband and wife.

As a final note, the block (family) effect is *not* significant here, since $F_2 = 1.50 < F_{.05,15,30} = 2.01$. This does not mean that including the block effect in the analysis was a mistake, since the samples were clearly *not* obtained independently. Furthermore, there is no guarantee that the block effect will once again turn out to be insignificant for the next set of data in this situation.

Constructing a Confidence Interval for the Difference between Two Population Means

Due to a possible block effect with this type of design, you cannot determine a confidence interval for an individual factor-level mean, μ_i. You can, however, construct a confidence interval for the difference between any *pair* of means, $\mu_i - \mu_j$. Remember: (1) We must determine which confidence intervals we will construct *before* observing the data (don't let the data dictate which confidence intervals to construct), and (2) this procedure is satisfactory provided you compare only a very small number of pairs (say, one or two pairs).

The second comment is very important! If you wish to compare a large number of population means, such as all possible pairs, a multiple comparisons procedure should be used (discussed following Example 11.8). In this way you can be sure that the probability of making one or more Type I errors (concluding that two means differ when, in fact, they are equal), is the predetermined significance level, α.

When using the randomized block design, our estimate of the common variance, σ^2, is now

$$s^2 = \text{estimate of } \sigma^2$$
$$= \text{MS(error)} = \frac{\text{SS(error)}}{(k-1)(b-1)}$$

11.27

Thus, a $(1 - \alpha) \cdot 100\%$ confidence interval for $\mu_i - \mu_j$ is

$$(\overline{X}_i - \overline{X}_j) - t_{\alpha/2,\text{df}} \cdot s \cdot \sqrt{\frac{1}{b} + \frac{1}{b}} \text{ to } (\overline{X}_i - \overline{X}_j) + t_{\alpha/2,\text{df}} \cdot s \cdot \sqrt{\frac{1}{b} + \frac{1}{b}}$$

11.28

where df = degrees of freedom for the t statistic (Table A.5) = $(k-1)(b-1)$; b = number of blocks; k = number of factor levels; and s is determined from equation 11.27.

EXAMPLE 11.8

Assume you have not yet observed the dental claim data in Example 11.7, and you decided to construct a 95% confidence interval for the difference between the average annual claim for the wife and the average annual claim per child. What does this confidence interval tell you?

Solution   Using the ANOVA table for these data,

$$s^2 = \text{MS(error)} = 3264.81$$

and so $s = 57.1385$. Also, $t_{.025,30} = 2.042$ using Table A.5. The resulting 95% confidence interval for $\mu_C - \mu_W$ is

$$(\overline{X}_C - \overline{X}_W) - t_{.025,30} \; s\sqrt{\frac{1}{16} + \frac{1}{16}} \quad \text{to} \quad (\overline{X}_C - \overline{X}_W) + t_{.025,30} \; s\sqrt{\frac{1}{16} + \frac{1}{16}}$$

$$= (230.94 - 153.25) - (2.042)(57.1385)(.3536) \quad \text{to}$$
$$(230.94 - 153.25) + (2.042)(57.1385)(.3536)$$
$$= 77.69 - 41.26 \quad \text{to} \quad 77.69 + 41.26$$
$$= 36.43 \quad \text{to} \quad 118.95$$

We are thus 95% confident that the average annual claim per child is between \$36.43 and \$118.95 *higher* than the average annual claim for the wife.

The Excel generated 95% confidence interval for $\mu_C - \mu_W$ is shown in Figure 11.12. To obtain this solution, enter the data in cells A1:D17, including the labels as shown in Figure 11.12, and then click on **KPK Data Analysis ➤ ANOVA.** In the resulting input screen (see Figure 11.6), enter "A1:D17" in the **Input Range** box and enter "E1" in the **Output Range** box. In the **Experimental Design** frame, click on **Randomized Block.** Be sure to click on the check box alongside **Confidence Interval for Difference Between Two Means** and enter 3 in the top box (First Group) and 2 in the bottom box (Second Group). The alpha value should be 5%. The resulting confidence interval in cells H37 and I37 agrees with the previous result.

Multiple Comparisons Procedure: Randomized Block Design

If the null hypothesis that the factor-level means are equal is rejected, then Tukey's multiple comparisons procedure (introduced in section 11.2) can be applied to the randomized block design. In this way, you can determine which

FIGURE

11.12

Excel spreadsheet with ANOVA table and confidence interval for Examples 11.7 and 11.8.

File Edit View Insert Format Tools Data KPK Data Analysis Window Help											_|&|×|
	A	B	C	D	E	F	G	H	I	J	K
1	Family	Husband	Wife	Child	Anova: Two-Factor Without Replication						
2	1	78	84	112							
3	2	105	80	274	SUMMARY	Count	Sum	Average	Variance		
4	3	95	184	305	1	3	274.0000	91.3333	329.3333		
5	4	85	158	280	2	3	459.0000	153.0000	11137.0000		
6	5	148	180	263	3	3	584.0000	194.6667	11110.3333		
7	6	284	208	145	4	3	523.0000	174.3333	9706.3333		
8	7	124	145	340	5	3	591.0000	197.0000	3523.0000		
9	8	118	75	130	6	3	637.0000	212.3333	4844.3333		
10	9	153	112	239	7	3	609.0000	203.0000	14187.0000		
11	10	143	204	262	8	3	323.0000	107.6667	836.3333		
12	11	84	110	182	9	3	504.0000	168.0000	4201.0000		
13	12	106	172	248	10	3	609.0000	203.0000	3541.0000		
14	13	218	185	320	11	3	376.0000	125.3333	2577.3333		
15	14	145	90	226	12	3	526.0000	175.3333	5049.3333		
16	15	175	304	152	13	3	723.0000	241.0000	4953.0000		
17	16	128	161	217	14	3	461.0000	153.6667	4680.3333		
18					15	3	631.0000	210.3333	6712.3333		
19					16	3	506.0000	168.6667	2024.3333		
20											
21					Husband	16	2189.0000	136.8125	2896.2958		
22					Wife	16	2452.0000	153.2500	3688.4667		
23					Child	16	3695.0000	230.9375	4832.4625		
24											
25											
26					ANOVA						
27					Source of Variation	SS	df	MS	F	P-value	F crit
28					Factor	80880.2917	2	40440.1458	12.3867	0.0001	3.3158
29					Blocks	73314.0000	15	4887.6000	1.4971	0.1687	2.0148
30					Error	97944.3750	30	3264.8125			
31											
32					Total	252138.6667	47				
33											
34											
35					95% CI FOR Child - Wife						
36					Difference	Critical t	Standard error	Lower Limit	Upper Limit		
37					77.6875	2.0423	20.2015	36.4305	118.9445		
38											

Sheet1 / Sheet2 / Sheet3 /

pairs of factor-level means are different while preserving your experimentwise significance level, α.

The number of means being compared is k, where k = the number of factor levels. For example, in Example 11.7, there are $k = 3$ different levels (husband, wife, child), and it was observed in the solution to this example that the per-child average cost in the sample appeared to be considerably different than the other two sample averages. The follow-up questions here are: Is $\mu_H \neq \mu_W$? Is $\mu_H \neq \mu_C$? Is $\mu_W \neq \mu_C$?

For the randomized block design, we use Table A.16 to find $Q_{\alpha,k,v}$, where α = the experimentwise significance level, k = number of factor-level means, and v = df associated with MS(error) = $(k-1)(b-1)$, where b is the number of blocks in the design. We conclude that any two population means (μ_i and μ_j) are unequal, provided

$$|\bar{X}_i - \bar{X}_j| > D$$

where

$$D = Q_{\alpha,k,(k-1)(b-1)} \sqrt{\frac{MS(error)}{b}}$$

In Example 11.7, $\alpha = .05$, $k = 3$, $b = 16$, and MS(error) = 3264.81. Referring to Table A.16, we first locate $Q_{.05,3,(3-1)(16-1)} = Q_{.05,3,30} = 3.49$. Next, we find

$$D = 3.49 \sqrt{\frac{3264.81}{16}} = 49.85$$

Examining the three sample means, we see that

$$\bar{X}_C - \bar{X}_H = 230.94 - 136.81 = 94.13 > 49.85$$

$$\bar{X}_C - \bar{X}_W = 230.94 - 153.25 = 77.69 > 49.85$$

$$\bar{X}_W - \bar{X}_H = 153.25 - 136.81 = 16.44 < 49.85$$

and so we conclude that the average per-child claim differs from the average claim for the husbands and the average claim for the wives, but we cannot distinguish between the average claims for the husband and wife populations. This is illustrated by an overbar connecting the husband and wife sample means.

$$\overline{\begin{array}{ccc} 136.81 & 153.25 \end{array}} \qquad 230.94$$
$$\begin{array}{ccc} \text{(H)} & \text{(W)} & \text{(C)} \end{array}$$

Using Excel to Carry Out a Randomized Block Analysis

Allied Container Corporation manufactures corrugated boxes that are sold to other businesses for use as shipping containers. It currently has three different brands of machine under consideration that are used to manufacture the boxes from corrugated sheets. It is about to purchase new machines, and it suspects that the average number of boxes produced per hour by an individual worker is not the same for each machine. To verify this, it conducted an experiment in which each of 20 randomly selected workers ran each machine (in random order) for one hour. At the end of each hour, the number of boxes produced on that particular machine was recorded. The results are in data set DATA11-9, where columns A, B, C contain the number of boxes produced on machines A, B, and C, respectively. The 20 rows consist of the blocks (workers), so that row 1 contains the boxes produced by worker 1 on the three machines, row 2 corresponds to worker 2, and so on.

Using a significance level of .05, what can you tell Allied about the average output of these three machines?

Solution

Begin by opening dataset DATA11-9. You should observe three columns of 20 values with corresponding labels, as shown in Figure 11.13. Click on **KPK Data Analysis ➤ ANOVA.** In the resulting input screen (see Figure 11.6), enter "A1:D21" in the **Input Range** box and enter "E1" in the **Output Range** box. Click on **Randomized Block** in the **Experimental Design** frame. Be sure to click on the checkbox alongside **Tukey Test for Difference Between Means** and leave the alpha value set at 5%. You will see the ANOVA table in cells E30:K36 in Figure 11.3, except rows 32 and 33 will be reversed. To swap these two rows, refer to the discussion of Figure 11.11, which mentioned that Excel's ANOVA table contains the block effect values in the first row and the factor effect values in the second row. After swapping these two rows, type "Factor (Machines)" in cell E32 and "Blocks (Workers)" in cell E33.

To carry out a multiple comparisons procedure, refer to cell F41, where Tukey's D value is 240.6. Which pairs of sample means differ by more than 240.6? These would be machines A and B, since 6388.05 – 6010.05 = 378, and machines A and C, since 6270.35 – 6010.05 = 260.3. Consequently, you are able to demonstrate that machines B and C are superior to machine A but are unable to show that machine B is superior to machine C. This is illustrated at the bottom of Figure 11.13 by the overbar connecting the sample means for machines B and C (no significant difference between these two machines), but there is no bar connecting machines A and B and machines A and C.

Recommendation. When purchasing new machines, remove machine A from consideration. Machines B and C are both outperforming machine A, but neither is clearly superior; so either brand machine should be considered for new purchases.

FIGURE

11.13

Excel solution for Example 11.9 using **KPK Date Analysis ➤ ANOVA.**

File Edit View Insert Format Tools Data KPK Data Analysis Window Help

Worker	MachineA	MachineB	MachineC
1	5652	5520	6310
2	6519	6459	5911
3	5814	6450	6457
4	6895	6730	6899
5	5832	6931	6457
6	6077	6466	5905
7	6419	6896	6868
8	6262	6352	5389
9	6134	6548	6573
10	5725	6281	5815
11	5572	6735	6360
12	6110	6875	6626
13	6438	6549	6664
14	5184	5696	5232
15	6082	6129	6493
16	6291	5552	6532
17	5790	6920	6152
18	6197	5817	6300
19	5774	6027	6261
20	5426	5818	6203

Anova: Two-Factor Without Replication

SUMMARY	Count	Sum	Average	Variance
1	3	17482.0000	5827.3333	174081.3333
2	3	18889.0000	6296.3333	112261.3333
3	3	18721.0000	6240.3333	136332.3333
4	3	20524.0000	6841.3333	9300.3333
5	3	19220.0000	6406.6667	303850.3333
6	3	18448.0000	6149.3333	82604.3333
7	3	20183.0000	6727.6667	71652.3333
8	3	18003.0000	6001.0000	282933.0000
9	3	19255.0000	6418.3333	60790.3333
10	3	17821.0000	5940.3333	99065.3333
11	3	18667.0000	6222.3333	352356.3333
12	3	19611.0000	6537.0000	152247.0000
13	3	19651.0000	6550.3333	12770.3333
14	3	16112.0000	5370.6667	79957.3333
15	3	18704.0000	6234.6667	50604.3333
16	3	19375.0000	6458.3333	21100.3333
17	3	18880.0000	6293.3333	335337.3333
18	3	18314.0000	6104.6667	64716.3333
19	3	18062.0000	6020.6667	59322.3333
20	3	17447.0000	5815.6667	150936.3333
MachineA	20	120201.0000	6010.0500	168450.4711
MachineB	20	127761.0000	6388.0500	184630.5763
MachineC	20	125407.0000	6270.3500	193008.6605

ANOVA

Source of Variation	SS	df	MS	F	P-value	F crit
Factor (Machine)	1496622.5333	2	748311.2667	7.6485	0.0016	3.2448
Blocks (Workers)	6657888.9833	19	350415.2096	3.5816	0.0004	1.8673
Error	3717815.4667	38	97837.2491			
Total	11872326.9833	59				

TUKEY MULTIPLE COMPARISON TEST

Critical Q	Distance	Alpha
3.44	240.6000	0.05

Means joined by a double line are not significantly different.

MachineA	MachineC	MachineB
6010.0498	6270.3501	6388.0498

DATA11-9

X Exercises 11.23–11.37

Understanding the Mechanics

11.23 The following ANOVA table for a randomized block design is partially filled in.

Source	df	SS	MS	F
Factor		140	20	
Blocks		105.6		
Error	21			
Total	31	336.4		

a. Complete the ANOVA table.

b. Is there a significant difference in the levels of the factor? Use a 10% significance level.

11.24 The following data were collected on a factor with two levels using 5 blocks.

Block	1	2	3	4	5
Factor Level 1	13	9	2	13	9
Factor Level 2	15	8	4	19	10

a. Specify the null and alternative hypotheses for testing whether a difference in factor levels exists.

b. Specify the null and alternative hypotheses for testing whether there is a block effect.

c. Compute the ANOVA table for this randomized block design.

d. What conclusions do the data support at the 5% significance level?

e. Use a paired t test to test for a difference in factor levels at the 5% significance level.

f. What is the relationship between the t test in part e and the F test in part c for testing whether a difference exists in the two factor levels?

11.25 The following block and factor level totals were computed from a randomized block design.

Blocks: $S_1 = 18$, $S_2 = 57$, $S_3 = 14$, $S_4 = 45$
Factor Levels: $T_1 = 24$, $T_2 = 25$, $T_3 = 31$, $T_4 = 54$

a. Compute the ANOVA table and assume that the total sum of squares is 477.75.

b. Is there a difference in the factor levels at the 5% significance level?

c. Is there sufficient evidence to conclude that blocking was effective in reducing the experiment error? Use a 5% significance level.

d. Use a multiple comparisons procedure to determine which pairs of factor-level means differ. Use a 5% significance level.

Applying the New Concepts

11.26 A travel agency is interested in the response time for receiving information from the tourism bureaus within various states in the Southeastern United States.

According to Harper's Hideaway Report newsletter, Hawaii has the shortest response time, but several states can take as long as three months. To determine if there is a difference in the time that it takes South Carolina, Georgia, and Florida to respond to tourist requests, six letters requesting information on various local state activities were sent to each of the states. The response times (in days) are recorded below.

Letter	South Carolina	Georgia	Florida
1	10	18	8
2	16	12	11
3	25	20	18
4	13	27	17
5	11	14	19
6	21	19	10

a. Why is this design considered a randomized block design? Determine whether the mean response time for a request from a potential tourist differs across the three states. Use a .05 significance level.

b. Should a multiple comparisons procedure be used to determine which pairs of states differ in their mean response time? If so, determine which states differ and use a significance level of .05.

c. What requirements on the data are necessary for the validity of the statistical test in part a?

(Adapted from "How Efficient Is Your State's Tourism Bureau?" *The Wall Street Journal,* July 17, 1998, p. W6.)

11.27 The study in Exercise 11.5 was modified such that only six secretaries were used. Each secretary had a different typing speed. Each secretary tested all three word processing software packages. The same task could not be used for testing all three packages, since the "learning effect" would come into play, so each secretary performed three separate tasks. However, the tasks were of essentially the same length and difficulty level. Furthermore, which task was assigned to which word processor was randomly determined, and the order in which the three word processors were tested was also randomly decided. The secretaries relaxed between tasks to avoid "fatigue effects." Thus, a randomized block design was achieved, with secretaries constituting blocks and the three observations (levels of the factor) within each block being randomized. The following data were obtained (the secretary's typing speed in words per minute is given in parentheses for reference purposes, and the body of the table contains the time taken to complete the tasks):

Secretary	Group 1 (Menu-Driven)	Group 2 (Command-Driven)	Group 3 (Mixed)
1 (75 wpm)	9	10	7
2 (65 wpm)	12	11	9
3 (55 wpm)	12	14	11
4 (50 wpm)	13	13	11
5 (45 wpm)	16	15	13
6 (30 wpm)	18	16	15

a. Compute the ANOVA table for the preceding data.

b. Conduct a hypothesis test to address the question of whether there is a difference between the three word processors (as measured by the performance of the secretaries). Use $\alpha = .10$.

c. Determine the *p*-value. Does the conclusion change at $\alpha = .05$ and at $\alpha = .01$?

d. Is the block (secretary's) effect significant at $\alpha = .01$?

11.28 An analyst with a marketing firm wished to know if there was a difference in the number of responses from advertising a certain product at three different times on television. Ten days were randomly selected to run a commercial with a call-in phone number at each of the three times. The number of responses was recorded for 16 products:

Product	Noon	5:00 P.M.	10:30 P.M.
1	12	18	14
2	12	30	22
3	5	4	3
4	21	20	24
5	13	19	14
6	17	16	15
7	35	37	33
8	20	29	20
9	7	5	8
10	35	39	37
11	17	15	16
12	31	45	40
13	15	25	21
14	18	29	18
15	7	10	6
16	20	17	18

a. At the .05 significance level, is there sufficient evidence to conclude that the mean number of responses at noon, 5:00 P.M., and 10:30 P.M. are different?

b. Find a 90% confidence interval for the difference in the mean number of responses for noon and 5:00 P.M.

11.29 In Exercise 11.28, subtract 3.0 from each of the observations in the table. Perform the ANOVA procedure at the .05 significance level and test the hypothesis that the three different times of day have no effect. Is the sum of squares the same for the coded data as for the original data? If any set of data is coded by adding (or subtracting) the same number to (or from) the value of each observation, how will the sum of squares be affected?

11.30 A quality-control engineer wishes to investigate the spray pattern delivered by three different windshield washer spray nozzles. The engineer uses eight different windshield designs with the three different spray nozzles. A score is given to each spray pattern to indicate the effectiveness of the spray pattern in cleaning the windshield. The experimental data are given below. Do the data provide sufficient evidence to indicate that there is a difference in the effectiveness of the three different windshield washer spray nozzles at the .05 significance level? Is there a significant difference due to blocks?

Windshield	Spray Nozzles 1	2	3
1	67.2	75.3	70.1
2	63.5	72.1	68.7
3	50.8	65.1	62.5
4	71.3	78.8	71.8
5	78.1	79.9	79.0

Windshield	Spray Nozzles		
	1	**2**	**3**
6	69.5	74.8	64.3
7	74.6	79.6	70.8
8	70.1	76.8	69.8

11.31 In a randomized block design, if the df for the error sum of squares is given as 12 and the df for the factor sum of squares is 3, can you find the number of blocks used in the experiment? If yes, how many were used? If the total sum of squares is given as 520, the error sum of squares as 110, and the sum of squares due to blocks as 280, can you find the F test for this experiment? If yes, what is it?

11.32 The number of reported injuries by employers appears to be declining. Widespread employer underreporting of injuries is a myth and not a key driver behind the reduction in claims frequency, experts said during the Ninth Annual Business Insurance Workers Compensation and Disability Management Conference in Coronado, California. A study of data from insurance policies in 37 states found that, on average, the frequency of reported injuries fell by 18% in the past few years. Suppose that the National Council on Compensation Insurance conducted a study at three similar-sized manufacturing plants in which three safety programs were implemented: Safety Program A consisting of educating managers and employees on safety and health, Safety Program B consisting of educating managers and supervisors only on safety and health, and Safety Program C consisting of making safety and health information available to those who are interested. Information on the number of reported injuries each quarter are documented for six quarters.

	2002 Q1	2002 Q2	2002 Q3	2002 Q4	2003 Q1	2003 Q2
Safety Program A	3	2	1	6	5	2
Safety Program B	6	3	2	9	7	4
Safety Program C	5	2	3	7	6	3

a. At the 10% significance level, test the hypothesis that there is no difference in the mean number of reported injuries for the three safety programs.

b. Is the test for blocks significant at the 10% significance level?

c. Determine a 90% confidence interval for the difference in the mean number of reported injuries for Safety Program A and Safety Program B.

(Source: "Experts View Shift in Claims Frequency," *Business Insurance*, vol. 35, no. 45, November 5, 2001, p. 48.)

11.33 When the Dow Jones Industrial Average drops several hundred points in a single day, journalists can choose either of two ways to present the news: a misleading but scary story or a valid but boring news story. For example, the 618-point drop on April 14, 2000, was the largest point decline up to that time, but its percentage drop of 6.7% barely made the top-10 one-day percentage declines and did not come close to the 22.6% plummet on October 19, 1987. On August 4, 1998, the Dow fell 299 points. The percentage drop was 3.4%—substantial, but smaller than hundreds of other one-day declines. Suppose a journalist wished to review if there was a difference in the way *The Baltimore Sun, Los Angeles Times,* and *St. Louis Post-Dispatch* covered the August 4 decline. A random sample of 10 business executives was selected to rate the presentation of this story on a scale from 1 to 10, with 1 representing "strongly agree that the story is misleading" and 10 representing "strongly disagree that the story is misleading." The results follow.

Business Executive	Baltimore Sun	Los Angeles Times	St. Louis Post-Dispatch
1	3	4	5
2	4	4	8
3	2	5	3
4	7	8	6
5	1	4	2
6	4	3	7
7	2	8	8
8	4	4	3
9	2	5	7
10	3	3	5

a. What makes this design a randomized block design? What are the blocks?

b. Assume that the necessary assumptions required for the randomized block design to be valid are satisfied. Do the data provide sufficient evidence at the .10 level of significance to conclude that the mean ratings by the business executives differ across newspapers?

c. Use the Tukey multiple-comparisons procedure to determine which pairs of treatment means differ in part a. Use a .05 significance level.

(Adapted from "When the Market Falls, Media Stoke Investors' Fear," *USA Today,* August 12, 1998, p. 13A; and "Dow Jones Industrial Average Milestones," http://www.finfacts.ie/Private/currency/djones.htm.)

11.34 Linoleum Unlimited is experimenting with three types of adhesives for laying linoleum. Each glue is tested on five different surfaces. The adhesiveness of the glue is measured, and the coded results are as follows. Construct the ANOVA table and test the hypothesis that there is no difference in the three types of adhesives at the .10 level of significance.

Surface	Adhesive 1	Adhesive 2	Adhesive 3
1	1.5	2.1	2.4
2	1.6	1.8	1.9
3	2.4	2.5	2.4
4	3.1	3.4	3.1
5	4.5	4.2	4.0

11.35 The Environmental Protection Agency (EPA) proposed that a new law be imposed on chemical companies that requires them to electronically report environmental data in a more timely fashion in accordance with three acts: National Environmental Policy Act (NEPA), the Clean Water Act (CWA), and the Clean Air Act (CAA). Some chemical companies claim that this will increase their costs. The EPA is interested in determining the effect that compliance with these acts has on a company's operational cost. Suppose that an environmental analyst at the EPA randomly sampled eight companies to determine if the percent increase in compliance costs differed across these three acts. The following table presents the percent increases in a company's operating costs for compliance with each of these acts.

Company	Percent Increase in Cost—NEPA	Percent Increase in Cost—CWA	Percent Increase in Cost—CAA
1	1.8	1.7	1.6
2	3.0	3.0	3.2
3	7.9	12.0	14.0
4	3.7	4.0	3.8
5	3.1	3.7	6.0
6	.7	.8	1.1
7	7.3	7.0	7.1
8	.4	.4	.5

a. Is there sufficient evidence to indicate a difference in the mean cost increase associated with complying with each of these acts? Test at the 10% significance level.

b. Is the effect of the blocks significant at the 10% level?

c. Construct a 90% confidence interval for the difference in the mean cost increase associated with complying with NEPA and CAA. Interpret this interval.

(Source: "Industry Opposes EPA Record Keeping Proposal on Cost Basis," *Chemical Market Reporter,* vol. 260, no. 18, November 12, 2001, p. 9.)

Using the Computer

11.36 [DATA SET EX11-36] *Variable description:*

WaitRestauA: Wait time at restaurant A

WaitRestauB: Wait time at restaurant B

WaitRestauC: Wait time at restaurant C

The manager of three steak restaurants would like to know if there is a difference in the length of time that a customer has to wait on Saturday evening to be seated. Data are recorded over a 24-week period and the average wait time per customer on a Saturday evening is recorded. Times are recorded in minutes.

a. Determine if there is sufficient evidence to conclude that a difference in waiting time exists among the three restaurants using a significance level of 5%.

b. Determine if there is a difference based on week using a significance level of 5%.

c. Which pairs of restaurants have different waiting times at a 5% significance level?

d. Do a "what if" analysis by eliminating week 13. Do any of the conclusions change?

11.37 [DATA SET EX11-37] *Variable description:*

Morale97: Morale of employee in 1997

Morale98: Morale of employee in 1998

Morale99: Morale of employee in 1999

The manager of a large factory is interested in determining if there has been a change in the morale of employees over the past three years. Thirty employees are randomly selected to provide a score between 1 and 10 indicating the morale level for each of the employees for each of the years 1997, 1998, and 1999. A score of 10 indicates the highest possible level of morale.

a. Test the hypothesis that the mean morale score has not changed over the three years. Use a 5% significance level.

b. Is there an effect due to blocks? Use a 5% significance level.

c. Should a multiple comparisons procedure be performed to determine which years differ with respect to morale?

11.5   THE TWO-WAY FACTORIAL DESIGN

The two-way factorial design was introduced in Section 11.3. For this type of experiment, the researcher is considering two factors of interest, say, factor A and factor B. Of concern will be whether the individual factors have a significant effect on the observed variable (called the dependent variable) as well as the combined effect of the two factors.

Consider a simple example in which the dependent variable is the score on a test designed to measure assertiveness and managerial potential. The factors are gender and marital status (single or married). Each of these two factors consists of two levels. Suppose we observed a significant difference between the male and female scores. Thus we would conclude that factor A (gender) is significant. The analysis procedure to investigate this hypothesis is described in this section. If a significant difference between the scores of the single and married subjects is observed, then we would conclude that factor B (marital status) is also significant.

FIGURE

11.14

Scores on
assertiveness/
managerial
potential exam.

	Single	Married
Male	Low	High
Female	High	Low

FIGURE

11.15

Layout for two-
way factorial
design.

	Factor B			
	1	2	...	b
1	x	x		x
2	x	x		x
Factor A ...				
a	x	x		x

Suppose that a closer look at the scores revealed that the married males and single females scored high, but the single males and married females scored low on the test, as illustrated in Figure 11.14.

Consequently, the relationship between gender and the dependent variable (exam score) *depends on the marital status,* since this relationship is different for the single and married groups. Similarly, the relationship between marital status and the dependent variable depends upon the particular level of factor A (gender). This example illustrates interaction between factors A and B. A method of detecting interaction using a simple graph, along with a statistical test of hypothesis, will be explained in this section.

Degrees of Freedom

In a two-way factorial design, each level of factor A is combined with each level of factor B when obtaining the sample data. Suppose that factor A has a levels and factor B has b levels, as shown in Figure 11.15. Each x represents a test score.

If we record one observation for each factor A and factor B combination (referred to as a *treatment*), then we have $n = ab$ total observations. The df for each factor is one less than the number of levels and the df for the interaction term is the product of the factor A df and the factor B df. Consequently,

$$\text{df for factor } A = a - 1$$

$$\text{df for factor } B = b - 1$$

$$\text{df for interaction} = (a - 1)(b - 1)$$

$$\text{df for total} = n - 1 = ab - 1$$

We have a bit of a problem here. This design, like all experimental designs, must contain a source of variation due to error, that is, the unexplained variation. Suppose $a = 4$ and $b = 3$. Then the remaining df for error is (df for total) − (df for factor A) − (df for factor B) − (df for interaction), which in this case is $11 - 3 - 2 - 6 = 0$. It can be shown that the error df is zero *regardless* of the values of a and b. Since

FIGURE

11.16

Illustration of two replicates in a two-way factorial design ($r = 2$).

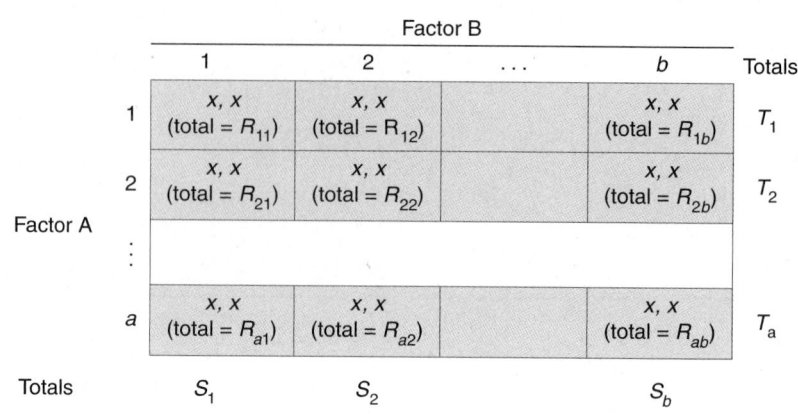

it will be necessary to measure this unexplained variation, this design requires that you obtain repeat observations (*replicates*) for each treatment. An illustration (using two replicates) including the various totals needed to carry out the analysis is shown in Figure 11.16. *In general, you will need two or more replicates at each treatment.* The number of replicates at each treatment need not be the same, but we consider here only the case where there are r replicates at each treatment.

In the replicated design, the degrees of freedom are

$$\text{df for factor A} = a - 1$$

$$\text{df for factor B} = b - 1$$

$$\text{df for interaction} = (a - 1)(b - 1)$$

$$\text{df for total} = \text{number of observations} - 1$$

$$= abr - 1$$

$$\text{df for error} = (abr - 1) - (a - 1) - (b - 1) - (a - 1)(b - 1)$$

$$= ab(r - 1)$$

Sum of Squares and Mean Squares

The necessary sums of squares can be computed in a manner similar to that used in the previous designs. Using Figure 11.16, the following expressions give the corresponding sums of squares.

$$\text{factor A:} \quad \text{SSA} = \frac{1}{br}[T_1^2 + T_2^2 + \cdots + T_a^2] - \frac{T^2}{abr} \qquad \text{11.29}$$

where T = total of all $n = abr$ observations (that is, $T = T_1 + T_2 + \cdots + T_a$).

$$\text{factor B:} \quad \text{SSB} = \frac{1}{ar}[S_1^2 + S_2^2 + \cdots + S_b^2] - \frac{T^2}{abr} \qquad \text{11.30}$$

$$\text{interaction:} \quad \text{SSAB} = \frac{1}{r}[\textstyle\sum R^2] - \text{SSA} - \text{SSB} - \frac{T^2}{abr} \qquad \text{11.31}$$

where the sum in the brackets is the sum of all the squares of the replicate totals, illustrated in Figure 11.16.

$$\text{total:} \quad \text{SS(total)} = \textstyle\sum x^2 - \frac{T^2}{abr} \qquad \text{11.32}$$

where $\sum x^2$ is the sum of the squares for each of the $n = abr$ observations. By subtraction,

$$SS(error) = SS(total) - SSA - SSB - SSAB \qquad 11.33$$

The corresponding mean squares can be obtained by dividing each sum of squares by the corresponding degrees of freedom. Thus we have

$$MSA = \frac{SSA}{a - 1} \qquad 11.34$$

$$MSB = \frac{SSB}{b - 1} \qquad 11.35$$

$$MSAB = \frac{SSAB}{(a - 1)(b - 1)} \qquad 11.36$$

$$MS(error) = \frac{SS(error)}{ab(r - 1)} \qquad 11.37$$

This analysis can be summarized in the following ANOVA table:

Source	df	SS	MS	F
Factor A	$a - 1$	SSA	$MSA = \dfrac{SSA}{a - 1}$	$F_1 = \dfrac{MSA}{MS(error)}$
Factor B	$b - 1$	SSB	$MSB = \dfrac{SSB}{b - 1}$	$F_2 = \dfrac{MSB}{MS(error)}$
Interaction	$(a - 1)(b - 1)$	SSAB	$MSAB = \dfrac{SSAB}{(a - 1)(b - 1)}$	$F_3 = \dfrac{MSAB}{MS(error)}$
Error	$ab(r - 1)$	SS(error)	$MS(error) = \dfrac{SS(error)}{ab(r - 1)}$	
Total	$abr - 1$	SS(total)		

The human resource director at Blackburn Industries is interested in examining the effect of gender and employee classification on the annual amount of dental claims for unmarried employees at Blackburn. Employee classifications range from category 1 (production-line workers) to category 4 (upper-level management). By utilizing a two-way factorial design, she can study the effect of gender (factor A) and employee classification (factor B), as well as the interaction effect between gender and employee classification, on the amount of the annual dental claims. These factors result in a 2×4 factorial design, since factor A consists of two levels and factor B has four levels. She decided to use three replicates for each of the eight treatment combinations, requiring annual claims from 24 different employees. The sample results are as follows, where the values in parentheses are the replicate totals for each of the treatments.

Gender (Factor A)		Category 1	Category 2	Category 3	Category 4	Total	Average
		Employee Classification (Factor B)					
Male		190, 225, 200 (615)	135, 180, 100 (415)	260, 330, 350 (940)	305, 275, 240 (820)	2,790	232.50
Female		235, 190, 270 (695)	275, 305, 285 (865)	160, 205, 140 (505)	155, 110, 75 (340)	2,405	200.42
Total		1,310	1,280	1,445	1,160	5,195	
Average		218.33	213.33	240.83	193.33		

Using the previous discussion, the necessary sums of squares can be derived.

$$SSA = \frac{1}{(4)(3)}(2790^2 + 2405^2) - \frac{5195^2}{24} = 6176.04$$

$$SSB = \frac{1}{(2)(3)}(1310^2 + 1280^2 + 1445^2 + 1160^2) - \frac{5195^2}{24} = 6853.12$$

$$SSAB = \frac{1}{3}(615^2 + 415^2 + 940^2 + 820^2 + 695^2 + 865^2 + 505^2 + 340^2)$$

$$-6176.04 - 6853.12 - \frac{5195^2}{24} = 98,578.13$$

$$S(\text{total}) = (190^2 + 225^2 + 200^2 + \cdots + 155^2 + 110^2 + 75^2) - \frac{5195^2}{24}$$

$$= 131,173.96$$

Consequently,

$$SS(\text{error}) = 131,173.96 - 6176.04 - 6853.12 - 98,578.13 = 19,566.67$$

The degrees of freedom here will be:

Gender factor: $a - 1 = 2 - 1 = 1$

Employee classification factor: $b - 1 = 4 - 1 = 3$

Interaction: $(a - 1)(b - 1) = (1)(3) = 3$

Error: $ab(r - 1) = (2)(4)(3 - 1) = 16$

Total: $abr - 1 = (2)(4)(3) - 1 = 24 - 1 = 23$

These calculations and the resulting mean squares can be summarized in the following ANOVA table.

Source	df	SS	MS	F
Gender	1	6,176.04	6,176.04	$F_1 = 6{,}176.04/1{,}222.92 = 5.05$
Employee classification	3	6,853.12	2,284.37	$F_2 = 2{,}284.37/1{,}222.92 = 1.87$
Interaction	3	98,578.13	32,859.38	$F_3 = 32{,}859.38/1{,}222.92 = 26.87$
Error	16	19,566.67	1,222.92	
Total	23	131,173.96		

Hypothesis Testing. When using a two-way factorial design, you can test for the significance of factor A, factor B, and the interaction of the two factors. For factor A, the null hypothesis is that the means are equal across the factor A levels. Written another way, we can define the following hypotheses:

$H_{0,A}$: factor A is not significant ($\mu_M = \mu_F$)

$H_{a,A}$: factor A is significant ($\mu_M \neq \mu_F$)

The corresponding test statistic is

$$F_1 = \frac{MSA}{MS(\text{error})}$$

11.38

and the testing procedure is to reject $H_{0,A}$ if

$$F_1 > F_{\alpha, v_1, v_2}$$

where F_{α, v_1, v_2} is from Table A.7, $v_1 =$ df for factor A $= a - 1$, and $v_2 =$ df for error $= ab(r - 1)$.

Similarly, to test for equal means of the factor B levels, we can define the hypotheses:

$H_{0,B}$: factor B is not significant ($\mu_1 = \mu_2 = \mu_3 = \mu_4$)

$H_{a,B}$: factor B is significant (not all μ_i's are equal)

The test statistic for determining the factor B effect is

$$F_2 = \frac{\text{MSB}}{\text{MS(error)}}$$

and factor B is significant ($H_{0,B}$ is rejected) if

$$F_2 > F_{\alpha,v_1,v_2}$$

where $v_1 =$ df for factor B $= b - 1$, and $v_2 =$ df for error $= ab(r - 1)$.

The final set of hypotheses is concerned with the interaction effect between the two factors. The hypotheses for this procedure can be stated

$H_{0,AB}$: there is no significant interaction between factor A and factor B

$H_{a,AB}$: there is significant interaction between factor A and factor B

The test statistic is the remaining F statistic in the ANOVA table, namely,

$$F_3 = \frac{\text{MSAB}}{\text{MS(error)}}$$

and the test procedure is to reject $H_{0,AB}$ if

$$F_3 > F_{\alpha,v_1,v_2}$$

where $v_1 =$ df for interaction $= (a - 1)(b - 1)$ and $v_2 =$ df for error $= ab(r - 1)$.

Multiple Comparisons Procedure: Two-Way Factorial Designs

The method of multiple comparisons discussed in section 11.2 for the one-factor ANOVA procedure (Tukey's method) can be used to examine pairwise differences between the various treatment means in two-way factorial designs. Since factor A has a levels and factor B has b levels, there are ab such means that can be compared, one pair at a time.

For the two-way factorial design, we use Table A.16 to find $Q_{\alpha,k,v}$, where α is the desired experimentwise significance level, $k = ab$ is the number of treatment means, and v is the degrees of freedom associated with MS(error). Any two (sample) treatment means differing by more than

$$D = Q_{\alpha,k,v} \cdot \sqrt{\frac{\text{MS(error)}}{r}}$$

will imply that the corresponding population means are unequal. This procedure is illustrated in the next example.

EXAMPLE 11.10

Using the previous ANOVA table constructed using the dental claims and the two factors, gender (factor A) and employee classification (factor B), determine whether (1) factor A is significant, (2) factor B is significant, (3) there is significant interaction between gender and employee classification, and (4) which pairs of the eight (population) treatment means are unequal. Use a significance level of .05.

Solution 1

The df for the F statistic are $v_1 = 1$ and $v_2 = 16$. Using Table A.7, $F_{.05,1,16} = 4.49$, and the test is to reject $H_{0,A}$ if $F_1 > 4.49$. Since $F_1 = 5.05 > 4.49$, we conclude that the gender factor *is* significant. Examining the raw data, we observe that the sample mean for the males is $2790/12 = 232.50$, and the female average is $2405/12 = 200.42$. Thus we conclude that the difference between these sample means *is* significant, with higher dental claims occurring in the male population.

Solution 2   For the employee classification factor, the df for the F statistic are $v_1 = 3$ and $v_2 = 16$, with a corresponding table value of $F_{.05,3,16} = 3.24$. Since $F_2 = 1.87 < 3.24$, the employee classification factor is *not* significant. Taking a closer look, we observe that the high (low) female values were balanced by the low (high) male values within each employee classification category. Consequently, there is insignificant variation in the means for the four employee classification groups, leading to the "fail to reject $H_{0,B}$" conclusion.

Solution 3   The discussion in the solution to part 2 indicates the presence of interaction between the two factors. The four male means are $615/3 = 205$ (category 1), $415/3 = 138.33$ (category 2), $940/3 = 313.33$ (category 3), and $820/3 = 273.33$ (category 4). The corresponding means for the female sample are 231.67, 288.33, 168.33, and 113.33. These means are shown in Figure 11.17(a), where interaction effect is very apparent, since the male and female lines are *not parallel.* When no interaction exists between the two factors, such a graph should contain lines that are *nearly parallel,* as illustrated in Figure 11.17(b).

The statistical test here supports this conclusion, since there is significant interaction provided F_3 is larger than $F_{.05,3,16} = 3.24$. Here, $F_3 = 26.87$, and so we once again conclude that there is significant interaction between gender and employee classification for this population.

Since the two lines in Figure 11.17(a) are not parallel, the relationship between employee classification and the amount of dental claims is not the same for males and females. In particular, the amount of dental claims is low for category 4 females and high for category 4 males. Also, the amount is high for category 2 females and low for category 2 males. *This type of discussion should always be included in the analysis whenever the interaction effect is significant.*

FIGURE

11.17

Illustration of interaction effect. (a) Interaction effect in Example 11.10. (b) Hypothetical situation containing no significant interaction between gender and employees classification.

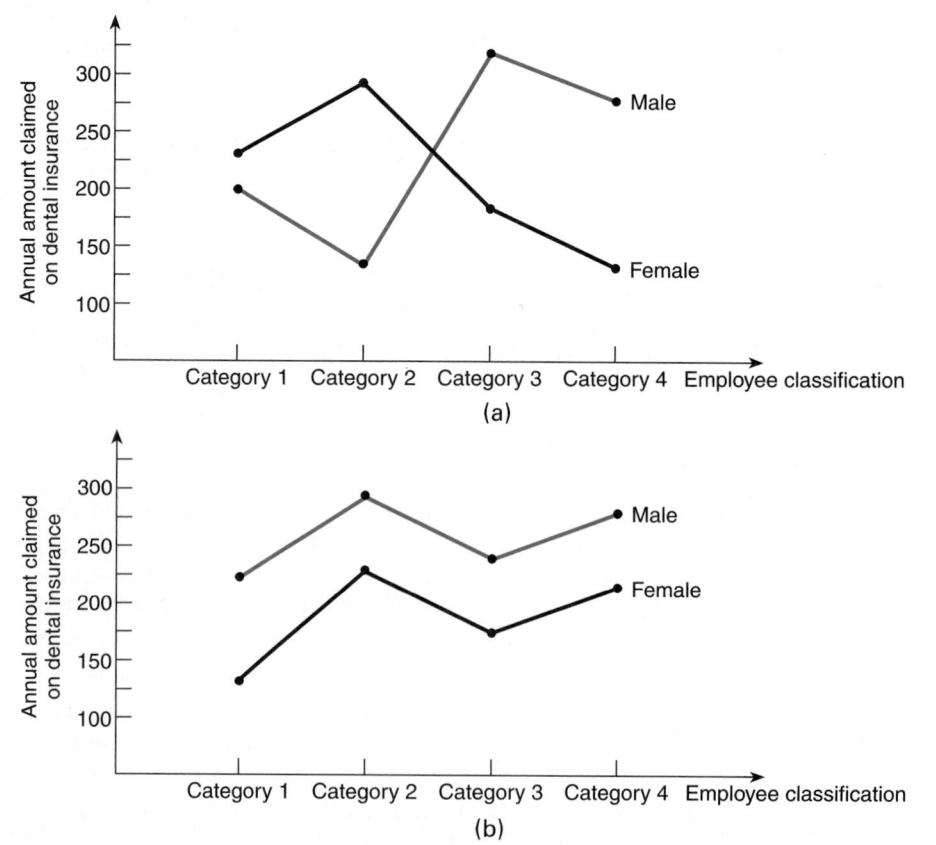

Solution 4

A multiple comparisons analysis will determine whether the average annual amount for category 1 males is the same as for category 4 males, the average for category 2 males is the same for category 3 females, and so forth. There are $2 \cdot 4 = 8$ means here, providing ${}_8C_2 = 28$ possible pairwise comparisons. In general, for a two-way factorial design there are ${}_{ab}C_2$ possible pairs of means that can be compared using the multiple comparisons procedure.

The critical value corresponding to $\alpha = .05$, $k = 8$, and $v = 16$ (the df associated with the error sum of squares) from Table A.16 is $Q_{.05,8,16} = 4.90$. Since MS(error) = 1,222.92 and there are $r = 3$ replicates at each treatment level, we next determine

$$D = Q_{\alpha,k,v} \cdot \sqrt{\frac{\text{MS(error)}}{r}}$$

$$= 4.90\sqrt{\frac{1222.92}{3}} = 98.93$$

Consequently, any pair of sample treatment means differing by more than 98.93 will imply that the corresponding population means are unequal.

The eight sample means are obtained by dividing the corresponding replicate totals (R) by $r = 3$. Placing them in order, we obtain

113.33	138.33	168.33	205.00	231.67	273.33	288.33	313.33
(F, 4)	(M, 2)	(F, 3)	(M, 1)	(F, 1)	(M, 4)	(F, 2)	(M, 3)

Here, M and F represent the gender (factor A) and 1, 2, 3, and 4 represent the employee classification (factor B).

Since $205.00 - 138.33 = 66.67 < 98.93$, we *cannot* conclude that $\mu_{M,1} \neq \mu_{M,2}$. This is represented by the overbar connecting these two sample means. Consider category 4 males and category 4 females. Here $273.33 - 113.33 = 160 > 98.93$, and so we conclude that there *is* a difference in the average amounts for these two groups; that is, $\mu_{M,4} \neq \mu_{F,4}$. This can be observed in the preceding sample means, since there is no overbar connecting these two means. Continuing this procedure, we arrive at the following summary for the multiple comparisons analysis:

males only: $\mu_{M,2} \neq \mu_{M,4}$, $\mu_{M,2} \neq \mu_{M,3}$, $\mu_{M,1} \neq \mu_{M,3}$

females only: $\mu_{F,4} \neq \mu_{F,1}$, $\mu_{F,4} \neq \mu_{F,2}$, $\mu_{F,3} \neq \mu_{F,2}$

males and females: $\mu_{F,4} \neq \mu_{M,4}$ $\mu_{F,4} \neq \mu_{M,3}$ $\mu_{F,2} \neq \mu_{M,2}$, $\mu_{F,3} \neq \mu_{M,4}$, $\mu_{F,3} \neq \mu_{M,3}$

Consequently, we observe three significant differences in each of the male and female populations and five significant differences in the amount of annual dental claims when comparing employee classifications across both genders.

The Excel solution for this example is shown in Figures 11.18 and 11.19. The data should be entered in cells A1:E7 using the format in Figure 11.18, with the

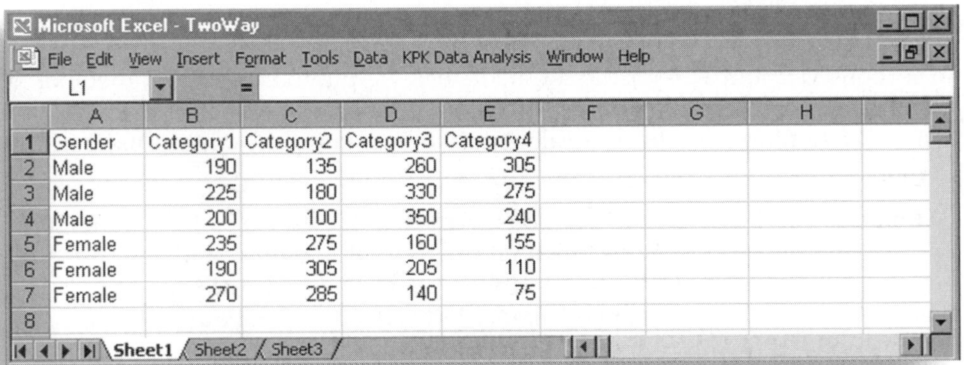

	A	B	C	D	E
1	Gender	Category1	Category2	Category3	Category4
2	Male	190	135	260	305
3	Male	225	180	330	275
4	Male	200	100	350	240
5	Female	235	275	160	155
6	Female	190	305	205	110
7	Female	270	285	140	75

FIGURE 11.18

Excel spreadsheet solution for Example 11.10 using **KPK Data Analysis ➤ ANOVA.**

FIGURE 11.19

Remainder of Excel solution to Example 11.10.

File Edit View Insert Format Tools Data KPK Data Analysis Window Help

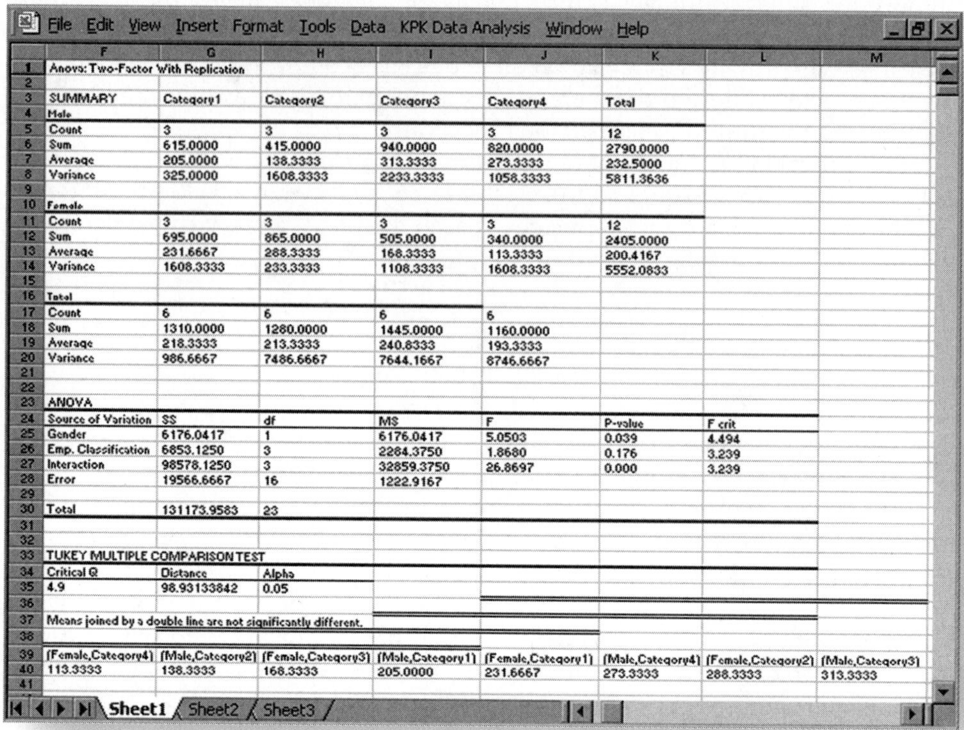

	F	G	H	I	J	K	L	M
1	Anova: Two-Factor With Replication							
2								
3	SUMMARY	Category1	Category2	Category3	Category4	Total		
4	Male							
5	Count	3	3	3	3	12		
6	Sum	615.0000	415.0000	940.0000	820.0000	2790.0000		
7	Average	205.0000	138.3333	313.3333	273.3333	232.5000		
8	Variance	325.0000	1608.3333	2233.3333	1058.3333	5811.3636		
9								
10	Female							
11	Count	3	3	3	3	12		
12	Sum	695.0000	865.0000	505.0000	340.0000	2405.0000		
13	Average	231.6667	288.3333	168.3333	113.3333	200.4167		
14	Variance	1608.3333	233.3333	1108.3333	1608.3333	5552.0833		
15								
16	Total							
17	Count	6	6	6	6			
18	Sum	1310.0000	1280.0000	1445.0000	1160.0000			
19	Average	218.3333	213.3333	240.8333	193.3333			
20	Variance	986.6667	7486.6667	7644.1667	8746.6667			
21								
22								
23	ANOVA							
24	Source of Variation	SS	df	MS	F	P-value	F crit	
25	Gender	6176.0417	1	6176.0417	5.0503	0.039	4.494	
26	Emp. Classification	6853.1250	3	2284.3750	1.8680	0.176	3.239	
27	Interaction	98578.1250	3	32859.3750	26.8697	0.000	3.239	
28	Error	19566.6667	16	1222.9167				
29								
30	Total	131173.9583	23					
31								
32								
33	TUKEY MULTIPLE COMPARISON TEST							
34	Critical Q	Distance	Alpha					
35	4.9	98.93133842	0.05					
36								
37	Means joined by a double line are not significantly different.							
38								
39	(Female,Category4)	(Male,Category2)	(Female,Category3)	(Male,Category1)	(Female,Category1)	(Male,Category4)	(Female,Category2)	(Male,Category3)
40	113.3333	138.3333	168.3333	205.0000	231.6667	273.3333	288.3333	313.3333
41								

Sheet1 / Sheet2 / Sheet3 /

factor A labels in column A and the factor B labels in the first row. The procedure to follow here is to click on **KPK Data Analysis ➤ ANOVA.** In the resulting input screen, click on "Two-Way Factorial" and "Tukey Test for Difference Between Means." Next, enter (1) "A1:E7" in the **Input Range** box, (2) "3" in the **Number of Replications** box, and (3) "F1" in the **Output Range** box. The resulting output in Figure 11.19 contains summary information and the ANOVA table in rows 23 through 30. In the ANOVA table, the word *Sample* was changed to *Gender,* *Columns* was changed to *Emp. Classification,* and *Within* was changed to *Error.*

The *p*-value for gender (factor A) is .039 and supports the earlier conclusion that the gender factor is significant, since .039 < .05. The employee classification factor (factor B) is not significant, as in the earlier solution, since its *p*-value (.176) exceeds .05. The Excel solution supports the finding that the interaction between these two factors is significant, since the *p*-value for the interaction effect is nearly zero. Also, Figure 11.19 contains the critical *F* values at the .05 significance level (in cells L25:L27), used in the earlier solution to Example 11.10.

Using a Calculator

In sections 11.2 and 11.4 (Using a Calculator), we provided shortcut methods of calculating the necessary sums of squares. For the two-way factorial design, you can use a similar procedure to calculate the four sums of squares used in this design.

SS(total)
1. Key in all *n* (= *abr*) observations (190, 225, 200, . . . , 155, 110, 75 in the previous illustration) as though you were determining the standard deviation of these *n* (= 24, here) values.
2. Press the sample standard deviation key on your calculator.

3. Square this value (press the x^2 key) to get the variance of these n observations.
4. Multiply by $n - 1$ (23, here). This is SS(total).

SSA
1. Key in the totals for factor A (2790 and 2405 for this illustration) as though you were finding the standard deviation of these values.
2. Press the sample standard deviation key on your calculator.
3. Square this value by pressing the x^2 key.
4. Multiply by $a - 1$ (1, here).
5. Divide this result by br ($= 4 \cdot 3 = 12$, here). This is SSA.

SSB
1. Key in the totals for factor B (1,310, 1,280, 1,445, 1,160 for this illustration) as though you were finding the standard deviation of these values.
2. Press the sample standard deviation key on your calculator.
3. Square this value by pressing the x^2 key.
4. Multiply by $b - 1$ (3, here).
5. Divide this result by ar ($= 2 \cdot 3 = 6$, here). This is SSB.

SSAB
1. Key in the ab replicate totals (615, 415, . . . , 505, 340 for this illustration) as though you were finding the standard deviation of these ab ($= 8$, here) values.
2. Press the sample standard deviation key on your calculator.
3. Square this value by pressing the x^2 key.
4. Multiply by $ab - 1$ (7, here).
5. Divide this result by r ($= 3$, here).
6. Subtract SSA and subtract SSB. This is SSAB.

SS(error) By subtraction, SS(error) = SS(total) − SSA − SSB − SSAB.

X Exercises 11.38–11.43

Understanding the Mechanics

11.38 The data for a 2×3 factorial experiment are presented here. For each factor-level combination there are two replicates.

		Level of Factor A		
		1	**2**	**3**
Level of	1	20.6, 22.6	21.3, 23.1	21.1, 20.1
Factor B	2	22.6, 23.4	24.3, 22.9	22.2, 23.4

a. Calculate the treatment means. Plot the treatment means using the y-axis for the value of the mean and the x-axis for the levels of factor A. Plot two curves, one for each level of factor B. Do you think the factors interact?

b. Construct an ANOVA table for the factorial experiment.

c. Is there sufficient evidence to conclude that there is interaction between the factors using a .05 significance level? Do the results of this test support what you observed visually in part a?

d. Is there sufficient evidence to conclude that the levels of factor A differ? Use a .05 significance level.

e. Is there sufficient evidence to conclude that the levels of factor B differ? Use a .05 significance level.

f. If appropriate, determine which treatment means differ by using a multiple comparisons procedure at the .05 significance level.

Applying the New Concepts

11.39 The comparative study of word processing software in Exercise 11.27 was modified to take into account different types of keyboards: enhanced keyboard, modified keyboard, and standard keyboard. Keyboard layout and type of software could not be assumed to be independent, because it was possible that a certain type of software might actually be enhanced by a certain type of keyboard (e.g., one with special function keys). In other words, interaction between factors was possible. Therefore, a 3×3 factorial design was implemented. The following table gives the completion time in minutes, with three replicates for each treatment "cell."

	Software Type		
Keyboard Type	**Group 1 (Menu-Driven)**	**Group 2 (Command-Driven)**	**Group 3 (Mixed)**
Enhanced	9, 8, 10	8, 7, 7	8, 10, 10
Modified	14, 14, 13	10, 14, 12	12, 10, 14
Standard	15, 18, 17	18, 16, 15	15, 15, 14

a. Calculate the ANOVA table for the preceding experiment.

b. Assume that the assumptions of an ANOVA have been satisfied. Is there a difference in the three word processors, as measured by the productivity of the secretaries? Use $\alpha = .05$.

c. Do the different keyboards seem to affect productivity, as measured by completion times? Use $\alpha = .05$.

d. Is there a significant interaction between software type and keyboard type, at $\alpha = .05$?

e. For parts b, c, and d, find the corresponding p-value for each test.

11.40 A manufacturer is interested in the number of defective components produced by its employees. A consultant recommends that each employee follow one of three proposed systematic procedures. To determine whether there was a difference in the three procedures, an experiment was conducted with one factor having three levels: less than a year of experience, 1 to 4 years' experience, and over 4 years' experience. The second factor was the systematic procedure, one level for each of the three proposed procedures. Data from the experiment, with three replicates per treatment, are as follows and show the average number of nondefective components produced per day over a one-week period for each employee:

Experience	Procedure		
	1	2	3
Less than a year	12.6, 15.7, 10.5	8.6, 9.9, 11.2	13.6, 12.8, 10.2
Between 1 and 4 years	13.7, 14.2, 15.8	9.2, 12.6, 13.1	12.1, 11.8, 14.1
Over 4 years	17.5, 19.8, 20.4	16.4, 17.1, 14.2	16.5, 18.7, 17.0

At the 10% significance level, is there a difference in the results of the three systematic procedures?

11.41 To investigate the effects of changes in inventory control policies for serial production systems, Dr. Henry Person collected data with the observed response being the number of units of system output in a 2×2 experiment. The factor CV (coefficient of variation of processing times at each work station) had two levels: CV = 5% and CV = 50%. The factor DT (down time rate at each work station) also had two levels: DT = 10% and DT = 30%. One hundred observations were collected in each combination of factor levels. The sum of squares for CV, DT, CV × DT, and Error were 11,718.06, 19,010.02, 632.52, and 671,215.97 respectively. Construct an ANOVA table and explain what conclusions can be drawn using a 5% significance level.

(Source: *Decision Sciences Institute 1998 Proceedings*, "Impacts of Inventory Controls on Just-In-Time and Push Systems," pp. 1181–83.)

11.42 A real estate broker wished to determine whether the Southern states and Midwestern states differ with respect to the median price of a new home for large and small metropolitan areas. Use the following data to test the location factor (Southern and Midwestern) and the city size factor (large and small metropolitan area) as well as the interaction of these two factors. Use a multiple comparisons test to examine pairwise differences. Use a significance level of 5%.

Midwestern and Small Metropolitan Area	Median Home Price
Cedar Rapids, Iowa	$106,700
Champaign-Urbana, Illinois	90,800
South Bend, Indiana	86,100
Peoria, Illinois	86,000
Moline, Illinois	81,900
Topeka, Kansas	80,800

Midwestern and Large Metropolitan Area	Median Home Price
Chicago, Illinois	$170,200
Columbus, Ohio	126,000
Cincinnati, Ohio	120,800
Des Moines, Iowa	109,700
St. Louis, Missouri	105,300
Lincoln, Nebraska	101,900

Southern and Small Metropolitan Area	Median Home Price
Baton Rouge, Louisiana	$104,900
Chattanooga, Tennessee	99,600
Little Rock, Arkansas	93,000
Corpus Christi, Texas	86,500
Amarillo, Texas	82,100
Ocala, Florida	72,000

Southern and Large Metropolitan Area	Median Home Price
Birmingham, Alabama	$128,800
Atlanta, Georgia	126,800
Dallas, Texas	126,000
New Orleans, Louisiana	108,600
Houston, Texas	108,500
Oklahoma City, Oklahoma	84,600

(Source: http://cgi.money.cnn.com/tools/citysearch/citysearch_bplive. html, accessed February 4, 2002)

Using the Computer

11.43 **[DATA SET EX11-43]** *Variable description:*

ExpLevel: Low (1) or High (2) experience level of operator

SpeedA: Number of nonconforming items for speed level A

SpeedB: Number of nonconforming items for speed level B

SpeedC: Number of nonconforming items for speed level C

SpeedD: Number of nonconforming items for speed level D

A quality engineer believes that there are two factors affecting the number of nonconforming items produced by a machine. The first factor is the experience level of the operator denoted by 1 and 2 for low and high experience, respectively. The variables SpeedA, SpeedB, SpeedC, and SpeedD are used to record the number of nonconforming items for four different machine speed levels. There are eight replicates for each of the factor level combinations.

a. Interpret the results of the two-way factorial experiment using a 5% significance level. How do you interpret the interaction term?

b. Which pairs of treatment means are significantly different? Use a significance level of 5%.

c. Do a "what if" analysis by deleting the last two replicates in each cell and performing the steps in parts a and b.

✓ Summary

The **one-factor analysis of variance (ANOVA)** procedure is a method of detecting differences between the means of two or more normal populations. The various populations represent the *levels* of a *factor* under observation. The factor might consist of, for example, different locations (does the crime rate differ among five cities?), brand (does one brand outsell the others?), or time periods (is average attendance the same each day of the week?).

Samples for this analysis must be obtained independently of each other. The ANOVA technique measures sources of variation among the sample data by computing various **sums of squares.** The variation from one level (population) to the next is measured by the factor sum of squares (SS(factor)), which is large when there is great variation among the sample means. The variation *within* the samples is measured by the error sum of squares (SS(error)). Each of these SS has a corresponding df, which is divided into the SS to produce a **mean square, MS.**

The ratio of MS(factor) to MS(error) produces an *F* statistic that is used to test for equal means within the various populations. If the *F* value is large (significant), we conclude that the means are not all the same, which implies that the factor of interest *does* have a significant effect on the variable under observation, called the **dependent** variable.

When we analyze the effect of a single factor, we perform a one-factor ANOVA and use a **completely randomized design.** The results of this analysis, including the various sums of squares, mean squares, and df, are summarized in an **ANOVA table.** If the ANOVA procedure concludes that the population means are not the same, a follow-up analysis can be conducted to determine which of the population means are unequal. This analysis is a **multiple comparisons procedure** and should be performed only in the event that the ANOVA null hypothesis of equal means is rejected. The multiple comparisons procedure discussed in this chapter is the **Tukey** test for multiple comparisons.

When samples are not obtained in an independent manner, a **randomized block design** often can be used to test for differences in the population means. Again, there is a single factor of interest, but to determine the effect of this factor, the sample data are organized into **blocks.** For this situation, the samples are not independently obtained, but data within the same block may be gathered from the same city or person or at the same point in time. By including a block effect in the ANOVA procedure, we can analyze the factor of interest (the population means) using an *F* test. In addition, another *F* statistic can be used for determining whether there is a significant block effect within the sample data. If the null hypothesis of equal factor-level means is rejected, a multiple comparisons procedure for the randomized block design should be carried out to determine which pairs of factor-level means are unequal.

The other experimental design that was discussed was the **two-way factorial design,** where the effect of two factors can be investigated. Observations are obtained for each combination of factor levels, called **treatments.** For such a design, it is necessary to obtain two or more independent **replicates** for each treatment. The two-way factorial design allows the researcher to investigate the effect of each factor individually, as well as the combined effect of the two factors, which is referred to as the **interaction effect.** A multiple comparisons analysis for the two-way factorial design will determine which pairs of treatment means are unequal.

Summary of Formulas

Completely Randomized Design (One-Factor ANOVA)

$$SS(factor) = \left[\frac{T_1^2}{n_1} + \frac{T_2^2}{n_2} + \cdots + \frac{T_k^2}{n_k} \right] - \frac{T^2}{n}$$

$$SS(total) = \sum x^2 - \frac{T^2}{n}$$

$$SS(error) = SS(total) - SS(factor)$$

$$MS(factor) = \frac{SS(factor)}{k-1}$$

$$MS(error) = \frac{SS(error)}{n-k} = s_p^2$$

where

    n = total number of observations

    k = number of groups (populations) to be compared

    T_i = total of sample values for the ith group

    T = grand total = $T_1 + T_2 + \cdots + T_k$

1. Test statistic:

$$F = \frac{MS(factor)}{MS(error)}$$

2. Confidence interval for μ_i:

$$\overline{X}_i \pm t_{\alpha/2, n-k} s_p \sqrt{\frac{1}{n_i}}$$

3. Confidence interval for $\mu_i - \mu_j$:

$$(\overline{X}_i - \overline{X}_j) \pm t_{\alpha/2, n-k} s_p \sqrt{\frac{1}{n_i} + \frac{1}{n_j}}$$

4. Multiple comparisons:

$$\mu_i \neq \mu_j \quad \text{provided } |\overline{X}_i - \overline{X}_j| > D$$

where

$$D = Q_{\alpha, k, v} \sqrt{\frac{MS(error)}{n_r}}$$

    v = df for error

    n_r = number of replicates in each sample.

Randomized Block Design

$$SS(factor) = \frac{1}{b} [T_1^2 + T_2^2 + \cdots + T_k^2] - \frac{T^2}{bk}$$

$$SS(blocks) = \frac{1}{k} [S_1^2 + S_2^2 + \cdots + S_b^2] - \frac{T^2}{bk}$$

$$SS(total) = \sum x^2 - \frac{T^2}{bk}$$

$$SS(error) = SS(total) - SS(factor) - SS(blocks)$$

$$MS(factor) = \frac{SS(factor)}{k-1}$$

$$MS(blocks) = \frac{SS(blocks)}{b-1}$$

$$MS(error) = \frac{SS(error)}{(k-1)(b-1)}$$

where

    b = number of blocks

    k = number of factor levels

    T = total of all bk observations

1. Test statistic for factor effect:

$$F_1 = \frac{MS(factor)}{MS(error)}$$

2. Test statistic for block effect:

$$F_2 = \frac{MS(blocks)}{MS(error)}$$

3. Confidence interval for $\mu_i - \mu_j$:

$$(\overline{X}_i - \overline{X}_j) \pm t_{\alpha/2, df} \cdot s \cdot \sqrt{\frac{1}{b} + \frac{1}{b}}$$

where

$$df = (k-1)(b-1)$$

$$s = \sqrt{MS(error)}$$

4. Multiple comparisons:

$$D = Q_{\alpha, k, (k-1)(b-1)} \sqrt{\frac{MS(error)}{b}}$$

Two-Way Factorial Design

$$SSA = \frac{1}{br} [T_1^2 + T_2^2 + \cdots + T_a^2] - \frac{T^2}{abr}$$

$$SSB = \frac{1}{ar} [S_1^2 + S_2^2 + \cdots + S_b^2] - \frac{T^2}{abr}$$

$$SSAB = \frac{1}{r} [\sum R^2] - SSA - SSB - \frac{T^2}{abr}$$

$$SS(total) = \sum x^2 - \frac{T^2}{abr}$$

$$SS(error) = SS(total) - SSA - SSB - SSAB$$

$$MSA = \frac{SSA}{a-1}$$

$$MSB = \frac{SSB}{b-1}$$

$$MSAB = \frac{SSAB}{(a-1)(b-1)}$$

$$MS(error) = \frac{SS(error)}{ab(r-1)}$$

where

a = number of levels for factor A

b = number of levels for factor B

r = number of replicates for each factor A, factor B combination (treatment)

R = sum of replicates for each treatment

T = grand total of all observations

1. Test statistic for factor A effect:

$$F_1 = \frac{MSA}{MS(error)}$$

2. Test statistic for factor B effect:

$$F_2 = \frac{MSB}{MS(error)}$$

3. Test statistic for interaction effect:

$$F_3 = \frac{MSAB}{MS(error)}$$

4. Multiple comparisons:

$$D = Q_{\alpha, ab, ab(r-1)} \sqrt{\frac{MS(error)}{r}}$$

X Review Exercises 11.44–11.65

11.44 A researcher wished to determine if there was a difference in the time required to complete three types of tasks. The data for the experiment are as follows. The time is given in units of minutes.

Task 1	Task 2	Task 3
66	80	49
90	58	60
75	79	56
63	61	68
71	68	53
72	73	58
80	77	59
55	82	70

a. How many factors are there in this experiment? How many factor levels are there? How many replicates for each level are there?

b. What is the name of this experimental design? Are the samples and observations within each factor level required to be independent for this design?

c. Construct the ANOVA table. What conclusion is supported by the data at the .05 significance level?

d. Compare all pairs of means by using a multiple comparisons procedure at the .05 significance level.

11.45 In 1998, political parties in Germany were interested in the projected economic expansion of that country because of the fall elections. German unemployment in April 1998 exceeded 12%, and this was the highest unemployment for that month since the 1930s. Assume that a political analyst working for the German government randomly sampled economists from each of the six economic institutes in Germany and asked for their estimate of the country's economic growth (in percentage) for 1999. A summary of the survey results are presented below.

Summary Group	Count	Sum	Average	Variance
Institute 1	4	9	2.25	0.07
Institute 2	4	10	2.5	0.026667
Institute 3	4	8	2	0.086667

Summary Group	Count	Sum	Average	Variance
Institute 4	4	9.6	2.4	0.053333
Institute 5	4	8.4	2.1	0.06
Institute 6	4	8.8	2.2	0.06

a. Assume that the SS(total) is equal to 1.758333. What conclusion can the political analyst draw from the data? Use a significance level of .05.

b. Test for the equality of group variances. Use a .05 significance level. What assumption concerning the population variances is required for an ANOVA procedure to be valid?

(Adapted from "German Growth Seen Accelerating in 1999," *The Wall Street Journal*, May 13, 1998, p. A15.)

11.46 A manager of an amusement park would like to know if there is a difference in the amount of time that park visitors spend waiting for four rides. A survey of six visitors from each ride revealed that the average waiting time for the four rides was 16, 14, 17, and 23 minutes, respectively, for rides 1, 2, 3, and 4. The MSE, using a completely randomized design, is 26.3. Perform a multiple comparisons procedure at the 5% significance level.

11.47 The following table gives scores on an index that measures leadership ability for respondents at three levels of management. It is assumed that the populations are normal and independent and the observations are randomly obtained. High scores represent greater leadership ability.

Supervisor	Middle-Level Manager	Upper-Level Manager
18	36	55
21	60	42
16	21	68
45	31	33
20	40	48

a. Compute the ANOVA table.

b. Is there a difference, on average, between the leadership scores of the three groups? Use $\alpha = .05$. Find the *p*-value.

c. What is the 95% confidence interval for the mean leadership score of middle-level managers?

d. What is the 99% confidence interval for the difference between mean scores for the upper-level managers and the middle-level managers?

e. Using a significance level of .05, perform a multiple comparisons procedure, if appropriate.

11.48 The study in Exercise 11.47 has been modified to cover the leadership scores of individual managers who advanced from the post of supervisor to upper-level manager. Fifteen persons were initially studied, but only 10 actually went all the way to upper-level managerial positions. Since the same managers were used, a randomized block design was obtained, with three scores for each manager. Assume that the populations are normally distributed. The following table lists the leadership scores for the 10 managers who completed the study.

Respondent	Supervisor	Middle-Level Manager	Upper-Level Manager
1	25	30	30
2	16	35	48
3	17	18	20
4	30	25	20
5	35	30	32
6	28	29	28
7	29	30	35
8	30	40	48
9	27	29	35
10	40	30	32

a. Compute the ANOVA table.

b. Test the hypothesis that the means for the three classes are equal, at $\alpha = .05$. Can you conclude that, on the average, leadership scores remain stable, or do they tend to change as the persons move up the managerial scale?

c. Is there a significant difference among the managers' mean leadership scores? Use $\alpha = .05$.

11.49 Exercise 11.47 was further modified to take into account the influence of gender. Thus, a 3×2 two-way factorial design was implemented. It was decided to have three replicates for each cell. The leadership ability scores are given in the following table.

Gender	Supervisor	Middle-Level Manager	Upper-Level Manager
Male	16, 17, 25	18, 25, 30	20, 30, 42
Female	18, 20, 28	20, 28, 30	30, 41, 55

a. Compute the ANOVA table.

b. At $\alpha = .10$, test for a significant difference in leadership scores among the three groups of managers.

c. At $\alpha = .10$, is there a difference between the leadership scores of males and females?

d. Test for interaction between managerial level and gender at $\alpha = .10$.

e. Find the p-value for the three preceding hypothesis tests. Do the conclusions change at $\alpha = .05$ or $\alpha = .01$?

11.50 A court decision in Chicago supported university students who did not want their mandatory fees to finance liberal campus groups. This decision currently affects Wisconsin, Illinois, and Indiana. But this action could eventually spark challenges from students in other universities across the nation. Suppose that two universities in Ohio—Ohio University and Ohio State University—were used to conduct an experiment to determine if senior students feel differently about this issue than freshmen students. Students were asked to respond on a scale from 1 to 7, with 1 representing "strongly opposed to any fees going to finance campus groups" and 7 representing "strongly support fees going to finance campus groups." The following table displays the results of the survey.

University	Seniors	Freshmen
Ohio University	3,3,1,3,2,3,3,4,1,2,3,5	4,3,6,4,7,2,5,3,6,6,4,7
Ohio State University	4,1,2,5,2,3,2,3,1,2,5,4	4,7,2,3,5,2,3,6,7,5,4,6

a. Construct the ANOVA table for this experiment.

b. Is there an interaction effect between universities and the classification of a student (senior versus freshman)? Use a significance level of .05.

c. Assume that the ANOVA assumptions are satisfied. Is there a difference between the students at the Ohio University and Ohio State University using a significance level of .05?

d. Is there an effect based on classification of student at the .05 significance level?

e. Graphically display the relationship between seniors' and freshmen's responses and the university they are attending.

(Source: "Court Rules Students Can Limit Who Gets Campus Funding," *USA Today*, August 12, 1998, p. 1A.)

11.51 A survey of four motels by 10 customers at each hotel yields 40 ratings, which resulted in the following partially complete ANOVA table. Test the null hypothesis that there is no difference in the average ratings of the four hotels. Use a 1% significance level.

Source	df	SS	MS	F
Factor				
Error			1.789	
Total		161.5		

11.52 An engineer wishes to design the flashlight batteries that provide the brightest light but do not burn out the light bulb prematurely. An experiment is conducted to determine the life of flashlight light bulbs at voltage levels of 3.5, 4.0, and 4.5. Ten light bulbs were used at each of these levels, and the data collected on the life of the light bulbs are as follows, in coded form.

Voltage Level 3.5	Voltage Level 4.0	Voltage Level 4.5
19	12	15
15	25	17
29	18	13
21	13	28
18	21	10
36	19	16
14	26	19
31	15	13
23	20	10
19	17	9

a. Compute the ANOVA table.

b. Is there a difference among the lifetimes of the light bulbs for the three groups? Use a .05 significance level.

c. What is a 95% confidence interval for the mean lifetime of the light bulbs in the group with the voltage level of 3.5?

d. What is the 99% confidence interval for the difference in mean lifetimes between the group with a voltage level of 3.5 and the group with a voltage level of 4.0?

e. Using a significance level of .05, perform a multiple comparisons procedure, if appropriate.

11.53 Travelers are single-minded when booking airline reservations: They want the best prices and they hop around to find them. Marketing analysts believe that travel Web sites will need to focus on customer loyalty to keep their customers from jumping ship. Web sites can accomplish this by improving customer service and by tracking customer preferences. The three Web sites that appear to be most frequently visited for purchasing travel tickets are Travelocity, Expedia, and Priceline.com. Suppose that eight weeks are randomly selected and the number of weekly visitors are recorded in thousands for each of these Web sites.

Week	1	2	3	4	5	6	7	8
Travelocity	523	570	595	480	501	525	475	532
Expedia	525	539	601	470	480	495	477	503
Priceline.com	499	527	598	440	445	494	470	497

a. Using a 5% significance level, determine whether the mean numbers of visitors to these three Web sites differ.

b. Use a multiple comparisons procedure, if appropriate, to determine which Web sites differ. Use a 5% significance level.

(Source: "Top Internet Travel Sites," *USA Today,* June 4, 2001, p. 2B.)

11.54 Suppose it is known in a randomized block design that the mean square for blocks is 75, the error mean square is 291, the total sum of squares is 5,083, and five blocks and four factor levels are used in the experiment. What would be the value of the F test for testing the hypothesis that there is no difference in the mean levels of the factor?

11.55 A two-way factorial experiment was performed using two factors: type of tire and inflation level. The tires were driven 10,000 miles and the amount of tire wear was recorded. The inflation levels were slightly under inflated, correctly inflated, and slightly over inflated. Four replications were used for each combination of factor levels. The following ANOVA table for this design is partially filled in.

Source	df	SS	MS	F
Type of Tires	2		8.361	
Inflation				
Interaction			4.102	
Error		110.75		
Total	35	420.972		

a. Complete the ANOVA table.

b. Is there a significant difference in the levels of the type-of-tire factor? Use a 10% significance level.

11.56 Fifteen university campuses of similar size were selected to determine which of three methods of advertising a blood-donation drive was most effective. Five randomly selected campuses advertised in the university newspaper (method 1). Another five advertised only by posters and signs around campus (method 2). The remaining five had each professor credit five points to the student's last test if the student contributed (method 3). The following table gives the percentage of the student body that contributed:

Method 1	.10	.15	.19	.21	.25
Method 2	.20	.18	.20	.23	.19
Method 3	.29	.20	.25	.30	.25

Do these data provide sufficient evidence at the .01 level of significance to reject the null hypothesis that there is no difference in the effectiveness of the three methods of advertising?

11.57 Sample data from three normally distributed populations were generated by a computer program for a simulation study. Do the data provide evidence to indicate that at least two of the population variances are not equal? Use a .05 significance level.

Sample 1	Sample 2	Sample 3	Sample 1	Sample 2	Sample 3
38	45	28	33	47	30
37	47	27	32	45	31
35	43	31	39	43	32
40	44	30	37	42	31
39	42	31	36	44	29
35	44	32	35	45	30
34	45	29			

11.58 Three different investment advisers were asked to give a performance rating from 0 to 100 on the risk-adjusted performances of 12 randomly selected aggressive growth mutual funds. From the following data, is there sufficient evidence to conclude that the three investment advisers differ in their mean performance ratings? Use a .05 significance level.

	Investment Advisers				Investment Advisers		
Mutual Funds	A	B	C	Mutual Funds	A	B	C
1	81	76	70	7	88	75	83
2	83	72	75	8	51	55	53
3	51	51	43	9	41	37	45
4	96	92	90	10	88	90	87
5	67	70	68	11	59	61	60
6	71	64	71	12	78	73	74

11.59 In a 3×3 factorial experiment with two replicates per treatment, how many error df are there? If a one-way ANOVA was used with three levels and six observations per level, how many error df are there? If the error df are very small for a two-way factorial experiment, how can one increase the error df?

11.60 Gage Repeatability & Reproducibility (GR&R) studies focus on identifying measurement variation caused by gages and appraisers. Using GR&R studies, it is possible to identify and reduce measurement variation for a more precise measurement. Ultimately, these results provide the information to differentiate between parts that are in and out of tolerance with a higher chance of being correct about measurement decisions. Suppose that a production manager performed an experiment with two factors—gages and experience. The factor gage consisted of two levels—older and newer gages. The factor experience of operator also consisted of two levels—less than three years experience and at least three years experience for the operator. In this experiment the manager measured the amount of time that it took the operator to adjust the gages so that they worked with a specified tolerance. Assume that the sum of squares for "gages," the sum of squares for "experience," and the total sum of squares were, respectively, 1.78, 13.05, and 332.28.

   a. Assume that in each cell of the factorial experiment, there were 28 operators and that the sum of squares for the interaction was 2.04. Construct the ANOVA table for this experiment.

   b. What conclusions do the data support with regard to the factors "gages" and "experience"? Use a 5% significance level.

   c. Under what conditions is the factorial experiment considered to be statistically valid?

(Source: "5 Ways to Verify Your Gages," *Quality*, vol. 39, no. 3, March 2000, pp. 38–42.)

11.61 A manager of Bookstop would like to determine if rankings of hardcover books are different across type (fiction and nonfiction) and cost (high [over $10] and low [$10 or less]). Consider the data on the next page to be a random sample of hardcover books and their sales rankings.

   a. Use an appropriate experimental design to analyze the two factors, type and cost, using a 5% significance level.

   b. Should you perform a multiple comparisons procedure? If so, use a 5% significance level.

   c. Do a what if analysis by dividing each ranking by 50 and analyzing the data. What changes occur in the ANOVA results?

Book Title	Fiction and over $10
All Through the Night	22
Rainbow Six	33
The Path of Daggers	2
Cold Mountain	31
The Present	34

	Fiction and $10 or less
Animorphs: The Pretender	19
Cat & Mouse	8
Special Delivery	48
Deception on His Mind	35
The MacGregor Grooms	7

	Nonfiction and over $10
Chicken Soup for The Teenage Soul II	3
In the Meantime	12
The 9 Steps to Financial Freedom	29
Sugar Busters	20
The Seat of the Soul	11

	Nonfiction and $10 or less
The Perfect Storm	46
Dr. Atkins' New Diet Revolution	4
The Virtues of Aging	26
Protein Powder	21
Don't Sweat the Small Stuff	25

(Source: "Best-Selling Books," *USA Today*, November 5, 1998, p. 8D.)

11.62 [DATA EX11-62] *Variable description:*

MutualFund: Name of mutual fund

AnnualExp: Annual expense ratio

LargeOrSmallGrowth: "Large" ("Small") indicates that the fund invests primarily in large (small) cap companies.

OverOrUnder1Billion: "Over" ("Under") indicates that the fund has more (less) than one billion in assets.

Operating expenses for a mutual fund are all the administrative, management, distribution and other costs that a fund company incurs in maintaining a mutual fund. These expenses are expressed as the "annual expense ratio" of the fund, a percentage figure that can be found in fund prospectuses. Some financial analysts believe the asset size of a mutual fund and the type of fund influence the annual expense ratio. Seven mutual funds of each type of fund (small or large cap fund) and each asset size (over or under $1 billion) are randomly selected.

    a. Use an appropriate experimental design to analyze two factors: type of companies in which the fund invests, and asset size. Use a 5% significance level.

    b. Should you perform a multiple comparisons procedure? If so, use a 5% significance level.

    c. Do a what-if analysis by multiplying each expense ratio by 1.5 and repeating part a. What changes occur in the ANOVA results?

(Source: "Mutual Funds: Quarterly Review," *The Wall Street Journal*, October 8, 2001, pp. R1–R44.)

11.63 [DATA SET EX11-63] *Variable description:*

Schedule1: productivity of each employee on work schedule 1.

Schedule2: productivity of each employee on work schedule 2.

Schedule3: productivity of each employee on work schedule 3.

The manager of an electronics factory wishes to determine the effect of three different work schedules on the productivity of assemblers of electrical components. Work schedule 1 is a five-day work week, 8 hours a day. Work schedule 2 is a week consisting of four days at 9 hours a day and 4 hours on the fifth day. Work schedule 3 is a four-day week, 10 hours a day. A random sample of eight employees was selected for each work schedule. The productivity of each employee was recorded for a week, and productivity was measured in terms of total dollar worth of units produced. The productivity figures are recorded using variables Schedule1, Schedule2, and Schedule3.

a. Consider the three histograms stacked in order from Schedule1 (first one) to Schedule3 (last one). From these histograms, what conclusions would you make?

b. Consider the Excel printout. What conclusions can you make assuming a 5% significance level? Is the Tukey procedure consistent with the results of the ANOVA table?

c. Suppose that observations 33 and 49 for Schedule 2 were mistyped as 25,341 and 25,473, and should have been 20,500 and 20,200. Do a "what if" analysis by changing these values and analyzing the data again. What changes take place in the variances of the three groups?

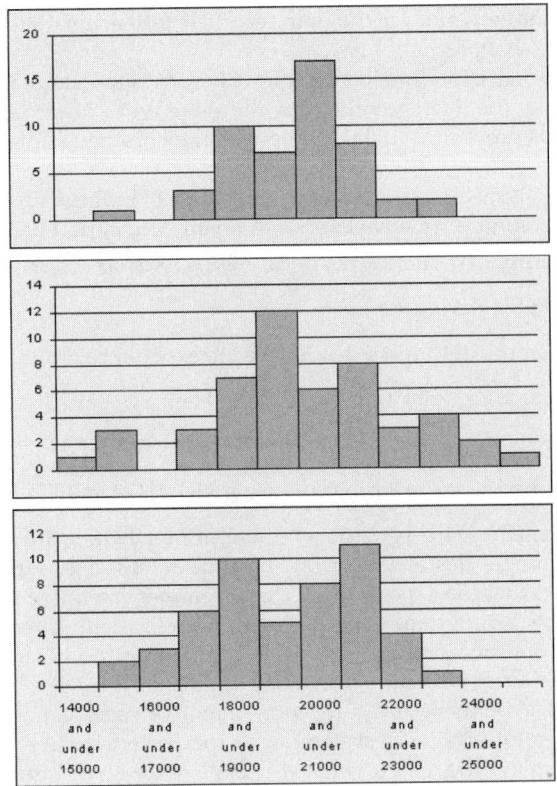

ANOVA

Source of Variation	SS	df	MS	F	P-value	F crit
Between Groups	10,148,561.45	2	50,743,280.7	1.21	0.30	3.06
Within Groups	615,589,918.92	147	4,187,686.5			
Total	625,738,480.37	149				

Tukey Multiple Comparisons Test

Critical Q	Distance	Alpha
3.36	972.39	0.05

Means joined by a double line are not significantly different.

Schedule3	Schedule1	Schedule2
19,628.00	20,056.70	20,250.54

Hartley Test for Homogeneity of Variance

Hartley Test	Critical Value	Alpha
2.31	1.85	0.05

11.64 [DATA EX11-64] *Variable description:*

TasteTester: One of 20 judges who rates three different tacos on a scale from 1 to 10 (highest).

FishTaco: rating for taco made with fish

ShrimpTaco: rating for taco made with shrimp

CalamariTaco: rating for taco made with calamari

American restaurants have become very creative in serving tacos. They are made using folded, warmed, or fried tortillas and traditionally are filled with a near-endless array of grilled or stewed meats and seafood, produce, and cheeses. Often tacos are topped with big-flavored salsas or a thickened cream. Chef Reed Hearon of San Francisco is a native of Austin, Texas, and author of the cookbook "La Parilla—The Mexican Grill." Suppose that three cooks used his cookbook to make one of three taco dishes—fish taco, shrimp taco, and calamari taco. Twenty judges rated each of the three dishes, and these ratings are recorded as the variables FishTaco, ShrimpTaco, and CalamariTaco.

a. Form a stem-and-leaf plot for the data recorded for each variable. How would you interpret these plots?

b. Use an appropriate experimental design with a 5% significance level to determine if there is a difference in the average rating for the three types of taco dishes. Use Tukey's multiple comparisons procedure to determine which dishes have difference ratings at the 5% significance level.

c. Do a what-if analysis by considering only the first 10 judges rather than the entire set of 20 observations. Comment on any changes that you note in part b.

(Source: "Expressive and Inexpensive, Tacos Are Hot Again," *Nation's Restaurant News,* August 13, 2001.)

11.65 [DATA EX11-65] *Variable description:*

Experience: A value from 1 through 4 describing the experience of the programmer

HelpSysA: Time required to write a program using Help System A

HelpSysB: Time required to write a program using Help System B

HelpSysC: Time required to write a program using Help System C

An information systems researcher wishes to determine whether the type of help system available to programmers has an effect on the time required to write a program. The researcher also knows that the experience of a programmer can influence the time (in minutes) required to write a program. An experiment is set up with three different help systems and four levels of programming experience (1 for almost no experience, 2 for no more than two years' experience but some previous experience, 3 for less than five years' but more than two years' experience, and 4 for more than five years' experience).

a. The mean times for each help system and experience level are presented below. In addition, a graph displays the means versus the experience level. Interpret this graph. Do you believe that there is an interaction effect?

b. Analyze the data using a significance level of 5%. Write a summary of your findings.

Exper	HelpSys A	HelpSys B	HelpSys C
1	31	34	39.5
2	33	30.5	30.5
3	26	25.5	23.5
4	24.5	23.5	18

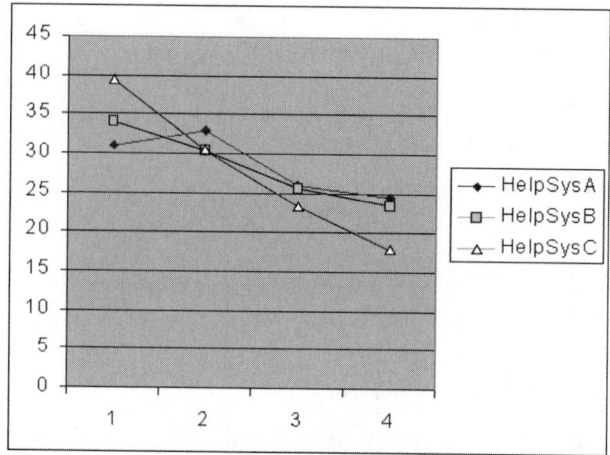

Computer Exercises Using the Databases

Exercise 1—Appendix F

From the database, randomly select 10 observations each from the NE sector, the NW sector, and SE sector (variable LOCATION). Using a .05 significance level, is there sufficient evidence to conclude that the mean house payment or apartment/house rent (variable HPAYRENT) is significantly different for the three locations? Include a multiple comparisons procedure, if appropriate.

Exercise 2—Appendix F

Select at random 12 observations for each level of two factors from the database. Factor A has two levels: a nonzero income from the secondary wage earner, and no secondary income (variable INCOME2). Factor B has two levels: own one's residence and rent one's residence (variable OWNORENT). Determine the effect of these two factors on house payment or house/apartment rent (variable HPAYRENT). Set up an ANOVA table that includes interaction. What conclusions can be drawn at the .05 significance level?

Exercise 3—Appendix G

From the database, select at random six observations from each bond rating and region combination. (Refer to variables BONDRATE and REGION.) Determine the effect of bond rating and region on the assets (variable ASSETS). Use a .05 significance level. Discuss the effect of interaction.

Exercise 4—Appendix G

Repeat Exercise 3, but determine the effect of bond rating (BONDRATE) and region (REGION) on the net income (NETINC) instead of assets.

Insights from Statistics in Action

MBA Programs: Making an Executive Decision to Master Your Career

At the beginning of this chapter, the Statistics in Action case study explained that the cost of many of the EMBA and global EMBA programs range from $50,000 to $100,000. Many corporate leaders wonder if it makes a difference whether a business employee earns a traditional MBA degree versus an executive MBA degree. If a business professional or company were to invest in one of these programs, would the salary change of participants from these three programs differ significantly—say, three years after completion of the program?

Surveys by *Business Week* magazine and academic researchers collect information on the salaries of participants in MBA programs to rate these programs for marketing purposes. Duke University's The Fuqua School of Business offers three MBA programs: The Global Executive, the Weekend Executive program, and the traditional MBA program. Suppose that a random sample of 30 students from each of these three programs at Duke University was selected and the number of years that it would take participants to break even after completing their degree was determined. The data are listed in StatInActChap11.xls.

1. What statistical procedure would you use to test for differences in the number of years that it would take a participant to break even across the traditional MBA, EMBA, and global EMBA programs after three years? State the null and alternative hypotheses.

2. Test for differences in the means across the three MBA programs. Use a significance level of 5%. Does this procedure allow you to make conclusions about which programs differ with respect to the number of years that it takes a participant to break even?

3. Use a multiple comparisons procedure with a 5% significance level to determine which MBA programs differ with respect to the number of years that it takes a participant to break even. How would you respond to a corporate executive asking the question, "Does the marketability of a

business professional differ significantly across these three programs?"

4. Construct a 95% confidence interval for the mean number of years that it takes a participant to break even for each of the three MBA programs. Interpret these confidence intervals.

5. Explain why a randomized block design would not be appropriate for analyzing the means across the three MBA programs.

(Source: "No Simple Answer: New Breed of Courses," *The Financial Times*, October 22, 2001, p. 9; "Minding Their Own Business," *The Washington Post*, March 22, 1998, p. W18; "No Restraints Even If You're Tied to the Job," *The London Times*, October 1, 2001, p. 13).

Appendix SPSS®

Chapter 11 Appendix: Data Analysis with SPSS

Analysis of Variance

To perform a one-factor analysis of variance, consider the breaking strength data in Example 11.6. Enter the breaking strengths of the nylon line for each of the five vendors in the first column ($25 \times 5 = 125$ values) and the corresponding 125 vendor indicators in the second column. Click on the **Variable View** tab and name these variables "value" and "vendor." Also, set the number of decimal places equal to zero for the vendor variable.

	value	vendor
1	25.3994	1
2	29.0130	1
3	25.2492	1
4	25.1491	1
5	24.1882	1
6	25.1491	1
7	24.2783	1
8	26.2402	1
9	23.6576	1
10	25.9299	1
11	23.4975	1
12	26.2702	1
13	24.5786	1
14	27.6716	1
15	27.0110	1
16	27.1912	1
17	26.1802	1
18	24.8889	1
19	24.8488	1
20	23.6176	1
21	27.4915	1
22	27.1511	1

Data View / Variable View

Click on **Analyze ➤ Compare Means ➤ One-Way ANOVA.** Move the value variable into the **Variable List** box and the vendor variable into the **Factor** box as shown on the next page. After clicking on **OK,** the output immediately following the **One-Way ANOVA** window will appear in the display pane. The resulting ANOVA table agrees with that obtained in the solution to Example 11.6. The factor sum of squares is labeled "Between Groups" and the error sum of squares is labeled "Within Groups."

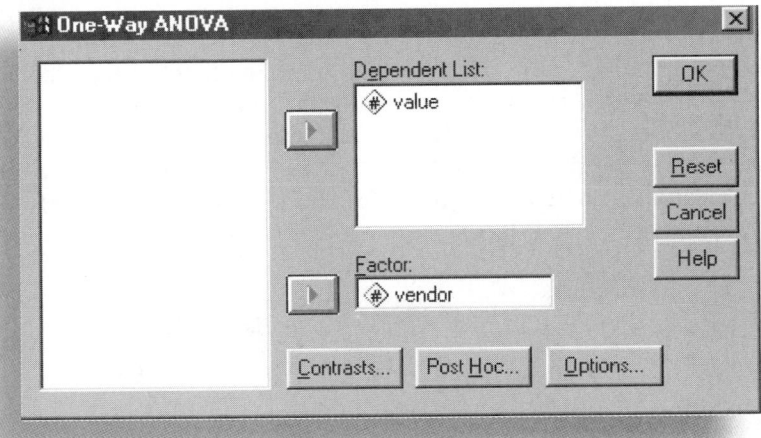

ANOVA

VALUE

	Sum of Squares	df	Mean Square	F	Sig.
Between Groups	388.437	4	97.109	39.049	.000
Within Groups	298.421	120	2.487		
Total	686.858	124			

Multiple Comparisons

SPSS provides a number of multiple comparisons procedures. To obtain the Tukey test for multiple comparisons, click on **Post Hoc** in the previous **One-Way ANOVA** window. In the window that appears, click on the check box alongside **Tukey** inside the **Equal Variances Assumed** frame. The output in the display pane from this procedure contains the following table. This table indicates that there is no evidence of a difference among the mean breaking strengths for the vendor 2, 3, and 5 populations because these three groups appear in a single column. Similarly, there is no evidence of a difference between the mean breaking strengths for vendors 1 and 4 because they appear together in a separate column. This table also contains the sample means.

Homogeneous Subsets

VALUE

Tukey HSD[a]

		Subset for alpha = .05	
VENDOR	N	1	2
2	25	21.343	
5	25	21.865	
3	25	22.122	
4	25		24.857
1	25		25.30
Sig.		.409	.294

Means for groups in homogeneous subsets are displayed.

a. Uses Harmonic Mean Sample Size = 25.000.

513

Randomized Block Design

To demonstrate the SPSS procedure for a randomized block design, consider the metal hinge hardness readings discussed in Section 11.4. Begin by putting the readings in the first column, the tip (1, 2, or 3) in the second column (this is the factor of interest), and the hinge value (1, 2, . . . , 10) in the third column (these are the block indicators). Name the columns "reading," "tip," and "hinge," as shown below.

	reading	tip	hinge
1	68	1	1
2	72	2	1
3	65	3	1
4	40	1	2
5	43	2	2
6	42	3	2
7	82	1	3
8	89	2	3
9	84	3	3
10	56	1	4
11	60	2	4
12	50	3	4
13	70	1	5
14	75	2	5
15	68	3	5
16	80	1	6
17	91	2	6
18	86	3	6
19	47	1	7
20	58	2	7
21	50	3	7
22	55	1	8

Data View   Variable View

Click on **Analyze ➤ General Linear Model ➤ Univariate.** Enter the variable names in the boxes as illustrated in the dialog box named Univariate. Next, click on **Model.** In this screen (named Univariate: Model) select the **Custom** option in the **Specify Model** frame. Move the variables tip and hinge into the **Model** box by selecting each one and clicking on the **Build Term(s)** pointer button. The option for the type of sum of squares will not affect the output. Click on **Continue** and then **OK.** In the illustrations to follow, the ANOVA table immediately after the **Univariate: Model** dialog box will appear in the display pane.

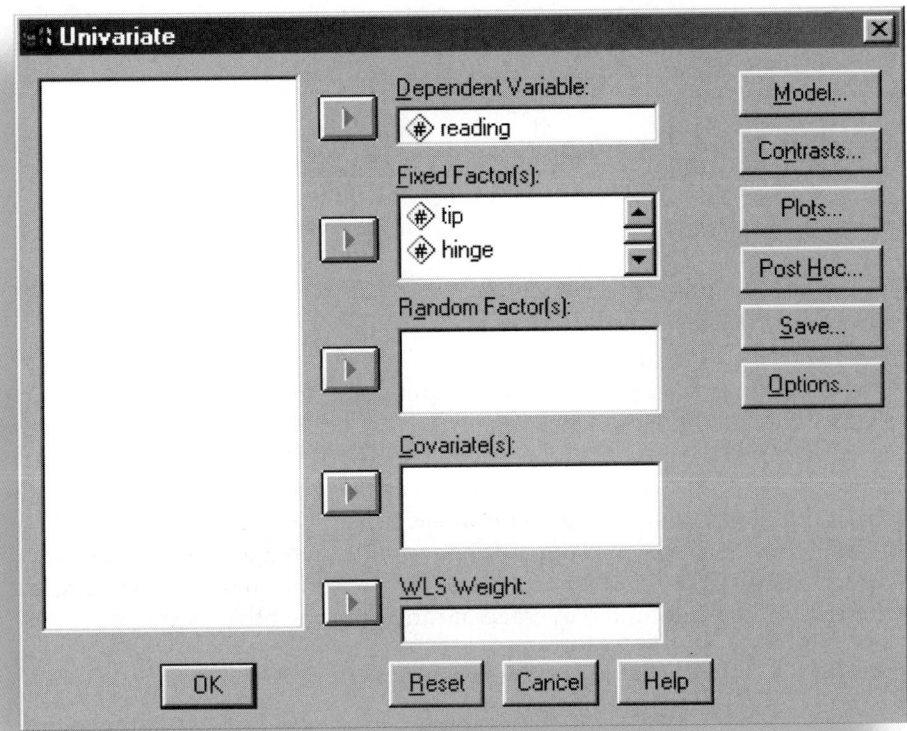

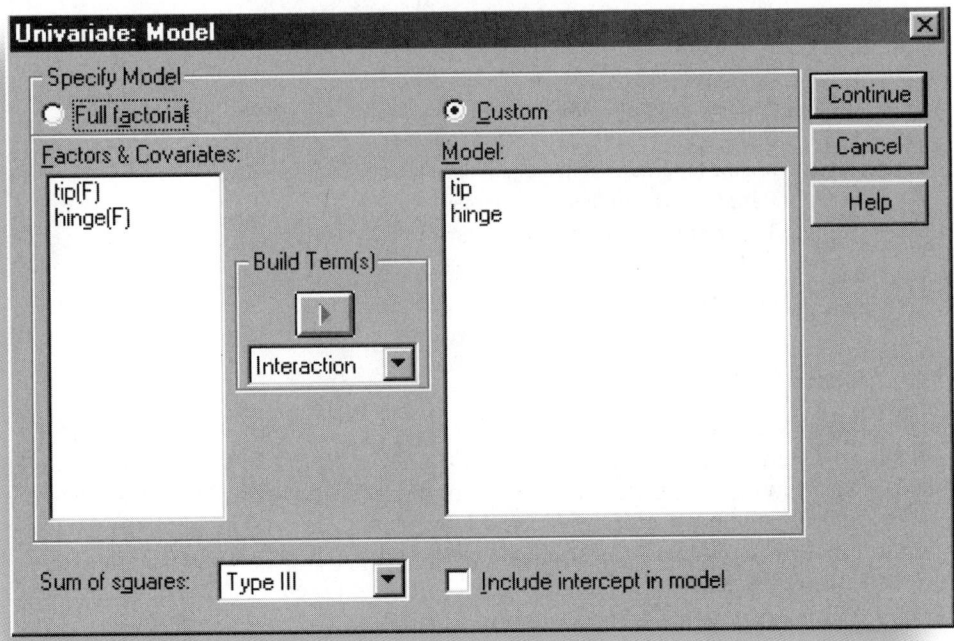

Tests of Between-Subjects Effects

Dependent Variable: READING

Source	Type III Sum of Squares	df	Mean Square	F	Sig.
Model	133931.867[a]	12	11160.989	1147.113	.000
TIP	304.200	2	152.100	15.633	.000
HINGE	5704.967	9	633.885	65.150	.000
Error	175.133	18	9.730		
Total	134107.000	30			

a. R Squared = .999 (Adjusted R Squared = .998)

The final window in this section is the output using the Tukey multiple comparisons procedure. To carry out this analysis, click on **Post Hoc** in the **Univariate** dialog box. Move the tip variable into the **Post Hoc Tests for** box by selecting this variable and clicking on the pointer. Click on the check box alongside **Tukey** inside the **Equal Variances Assumed** frame. Click on **Continue** and **OK.** This output indicates that there is no difference between the average hardness reading for tips 1 and 3 (they occur together in a single **Subset** column) but the average hardness for tip 2 is larger than the average hardness for the other two tips.

Homogeneous Subsets

READING

Tukey HSD[a,b]

TIP	N	Subset 1	Subset 2
1	10	62.90	
3	10	63.20	
2	10		69.80
Sig.		.975	1.000

Means for groups in homogeneous subsets are displayed.
Based on Type III Sum of Squares
The error term is Mean Square(Error) = 9.730.
a. Uses Harmonic Mean Sample Size = 10.000.
b. Alpha = .05.

Two-Way Factorial Design

This analysis is carried out much like that used for a randomized block design. Consider the dental claim data used in section 11.5. The data are entered into three columns as shown in the data window immediately following. The columns were named "claim," "gender" (factor A), and "empclass" (factor B). Click on **Analyze ➤ General Linear Model ➤ Univariate.** Move the claim variable to the **Dependent Variable** box. Move the gender variable to the **Fixed Factor(s)** box and then move variable empclass to this same box. There is no need to click on the **Model** button to carry out a two-way factorial design because the default options will be used. The ANOVA table immediately following the data window will appear in the display pane. Rows 3, 4, 5, 6, and 8 match up with the ANOVA table format used in section 11.5 and discussed in Example 11.10. Using a significance level of .05, the gender factor and the interaction between gender and the employee classification are seen to be significant since their p-values (in the column labeled "Sig.") are less than .05.

For this example, a multiple comparisons test can be carried out to compare the means for the four employee classifications. *Note:* There is no need to carry out post-test for the gender variable since there are only two levels here (male and female), and this variable has already been demonstrated to be significant. To compare the four means for employee classification, click on **Post Hoc** in the **Univariate** dialog box. Move the empclass variable into the **Post Hoc Tests for** box by selecting this variable and clicking on the pointer. Click on the check box alongside **Tukey** inside the **Equal Variances Assumed** frame. Click on **Continue** and **OK.** The resulting output (not shown) indicates that there is no difference between the average dental claim amount for the four employee classifications since all four groups appear together in a single column under **Subset.** *Note:* If significant interaction is indicated, it is not recommended to perform multiple comparisons on one factor.

	claim	gender	empclass
1	190	1	1
2	225	1	1
3	200	1	1
4	135	1	2
5	180	1	2
6	100	1	2
7	260	1	3
8	330	1	3
9	350	1	3
10	305	1	4
11	275	1	4
12	240	1	4
13	235	2	1
14	190	2	1
15	270	2	1
16	275	2	2
17	305	2	2
18	285	2	2
19	160	2	3
20	205	2	3
21	140	2	3
22	155	2	4

▸ **Data View** ╱ Variable View ╱

Tests of Between-Subjects Effects
Dependent Variable: CLAIM

Source	Type III Sum of Squares	df	Mean Square	F	Sig.
Corrected Model	111607.292	7	15943.899	13.038	.000
Intercept	1124501.042	1	1124501.042	919.524	.000
GENDER	6176.042	1	6176.042	5.050	.039
EMPCLASS	6853.125	3	2284.375	1.868	.176
GENDER *EMPCLASS	98578.125	3	32859.375	26.870	.000
Error	19566.667	16	1222.917		
Total	1255675.000	24			
Corrected Total	131173.958	23			

R Squared = .851 (Adjusted R Squared = .786)

On the CD . . .
Chapter 11 Appendix: Data Analysis with MINITAB

chapter

12

Quality Improvement X

During 2000, surveys by Consumer Reports and J. D. Power & Associates revealed that overall quality and customer satisfaction for Ford cars lagged the competition. This was a reversal from the 1980s, when Ford had a substantial lead in quality. In fact, Dr. W. Edwards Deming was recruited to jump-start Ford's quality movement. Commitment to Deming's principles of total quality management is credited for a series of home runs at Ford, including the aerodynamic Taurus-Sable's rise to best-selling car in America and Ford's achievement as the most profitable American auto company during the 1980s. Ford's hard-won reputation for quality was tarnished by a series of setbacks, from the controversy over deadly rollovers of Ford Explorers equipped with Firestone tires to costly recalls of several models.

What is Ford's chief executive officer (CEO) counting on to put Ford back on track? *Six Sigma.* Employees understand that sigma is a Greek symbol representing a statistical unit that measures how much something varies from perfection. Most U.S. companies operate at Three Sigma—about 66,800 defects per million opportunities. Six Sigma quality is virtually flawless—3.4 defects per million opportunities.

Ford's approach is quality oriented, but with a bottom-line orientation, whereas the total quality management approach of the 1980s focused primarily on improving processes with the thought that profits automatically follow. A typical project is assigned to a manager who has to improve processes 70 percent and produce $250,000 in cost savings. Middle managers, known as Black Belts, are committed to working on quality-improvement projects for two years.

Ford's CEO painfully realizes that consistency is the ultimate test of any quality program—and, perhaps, Ford's greatest failing. He believes that had Ford stuck with total quality management, it might have avoided many of the problems that have plagued the company. As the years rolled by, the concept faded into the background at Ford. Its champions retired and were replaced by executives who had other priorities. U.S. automakers had so much confidence that they felt they had achieved quality and didn't need to focus on it anymore.

When you have completed this chapter, you will have a firm grasp in understanding how qual-

ity improvement tools can provide a company with a greater competitive advantage. When you have completed this chapter, you will be able to

- Discuss the essential concepts behind total quality management (TQM) and the Malcolm Baldrige National Quality Award.
- Construct control charts that monitor the stability of a process.
- Determine if a particular process is capable of meeting the corresponding process specifications.

A Look Back/Introduction

What if you could be 99% mistake-free in your job? How about 99.9%? In many job areas, that is just good enough to get you a place in the unemployment line. Because if 99.9% was good enough, then . . .

- 22,000 checks per hour would be deducted from the wrong bank accounts.
- Two million documents would be lost by the IRS this year.
- 12 babies born today would be given to the wrong parents.
- 18,322 pieces of mail would be mishandled in the next hour.
- 20,000 drug prescriptions would be written incorrectly this year.

It should be clear from these statistics that there is a great need to ensure quality in our goods and services.

Previous chapters have introduced you to various statistical measures, such as the sample mean (a measure of *location*) and the sample range (a measure of *dispersion* or *variation*). When examining a population, knowledge of these measures can tell you a great deal about the population. For example, if your company advertises 10-pound bags of dog food but a large random sample of bags produces an average ($\overline{x}$) of 8.7 pounds, the company will undoubtedly encounter many angry consumers and may well be out of the dog food business if the sample is representative of all bags being produced.

Similarly, too much variation in the bag weights would indicate that the *production process* is too erratic. The company would then lose money due to dissatisfied customers (whose bags weigh under 10 pounds) or excess product being packaged (in bags that weigh over 10 pounds). Ideally, this production process could be fine-tuned to always produce 10-pound bags with no variation, but realistically, such a goal is nearly impossible. Our example, however, points out the need to be *on target* and *consistent*.

In part, *quality improvement is the study of variability*. Recently, it has received a great deal of national attention, as more and more companies are facing competitors who focus on quality and offer less expensive, more reliable products. This chapter will examine the human side of quality management along with many of the popular tools for implementing quality standards in manufacturing and service industries. Many of the statistical measures and procedures from the earlier chapters will be used to develop simple, yet powerful, methods of monitoring and controlling process location and variation.

QUALITY IMPROVEMENT:
THE PAST, PRESENT, AND FUTURE

Rarely a day goes by in which we are not bombarded by such statements as, "Quality is our most important job at Company A," or "Company B is a leader in quality." It is safe to say that a focus on quality is taking over U.S. business; however, using the word *quality* in one's advertising is not what this movement is all about. Rather, the focus on quality represents a change in the entire corporate culture, from the top on down, ranging from a dramatic change in how we manage and treat company employees all the way to using statistical methods to monitor and improve a production or service process.

New ideas within U.S. business organizations generally encounter a great deal of resistance. The "Doing business as usual" and "If it ain't broke, don't fix it" philosophies have prevailed, we would argue, for too long. New ideas require change. Change means more work, and we all seem to have enough work. American manufacturing organizations were first to notice that, in fact, many parts of their businesses were broken. As they began to lose an ever-increasing share to overseas' competition, they began to take a closer look at their manufacturing processes and management styles. It has become clear to an increasing number of both manufacturing and service organizations that what worked in the past may not be the ideal path for the twenty-first century.

At the dawn of the twentieth century, most of the products in the marketplace today didn't even exist. There were no airplanes, televisions, computers—or even bottled soft drinks. As we began to efficiently mass produce goods, organizations were created that contained multilayered management hierarchies under top-down control, as exemplified by General Motors in the 1920s. The General Motors model consisted of semiautonomous divisions (Chevrolet, Buick, Oldsmobile, Cadillac, and Pontiac) managing their own affairs while headquarters maintained financial control over the organization as a whole.

Today, nearly every business organization reflects these roots to some degree, and it was in this world that the quality profession developed. Their early efforts focused on creating statistical tools to help produce mass quantities of nearly identical goods. Prior to the late 1970s, *quality* meant *quality control.* In fact, the original name of the American Society for Quality was the American Society for Quality Control. Quality efforts encompassed inspection, conformance, and sorting out defects. Little effort was placed on monitoring work processes or preventing problems. Inspection—both incoming and outgoing—and 100% testing were the predominant methods of controlling quality.

Quality improvement hit center stage in the 1970s, when U.S. industry was faced with increased competition from the Japanese on the basis of product quality, price, and overall product reliability. In the 1980s, defect prevention (largely spearheaded by the U.S. automotive industry) rapidly evolved and expanded. The early results were favorable, spurring additional expansion of the quality movement.

The word *quality* began to fall into disfavor in the early 1990s as evidenced by the fact that many organizations seemed to be talking less about their quality improvement programs. There were a number of reasons behind this phenomenon:

* There were oftentimes bitter memories for many employees from the 1980s when quality initiatives were popular, leading employees to believe that they would have control over their work and be able to work on problems of significance to the organization.

521

- Senior leaders within the organization had little training in the concepts and tools behind an effective and comprehensive quality improvement program. Consequently, under stress they fell back into old habits and management approaches.
- When leaders were under pressure to achieve rapid results, they often abandoned quality initiatives that typically took time to implement before producing a gain in the corporate bottom line.

However, a large number of organizations were quiet on the subject of quality improvement simply because quality control and statistical process control (SPC) had already become integrated into the business strategy. These concepts moved from being new ideas into an accepted part of the organizational strategy. Quality concepts, tools, and methods were intertwined with the work of the organization, and use of this methodology became part of the job.

Even as we continue to use command-and-control techniques in our organizations, the emphasis in the twenty-first century is shifting toward allowing greater freedom. Layer after layer of bureaucracy and hierarchy is being stripped away, allowing for ever-increasing creativity and productivity. It has taken organizations a long time to realize that the level of external customer satisfaction is related to the level of employee satisfaction. This is especially true for industries such as health care and retail trade, where the customer is an integral part of the work process. As a result, discussion of quality improvement can no longer set aside the social, psychological, and emotional needs of employees.

This concept forms the basis of the **total quality management (TQM)** movement that has produced positive results for many U.S. manufacturing and service organizations. The TQM approach represents a basic change for many businesses in how they view employees, competition, training, and business strategies. What these businesses have discovered is that we live at a time when changes are occurring constantly and institutions that do not allow reaction to such changes have difficulty surviving.

What is TQM? There are a number of definitions of TQM in the literature, but essentially, TQM embraces a management philosophy that will allow a firm to meet or surpass customer expectations. TQM focuses on continuous quality improvement, teamwork, and paying close attention to the voice of the customer. TQM is an integrated management system that involves everyone in the organization (as well as outside suppliers) and uses quantitative methods to monitor and continuously improve the quality of a process.

Despite TQM being a hot topic for the past 15 years, it has its critics. Unrealistic expectations, quick-fix mentality, and competition from other tools are some reasons why many firms have soured on TQM. It was expected to turn lead into gold and reverse poor performance. Often TQM efforts were measured against short-term financial performance. When short-term improvements did not materialize, many firms became disillusioned.

Proponents of TQM examine these arguments and are quick to point out that the case against TQM is based on haphazard studies that merely report managers' perceptions about whether TQM had a significant financial impact on their organizations. Such studies are rarely based on objective data and statistically valid analyses. They also maintain that while most firms will claim they have implemented TQM, few are doing it effectively. Effectively implementing TQM means that the key principles of TQM—such as focus on customer satisfaction, employee involvement, and continuous improvement—are well accepted, practiced, and deployed within a firm.

One thing is clear—to get the maximum benefits from TQM, one must be patient. Managers who embrace TQM for quick gains will be disappointed because TQM is *not* a quick fix. It improves performance in the long haul. Even after effective implementation, it still takes two to three years before financial performance begins to improve.

The Quality Gurus

Surprising to many people is that the quality message has been preached in the United States for many years. People simply ignored the message because there was little foreign competition. The corporate mindset was "we are invincible" and the corporate strategy became "new challenge, old response." The early quality messengers, most notably **W. Edwards Deming** and **Joseph M. Juran,** warned that past success does not guarantee survival tomorrow. In 1979, another quality expert, **Philip B. Crosby,** began offering organizations a quality-management/improvement program. Although these three individuals appear to have different messages, there are many similarities in their guidelines for building quality-focused organizations. We will briefly examine the key points of the Deming, Juran, and Crosby quality-improvement programs.

W. Edwards Deming. The year 1993 marked the end of an era in the world of quality improvement as Dr. W. Edwards "Ed" Deming passed away at the age of 93. He was lecturing and delivering his typically unflattering message to corporate executives up until shortly before his death. A classic quote from Dr. Deming is, "The basic cause of sickness in American industry and resulting unemployment is failure of top management to manage." Deming insisted on working with top management of companies seeking his services, and, as the previous quote makes clear, he was quick to point out that they were a significant part of any corporate difficulties. He denounced production quotas, performance ratings, and individual bonuses as being detrimental to quality improvement.

Dr. Deming mellowed slightly during his final years but was best known for his confrontive style and often sarcastic response to what he considered a less-than-intelligent question. This is perhaps due to the fact that he was largely ignored in this country for decades. In 1950, he took his message to Japan and was very instrumental in turning Japanese industry into a world economic power. When he was "discovered" much later in the United States, his presence filled lecture halls with people anxious to hear what these "new" ideas were all about. In fact, they were the same ideas he had advocated many years before.

Deming's philosophy centers around a 14-point program on managing productivity and quality. This program is discussed at length in his book *Out of the Crisis,* in which he paints a rather gloomy picture about the survival of American business if it does not make changes. Deming's 14 points are as follows:

1. Create constancy of purpose for improvement of product and service.

2. Adopt the new philosophy.

3. Cease dependence on inspection to achieve quality.

4. End the practice of awarding business on the basis of price tag alone. Instead, minimize total cost by working with a single supplier.

5. Improve, constantly and forever, every process for planning, production, and service.

6. Institute training on the job.

7. Adopt and institute leadership.

8. Drive out fear.

9. Break down barriers between staff areas.

10. Eliminate slogans, exhortations, and targets for the workforce.

11. Eliminate numerical quotas for the workforce and numerical goals for management.

12. Remove barriers that rob people of pride of workmanship. Eliminate the annual rating or merit system.

13. Institute a vigorous program of education and self-improvement for everyone.

14. Put everybody in the company to work to accomplish the transformation.

Deming advocates the use of statistical methods and statistical charts (discussed in sections 12.4, 12.5, and 12.6) to monitor and correct production processes. While continuous improvement is also preached by Juran and Crosby, Deming stresses that continuous improvement is the only way to retain customers. Ford Motor Company has used the Deming approach since 1981 and has been praised for the improved quality of its automobiles. But, as stressed by Deming's fifth point, this is a neverending process whereby Ford Motor Company should constantly strive to improve their products.

Joseph M. Juran. Juran's quality philosophy urges managers to adopt a more internal focus on quality improvement. The *customer* might be the next person down the production line, and it is important to realize that each step in a process affects the next. Juran calls this "identifying the customer." It is important from Juran's point of view to examine the entire production process for problems and to train employees to do the same. He is an advocate of using quality teams for problem solving and for helping the company internalize the "quality first" mindset. Both Juran and Crosby believe that by concentrating on reducing waste and minimizing the number of defective products, the quality focus can lead to savings that far exceed the cost of implementing and sustaining such a program.

The core of Juran's philosophy is contained in the *Juran Trilogy*—quality planning, quality control, and quality improvement. Quality planning concentrates on (1) identifying who the customers are and their needs; (2) developing product features that respond to those needs, and processes that can produce those product features; and (3) transferring this plan throughout the entire organization. Quality control measures the performance of the production or service process against the quality goals and then acts on those differences. The quality-improvement phase emphasizes the importance of achieving continuous quality improvement for the entire life of the product or service.

Philip B. Crosby. Crosby's methods are filled with catchy slogans, such as "zero defects" and "quality is free." The latter slogan is the title of his first and most popular book. This particular aspect of Crosby's approach goes against the grain of Deming's tenth point (Eliminate slogans, exhortations, and targets for the work force), but has made Crosby's message a very popular one. Unlike Deming and Juran, Crosby is an excellent motivational speaker, and his enthusiastic approach has produced a great many quality "converts."

Crosby's approach is largely nontechnical. Similar to Deming, he also has a 14-point program, which addresses such issues as management commitment, quality-improvement teams, quality measurement, corrective action, quality awareness, goal setting, and the importance of employee recognition. His particular style and message have been very instrumental in helping organizations adjust their attitude toward quality. He emphasizes early training for *all* managers, and his program provides them, many would argue, with an excellent guide for becoming better employee leaders rather than merely employee managers.

Similarities and Differences. Deming, Juran, and Crosby all agree on one thing: For a quality program to succeed, the quality commitment must cut across the entire organization. They also agree on the following points.

- Attack the system, not the employee.
- Identify the customer—internal or external.
- Satisfy or exceed customer requirements.
- Teamwork and training are essential.
- Create an atmosphere of continuous improvement.
- Management, not the front-line worker, is responsible for poor quality.

Some areas where these three individuals differ include the following.

- Juran and Deming rely heavily on statistical methods; Crosby does not.
- Crosby's nontechnical approach focuses on getting an organization started on quality improvement and committed to this purpose. Deming and Juran have a more nuts-and-bolts approach to achieving this end.
- Deming believes in starting with top management commitment, whereas Juran believes this effort can begin with middle management and filter up and down the organization.
- Deming places a great deal of emphasis on studying variation (see section 12.4).
- Deming describes fear in negative terms when he discusses eliminating fear in the workplace. Juran believes that fear can bring out the best in people when they are confronted with the possibility of their company's going under.

As a final word, we would argue that it is more beneficial to concentrate on the similarities of these (or any espoused) quality philosophies. It is more important to do *something* in the area of quality improvement than to spend countless hours arguing which program is superior. In fact, most quality programs that are implemented end up as a hybrid of these ideas and the company's own contributions when the final quality-improvement strategy is agreed upon.

Some Key Definitions

As we have seen, the term *quality* means slightly different things to different people. We will define a **quality product or service** to be one that meets or surpasses the needs and expectations of the customer; that is, quality means general excellence in the eyes of the customer. However, as Deming was quick to point out, "It will not suffice to have customers who are merely satisfied. A satisfied customer may switch. . . . It is necessary to innovate, to predict the needs of the customer, to give him more." It is important to understand that quality improvement does not just apply to businesses. It also works in nonprofit organizations, such as schools, health care and social services, and government agencies. Here are other key terms that will be used in the sections to follow.

Process. Any combination of people, machinery, material, and methods that is intended to produce a product or service.

Quality Characteristics. Features of a product that describe its fitness for use, such as length, weight, taste, appearance, reliability. For a service organization these could include promptness of service (e.g., check-in time at a hotel, response time to a police call), number of customer complaints, or level of employee attitude.

Statistical Process Control (SPC). The application of statistical quality-control methods to measuring and analyzing the variation found in processes.

Control Chart. A statistical chart used to monitor various aspects of a process (such as the process average) and to determine if the process is in control (stable) or out of control (unstable).

12.2

THE MALCOLM BALDRIGE NATIONAL QUALITY AWARD AND ISO 9000 REGISTRATION

Malcolm Baldrige Award

The **Malcolm Baldrige National Quality Award** (MBNQA) was established by Congress in 1987. The award was named after the former Secretary of Commerce, who was killed in a rodeo accident earlier the same year. The MBNQA was modeled, in part, after the Deming Award, named after W. Edwards Deming, presented annually in Japan for more than 45 years to the organization that best demonstrates dramatic quality improvement. After the MBNQA was created, 37 countries, Puerto Rico, and Western Europe developed national quality awards, many of which were modeled after the Baldrige award.

Annually, about 30,000 organizations request copies of the MBNQA criteria and application forms (available at the Baldrige organization Web site at www.quality.nist.gov). Recent winners of the MBNQA, through 2000, are listed in Table 12.1. There can be at most two winners each year within each of three categories—manufacturing companies, small businesses, and service companies. Federal Express was the first service company winner in 1990; in 1992, AT&T became the only company to win two Baldrige awards in the same year. Also, 1992 marked the first time two service companies won the award. In 1997, Xerox joined the group of two-time winners, and in 1994, AT&T became the only three-time winner. The examination process includes on-site visits for those companies passing an initial screening. As you can see from Table 12.1, there need not be an MBNQA winner within all three categories if the Baldrige examiners find no company in a particular category (such as small businesses, 1997 and service companies, 1998) that meet the rather strict, yet very objective, criteria.

TABLE

12.1

Recent Winners of the Malcolm Baldrige National Quality Award.

	Manufacturing Companies	Small Business	Service Companies
1990	Codillac Motor Car Div. IBM Rochester	Wallace Co. Inc.	Federal Express
1991	Solectron Corp. Zytec Corp.	Marlow Industries	

1992	AT&T Network Systems Group—
	    Transmission Systems Business Unit
	Texas Instruments Inc.—Defense
	    Systems & Electronics Group
		Granite Rock Co.	AT&T Universal Card Services
			
			The Ritz-Carlton Hotel Co.

1993	Eastman Chemical Company (a division of Eastman Kodak Company)	Ames Rubber Corporation	
1994		Wainwright Industries, Inc.	AT&T Consumer Communications Services GTE Directories Corporation

1995	Armstrong World Industries Building
	    Products Operations
	Corning Telecommunications Products
	    Division		

1996	ADAC Laboratories	Custom Research, Inc. Trident Precision Manufacturing, Inc.	Dana Commercial Credit Corp.
1997	3M Dental Products Division Solectron Corp.		Merrill Lynch Credit Corp. Xerox Business Services
1998	Boeing Airlift and Tanker Programs Solar Turbines, Inc.	Texas Nameplate Co. Inc.	
1999	STMicroelectronics, Inc.— Region Americas	Sunny Fresh Foods	BI

2000	Dana Corporation—
	    Spicer Driveshaft Division
		Los Alamos National
		    Bank
			Ritz-Carlton Hotel Company, L.L.C.
			Operations Management
			    International, Inc.

2001	Clarke American Checks, Inc.	Pal's Sudden Service	

The MBNQA was established to raise awareness about quality management in the United States, and to recognize U.S. companies that have a world-class system for managing their operations and people and for satisfying their customers. A company applying for this award must provide evidence, in minute detail, describing its achievements and improvements in the following areas:

- Leadership
- Strategic planning
- Customer and market focus
- Information and analysis
- Human resource focus
- Process management
- Business results

Each of these seven categories receives a score, ranging from 85 (strategic planning, customer and market focus, human resource focus, and process management) to 450 (business results). The total score is 1,000 points. Figure 12.1 also contains a breakdown of the points within each category. For example, the 85 points within category 3 (Customer and Market Focus) is broken down into two subcategories: customer and market knowledge (40 points) and customer relationships and satisfaction (45 points).

The seven categories and their characteristics are described as follows.

Category 1: Leadership
- How the organization's senior leaders address values and performance expectations
- Empowerment, innovation, learning, and organizational directions

Category 2: Strategic Planning
- The organization's strategic development process, including how the organization develops strategic objectives, action plans, and related human resource plans
- How plans are deployed and how performance is tracked

Examination Categories	Points	
1.0 Leadership		120
1.1 Organizational leadership	80	
1.2 Company responsibility and citizenship	40	
2.0 Strategic planning		85
2.1 Strategy development	40	
2.2 Strategic deployment	45	
3.0 Customer and market focus		85
3.1 Customer and market knowledge	40	
3.2 Customer relationships and satisfaction	45	
4.0 Information and analysis		90
4.1 Measurement and analysis of organizational performance	50	
4.2 Information analysis	40	
5.0 Human resource focus		85
5.1 Work systems	35	
5.2 Employee education, training, and development	25	
5.3 Employee well-being and satisfaction	25	
6.0 Process management		85
6.1 Product and service processes	45	
6.2 Business processes	25	
6.3 Support processes	15	
7.0 Business results		450
7.1 Customer-focused results	115	
7.2 Financial and market results	115	
7.3 Human resource results	80	
7.4 Supplier and partner results	25	
7.5 Organizational effectiveness results	115	
TOTAL POINTS		1,000

FIGURE 12.1

Categories and maximum points awarded for the Malcolm Baldrige National Quality Award.

Category 3: Customer and Market Focus
- How the organization determines requirements, expectations, and preferences of customers and markets
- How the organization builds relationships with customers and determines their satisfaction

Category 4: Information and Analysis
- The organization's performance measurement system
- How the organization analyzes performance data and information

Category 5: Human Resources Focus
- How the organization enables employees to develop and utilize their full potential, aligned with the organization's objectives
- The organization's efforts to build and maintain a work environment and an employee support climate conducive to performance excellence, full participation, as well as personal and organizational growth

Category 6: Process Management
- The key aspects of the organization's process management, including customer-focused design as well as product and service delivery
- The supplier and partnering processes involving all work units

Category 7: Business Results
- The organization's performance and improvement in key business areas—customer satisfaction, product and service performance, financial and marketplace performance, human resource results, supplier and partner results, and operational performance
- Performance levels relative to competitors

The Baldrige criteria can be used to *quantify* and *measure* the more human attributes of your organization, such as attitudes, perceptions, emotions, values, motivation, and morale. The guiding force behind such changes must be the corporate managers. However, successful implementation of this program does not depend entirely on management expertise, but also on the cooperation of other people, including line operators, vendors, customers, and the CEO, who interact within the organizational system.

Few awards or programs have affected U.S. business as the Baldrige Award has. Initiated in obscurity, it has rapidly become a glittering prize for executives, who see it as an official recognition of their behind-the-scenes efforts to improve quality. Companies considering applying for this award must examine their motives carefully. If this is merely an attempt for the company to look good, and management is not fully aligned with the values of quality, the application process and resulting disappointment can have a serious negative (and often costly) effect on the organization.

An important point to be made here is that the principal benefit of the application process is the internal changes required, not the award itself, as Baldrige winners are quick to point out. Companies are using these criteria as a self-assessment tool. Whether or not they win the award, such quality-driven companies undoubtedly will be better able to survive and thrive in an increasingly competitive and quality-conscious marketplace.

ISO 9000 Registration

As the emerging global economy invites new and expanded international trade and business, corporations are finding that continued success requires doing business beyond the borders of their host country. As new worldwide markets bring together once foreign customers and companies, standardized business practice will facilitate successful business relations. Industry standards and practices unique to individual countries and continents become a problem when expanding markets, much like a language barrier.

Acknowledging, controlling, and reducing process variation lies at the heart of most quality-control endeavors. Conflicting business practices among various international industries represent one possible source of variation. In response to this problem, the International Organization for Standards for Quality Management issued the **ISO 9000 standards** as a series of guidelines. Revised in 2000, the ISO 9000 standards now represent the worldwide benchmark standards for process quality systems. ISO 9000 does not specify how business and industry processes must be performed but instead defines required actions that must be carried out within those processes to ensure quality products. Businesses and corporations that subscribe to ISO practices operate their systems in like fashion. In this sense, ISO 9000 significantly reduces process variation among companies in the worldwide business community.

The ISO 9000 set of standards contains the following three core documents.

1. *ISO 9000:2000.* "Quality Management Systems—Fundamentals and vocabulary." This document describes quality management system fundamentals and terminology.

2. *ISO 9001:2000.* "Quality Management Systems—Requirements." This document defines the requirements and is used to demonstrate an organization's capability to provide products or services that meet customer and applicable regulatory requirements.

3. *ISO 9004:2000.* "Quality Management Systems—Guidelines for Performance Improvement." This document provides guidance on quality management systems for those organizations that wish to move beyond the requirements of ISO 9001:2000.

The intent of ISO 9001:2000 is to shift an organization's focus from functional management thinking to process management thinking. It is structured to facilitate the idea that all processes are linked within the company.

ISO 9000 requires companies to establish and maintain procedural control by concentrating on procedure documentation. Employee training and awareness in quality procedures is required and documented. ISO 9000 mandates that ISO registered businesses have written procedures that are understood and followed by all company employees. ISO requires a documented and established system as well as universal conformance to that system.

Registration to ISO 9000 standards is increasingly becoming a prerequisite for doing business. Nonregistered companies are often blocked from entering the competition. The European business community led the adoption of ISO standards and is now nearly an exclusively ISO community. Major U.S. corporations are following suit. Required ISO registration of suppliers is commonplace, and in many instances an invitation to bid on a contract is predicated upon ISO registration. ISO 9000 registration requires application to a register, quality system documentation reviews, pre-assessment to identify noncompliant procedures, final assessment and registration or corrective action, and periodic surveillance audits for verifying continued compliance.

It is worth noting that ISO 9000 registration does not necessarily imply that the registered companies have good product quality. The ISO standards do not require a company to supply references to quality results or customer satisfaction. A registered company is not required to document attempted improvements in the product quality. As a result, ISO 9000 registration does not mean that all registered companies have similar levels of product quality.

Comparing the Baldrige Award and ISO 9000 Registration

Quite often, the Baldrige Award criteria and the ISO 9000 standards are considered to be equivalent in their purpose and content. Such is not the case, however, since there are many notable differences. In particular, the Baldrige Award depends heavily on results and customer satisfaction, whereas ISO 9000 registration is less outcome-oriented. It should be noted, however, that the focus of ISO 9000:2000 was revised to allow organizations to demonstrate their ability to enhance customer satisfaction through continual improvement and prevention of nonconformity. The Baldrige Award is just that—an *award* or form of recognition. On the other hand, ISO 9000 registration provides customers with some assurance that a registered supplier has a documented quality system in place and is following it. Although many companies are using the Baldrige Award and ISO 9000 standards compatibly, there is no guarantee that an ISO registration will translate into a high Baldrige Award assessment score.

X Exercises 12.1–12.8

12.1 What are the basic elements of TQM?

12.2 Briefly detail the areas of common agreement between Deming, Juran, and Crosby.

12.3 Cite the appropriate term associated with each of the following definitions.

   a. A feature/characteristic of a product or service that imparts its fitness for use.

   b. A chart used to monitor and control some aspect of a process.

   c. A combination of people, machinery, material, and methods used to produce a product or service.

12.4 For each of the following statements, indicate to which of the seven MBNQA categories the statement corresponds.

   a. Companies should have well-defined programs for developing their employees and involving them in quality-improvement activities.

   b. Firms must have well-established and well-documented systems for collecting and analyzing data concerning product/service quality.

   c. Top management must signal a commitment to quality values by being responsible members of society through fulfilling their societal or public obligations.

   d. Firms should be able to establish that their levels of quality meet or exceed those of direct product/service competitors.

12.5 If a firm is unsuccessful in winning the Baldrige Award, its efforts will have been wasted. Do you agree or disagree with this statement, and why?

12.6 What are the three documents in the ISO 9000 set of standards? Which of these would be used to demonstrate an organization's capability of providing quality products or services?

12.7 Roughly half of the MBNQA point total comes from which category? Consider a company or business you have worked for (in any capacity) prior to or during your college years. How does this category apply to this company, and what advice would you offer the company to improve in this area?

12.8 Do you see the seven examination categories for the MBNQA as distinct and nonoverlapping? Would you expect efforts within certain categories to have an impact on improvement efforts in other categories? If so, which categories?

12.3   QUALITY-IMPROVEMENT TOOLS

This textbook has emphasized the use of statistical graphs for examining sample data. This is especially important in the quality area, where such graphs allow you to understand the reasons for quality problems and to find solutions for eliminating them. They provide a means of conveying information that is more easily understood by a group of people, such as those attending a staff meeting or a team assigned to examine a particular quality problem. They allow you to see an entire process or to focus on a particular problem area within the process.

Recall that we defined a *process* as any combination of people, machinery, material, and methods intended to produce a product or service. The use of statistical graphs can provide you with various recordings of this process, ranging from an instant snapshot, such as a **histogram,** to charts recorded over time. This latter category of graphs includes control charts, the subject of the remaining sections of this chapter. Histograms, introduced in Chapter 2, provide a summary of a set of sample data, constructed by condensing the data into classes (groups) and constructing bars of height equal to the frequency (or relative frequency) of each class.

Another popular quality-improvement tool, the **Pareto chart,** was introduced in the Chapter 2 exercises (see Exercises 2.33, 2.34, and 2.57). This is an enhanced bar chart useful for identifying quality problems with the largest impact, and for displaying the relative importance of different categories of information. Another statistical graph in the category of quality-improvement tools is the *scatter diagram*. The scatter diagram is useful whenever your sample observations contain information on two variables, say X = percent of steel used in a rubber tire mixture and Y = corresponding tire durability. (The scatter diagram will be explained in Chapter 14, which also analyzes the relationship between these two variables.)

Two other methods of graphing a process include the **flowchart** and the **cause-and-effect diagram** (also known as the *fishbone* or *Ishikawa diagram*). The best way to understand a process is to draw a picture of it—that is basically what a flowchart is. The purpose of a cause-and-effect diagram is to examine a phase of the process in more detail and to relate causes and effects within the process.

Flowcharts

When a product moves down an assembly line, the process flow is readily apparent, so a flowchart likely is not necessary. However, if the flow of material during a production process is unpredictable (as in a job-shop manufacturing facility), or is not flowing smoothly, such a chart can be very useful in studying the process. While not statistical in nature, a flowchart can often identify key areas where a data collection and/or analysis would be beneficial. A popular use of flowcharts is to analyze the delivery of a service for which the flow of paper and sequence of actions may not be readily apparent.

Flowcharts should be used as a first-step examination of a process. In this way, all people who work in the process can understand it. Better understanding leads to more suggestions for improvement and more enthusiasm, since employees can see better how they fit into the overall picture. The flowchart provides a basic diagram of the *entire* process and so leads to better communication among everyone involved. Let's examine an example.

Metro Delivery Service provides package delivery services in a large metropolitan area. It has a money-back guarantee that any package brought to any of its dropoff stations will be delivered to anywhere within its area in 90 minutes or less. Metro achieved initial success with its innovative use of bicycles and motorbikes for delivering small packages. The bulk of its business, however, consists of delivering larger packages requiring an automobile or van. Lately, the owner of Metro had noticed a lack of consistency in meeting the 90-minute deadline. Metro management immediately began to blame the problem on what it perceived to be a careless attitude among the company drivers. However, the owner of Metro had attended several quality-improvement seminars and suspected that company performance could best be improved by making changes to the process itself.

A team of employees from all phases of the delivery process was formed and charged with taking a *systematic* look at the entire delivery process, beginning with a customer's arrival at a dropoff station and ending with the package's delivery. The flowchart in Figure 12.2 was the result.

The chart is basic and doesn't provide a great deal of detail. Nevertheless, it is a good starting point for the team to begin discussing the various operations and potential bottlenecks (the points at which the flow is constricted) within the delivery process. Final versions of a flowchart most often are *very* detailed, so that each employee can see precisely where his or her job fits into the flow of the entire process.

531

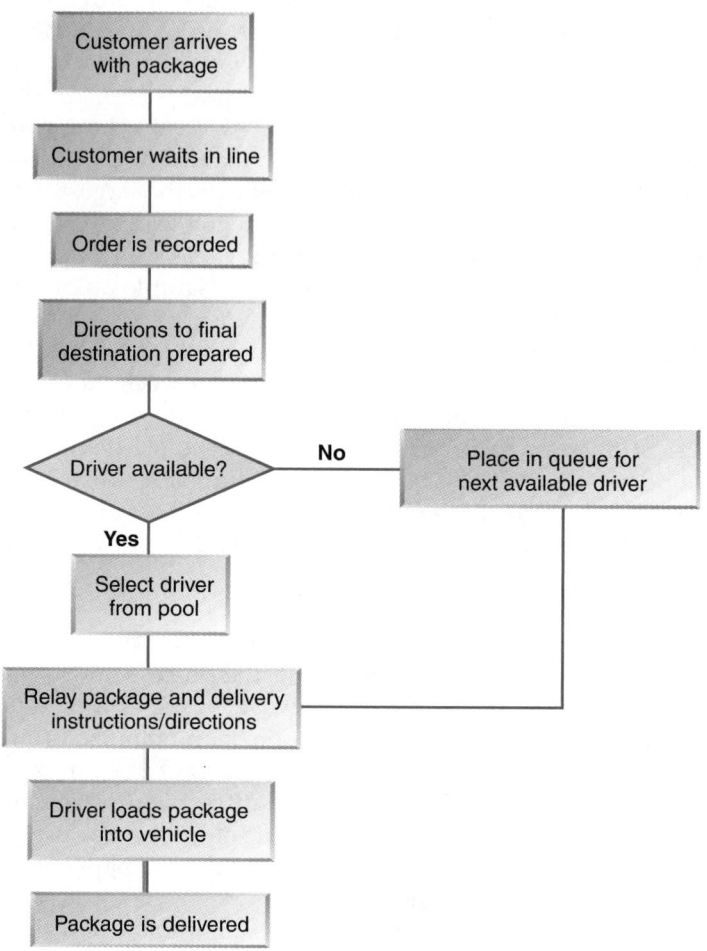

FIGURE

12.2

Flowchart of package delivery process for Metro Delivery Service.

The symbols used in Figure 12.2 consist of rectangular boxes (□) and diamond boxes (◇). The rectangles represent each step of the process; the diamonds are points where a decision must be made, typically requiring a yes or no response. A decision point does occur in this flowchart, since the dispatch supervisor must determine whether a driver is available at the time a package is due to leave the station.

The quality-improvement team at Metro was able to use this flowchart to discuss the delivery operation and to study potential problem areas. Their next concern was to explore why a package arrived late at its destination—a topic best examined using a cause-and-effect diagram.

Cause-and-Effect Diagrams

Cause-and-effect diagrams are often called fishbone diagrams or *Ishikawa diagrams*, named after their originator, Dr. Kaoru Ishikawa. In the 1940s, Ishikawa found that many Japanese plant personnel were overwhelmed by the many factors that could influence the outcome of a particular process. He created this very powerful diagram to represent the relationships between potential problems and their sources.

The basic form of a cause-and-effect diagram is shown in Figure 12.3. It has three features:

1. A horizontal arrow with the problem to be studied in a box at its far right

2. Major branches off the horizontal arrow representing the primary (main) causes contributing to this problem

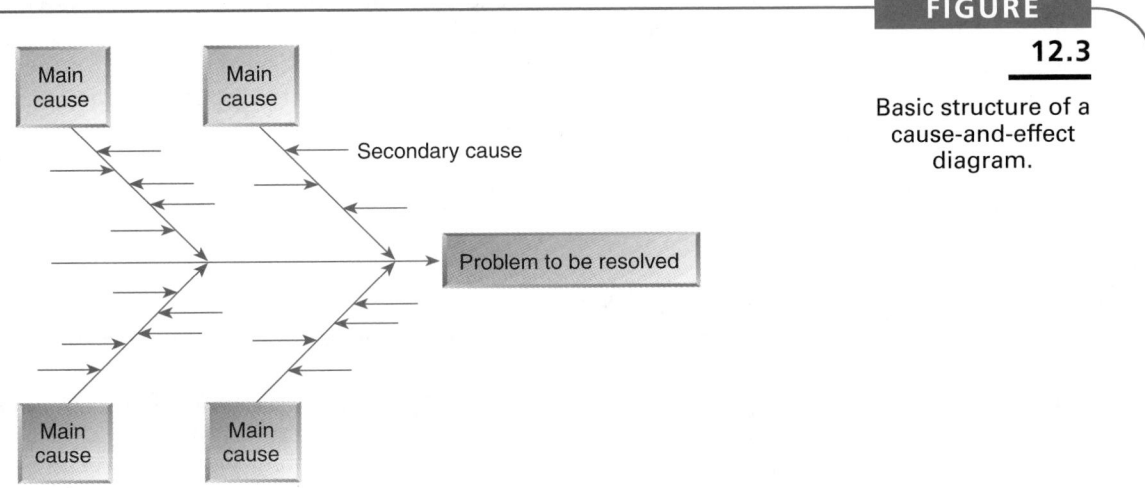

FIGURE

12.3

Basic structure of a cause-and-effect diagram.

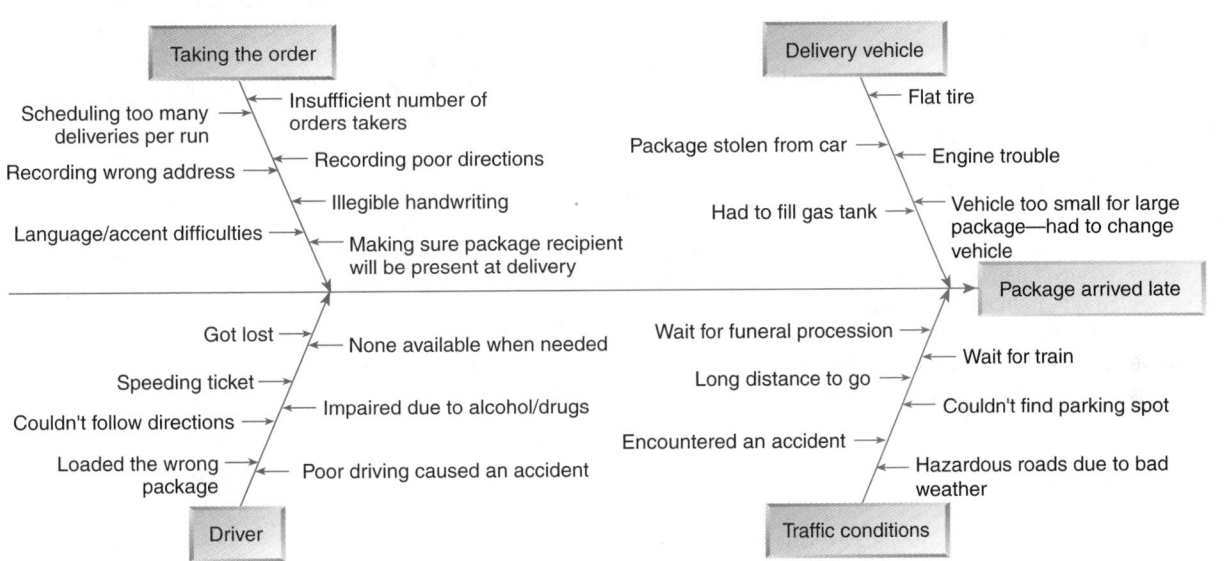

FIGURE

12.4

Cause-and-effect diagram for Metro Delivery Service.

3. Additional arrows within each major branch making up the secondary causes that contribute to the main problem within that major branch

If you examine the shape of Figure 12.3, you will see that it does indeed resemble the skeleton of a fish, which is why *fishbone diagram* is the more popular name for this chart. Although Figure 12.3 shows only two levels of arrows off the horizontal arrow (primary and secondary causes), this procedure of subdividing the possible causes can be continued for additional levels in Step 3 until all variables have been accounted for.

The team at Metro Delivery Service began by identifying four primary causes for the late delivery of a package: taking the order; assigning the driver to the order; traffic conditions; and the delivery vehicle. Secondary causes within each of these primary branches were brainstormed; the result of this effort was the cause-and-effect diagram in Figure 12.4. While developing this chart, the individuals on the team discovered (1) there was a feeling that everyone was working together (a true "team spirit"); (2) the chart enabled them to discuss the delivery process better; and (3) they were able to view the entire delivery process as a system rather than as a collection of disjointed activities.

A final word regarding this example: The logical next step for Metro would be to observe the process (obtain sample data) and construct a Pareto chart for each of the four major branches, summarizing the frequency of secondary causes within each branch. In this way, they could attack the problem by putting their resources into those areas that would bring about the greatest improvement in performance.

X Exercises 12.9–12.19

12.9 Describe reasons for using each of the following graphical quality improvement tools. What information does each graph best present?

  a. Pareto chart
  b. Fishbone diagram
  c. Flowchart
  d. Control chart
  e. Scatter diagram

12.10 For each of the following scenarios, select the graphical tools noted in Exercise 12.9 as the most appropriate for analyzing the given scenario. Explain the reasons for each of your selections.

  a. A university is interested in the relationship between a student's grade point average and the student's starting salary after graduating from college. The university's assessment office has interviewed students prior to and after earning a degree. How can this office show this relationship?

  b. An appliance manufacturer maintains records for all warranty services performed. Data analysis for warranty service related to their stoves and ovens has revealed cooking temperature problems generate over 60 percent of the warranty calls. The service manager wishes to investigate possible causes for the temperature problems. What analysis should the manager next perform?

  c. A production supervisor has listed all operations required in a manufacturing facility for each product. The supervisor wishes to examine methods for streamlining production. How should the supervisor compile and present the operations?

  d. A restaurant manager notices that the catering service provided by the restaurant has received numerous complaints. Problems occur during recording of orders as well as with delivery of the food. What type of chart should the manager use to understand the many factors that could influence the quality of the catering service?

  e. Every hour an inspector randomly selects five bearings and measures their inside and outside diameters. The inspector wishes to investigate the ability of the manufacturing process to produce dimensionally acceptable bearings. What graphical technique should be used?

12.11 Create a flowchart showing the steps that a customer would follow to apply for a mortgage loan. Include decision symbols that ask the following questions: (1) Is this a small loan or a large loan? (2) Do I qualify for the loan? (3) Will the home appraise for more than the loan amount? (4) Is the proposed down payment sufficient? (5) Will the loan be granted?

12.12 Small and specialized production companies often do not produce in sufficient quantity to provide a statistically significant number of observations. Some special order products may be produced in lots of less than 10. Single unit production is not rare. Although process control charts may be of little use in these instances, statistical quality control procedures can help identify problem areas. Identifying each step in the manufacturing process and then recording instances of error or difficulty in those areas permit the use of Pareto analysis for identifying improvement opportunities. Ten operations were identified, and the number of defects or problems with the operations was recorded over a 10-week period.

Operation	Number of Defects
Milling	11
Lathe operations	21
Drilling	4
Heat treating	9
Surface preparation	27
Testing	10
Surface coating	32
Layout operations	18
Metallurgy	16
Dimensional tolerance	19

Construct a Pareto chart for the above data and note operations where further investigation and analysis may be needed.

(Source: Adapted from "Tracking Attribute Data Improves Supplier Rating," *Quality*, October 1997, pp. 46–48.)

12.13 Review Web home pages of major corporations, such as Ford and IBM. Create categories for items that are missing from their home page. For example, does the home page have a search index? Is there online help? Is there an FAQ section? Is there a copyright and privacy statement? Is there contact information? Is there a link to financial news about the company? Is there a link to career information for jobs within the company? Which of these categories has the highest frequency of missing items? Which categories appear to have very few missing items?

12.14 The process of purchasing a new car can be very frustrating to the careful buyer. Construct a fishbone diagram to show potential causes of a car buyer being frustrated with the car-buying process. Consider the initial stage of viewing a car and the final stage of negotiating a contract on a car. Pursue each line of causality back to its root cause. Consider grafting relatively empty branches onto others.

12.15 Construct a fishbone diagram to show the potential causes of a customer being unsatisfied with a meal served at a fine restaurant. Consider root causes, starting with the chef, management, training of employees, and the facility. Split up any overcrowded branches.

12.16 Manufacturing companies probably provided the first American applications of the statistical quality control principles advanced by Deming and others. Successes achieved in the manufacturing sector have prompted the adoption of quality practices in other segments of U.S. enterprise. Many service industries now use quality control tools for understanding their processes, their customers, and for providing consistent and quality service. A hospital utilized fishbone diagrams as part of their analysis in efforts to reduce pain in cases of outpatient surgery. The sources and causes they identified are given below.

Main Causes of Outpatient Discomfort	Elements of Each Main Cause
Environment	a. Temperature
	b. Cleanliness
	c. Humidity
	d. Ventilation
	e. Lighting
Equipment	a. Operating table
	b. Headlight
	c. Rolling sitting stool
	d. Instrument sets
	e. Power drill
	f. Suction pump
	g. Standing stool
People	a. Same-day surgery nurses
	b. Surgeon
	c. Anesthesiologist
	d. Scrub nurse
	e. Patient
	f. Circulating nurse
Supplies	a. Disposables
	b. Irrigants
	c. Sutures
	d. Local anesthetics
Methods	a. Intravenous
	b. By mouth
	c. Antinausea
	d. Intramuscular
	e. Reversal medications
	f. Sedative
Measurements	a. State of consciousness
	b. Oxygen saturation
	c. Vital signs
	d. Pain

  a. Use the above causes and elements to construct a cause-and-effect diagram that can be used to better understand causes of patient discomfort.
  b. What steps should hospital staff take next for improved patient comfort?

(Source: "Charting New Territory," *Quality Progress*, vol. 30, no. 2, February 1997, pp. 63–66.)

12.17 It so happens that pizza is the preferred food of most college students. Chances are good that you are a pizza expert. Create a flowchart of the process that the local pizzeria must go through to make and deliver your pizza. Include decision symbols that ask the following questions: (1) Does the local pizzeria accept online orders? (2) How long will it be until they can deliver your pizza? (3) Is the delivered pizza what you ordered? (4) What form of payment will the delivery person accept? After creating this flowchart, see if you can determine what potential bottlenecks exist in the pizza making/delivery process.

12.18 A major crisis facing education today is the dropout rate for high school students. As a concerned citizen, you have volunteered to help examine this problem and to try to identify root causes of student dropout.
  a. Construct a fishbone diagram where the primary causes are Students, Faculty/Staff, Curriculum, and Family.
  b. For the Student branch, what are some possible secondary causes (e.g., low self-esteem and peer pressure)?
  c. For the Faculty/Staff branch, possible secondary causes are disinterest of teachers and class size. What are some others?
  d. Secondary causes for the Curriculum branch might include lack of basic skills and language barriers. Can you think of other causes?
  e. Possible secondary causes for the Family branch are lack of parental interest in education and truancy not being monitored. What are some others?

12.19 In November 2001, new telephone codes went into effect for long-distance phone calls in Mexico. Authorities did not announce the new dialing arrangement until the month before the new codes became effective. Under the new system, a long-distance phone call from Dallas to Mexico City will require 15 digits. Under this new system, phone calls to Mexico's three largest cities require an extra two digits, but to the rest of the country an extra three digits is needed. Many customers have phoned the operator complaining about the new system. Even operators were not sure of the correct phone numbers in some cases. The following table categorizes causes of problems with the new system. Using the information in this table, construct a cause-and-effect diagram that can be used to improve the implementation of the new telephone codes in Mexico.

Main Causes of Delay in Making Long Distance Call	Elements of Each Main Cause
Customer	a. Customer did not receive information about the new telephone codes.
	b. Customer was unfamiliar with dialing to Mexico.
	c. Customer incorrectly dialed the new telephone code.
	d. Customer knew of the new telephone codes, but thought that the old code would still work.

Main Causes of Delay in Making Long Distance Call	Elements of Each Main Cause	Main Causes of Delay in Making Long Distance Call	Elements of Each Main Cause
Operator	a. Operator gave customer wrong advice on how to dial using the new telephone codes. b. Operator kept getting a busy signal when trying to connect the customer to the phone line using the new telephone code. c. Customer did not give operator enough information to dial the phone number. d. Operator connected customer to a phone connection other than the one he/she requested.	Hardware Language	a. There was a hardware malfunction. b. Third-party interfered with the phone connection. a. Operator could not understand the language in which the customer was speaking. b. Explanation given by operator was too complicated.

(Source: "Mexico's New Dialing Codes Could Confuse Phone Callers," *Dallas Morning News,* October 31, 2001, p. 10D.)

12.4   STATISTICAL PROCESS CONTROL, PROCESS VARIATION, AND CONTROL CHARTS

A **process** is a combination of resources such as people, machines, or material that lead to a specific product. **Statistical Process Control** (SPC) was previously defined as the application of statistical quality-control methods to measuring and analyzing the variation found in processes. Before a company can successfully implement SPC techniques, it is important that all workers (including management) have a clear understanding of process variation and the value of reducing variation and keeping it reduced. SPC is not a tool to steer a process, but is a means of gaining process understanding to reduce process variation.

Variation exists in every process and in nearly every sample of measurements. Even the best automatic machine tools cannot make every unit exactly the same. Along with machine inconsistencies, process variation is introduced due to people, materials, production methods, and the environment, for example. These sources of variation also are the key components of any cause-and-effect (fishbone) diagram.

Consequently, the measured quality of a manufacturer's product is always subject to a certain amount of variation as a result of chance. We refer to this situation as a *stable* system of *chance causes* of variation. Variation within this stable pattern is random and inevitable. Variations *outside* this stable pattern is another matter. Once discovered, causes for such variation (called *assignable causes*) should be searched out and corrected. Detection of such variation is a key objective of quality control, and is the subject of the remaining sections in this chapter.

For a production process, one of the goals of a quality-improvement program is to reduce the variability in the process, with an eye toward eliminating this process variation—an impossible task, but a goal, nonetheless. By keeping a close watch on process variation and not overreacting to chance variation, a company can bring about dramatic improvements in product quality and a reduction of line stoppages, scrap, and rework. This can be illustrated in a very striking and entertaining way using a favorite device of Dr. Deming—the funnel experiment.

The Deming Funnel Experiment

The **funnel experiment** was often used by Dr. W. Edwards Deming in his lectures to illustrate that reacting to chance (random) variation has an adverse effect on overall process variation. Despite the good intentions of a machine operator to "fix" the system and move it closer to the process target, such manipulations only make matters worse. In fact, the more diligent the operator, the worse the result.

The device used by Deming was a funnel, mounted on a stand, that is placed directly over a target having a bull's-eye directly in the center, illustrated in Figure 12.5a. A marble is dropped through the funnel, hits the target, and rolls a short distance away. The target bull's-eye represents the process target (such as a stated length or weight), and the final resting place of the marble represents the value of

FIGURE

12.5

Deming funnel experiment (panel *a*) and MINITAB
simulation output using control strategies 1, 2, and 3 (panels *b, c,* and *d*).

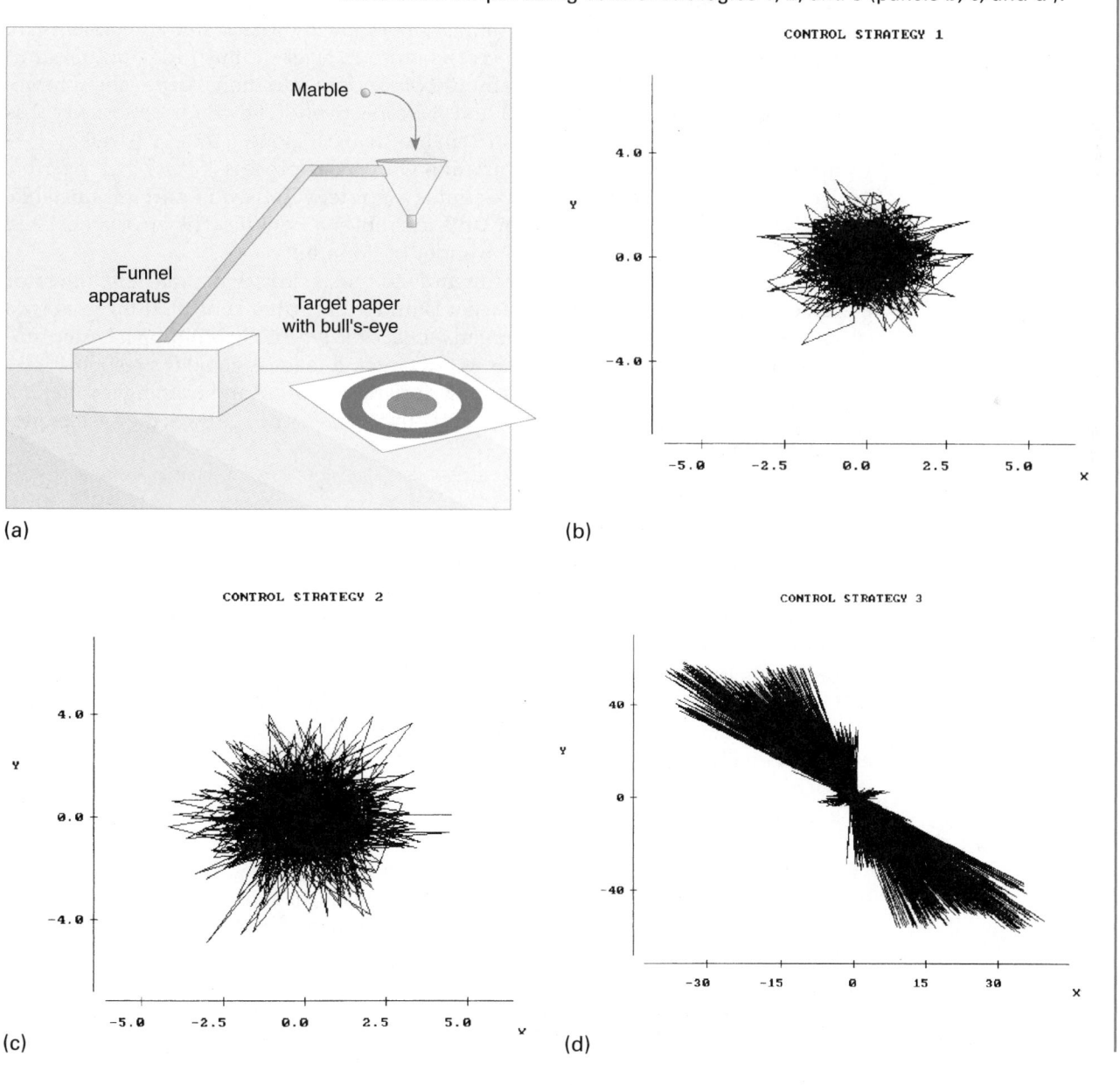

(a)

(b)

(c)

(d)

the final product. The direction and distance from the bull's-eye represent random variation within the manufacturing process. Despite the operator's best efforts, the marble will not come to rest directly on the bull's-eye each time.

Strategy 1. The recommended strategy would be not to react to this random variation and not to move the funnel. The diligent operator, on the other hand, could measure the distance and direction that the marble strayed from the bull's-eye and move the funnel that distance in the opposite direction. Two possible alternative strategies here would be the following.

Strategy 2. Measure the distance from the marble's resting place to the bull's-eye. Move the funnel an equal distance, but in the opposite direction. This will be called the "error relative to the previous position" strategy.

Strategy 3. Measure the distance from the marble's resting place to the bull's-eye. Move the funnel this distance, in the opposite direction, starting at the bull's-eye. This procedure could be called the "error relative to the bull's-eye" strategy.

A sequence of MINITAB commands was used to simulate this funnel experiment 1000 times; the results are given in Figure 12.5.* The bull's-eye is in the center of each graph, at the point $X = 0$, $Y = 0$. Control strategy 1 is where we do not react to chance variation and the funnel is not moved (no machine adjustments are made in an attempt to fix the process). Figure 12.5*b* is an illustration of this strategy, with, as expected, a certain amount of random variation. Parts *c* and *d* represent the outcome of strategies 2 and 3, respectively. The result of strategy 2 is stable, but contains more variation than the "leave it alone" strategy (strategy 1)—in fact, it can be shown that the variation within this process is *twice* that in part *b*. The error relative to the bull's-eye strategy (strategy 3) used in part *d* is unstable, contains a great deal of variation, and resembles a bow tie. The error associated with this strategy will eventually wander off to infinity.

The point of the funnel experiment is to make clear that a machine operator can only be held accountable for what is under his or her control. If the goal is to reduce process variation, then we can *improve the process* by building a better funnel or by moving the funnel closer to the target. It is management's responsibility to examine the process carefully and to provide resources and training for making process improvements. As Deming, and others, have said, "Attack the system, not the employee."

Control Charts

In a sense, **control charts** form the foundation of the inspection side of Statistical Process Control. These charts were first introduced by W. A. Shewhart at Bell Telephone Laboratories in 1924. Essentially, control charts allow you to monitor a process (usually, but not necessarily, a manufacturing process) to determine if the process is **in control** or **out of control.** A process is *in control* if the observed variation is due to inherent or natural variability. This variability is the cumulative effect of many small, essentially uncontrollable, causes. A process is *out of control* if a relatively large variation is introduced that can be traced to an *assignable cause.* Such causes are generally the result of an improperly adjusted machine, an operator error, or defective raw material.

It is important to note that a process may be in control yet entirely unsatisfactory. For example, your process of producing 10-pound bags of dog food might be perfectly in control, with little variation, yet a closer look might reveal that the process appears to be centered at 8.7 pounds, which would certainly be unacceptable to dog owners who check the weight of the bags.

---

*This sequence of MINITAB commands (a MINITAB macro) is in the MINITAB Macros folder in the textbook CD. If the file has been copied into say, C:\Temp, then type EXECUTE "C:\Temp\funnel" while in MINITAB. The result will be modified versions of Figure 12.5(b), (c), and (d). This macro is a revised version of the one in the *MINITAB Users' Group Newsletter,* 14, October 1991.

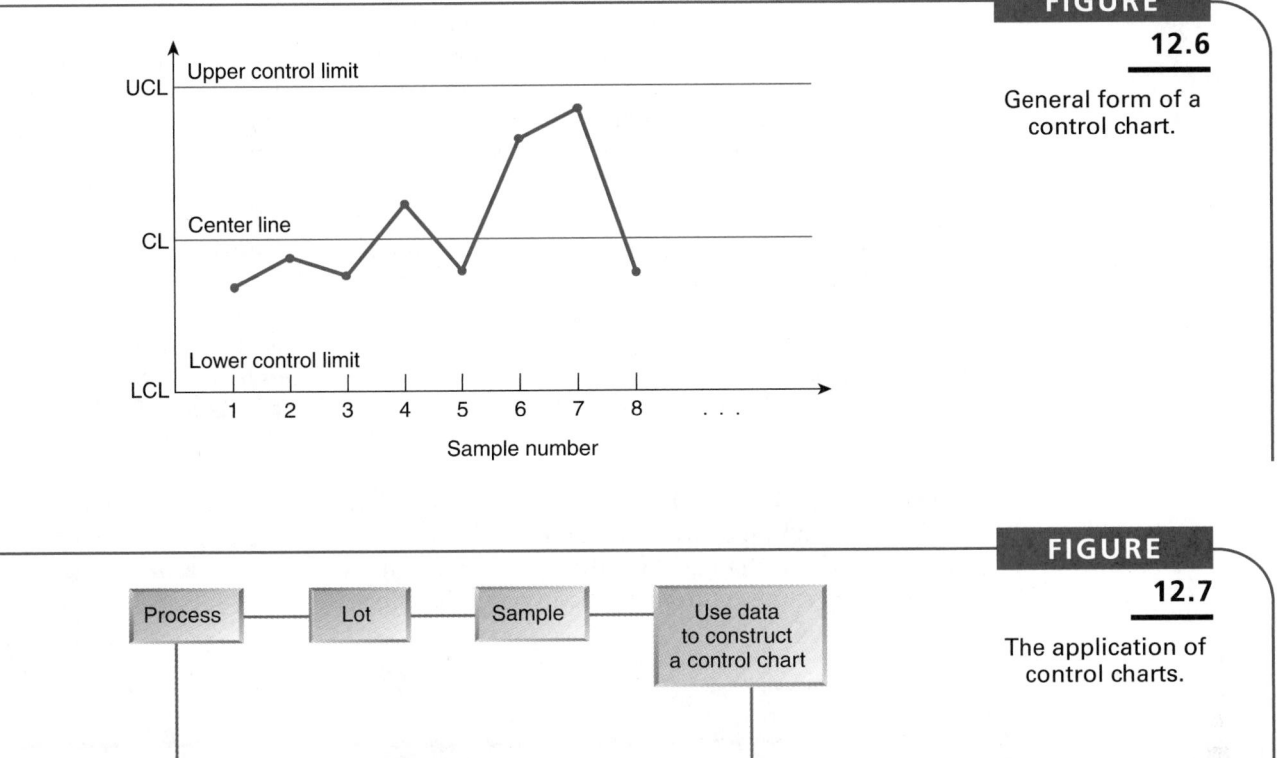

FIGURE

12.6

General form of a control chart.

FIGURE

12.7

The application of control charts.

During the in-control state, we say that the variation is due to **chance cause.** Such variation can be reduced by careful analysis of the process, but it can never be completely eliminated. On the other hand, variation during an out-of-control state is due to one or more **assignable causes.** Such causes are avoidable and cannot be overlooked.

The purpose of the control chart is to detect the presence of an out-of-control state, during which a large portion of the process output will not be conforming to requirements. If an assignable cause can be determined, corrective action is taken and an attempt is made to return the process to an in-control state. As Figure 12.5 illustrates, while a process is believed to be in control it should not be adjusted or tampered with, since such well-meaning adjustments generally result in an *increase* in process variation.

The general form of a control chart is shown in Figure 12.6. The chart contains a **center line (CL),** which represents the average value of the quality characteristic corresponding to the in-control state. The other two horizontal lines are the *control limits;* the **upper control limit** (UCL) and the **lower control limit** (LCL) are the same distance from the center line. *These limits are chosen so that if the process is in control, nearly all the plotted points will be between the two control limits.* For example, a plotted point might represent the average weight of a sample of five filled coffee cans. As long as the plotted averages fall within the control limits, the process is determined to be in control, with only chance variation present. The process of using a control chart to monitor and improve process quality is shown in Figure 12.7.

When measuring a *quality characteristic* such as the weight of a filled coffee can, the resulting data are referred to as **variables data.** Conversely, when counting the number of solder defects in the coffee can, such data are referred to as **attribute data.** Chapter 1 referred to variables data as *continuous* data and to attribute data as *discrete* data. The type of control chart that is needed for a particular situation depends on what quality characteristic is being measured and what type of data is being collected. For the filled weight of the coffee cans, we would undoubtedly be interested in the average weight of each sample of five cans and would construct a control chart referred to as an $\overline{X}$ **chart** ($\overline{X}$ is read as "X bar"). We would also want to maintain a control chart for the *variation* within each sample. The control chart to use for this situation would be an **R chart,** where R represents the sample range.

Since control charts are typically used to monitor *small* samples, the sample range is generally used to measure sample variation. The range is easier to calculate than is the sample standard deviation (s), and provides nearly as much information about the sample variation for sample sizes under 10. For sample sizes of 10 or more, the sample standard deviation should be used to measure sample variation, producing $\overline{X}$ and s charts. For a more thorough discussion of these charts, refer to the book by D. C. Montgomery in the list of Further Reading later in the chapter.

One cautionary note regarding the use of control charts: Most processes cannot be expected to remain stable over an extended period of time. A change in raw materials, tooling, or work shifts or any other major change in process operating conditions can change the process distribution. New control limits should be determined if the control chart is to retain its effectiveness.

12.5   CONTROL CHARTS FOR VARIABLES DATA: THE $\overline{X}$ AND *R* CHARTS

Variables data are obtained by observing a continuous variable, which has *no gaps* in the values it can have, over the range of possible values. A corresponding control chart could be constructed for controlling and analyzing a process whose quality characteristic is a continuous variable, such as weight, length, or concentration.

The first step is to obtain data for construction of the control chart. A number of preliminary samples (say, *m* of these) is obtained, each of size *n*, when the process is thought to be in control. Typically, *m* ranges from 20 to 25, and the sample size, *n*, is 4, 5, or 6. Define $\overline{X}_1, \overline{X}_2, \ldots, \overline{X}_m$ to be the *m* sample averages. Also define $R_1, R_2, \ldots, R_m$ to be the *m* sample ranges.

For example, suppose the quality characteristic is the weight of a filled coffee can produced by International Food Products. The first three samples are (data in ounces):

Sample	Data	$\overline{X}$	R
1	19.8, 20.1, 20.2, 19.9, 20.0	20.00	20.2 – 19.8 = .4
2	20.3, 19.9, 19.8, 19.8, 20.1	19.98	20.3 – 19.8 = .5
3	20.0, 19.7, 20.2, 19.8, 19.7	19.88	20.2 – 19.7 = .5

For these samples, $\overline{X}_1 = 20.00$, $\overline{X}_2 = 19.98$, $\overline{X}_3 = 19.88$, $R_1 = .4$, $R_2 = .5$, and $R_3 = .5$. These results and those for the next 17 samples are shown in Table 12.2.

In the quality-control context, the population consists of the *process* values. Thus we speak of the process mean, the process standard deviation, and so on. The best estimator of μ, the process mean, is

$$\overline{\overline{X}} = \frac{\overline{X}_1 + \overline{X}_2 + \cdots + \overline{X}_m}{m}$$

12.1

TABLE

12.2

Preliminary sample results.

Sample	1	2	3	4	5	6	7	8	9	10
$\bar{X}$	20.00	19.98	19.88	19.94	20.04	20.06	20.02	19.82	20.02	20.06
R	.4	.5	.5	.4	.6	.3	.4	.4	.5	.7
Sample	11	12	13	14	15	16	17	18	19	20
$\bar{X}$	19.94	19.86	19.90	20.12	19.92	20.04	20.06	19.98	19.88	20.08
R	.4	.3	.2	.5	.5	.4	.3	.5	.6	.4

TABLE

12.3

Factors for constructing on R chart.

n	d_2	d_3	D_3	D_4
2	1.128	.853	0	3.267
3	1.693	.888	0	2.574
4	2.059	.880	0	2.282
5	2.326	.864	0	2.114
6	2.534	.848	0	2.004
7	2.704	.833	.076	1.924
8	2.847	.820	.136	1.864
9	2.970	.808	.184	1.816
10	3.078	.797	.223	1.777

For our coffee-can filling example, the process consists of taking empty coffee cans and filling them with a prescribed amount of coffee. The quality characteristic is the filled weight of the can. The estimate of the process average is

$$\bar{\bar{X}} = \frac{20.00 + 19.98 + \cdots + 20.08}{20}$$

$$= \frac{399.60}{20} = 19.98 \text{ ounces}$$

We also need an estimate of the process standard deviation (σ). As mentioned earlier, there is more than one way to estimate this parameter, but since the sample sizes are small (under 10), the best way to proceed is to use the sample ranges (R) and carry out the following steps:

1. Determine the average of the m values of R. Call this $\bar{R}$.

2. Select the value of d_2 from Table 12.3 using the corresponding sample size, n.

3. Estimate σ using

$$\hat{\sigma} = \frac{\bar{R}}{d_2}$$

12.2

For the coffee-can illustration,

$$\bar{R} = \frac{.4 + .5 + \cdots + .4}{20}$$

$$= \frac{8.8}{20} = .44$$

Using Table 12.3, the estimate of the process standard deviation is

$$\hat{\sigma} = \frac{\overline{R}}{d_2} = \frac{.44}{2.326} = .189 \text{ ounce}$$

In Chapter 7, a procedure was outlined for constructing a confidence interval for the population mean using the results of a *single* sample. When constructing a control chart for the process average, a similar procedure is followed using the results of *multiple* samples (*m* of them). The center line and control limits are defined below:

$$UCL = \overline{\overline{X}} + 3\frac{\hat{\sigma}}{\sqrt{n}} = \overline{\overline{X}} + 3\frac{(\overline{R}/d_2)}{\sqrt{n}}$$

$$\text{Center Line} = \overline{\overline{X}}$$

$$LCL = \overline{\overline{X}} - 3\frac{\hat{\sigma}}{\sqrt{n}} = \overline{\overline{X}} - 3\frac{(\overline{R}/d_2)}{\sqrt{n}}$$

12.3

Notice that the control limits take on the appearance of a confidence interval where the value 3 replaces the value previously obtained from the standard normal (Z) table or the *t* table. The resulting control limits are referred to as the **three-sigma control limits.** It should be mentioned that the value 3 can be changed to fit the quality requirements of the process. Essentially, using this value produces control limits that will be exceeded approximately 27 times in 10,000 (.0027) if the process average and variation remain stable. Assuming a normal (or nearly normal) process, the value .0027 is obtained by finding the combined tail area under a standard normal curve outside ±3 (see Figure 12.8). In Chapter 7, a confidence interval for a population mean was constructed using a single sample. Control limits in a control chart are derived using many small samples instead of a single larger sample. Tying these two topics together, it may be helpful for you to view an $\overline{X}$ chart as a 99.7% confidence interval for the population mean derived using many small samples. Here, 99.7% is (1 − .0027) × 100%, where .0027 is the probability of a sample mean lying outside the control limits if the process is on target (centered correctly) and remains stable.

For the coffee-can illustration, $\overline{\overline{X}} = 19.98$ and $\hat{\sigma} = .189$, so the control limits would be

$$UCL = 19.98 + 3\frac{.189}{\sqrt{5}} = 19.98 + .25 = 20.23$$

$$\text{Center Line} = 19.98$$

$$LCL = 19.98 - 3\frac{.189}{\sqrt{5}} = 19.98 - .25 = 19.73$$

The control chart is shown in Figure 12.9. Notice that all 20 of the sample means are within the control limits, indicating that the control chart is ready for use. If one or more of the sample means falls outside the control limits, a search should be made to determine whether there is an assignable cause behind these extreme sample values. If such a cause is found, this sample should be removed and the control limits (including the center line) should be rederived.

The *R* Chart

To monitor the process variability, we use an *R* chart to plot values of the sample range, *R*. As we do with the $\overline{X}$ chart, we conclude that the sample *variability* is out of control when a sample range falls outside the control limits of the *R* chart. If the

FIGURE

12.8

Tail area outside ±3 for the standard normal curve.

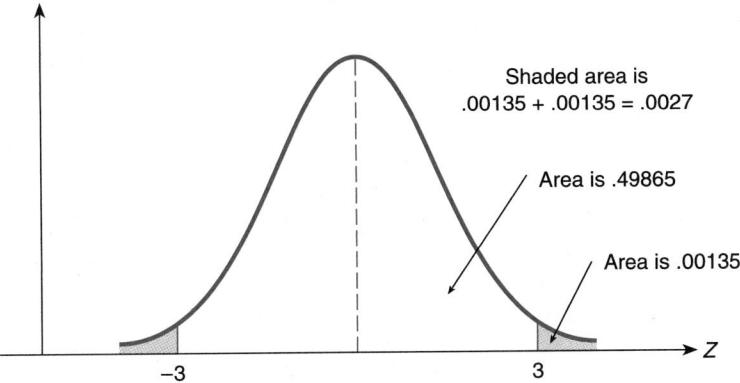

FIGURE

12.9

$\bar{X}$ chart for coffee-can example.

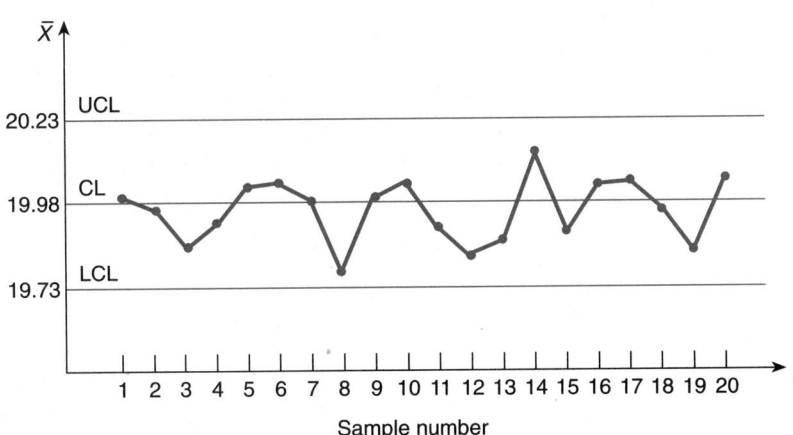

sample range falls within the control limits, the process variation is in control, that is, stable. Note that it is possible for a sample range to be out of control while the corresponding sample mean ($\bar{X}$) is well in control; that is, a sample can contain extreme variation but be centered properly.

The center line for the R chart is the average ($\bar{R}$) of the m ranges. For the summary data in Table 12.2, we have already determined that $\bar{R} = .44$. The three-sigma control limits are derived by again adding and subtracting three times the estimated standard deviation of $\bar{R}$, say, $s_{\bar{R}}$. The value of $s_{\bar{R}}$ can be derived using

$$s_{\bar{R}} = \bar{R}\left(\frac{d_3}{d_2}\right)$$

12.4

where the values of d_2 and d_3 are provided in Table 12.3.

The control limits for the R chart are

$$\text{UCL} = \bar{R} + 3s_{\bar{R}} = \bar{R} + 3\bar{R}\left(\frac{d_3}{d_2}\right) = \left(1 + 3\frac{d_3}{d_2}\right)\bar{R}$$

$$\text{LCL} = \bar{R} - 3s_{\bar{R}} = \bar{R} - 3\bar{R}\left(\frac{d_3}{d_2}\right) = \left(1 - 3\frac{d_3}{d_2}\right)\bar{R}$$

By defining

$$D_3 = 1 - 3\frac{d_3}{d_2} \quad \text{and} \quad D_4 = 1 + 3\frac{d_3}{d_2}$$

12.5

the R chart can be defined using

$$UCL = D_4\bar{R}$$
$$\text{Center line} = \bar{R}$$
$$LCL = D_3\bar{R}$$

12.6

Comments

1. Values of D_3 and D_4 are provided in Table 12.3.

2. Since a sample range is never negative, D_3 is defined to be zero whenever the expression in equation (12.5) is negative, that is, for $n = 2, 3, 4, 5$, and 6.

For our previous example, in which the quality characteristic is the filled weight of a coffee can, the limits for the R chart are easily found:

$$UCL = (2.114)(.44) = .93$$

$$\text{Center line} = .44$$

$$LCL = 0$$

This R chart is shown in Figure 12.10. Note that all the sample ranges appear to be in control, so the R chart is ready for use. If future range values fall within these limits, we conclude that the process variation is in control. Our procedure is the same as for the $\bar{X}$ chart: If any of the values in Figure 12.10 had fallen outside the control limits, a search would have been made for an assignable cause (or causes) for these sample points. Samples for which such a cause is found should be removed and the R chart derived again.

FIGURE 12.10

R chart for the coffee-can example.

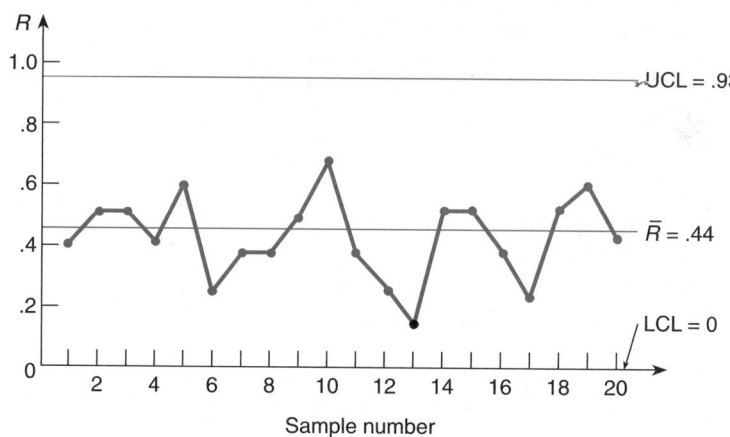

EXAMPLE
12.1

Following the construction of the control charts using the data in Table 12.2 (shown in Figures 12.9 and 12.10), samples of five filled coffee cans were obtained every half hour over a three-hour period. The data for these samples are as follows (in ounces).

Sample	Data
1	19.9, 19.7, 19.9, 20.2, 20.3
2	20.1, 20.3, 19.6, 19.8, 19.5
3	19.9, 20.1, 20.3, 19.9, 19.9
4	20.1, 19.9, 20.0, 20.1, 20.3
5	20.0, 19.5, 19.5, 20.1, 20.2
6	19.7, 19.8, 20.3, 19.7, 20.1

Using the proper control charts, determine whether the process location and variability are in control during this three-hour period.

Solution

The first step is to find the sample averages and ranges.

Sample	1	2	3	4	5	6
$\bar{X}$	20.00	19.86	20.02	20.08	19.86	19.92
R	.6	.8	.4	.4	.7	.6

Each sample mean is plotted in the $\bar{X}$ chart and each sample range in the R chart. Both charts are shown in Figure 12.11. Since all points in the two charts are within the control limits, we conclude that the process is in control (stable) and that no adjustments to the process are necessary.

FIGURE
12.11

Control charts for Example 12.1.

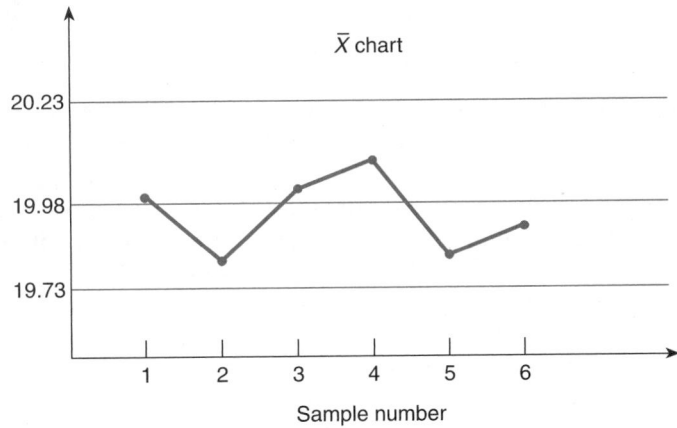

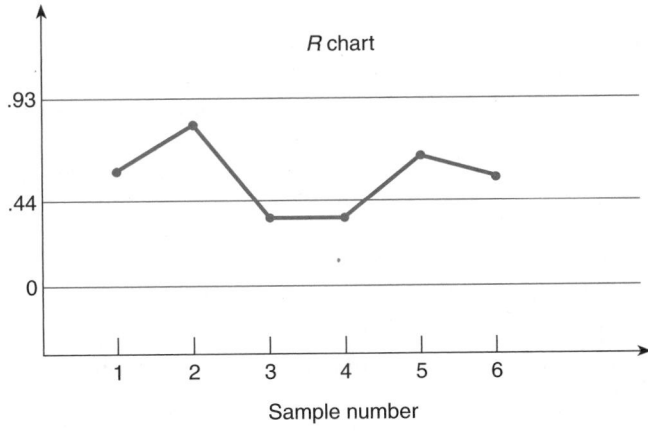

Steps for Making $\bar{X}$ and R Charts

1. Collect m samples of data, each of size n (in our first example, $m = 20$ samples of $n = 5$ observations each).

2. Compute the average of each subgroup $(\bar{X}_1, \bar{X}_2, \bar{X}_3, \ldots, \bar{X}_m)$.

3. Compute the range for each subgroup $(R_1, R_2, R_3, \ldots, R_m)$.

4. Find the overall mean, $\bar{\bar{X}}$, where $\bar{\bar{X}}$ is the average of the m values of $\bar{X}$.

5. Find the average range, $\bar{R}$, where $\bar{R}$ is the average of the m values of R.

6. To estimate σ (say, $\hat{\sigma}$), compute $\bar{R}/d_2$, where d_2 can be found using Table 12.3.

7. Compute the 3-sigma control limits for the $\bar{X}$ control chart:

$$\text{UCL} = \bar{\bar{X}} + 3\frac{\hat{\sigma}}{\sqrt{n}}$$

$$\text{CL} = \bar{\bar{X}}$$

$$\text{LCL} = \bar{\bar{X}} - 3\frac{\hat{\sigma}}{\sqrt{n}}$$

8. Compute the 3-sigma control limits for the R control chart.

$$\text{UCL} = D_4\bar{R} \qquad \text{(using Table 12.3)}$$

$$\text{CL} = \bar{R}$$

$$\text{LCL} = D_3\bar{R} \qquad \text{(using Table 12.3)}$$

9. Construct the control charts by plotting the $\bar{X}$ and R points for each subgroup on the same vertical line.

Pattern Analysis for $\bar{X}$ Charts

So far, our discussion of control charts has focused on determining out-of-control conditions by identifying a point beyond the three-sigma control limits on the $\bar{X}$ or R charts. For $\bar{X}$ charts, a closer look at the pattern of the control chart points (all of which may be within the control limits) may also reveal a process that is out of control and requiring attention. For example, six points in a row, all increasing or decreasing, indicates an out-of-control process, possibly due to a gradual wearing down of a machine part or due to operator fatigue. While the process may be not outside the control limits, it can be improved by identifying and eliminating this source of variation (an assignable cause).

Pattern analysis is concerned with recognizing systematic or nonrandom patterns in an $\bar{X}$ control chart and identifying the source of such process variation. To help us detect nonrandom patterns in $\bar{X}$ charts, we divide each chart into zones:

- *Zone A* contains the area between the two- and the three-sigma limits, both above and below the center line.
- *Zone B* contains the area between the one- and the two-sigma limits, both above and below the center line.
- *Zone C* contains the area between the center line and the one-sigma limit, both above and below the center line.

Specific patterns indicating nonrandom variation can be summarized as follows:*

Pattern	Description
1	One point beyond zone A
2	Nine points in a row in zone C or beyond, all on one side of the center line

*There is no general agreement about the set of nonrandom patterns. This set is used by MINITAB.

3	Six points in a row, all increasing or all decreasing
4	Fourteen points in a row, alternating up and down
5	Two out of three points in a row in zone A or beyond
6	Four out of five points in a row in zone B or beyond (on one side of center line)
7	Fifteen points in a row in zones C (above or below center line)
8	Eight points in a row beyond zones C (above or below center line)

These patterns are illustrated in Figure 12.12, where A, B, and C refer to zones A, B, and C. Note that pattern 1 illustrates what we have, up to this point, identified as an out-of-control state.

We will not attempt in this discussion to interpret the causes behind these nonrandom patterns; rather, these patterns should point out to you that *there is more to control chart inspection than looking for points outside the control limits.* The

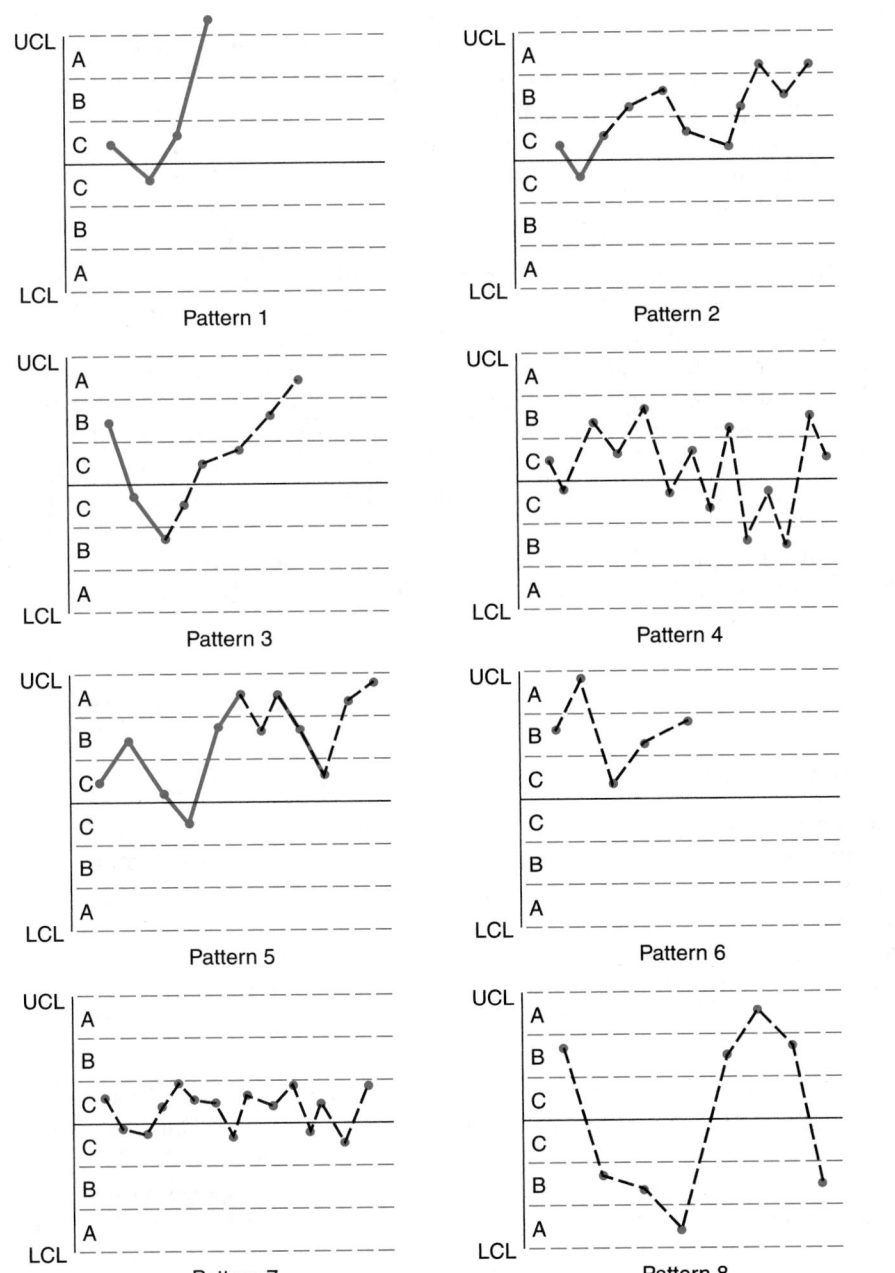

FIGURE 12.12

Eight patterns requiring a search for assignable causes due to nonrandom variation. The dotted lines indicate the nonrandom pattern.

FIGURE

12.13

MINITAB $\bar{X}$ chart with zones A, B, and C, containing three nonrandom patterns.

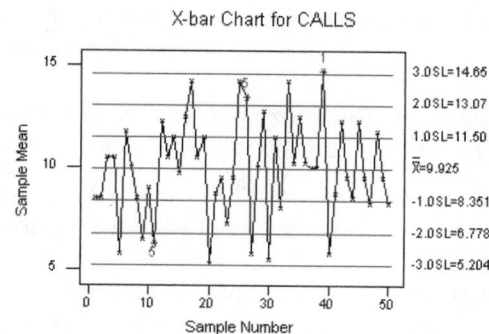

ability to interpret a particular pattern in terms of assignable causes requires a great deal of experience and knowledge of the process. For more information on pattern interpretation, see the textbook by Montgomery listed in the Further Reading section at the end of this chapter.

MINITAB will construct these zones in the $\bar{X}$ chart and will search for the eight patterns. The instructions for carrying out this analysis are contained in the MINITAB appendix for this chapter in the textbook CD. If MINITAB does detect a pattern, the sample at which the pattern is completed is flagged by placement of a value (1 for pattern 1, 2 for pattern 2, and so forth) directly above or below the plotted point.

Suppose that Home Security Protection is a company that installs and maintains home security systems. It is interested in monitoring the number of calls that come into its office as a result of a home system triggering an alarm because of an intruder or false alarm. The company obtains a sample of 50 consecutive days and records the number of calls between midnight and 6 A.M., 6 A.M. and noon, noon and 6 P.M., and 6 P.M. and midnight—a total of four observations for each of the 50 days. The resulting $\bar{X}$ chart is shown in Figure 12.13, where several nonrandom patterns are detected. The glaring pattern occurs in sample 39, where the plotted mean lies above the upper control limit (pattern 1). Two instances of pattern 5 (two out of three points in a row in zone A or beyond) are observed in samples 9, 10, 11 and in samples 24, 25, 26. Home Security Protection clearly has a process that is not in control, and it should take a closer look at what assignable causes are contributing to this excessive variation.

Microsoft® Excel Application Use DATA12-2

EXAMPLE

12.2

Excel-Generated $\bar{X}$ and R Charts

The control charts in Figures 12.9 and 12.10 were derived for the 20-ounce cans of ground coffee produced by International Food Products. Management decided to repeat this procedure on their 50-ounce coffee cans, sold mostly to restaurants and hospitals. Twenty samples of five cans each were obtained every 30 minutes, and the resulting 100 observations are contained in a single column. Analyze these data by first constructing an R chart using Excel and, if in control, then constructing the $\bar{X}$ chart. Are these control charts ready for use?

Solution

Excel does not have the capability of constructing control charts using its built-in graphical tools, but they are constructed easily using the KPK Data Analysis macros that accompany this textbook. Begin by opening file DATA 12-2. The first 7 observations are shown in Figure 12.14. To obtain the R chart, click on **KPK Data Analysis ➤ Quantitative Data Charts/Tables ➤ Control Charts.** Select **R Chart** and enter "A1:A100" in the **Input Range** box and "B1" in the **Output Range** box. Also, enter "5" in the **Sample Size** box and "R Chart for Coffee Cans" as the chart title.

FIGURE

12.14

Excel spreadsheet using KPK Data Analysis (Example 12.2).

	A	B	C	D	E	F	G	H	I	J	K
1	49.89	R Chart			X-Bar Chart						
2	50.13	Limit	Value		Limit	Value					
3	49.73	UCL	1.918		UCL	50.54					
4	50.77	CL	0.907		CL	50.02					
5	49.26	LCL	0.000		LCL	49.50					
6	49.85										
7	50.39										

R Chart / X-Bar Calc / X-Bar Chart \ DATA12-2

FIGURE

12.15

Excel R chart using KPK Data Analysis (Example 12.2).

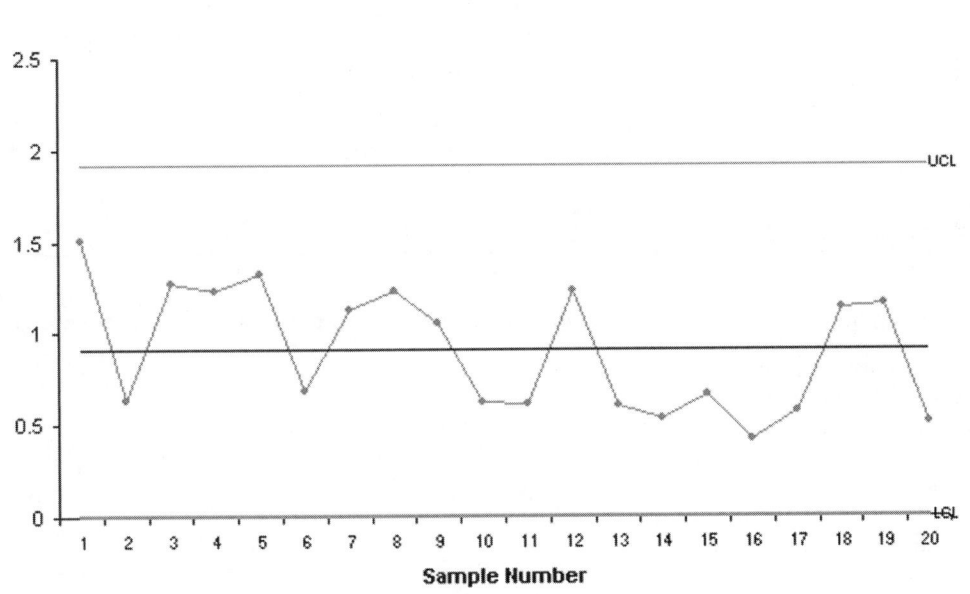

R Chart for Coffee Cans

Discussion. The resulting summary information is in columns B and C in Figure 12.14 and the corresponding R chart is in Figure 12.15. All 20 of the sample ranges lie between the upper control limit of 1.918 and the (inactive) lower control limit of zero. From a variability standpoint, this process is in control. In general, *if the R chart signals an out-of-control process, there is no point in continuing and attempting to interpret the corresponding $\bar{X}$ chart.*

To construct the $\bar{X}$ chart using Excel, repeat the preceding procedure, except select **X Bar Chart** in the input screen and enter "X-Bar Chart for Coffee Cans" as the chart title. Enter "E1" in the **Output Range** box. The resulting summary information is in columns E and F in Figure 12.14 and the $\bar{X}$ chart is shown in Figure 12.16. None of the samples indicate an out-of-control condition since all the plotted means lie between 49.50 and 50.54. A closer look at the $\bar{X}$ chart fails to uncover any nonrandom patterns.* The R chart and $\bar{X}$ chart for this process are ready for use.

---

*This conclusion is supported when the authors used MINITAB to search for nonrandom patterns in the $\bar{X}$ chart using this set of data.

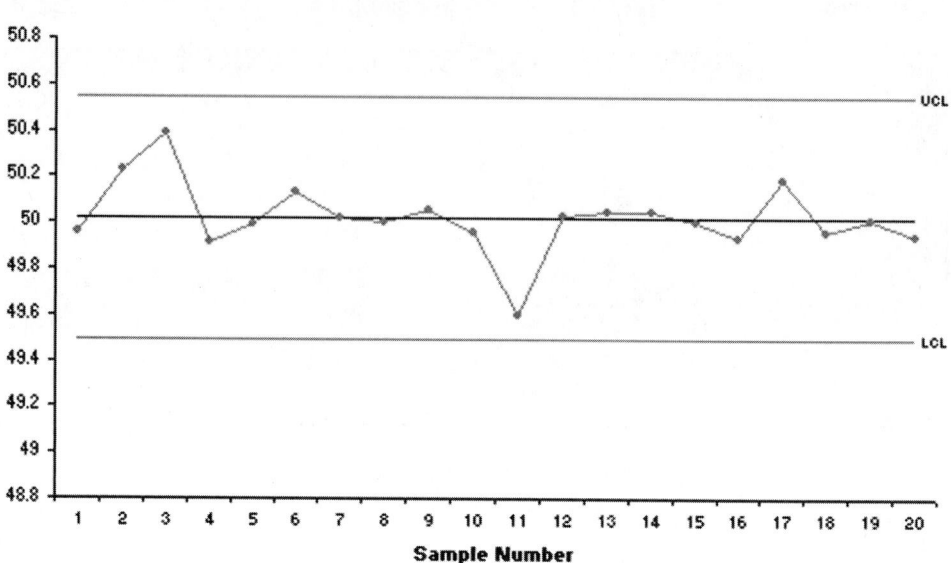

FIGURE

12.16

Excel $\bar{X}$ chart using KPK Data Analysis (Example 12.2).

X-Bar Chart for Coffee Cans

Exercises 12.20–12.32

Understanding the Mechanics

12.20 Thirty samples of size 5 are drawn from a process. The mean of the sample means for the batches of size 5 is equal to 130 and the mean of the sample ranges is equal to 10.

a. Find the center line and control limits for the $\bar{X}$ chart.

b. Find the boundaries for the A, B, and C zones of the $\bar{X}$ chart.

c. Find the center line and control limits for the R chart.

d. Would the process be in control for the following set of future sample means?

125.7   126.5   128.0   129.7   132.3   134.5

12.21 Construct an $\bar{X}$ and R chart for the following data, assuming a sample size of 5.

Sample Number	Sample Mean	Sample Range
1	380	27
2	420	28
3	435	31
4	425	42
5	422	33
6	433	36
7	430	18
8	445	42
9	430	38
10	409	38
11	403	33
12	418	28
13	400	22

Sample Number	Sample Mean	Sample Range
14	401	25
15	409	35
16	450	70
17	429	31
18	490	85
19	412	21
20	500	95

12.22 Samples of five cups of beer are taken at five-hour intervals from various depths in the brew kettle, and the alcohol content, as a percentage of volume, is measured. The following table relates the sample means and ranges for the last 10 samples.

Sample	Mean	Range	Sample	Mean	Range
1	2.8	0.9	6	3.3	0.2
2	4.2	0.2	7	2.9	0.9
3	3.7	0.6	8	2.7	0.3
4	3.9	1.1	9	3.4	0.5
5	2.6	0.5	10	2.8	1.0

a. Construct an R chart that can be used to control the alcohol content of the beer.

b. Construct an $\bar{X}$ chart that can be used to control the alcohol content of the beer.

c. Perform a pattern analysis of the $\bar{X}$ chart from part b by checking for nonrandom patterns.

12.23 A drill press operator selects samples of eight metal bushings and measures and records the internal diameter of the bushings at 15-minute intervals for the first two hours of her shift. The following are the sample ranges of the internal diameter measurements:

Sample	Range (mm)	Sample	Range (mm)
1	1.26	5	1.42
2	1.20	6	1.44
3	1.39	7	0.99
4	1.62	8	1.21

a. Construct an R chart using these data.
b. What are your observations concerning the pattern of these data?

Applying the New Concepts

12.24 Concerned with reducing costs, a delivery manager uses control charts for monitoring gas mileage of delivery fleet vehicles. Each week the manager randomly selects mileage and fuel records for five vehicles. The fleet of delivery vehicles consists of identical make and model trucks. Data for 25 weeks follow:

Week	Miles per Gallon
1	12.3, 13.1, 10.2, 11.6, 12.2
2	9.3, 10.5, 13.1, 12.2, 10.3
3	11.3, 12.6, 9.9, 10.6, 11.4
4	12.0, 11.3, 10.2, 10.6, 11.6
5	11.2, 12.3, 10.9, 11.5, 11.8
6	13.1, 12.2, 11.8, 11.2, 9.4
7	11.2, 11.7, 10.8, 10.1, 12.4
8	12.6, 11.3, 10.4, 11.7, 13.2
9	11.5, 12.6, 9.7, 10.5, 10.7
10	13.1, 12.7, 11.6, 12.3, 12.8
11	12.3, 11.2, 11.6, 13.4, 9.4
12	11.3, 12.6, 9.8, 10.7, 11.1
13	10.4, 11.3, 12.3, 12.6, 11.9
14	12.4, 13.5, 10.8, 11.6, 10.7
15	13.1, 12.0, 10.9, 11.8, 11.1
16	11.5, 11.3, 12.2, 10.9, 11.8
17	11.3, 12.6, 12.1, 10.9, 11.8
18	12.4, 10.7, 9.6, 13.6, 11.1
19	11.5, 12.3, 12.2, 11.8, 11.6
20	11.3, 10.8, 11.4, 12.0, 11.9
21	12.6, 10.2, 13.5, 12.1, 12.8
22	10.9, 11.4, 10.5, 13.2, 12.7
23	13.2, 12.8, 11.9, 12.7, 13.1
24	9.4, 11.6, 12.8, 13.0, 12.3
25	12.2, 11.5, 12.9, 10.6, 10.1

a. Construct an R chart for gasoline mileage.
b. Construct an $\bar{X}$ chart for gasoline mileage.
c. Comment on any nonrandom patterns in the $\bar{X}$ chart.

12.25 A drill press operator selects samples of eight bronze bushings and measures and records the internal diameter of the bushings at 15-minute intervals for the first two hours of her shift. The following are the sample ranges of the internal diameter measurements:

Sample	Range (in.)	Sample	Range (in.)
1	.016	5	.007
2	.014	6	.010
3	.012	7	.012
4	.010	8	.013

a. Construct an R chart using these data.
b. What are your observations concerning the pattern of these data?

12.26 The drill press operator in Exercise 12.25 continues to sample eight bushings for the next two hours of her shift and gathers the following internal diameter sample ranges:

Sample	Range (in.)	Sample	Range (in.)
1	.013	5	.019
2	.015	6	.021
3	.015	7	.022
4	.018	8	.023

a. What pattern has emerged during the last two hours of operation?
b. What are the likely consequences if nothing is done to correct the process?
c. What are some possible causes for the new pattern of variation?

12.27 Selit Corporation's vice president of sales uses control charts for analyzing regional sales activity. Five sales representatives are assigned to each region, and the mean quarterly sales volumes for each region's sales representatives are given below. If the Mid-Atlantic region is considered to be a southern region, then there are three northern and three southern regions. Compute the mean total northern and southern quarterly sales, and construct an $\bar{X}$ chart for northern sales and for southern sales.

Mean Sales by Region ($1000)

Yr/ Qtr	North- east	South- west	North- west	North Central	Mid- Atlantic	South Central
92Q1	$924	$1056	$1412	$431	$539	$397
92Q2	928	1048	1280	470	558	391
92Q3	956	1129	1129	439	591	414
92Q4	1222	1073	1181	431	556	407
93Q1	748	1157	1149	471	540	415
93Q2	962	1146	1248	496	590	442
93Q3	983	1064	1103	506	606	384
93Q4	1024	1213	1021	573	643	448
94Q1	991	1088	1085	403	657	441
94Q2	978	1322	1125	440	602	366
94Q3	1040	1256	910	371	596	470
94Q4	1295	1132	999	405	640	426
95Q1	765	1352	883	466	691	445
95Q2	1008	1353	851	536	723	455
95Q3	1038	1466	997	551	701	363
95Q4	952	1196	878	670	802	462
96Q1	1041	1330	939	588	749	420
96Q2	1020	1003	834	699	762	454
96Q3	976	1197	688	743	807	447
96Q4	1148	1337	806	702	781	359

(Source: "How to Teach Others to Apply Statistical Thinking," *Quality Progress*, June 1997, pp. 67–79.)

12.28 Refer to the data for the six regions in Exercise 12.27.
a. Construct an $\bar{X}$ chart for the six regions combined.
b. Compare the chart from part a with the charts constructed in Exercise 12.27.

Using the Computer

12.29 **[DATA SET EX12-29]** *Variable description:*

DelivTimes: Time in minutes that it takes to deliver a pizza

The owner of Pizza New York has built a solid business by promising timely and consistent home delivery service. She maintains a control chart procedure for monitoring these delivery times and searches for an assignable cause whenever an out-of-control condition appears. The data recorded in the variable DelivTimes are the delivery times for 200 trips over 50 randomly selected days, with four trips observed on each day. Use appropriate control charts to determine if this process is out of control.

12.30 [DATA SET EX12-30] *Variable description:*

BoltLen: Length of a bolt produced for a military aircraft

A quality engineer is interested in the precision of the production of bolts for a tactical military aircraft. A special computerized instrument is used to measure the exact length of the bolts. Forty samples of size 10 each are randomly selected, and the length is recorded in centimeters. The ideal length is 9 centimeters.

    a. Construct an $\bar{X}$ chart and an R chart.

    b. What is the first indication (if any) of the process being out of control?

12.31 [DATA SET EX12-31] *Variable description:*

BatteryLife: Life of a 12-volt battery in hours from accelerated life testing

The production plant manager has used control charts to monitor the quality of 12-volt batteries manufactured at the plant. A sample of three 12-volt batteries is selected every hour. These batteries are subjected to an accelerated life testing procedure. The life of each of the 120 samples of batteries of size 3 is recorded in BatteryLife. Construct the necessary charts to determine if you have any reservations about this process based on these charts.

12.32 Assume that a manufacturing process produces axle shafts having a mean diameter of 3.5 inches and a standard deviation of .01 inches. If the axle diameter from this process is a normally distributed random variable and 20 samples of 10 axles are periodically checked, estimate the upper and lower process control limits. Now use Excel's random number generator to produce 20 samples of 10 axles from a normal distribution having a mean of 3.5 and a standard deviation equal to .01. Construct an $\bar{X}$ chart for these observations and compare the control limits to the ones you estimated above.

12.6   CONTROL CHARTS FOR ATTRIBUTE DATA: THE *p* AND *c* CHARTS

Many quality characteristics cannot be measured. In these situations, an item is typically classified as either conforming or nonconforming, where the word *conforming* implies that the item conforms to specifications imposed upon the process (such as no surface scratches). Such quality characteristics are called *attributes.* The data gathered on these characteristics consist of counts or values based on counts, such as proportions. Examples of such data would be the proportion of nonconforming computer chips in a container of 200 chips (monitored using a *p* chart) or the number of blemishes in a square yard of sheet metal (monitored using a *c* chart).

Control Chart for the Proportion Nonconforming: The *p* Chart

The proportion nonconforming is defined as the number of nonconforming items in a population divided by the population size. It is denoted by *p,* and it corresponds to the binomial parameter *p* discussed in Chapters 5 and 10, where (as in Chapter 10) the value of *p* is unknown. Consequently, the process involved must satisfy the assumptions behind a binomial situation, described in Chapter 5, section 4 (page 183). When using a *p* **chart,** we concentrate on the parameter *p* and observe when this proportion appears to be out of control. If an item is judged on more than one quality characteristic, it is said to be nonconforming if the item does not conform to standard on one or more of these characteristics.

    The reasons for using a *p* chart include the following:

1. Quality measurements are not possible.

2. Quality measurements are possible, but not practical (such as determining the atmospheric pressure at which an electrical component is destroyed).

3. Many characteristics on each part are being judged during inspection.

4. The main question of interest is, "will the process be able to produce conforming products over time?"

The construction of a *p* chart is done in basically the same way as for an $\overline{X}$ or an *R* chart. A collection of samples (usually, 20 to 25) is obtained while the process is believed to be in control. Let T_i be the number of nonconforming items in the *i*th sample, and let *n* be the sample size. The resulting proportion nonconforming is $p_i = T_i/n$. For example, if sample 4 contains 150 items, 3 of which are nonconforming, then $n = 150$, $T_4 = 3$, and $p_4 = 3/150 = .02$.

The five-step procedure for constructing a *p* chart follows, and is illustrated in the next example.

Steps for Making *p* Charts (Constant Sample Size)

1. Collect *m* samples of data (typically, 20 to 25), each of size *n*.

2. Determine the proportion nonconforming for each sample. Call this value p_i.

$$p_i = \frac{T_i}{n}$$

where T_i is the number of nonconforming items in sample *i* and *n* is the sample size.

3. Find $\bar{p}$, the overall proportion nonconforming.

$$\bar{p} = \frac{\text{total number of nonconforming units}}{\text{total sample size}}$$

That is,

$$\bar{p} = \frac{\sum T_i}{mn}$$

Note: $\bar{p}$ is merely the average of the *m* values of p_i.

4. Compute the 3-sigma control limits:

$$\text{UCL} = \bar{p} + 3\sqrt{\frac{\bar{p}(1-\bar{p})}{n}}$$

$$\text{CL} = \bar{p}$$

$$\text{LCL} = \bar{p} - 3\sqrt{\frac{\bar{p}(1-\bar{p})}{n}}$$

12.7

5. Draw in the control lines and plot the values of p_i.

EXAMPLE 12.3

Repeated samples of 150 coffee cans are inspected to determine whether a can is out of round (the cylindrical shape of the can has been distorted) or whether it contains leaks due to improper construction. Such a can is said to be nonconforming, and *p* represents the proportion of nonconforming cans in the population. Twenty preliminary samples (150 cans each) are obtained.

Sample Number	Number of Nonconforming Cans	p_i
1	7	.047
2	4	.027
3	1	.007

Sample Number	Number of Nonconforming Cans	p_i
4	3	.020
5	4	.027
6	8	.053
7	10	.067
8	5	.033
9	2	.013
10	7	.047
11	6	.040
12	8	.053
13	0	.000
14	9	.060
15	3	.020
16	1	.007
17	4	.027
18	5	.033
19	7	.047
20	2	.013
	96	

Construct the p chart for these data.

Solution   Steps 1 and 2 have been completed. The next step is to determine the overall proportion nonconforming, $\bar{p}$, which is found by dividing the total number of nonconforming items (96) by the total sample size (20 · 150 = 3,000). Consequently,

$$\bar{p} = \frac{96}{3000} = .032$$

The control limits are then easily derived:

$$UCL = .032 + 3\sqrt{\frac{(.032)(.968)}{150}} = .075$$

Center line = .032

$$LCL = .032 - 3\sqrt{\frac{(.032)(.968)}{150}} = -.011 \quad (\text{set LCL} = 0)$$

Since a negative proportion is impossible, the LCL is set equal to zero and is inactive. The resulting p chart is shown in Figure 12.17. Since none of the 20 sample proportions are outside the control limits, the p chart has been established and is ready for use.

FIGURE

12.17

p chart for Example 12.3.

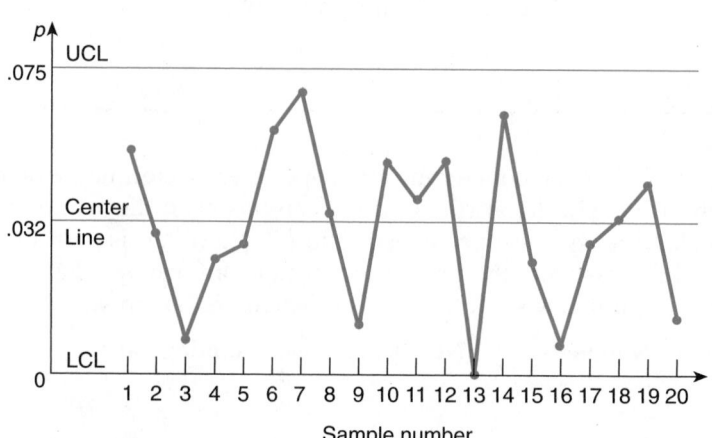

FIGURE

12.18

Excel *p* chart using
KPK Data Analysis
(Example 12.3).

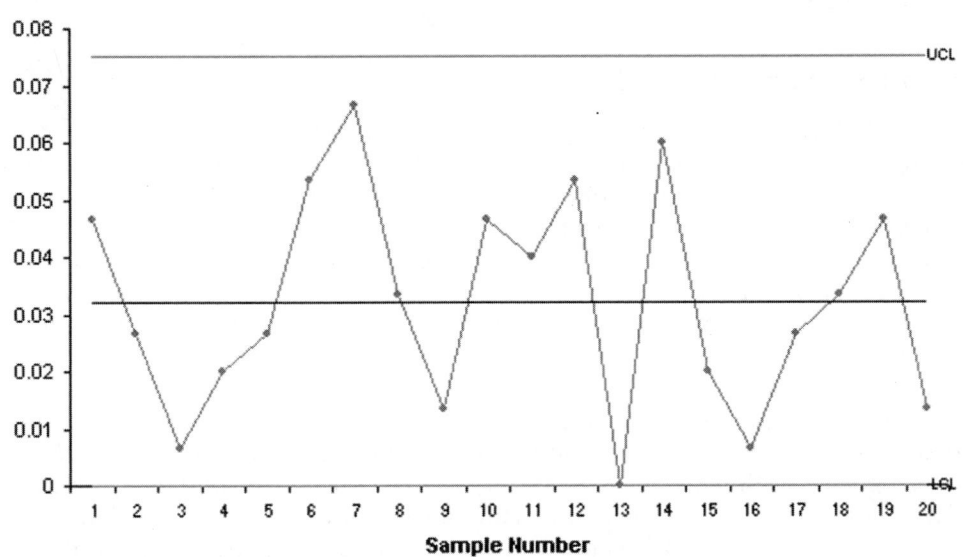

The KPK Data Analysis macros provide an easy-to-use procedure for constructing a *p* chart. Begin by entering the number of nonconforming cans (7, 4, 1, . . .) in column A. Click on **KPK Data Analysis ➤ Quantitative Data Charts/Tables ➤ Control Charts.** Select **p Chart** and enter "A1:A20" in the **Input Range** box and "B1" in the **Output Range** box. Also, enter "150" in the **Sample Size** box and "p Chart for Coffee Cans" as the chart title. Select "counts" in the **Type of Input Data** section because the data consist of the *number* of nonconforming cans in each sample of 150 rather than the *proportion* of nonconforming cans in each sample. The resulting chart in Figure 12.18 agrees with the one in Figure 12.17, so once again we conclude that the process is in control, and the *p* chart is ready for use.

EXAMPLE

12.4

Continuing with Example 12.3, the next five coffee can samples (each of size 150) produced 5, 2, 11, 6, and 8 nonconforming cans, respectively. Do the sample proportions indicate that the process is in control for each of these samples?

Solution

The five sample proportions are

$$5/150 = .033$$
$$2/150 = .013$$
$$11/150 = .073$$
$$6/150 = .040$$
$$8/150 = .053$$

Each of these proportions falls within the control limits in Figure 12.17, so the conclusion would be that the process is in control during this period.

Notice that the third sample came close to exceeding the upper control limit of .075, and it might be tempting to react and start tampering with the process to fix it. But this action would defeat the purpose of a control chart, since we conclude that the occurrence of 11 nonconforming cans is due simply to chance variation and no process adjustment is called for. As was pointed out earlier, such well-meaning overadjustments result in *increased* process variation rather than improved product quality.

Control Chart for Number of Nonconformities: The c Chart

The p chart dealt with monitoring the proportion (or in a sense, the number) of *nonconforming units* in a sample of n units. Since it is quite possible for a unit to have more than one nonconformity, we must also consider the *number of nonconformities per unit*. The c **chart** can be used for controlling a single type of nonconformity or for controlling all types of nonconformities without distinguishing between types. Situations in which a c chart could be used would include monitoring the number of scratches on a CRT casing, the number of minor blemishes on a rubber tire, the number of loose bolts on a manufactured assembly, and so forth.

The assumption behind the process is that the number of nonconformities occurring in a unit satisfies the assumptions behind the Poisson process, described in Chapter 5, section 6, page 198. An important characteristic of the Poisson random variable is that the mean and variance are identical, and so the standard deviation is the square root of the mean. Therefore, the control chart for the number of nonconformities per unit (say, c) is easy to construct. The method for constructing a c chart is described in the following five-step procedure.

Steps for Making a c Chart

1. Collect m samples of data (typically, 20 to 25 units), where each sample is obtained by observing a single unit.

2. Determine the number of nonconformities for the ith unit. Call this value c_i.

3. Find the *average* number of nonconformities per unit, $\bar{c}$, where

$$\bar{c} = \frac{\sum c_i}{m}$$

4. Compute the 3-sigma control limits:*

$$\text{UCL} = \bar{c} + 3\sqrt{\bar{c}}$$
$$\text{Center line} = \bar{c}$$
$$\text{LCL} = \bar{c} - 3\sqrt{\bar{c}}$$

12.8

5. Construct the control chart by drawing in the control lines and plotting the values of c_i.

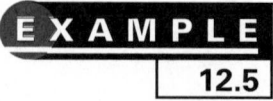

EXAMPLE 12.5

An automobile assembly worker is interested in monitoring and controlling the number of minor paint blemishes appearing on the outside door panel on the driver's side of a certain make of automobile. The following data were obtained, using a sample of 25 door panels.

---

*If the mean of the process is known, its value may be substituted for $\bar{c}$ in the control limits and center line.

Panel	1	2	3	4	5	6	7	8	9	10	11	12	13	14
Number of Paint Blemishes	1	0	3	3	1	2	5	0	2	1	2	0	8	0

Panel	15	16	17	18	19	20	21	22	23	24	25
Number of Paint Blemishes	2	1	4	0	2	4	1	1	0	2	3

Construct the control chart for this situation and determine whether all the plotted points are in control.

Solution

The average number of nonconformities (minor paint blemishes) for the sample of 25 door panels is $\bar{c}$ where

$$\bar{c} = \frac{1 + 0 + 3 + \cdots + 2 + 3}{25}$$

$$= \frac{48}{25} = 1.92$$

The limits and center line for the resulting c chart are

$$\text{UCL} = 1.92 + 3\sqrt{1.92} = 6.08$$

$$\text{Center line} = 1.92$$

$$\text{LCL} = 1.92 - 3\sqrt{1.92} = -2.24 \quad (\text{set LCL} = 0)$$

Since the Poisson variable is never negative, the LCL is set equal to zero here and is inactive.

You can easily construct a c chart using KPK Data Analysis. Begin by entering the number of paint blemishes (1, 0, 3, 3, . . .) in column A. Click on **KPK Data Analysis ➤ Quantitative Data Charts/Tables ➤ Control Charts.** Select **c Chart** and enter "A1:A25" in the **Input Range** box and "B1" in the **Output Range** box. Also, enter "c Chart for Door Panels" as the chart title. The resulting c chart is shown in Figure 12.19. Notice that the thirteenth sample contains an out-of-control observation. If control limits for current or future production are to be meaningful, they must be based on data from a process that is *in control.*

FIGURE

12.19

Excel c chart using KPK Data Analysis (Example 12.5).

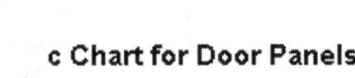

c Chart for Door Panels

The next step here would be to examine the thirteenth observation to determine if an assignable cause can be located. If it can, the observation should be removed, the control limits recomputed (using 24 samples), and the procedure continued until all observations are in control. If no assignable cause is found, you have one of two choices: (1) retain this observation and keep the control limits, or (2) drop this observation, assuming that an assignable cause exists but was not identified.

EXAMPLE 12.6

It was discovered that defective paint was used during sample number 13 in Example 12.5. Since this is a legitimate assignable cause, the observation was removed from the sample. Construct the modified control limits for the c chart, and determine if the control chart is ready for use.

Solution

Removing the thirteenth observation produces a new total of $48 - 8 = 40$ and an average of

$$\bar{c} = \frac{40}{24} = 1.67$$

The resulting control limits are

$$UCL = 1.67 + 3\sqrt{1.67} = 5.55$$

$$\text{Center line} = 1.67$$

$$LCL = 1.67 - 3\sqrt{1.67} = -2.21 \quad (\text{set } LCL = 0)$$

Reviewing the 24 samples, all of the number of nonconformities fall within the revised control limits, so the c chart has been established.

Comments

1. At first glance, it might seem strange that lower control limits are used for p charts and c charts. After all, why should we be concerned when, say, a sample proportion (p_i) falls below the lower control limit? Keep in mind that a plotted point outside a control limit does not necessarily indicate that something *bad* happened, merely that something *unusual* occurred. Whether this point lies above the UCL or below the LCL, a search should be made for an assignable cause. Perhaps this small proportion is due to extremely good raw material or to a change in operator skill/attitude. In either case, management should investigate the reasons behind this unusual event.

2. Any control chart should be modified when it appears that a substantial decrease in variability has produced a process that is more consistent. As product quality improves, the definition of what is in control should also change to reflect the new standards resulting from the improved process. One always hopes that *this year's control limits will not be acceptable on next year's control chart.*

X Exercises 12.33–12.44

Understanding the Mechanics

12.33 The p chart and c chart are commonly used when quality measurements are not practical. How do these charts differ? Which chart uses the assumption of a Poisson process to obtain its control limits? Which chart is appropriate for observing the proportion of nonconforming items?

12.34 Indicated whether a p or c chart would be appropriate for controlling the following:

    a. The number of defective fuses in a sample of 25.

    b. The number of defective sectors on a disk drive.

    c. The number of times that a computer software program malfunctions in a month.

    d. The number of overripe tomatoes in a carton of 50 tomatoes.

    e. The number of knots on a sheet of paneling.

12.35 Fifty samples of 100 items each were inspected for an in-control process. In the 50 samples, a total of 250 items were found to be defective.

   a. What is an estimate of the proportion of defective items?

   b. What is the upper and lower control limits for a *p* chart?

12.36 Surface defects have been counted on 18 circular steel plates. Using the following data, set up the appropriate control chart and comment on whether the process is in control.

Plate	1 2 3 4 5 6 7 8 9 10 11 12 13 14 15 16 17 18
No. of non-conformities	1 4 0 3 2 5 1 0 8 1 1 3 5 2 4 2 1 3

Applying the New Concepts

12.37 Consider a hospital that uses control charts for monitoring patient sedation. After administering sedation, nurses record their impressions of the patients at 10- to 15-minute intervals. Patients who were asleep or awake and pain free were considered acceptable and fulfilled the objective of conscious sedation. Other patient conditions were deemed unacceptable. Twenty-five entries each day over a 15-day period are given below:

Day

1	2	3	4	5	6	7	8	9	10	11	12	13	14	15

Unacceptable

17	7	5	9	5	14	5	0	6	7	13	14	8	5	0

p

.680 .280 .200 .360 .200 .560 .200 0.00 .240 .280 .520 .560 .320 .200 0.00

   a. Construct a *p* chart using these data.

   b. Is this process in control?

   c. What assignable cause might be the cause of any out-of-control observations? What should the hospital do?

12.38 Six operators produce boots at a leather goods manufacturing facility. Each day 50 pairs of boots are inspected from each worker and the number of defects are recorded. Data collected during the past two weeks follow.

Operator	Mon.	Tue.	Wed.	Thu.	Fri.	Total
Steve	2	1	2	2	2	
	0	2	1	2	3	17
Mary	1	3	0	2	1	
	4	2	0	0	2	15
Carlos	2	0	1	0	1	
	2	0	2	1	1	10
John	4	4	5	5	6	
	4	3	4	5	6	46
Andrew	2	1	1	0	2	
	2	1	1	0	2	12
Bethany	2	0	0	1	3	
	2	1	0	0	2	11

   a. Construct an appropriate type of control chart for the number of defects using the 10 data points for the two-week period. Note that 300 pairs of boots are inspected each day.

   b. Can the process be considered as in control?

   c. Construct Pareto charts for the number of defects by worker.

   d. What corrective measures do you suggest?

12.39 Web design experts believe that the greatest mistake exhibited by Web sites today is poor information architecture. Research strongly indicates that 80% of usability problems are directly related to the structure of a Web site. Poor structure causes broken links and error messages that don't tell users what to do next. Suppose that a company has a large intranet Web site and uses software to detect broken links and error messages. Assume that this software is run weekly at the company and the number of broken links and error messages obtained from going to a location linked to a Web page are noted. These data are present for 14 weeks.

Week	1	2	3	4	5	6	7	8	9	10	11	12	13	14
Broken Links	2	1	0	1	3	0	0	0	1	3	4	5	8	4

   a. What type of control chart is appropriate to use in this instance? Why?

   b. Construct the appropriate control chart for these data. Is this process in control?

(Source: "Giving Web Users a Break," *Marketing Magazine*, 106, no. 37, September 2001, p. 13.)

12.40 Bill 3 was passed in November 1989 in the province of Manitoba, Canada. Bill 3 was among the most stringent drinking-and-driving legislation ever enacted in North America. Its proponents pointed to the decrease in alcohol-related traffic fatalities in the year following the passage of Bill 3. Its critics, however, maintained that the decrease in alcohol-related fatalities was due simply to random chance. The following data represent the proportion of total traffic fatalities that were alcohol-related for the 1973 to 1990 time period. For the sake of simplicity, assume that there was a constant 250 traffic fatalities per year for the period in question.

Year	Alcohol-Related Fatalities	Year	Alcohol-Related Fatalities
1973	0.4940	1982	0.4500
1974	0.4455	1983	0.4000
1975	0.5354	1984	0.3916
1976	0.5398	1985	0.4440
1977	0.4865	1986	0.5380
1978	0.4038	1987	0.4301
1979	0.6425	1988	0.4744
1980	0.4457	1989	0.4277
1981	0.5357	1990	0.4211

   a. Construct a *p* chart for these data.

   b. Does the *p* chart in part a indicate an in-control state?

   c. Would you agree with the proponents of Bill 3 that the legislation was successful in significantly reducing alcohol-related traffic fatalities?

(Source: Fred A. Spring, "A Bill's Effect on Alcohol-Related Traffic Fatalities," *Quality Progress* 27, no. 2, February 1994, pp. 35–38.)

Using the Computer

12.41 [DATA SET EX12-41] *Variable description:*

NumAirBubbles: Number of air bubbles in the production of picture windows

A quality engineer is interested in the quality of picture windows produced at his plant. Every fiftieth window produced is selected, and a sample of 40 windows is obtained where the number of air bubbles is recorded. Construct a control chart to determine those samples where the chart indicates that the process is out of control.

12.42 [DATA SET EX12-42] *Variable description:*

NumAbsences: Number of absences per day from a plant with 200 employees

The production manager of a plant is concerned about the affect that too many absences may have on the productivity of a plant. The manager does not mind some absences per day, as employees may use sick time, personal leave, or comp time. If too few absences are occurring, this might indicate that in the future too many employees will be absent on the same day. Also many absences are sometimes followed by very few absences. The manager would like to gain insight into the process from a control chart of the number of absences per day from a total of 200 employees over 30 working days. What conclusions can you reach?

12.43 [DATA SET EX12-43] *Variable description:*

NumErrAcct: Number of errors found in purchase orders

A manager of an accounting office is concerned that purchase orders may contain too many errors and hence result in excessive returned merchandise. To gain insight into the process in which purchase orders are filled out, 35 purchase orders are randomly selected and the number of errors are recorded in the variable NumErrAcct. What control chart is appropriate for this situation? Construct this chart and discuss the results.

12.44 [DATA SET EX12-44] *Variable description:*

SuppA: Number of defective cases in sampled batch of 150 cases from supplier A

SuppB: Number of defective cases in sampled batch of 120 cases from supplier B

A recording studio and production company use two suppliers for their clear plastic cassette tape cases. A case is considered defective if it is scratched, cloudy, cracked, or otherwise unusable. Data from 50 samples collected from each of the two suppliers are recorded in the variables SuppA and SuppB.

   a. Construct the appropriate control chart for each of the two suppliers.

   b. Do either of these two processes indicate an out-of-control condition?

   c. Comment on the performance of the two suppliers. Which would you prefer to use?

12.7   PROCESS CAPABILITY

We have dealt with control charts that monitor a process to determine whether it is operating in control. But the term "in control" merely indicates that the process is performing within natural variation *as measured by past performance*. It is entirely possible that the process might be in control but not be *capable* of meeting the process requirements, referred to as **specification limits.**

For example, suppose the process that produces piston rings is operating in control, with the inside diameter of the rings centered at 12.1 cm with a standard deviation of .03 cm. However, the product specifications state that in order to be of acceptable quality, the piston rings must have an inside diameter between 11.95 and 12.05 cm. The value 11.95 is called the *lower spec limit* (LSL) and 12.05 is the *upper spec limit* (USL). From this information, we would have to conclude that the piston rings process is incapable of meeting the required specifications (specs) (see Figure 12.20).

In Figure 12.20, the difference between 12.19 and 12.01 is 6 standard deviations (estimated) and is referred to as the **process spread:**

$$\text{process spread} = 6\hat{\sigma}$$

12.9

For this illustration, $6\hat{\sigma} = 12.19 - 12.01 = .18$ cm.

FIGURE

12.20

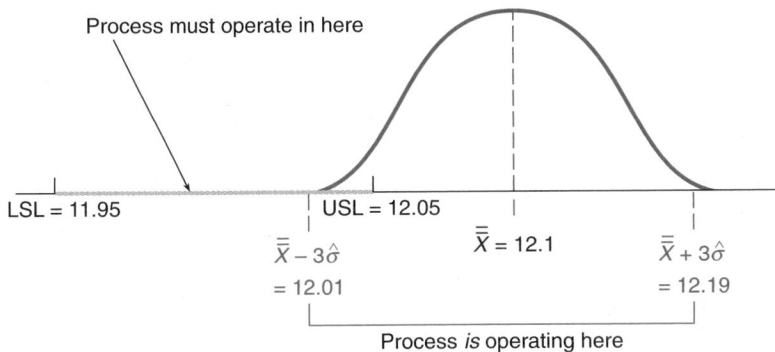

FIGURE

12.21

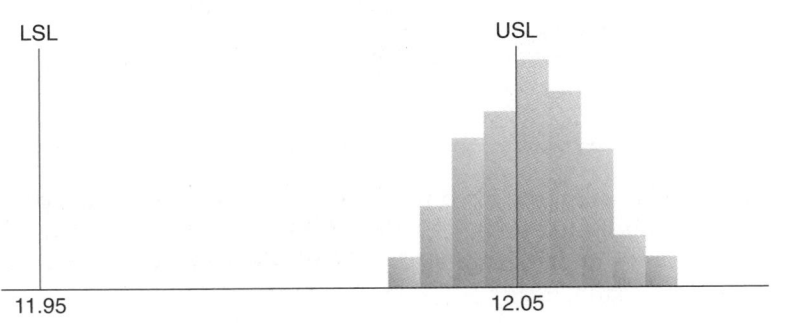

A visual method of checking process capability is to obtain a fairly large sample and plot a histogram against the required spec limits. In the preceding example, the quality characteristic of interest is the inside diameter of a piston ring; suppose that the histogram of inside diameters looks like the one in Figure 12.21. Visually, it is clear that the process is centered at a value much too large and that the process is not capable of meeting the required specifications.

This section will introduce three descriptors of **process capability** that *measure* how well the process is conforming to the required specifications. We will move away from a subjective visual assessment of process capability toward an objective measure that is based on facts (sample information) rather than opinion.

Process Capability Ratios, C_p and C_{pk}

When computing the first measure (C_p), there are three assumptions:

1. The process output is centered within specification.

2. The process is normally distributed.

3. The process is stable (in control).

The measure C_p is simply a comparison of the process capability with the specifications, and it is a valid indicator *only* if the above assumptions are true. It is clear from Figure 12.21 that assumption 1 is violated for the piston ring illustration, since the process is centered at a value much larger than 12 cm (the center of the spec limits).

Determining the ratio C_p is similar to comparing the width of a car driving down the center of a road to the width of the road, where the width of the car is the process spread, $6\hat{\sigma}$, and the width of the road is the width of the process specs

(USL – LSL). The process capability ratio C_p for a two-sided spec limit is found by dividing these two widths:

$$C_p = \frac{USL - LSL}{6\hat{\sigma}}$$

12.10

Often, process specifications are one-sided, specifying only a lower spec limit (for example, the bursting strength of a glass bottle) or an upper spec limit (for example, the number of missing rivets in an aircraft assembly). For these situations, we compare the distance between the sample mean and the spec limit with three standard deviations:

$$C_p = \frac{USL - \overline{X}}{3\hat{\sigma}} \qquad \text{(upper spec limit only)}$$

12.11

$$C_p = \frac{\overline{X} - LSL}{3\hat{\sigma}} \qquad \text{(lower spec limit only)}$$

12.12

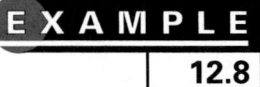

12.7

The specification limits for the filled weight of a coffee can are 20 ± 1 (ounces); that is, the USL is 21 ounces and the LSL is 19 ounces. A sample of 100 cans provides a mean of 19.98 ounces and an estimated standard deviation of 0.189 ounce. Determine the capability ratio, C_p.

Solution   The process spread is $(6)(.189) = 1.134$ ounce. The value of C_p can be found from equation 12.10:

$$C_p = \frac{21 - 19}{1.134} = 1.76$$

E X A M P L E

12.8

The bursting strength of a particular soft-drink container has a lower spec limit of 200 psi (pounds per square inch). A sample of 100 containers produced a sample mean of 226 psi and a standard deviation of 11.3 psi. What is the capability ratio, C_p?

Solution   Using equation 12.12,

$$C_p = \frac{226 - 200}{3(11.3)} = \frac{26}{33.9} = .77$$

Interpreting C_p

A general rule for interpreting C_p is as follows:*

$C_p \geq 1.33$	good
$1 \leq C_p < 1.33$	adequate
$C_p < 1$	inadequate

For Example 12.7, the value of $C_p = 1.76$ would be in the "good" category, and we would conclude that the *potential* capability of the coffee-can process to meet the

---

*A more precise interpretation of C_p should consider whether the process is new or existing and whether the quality characteristic is of critical importance (such as one related to consumer safety). See the reference by Montgomery in the Further Reading section for more detail.

product specs is very good, with little chance of producing a nonconforming (out-of-spec) product. The term *potential* is needed here, since *no attention has been paid to where the process is centered when determining this capability ratio.* The C_{pk} capability ratio (discussed next) considers this very important aspect of the process performance.

A value of $C_p = .77$ was determined for Example 12.8, indicating that this process has a tendency to operate dangerously close to the lower spec limit. We can expect that an unsatisfactory number of containers will have a bursting strength below the lower spec limit of 200 psi.

Consideration of Process Location: Use of C_{pk}

When determining the C_p ratio, we used the analogy of comparing the width of a car (the process spread) to the width of the road (the difference between the spec limits), while *assuming* that the car is traveling down the center of the road. The C_p ratio is a measure of potential capability.

The C_{pk} process capability ratio not only compares the width of the car to the width of the road but also questions whether the car is on or off the center stripe. This ratio examines the distance from the process center to the *nearest* spec limit (assuming both an upper and a lower spec limit), as illustrated in Figure 12.22.

There are four assumptions behind the use of the C_{pk} ratio:

1. The process may or may not be centered in spec.

2. The process is normally distributed.

3. The process is stable.

4. Control charts will be used to monitor the process over time.

Procedure for Finding C_{pk}.

1. Determine $R_L = \dfrac{\overline{X} - \text{LSL}}{3\hat{\sigma}}$

2. Determine $R_U = \dfrac{\text{USL} - \overline{X}}{3\hat{\sigma}}$

3. $C_{pk} = $ Minimum of R_L and R_U

Referring to Example 12.7, we have $\bar{x} = 19.98$ ounces, $\hat{\sigma} = .189$ ounce, LSL $= 19$ ounces, and USL $= 21$ ounces. Consequently,

$$R_L = \frac{19.98 - 19}{3(.189)} = 1.73$$

$$R_U = \frac{21 - 19.98}{3(.189)} = 1.80$$

and so C_{pk} is the minimum of 1.73 and 1.80, that is, $C_{pk} = 1.73$.

The value of C_{pk} will always be less than or equal to the corresponding value of C_p. *A generally acceptable value of C_{pk} is 1.* Consequently, the coffee-can process

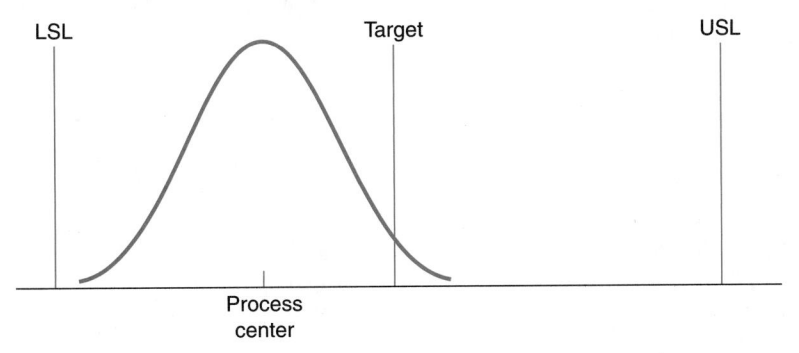

LSL   Target   USL

Process center

FIGURE

12.22

The C_{pk} ratio considers the distance from the process center to the nearest spec limit.

563

in Example 12.7 is well centered and operating well within the upper and lower spec limits.

Taking C_{pk} One Step Further. If the process is capable ($C_{pk} > 1$):

1. Monitor the process.

2. Pursue continuous improvement.

If the process is not capable ($C_{pk} \leq 1$):

1. Monitor the process.

2. Pursue continuous improvement.

3. Invest time, money, and resources to reduce process variation.

4. Consider removing this product from production.

Although the fourth statement under $C_{pk} \leq 1$ may appear to be a bit drastic, it is worthy of serious consideration, given the present world of increasing product quality requirements and consumer quality demands.

Consideration of the Process Target: Use of C_{pm}

When using the C_p ratio or the C_{pk} ratio, we divide by either $3s$ or $6s$, where s is the sample standard deviation. The value of s is a measure of the variation about the process mean (center). An alternative here is to replace s with an estimate of the variation about the process *target* (T), assumed here to be midway between the upper spec limit and the lower spec limit; that is, $T = (USL + LSL)/2$. Denoting this estimate by s', then,

$$
\begin{aligned}
s' &= \sqrt{\frac{\Sigma(x - T)^2}{n - 1}} \\
&= \sqrt{\frac{\Sigma(x - \bar{x})^2}{n - 1} + \frac{n(\bar{x} - T)^2}{n - 1}} \\
&= \sqrt{s^2 + \frac{n(\bar{x} - T)^2}{n - 1}}
\end{aligned}
$$

12.13

Consider the ratio defined by

$$
C_{pm} = \frac{USL - LSL}{6s'}
$$

12.14

This index will decrease as s' increases, due to a shift from the process target. When the process variance (s^2) changes and the process mean drifts from T concurrently, the C_{pm} index has the ability to detect these changes. We suggest you interpret the C_{pm} index using the same guidelines for interpreting the C_p ratio discussed previously. In particular, this implies that a C_{pm} ratio less than 1 is an indicator of a process that cannot adequately meet the process specifications.

E X A M P L E

12.9

Determine the C_{pm} ratio for the coffee-can illustration in Example 12.7.

Solution   The sample size is $n = 100$, the target value is $T = 20$ ounces, the sample mean is $\bar{x} = 19.98$ ounces, and the sample standard deviation is $s = .189$ ounce. Consequently,

$$s' = \sqrt{.189^2 + \frac{100(19.98 - 20)^2}{99}} = .1901$$

and

$$C_{pm} = \frac{21 - 19}{6(.1901)} = \frac{2}{1.141} = 1.75$$

Since 1.75 > 1.33, we once again conclude that this process is capable of meeting the process specifications.

Determining the Percent Nonconforming

Another method of measuring process capability is to estimate the number of nonconforming units, that is, those outside the spec limits. The basic assumption behind this procedure is that we have reason to believe that the process is *normally distributed*. If there is reason to doubt this assumption (such as, when a process has been shown to be out of control), then the results of this section are unreliable. There is nothing new about the procedure we will use here, since we learned in Chapter 6 that the percent nonconforming can be determined by finding the corresponding area under a normal curve. The mean and standard deviation are estimated using the sample statistics, again assuming that the process is in control during the collection of this sample. This procedure is illustrated in the following example.

EXAMPLE 12.10

A machine is used to fill plastic containers of motor oil, each of which is supposed to contain 32 fluid ounces. The process specs are 32 ± .5 fluid ounces. A sample of 75 containers produces a mean of $\bar{x} = 31.92$ fluid ounces and a standard deviation of $s = .16$. Describe the process capability.

Solution

The sample standard deviation is the estimated process standard deviation, that is, $\hat{\sigma}$. First we determine the process capability ratio C_{pk}.

$$R_L = \frac{31.92 - 31.5}{3(.16)} = \frac{.42}{.48} = .88$$

$$R_U = \frac{32.5 - 31.92}{3(.16)} = \frac{.58}{.48} = 1.21$$

Consequently,

$$C_{pk} = \text{minimum of .88 and 1.21}$$
$$= .88$$

which is an unacceptable value.

To find the value of C_{pm}, we use equation 12.13 to calculate the variation about the process target, $T = 32$. This is

$$s' = \sqrt{(.16)^2 + \frac{75(31.92 - 32)^2}{74}} = .179$$

The resulting ratio is

$$C_{pm} = \frac{32.5 - 31.5}{6(.179)} = .93 < 1$$

So, both the C_{pk} and C_{pm} ratios indicate a process incapable of meeting process specifications. The small value of C_{pm} is due to the variation about the process center, as measured by $s = .16$, and the slight drift from the process target equal to $\bar{x} - T = 31.92 - 32 = -.08$.

To estimate the percent nonconforming, we examine the tails of a normal curve outside the lower and upper spec limits of 31.5 and 32.5. These tail areas are shaded in Figure 12.23, where the curve is centered at $\bar{x} = 31.92$ with a standard deviation of $\hat{\sigma} = .16$.

The standardized values for the spec limits are

$$\text{standardized LSL} = \frac{31.5 - 31.92}{.16} = -2.62$$

$$\text{standardized USL} = \frac{32.5 - 31.92}{.16} = 3.62$$

The proportion nonconforming will be

(the proportion to the left of –2.62 under a Z curve)

+ (the proportion to the right of 3.62 under a Z curve)

= .0044 + .0002 (approximately) = .0046

So, an estimated .46% of the oil containers will be nonconforming. At first glance, this appears to be a reasonably "small" number. However, when discussing the proportion of units nonconforming, it is common to talk in terms of number of units nonconforming *per million* units produced. For this example, the estimated number of nonconforming oil containers per million produced is (.0046)(1,000,000) or 4,600, a number that should be large enough to get management's attention.

The expected number of nonconforming units per million produced, *provided the process is centered in the specs*, can be estimated roughly from the value of C_{pk} using Table 12.4. This table is constructed using the procedure discussed in the previous example.

Since Table 12.4 assumes the process is centered exactly on target (midway between the spec limits), it provides a measure of the potential number of non-

---

FIGURE

12.23

Tail areas represent the proportion of nonconforming units.

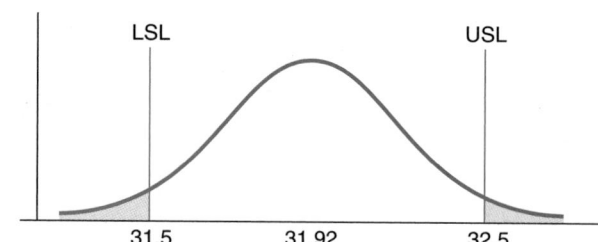

TABLE

12.4

Determining the number of nonconforming units per million produced using C_{pk}.

C_{pk}	Number of Nonconforming Units per Million Produced
.5	133,614
.75	24,448
1.00	2,700
1.30	96
1.50	6.8
2.00	.002

conforming units per million produced, given the variation of the process. Since the process in the previous example was very nearly centered on target (32 fluid ounces) with a C_{pk} of .88, we would expect Table 12.4 to provide a crude estimate of the number nonconforming, namely, between 2,700 and 24,448. The actual number of nonconforming units per million produced was estimated to be 4,600.

X Exercises 12.45–12.55

Understanding the Mechanics

12.45 What phenomena do process capability indices measure? If a process is in control, does that imply that the process is capable of meeting process requirements? Explain.

12.46 How does the measure of process capability C_{pm} differ from both C_p and C_{pk}?

12.47 For each of the following well-centered processes (i.e., A–D), a sample of size 325 is collected and the standard deviation of the process estimated. Calculate C_p, and indicate whether you believe the process capability to be "good," "adequate," or "inadequate."

Process	Specifications	Sample Standard Deviation
A	0.65 ± 0.07	0.030
B	29.3 ± 2.5	0.740
C	99.5 ± 7.2	1.110
D	0.25 ± 0.02	0.006

12.48 For each of the following processes (i.e., A–D), a sample of size 400 is collected in order to estimate the process mean and variability.

Process	Specifications	Mean	Sample Standard Deviation
A	124.0 ± 8.5	117.6	2.560
B	0.66 ± 0.08	0.67	0.022
C	89.2 ± 2.0	90.0	0.720
D	0.13 ± 0.03	0.132	0.009

a. Indicate which measure of process capability (C_p vs. C_{pk}) appears the more appropriate to use for each process, and state why.

b. Compute the appropriate measure of process capability for each process.

c. Using Table 12.4, estimate the number of nonconforming units per million for processes B and D.

12.49 Verify in equation 12.13 that

$$\frac{\Sigma(x-T)^2}{n-1} = s^2 + \frac{n(\bar{x}-T)^2}{n-1}$$

Applying the New Concepts

12.50 A process used to fill small cartridges with CO_2 has an upper specification limit of 250 psi (i.e., pounds per square inch). A sample of 150 CO_2 cartridges produces a sample mean of 228.8 psi and a standard deviation of 6.2 psi.

a. What is the capability ratio C_p for this process?

b. What proportion of the CO_2 cartridges will exceed the upper specification limit?

12.51 Answer the following questions using the data from Exercise 12.50.

a. Assuming that the process target is 225 psi, compute C_{pm}, considering only the upper specification limit.

b. Assuming that the process target is 229 psi, compute C_{pm}, considering only the upper specification limit.

c. What happens to C_{pm} as the process mean and target converge (i.e., get closer to one another), given a constant process variability?

12.52 Printed circuit boards are manufactured using several processes. One process applies an etch-resist ink to a panel that is composed of a copper-clad laminate. The etch-resist ink is printed on the panel by passing a squeegee over a screen that contains a template of the desired circuit image. The size of the image that is printed on the panel is a critical factor. If the image is either too large or too small, substantial problems in component assembly are encountered. Consider the specification of the height of the image to be 1.34 ± .04 mm. A sample of 300 printed circuit boards is randomly collected. The sample mean was found to be 1.35 with a standard deviation of .009 mm.

a. What is the value of C_p for this process? How would you interpret this value?

b. What is the value of C_{pk} for this process? How would you interpret this value?

c. Using Table 12.4, estimate the number of nonconforming units per million for this process.

(Source: "Process Capability: A Criterion for Optimizing Multiple Response Product and Process Design," *IIE Transactions*, 33, 2001, pp. 497–509.)

12.53 A decision must be made between two experimental processes for producing silicon chips. The specification limits on the thickness of the chips is .125 ± .003 mm. Samples of 500 chips are drawn from experimental runs for each process, and means and standard deviations are recorded:

Process	Sample Mean	Sample Standard Deviation
A	0.1254	0.0008
B	0.1231	0.0003

a. Which of the two processes is better centered?

b. Calculate C_{pk} for both processes.

c. Which process do you recommend, and why?

12.54 Three processes in your manufacturing facility have been producing unacceptably high numbers of nonconforming parts. You have drawn normally distributed samples of 375 from each process. The sample means and standard deviations are as follows:

Process	Specifications	Sample Mean	Sample Standard Deviation
A	51.0 ± 1.2	51.2	1.1
B	102.5 ± 8.9	108.1	2.3
C	3.4 ± 0.5	3.7	0.4

a. Calculate the *z*-scores for the specification limits and the spread between specification limits (in standard deviations) for each process.

b. The plant manager wants to know your thoughts regarding this predicament. Considering the calculated *z*-scores and spreads, do you believe that the problem is attributable to improper centering of the process, excessive process variability, or both? Discuss your answer for each process individually.

12.55 [DATA SET EX12-55] *Variable Description:*

Diameter: The diameter of a fastening hole for an aluminum body cover

A random sample of 15 fastening holes for an aluminum body cover was recorded in a Ford manufacturing plant to determine the process capability. The diameters of these holes are given in units of millimeters. Specification limits are 8.975 ± .105 mm. The target value is 8.975 mm. Determine the capability indices for this process. What are your recommendations?

(Source: "Simple Process Capability," *Quality*, February 2001, pp. 34–38.)

Summary

American manufacturing and service industries are continuing to undergo an evolution that emphasizes quality. The need for tools to monitor quality has sparked a renewed interest in the everyday application of statistical thinking. Decisions are routinely based on *facts* gathered from sample data.

This chapter has examined both the management and the statistical sides of quality improvement. **Total Quality Management (TQM)** is a customer-focused management strategy that emphasizes a respect for employees and a constant effort at improving product or service quality. A **quality product or service** is one that meets or surpasses the needs and expectations of the customer. The basic philosophies of the early quality pioneers, **Deming, Juran,** and **Crosby,** were explained, noting both similarities and differences in their approaches to quality improvement.

Companies in the United States demonstrating a high degree of quality emphasis both internally and externally are recognized each year through the **Malcolm Baldrige National Quality Award** (MBNQA). Recipients of this award have exhibited and documented that they have a world-class system for managing their operations/employees and satisfying their customers. The **ISO 9000 standards** require businesses to provide evidence of the establishment of a quality system that is understood and followed by all company employees. Registration to ISO 9000 standards increasingly is becoming a prerequisite for doing business. The Baldrige Award criteria are more customer focused, whereas ISO 9000 registration provides a common basis for assuring buyers that specific (documented) quality practices are being followed by their suppliers.

A **process** can be any combination of resources, such as people, machines, and/or material that lead to a product or service. **Statistical process control** (SPC) is the application of statistical procedures intended to measure, analyze, and control this process.

To monitor a process, you must first define what it is you wish to measure or count. For measurement data, what you are measuring is the *quality characteristic* and such measurements result in **variables data.** Examples of variables data include the weight or length of a manufactured unit. When counting, you obtain **attribute data,** such as the number of nonconformities per unit.

Two of the quality-improvement tools were explained in Chapter 2, namely, the **histogram** and **Pareto chart.** Two additional tools for describing a process were introduced in this chapter, the flowchart and the cause-and-effect diagram. A **flowchart** is a diagram of an entire process that can be used to view the process as a system and allow you to search for potential problem areas or opportunities for improvement. The **cause-and-effect diagram** can be used to represent the relationships between potential problems within a process and their possible causes.

Another quality-improvement tool, a **control chart,** can be set up to monitor a process to determine whether it is **in control** (stable) or **out of control** (unstable). Provided the plotted points for a control chart stay within the **upper control limit** (UCL) and the **lower control limit** (LCL), the process is exhibiting natural variation and is said to be in control. The **center line (CL)** represents the average value of the quality characteristic corresponding to the in-control state. If a plotted point exceeds either of the limits, a search is made for an **assignable cause,** that is, an explanation (such as defective raw material) for this extreme value in the control chart. Control charts for variables data consist of the $\overline{X}$ **chart** for monitoring the process center and the **R chart** for monitoring the process variation. For attribute data, the most commonly used control charts are the **p chart** for observing and controlling the proportion of nonconforming units and the **c chart** for the number of nonconformities per unit.

Control charts enable the front-line worker to distinguish between random variation (**chance cause**) and that due to an assignable cause. One of Deming's main points is that a process should not be "tampered with" when it is exhibiting chance variation. This was illustrated using his **funnel experiment,** which demonstrated how such manipulations will actually have an adverse effect on process variation. Systematic and nonrandom patterns can be detected in an $\overline{X}$ control chart by conducting a **pattern analysis.**

For most production situations, a process must conform to certain requirements referred to as **specification limits.** These may be imposed by an outside purchaser or internally by the company's engineering staff. The ability of the process to conform to these specifications is the **process capability.** If a large percentage of the units produced can be expected to lie outside the spec limits, we would conclude that the process is not capable of performing to specification. Measures of process capability consist of the C_p ratio, which does not consider where the process is centered, the C_{pk} ratio, which does, and the C_{pm} ratio, which includes the effect of a drift away from the process target. The C_p ratio measures how well the process *should* perform (the difference of the spec limits) compared with how well the process *is* performing (the **process spread,** defined as six standard deviations).

✓ Summary of Formulas

Control Charts

1. $\overline{X}$ Chart:

$$\text{UCL} = \overline{\overline{X}} + 3\frac{\hat{\sigma}}{\sqrt{n}}$$

$$\text{CL} = \overline{\overline{X}}$$

$$\text{LCL} = \overline{\overline{X}} - 3\frac{\hat{\sigma}}{\sqrt{n}}$$

where $\overline{\overline{X}} = \sum \overline{X}_i/m$ and $\hat{\sigma} = \overline{R}/d_2$ (values of d_2 provided in Table 12.3).

2. R chart:

$$\text{UCL} = D_4\overline{R}$$

$$\text{CL} = \overline{R}$$

$$\text{LCL} = D_3\overline{R}$$

(values of D_3 and D_4 provided in Table 12.3).

3. p chart:

$$\text{UCL} = \overline{p} + 3\sqrt{\frac{\overline{p}(1-\overline{p})}{n}}$$

$$\text{CL} = \overline{p}$$

$$\text{LCL} = \overline{p} - 3\sqrt{\frac{\overline{p}(1-\overline{p})}{n}}$$

4. c chart:

$$\text{UCL} = \overline{c} + 3\sqrt{\overline{c}}$$

$$\text{CL} = \overline{c}$$

$$\text{LCL} = \overline{c} - 3\sqrt{\overline{c}}$$

where $\overline{c}$ = average number of nonconformities per unit.

Process Capability

1. Process spread: $6\hat{\sigma}$ where $\hat{\sigma} = s$ (sample standard deviation).

2. $C_p = \dfrac{\text{USL} - \text{LSL}}{6\hat{\sigma}}$ (two-sided spec limit)

$C_p = \dfrac{\text{USL} - \overline{X}}{3\hat{\sigma}}$ (upper spec limit only)

$C_p = \dfrac{\overline{X} - \text{LSL}}{3\hat{\sigma}}$ (lower spec limit only)

3. C_{pk} = minimum of R_L and R_U where

$$R_L = \frac{\overline{X} - \text{LSL}}{3\hat{\sigma}} \qquad R_U = \frac{\text{USL} - \overline{X}}{3\hat{\sigma}}$$

4. $C_{pm} = \dfrac{\text{USL} - \text{LSL}}{6s'}$ where

$$s' = \sqrt{s^2 + \frac{n(\overline{x} - T)^2}{n-1}}$$

and T = process target = $(\text{USL} + \text{LSL})/2$.

Further Reading

Cianfrani, Charles, *ISO 9001:2000 Explained,* Milwaukee, Wis.: American Society for Quality, 2001

Crosby, Philip, *Quality and Me: Lessons from an Evolving Life,* San Francisco: Jossey-Bass, 1999

Crosby, Philip, *Quality Is Still Free: Making Quality Certain in Uncertain Times,* New York: McGraw-Hill, 1996

Deming, W. Edwards, *Out of the Crisis,* Cambridge, Mass.: MIT Press, 2000

Dobyns, Lloyd, and Clare Crawford-Mason, *Quality or Else: The Revolution in World Business,* Boston: Houghton-Mifflin, 1993

Juran, J. M., *Juran on Leadership for Quality,* New York: Free Press, 1989

———, *Juran on Quality by Design,* New York: Free Press, 1992

———, *Quality Control Handbook,* 5th ed., New York: McGraw-Hill, 1999

Juran, J. M., and Frank M. Gryna, *Quality Planning and Analysis,* New York: McGraw-Hill, 1993

Kane, V. E., "Process Capability Indices," *Journal of Quality Technology,* 18, no. 1, 1986: 41

Kanholm, Jack, *ISO 9000:2000 New Requirements,* Pasadena, Calif.: AQA Press, 2000

Ketola, Jeanne, and Kathy Roberts, *ISO 9000:2000 in a Nutshell,* Chico, Calif.: Paton Press, 2001

Montgomery, D. C., *Introduction to Statistical Quality Control,* 4th ed., New York: Wiley, 2000

Rosander, A. C., *Deming's 14 Points Applied to Services,* Houston: Marcel-Dekker, 1991

Shewhart, W. A., "Quality Control Charts," *Bell System Technical Journal,* 1926

Walton, Mary, *The Deming Management Method,* New York: Perigee Books, 1988

Information on the Malcolm Baldrige National Quality Award: Malcolm Baldrige National Quality Award Office, NIST, Administration Bldg., Rm. A537, Gaithersburg, MD 20899-0001, (301) 975-2036. Website is http://www.quality.nist.gov.

X Review Exercises 12.56–12.73

12.56 What is the difference between chance causes and assignable causes? Explain the objective of control charts with respect to these two causes.

12.57 Identify the quality guru(s) associated with each of the following notions or terms.
   a. Management, particularly top management, is most responsible for poor quality.
   b. Fear can be channeled constructively into quality-improvement efforts.
   c. Zero defects
   d. The problem is the system, not the people.
   e. Quality is free.
   f. The use of statistical methods is imperative to quality improvement.
   g. The overriding objective of quality improvement is to exceed customer requirements and expectations.

12.58 Under what conditions would C_p, C_{pk}, and C_{pm} all be equal?

12.59 Briefly explain, in one sentence each, the seven categories of the Malcolm Baldrige National Quality Award. Which categories carry the most points during the examination phase of a company?

12.60 Control charts have upper and lower limits just as confidence intervals have upper and lower endpoints. Explain the similarity between the calculation of the limits for control charts and the endpoints of a confidence interval.

12.61 Differentiate between specification limits and control limits. Is there a measure that conveys the relationship between the two? Explain.

12.62 Classify the following as attribute or variables data:
  a. The weight of a bat manufactured for professional baseball
  b. The number of broken links on a Web home page
  c. The number of defective sectors on a hard drive manufactured for personal computers
  d. The voltage output of a transformer
  e. The thickness of a razor manufactured for shaving

12.63 Explain the primary difference between the measures of process capability C_p and C_{pm}. Which do you think will usually be larger? Why?

12.64 The specification limits for the tear strength of a cardboard container are 150 ± 2 ft-lb. A normally distributed sample of 100 containers yields a mean tear strength of 150.3 ft-lb with a standard deviation of 0.7 ft-lb.
  a. Calculate C_{pk}.
  b. Estimate the number of containers nonconforming per million by using Table 12.4.
  c. Calculate the number of containers nonconforming per million.

12.65 Health care executives are using statistical process control to provide insight into medical group performance. One of the primary care performance indicators that they are charting is the net revenue per relative value unit (RVU) production from a full-time equivalent provider. The upper and lower control limits for the average value per month are 84 and 48, respectively. Using the eight patterns for detecting assignable causes, at what point would you consider the process to be out of control, using the following 18 values?

Month	1	2	3	4	5	6	7	8	9
RVU	55	67	72	73	77	85	44	64	65

Month	10	11	12	13	14	15	16	17	18
RVU	74	61	66	60	59	66	67	64	76

(Source: "The Synergistic Effect of Linking Statistical Process Control and Profit and Loss," *Journal of Health Care Finance*, 27, no. 3, Spring 2001, pp. 64–75.)

12.66 Indicate whether an $\bar{X}$, R, p, or c chart would be the best for controlling:
  a. the number of defective resistors in a container of 500 resistors
  b. the mean cranking amperage of a sample of car batteries
  c. the discrepancy in time it takes to perform an identical oil change
  d. the number of scratches and other imperfections in an 8-foot × 4-foot sheet of paneling
  e. the mean length of a sample of bolts
  f. the number of nonconforming sprocket sets in a container of 250

12.67 A number of graphical tools for quality improvement were mentioned in this chapter. The following statements correspond to one of these tools. Identify the graphical tool associated with each statement.
  a. This tool shows the relationship, if any, between two variables.
  b. This tool graphically illustrates a process by showing the activities engaged in and decisions made.
  c. This tool can be used to monitor and control a process over time.
  d. This tool is used to identify the quality problem(s) with the largest impact.
  e. This tool shows the main/subcauses responsible for a quality problem.

12.68 Hillerich & Bradsby crafts each professional bat to be within ±.0003 inches in five key diameters: barrel, midbarrel, midhandle, handle, and knob. Assume that the target diameter of the midhandle is .75000 inches and that a random sample of 20 bats yields a sample mean of .75003 with a standard deviation of .00005.
  a. What is the value of C_p for this process? How would you interpret this value?
  b. What is the value of C_{pm} for this process? How would you interpret this value?
  c. What is the value of C_{pk} for this process? How would you interpret this value?
  d. Using Table 12.4, estimate the number of nonconforming units per million for this process.

(Source: "Making Bats for the Pros," *Quality Progress*, 34, no. 8, August 2001, p. 30.)

12.69 **[DATA SET EX12-69]** *Variable description:*

Sample Number: Samples are numbered from 1 to 20

Breaking Strength1 through Breaking Strength4: the breaking points of a single strand of fabric in a sample of size 4

During most fabric production processes, fabric tensile and tear strength are checked before the weaving of fabric. Control charts have replaced many inspection procedures in an attempt to produce quality fabric. Quality-control procedures are conducted during every phase of the production process, from the fiber opening to the spinning and weaving. Twenty samples of size four are selected from a fabric production process. Develop appropriate control charts to determine whether this process is in control. What are your recommendations?

(Source: "Box-Chart: Combining X-bar and S Charts," *Total Quality Management*, July 2000, p. 857.)

12.70 The lower specification limit for an inflatable air bladder to be used in an automobile seat is 230 psi. A sample of 100 bladders failed at a mean of 236.1 psi with a standard deviation of 1.8 psi.
  a. Calculate the process capability ratio C_p.
  b. What proportion of the air bladders will fail at less than 230 psi?

12.71 The Palmer House, a landmark Chicago hotel, periodically receives complaints from guests regarding low water pressure. To remedy the problem, the engineering department can adjust the flow of water, therefore water pressure, to the various floors of the hotel. Management wishes to establish a control chart to control the number of complaints about low water pressure. It is decided that the number of complaints received per day will be recorded by floor of the hotel. The following are the number of complaints received per floor (10 in all) for the last two days.

Sample	Complaints	Sample	Complaints	Sample	Complaints
1	3	8	2	15	4
2	1	9	1	16	4
3	0	10	0	17	0
4	2	11	4	18	2
5	5	12	3	19	2
6	0	13	2	20	1
7	2	14	1		

  a. What type of chart is appropriate to use in this instance?
  b. Construct the appropriate control chart.
  c. Plot the data and control limits. Is this process in control or out of control?

12.72 Rural ambulance and rescue squads are largely staffed by volunteer emergency medical technicians (EMTs). As the number of rural jobs decline and EMTs begin commuting to work in more populated areas, ambulance and rescue services find it increasingly difficult responding to all calls. The chief of one such rural squad used control charts to gain a better understanding of her community's need for service and to improve the squad's ability to respond to all calls. The following control chart shows the number of daily calls for which the squad was unable to respond ("dropped calls") over a seven-week period. Comment on any patterns that you observe. What recommendations would you make? (*Hint:* Look for a cyclical pattern.) Note that this example illustrates that control charts are useful to service organizations as well as to manufacturing-oriented organizations.

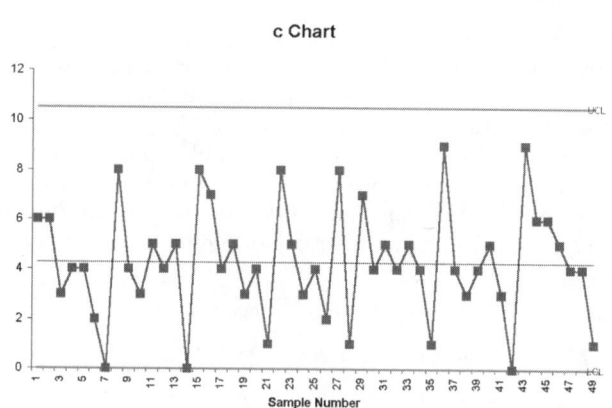

c Chart

12.73 [DATA SET EX12-73] *Variable description:*

WidthCircuit: The width of a circuit path in a computer chip (in microns)

A computer chip manufacturer monitors the quality of its computer chips by selecting a batch of 10 computer chips and measuring the width of the circuit path. If this path is too wide or too narrow, the computer CPU might malfunction. Is there a pattern that might indicate that the following $\bar{X}$ chart, in which 30 batches were sampled, is out of control? Construct an R chart and explain if there is a similar indication that the process is out of control.

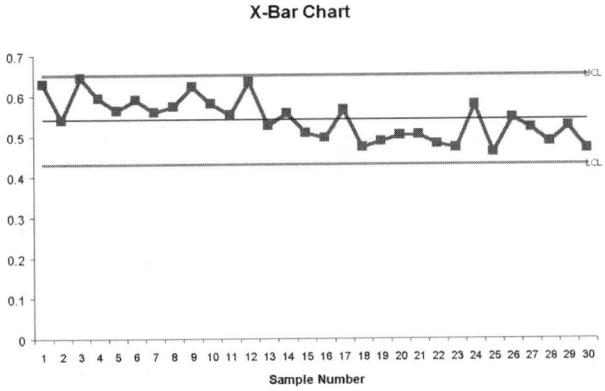

X-Bar Chart

Sample Number

Insights from Statistics in Action

Business Excellence: Banking on Six Sigma to Keep Quality Job One

At the beginning of this chapter, the Statistics in Action case study discussed the efforts of Ford Motor Company to implement the six-sigma concept in its production processes. In essence, this policy states that a single-sided spec limit is at least six standard deviations (sigmas) away from the mean, allowing for a 1.5 sigma shift for the process average. For a K-sigma quality process, one would subtract 1.5 from the value of K and then examine the standard normal (Z) curve to the right of $K - 1.5$. For example, for a six-sigma policy, examine the area to the right of $6 - 1.5 = 4.5$ under the Z curve. This is .0000034, which translates to 3.4 nonconforming parts per million, or "being 99.9997% perfect." Similarly, for $K = 4$, the number of nonconforming items in a four-sigma plan is $P(Z > 2.5) \times 10^6 = 6,210$ parts per million.

As explained in "Six Sigma's Missing Link" in *Quality Progress*, K-sigma plans can be implemented for service industries as well. The example used in that article is one involving mortgage customers who expect their applications to be processed in 10 days after filing. Suppose all the defects (loans in a monthly sample taking more than 10 days to process) are counted and it is determined that 150 loans in the 1,000 applications processed in that month do not meet this customer requirement. Now, 150/1,000 defects translates into 850/1,000 defect-free applications. Let $z_{.85}$ represent the z value such that 85% of the area to its left is equal to .85. From a normal distribution table or using the inverse normal probability function on a statistical computer program, $z_{.85}$ can be found to be 1.036. Adding 1.5 to 1.036 gives a process stigma of 2.5, which is well below the value of 6 for a six-sigma plan.

1. Consider a process in which an electronic component is measured in units of $1/128$ inch. The process target is 31 units and the specification limits are set at $31 - 16 = 15$ and $31 + 16 = 47$. If this process was on target (that is, the sample mean is midway between the spec limits) and the standard deviation of the process was 5.33, what is C_{pk}? From Table 12.4, what is the estimate of the number of nonconforming units per million?

2. To achieve six-sigma quality, C_{pk} must be equal to 1.54. What would the standard deviation have to be for the process in question 1 to achieve six-sigma quality?

3. Suppose that the sample mean is 33.5 in question 1 and that the process target is midway between the specification limits. What is the value of C_{pm}? How would you interpret this value?

4. A six-sigma policy translates into 3.4 nonconforming parts per million and a four-sigma policy translates into 6,210 nonconforming parts per million. How many nonconforming parts per million would there be for a five-sigma program?

5. Suppose that a hotel manager is monitoring the number of complaints that customers have about their rooms. If 1,000 customers are sampled and it is determined that five customers had legitimate complaints, at what process sigma level would the hotel be operating?

(Source: "Ford Embraces Six Sigma," *The New York Times*, June 13, 2001, p. C5; "Six Sigma's Missing Link," *Quality Progress*, November 2000, p. 77.)

Appendix SPSS®

Chapter 12 Appendix: Data Analysis with SPSS

$\overline{X}$ and R Control Charts

To illustrate the construction of $\overline{X}$ and R charts, the coffee-can weights used in Example 12.2 will be used. Enter the coffee-can weights in the first column (named "weight"). The subgroup size is five for this example because five measurements were obtained in each of the 20 samples. Consequently, enter five values of "1," five values of "2," . . . , five values of "20" in the second column (named "group"). Click on **Graphs ➤ Control ➤ X-Bar, R, s.** Click on **Define** and enter the variable labeled "weight" in the **Process Measurement** box and the variable labeled "group" in the **Subgroups Defined by** box. By clicking on **OK,** the R chart (first) and the $\overline{X}$ chart (second) immediately following this dialog window will appear in the display pane.

	weight	group
1	49.89	1
2	50.13	1
3	49.73	1
4	50.77	1
5	49.26	1
6	49.85	2
7	50.39	2
8	50.09	2
9	50.35	2
10	50.49	2
11	51.23	3
12	50.41	3
13	50.06	3
14	49.96	3
15	50.29	3
16	50.06	4
17	50.40	4
18	50.13	4
19	49.17	4
20	49.80	4
21	49.73	5
22	50.80	5

◀ ▶ \ **Data View** ⁄ Variable View ⁄

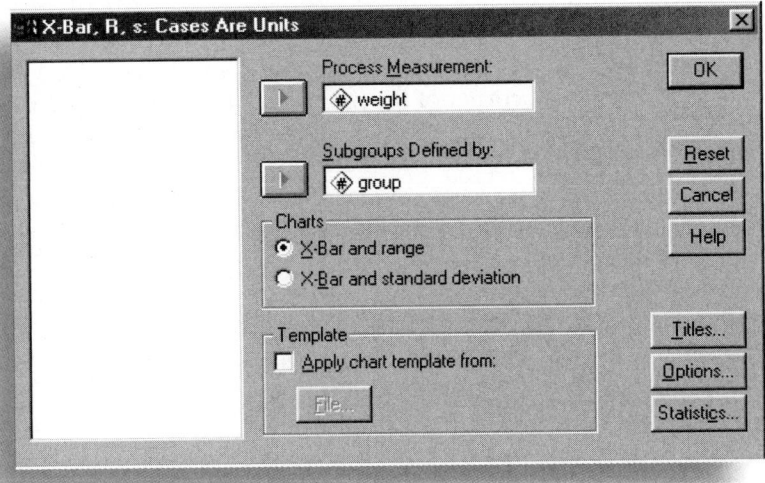

Control Chart: WEIGHT

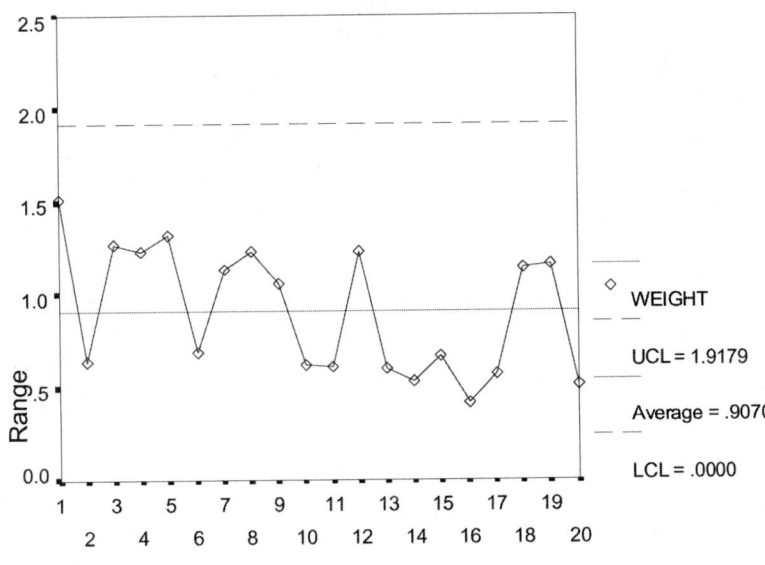

Sigma level: 3

Control Chart: WEIGHT

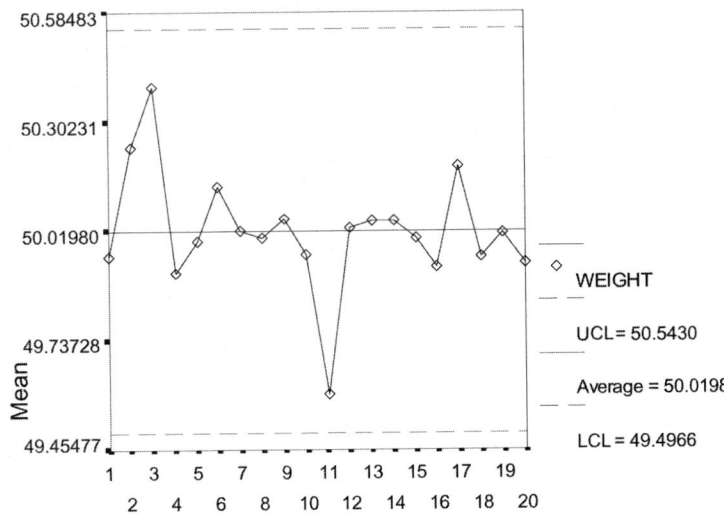

Sigma level: 3

Process Capability

To have SPSS compute the various process capability indices, click on the **Statistics** button in the lower-right corner of the previously illustrated input dialog box. Enter the specification limits and target value, as illustrated below. Click on the check boxes for C_p, C_{pk}, and C_{pm} and the check box for **Actual % outside specification limits.** Notice that the process standard deviation was estimated using the average of the sample ranges ($\bar{R}/d_2$) since this illustration contains 20 samples of five coffee cans each, rather than a single random sample of 100 cans. The resulting process capability ratios immediately follow the input dialog box. Since all the ratios are under one and 1% of the can weights (10,000 per million) are outside the specification limits, this process is clearly incapable of meeting the process specifications.

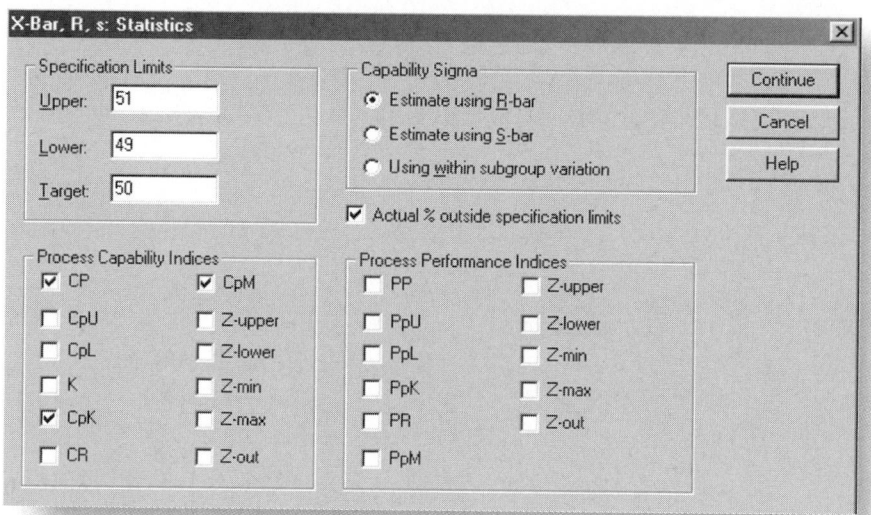

Process Statistics

	Act. % Outside SL	1.0%
Capability	CP[a]	.855
Indices	CpK[a]	.838
	CpM[a,b]	.854

The normal distribution is assumed. LSL = 49 and USL = 51.
a. The estimated capability sigma is based on the mean of the sample group ranges.
b. The target value is 50.

p Charts

Consider the data used in Example 12.3. Enter the number of nonconforming cans in each of the samples (7, 4, 1, . . . , 2) in the first column and name this column "cans." To construct the corresponding *p* chart, click on **Graphs ➤ Control ➤ p, np.** Be sure to check the box alongside **Cases are subgroups** in the **Data Organization** frame. Click on **Define.** Move the variable labeled cans into the **Number Nonconforming** box and in the **Sample Size** frame, enter 150. After clicking on **OK,** the SPSS version of the *p* chart in Figure 12.17 will appear in the display frame.

c Charts

Consider the data used in Example 12.5. Enter the number of paint blemishes for each of the door panels (1, 0, 3, . . . , 3) in the first column and name this column "number." To construct the corresponding c chart, click on **Graphs ➤ Control ➤ c, u.** Be sure to check the box alongside **Cases are subgroups** in the **Data Organization** frame. Click on **Define.** Move the variable labeled number into the **Number of Nonconformities** box and in the **Sample Size** frame, enter 1. After clicking on **OK,** the SPSS version of the c chart in Figure 12.19 will appear in the display frame.

On the CD . . .
Chapter 12 Appendix: Data Analysis with MINITAB

Applications of the Chi-Square Statistic

X

Statistics in Action
Data Mining: The Art and Science of Customer Relationship Management

"You have been selected to qualify for an amazing vacation!" Many consumers have been targeted with mail offering exciting purchasing opportunities. Companies are studying consumer DNA and attempting to anticipate, rather than react to, customer needs. Dramatic advances in data capture and storage capabilities are enabling organizations to integrate their various databases to learn characteristics about their customers, such as their demographics, geography, product usage, and purchasing patterns. *Data mining* pertains to the use of technologies and techniques for recognizing and tracking patterns within these data to help businesses sift through layers of seemingly unrelated data for meaningful relationships to build a model of customer behavior. Companies can leverage this knowledge to create intelligent, proactive pathways back to the customer.

Why is the term *data mining* used in determining consumer behavior? This term is used to indicate that an information extraction activity, such as statistical analysis, is being used to discover hidden facts contained in databases. To be sure, data mining and customer behavior modeling tools are far from exact in predicting what a customer will buy or do in the future. Data mining might be good at breaking down customers' behavior based on what they have done or bought in the past but that does not necessarily predict what clients will want to buy in the future. Marketing researchers say that the information gained from data mining is a start-

ing point on which to base decisions in managing customer relationships.

Who uses data mining? Blockbuster Entertainment mines its video rental history database to recommend rentals to individual customers. American Express can suggest products to its cardholders based on analysis of their monthly expenditures. Wal-Mart is pioneering massive data mining to transform its supplier relationships. Wal-Mart captures point-of-sale transactions from more than 2,900 stores in six countries and continuously transmits this data to its massive 7.5 terabyte data warehouse. The database for Avis Rental Agency is used to market directly to frequent customers fitting certain demographics and psychographics.

Psychographic profiling is a process used by many companies to group customers via lifestyle choices, personality, activities, beliefs, and values. Clusters of homogeneous individuals identified in data-mining studies are often examined to determine if a relationship exists between the clusters and various psychographic profiles. When you have completed this chapter, you will have a firm grasp in understanding how tests of independence will enable you to

- Determine if two classifications, such as their willingness to make a purchase spontaneously and their age, are independent (not related).
- Measure the strength of the relationship between two classifications using a test of hypothesis and corresponding *p*-value.
- Determine if the proportions of consumers with certain lifestyles differ across categories of consumer behavior.

A Look Back/Introduction

We have now examined several topics in *descriptive* and *inferential* statistics. The descriptive area introduced you to both the numeric methods (for example, mean, median, and variance) and the graphic methods (for example, histogram and scatter diagram) of describing data. In inferential statistics, we discussed point estimation, confidence intervals, and tests of hypothesis. In the remaining chapters, we turn our attention to other applications of the material from these earlier chapters.

In Chapter 8, we introduced the chi-square (χ^2) distribution. We used this distribution to test that the variance of a normal distribution was equal to a specified value. The shape of the chi-square distribution is skewed right (with a right tail) and is nonnegative. The shape of a chi-square curve and areas (probabilities) under such a curve are contained in Table A.6. The test statistic in Chapter 8 had a chi-square distribution. This chapter introduces you to additional applications of statistics by using the chi-square distribution to answer such questions as these:

Do reported percentages of market share accurately describe the product mix for the new cars sold this past year in Minneapolis, Minnesota?

Does a person's age have an influence on buying behavior?

13.1

CHI-SQUARE GOODNESS-OF-FIT TESTS

The Binomial Situation

In the binomial situation (introduced in Chapter 5) the following four conditions must be satisfied:

1. The experiment consists of *n* repetitions, called *trials.*

2. The trials are *independent.*

3. Each trial has two (and only two) possible outcomes, referred to as *success* and *failure.*

4. The probability of a success for each trial is p, where p remains the same for each trial. For a large finite population, p is the *proportion* of successes in this population.

Consequently, the binomial distribution applies to applications where there are only two possible outcomes, such as:

- The person selected is a male or a female.
- The product tested is either defective or not defective.
- A new-car buyer buys either an American-made car or a foreign-made car.

Inferences for the Binomial Situation

Estimating the binomial parameter, p, was covered in Chapter 10. We obtained a random sample of size n and observed the number of successes, x. The estimator of p, the proportion of successes in the *population*, was $\hat{p} = x/n =$ the proportion of successes in the *sample*. We also discussed hypothesis testing for p. For example, we discussed a binomial situation in which a calculator was either defective (with probability p) or not defective. The hypothetical value of p was .04, and we determined whether the results of the sample (13 defectives out of 150) indicated a departure from this percentage. Here $\hat{p} = 13/150 = .0867$. So, 8.67% of the sampled calculators were defective. Is this percentage large enough for us to conclude that p is different from .04, or is this large value of $\hat{p}$ just due to the fact that we tested a sample and not the entire population—that is, is this sampling error?

The resulting value of the test statistic was

$$Z^* = \frac{\hat{p} - .04}{\sqrt{\dfrac{(.04)(.96)}{150}}} = \frac{.0867 - .04}{.016} = 2.92$$

By comparing $Z^* = 2.92$ with the value 1.96 in Table A.4, we rejected H_0 using $\alpha = .05$; that is, the proportion of defective calculators was not 4%. The corresponding p-value was .0036.

Another Test for H_0: $p = p_0$ versus H_a: $p \neq p_0$

There is another test for a *two-tailed* test on p. This new test extends easily to a situation in which there are *more than two possible outcomes* for each trial: the **multinomial situation.**

To demonstrate this new testing procedure, the **chi-square goodness-of-fit test,** let's look at the lot sampling example. Note that the population consists of two *categories*—defective (category 1) and nondefective (category 2). Let $p_1 =$ the proportion of defectives in the population and $p_2 =$ the proportion of nondefectives in the population. In the previous solution, $p_1 = p$ and $p_2 = 1 - p$.

The **observed frequency** is the number of observations in a category. In this case, we observed 13 sample values in category 1 (defective) and 137 in category 2. So we define

$$O_1 = 13$$
$$O_2 = 137$$

The **expected frequency** is the number of observations we *expect* to see in a category if H_0 is true. How many units do we expect to see in each category if H_0 is *true?* The hypotheses here can be written

$$H_0: p_1 = .04, p_2 = .96$$
$$H_a: p_1 \neq .04, p_2 \neq .96$$

This means that if H_0 is true, then, on average, 4% of the sample values should be defective (category 1) and 96% should be nondefective (category 2). Define

E_1 = expected number of sample values in category 1 if H_0 is true

$= (150)(.04) = 6.0$

E_2 = expected number of sample values in category 2 if H_0 is true

$= (150)(.96) = 144.0$

We next define a test statistic that has an approximate chi-square distribution:

$$\chi^2 = \sum \frac{(O - E)^2}{E}$$

13.1

where the summation is over all categories (two here). In previous uses of this distribution, its shape depended on the sample size, specified by the degrees of freedom (df). Now the shape depends on the number of categories, and

df = number of categories − 1

For the binomial situation,

$$df = 2 - 1 = 1$$

Therefore, for any *binomial* application, the test statistic in equation 13.1 has a *chi-square distribution with 1 df*.

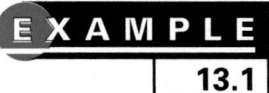

EXAMPLE 13.1

Analyze the lot sampling data using the chi-square test statistic and a significance level of $\alpha = .05$.

Solution   **Step 1.** The hypotheses are

$$H_0: p_1 = .04, p_2 = .96$$
$$H_a: p_1 \neq .04, p_2 \neq .96$$

Step 2. The test statistic is

$$\chi^2 = \sum \frac{(O - E)^2}{E}$$
$$= \frac{(O_1 - E_1)^2}{E_1} + \frac{(O_2 - E_2)^2}{E_2}$$

Step 3. If H_0 is not true (H_a is true), we expect the observed values to be different from the expected values, resulting in a *large* value for χ^2. So the procedure is to reject H_0 if the chi-square test statistic lies in the *right* tail. Consequently, we

reject H_0 if $\chi^2 > \chi^2_{.05,1}$

where $\chi^2_{.05,1}$ is the χ^2 value having a right-tail area of .05 with 1 df. Using Table A.6, this value is 3.84. Therefore, we

reject H_0 if $\chi^2 > 3.84$

Step 4. We have

$O_1 = 13$ $\qquad$ $E_1 = 6$

$O_2 = 137$ $\qquad$ $E_2 = 144$

(Note that $O_1 + O_2 = E_1 + E_2 = n = 150$.) The calculated value of the test statistic is

$$\chi^{2*} = \frac{(13-6)^2}{6} + \frac{(137-144)^2}{144}$$
$$= 8.17 + .34 = 8.51$$

This value is larger than 3.84, so we rejected H_0.

Step 5. We conclude, as before, that the proportion of defectives (p_1) is not .04.

The *p*-value for Example 13.1 using the chi-square analysis is shown in Figure 13.1; it is the shaded area to the right of 8.51. Using Table A.6, all we can say is that this value is less than .005. The actual value is .0036 (calculated using Excel or a statistical software package). This is the *same p*-value we obtained when Z^* was used to perform this test of hypothesis.

In the lot sampling example, we observe some quite fascinating (would you believe mildly interesting?) parallels with Chapter 11. In Chapter 11, we noted that when using the *F* test from the ANOVA procedure to test $H_0: \mu_1 = \mu_2$, we obtained an *F* value that was the *square* of the *t* value obtained using the corresponding *t* test. Also, the value from the *F* table used to define the rejection region was the square of the corresponding *t* value. This relationship held only when testing the equality of two means. Finally, the *p*-values from the two tests were identical; it made no difference which test we used for a two-tailed test on two means because the results were the same for both procedures. However, the ANOVA technique also could be used for comparing the means of more than two populations.

Using the results from the lot-sampling example in this chapter, we again find that:

1. $\chi^{2*} = 8.51 = (2.92)^2 = (Z^*)^2$.

2. The table values for the rejection region are 1.96 for the Z test and $3.84 = (1.96)^2$ for the χ^2 test.

3. The *p*-value for each test was the same.

So again we have two testing procedures that produce identical conclusions. *The chi-square test, however, extends easily to the multinomial situation.* The chi-square goodness-of-fit test is an *extension* of the Z test used to test a binomial parameter. Furthermore, there is a definite relationship between the standard normal distribution (Z) and the chi-square distribution: the *square* of Z always is a chi-square random variable with 1 df.

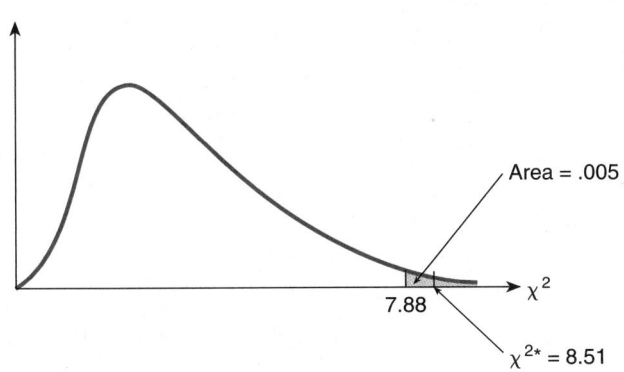

FIGURE

13.1

p-value for Example 13.1 using the chi-square analysis.

TESTING H_0: $p = p_0$ VERSUS H_a: $p \neq p_0$

Using Z Test
Test statistic:

$$Z = \frac{\hat{p} - p_0}{\sqrt{\dfrac{p_0(1 - p_0)}{n}}}$$

Rejection region:
reject H_0 if $|Z| > Z_{\alpha/2}$
(Use Table A.4.)

Using χ^2 Test
Test statistic:

$$\chi^2 = \frac{(O_1 - E_1)^2}{E_1} + \frac{(O_2 - E_2)^2}{E_2}$$

$$= \sum \frac{(O - E)^2}{E}$$

Rejection region:
reject H_0 if $\chi^2 > \chi^2_{\alpha,1}$
(Use Table A.6.)

The Multinomial Situation

The multinomial situation is identical to the binomial situation, except that there are k possible outcomes on each trial rather than two. Here, k is any integer that is at least 2.

Suppose that the management of Tucker Industries is concerned with how company employees feel about management; in particular, do the employees feel that management is responsive to employee suggestions? A quality consultant has informed the Tucker team charged with examining this situation that traditionally the following percentages are observed in companies of this size:

Category	Description	Percentage of Employees in This Category
1	Management is extremely responsive to employee suggestions	.05
2	Management is somewhat responsive to employee suggestions	.30
3	No opinion	.20
4	Management is usually not responsive to employee suggestions	.40
5	Management is rarely responsive to employee suggestions	.05

The Tucker team would like to verify these percentages among its own employees and obtains responses to the question, "Is management responsive to employee suggestions?" from a random sample of 500 employees. Possible responses to this question are the five categories just listed, and the following frequencies are observed in each category for this sample:

Category	Frequency
1	32
2	142
3	87
4	221
5	18
	500

The assumptions necessary for a multinomial experiment are as follows:

1. The experiment consists of n independent repetitions (trials).

2. Each trial outcome falls in exactly one of k categories.

3. The probabilities of the k outcomes are denoted by $p_1, p_2, \ldots, p_k$, where these probabilities (proportions) remain the same on each trial. Also, $p_1 + p_2 + \cdots + p_k = 1$.

For this situation, we can define k random variables as the k observed values, where

$$O_1 = \text{observed number of sample values in category 1}$$
$$O_2 = \text{observed number of sample values in category 2}$$
$$\vdots$$
$$O_k = \text{observed number of sample values in category } k$$

For our example, $n = 500$ trials, where each trial consists of obtaining an employee response to the question dealing with management response to employee suggestions. There are $k = 5$ possible responses (categories) for this experiment. Assuming these 500 Tucker Industries employees constitute a random sample, then these trials are independent. Also, let

$$p_1 = \text{proportion of people responding in category 1}$$
$$p_2 = \text{proportion of people responding in category 2}$$
$$\vdots$$
$$p_5 = \text{proportion of people responding in category 5}$$

The five random variables in our example are

$$O_1 = \text{observed number of Tucker employees in the sample responding in category 1}$$
$$\vdots$$
$$O_5 = \text{observed number of Tucker employees in the sample responding in category 5}$$

Thus, this example fits the assumptions for the multinomial situation.

Hypothesis Testing for a Multinomial Situation

The hypotheses for the Tucker Industries example are

$$H_0: p_1 = .05, p_2 = .30, p_3 = .20, p_4 = .40, p_5 = .05$$
$$H_a: \text{at least one of the } p_i\text{'s is incorrect}$$

Notice that H_a is *not* $p_1 \neq .05$, $p_2 \neq .30$, $\ldots$, $p_5 \neq .05$. This hypothesis is too strong and is not the opposite of H_0.

Let $p_{1,0}$ be any specified value of p_1, $p_{2,0}$ any specified value of p_2, and so on. The hypotheses to test the multinomial parameters are

$$H_0: p_1 = p_{1,0}, p_2 = p_{2,0}, \ldots, p_k = p_{k,0}$$
$$H_a: \text{at least one of the } p_i\text{'s is incorrect}$$

Using the observed values ($O_1, O_2, \ldots$), the point estimates here are

$$\hat{p}_1 = \text{estimate of } p_1 = O_1/n$$
$$\hat{p}_2 = \text{estimate of } p_2 = O_2/n$$
$$\vdots$$

To test H_0 versus H_a, we use the previously stated chi-square statistic. To define the rejection region, notice that when H_a is true, we would expect the O's and E's to be "far apart," because the E's are determined by assuming that H_0 is true. In other words, if H_a is true, the chi-square test statistic should be large. Consequently, we always reject H_0 when χ^{2*} lies in the *right tail* when using this particular statistic.

To test H_0 versus H_a, compute

$$\chi^2 = \sum \frac{(O - E)^2}{E}$$

where

1. The summation is across all categories (outcomes).

2. The O's are the *observed* frequencies in each category using the sample.

3. The E's are the *expected* frequencies in each category if H_0 is true, so

$$E_1 = np_{1,0}$$
$$E_2 = np_{2,0}$$
$$E_3 = np_{3,0}$$
$$\vdots$$

4. The df for the chi-square statistic are $k - 1$, where k is the number of categories.

To carry out the test,

$$\text{reject } H_0 \text{ if } \chi^2 > \chi^2_{\alpha,df}$$

Notice that the hypothetical proportions (probabilities) for each of the categories are specified in H_0. Consequently, we will complete the analysis by concluding that at least one of the proportions is incorrect (we reject H_0) or that there is not enough evidence to conclude that these proportions are incorrect (we fail to reject H_0). We do not *accept* H_0; we never conclude that these specified proportions *are* correct. We act like the juror who acquits a defendant not because he or she is convinced that this person is innocent but because there was not sufficient evidence for conviction.

When we introduced the ANOVA technique, we mentioned that this procedure allowed us to determine whether many population means were equal using a *single* test. This technique was preferable to using many t tests to test the equality of two means, one pair at a time, because these tests would not be independent, and the overall significance level would be difficult to determine. We encounter the same situation here. *It is much better to use a chi-square goodness-of-fit test to test all of the proportions at once rather than using many Z tests to test the individual proportions.*

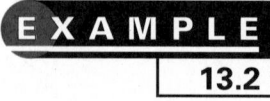

EXAMPLE 13.2

What do the observed number of Tucker Industries employees in each category for the sample of 500 employees tell us about the mix of responses to this question for all Tucker employees? Do they conform to the percentages cited by the quality consultant? Use a significance level of .05.

Solution **Step 1.** Let p_1 = proportion of all Tucker employees that would respond in category 1 to this question; that is, they feel that management is extremely responsive to employee suggestions. Similarly, define p_2, p_3, p_4, and p_5 to be the corresponding percentages for categories 2, 3, 4, and 5. The hypotheses under investigation are

$$H_0: p_1 = .05, p_2 = .30, p_3 = .20, p_4 = .40, p_5 = .05$$

$$H_a: \text{at least one of these } p_i\text{'s is incorrect}$$

Step 2. The test statistic is

$$\chi^2 = \sum \frac{(O-E)^2}{E}$$

where the summation is over the five categories.

Step 3. Your test procedure here is to

$$\text{reject } H_0 \text{ if } \chi^2 > \chi^2_{\alpha,df}$$

The df is (number of categories) – 1, so df = 5 – 1 = 4. The chi-square value from Table A.6 is $\chi^2_{.05,4} = 9.49$, and we

$$\text{reject } H_0 \text{ if } \chi^2 > 9.49$$

Step 4. The observed values are

$$O_1 = 32, O_2 = 142, O_3 = 87, O_4 = 221, O_5 = 18$$

The expected values when H_0 is true are obtained by multiplying $n = 500$ by each of the proportions in H_0. So

$$E_1 = (500)(.05) = 25$$
$$E_2 = (500)(.30) = 150$$
$$E_3 = (500)(.20) = 100$$
$$E_4 = (500)(.40) = 200$$
$$E_5 = (500)(.05) = 25$$

In general, do not round the expected values, because they are averages. The computed value of the chi-square test statistic is

$$\chi^{2*} = \frac{(32-25)^2}{25} + \frac{(142-150)^2}{150} + \frac{(87-100)^2}{100} + \frac{(221-200)^2}{200} + \frac{(18-25)^2}{25}$$
$$= 8.242$$

Because 8.242 does not exceed 9.49, we fail to reject H_0.

Step 5. There is insufficient evidence to indicate that the proportion of Tucker employees in each response category differs from the proportions stated by the quality consultant. In other words, the observed values were "close enough" to the expected values under H_0 to let this hypothesis stand. Examining categories 4 and 5, this indicates that 45% of the Tucker employees feel that management is not responsive on some level to employee suggestions. Obviously, there is a great deal of room for improvement in this area of management relations.

In Example 13.2, the proportions under investigation were specified directly. We can also use the chi-square statistic when the proportions are implied.

EXAMPLE 13.3

Allied Health Corporation owns and operates hospitals in the southeast. Three of their hospitals were recently audited by federal auditors to determine if the three hospitals were in compliance with Medicare billing regulations. According to the auditors, a billing selected for audit had an equal probability of being from each of the three hospitals. A random sample of the audited billings revealed the following number of billings selected from each hospital: hospital 1: 485, hospital 2: 405, hospital 3: 310; total = 1,200. Using a significance level of .01, what can you conclude about the auditors' selection of billings?

Solution   **Step 1.** Let p_1 = proportion of audited billings from hospital 1, p_2 = proportion from hospital 2, and p_3 = proportion from hospital 3. If an audited billing has an equal probability of belonging to each hospital, then each of these proportions will be 1/3, providing the values for H_0:

$$H_0: p_1 = 1/3, p_2 = 1/3, p_3 = 1/3$$

H_a: at least one of these proportions is incorrect

Steps 2 and 3. The test procedure will be to

$$\text{reject } H_0 \text{ if } \chi^2 > \chi^2_{.01,2} = 9.21$$

because df $= k - 1 = 3 - 1 = 2$. The value of χ^2 is determined from equation 13.2.

Step 4. The observed and expected values are

O	E (if H_0 is true)	$\hat{p}$
$O_1 = 485$	$E_1 = (1200)(1/3) = 400$	$485/1200 = .404$
$O_2 = 405$	$E_2 = (1200)(1/3) = 400$	$405/1200 = .338$
$O_3 = \underline{310}$	$E_3 = (1200)(1/3) = \underline{400}$	$310/1200 = \underline{.258}$
1,200	1,200	1.0

$$\chi^{2*} = \frac{(485-400)^2}{400} + \frac{(405-400)^2}{400} + \frac{(310-400)^2}{400}$$

$$= 18.06 + .06 + 20.25 = 38.4$$

So we reject H_0 because $38.4 > 9.21$.

Step 5. There *is* an unequal distribution of hospital selection here. Your next step should be to examine the three values making up this large χ^2 value. This large value is due to the 18.06 (the number of billings from hospital 1 was larger than expected under H_0) and the 20.25 (the number of billings from hospital 3 was smaller than expected under H_0). This discrepancy can also be seen in the values of $\hat{p}$ from step 4.

The p-value for the results in Example 13.3 is shown in Figure 13.2. Using Table A.6 and 2 df, the largest value here is 10.6, with a corresponding right-tail area of .005. All you can say using this table is that the p-value is less than .005. At any rate, it is small and would lead you to reject H_0 for the most common values of α.

Pooling Categories

When using the chi-square procedure of comparing observed and expected values, we determine the difference between these two values for each category, square it, and *divide by the expected value, E.* If one value of E is very small (say, less than 5), then this computation produces an extremely *large* contribution to the final χ^2 value from this category. In other words, this small expected value pro-

---

FIGURE

13.2

Shaded area is p-value for Example 13.3.

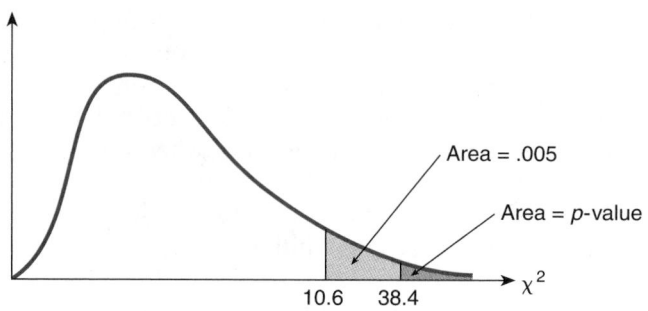

duces an inflated chi-square value, with the result that we reject H_0 when perhaps we should not have. To prevent this from occurring, we use the following rule: When using equation 13.2, each expected value, E, should be at least 5.*

If you encounter an application where one or more of the expected values is less than 5, you can handle this situation by **pooling** your categories such that each of the new categories has an expected value that is at least 5.

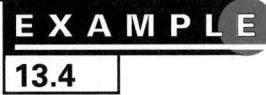

The analysis in Example 13.2 was repeated for Metro Elevators, a small subsidiary of Tucker Industries. Metro installs and repairs escalators and elevators for use in commercial buildings. Independent of the Tucker sample in Example 13.2, Metro obtained a random sample of 75 of their employees, since it suspected that its responses to the question dealing with how well management responds to employee suggestions would be considerably different from the stated proportions in Example 13.2. The following data were obtained:

Category	Frequency
1	9
2	31
3	12
4	18
5	5
	75

Do the data from Metro appear to contradict the stated proportions in Example 13.2? Use $\alpha = .05$.

Solution

Category	Observed (O)	Expected (E), if H_0 Is True
1	$O_1 = 9$	$E_1 = (75)(.05) = 3.75$
2	$O_2 = 31$	$E_2 = (75)(.30) = 22.50$
3	$O_3 = 12$	$E_3 = (75)(.20) = 15.00$
4	$O_4 = 18$	$E_4 = (75)(.40) = 30.00$
5	$O_5 = 5$	$E_5 = (75)(.05) = 3.75$

Notice that the first and last expected values are less than 5. As a result, it will be necessary to pool (combine) categories 1 and 2 and categories 4 and 5. The new summary is obtained by summing O_1 and O_2 ($= 40$), E_1 and E_2 ($= 26.25$), O_4 and O_5 ($= 23$), and E_4 and E_5 ($= 33.75$).

New Category	Name	Observed (O)	Expected (E), if H_0 Is True
1	Management is responsive	40	26.25
2	No opinion	12	15.00
3	Management is not responsive	23	33.75
		75	75

Now each of the expected values is at least 5, and we can continue the analysis. The hypotheses using the new categories are

$$H_0: p_1 = .35, p_2 = .20, p_3 = .45$$

H_a: at least one of these proportions is incorrect

The value of $p_1 = .35$ is obtained by summing the previous first two proportions ($.05 + .30$), and the value of $p_3 = .45$ is the sum of the previous last two proportions ($.40 + .05$).

---

*This rule is somewhat arbitrary and a bit conservative, but is commonly used. Another procedure for pooling requires that all the expected values be 3 or more, while yet another procedure requires that no more than 20% of all the expected values be less than 5, with none less than 1.

The computed chi-square value is now

$$\chi^{2*} = \frac{(40 - 26.25)^2}{26.25} + \frac{(12 - 15)^2}{15} + \frac{(23 - 33.75)^2}{33.75}$$
$$= 7.202 + .600 + 3.424 = 11.226$$

This value exceeds the Table A.6 value of $\chi^2_{.05,2} = 5.99$, so we reject H_0 and conclude that the mix of responses to this question at Metro Elevator is not the same as the proportions stated in Example 13.2. The main contributors to this large chi-square value came from the first and third categories, since we observed more people stating that management is responsive than we expected under H_0 (40 versus 26.25) and fewer people stating that management is not responsive than expected (23 versus 33.75).

Using Excel to Perform a Multinomial Goodness-of-Fit Test

The KPK Data Analysis package provides an easy method of carrying out a multinomial goodness-of-fit test. We will illustrate this procedure using Example 13.2, which tested five proportions. First, enter the five observed values (32, 142, 87, 221, 18) in column A and the five proportions (.05, .30, .20, .40, .05) in column B. Click on **KPK Data Analysis ➤ Chi Square Tests.** Enter "A1:A5" for the **Input Range of Observed Frequencies** and "B1:B5" for the **Input Range of Hypothesized Proportions.** You can enter "C1" for the **Output Range.** The default alpha value is 5%, and so there is no need to change this value.

The resulting output is shown in Figure 13.3, where column J (a blank column) is hidden. The computed chi-square value (8.242) is the same as that obtained in the solution to Example 13.2, and based on the p-value of .0831 (in cell L9), we again fail to reject H_0 since the p-value exceeds $\alpha = .05$. As a reminder, you should follow up this conclusion with a discussion of why the large chi-square value occurred, as was done in step 5 of the Example 13.2 solution.

Testing a Hypothesis about a Distributional Form

In this discussion of the goodness-of-fit test, we examine such questions as the following:

- Is it true that these data came from a binomial distribution with probability of success, p, equal to .2?

FIGURE

13.3

Excel spreadsheet for chi-square multinomial goodness-of-fit test using KPK Data Analysis (Example 13.2).

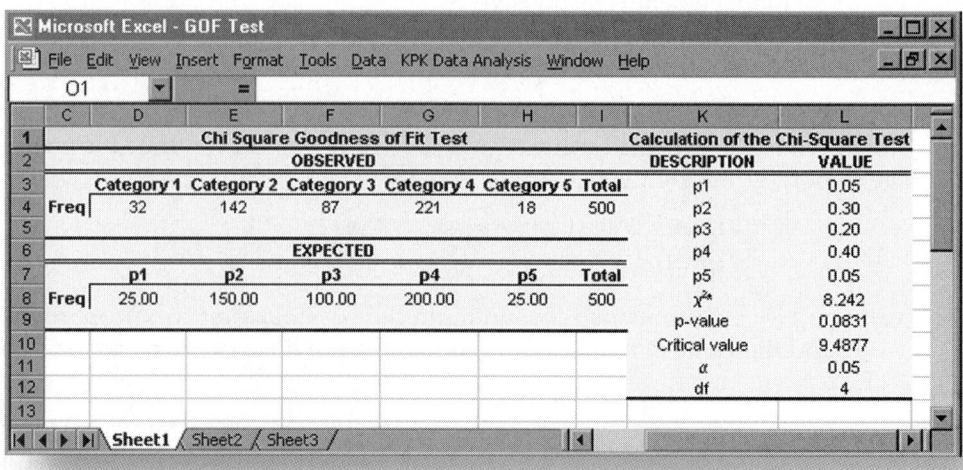

- Does this particular set of data violate the assumption that the number of defects in this product follow a Poisson distribution?
- Is there any reason to doubt the assumption that the weights of all Rice Krinkle cereal boxes follow a normal distribution using a recently obtained sample of boxes?

The first two questions concern *discrete* distributions (binomial and Poisson). The final question is concerned with whether the data came from a particular *continuous* (in this case, normal) distribution. We illustrate the chi-square technique using a goodness-of-fit test for a discrete situation. (The goodness-of-fit test for the normal distribution is illustrated in Exercise 13.13.)

Suppose that Blitz laundry detergent is well known for its obnoxious commercials, which advertise that 20% of all Blitz boxes contain a valuable discount coupon. The commercials also claim that the boxes containing coupons are randomly distributed across all stores carrying the product. A recent study obtained a random sample of 10 Blitz boxes from each of 100 different stores. The results were

Of 10 Boxes, Number Containing Coupons	Number of Stores
0	9
1	31
2	29
3	18
>3	13
	100

We wish to know whether these data appear to come from a binomial distribution with $p = .2$, using $\alpha = .05$.

Your immediate reaction may well be that this problem does not fit a multinomial situation. However, there are 100 independent trials, each trial consisting of randomly selecting 10 boxes of Blitz detergent. Also, we can set up five categories here, namely:

Category 1: Observe 0 coupons in the 10 boxes (probability p_1)

Category 2: Observe 1 coupon in the 10 boxes (probability p_2)

Category 3: Observe 2 coupons in the 10 boxes (probability p_3)

Category 4: Observe 3 coupons in the 10 boxes (probability p_4)

Category 5: Observe > 3 coupons in the 10 boxes (probability p_5)

So we *do* have a multinomial situation here. The hypotheses can be stated as

H_0: the data follow a binomial distribution with $p = .2$

H_a: the data do not follow a binomial distribution with $p = .2$

If H_0 is true, how often should we observe zero coupons in 10 boxes? Each multinomial trial fits a binomial situation, where a success consists of a box containing a coupon. We repeat the trial 10 times and count the number of successes (coupons). According to Table A.1, with $n = 10$ and probability of success $p = .2$, you should observe zero coupons out of 10 boxes 10.7% of the time. So, if H_0 is true, $p_1 = .107$. Similarly, if H_0 is true, we should see 1 success out of 10 trials 26.8% of the time. In other words, $p_2 = .268$. Therefore, another way to state your hypotheses is

H_0: $p_1 = .107$, $p_2 = .268$, $p_3 = .302$, $p_4 = .201$, $p_5 = .122$

H_a: at least one of these p_i's is incorrect

We obtain p_5 by finding the probability of more than three successes in 10 trials:

$$1 - (\text{probability of 3 or less}) = 1 - (p_1 + p_2 + p_3 + p_4)$$

$$= 1 - .878 = .122$$

So this is a multinomial test of hypothesis in disguise. Next, we compute the expected values, E.

Category	Observed (O)	Expected (E), if H_0 Is True
0 boxes	9	$(100)(.107) = 10.7$
1 box	31	$(100)(.268) = 26.8$
2 boxes	29	$(100)(.302) = 30.2$
3 boxes	18	$(100)(.201) = 20.1$
>3 boxes	13	$(100)(.122) = 12.2$
	100	100

Make sure that all the E's (do not worry about the O's) are at least 5. In this case, all E's are greater than 5, so no pooling of categories is necessary.

To define the rejection region, we notice that there are $k =$ five categories. So the df in the chi-square statistic is df $= k - 1 = 4$. Also, $\chi^2_{.05,4} = 9.49$, and so the test procedure will be to

$$\text{reject } H_0 \text{ if } \chi^2 > 9.49$$

The value of our test statistic is

$$\chi^{2}* = \frac{(9 - 10.7)^2}{10.7} + \frac{(31 - 26.8)^2}{26.8} + \cdots + \frac{(13 - 12.2)^2}{12.2}$$
$$= 1.25$$

Because 1.25 is less than 9.49, we fail to reject H_0 and conclude that there is no evidence to suggest that these data have violated the binomial assumption. These 100 observations suggest that we have no reason to accuse Blitz of false advertising for their claim that 20% of their boxes contain coupons.

In summary, you can refer to the following guidelines if you are trying to perform a test of hypothesis on a binomial parameter, p (for example, H_0: $p = .2$).

1. If you have a *single* sample of size n, then the results of Chapter 10 apply; you have a binomial experiment.

2. If you have *many* samples of size n, then the results of this section apply; this problem can be expressed as a multinomial experiment. The chi-square goodness-of-fit procedure allows you to perform a test on the population proportion, p, as well as determine if the population follows a binomial distribution. The previous example illustrates this type of situation.

Distributional Form with Unknown Parameters

In the Blitz cereal example, H_0 not only stated that the data followed a binomial distribution, it also specified a value of the binomial parameter p (namely, $p = .2$). Often your only concern is whether the data follow a particular distribution (such as binomial, Poisson, or normal), and the values of the corresponding parameters are not present.

For example, suppose that the manager of Case Electronics has always assumed that the weekly sales of Case's top-of-the-line telephone answering machine followed a Poisson distribution. Data from a 50-week period were gathered, with the following results:

Units Sold	Number of Weeks	Units Sold	Number of Weeks
0	1	5	7
1	3	6	5
2	6	7	3
3	11	8	4
4	10	>8	0
			50

How can we test the hypothesis that the number of units sold follows a Poisson distribution, using $\alpha = .1$?

The correct hypotheses here are

H_0: weekly sales follow a Poisson distribution

H_a: weekly sales do not follow a Poisson distribution

The probability function for the Poisson distribution has one parameter, μ, because this function (from equation 5.15) is given by

$$P(X = x) = \frac{\mu^x e^{-\mu}}{x!}$$

for $x = 0, 1, 2, \ldots$, where $x =$ the number of units sold during a particular week.

However, the value of μ was not specified in H_0. In this case, we estimate any unknown parameter (μ, here) from the sample information and replace each parameter by its estimate in the probability function. In this way, we can estimate all the expected frequencies ($E_1, E_2, E_3, \ldots$).

Whenever you estimate unknown parameters for use with the chi-square test, *you need to adjust the corresponding degrees of freedom,* df. In general, the df for the chi-square goodness-of-fit statistic is given by

df = (number of classes) – 1 – (number of estimated parameters)

For the Poisson situation, you are estimating only one parameter, μ, and so the df = (number of classes) – 1 – 1 = (number of classes) – 2. The same argument holds true for a test of hypothesis on a binomial distribution where the single parameter, p, is unspecified in H_0 and is instead estimated from the sample information.

Estimating μ

Because μ is the mean of the telephone answering machine sales population, we estimate it using the average (mean) of the sample. In the sample, we observe 1 value of zero, 3 values of one, 6 values of two, and so on for all 50 values. The sample average, our estimate of μ, will be

$$\hat{\mu} = \frac{(0)(1) + (1)(3) + (2)(6) + \cdots + (8)(4)}{50}$$

$$= \frac{206}{50} = 4.12$$

Rounding this to $\hat{\mu} = 4.1$, the estimated probability function is

$$P(X = x) = \frac{(4.1)^x e^{-4.1}}{x!}$$

for $x = 0, 1, 2, \ldots$.

We can now use Table A.3 (the Poisson table) to estimate the expected number of weeks with zero sales, with one sale, and so on. We are *estimating* each expected value, so we denote each of them as $\hat{E}$.

X	P(X = x)	$\hat{E}$	O
0	.0166	(.0166)(50) = .83	1
1	.0679	(.0679)(50) = 3.39	3
2	.1393	(.1393)(50) = 6.97	6
3	.1904	(.1904)(50) = 9.52	11
4	.1951	(.1951)(50) = 9.76	10
5	.1600	(.1600)(50) = 8.00	7
6	.1093	(.1093)(50) = 5.46	5
7	.0640	(.0640)(50) = 3.20	3
8	.0328	(.0328)(50) = 1.64	4
>8	.0246	(.0246)(50) = 1.23	0
	1.0000	50.00	50

Notice that, for the category $X > 8$, the corresponding probability is $1 - (.0166 + .0679 + \cdots + .0640 + .0328) = .0246$.

The next step always is to check your expected frequencies ($\hat{E}$) to see if pooling is necessary. Each $\hat{E}$ value must be at least 5, so it is necessary to pool the first three classes ($.83 + 3.39 + 6.97 = 11.19$) and the last three classes ($3.20 + 1.64 + 1.23 = 6.07$). Now you can evaluate the chi-square statistic.

X	$\hat{E}$	O	$(O - \hat{E})$	$(O - \hat{E})^2/\hat{E}$
≤ 2	11.19	10	−1.19	.127
3	9.52	11	1.48	.230
4	9.76	10	.24	.006
5	8.00	7	−1.00	.125
6	5.46	5	−.46	.039
≥ 7	6.07	7	.93	.142
	50.00	50	0.00	.669

(check)

$$\chi^2 = \sum \frac{(O - \hat{E})^2}{\hat{E}} = .669$$

The degrees of freedom for the corresponding test are

$$df = (\text{number of classes}) - 1 - (\text{number of estimated parameters})$$

$$= 6 - 1 - 1 = 4$$

The resulting test, using Table A.6 and $\alpha = .1$, is

reject H_0 if $\chi^2 > 7.779$

Because $.669 < 7.779$, we fail to reject H_0 and conclude that there is not enough evidence to indicate that the Poisson distribution assumption is incorrect.

X Exercises 13.1–13.15

Understanding the Mechanics

13.1 Using the following data, test with a significance level of 10% that the probabilities are the same in every category.

Category	A	B	C	D
Observed Frequency	58	37	44	61

13.2 Consider a multinomial experiment with five categories and a sample of size 50. Test H_0: $p_1 = .1$, $p_2 = .2$, $p_3 = .2$, $p_4 = .2$, $p_5 = .3$. Use a 5% signifiance level. Do all the cells have an expected frequency of at least 5?

Category	1	2	3	4	5
Observed Frequency	3	12	20	5	10

13.3 Do the following data appear to come from a binomial distribution with $p = .5$? Test using a .05 significance level.

Value of Binomial Random Variable	Observed Frequency
0	2
1	11
2	34
3	31
4	18
5	5

Applying the New Concepts

13.4 The credit card industry is very competitive, with about 3 billion solicitations each year. In 1998, Visa had about 47% of the market, compared with nearly 26% for Mastercard, 20% for American Express, and 7% for other credit cards. Suppose that a financial analyst wished to determine if these percentages still held. Assume that the financial analyst randomly sampled 200 households and asked which credit card they primarily used. The results were as follows.

Visa	Mastercard	American Express	Other
110	40	39	11

a. What are the expected values for each category? Should the expected values be above a certain value for the chi-square test to be valid?

b. Does this survey indicate that the population percentages using these credit cards differ from the previous year? Use a .10 significance level.

(Source: "Credit Card Firms Face Justice Suit," *USA Today,* July 17, 1998, p. 1B.)

13.5 A stockbroker believes that when too many of the stock market newsletters are bullish on the market (that is, they predict that stock prices will go higher), the stock market will most likely fall. Thirty-two randomly selected stock market newsletters were each placed in one of three categories:

Bearish on Stock Market	Neutral on Stock Market	Bullish on Stock Market
9	10	13

Test the null hypothesis that the newsletters are equally divided among the three categories. Use a .05 significance level.

13.6 Economists believe that the average holiday spending for Americans is $800. The amount of time to pay off this holiday expense is two months or less for about 35% of the population and more than two months for the rest of the population. To check this claim, suppose that a random sample of 500 American adults was selected, and the following results were recorded.

Two Months or Less to Pay Off Holiday Bills	More than Two Months to Pay Off Holiday Bills
165	335

a. Is there sufficient evidence indicating that the percentage of the population paying off their holiday bills in two months or less differs from 35%?

b. Use the Z test to test the belief in part a. Use a 10% significance level.

c. What relationship exists between the test statistic in parts a and b?

(Source: "Holiday Hangover," *USA Today*, December 15, 1998, p. 1B.)

13.7 Seven manufacturers virtually dominate the market for residential central air conditioners. The proportion of the market captured by each manufacturer has been fairly constant over the past few years with Carrier, Goodman, Trane, Rheem, Lennox, York, and Nordyne having 29%, 18%, 15%, 13%, 13%, 7%, and 5%, respectively. However, marketing analysts believe that the market share by these manufacturers is changing due to new government-mandated efficiency standards for residential air-conditioning systems. Suppose that a survey of 200 newly constructed residential homes in the Atlanta area revealed the following number of central air conditioners installed by the seven manufacturers. Do the data indicate that the market share by these seven manufacturers has changed? Use a 5% significance level.

Carrier	Goodman	Trane	Rheem	Lennox	York	Nordyne
50	55	25	29	24	9	8

(Source: "Air Conditioner Makers Clash over New Efficiency Standards," *Dallas Morning News*, June 19, 2001, p. 1D.)

13.8 Electrical fuses are packaged in lots of 20. The quality-control department claims that on the average only about 10% of the fuses in each package of 20 fuses are defective. A random sample of 40 packages was selected and the results were:

Defective Fuses	Packages
0	7
1	12
2	10
3	7
4	1
5	1
>5	2

Do these data appear to have come from a binomial distribution with $p = .10$? Use a significance level of .05.

13.9 A temporary manpower service has 20 competent computer programmers that can be assigned to a company on a weekly basis. The manager of the manpower service agency believes that the number of programmers assigned to a job during a week follows a binomial distribution with $p = .05$. A random sample of 100 weeks is selected. Seven classes are used to summarize the frequency of different numbers of programmers assigned to a job during a week. Test that the following data follow a binomial distribution with $p = .05$. Use a .10 significance level.

Class	Number of Programmers Assigned to a Job During a Week	Observed Frequencies
1	0	29
2	1	40
3	2	18
4	3	9
5	4	3
6	5	1
7	6 or more	0

13.10 An auditor believes that the number of errors per 25 invoices in the records of a discount furniture store chain follow a Poisson distribution with a mean of 2.2. To test the auditor's belief, 25 stores were randomly selected and the number of errors were tabulated.

Errors per 25 Invoices	Stores	Errors per 25 Invoices	Stores
0	3	4	2
1	5	5	2
2	7	6	1
3	4	>6	1

Do these data appear to have come from a Poisson distribution with a mean of 2.2? Use a .10 significance level.

13.11 On each flight of Astral Airways, 12 randomly selected passengers are asked if they would be willing to pay a 5% airfare increase to fly on an airline that offered iris-scan security IDs that permitted speedy passage through the security checks. Results of the survey from 50 different flights were as follows:

Yes Answers	Flights	Yes Answers	Flights
0	3	4	7
1	10	5	3
2	13	6	2
3	12	>6	0

Use a chi-square goodness-of-fit test to determine whether these data came from a binomial distribution. Let the significance level be .05. [*Hint:* p must be estimated using (total number of people who said yes)/(total number asked).]

13.12 An assembly-line operation coats moving sheets of steel with a plastic film. If the thickness of the plastic coating at any point is less than 5mm, then a nonconformity is present. A quality inspector samples 150 lots of 1-meter by 10-meter sheets that have been coated. The number of nonconformities is believed to follow a Poisson distribution. Eight classes are used to classify the frequencies of each number of nonconformities per lot. Test the hypothesis that the data follow a Poisson distribution. Use a .05 significance level.

Class	Number of Nonconformities per Lot	Observed Frequency
1	0	21
2	1	43
3	2	37
4	3	25
5	4	12
6	5	7
7	6	5
8	7 or more	0

13.13 To perform certain statistical tests on a set of data, the assumption of normality is required. It is thought that the percentage gain over the past three years in mutual funds that have balanced portfolios of both long-term growth stocks and income-oriented stocks is normally distributed, with a mean of 35% and a standard deviation of 10%. A sample of 75 mutual funds of this type is selected to test this assumption of normality using a chi-square goodness-of-fit test. For the intervals listed, probabilities can be found from the normal table (Table A.4). To find the expected frequencies in the third column, the sample size is multiplied by each probability. If the differences between the observed and expected frequencies are large, then the chi-square statistic based on the observed and expected frequencies would be large and would cause the null hypothesis (that the data were sampled from a normally distributed population with mean = 35 and standard deviation = 10) to be rejected.

Percentage Gain Interval	Probability	Expected Frequency	Observed Frequency
less than 20	.0668	5.01	7
20 and less than 30	.2417	18.1275	15
30 and less than 40	.3830	28.725	26
40 and less than 50	.2417	18.1275	21
50 or more	.0668	5.01	6

At the 5% significance level, complete the chi-square goodness-of-fit test by calculating the chi-square statistic presented in this chapter and by using a tabulated chi-square value for the critical value of the rejection region. The degrees of freedom is taken to be equal to the number of intervals minus one.

Using the Computer

13.14 [DATA SET EX13-14] *Variable description:*

CareerDev: Responses of "Agree," "Indifferent," or "Disagree" to the statement "Telecommuters have an equal chance of being promoted"

According to the International Telework Association and Council, 19.6 million U.S.-based employees telecommuted in 1999. The perceived benefits to the employees include an expected better quality of life and more flexible work schedules, since these employees work at home and have a substantially reduced travel schedule. However, the perceived benefits of promotion are not as easy to assess. One company that has touted its successful telecommuting program is AT&T. Suppose AT&T surveyed 200 of its employees and asked them to respond to the statement, "Telecommuters have an equal chance of being promoted."

a. Use the data in CareerDev to form a contingency table and form a bar chart to display the responses of "Agree," "Indifferent," or "Disagree." (In Excel, click on **KPK Data Analysis ➤ Qualitative Data Charts/Tables ➤ Contingency Tables,** after creating a column of ones for the second variable of the table. In SPSS, select **Transform ➤ Count** to create a table of frequencies. In MINITAB, click on **Stat ➤ Tables ➤ Tally** to construct a table of frequencies.)

b. Assume that a manager at AT&T would like to test the null hypothesis that the proportion of responses for each of these categories is equal. Perform the necessary test using a significance level of 5%. (In Excel, click on **KPK Data Analysis ➤ Chi Square Tests** and select the Multinomial Goodness of Fit test using the frequency table constructed in part a. In SPSS, first replace the words "Agree," "Indifferent," and "Disagree" in the untabulated data with the numbers 1, 2, and 3. This can be performed in Excel using the **If worksheet** function. Select **Analyze ➤ Nonparametric Tests ➤ Chi Square** and select "all categories are equal." In MINITAB, a table of frequencies can be created as in part a. Refer to the Chapter 13 MINITAB appendix on the textbook CD to calculate the chi-square test for a multinomial experiment.)

(Source: "Exploring the Telecommuting Paradox," *Communications of the ACM,* 43, no. 3, March 2000, pp. 29–31.)

13.15 [DATA SET EX13-15] *Variable description:*

LateFlights: Number of late flights per day

A manager for Easy Fly Airlines believes that the number of late flights per day between Boston and New York follows a binomial distribution, with $p = .35$. Easy Fly airlines schedules 10 shuttle flights per day between these cities. A random sample of 100 days was selected, and the number of late flights was recorded for each day.

a. Obtain a discrete histogram for the variable LateFlights.

b. Obtain the binomial probabilities for $n = 10$ and $p = .35$. Using Excel, type "0" through "10" in column C. In D1 type "=Binomdist(C1,10,.35,False)" and drag down through cell D11.

c. Using the probabilities in part b, obtain a column of expected values. Pool cells if necessary.

d. Test that the variable LateFlights follows a binomial distribution, with $p = .35$. Use a 5% significance level.

e. Do a what-if analysis by using a value of $p = .20$ and repeating the analysis. What conclusion do you reach?

CHI-SQUARE TESTS OF INDEPENDENCE

In the previous section, we classified each member of a population into one of many categories. This classification was one-dimensional, because each member was classified using only *one* criterion (brand, color, and so on). In this section, we extend classification to a two-dimensional situation, in which each element in the population is classified according to two criteria, such as gender and income level (high, medium, or low). The question of interest is, are these two variables (classifications) *independent?* For example, if gender and income level are not independent, perhaps gender discrimination is present in the salary structure of a company. If a person's salary is not related to gender, these two classifications *would* be independent.

In Chapter 4, we examined a survey concerned with the age and gender of the purchasers of a recently released microcomputer. The results were summarized in a *contingency* (or *cross-tab*) table. This table consisted of **cells,** where each cell contains the *frequency* of people in the sample who satisfy each of the various cross-classifications:

Gender	Age <30	Age 30–45	Age >45	Total
Male	60	20	40	120
Female	40	30	10	80
Total	100	50	50	200

This 2×3 contingency table shows that there were 60 people who were both male *and* under 30. In Chapter 4, we determined various probabilities for a person selected at random from this group of 200, such as the probability that this person is both a male and over 45 years. Now we will view these data as the results of a particular experiment (survey) and attempt to determine whether the variables—age and gender—are independent for this application. Put another way, is the age structure of the male buyers the same as that of the female purchasers? The hypotheses are

H_0: the classifications (age and gender) are independent

H_a: the classifications are dependent

This problem can also be viewed as a multinomial experiment containing 200 trials and $(2)(3) = 6$ possible categories for each trial outcome.

Deriving a Test of Hypothesis for Independent Classifications

We want to decide whether the data about the purchasers exhibit random variation or a pattern of some type due to a dependency between age and gender. If these classifications *are* independent (H_0 is true), how many people would you expect in each cell? Consider the upper right cell, which shows males over 45 years. The expected number of sample observations in this cell is $200 \cdot P$(sampled purchaser is a male and over 45). Assuming independence, this is $200 \cdot P$(sampled purchaser is a male) $\cdot P$(sampled purchaser is over 45), using the multiplicative rule for independent events discussed in Chapter 4.

What is P(sampled purchaser is a male)? We do not know, because we do not have enough information to determine what percentage of *all* purchasers are male. However, we can *estimate* this probability using the percentage of males in the sample: $120/200 = .6$.

Similarly, P(sampled purchaser is over 45) can be estimated by the fraction of people over 45 in the sample—namely, 50/200. So, our estimate of the expected number of observations for this cell is

$$\hat{E} = 200 \cdot \frac{120}{200} \cdot \frac{50}{200} = \frac{(120)(50)}{200} = 30$$

So, for this cell, the observed frequency is $O = 40$, and our estimate of the expected frequency (if H_0 is true) is $\hat{E} = 30$. In general,

$$\hat{E} = \frac{(\text{row total for this cell}) \cdot (\text{column total for this cell})}{n}$$

where n = total sample size. A summary of the calculations can be tabulated as follows.

Gender	Age	Observed (O)	Expected ($\hat{E}$), If H_0 Is True
Male	<30	60	(120)(100)/200 = 60
	30–45	20	(120)(50)/200 = 30
	>45	40	(120)(50)/200 = 30
Female	<30	40	(80)(100)/200 = 40
	30–45	30	(80)(50)/200 = 20
	>45	10	(80)(50)/200 = 20
		200	200

The easiest way to represent these 12 values is to place the expected value in parentheses alongside the observed value in each cell:

Gender	Age <30	Age 30–45	Age >45	Total
Male	60 (60)	20 (30)	40 (30)	120
Female	40 (40)	30 (20)	10 (20)	80
Total	100	50	50	200

Pooling

At this point, you need to check your expected values. If any one of them is less than 5, you need to combine, or *pool*, the column (or row) in which this small value occurs with another column (or row) to comply with our earlier requirement that all expected values in the chi-square statistic are at least 5. The observed and expected values for this new column (row) are obtained by summing the values for the two columns (rows).

The Test Statistic

The test statistic for testing H_0: the classifications are independent versus H_a: the classifications are dependent is the usual chi-square statistic, which in this case compares each *observed* frequency with the corresponding *expected* frequency estimate.

$$\chi^2 = \sum \frac{(O - \hat{E})^2}{\hat{E}}$$

13.3

where the summation is over all cells of the contingency table.

Degrees of Freedom

In the multinomial situation, the degrees of freedom for the chi-square statistic were $k - 1$, where k = the number of categories (outcomes). In this situation, there were k values of $(O - \hat{E})$. However, because the sum of the observed frequencies is

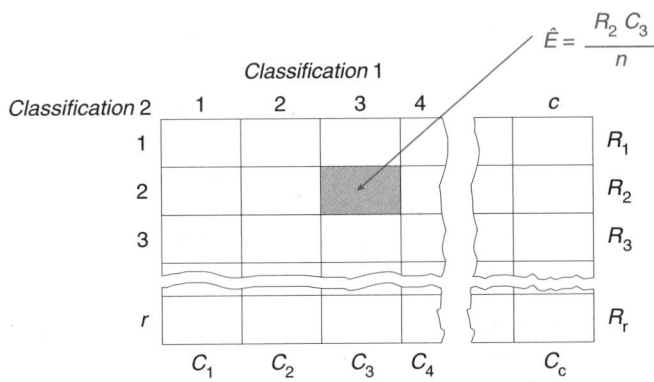

FIGURE

13.4

Expected value estimates for an $r \times c$ contingency table.

the same as the sum of the expected frequencies, the sum of the k values of $(O - \hat{E})$ is *always zero*. This means that, of these k values, only $k - 1$ are free to vary, resulting in $k - 1$ df for the chi-square statistic.

Take a close look at the observed and expected frequencies in the contingency table for age and gender of purchasers. Notice that (1) for each row, sum of O's = sum of $\hat{E}$'s and (2) for each column, sum of O's = sum of $\hat{E}$'s. In general, if classification 1 has c categories and classification 2 has r categories, you construct an $r \times c$ **contingency table** (Figure 13.4). Of the c values of $(O - \hat{E})$ in each row, only $c - 1$ are free to vary. Similarly, only $r - 1$ of the values in each column are free to assume any value. So, for this contingency table, only $(r - 1)(c - 1)$ values are free to vary. Therefore, for the chi-square test of independence,

$$df = (r - 1)(c - 1)$$

13.4

Testing Procedure

When H_0 is not true, the expected frequencies and observed frequencies will be very different, producing a large χ^2 value. We again reject H_0 if the value of the test statistic falls in the *right-tail* rejection region, so we

$$\text{reject } H_0 \text{ if } \chi^2 > \chi^2_{\alpha,df}$$

where $df = (r - 1)(c - 1)$.

In summary, the chi-square test of independence hypotheses are

H_0: the row and column classifications are independent (not related)

H_a: the classifications are dependent (related or associated in some way)

The test statistic is

$$\chi^2 = \sum \frac{(O - \hat{E})^2}{\hat{E}}$$

where

1. The summation is over all cells of the contingency table consisting of r rows and c columns.

2. O is the observed frequency in this cell.

3. $\hat{E}$ is the estimated expected frequency for this cell.

$$\hat{E} = \frac{\left(\begin{array}{c} \text{total of row in} \\ \text{which the cell lies} \end{array} \right) \times \left(\begin{array}{c} \text{total of column in} \\ \text{which the cell lies} \end{array} \right)}{(\text{total of all cells})}$$

4. The degrees of freedom for the chi-square statistic are df $= (r - 1)(c - 1)$.

The test procedure is (using Table A.6):

$$\text{reject } H_0 \text{ if } \chi^2 > \chi^2_{\alpha,df}$$

We can now return to our question of whether the age and gender of micro-computer purchasers are independent. Step 1 (statement of hypotheses) and step 2 (definition of test statistic) of our five-step procedure have been discussed already. Assume that a significance level of $\alpha = .1$ was specified. For step 3, the df are $(2 - 1)(3 - 1) = 2$. Using Table A.6, $\chi^2_{.1,2} = 4.61$. So we will reject H_0 if $\chi^2 > 4.61$. For step 4, referring to the contingency table,

$$\chi^{2*} = \frac{(60 - 60)^2}{60} + \frac{(20 - 30)^2}{30} + \frac{(40 - 30)^2}{30} + \frac{(40 - 40)^2}{40}$$
$$+ \frac{(30 - 20)^2}{20} + \frac{(10 - 20)^2}{20}$$
$$= 0 + 3.33 + 3.33 + 0 + 5 + 5$$
$$= 16.66$$

This exceeds the table value of 4.61, so we reject H_0. We thus conclude that the age and gender classifications are *not* independent (step 5).

If the results of the chi-square test lead to a conclusion that the classifications are not independent, a closer look at the individual terms in the chi-square statistic can often reveal what the relationship is between these two variables.

Examining the six terms, we observe four large values, namely, 3.33 (male/age 30–45), 3.33 (male/age over 45), 5 (female/age 30–45), and 5 (female/age over 45). We obtained more men (and fewer women) over 45 years than we would expect if there was no dependency. Similarly, there were fewer men (and more women) between 30 and 45 years.

We can find the *p*-value for this situation also, given $\chi^{2*} = 16.66$. Using a χ^2 curve with 2 df, the area to the right of 16.66, using Table A.6, is <.005. The *p*-value indicates the *strength* of the dependency between two classifications. *The smaller the p-value, the more you tend to support the alternative hypothesis, which indicates a stronger dependency between the two variables.* For the age and gender illustration, $p < .005$, so we conclude that the age and gender of these purchasers are strongly related.

It is worth mentioning at this point that it is possible that examining one category (such as gender) can fail to show any differences among subcategories (male versus female), but when the category is examined along with another category (such as age classification), patterns can emerge. Such a technique is often useful in detecting job discrimination within companies. For example, no gender discrimination may be evident in a sample, but when it is examined along with race or age categories, certain discriminatory practices can be identified.

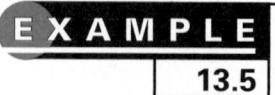

13.5

The personnel director at PCSoft, a computer software development firm, is interested in determining whether an employee's educational level has an effect on his or her job knowledge. An exam was given to a sample of 120 employees, and the director would like to know whether there is a difference in exam performance among three groups: (1) those with a high school diploma only, (2) those with a bachelor's degree only, and (3) those with a master's degree.

Rather than using the actual exam scores and performing a one-factor analysis of variance (ANOVA, discussed in Chapter 11), she rated each person's exam performance as high, average, or low. The results of the study are as follows:

	High	Average	Low	Total
Master's degree	4	20	11	35
Bachelor's degree	12	18	15	45
High school diploma	9	22	9	40
Total	25	60	35	120

Does job knowledge as measured by the exam appear to be related to the level of an employee's education, at this particular firm? Use $\alpha = .05$.

Solution

Step 1. This problem calls for a chi-square test of independence, with hypotheses

H_0: exam performance is independent of educational level

H_a: these classifications are dependent

Steps 2 and 3. Your test statistic is the chi-square statistic in equation 13.3. The table of frequencies here is a 3×3 contingency table, which means that the degrees of freedom are df $= (3 - 1)(3 - 1) = 4$. From Table A.6, we determine that $\chi^2_{.05,4} = 9.49$, so the testing procedure is to

reject H_0 if $\chi^2 > 9.49$

Step 4. Computing the expected frequency estimates in the usual way, we arrive at the following table:

	High	Average	Low	Total
Master's degree	4 (7.29)	20 (17.5)	11 (10.21)	35
Bachelor's degree	12 (9.38)	18 (22.5)	15 (13.12)	45
High school diploma	9 (8.33)	22 (20.0)	9 (11.67)	40
Total	25	60	35	120

To illustrate the calculations, the 11.67 in the lower right cell is $(40 \times 35)/120$. The computed chi-square value is

$$\chi^{2*} = \frac{(4 - 7.29)^2}{7.29} + \frac{(20 - 17.5)^2}{17.5} + \cdots + \frac{(9 - 11.67)^2}{11.67} = 4.67$$

This value is less than 9.49, and so we fail to reject H_0.

Step 5. We see no evidence of a relationship between job knowledge as measured by the exam and level of education.

We do not conclude that these data demonstrate that the two classifications are clearly *independent*, because this would amount to accepting H_0. We are simply unable to demonstrate that a relationship exists.

You can carry out a test of independence using Excel, but you will need to first construct a table of the expected frequencies—a somewhat tedious procedure. The analysis is much simpler using the macro contained in KPK Data Analysis. We will illustrate this procedure using Example 13.5. Begin by entering the nine observed frequencies in cells A1:C3 by placing "4," "12," and "9" (the HIGH values) in column A, the three AVERAGE frequencies ("20," "18," "22") in column B and the LOW frequencies ("11," "15," "9") in column C. Click on **KPK Data Analysis ➤ Chi Square Tests** and select **Independence of Rows and Columns.** Enter "A1:C3" in the **Input Range of Observed Frequencies** box and "D1" for the **Output Range.** The default alpha value is 5%, and so there is no need to change this value.

The resulting output in Figure 13.5 agrees with the previous solution—namely, there is no evidence of a relationship between exam score (job knowledge) and level of education. Excel also provides a *p*-value of .323 in Figure 13.5 (cell K4), and so once again we fail to reject H_0, since this value is larger than $\alpha = .05$.

FIGURE

13.5

Excel spreadsheet for chi-square test of independence using KPK Data Analysis (Example 13.5).

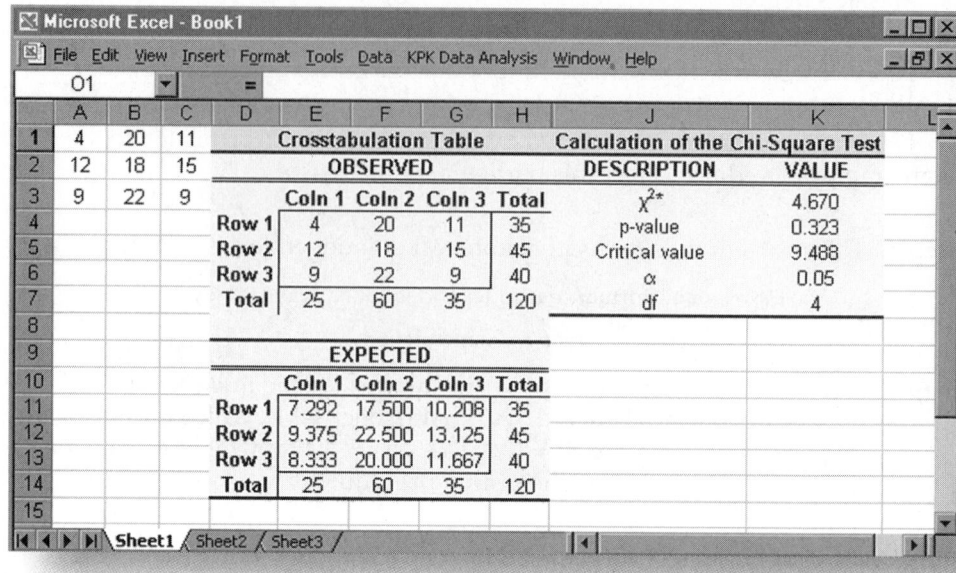

Comments

In Example 13.5, the personnel director recorded the exam performance as high, average, or low rather than listing the actual exam score. Why would anyone take *interval/ratio* data (the exam scores) and convert them to seemingly weaker *ordinal* data (the exam performance classifications)? Do you lose useful information by doing this? When using the ANOVA procedure in Chapter 11, we were forced to assume that these data came from *normal* populations with equal variances. In this chapter, *no* assumptions regarding the populations (aside from the randomness of the sample) were necessary. So, by converting the exam scores to a form suitable for a contingency table and using the chi-square test of independence, we can avoid the assumptions of normality and equal variances.

This question introduces *nonparametric statistics*, often called *distribution-free* statistics. The beauty of these procedures is that they require only very weak assumptions regarding the populations. However, if the data *do* satisfy the requirements of the ANOVA procedure (or nearly so), the nonparametric test is less sensitive to differences among the populations (such as educational level) and so is less *powerful* than the ANOVA *F* test. Additional nonparametric tests of hypothesis are discussed in Chapter 18.

Microsoft® Excel Application Use DATA13-6

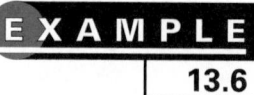

EXAMPLE 13.6

An Excel Test of Independence and Corresponding *p*-Value

In Example 4.3, a quality engineer at Microtek obtained a random sample of 200 electrical components produced over a one-week period. Each component was inspected and classified as (1) OK, (2) OK after rework (repair), or (3) scrap (unusable). Which of the three Microtek plants produced the part (Memphis, Miami, Pittsburgh) was also recorded. The same sample results are stored in columns A and B of data set DATA13–6, where

Column A = city producing the component: 1 = Memphis
2 = Miami
3 = Pittsburgh

FIGURE

13.6

Excel contingency table for Example 13.6.

	A	B	C	D	E	F	G	H	I	J
1	City	Quality		Contingency Table						
2	2	2			Quality					
3	1	1	City	OK	OK-Rework	Scrapped	Grand Total			
4	2	2	Memphis	60	15	5	80			
5	1	1	Miami	35	20	10	65			
6	2	3	Pittsburgh	25	15	15	55			
7	1	1	Grand Total	120	50	30	200			
8	2	2								
9	1	1		Crosstabulation Table					Calculation of the Chi-Square Test	
10	2	1		OBSERVED					DESCRIPTION	VALUE
11	2	2		Coln 1	Coln 2	Coln 3	Total		χ^{2*}	17.1911
12	3	1	Row 1	60	15	5	80		p-value	0.0018
13	2	2	Row 2	35	20	10	65		Critical value	7.7794
14	3	2	Row 3	25	15	15	55		α	0.1
15	2	2	Total	120	50	30	200		df	4
16	1	2								
17	1	1		EXPECTED						
18	1	2		Coln 1	Coln 2	Coln 3	Total			
19	3	3	Row 1	48.000	20.000	12.000	80			
20	1	2	Row 2	39.000	16.250	9.750	65			
21	2	1	Row 3	33.000	13.750	8.250	55			
22	2	1	Total	120	50	30	200			
23	2	1								

Column B = component quality: 1 = OK
                               2 = OK after rework
                               3 = scrapped

Using Excel, construct a contingency table. This will be the same contingency table derived in Example 4.3. Using a significance level of .10, determine whether these two categories (city and product quality) are independent. What is the resulting *p*-value?

Solution

To construct the contingency table using Excel, first open the Excel file DATA13–6. You should then see the first two columns labeled **City** and **Quality** in Figure 13.6. The Excel Tool Pack does not contain a procedure for constructing a contingency table from these two columns; however, the KPK Data Analysis add-ins do allow you to do this. Click on **KPK Data Analysis ➤ Qualitative Data Charts ➤ Contingency Table.** It is important when using this procedure to make sure that the two columns of data contain labels in the top row (**City** and **Quality** here). Enter "A1:A201" in the top box. This is the input range for the row variable (**City**) and includes the label. Repeat this for the column variable (**Quality**) by typing "B1:B201" in the second box. Enter "C1" as the **Output Range** and click on **OK.** You will then obtain the output shown in Figure 13.6. To make this table easier to interpret, enter the city names in cells C4, C5, and C6 and the quality labels in cells D3, E3, and F3 (as in Figure 13.6).

To carry out the test of independence, click on **KPK Data Analysis ➤ Chi Square Tests,** and select **Independence of Rows and Columns** in the top list. Enter "D4:F6" in the **Input Range of Observed Frequencies** box. These are the nine observed values in Figure 13.6, created by the preceding procedure. Enter "C9" for the **Output Range.** Also, the value of alpha needs to be changed from the default value of 5% to 10%. The resulting output is shown below the previously created contingency table in Figure 13.6. The computed chi-square value is seen to be 17.1911, with a corresponding p-value of .0018.

Since the p-value is less than .10, we conclude that these two categories (city and product quality) are dependent; that is, they are related in some way. Also, due to the small size of this p-value, we can say that the categories are *strongly* related. To determine this relationship, we compare the observed and expected values. Notice that (1) a superior product is coming from Memphis, since we observed more "OK" and fewer "scrap" components than expected under H_0, and (2) an inferior product is being produced in Pittsburgh, since we observed fewer "OK" and more "scrap" components than expected under H_0. Our advice to Microtek would be to examine these two production processes (Memphis and Pittsburgh) to determine why there is this pattern of product quality.

Test of Independence with Fixed Marginal Totals (Test of Homogeneity)

We use a slightly different interpretation of the previous chi-square procedure when we determine *in advance* the number of observations to be sampled within each column (or row). In the previous discussion, the row and column totals were random variables because we had no way of knowing what they would be before the sample was obtained. In this discussion, the contingency table is the same, except that the column (or row) totals are predetermined.

Assume Delmar International, a textile manufacturer, has facilities located in Dallas, Boston, Seattle, and Toronto. Over the years, Delmar has gone to great lengths to discourage the formation of labor unions at these plants, including constructing employee recreational centers and offering better-than-average employee benefits. Management suspects, however, that there is growing interest among the employees in forming a union. Of particular interest is whether employee interest in a union differs among the four plants.

The Dallas and Toronto plants are considerably larger than the other two, so Delmar obtains a random sample of 200 employees from each of these two plants and 100 from each of the two smaller facilities. The results of the survey are as follows:

	Dallas	Boston	Seattle	Toronto	Total
Interested	120	41	45	112	318
Not interested	35	38	40	36	149
Indifferent	45	21	15	52	133
Total	200	100	100	200	600

In the previous tests of independence, we had a *single* population, where each member was classified according to two criteria, such as age and gender. Now we have four distinct populations—namely, the Delmar employees in each of the four cities. Consequently, we obtained a random sample from each one. The column totals (sample sizes) were determined in advance. This example differs from our previous ones, where we had no idea what the row or column totals would be before the sample was obtained.

The question of interest here becomes, is interest in a labor union the same in each of the four cities? In other words, we are trying to determine whether these four populations can be viewed as belonging to the *same* population (in terms of this criterion). Identical populations are said to be **homogeneous.** Consequently, the test of hypothesis here is a **test of homogeneity** as well as a test for independence. The null hypothesis can be written as

H_0: the four populations are homogeneous in their interest in a union

The procedure for analyzing a contingency table is the *same* whether or not the column (or row) totals are fixed in advance.

FIGURE

13.7

Excel spreadsheet for chi-square test of homogeneity using KPK Data Analysis.

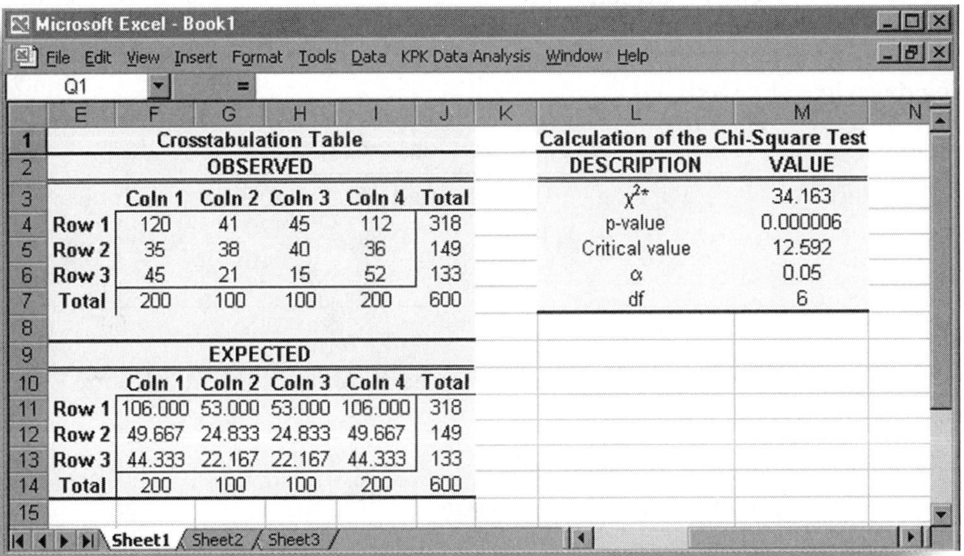

Microsoft Excel - Book1

File Edit View Insert Format Tools Data KPK Data Analysis Window Help

Q1 =

Crosstabulation Table

OBSERVED

	Coln 1	Coln 2	Coln 3	Coln 4	Total
Row 1	120	41	45	112	318
Row 2	35	38	40	36	149
Row 3	45	21	15	52	133
Total	200	100	100	200	600

EXPECTED

	Coln 1	Coln 2	Coln 3	Coln 4	Total
Row 1	106.000	53.000	53.000	106.000	318
Row 2	49.667	24.833	24.833	49.667	149
Row 3	44.333	22.167	22.167	44.333	133
Total	200	100	100	200	600

Calculation of the Chi-Square Test

DESCRIPTION	VALUE
χ^{2*}	34.163
p-value	0.000006
Critical value	12.592
α	0.05
df	6

Sheet1 / Sheet2 / Sheet3

An Excel solution using $\alpha = .05$ is provided in Figure 13.7.* The expected cell frequencies are computed by finding

$$\hat{E} = \frac{\text{(row total)(column total)}}{600}$$

The computed chi-square value is

$$\chi^{2*} = \frac{(120 - 106.0)^2}{106} + \frac{(41 - 53.0)^2}{53} + \cdots + \frac{(52 - 44.333)^2}{44.333} = 34.163$$

The degrees of freedom here are $(3 - 1)(4 - 1) = 6$, so we reject H_0 if $\chi^2 > 12.59$, where 12.59 is $\chi^2_{.05,6}$. The computed value (34.163) exceeds the tabled value, so we reject H_0. We conclude that these four populations are *not* homogeneous. The employee interest in a labor union is not identical at each of the four locations.

Examining the individual terms of the chi-square value in Figure 13.7, we note that the larger plants (Dallas and Toronto) had a higher proportion of employees interested in forming a union. In Dallas, for example, if these classifications were independent, we would expect 106 employees to be interested; instead, we observed 120. The same argument applies to the Toronto plant.

The p-value for this analysis is .000006, contained in cell M4, Figure 13.7. Because of this extremely small value, we reject H_0 and conclude that employees at these four plants have considerably different views in regard to the formation of a labor union.

EXAMPLE 13.7

Masuturi, a manufacturer of printed circuit boards, has determined that boards classified as nonconforming nearly always have one of three defects: a component on the board is either missing, damaged, or raised (installed improperly). The boards are produced on three machines (A, B, and C). Machine A is 90% computer-controlled and produces twice as many boards per day as machines B and C, which

*To obtain this solution, follow the procedures used in the Excel solution to Example 13.5. Enter "A1:D3" in the Input Range box.

are 50% computer-controlled. To determine whether there is a relationship between the type of nonconformity and the machine, a sample of 500 nonconforming boards was obtained, 250 from machine A and 125 each from machines B and C, since machine A produces twice as many boards as machines B and C. The following data were obtained:

Type of Nonconformity

Machine	Missing	Damaged	Raised	Total
A	50	80	120	250
B	60	55	10	125
C	65	45	15	125
Total	175	180	145	500

Is the type of nonconformity related to the machine used for production? Use a significance level of .10.

Solution   **Step 1.** The hypotheses for this test of homogeneity are

H_0: the three machine populations are homogeneous in the types of nonconformity produced

H_a: the three machine populations are not homogeneous in the types of nonconformity produced

Steps 2 and 3. Your test statistic is the chi-square statistic in equation 13.3 with degrees of freedom $(3 - 1)(3 - 1) = 4$. Using Table A.6, the testing procedure is to

$$\text{reject } H_0 \text{ if } \chi^2 > 7.78$$

Step 4. Computing the expected frequencies in the usual way produces the following table:

Type of Nonconformity

Machine	Missing	Damaged	Raised	Total
A	50 (87.5)	80 (90.0)	120 (72.5)	250
B	60 (43.75)	55 (45.0)	10 (36.25)	125
C	65 (43.75)	45 (45.0)	15 (36.25)	125
Total	175	180	145	500

The computed chi-square value is

$$\chi^{2*} = \frac{(50 - 87.5)^2}{87.5} + \frac{(80 - 90)^2}{90} + \cdots + \frac{(15 - 36.25)^2}{36.25}$$

$$= 16.071 + 1.111 + 31.121 + 6.036 + 2.222 + 19.009 + 10.321 + 0.000 + 12.457$$

$$= 98.35$$

This value is greater than 7.78, so we reject H_0.

Step 5. There is evidence to indicate that the three machine populations are not homogeneous; that is, the type of nonconformity *is* related to the machine used for production of the circuit boards. Comparing the observed and expected values, we observed more raised component nonconformities than expected on machine A and fewer than expected on machines B and C. Also, we observed fewer missing-component nonconformities than expected on machine A and more than expected on machines B and C.

Exercises 13.16–13.25

Understanding the Mechanics

13.16 The following table contains observed frequencies for row and column categories.

Row Categories	Column Categories	
	Category 1	Category 2
Category 1	11	21
Category 2	9	12
Category 3	10	7

a. Formulate the hypotheses for a chi-square test of independence.
b. Calculate the expected cell frequencies.
c. Calculate the chi-square statistic.
d. At the 5% significance level, do the data support the conclusion that the categories are not independent?

13.17 Test the null hypothesis of independence of the two classifications A and B in the accompanying table. Combine any row or column to comply with the requirement that all expected cell frequencies are at least 5. Base your conclusions on the *p*-value.

A	B			
	B_1	B_2	B_3	B_4
A_1	10	6	3	2
A_2	13	7	8	4
A_3	3	15	2	1

13.18 A survey included 100 males and 100 females. Thirty-five percent of the females voted for an issue, whereas 50% of the males voted for the issue.
a. Construct a contingency table.
b. State the appropriate null and alternative hypotheses that would be of interest.
c. Do the data support that males and females are not homogeneous in their support of this issue? Use a 5% significance level.

13.19 A survey of 100 customers from stores A, B, and C recorded the form of payment for each customer. The results are tabulated as follows:

	Store A	Store B	Store C
Cash	40	35	20
Credit Card	40	30	30
Check	20	35	60

a. State appropriate null and alternative hypotheses for this problem.
b. Should any cells be pooled?
c. Calculate the chi-square statistic.
d. Is there sufficient evidence to reject the null hypothesis in part a with a 1% significance level?

13.20 Lipton aired a commercial showing Loni Anderson and Mr. T spoofing how "real families" behave while enjoying "real cooking." However, a poll indicates that overall, only about a third of the audience enjoyed the ad. The following table presents the number of individuals who liked the ad among males and females.

	Liked the Ad	Did Not Like the Ad
Male	13	25
Female	20	42

a. State appropriate null and alternative hypotheses to test if a relationship exists between the gender of the viewer and whether a viewer liked the ad.
b. What conclusion can you make about the hypotheses in part a? Use the *p*-value to determine your response.

(Source: "Unreal Ad Families Tout Real Lipton Fare," *USA Today*, June 11, 2001, p. 4B.)

13.21 The Meyers–Briggs Type Indicator (MBTI) is a personality scale that can be used to classify qualities like Extrovert (E), Introvert (I), Intuitive (N), Feeling (F), Sensing (S), Thinking (T), Judging (J), Perceptive (P). Thus, EN means extrovert-intuitive, SP means sensing-perceptive. Consider the following hypothetical frequencies for a cross-tabulation of four types of personality using the MBTI against profession.

Profession	Personality (MBTI)				
	EN	IF	SP	JT	Total
Computer programmer	4	6	5	6	21
Accountant	3	7	5	5	20
Marketer	9	3	7	4	23
Educator	5	5	5	5	20
Total	21	21	22	20	84

a. From the table, can you conclude at a 1% significance level, whether personality type and profession are related?
b. State the *p*-value for your test.

13.22 A quality manager was interested in whether three shifts were homogeneous with respect to the number of resulting defects when producing products A, B, and C. Four hundred defects from the past three months were sampled from each of the three shifts.
a. What conclusion can you give the quality manager using the following data? Use a 10% significance level.
b. Do a what-if analysis by using only shifts 1 and 2. What conclusion do you reach using a 10% significance level?

	Product A	Product B	Product C	Total
Shift 1	120	138	142	400
Shift 2	115	142	143	400
Shift 3	155	120	125	400

13.23 The U.S. Civil Rights Commission investigated voting equipment used in Florida during the 2000 presidential election to determine whether there was evidence of intentional discrimination. A survey was conducted of above-poverty-level neighborhoods and below-poverty-level neighborhoods to examine if there are indications of disparity in the types of voting equipment used in these neighborhoods. Suppose that the following are the frequencies for types of voting machines found in 300 above-poverty-level neighborhoods and 300 below-poverty-level neighborhoods.

	Punch Card	Optical Scan	Datavote	Lever Machine	Paper Ballots
Above poverty level	170	82	28	12	8
Below poverty level	185	71	29	10	5

a. What conclusion can you give to the U.S. Civil Rights Commission regarding whether the above-poverty-level neighborhoods and below-poverty-level neighborhoods are homogeneous with respect to the different types of voting equipment used for the election? Use the p-value to make your conclusion.

b. Do a what-if analysis by changing the number of punch card machines and optical scan machines for the above-poverty-level neighborhood to 150 and 102, respectively. What would be your conclusion to part a if you were using a 5% significance level?

(Source: "Rights Report on 2000 Vote Fuels Debate Clouded by Ambiguities," *The Wall Street Journal*, June 11, 2001, p. A24.)

Using the Computer

13.24 [DATA SET EX13-24] *Variable description:*

Airport: Either New York Kennedy Airport, New York LaGuardia Airport, or Newark New Jersey Airport

IncidentCategory: One of four classifications of runway incidents denoted by an A, B, C, or D

The Federal Aviation Administration classifies runway incidents at airports into one of four categories. Category A incidents are incidents in which extreme action is taken to narrowly avoid a collision. Category B incidents

are incidents in which there is substantial potential for a collision. Category C incidents are incidents in which there is ample time and distance to avoid a collision. Category D incidents are incidents in which there is little or no chance for collision but meets the definition of a runway incursion. Suppose that data are collected for the three major airports serving New York City.

a. Form a contingency table for these data and compute the expected values for each cell. Pool (combine) the necessary rows or columns so that no cell has an expected value less than five.

b. Using the table in part a, test that a relationship exists between the three major airports serving New York City and the type of incidences that can occur on a runway. Use a 10% significance level.

c. What would be the conclusion to part b had the frequency table been used without pooling any rows or columns?

(Source: "Runway Close Calls," *Dallas Morning News*, June 21, 2001, p. 20A.)

13.25 [DATA SET EX13-25] *Variable description:*

Salary: Row categories listed under Salary are "Less than $40,000," "Between $40,000 and less than $70,000," and "More than $70,000"

GM: Frequency of individuals preferring GM cars for each row

Ford: Frequency of individuals preferring Ford cars for each row

Imports: Frequency of individuals preferring import cars for each row

Market analysts are interested in the relationship between buyers' income and the type of car they prefer to drive. A study in which 500 recent automobile buyers were randomly selected revealed a possible relationship between a buyer's preference and his/her income bracket.

a. Is there sufficient evidence to indicate that a relationship exists between automobile preference and salary level using a 5% significance level?

b. Do a what-if analysis by considering only GM and Ford. Does this change your response to part a?

✓ Summary

When performing a two-tailed test of hypothesis on a binomial parameter (for example, $p = .75$) we can use a chi-square test statistic. The advantage of this approach is that it extends easily to the **multinomial situation,** where each trial can result in any specified number of outcomes. For example, the roll of a single die has six possible outcomes on each roll.

In the multinomial situation, the probability of observing each possible outcome may be specified (such as one-sixth for each outcome in the single die illustration). To test the hypothesis, a random sample of observations is obtained, and a chi-square test

statistic is evaluated either to reject or to fail to reject this set of probabilities (percentages). Such a test is referred to as a **chi-square goodness-of-fit test.** The form of this chi-square test statistic is

$$\chi^2 = \sum \frac{(O - E)^2}{E}$$

where

1. O represents the **observed frequency** of observations in a particular category (such as the observed number of 3s in 60 rolls of a single die).

2. E is the **expected frequency** for this category. For example, we would expect to see $60 \cdot 1/6 = 10$ values of 3 in the die illustration.
3. The chi-square value is obtained by summing over all categories of the multinomial random variable.
4. Categories must be **pooled** together whenever an expected value (E) for a particular category is less than 5.

The chi-square goodness-of-fit procedure can be used to determine whether a certain set of sample data came from a specified probability distribution. For example, you might attempt to determine whether the number of nonconformities in a particular product follows a Poisson distribution. By collecting a random sample and counting the number of nonconformities in each product, you can compare the frequency of observed values (how many 0's, how many 1's, and so on) with what you would expect if the null hypothesis (H_0: the data are from a Poisson distribution) is true. If the calculated chi-square value is significantly large (in the right tail), this hypothesis will be rejected. Whenever any of the parameters for this distribution are unknown (such as μ for the Poisson illustration), they can be estimated using the sample data. The degrees of freedom of the chi-square test statistic are reduced by one for *each* estimated parameter.

Finally, this chi-square statistic can be used to test whether two classifications (such as age and performance) used to define a **contingency table** are independent. This is the **chi-square test of independence.** The expected value within each **cell** of the contingency table is determined under the assumption that H_0 is true, for H_0: the row and column classifications are independent. This also leads to a right-tailed rejection region using the chi-square statistic.

This procedure can be used as a **test for homogeneity** when fixed sample sizes are used for each row or column of the table. If the column totals are fixed in advance, this test will determine whether the populations defined by the column categories are **homogeneous** (identical) with respect to the variable defining the rows. A similar argument applies when the row totals are predetermined. The test statistic used for a test of homogeneity is the same chi-square statistic used in the test of independence.

 ## Summary of Formulas

Chi-Square Test Statistic:

$$\chi^2 = \sum \frac{(O - E)^2}{E}$$

summed over all categories for a goodness-of-fit test and over all cells for a test of independence or homogeneity. In the latter case, each expected value (E) is replaced by its estimate, $\hat{E}$.

Estimated Expected Value for a Test of Independence/Homogeneity:

$$\hat{E} = \frac{(\text{row total for cell})(\text{column total for cell})}{n}$$

where n is the total of all cells in the contingency table.

X Review Exercises 13.26–13.52

13.26 Sears charges a 21% annual rate with the proprietary Sears credit card. Historically, 5% of all accounts end up not being closed out without being paid in full. Suppose that a financial analyst wished to determine if the current percentage of accounts that have not been paid in full is different from 5%.

a. What conclusion can the analyst make using a 5% significance level if a random sample of 100 accounts revealed that eight accounts were closed out and had not been paid in full? Use the Z test.

b. Use the chi-square goodness-of-fit test instead of the Z test in part a.

c. What is the relationship between the test statistics in parts a and b?

(Adapted from "Come See the Softer Side of Sears—Its Earnings," *The Wall Street Journal,* July 23, 1998, p. B1.)

13.27 Russia's last czar, Nicholas II, and his family were buried in St. Petersburg's Peter and Paul Fortress in July 1998 on the anniversary of their murder. In a survey of Russian citizens across several major cities in Russia, respondents were asked how they primarily view the czar. The results are as follows:

25% Innocent victim of Bolsheviks
22% Not good ruler but redeemed by martyr's death
16% Brought poverty, catastrophe to Russia
15% Responsible for what happened after 1917
22% No opinion on the czar

Suppose that a political analyst wished to determine if these same percentages held for the residents of St. Petersburg. Two hundred residents of St. Petersburg were selected for the survey. Using the following data, test that the distribution of the responses appears to be the same as the distribution in the national survey. Use a 1% significance level.

Category	Number of Respondents Selecting This Category
Innocent victim of Bolsheviks	45
Not good ruler but redeemed by martyr's death	50
Brought poverty, catastrophe to Russia	40
Responsible for what happened after 1917	34
No opinion on the czar	31

(Source: "Russia's Last Royal Burial," *USA Today,* July 17, 1998, p. A1.)

13.28 A large department store in New York City has five entrances and exits. It is believed that the proportion of shoppers entering or leaving the store is approximately the same for each of the five doorways on any single day. The number of customers entering or leaving the store is tallied at each doorway for three randomly selected days:

Doorways	Customers
1	150
2	123
3	126
4	163
5	152

Do the data justify the statement that all five entrances and exits are used equally often? Use a 5% significance level.

13.29 Six automotive manufacturers hold approximately 85% of the market share of automobiles sold in the United States. In September 2001, the market share held by General Motors, Ford, DaimlerChrysler, Toyota, Honda, and Nissan were 29.7%, 21.8%, 11.8%, 9.8%, 7.3%, and 4.6%, respectively. Suppose that with the slower economy in 2002, a survey of 1,000 recently sold automobiles shows the results in the following table. Would you conclude that the market share held by these six automotive manufacturers has changed? Use a 5% significance level.

General Motors	Ford	DaimlerChrysler	Toyota	Honda	Nissan	Other
325	201	120	102	64	39	149

(Source: "DaimlerChrysler Turnaround Seems to Be Going in Reverse," *The Wall Street Journal,* October 11, 2001, p. B4.)

13.30 A car-rental company has 15 cars to rent. The owner believes that the number of cars rented daily is binomially distributed. He also believes that each car has a 30% chance of being rented each day. Forty-five randomly selected days are chosen and the number of cars rented are recorded. From the data, test the hypothesis that the daily rental of cars is binomially distributed with $p = .30$. Use a 5% significance level.

Cars Rented	Days Occurred	Cars Rented	Days Occurred
0	0	5	12
1	3	6	6
2	3	7	3
3	6	≥8	3
4	9		

13.31 An advertising firm believes that the number of daily responses to an advertisement in the *Wall Street Journal* follows a Poisson distribution. Forty days were randomly selected, and the following data were collected:

Responses	Days	Responses	Days
0	0	4	6
1	8	5	6
2	8	6	2
3	10		

Can you conclude that the data did come from a Poisson distribution? Use a 1% level of significance.

13.32 The assistant dean of the College of Business at Oceanside University believes that the number of students dropping a class is Poisson distributed. Fifty classes, all containing the same number of students, were randomly selected. The number of withdrawals from the classes was recorded. Based on the following data, what conclusion can be drawn about whether these data come from a Poisson distribution? Use a significance level of 5% to justify your conclusion.

Drops	Classes	Drops	Classes
0	0	5	4
1	2	6	6
2	6	7	4
3	10	>7	0
4	18		

13.33 Favin Copiers Inc. has repairpersons who are used to traveling to sites where a Favin copier needs repair. For a certain metropolitan area, the company has 10 repairpersons who stand by for calls to repair a copier. A manager believes that the number of repairpersons used each day is binomially distributed with $p = .3$, where p is the probability that a repairperson is sent out on any given day. One hundred days of operation yielded the following results:

Number of Repairpersons Sent Out	Days with the Number of Repairpersons Sent Out
0	4
1	10
2	21
3	27
4	18
5	12
6	5
7	3
8 or more	0

Test the goodness-of-fit of the data to a binomial distribution with $p = .3$. Use a significance level of .05.

13.34 A computer generates 100 observations from a normally distributed population with mean 35 and standard deviation 2. The results of the 100 observations generated are:

Interval	Observed Frequency	Interval	Observed Frequency
less than 32	6	35 but less than 36	19
32 but less than 33	9	36 but less than 37	15
33 but less than 34	12	37 but less than 38	11
34 but less than 35	23	38 or more	5

Use the chi-square goodness-of-fit procedure in Exercise 13.13 to test whether there is enough evidence to support the conclusion that the generated numbers did not come from a normally distributed population with mean = 35 and standard deviation = 2. Use a 1% significance level.

13.35 The vice president of a national firm wants to know the response of workers at a certain plant to a proposal to relocate the plant. Forty workers were randomly selected from each of the five divisions at the plant and asked if they favored a relocation of the plant.

Division	Favored	Do Not Favor	Total
A	15	25	40
B	18	22	40
C	24	16	40
D	17	23	40
E	20	20	40

Do the data indicate that the divisions are not homogeneous with respect to the proportion of workers who favor a relocation of the plant? Use a .05 significance level.

13.36 Computer-controlled cameras are being used experimentally to ticket automobile drivers for speeding and running red lights. These devices are operated by private firms and have an incentive to pull in as many drivers as they can. Although approximately 70% of the motorists stoically accept and pay these tickets, others resent this procedure and fight the tickets. Assume that the actions of 200 motorists who received a ticket from a computer-controlled camera produced the following results. Do the data indicate that whether a person pays their traffic ticket is dependent on the type of traffic violation? Use a 10% significance level.

Traffic Violation	Pay Ticket	Fight Ticket
Run Red Light	40	20
Spceding	100	40

(Source: "Speeders, Say Cheese," *Time*, 158, no. 11, September 17, 2001, p. 32.)

13.37 An immigration attorney was investigating which industries to target for obtaining new clients who might have problems with changes in the immigration laws. Five industries were selected. Twenty workers were chosen in each industry, and their visa status was verified. The data are summarized as follows:

Visa Status	Industry A	B	C	D	E	Total
Illegal alien	8	10	5	10	1	34
Legal resident	4	2	6	4	9	25
U.S. citizen	8	8	9	6	10	41
Total	20	20	20	20	20	100

a. Are the five industries homogeneous with respect to the visa status of their workers? Use $\alpha = .05$.

b. State the p-value.

13.38 The Federal Aviation Administration (FAA) issued 625,581 pilot certificates in 2000. More than 250,000 were for private pilot certificates. The percentages of different types of pilot certificates issued in 2000 were 40%, 23%, 19%, and 18% for private pilot license, airline transport pilot license, commercial airline pilot license, and student pilot license, respectively. Suppose that the FAA surveyed 300 new applicants for pilot licenses to determine if these percentages still hold. The data from this survey follow. What conclusion would you give to the FAA after analyzing the data? Use a 5% significance level.

Private Pilot License	Airline Transport Pilot License	Commercial Airline Pilot License	Student Pilot License
105	70	60	65

(Source: "Who's Licensed to Fly?" *USA Today*, December 3, 2001, p. 1A.)

13.39 Employers have expanded benefits for workers over the past several years to make recruiting easier and to increase morale. Among the benefits have been full or partial school tuition reimbursement and up to three months leave of absence unrelated to the Family Medical and Leave Act. Suppose that a study is conducted using 200 randomly selected companies, and their policy on tuition reimbursement, as well as their policy on family leave, are recorded.

	At Least 3 Months of Leave Allowed	Less than 3 Months of Leave Allowed
No Tuition Reimbursement	10	15
Partial Tuition Reimbursement	60	50
Full Tuition Reimbursement	50	15

a. What null and alternative hypothesis would be of interest in determining if a relationship exists between a company's tuition reimbursement policy and its policy on family leave?

b. Test the hypotheses developed in part a. What is your conclusion at the 5% significance level?

(Source: "Employers Expand Benefits," *USA Today*, June 28, 2001, p.1B.)

13.40 Marketing analysts are interested in age groups to target in advertisements. Internet studies indicate that the majority of home Internet users are less than 30 years of age. To investigate the relationship between the age of Internet users and how often they view Internet advertising, a survey of 396 Internet users was conducted.

Age	No More than Once a Month	Several Times a Month	Once a Week	Several Times a Week	Every Day
18–24	24	7	20	19	10
25–34	33	18	23	27	20
35–44	33	9	14	29	19
45–54	19	5	14	12	10
55–64	17	1	3	7	3

a. What are the null and alternative hypotheses of interest to a marketing analyst examining these data?

b. Do the data support that a relationship exists between the age of Internet users and how often they view Internet advertising? Use a 5% significance level. Do all cells have expected values of five or more?

(Source: "Survey of Internet Users' Attitudes toward Internet Advertising," *Journal of Interactive Marketing*, 13, no. 3, pp. 34–54.)

13.41 A record company wanted to survey its customers regarding music preferences. A random sample of 258 frequent customers of the record company was selected, and information was gathered on their music preference and job classification. From the following data, can the null hypothesis of independence between type of music preferred and working status be rejected at the 10% significance level?

Job Classification	Country and Western	Rock	Classical	Jazz	Total
Clerical	25	40	17	5	87
Managerial	21	25	29	15	90
Blue collar	27	33	14	7	81
Total	73	98	60	27	258

13.42 The personnel department of a particular firm wants to know if an employee's age is associated with productivity (given in items per hour). The manager of the personnel department draws a random sample of 60 employees from each of the age classifications listed. Do the data support the hypothesis that the five age categories are not homogeneous with respect to productivity? Use a 10% significance level.

Age	4–5 Items	6–7 Items	≥8 Items	Total
20 and under 30	15	25	20	60
30 and under 40	13	29	18	60
40 and under 50	16	26	18	60
50 and under 60	19	26	15	60
60 and under 70	22	24	14	60

13.43 A recent survey in ownership of home entertainment products shows that Sanyo is the leading brand of television sets sold in America. Samsung and Zenith have notably lagged the home entertainment products industry in terms of market share. Suppose that an executive at Zenith wishes to determine if there is a relationship between sales of television sets and income of the customer. Such a relationship would suggest targeting income groups in their advertisements. The following table displays the brand of television sets owned by 185 families with less than $60,000 annual income and by 185 families with at least $60,000 annual income. Do the data indicate a lack of homogeneity among the two income groups with respect to the brand of television set purchased? Use a 5% significance level.

Television Brand	Family Income Less than $60,000	Family Income at Least $60,000
Sanyo	27	48
RCA	26	39
Sony	24	36
Panasonic	32	25
General Electric	34	15
Samsung	20	12
Zenith	22	10

(Source: "Zenith Sees Its Future in Digital TV," *USA Today,* July 20, 2001, p. 7B.)

13.44 Axiom Market Research published the following data concerning education level and attendance at "regular" theater performances. A sample size of 950 was selected. Do the data indicate, at the .05 significance level, a relationship between level of education and regular theater attendance?

Education	Attend More than Once per Year	Attend No More than Once per Year	Total
College graduate	82	120	202
Some college	75	131	206
High school graduate	106	215	321
Not a high school graduate	51	170	221

13.45 A sample of households classified as having incomes below the poverty level revealed the following distribution of persons by age:

Age	Frequency
0 to <5	27
5 to <18	53
18 to <22	16
22 to <45	60
45 to <65	26
65 to <72	18
Total	200

a. Compute the mean and standard deviation for this distribution.

b. Using a 10% significance level, determine with a chi-square test whether the data fit a normal population.

c. Find the p-value for the test.

d. Does your conclusion change if $\alpha = .05$ or $\alpha = .01$?

13.46 In an effort to monitor the service of its employees, a parcel-delivery firm keeps a tally of the number of packages misrouted each week at each of its 25 distribution centers, with the following results:

Misrouted Packages	Distribution Centers
0	5
1	6
2	8
3	6
>3	0

Do these data appear to come from a Poisson distribution? Use a .05 significance level.

13.47 In the field of organizational psychology, extensive study has been made of different leadership styles. One researcher refers to two extremes as authoritarian versus democratic; another refers to task-oriented versus people-oriented; yet others have their own labels for these qualities. Whatever the label, do these different styles affect the morale of the subordinates? To address this issue, a researcher established a ranking scale for worker morale, based on interviews, and grouped the workers into low, acceptable, and high morale categories. These were cross-classified against the leadership style of the supervisor. The following contingency table summarizes the results.

| Worker Morale | Leadership Style | | Total |
	Authoritarian	Democratic	
Low	10	5	15
Acceptable	8	12	20
High	6	9	15
Total	24	26	50

a. Apply the chi-square test of independence to these data, at a 5% significance level.

b. State the p-value for your test.

c. Is worker morale related to the supervisor's leadership style, or are these qualities independent?

13.48 Kingston Pencils is considering a new bonus plan. Under the current bonus plan, the amount of bonus is not linked to production but only linked to profits. According to the proposed bonus plan, the amount of bonus will be linked to the quantity produced but will be subject to the amount of profits. The controller of Kingston is interested in examining whether employee opinion of the bonus plan is independent of job classification.

Employee	Favorable	Unfavorable
White collar	67	28
Blue color	43	19

Calculate the p-value and interpret it.

13.49 Proponents of a proposal for individuals to invest some of their Social Security taxes in private accounts are sometimes accused of scare tactics about Social Security's solvency to force the issue of private accounts. Polls reveal that professionals are evenly split on the benefits of privatization of Social Security and that only about 20% of the senior citizens are for it. Political analysts suggest that issues on Social Security may be divided along partisan lines. Suppose that a survey of 400 voting adults in the Washington, D.C., area revealed the following results. At the 5% significance level, do the data provide sufficient evidence to indicate that issues on the privatization of Social Security are related to a person's political affiliation?

	Favor Private Accounts	Favor Partial Privatization	Favor Using General Tax Revenue to Maintain Social Security System
Democrats	70	30	118
Republicans	75	36	71

(Source: "Wall Street Ponies Up to Back Bush's Social Security Plan," *The Wall Street Journal*, June 12, 2001, p. A24.)

13.50 The percentage of time that each of the following carriers has been on time has been reported to be from 70% to 80%: United, Northwest, Alaska, America West, and TWA. Suppose that an airline consultant wished to determine if these carriers are homogeneous with respect to the number of times that they are on time. A random sample of 50 flights from each of these airlines was selected, and the number of times that the airline was on time was recorded. The contingency table below shows the observed frequencies. At a .10 significance level, is there evidence to support the statement that these airlines are not homogeneous with respect to being on time?

	On Time	Not On Time
United	35	15
Northwest	31	19
Alaska	45	5
America West	38	12
TWA	33	17

(Source: "Worst On-Time Arrivals in May," *USA Today*, July 17, 1998, p. B1.)

13.51 [DATA SET EX13-51] *Variable description:*

DouglasorNoble: Indicates whether an online buyer purchases a Douglas fir or a Noble fir

OnlineSite: Indicates which of the four online sites that the buyer used in purchasing a Christmas tree

While Internet sales of Christmas trees still only represent about 5% of the Christmas tree market, experts say that this market segment could potentially grow rapidly. Some online buyers like the home-delivery aspect of the service, particularly if they are too busy to shop for a tree. To better understand the relationship between the type of tree and the online site where buyers purchase their trees, a random sample of 300 online buyers was selected, and the data in DouglasorNoble and OnlineSite were collected.

a. Form a contingency table of the data.

b. Can you conclude that the type of tree ordered and the online site are independent at the 5% significance level?

c. Do a what-if analysis by removing the site www.mtnstarfarms.com from the contingency table. Does this change your conclusion in part b?

13.52 [DATA SET EX13-52] *Variable description:*

Return: Percentage return on equity

An analyst for the computer industry believes that the distribution of the percentage return on equity for all computer software firms is approximately normally distributed. A random sample of 250 firms with at least some software business was selected to verify this belief.

a. Find the mean and standard deviation of the data.

b. Standardize the data by subtracting the mean and dividing by the standard deviation.

c. Construct a histogram of the data using a class width of 1.

d. Under the assumption of a standard normal distribution, find the expected probabilities for the intervals of data, keeping in mind that the first and last intervals are open intervals.

e. Compute the chi-square goodness-of-fit test statistic.

f. What conclusion can you draw using a 5% significance level?

Computer Exercises Using the Databases

Exercise 1—Appendix F

Randomly select 100 observations from the database. Determine whether the variable family size (FAMLSIZE) has a distribution that is significantly different from the binomial distribution. Use a .05 significance level.

Exercise 2—Appendix F

Randomly select 200 observations from the database. Are the categories own or rent one's residence (variable OWNORENT) and family size (variable FAMLSIZE) independent? Use a .05 significance level.

Exercise 3—Appendix G

Randomly select 100 observations from the database. Determine whether the total asset value (variable TOTAL) has a distribution that is significantly different from the normal distribution. Use a .05 significance level. (*Hint:* See Exercise 13.13.)

Exercise 4—Appendix G

Randomly select 100 observations from the database. Are the categories bond rating (BONDRATE) and positive or negative net income (NETINC) independent? Use a .05 significance level.

Insights from Statistics in Action

Data Mining: The Art and Science of Customer Relationship Management

At the beginning of this chapter, the Statistics in Action case study discussed the interest that companies have in data mining to determine if relationships exist between the profiles of certain individuals and their purchasing behavior. Psychographic profiles of consumers are often studied to determine which group of people to target in advertising. Suppose that an airline company wishes to determine if there is a relationship between the number of frequent-flyer miles that a customer has and the following five types of consumers:

1. *Uninvolved* People who don't care about the product; they just want it to do the job

2. *Functionalists* Satisfied users who want high performance and quality; repeat customers

3. *Searchers* People looking for new and exciting products that are fun to use

4. *Young expressives* Youthful in attitude; people who like a personal stamp on things

5. *Demanding pros* Highly ambitious, image-conscious, early adapters to new products

Use the data in StatInActChap13.xls to answer the following questions regarding the relationship between the type of consumer and the number of frequent-flyer miles that a customer has.

1. Find the expected frequency for each combination of type of consumer and the number of frequent-flyer miles category. Are any expected frequencies less than five? If there are, which rows or columns would you combine? Why?

2. What are the null and alternative hypotheses associated with a chi-square test on the observed frequency data?

3. Perform a chi-square test to determine if the data support the conclusion that a relationship exists between *type of consumer* and the *number of frequent-flyer miles* that the customer has. Do not combine any rows or columns. Use a 10% significance level.

4. Combine the rows or columns to maximize the degrees of freedom and eliminate cell(s) with an expected frequency less than five. What is the result of the statistical analysis for testing independence of the two categories *type of consumer* and *number of frequent-flyer miles?* Use a 10% significance level. What conclusion would you suggest to the marketing department at the airline company?

5. Suppose that the rows and columns are combined so that the degrees of freedom are not maximized. Would the conclusion in question 3 change?

Sources: "CRM Shifts to Data Mining to Keep Customers," *Global Finance*, 15, issue 11, October 2001, p. 97. "Data Mining Application Helps BB&T Increase Cross-Sell Ratio," *Bank Systems & Technology*, 38, issue 6, June 2001, p. 66. "Finding Pearls in an Ocean of Data," *Computerworld*, 35, issue 30, 2001, p. 49.

Appendix SPSS®

Chapter 13 Appendix: Data Analysis with SPSS

Test of Independence

The SPSS procedure to carry out a chi-square test of independence must begin with data that are not yet tabulated (as in Example 13.6). If the data are already tabulated (as in Example 13.5), the first step is to construct two columns containing the untabulated data. For example 13.5, let

M = employee's top level of education is a master's degree

B = employee's top level of education is a bachelor's degree

HS = employee's top level of education is a high school diploma

and

H = employee's exam performance was rated as high

A = employee's exam performance was rated as average

L = employee's exam performance was rated as low

A data set containing 120 rows is constructed using the first two columns of the data sheet, as illustrated on the next page. Click on the **Variable View** tab and name these variables "degree" and "perform." For example, the first four rows represent the four individuals with a master's degree and a high exam performance rating. The next 20 rows represent the 20 individuals with a master's degree and an average exam performance rating, and so on. The final nine rows contain "HS L" for the nine individuals with a high school diploma and a low exam performance rating.

	degree	perform	var
1	M	H	
2	M	H	
3	M	H	
4	M	H	
5	M	A	
6	M	A	
7	M	A	
8	M	A	
9	M	A	
10	M	A	
11	M	A	
12	M	A	
13	M	A	
14	M	A	
15	M	A	
16	M	A	
17	M	A	
18	M	A	
19	M	A	
20	M	A	
21	M	A	
22	M	A	

Data View   Variable View

Click on **Analyze ➤ Descriptive Statistics ➤ Crosstabs.** Move the degree variable into the **Row(s)** box and the perform variable into the **Column(s)** box. Click on the **Statistics** button and on the box alongside **Chi-square statistic** in the screen that appears. Click on **Continue** and then **OK.** The output immediately following the **Crosstabs** window will appear in the display pane. The resulting table of observed frequencies and corresponding value of the chi-square statistic agree with the solution to Example 13.5 (except for the order of the rows and columns). Note that the chi-square value is labeled **Pearson Chi-Square** in the SPSS output. The *p*-value (on the far right) is .323. Since this value is greater than .05, there is insufficient evidence to indicate that a relationship exists between exam performance and level of education.

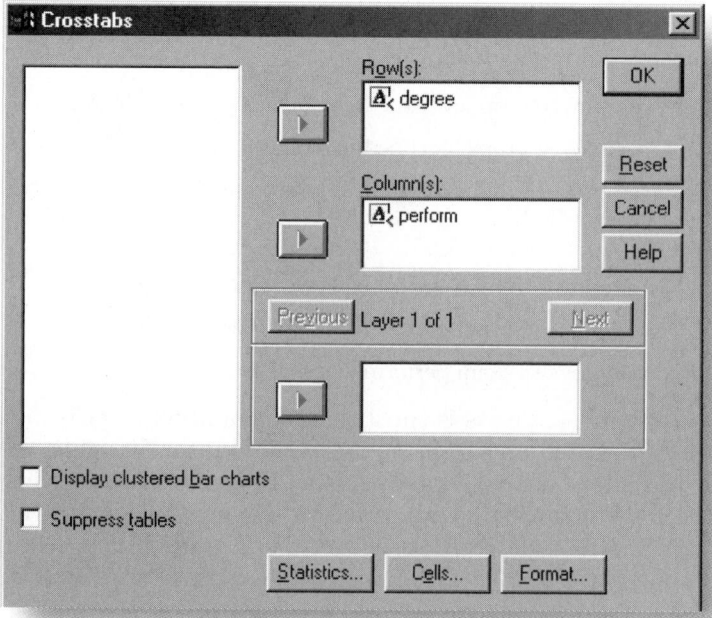

DEGREE * PERFORM Crosstabulation

Count

		PERFORM			
		Group Label			
		A	H	L	Total
DEGREE	B	18	12	15	45
	HS	22	9	9	40
	M	20	4	11	35
Total		60	25	35	120

Chi-Square Tests

	Value	df	Asymp. Sig. (2-sided)
Pearson Chi-Square	4.670[a]	4	.323
N of Valid Cases	120		

a. 0 cells (.0%) have expected count less than 5. The minimum expected count is 7.29.

On the CD . . .

Chapter 13 Appendix: Data Analysis with MINITAB

Correlation and Simple Linear Regression   X

Statistics in Action
Alpha Beta Soup for the Investor's Soul: Recipe Includes Regression Analysis

The prospectus for Rydex Ursa reads: "Rydex Series Trust Ursa Fund seeks to provide investment results that inversely correlate with the performance of the S&P 500." This fund makes a market for itself by appealing to investors who believe that the S&P 500 stock index is ready to head south. The fund is able to move in a direction opposite to the S&P 500 index by engaging in short sales and futures contracts. In financial parlance, this mutual fund would have a negative beta. Knowing the alpha and beta of a mutual fund can assist investors in selecting mutual funds in accordance with their risk tolerance to hopefully prevent a bad case of financial heartburn.

Morningstar describes alpha as "a measure of the difference between a fund's actual returns and its expected performance, given its level of risk as measured by beta." The beta value of a stock characterizes the stock's response to fluctuations in the market portfolio. To better understand alpha and beta, consider the equation: mutual fund return = alpha + beta × index return. This equation implies that the performance of a mutual fund can be measured against the performance of an index, typically the S&P 500 stock index. Suppose the market index return is 2% and a stock's beta is 1.5 and its alpha is 1. The stock return would then be 4% (i.e., 1% + 1.5 × 2% = 4%). Thus, a higher beta value means that a mutual fund could outperform the general market if the market were to rally or it could underperform the market if the market were to decline.

Morningstar, started 14 years ago as a newsletter, now has annual revenues of $45 million. Its star ratings and information on the investment style of a fund are widely used by investors to assess a fund's performance. However, a mutual fund manager might change his or her investment approach over time. For example, a manager might switch to riskier stocks because the manager believes the economy is poised to rebound. Investors can detect this switch in a manager's investing style by monitoring the fund's beta. If investors could foretell that the stock market would rally, they would load up on high-beta mutual funds. However, the quest for a variable that can foretell the stock market's future performance is the modern-day version of searching for the Holy Grail. To protect themselves, investors can balance their portfolios with mutual funds having high betas and low betas to keep a diversified portfolio.

Fidelity Dividend Growth fund had an alpha and a beta of 6.20 and .85, respectively, for the last three years. The beta value of .85 indicates that this fund is less volatile than the S&P 500. This type of fund would appeal to a somewhat conservative investor, perhaps one that understood that high-beta funds are a two-edged sword. The alpha value

is positive for this fund, and this value represents the contribution made by the fund manager to the fund's performance. Mutual funds with high alpha values tend to be the higher-performing funds.

Statistical analysis provides investors with a variety of tools to evaluate their investment. When you have completed this chapter, you will be able to

- Use regression analysis to develop an equation with two variables, such as an equation involving the performance of a mutual fund and the performance of the S&P 500 index.
- Measure the strength of a linear relationship between two variables.
- Determine which observations, say values of mutual fund performance and S&P 500 performance, would be considered outliers and which observations, if removed, would have a dramatic effect on the best line through the observations.

A Look Back/Introduction

The early chapters discussed methods of reducing a set of values for one variable to a graph (such as a histogram) or a numerical measure (such as a mean). A **variable** here is a characteristic of the population being measured or observed. For example, the variable of interest might be an individual's height or income. The sample then consists of random observations of the variable describing a given population.

In this chapter we discuss the situation in which the population and sample consist of measurements not of *one* variable but of *two.* As a result, we not only can describe each variable individually—we can also describe how the two variables are related. The relationship between the two variables can be described using a simple graph or a numerical measure (statistic). We can then use the sample results to form a conclusion about the population from which the sample was obtained. If we believe that a linear relationship between the two variables exists, the next step is to construct the "best-fitting" line through the points defined by the sample bivariate data.

Finally, we turn our attention to the question of what we are estimating when sampling from a population of bivariate data. How can we determine whether a significant linear relationship exists? To answer this question, we introduce the concept of a **statistical model** and the assumptions behind it. Various tests of hypothesis examine the adequacy of this model (is it a good one?), and an assortment of confidence intervals measure the reliability of the corresponding estimates using this model.

14.1

BIVARIATE DATA AND CORRELATION

With bivariate data, each observation consists of data on two variables. For example, you obtain a sample of people and record their ages (X) and liquid assets (Y). Or, for each month, you record the average interest rate (X) and the number of new housing starts (Y). These data are *paired.*

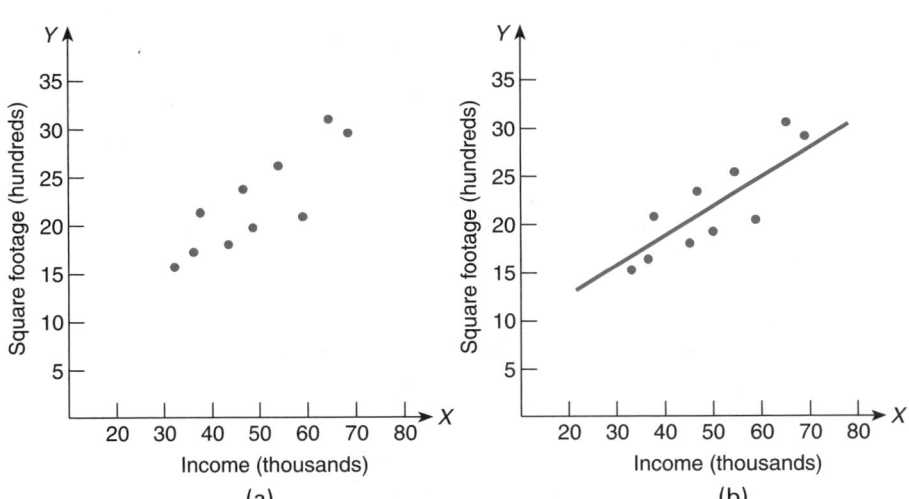

FIGURE

14.1

Scatter diagram of real-estate data. (a) Scatter diagram of sample data. (b) Line through sample data.

Suppose that a real-estate developer is interested in determining the relationship between family income (X, in thousands of dollars) of the local residents and the square footage of their homes (Y, in hundreds of square feet). A random sample of 10 families is obtained with the following results:

Income (X)	32	36	55	47	38	60	66	44	70	50
Square footage (Y)	16	17	26	24	22	21	32	18	30	20

Bivariate data can be represented graphically using a **scatter diagram.** In this graph, each observation is represented by a point, where the X-axis is always horizontal and the Y-axis is vertical. A scatter diagram of the real-estate data is shown in Figure 14.1*a*. The underlying pattern here appears to be that larger incomes (X) are associated with larger home sizes (Y). In this example X and Y have a **positive (direct) relationship.** A **negative (inverse) relationship** occurs when Y decreases as X increases—for example, when Y is the demand for a particular consumer product and X is the selling price.

We next try to determine whether we can estimate this relationship by means of a straight line. One possible line is sketched in Figure 14.1*b*; it passes among these points and has a positive slope. To measure the strength of the linear relationship between these two variables, we determine the coefficient of correlation.

Coefficient of Correlation

It is often difficult to determine whether a *significant* linear relationship exists between X and Y by inspecting a scatter diagram of the data. A second procedure is to include a *measure* of this linearity—the sample coefficient of correlation. It is computed from the sample data by combining these pairs of values into a single number, written as r. The sample **coefficient of correlation, r,** measures the strength of the linear relationship that exists within a sample of n bivariate data. Its value is given by

$$r = \frac{\sum(x - \bar{x})(y - \bar{y})}{\sqrt{\sum(x - \bar{x})^2}\sqrt{\sum(y - \bar{y})^2}}$$

$$= \frac{\sum xy - (\sum x)(\sum y)/n}{\sqrt{\sum x^2 - (\sum x)^2/n}\sqrt{\sum y^2 - (\sum y)^2/n}}$$

14.1

14.2

where $\sum x$ = sum of X values, $\sum x^2$ = sum of X^2 values, $\sum y$ = sum of Y values, $\sum y^2$ = sum of Y^2 values, $\sum xy$ = sum of XY values, $\bar{x} = \sum x/n$, and $\bar{y} = \sum y/n$. Note that X and Y represent the variables on the horizontal and vertical axes, respectively, whereas x and y represent specific observations of the X and Y variables. When using a calculator to determine a coefficient of correlation, equation 14.2 provides a computationally easier procedure. Notice that the summations in the denominator of equation 14.1 are the numerators for the sample variances of x and y.

Sum of Squares

We will introduce a shorthand notation at this point, related to the notation in Chapter 11 for ANOVA. Let

$$
\begin{aligned}
SS_X &= \text{sum of squares for } X \\
&= \sum(x - \bar{x})^2 \\
&= \sum x^2 - \frac{(\sum x)^2}{n} \quad\quad (14.3)\\
SS_Y &= \text{sum of squares for } Y \\
&= \sum(y - \bar{y})^2 \\
&= \sum y^2 - \frac{(\sum y)^2}{n} \quad\quad (14.4)\\
SCP_{XY} &= \text{sum of cross products for } XY \\
&= \sum(x - \bar{x})(y - \bar{y}) \\
&= \sum xy - \frac{(\sum x)(\sum y)}{n} \quad\quad (14.5)
\end{aligned}
$$

Using this notation, we can write r as

$$
r = \frac{SCP_{XY}}{\sqrt{SS_X}\,\sqrt{SS_Y}} \quad\quad (14.6)
$$

The following are some important properties of the sample correlation coefficient r.

1. r ranges from -1.0 to 1.0.

2. The larger $|r|$ (absolute value of r) is, the stronger is the linear relationship.

3. r near zero indicates that there is no linear relationship between X and Y, and the scatter diagram *typically* (although not necessarily) appears to have a shotgun effect (Figure 14.2a). Here, X and Y are uncorrelated.

4. $r = 1$ or $r = -1$ implies that a perfect linear pattern exists between the two variables in the sample, that is, a single line will go *through* each point. Here we say that X and Y are **perfectly correlated** (Figure 14.2b and c).

5. Values of $r = 0$, 1, or -1 are rare in practice. Several other values of the correlation coefficient are illustrated in Figure 14.2d, e, and f.

6. The sign of r tells you whether the relationship between X and Y is a positive (direct) or a negative (inverse) one.

7. The value of r tells you very little about the slope of the line through these points (except for the sign of r). If r is positive, the line through these points has positive slope, and similarly, this line will have negative slope if r is negative.

FIGURE

14.2

Scatter diagrams for various values of the sample correlation coefficient.

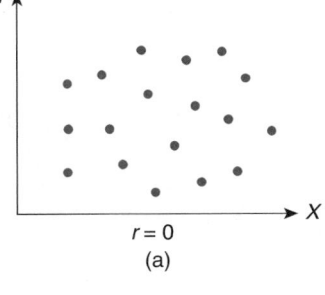

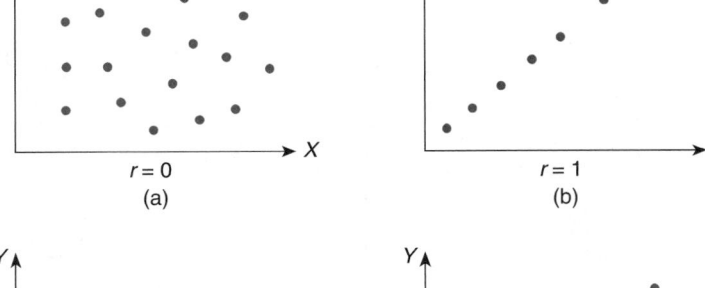

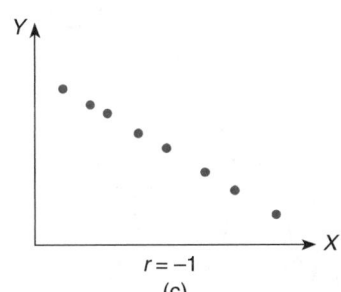

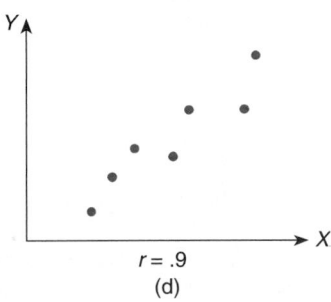

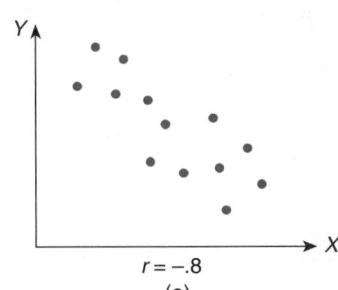

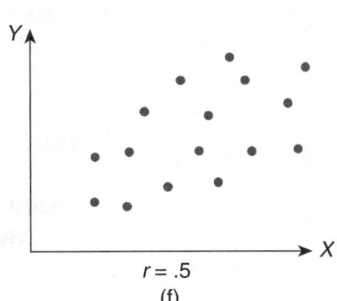

FIGURE

14.3

Although (a) has a large slope and (b) has a small slope, both are scatter diagrams for $r = .9$.

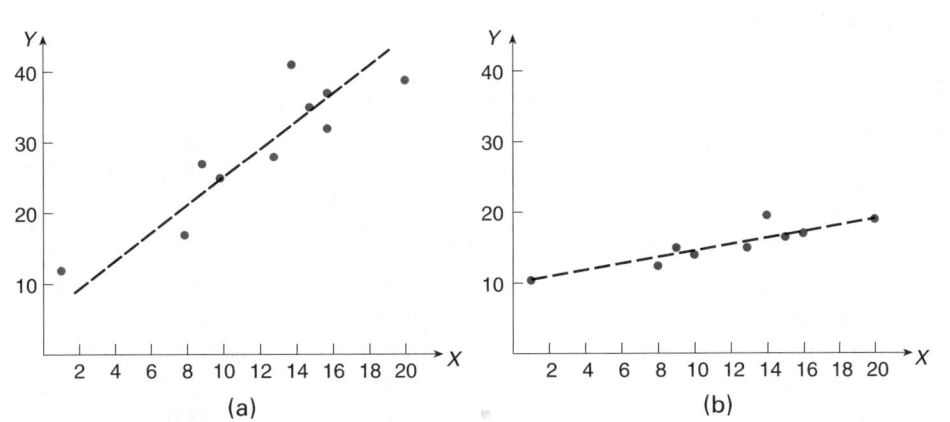

However, a set of data with $r = .9$ will not necessarily have a steeper line passing through it than will a set of data with $r = .4$. All you will observe in the first data set is a set of points that is very close to some straight line with positive slope, but you know nothing (except for the sign) about the slope of this line. See Figure 14.3, where both sets of data have an r value of .9.

EXAMPLE

14.1

Determine the sample correlation coefficient for the real-estate data in Figure 14.1.

Solution   Your calculations can be organized as follows:

Family	X (Income)	Y (Square Footage)	XY	X^2	Y^2
1	32	16	512	1,024	256
2	36	17	612	1,296	289
3	55	26	1,430	3,025	676
4	47	24	1,128	2,209	576
5	38	22	836	1,444	484
6	60	21	1,260	3,600	441
7	66	32	2,112	4,356	1,024
8	44	18	792	1,936	324
9	70	30	2,100	4,900	900
10	50	20	1,000	2,500	400
	498	226	11,782	26,290	5,370

Using the totals from this table,

$$SS_X = 26{,}290 - \frac{(498)^2}{10} = 1489.6$$

$$SS_Y = 5370 - \frac{(226)^2}{10} = 262.4$$

$$SCP_{XY} = 11{,}782 - \frac{(498)(226)}{10} = 527.2$$

This value of the sample correlation coefficient is

$$r = \frac{SCP_{XY}}{\sqrt{SS_X}\sqrt{SS_Y}}$$

$$= \frac{527.2}{\sqrt{1489.6}\sqrt{262.4}} = \frac{527.2}{625.2} = .843$$

Using Excel. For large data sets, the easiest way to obtain a scatter diagram and calculate the value of r is to use a computer. At the end of the chapter, we will show you how to do this using SPSS and MINITAB. The Excel result is shown in Figure 14.4. To obtain this output, follow this sequence:

1. Click on the **Chart Wizard** icon (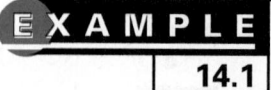) ➤ **XY (Scatter)** ➤ **Next.** Enter "A1:B10" in the **Data Range** box (click on **Next**). Click on the **Titles** tab and enter "Real Estate Data" for the chart title, "Income" in the **Value (X) Axis** box, and "Footage" in the **Value (Y) Axis** box. Click on **Finish.**

2. Drag the plot so that the upper-left corner is in cell C1 as shown in Figure 14.4. The resulting plot will begin the X and Y axes at zero. To obtain the more focused plot in Figure 14.4, *right* click on any of the values along the X axis, click on **Format Axis,** and then click on the **Scale** tab. Set the minimum value to 30 and the maximum value to 75. Repeat this for the Y axis by right clicking on any of the Y axis values, clicking on the **Scale** tab, and setting the minimum value to 15 and the maximum value to 35.

3. Enter "Correlation Coefficient" in cell A11. Click on (activate) cell A12 and click on the **Paste** function icon (f_x) ➤ **Statistical** ➤ **CORREL.** Enter "A1:A10" for **Array 1** and "B1:B10" for **Array 2.** The resulting correlation coefficient ($r = .843$) should appear in cell A12.

FIGURE

14.4

Excel-generated
scatter diagram
and correlation
coefficient for real
estate data.

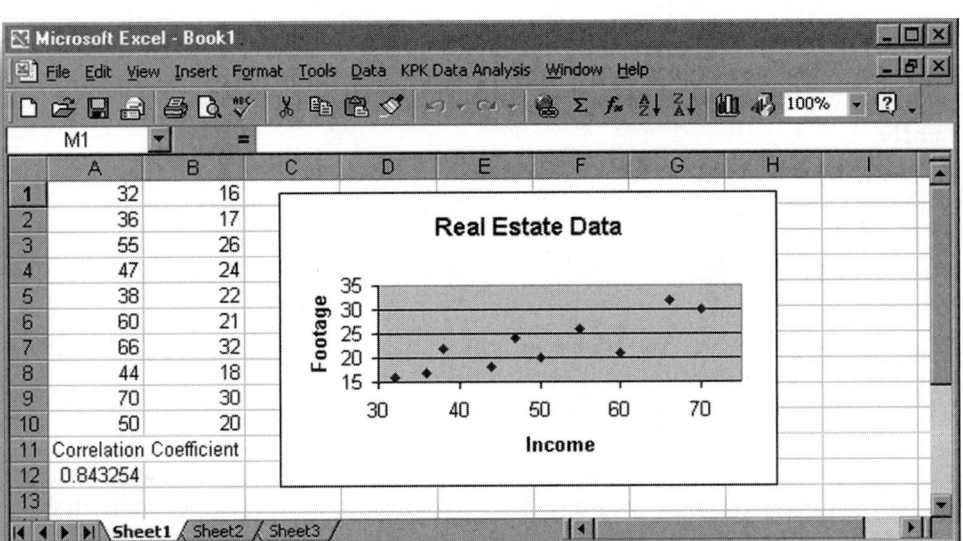

Covariance

Another commonly used measure of the association between two variables, X and Y, is the sample covariance, written cov(X, Y). It is similar to the sample correlation between these two variables. For one thing, the covariance and correlation always have the *same sign*. Consequently, if large values of X are associated with large values of Y, then both the covariance and correlation are positive. Similarly, both values are negative whenever large values of X are associated with small values of Y. For any two variables, X and Y, the sample **covariance** between these variables is defined in the following box.

DEFINITION

The sample covariance between two variables, cov(X, Y) is a measure of the joint variation of the two variables, X and Y, and is defined to be

$$\text{cov}(X, Y) = \frac{1}{n-1}\Sigma(x - \bar{x})(y - \bar{y})$$

$$= \frac{1}{n-1}\text{SCP}_{XY}$$

14.7   14.8

In Example 14.1, the sample covariance between income (X) and home size (Y) is

$$\text{cov}(X, Y) = \frac{1}{n-1}\text{SCP}_{XY} = \frac{1}{9}(527.2) = 58.58$$

To see how the sample covariance and sample correlation (r) are related, let

$$s_X = \text{standard deviation of the } X \text{ values } = \sqrt{\frac{\text{SS}_X}{n-1}}$$

and

$$s_Y = \text{standard deviation of the } Y \text{ values } = \sqrt{\frac{\text{SS}_Y}{n-1}}$$

Then

$$r = \text{sample correlation between } X \text{ and } Y$$
$$= \frac{\text{cov}(X, Y)}{s_X s_Y}$$

In Example 14.1,

$$s_X = \sqrt{\frac{1489.6}{9}} = 12.865 \qquad \text{and} \qquad s_Y = \sqrt{\frac{262.4}{9}} = 5.400$$

so

$$r = \frac{58.58}{(12.865)(5.400)} = .843 \qquad \text{(as before)}$$

The correlation between two variables is used more often than the covariance because r always ranges from –1 to 1. The covariance, on the other hand, has no limits and can assume any value. Furthermore, the units of measurement for a covariance are difficult to interpret. For example, the previously calculated covariance is 58.58 (thousands of dollars) × (hundreds of square feet)—a somewhat meaningless unit of measurement. So, in a sense, the correlation is a scaled version of the covariance and has no units of measurement (a nice feature). To illustrate, the sample correlation between body weight and height will be the same whether you use the metric or the English systems to obtain the sample data. The covariance, however, will *not* be the same for these two situations. The covariance does have its applications, however, particularly in financial analyses, such as determining the risk associated with a number of interrelated investment opportunities.

As a final look at these two measures, you can consider the correlation between two variables to be the covariance between the **standardized** variables. By defining

$$X' = \frac{X - \overline{X}}{s_X} \qquad \text{and} \qquad Y' = \frac{Y - \overline{Y}}{s_Y}$$

then

$$\text{cov}(X', Y') = \text{correlation between } X \text{ and } Y = r$$

Least Squares Line

If we believe that two variables do exhibit an underlying linear pattern, how can we determine a straight line that best passes through these points? So far, we have demonstrated only the calculations necessary to compute a correlation coefficient. We next illustrate how to construct a line through a set of points exhibiting a linear pattern; we look at the assumptions behind this procedure in the next section.

Look at the scatter diagram in Figure 14.1*b*, which shows one possible line through these points. The scatter diagram and line are repeated in Figure 14.5, which also shows the vertical distances from each point to the line ($d_1, d_2, \ldots$).

Is line L the best line through these points? Because we would like the distances $d_1, d_2, \ldots, d_{10}$ to be small, we define the best line to be the one that minimizes

$$\Sigma d^2 = d_1^2 + d_2^2 + d_3^2 + \cdots + d_{10}^2$$

We square each distance because some of these distances are positive (the point lies *above* line L) and some are negative (the point lies *below* line L). If we did not

FIGURE

14.5

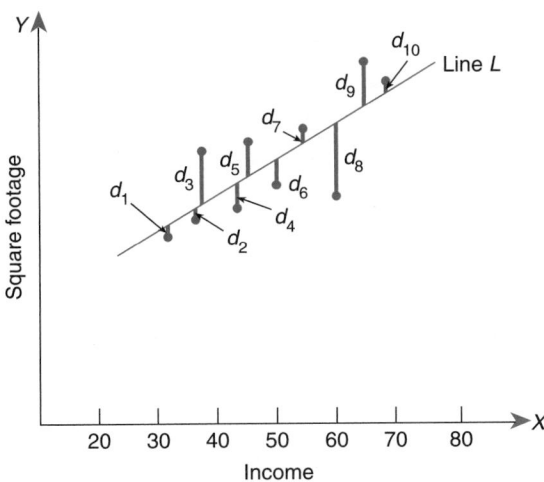

Vertical distances from line L to real-estate data (Example 14.1), represented by $d_1, d_2, \ldots, d_{10}$.

square each distance, d, the positive d's might cancel out the negative ones. This means that using $(d_1 + d_2 + \cdots + d_{10})$ as a *measure of fit* is *not* a good idea. A better method is to determine which line makes equation 14.10 as small as possible; this line is called the **least squares line.** Deriving this line in general requires the use of calculus (derivatives, in particular).*

Because we intend to use this line to predict Y for a particular value of X, we use the notation $\hat{Y}$ (Y-hat) to describe the equation of the line. We can now define, for the least squares line, the b_0 and b_1 that minimize $(d_1^2 + d_2^2 + \cdots + d_n^2)$, given by

$$b_1 = \frac{\text{SCP}_{XY}}{\text{SS}_X}$$

$$b_0 = \bar{y} - b_1\bar{x}$$

14.11 14.12

where SS_X and SCP_{XY} are as defined in equations 14.3 and 14.5. Also, $\bar{x} = \sum x/n$ and $\bar{y} = \sum y/n$. The resulting least squares line is

$$\hat{Y} = b_0 + b_1 X$$

In Figure 14.6, notice that each distance, d, is actually $Y - \hat{Y}$ and consists of the **residual,** encountered by using the straight line to estimate the value of Y at this point. So

$$\sum d^2 = \sum (y - \hat{y})^2$$

This term is the **sum of squares of error** (or *residual sum of squares*) and is written **SSE.** Consequently, the least squares line is the one that makes SSE as small as possible.

---

*For the mathematically curious, we provide a condensed derivation of these coefficients. To minimize $\sum d^2$, first write this expression as

$$f(b_0, b_1) = \sum d^2 = \sum (y - \hat{y})^2$$

$$= \sum (y - b_0 - b_1 x)^2$$

because $\hat{y} = b_0 + b_1 x$.

To minimize this function, determine the partial derivatives with respect to b_0 (written as f_{b_0} and with respect to b_1 (written as f_{b_1}). These are

$$f_{b_0} = 2\sum (y - b_0 - b_1 x)(-1) = -2[\sum y - nb_0 - b_1\sum x]$$

$$f_{b_1} = 2\sum (y - b_0 - b_1 x)(-x) = -2[\sum xy - b_0\sum x - b_1\sum x^2]$$

Setting $f_{b_0} = f_{b_1} = 0$ and solving for b_0 and b_1 results in equations 14.11 and 14.12.

14.6

The least squares line for Example 14.1. Each $d = Y - \hat{Y}$, the error encountered by using the straight line to estimate the value of Y at the corresponding point.

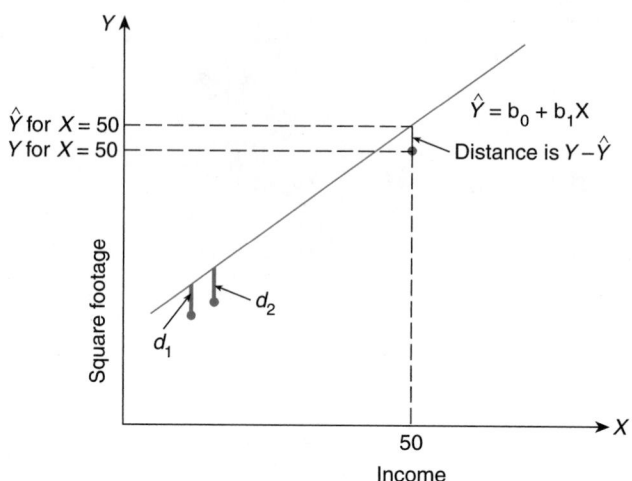

$$SSE = \Sigma d^2 = \Sigma(y - \hat{y})^2$$

14.13

There is another method of determining SSE when using the least squares line, which avoids having to determine the value of $\hat{Y}$ at each point:

$$SSE = SS_Y - \frac{(SCP_{XY})^2}{SS_X}$$

14.14

EXAMPLE 14.2

Determine the least squares line for the real-estate data we used in Example 14.1. What is the SSE?

Solution Using the calculations from Example 14.1, $SCP_{XY} = 527.2$, $SS_X = 1489.6$, and $SS_Y = 262.4$, leading to

$$b_1 = \frac{SCP_{XY}}{SS_X}$$

$$= \frac{527.2}{1489.6} = .3539$$

and

$$b_0 = \bar{y} - b_1\bar{x}$$

$$= 22.6 - \left(\frac{527.2}{1489.6}\right)(49.8) = 4.975$$

because

$$\bar{y} = \frac{\Sigma y}{n} = \frac{226}{10} = 22.6 \qquad \text{and} \qquad \bar{x} = \frac{\Sigma x}{n} = \frac{498}{10} = 49.8$$

So the equation of the best (least squares) line through these points is

$$\hat{Y} = 4.975 + .3539X$$

This equation tells us that in the sample data an increase of $1,000 in income ($X$ increases by 1) is accompanied by an increase of 35.39 square feet in home size

FIGURE

14.7

Least squares line
for real-estate data
(Example 14.2).

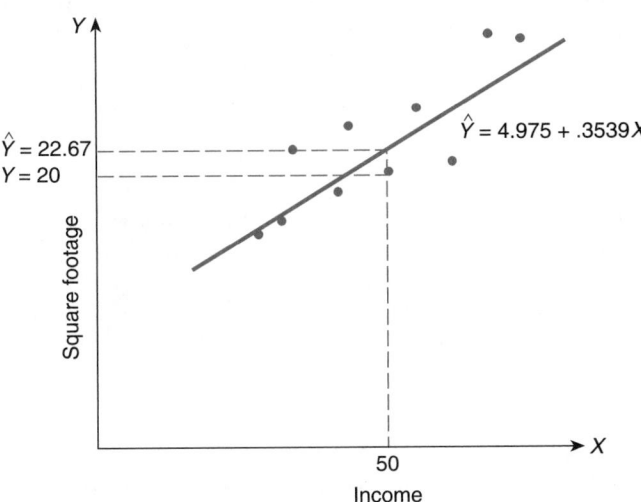

(Y increases by .3539), on the average. For this illustration (and many others in practice), the *intercept, b_0*, has no real meaning because it corresponds to an income of zero dollars. Furthermore, an income of zero is considerably outside the range of the incomes in the sample. It is unsafe to assume that the linear relationship between X and Y present over the range of sample incomes ($32,000 to $70,000) exists outside this range—in particular, all the way to an income of zero. The **slope, b_1**, generally is the more informative value.

In Figure 14.7, the actual value of Y (in the sample data) for X = 50 is Y = 20 (the last pair of X, Y values). The predicted value of Y using the least squares line is

$$\hat{Y} = 4.975 + (.3539)(50) = 22.670$$

The residual at this point is

$$\text{residual} = Y - \hat{Y} = 20 - 22.670 = -2.670$$

Repeating this for the other nine points leads to the following results. Notice that the sum of the residuals when using the least squares line is zero. This is always true.

X	Y	$\hat{Y}$	$Y - \hat{Y}$	$(Y - \hat{Y})^2$
32	16	16.300	−0.300	0.090
36	17	17.715	−0.715	0.511
55	26	24.440	1.560	2.434
47	24	21.608	2.392	5.722
38	22	18.423	3.577	12.795
60	21	26.209	−5.209	27.134
66	32	28.332	3.668	13.454
44	18	20.547	−2.547	6.487
70	30	29.748	0.252	0.064
50	20	22.670	−2.670	7.129
			0	75.82

↰ Rounded

As you can see, calculating the SSE (= 75.82) using the table and equation 14.13 is tedious. Using equation 14.14 instead leads to

$$\text{SSE} = 262.4 - \frac{(527.2)^2}{1489.6}$$

$$= 262.4 - 186.59$$

$$= 75.81$$

This calculated SSE value is slightly more accurate than the value obtained by summing the squared residuals and will be used in the examples to follow.

Remember, however, that equation 14.13 applies to *any* line that you choose to construct through these points, whereas equation 14.14 applies only to the SSE for the least squares line.

In Example 14.2, we attempted to predict the size of a home (Y) using the corresponding income (X). The variable Y is the **dependent variable,** and X is the **independent variable.** By passing a straight line through the sample points with Y as the dependent variable, we are **regressing** Y on X. *In linear regression, you regress the dependent variable, Y, which you are trying to predict, on the independent (or predictor or explanatory) variable, X.*

X Exercises 14.1–14.12

Understanding the Mechanics

14.1 Consider the following table.

X	Y	XY	X²	Y²
3	8			
10	22			
2	6			
5	9			
4	8			

Totals $\Sigma x =$ ___ $\Sigma y =$ ___ $\Sigma xy =$ ___ $\Sigma x^2 =$ ___ $\Sigma y^2 =$ ___

a. Find the totals for each column in the table.
b. Use the totals in the table to calculate the slope and the intercept for the least squares line.
c. Calculate the sample correlation of X and Y.

14.2 The following pairs of observations were collected.

X	1	2	3	4	5
Y	2	6	4	10	15

a. Plot the values of X and Y. What relationship does the scatter diagram suggest?
b. Find the least squares line.
c. Find the predicted value for each value of X.
d. Find the residual for each predicted value of Y.
e. Verify that the sum of the residuals in part d is zero.

Applying the New Concepts

14.3 Nationwide, about 27% of mortgage-paying homeowners spent 30% or more of their income on housing costs. Hawaiians paid the largest percentage at 41% and South Dakotans the smallest at 17.5%. Eight states were randomly selected, and the median household income (X) in thousands and the percentage of mortgage-paying homeowners whose housing costs exceed 30% of their income (Y) are as follows.

State	California	Hawaii	Idaho	Maine	Oklahoma	South Dakota	Utah	West Virginia
X	46.5	51.1	37.1	36.4	33.5	35.2	45.6	28.6
Y	37.2	41.0	20.6	24.3	22.0	17.5	30.0	23.0

a. Graph the data and draw a line through the points. Would you say that the data appear to demonstrate a linear relationship between X and Y?
b. Calculate the least squares line. How does it compare to the line in part a?

(Source: "Snapshot of U.S. Commuting, Income, Housing," *USA Today,* August 6, 2001, p. 2A.)

14.4 The supervisor of a group of assembly-line workers wanted to compare last year's productivity (X) to this year's productivity (Y) for each of the 20 employees that she supervises. In the past, an approximate linear relationship has existed between these two variables. Last year the average productivity per worker was 9.5 items per hour. This year, the average productivity per worker is 12.1 items per hour. The supervisor found the following sums for her 20 employees:

$$SCP_{XY} = 0.4$$
$$SS_X = 0.3$$
$$SS_Y = 0.8$$

a. Calculate the correlation coefficient.
b. Calculate the least squares line.
c. Calculate the sum of squares for error.

14.5 Because $b_0 = \bar{y} - b_1\bar{x}$, we can replace b_0 in $\hat{Y} = b_0 + b_1X$ by $\bar{y} - b_1\bar{x}$). Hence, we have $\hat{Y} = \bar{y} + b_1(X - \bar{x})$. From this equation, show that the point $(\bar{x}, \bar{y})$ always falls on the least squares line.

14.6 Compare the formulas for the sample correlation, r, and the slope of the least squares line, b_1, and verify that $b_1 = r\sqrt{SS_Y/SS_X}$. What can we say about the sign of r and b_1?

14.7 Generale Bank agreed to a takeover from the Dutch-Belgian bank and insurance concern, named Fortis Group. This acquisition would propel Fortis to the top league of Europe's largest financial institutions and speed up other cross-border mergers in the European financial-services sector, an industry roiled by mounting competition and the launch of the euro. Generale Bank management advisor is interested in the relationship between the market capitalization of Europe's main bank insurance concerns and their total assets. The following data are listed as a random sample of these European companies with their market capitalization and total assets in billions of dollars.

European Bank Insurance Firm	Market Capitalization	Total Assets
Deutsche Bank	46.3	585.0
Credit Suisse	59.1	370.0
ING Group	49.4	309.4
Benelux Bank	23.8	168.0
Generale Bank	9.8	160.8
CGER-ASLK	33.6	328.8

a. Graph the data. Estimate the intercept and slope of the regression equation from viewing the graph. Also, estimate the correlation coefficient.

b. Calculate the least squares line. Interpret the coefficients of the regression equation. How closely do the calculated values of the least squares line agree with your estimates from part a?

c. Calculate the correlation coefficient and compare to your estimate from part a.

(Source: "Belgium's Largest Bank Agrees to Be Acquired by Fortis Group," *The Wall Street Journal*, May 13, 1998, p. C14.)

14.8 The owner of Grandmother's Cake Shop would like to predict the quantity of cakes sold when they are marked at low prices. There are no restrictions on the quantity, because the shop can easily bake several cakes in an hour if the demand is stronger than predicted. Past data show the following results.

Number of Cakes Sold (Y)	Price of Cake (X)	Number of Cakes Sold (Y)	Price of Cake (X)
14	2.30	16	1.99
16	2.10	17	1.90
17	1.80	15	2.25
17	1.89	14	2.39
13	2.50	13	2.70
12	2.80		

a. Find the least squares line for X and Y.

b. Graph the data and the least squares line.

c. Suppose that the manager believes that there is a strong linear relationship between Y and X^2. Find the prediction equation for Y using X^2 only.

d. Compare the SSE for the least squares line found in part a with the least squares line found in part c.

14.9 Lottieries remain the most pervasive form of gambling in the United States. Surveys show that more than half of all American households have bought lottery tickets at some time. The Texas Lottery Commission is interested in the revenue generated by the Texas Lotto, in which players pick 6 numbers, and also the Texas lotteries in which players pick less than 6 numbers (Cash 5, Pick 3, and Texas 2 step). The revenue for the years 1992 to 2000 are presented in units of billions of dollars.

Year	Texas Lotto (X)	Texas Games Choosing Less than Six Numbers (Y)
1992	0.01	0.51
1993	0.75	0.95
1994	1.05	1.70

Year	Texas Lotto (X)	Texas Games Choosing Less than Six Numbers (Y)
1995	1.05	1.95
1996	0.85	2.55
1997	0.90	2.85
1998	0.75	2.25
1999	0.70	1.80
2000	0.52	2.14

a. Plot the values of X and Y. What is your estimate of the correlation coefficient?

b. Compute the sample correlation coefficient and compare it to your response in part a.

c. Find the least squares lines for X and Y and interpret the coefficients of the regression line in the context of this problem.

Using the Computer

14.10 [**DATA SET EX14-10**] *Variable description:*

State: Name of state in U.S.

2000Pop: Population of state at the end of the year 2000

1990Pop: Population of state at the end of the year 1990

For the first decade since 1870, every state in the United States gained population for the decade ending in 2000. Overall, the U.S. population grew by 13.2%. Not all states grew evenly; Nevada gained the most at 66.3% and North Dakota gained the least at .5%.

a. Plot Y = 2000Pop and X = 1990Pop. Would you say that the plot indicates a linear relationship between X and Y?

b. What is the correlation coefficient? Do you think that value indicates a linear trend?

c. Using the least squares line, what is the predicted value for the population of North Carolina at the end of the year 2000? Would you say this is a good estimate?

14.11 [**Simulation Exercise**] The method of least squares is a technique used to compute the "best" straight line fit to a set of data points plotted on a graph. To better visualize this technique, in Excel click in **KPK Data Analysis ➤ Simulation Exercise** and select **Draw Least Squares Line**. In this simulation exercise, the value of the correlation and the sample size of the data set to be generated is specified by the user. A graph of the data is presented to illustrate the shape of the data for the specified correlation and sample size. The user can move the line sitting above the graph inside the sample points so that it best "slices through" the data. Then the user can view the actual least squares line to see how closely it matches it to the user's line.

a. Using a sample size of 20, generate data having correlations of –.9, –.5, –.2, 0, .2, .5., and .9. Comment on the shape of the data for each correlation.

b. Select various combinations of high and low correlations with high and low sample sizes, and demonstrate your expertise at fitting a straight line through the data by moving the line sitting above the graph so that it appears to be the "best" linear predictor. Is the actual least squares line close to your line? For which combinations of correlations and sample sizes do you find this to be easy?

14.12 [DATA SET EX14-12] *Variable description:*

AskPrice: Asking price of a car

SellPrice: Selling price of a car

A car dealer is interested in the relationship between the original asking price of a new car and the final selling price of the car. The car dealer selected a random sample of 50 car deals. The asking and selling prices were recorded as variables AskPrice and SellPrice, respectively. The units of the data are in thousands of dollars.

a. Graph the data. Estimate the intercept and slope of the regression equation from viewing the graph. Estimate the value of the correlation from viewing the graph.

b. Calculate the correlation coefficient and find the coefficients of the least squares line. Compare your answers to that in part a.

14.2

THE SIMPLE LINEAR REGRESSION MODEL

When we construct a straight line through a set of data points, we are attempting to predict the behavior of a dependent variable, Y, using a straight line equation with one predictor (independent) variable, X. Examples 14.1 and 14.2 examined the relationship in a particular community between the square footage (Y) of a particular home and the income of the owner (X).

Another applicant is attempting to predict the sales (Y) of a certain brand of shampoo using the amount of advertising expenditure (X) as the independent variable. We expect that as more advertising dollars are spent, the sales will increase. In other words, we expect a *positive* relationship for this situation.

Regression analysis is a method of studying the relationship between two (or more) variables, one purpose being to arrive at a method for predicting a value of the dependent variable. In **simple linear regression,** we use only *one* predictor variable, X, to describe the behavior of the dependent variable, Y. Also, the relationship between X and Y is assumed to be basically linear.

We have learned the mechanics of constructing a line through a set of bivariate sample values. We are now ready to introduce the concept of a statistical model.

Defining the Model

Return to Example 14.2 and Figure 14.4. This set of sample data contained a value of $X = 50$ and $Y = 20$. Consider the population of *all* houses in this community where the owner's income is 50 (that is, $50,000). Will they all have the same square footage? Unless this is a very boring-looking neighborhood, certainly not. Does this mean that the straight line predictor is of no use? The answer again is no; we do not expect things in this world to be that perfectly predictable. When you use the equation of a straight line to predict the square footage, you should be aware that there will be a certain amount of *error* present in this estimate. This is similar to the situation in which we estimate the mean, μ, of a population and the sample mean, $\overline{X}$, always estimates this parameter with a certain amount of inherent error.

When we elect to use a straight-line predictor, we employ a **statistical model** of the form

$$Y = \beta_0 + \beta_1 X + e$$

14.15

where (1) $\beta_0 + \beta_1 X$ is the *assumed* line about which *all* values of X and Y will fall, called the **deterministic** portion of the model, and (2) e is the error component, referred to as the **random error** part of the model.

In other words, there exists some (unknown) line about which all X, Y values can be expected to fall. Notice that we said "about which," not "on which"—hence the necessity of the error term, e, which is the unexplained error that is part of the simple linear model. Because this model considers only one independent variable, the effect of other predictor variables (perhaps unknown to the analyst) is contained in this error term.

We emphasize that the deterministic portion, $\beta_0 + \beta_1 X$, refers to the straight line for the *population* and will remain unknown. However, by obtaining a random sample of bivariate data from this population, we are able to estimate the unknown parameters, β_0 and β_1. Thus b_0 is the *intercept* of the sample regression line and is the estimate of the population intercept, β_0. The value of b_0 can be calculated using equation 14.12. Similarly, b_1 is the *slope* of the sample regression line and is the estimate of the population slope, β_1. The value of b_1 can be calculated using equation 14.11.

Assumptions for the Simple Linear Regression Model

We can construct a least squares line through *any* set of sample points, whether or not the pattern is linear. We could construct a least squares line through a set of sample data exhibiting no linear pattern at all. However, to have an effective predictor and a model that will enable us to make statistical decisions, certain assumptions are necessary.

We treat the values of X as fixed (nonrandom) quantities when using the simple linear regression model. For any given value of X, the only source of variation comes from the error component, e, which is a random variable. In fact, there are many random variables here, one for each possible value of X. The assumptions used with this model are concerned with the nature of these random variables.

The first three assumptions are concerned with the behavior of the error component for a fixed value of X. The fourth assumption deals with the manner in which the error components (random variables) affect each other.

Assumption 1. *The mean of each error component is zero.* This is the key assumption behind simple linear regression. Look at Figure 14.8, where we once again examine a value of $X = 50$. Considering all homes (in this community) whose owners have an income of $50,000 ($X = 50$), we have already decided that these homes do not all have the same square footage, Y. In fact, the square-footage values will be scattered about the (unknown) line $Y = \beta_0 + \beta_1 X$, with some values lying above the

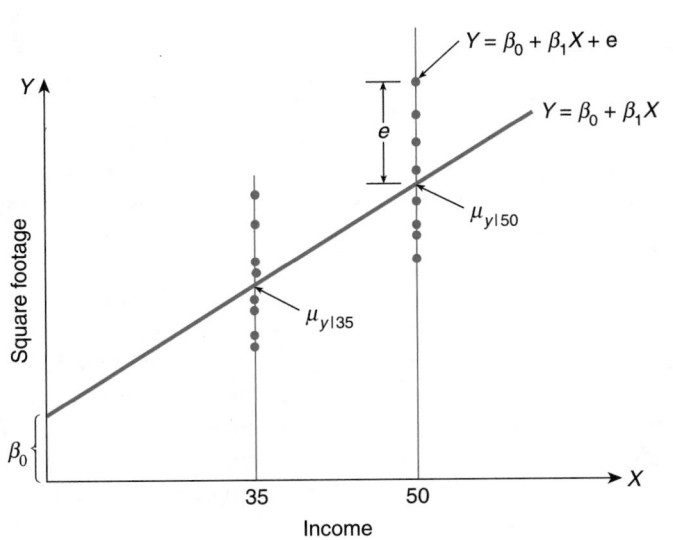

FIGURE

14.8

Illustration of assumption 1; see text.

FIGURE

14.9

A violation of assumption 3; see text.

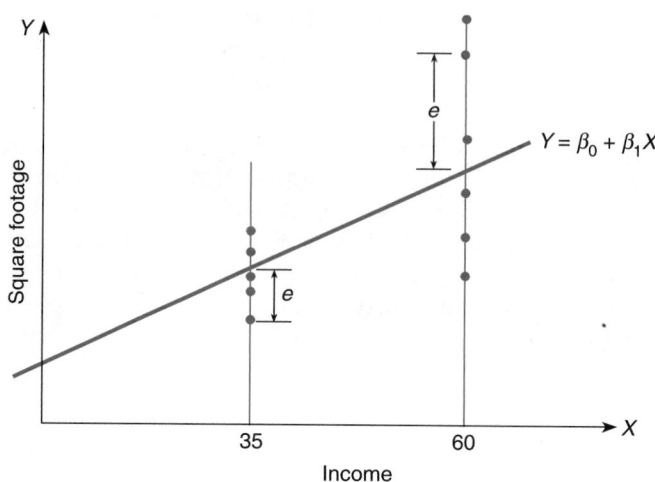

line (*e* is positive) and some falling below it (*e* is negative). Consider the average of *all* Y values with $X = 50$. This is written as

$$\mu_{Y|50}$$

which is the mean of Y *given* $X = 50$. Our assumption here is that the point $(50, \mu_{Y|50})$ *lies on this line;* that is, for *any* value of X, the point $(x, \mu_{Y|x})$ *lies on the line* $Y = \beta_0 + \beta_1 X$ (such as $\mu_{Y|35}$ in Figure 14.8). Put another way, the error is zero, *on average.*

Assumption 2. *Each error component (random variable) follows an approximate normal distribution.* In our sample of 10 homes and incomes, we had one family with $X = 50$ and $Y = 20$. Figure 14.8 illustrates what we might expect if we were to examine other homes whose owners had an income of $50,000. We assume here that if we were to obtain 100 homes, for example, whose owners had this income, a histogram of the resulting errors (*e*) would be bell-shaped in appearance. So we would expect a concentration of errors near zero (from assumption 1), with half of them positive and half of them negative.

Assumption 3. *The variance of the error component,* σ_e^2, *is the same for each value of X.* For each value of X, the errors illustrated in Figure 14.8 have so far been assumed to follow a normal distribution with a mean of zero. So each error, *e*, is from such a normal population. The variance of this population is, σ_e^2. The assumption here is that, σ_e^2 *does not change* as the value of X changes. This is the assumption of **homoscedasticity.** A situation where this assumption is violated is illustrated in Figure 14.9, where we once again consider what might occur if we *were* to obtain (we will not, actually) many values of Y for $X = 35$ and also for $X = 60$. If Figure 14.9 were the result, assumption 3 would be violated, because the errors would be much larger (in absolute value) for the $60,000-income homes than they would for the $35,000-income homes. Figure 14.9 illustrates **heteroscedasticity,** which does pose a problem when we try to infer results from a linear regression equation.

You might argue that, proportionally, the errors for $X = 60$ seem about the same as those for $X = 35$, which means that you would expect larger errors for larger values of X here. If this is the case, the confidence intervals and tests of hypothesis that we are about to develop for the simple linear regression model are *not appropriate.* There are methods of "repairing" this situation, by applying a *transformation* to the dependent variable, Y, such as $\sqrt{Y}$ or $\log(Y)$. By using this "new" dependent variable rather than the original Y, the resulting errors often will exhibit a nearly constant variance. Such transformations, however, are beyond the scope of this text.

FIGURE

14.10

Illustration of assumptions 1, 2, 3; see text.

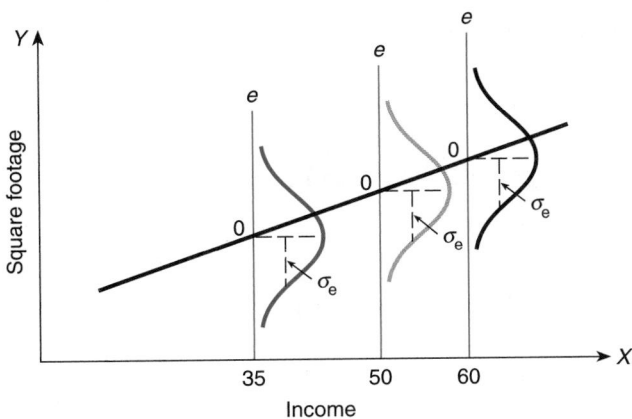

A summary of the first three assumptions is shown in Figure 14.10. Note that the distribution of errors is *identical* for each illustrated value of X; namely, it is a normal distribution with mean = 0 and variance σ_e^2.

Assumption 4. *The errors are independent of each other.* This implies that the error encountered for one value of Y is unaffected by the error for any other value of Y. To illustrate, consider the real-estate data and suppose that the sample is *not* random but that instead the sample houses are all located on a certain street. The first house has a positive error when predicting the square footage. If the probability is greater than .5 that the next house in the sample also has a positive error (that is, if its location makes it probable that it will be a certain size), then the assumption of independence is violated. In other words, the sample was poorly chosen because the houses on one street are likely to be more or less the same size and their owners are likely to have similar incomes. The nonrandom sample led to a violation of assumption 4.

We can draw two conclusions from these assumptions. First, each value of the dependent variable, Y, is a normal random variable with mean = $\beta_0 + \beta_1 X$ and variance σ_e^2. Second, the error components come from the same normal population, *regardless of the value* of X. In other words, it makes sense to examine the residuals resulting from each value of X in the sample, to construct a histogram of these residuals, and to determine whether its appearance is bell-shaped (normal), centered at zero. A key assumption when using simple linear regression is that the errors follow a normal distribution with a mean of zero. Constructing a histogram of the sample residuals provides a convenient method of determining whether this assumption is reasonable for a particular application.

This discussion is continued in section 14.6 ("Examining the Residuals"). This section will demonstrate graphical methods for checking these assumptions (including a histogram of the residuals), along with various numerical measures that identify *unusual* and *influential observations* in the sample data.

Estimating the Error Variance, σ_e^2

The variance of the error components, σ_e^2, measures the variation of the error terms resulting from the simple linear regression model. The value of σ_e^2 severely affects our ability to use this model as an effective predictor for a given situation. Suppose, for example, that σ_e^2 is very large in Figure 14.10. This means that if we were to obtain many observations (square footage values, Y) for a *fixed* value of X (say, income = \$50,000), these Y values would vary a great deal, decreasing the accuracy of our model; we would prefer that these values were grouped closely about the mean, $\mu_{Y|50}$.

In practice, σ_e^2 typically is unknown and must be estimated from the sample. To estimate this variance, we first determine the sum of squares of error, SSE, using $SSE = \Sigma(y - \hat{y})^2$ or equation 14.14. Estimating β_0 and β_1 for the simple regression model results in a loss of 2 df, leaving $n - 2$ df for estimating the error variance. Consequently,

$$s^2 = \hat{\sigma}_e^2 = \text{estimate of } \sigma_e^2 = \frac{SSE}{n - 2}$$

14.16

where

$$SSE = \Sigma(y - \hat{y})^2 = SS_Y - \frac{(SCP_{XY})^2}{SS_X}$$

Note that SSE is the expression that was minimized in Figure 14.5 when determining the "best" line through the sample points. In Figure 14.5, each distance d corresponds to $y - \hat{y}$.

We can determine the estimate of σ_e^2 and σ_e for the real-estate data in Example 14.2, where we calculated the value of SSE to be 75.81. Our estimate of σ_e^2 is

$$s^2 = \frac{SSE}{n - 2} = \frac{75.81}{8} = 9.476$$

and so $s = \sqrt{9.476} = 3.078$ provides an estimate of σ_e. The values of s^2 and s are a measure of the variation of the Y values about the least squares line.

Comments

We know from the empirical rule that approximately 95% of the data from a normal population should lie within two standard deviations of the mean. For this example, this rule implies that approximately 95% of the residuals should lie within $2(3.078) = 6.16$ of the mean. In the table in Example 14.2, the sample residuals are in the fourth column. Their sum is *always* zero, when using the least squares line; therefore, their mean is *zero*. So, approximately 95% of the residuals should be no larger (in absolute value) than 6.16. In fact, all of them are less than 6.16—not a surprising result, given that we had only 10 values in the sample.

X | Exercises 14.13–14.22

Understanding the Mechanics

14.13 The residuals of a least squares line are as follows.

$Y - \hat{Y}$:   .4 .2   3 –.1   .2   .1 –.3 –.4 –.2 –3 .1 .3 .4

      –3 .3 –.1   3 –.2 –.3 –.4

   a. Find the estimate of the error variance, s^2.

   b. Are approximately 95% of the residuals within $2s$ of the mean of the residuals? What does your answer indicate about the appropriateness of the data for a regression analysis procedure?

14.14 Consider the following set of residuals, resulting from a regression analysis.

$Y - \hat{Y}$	X	$Y - \hat{Y}$	X
.4	1.0	2.0	4.0
–.4	1.5	–3.0	5.0
–1.0	1.6	4.2	6.0
1.2	2.0	–3.4	7.0
–1.6	2.5	–5.0	8.0
–1.0	3.0	7.6	9.0

   a. Construct a graph of the residuals versus the X values.

   b. Does it appear that the equal variance assumption of regression analysis is violated?

Applying the New Concepts

14.15 The following data show the number of total annual bankruptcy petitions filed in the northern district of a southern state (in thousands) and the size of the permanent staff at the U.S. Bankruptcy Court for that district.

Bankruptcies in Thousands (X)	Permanent Staff at U.S. Bankruptcy Court (Y)
2.1	15
3.8	18
4.1	18
10.0	59
3.2	14
3.9	18
6.1	24

a. Compute the least squares line.

b. Identify the values of the slope and the intercept for the simple linear regression model.

c. Estimate the variance of the error for the model.

d. Find the residuals $(Y - \hat{Y})$ for all the Y values.

14.16 What assumptions need to be made about the error component of a linear model in order that statistical inference can be used?

14.17 The following is a list of sample errors $(Y - \hat{Y})$ from a linear regression application:

2.1, −.3, 1.4, −2.8, −3.9, 4.2, 3.6, 4.3, 1.8, −2.7, −.8, 1.2, .9, −1.1, −4.5, −5.2, −1.3, .5, .9, −.6, 1.5, 2.1, −2.2, .9

Do the data appear to conform to the empirical rule that approximately 95% of the errors should lie within two standard deviations of the mean? Construct a histogram for the residuals.

14.18 Let X be the distance an employee lives from his or her job. Let Y be the average time that it takes the employee to drive to work. Data from 30 employees gave the following sample statistics.

$$SCP_{XY} = 8.4 \qquad SS_X = 9.4 \qquad SS_Y = 12.2$$

a. Find the estimate of the error variance.

b. Find the interval in which approximately 68% of the error values should fall.

14.19 At Toys 'R' Us in Frankfurt, Germany, the manager converted toys that were previously priced in terms of marks into prices marked with euros. However, consumers believe that prices were not all converted evenly and that some prices were increased.

Retail Item	Original Price in Marks	Changed Price in Euros
Lego Life on Mars 7315	64.95	34.69
Black & Decker Drill KR 700	169	89.95
Wash & Go Shampoo 2 in 1	4.99	2.69
Original Kaisers Muffin Pan	16.95	8.99
Wileda Mop	9.99	5.49
Uno card game	16.99	8.99
Margaret Astor Powder Blush	16.95	8.99
Barbie Princess	32.95	18.49

a. Find the least squares line for predicting the changed price in euros using the original price in marks for the eight products listed.

b. Compute the correlation coefficient and interpret it.

c. Compute the residuals for each product. Based on the values of the residuals, which product would you say has been increased in price?

(Source: "Marketer's Friend, .99, Hits the Euro Zone," *The Wall Street Journal*, July 31, 2001, p. A14.)

14.20 Why is $\Sigma(y - \hat{y})^2$ used in estimating the variance of the error term instead of $\Sigma(y - \hat{y})$?

Using the Computer

14.21 [DATA SET EX14-21] *Variable description:*

InterpersonalScore: Employer's rating of an employee's interpersonal skills

JobPerformScore: Employer's rating of an employee's performance on the job

C-Cubed is a collaboration between the Fort Worth, Texas, Chamber of Commerce and the local school district. This partnership is designed to provide local businesses with successful employees according to "Learn to Work," an article in *The Fort Worth Star-Telegram*, June 29, 1997, p. 1E. One skill that often is not taught in school, but that appears to be essential to long-term job success is interpersonal skills. Suppose that in a survey of Fort Worth businesses, 70 employees who obtained jobs through the C-Cubed effort were selected. The employers were asked to rate the employees on interpersonal skills and on job performance on a scale from 1 to 10, with 10 representing perfect satisfaction.

a. Find the least squares line for predicting JobPerformScore from InterpersonalScore. Interpret the slope of this line.

b. Construct a histogram of the residuals. Do the residuals appear to follow a normal distribution?

14.22 [DATA SET EX14-22] *Variable description:*

SpecialNumber: Number of special parts ordered

SpecialCost: Dollar cost of special parts ordered

A sales manager for a car dealership mails an order for special parts each week. The manager is interested in the relationship between the number of special parts ordered and the total cost of the special order. One hundred special parts orders were randomly selected. The number of special parts and the total cost of these parts are recorded as variables SpecialNumber and SpecialCost, respectively.

a. Find the least squares line and interpret the coefficients.

b. What is the shape of the histogram of the residuals?

c. Sometimes researchers make a transformation on the data to make the residuals conform better to a normal distribution. Suppose that the square of SpecialCost is used instead of the original values. Describe the shape of the histogram in which this value is used as the dependent variable. Would you say that the error component of this regression model follows an approximately normal distribution?

14.3

INFERENCE ON THE SLOPE, β_1

Performing a Test of Hypothesis on the Slope of the Regression Line

Under the assumptions of the simple linear regression model outlined in the previous section, we are now in a position to determine whether a linear relationship exists between the variables X and Y. Examining the estimate of the slope, b_1, will provide information as to the nature of this relationship.

Consider the *population* slope, β_1. Three possible situations are demonstrated in Figure 14.11. What can you say about using X as a predictor of Y in Figure 14.11a? When $\beta_1 = 0$, the population line is perfectly horizontal. As a result, the value of Y is the *same* for each value of X, and so X is not a good predictor of Y; the value of X provides no information regarding the value of Y. In the event $\beta_1 = 0$, the best predictor of Y is given by $\hat{Y} = \bar{y}$, and so $\beta_1 \neq 0$ is equivalent to saying that $\hat{Y}$ (using X as a predictor) is superior to using the sample mean ($\hat{Y} = \bar{y}$) as a predictor.

To determine whether X provides information in predicting Y, the hypotheses are

$$H_0: \beta_1 = 0 \qquad (X \text{ provides no information})$$

$$H_a: \beta_1 \neq 0 \qquad (X \text{ does provide information})$$

Other Alternative Hypotheses. If we are attempting to demonstrate that a significant *positive* linear relationship exists between X and Y, the appropriate alternative hypothesis would be $H_a: \beta_1 > 0$. For example, do the data in Example 14.1 support the hypothesis that owners with large incomes have larger homes?

When the purpose of the analysis is to determine whether a *negative* linear relationship exists between X and Y, the alternative hypothesis should be $H_a: \beta_1 < 0$. For example, you would expect such a relationship between the number of new housing starts (Y) and the interest rate (X) (as the interest rate increases, you would expect the number of new houses under construction to decrease).

The Test Statistic. We use the point estimate of β_1 (that is, b_1) in the test statistic to determine the nature of β_1. What is b_1? a constant? a variable? Suppose that we obtained a different set of data and recalculated b_1. The new value would not be exactly the same as the previous value, implying that b_1 is actually a variable. To be more precise, under the assumptions of the previous section, b_1 is a *normal* random variable with mean $= \beta_1$ and variance $= \sigma_{b_1}^2 = \sigma_e^2 / SS_X$. Notice that b_1 is, on the average, equal to β_1; that is, b_1 is an *unbiased* estimator of β_1. The variance $\sigma_{b_1}^2$ is a parameter describing the variation in the b_1 values if we were to obtain random samples of n observations indefinitely.

FIGURE

14.11

Three possible population slopes (β_1).

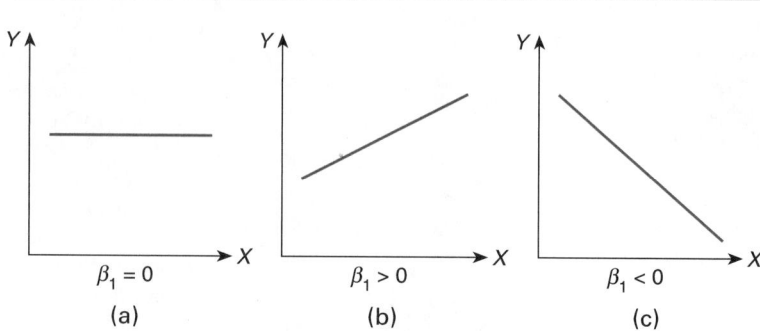

$\beta_1 = 0$ $\beta_1 > 0$ $\beta_1 < 0$

(a)   (b)   (c)

If we replace the unknown σ_e^2 by its estimate, s^2, then the *estimated* variance of b_1 is $s_{b_1}^2 = s^2/SS_X$. As a result

$$t = \frac{b_1 - \beta_1}{s/\sqrt{SS_X}} = \frac{b_1 - \beta_1}{s_{b_1}}$$

14.17

has a t distribution with $n - 2$ df. If the null hypothesis is $H_0: \beta_1 = 0$, the test statistic becomes

$$t = \frac{b_1}{s/\sqrt{SS_X}}$$

14.18

A summary of the testing procedure is shown in the accompanying box.

TEST OF HYPOTHESIS ON THE SLOPE OF THE REGRESSION LINE

Two-Tailed Test

$$H_0: \beta_1 = 0$$
$$H_a: \beta_1 \neq 0$$

Test statistic:

$$t = \frac{b_1}{s_{b_1}}$$

where $s_{b_1} = s/\sqrt{SS_X}$ and df $= n - 2$.

Test:

reject H_0 if $|t| > t_{\alpha/2, n-2}$

One-Tailed Test

$H_0: \beta_1 \leq 0$	$H_0: \beta_1 \geq 0$
$H_a: \beta_1 > 0$	$H_a: \beta_1 < 0$

Test statistic: | Test statistic:

$$t = \frac{b_1}{s_{b_1}} \qquad\qquad t = \frac{b_1}{s_{b_1}}$$

where $s_{b_1} = s/\sqrt{SS_X}$ | where $s_{b_1} = s/\sqrt{SS_X}$
and df $= n - 2$. | and df $= n - 2$.

Test: | Test:
reject H_0 if $t > t_{\alpha, n-2}$ | reject H_0 if $t < -t_{\alpha, n-2}$

EXAMPLE 14.3

Is there sufficient evidence, using the real-estate data in Example 14.1, to conclude that a positive linear relationship exists between income (X) and home size (Y)? Use $\alpha = .05$.

Solution

Step 1. The hypotheses indicated here are

$$H_0: \beta_1 \leq 0$$
$$H_a: \beta_1 > 0$$

FIGURE

14.12

t curve with 8 df showing rejection region (shaded) for Example 14.3.

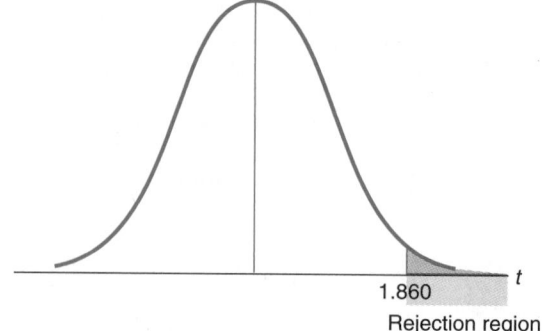

1.860 *t*

Rejection region

FIGURE

14.13

Excel input screen using **Tools ➤ Data Analysis ➤ Regression**.

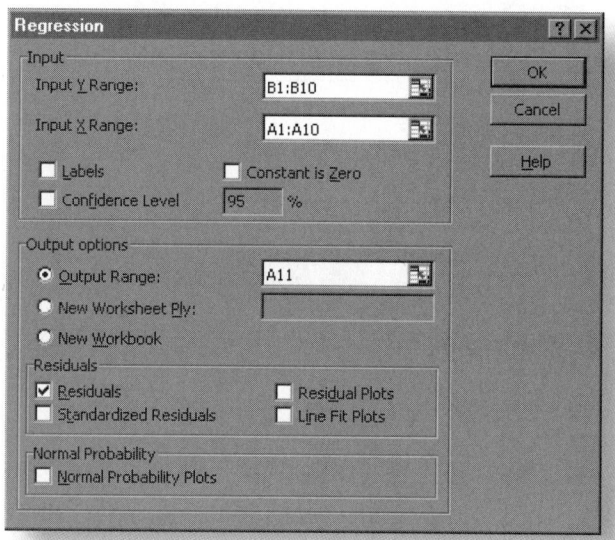

Step 2. The test statistic is

$$t = \frac{b_1}{s_{b_1}}$$

which has a *t* distribution with $n - 2 = 8$ df.

Step 3. The testing procedure is to

reject H_0 if $t > t_{.05,8} = 1.860$

The *t* curve is shown in Figure 14.12.

Step 4. We previously determined that $SS_X = 1489.6$, $b_1 = .3539$, and $s = 3.078$. The calculated test statistic is then

$$t^* = \frac{.3539}{3.078/\sqrt{1489.6}} = \frac{.3539}{.0797} = 4.44$$

where $s_{b_1} = .0797$. Because $4.44 > 1.86$, we reject H_0.

Step 5. Based on these 10 observations, we conclude that a positive linear relationship does exist between income and home size.

Using Excel. An Excel solution to Example 14.3 is shown in Figures 14.14 and 14.15. After clicking on **Tools ➤ Data Analysis ➤ Regression,** enter the input and output ranges as shown in Figure 14.13. Be sure to click on the **Residuals** box.

FIGURE

14.14

Excel solution to
Example 14.3.

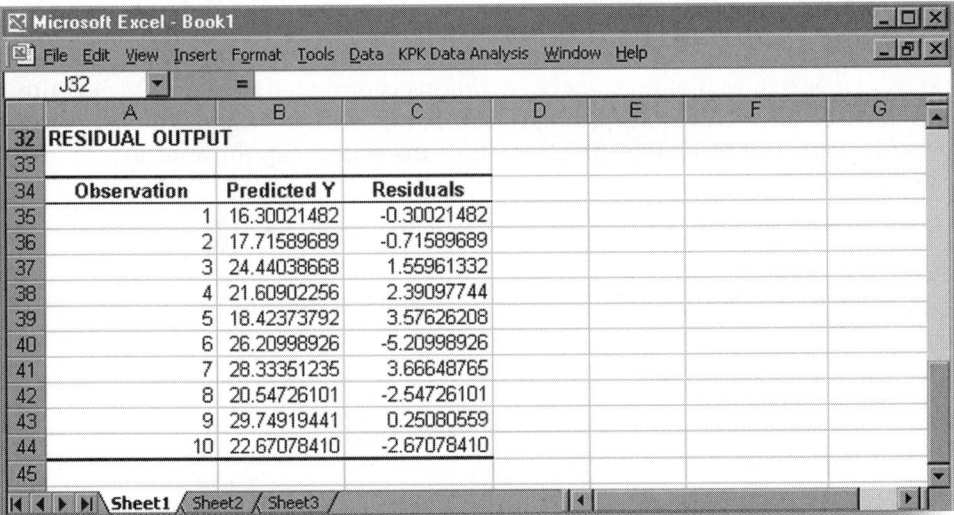

FIGURE

14.15

Excel-generated
predicted Y values
and residuals
(Example 14.3).

Some of the more interesting portions of the output are highlighted (shaded) in
Figure 14.14 and are discussed below. The construction of this ANOVA table is discussed in Chapter 15.

Cell(s)	Contents
B27, B28	The least squares equation is $\hat{Y} = 4.975 + .3539X$.
C28	The standard deviation of b_1 is $s_{b_1} = .07976$.
D28	The value of the test statistic is $t^* = b_1/s_{b_1} = 4.44$.
E28	The p-value for the t test is .0022. Since this value is less than .05 (α), we can conclude that a positive linear relationship exists between income and home size.
B17	The estimated standard deviation of the error components is $s = 3.078$.
C23	The value of SSE is 75.81.

The 10 predicted Y values ($\hat{Y}$ values) and corresponding residuals ($Y - \hat{Y}$ values) are shown in Figure 14.15. These values were previously calculated without the use of a computer in the solution to Example 14.2. The Excel calculated residuals contain more accuracy but do agree with the values in the Example 14.2 solution to two decimal places.

EXAMPLE 14.4

The firm of Smithson Financial Consultants has been hired by Blackburn Industries to determine whether a relationship exists between the age of unmarried male Blackburn employees (that is, never married, divorced, or widowed male employees) and the amount of individual liquid assets. The main question of interest is whether a linear relationship exists between these two variables, where X is defined as the age of the employee and Y is the *percentage* of annual income allocated to liquid assets (such as cash, savings accounts, and tradable stocks and bonds). A random sample of 12 unmarried male employees is selected, and the following data are obtained:

Age (X)	Liquid Assets (Y, Percentage of Annual Income)	Age (X)	Liquid Assets (Y, Percentage of Annual Income)
38	16	58	13
48	12	31	13
38	10	42	20
28	7	35	10
40	9	54	18
50	22	62	25

A scatter diagram of these 12 observations is provided in Figure 14.16, with a summary of the calculations. Using $\alpha = .10$, do you think that an employee's age provides useful information for predicting the percentage of total income allocated to liquid assets?

FIGURE 14.16

Scatter diagram and least squares line for age (X) and percentage of annual income invested in liquid assets (Y).

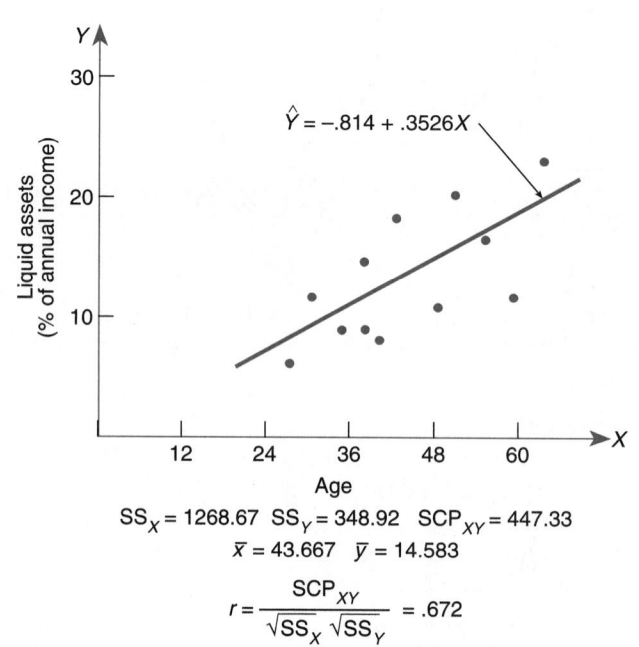

$SS_X = 1268.67$ $SS_Y = 348.92$ $SCP_{XY} = 447.33$

$\bar{X} = 43.667$ $\bar{Y} = 14.583$

$$r = \frac{SCP_{XY}}{\sqrt{SS_X}\ \sqrt{SS_Y}} = .672$$

To derive the least squares regression line, we determine

Solution

$$b_1 = \frac{\text{SCP}_{XY}}{\text{SS}_X} = \frac{447.33}{1268.67} = .3526$$

and

$$b_0 = \bar{y} - b_1\bar{x}$$
$$= 14.583 - (.3526)(43.667) = -.814$$

Consequently, the least squares line is

$$\hat{Y} = -.814 + .3526X$$

Notice that the slope of this line is positive. As the following test of hypothesis will conclude, this slope is significant. Consequently, a higher percentage invested in liquid assets is associated with the *older* employees. According to these data, each additional year of age is accompanied by an increase of .35 percent of income allocated to liquid assets, on the average, for the unmarried male population at Blackburn.

To carry out a test of hypothesis, we follow the usual five-step procedure.

Step 1. Because the suspected direction of the relationship between these two variables (positive or negative) is unknown before the data are obtained, a two-tailed test is appropriate. The hypotheses are

$$H_0: \beta_1 = 0$$
$$H_a: \beta_1 \neq 0$$

Step 2. The test statistic is $t = b_1/s_{b_1}$, which has $n - 2 = 10$ df.
Step 3. The test procedure is to

$$\text{reject } H_0 \text{ if } |t| > t_{.10/2,10} = t_{.05,10} = 1.812$$

Step 4. Based on the data summary in Figure 14.16 and using equation 14.14,

$$\text{SSE} = \text{SS}_Y - \frac{(\text{SCP}_{XY})^2}{\text{SS}_X}$$
$$= 348.92 - \frac{(447.33)^2}{1268.67}$$
$$= 348.92 - 157.73 = 191.19$$

Consequently,

$$s^2 = \frac{\text{SSE}}{n - 2} = \frac{191.19}{10} = 19.12$$

and so

$$s_{b_1} = \frac{s}{\sqrt{\text{SS}_X}} = \frac{\sqrt{19.12}}{\sqrt{1268.67}} = .1228$$

The computed value of the test statistic is therefore:

$$t^* = \frac{b_1}{s_{b_1}}$$
$$= \frac{.3526}{.1228} = 2.87$$

Because $t^* = 2.87$ exceeds the table value of 1.812, we reject H_0 in support of H_a.

Step 5. Our conclusion is that age is a useful (although imperfect) predictor of percentage of income invested in liquid assets for this particular population.

One thing to keep in mind is that *statistical* significance does not always imply *practical* significance. In other words, rejection of H_0: $\beta_1 = 0$ (statistical significance) does not mean that precise prediction (practical significance) follows. It *does* demonstrate to the researcher that, within the sample data at least, this particular independent variable has an association with the dependent variable.

Confidence Interval for β_1

Following our usual procedure of providing a confidence interval with a point estimate, we use the t distribution of the previous test statistic and equation 14.17 to define a confidence interval for β_1. The narrower this confidence interval is, the more faith we have in our estimate of β_1 and in our model as an accurate, reliable predictor of the dependent variable. A $(1 - \alpha) \times 100\%$ confidence interval for β_1 is

$$b_1 - t_{\alpha/2, n-2} s_{b_1} \qquad \text{to} \qquad b_1 + t_{\alpha/2, n-2} s_{b_1}$$

EXAMPLE 14.5

Construct a 90% confidence interval for the population slope, β_1, using the real-estate data in Examples 14.1 and 14.3.

Solution   All the necessary calculations have been completed; $b_1 = .3539$ and $s_{b_1} = .0797$ (from Example 14.3). Using $t_{.05,8} = 1.860$, the resulting confidence interval is

$$.3539 - (1.860)(.0797) \qquad \text{to} \qquad .3539 + (1.860)(.0797)$$
$$= .3539 - .148 \qquad \text{to} \qquad .3539 + .148$$
$$= .206 \qquad \text{to} \qquad .502$$

So we are 90% confident that the value of the estimated slope ($b_1 = .3539$) is within .148 of the actual slope, β_1. The large width of this interval is due in part to the lack of information (small sample size) used to derive the estimates; a larger sample would decrease the width of this confidence interval.

Comments

A failure to reject H_0 when performing a hypothesis test on β_1 does not always indicate that no relationship exists between the two variables. Some form of nonlinear relationship may exist between these variables. For example, in Figure 14.17, there is clearly a strong curved (*curvilinear*) relationship between X and Y. However, the least squares line through these points is horizontal, leading to a t value equal to zero and a failure to reject H_0. Furthermore, the sample correlation coefficient, r, for these data is zero.

FIGURE 14.17

Curvilinear relationship. The horizontal line is the least squares line.

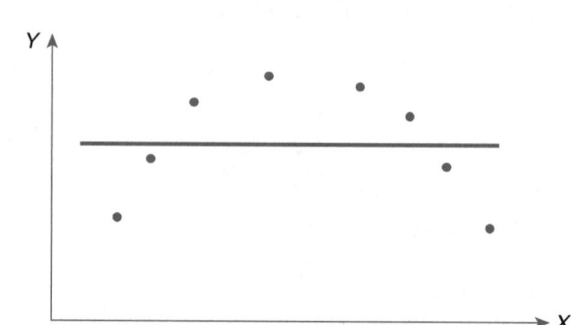

Of course, you may fail to reject H_0 as the result of a type II error. In other words, you failed to reject H_0 when in fact a significant linear relationship does exist. This situation is more apt to occur when using a small sample to test the null hypothesis.

More often, a failure to reject H_0 occurs when there is no visible relationship between the two variables within the sample data. To determine whether there is no relationship or if there is a nonlinear one, you should inspect either a scatter diagram of the data, a scatter diagram of the residuals, or, better yet, both. The latter diagram is a picture of the residuals $(Y - \hat{Y})$ plotted against the independent variable, X. Residual plots are discussed further in Section 14.6 and in Chapter 15.

In many situations, a business analyst has the opportunity to select the values of the independent variable, X, *before* the sample is obtained. At first glance, it might appear that the precision of b_1 (as an estimator of β_1) is unaffected by the X values. This is partially but not completely true. Because a narrow confidence interval for β_1 lends credibility to our model, we may choose to decrease the width of this confidence interval by decreasing s_{b_1}. Now $s_{b_1} = s / \sqrt{SS_X}$, so if we make SS_X large, the resulting s_{b1} will be small. Therefore, given the opportunity, select a set of X values having a *large variance*. You can accomplish this by choosing a great many X values on the lower end of your range of interest, a large number of values at the upper end, and some values in between to detect any curvature that exists (as in Figure 14.17).

X Exercises 14.23–14.32

Understanding the Mechanics

14.23 The following statistics were obtained from 21 pairs of observations.

$$b_0 = -10.8 \qquad b_1 = 3.0 \qquad s_{b_1} = 1.6$$

a. Test that the slope of the population regression line differs from zero. Use a 1% significance level.
b. Find a 99% confidence interval for the slope of the population regression line.

14.24 Five observations collected in a regression study are as follows.

X	2	4	6	8	10
Y	1	3	4	15	20

a. Is there sufficient evidence using the observed data to conclude that a positive linear relationship exists between X and Y? Use a 5% significance level.
b. Compute the 95% confidence interval for the slope of the population regression line.

Applying the New Concepts

14.25 It is believed that the size of the U.S. population (X) is a variable that influences personal consumption expenditure for housing (Y). However, the relationship historically does not appear to be linear. Therefore, a log transformation of housing expenditure is used. Fifteen observations are taken over previous years. The units of Y are millions and the units of X are billions.

X	Log Y	X	Log Y	X	Log Y
183.69	3.935	196.56	4.241	207.66	4.631
186.54	4.001	198.71	4.305	209.90	4.722
189.24	4.060	200.71	4.379	211.91	4.818
191.89	4.117	202.68	4.465	213.85	4.923
194.30	4.182	205.05	4.542	215.97	5.009

From the data, does there appear to be a significant positive linear relationship between X and log Y? Use a significance level of .05.

14.26 The life of a lawnmower engine can be extended by frequent oil changes. An experiment was conducted in which 20 lawn mowers were used over many years with different time intervals between oil changes. Let X be the number of hours of operation between oil changes. Let Y be the number of years that the engine was able to perform adequately.

X	Y	X	Y	X	Y
11.25	12.1	22.0	9.5	25.5	6.1
15.5	11.8	22.5	9.2	26.0	5.4
17.5	11.5	23.0	8.4	26.5	4.8
20.5	10.1	23.5	8.8	27.0	4.6
19.5	9.9	24.0	7.1	28.0	4.8
18.5	9.7	24.5	7.2	30.0	4.1
21.5	10.1	25.0	5.8		

a. Graph the data and the least squares line.
b. Is there sufficient evidence to conclude, at the 10% significance level, that a negative linear relationship exists between Y and X? What is the critical region?

14.27 Gas mileage of vehicles depends on a number of factors such as weight of the vehicle, driving habits, and air system restrictions. As a general rule, more horsepower results in lower gas mileage. A random sample of seven large pickups was selected, and the horsepower and miles per gallon (mpg) were recorded. Is there sufficient evidence using the observed data to conclude that a negative relationship exists between horsepower and mpg? Use a 5% significance level.

Pickup	Horsepower (X)	Highway MPG (Y)
Cadillac Escalade	345	15
Chevrolet Silverado 1500	200	21
Dodge Ram 2500	245	17
Ford F-250	260	16
GMC Sierra 1500	270	21
Lincoln Blackwood	300	17
Toyota Tundra Regular	190	18

(Source: "Rolling On," *Kiplinger's Personal Finance,* December 2001, pp. 122–129.)

14.28 Monthly charges for wireless phone service have decreased as worldwide subscribers have increased. Is there sufficient evidence to conclude that a negative relationship exists between the monthly charges for wireless phone service and the number of worldwide subscribers, using the following data? Use a 5% significance level. What are the necessary assumptions for your conclusions to be valid?

Year	Number of Wireless Subscribers	Monthly Charges for Wireless Phone Service
2001	610	35
2000	502	37
1999	410	38
1998	292	40
1997	255	45
1996	175	53
1995	150	60

(Source: "Emerging Mobile and Wireless Networks," *Communications of the ACM,* June 2000, pp. 73–81.)

14.29 The soft drink 7Up fell hard from its one-time perch as the world's third-best-selling soft drink. Sprite, the leader in the lemon-lime soft drink segment, has grown to three times 7Up's size in recent years. The market share of 7Up appears to have leveled off in recent years and the market share of Sprite appears to have dropped slightly for the first time in a decade. Marketing analysts at Dr. Pepper/7Up are interested in the relationship between the market share of Sprite and 7Up as they believe that a substantial increase in Sprite's market share will make 7Up more difficult to market.

Year	Sprite's Market Share	7Up's Market Share
1991	4.0	2.6
1992	4.2	2.7
1993	4.3	2.8
1994	4.5	2.9
1995	5.2	2.5
1996	5.9	2.3
1997	6.4	2.4
1998	6.6	2.3
1999	7.1	2.2
2000	6.1	2.0

a. Find a 99% confidence interval for the slope of the regression line with Y = 7Up's market share and X = Sprite's market share.

b. Use the confidence interval in part a to determine if a linear relationship exists between X and Y at the 1% significance level.

(Source: "Bottling Industry Thinks 7Up Might Be on Its Way Back," *Dallas Morning News,* June 16, 2001, p. 1F.)

14.30 An investment counselor wanted to know the relationship between the price/earnings ratio (Y) and the yield (X) for high-yield stocks. If a stock yielded over 5.5%, it was considered to be a high-yield stock. Twenty-five high-yield stocks were randomly selected. The following sample statistics were found:

$$SCP_{XY} = -10.4$$

$$SS_X = 11.4$$

$$SS_Y = 21.4$$

a. Test that the slope of the regression equation used to predict the price/earnings (P/E) ratio from the yield of a stock is negative. Use a 10% significance level.

b. Find a 95% confidence interval for the slope in part a.

Using the Computer

14.31 **[DATA SET EX14-31]** *Variable description:*

FurniturePrice: Price of furniture sold

TimeToSell: Time that it took for a furniture item to sell

Experience: Length of time the salesperson has been in sales

The furniture store business can be tricky. "Furniture customers are fickle, with tastes varying widely across the country. They enter a store to get ideas and browse, not necessarily to buy," says Troy Peery Jr., president of Heilig-Meyers Company. Suppose that a furniture manager wished to determine if there is a linear relationship between the selling price of furniture and either the amount of time that it took for the furniture to sell or the number of years of experience of the salesperson who sold the furniture. The units for TimeToSell are months and the units for Experience are years.

a. Look at a plot of FurniturePrice and TimeToSell and a plot of FurniturePrice and Experience. Comment on the linear relationship in each plot. Which would you use to construct a prediction equation?

b. For the variables selected in part a to construct a prediction equation, is there sufficient evidence to conclude that a positive relationship exists at a 1% significance level?

c. Do a what-if analysis by multiplying TimeToSell by 2 and find the test statistic for testing whether a positive relationship exists. Compare this to your result in part b.

(Source: "Sofa with Your Stereo, Sir," *Forbes,* July 7, 1997, p. 46.)

14.32 [DATA SET EX14-32] *Variable description:*

ExpenditureR&D: Percentage of total revenue spent on research and development (R&D)

PEratio: Price/earnings ratio for a company

A financial analyst is interested in the relationship between a company's P/E (price/earnings) ratio and the percentage of total revenue spent by the company on R&D. A random sample of 100 companies was selected

and the data were recorded in variables ExpenditureR&D and PEratio, respectively.

a. Plot the variables X = ExpenditureR&D and Y = PEratio. Estimate the intercept and slope and interpret these values.

b. Find 90%, 95%, and 99% confidence intervals for the slope of the regression line. How much does the width of the confidence interval change as the confidence level is increased?

MEASURING THE STRENGTH OF THE MODEL

14.4

We have already used the sample coefficient of correlation, r, as a measure of the amount of linear association within a sample of bivariate data. The value of r is given by

$$r = \frac{SCP_{XY}}{\sqrt{SS_X}\,\sqrt{SS_Y}}$$

14.19

The possible range for r is –1 to 1.

Comparing the equations for r and b_1 we see that

$$r = b_1 \sqrt{\frac{SS_X}{SS_Y}}$$

Because SS_X and SS_Y are *always greater than zero*, r and b_1 have the same sign. Thus, if a positive relationship exists between X and Y, then both r and b_1 will be greater than zero. Similarly, they are both less than zero if the relationship is negative.

When you determine r, you use a sample of observations; r is a *statistic*. What does r estimate? It is actually an estimate of ρ (rho, pronounced "roe"), the **population correlation coefficient.** To grasp what ρ is, imagine obtaining *all* possible X, Y values and using equation 14.19 to determine a correlation. The resulting value is ρ.

The population slope, β_1, and ρ are closely related. In particular, $\beta_1 = 0$ if and only if $\rho = 0$. This leads to another method of determining whether the simple linear regression model (using X to predict Y) is satisfactory. The hypotheses are

$H_0: \rho = 0$ (no linear relationship exists between X and Y)

$H_a: \rho \neq 0$ (a linear relationship does exist)

In a similar manner, alternative hypotheses can be set up to demonstrate a positive relationship ($H_a: \rho > 0$) or a negative relationship ($H_a: \rho < 0$). The test statistic uses the point estimate of ρ (that is, r) and is defined by

$$t = \frac{r}{\sqrt{\dfrac{1 - r^2}{n - 2}}}$$

14.20

where n = the number of observations in the sample. It is also a t statistic with $n -$ 2 df. Although equations 14.18 and 14.20 appear to be unrelated, the two are algebraically equivalent and *their values for* t *are always the same.*

Thus, the t tests for H_0: $\beta_1 = 0$ *and* H_0: $\rho = 0$ produce identical results, *provided both tests use the same level of significance.* Performing both tests is therefore unnecessary; they both produce the same conclusion. Remember, if you have already computed the sample correlation coefficient, r, equation 14.20 offers a much easier method of determining whether the simple linear model is statistically significant. Notice also in equation 14.20 that the significance of the t value depends on the sample size, n. As a result, *if the sample size is large enough, then virtually any value of r can produce a significantly large value of* t.

EXAMPLE 14.6

Use equation 14.20 to determine whether a positive linear relationship exists between X = income and Y = home square footage, based on the real-estate data from Example 14.1. Use $\alpha = .05$.

Solution   The hypotheses to be used here are H_0: $\rho \leq 0$ versus H_a: $\rho > 0$. In Example 14.1, we found that $r = .843$. This leads to a computed test statistic value of

$$t^* = \frac{r}{\sqrt{\dfrac{1-r^2}{n-2}}} = \frac{.843}{\sqrt{\dfrac{1-(.843)^2}{8}}}$$

$$= \frac{.843}{.190} = 4.44$$

Because this value is the same as the one obtained in Example 14.3 (testing H_0: $\beta_1 \leq 0$ versus H_a: $\beta_1 > 0$), we draw the same conclusion. A positive linear relationship *does* exist between these two variables. In other words, r is large enough to justify this conclusion.

Remember, there is no harm in using equation 14.20 as a substitute for equation 14.18 with H_0: $\beta_1 = 0$ (or ≤ 0, or ≥ 0), particularly if you have already determined the value of r.

Danger of Assuming Causality

A word of warning is in order here—namely, that high statistical correlation does not imply *causality*. Even if the correlation between X and Y is extremely high (say, $r = .95$), a unit increase in X does not necessarily *cause* an increase in Y. All we know is that in the sample data, as X increased, so did Y. As a simple example, consider X = percentage of gray hairs and Y = blood pressure. One might expect to observe a high correlation between these two variables, but it is probably absurd to say that an additional gray hair will *cause* a person's blood pressure to increase. What is actually happening is that there is another variable, in this case age, that is causing both percentage of gray hair and blood pressure to increase.

In many business and economics applications, we observe highly correlated variables when each pair of observations corresponds to a particular time period. For example, we would expect a high correlation between average annual wages (X) and the U.S. gross national product (GNP; Y) when measured over time. Even though wages may be a good predictor of GNP, this correlation does not imply that an increase in wages *causes* an increase in GNP. It is much more likely that a third factor—inflation—caused both wages and GNP to increase.

Coefficient of Determination

In our earlier discussion of ANOVA techniques, we used the expression SS(total) $= \Sigma(y - \bar{y})^2$ to measure the tendency of a set of observations to group about the mean. If this value was large, then the observations (data) contained much variation and were *not* all clustered about the mean, $\bar{y}$.

In the simple linear regression model, $SS_Y = \Sigma(y - \bar{y})^2$ is computed in the same way and (as before) measures the total variation in the values of the dependent variable.

SS_Y = total variation of the dependent variable observations

When comparing the sum of squares of error, SSE, to the total variation, SS_Y, we use the ratio SSE/SS_Y. If all $\hat{Y}$ values are equal to their respective Y values, there is a perfect fit, with $SSE = 0$ and $r = 1$ or -1. Our model explains 100% of this total variation, and the unexplained variation is zero.

In general, SSE/SS_Y (expressed as a percentage) is the *percentage of unexplained variation.* Recall from equations 14.14 and 14.19 that

$$SSE = SS_Y - \frac{(SCP_{XY})^2}{SS_X} \qquad \text{and} \qquad r^2 = \frac{(SCP_{XY})^2}{SS_X SS_Y}$$

Thus

$$r^2 = 1 - \frac{SSE}{SS_Y}$$

As a result, r^2 may be interpreted as a measure of the *explained variation* in the dependent variable using the simple linear model; r^2 is the **coefficient of determination.**

r^2 = coefficient of determination

$$= 1 - \frac{SSE}{SS_Y}$$

= percentage of explained variation in the dependent variable using the simple linear regression model

14.21

For this model, we can determine r^2 simply by squaring the coefficient of correlation. In Chapter 15, we will predict the dependent variable, Y, using *more than one* predictor (independent) variable. To derive the coefficient of determination in this case, we must first calculate SSE and then use equation 14.21. So, although this definition may appear to be unnecessary, it will enable us to compute this value when we use a multiple linear regression model.

EXAMPLE 14.7

What percentage of the total variation of the home sizes is explained by means of the single predictor, income, using the real-estate data from Example 14.1?

Solution

We previously calculated r to be .843, so the coefficient of determination is

$$r^2 = (.843)^2 = .71$$

Therefore, we have accounted for 71% of the total variation in the home sizes by using income as a predictor of home size.

Notice that we could have determined this value by using the calculations from Examples 14.1 and 14.2, where

$$r^2 = 1 - \frac{SSE}{SS_Y}$$

$$= 1 - \frac{75.81}{262.4} = .71$$

FIGURE

14.18

Splitting $(y - \bar{y})$ into two deviations, $(\hat{y} - \bar{y}) + (y - \hat{y})$.

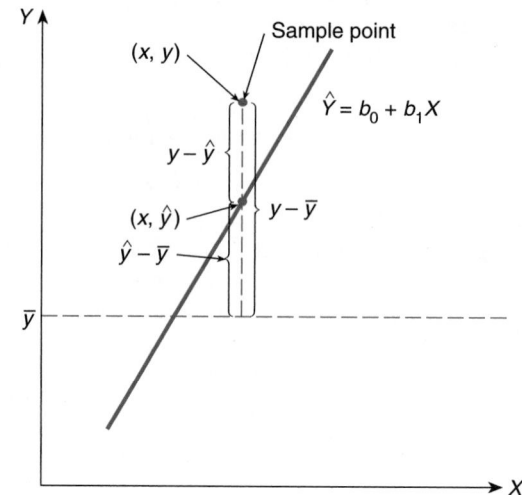

Total Variation, SS_Y

In Chapter 11, when discussing the ANOVA procedure, we partitioned the total variation in the observations, measured by SS(total), into two sums of squares, namely, SS(factor) and SS(error). The resulting equation was

$$SS(total) = SS(factor) + SS(error)$$

In a similar fashion, we can partition the total variation of the Y values in linear regression, measured by SS_Y, into two other sums of squares. In Figure 14.18, notice that the value of $y - \bar{y}$ can be written as the sum of two deviations, namely,

$$y - \bar{y} = (\hat{y} - \bar{y}) + (y - \hat{y})$$

By squaring and summing over *all* the data points in the sample, we can show that*

$$\Sigma(y - \bar{y})^2 = \Sigma(\hat{y} - \bar{y})^2 + \Sigma(y - \hat{y})^2$$

The summation on the left of the equals sign is SS_Y. The second summation on the right is the sum of squares of error, SSE. The first summation on the right is defined to be the *sum of squares of regression, SSR*.

$$\Sigma(\hat{y} - \bar{y})^2 = SSR$$

As a result, we have

$$SS_Y = SSR + SSE$$

14.22

By comparing equations 14.14 and 14.22, we see that a simple way to calculate the sum of squares of regression is

$$SSR = \frac{(SCP_{XY})^2}{SS_X}$$

14.23

The regression sum of squares, SSR, measures the variation in the Y values that would exist if differences in X were the *only* cause of differences among the

---

*This result follows since it can be shown that $\Sigma(\hat{y} - \bar{y})(y - \hat{y}) = 0$ when using the least squares line.

Y's. If this were the case, then all the (X, Y) points would lie exactly on the regression line. In practice, this does not happen when using a simple linear regression model. Otherwise, we would have a deterministic phenomenon, not an object of statistical investigation. Consequently, the sample points can be assumed to lie about the regression line rather than on this line. This variation *about* the regression line is measured by the error sum of squares, SSE.

X Exercises 14.33–14.42

Understanding the Mechanics

14.33 The following data were collected on two variables X and Y.

X	1	2	4	6	10	12
Y	20	15	12	10	5	1

a. Specify the null and alternative hypotheses for testing that the population correlation is negative.

b. Calculate the estimate of the population correlation coefficient between X and Y.

c. Calculate the coefficient of determination.

d. Using a 5% significance level, test the hypothesis in part a.

Applying the New Concepts

14.34 The manager of a company that relies on traveling salespersons to sell the company's products wants to examine the relationship between sales and the amount of time a salesperson spends with each established customer who regularly orders the company's products. The manager collects data on 12 salespersons. Let Y represent sales per month and X represent hours spent with customers per month.

X	Y	X	Y	X	Y
3.2	412	6.1	715	5.1	570
4.6	500	4.2	500	7.1	800
3.9	450	5.6	610	6.5	725
5.3	610	5.3	600	7.8	850

Can one conclude that the population correlation coefficient between X and Y is positive? Use a 10% significance level. Can one conclude that spending more time with customers increases sales?

14.35 From 1987 to 1996, the revenue and the number of employees at Electronic Data Systems Corp. (EDS) have generally been in an uptrend. To understand the relationship between revenue and number of employees, construct a prediction equation of revenue from number of employees. What percentage of the total variation in revenue is explained using the number of employees? Does this indicate there is a linear relationship between revenue and number of employees? Use a 5% significance level.

Year	Number of Employees (in Thousands)	Revenue (in Billions)
1987	43.4	4.33
1988	50.4	4.74
1989	56.9	5.37
1990	61.5	6.02
1991	65.2	7.03
1992	71.0	8.16
1993	69.7	8.51
1994	81.5	9.96
1995	96.0	12.4
1996	100.5	14.4

(Source: "Reinventing EDS," *Dallas Morning News*, July 1, 1997, Business Section, p. 1.)

14.36 The demand and supply of new apartments are typically not in balance in most large cities across the United States. For example, in Dallas, the demand for new apartments has generally been greater than the supply of new units. However, in some years, the supply of new units exceeds demand, which has kept rental prices stable. Consider the data below to be a random sample of yearly data listing the demand for new apartments and the supply of new units. The data are in units of thousands.

Demand for New Apartment Units	Supply of New Apartment Units
4.1	9.5
9.2	3.1
10.5	1.8
3.2	.7
−3.0	3.8
5.5	2.5
8.1	2.8
5.3	3.8
7.1	6.0
11.0	12.1
10.3	11.5
10.0	14.5

a. Calculate the correlation coefficient between the demand and supply of apartment units.

b. What is the coefficient of determination for predicting the demand of apartment units from the supply of new units? Interpret this value.

c. Do the data support the belief that a nonzero correlation exits? Use a .10 significance level.

(Source: "Apartment Pipeline," *Dallas Morning News*, August 8, 1997, p. D1.)

14.37 Ten cards numbered 1 through 10 are shuffled, and a person is asked to pick one. The card is replaced and the deck reshuffled. Then the person is asked to draw a second card. If the second card is higher than the first, the dealer gives $.85 to the player. If the second card is not higher than the first, the player pays $1.15 to the dealer. A sample of 15 pairs of draws is taken to see whether there is any correlation between the first and the second cards.

a. Would you expect to observe significant correlation here? Why or why not?

b. Find the coefficient of determination for the following data, and test using a 5% significance level that there is no correlation between the first and the second cards. Interpret the value of the coefficient of determination.

First Card (X)	Second Card (Y)	First Card (X)	Second Card (Y)
7	3	10	5
3	10	3	6
8	2	4	3
5	8	6	1
2	7	7	8
7	9	8	4
9	4	2	6
1	1		

14.38 Refer to Exercise 14.25. Use equation 14.20 to test that there is no linear relationship between the size of the U.S. population and the logarithm of personal consumption expenditure on housing. Use a significance level of 5%.

14.39 For the data in Exercise 14.26, test that there is no linear relationship between the number of hours of operation between oil changes and the number of years that the engine was able to perform adequately. Use equation 14.20 and test with a 10% significance level. Is the result the same as in Exercise 14.26?

14.40 A sample of 35 pairs of observations is taken, and a sample correlation coefficient is computed to be $r = .48$. Do the data provide sufficient evidence to reject the null hypothesis of no correlation? Use a 1% significance level.

Using the Computer

14.41 [DATA SET EX14-41] *Variable description:*

SatDishAdv: Amount spent on local advertising (excludes national advertising)

SatDishSales: Annual sales of satellite dishes

Tandy Corp.'s Radio Shack units have used their marketing muscle to promote many of their products. Through Radio Shack's ubiquitous neighborhood stores, Tandy has become a leading retailer for home satellite equipment. Suppose that a company analyst wished to determine if there is a linear relationship between the amount spent on local advertising (SatDishAdv) and the annual sales of satellite dishes (SatDishSales). Fifty stores are randomly selected and the data are recorded in units of thousands of dollars.

a. Find the correlation between X = SatDishAdv and Y = SatDishSales. Based on this value, do you think that the data will support the alternative hypothesis that the population correlation is positive? Use a 5% significance level.

b. Find the value of the t statistic for testing that the slope of the regression equation is greater than zero. What conclusion can you make using a 5% significance level? Compare the value of this t statistic with that calculated in part a.

c. Find the predicted values of SatDishSales. What is the correlation between these values and the original values of SatDishSales? Compare this to the correlation obtained in part a.

(*Source:* "Radio Shack No. 1 for Dishes," *Dallas Morning News,* July 14, 1997, p. D2.)

14.42 [DATA SET EX14-42] *Variable description:*

AnnualInc: Yearly income

VacationExp: Expenditure on vacation

A marketing analyst is interested in the relationship between the yearly income of recently married couples and their vacation expenditure for the year. A random sample of 100 married couples is selected, and the data are recorded in variables AnnualInc and VacationExp in units of thousands of dollars. If a relationship exists, the marketing analyst will use an estimate of a married couple's income to determine which type of promotional vacation information to mail to them.

a. Test whether a linear relationship exists between the variables Y = VacationExp and X = AnnualInc. Use a 1% significance level.

b. Sometimes a transformation of one of the variables will result in a better linear relationship with the other variable. Take the natural log of AnnualInc. Find the correlation between these values and VacationExp. Is there sufficient evidence to conclude that a nonzero correlation exists at the 1% significance level?

14.5

ESTIMATION AND PREDICTION USING THE SIMPLE LINEAR MODEL

We have concentrated on predicting a value of the dependent variable (Y) for a given value of X. In the previous examples, we used a person's income, X, to predict the size of that person's home (Y). Notice in Figure 14.8 that we can also use the least squares line to estimate the *average* (*mean*) value of Y for a specified value of X. So we can use this line in two different situations.

Situation 1. The regression equation $\hat{Y} = b_0 + b_1 X$ estimates the *mean* value of Y for a specified value of the independent variable, X. For $X = x_0$, this value would be written $\mu_{Y|x_0}$ (the mean of Y given $X = x_0$).

For example, the least squares line passing through the real-estate data in Example 14.1 is $\hat{Y} = 4.975 + .3539X$. The average square footage for *all* homes in the population with an income of \$50,000 ($X = 50$) is $\mu_{Y|50}$. Its estimate is provided by the corresponding value on the least squares line, namely,

$$\hat{Y} = 4.975 + (.3539)(50) = 22.67$$

So the estimate of the average square footage of all such homes is 2,267 square feet (Figure 14.7).

Situation 2. An *individual* predicted value of Y also uses the regression equation $\hat{Y} = b_0 + b_1 X$ for a specified value of X. This value of Y is denoted Y_{x_0} for $X = x_0$. This application is the more common one in business, because a regression equation is generally used for individual forecasts.

For example, assume the Jenkins family resides in our sample community and has an income of \$50,000. A prediction of their home size (Y_{50}) is also

$$\hat{Y} = 4.975 + (.3539)(50) = 22.67$$

which is 2,267 square feet (Figure 14.7).

We see that the least squares line can be used to estimate average values (situation 1) or predict individual values (situation 2). Since $\mu_{Y|50}$ is a parameter, we use $\hat{Y}$ to estimate this value. On the other hand, Y_{50} represents a particular value of a dependent (random) variable, and so $\hat{Y}$ is used to *predict* this value. In the first situation, we can determine a *confidence* interval for $\mu_{Y|50}$; in the second situation, we determine a *prediction* interval for Y_{50}.

Confidence Interval for $\mu_{Y|x_0}$ (Situation 1)

We have already established that the point estimate of $\mu_{Y|x_0}$ is the corresponding value of $\hat{Y}$. The reliability of this estimate depends on (1) the number of observations in the sample, (2) the amount of variation in the sample, and (3) the value of $X = x_0$. A confidence interval for $\mu_{Y|x_0}$ takes all three factors into consideration.

A $(1 - \alpha) \times 100\%$ confidence interval for $\mu_{Y|x_0}$ is

$$\hat{Y} - t_{\alpha/2, n-2} s \sqrt{\frac{1}{n} + \frac{(x_0 - \bar{x})^2}{SS_X}} \quad \text{to} \quad \hat{Y} + t_{\alpha/2, n-2} s \sqrt{\frac{1}{n} + \frac{(x_0 - \bar{x})^2}{SS_X}} \qquad \text{14.24}$$

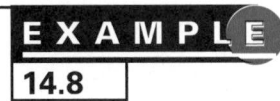

EXAMPLE 14.8

Determine a 95% confidence interval for the average home size of families with an income of \$45,000, using the real-estate data from Example 14.1.

Solution

We previously determined that $n = 10$, $\bar{x} = 49.8$, $SS_X = 1489.6$, and $s = 3.078$. The point estimate for the average square footage, $\mu_{Y|45}$, is

$$\hat{Y} = 4.975 + .3539(45)$$

$$= 20.90 \ (2{,}090 \text{ square feet})$$

Obtaining $t_{.025,8} = 2.306$ from Table A.5, the 95% confidence interval for $\mu_{Y|45}$ is

$$20.90 - (2.306)(3.078)\sqrt{\frac{1}{10} + \frac{(45 - 49.8)^2}{1489.6}} \quad \text{to} \quad 20.90 + (2.306)(3.078)\sqrt{\frac{1}{10} + \frac{(45 - 49.8)^2}{1489.6}}$$

$$= 20.90 - (2.306)(3.078)(.340) \quad \text{to} \quad 20.90 + (2.306)(3.078)(.340)$$

$$= 20.90 - 2.41 \quad \text{to} \quad 20.90 + 2.41$$

$$= 18.49 \quad \text{to} \quad 23.31$$

We are thus 95% confident that the average home size for families earning $45,000 is between 1,849 and 2,331 square feet.

Using Excel to Construct Confidence Intervals. Excel does not provide confidence and prediction intervals in its statistical tool package, but the KPK Data Analysis add-ins will allow you to compute these intervals. To carry out this analysis, enter "Income" in cell A1 and "Footage" in cell B1. Next, enter the income values in cells A2:A11 and the square footage values in cells B2:B11 and then click on **KPK Data Analysis ➤ Regression.** Enter "B1:B11" in the **Y Range** box and "A1:A11" in the **Contiguous X Range** box.* Specify C1 in the **Output Range** box. At the bottom of the form, click on the check box inside the **Confidence Intervals for the Mean of Y and Prediction Intervals for Y** frame and enter "A2:A11" in the accompanying box. The only available confidence level is 95%. The resulting output is shown in Figure 14.19.

The column labeled **Std. Error Prediction** contains the standard deviation of the predicted Y values. Writing this as $s_{\hat{Y}}$,

$$s_{\hat{Y}} = s\sqrt{\frac{1}{n} + \frac{(x_0 - \bar{x})^2}{SS_X}}$$

14.25

For each value of X *in the sample* (say, x_0), the corresponding confidence interval for $\mu_{Y|x_0}$ is

$$\hat{Y} - t \cdot s_{\hat{Y}} \quad \text{to} \quad \hat{Y} + t \cdot s_{\hat{Y}}$$

where $t = t_{\alpha/2, n-2}$, as before, and $\hat{Y}$ is contained in the column labeled **Predicted Value.**

Using the Excel output in Figure 14.19, we can find the confidence intervals corresponding to X values of 32 and 50. The remaining eight confidence intervals are constructed in a similar manner.

For $X = 32$ in the first row, the confidence interval is

$$16.300 - (2.306)(1.721) \quad \text{to} \quad 16.300 + (2.306)(1.721)$$

$$= 12.33 \quad \text{to} \quad 20.27$$

For $X = 50$ in the last row, the confidence interval is

$$22.671 - (2.306)(.974) \quad \text{to} \quad 22.671 + (2.306)(.974)$$

$$= 20.43 \quad \text{to} \quad 24.92$$

Notice that the confidence interval is much wider for $X = 32$ than for $X = 50$.

All 10 confidence intervals are shown in columns F and G in Figure 14.19 under the headings **Lower 95% Mean** and **Upper 95% Mean.** The intervals in the first and last rows (for $X = 32$ and $X = 50$) agree with the previously calculated confidence intervals for the average square footage using these two incomes. For values of X not in the sample, simply construct a new column containing these values and enter this range in the **Contiguous X Range** box.

By connecting the upper end of the confidence intervals for all 10 data points and connecting the lower limits, we obtain Figure 14.20. Equation 14.23 indicates that the confidence interval is narrowest when $(x_0 - \bar{x})^2 = 0$, that is, at $X = x_0 = \bar{x}$. For values of X to the left or right of $\bar{x}$, the confidence interval is wider. In other words, *the farther x_0 is from $\bar{x}$, the less reliable is the estimate.*

---

*Chapter 15 will explore the use of more than one independent (explanatory) variable. These columns may or may not be adjacent (contiguous) in your spreadsheet. The KPK Data Analysis regression procedure, unlike the standard Excel procedure, allows for either option. In this chapter, always use the **Contiguous X Range** box.

FIGURE

14.19

Excel confidence and prediction intervals for real estate data using KPK Data Analysis (see Figure 14.4).

C	D	E	F	G	H	I
X Variable 1	Predicted Value	Std Error Prediction	Lower 95% Mean	Upper 95% Mean	Lower 95% Predict	Upper 95% Predict
32	16.300	1.721	12.331	20.270	8.167	24.434
36	17.716	1.469	14.327	21.104	9.850	25.582
55	24.440	1.058	22.000	26.880	16.934	31.947
47	21.609	0.999	19.306	23.912	14.146	29.072
38	18.424	1.354	15.301	21.546	10.669	26.179
60	26.210	1.269	23.284	29.136	18.532	33.888
66	28.334	1.618	24.603	32.064	20.314	36.353
44	20.547	1.078	18.062	23.033	13.026	28.069
70	29.749	1.882	25.408	34.090	21.428	38.070
50	22.671	0.974	20.426	24.916	15.225	30.116

FIGURE

14.20

95% confidence intervals for the real-estate data derived from Excel output shown in Figure 14.19.

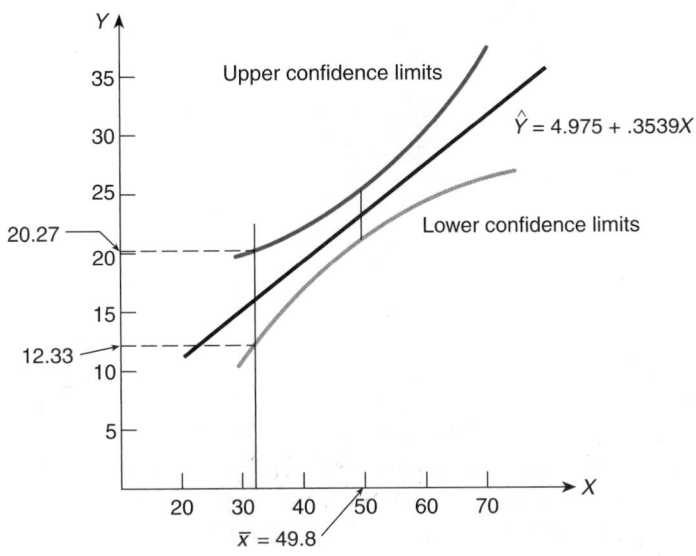

The Danger of Extrapolation. *Extrapolation* is the process of calculating an estimate corresponding to a value of X outside the range of the data used to derive the prediction equation (the least squares line). For example, in Figure 14.20 the least squares line could be used to estimate the average home size for families with an income of \$100,000. Although we *can* estimate $\mu_{Y|100}$, the corresponding confidence interval for this parameter will be extremely wide, so the point estimate, $\hat{Y}$, will have little practical value.

To use the simple regression model effectively for estimation, you need to stay within the range of the sampled values for the independent variable, X. This process is called *interpolation.* If you use values outside this range, you need to be aware that given *another* set of data, you would quite likely obtain a considerably different estimate. Furthermore, you have no assurance that the linear relationship still holds outside the range of your sample data.

Prediction Interval for Y_{x_0} (Situation 2)

The procedure of predicting individual values is used more often in business applications. The regression equation is generally used to *forecast* (predict) a future value of the dependent variable for a particular value of the independent variable. When attempting to predict a single value of the dependent variable, Y, using the simple linear regression model, we begin, as before, with $\hat{Y}$. Substituting $X = x_0$ into the regression equation provides the best prediction of Y_{x_0}. For example, if the Johnson family has an income of $45,000, our best guess as to their home size (using this particular model) is $\hat{Y}$ for $X = 45$. From the results of Example 14.8, this is 20.90, or 2,090 square feet.

We do not use the term *confidence interval* for this procedure because what we are estimating (Y_{x_0}) is not a parameter. It is a value of a random variable, so we use the term **prediction interval.**

The variability of the error in predicting a single value of Y is more than that for estimating the average value of Y (situation 1). It can be shown that an estimate of the variance of the error $(Y - \hat{Y})$, when using $\hat{Y}$ to predict an individual Y for $X = x_0$, is

$$s_Y^2 = s^2\left(1 + \frac{1}{n} + \frac{(x_0 - \bar{x})^2}{SS_X}\right)$$

14.26*

This result can be used to construct a $(1 - \alpha) \times 100\%$ prediction interval for Y_{x_0}, as follows:

$$\hat{Y} - t_{\alpha/2, n-2}s\sqrt{1 + \frac{1}{n} + \frac{(x_0 - \bar{x})^2}{SS_X}} \quad \text{to}$$

$$\hat{Y} + t_{\alpha/2, n-2}s\sqrt{1 + \frac{1}{n} + \frac{(x_0 - \bar{x})^2}{SS_X}}$$

14.27

Notice that the only difference between this prediction interval and the confidence interval in equation 14.24 is the inclusion of "1+" under the square root sign. The other two terms under the square root are usually quite small, so this "1+" has a large effect on the width of the resulting interval. Be aware that our warning about extrapolating outside the range of the data applies here as well. In equations 14.26 and 14.27, the distance from the mean $(x_0 - \bar{x})$ is squared, which increases the risk of predicting beyond the range of the sampled data.

EXAMPLE 14.9

We previously determined that if the Johnson family has an income of $45,000, the best prediction of their home size is $\hat{Y} = 20.90$. Determine a 95% prediction interval for this situation.

Solution   We can use the calculations from Example 14.8 to derive the prediction interval for Y_{45}. The result is

$$20.90 - (2.306)(3.078)\sqrt{1 + \frac{1}{10} + \frac{(45 - 49.8)^2}{1489.6}} \quad \text{to}$$

$$20.90 + (2.306)(3.078)\sqrt{1 + \frac{1}{10} + \frac{(45 - 49.8)^2}{1489.6}}$$

$$= 20.90 - (2.306)(3.078)(1.056) \quad \text{to} \quad 20.90 + (2.306)(3.078)(1.056)$$

$$= 20.90 - 7.49 \quad \text{to} \quad 20.90 + 7.49$$

$$= 13.41 \quad \text{to} \quad 28.39$$

---

*This follows since $Y = \hat{Y} + e$ and, as a result, $s_Y^2 = s_{\hat{Y}}^2 + s_e^2$. Substituting equation 14.25 for $s_{\hat{Y}}^2$ and s^2 for s_e^2 produces the desired results.

FIGURE
14.21

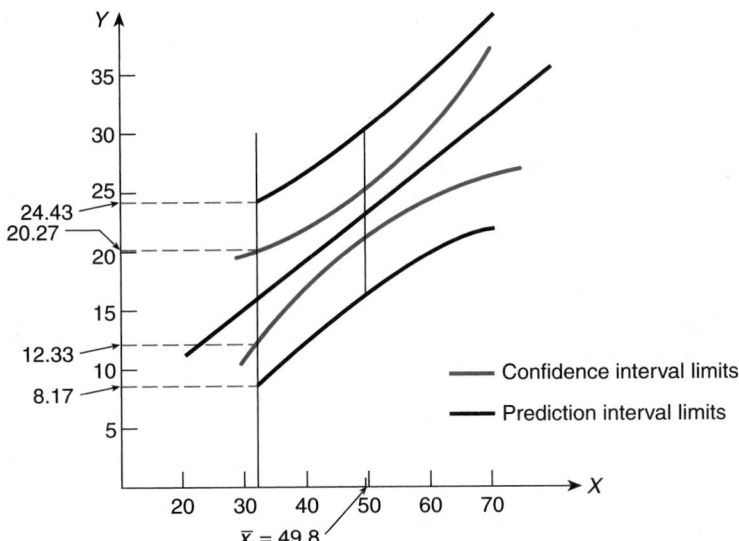

The 95% prediction and confidence intervals for the real-estate data. Calculated values on the Y axis are for $X = 32$.

Comparing this interval to the confidence interval for $\mu_{Y|45}$ in Example 14.8, we see that individual predictions are considerably less accurate than estimations for the mean home size. Of course, we could reduce the width of this interval by obtaining additional data. Expecting accurate results from a sample of 10 observations is being a bit optimistic.

Using Excel for Constructing Prediction Intervals. Prediction intervals can be determined without any calculations by using the **KPK Data Analysis ➤ Regression** procedure discussed immediately following the solution to Example 14.8. From Figure 14.19, we observe the following prediction intervals:

$$X = 32: \text{prediction interval for } Y_{32} \text{ is from 8.167 to 24.434}$$

$$X = 50: \text{prediction interval for } Y_{50} \text{ is from 15.225 to 30.116}$$

Notice that these intervals are considerably wider than the corresponding confidence intervals.

Figure 14.21 shows the prediction intervals for all 10 data points; the upper and lower limits have been connected. The increased width of a prediction interval versus a confidence interval is quite apparent from this graph. Also, like the width of a confidence interval, the width of a prediction interval increases as the value of X strays from $\bar{x}$.

14.6

EXAMINING THE RESIDUALS

Checking the Model Assumptions

When using a linear regression model, you should keep two things in mind. First, no distributional assumptions are necessary to derive the least squares estimates of β_0 and β_1. The regression coefficients b_0 and b_1 from the sample regression line are the "best" estimates in the least squares sense.

Second, several key assumptions *are* required for the validity of any constructed confidence intervals and tests of hypothesis. If these assumptions are violated, you may still have an accurate prediction, $\hat{Y}$, but the validity of the inference procedures will be highly questionable.

Your final step in any regression analysis should be to verify your assumptions.

Assumption 1. *The errors are normally distributed with a mean of zero.* An easy method to determine whether the errors follow a normal distribution centered at zero is to let the computer construct a histogram of the sample residuals $(Y - \hat{Y})$. Since the residuals *always* sum to zero when using the least squares line, the residual histogram is typically centered at zero. The plot should reveal whether the distribution of residuals is severely skewed. Remember that an exact normal distribution is not necessary here; problems arise only when the distribution is severely skewed and does not resemble a normal distribution. (The Excel procedure to obtain this histogram is illustrated in upcoming Example 14.10.)

More sophisticated methods of checking this assumption involve the use of a *probability plot* or a *chi-square goodness-of-fit test.* We do not discuss the probability plot technique here, except to say that you plot the residuals in a specialized type of graph. If the resulting graph is linear in appearance, the normality assumption has been verified.

The goodness-of-fit test was discussed in Chapter 13, where we used a chi-square statistic to test the hypothesis that a particular set of data (in this case, the regression residuals) came from a specific (normal, here) distribution. Exercise 13.13 at the end of Section 13.1 discusses how to use the chi-square test for a suspected *normal* population.

If you have reason to believe that this assumption of your model has been violated, then you need to search for another model. This new model may include additional predictor variables (the subject of Chapter 15) that have been overlooked. Another possibility is to transform the dependent variable (for example, use $\sqrt{Y}$ rather than Y) or to transform the independent variable. As your model tends to "improve," you should observe the residuals tending toward a normal distribution.

Assumption 2. *The variance of the errors remains constant.* For example, you should not observe larger errors associated with larger values of X. When the residuals $(Y - \hat{Y})$ are plotted against the independent variable, X, we hope to observe *no pattern* (a "shotgun blast" appearance) in this graph, as in Figure 14.22a. Remember—the assumption is essentially that the errors consist of what engineers call *noise,* with no observable pattern.

A common violation of this assumption of equal variances occurs when the value of the residual increases as X increases, as illustrated in Figure 14.22b. In this graph, the variance of the residual increases with X, producing a funnel appearance. This has a serious effect on the validity of the t tests discussed in this chapter, which determine the strength of the regression model.

When you encounter a violation of this type, you need to resort to more advanced modeling techniques, such as *weighted least squares* or *transformations* of your dependent variable.*

Assumption 3. *The errors are independent.* Examining this assumption after the regression equation has been determined involves using the residual from each of the sample observations. For given values of X, the actual error is

$$e = Y - (\beta_0 + \beta_1 X)$$

The β's are unknown, so we estimate the error by using the residual for this particular observation,

$$Y - \hat{Y} = Y - (b_0 + b_1 X)$$

---

*See J. Neter, M. Kutner, and C. Nachtschein, *Applied Linear Regression Models,* 3rd ed. (Homewood, Ill.: Richard D. Irwin, 1996).

FIGURE

14.22

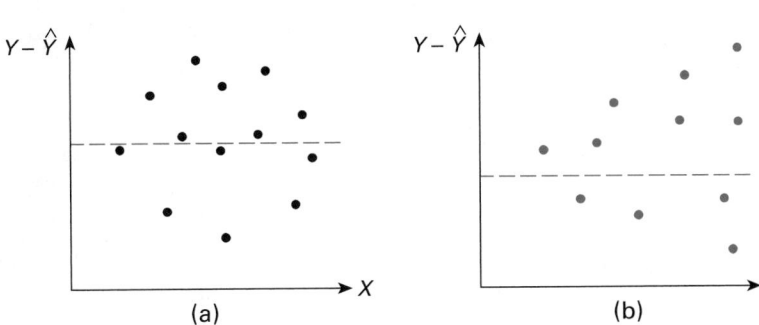

FIGURE

14.23

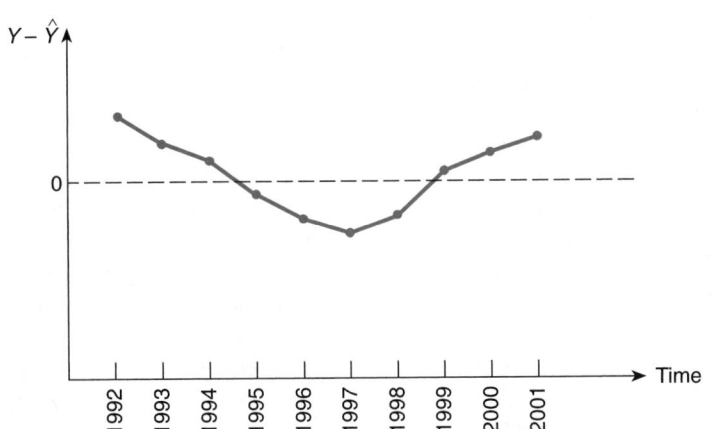

When your regression data consist of *time-series* data, your errors often are not independent. This type of data has the following appearance:

Time	Y	X
1992	#	#
1993	#	#
1994	#	#
⋮	⋮	⋮

(# denotes a numeric value)

Also remember that your error component includes the effect of variables missing from your model. Chapter 15 deals with regression models containing more than one predictor variable. In many business applications, there is a positive relationship between time-related predictor variables, such as prices and wages, because they increase over time.

This relationship can produce a set of residuals in your regression analysis that are not independent of one another but instead display a pattern similar to the one in Figure 14.23. This plot contains the sample residuals on the vertical axis and time on the horizontal axis. If this assumption were *not* violated here, we would observe the shotgun appearance as in Figure 14.22*a*. Instead we notice that adjacent residuals have roughly the same value and so are correlated with each other. This is *autocorrelation*.

To be more specific, the pattern in Figure 14.23 is one of *positive* autocorrelation. Negative autocorrelation exists when most of the neighboring residuals are very unequal in size (such as a positive residual, followed by a negative residual, followed by a positive residual, and so on). The amount of autocorrelation that exists in residuals is measured by the *Durbin-Watson statistic*. Chapter 17 discusses the calculation of this statistic and its use in detecting autocorrelated residuals.

The problem of autocorrelated errors is the most difficult of the three assumptions to correct. The error term is not noise, as we originally assumed, but instead has a definite pattern (as in Figure 14.23). Several ways of treating this problem are discussed in Chapter 17.

Comment

Practically all computer packages can provide the value of the Durbin-Watson statistic when performing a linear regression analysis. When your data are *not* collected over time (but rather from different families, cities, companies, or the like), this statistic is meaningless and should be ignored. For this situation, assumption 3 is not of vital concern and is often taken for granted.

Checking for Outliers and Influential Observations

A closer look at the regression data and computer solution can reveal some rather interesting and important details concerning the least squares line. Of particular interest is whether there are one or more **outliers** in the sample observations. These points are generally fairly obvious in a scatter diagram, since such points do not seem to "fit" with the remaining observations. An outlier can have a dramatic effect on the least squares line, because the regression line will be pulled in the direction of the outlier, reducing the effectiveness of the regression line as a predictor. Such observations need to be detected and studied to determine if an error was made in the recording of this data point and whether this observation should be corrected or removed from the sample data.

Also of interest is the determination of whether the sample outliers are very influential in determining the fitted regression line (the least squares line). A point is said to have a *strong influence* on the regression line if removal of this observation produces a dramatic shift in the regression line if the line is recalculated from the remaining points. These observations may be extreme in their X value, Y value, or both.

Figure 14.24 contains three outliers (points A, B, and C). Point A has an X value close to the average of the X values in the sample, but has an extremely large Y value. As we will demonstrate, this observation will not have a large influence on the regression line, due to the number of sample observations having similar X values. Point B has a large X value, but the Y value is consistent with the line determined from the remaining observations; it will not have a very strong influence on the regression line. Point C is another matter—it has an extremely large X value and a Y value that is not consistent with the regression line through the remaining observations. Removal of this observation would produce a drastically different least squares line; this point is an **influential observation.**

Identifying Outlying Values of the Independent Variable. Observations having extremely large or small values of the independent variable (X) can be detected by computing **sample leverages.** An observation whose value of the independent variable is distant from the sample mean of the X values ($\bar{x}$) is said to have high leverage. In Figure 14.24, point C would be a high-leverage observation and point B has a potentially high leverage. The leverage of the ith observation is measured by h_i, where

$$h_i = \frac{1}{n} + \frac{(x_i - \bar{x})^2}{SS_X}$$

14.28

and $SS_X = \Sigma x^2 - (\Sigma x)^2/n$.

FIGURE

14.24

Excel illustration of outliers and influential observations.

Consider the real-estate data in Examples 14.1, 14.2, and 14.3. Suppose one additional observation is added to this data set. In Figure 14.25a, this observation is $X = 115$ and $Y = 48$ (a family with a large income and a large house). In Figure 14.25b, the additional observation is $X = 115$ and $Y = 29$ (a family with a large income and a small house for this income). The leverage value for the additional observation *will be the same* in both cases because it depends on the X value only. In either case, the average of the 11 X values in the sample is now

$$\bar{x} = 55.727$$

Also,

$$SS_X = 39{,}515 - \frac{(613)^2}{11} = 5354.18$$

Consequently, the leverage of the new observation is

$$h_{11} = \frac{1}{11} + \frac{(115 - 55.727)^2}{5354.18} = .747$$

Commonly accepted procedures for simple linear regression are to conclude that a sample observation has an outlying X value if its leverage value is larger than 4/n or larger than 6/n, where n is the number of sample observations. MINITAB uses the "larger than 6/n" rule, and we will accept that decision rule in our discussion. Here, $6/n = 6/11 = .545$; and since $.747 > .545$, we conclude that the 11th observation does have an unusually large income (X). Since the leverage value depends strictly on the X value, it is impossible to say whether the new observation exerts a large influence on the regression equation. We will demonstrate shortly that the new observation in Figure 14.25a is *not* an influential observation, whereas in Figure 14.25b it is.

Compare the leverage value in equation 14.28 and the confidence interval for the mean value of Y at $X = x_0$ given in equation 14.24. If a confidence interval is calculated at the ith observation (x_i, y_i), then the leverage for this observation, h_i, is the quantity under the square root sign in equations 14.24 and 14.25. As a result, the standard deviation of the predicted Y value in equation 14.25 can be written

$$s_{\hat{Y}} = s\sqrt{h_i}$$

14.29

FIGURE

14.25

(a) Original real-estate data, with a new observation ($X = 115$, $Y = 48$).
(b) Original real-estate data, with a new observation ($X = 115$, $Y = 29$).

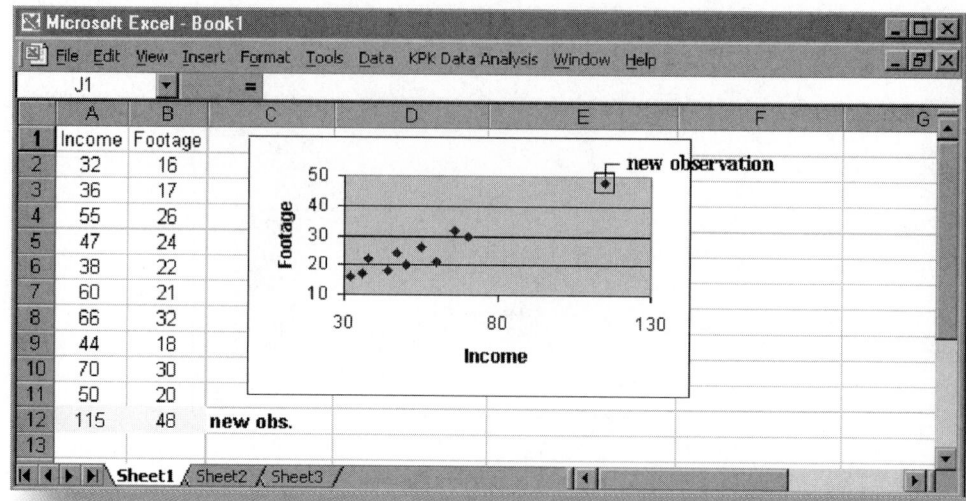

(a)

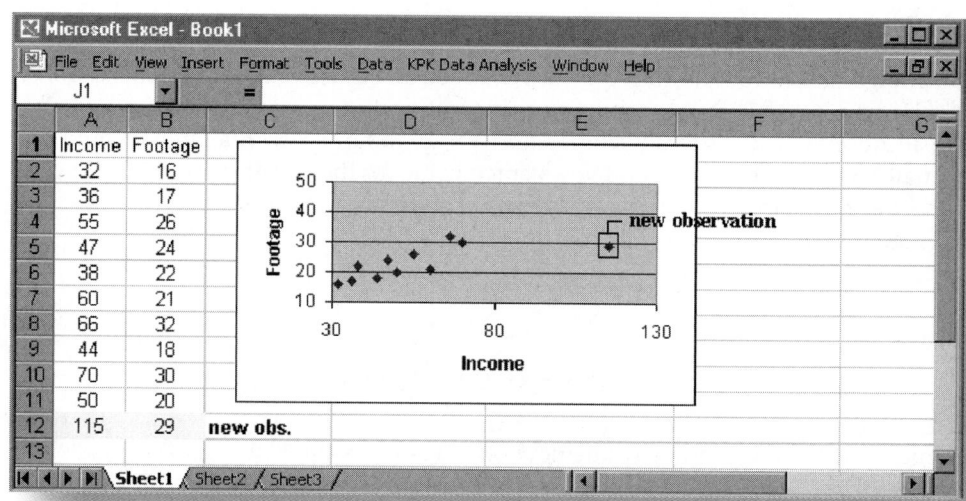

(b)

The corresponding confidence interval for $\mu_{Y|x_i}$ is

$$\hat{Y} - t_{\alpha/2,n-2}s\sqrt{h_i} \qquad \text{to} \qquad \hat{Y} + t_{\alpha/2,n-2}s\sqrt{h_i}$$

14.30

and the prediction interval for Y_{x_i} in equation 14.27 is

$$\hat{Y} - t_{\alpha/2,n-2}s\sqrt{1 + h_i} \qquad \text{to} \qquad \hat{Y} + t_{\alpha/2,n-2}s\sqrt{1 + h_i}$$

14.31

Consequently, as the leverage of the ith observation increases (x_i moves farther from $\bar{x}$), the confidence interval for $\mu_{Y|x_i}$ and the prediction interval for Y_{x_i} become wider. The smallest possible leverage value is $h_i = 1/n$, and this occurs only if $x_i = \bar{x}$.

Identifying Outlying Values of the Dependent Variable. Sample observations having unusually large or small values of the dependent variable (Y) can generally be detected using the sample **standardized residuals.** Recall that the residual at the ith observation is $Y - \hat{Y}$, and that this residual estimates the error in the model at this observation. Since one of the model assumptions is that each error has a mean of zero, then to standardize the ith residual we simply divide by its estimated standard deviation. The estimated standard deviation of the ith residual can be written as

$$s\sqrt{1-h_i}$$

14.32

where h_i is the leverage for this observation, defined in equation 14.28, and s (rather, s^2) is defined in equation 14.16. Consequently,

$$\text{standardized residual} = \frac{Y_i - \hat{Y}_i}{s\sqrt{1-h_i}}$$

14.33

A recommended procedure is to identify an observation as having an outlying value of Y if its standardized residual is larger than 2 or less than –2. MINITAB will automatically inform you which (if any) of your observations have standardized residuals larger than 2 in absolute value.

Using Excel, SPSS, or MINITAB and Figure 14.25a, the following results can be obtained:

$$\text{Least squares line: } \hat{Y} = 3.752 + .3796X$$

$$\text{SSE} = 77.18 \quad \text{and} \quad s = \sqrt{\frac{77.18}{9}} = 2.93$$

For $X = 115$, $\hat{Y} = 47.41$, and

$$\text{Standardized residual of observation } 11 = \frac{48 - 47.41}{2.93\sqrt{1-.747}} = .40$$

Consequently, observation 11 does not contain an extreme value of the dependent variable. We would still classify this observation as an outlier due to the large value of the independent variable ($X = 115$) and the correspondingly large leverage value ($h_{11} = .747$).

For Figure 14.25b, the results are:

$$\text{Least squares line: } \hat{Y} = 13.746 + .1693X$$

$$\text{SSE} = 146.14 \quad \text{and} \quad s = \sqrt{\frac{146.14}{9}} = 4.03$$

For $X = 115$, $\hat{Y} = 33.22$, and

$$\text{Standardized residual of observation } 11 = \frac{29 - 33.22}{4.03\sqrt{1-.747}} = -2.08$$

Since $-2.08 < -2$, observation 11 is extreme in both the Y value *and* the X value.

Identifying Influential Observations. On occasion, you may have one or two observations that have a very large impact on the sample regression line. If such an observation were deleted from the sample, the new values of the intercept (b_0) and/or the slope (b_1) would be much different. If such an observation exists, a little investigation may be in order to determine if this sample value should be modified or removed. If an error was made while recording this observation, then, if possible, the regression analysis should be rerun using the corrected value.

Often, it is impossible to recapture this observation. For example, it might have been recorded during an expensive experiment, which would necessitate rerunning the experiment. Perhaps, this observation occurred during a point in time that has since passed. For such situations, you could remove this observation and rerun the regression analysis.

On the other hand, if this observation was recorded correctly, simply removing this observation from the data set is ill-advised. This observation might be revealing something; in particular, your model (using a straight line to predict Y) may be inappropriate, or the situation you're attempting to model is simply not as predictable as you expected. Perhaps additional independent variables should be considered (discussed in Chapter 15).

Determining influential observations uses the strategy for identifying outliers that was just discussed, since such observations are characterized by large leverage values (unusual values of X) and/or large standardized residuals (unusual values of Y).

A commonly used measure of influence is **Cook's distance measure,** which combines the leverage value and standardized residual into one overall value. Cook's distance measure for the ith observation is given by

$$D_i = \frac{1}{2} \frac{h_i}{1 - h_i} \text{ (standardized residual)}^2$$

$$= \frac{(Y_i - \hat{Y}_i)^2}{2s^2} \left(\frac{h_i}{(1 - h_i)^2} \right)$$

14.34

For example, in Figure 14.25a, at observation 11,

$$Y = 48, \qquad \hat{Y} = 47.41, \qquad s = 2.93, \qquad h_{11} = .747$$

and so

$$D_{11} = \frac{(48 - 47.41)^2}{2(2.93)^2} \left(\frac{.747}{(1 - .747)^2} \right) = .24$$

For Figure 14.25b, at observation 11,

$$Y = 29, \qquad \hat{Y} = 33.22, \qquad s = 4.03, \qquad h_{11} = .747$$

and

$$D_{11} = \frac{(29 - 33.22)^2}{2(4.03)^2} \left(\frac{.747}{(1 - .747)^2} \right) = 6.40$$

For simple linear regression, we recommend you conclude that the ith observation is influential if the corresponding D_i measure is larger than .8.* For Figure 14.25a, the new observation is *not* considered influential: .24 < .8, and so, despite the large leverage value, this observation would not seriously affect the regression results if it were removed from the sample. In Figure 14.25b, the new observation *would* be labeled as influential, because 6.40 > .8.

A final look at Figure 14.24 is contained in Figure 14.26, where the leverage value, standardized residual, and Cook's distance measure are shown for each of the three outliers. These results are summarized in Table 14.1, where the cutoff for the leverage values is $h_i = 6/n = 6/15 = .4$.

---

*The cutoff value for Cook's distance measure in simple linear regression can also be defined using the F distribution: tail area = .5, df = 2 and $n - 2$. For nearly all sample sizes, the value .8 provides a reliable, and slightly conservative, approximation to this F-value.

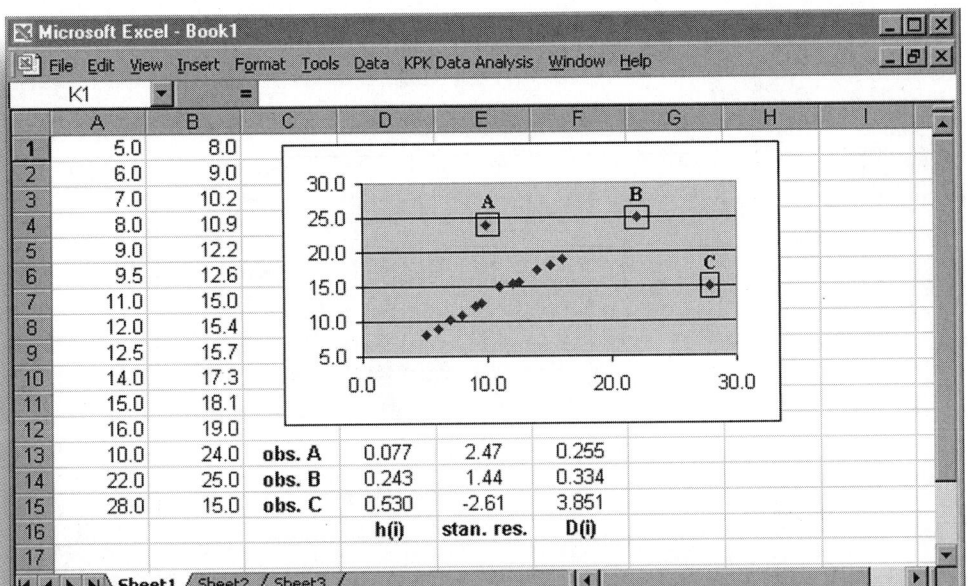

FIGURE

14.26

Another look at Figure 14.24, with calculated leverages, standardized residuals, and Cook's distance measures.

TABLE

14.1

Summary of Figures 14.24 and 14.26.

Point	Outlying in X Value ($h_i > .4$)	Outlying in Y Value ($|$ stand. res. $| > 2$)	Influential Observation ($D_i > .8$)
A	No	Yes	No
B	No	No	No
C	Yes	Yes	Yes

Microsoft® Excel Application Use DATA14-10

A Full Excel Simple Linear Regression Analysis

EXAMPLE

14.10

The editor of a monthly automotive magazine is interested in determining how well automotive manufacturers are meeting federal mandates concerning the average fuel economy that a manufacturer's fleet of cars must reach. The editor suspects that a linear relationship exists between X = engine capacity (in liters) and Y = miles per gallon (mpg). A sample of 60 different models was obtained (all models having a manual transmission) and is found in data set DATA14-10. The engine capacities (X values) are in column A, and the miles per gallon (Y values) are in column B.

Determine the appropriateness of the simple linear regression model, and examine the residuals (1) to detect any outliers, (2) to determine if any outliers would be classified as influential observations, and (3) to verify the model assumptions.

Solution

Begin by opening data file DATA14-10 into columns A and B. The labels **Capacity** and **MPG** should be in cells A1 and B1, as shown in Figure 14.27. To obtain a scatter diagram of the observations, click on the **Chart Wizard** icon and select **XY(Scatter)** ➤ **Next**. If necessary, enter the data range as "A1:B61," and click on

FIGURE

14.27

Excel plot of
X = engine
capacity versus
Y = miles
per gallon
(Example 14.10).

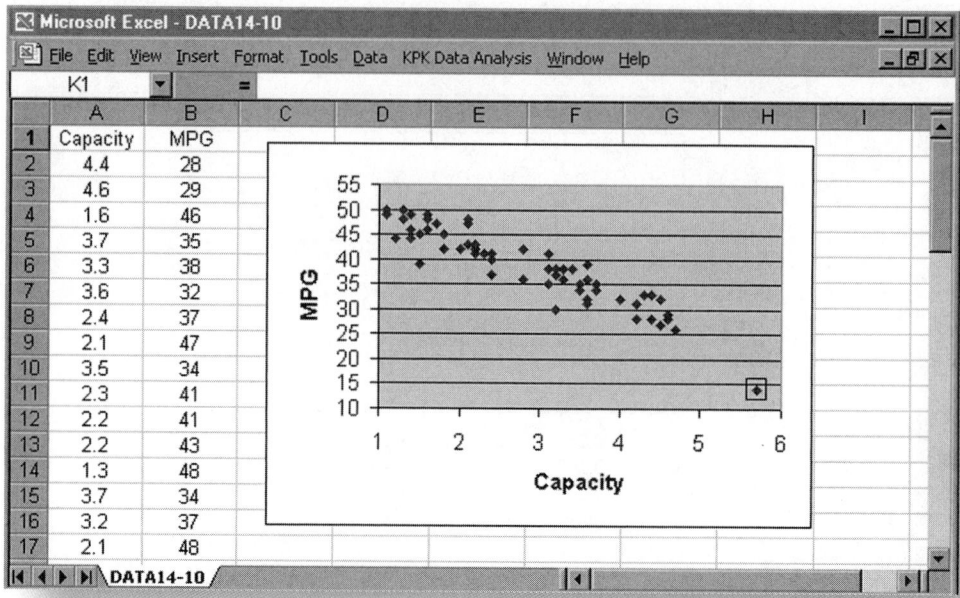

Next. Click on the **Titles** tab and enter **Capacity** as the X axis title and **MPG** as the Y axis title. You may enter a chart title if you wish. After clicking on **Finish,** you will see the scatter diagram in Figure 14.27, where a negative relationship is observed between X = capacity and Y = miles per gallon. There is one unusual observation (boxed).

To obtain the regression equation, use the KPK Data Analysis option since it identifies outliers and influential observations. Click on **KPK Data Analysis ➤ Regression** and enter "B1:B61" in the **Y Range** box and "A1:A61" in the **X Range** box. Enter "C18" as the output range, directly below the previously created scatter diagram. Select **Residuals, Standardized Residuals, Leverages,** and **Cook's Ds** in the **Data** frame, and **Residual Plots** in the **Plots** frame. The resulting regression equation from Figure 14.28 is $\hat{Y} = 55.494 - 5.981X$. Since the X coefficient is negative, there is indeed a negative relationship, and each additional liter of engine capacity in the data is accompanied by a decrease of approximately six miles per gallon (on the average).

A scan of the standardized residuals and Cook's distance measures reveals three "suspicious" or "interesting" observations—namely, observations 28, 51, and 60. These three observations are highlighted in Figure 14.29, which contains an abbreviated listing of the residuals, standardized residuals, leverages, and Cook's measures. The leverage cutoff here is $6/60 = .1$ and a complete scan of the leverage column indicates that observation 28 is the only observation with a leverage value exceeding .1. It also has a standardized residual larger than 2 in absolute value, and so this observation contains outlying values of both the independent and dependent variables. This is, in fact, the "unusual" observation identified in the lower-right corner of the scatter diagram (Figure 14.27). Observations 51 and 60 also contain outlying values of Y, since their standardized residuals exceed 2 in absolute value.

All of the Cook's D values are under .8. Upon closer examination, it was discovered that observation 28 was from a Lamborghini and was, in fact, correctly recorded. No recording error was discovered for observations 51 and 60.

FIGURE

14.28

Excel regression
equation for
Example 14.10.

FIGURE

14.29

Excel output
containing
standardized
residuals,
leverages, and
Cook's distance
measures using
KPK Data Analysis.

Figure 14.30 is a plot of the residuals, where the $Y - \hat{Y}$ values are plotted against the corresponding X values. The three boxed values correspond to observations 28 (labeled C), 51 (labeled B), and 60 (labeled A). In this plot, the three large residuals are obvious. No pattern is detected in the residual plot, and assumption 2 appears to be satisfied.

A histogram of the residuals is shown in Figure 14.31. First, locate the residuals in your spreadsheet. Similar to Figure 14.29, the *full* set of residuals would occupy cells E42:E101. To obtain the residual histogram in Figure 14.31, click on **KPK Data Analysis ➤ Quantitative Data Charts/Tables ➤ Histogram/Freq.**

FIGURE

14.30

Excel residual plot using KPK Data Analysis (Example 14.10).

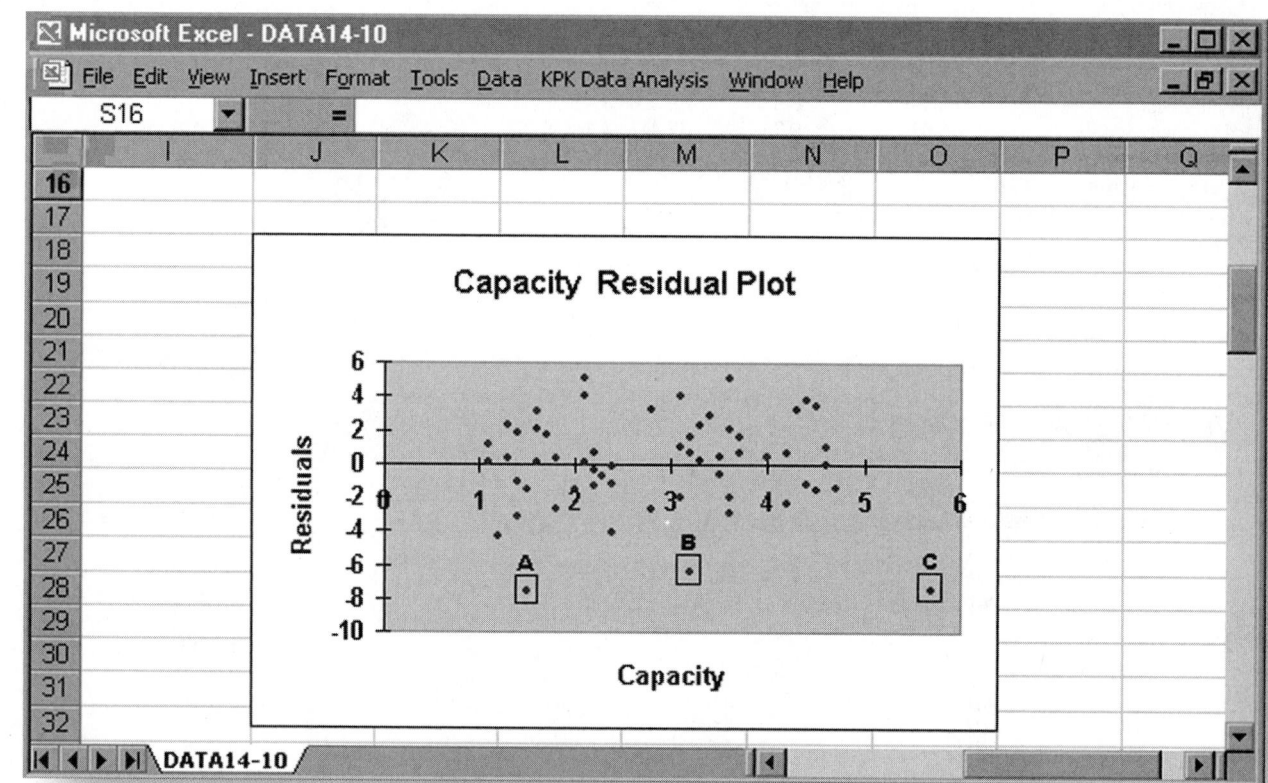

FIGURE

14.31

Histogram of residuals using KPK Data Analysis (Example 14.10).

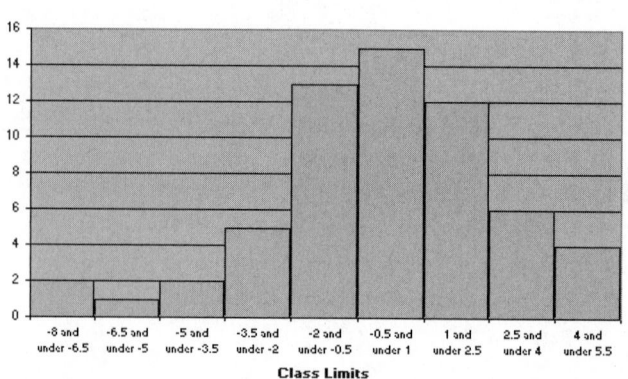

Charts. Enter "E42:E101" in the **Input Range** box, "J1" in the **Output Range** box, and "8" in the **Number of Classes** box. Finally, click on the check boxes for **Frequencies** and **Frequency Histogram,** and then **OK.** The resulting histogram in Figure 14.31 appears to be approximately normally distributed with a mean of zero (assumption 1). The three residuals in the left-most two boxes correspond to observations 28, 51, and 60. There is no need to check assumption 3, since the regression data were not time-ordered.

Conclusion. The model appears to be an excellent one, providing a highly significant t statistic ($t = -19.46$, p-value ≈ 0) and $r^2 = 86.7\%$; that is, engine capacity explains 86.7% of the variation in the mpg values. All of the model assumptions appear to be satisfied. All three of the apparent outliers could be retained in the model, since none of these observations produced a significant Cook's distance measure, and no error was made in the recording of these values. Consideration could be given to removing the Lamborghini from the population and from the sample, and restricting the discussion to less exotic automobiles.

X Exercises 14.43–14.57

Understanding the Mechanics

14.43 Data for X and Y are presented below.

X	12	15	20	25	30
Y	2	6	10	20	50

a. Calculate the least squares line.
b. Determine a 90% confidence interval for the mean value of Y using $X = 10$.
c. Determine a 90% prediction interval for Y using $X = 10$.
d. Calculate the standardized residual, the leverage value, and value of Cook's D for each observation.
e. Would any observation be considered influential?

14.44 Which observation in the following data set would you consider to be influential?

X	1	6	12	20	30	40	50
Y	50	7	22	30	50	100	120

Applying the New Concepts

14.45 For the data in Exercise 14.3, find a 95% confidence interval for the mean percentage of mortgage-paying homeowners whose housing costs exceed 30% for an X value equal to a median income of $35,000. Interpret this interval. For the same value of X, find a 95% prediction interval for the percentage of mortgage-paying homeowners whose housing costs exceed 30%. Interpret this interval.

14.46 For the data in Exercise 14.8, find a 90% confidence interval for the mean number of cakes sold when the independent variable $X^2 = (2.00)^2 = 4.00$. Determine if any observation can be considered influential for the simple regression model in which Y is regressed on X^2.

14.47 For the data in Exercise 14.15, find a 95% confidence interval for the mean size of the permanent staff for 6,000 annual bankruptcies. Calculate the standardized residual, the leverage value, and the value of Cook's D for each observation. Comment on these values.

14.48 For the data in Exercise 14.19 in which the new price in euros is predicted using the original price in marks for eight products, calculate the standardized residual, the leverage value, and the value of Cook's D for each observation. Comment on these values. Would any observation be considered influential?

14.49 For the data in Exercise 14.25, find the 90% prediction interval for the log of personal consumption expenditure for an X value of 200 billion people. Transform the interval, by replacing each endpoint by 10^z, where z is the value of the endpoint. What does this transformed prediction interval represent?

14.50 *Consumer Reports* rates the performance of bookshelf speakers. Speakers are tested by placing them in an echo-free chamber and feeding them test signals containing all audible frequencies. Ratings range from 0 to 100, with 100 being a perfect score. Consumers often want to know if price is any reflection of the quality of the product. To understand if a linear relationship exists between the rating and the price of bookshelf speakers, the following data were collected.

Speakers	Price	Rating
NHT Model 1.5	600	76
B&W DM 602 S2	550	78
Polk Audio RT55i	550	61
JBL Northridge Series N28	400	75
Polk Audio RT35i	335	70
JBL Studio Series S26	300	61
DCM DCM6	200	50
Yamaha NS-A638	125	67
Bose 141	100	64
KLH 911B	100	47

a. Let the dependent variable be the price of a bookshelf speaker and the independent variable be the rating. Do the data support the conclusion that there is a linear relationship between these two variables? What is your conclusion at the 5% significance level? What would it be at the 1% significance level?

b. Based on the values of the standardized residuals, would you say that there are any outliers?

(Source: "Loudspeaker Ratings," *Consumer Reports,* August 2001, p. 36.)

14.51 For the data in Exercise 14.26, find the 99% confidence interval for the average number of years that a lawn mower will be able to function properly if the number of hours of operation between oil changes is 23 hours. What is the standard deviation for the predicted value of the number of years that a single lawnmower will be able to perform adequately if the number of hours of operation between oil changes is 23?

14.52 For a fixed value of X, which interval is larger, the confidence interval for the mean value of Y at X (equation 14.24) or the prediction interval for a predicted value of Y at X (equation 14.27)? What value can you assign to X to achieve the narrowest confidence interval for the mean value of Y at X or for the predicted value of Y at X?

14.53 A sample of 200 executives who work in Chicago was taken to find out how much of their own money the executives invest each year in stock of the company that they work for. The following regression equation was developed, where X is the income (in thousands) of an executive and Y is the amount of money (in thousands) he or she invests each year in the company. The prediction equation is

$$\hat{Y} = 9.5 + 0.05X$$

Based on the regression equation, can the following statement be made? A Chicago-area executive who earns $15,000 a year would invest about $10,250 in company stock. Comment.

Using the Computer

14.54 **[DATA SET EX14-54]** *Variable description:*

MortgageLender: Name of lending institution

Location: City and state of institution

MortgageLoans01: Amount of mortgage loans approved during 2001 in millions of dollars

MortgageLoans00: Amount of mortgage loans approved during 2000 in millions of dollars

In 2001, America's residential lenders were awash in refinancings. The total mortgage packages approved exceeded $1.5 trillion. However, refinancings were not uniform across the United States. Twenty major mortgage institutions were randomly selected, and the amount of mortgage refinancing was recorded for 2001 and 2000.

a. Plot $Y = $ MortgageLoans01 and $X = $ Mortgage-Loans00. Comment on how linearly related you think the two variables are.

b. Do the data support the hypothesis that there is a linear relationship between X and Y? Base your response on the *p*-value.

c. Determine a 95% prediction interval for the amount of mortgage loans approved in 2001 if the institution serviced $150,000 million of mortgages in 2000.

d. Determine if any observations are influential.

(Source: "Refi Boom Headaches," *U.S. Banker,* June 2001, p. 58.)

14.55 **[DATA SET EX14-55]** *Variable description:*

NumberTourist: Number of tourists visiting water park daily

AmountSpent: Amount spent by the tourists daily

The manager of a water park would like to investigate the relationship between the number of tourists who visit her water park daily and the amount of revenue generated. A random sample of 40 days is selected, and data on daily attendance (X) and amount spent by tourists (Y) are recorded. The amount spent is in units of thousands.

a. Find the predicted values and the residual values. Verify that the residuals sum to zero.

b. Do any of the observations have an unusually large value for Cook's D?

c. Construct a residual plot of AmountSpent and the residuals. Do you notice any pattern? Does this violate any assumptions of the regression analysis model?

14.56 **[DATA SET EX14-56]** *Variable description:*

WebSalary: Salary paid to the Web general manager

ComputerExp: Years experience working in a computer environment

The average size of the Internet staff at companies surveyed by Buck Consultants in Stamford, Conn., is approximately 14. The salary of the Web general manager averages $73,000, but this varies by experience. Suppose that a consultant wished to determine if there is a linear relationship between WebSalary and ComputerExp. Data were collected on 60 Web general managers with salary recorded in thousands of dollars and computer experience recorded in years.

a. Plot $Y = $ WebSalary and $X = $ ComputerExp. Comment on the fit. Do you notice any outliers or influential observations?

b. Calculate the leverage values, standardized residuals, and Cook's D values to identify unusual observations. Compare these to those found in part a. Which observation appears to be the most influential?

(Source: "Companies Forming Web Site Departments to Handle Online Work," *Dallas Morning News,* July 9, 1997, p. 10D.)

14.57 **[DATA SET EX14-57]** *Variable description:*

CEO_Compens: Total compensation of the chief executive officer (CEO)

CompanyProfit: Annual company after-tax profit

A financial researcher is interested in the relationship between the total compensation of the CEO of a corporation and the after-tax profit of the company. A random sample of 50 CEOs was selected. Total compensation includes salary, bonus, and stock options in thousands of dollars, and company profit is measured in units of millions of dollars.

a. Plot Y = CEO_Compens and X = CompanyProfit. Comment on the fit of the data.

b. Calculate the leverage values, standardized residuals, and Cook's D to identify unusual observations.

c. Eliminate the most influential observation and perform part b again. What changes, if any, do you note.

Summary

When dealing with a pair of variables (say, X and Y), we generally are interested in determining whether the variables are related in some manner. If a relationship does exist, perhaps the **independent variable** (X) can be used to predict values of the **dependent variable** (Y). If a significant linear relationship exists within the sample data, both the direction (positive or negative) and the strength of this linear relationship can be measured using the sample **coefficient of correlation,** r. The sample correlation coefficient is an estimate of the **population coefficient of correlation,** ρ. Another commonly used measure of association between two variables is the sample **covariance.**

Whenever a sample of bivariate data contains a significant linear pattern, we determine the **least squares line** through the data points and generate an equation that can be used to predict values of the dependent variable. To describe accurately the assumptions behind this procedure, we introduced the concept of a **statistical model** consisting of a **deterministic** portion (the straight line) and a **random error** component. This model can be written as $Y = \beta_0 + \beta_1 X + e$, where $\beta_0 + \beta_1 X$ is the deterministic component and e represents the error component. When we perform any test of hypothesis regarding the underlying bivariate population, we must be careful to satisfy the necessary assumptions behind this procedure. For example, we assume **homoscedasticity,** the assumption that the variance of the error component does not change as the independent variable changes. **Heteroscedasticity,** in which the variance of the error component *does* change, would invalidate any of the hypothesis tests associated with a linear regression model.

By regressing Y on X we are able to determine the least squares line, $\hat{Y} = b_0 + b_1 X$. The value of b_0 is the **intercept** of the least squares line and estimates the population intercept β_0. The **slope** of the least squares line, b_1, estimates the population slope β_1. One question of interest is, if we **regress** X on Y (that is, switch the independent and dependent variables), can we rearrange the previous equation and say that $\hat{X} = (-b_0/b_1) + (1/b_1)Y$? The answer is no, although the coefficient of correlation, r, is the same in either case.

Various methods for determining the utility of the model as a predictor of the dependent variable include: (1) a t test for detecting a significant slope,

b_1 (a value of $\beta_1 = 0$ indicates that X has no predictive ability); (2) a t test for determining whether the sample correlation, r, is significantly large (a value of $\rho = 0$ indicates that there is no linear relationship between the two variables); and (3) a confidence interval for the slope, β_1. The two t tests appear to be quite different, but their computed values (and df) are *identical*; there is no point in performing both tests.

Another measure of how well the model provides estimates that fit the sample data is given by the **coefficient of determination,** r^2. For **simple linear regression** (one independent variable), this is the square of the correlation coefficient. Another definition of the coefficient of determination can also be used to examine more than one independent variable (called multiple linear regression), namely, $r^2 = 1 - (SSE/SS_Y)$. Here, **SSE** is the **sum of squares of error** and SS_Y represents the total variation in the sample Y values. For example, if $r^2 = .85$, then 85% of the variation in the sample Y values has been explained using this model.

The value of $\hat{Y}$ from the least squares regression line at a specific value of X (say, $X = x_0$), can be used to estimate an *average* value of Y, given this value of X (written $\mu_{Y|x_0}$). The value of $\hat{Y}$ centers a *confidence interval* for $\mu_{Y|x_0}$. Similarly, we can use the $\hat{Y}$ value to center a **prediction interval** for an individual value of the dependent variable, given this specific value of X (written Y_{x_0}). The value of $\hat{Y}$ can be used to *estimate* the value of $\mu_{Y|x_0}$ or *predict* the value of Y_{x_0}.

Examination of the **residuals** [values of $(Y - \hat{Y})$] is an important step during a **regression analysis.** These values can be used to verify the model assumptions as well as to indicate sample observations that appear to be **outliers** or observations that are very influential in determining the least squares line. The calculated **sample leverages** will identify observations that have unusual values of the independent variable, X; that is, such observations have values of X that are distant from the sample mean of the X values ($\bar{x}$). Observations that have unusually large or small values of the dependent variable, Y, can generally be detected during an inspection of the **standardized residuals.** Observations that have a large impact in the calculation of the least squares line are referred to as **influential observations.** These sample points can be determined using the calculated **Cook's distance measures.**

Summary of Formulas

Correlation Between Two Variables

$$r = \frac{\text{SCP}_{XY}}{\sqrt{\text{SS}_X}\,\sqrt{\text{SS}_Y}}$$

where

$$\text{SCP}_{XY} = \sum xy - \frac{(\sum x)(\sum y)}{n}$$

$$\text{SS}_X = \sum x^2 - \frac{(\sum x)^2}{n}$$

$$\text{SS}_Y = \sum y^2 - \frac{(\sum y)^2}{n}$$

Least Squares Line

$$\hat{Y} = b_0 + b_1 X$$

where

$$b_1 = \frac{\text{SCP}_{XY}}{\text{SS}_X} \qquad \text{and} \qquad b_0 = \bar{y} - b_1 \bar{x}$$

Estimate of the Residual Variance

$$\hat{\sigma}_e^2 = s^2 = \frac{\text{SSE}}{n-2}$$

where

$$\text{SSE} = \sum (y - \hat{y})^2$$

$$= \text{SS}_Y - \frac{(\text{SCP}_{XY})^2}{\text{SS}_X}$$

t Statistic for Detecting a Significant Slope

$$t = \frac{b_1}{s_{b_1}}$$

(df $= n - 2$), where

$$s_{b_1} = \frac{s}{\sqrt{\text{SS}_X}}$$

Confidence Interval for the Slope, β_1

$$b_1 - t_{\alpha/2, n-2} s_{b_1} \qquad \text{to} \qquad b_1 + t_{\alpha/2, n-2} s_{b_1}$$

t Statistic for Detecting a Significant Correlation

$$t = \frac{r}{\sqrt{\dfrac{1 - r^2}{n - 2}}}$$

(df $= n - 2$)

Coefficient of Determination

$$r^2 = \text{square of correlation coefficient}$$

$$= 1 - \frac{\text{SSE}}{\text{SS}_Y}$$

Confidence Interval for the Average Value of X at a Specific Value of X (Say x_0)

$$\hat{Y} \pm t_{\alpha/2, n-2} s \sqrt{\frac{1}{n} + \frac{(x_0 - \bar{x})^2}{\text{SS}_X}}$$

Prediction Interval for a Particular Value of Y at a Specific Value of X (say, x_0)

$$\hat{Y} \pm t_{\alpha/2, n-2} s \sqrt{1 + \frac{1}{n} + \frac{(x_0 - \bar{x})^2}{\text{SS}_X}}$$

Leverage of the ith Observation

$$h_i = \frac{1}{n} + \frac{(x_i - \bar{x})^2}{\text{SS}_X}$$

Standardized Residual of the ith Observation

$$\frac{Y_i - \hat{Y}_i}{s\sqrt{1 - h_i}}$$

Cook's Distance Measure for the ith Observation

$$D_i = \frac{(Y_i - \hat{Y}_i)^2}{2s^2} \left(\frac{h_i}{(1 - h_i)^2} \right)$$

Review Exercises 14.58–14.73

14.58 The following statistics were calculated from pairs of observations where X represents the independent variable and Y represents the dependent variable.

$$\Sigma x = 511 \qquad \Sigma y = 314 \qquad \Sigma xy = 19{,}064$$

$$\Sigma x^2 = 34{,}234.5 \qquad \Sigma y^2 = 13{,}036 \qquad n = 8$$

  a. Determine the least squares line.
  b. Determine the sample correlation coefficient between X and Y.
  c. Determine if there is a linear relationship between X and Y at the .10 significance level.
  d. Find a 90% confidence interval for the slope of the regression line.
  e. Find a 90% confidence interval for the mean of Y if $X = 60$.
  f. Find a 90% prediction interval for Y if $X = 60$.
  g. What are the necessary assumptions for the validity of the procedure in parts c, d, e, and f?

14.59 Arena football has experienced enormous growth since 1987, when only 12 indoor football games were played. To understand the relationship between the attendance (in millions) and number of games, data from 1991 to 2000 are listed below.

Year	1991	1992	1993	1994	1995	1996	1997	1998	1999	2000
Attendance	.41	.74	.69	.70	.88	1.13	1.07	1.04	1.06	1.15
Games	40	60	60	66	78	105	98	98	105	119

  a. Find the least squares line for the data using $X = $ number of games and $Y = $ attendance (in millions). Interpret the slope of the regression equation.
  b. Test that there is a linear relationship. Use the p-value to base your conclusion.
  c. Find a 95% confidence interval for the slope of the regression line. Interpret the interval in the context of this problem.
  d. Find a 95% prediction interval for the attendance when the number of games is 110.
  e. What assumptions are necessary for the validity of the responses to parts b, c, and d?

14.60 Dolls-R-Us believes that television advertising is the most effective way to market its new line of dolls. The sales manager recorded the amount of money spent on advertising and the amount of sales for 20 randomly selected months. The average cost for television advertising for the 20 months was $110,000. The average sales volume for the 20 months was $675,000. The following sample statistics were found from the data for the 20 months.

$$\text{SCP}_{XY} = 198.4 \qquad \text{SS}_X = 205.3 \qquad \text{SS}_Y = 341.6$$

where Y represents the sales volume (in thousands) and X represents the television advertising costs (in thousands of dollars).
  a. Calculate the least squares line.
  b. Calculate the coefficient of determination.
  c. Calculate the sum of squares of error.
  d. What is the estimate of the variance of the error component for the model?
  e. Is there sufficient evidence from the data to conclude at the .01 significance level that a positive relationship exists between X and Y?
  f. Find a 95% prediction interval for the monthly sales volume if the television advertising expenditure during one particular month is $120,000.

14.61 A car rental agency has a fleet of 200 cars available for rent at Kennedy airport in New York City. The owner of the agency uses a regression equation for estimating the company's daily revenue based on the number of incoming flights that day. The regression equation is $\hat{Y} = 2500 + 21.4X$, where X is the number of daily incoming flights and Y is the daily revenue in dollars. The data used to find the least squares line are based on a sample of 100 randomly selected days in 1998. Can the following statement be made based on regression analysis? If Kennedy airport increases its daily incoming flights by 50 flights next year, then the car agency can expect to make an additional daily revenue of $1,070. Comment.

14.62 Each week, a realtor advertises the houses she manages that are available for rent. The number of telephone calls from people inquiring about the advertisement were recorded for several weeks, during which various sizes of the advertisement were used. Is there sufficient evidence from the following data to conclude at the .10 significance level, that a nonzero correlation exists?

X (Height of Ad, Inches)	Y (Number of Inquiries)	X (Height of Ad, Inches)	Y (Number of Inquiries)
0.5	3	2.5	10
1.0	4	3.0	14
1.5	6	3.5	12
2.0	5	4.0	18

14.63 The manager of a firm that specializes in assisting individuals in filling out federal income tax forms obtained data from the Internal Revenue Service pertaining to deductions for charitable contributions. The following table provides a distribution of charitable contributions of eight groups with different adjusted gross incomes.

Median Adjusted Gross Income (in Thousands of Dollars) (X)	Percentage in Group Making Charitable Contributions (Claiming Itemized Deductions) (Y)
5.0	17.0
7.5	36.0
12.5	40.5
17.5	38.5
25.0	29.2
40.0	14.0
75.0	4.2
100.0	1.5

a. Obtain the least squares line for these data.

b. Identify the values of the intercept, the slope, and the variance of the error for the simple linear regression model.

c. Find the residuals for all the Y values.

d. If the correlation between X and Y above was very strong, would it then be correct to conclude that an increase in income causes people to become less charitable?

14.64 The toughness of a paint is usually a good indication of how long it will last. Generally, the low-luster paints tend to be tougher than the fiat paints, especially in their ability to resist staining. *Consumer Reports* rates paints on their toughness and also provides an overall rating for each paint. Twelve flat paints and their overall rating (higher scores are better) and their toughness rating (lower scores are better) are shown below. Find a 95% prediction interval for the overall score of a paint with a toughness rating of 6. Interpret this interval.

Flat Paints	Overall Score	Toughness
Valspar American Tradition (Lowe's)	80	3
Sherwin Williams Everclean Interior	70	4
Ralph Lauren Premium Quality	63	5
Sears Best Easy Living	63	8
Glidden Dulux Inspirations	62	4
Behr Premium Plus (Home Depot)	61	5
Martha Stewart Everyday Colors	61	5
Color Place Premium (Wal-Mart)	60	7
Dutch Boy Fresh Look (Kmart)	60	8
Benjamin Moore Regal Wall Satin	60	9
Kelly Moore Super	55	7
Glidden Evermore (Home Depot)	52	12

(Source: "Picking the Best Paint," *Consumer Reports,* June 2001, pp. 36–38.)

14.65 One management policy is based on the hypothesis that the more productive a worker is, the more satisfied the worker will be. A scale from 1 to 10 is used to measure productivity, with 10 being assigned to an extremely productive worker. A second scale from 1 to 10 is used to measure satisfaction. The worker assigns him- or herself a 10 if he or she is satisfied in every aspect of the job. Twenty employees were selected randomly from the production-and-research department of Tellon Oil. The results of the data collection are as follows:

Satisfaction (Y)	Productivity (X)	Satisfaction (Y)	Productivity (X)
5	4	9	7
2	3	7	5
9	8	4	4
9	9	8	7
5	6	9	8
3	5	10	9
5	4	5	6
7	7	1	2
9	8	7	8
2	3	9	9

a. Draw a scatter diagram of the data.

b. Test the hypothesis, at a 5% significance level, that there is a positive linear relationship between productivity and satisfaction.

c. Find a 99% confidence interval for the slope of the regression equation.

d. Calculate the coefficient of determination.

e. Find a 99% prediction interval for the satisfaction of a particular worker whose measure of productivity is 7.

14.66 Stock brokerage firms receive a score called their *batting average*. This value is obtained by dividing the firm's total number of awards for various categories such as forecasting earnings of companies by the number of analysts used by that firm. The following data represent the stock-picking awards of eight stock brokerage firms and their batting average.

Securities Firm	Number of Stock-Picking Awards	Batting Average
Salomon Smith Barney	21	.574
Merrill Lynch	8	.359
Morgan Stanley	15	.410
Lehman Brothers	11	.522
Goldman Sachs	11	.344
A. G. Edwards	10	.477
Credit Suisse First Boston	8	.273
J. P. Morgan Chase	6	.313

a. Plot Y = batting average and X = number of stock picking awards. Do you think that the data demonstrate a linear relationship between X and Y?

b. Calculate the coefficient of determination. Interpret this value.

c. Find a 90% prediction interval for the batting average of a securities firm that has 12 stock-picking awards. Interpret this interval.

(Source: "Firm by Firm: Tally of Awards Ranks 82 Research Houses," *The Wall Street Journal*, June 26, 2001, p. R16.)

14.67 Diane's Beauty Salon is currently hiring beauticians at its new location in a popular mall. Diane wants to know what percentage of commission to pay the beauticians based on experience. A survey of 12 licensed beauticians was taken with the following results.

Percentage of Commission (Y)	Years of Experience (X)	Percentage of Commission (Y)	Years of Experience (X)
24	2	25	4
18	1	44	12
30	5	33	8
41	10	24	3
35	8	20	1
35	7	40	10

a. Find the least squares line.

b. Calculate the sum of squares due to error.

c. Test the null hypothesis that there is no linear relationship between years of experience and percentage of commissions paid. Use a significance level of .05.

d. Find a 90% confidence interval for the slope of the regression line.

14.68 A regression line is fitted to a set of data and the values of $(Y - \hat{Y})$ are calculated. Does the following set of sample errors appear to conform to the empirical rule that 95% of the data should lie within two standard deviations of the mean? Construct a histogram for the residuals. Comment on the shape of the histogram.

1.1, –0.8, 2.6, 1.5, 0.2, –0.4, 0.8, –1.8, –2.3, 0.9, –2.7, 3.1, –1.0, 0.9, 4.5,
–3.4, –0.1, –0.2, 2.4, –1.7, –0.7

14.69 **[DATA SET EX14-69]** *Variable description:*

ChinaEmissions: China's carbon dioxide emissions in millions of metric tons of carbon

US_Emissions: United States' carbon dioxide emissions in millions of metric tons of carbon

Only a few years ago, many studies projected that China would emerge as the world's leading source of carbon dioxide by 2020, but recent developments appear to have put off that day by years. Although the United States has improved its energy efficiency since the oil crises of the 1970s, the growth in gas-guzzling vehicles continues to push the carbon dioxide emissions of the United States to new highs. China is second to the United States because it makes such enormous inefficient use of coal. Data are collected on the carbon dioxide emissions of both countries from 1980 to 1999.
   a. Plot the values of the carbon dioxide emissions of China and the carbon dioxide emissions of the United States.
   b. Develop a regression equation to predict the carbon dioxide emissions of China using the carbon dioxide emissions of the United States.
   c. For which years does the regression equation appear to predict well?
   d. What observations (if any) would you identify as influential?

(Source: "China Said to Reduce Carbon Dioxide Emissions," *New York Times,* June 15, 2001, p. 65.)

14.70 **[DATA SET EX14-70]** *Variable description:*

ApprecRank: Rank of stock in 30 DJI with regard to performance

DividendRank: Rank of stock in 30 DJI with regard to dividend growth

Some security analysts believe that share prices are a function of future dividend flows. Fads and fashions may come and go, but this relationship appears to have withstood the test of time. To confirm the wisdom of this belief, consider the 30 Dow Jones Industrial (DJI) stocks ranked by appreciation ApprecRank and by dividend growth as given in variable DividendRank.
   a. Plot the values of $Y =$ ApprecRank and $X =$ DividendRank. Does the least squares line appear to be a good fit when eyeballing the scatterplot?
   b. Test that there is a linear relationship between X and Y. Use a 5% significance level.
   c. Construct a histogram of the residuals. Do they appear to be approximately normally distributed?

14.71 **[DATA SET EX14-71]** *Variable description:*

Total: Total amount of soup purchased over the past six months

Campbell: Amount of Campbell soup purchased over the past six months

Pet: Amount of Pet soup purchased over the past six months

Private: Amount of soup with a private label purchased over the past six months

"Never underestimate the power of marketing" is Campbell Soup Company's motto. Campbell increased its ad budget for its soups by 30% to 40% in 1994. The company has used Olympic medal winners to promote its soup. Suppose that an analyst for the food industry is interested in the relationship of the total purchase of soup by a family and the purchase of three types of soup. The analyst randomly selected 50 soup-eating families in the Philadelphia area, and over a six-month period, each family's total purchase of soups, the amount purchased of Campbell Soup, the amount purchased of Pet Soup, and the amount purchased of soups with a private store label were recorded. The correlations of these variables are displayed below in a matrix format using the **Correl** function in Excel.
   a. Interpret the values of the correlations in this matrix. Which correlations are different from zero at the 5% significance level?
   b. Would you say that the variable Campbell is a good predictor of Private? Why?
   c. Which variable would you say is the best predictor of the total amount of soup purchased over the past six months?

d. Interpret the slope of the regression equation for the predictor selected in part c. What is a 95% confidence interval for the slope of the regression line?

(*Source:* "Campbell's New Ads Heat Up Soup Sales," *The Wall Street Journal,* March 17, 1994, p. B5.)

	A	B	C	D	E	F	G	H
1	Total	Campbell	Pet	Private				
2	336.61	133.93	91.51	43.32				
3	347.2	137.2	116.26	41.85		Total	Campbell	Pet
4	376.53	161.16	129.21	73.97	Campbell	0.826098		
5	368.04	159.01	111.81	70.39	Pet	0.587812	0.310694	
6	379.81	178.23	101.29	78.39	Private	0.297726	-0.0508	0.111523
7	373.76	161.55	143.02	42.46				
8	335.35	135.44	80.6	49.33				
9	283.75	50.8	109.59	39.35				
10	338.78	151.66	70.13	32.3				

14.72 [DATA SET EX14-72] *Variable description:*

OverallScore: Overall rating for portable CD players

HeadPhone ErrCorr: Score on headphones and error detection for portable CD players

BumpImm_Controls: Score on bump immunity and controls for portable CD players

Consumer Reports rates portable CD players so that a consumer can judge which CD player is the best value. An overall rating is given to each CD player that is tested. Ratings are also given to headphones and error correction to reflect a CD player's accuracy in reproducing sound and how well the CD handled damaged discs. In addition, ratings are provided on "bump immunity" and controls to reflect how well a CD resisted skipping when jostled and the ease of using the buttons and reading the LCD panel.

    a. Develop the estimated regression equation that can be used to predict the overall rating for a portable CD player using the score on headphones and error detection. Assess the fit of this equation using a 5% significance level.

    b. Repeat part a using the score on bump immunity and controls to predict the overall rating.

    c. Compare the regression equations in parts a and b. Which variable, score on headphones and error detection or score on bump immunity and controls, would you say is a better predictor of the overall score for portable CD players?

    d. For the equation that you selected in part c, find the observation with the largest standardized residual. Remove that observation and estimate the regression equation on the remaining data. By how much does the coefficient of determination change?

(Source: "Portable CD Players," *Consumer Reports,* July, 2001, p. 214.)

14.73 [DATA SET EX14-73] *Variable description:*

Model: Model name of luxury automobile

SugRetailPrice: Suggested retail price of new luxury model automobile

DealerCost: Dealer's cost for automobile model

Twenty new luxury automobiles were randomly selected and their suggested retail price and dealer's cost recorded. Generally, subtracting about 8 to 9% of the suggested retail price is an approximation of the dealer's cost. However, for luxury models, the dealer's cost tends to vary more than for the lower-priced models.

    a. The following plot displays the dealer's cost and the suggested retail price of the 20 luxury model automobiles in this data set. Which point would you say is an influential observation? Why?

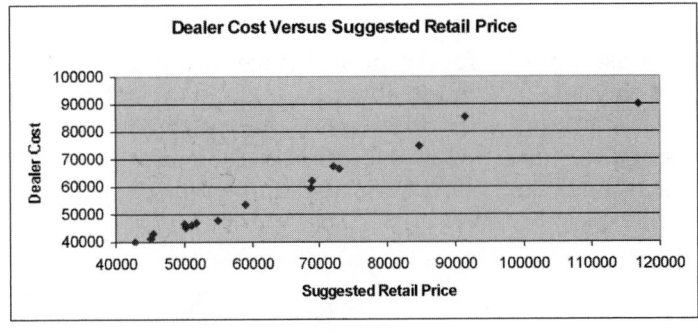

b. Find the regression equation to predict dealer's cost using the suggested retail price. What is the coefficient of determination? Interpret this value.

c. What is the value of Cook's D for the point selected in part a? Remove the observation with the largest value of Cook's D and find the regression equation using the remaining data. Compare the coefficient of determination with that obtained in part b.

d. What is the predicted value for the dealer's cost for a Mercedes-Benz CL500 using the regression equation developed in part b? What is it using the regression equation in part c? Which prediction is more accurate?

(Source: "Rolling On," *Kiplinger's Personal Finance,* December 2001, pp. 103–128.)

Computer Exercises Using the Databases

Exercise 1—Appendix F

From the database, randomly select 50 observations. Compute the sample correlation between the variable HPAYRENT (house payment or rent) and the variable UTILITY (monthly utility expenditure). Is there evidence to conclude that a positive correlation exists? Use a .05 significance level.

Exercise 2—Appendix F

Randomly select 50 observations from the database. Plot the values of total indebtedness (TOTLDEBT) and total income (INCOME1 + INCOME2). Also plot the values of TOTLDEBT and HPAYRENT (house payment or rent). Choose the graph that appears to have a stronger linear relationship between the graphed variables. Test to determine if the predictor variable significantly contributes to the prediction of total indebtedness. Use a significance level of .10.

Exercise 3—Appendix G

Randomly select 50 observations from the database. Compute the sample correlation between the variable NETINC (net income) and each of the variables SALES (gross sales) and COSTSALE (cost of sale). Select the variable from the latter two that has the highest correlation with net income. Regress net income on this variable and determine if this variable significantly contributes to the prediction of net income. Use a .05 significance level.

Exercise 4—Appendix G

Randomly select 50 observations from the database. Compute the regression line for predicting total assets (TOTAL) from current assets (ASSETS). Also compute the regression line for predicting total assets using current liabilities (LIABIL). Test for the adequacy of the fit of these two regression lines to the data. Use a .10 significance level. Which of these two regression lines has a higher value for the coefficient of determination and what does the higher value indicate?

Insights from Statistics in Action

Alpha Beta Soup for the Investor's Soul: Recipe Includes Regression Analysis

The Statistics in Action introductory case study mentioned that investors use the alpha and beta of a mutual fund to assess the volatility of the fund. These values are the intercept and slope, respectively, of a regression equation in which a mutual fund's performance is regressed on the S&P 500 index. If beta were zero (or not significantly different from zero), the performance of a mutual fund when compared to the performance of the S&P 500 stock index would be represented as having a constant rate of return. If the beta were between 0 and 1, the mutual fund (e.g., a mutual fund investing in utility stocks) would be less volatile than the stock market. A beta equal to 1 would indicate a match in performance with the S&P 500 and a value above 1 indicates a fund that is more volatile than the general market. Suppose that an investor is monitoring two mutual funds, the Heritage Fund and the Eagle Fund, and wishes to compare their performance to the S&P 500 index. Each of these funds has returned 31% over the past 30 weeks, and the weekly percentage increase or decrease in performance is recorded for each fund and for the S&P 500 index in the data file StatInActChap14.xls.

1. Graph the data for the Heritage Fund and the S&P 500 index. Also graph the data for the Eagle Fund and the S&P 500 index. Do you believe that a linear trend exists for each graph?

2. Find the regression equation for each graph in part a. Do you consider the regression lines to be an acceptable fit to the data? Use the *p*-value as a basis for your conclusion.

3. How would you interpret the intercept and slope for each regression line? Which mutual fund would a conservative investor prefer?

4. Using the regression analysis for the Heritage Fund and the regression analysis for Eagle Fund, which observation has the largest standardized residual? Delete this observation from the data set and find the resulting regression equation.

5. Compare the r^2 for the regression line with and without the deleted observation in part 4. Look at the observation that was deleted. Why do you believe that it is an influential observation?

Sources: "The Alpha Advantage," *Financial Planning* 31, issue 8, September 2001, p. 59; and "The Ratings Game," *Money* 30, issue 1, January 2001, p. 59.

Appendix **SPSS**®

Chapter 14 Appendix: Data Analysis with SPSS

Correlation and Simple Linear Regression

The SPSS procedure to obtain the correlation between two variables and carry out a simple linear regression analysis will be illustrated using the real-estate data in Example 14.1, as illustrated below.

	income	footage
1	32	16
2	36	17
3	55	26
4	47	24
5	38	22
6	60	21
7	66	32
8	44	18
9	70	30
10	50	20

To carry out the analysis, click on **Analyze ➤ Regression ➤ Linear.** Move the footage variable into the **Dependent** box and the income variable into the **Independent(s)** box.

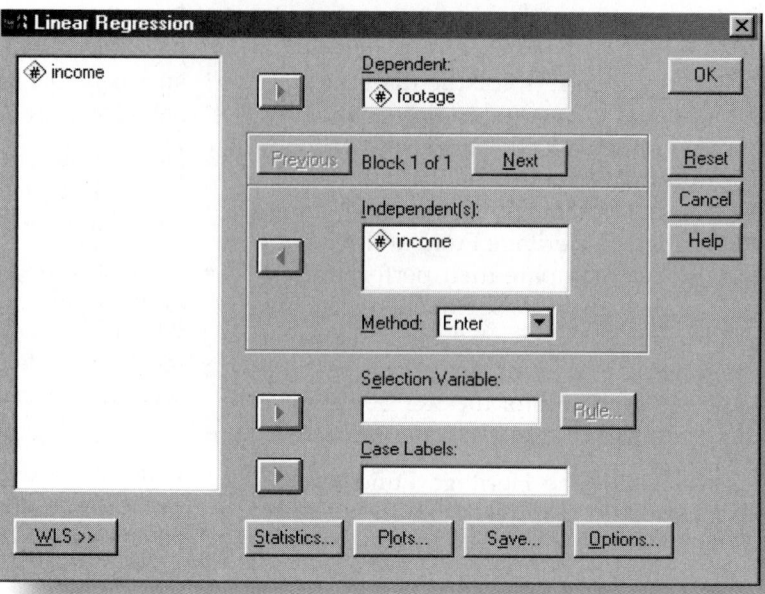

At this point there are a number of options available by clicking on **Save**. To obtain:

1. the predicted Y values, click on **Predicted Values ➤ Unstandardized.**

2. the standardized residuals, click on **Residuals ➤ Studentized.** *Note:* SPSS refers to the standardized residuals defined in equation 14.33 as studentized residuals, rather than standardized residuals.

3. the Cook's distance measures, click on **Distances ➤ Cook's.**

4. the sample leverages, click on **Distances ➤ Leverage values.**

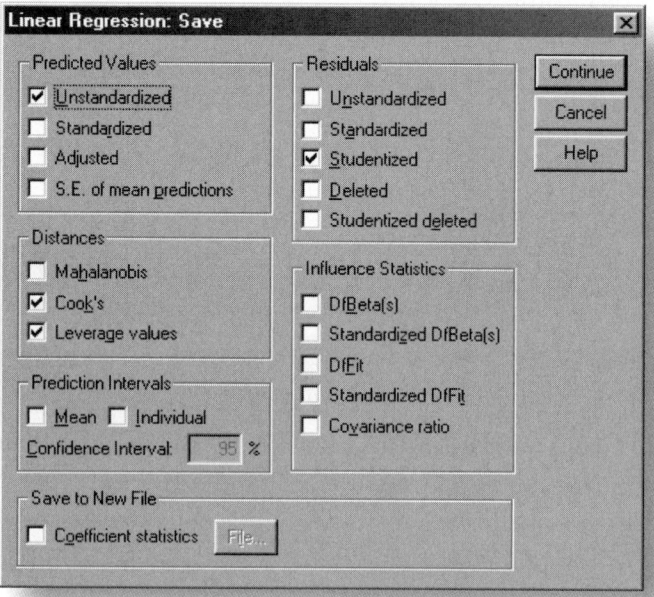

The following window will appear in the data window. The predicted Y values are in the pre_1 column, the standardized/studentized residuals are in the sre_1 column, the Cook's distance measures are in the coo_1 column, and the sample leverages are in the lev_1 column. The far-right column named leverage will be explained in the discussion to follow.

	income	footage	pre_1	sre_1	coo_1	lev_1	leverage
1	32	16	16.30021	-.11763	.00315	.21270	.31270
2	36	17	17.71590	-.26465	.01033	.12785	.22785
3	55	26	24.44039	.53950	.01950	.01815	.11815
4	47	24	21.60902	.82111	.03966	.00526	.10526
5	38	22	18.42374	1.29358	.20071	.09347	.19347
6	60	21	26.20999	-1.85750	.35296	.06984	.16984
7	66	32	28.33351	1.39994	.37390	.17618	.27618
8	44	18	20.54726	-.88337	.05451	.02258	.12258
9	70	30	29.74919	.10297	.00317	.27393	.37393
10	50	20	22.67078	-.91453	.04648	.00003	.10003

The following regression output will appear in the display pane. The correlation between the two variables ($r = .843$) is in the **Model Summary** table in the column labeled R. The resulting prediction equation is $\hat{Y} = 4.975 + .354X$. In the **Residuals Statistics** table, the minimum and maximum values for the studentized residuals and for the Cook's distance measures have been highlighted.

Coefficient of correlation

Model Summary[b]

Model	R	R Square	Adjusted R Square	Std. Error of the Estimate
1	.843[a]	.711	.675	3.08

a. Predictors: (Constant), INCOME

b. Dependent Variable: FOOTAGE

ANOVA[b]

Model		Sum of Squares	df	Mean Square	F	Sig.
1	Regression	186.587	1	186.587	19.689	.002[a]
	Residual	75.813	8	9.477		
	Total	262.400	9			

a. Predictors: (Constant), INCOME

b. Dependent Variable: FOOTAGE

Coefficients[a]

Model		Unstandardized Coefficients		Standardized Coefficients		
		B	Std. Error	Beta	t	Sig.
1	(Constant)	4.975	4.090		1.216	.258
	INCOME	.354	.080	.843	4.437	.002

a. Dependent Variable: FOOTAGE

Residuals Statistics[a]

	Minimum	Maximum	Mean	Std. Deviation	N
Predicted Value	16.30	29.75	22.60	4.55	10
Std. Predicted Value	-1.384	1.570	.000	1.000	10
Standard Error of Predicted Value	.97	1.88	1.34	.32	10
Adjusted Predicted Value	16.44	29.60	22.52	4.50	10
Residual	-5.21	3.67	-2.84E-15	2.90	10
Std. Residual	-1.692	1.191	.000	.943	10
Stud. Residual	-1.858	1.400	.012	1.041	10
Deleted Residual	-6.28	5.07	8.30E-02	3.55	10
Stud. Deleted Residual	-2.304	1.507	-.016	1.154	10
Mahal. Distance	.000	2.465	.900	.860	10
Cook's Distance	.003	.374	.110	.145	10
Centered Leverage Value	.000	.274	.100	.096	10

a. Dependent Variable: FOOTAGE

Note on the SPSS Leverage Values. SPSS does not include the term $\frac{1}{n}$ in equation 14.28 when defining sample leverages. Consequently, the SPSS sample leverage for the ith observation is $\frac{(x_i - \bar{x})^2}{SS_X}$. To obtain the leverage values that agree with equation 14.28 (used in the KPK Excel macros and MINITAB), click on **Transform ➤ Compute.** Enter "leverage" in the **Target Variable** box and "lev_1 + 1/10" in the **Numeric Expression** box. After clicking on **OK** the leverage column shown in the preceding data window should appear. Using the bottom (Centered Leverage Value) row in the preceding **Residuals Statistics** table, these values will range from .1 + .000 to .1 + .274; that is, from .100 to .374.

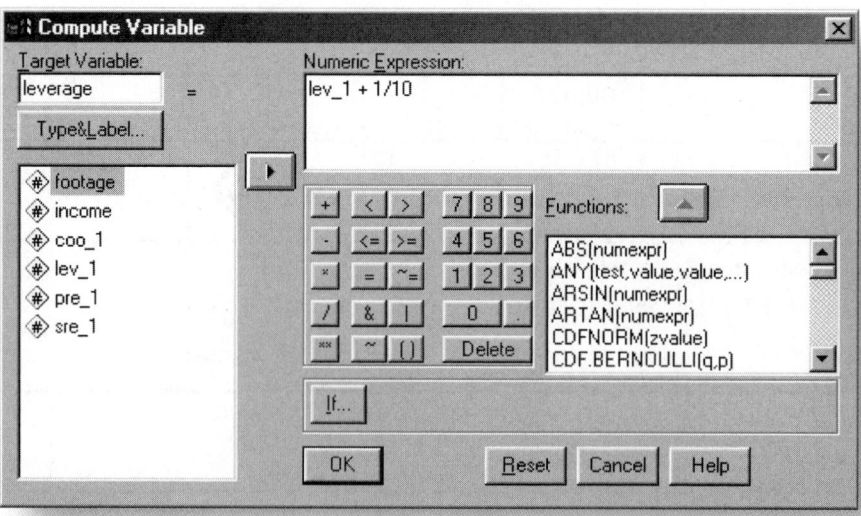

Confidence and Prediction Intervals

Examples 14.8 and 14.9 were concerned with deriving a 95% confidence interval for the mean home size for families earning $45,000 and a 95% prediction interval for a particular family having an income of $45,000. To derive these intervals using SPSS, enter 45 in the eleventh row under income but leave the corresponding value under the footage column blank. Carry out the analysis as described previously but after clicking on **Save,** click on **Unstandardized** in the **Predicted Values** frame and **Mean** and **Individual** in the **Prediction Intervals** frame. The default confidence level is 95%. After clicking on **OK,** the following columns will appear in the data window. The predicted Y values are in the pre_1 column, the lower and upper limits for the confidence intervals are in the lmci_1 and umci_1 columns, and the lower and upper limits for the prediction intervals are in the lici_1 and uici_1 columns. Note that the predicted value using $X = 45$ (20.90) and the corresponding confidence and prediction intervals appear in the last row.

	income	footage	pre_1	lmci_1	umci_1	lici_1	uici_1
1	32	16	16.30021	12.33057	20.26986	8.16685	24.43358
2	36	17	17.71590	14.32739	21.10440	9.84980	25.58199
3	55	26	24.44039	22.00028	26.88049	16.93388	31.94689
4	47	24	21.60902	19.30586	23.91219	14.14591	29.07214
5	38	22	18.42374	15.30126	21.54622	10.66852	26.17895
6	60	21	26.20999	23.28440	29.13557	18.53193	33.88804
7	66	32	28.33351	24.60286	32.06416	20.31408	36.35294
8	44	18	20.54726	18.06182	23.03270	13.02590	28.06862
9	70	30	29.74919	25.40829	34.09010	21.42832	38.07007
10	50	20	22.67078	20.42563	24.91593	15.22537	30.11620
11	45	.	20.90118	18.48896	23.31340	13.40370	28.39867

Confidence Interval for the Population Slope

To obtain a 95% confidence interval for the population slope, β_1, click on **Statistics** in the **Linear Regression** window. Click on **Confidence intervals** in the **Regression Coefficients** frame. The resulting 95% confidence interval will be contained as part of the regression output in the display pane inside the box titled **Coefficients.**

On the CD . . .
Chapter 14 Appendix: Data Analysis with MINITAB

chapter

Multiple Linear Regression X

Statistics in Action
Getting Framed Right Before Your Eyes: Evaluating the Price You Will Pay

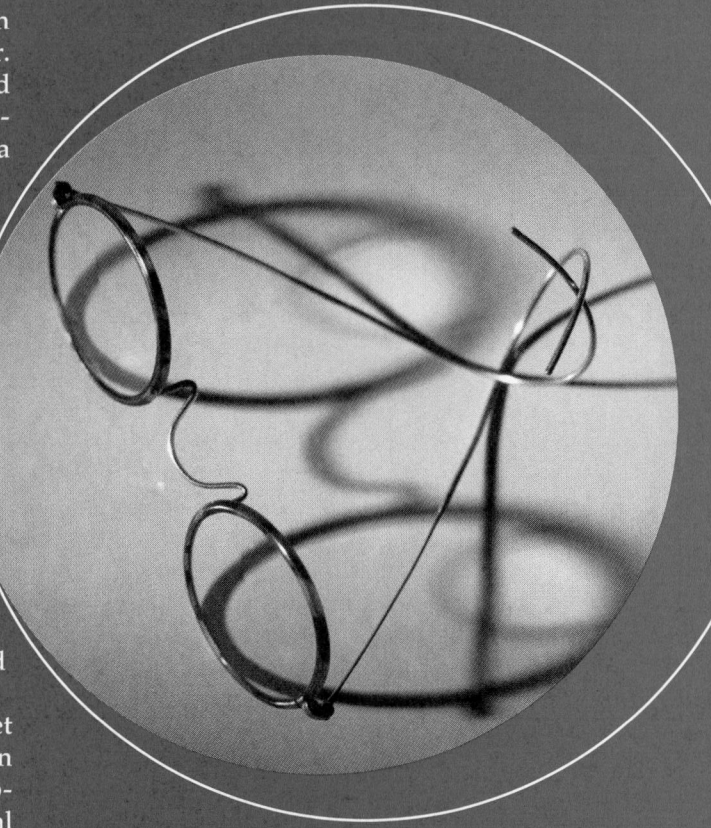

Nearly 60 percent of Americans, 161 million people, depend on prescription eyewear. Choosing eyewear can be a complicated process: Working within the constraints of prescription requirements, consumers try to find a style that is both flattering and fashionable. Often, they have the added complication of not being able to actually *see* what they look like in the frames when making their purchasing decision. That is, the eyewear must be glazed with the prescription lenses before the consumer can truly view what they have bought. If the eyewear doesn't feel right or the buyer believes that the spectacles really do have that nerd look, then a potential conflict can brew with customer service. Some frame companies are using the Internet to help consumers see themselves in their frames before they buy them. They allow consumers to upload a picture of themselves and then "try the frames" on their photo.

Eyewear is big business. In 2001, the market for eyeglasses was approximately $14 billion according to Jobson Optical Group, a trade publisher and research company for the optical industry. Optical companies have become fiercely competitive for this market. The markup on eyewear is about two and a half times their wholesale cost. There are approximately 20 optical chains in the United States. Two chains promise to make eyeglasses while you wait. LensCrafters and EyeMasters have the capability of manufacturing prescription eyewear in about an hour. Most optical stores tout product selection, insurance benefits, competitive prices, high quality, and fast service. Doctors of optometry are even located inside some of the stores. Companies are conducting research in which a wearer can one day adjust the lenses to fit his or prescription in minutes.

687

"The Internet is still an inconsequential part of the market," notes Jeffrey Stein, a retail analyst at McDonald Investments. Most eye-care companies hope that it stays that way. Salespeople at optical stores explain eyewear needs to be customized for each person's vision and face. They explain that even if lenses are ordered as the doctor prescribed, small errors in calculating pupil distances or in positioning frames on one's face may turn what appears to be a friendly dog into a hungry bear.

Three companies—Luxottica, Safilo, and Marchon—make almost half of all eyeglass frames in the United States. Many of these frames are quite similar. Consumers often see one frame cost $250 and a look-alike frame cost about $125. In some cases, the metal can be more expensive, such as the case with titanium frames. But often, the price differential comes from the way the eyewear is marketed or from the frame design. Hypoallergenic frames typically command a higher price.

Statistical analysis can be used to determine those variables that make a difference in the pricing of eyewear. *Consumer Reports* surveyed 64,000 consumers to evaluate variables such as service, quality, satisfaction, and speed in delivering the product. When you have completed this chapter, you will be able to

- Construct a prediction equation involving more than one predictor, such as predicting the price of eyeglasses using several variables recorded in a consumer survey.
- Construct a regression model that includes interactions between the predictor variables and includes transformations of predictor variables, such as the square of a variable.
- Classify an observation as *influential.*
- Verify model assumptions necessary for the validity of testing the contribution of independent variables in a prediction equation.

A Look Back/Introduction

We used the technique of simple linear regression in Chapter 14 to explain the behavior of a dependent variable using a single predictor (independent) variable. For example, we can attempt to explain the amount of new housing construction using the interest rate as a predictor variable.

To define this procedure in statistical terms, we introduced the concept of a statistical model. This model consists of two parts. The first part, the deterministic component, is assumed to be $Y = \beta_0 + \beta_1 X$ (a straight line), implying that the underlying pattern for the X and Y variables is linear. If a simple linear regression model is appropriate for the construction illustration, a scatter diagram of the new housing starts (Y) and the corresponding interest rates (X) should reveal a basic linear pattern. We never expect all the sample data to lie *exactly* on a straight line; we realize that with any statistical model there is error involved. This error makes up the random component. The actual model used for simple linear regression is $Y = \beta_0 + \beta_1 X + e$, where e represents the distance from the actual Y value to the line passing through all X, Y values. The value of e is the error and represents the error component of the model. The assumptions behind the use of this model deal with the behavior of these error terms—are they normally distributed, centered at zero, with the same variance? Are they independent?

In the construction example, it seems reasonable to assume that the volume of housing construction is affected not only by the interest rate but also by many other factors (variables) as well, including cost of materials, geographic location, and unemployment rate in the area. We next look at statistical models that predict the dependent variable (such as $Y =$ the number of new housing starts) as a function of *more than one* independent variable. The concept and assumptions are the same as before—now we are merely concerned with more than one predictor variable. When we include these additional variables, the predictive ability of the model should be significantly improved. This procedure is called multiple linear regression, and it is a very useful statistical technique.

15.1

THE MULTIPLE LINEAR REGRESSION MODEL

Prediction Using More than One Variable

To explain or predict the behavior of a certain dependent variable using more than one predictor variable, we use a **multiple linear regression** model. The form of this model is

$$Y = \beta_0 + \beta_1 X_1 + \beta_2 X_2 + \cdots + \beta_k X_k + e$$

15.1

where $X_1, X_2, \ldots, X_k$ are the k independent (predictor) variables and e is the error associated with this model.

Notice that equation 15.1 is similar to the equation for the simple linear regression model (equation 14.15) except that the *deterministic component* is now

$$\beta_0 + \beta_1 X_1 + \cdots + \beta_k X_k$$

15.2

rather than $\beta_0 + \beta_1 X$. Once again the error term, e, is included to provide for deviations about the deterministic component.

What is the appearance of the deterministic portion in equation 15.2? In Chapter 14, where we discussed simple linear regression, the deterministic portion was a straight line. In the case of multiple linear regression, the deterministic portion is more difficult (usually impossible) to represent graphically. If your model contains two predictor variables, X_1 and X_2, the deterministic component becomes a plane, as shown in Figure 15.1. Consequently, the key assumption behind the use of this particular model is that the Y values will lie in this plane, *on the average,* for any particular values of X_1 and X_2.

In Chapter 14, we examined the relationship between the square footage of a home (Y) and the corresponding household income (X). The results were:

- least squares line: $\hat{Y} = 4.975 + .3539X$
- correlation between X and Y: $r = .843$
- coefficient of determination: $r^2 = .711$
- a significant linear relationship exists

FIGURE

15.1

The multiple linear regression model (two independent variables).

We now want to include two additional variables in this model. The real-estate developer performing the study suspects that (1) larger families have larger homes and (2) the size of the home is affected by the amount of formal education (years of college) of the wage earner(s) in the home. We now have three independent variables:

X_1 = annual income (thousands of dollars)

X_2 = family size

X_3 = combined years of formal education (beyond high school) for all household wage earners

The same 10 families introduced in Example 14.1 were used in the study, but data were collected on the two additional variables, X_2 and X_3.*

Family	Y (Home Square Footage)	X_1 (Income)	X_2 (Family Size)	X_3 (Years of Formal Education)
1	16	32	2	4
2	17	36	2	8
3	26	55	3	7
4	24	47	4	0
5	22	38	4	2
6	21	60	3	10
7	32	66	6	8
8	18	44	3	8
9	30	70	5	2
10	20	50	3	6

The data configuration now has four columns (including Y) and 10 rows (called *observations*). Our task is to use the data on all *three* variables (X_1, X_2, and X_3) to provide a better estimate of home size (Y).

The Least Squares Estimate. Using Figure 15.1, we proceed as we did for simple regression and determine an estimate of the β's that will make the sum of squares of the residuals as small as possible. A *residual* is defined as the difference between the actual Y value and its estimate; that is, $Y - \hat{Y}$. In other words, we attempt to find the $b_0, b_1, \ldots, b_k$ that minimize the sum of squares of error,

$$SSE = \Sigma(Y - \hat{Y})^2$$

15.3

where now $\hat{Y} = b_0 + b_1X_1 + b_2X_2 + \cdots + b_kX_k$ and $b_0, b_1, \ldots, b_k$ are called the *least squares estimates* of $\beta_0, \beta_1, \ldots, \beta_k$.

By determining the estimated *regression coefficients* ($b_0, b_1, \ldots, b_k$) that minimize SSE rather than $\Sigma(Y - \hat{Y})$, we once again avoid the problem of positive errors canceling out negative ones. Another advantage of this procedure is that, by means of a little calculus, we can show that a fairly simple expression exists for these sample regression coefficients. Because this expression involves the use of *matrix notation*, we omit this result.[†]

There is only one way to solve a multiple regression problem in practice, and that is with the help of a computer. All computer packages determine the values of $b_0, b_1, \ldots, b_k$ in the same way—namely, by minimizing SSE. As a result, these values will be identical (except for numerical rounding errors), regardless of which computer program you use.

---

*A sample of size 10 is unrealistically small in practice.

[†]Information on this expression is presented in T. Sincich and W. Mendenhall, *A Second Course in Business Statistics: Regression Analysis,* 5th ed. (Upper Saddle River, NJ: Prentice-Hall, 1996); J. Neter, M. Kutner, and C. Nachtscheim, *Applied Linear Regression Models,* 3rd ed. (Homewood, Ill.: Richard D. Irwin, 1996).

FIGURE

15.2

Excel multiple regression solution to predicting house size using three predictor variables.

In the example where we attempt to predict home size using the three predictor variables, the prediction equation is

$$\hat{Y} = b_0 + b_1 X_1 + b_2 X_2 + b_3 X_3$$

where

$$\hat{Y} = \text{predicted home size}$$

$$X_1 = \text{income}$$

$$X_2 = \text{family size}$$

$$X_3 = \text{years of education}$$

and b_0, b_1, b_2, and b_3 are the least squares estimates of β_0, β_1, β_2, and β_3.

Figure 15.2 contains the Excel solution using the data we presented. To obtain this solution, type "Footage", "Income", "FamSize", and "YrsEduc" in cells A1:D1 and enter the 10 rows of data in cells A2:D11. Click on **Tools ➤ Data Analysis ➤ Regression,** and enter "A1:A11" as the **Input Y Range,** "B1:D11" as the **Input X Range,** and "E1" as the **Output Range.** Be sure to click on the box alongside **Labels,** since there are labels in the first row. According to this output, the best prediction equation (in the least squares sense) for home size is

$$\hat{Y} = 5.657 + .194 X_1 + 2.338 X_2 - .163 X_3$$

So this solution minimizes SSE. But what is the SSE here? We need to determine how well this equation "fits" the 10 observations in the data set. Consider the first family, where $X_1 = 32$ (income = $32,000), $X_2 = 2$ (family size = 2, such as an adult couple with no children), and $X_3 = 4$ (combined years of college = 4). The predicted home size here is

$$\hat{Y} = 5.657 + .194(32) + 2.338(2) - .163(4) = 15.886$$

Consequently, the predicted home size is 1,589 square feet. The actual square footage for this observation is 1,600 ($Y = 16$), so the sample residual here is $Y - \hat{Y}$ = 16 − 15.886 = .114.

Using this procedure on the remaining nine observations, we get the following results:

Y	$\hat{Y}$	$Y - \hat{Y}$	$(Y - \hat{Y})^2$
16	15.886	0.114	0.01300
17	16.010	0.990	0.98010
26	22.195	3.805	14.47803
24	24.121	−0.121	0.01464
22	22.051	−0.051	0.00260
21	22.676	−1.676	2.80898
32	31.179	0.821	0.67404
18	19.900	−1.900	3.61000
30	30.593	−0.593	0.35165
20	21.388	−1.388	1.92654
		0	24.86 = SSE

└─approximately

The computed value for the error sum of square is SSE = 24.86. This value also is high-lighted in cell G13 in Figure 15.2. This result implies that for *any* other values of b_0, b_1, b_2, and b_3, if we were to find the corresponding $\hat{Y}$'s and the resulting SSE = $\Sigma(Y - \hat{Y})^2$ using these values, this new SSE would be *larger* than 24.86. Thus, $b_0 = 5.657$, $b_1 = .194$, $b_2 = 2.338$, and $b_3 = -.163$ minimize the error sum of squares, SSE. Put still another way, these values of b_0, b_1, b_2, and b_3 provide the *best fit* to our data.

Using only income (X_1) as a predictor in Chapter 14, we found the SSE to be 75.81 in our table. By including the additional two variables, the SSE has been reduced from 75.81 to 24.86 (a 67% reduction). It appears that either family size (X_2), years of education (X_3), or both contribute, perhaps significantly, to the prediction of Y.

Interpreting the Regression Coefficients.   When using a multiple linear regression equation, such as $Y = \beta_0 + \beta_1 X_1 + \beta_2 X_2 + \beta_3 X_3 + e$, what does β_2 represent? Very simply, it reflects the change in Y that can be expected to accompany a change of one unit in X_2, *provided all other variables* (namely, X_1 and X_3) *are held constant.*

In the previous example, the sample estimate of β_2 was $b_2 = 2.338$. Can we expect an increase of 2.338 on the average as X_2 (the family size) increases by one if X_1 and X_3 are held constant? This type of argument is filled with problems, as we demonstrate later. The primary problem is that a change in one of the predictor variables (such as X_2) always (or almost always) is accompanied by a change in one of the other predictors (say, X_1) in the sample observations. Consequently, variables X_1 and X_2 are related in some manner, such as $X_1 \cong 1 + 5X_2$. In other words, a situation in which X_2, for instance, changed and the others remained constant would not be observed in the sample data.

In the case (typically not observed in business applications) where the predictor variables *are* totally unrelated, a unit change in X_2, for example, can be expected to be accompanied by a change of β_2 in the dependent variable.

In general, it is not safe to assume that the predictor variables are unrelated. As a result, the b's usually do not reflect the true "partial effects" of the predictor variables, and you should avoid such conclusions. Section 15.4 discusses methods of dealing with this type of situation.

The Assumptions behind the Multiple Linear Regression Model

The form of the multiple linear regression model is given by equation 15.1, which contains a linear combination of the k **predictor (independent) variables** as well as the error component, e, to predict the behavior of a particular **dependent variable,** Y. The assumptions for the case of $k > 1$ predictors are exactly the same as for

FIGURE

15.3

The errors in multiple linear regression ($k = 2$).

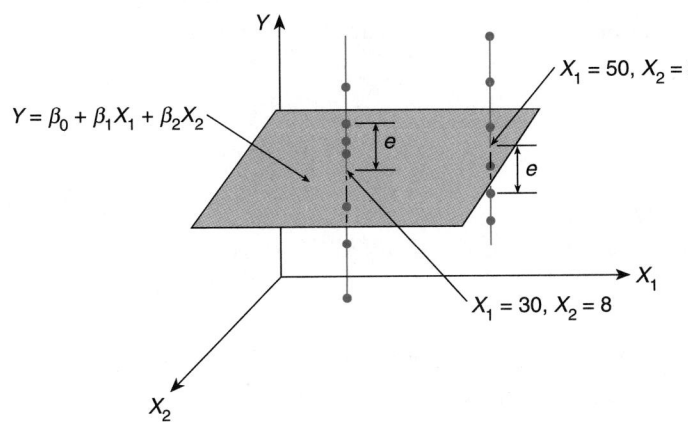

$k = 1$ independent variable (simple linear regression). Two assumptions were discussed in Chapter 14:

1. The errors follow a normal distribution, centered at zero, with common variance, σ_e^2.

2. The errors are (statistically) independent.

The case for $k = 2$ predictor variables can be represented graphically, as shown in Figures 15.1 and 15.3. Using Figure 15.3, consider the situation in which $X_1 = 30$ and $X_2 = 8$. If you *were* to obtain repeated values of Y for these values for X_1 and X_2, you would obtain some Y's above the plane and some below. The assumptions are that the *average* value of Y with $X_1 = 30$ and $X_2 = 8$ lies *on* the plane and that, moreover, these errors are normally distributed.

The final part of assumption 1 is that the variation about this plane does not depend on the values of X_1 and X_2. You should see roughly the same amount of variation if you obtain repeated values of Y corresponding to $X_1 = 50$ and $X_2 = 2$ as you observed for $X_1 = 30$ and $X_2 = 8$. The variance of these errors, if you could observe Y indefinitely, is σ_e^2.

Finally, assumption 2 means that the error encountered at $X_1 = 50$ and $X_2 = 2$, for instance, is not affected by a known error at any other point, such as $X_1 = 30$ and $X_2 = 8$. The error associated with one pair of X_1, X_2 values has no effect on any other error.

An Estimate of σ_e^2. When using a straight line to model a relationship between Y and a single predictor, the estimate of σ_e^2 was given by equation 14.16, where

$$s^2 = \hat{\sigma}_e^2 = \frac{\text{SSE}}{n - 2}$$

In general, for k predictors and n observations, the estimate of this variance is

$$s^2 = \hat{\sigma}_e^2 = \frac{\text{SSE}}{n - (k + 1)} = \frac{\text{SSE}}{n - k - 1}$$

15.4

The value of s^2 is critical in determining the reliability and usefulness of the model as a predictor. If $s^2 = 0$, then SSE $= 0$, implying that $Y = \hat{Y}$ for each of the observations in the sample data. This rarely happens in practice, but it does point out that a small s^2 is desirable. As s^2 increases, you can expect more error when predicting a value of Y for specified values of $X_1, X_2, \ldots, X_k$. In the next section, we use s^2 as a key to determining whether the model is satisfactory and which of the independent variables are useful in the prediction of the dependent variable. The square root of this estimated variance is the **residual standard deviation.**

$$s = \sqrt{\frac{SSE}{n - k - 1}}$$

15.5

In the Excel solution in Figure 15.2, the value of s is highlighted in cell F7. The residual standard deviation is often called the **standard error.**

EXAMPLE 15.1

Determine the estimate of σ_e^2 and the residual standard deviation (standard error) for the real-estate data on page 692.

Solution   This example contained $n = 10$ observations and $k = 3$ predictor variables. The resulting error sum of squares was SSE = 24.86 (from Figure 15.2). Therefore,

$$s^2 = \hat{\sigma}_e^2$$

$$= \frac{24.86}{10 - 3 - 1} = \frac{24.86}{6} = 4.14$$

and

$$s = \sqrt{4.14} = 2.035$$

That is, the residual standard deviation is 203.5 square feet.

If a particular regression model meets all the required assumptions, then the next question of interest is whether this set of independent variables provides an accurate method of predicting the dependent variable, Y. The next section shows how to calculate the predictive ability of your model and determine which variables contribute significantly to an accurate prediction of Y.

X Exercises 15.1–15.8

Understanding the Mechanics

15.1 The least squares regression equation using 20 observations is $\hat{Y} = 3 - 10X_1 + 20X_2 - X_3$.
   a. What is the error degrees of freedom?
   b. If X_1 is increased by 1, X_2 increased by 2, and X_3 remains unchanged, what is the net change in the predicted value of Y?

15.2 The following data were collected.

Y	X_1	X_2
5.4	11	3.1
7.7	14	5.1
9.1	17	5.4
8.8	17	4.4
6.2	11	3.5
7.0	12	3.8
8.4	14	4.9
7.1	13	4.0

The regression equation for this data is $\hat{Y} = .214 + .341X_1 + .608X_2$. Calculate the estimate of the variance of the error component of the model.

Applying the New Concepts

15.3 An oil-service company decided to fit a least squares equation to a set of data to predict the total cost of building a well. The independent variables are $X_1 =$ drilling days, $X_2 =$ total depth, and $X_3 =$ intermediate casing depth. After calculating the least squares equation, the residuals were calculated to find out whether the assumptions of regression analysis are satisfied. The following are the residuals from 20 observations:

−0.8, 1.5, −3.7, 4.1, −3.1, −5.2, 4.3, −2.1, −1.6, 4.1, 0.9, −0.3, 4.5, −4.2, 3.2, −2.7, 1.7, −2.2, 3.4, −1.8

Do the residuals $Y - \hat{Y}$ appear to conform to the empirical rule that approximately 95% of the data should lie within two standard deviations of the mean?

15.4 What are the standard assumptions about the error component of a multiple linear regression model for inference results about the model to be valid?

15.5 Tony owns a used-car lot. He would like to predict monthly sales volume. Tony believes that sales volume (given in thousands) is directly related to the number of salespeople employed and the number of cars on the lot for sale. The following data were collected over a period of 10 months:

Monthly Sales Volume (Y)	Salespeople (X_1)	Cars (X_2)
5.8	4	20
7.5	5	15
11.4	7	25
7.0	3	17
5.1	2	18
8.1	4	25
13.3	8	30
15.0	9	35
8.3	5	20
6.8	4	23

   a. Using a computerized statistical package, determine the least squares prediction equation for these data.
   b. Find the value of SSE.

15.6 Using the regression equation $\hat{Y} = 100 - 4X_1 + 12X_2 - 2X_3$, where do you expect the average value of Y to be for $X_1 = 10$, $X_2 = 5$, and $X_3 = 20$?

Using the Computer

15.7 **[DATA SET EX15-7]** *Variable description:*

Model: Brand and description of laptop

Price: Retail price of laptop

Rating: Overall score by *Consumer Reports*

Features: A score of 1, 2, or 3 with low values indicating more features

Laptops now belong in the same league as desktop computers, thanks to brighter and larger displays, faster processors, and more-efficient batteries. Expanding a laptop's advantages is the growing availability of high-speed wireless Internet access at airports. For recommendations on which laptop to purchase, consumers look toward the ratings provided by *Consumer Reports*. A sample of 12 laptops was selected and the rating and score on the laptop's features are recorded.

   a. Find the prediction equation for the price of a laptop using rating and features. What is the value of the residual standard deviation?
   b. If the value of SSE were equal to zero for this problem, what would that imply?

(Source: "Is This Your Next Computer?" *Consumer Reports,* 66, issue 6, June 2001, p. 20.)

15.8 **[DATA SET EX15-8]** *Variable description:*

SuburbCity: A suburban city in California

City: The largest city which lies closest to the suburban city

Age: The age of the suburban city

InitialPop: The population of the suburban city when the suburb was first recognized as a suburban city

2000Pop: Population of the suburban city in the year 2000

Many suburbs in California have grown into large cities, but are often not thought of as cities because they are in the shadow of a major city. Urban experts recognize suburbs having either a large population or having a substantial growth spurt as suburban cities. These suburban cities often have more homes than jobs and are sometimes called *boomburbs*. Fourteen suburban cities are sampled and their age as a suburban city, the initial population of the suburban city when it was first recognized as a city, and the population size of the city in the year 2000 were recorded.

   a. Find the regression equation to predict 2000Pop using the predictors Age and InitialPop. If InitialPop is held constant but the age of the suburban city changes by one year, by how much does the predicted population size change?
   b. Verify that the sum of the residuals is zero. What is the mean of the residuals? Do approximately 95% of the residuals lie within two standard deviations of the mean?

(Source: "Boomburbs' Growth Skyrockets," *USA Today,* June 22, 2001, p. 11A.)

15.2

HYPOTHESIS TESTING AND CONFIDENCE INTERVALS FOR THE β PARAMETERS

Multiple linear regression is a popular tool in the application of statistical techniques to business decisions. However, this modeling procedure does not always result in an accurate and reliable predictor. When the independent variables that you have selected account for very little of the variation in the values of the dependent variable, the model (as is) serves no useful purpose.

The first thing we demonstrate is how to determine whether your overall model is satisfactory. We begin by summarizing a regression analysis in an analysis of variance (ANOVA) table, much as we did in Chapter 11.

The ANOVA Table

The summary ANOVA table contains the usual headings.

Source	df	SS	MS	F
Regression	k	SSR	MSR	MSR/MSE
Residual	$n - k - 1$	SSE	MSE	
Total	$n - 1$	SST		

where n = number of observations and k = number of independent variables.

$$SST = \text{total sum of squares}$$
$$= SS_Y$$
$$= \Sigma(Y - \bar{Y})^2 = \Sigma Y^2 - \frac{(\Sigma Y)^2}{n}$$
$$SSE = \text{sum of squares for error}$$
$$= \Sigma(Y - \hat{Y})^2$$
$$SSR = \text{sum of squares for regression}$$
$$= \Sigma(\hat{Y} - \bar{Y})^2$$
$$= SST - SSE$$
$$MSR = \text{mean square for regression}$$
$$= \frac{SSR}{k}$$
$$MSE = \text{mean square for error}$$
$$= \frac{SSE}{n - k - 1}$$

15.6   15.7   15.8   15.9   15.10

Practically all computer packages provide you with this ANOVA summary as part of the standard output. The ANOVA section of the Excel solution for the real-estate model is in Figure 15.4A. Notice that

$$SST = SS_Y$$

$$= (16^2 + 17^2 + \cdots + 20^2) - \frac{(16 + 17 + \cdots + 20)^2}{10} = 262.4$$

This is the same value of SS_Y we obtained for the same example in Chapter 14, when we used only income (X_1) as the predictor variable. This is hardly surprising because *this value is strictly a function of the Y values* and is unaffected by the model that we are using to predict Y. The total sum of squares (SST) measures the total variation in the values of the dependent variable. Its value is the same, regardless of which predictor variables are included in the model.

The df for the regression source of variation is k = the number of predictor variables in the analysis. The df for the error sum of squares is $n - k - 1$, where n = the number of observations in the sample data.

As in the case of simple linear regression, the sum of squares of regression (SSR) measures the variation *explained* by the model—the variation in the Y values that would exist if differences in the values of the predictor variables were the only cause of differences among the Y's. On the other hand, the sum of squares of error (SSE) represents the variation *unexplained* by the model. The easiest way to determine the sum of squares of regression is to subtract:

$$SSR = SST - SSE$$

FIGURE
15.4

Excel output (see Figure 15.2).
A. Prediction equation and ANOVA table using X_1, X_2, and X_3.
B. Prediction equation and ANOVA table using X_1 and X_2.

The error mean square is MSE = SSE/$(n - k - 1)$ = 24.858/(10 − 4) = 4.14. This is the same as the *estimate* of σ_e^2 determined in Example 15.1. So,

$$s^2 = \hat{\sigma}_e^2 = \text{MSE}$$

A Test for H_0: All β's = 0

We have yet to make use of the F value calculated in the ANOVA table, where

$$F = \frac{\text{MSR}}{\text{MSE}}$$

15.11

When using the simple regression model, we previously argued that one way to determine whether X is a significant predictor of Y is to test H_0: $\beta_1 = 0$, where β_1 is the coefficient of X in the model $Y = \beta_0 + \beta_1 X + e$. If you reject H_0, the conclusion is that the independent variable X *does* contribute significantly to the prediction of Y. For example, in Example 14.3, by rejecting H_0: $\beta_1 = 0$, we concluded that income (X_1) was a useful predictor of home size (Y) using the simple linear model.

We use a similar test as the first step in the multiple regression analysis, where we examine the hypotheses

$$H_0: \beta_1 = \beta_2 = \cdots = \beta_k = 0$$

$$H_a: \text{at least one of the β's} \neq 0$$

If we *reject* H_0, we can conclude that at least one (but maybe not all) of the independent variables contributes significantly to the prediction of Y. If we *fail to reject* H_0, we are unable to demonstrate that any of the independent variables (or combination of them) helps explain the behavior of the dependent variable, Y. For example, in our housing example, if we were to fail to reject H_0, this would imply that we are unable to demonstrate that the variation in the home sizes (Y) can be explained by the effect of income, family size, and years of education.

FIGURE 15.5

F curve with k and $n - k - 1$ df. The lightly shaded area is the rejection region.

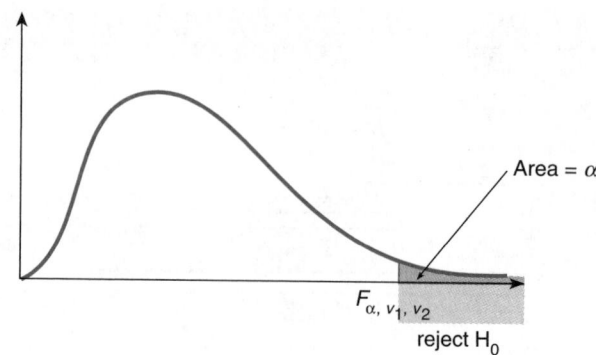

Area = α

$F_{\alpha,\,v_1,\,v_2}$

reject H_0

Test Statistic for H_0 versus H_a. The test statistic used to determine whether our multiple regression model contains at least one explanatory variable is the F statistic from the preceding ANOVA table.

When testing H_0: all β's = 0 (this set of predictor variables is no good at all) versus H_a: at least one $\beta \neq 0$ (at least one of these variables is a good predictor), the test statistic is

$$F = \frac{\text{MSR}}{\text{MSE}}$$

which has an F distribution with k and $n - k - 1$ df. The expression $n - k - 1$ can be written as $n - (k + 1)$, where $k + 1$ is the number of coefficients (β's) estimated including the constant term.

Notice that the df for the F statistic comes directly from the ANOVA table. The testing procedure is to

$$\text{reject } H_0 \text{ if } F > F_{\alpha,v_1,v_2}$$

where (1) $v_1 = k$, $v_2 = n - k - 1$ and (2) F_{α,v_1,v_2} is the corresponding F value in Table A.7 having a *right-tail area* = α (Figure 15.5).

EXAMPLE 15.2

Using the real-estate data and the model we developed, what can you say about the predictive ability of the independent variables, income (X_1), family size (X_2), and years of education (X_3)? Use $\alpha = .10$.

Solution   **Step 1.** The hypotheses are

$$H_0: \beta_1 = \beta_2 = \beta_3 = 0$$

$$H_a: \text{at least one } \beta \neq 0$$

Remember that your hope here is to reject H_0. If you are unable to demonstrate that any of your independent variables have any predictive ability, then you will fail to reject H_0.

Step 2. The test statistic is

$$F = \frac{\text{MSR}}{\text{MSE}}$$

The mean squares are obtained from the ANOVA summary of the regression analysis (see Figure 15.4).

Step 3. The df for the F statistic are $k = 3$ and $n - k - 1 = 10 - 3 - 1 = 6$. So we will

$$\text{reject } H_0 \text{ if } F > F_{.10,3,6} = 3.29$$

Step 4. According to Figure 15.4A, the computed F value is

$$F^* = \frac{79.18}{4.14} = 19.1$$

Because $F^* > 3.29$, we reject H_0.

Step 5. The three independent variables *as a group* constitute a good predictor of home size. This does *not* imply that all three variables have significant predictive ability; however, at least one of them does. The next section shows how you can tell *which* of these predictor variables significantly contributes to the prediction of home size.

A Test for H_0: $\beta_i = 0$

Assuming that you rejected the null hypothesis that all of the β's are zero, the next logical question would be, which of the independent variables contributes to the prediction of Y?

In Example 15.2, we rejected the null hypothesis, so at least one of these three independent variables affects the variation of the 10 home sizes in the sample. To determine the contribution of each variable, we perform three separate t tests:

$$H_0: \beta_1 = 0 \ (X_1 \text{ does not contribute})$$

$$H_a: \beta_1 \neq 0 \ (X_1 \text{ does contribute})$$

$$H_0: \beta_2 = 0 \ (X_2 \text{ does not contribute})$$

$$H_a: \beta_2 \neq 0 \ (X_2 \text{ does contribute})$$

$$H_0: \beta_3 = 0 \ (X_3 \text{ does not contribute})$$

$$H_a: \beta_3 \neq 0 \ (X_3 \text{ does contribute})$$

One-tailed tests also can be used here, but we will demonstrate this procedure using two-tailed tests. This means that we are testing to see whether this particular X contributes to the prediction of Y, but we are not concerned about the direction (positive or negative) of this relationship.

When income (X_1) was the only predictor of home size (Y), we used a t test to determine whether the simple linear regression model was adequate. In Example 14.3, the value of the test statistic was derived, where

$$t = \frac{b_1}{s_{b_1}}$$

15.12

Also, b_1 is the estimate of β_1 in the simple regression model, and s_{b_1} is the (estimated) standard deviation of b_1. Excel refers to s_{b_1} as the *standard error* of b_1.

All computer packages provide both the estimated coefficient (b_1) and its standard error (s_{b_1}). In Example 14.3, the computed value of this t statistic was $t^* = 4.44$. This result led us to conclude that income was a good predictor of home size because a significant positive relationship existed between these two variables.

We use the same t statistic procedure to test the effect of the individual variables in a multiple regression model. When examining the effect of an individual independent variable, X_i, on the prediction of a dependent variable, the hypotheses are

$$H_0: \beta_i = 0$$

$$H_a: \beta_i \neq 0$$

The test statistic is

$$t = \frac{b_i}{s_{b_i}}$$

where (1) b_i is the estimate of β_i, (2) s_{b_i} is the (estimated) standard error of b_i, and (3) the df for the t statistic is $n - k - 1$.

The test of H_0 versus H_a is to

$$\text{reject } H_0 \text{ if } |t| > t_{\alpha/2, n-k-1}$$

where $t_{\alpha/2, n-k-1}$ is obtained from Table A.5.

We can now reexamine the real-estate data in Example 15.2.

X_1 = Income. Consider the hypotheses

$$H_0: \beta_1 = 0$$

$$H_a: \beta_1 \neq 0$$

As in Example 15.2, we use $\alpha = .10$.

According to Figure 15.4A, $b_1 = .194$ and $s_{b_1} = .0877$. Also contained in the output is the computed value of

$$t^* = \frac{b_1}{s_{b_1}} = \frac{.194}{.0877} = 2.21$$

Why is this value of t^* *not* the same as the value of t calculated for this variable in Chapter 14, when income was the only predictor of Y? When there are three predictors in the model, t^* for income is 2.21. When income is the only predictor in the model, $t^* = 4.44$. The difference in the two values is simply that $t^* = 2.21$ provides a measure of the contribution of X_1 = income, *given that X_2 and X_3 already have been included in the model.* A large value of t^* indicates that X_1 contributes significantly to the prediction of Y, even if X_2 and X_3 have been included previously as predictors.

The hypotheses can better be stated as

H_0: income *does not* contribute to the prediction of home size, *given* that family size and years of education already have been included in the model

H_a: income *does* contribute to this prediction, given that family size and years of education already have been included in the model

or as

$$H_0: \beta_1 = 0 \qquad \text{(if } X_2 \text{ and } X_3 \text{ are included)}$$

$$H_a: \beta_1 \neq 0$$

Because $t^* = 2.21$ exceeds the table value of $t_{\alpha/2, n-k-1} = t_{.05, 10-3-1} = t_{.05, 6} = 1.943$, we conclude that income contributes significantly to the prediction of home size and should be kept in the model. An easier procedure to use here is to compare the corresponding p-value to the significance level (α). The p-value is in cell I18 in Figure 15.4A and is equal to .069. Since this is less than $\alpha = .10$, we reject H_0 and again conclude that income is a significant predictor.

X_2 = Family Size. Using a similar argument, the following test of hypothesis will determine the contribution of family size, X_2, as a predictor of the home square footage, given that X_1 and X_3 already have been included. The hypotheses here are

$$H_0: \beta_2 = 0 \qquad \text{(if } X_1 \text{ and } X_3 \text{ are included)}$$

$$H_a: \beta_2 \neq 0$$

According to Figure 15.4A, the computed t statistic here is

$$t^* = \frac{b_2}{s_{b_2}} = \frac{2.3381}{.9078} = 2.576$$

This value also exceeds $t_{.05, 6} = 1.943$ (p-value of .042 is less than .10), and so family size provides useful information in predicting the square footage of a home. We conclude that we should keep X_2 in the model.

$X_3 =$ **Years of Education.** To test

$$H_0: \beta_3 = 0 \quad \text{(if } X_1 \text{ and } X_2 \text{ are included)}$$

$$H_a: \beta_3 \neq 0$$

we once again use the t statistic.

$$t = \frac{b_3}{s_{b_3}}$$

Using Figure 15.4, the computed value of this statistic is

$$t^* = \frac{-.1628}{.2441} = -.67$$

Because $|t^*| = .67$, which does not exceed $t_{.05,6} = 1.943$, we fail to reject H_0. Here, the p-value of .530 exceeds the significance level of .10. We conclude that, given the values of $X_1 =$ income and $X_2 =$ family size, the level of a family's education appears not to contribute to the prediction of the size of their home. This means that X_3 can be ignored in the final prediction equation, leaving only X_1 and X_2.

Comments

As a word of warning, you should *not* simply remove this term from the equation containing all three variables. Since the predictor variables are typically related in some manner, the sample regression coefficients ($b_0, b_1, \ldots$) change as variables are added to or deleted from the model. Referring to Figure 15.4A, the final prediction equation is not $\hat{Y} = 5.657 + .194X_1 + 2.338X_2$. Instead, the coefficients of X_1 and X_2 should be derived by repeating the analysis using only these two variables. According to Figure 15.4B, this prediction equation is $\hat{Y} = 5.091 + .165X_1 + 2.657X_2$.

A Confidence Interval for β_i

Using what you believe to be the "best" model, you can easily construct a $(1 - \alpha) \times 100\%$ confidence interval for β_i based on the previous t statistic:

$$b_i - t_{\alpha/2, n-k-1} s_{b_i} \quad \text{to} \quad b_i + t_{\alpha/2, n-k-1} s_{b_i} \qquad \textbf{15.13}$$

Once again, k represents the number of predictor variables used to estimate β_i.

**EXAMPLE
15.3**

Suppose you decide to retain only $X_1 =$ income and $X_2 =$ family size in the prediction equation. Referring to Figure 15.4B, construct a 90% confidence interval for β_2, the coefficient for X_2.

Solution

Since this model contains $k = 2$ predictor variables, we first find $t_{\alpha/2, n-k-1} = t_{.05,7} = 1.895$. Using cells F40 and G40 (highlighted) in Figure 15.4B, the confidence interval for β_2 is

$$2.6569 - (1.895)(.7405) \quad \text{to} \quad 2.6569 + (1.895)(.7405)$$

$$= 2.6569 - 1.4032 \quad \text{to} \quad 2.6569 + 1.4032$$

$$= 1.25 \quad \text{to} \quad 4.06$$

Therefore, we are 90% confident that the estimate of β_2 (that is, $b_2 = 2.6569$) is within 1.4032 of the actual value of β_2. Notice that this is an extremely wide confidence interval. As usual, increasing the sample size would help to reduce the width of this confidence interval. When creating Figure 15.4B, if you enter 90% as the confidence level, Excel will determine this confidence interval for you (cells L40 and M40 in Figure 15.4B).

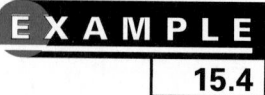

EXAMPLE 15.4

An Excel Multiple Regression Analysis

The management of BB Investments decided to develop a model to predict the amount of money invested by various clients in their portfolio of high-risk securities. It was generally agreed that the income of the investor should be a major factor in predicting his or her annual investment and would explain a major portion of the variability in the amount invested. In addition, the investor's willingness to assume risk also was influenced by the investor's view of current and future economic conditions. On the assumption that the investors would use economic forecasts and economists' indices of future expectations, the financial group at BB Investments constructed an economic index that ranged from 0 to 100. When applied to any particular point in time, this index was tied to the expected increase in interest rates and borrowing levels, the expected increase in manufacturing costs because of the rate of inflation, and the expected level of price inflation at the retail level. This meant that the *lower* the index, the *better* the future economic conditions were expected to be.

Data were obtained by randomly selecting 50 high-risk portfolio customers and recording their incomes and the amounts of their investments. The income figures represent annual incomes and the economic index values are the index values at the time the investment was made. Determine the adequacy of this model and the predicted investment for an investor with an income of $48,500 at a time when the economic index has a value of 72.

Solution

The Excel regression solution is shown in Figure 15.6. To obtain this solution, first open data set DATA15-4. The first 20 rows are shown in columns A, B, and C in Figure 15.6. Next, click on **Tools ➤ Data Analysis ➤ Regression,** and enter "A1:A51" as the **Input Y Range,** "B1:C51" as the **Input X Range,** and "D1" as the **Output Range.** Finally, click on the box alongside **Labels** (since there are labels in the first row) and on **OK.**

FIGURE 15.6

Excel regression solution for Example 15.4.

Invest	Index	Income	SUMMARY OUTPUT					
2500	86	55800						
3700	54	60400	Regression Statistics					
3900	21	72700	Multiple R	0.94784179				
1700	91	41700	R Square	0.89840406	← R^2			
1000	72	35200	Adjusted R Square	0.89408082				
1700	16	41800	Standard Error	283.03313234				
2500	81	43700	Observations	50				
3400	32	67900						p-value for F test
2500	37	53700	ANOVA			MSR	MSE	
2900	89	57400		df	SS	MS	F	Significance F
2100	48	47100	Regression	2	33294135.56	16647067.8	207.8084	4.5877E-24
2600	61	55300	Residual	47	3765064.438	80107.754		
1700	33	40000	Total	49	37059200			
2100	82	40200						
1500	95	36900		Coefficients	Standard Error	t Stat	P-value	
1700	73	40700	Intercept	-1183.3183	219.3703591	-5.3942	2.19E-06	
1400	9	35100	Index	-0.1271481	1.54705816	-0.0822	0.934847	
2400	42	50900	Income	0.07199484	0.003588211	20.0643	1.10E-24	
1000	74	36300						

The least squares equation (highlighted) is

$$\hat{Y} = -1183.3 - .127X_1 + .072X_2$$

The predicted investment is

$$\hat{Y} = -1183.3 - .127(72) + .072(48,500)$$

$$= -1183.3 - 9.1 + 3492.0 = 2299.6$$

that is, approximately $2,300. Note that, following the same argument used in Chapter 14, $2,300 also serves as an estimate of the average investment whenever $X_1 = 72$ and $X_2 = \$48,500$. This topic is explored further in Section 15.5, where we discuss the construction of a confidence interval for an *average* investment or a prediction interval for an *individual* investment.

The first test of hypothesis determines whether these two variables *as a group* provide a useful model for predicting the amount of an investment:

$$H_0: \beta_1 = \beta_2 = 0$$

$$H_a: \beta_1 \neq 0, \beta_2 \neq 0, \text{ or both} \neq 0$$

Using the ANOVA table, the value of the F statistic is

$$F^* = \frac{\text{MSR}}{\text{MSE}} = \frac{16,647,067.78}{80,107.754} = 207.81$$

The df here are $v_1 = k = 2$ and $v_2 = n - k - 1 = 50 - 2 - 1 = 47$. Because $F_{.10,2,47}$ is not in Table A.7a, we use the nearest value, $F_{.10,2,40} = 2.44$. The computed F^* exceeds this value, so we reject H_0 and conclude that at least one of these two independent variables is a significant predictor of investment amounts. We could have avoided any table look-up here by simply comparing the p-value for the F test (nearly zero) to the significance level of $\alpha = .10$. Since the p-value is less than α, H_0 is rejected rather soundly and we arrive at the same conclusion.

The t Tests. Because we rejected $H_0: \beta_1 = \beta_2 = 0$, the next step is to examine the t tests to determine which of the two independent variables are useful predictors. The t value from Table A.5 is $t_{\alpha/2,n-k-1} = t_{.05,47} \approx 1.684$. We can either compare the t values to 1.684 or compare the corresponding p-values to $\alpha = .10$. The p-value for $X_1 = $ economic index is $.935 > .10$, and the p-value for $X_2 = $ income is approximately zero and is $< .10$. The large p-value (and small t statistic) for X_1 implies that, given the presence of X_2 in the model, X_1 does not contribute useful information to the prediction of the amount of an investment. Conversely, for X_2, the small p-value (and large t statistic of 20.06) indicates that the investor's income *is* an excellent predictor of the amount of an investment. It was the contribution of this variable and not of X_1 that produced the extremely large F value obtained previously.

As we have seen, a quick glance at the computer output allows you to determine whether your model is useful as a whole and, furthermore, which variables are useful predictors. But beware—the analysis is not over! *Before you form your conclusions from this analysis and make critical decisions based on several tests of hypotheses, you need to be sure that none of the assumptions of the multiple linear regression model (discussed earlier) have been violated.* We will discuss this problem in the final section of this chapter, where we conclude the analysis by examining the sample *residuals*, $Y - \hat{Y}$.

The use of t tests allows you to determine the predictive contribution of each independent variable, provided you want to examine the contribution of *one* such variable while assuming that the remaining variables are included in the equation. The next section shows you how to extend this procedure to a situation in which you wish to determine the contribution of any *set* of predictor variables by using a single test.

☒ Exercises 15.9–15.20

Understanding the Mechanics

15.9 The following regression equation was calculated from a data set of 20 observations: $\hat{Y} = -1.0 + 2.5X_1 + 4.0X_2$. The value of MSR and MSE are .465 and .004, respectively. The standard deviations of the regression coefficients of X_1 and X_2 are .26 and .21, respectively.

a. Test the hypothesis that at least one of the regression coefficients is not equal to zero. Use a .05 significance level.

b. Test H_0: $\beta_1 = 0$ versus H_a: $\beta_1 \neq 0$. Use a .05 significance level.

c. Test H_0: $\beta_2 = 0$ versus H_a: $\beta_2 \neq 0$. Use a .05 significance level.

15.10 A researcher wished to test that a model with five independent variables contributed to the prediction of a certain dependent variable. From 51 observations, the researcher calculated SST to be equal to 215 and SSE to be equal to 180. Construct an ANOVA table.

Applying the New Concepts

15.11 Many chief executives (CEOs) have been under serious criticism from organized labor for the fat paychecks that CEOs take home. Many of the CEOs have advocated sacrifice and leaner paychecks for large groups of employees of their companies. An experiment was set up in which 15 observations were taken on the variables:

Y = CEOs pay (in thousands of dollars)

X_1 = company's net profit (in millions of dollars)

X_2 = number of employees (in thousands)

A computer package gave the following sample statistics:

$$b_1 = .1336 \qquad b_2 = -.86$$

$$s_{b_1} = .0424 \qquad s_{b_2} = .39$$

a. Given that X_2 is in the model, does X_1 contribute to predicting the dependent variable at the .05 significance level?

b. Given that X_1 is in the model, does X_2 contribute to predicting the dependent variable at the .05 significance level?

15.12 Brown and Gilbert's law firm would like to predict the salary for a legal secretary based on years of college education (X_1), typing speed in words per minute (X_2), and years of experience (X_3). The following data were collected:

Y	X_1	X_2	X_3	Y	X_1	X_2	X_3
15,120	2	65	2	12,500	0	45	.5
12,500	1	45	2	15,800	2.5	60	2
26,000	3.5	85	9	19,600	1	70	3
19,000	0	55	11	21,800	3	75	6
16,000	4	85	1	12,400	0	60	.5
15,000	0	65	1	22,500	2	75	7

a. Using a computerized statistical package, determine the least squares prediction equation.

b. What is the value of the residual standard deviation?

c. Do the variables X_1, X_2, and X_3 contribute to predicting salaries at the .10 significance level?

d. Find a 90% confidence interval for β_1.

e. Test the null hypothesis that $\beta_1 = 0$ at the 10% significance level.

f. Interpret the results of the hypothesis test in part e.

15.13 Highway miles per gallon (mpg) for large pickups range from 14 to 21. Typically, the more horsepower and the larger the engine size, the lower the mpg. A random sample of eight pickups is selected. Find the 95% confidence intervals for the regression coefficients of a model using horsepower and engine size to predict mpg. Interpret these two confidence intervals.

Pickup	MPG	Horsepower	Engine Size
Chevrolet Avalanche	15	285	5.3
Chevrolet Silverado 2500	16	300	6.0
Dodge Ram 1500	19	215	3.7
F-150 Regular Cab	21	202	4.2
GMC1500 Regular Cab	23	200	4.3
GMC Sierra Denali	14	325	6.0
Lincoln Blackwood	17	300	5.4
Toyota Tundra Regular	19	190	3.4

(Source: "2002 Car Guide," *Kiplinger's Personal Finance*, December 2001, p. 128.)

15.14 The regression equation $\hat{Y} = 11 + .5X_1 + .2X_2$ was computed using 20 data points to predict the price/earnings ratio (P/E) of a stock from the independent variables gross profit margin (X_1) and the sales growth of the company (X_2). The independent variables are expressed in terms of percentages. Assume that the standard deviations of the estimates for β_1 and β_2 are .16 and .21, respectively.

a. What is the 95% confidence interval for β_1? Interpret this interval.

b. What is the 95% confidence interval for β_2? Interpret this interval.

15.15 The tensile strength (Y) of a paper product is related both to the amount of hardwood in the pulp (X_1) and to the amount of time the paper spent soaking in a preparatory solution prior to cutting (X_2). A quality engineer collected ten samples of the variables Y, X_1, and X_2. Complete the following ANOVA table to test the null hypothesis that the independent variables X_1 and X_2 are not useful predictors of the tensile strength of the paper product.

Source	df	SS	MS	F
Regression			582.83	
Error				
Total		1300.90		

15.16 Datamatics Equipment, a Seattle-based electronics firm, is interested in identifying variables in the manufacturing environment that have a linear relationship with the number of line shortages on the manufacturing floor. The sample data used in a regression analysis are as follows:

Week	Y	X_1	X_2	X_3	Week	Y	X_1	X_2	X_3
1	293	205	5.936	343	9	420	365	4.780	453
2	348	215	5.815	259	10	407	329	4.905	460
3	416	227	4.983	250	11	397	345	5.009	426
4	445	301	4.841	236	12	430	249	4.869	408
5	453	362	4.755	243	13	497	356	4.791	324
6	392	358	4.775	303	14	534	424	4.754	330
7	382	302	4.813	411	15	547	430	4.598	283
8	365	246	4.909	420					

where

Y = number of line shortages with back-order status for a given week

X_1 = number of delinquent purchase orders for a given week

X_2 = inventory level (in millions of dollars) for prior weeks

X_3 = number of purchased items for prior weeks

The least squares regression equation was found to be:

$$\hat{Y} = 710.9 + 0.4767X_1 - 70.90X_2 - 0.2525X_3$$

a. Does the complete model significantly contribute to predicting the dependent variable? Use a 10% significance level.

b. If s_{b_2} is 36.886, find a 95% confidence interval for β_2.

c. Interpret the results of the hypothesis test in part a, and interpret the confidence interval in part b.

15.17 A district manager is interested in predicting district sales of an exclusively sold home water filter. As part of a marketing feasibility study, the manager selects 10 home improvement stores to market the water filter and collects data on the sales (Y), the size of the target population (X_1), and the per capita income of the local area (X_2). The sample residuals were: 350, 1,250, –3,500, 290, 1,500, –150, 4,500, –1,480, –1,250, –1,510. Given that the value of SST is 91,231,286, test the hypothesis that the variables X_1 and X_2 contribute to predicting sales. Use a 5% significance level.

15.18 *Money* magazine picks selected stocks and lists their five-year projected earnings growth, their price/earnings (P/E) ratio, and their target return. All units are percentages. A rationale is also provided as to why each stock will outperform the market. For example, Cisco systems is cited as driving technological change as opposed to being driven by it. Cisco systems has a research and development (R & D) budget of more than $500 million.

Stock	Five-Year Earnings Growth	Price/ Earnings	Target Return
AirTouch Comm	38	41	57
Amgen	16	20	19
Cisco Systems	35	20	45
Coca-Cola	18	37	11
Colgate-Palmolive	13	22	15
CUC International	25	22	48
Enron	15	14	30
Hewlett-Packard	16	15	25
Home Depot	25	23	12
Intel	20	16	14
Johnson & Johnson	15	24	13
Merck	14	23	24
Monsanto	17	23	14
Nike	18	17	43
Sun Microsystems	20	13	39

a. Find the regression equation for predicting a stock's target return from its five-year earnings growth and P/E ratio.

b. Given that P/E is in the model, does a stock's five-year earnings growth contribute to the prediction of the target return? Use a 5% significance level.

c. Given that a stock's five-year earnings growth is in the model, does P/E contribute to the prediction of the target return? Use a 5% significance level.

d. Find a 95% confidence interval for the regression coefficient of five-year earnings growth variable.

(Source: "Our Picks for the 21st Century," *Money*, June 1997, p. 60.)

Using the Computer

15.19 [DATA SET EX15-19] *Variable description:*

CellularBill: Bill for monthly use of cellular phone

MinutesTalked: Total number of minutes that the cellular phone was used

MonthlyCharge: Fixed monthly charge for making phone calls

The wireless phone market is taking a bigger and bigger share of the total phone market. Many phone companies are offering free off-peak calls. Many companies are launching PCS—short for personal communications services. Suppose that a communications consultant wished to determine the relationship between the variables CellularBill and the independent variables MinutesTalked and MonthlyCharge.

a. Perform a regression analysis on these data and explain what conclusions the data support at a 5% significance level.

b. Construct a histogram of the residuals and comment on the shape of the distribution.

(Source: "Talk Keeps Getting Cheaper," *Business Week,* June 16, 1997, p. 37.)

15.20 [DATA SET EX15-20] *Variable description:*

ProficiencyStart: Proficiency of newly hired employee

Proficiency6mo: Proficiency of employee after six months

Proficiency1yr: Proficiency of employee after one year

An operations manager is interested in predicting the proficiency of an employee after being on the job for one year. The manager uses two predictors—proficiency when hired and proficiency after six months.

a. Find the estimated regression equation using ProficiencyStart and Proficiency6mo to predict Proficiency1yr.

b. Test that ProficiencyStart does not contribute to the prediction of Proficiency1yr, given that Proficiency6mo is included in the model. Use a 5% significance level.

c. Find the regression coefficient for Proficiency6mo and interpret this interval. Use a 95% confidence interval.

d. Test that Proficiency6mo does not contribute to the prediction of Proficiency1yr, given that ProficiencyStart is included in the model. Use a 5% significance level.

e. Find a 95% confidence interval for the regression coefficient of ProficiencyStart and interpret this interval.

15.3   DETERMINING THE PREDICTIVE ABILITY OF CERTAIN INDEPENDENT VARIABLES

We can extend the procedure we used to examine the contribution of each independent variable, one at a time, using a t test.

Assume that the personnel director of an accounting firm has developed a regression model to predict an individual's performance on the CPA exam. The multiple linear regression model contains eight independent variables, three of which (say, X_6, X_7, X_8) describe the physical attributes of each individual (say, height, weight, and age). Can all three of these variables be removed from the analysis without seriously affecting the predictive ability of the model?

To answer this question, we return to a statistic described in Chapter 14 that measures how well a model captures the variation in the values of the dependent variable.

Coefficient of Determination

The total variation of the sampled dependent variable is determined by

$$SST = \text{total sum of squares}$$
$$= SS_Y$$
$$= \Sigma(Y - \overline{Y})^2$$
$$= \Sigma Y^2 - \frac{(\Sigma Y)^2}{n}$$

where n = number of observations. To determine what percentage of this variation has been explained by the predictor variables in the regression equation, we determine the **coefficient of determination, R^2.**

$$R^2 = 1 - \frac{SSE}{SST}$$

15.14

The range for R^2 is 0 to 1. If $R^2 = 1$, then 100% of the total variation has been explained, because in this case SSE = $\Sigma(Y - \hat{Y})^2 = 0$, and so $Y = \hat{Y}$ for each observation in the sample; that is, the model provides a *perfect predictor*. This does not occur in practice, but the main point is that a large value of R^2 is generally desirable for a regression application. It should be mentioned that $R^2 = 1$ whenever the number of observations (n) is equal to the number of estimated coefficients ($k + 1$). This does not mean that you have a "wonderful" model; rather, you have inadequate data. As a result, you need to guard against using too small a sample in your regression analysis. *A general rule of thumb is to use a sample containing at least three times as many (unique) observations as the number of predictor variables (k) in the model.*

H_0: **All β's = 0.** A test statistic for testing H_0: all β's = 0 was introduced in equation 15.11, which used the ratio of two mean squares from the ANOVA table. Another way to calculate this F value is to use

$$F = \frac{R^2/k}{(1-R^2)/(n-k-1)}$$

15.15

This version of the F statistic is used to answer the question, Is the value of R^2 significantly large? If H_0 is rejected, then the answer is yes, and so this group of predictor variables has at least some predictive ability for predicting Y.

The F value computed in this way will be exactly the *same* as the one computed using $F = $ MSR/MSE, except for possible rounding error (see Example 15.5).

Once again, remember that *statistical* significance does not always imply *practical* significance. A large value of R^2 (rejecting H_0) does not imply that precise prediction (practical significance) will follow. However, it does inform the researcher that these predictor variables, as a group, are associated with the dependent variable.

EXAMPLE 15.5

In Chapter 14, we determined that X = income explained 71% of the total variation of the home sizes (Y) in the sample, since the computed value of r^2 was .711. What percentage is explained using all three predictors (income, family size, and years of education)?

Solution

The coefficient of determination using X_1 only is .711. Using the Excel solution in Figure 15.4A, the coefficient of determination using X_1, X_2, and X_3 is

$$R^2 = 1 - \frac{\text{SSE}}{\text{SST}}$$

$$= 1 - \frac{24.858}{262.4} = .905$$

Consequently, 90.5% of this variation has been explained using the three independent variables.

The F value determined in Example 15.2 for testing H_0: $\beta_1 = \beta_2 = \beta_3 = 0$ can be duplicated using equation 15.15 because

$$F = \frac{.905/3}{(1-.905)/(10-3-1)} = \frac{.905/3}{.095/6} = 19.1 \text{ (as before)}$$

Comments

1. In Example 15.5, notice that the value of R^2 *increased* when we went from using one independent variable to using three. As you add variables to your regression model, R^2 *never decreases*. However, the increase may not be a significant one. If adding 10 more predictor variables to your model causes R^2 to increase from .91 to .92, this is not a *significant* increase. Therefore, do not include these 10 variables; they clutter up your model and are likely to add spurious predictive ability to it.

2. Nearly every computer package (including Excel, SPSS, and MINITAB) will provide a value in the output, referred to as the **adjusted R^2**. This particular statistic does *not* necessarily increase as additional predictor variables are added to the model, and many researchers use this value to

determine the predictive contribution of a variable added to the model. The adjusted R^2 is found by dividing SSE and SST by their respective degrees of freedom.

$$R^2(\text{adj}) = 1 - \frac{\text{SSE}/(n - k - 1)}{\text{SST}/(n - 1)}$$

15.16

Referring to Example 15.5 and Figure 15.4A, the adjusted R^2 value is

$$R^2(\text{adj}) = 1 - \frac{24.858/6}{262.4/9} = 1 - \frac{4.143}{29.156} = .858$$

which is also given in cell F6 in Figure 15.4A.

How can we tell if adding (or removing) a certain set of X variables causes a *significant* increase (or decrease) in R^2?

The Partial F Test

Consider the situation in which the personnel director is trying to determine whether to retain three variables (X_6 = height, X_7 = weight, X_8 = age) as predictors of a person's performance on a CPA exam. We know one thing—R^2 *will* be higher with these three variables included in the model. If we do not observe a *significant* increase, however, our advice would be to remove these variables from the analysis. To determine the extent of this increase, we use another F test.

We define two models—one contains X_6, X_7, and X_8, and one does not:

Complete model: uses all predictor variables, including X_6, X_7, and X_8

Reduced model: uses the same predictor variables as the complete model except X_6, X_7, and X_8

Also, let

R_c^2 = the value of R^2 for the complete model

R_r^2 = the value of R^2 for the reduced model

Do X_6, X_7, and X_8 contribute to the prediction of Y? We will test

H_0: $\beta_6 = \beta_7 = \beta_8 = 0$ (they do not contribute)

H_a: at least one of the β's $\neq 0$ (at least one of them does contribute)

The test statistic here is

$$F = \frac{(R_c^2 - R_r^2)/v_1}{(1 - R_c^2)/v_2}$$

15.17

where v_1 = number of β's in H_0 and $v_2 = n - 1 - $ (number of X's in the complete model).

For this illustration, $v_1 = 3$ because there are three β's in H_0. Assuming that there are eight predictor variables in the complete model, then $v_2 = n - 1 - 8 = n - 9$. Here, n is the total number of observations (rows) in the data. This F statistic measures the *partial* effect of these three variables; it is a *partial F test.*

Equation 15.17 resembles the F statistic given in equation 15.15, which we used to test H_0: all β's = 0. If all the β's are zero, then the reduced model consists of only a constant term, and the resulting R^2 will be zero; that is, $R_r^2 = 0$. Setting $R_r^2 = 0$ in equation 15.17 produces equation 15.15, where $v_1 = k$ and $v_2 = n - k - 1$.

These variables (as a group) contribute significantly if the computed partial F value in equation 15.17 exceeds F_{α,v_1,v_2} from Table A.7.

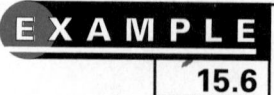

EXAMPLE
15.6

The personnel director gathered data from 30 individuals using all eight independent variables. These data were entered into a computer, and a multiple linear regression analysis was performed. The resulting R^2 was .857.

Next, variables X_6, X_7, and X_8 were omitted, and a second regression analysis was performed. The resulting R^2 was .824. Do the variables X_6, X_7, and X_8 (height, weight, and age) appear to have any predictive ability? Use $\alpha = .10$.

Solution

Here, $n = 30$ and

$$R_c^2 = .857 \text{ (complete model)}$$

$$R_r^2 = .824 \text{ (reduced model)}$$

Based on the previous discussion, the value of the partial F statistic is

$$F^* = \frac{(.857 - .824)/3}{(1 - .857)/(30 - 1 - 8)} = \frac{.033/3}{.143/21} = 1.61$$

The procedure is to reject H_0: $\beta_6 = \beta_7 = \beta_8 = 0$ if $F^* > F_{.10,3,21} = 2.36$. The computed F value does not exceed the table value, so we fail to reject H_0. We conclude that these variables should be removed from the analysis because including them in the model fails to produce a significantly larger R^2.

The partial F test also can be used to determine the effect of adding a *single* variable to the model.

EXAMPLE 15.7

Using the real-estate data analyzed in Example 15.2, determine whether $X_2 = $ family size contributes to the prediction of home size, given that $X_1 = $ income and $X_3 = $ years of education are included in the model. Use a significance level of $\alpha = .10$.

Solution

We test the hypotheses

$$H_0: \beta_2 = 0 \quad \text{(if } X_1 \text{ and } X_3 \text{ are included)}$$

$$H_a: \beta_2 \neq 0$$

The complete model uses X_1, X_2, and X_3. Using Example 15.5,

$$R_c^2 = .905$$

The reduced model uses only X_1 and X_3. Figure 15.8 contains the Excel solution using this model and the KPK Data Analysis regression procedure. When using the standard Excel regression analysis, the X variables must be in adjacent (contiguous) columns, whereas the KPK Data Analysis procedure does not have this restriction. To obtain the output in Figure 15.8, click on **KPK Data Analysis ▶ Regression.** You will then see the input form shown in Figure 15.7. When using this form, you *must* have labels in the first row for all of your variables. Enter "A1:A11" as the **Y Range,** which includes the label in cell A1. Next, click on **Noncontiguous X Range** and enter "2" as the number of X variables, "B1:B11" for **X Column 1,** and "D1:D11" for **X Column 2.** Finally, enter "E1" as the **Output Range.** Using the Figure 15.8 output, the coefficient of determination using the reduced model is

$$R_r^2 = .801$$

The value of the partial F statistic is

$$F^* = \frac{(.905 - .801)/1}{(1 - .905)/(10 - 1 - 3)} = \frac{.104/1}{.095/6} = 6.6$$

The 1 in the numerator indicates that there is one β in H_0; subtracting the 3 in the denominator indicates that there are three X's in the complete model.

FIGURE

15.7

Input screen using **KPK Data Analysis ➤ Regression.**

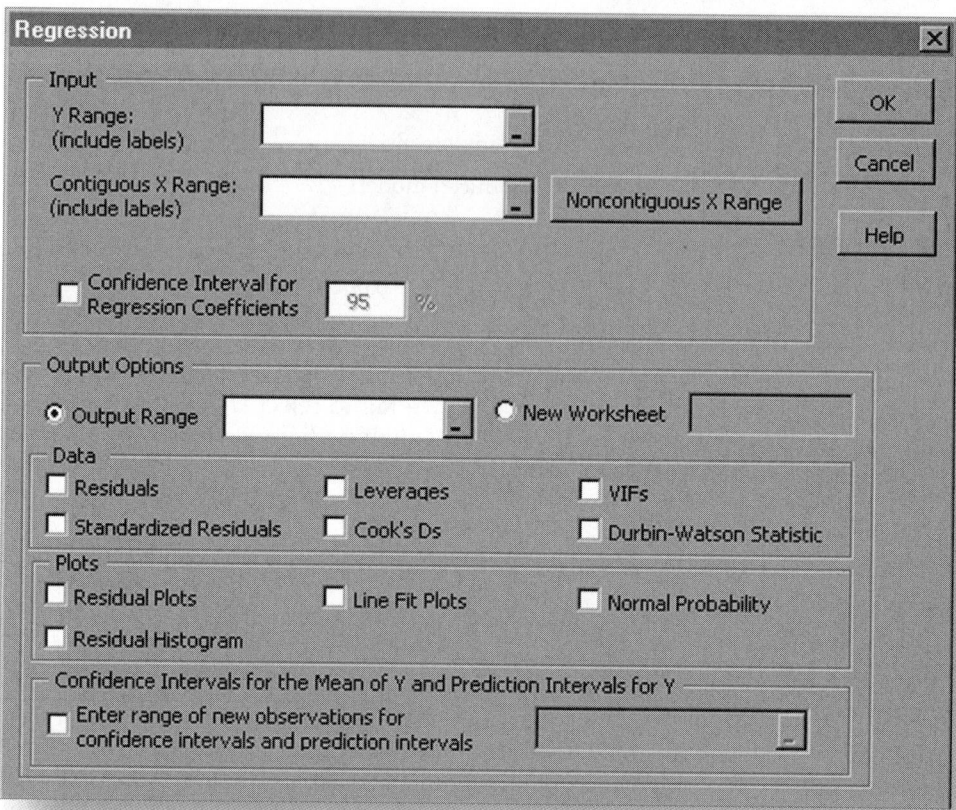

FIGURE

15.8

Excel output using X_1 = income and X_3 = years of education as predictors.

	A	B	C	D	E	F	G	H	I	J
1	Footage	Income	FamSize	YrsEduc	**SUMMARY OUTPUT**					
2	16	32	2	4						
3	17	36	2	8	**Regression Statistics**					
4	26	55	3	7	Multiple R	0.895				
5	24	47	4	0	R Square	0.801	$\leftarrow R^2_r$			
6	22	38	4	2	Adjusted R Square	0.744				
7	21	60	3	10	Standard Error	2.735				
8	32	66	6	8	Observations	10				
9	18	44	3	8						
10	30	70	5	2	**ANOVA**					
11	20	50	3	6		df	SS	MS	F	Significance F
12					Regression	2	210.0575	105.0288	14.0460	0.003545
13					Residual	7	52.3425	7.4775		
14					Total	9	262.4			
15										
16						Coefficients	Standard Error	t Stat	P-value	
17					Intercept	6.7333	3.7659	1.7879	0.1169	
18					Income	0.3731	0.0717	5.2060	0.0012	
19					YrsEduc	-0.4938	0.2787	-1.7717	0.1197	
20										

This value does exceed $F_{.10,1,6} = 3.78$, and so X_2 = family size does (as suspected from the earlier t test) significantly improve the model's predictive ability when included with X_1 and X_3. In other words, there is a significant increase in R^2 (from .801 to .905) when X_2 is added to the model, and as a result, our conclusion is to retain this variable in the model.

Comments

Both Example 15.7 and the t test for X_2 discussed on page 700 dealt with testing H_0: $\beta_2 = 0$ versus H_a: $\beta_2 \neq 0$. Both tests attempted to determine whether X_2 should be included as a predictor given that X_1 and X_3 were already included as predictor variables. *Note:* (1) the partial F value = 6.6 = $(2.576)^2$ = $(t \text{ value})^2$, and (2) the p-value using the t test (.042) = the p-value using the F test (not shown).

We can see that these tests are *identical:* they result in exactly the same p-value and the same conclusion. This result demonstrates that to determine the predictive ability of an individual independent variable, we can compute the partial F statistic or the somewhat simpler t statistic. Some computer packages use the F statistics to summarize the individual predictors, whereas others (such as Excel, SPSS, and MINITAB) use the t values to measure the influence of each predictor. You should use whatever is provided (the F statistic or t statistic) to measure the partial effect of each variable; both sets of statistics accomplish the same thing.

Using Curvilinear Models: Polynomial Regression

Motormax produces electric motors for use in home furnaces. The company has formed a team of employees to examine the relationship between the dollars spent per week in inspecting finished products (X) and the number of motors produced during that week that were returned to the factory by the customer (Y). Motormax suspects that the number of returned motors will decrease as the amount spent on inspection increases but that after a certain point the decrease will slow down—that is, the number of returned motors will continue to decrease but at a slower rate. In other words, after spending a certain amount on inspecting finished product, they will reach a point where there will be little decrease in the number of returned motors, even though they spend a much larger amount on inspection.

The following data were gathered from company records covering 15 (non-consecutive) weeks (the inspection expenditure (X) is in thousands of dollars):

Week	Units Returned (Y)	Inspection Expenditures (X)	Week	Units Returned (Y)	Inspection Expenditures (X)
1	32	5.1	9	25	8.5
2	16	13.5	10	26	6.8
3	48	2.1	11	28	6.4
4	24	8.0	12	15	14.7
5	21	10.6	13	38	3.6
6	14	15.4	14	23	9.7
7	42	2.8	15	21	11.5
8	18	12.8			

The sample values and scatter diagram are shown in Figure 15.9. This chart can be obtained using Excel's Chart Wizard and selecting the **XY (Scatter)** option. The data range is A1:B16. Once you have the plot, you can right click on any of the 15 plotted points and click on **Add Trendline ➤ Linear** to obtain the trend line in Figure 15.9. The last five values are above the trend line, and so it appears that Motormax has a point—the number of returned motors does appear to level off after a certain amount of inspection expense.

Does the simple linear model $Y = \beta_0 + \beta_1 X + e$ capture the relationship between inspection expenditure (X) and number of units returned (Y)? Although Y does decrease as X increases here, the linear model does not capture the "slowing down" of Y for larger values of X. The least squares line (contained in Figure 15.9) overpredicts Y for the middle range of X but underpredicts Y for small or large values of X.

Figure 15.10 shows **quadratic curves** rather than straight lines. If we include X^2 in the model, we can describe the curved relationship that seems to exist between the number of returned motors and inspection expense. More specifically, the left half of Figure 15.10*a* resembles the shape of the scatter diagram in Figure 15.9.

Consider the model

$$Y = \beta_0 + \beta_1 X + \beta_2 X^2 + e \qquad \text{15.18}$$

Is this a linear regression model? At first glance, it would appear not to be. However, by the word *linear* we really mean that the model is *linear in the unknown* β's, not in X. In equation 15.18, there is no term such as β_1/β_2 or $\beta_1\beta_2$. So the model is linear in the β's, and this is a (multiple) linear regression application.

The model in equation 15.18 is a **curvilinear model** and is an example of *polynomial regression*. Such models are very useful when a particular independent variable and dependent variable exhibit a definite increasing and/or decreasing relationship that is nonlinear.

FIGURE

15.9

Excel scatter diagram of data and least squares trend line for inspection expense example.

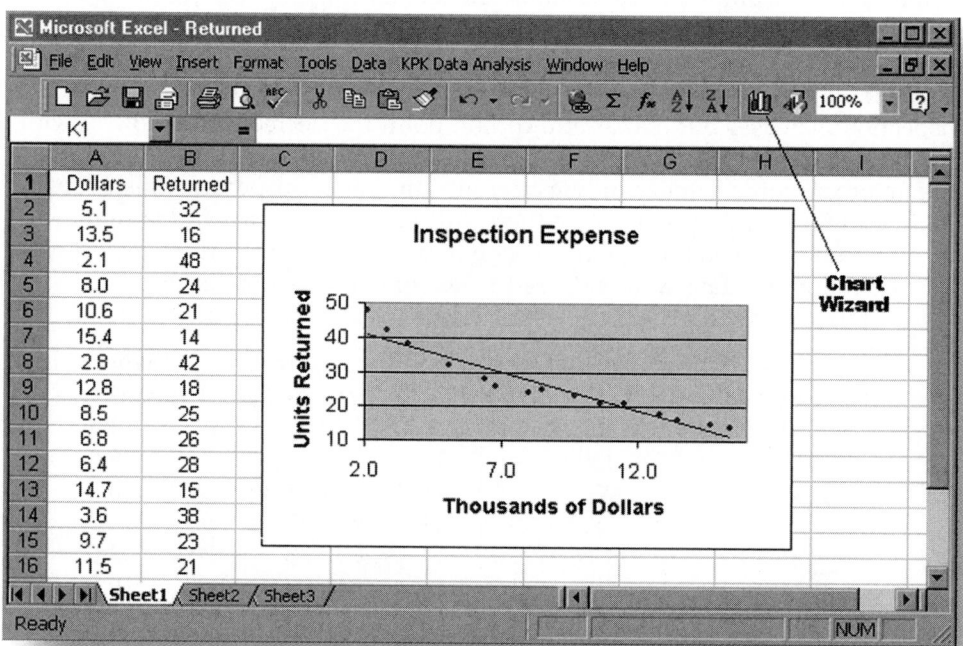

FIGURE

15.10

Quadratic curves.
(a) Graph of
$Y = 34 - 12X + 2X^2$.
In general, this is the shape of
$Y = \beta_0 + \beta_1 X + \beta_2 X^2$,
where $\beta_2 > 0$.
(b) Graph of
$Y = 6 + 12X - 2X^2$.
In general, this is the shape of
$Y = \beta_0 + \beta_1 X + \beta_2 X^2$,
where $\beta_2 < 0$.

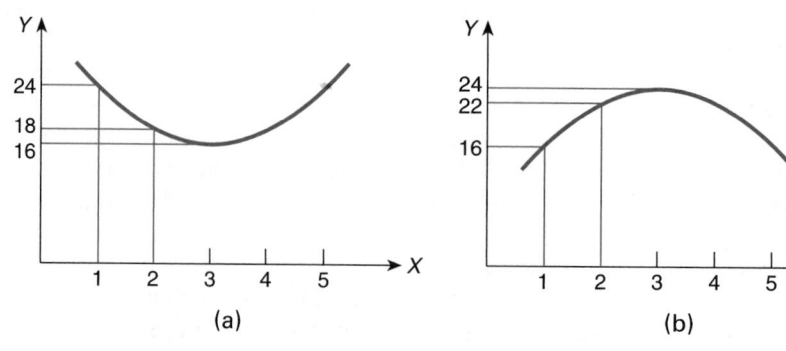

Solving for β_0, β_1, and β_2. Equation 15.18 represents a multiple regression model containing two predictors, namely, $X_1 = X$ and $X_2 = X^2$. The data for the model then are

Y	X_1	X_2
32	5.1	26.01 (= 5.1^2)
16	13.5	182.25 (= 13.5^2)
48	2.1	4.41
⋮	⋮	⋮
23	9.7	94.09
21	11.5	132.25

These data for Y, X_1, and X_2 are your input to the multiple linear regression computer program. You can simplify this task by letting the computer build the $X_2 = X^2$ column of data by squaring the entries in the $X_1 = X$ column.

EXAMPLE 15.8

Determine the Excel solution using the model $Y = \beta_0 + \beta_1 X + \beta_2 X^2 + e$ for the Motormax data shown in Figure 15.11. Also,

1. Predict the number of returned motors for a week in which Motormax spends $20,000 on inspecting final product.

2. What do the F test and t test tell you about this model? Use $\alpha = .10$.

Solution 1

To obtain the Excel solution in Figure 15.11, enter the data and labels in cells A1:B16 as shown. In cell C1, type "DollarsSQ" and in cell C2, type "= B2*B2". Drag cell C2 down through cell C16. This will produce the X^2 values in column C. Next, click on **Tools ➤ Data Analysis ➤ Regression,** and enter "A1:A16" as the **Input Y Range,** "B1:C16" as the **Input X Range,** and "D1" as the **Output Range.** Finally, click on the box alongside **Labels** (since there are labels in the first row) and on **OK.**

The regression coefficients are in cells E17:E19 (highlighted). The predicted number returned for $X_1 = 20$ (thousand) is

$$\hat{Y} = 54.8 - 4.96(20) + .156(20)^2 = 18.0$$

The model predicts that 18 motors will be returned during this particular week.

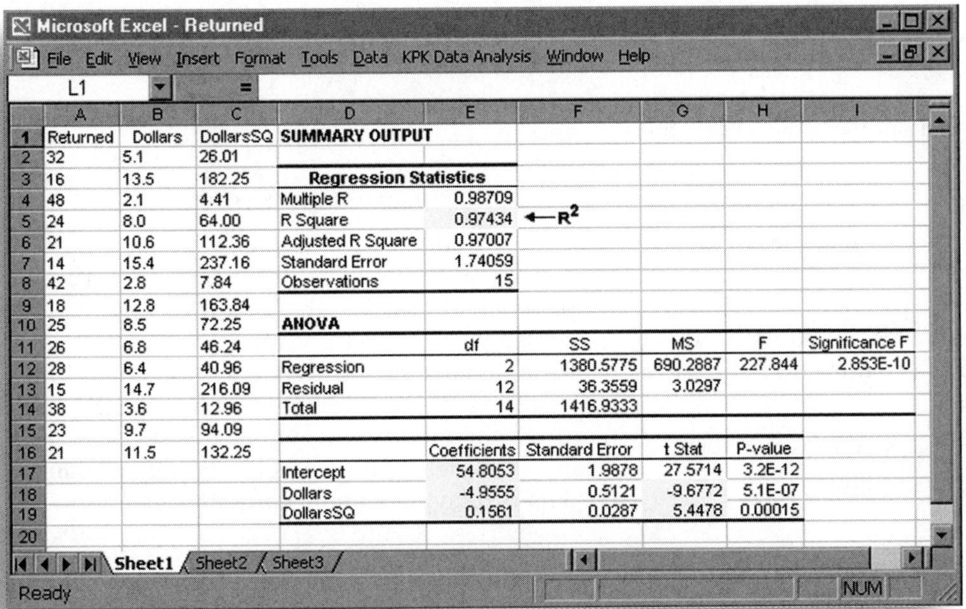

FIGURE 15.11

Excel solution to Example 15.8 using $Y = \beta_0 = \beta_1 X + \beta_2 X^2$.

	A	B	C	D	E	F	G	H	I
1	Returned	Dollars	DollarsSQ	SUMMARY OUTPUT					
2	32	5.1	26.01						
3	16	13.5	182.25	**Regression Statistics**					
4	48	2.1	4.41	Multiple R	0.98709				
5	24	8.0	64.00	R Square	0.97434	←R²			
6	21	10.6	112.36	Adjusted R Square	0.97007				
7	14	15.4	237.16	Standard Error	1.74059				
8	42	2.8	7.84	Observations	15				
9	18	12.8	163.84						
10	25	8.5	72.25	ANOVA					
11	26	6.8	46.24		df	SS	MS	F	Significance F
12	28	6.4	40.96	Regression	2	1380.5775	690.2887	227.844	2.853E-10
13	15	14.7	216.09	Residual	12	36.3559	3.0297		
14	38	3.6	12.96	Total	14	1416.9333			
15	23	9.7	94.09						
16	21	11.5	132.25		Coefficients	Standard Error	t Stat	P-value	
17				Intercept	54.8053	1.9878	27.5714	3.2E-12	
18				Dollars	-4.9555	0.5121	-9.6772	5.1E-07	
19				DollarsSQ	0.1561	0.0287	5.4478	0.00015	
20									

Solution 2 We first examine the F test. Our first test of hypothesis determines whether the overall model has predictive ability.

$$H_0: \beta_1 = \beta_2 = 0$$

$$H_a: \text{at least one of the } \beta\text{'s} \neq 0$$

Using the R^2 value from Figure 15.11 (in cell E5) and equation 15.15,

$$F^* = \frac{.97434/2}{.02566/(15-2-1)} = \frac{.97434/2}{.02566/12} = 227.8$$

As we might have suspected, this model does have significant predictive ability; $F^* = 227.8$ exceeds $F_{\alpha,k,n-k-1} = F_{.10,2,12} = 2.81$ from Table A.7.

Now we want to look at the t tests (same as partial F tests). Here, we examine each variable in the model, namely, X and X^2. The t value from Table A.5 is $t_{.10,12} = 1.356$ for a one-tailed test. We want to determine first whether $X_1 = $ inspection expenditure should be included in the model. Increased expenditure should be associated with decreased returns, so β_1 should be less than zero. We will therefore use a one-tailed procedure to test $H_0: \beta_1 \geq 0$ versus $H_a: \beta_1 < 0$.

According to Figure 15.11, the computed t statistic is $t^* = b_1/(\text{standard deviation of } b_1) = -9.68$ (highlighted). Now, $t^* = -9.68 < -1.356$, which means that the expenditure variable should be retained as a predictor of returns.

Next, we want to determine whether $X_2 = $ (inspection expenditures)^2 contributes significantly to the prediction of number returned. We are asking whether including the *quadratic term* was necessary. If this model is the correct one, then according to Figure 15.10a, β_2 should not only be unequal to zero but also, more specifically, should be greater than zero. This follows because if the number of returned motors does, in fact, level off after a certain amount of inspection expenditures, the curve should resemble the left half of the quadratic curve in Figure 15.10a.

The appropriate hypotheses are

$$H_0: \beta_2 \leq 0$$

$$H_a: \beta_2 > 0$$

We reject H_0 if $t > t_{.10,12} = 1.356$.

From Figure 15.11, we see that $t^* = b_2/(\text{standard deviation of } b_2) = 5.45$ (highlighted). This value lies in the rejection region, so we conclude that $\beta_2 > 0$, which means that the quadratic term, X^2, contributes significantly and in the correct direction.

Comments

There are three points you should note about the curvilinear model.

1. Curvilinear models often are used for situations in which the rate of increase or decrease in the dependent variable is not constant when plotted against a particular independent variable. The use of X^2 (and in some cases, X^3) in your model allows you to capture this nonlinear relationship between your variables.

2. There are other methods available for modeling a nonlinear relationship, including

$$Y = \beta_0 + \beta_1\left(\frac{1}{X}\right) + \text{error}$$

and

$$Y = \beta_0 + \beta_1 e^{-x} + \text{error}$$

These models also are (simple, here) linear regressions; they are linear in the unknown parameters. Unlike the quadratic model discussed previously, these models involve a **transformation** of the independent variable, X. When replacing X by the transformed X (such as $1/X$ or e^{-x}) in the model, one obtains many other curvilinear models that may better fit a set of sample data displaying a nonlinear pattern.

3. Avoid using the model $Y = \beta_0 + \beta_1 X + \beta_2 X^2 + e$ for values of X outside the range of data used in the

FIGURE

15.12

Error resulting
from extrapolation.
See text and
Figure 15.10*a*.

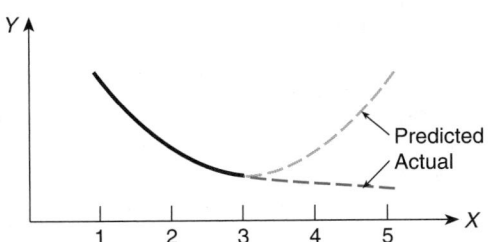

analysis. Extrapolation is extremely dangerous when using this modeling technique. Consider Figure 15.10*a*, and suppose that values of X between 1 and 3 were used to derive the estimate of β_0, β_1, and β_2. Figure 15.12 shows the results. For values of X larger than 3, the predicting equation will turn up, whereas the actual relationship will probably continue to level off. So this model works for interpolation (for values of X between 1 and 3, here) but is extremely unreliable for extrapolation.

X Exercises 15.21–15.30

Understanding the Mechanics

15.21 The SSE and SST for a regression equation with three independent variables were found to be 26 and 250, respectively. The number of observations was 10.
  a. Calculate the R^2 value.
  b. Calculate the adjusted R^2 value.

15.22 A researcher collected data from 28 individuals. Seven independent variables were used to predict a dependent variable. The value of R^2 for this model was .87. When the variables X_1 and X_3 were omitted from the model, R^2 was .84. Do the variables X_1 and X_3 contribute to the prediction of the dependent variable? Use a .10 significance level.

Applying the New Concepts

15.23 The manager of the personnel department of a computer firm is interested in knowing the relationship between the pay raise (Y) given to an employee of the firm and the following variables: yearly performance evaluation (X_1), years with the company (X_2), and number of credit hours of computer courses that the employee has taken in college (X_3). After observing 50 employees under different values of X_1, X_2, and X_3, the manager wishes to test that X_2 and X_3 contribute to predicting the variation in pay raises. The coefficient of determination for the model involving just Y and X_1 is .71. The coefficient of determination for the model with X_1, X_2, and X_3 is .82. Do the additional independent variables contribute significantly to the model? Use a 5% significance level.

15.24 According to Professor David Douglas of the University of Arkansas in "The Changing Language Mix in Information Systems Curricula" in the *1998 Proceedings of*

Decision Sciences Institute, the computer programming courses of COBOL, C, C++, Java, and Visual Basic will be among the dominant programming languages expected of future information systems graduates. Suppose that a career placement director wished to determine the relationship between a student's starting salary and two independent variables: a proficiency score in programming languages and a score measuring interpersonal skills. Data collected from 83 graduates of an information systems program yielded a coefficient of determination of .64.
  a. Using a significance level of 1%, what conclusion can you make about the contribution that these two prediction scores make to the prediction of starting salaries?
  b. What is the value of the adjusted R^2? How does this compare with the value of R^2?

15.25 The dean of the college of business at Fargo University would like to see whether several variables affect a student's grade point average. Thirty first-year students were randomly selected and data were collected on the following variables:

  Y = grade point average for the first year

  X_1 = average time spent per month at fraternity or sorority functions

  X_2 = average time spent per month working part time

  X_3 = total number of hours of coursework attempted

The SSE for the least squares line involving only Y and X_1 was found to be 5.21. The SSE for the complete model was found to be 4.31. The SST is 24.1. At the 5% significance level, test the null hypothesis that the independent variables X_2 and X_3 do not contribute to predicting the variation in Y, given that X_1 is already in the model.

15.26 The market capitalization of major oil companies is partly driven by the company's oil/gas reserves. Royal Dutch Shell Group has by far the largest amount of oil/gas reserves, exceeding 19 billion barrel equivalents of oil and gas. This company also has the largest market capitalization. Suppose that an energy consultant wished to determine the relationship between an oil company's oil/gas reserves (in units of billions of barrel equivalents of oil and gas) and market capitalization (in units of billions of dollars).

Oil Company	Market Capitalization (Y)	Oil/Gas Reserves (X)	Square of Oil/ Gas Reserves (X^2)
Enron	13.1	1.2	1.44
Repsol	12.3	1.4	1.96
Phillips	12.0	2.5	6.25
Arco	13.8	4.2	17.64
Texaco	25.3	4.8	23.04
Amoco	31.1	6.8	46.24
Chevron	51.3	7.1	50.41
Mobil	53.2	7.4	54.76
Exxon	174.9	14.2	201.64
RD Shell Group	181.7	19.4	376.36

a. The R^2 for the regression equation $\hat{Y} = -18.035 + 10.856X$ is 91.78%. Test that the variable oil/gas reserves contributes to the prediction of market capitalization. Use a 1% significance level.

b. The R^2 for the regression equation $\hat{Y} = -9.045 + 7.857X + .150X^2$ is 92.29%. Test that the variable oil/gas reserves and the square of this variable contribute to the prediction of market capitalization. Use a 1% significance level.

c. What is the adjusted value of R^2 for the model in parts a and b? Since the value of the adjusted R^2 does not increase in value for the model in part b, what conclusion can you make about the appropriateness of adding the square term to the model?

(Source: "BP-Amoco Would Set New Standards," *The Wall Street Journal*, August 13, 1998, p. A3.)

15.27 Professor Xenophon Koufteros of The University of Texas at El Paso and Professors Mark Vonderembse and William Doll of The University of Toledo have performed a large-scale study to understand the impact that manufacturing practices have on throughput time reduction. A random sample of 244 firms was used to collect data on throughput time (TT) as well as on pull production (PP) and quality improvement effort (QI). For the regression equation predicting TT using PP and QI, the MSE was .85851 and the total sum of squares was 242.67012. Use the following table to determine which independent variables should be included in the model assuming a 5% significance level. What is the value of R^2? How does this compare to the value of the adjusted R^2?

Variable	Coefficient	Standard Deviation
Pull Production (PP)	−.1268	.0586
Quality Improvement Effort (QI)	−.291539	.2061

(Source: "How to Cut Manufacturing Throughput Time," *1998 Proceedings of the Decision Sciences Institute*, pp. 1433–35.)

15.28 An economist would like to examine the relationship between personal savings and the following independent variables:

X_1 = total personal income

X_2 = yield on U.S. government securities

X_3 = consumer price index

The following data were collected for 14 randomly selected months:

Y	X_1	X_2	X_3	Y	X_1	X_2	X_3
80.2	2077.2	12.036	233.2	107.4	2179.4	9.259	249.4
91.6	2086.4	12.814	236.4	116.8	2205.7	10.321	252.7
87.4	2101.0	15.526	239.8	102.1	2234.3	11.580	253.9
104.9	2102.1	14.003	242.5	97.9	2257.6	13.888	256.2
116.2	2114.1	9.150	244.9	93.3	2276.6	15.661	258.4
109.1	2127.1	6.995	247.6	83.6	2300.7	14.724	260.5
110.1	2161.2	8.126	247.8	91.0	2318.2	14.905	263.2

a. Using a computerized statistical package, determine the least squares equation for these data.

b. Use only the variables X_1 and X_2. What is the new prediction equation?

c. Does the variable X_3 contribute to predicting the variation in personal savings, given that X_1 and X_2 are in the model? Use a 10% significance level.

Using the Computer

15.29 **[DATA SET EX15-29]** *Variable description:*

CompPerf: Computer performance

CompEffic: Self-perception of computer self-efficacy

Loyalty: Self-perception of company loyalty

CompanyYrs: Number of years with the company

Professor Bassam Hasan of Macon State College and Professor Brian Reithel of University of Mississippi have investigated computer performance with measures of self-efficacy. They employ social cognitive theory (SCT) to develop a model to predict computer performance. Self-efficacy refers to "people's judgments of their capabilities to organize and execute courses of action required to attain designated types of performance," according to their study in "Performance In Computer Training: Identifying Critical Factors," in the *1998 Proceedings of Decision Sciences Institute*. Suppose that a random sample of 25 employees working in the Information Technology Department of a corporation are sampled. The dependent variable is computer performance, and the independent variables are measures of computer self-efficacy, company loyalty, and number of years with the company. The variables computer self-efficacy and loyalty are measured on a scale from 1 to 7, and computer performance is a score from 1 to 100.

a. Find the regression equation predicting CompPerf using CompEffic. Comment on the fit of the regression line to the data.

b. Find the regression equation predicting CompPerf using CompEffic, Loyalty, and CompanyYrs. Using a 5%

significance level, do the variables Loyalty and CompanyYrs contribute to the prediction of CompPerf, given that CompEffic is in the model?

15.30 [DATA SET EX15-30] *Variable description:*

NintendoExpend: Amount of money spent by a family on Nintendo games

GamesExpend: Amount of money spent by a family on computer games other than Nintendo

TimeOwnGames: Length of time that a family has owned computer games

In 1994, Nintendo of Canada Ltd. reported an 11% drop in hardware sales after six strong years of double-digit increases. The company claimed that more than one in three Canadian families owned a Nintendo system. Suppose that an analyst wished to determine the relationship between the amount of money spent on Nintendo games (NintendoExpend) and the independent variables GamesExpend and TimeOwnGames. A random sample of 35 Canadian families who had purchased Nintendo games was obtained.

a. Do the variables GamesExpend and TimeOwnGames contribute to the prediction of NintendoExpend? Use a 5% significance level.

b. Take the natural logarithm of NintendoExpend and use this variable as the dependent variable in part a. Do you believe that this model explains the relationship between the dependent and independent variables better than in part a?

(Source: "Nintendo Sales Miss Intended Mark," *Toronto Star*, January 5, 1994, p. D2.)

THE PROBLEM OF MULTICOLLINEARITY

15.4

Another possible title for this section is: What do the individual b_i's tell you? We discuss one of the common problems in the use (or misuse) of multiple linear regression—namely, trying to extract more information from the results than they actually contain.

We examine the validity of such statements as: Because $b_1 = 10$, increasing X_1 by 1 *while holding X_2 constant* will result in an increase of 10 in Y.

Assume that a sample of 10 employees at Bellaire Industries was examined in an effort to determine the ability of age (X_1) and years of experience (X_2) to predict an employee's salary (Y). The following data were obtained:

Employee	Y (Salary)	X_1 (Age)	X_2 (Years of Experience)
1	62	52	33
2	45	47	21
3	55	38	14
4	38	25	3
5	52	44	18
6	70	55	30
7	41	36	8
8	48	40	15
9	43	32	7
10	58	50	27

First, we can ask how well X_1 (age) predicts Y (salary).

An Excel solution using the model $Y = \beta_0 + \beta_1 \cdot (\text{age}) + e$ is shown in Figure 15.13. Notice the computed t value. Now, $k = 1$ because this model considers only one independent variable, so the tabulated value for comparison (using $\alpha = .10$) is $t_{\alpha/2,n-k-1} = t_{.05,10-1-1} = t_{.05,8} = 1.860$. The value of $t^* = 4.60$ is considerably larger than 1.86, so X_1 (age) is an excellent predictor of Y (salary).

What is the correlation between X_1 and Y? It seems reasonable that it would be quite large, because age has been shown to be a good predictor. This correlation is highlighted in cell G3 in Figure 15.13, and its value is .852. To obtain the array of correlations in cells G3, G4 and H4, click on **Tools ➤ Data Analysis ➤ Correlation** and enter "A1:C11" as the **Input Range** and "F1" as the **Output**

FIGURE

15.13

Excel solution to
$\hat{Y} = b_0 + b_1 \cdot$ (age).
Correlation
between salary
and age is in
cell G3.

Range. Be sure to click on the box alongside **Labels** (there are labels in the first row). Since the correlation between these two variables is .852, we conclude that there is a *positive* relationship between age and salary, as we would expect.

Next, we determine how well X_2 (years of experience) predicts Y (salary). The solution using $Y = \beta_0 + \beta_1 \times$ (years of experience) $+ e$ is shown in Figure 15.14. Once again, the computed t value $= t^* = 5.21$ is much larger than $t_{.05,8} = 1.860$, and the correlation between these two variables (highlighted in cell G4) is .879. This result is not surprising; we might expect people with more years of experience to have higher salaries. Consequently, a significant positive relationship appears to exist between these two variables.

Finally, we turn to the question, how well do both X_1 (age) and X_2 (years of experience) predict salary? The model here is $Y = \beta_0 + \beta_1 X_1 + \beta_2 X_2 + e$. The least squares solution is shown in Figure 15.15.

$$\hat{Y} = 36.1 - .014 X_1 + .890 X_2$$

A few seemingly bizarre things show up here.

The coefficient of X_1 is $b_1 = -.014$. This result would appear to indicate that larger values of X_1 (older people) produce smaller salaries. But we know from our first analysis that the *opposite* is true. We would have expected a *positive* value of b_1 here, and so the coefficient of X_1 appears to have the wrong sign.

The small t values also are puzzling. The value of the F statistic (using Figure 15.15) is

$$F^* = \frac{R^2/2}{(1 - R^2)/(10 - 1 - 2)} = \frac{.7726/2}{.2274/7} = 11.89$$

This value is also contained in the ANOVA table, where

$$F^* = \frac{MSR}{MSE} = \frac{357.55}{30.07} = 11.89$$

Using $\alpha = .10$, this value is much larger than $F_{.10,2,7} = 3.26$, and so the model does provide a very good predictor of Y. The coefficient of determination is $R^2 = .77$; these two predictor variables explain 77% of the total variation in the ten salary values.

FIGURE

15.14

Excel solution to $\hat{Y} = b_0 + b_1 \cdot$ (years of experience). Correlation between salary and years of experience is in cell G4.

FIGURE

15.15

Excel solution to $\hat{Y} = b_0 + b_1 \cdot$ (age) $+ b_2 \cdot$ (years of experience). Correlation between age (X_1) and years of experience (X_2) is in cell H4.

The t values are very small; both are smaller in absolute value than $t_{\alpha/2, n-k-1} = t_{.05, 10-2-1} = t_{.05, 7} = 1.895$. Does this imply that both predictors are weak and should be removed from the model? Certainly not, as our previous analysis made clear.

This example demonstrates the problem of **multicollinearity.** In multiple regression models, it is desirable for each independent variable, X, to be highly correlated with Y, but it is *not* desirable for the X's to be highly correlated *with each other.* In business applications of multiple linear regression, the independent variables typically have a certain amount of pairwise correlation (usually positive). Extremely high correlation between any pair of variables can cause a variety of problems, as we will show.

The (sample) correlation between X_1 and X_2 is

$$r = \frac{\sum X_1 X_2 - (\sum X_1)(\sum X_2)/n}{\sqrt{\sum X_1^2 - (\sum X_1)^2/n}\ \sqrt{\sum X_2^2 - (\sum X_2)^2/n}}$$

This value, using the highlighted correlation in Figure 15.15, is $r = .970$. Notice in the data set that nearly every time X_1 increases, so does X_2; X_1 and X_2 are highly correlated. As a result, these data contain a great deal of multicollinearity.

Implications

First of all, the correlation of X_1 and X_2 explains the small t values. Remember that each t value describes the contribution of that particular independent variable *after* all other independent variables have been included in the model. X_1 is very nearly a linear function of X_2 (as evidenced by $r = .970$), so it contributes very little to the prediction of Y, given that X_2 is in the model. The same argument applies to X_2. This means that neither X_1 nor X_2 is a strong predictor given that the other variable is included—not that each one is a weak predictor by itself.

The second implication of the multicollinearity is that the situation in which X_1 increases by 1 while X_2 remains constant never occurred in the sample data—as X_1 increased by 1, X_2 always changed also, because X_1 and X_2 are highly correlated.

Finally, the sample coefficients (b_1 and b_2) of our independent variables have very large variances. If we took another sample from this population, the values of b_1 and b_2 probably would change dramatically—this is not a good situation. In fact, as this example has demonstrated, these coefficients can even have the "wrong" sign, a sign different from that obtained when regressing X_1 or X_2 alone on Y.

Detecting Multicollinearity: Variance Inflation Factors

Whenever you perform a multiple regression analysis, it is always a good idea to examine the pairwise correlations between all of your variables, including the dependent variable. In this way, you can often detect two variables that are contributing to the multicollinearity problem.

These correlations can be obtained using a single command with most computer packages. The Excel procedure to generate a table (often called a *correlation matrix*) of pairwise correlations was discussed in the creation of Figure 15.13. This output indicates that the correlation between Y and X_1 is .852, that between Y and X_2 is .879, and that between X_1 and X_2 is .970. The high correlation between X_1 and X_2 is the reason multicollinearity exists for this illustration.

Since the correlation of any variable with itself is 1, this particular correlation matrix can be written as

$$\begin{array}{c}Y\\X_1\\X_2\end{array}\begin{array}{ccc}Y & X_1 & X_2\\ \begin{bmatrix}1.0 & .852 & .879\\ .852 & 1.0 & .970\\ .879 & .970 & 1.0\end{bmatrix}\end{array}$$

An examination of pairwise correlations is not a foolproof method of detecting multicollinearity problems, since a particular independent variable may be nearly a linear combination of several other independent variables, but still not be highly correlated pairwise with any of them. Consequently, an examination of the correlation matrix would fail to detect this relationship.

Suppose a regression analysis contains 10 predictor variables and that variable X_6 is nearly a linear combination of X_3, X_5, and X_9. Consequently,

$$X_6 \approx a_0 + a_1 X_3 + a_2 X_5 + a_3 X_9$$

for some set of constants a_0, a_1, a_2, and a_3. How can we detect if such a relationship exists? This is accomplished very simply, by treating X_6 as a dependent variable and using variables X_3, X_5, and X_9 as independent variables in a regression analysis. If this relationship is present in the data, the resulting R^2 will be very high. This large value of R^2 is your warning that this independent variable is contributing to the multicollinearity problem.

Fortunately, it is not necessary to examine each independent variable in this way. Most computer packages will compute a statistic referred to as a **variance inflation factor** for each independent variable. The variance inflation factor for variable X_j is defined as

$$VIF_j = \frac{1}{1 - R_j^2}$$

15.19

where R_j^2 is the coefficient of determination obtained by regressing X_j on the remaining $k - 1$ independent variables. If R_j^2 is large (close to 1.0), then VIF_j will be large. *A commonly used procedure here is to conclude that severe multicollinearity exists in the sample data if the maximum VIF_j is larger than 10.*

The Excel regression procedure does not provide the variance inflation factors, but these values are available when using **KPK Data Analysis ➤ Regression**. Using this on the previous illustration with age and years of experience as predictors of salary (see Figure 15.15), enter "A1:A11" in the **Y Range** box and "B1:C11" as the **Contiguous X Range**. These ranges *must* include labels in the first row. Next, enter "D1" as the **Output Range** and be sure to click on the box alongside **VIFs**. The resulting output is shown in Figure 15.16, where the VIFs (both equal to 16.9) are highlighted in cells K18 and K19. Note that the VIFs for both X_1 and X_2 are equal (such is always the case when using only two predictor variables), and both exceed 10. In Figure 15.15, we saw that the correlation between X_1 and X_2 is .970. When regressing X_1 on X_2 (or vice versa), the resulting R^2 is the square of this correlation; that is, $R_1^2 = R_2^2 = (.970)^2 = .941$. The resulting values for VIF_1 and VIF_2 are

$$VIF_1 = VIF_2 = \frac{1}{1 - .941} = 16.9$$

FIGURE

15.16

Excel solution to $\hat{Y} = b_0 + b_1 \cdot$ (age) $+ b_2 \cdot$ (years of experience) using KPK Data Analysis regression procedure, including calculation of variance inflation factors.

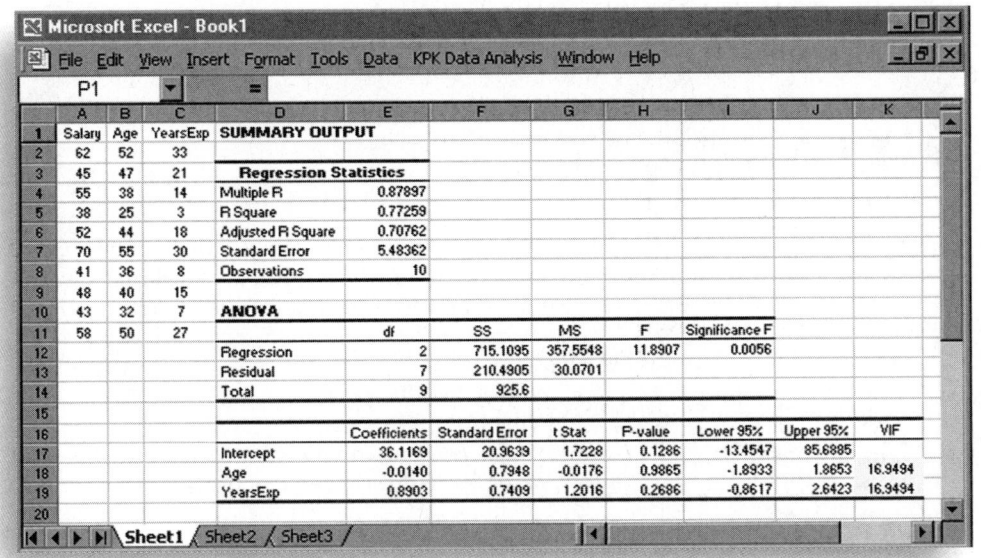

which agree with the Excel results. The easiest way out of this dilemma is to remove one of these predictor variables from the model. The best procedure here would be to retain X_2 = years of experience, because it has the highest correlation with Y.

A Final Look at Multicollinearity

Another method of eliminating correlated predictor variables is to use a **stepwise** selection procedure. This technique of selecting the variables to be used in a multiple linear regression equation is discussed in the next section. Essentially, it selects variables one at a time and generally (although not always) does not insert into the regression equation a variable that is highly correlated with a variable already in the equation. In the previous example, a stepwise procedure would have selected variable X_2 (the single best predictor of Y) and then informed the user that X_1 did not significantly improve the prediction of Y, given that X_2 was already included in the prediction equation.

Other, more advanced methods of detecting and treating the multicollinearity problem are beyond the scope of this text. One of the more popular procedures is *ridge regression.**

We have seen that the problem of multicollinearity enters into our regression analysis when an independent variable is highly correlated with one or more other independent variables. Multicollinearity produces inflated regression coefficients that can even have the wrong sign. Also, the resulting t statistics can be small, making it difficult to determine the predictive ability of an individual variable. Therefore, $b_1, b_2, \ldots$ tell us nothing about the partial effect of each variable, unless we can demonstrate that there is no correlation among our predictor variables. In business applications, correlation (in particular, *positive* correlation) among the independent variables is far from unusual.

As a final note, care should be taken in the selection of a model not to include variables that will be likely to produce multicollinearity. The detection and correction of the multicollinearity problem is often difficult to accomplish, and the methods discussed in this section are open to debate. The treatments of multicollinearity discussed so far are highly data dependent; that is, a new set of data could very well produce different results. Also, examining pairwise correlations may well miss the presence of multicollinearity, since multicollinearity will exist when one predictor variable is nearly a linear combination of two or more predictor variables and is not highly correlated with either of them. *In short, there is no easy way out of the multicollinearity problem.*

---

*For an excellent discussion of this topic, see J. Neter, M. Kutner, and C. Nachtscheim, *Applied Linear Regression Models*, 3rd ed. (Homewood, Ill.: Richard D. Irwin, 1996).

X Exercises 15.31–15.38

Understanding the Mechanics

15.31 Which independent variables appear to contribute to high multicollinearity? Use the following correlation matrix.

	Y	X_1	X_2	X_3	X_4	X_5
Y	1.00	.80	.95	.32	.41	.50
X_1	.80	1.00	.98	.03	.25	.41
X_2	.95	.98	1.00	.12	.22	.03
X_3	.32	.03	.12	1.00	.10	.27
X_4	.41	.25	.22	.10	1.00	.97
X_5	.50	.41	.03	.27	.97	1.00

15.32 A regression equation uses three independent variables to predict Y. The coefficient of determination for regressing X_1 on variables X_2 and X_3 is .95. The coefficient of determination for regressing X_2 on variables X_1 and X_3 is .85.

a. What is the VIF for X_1?

b. What is the VIF for X_2?

c. Would you say multicollinearity may present a problem for this regression equation?

Applying the New Concepts

15.33 The following table displays the top 10 prime-time television programs in April 1998 along with their rating and share of the market (both in units of percentage). Market share is defined as the percentage of all switched-on sets turned to the show in question.

Program Name	Rating	Share of Market
ER	30.6	33
Seinfeld	18.9	23
CBS Sunday movie,		
The Echo of Thunder	16.4	26
Veronica's Closet	15.9	24
Friends	15.3	26
Just Shoot Me	14.4	24
60 Minutes	12.5	23
Dateline NBC Tuesday	12.0	21
Law and Order	11.9	20
Dateline NBC Monday	11.5	20

a. In the computer printout, with share of market regressed on rating and the square of rating, is multicollinearity a concern?

b. From the correlation between rating and the square of rating, calculate the VIF for each of the independent variables.

c. Can one calculate the VIFs from the correlation values if there are more than two independent variables?

(Source: "Top 10 Prime-Time Programs," *The Wall Street Journal*, April 23, 1998, p. A16.)

Summary Output for Exercise 15.33

SUMMARY OUTPUT

Regression Statistics	
Multiple R	0.91045
R Square	0.82891
Adjusted R Square	0.78003
Standard Error	1.79618
Observations	10

ANOVA

	df	SS	MS	F	Significance F
Regression	2	109.41628	54.70814	16.95721	0.00207
Residual	7	22.58372	3.22625		
Total	9	132			

	Coefficients	Standard Error	t Stat	P-value	Lower 95%	Upper 95%
Intercept	11.64160	7.30247	1.59420	0.15492	-5.62598	28.90919
Rating	0.89455	0.77799	1.14982	0.28798	-0.94511	2.73421
Rating Squared	-0.00671	0.01838	-0.36531	0.72567	-0.05018	0.03675

Correlation between Rating and Rating Squared	0.99077

15.34 A manager collected 40 observations on three variables to predict worker proficiency. The manager computed the least squares equation to be $\hat{Y} = 30 - 501X_1 + 300X_2 + 1.8X_3$. The manager collected another set of observations using the same variables and found the least squares equation to be $\hat{Y} = -20 + 204X_1 - 98X_2 + 1.9X_3$. Is there any explanation for these two different prediction equations?

15.35 A financial analyst uses four independent variables to predict the earnings of a company. Construct a correlation matrix to determine if multicollinearity appears to be a problem with using all four independent variables. Compute the least squares equation using independent variables that do not contribute to the multicollinearity problem.

Y	X_1	X_2	X_3	X_4
40	3	5	12	18
40	4	6	14	21
47	5	8	15	23
47	6	9	13	22
45	5	7	17	27
36	4	6	21	34
27	6	9	32	48
29	8	12	42	63
36	3	5	18	27
35	4	6	25	40

15.36 Consider the following set of data for 12 emerging growth-oriented companies. Y represents the growth rate of a company for the current year, X_1 represents the growth rate of the company for the previous year, and X_2 represents the percent of the market that does not use the company's product or a similar product. All values are percentages.

Y	X_1	X_2	Y	X_1	X_2
20	10	30	30	15	60
24	12	35	36	42	38
18	15	25	47	45	40
33	30	40	35	32	32
27	19	32	28	24	31
20	24	20	32	20	50

a. Construct the correlation matrix for the variables. Does multicollinearity appear to be a problem?

b. Find the coefficient of determination for the model with only X_1 included in the model.

c. Find the coefficient of determination for the model with only X_2 in the model.

d. The coefficient of determination for the complete model is .896. Does it appear from observing the values of the coefficient of determination in parts a and b that both variables X_1 and X_2 should stay in the model?

Using the Computer

15.37 [DATA SET EX15-37] *Variable description:*

StockPercent: Percentage of portfolio in stocks

BondPercent: Percentage of portfolio in bonds

Performance: Percentage return of the portfolio six months later

During the 11 years that the *Wall Street Journal* has tracked asset-allocation advice offered by major investment firms, strategists have recommended holding an average of 12% cash. In 1998, the average was only 6% Suppose that 50 financial strategists were asked what percentage of their portfolio should be in stocks and bonds. The performance of the corresponding portfolio was recorded six months later.

a. Regress Performance on StockPercent and BondPercent. Does the model contribute to the prediction of Performance using a 5% significance level?

b. Does each of the independent variables contribute to the prediction of Performance assuming the other independent variable is included in the model? Use a 5% significance level.

c. Find the VIF of StockPercent and BondPercent. Do you believe that there is a multicollinearity problem within the data?

(Source: "The Wisdom of Wall Street Is Decidedly Short on Cash," *The Wall Street Journal,* April 30, 1998, p. C1.)

15.38 [DATA SET 15-38] *Variable description:*

SalesMonth: Sales of discount department store during the previous month

AgeStore: Age of the store

ExperManager: Years of experience of store manager

Many of the newly opened discount department stores sell more merchandise than similar older stores. However, over time these stores' sales tend to level off. To understand the relationship between the sales of a discount department store and the age of a store, a manager randomly selected 35 stores with approximately the same square footage. The sales of the previous month and the age of the store are recorded as variables SalesMonth (in thousands of dollars) and AgeStore (in years). A regional executive is interested in the relationship between SalesMonth and the independent variables AgeStore and ExperManager (years of experience of store manager).

a. Construct the model in which the regional executive is interested. Comment on the contribution of the independent variables used to predict SalesMonth assuming a significance level of 5%.

b. Add the squares of the variables AgeStore and ExperManager to the model in part a and comment on the appropriateness of adding these terms.

c. Find the correlations between the independent variables in part b. What conclusion can you make about possible problems with multicollinearity?

d. Find the VIFs for the independent variables in part b. What conclusion can you make about the level of multicollinearity?

15.5

DUMMY VARIABLES AND ADDITIONAL TOPICS IN MULTIPLE LINEAR REGRESSION

The use of **dummy,** or **indicator, variables** in a regression analysis allows you to include *qualitative* variables in the model. For example, if you wanted to include an employee's gender as a predictor variable in a regression model, define

$$X_1 = \begin{cases} 1 & \text{if female} \\ 0 & \text{if male} \end{cases}$$

Note that the choice of which gender is assigned the value of 1, male or female, is arbitrary. The estimated value of Y will be the same, regardless of which coding procedure is used.

Returning to the data we used in Example 15.2, the real-estate developer noticed that all the houses in the population were from three neighborhoods, A, B, and C. Taking note of which neighborhood each of the sampled houses was from led to the following data (in the discussion following Example 15.2, $X_3 = $ years of education was shown to be a weak predictor and so is removed from the model here):

Family	Home Square Footage (Y)	Income (X_1)	Family Size (X_2)	Neighborhood
1	16	32	2	B
2	17	36	2	C
3	26	55	3	A
4	24	47	4	C
5	22	38	4	B
6	21	60	3	C
7	32	66	6	B
8	18	44	3	B
9	30	70	5	A
10	20	50	3	A

Using these data, we can construct the necessary dummy variables and determine whether they contribute significantly to the prediction of home size (Y).

One way to code neighborhoods would be to define

$$X_3 = \begin{cases} 0 & \text{if neighborhood A} \\ 1 & \text{if neighborhood B} \\ 2 & \text{if neighborhood C} \end{cases}$$

However, this type of coding has many problems. First, because $0 < 1 < 2$, the codes imply that neighborhood A is smaller than neighborhood B, which is smaller than neighborhood C. Furthermore, any difference between neighborhoods A and C receives twice the weight (because $2 - 0 = 2$) of any difference between neighborhoods A and B or B and C. So this coding transforms data that are actually *nominal* to data that are *interval*, a much stronger type.

A better procedure is to use the necessary number of dummy variables (coded 0 or 1) to represent the neighborhoods. We needed one dummy variable with two categories (male and female) to specify a person's gender. To represent the three neighborhoods, we use two dummy variables by letting

$$X_3 = \begin{cases} 1 & \text{if house is in A} \\ 0 & \text{otherwise} \end{cases} \quad \text{and} \quad X_4 = \begin{cases} 1 & \text{if house is in B} \\ 0 & \text{otherwise} \end{cases}$$

Note that as for the male/female dummy variable, this coding is arbitrary as far as the prediction, $\hat{Y}$, is concerned. We could have assigned $X_3 = 0$ and $X_4 = 0$ to neighborhood A, with $X_3 = 1$ for B and $X_4 = 1$ for C.

What happened to neighborhood C? It is not necessary to develop a third dummy variable here because we have the following scheme:

House Is in Neighborhood	X_3	X_4
A	1	0
B	0	1
C	0	0

In fact, it can be shown that a third dummy variable is not only unnecessary, it is very important that you not include it. If you attempted to use three such dummy variables in your model, you would receive a message in your computer output informing you that "no solution exists" for this model. Suppose we had introduced a third dummy variable (say, X_5) that was equal to 1 if the house was in neighborhood C. For each observation in the sample, we would have

$$X_5 = 1 - X_3 - X_4$$

Whenever any one predictor variable is a linear function (including a constant term) of one or more other predictors, then mathematically *no solution* exists for the least squares coefficients, since you have multicollinearity at its

FIGURE

15.17

Excel solution (partial output) to real-estate dummy variable problem. (A) Solution using X_1, X_2, X_3, and X_4. (B) Solution using variables X_1 and X_2.

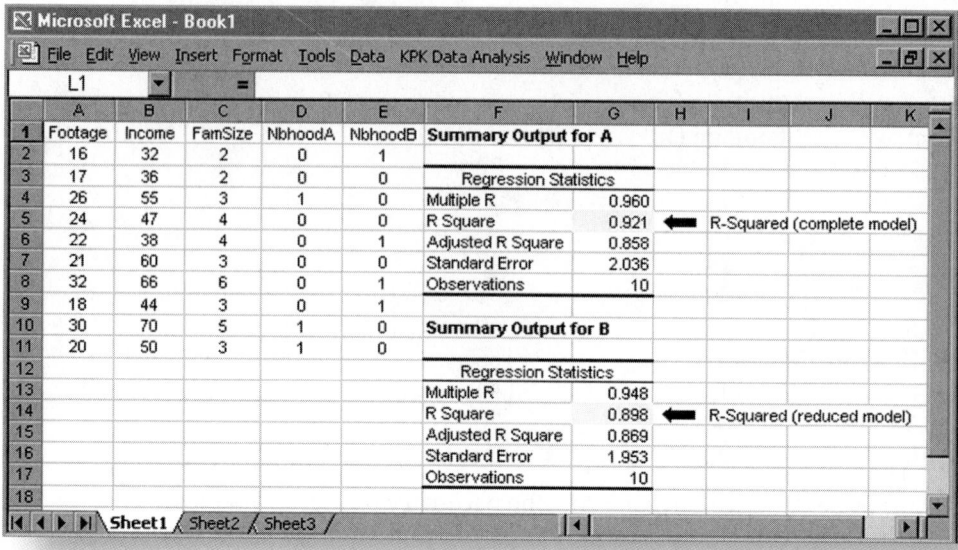

worst. To arrive at a usable equation, any such predictor variable must not be included.

The resulting model here is*

$$Y = \beta_0 + \beta_1 X_1 + \beta_2 X_2 + \beta_3 X_3 + \beta_4 X_4 + e$$

The final array of data (ready for input into a computer program) is

Row	Y	X_1	X_2	X_3	X_4	Row	Y	X_1	X_2	X_3	X_4
1	16	32	2	0	1	6	21	60	3	0	0
2	17	36	2	0	0	7	32	66	6	0	1
3	26	55	3	1	0	8	18	44	3	0	1
4	24	47	4	0	0	9	30	70	5	1	0
5	22	38	4	0	1	10	20	50	3	1	0

where Y = square footage of home, X_1 = income, X_2 = family size, $X_3 = 1$ if neighborhood A, and $X_4 = 1$ if neighborhood B.

An abbreviated Excel solution using all four predictors is shown in Figure 15.17A. To determine whether the particular neighborhood has any effect on the prediction of home size, we test

$$H_0\colon \beta_3 = \beta_4 = 0 \quad \text{(if } X_1 \text{ and } X_2 \text{ are included)}$$

$$H_a\colon \beta_3 \text{ or } \beta_4 \text{ (or both)} \neq 0$$

In the complete model, the variables are X_1, X_2, X_3, and X_4, and from Figure 15.17A,

$$R_c^2 = .921$$

In the reduced model, the variables are X_1 and X_2 only, and from Figure 15.17B,

$$R_r^2 = .898$$

---

*Models that include dummy variables typically contain terms that reflect any interaction between the dummy variables and the other quantitative variables. For this model, this would amount to adding four additional terms to the model, namely, $X_1 X_3$, $X_1 X_4$, $X_2 X_3$, and $X_2 X_4$. Such a model would require a larger sample size (n) than that used in this illustration, since the model would then contain $k = 8$ predictor variables. This topic is explored further in Section 15.6.

At first glance, it does not appear that X_3 and X_4 produced a significant increase in R^2. The partial F test will determine whether this is true.

$$F = \frac{(R_c^2 - R_r^2)/(\text{number of } \beta\text{'s in } H_0)}{(1 - R_c^2)/[n - 1 - (\text{number of } X\text{'s in the complete model})]}$$

$$= \frac{(.921 - .898)/2}{(1 - .921)/(10 - 1 - 4)} = \frac{.023/2}{.079/5} = .73$$

Using $\alpha = .10$, this result is considerably less than $F_{.10,2,5} = 3.78$, so there is no evidence that the neighborhood dummy variables significantly improve the prediction of home size.

In this example, the dummy variables were not significant predictors in the model. However, do not let this mislead you. In many business applications, dummy variables representing location, weather conditions, yes/no situations, time, and many other variables can have a tremendous effect on improving the results of a multiple regression model.

Stepwise Procedures

Assume you wish to predict annual divisional profits for a large corporation using, among other techniques, a multiple linear regression model. Your strategy is to consider any variable that you think *could* have an effect on these profits. You have identified twelve such variables.

One possibility is to include all these variables in your model and to use the t tests to decide which variables are significant predictors. However, this procedure invites multicollinearity, because your model is more apt to include correlated predictors, severely hindering the interpretation of your model. In particular, two independent variables that are very highly correlated may both have small t values (as we saw in Section 15.4), causing you possibly to discard both of them from the model—this is *not* the right thing to do because you possibly should have retained one of them.

A better way to proceed here is to use one of the several stepwise selection procedures. These techniques either choose or eliminate variables, one at a time, in an effort not to include those variables that either have no predictive ability or are highly correlated with other predictor variables. A word of caution—these procedures do not provide a guarantee against multicollinearity; however, they greatly reduce the chances of including a large set of correlated independent variables.

These procedures consist of three different selection techniques: (1) forward regression, (2) backward regression, and (3) stepwise regression.

Forward Regression. The **forward regression** method of model selection puts variables into the equation, one at a time, beginning with that variable having the highest correlation (or R^2) with Y. For sake of argument, call this variable X_1.

Next, it examines the remaining variables for the variable that, when included with X_1, has the highest R^2. That predictor (with X_1) is inserted into the model. This procedure continues until adding the "best" remaining variable at that stage results in an insignificant increase in R^2 according to the partial F test.

Backward Regression. **Backward regression** is the opposite of forward regression: it begins with *all* variables in the model and, one by one, removes them. It begins by finding the "worst" variable—the one that causes the smallest decrease in R^2 when removed from the complete model. If the decrease is insignificant, this variable is removed, and the process continues.

The variable among those remaining in the model that causes the smallest decrease in the new R^2 is considered next. You continue this procedure of removing variables until a significant drop in R^2 is obtained, at which point you replace this significant predictor and terminate the selection.

FIGURE

15.18

Possible solution using stepwise regression on divisional profits data.

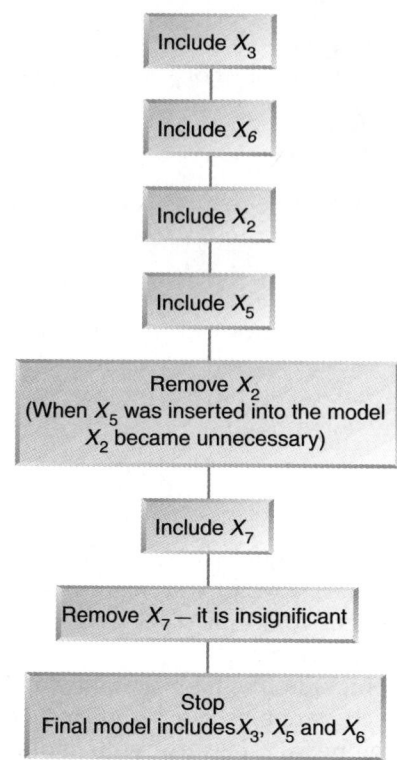

Will the model resulting from a backward regression be the same as that obtained using forward regression? Not necessarily; usually, however, the resulting models are very similar. Of course, if two variables are highly correlated, the forward procedure could choose one of the correlated predictors, whereas the backward procedure could choose the other.

Stepwise Regression.   The **stepwise regression** method is a modification of forward regression. *It is the most popular and flexible of the three selection techniques.* It proceeds exactly as does forward regression, except that at each stage it can *remove* any variable whose partial F value indicates that this variable does not contribute, given the present set of independent variables in the model. Like forward regression, it stops when the "best" variable among those remaining produces an insignificant increase in R^2.

Figure 15.18 illustrates this procedure for the example on predicting divisional profits (the data are not shown). Data from all 12 independent variables, as well as from Y, are used as input to a stepwise regression program. One possible outcome from this analysis is shown in Figure 15.18.

The stepwise solution for the data we used to predict home size is contained in the end-of-chapter SPSS appendix. As we previously determined, $X_3 =$ educational level does not contribute significantly, and so the resulting prediction equation includes only $X_1 =$ income and $X_2 =$ family size. This equation is

$$\hat{Y} = 5.091 + .165X_1 + 2.66X_2$$

Using Dummy Variables in Forward or Stepwise Regression.   We emphasized that $C - 1$ dummy variables should be used to represent C categories if *all* the dummy variables were to be inserted into the regression equation. When using a forward or stepwise regression procedure, this may not be the best way to proceed, as the following illustration shows.

Suppose you are using nine dummy (indicator) variables to represent 10 cities. The dependent variable is monthly sales, and the purpose is to determine which city (or cities) exhibits very large or very small sales. If a forward or stepwise selection procedure is used, then including one of these dummy variables indicates that specifying this particular city significantly improves the prediction of sales. In other words, it indicates that sales for this city are not just average but are much higher (its coefficient will be positive) or lower (its coefficient will be negative) than average.

When you use the forward or stepwise techniques, you probably will not include all nine dummy variables in the model. Your ability to predict sales (Y) is unaffected by not defining a tenth dummy variable and, in fact, as pointed out earlier, the regression analysis will not accept all 10 dummy variables.

For this situation, however, there is the danger of not detecting extremely high or low sales in the tenth city, which did not receive a dummy variable. When including these variables one at a time in the regression equation using a forward or stepwise procedure, we can allow the regression model to examine the effect of all 10 cities. We do this by defining 10 such dummy variables, one for each city.*

Because a forward regression procedure generally will not attempt to include all 10 dummy variables, you are able to investigate the existence of high or low sales in each of the 10 cities. When using dummy variables in a forward or stepwise regression procedure, it is perfectly acceptable to use C such variables to represent C categories.

Examining the Residuals

The topic of examining the sample residuals (values of $Y - \hat{Y}$) was introduced in Section 14.6 for the linear regression model containing one predictor variable. These values can be plotted in **residual plots** to verify the model assumptions discussed on page 692 as well as to identify outliers and observations that are very influential in determining the least squares prediction equation. The process for constructing a residual plot is discussed as it pertains to verifying the model assumptions.

Checking the Model Assumptions. An important step in a regression analysis is to verify the model assumptions. If one or more of these assumptions are violated, the results of the F test and the t tests discussed in this chapter are, at best, questionable. The procedure for verifying these assumptions is nearly identical to that used in simple linear regression, described in detail in Section 14.6.

- **Checking Assumption 1:** *The errors are normally distributed, with a mean of zero.* Construct a histogram of the sample residuals. This plot should resemble a normal curve centered at zero. Remember that an exact normal curve is not necessary here, but the inference results from this chapter are suspect if this distribution is severely skewed.
- **Checking Assumption 2:** *The variance of the errors remains constant.* In Chapter 14, the sample residuals were plotted against the independent variable, X. For the multiple regression analysis, there is more than one independent variable and so one alternative is to plot the residuals versus the predicted ($\hat{Y}$) values. This plot should contain no pattern. This is the "shotgun blast" appearance illustrated in Figure 14.22a, where now the horizontal axis is $\hat{Y}$ rather than X. Beware of situations where the larger residuals are associated with the larger $\hat{Y}$ values, as illustrated in Figure 14.22b, where again the horizontal axis is $\hat{Y}$.

---

*This problem is discussed in D. Dorsett and J. T. Webster, "Guidelines for Variable Selection Problems When Dummy Variables Are Used," *The American Statistician*, 37, no. 4 (1983): p. 337.

- **Checking Assumption 3:** *The errors are independent.* This is an important assumption whenever the sample data are obtained in a sequential manner—in particular, across time. Such data are referred to as *time series data*, where, for example, each row (value of Y and the predictor variables) corresponds to a particular year. This assumption can be tested using the *Durbin-Watson statistic,* defined in Chapter 17, which discusses the use of multiple linear regression models on time series data.

Detecting Sample Outliers. As in Chapter 14, we will:

- Detect sample observations with outlying values of the predictor variables using **sample leverages.**
- Detect observations with outlying values of the dependent variable, Y, using the **standardized residuals.**
- Classify an observation as "influential" using the corresponding **Cook's distance measure.**

For the multiple linear regression model, no simple formula exists for the leverage value (h_i) of the ith observation. Nearly all computerized statistical packages will provide you with these leverage values via a simple command. The instructions when using SPSS and MINITAB are contained in the end-of-chapter appendices for Chapter 14. The output using Excel will be shown in upcoming Example 15.9. *A suggested procedure here is to conclude that an observation has outlying values of the predictor variables if its leverage value is larger than $2(k+1)/n$ or larger than $3(k+1)/n$, where k is the number of predictor variables and n is the number of observations (rows of data).* Since MINITAB and the KPK Data Analysis regression procedure within Excel use the "larger than $3(k+1)/n$" rule, we will use this decision rule in the discussion to follow.

The standardized residual, as in Chapter 14, is defined as

$$\text{Standardized residual} = \frac{Y_i - \hat{Y}_i}{s\sqrt{1 - h_i}} \qquad 15.20$$

where $s = \sqrt{\text{MSE}}$ and MSE is as defined in equation 15.10. *A recommended procedure is to identify an observation as having an outlying value of Y if its standardized residual is larger than 2 or less than –2.* MINITAB will flag automatically any observation having such a standardized residual.

Influential observations are those that, if removed, result in a considerably different regression equation. Such observations may have been improperly recorded (an error was made) or, if recorded correctly, may be a signal that your model is inadequate. A search for additional predictor variables could be made that, when inserted into the existing model, results in a better "model fit." Influential observations will be identified by using Cook's distance measure, where this measure for the ith observation is defined as

$$D_i = \left(\frac{1}{k+1}\right)\left(\frac{h_i}{1-h_i}\right)(\text{standardized residual})^2$$

$$= \frac{(Y_i - \hat{Y}_i)^2}{(k+1)s^2}\left[\frac{h_i}{(1-h_i)^2}\right] \qquad 15.21$$

A suggested procedure here is to conclude that the ith observation is influential if the corresponding D_i measure is larger than DMAX, where DMAX depends on the number of predictor variables and is as specified in Table 15.1. For a more accurate procedure, you can set $DMAX = F_{.5,k+1,n-k-1}$. The values in Table 15.1 closely approximate these median F values.

TABLE

15.1

k	1 or 2	3 or 4	≥ 5
DMAX	.8	.9	1.0

FIGURE

15.19

Excel regression output using KPK Data Analysis (Example 15.9).

	A	B	C	D	E	F	G	H	I
1	Invest	Index	Income	**SUMMARY OUTPUT**				**Maximum**	
2	2500	86	55800					Stand. Resid.	1.99005
3	3700	54	60400		Regression Statistics			Leverage	0.13557
4	3900	21	72700	Multiple R	0.9478			Cook's D	0.11589
5	1700	91	41700	R Square	0.8984				
6	1000	72	35200	Adjusted R Square	0.8941				
7	1700	16	41800	Standard Error	283.0331				
8	2500	81	43700	Observations	50				
9	3400	32	67900						
10	2500	37	53700	**ANOVA**					
11	2900	89	57400		df	SS	MS	F	Significance F
12	2100	48	47100	Regression	2	33294135.56	16647067.78	207.808	4.5877E-24
13	2600	61	55300	Residual	47	3765064.438	80107.754		
14	1700	33	40000	Total	49	37059200			
15	2100	82	40200						
16	1500	95	36900		Coefficients	Standard Error	t Stat	P-value	Lower 95%
17	1700	73	40700	Intercept	-1183.3183	219.3704	-5.3942	2.194E-06	-1624.6341
18	1400	9	35100	Index	-0.1271	1.5471	-0.0822	9.348E-01	-3.2394
19	2400	42	50900	Income	0.0720	0.0036	20.0643	1.096E-24	0.0648
20	1000	74	36300						
21	3200	31	63700						
22	2500	12	46800						
23	4500	25	75200	**RESIDUAL OUTPUT**					
24	2400	24	42400						
25	2000	88	42000	Observation	Predicted Invest	Residuals	Standardized Residuals	Leverages	Cook's D
26	2900	53	54600	1	2823.0588	-323.0588	-1.1797	0.0639	0.0317
27	3600	40	61600	2	3158.3038	541.6962	1.9445	0.0312	0.0406
28	2800	81	60000	3	4048.0362	-148.0362	-0.5500	0.0958	0.0107
29	2200	44	50600	4	1807.2959	-107.2959	-0.3951	0.0793	0.0045
30	3800	36	66300	5	1341.7453	-341.7453	-1.2549	0.0742	0.0420
31	4300	50	70900	6	1824.0315	-124.0315	-0.4572	0.0812	0.0062
32	3300	95	66600	7	1952.5570	547.4430	1.9901	0.0553	0.0773

DATA15-4

Microsoft® Excel Application Use DATA15-4

EXAMPLE

15.9

An Excel Residual Analysis

An Excel analysis of the residuals using the investment data in Example 15.4 follows. Since this sample consists of a random sample of 50 investment clients, and is not time ordered, assumption 3 was not investigated.

To obtain the Excel output in Figure 15.19, click on **KPK Data Analysis ➤ Regression.** Referring to the input screen in Figure 15.7, enter "A1:A51" in the **Y Range** box, "B1:C51" in the **Contiguous X Range** box, and "D1" in the **Output Range** box. Be sure to click on the boxes for **Residuals, Standardized Residuals, Leverages,** and **Cook's Ds.** The maximum standardized residual, leverage value, and Cook's D are provided in cells I2:I4. To obtain these values, first type in the labels in cells H1:H4 of Figure 15.19. In cell I2, type "=max(G26:G75)" to obtain the

Solution

maximum standardized residual, since these values occupy cells G26:G75 in Figure 15.19. Repeat this using "=max(H26:H75)" in cell I3 for the maximum leverage and "=max(I26:I75)" in cell I4 for the maximum Cook's D.

A histogram of the residuals is shown in Figure 15.20. To obtain the histogram, click on **KPK Data Analysis ➤ Quantitative Data Charts/Tables ➤ Histogram/Freq. Charts.** Enter "F26:F75" in the **Input Range** box, "K1" in the **Output Range** box, and "8" in the **Number of Classes** box. Finally, click on the check boxes for **Frequencies** and **Frequency Histogram,** and then **OK.** Except for a very slight positive skew, the residuals appear to be approximately normally distributed, centered at zero, and so we conclude that assumption 1 is satisfied.

The residuals are plotted against the predicted Y values ($\hat{Y}$ values) in Figure 15.21. This plot can be obtained by clicking on **Excel Chart Wizard ➤ XY (Scatter) ➤ Next.** The data range is E26:F75, since the predicted Y values are in cells E26:E75, and the residuals are in F26:F75. Using Figure 15.21 as a guide, you can input the various titles by clicking on the **Titles** tab. Once you have clicked on **Finish,** and you have the plot on your spreadsheet, the minimum and maximum val-

FIGURE

15.20

Excel histogram of residuals using KPK Data Analysis (Example 15.9).

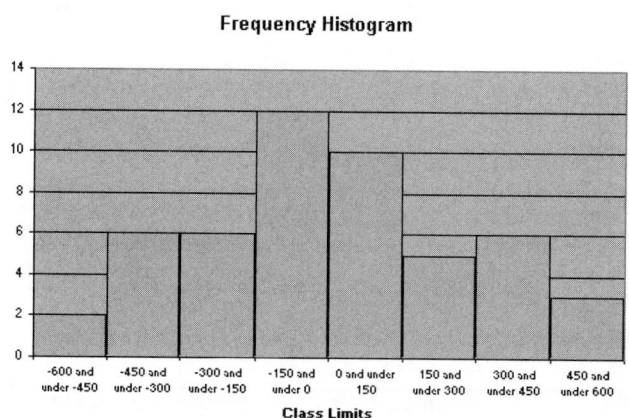

FIGURE

15.21

Excel residual plot for Example 15.9.

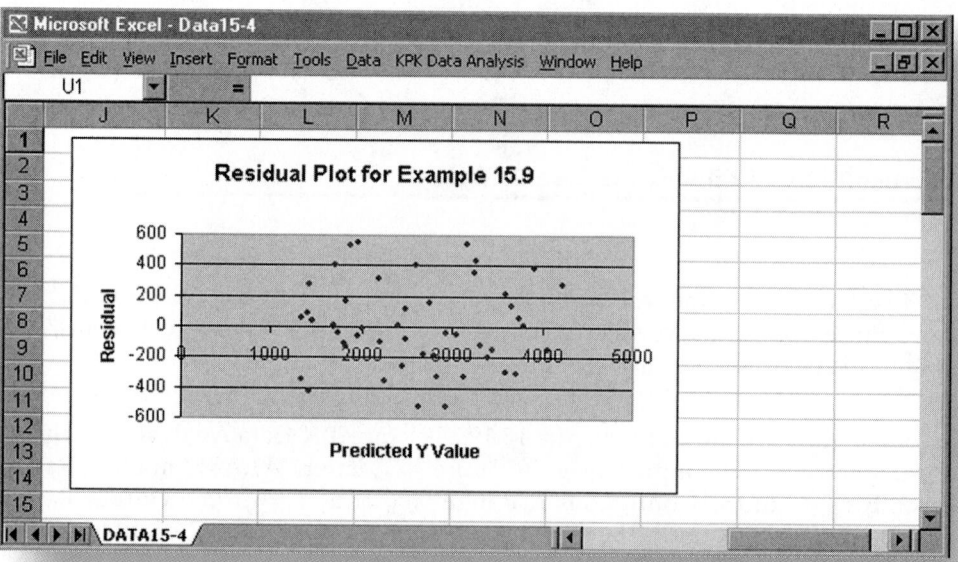

ues on the vertical axis can be set at –600 and 600, respectively, by right clicking on this axis and then clicking on **Format Axis** and the **Scale** tab. Also, the decimal places can be set at zero for both axes by repeating this procedure on both axes using the **Number** tab. No pattern is observed in this plot, and assumption 2 appears to be satisfied.

Using the maximum values in I2:I4 in Figure 15.19, we see that none of the standardized residuals is greater than 2 in absolute value, and so there are no observations with an outlying Y value. None of the leverage (h_i) values exceed $3(2 + 1)/50 = 9/50 = .18$, and so there are no observations with unusually large or small values of the predictor variables. Finally, there are no influential observations, since all of the Cook's distance measures are less than .8 (from Table 15.1).

Prediction Using Multiple Regression

Once a regression equation has been derived, its primary application generally is to derive predicted values of the dependent variable. Computer packages provide an easy method of deriving such an estimate. To illustrate, consider the regression equation we developed for the real-estate data. For this illustration we include X_3 = years of formal education, although, as we demonstrated in Section 15.2, this variable could be dropped without any significant loss in the prediction of home size. The resulting prediction equation was

$$\hat{Y} = 5.657 + .194X_1 + 2.338X_2 - .163X_3$$

Consider a situation in which

$$X_1 = \text{income} = 46 \text{ (thousands of dollars)}$$
$$X_2 = \text{family size} = 4$$
$$X_3 = \text{years of formal education} = 8 \text{ (years)}$$

The predicted home size (Y) here is

$$\hat{Y} = 5.657 + .194(46) + 2.338(4) - .163(8) = 22.63 \text{ (2,263 square feet)}$$

Prediction Using Excel. The standard statistical tool package with Excel does not allow for new value prediction. However, the KPK Data Analysis add-ins will allow you to predict values of the dependent variable using one or more new observations. For each observation, it will also provide the estimated standard deviation (standard error) of the predicted Y, along with a confidence interval and prediction interval. The easiest way to accomplish this is to simply attach the new observations at the end of your sample values. Referring to Figure 15.2, the new observation ($X_1 = 46$, $X_2 = 4$, $X_3 = 8$) can be typed into cells B12, C12, and D12. Click on **KPK Data Analysis ➤ Regression**. Using the input screen in Figure 15.7, the **Y Range** is "A1:A11," and the (contiguous) **X Range** is "B1:D11." Click on the box inside **Confidence Intervals for the Mean of Y and Prediction Intervals for Y** at the bottom of the input form and enter "B12:D12" as the range of new observations. The regression output using this input information is shown in Figure 15.22. The predicted Y value in cell H25 is $\hat{Y} = 22.625$ and agrees with the previous result.

Confidence and Prediction Intervals. In the preceding illustration, what does $\hat{Y} = 22.625$ estimate? For ease of notation, let X_0 represent the set of X values used for this estimate; that is, $X_0 = (46, 4, 8)$, where $X_1 = 46$, $X_2 = 4$, and $X_3 = 8$. This value of $\hat{Y}$ estimates (1) the *average* home size of all families with this specific set of X values, written $\mu_{Y|X_0}$ and (2) the home size for an *individual* family having this specific set of X values, written Y_{X_0}.

Using the notation from Chapter 14, let

$$s_{\hat{Y}} = \text{standard deviation (standard error) of the predicted } Y \text{ mean}$$

FIGURE

15.22

Prediction for new data using Excel and KPK Data Analysis. For the input data, see Figure 15.2.

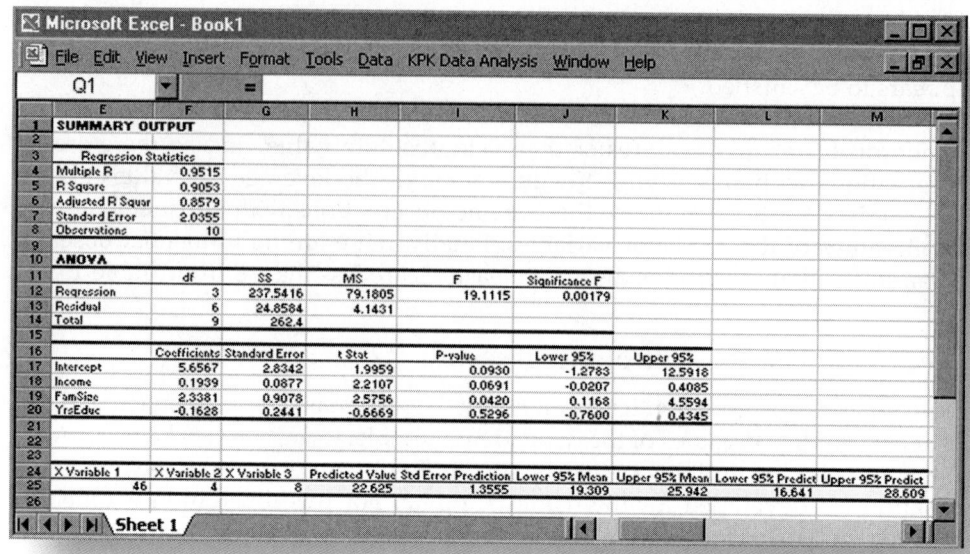

To determine the reliability of this particular point estimate, $\hat{Y}$, you can (1) derive a **confidence interval** for $\mu_{Y|X_0}$ if your intent is to estimate the *average* value of Y given X_0 (not the usual situation) or (2) derive a **prediction interval** for Y_{X_0} if the purpose is to forecast an *individual* value of Y given this specific set of values for the predictor variables. In business applications, deriving a specific forecast is, by far, the more popular use of linear regression.

These intervals are summarized as follows. A $(1 - \alpha) \cdot 100\%$ confidence interval for $\mu_{Y|X_0}$ is

$$\hat{Y} - t_{\alpha/2,n-k-1}s_{\hat{Y}} \qquad \text{to} \qquad \hat{Y} + t_{\alpha/2,n-k-1}s_{\hat{Y}}$$

15.22

A $(1 - \alpha) \cdot 100\%$ prediction interval for Y_{X_0} is

$$\hat{Y} - t_{\alpha/2,n-k-1}\sqrt{s^2 + s_{\hat{Y}}^2} \qquad \text{to} \qquad \hat{Y} + t_{\alpha/2,n-k-1}\sqrt{s^2 + s_{\hat{Y}}^2}$$

15.23

where s^2 is the MSE value in the regression ANOVA table and is defined in equation 15.4.

Using Excel to Determine the Intervals. In Figure 15.22 (cell I25), the standard deviation of the predicted Y mean is labeled **StdErrorPrediction** and is equal to $s_{\hat{Y}} = 1.3555$. The 95% confidence interval for $\mu_{Y|X_0}$ is derived by first using Table A.5 to obtain $t_{\alpha/2,n-k-1} = t_{.025,10-3-1} = t_{.025,6} = 2.447$. The resulting confidence interval is

$$22.625 - (2.447)(1.3555) \qquad \text{to} \qquad 22.625 + (2.447)(1.3555)$$

$$= 22.625 - 3.317 \qquad \text{to} \qquad 22.625 + 3.317$$

$$= 19.308 \qquad \text{to} \qquad 25.942$$

Consequently, we have estimated the average home size for families with $X_1 = 46$, $X_2 = 4$, $X_3 = 8$ to within 331.7 square feet of the actual mean with 95% confidence. The KPK Data Analysis regression procedure within Excel computes this interval for you and is contained in cells J25 and K25 in Figure 15.22.

The prediction interval from equation 15.23 is derived by using MSE = 4.1431 from Figure 15.22 to obtain

$$22.625 - 2.447\sqrt{4.1431 + (1.3555)^2} \quad \text{to} \quad 22.625 + 2.447\sqrt{4.1431 + (1.3555)^2}$$

$$= 22.625 - 5.984 \quad \text{to} \quad 22.625 + 5.984$$

$$= 16.641 \quad \text{to} \quad 28.609$$

This means that we have predicted the home size of an individual family with $X_1 = 46$, $X_2 = 4$, and $X_3 = 8$ to within 598.4 square feet of the actual value with 95% confidence. This same prediction interval will be provided by the KPK Data Analysis regression procedure and is contained in cells L25 and M25 in Figure 15.22.

Exercises 15.39–15.54

Understanding the Mechanics

15.39 Let Y be the annual salary, in thousands of dollars, of a salesperson. Let X_1 be the years of experience of the salesperson. A salesperson's pay can come from salary, commission, or a combination of the two. Let $X_2 = 1$ if the salesperson is strictly on commission and $X_2 = 0$ if not. Let $X_3 = 1$ if the salesperson is on a combination of salary and commission and $X_3 = 0$ if not. From 20 observations a prediction equation was found to be $\hat{Y} = 7 + 5X_1 + 4X_2 + 7X_3$.

a. What is the predicted salary of a salesperson with five years' experience who is working strictly on commissions?

b. What is the predicted salary of a salesperson with five years' experience who is working on a combination of salary and commissions?

c. What is the predicted salary of a salesperson with five years' experience who is working strictly on salary?

d. Test the hypothesis that the dummy variables improve the prediction of a salesperson's salary. Assume that R^2 for the model including only X_1 is .70 and that R^2 for the complete model is .80. Use a .05 significance level.

Applying the New Concepts

15.40 If an economist is interested in examining the relationship between household income and household recreational expenses over time, then the economist would use *time series* data. However, if an economist is interested in estimating household recreational expenses as a function of household income, then he or she would use *cross-sectional* data. A set of cross-sectional data were collected from a sample of 30 households in a large metropolitan area. The independent variables are yearly household income (in thousands), X_1, and house payment (either rent or mortgage), X_2. The dependent variable was annual household recreational expenses. The least squares line is $\hat{Y} = 51.3 + 12.3X_1 + .11X_2$. Given that the standard deviations of the estimates of the coefficients of X_1 and X_2 are 5.59 and .048, test the hypothesis that the variable X_1 contributes to the prediction of Y, given that X_2 is in the model. Also, test that X_2 contributes to the prediction of Y, given that X_1 is in the model. Use a .05 significance level.

15.41 An operations manager has collected data on four variables used to predict the cost of employee turnover (Y). Perform a backward regression procedure using a significance level of 10% to determine which variables contribute to the prediction of Y. Start by developing a model with all the independent variables in the model. Then remove the independent variable with the largest p-value provided that the p-value is greater than .10 and create a new model with the remaining independent variables. Repeat this procedure with the new model by removing the independent variable with the largest p-value that is greater than .10 and again developing a new model with the remaining variables. When all the independent variables have p-values less than .10, then this is the final model selected using the backward regression procedure.

Y	X_1	X_2	X_3	X_4
27	3	3	12	23
23	5	4	14	25
30	6	5	17	20
24	7	6	22	22
27	7	7	28	33
22	5	7	45	39
11	4	8	34	50
22	3	3	25	60
16	2	6	22	76
11	1	8	25	88

15.42 Data are collected for the variables Y, X_1, and X_2. A computer printout of the correlation matrix is:

$$\begin{array}{c} \\ Y \\ X_1 \\ X_2 \end{array} \begin{array}{c} \begin{array}{ccc} Y & X_1 & X_2 \end{array} \\ \begin{bmatrix} 1 & .49 & .30 \\ .49 & 1 & .12 \\ .30 & .12 & 1 \end{bmatrix} \end{array}$$

a. Which independent variable, X_1 or X_2, would be selected first in a forward regression procedure?

b. Which independent variable, X_1 or X_2, would be a better predictor of Y? Why?

15.43 The following is a correlation matrix for three independent variables and one dependent variable:

$$\begin{array}{c|cccc} & Y & X_1 & X_2 & X_3 \\ \hline Y & 1 & .25 & .36 & .59 \\ X_1 & .25 & 1 & .54 & .22 \\ X_2 & .36 & .54 & 1 & .31 \\ X_3 & .59 & .22 & .31 & 1 \end{array}$$

a. Which independent variable would be chosen for the first stage of a forward regression procedure?

b. Which independent variable would be chosen for the first step of a stepwise regression procedure?

15.44 The least squares regression equation

$$\hat{Y} = 1.5 + 3.5X_1 + 7.5X_2 - 150X_3$$

has the following t values for the independent variables:

Null Hypothesis	t Statistic
$\beta_1 = 0$	4.5
$\beta_2 = 0$	1.89
$\beta_3 = 0$	1.52

Twenty observations were used in calculating the least squares equation. In the first stage of a backward selection procedure, which independent variable would be eliminated first? Use a 5% level of significance.

15.45 Describe the main difference between the forward selection procedure and the stepwise selection procedure in regression analysis.

15.46 Football team valuation experts assess the value of a team on several factors, including the stadium in which they play. Several teams have increased their value by moving into taxpayer-paid stadiums. Gate receipts contribute to revenue and player costs affect operating income. The following table presents the current value of 10 randomly selected football franchises, their current value, annual revenue in millions of dollars, and operating income in millions of dollars.

Franchise	Current Value	Revenue	Operating Income
Tampa Bay Buccaneers	582	146	35.5
Tennessee Titans	536	134	41.5
Cincinnati Bengals	479	120	14.5
St. Louis Rams	448	124	25.2
New York Jets	423	121	17.1
San Francisco 49ers	419	120	26.1
Philadelphia Eagles	405	116	6.7
Chicago Bears	362	113	3.3
Arizona Cardinals	342	107	5.1
Atlanta Falcons	338	113	5.0

a. Do the variables revenue and operating income contribute to the prediction of the current value of a football franchise. Use a 5% significance level.

b. Compute the coefficient of determination for the model obtained in part a and interpret it.

c. Find the standardized residual for each observation.

d. Remove any observation having a standardized residual less than –2 or greater than 2 and use the remaining observations to compute the least squares line. How does the coefficient of variation for this model compare to that obtained in part b?

e. Using the model obtained in part d, find a 95% prediction interval for the current value of a franchise with a revenue of $120 million and operating income of $20 million.

(Source: "Team Valuations," *Forbes*, September 2001, pp. 82–86.)

15.47 Which of the standard assumptions of regression appear to have been violated in the data from the following table, which lists the dependent variable and the residual values?

$\hat{Y}$	$Y - \hat{Y}$	$\hat{Y}$	$Y - \hat{Y}$
1.5	.12	5.0	−1.45
2.1	−.70	5.5	1.61
3.5	−.91	6.0	1.79
4.0	1.02	7.0	−2.40
4.5	−1.18	7.5	2.10

15.48 How should a graph of the residuals $(Y - \hat{Y})$ plotted against the predicted values $\hat{Y}$ look if the standard assumptions of regression are satisfied?

15.49 A set of 20 observations is used to obtain the least squares line

$$\hat{Y} = 1.5 + 3.6X_1 + 4.9X_2$$

a. Given that the estimated standard deviation of Y at $X_1 = 1.0$ and $X_2 = 2.0$ is 3.4, find a 90% confidence interval for the mean value of Y at $X_1 = 1.0$ and $X_2 = 2.0$.

b. Given that the MSE from this analysis is 21.5, then, using the information in part a, find a 90% prediction interval for an individual value of Y at $X_1 = 1.0$ and $X_2 = 2.0$.

15.50 The first quarter of 1998 saw the Standard & Poor's 500 Index surge nearly 14%. Nine of the 14 major brokerage firms did even better than the index in recommending companies to investors. Investors are often interested in whether a brokerage firm's previous performance can be used to predict current performance. Let Y represent the current quarter's performance. Let X_1 and X_2 represent the performance for one year and five years, respectively. Consider the performance data below for 14 major brokerage houses. Performance is measured in percentage.

Firm	Quarter Ending 3/31/98 (Y)	One Year Performance (X_1)	Five-Year Performance (X_2)
Lehman Brothers	16.6	62.4	162.4
Everen	12.5	59.4	177.0
A. G. Edwards	18.0	58.1	239.7
Wheat First	22.6	57.8	175.0
Edwards Jones	15.8	56.8	152.4
Raymond James	16.5	56.4	247.4
Prudential	14.7	56.0	127.6
Paine Weber	21.0	53.1	292.2
Goldman Sachs	12.6	50.1	169.4
Merril Lynch	14.5	46.2	200.1
Credit Suisse F. B.	11.6	46.2	178.3
Bear Stearns	14.4	45.7	177.9
Salomon S. B.	11.5	44.3	172.0
Morgan Stanley	13.6	39.0	125.4

a. The prediction equation for these data is $\hat{Y} = -.342 + .1982X_1 + .0291X_2$. Predict Y for each of the brokerage houses.

b. Calculate the residuals $Y - \hat{Y}$ for each firm.

c. Calculate the residual standard deviation.

d. How many residuals lie within two standard deviations of the mean of the error terms? How many observations would you expect to lie outside of two standard deviations, assuming that the residuals are approximately normally distributed?

(Source: "Brokerage Houses' Stock Picks Sparkle," *Wall Street Week,* May 7, 1998, p. C1.)

15.51 Explain the difference between a confidence interval for the mean value of Y at particular values of the independent variables and a prediction interval for a future value of Y at particular values of the independent variables. Will the prediction interval for Y always be larger than the corresponding confidence interval for particular values of the independent variables?

Using the Computer

15.52 **[DATA SET EX15-52]** *Variable description:*

Location: Location of exclusive property in the Houston and surrounding area

Price: Price for exclusive property advertised in *The Wall Street Journal*

Bedrooms: Number of bedrooms in the house

Sqfootage: Square footage of living space in the house

Real-estate agents use *The Wall Street Journal* to advertise exceptional properties to gain maximum exposure to potential buyers outside a local area. A random sample of 20 properties in the Houston metropolitan area are selected, and the price, number of bedrooms, and square footage are recorded.

a. Create a dummy variable that is equal to 1 if the property has five or more bedrooms and 0 if it has less than five bedrooms. Do Sqfootage and the dummy variable contribute to the prediction of the price of the property? Use a 10% significance level.

b. What is a 95% prediction interval for a six-bedroom house with 4,700 square feet?

c. Can you identify any observations with a standardized residual larger than 2 or less than –2?

(Source: "Distinctive Properties & Estates," *The Wall Street Journal,* June 22, 2001, p. W15F.)

15.53 **[DATA SET EX15-53]** *Variable description:*

Magazine: Name of widely circulated magazine

TotalRev: Total revenue for the magazine from all sources

AdRev: Revenue from advertisements in the magazine

SubscriberRev: Revenue for the magazine from subscribers

Magazines obtain revenue from advertisements, subscribers, newstands, and general circulation. The amount of revenue from advertisements and subscribers tends to be rather stable for most widely circulated magazines. To understand the relationship between AdRev and SubscriberRev in predicting TotalRev, 16 widely circulated magazines were randomly selected. Data for each of the variables were recorded in units of thousands of dollars.

a. Using a significance level of 1%, comment on the contribution of AdRev and SubscriberRev in predicting TotalRev.

b. Interpret the 95% prediction interval for a magazine's total revenue given that the revenue from advertisements is $200,000 and the revenue from subscribers is $100,000.

c. Are there any influential observations? If so, eliminate the most influential observation and comment on the increase or decrease in the coefficient of determination.

(Source: "Top 300 Magazines by Gross Revenue," *Advertising Age,* June 16, 1997, p. S6.)

15.54 **[DATA SET EX15-54]** *Variable description:*

Funding: Level of funding approved for research proposal

Theory: Score on theoretical soundness

Usefulness: Score on usefulness of applications

Reviewer: 1 if reviewer is from the business research institute and 0 if the reviewer is external to the institute

A business research institute receives research proposals for possible funding. These research proposals come from universities engaged in long-term business projects. Each proposal is evaluated in two areas: theoretical soundness and usefulness of applications. The proposal is reviewed by either someone at the business research institute or someone externally. A committee within the institute considers the scores and qualifications of the reviewer and then may approve some level of funding. A researcher wished to determine the relationship of the level of funding with the scores given by the reviewer and with whether the reviewer is from the business research institute or external to it. The researcher randomly sampled 35 proposals that have received some level of funding. The level of funding is recorded in units of thousands of dollars.

a. Find a 95% confidence interval for the mean level of funding for a proposal with scores of 7 for theoretical soundness and 7 for applications by a reviewer in the business research institute. Interpret the interval in the context of the problem.

b. In part a, if the confidence interval for the mean level of funding was changed to a prediction interval for the same values of the scores by a reviewer in the business research institute, what is the resulting interval and how would you interpret it?

c. From the histogram of the residuals, does it appear that the errors are approximately normal?

d. Do any of the observations have values of Cook's D greater than .9?

15.6 MODEL BUILDING

Linear regression models can provide you with a variety of predictive equations that attempt to explain the behavior of a particular dependent variable. These go beyond the straight line obtained in Chapter 14 and the flat plane of this chapter, using two independent (predictor) variables, illustrated in Figure 15.1. This section will introduce you to the more flexible linear models, which include the effect of **interaction terms** and **quadratic terms.**

Interaction Effects

An interaction effect between two predictor variables, say, X_1 and X_2, implies that how these two variables occur *together* has an impact on the prediction of the dependent variable. This is the same type of effect observed in two-way factorial designs, discussed in Chapter 11, where the effect of one factor on the dependent variable depends on the level of the second factor. A linear regression model containing two predictor variables and an interaction term can be written

$$Y = \beta_0 + \beta_1 X_1 + \beta_2 X_2 + \beta_3 X_1 X_2 + e$$

15.24

where the *interaction term* is the product of X_1 and X_2, and e is the error associated with the model. Since the error term is assumed to have a mean of zero, an alternate form of this model is

$$\mu_Y = \beta_0 + \beta_1 X_1 + \beta_2 X_2 + \beta_3 X_1 X_2$$

15.25

where μ_Y is the mean of the random variable Y.

To illustrate an interaction effect, consider the model

$$\mu_Y = 10 + 15X_1 + 4X_2 - 5X_1 X_2$$

Suppose we set $X_2 = 2$. Then we have

$$\mu_Y = 10 + 15X_1 + 4(2) - 5X_1(2)$$
$$= 10 + 15X_1 + 8 - 10X_1$$
$$= 18 + 5X_1$$

For $X_2 = 5$, the model becomes

$$\mu_Y = 10 + 15X_1 + 4(5) - 5X_1(5)$$
$$= 10 + 15X_1 + 20 - 25X_1$$
$$= 30 - 10X_1$$

These two lines are shown in Figure 15.23a. Due to presence of the interaction term, the relationship between Y and X_1 is highly dependent on the value of X_2. This is not the case if the interaction effect is missing from the model, illustrated in Figure 15.23b. Without the interaction term, the model becomes

$$\mu_Y = 10 + 15X_1 + 4X_2$$

where for $X_2 = 2$, we have $\mu_Y = 10 + 15X_1 + 4(2) = 18 + 15X_1$ and for $X_2 = 5$, the model becomes $\mu_Y = 10 + 15X_1 + 4(5) = 30 + 15X_1$. Notice in Figure 15.23b that the two lines are parallel, indicating the absence of an interaction effect between these two variables.

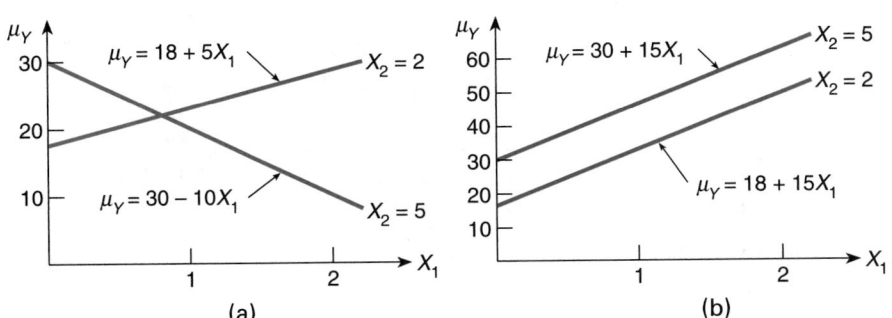

FIGURE

15.23

Illustration of interaction effect. (a) Interaction is present in the model $\mu_Y = 10 + 15X_1 + 4X_2 - 5X_1X_2$. (b) Interaction is absent in the model $\mu_Y = 10 + 15X_1 + 4X_2$.

Quadratic Effects

Quadratic effects were discussed in Section 15.3, which introduced curvilinear models. An example of a curvilinear model using a single predictor variable (say, X_1) is

$$Y = \beta_0 + \beta_1 X_1 + \beta_2 X_1^2 + e$$

15.26

Such a model is useful whenever the effect of X_1 is nonlinear; in particular, the change in Y for a given change in X_1 tends to increase or decrease as X_1 gets larger. Such a relationship can be seen in Figure 15.9, where the change in Y tends to "slow down" for larger values of the predictor variable. Including quadratic terms in the multiple regression model allows you to capture such relationships between the dependent variable and the various predictor variables.

Second-Order Models

The multiple linear regression model introduced in equation 15.1 is

$$Y = \beta_0 + \beta_1 X_1 + \beta_2 X_2 + \cdots + \beta_k X_k + e$$

This model is referred to as a **first-order model,** since no interaction terms or quadratic terms are included.

A **complete second-order model** is one that includes all possible interaction and quadratic terms. For the cases of two and three predictor variables, this model becomes

$$Y = \beta_0 + \beta_1 X_1 + \beta_2 X_2 + \beta_3 X_1 X_2 + \beta_4 X_1^2 + \beta_5 X_2^2 + e$$

$$Y = \beta_0 + \beta_1 X_1 + \beta_2 X_2 + \beta_3 X_3 + \beta_4 X_1 X_2 + \beta_5 X_1 X_3 + \beta_6 X_2 X_3$$
$$+ \beta_7 X_1^2 + \beta_8 X_2^2 + \beta_9 X_3^2 + e$$

15.27   15.28

Such a model is linear in the unknown β parameters, and so is considered to be a multiple linear regression model. It will provide you with a much more powerful modeling tool than will a first-order model. Construction of a second-order model is illustrated in Example 15.10.

Microsoft® Excel Application   Use DAT15-10

Construction of a Second-Order Model

EXAMPLE 15.10

A financial analyst at a major lending institution is interested in predicting the annual sales for defense-related companies. As a possible set of predictor variables, she decides to use the number of employees, current assets, current liabilities, and total assets. Data from a random sample of 50 such industries is contained in dataset DAT15-10, where each column of data is described as follows:

Column	Contains
A	Y = annual sales (units of \$10,000,000)
B	X_1 = number of employees (units of 100)
C	X_2 = current assets (units of \$100,000)
D	X_3 = current liabilities (units of \$100,000)
E	X_4 = total assets (units of \$100,000)

Construct an appropriate second-order model based on this set of sample data. Use a significance level of .10.

Solution

The first look at the data will be a first-order model containing all four predictor variables. The Excel solution using these variables is shown in Figure 15.24. This output, which includes the four variance inflation factors, can be obtained by clicking on **KPK Data Analysis ➤ Regression.** The **Y Range** is "A1:A51," and the (contiguous) **X Range** is "B1:E51." Both ranges must include labels in the first row. It will be necessary to click on the box alongside **VIFs.** The variance inflation factors for X_1 and X_3 (highlighted) are both larger than 10, indicating a high correlation between these two variables. This correlation (highlighted in cell G23) is .949. This correlation can be obtained by typing "= correl(B2:B51,D2:D51)" in cell G23. As a result, it was decided to drop X_3 (current liabilities) from the model, since the analyst, rather arbitrarily, elected to keep the number of employees (X_1) in the prediction equation.

The regression analysis was repeated using predictor variables, X_1, X_2, and X_4 in Figure 15.25. Since the range of the predictor variables is noncontiguous, it was necessary to use the KPK Data Analysis regression procedure. By (1) clicking on **KPK Data Analysis ➤ Regression;** (2) entering "A1:A51" as the **Y Range;** (3) clicking **Noncontiguous X Range;** (4) entering "3" as the number of X variables (followed by **OK**) with ranges B1:B51, C1:C51, and E1:E51; and (5) entering "F1" as the **Output Range,** the Excel output in Figure 15.25 was obtained. All of the variance inflation factors are now well under 10. Due to the large p-value for X_4 = total assets (highlighted in cell J20), this variable was dropped from the

FIGURE

15.24

Excel regression solution using KPK Data Analysis and all four predictor variables.

(Figure: Microsoft Excel - DAT15-10 screenshot)

	Regression Statistics	
Multiple R	0.96224	
R Square	0.92590	
Adjusted R Square	0.91931	
Standard Error	0.52817	
Observations	50	

ANOVA

	df	SS	MS	F	Significance F
Regression	4	156.8559	39.2140	140.5677	0.000000
Residual	45	12.5536	0.2790		
Total	49	169.4095			

	Coefficients	Standard Error	t Stat	P-value	Lower 95%	Upper 95%	VIF
Intercept	-0.0098	0.3016	-0.0326	0.9741	-0.6172	0.5975	
Employees	0.2178	0.0302	7.2193	0.0000	0.1571	0.2786	10.9718
CurAssets	-0.0162	0.0075	-2.1631	0.0359	-0.0313	-0.0011	1.0738
CurLiabil	-0.0102	0.0883	-0.1151	0.9089	-0.1879	0.1676	10.8690
TotAssets	0.0020	0.0033	0.6261	0.5344	-0.0045	0.0086	1.1321

Corr(X1 and X3)   0.949

Data columns (Sales, Employees, CurAssets, CurLiabil, TotAssets):

Sales	Employees	CurAssets	CurLiabil	TotAssets
2.6	17.9	37.0	6.6	67.4
5.1	24.9	8.8	7.4	26.1
1.9	12.9	13.3	2.5	40.1
2.2	11.3	17.7	3.3	56.6
4.4	18.8	21.8	6.2	80.7
2.4	13.6	17.9	2.8	12.3
3.1	16.1	27.2	5.6	75.9
5.1	25.4	15.8	7.6	24.7
5.3	23.4	15.1	7.0	13.4
2.3	15.5	24.5	5.2	27.8
6.8	32.9	23.7	10.3	28.3
2.5	13.1	49.3	3.2	100.5
4.7	24.4	23.9	8.2	39.3
4.8	20.4	17.7	5.9	71.6
3.8	17.9	3.2	6.6	69.9
4.4	23.9	9.4	5.8	48.3
1.9	10.8	20.5	4.1	78.5
2.7	13.6	37.2	5.3	23.9
4.6	21.6	10.7	8.5	55.0
5.9	27.9	14.8	8.8	20.7
4.8	18.5	18.6	5.6	46.9
9.4	42.8	23.4	13.8	72.2
3.6	19.0	29.2	5.9	57.5

DAT15-10

model. *Note:* It is possible that an interaction effect exists between X_1 and X_4 or between X_2 and X_4, which will not be detected once X_4 is dropped from the model.

In Figure 15.26, the interaction effect between X_1 and X_2 (that is, X_1X_2) along with the quadratic terms (X_1^2 and X_2^2) were included. The interaction column can be obtained by typing "=B2*C2" in cell D2 and dragging this cell down through cell D51. The quadratic column for X_1 can be built by typing "=B2*B2" in cell E2 and dragging down through cell E51. This should be repeated for the second quadratic term by typing "=C2*C2" in cell F2 and dragging down through cell F51. The titles "Emp*Assets", "EmpSQ", and "AssetsSQ" should be typed in the top row (cells D1, E1, and F1). Referring to the highlighted *p*-values in Figure 15.26, the *p*-values for the quadratic terms appear quite large, and so the analyst decided to re-run the regression analysis without these terms in the model. This output is shown in Figure 15.27.

The R^2 value using the five predictors in Figure 15.26 is .933. The R^2 value with the quadratic terms removed is .932 (highlighted in Figure 15.27). Consequently,

Microsoft Excel - DAT15-10

File Edit View Insert Format Tools Data KPK Data Analysis Window Help

Q1 =

	A	B	C	D	E	F	G	H	I	J	K	L	M
1	Sales	Employees	CurAssets	CurLiabil	TotAssets	SUMMARY OUTPUT							
2	2.6	17.9	37.0	6.6	67.4								
3	5.1	24.9	8.8	7.4	26.1	Regression Statistics							
4	1.9	12.9	13.3	2.5	40.1	Multiple R	0.96222						
5	2.2	11.3	17.7	3.3	56.6	R Square	0.92588						
6	4.4	18.8	21.8	6.2	80.7	Adjusted R Square	0.92104						
7	2.4	13.6	17.9	2.8	12.3	Standard Error	0.52248						
8	3.1	16.1	27.2	5.6	75.9	Observations	50						
9	5.1	25.4	15.8	7.6	24.7								
10	5.3	23.4	15.1	7.0	13.4	ANOVA							
11	2.3	15.5	24.5	5.2	27.8		df	SS	MS	F	Significance F		
12	6.8	32.9	23.7	10.3	28.3	Regression	3	156.8522	52.2841	191.528	5.412E-26		
13	2.5	13.1	49.3	3.2	100.5	Residual	46	12.5573	0.2730				
14	4.7	24.4	23.9	8.2	39.3	Total	49	169.4095					
15	4.8	20.4	17.7	5.9	71.6								
16	3.8	17.9	3.2	6.6	69.9		Coefficients	Standard Error	t Stat	P-value	Lower 95%	Upper 95%	VIF
17	4.4	23.9	9.4	5.8	48.3	Intercept	-0.0035	0.2932	-0.0118	0.9906	-0.5937	0.5868	
18	1.9	10.8	20.5	4.1	78.5	Employees	0.2145	0.0091	23.6925	0.0000	0.1963	0.2327	1.0096
19	2.7	13.6	37.2	5.3	23.9	CurAssets	-0.0163	0.0074	-2.2005	0.0328	-0.0312	-0.0014	1.0684
20	4.6	21.6	10.7	8.5	55.0	TotAssets	0.0020	0.0032	0.6227	0.5365	-0.0044	0.0083	1.0745
21	5.9	27.9	14.8	8.8	20.7								

DAT15-10

FIGURE 15.25

Excel regression solution using KPK Data Analysis and X_1, X_2, and X_4.

Microsoft Excel - DAT15-10

File Edit View Insert Format Tools Data KPK Data Analysis Window Help

P1 =

	A	B	C	D	E	F	G	H	I	J	K	L
1	Sales	Employees	CurAssets	Emp*Assets	EmpSQ	AssetsSQ	SUMMARY OUTPUT					
2	2.6	17.9	37.0	662.3	320.4	1369.0						
3	5.1	24.9	8.8	219.12	620.0	77.4	Regression Statistics					
4	1.9	12.9	13.3	171.57	166.4	176.9	Multiple R	0.96610				
5	2.2	11.3	17.7	200.01	127.7	313.3	R Square	0.93335				
6	4.4	18.8	21.8	409.84	353.4	475.2	Adjusted R Square	0.92578				
7	2.4	13.6	17.9	243.44	185.0	320.4	Standard Error	0.50656				
8	3.1	16.1	27.2	437.92	259.2	739.8	Observations	50				
9	5.1	25.4	15.8	401.32	645.2	249.6						
10	5.3	23.4	15.1	353.34	547.6	228.0	ANOVA					
11	2.3	15.5	24.5	379.75	240.3	600.3		df	SS	MS	F	Significance F
12	6.8	32.9	23.7	779.73	1082.4	561.7	Regression	5	158.1189	31.6238	123.239	1.0143E-24
13	2.5	13.1	49.3	645.83	171.6	2430.5	Residual	44	11.2906	0.2566		
14	4.7	24.4	23.9	583.16	595.4	571.2	Total	49	169.4095			
15	4.8	20.4	17.7	361.08	416.2	313.3						
16	3.8	17.9	3.2	57.28	320.4	10.2		Coefficients	Standard Error	t Stat	P-value	
17	4.4	23.9	9.4	224.66	571.2	88.4	Intercept	1.1075	0.6910	1.6029	0.1161	
18	1.9	10.8	20.5	221.4	116.6	420.3	Employees	0.1328	0.0444	2.9901	0.0046	
19	2.7	13.6	37.2	505.92	185.0	1383.8	CurAssets	-0.0394	0.0419	-0.9422	0.3512	
20	4.6	21.6	10.7	231.12	466.6	114.5	Emp*Assets	0.0023	0.0015	1.5370	0.1314	
21	5.9	27.9	14.8	412.92	778.4	219.0	EmpSQ	0.0007	0.0009	0.7789	0.4402	
22	4.8	18.5	18.6	344.1	342.3	346.0	AssetsSQ	-0.0003	0.0005	-0.5310	0.5981	
23	9.4	42.8	23.4	1001.52	1831.8	547.6						

DAT15-10

FIGURE 15.26

Excel regression solution using X_1, X_2, X_1X_2, and quadratic terms.

FIGURE

15.27

Excel regression solution using X_1, X_2, and X_1X_2.

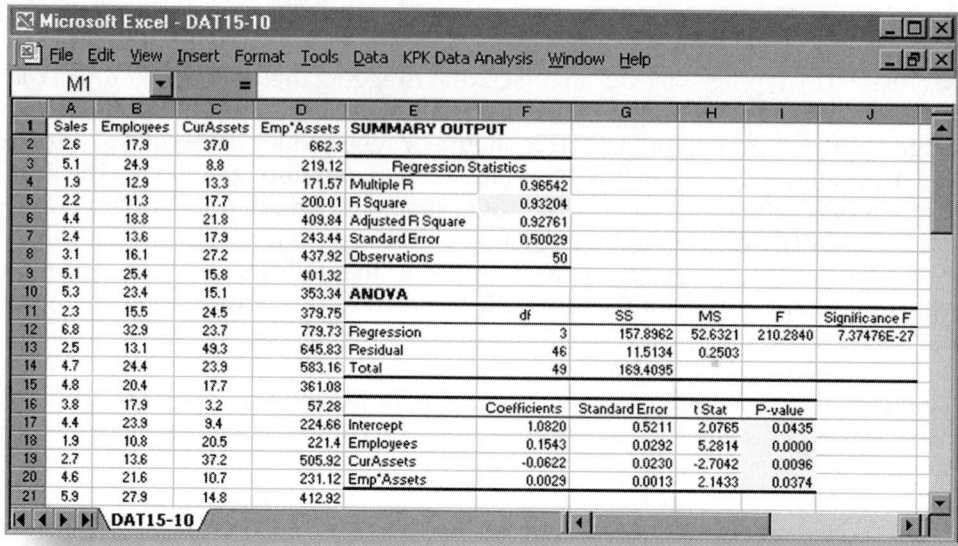

the two quadratic terms do not contribute significantly to the prediction of sales. This is confirmed using the partial F value, where

$$F = \frac{(.933 - .932)/2}{(1 - .933)/(50 - 1 - 5)} = .33$$

which is less than $F_{.10,2,44} \approx 2.44$. The p-values for the remaining three predictors are less than .10, and so the resulting prediction equation is

$$\hat{Y} = 1.0820 + 0.1543X_1 - 0.0622X_2 + 0.0029X_1X_2$$

The final step in the analysis would be to examine the residuals, as outlined in Example 15.9.

X Exercises 15.55–15.60

Understanding the Mechanics

15.55 Consider a regression model with a continuous independent variable X_1 and with an independent variable X_2 that is equal to 1 for training method A and 0 for training method B. Twenty observations were used to yield the following prediction equation.

$$\hat{Y} = 10.1 + 5X_1 + 8X_2 - 10X_1X_2$$

a. For training method A, what is the prediction equation?

b. For training method B, what is the prediction equation?

c. Are the prediction lines parallel in parts a and b?

15.56 Consider the following two regression models that were fit using 25 observations:

Model 1: $\hat{Y} = 13 + 2X_1 + 3X_2 + 6X_1^2 + 7X_2^2 - 20X_1X_2$

Model 2: $\hat{Y} = 10 + 14X_1 + 2X_2$

a. What terms in Model 1 indicate a quadratic effect?

b. If the coefficients of determination for Model 1 and Model 2 are .61 and .52, respectively, do the second-order terms contribute to the prediction of Y in Model 1? Use a .05 significance level.

Applying the New Concepts

15.57 A marketing researcher is interested in whether the interaction of advertising and price affect sales. The following computer printout displays a regression analysis of the contribution of advertising and price on sales. Comment on the appropriateness of the resulting linear relationship. A regression analysis is also provided for the same model but includes the interaction of advertising and price. Why do you think that the p-value associated with advertising has changed in the model that includes interaction? Do you think that the interaction term contributes to the prediction of sales when advertising and price are in the model? Use a 10% significance level.

Summary Output for Exercise 15.57

Regression Statistics

Multiple R	0.984261019
R Square	0.968769754
Adjusted R Square	0.963091528
Standard Error	111.4304063
Observations	14

ANOVA

	df	SS	MS	F	Significance F
Regression	2	4236871.4	2118435.7	170.6113	5.25007E-09
Residual	11	136584.09	12416.7354		
Total	13	4373455.49			

	Coefficients	Standard Error	t Stat	P-value	Lower 95%	Upper 95%	VIF
Intercept	−3487.886	402.32131	−8.6694041	3.02E-06	−4373.389681	−2602.3823	
price	26.61620811	4.90601983	5.42521414	0.000209	15.81812582	37.4142904	1.00259
ad	6.844391846	0.39427939	17.3592434	2.43E-09	5.976588329	7.71219536	1.00259

Summary Output

Regression Statistics

Multiple R	0.99179144
R Square	0.98365026
Adjusted R Square	0.97874534
Standard Error	84.5605478
Observations	14

ANOVA

	df	SS	MS	F	Significance F
Regression	3	4301950.63	1433983.54	200.5435008	3.141E-09
Residual	10	71504.8624	7150.48624		
Total	13	4373455.49			

	Coefficients	Standard Error	t Stat	P-value	Lower 95%	Upper 95%	VIF
Intercept	2200.1765	1909.99153	1.15192998	0.276145139	−2055.550566	6455.90356	
price	−51.93048	26.3008498	−1.9744792	0.076572324	−110.5324354	6.67147522	50.035
ad	−3.6836857	3.50256396	−1.0517112	0.317682354	−11.48788591	4.12051447	137.39
price*ad	0.14531379	0.04816743	3.01684784	0.012965072	0.037990063	0.25263752	194.73

15.58 Stocks with fast-growing earnings are usually classified as growth stocks. Stocks that have low P/E ratios and that are believed to be undervalued are categorized as value stocks. A sample of 16 top-performing midcap mutual funds—eight value-oriented mutual funds and eight growth-oriented mutual funds—are selected. The following table displays the percent return of these mutual funds during the second quarter of 2001 and during the first six months of 2001.

Midcap Growth	Six-Month Return	Quarterly Return
Baron Growth	9.4	18.7
Wasatch Ultra Growth	9.4	36.5
Westcore Select	9.3	21.4
Federated Kaufmann K	7.5	14.4

Midcap Growth	Six-Month Return	Quarterly Return
Oak Ridge Sm Cap Eqty A	3.5	14.7
Value Line Emerg Opptys	2.5	18.2
Heritage Aggr Growth A	1.9	13.7
Quant Sm Cap Shs	1.8	14.3
Midcap Value		
CGM Tr Focus Fund	26.0	19.7
Columbia Strategic Value	24.4	16.5
Al Frank Fund	22.8	14.9
MassMutual Inst Foc VI A	21.8	14.1
TCW Galileo Val Op Instl	20.4	16.7
Diamond Hill Focus A	19.7	12.0
Merrill Mid Cap Val A	18.1	15.2
Legg Maso Inv Oppty Prm	17.7	11.5

a. Is there sufficient evidence that a dummy variable representing the classification of growth or value orientation and the variable representing quarterly return contribute to the prediction of a mutual fund's six-month return? Use a 5% significance level.

b. Add the square of quarterly return and the interaction of the dummy variable representing growth or value classifications with quarterly return to the model in part a. Test that these additional terms contribute to the model when the dummy variable and the quarterly return variable are in the model. Use a 5% significance level.

(Source: "USA Today's Midyear Stock Mutual Fund Report," *USA Today,* July 5, 2001, p. 7B.)

15.59 [DATA SET EX15-59] *Variable description:*

Age: Age in years of person applying for term insurance

InsuranceLevel: Indicator variable equal to 0 or 1 for $100,000 or $500,000 of insurance, respectively

Gender: Indicator variable equal to 0 or 1 for male or female, respectively

MonthlyRate: Monthly premium for insurance

Term insurance rates have trended lower over the past couple of decades as the life expectancy of Americans has increased. A sample of term insurance quotes for 63 randomly selected individuals was collected. These rates assume that individuals are healthy and are nonsmokers.

a. Construct quadratic and interaction terms to predict the monthly premium of an individual. In the model include the independent variables Age, InsuranceLevel, Gender, the square of Age, the interaction of Age and InsuranceLevel, and the interaction of Age and Gender. Use the *p*-values to determine whether these independent variables contribute to the prediction of the monthly premium.

b. Remove the two observations that you believe are the most influential and repeat part a. Compare the MSE for this model with the regression model in part a.

(Source: "Affordable Life Insurance," *Kiplinger's Personal Finance,* August 2001, p. 61.)

15.60 [DATA SET EX15-60] *Variable description:*

Tasktime: Time required to complete a task

Aptitude: Score on aptitude test

Exper: On-the-job experience

A manager in charge of a production process is interested in the amount of time, Y, in minutes (Tasktime) that it takes a production worker to perform a certain task relative to his or her score on an aptitude test (Aptitude) and relative to the person's on-the-job experience (Exper) in years. The manager uses a first-order regression model with Aptitude and Exper to predict Tasktime. In addition, the manager uses a second-order regression model with Aptitude, the square of Aptitude, Exper, the square of Exper, and the interaction of Aptitude and Exper. Test that the second-order terms contribute to the model using a 5% significance level.

✓ Summary

Multiple linear regression offers a method of predicting (or modeling) the behavior of a particular **dependent variable** (Y) using two or more **independent (predictor) variables.** As in the case of simple linear regression, which uses one predictor variable, the regression coefficients are those that minimize

$$\text{SSE} = \text{sum of squares of error} = \Sigma(Y - \hat{Y})^2$$

To use this technique properly, you must pay special attention to the assumptions behind it: (1) the regression errors follow a normal distribution, centered at zero, with a common variance and (2) the errors are statistically independent. An estimate of this common variance is

$$\hat{\sigma}_e^2 = s^2 = \text{MSE} = \frac{\text{SSE}}{n - k - 1}$$

The square root of this variance is the **residual standard deviation,** or the **standard error.** To determine the adequacy of the regression model, you can test the entire set of predictor variables using an *F*-test with k and $n - k - 1$ degrees of freedom:

$$F = \frac{\text{MSR}}{\text{MSE}} = \frac{R^2/k}{(1 - R^2)/(n - k - 1)}$$

The contribution of an individual predictor variable (say, X_i) can be tested using a *t* statistic with $n - k - 1$ df:

$$t = \frac{b_i}{s_{b_i}}$$

where s_{b_i} represents the estimated standard deviation of b_i. Here b_i is the least squares estimate of the population parameter, β_i, and centers the confidence interval for this parameter.

The **coefficient of determination, R^2,** describes the percentage of the total variation in the sample Y values explained by this set of predictor variables. To determine the contribution of a particular subset of the predictor variables—such as X_2 and X_4—R^2 is computed with X_2 and X_4 included and then with X_2 and X_4 excluded from the regression equation. A **partial *F* test** is then used to determine whether the resulting decrease in R^2 is significant. The **adjusted value of R^2, R^2(adj),** is a statistic that, unlike R^2, does not necessarily increase as variables are added to the model. R^2(adj) helps distinguish variables that significantly improve the model from those that do not.

When a **curvilinear** pattern exists between two variables, X and Y, this nonlinear relationship often can be modeled by including an X^2 term in the regression equation. The resulting equation is

$$\hat{Y} = b_0 + b_1 X + b_2 X^2$$

This type of model often works well in situations where Y (for example, sales) appears to increase more slowly as the independent variable, X (for example, the amount of shelf space devoted to this product) continues to increase.

The problem of **multicollinearity** arises in the application of multiple linear regression whenever one or more of the predictor variables are a nearly linear combination of the remaining predictor variables. The most common form of multicollinearity occurs when two predictor variables are highly correlated. The resulting regression equation contains coefficients that are highly inflated (have a large variance), with t statistics that are extremely small, despite the fact that one or more of these seemingly insignificant variables are very useful predictors. The presence of multicollinearity within a specific data set can be detected by computing a **variance inflation factor** for each predictor variable. This value is large (>10) whenever the corresponding predictor variable produces a large R^2 value when regressed on the remaining predictor variables.

Stepwise techniques allow you to insert variables one at a time into the equation **(forward regression),** remove them one at a time after initially including all variables in the equation **(backward regression),** or perform a combination of the two by inserting variables one at a time but removing a variable that has become redundant at any stage **(stepwise regression).** Once the variables for the model have been selected, **residual plots** should be obtained (1) to examine the underlying assumptions that are necessary in a regression analysis, and (2) to search for outlying and influential observations. Sample observations that have unusually large or small values for the predictor variables can be detected using **sample leverages** (h_i). By computing the **standardized residuals,** you can identify observations having an outlying value of the dependent variable, Y. **Cook's distance measures** (D_i) can be used to determine if any of the sample observations have a large effect on determining the regression equation.

Dummy variables can be used in a regression application to represent the categories of a qualitative variable (such as city). If all dummy variables are to be inserted into the equation, then $C - 1$ such variables should be defined to represent C categories. If a forward or stepwise selection procedure is used to define the final regression equation, then a better procedure is to define C dummy variables to represent this situation.

Use of a computer package is essential in the derivation of a multiple regression equation. In this chapter, we use Excel, SPSS, and MINITAB. They provide the sampling coefficients (b_0, b_1, b_2, . . .), the statistics necessary to perform any test of hypothesis, and those needed for the prediction and confidence intervals for any specific set of predictor variable values. A **confidence interval** is derived whenever the predicted Y value is used to estimate the average value of the dependent variable for a specific set of X values. When the predicted Y value is used to predict an individual value of Y for a specific set of X values, a **prediction interval** can be used to place bounds on the actual Y value.

A linear regression model containing a strictly linear combination of the predictor variables (such as $Y = \beta_0 + \beta_1 X_1 + \beta_2 X_2 + e$) is a **first-order model.** A **complete second-order model** (such as $Y = \beta_0 + \beta_1 X_1 + \beta_2 X_2 + \beta_3 X_1 X_2 + \beta_4 X_1^2 + \beta_5 X_2^2 + e$) includes **interaction terms** (such as $\beta_3 X_1 X_2$) and **quadratic terms** (such as $\beta_4 X_1^2$). The second-order model provides an extremely powerful modeling device, since any curvilinear effects of the predictor variables (using the quadratic terms) and any interactive effects between the predictor variables can be captured.

 # Summary of Formulas

H_0: all β's $= 0$	H_0: $\beta_i = 0$
H_a: at least one $\beta \neq 0$	H_a: $\beta_i \neq 0$
	(or H_a: $\beta_i > 0$)
$F = \dfrac{\text{MSR}}{\text{MSE}} = \dfrac{R^2/k}{(1 - R^2)/(n - k - 1)}$	(or H_a: $\beta_i < 0$)
(df $= k$ and $n - k - 1$)	$t = \dfrac{b_i}{s_{b_i}}$
	(df $= n - k - 1$)

Confidence Interval for β_i

$$b_i - t_{\alpha/2,n-k-1}s_{b_i} \quad \text{to} \quad b_i + t_{\alpha/2,n-k-1}s_{b_i}$$

Coefficient of Determination

$$R^2 = 1 - \frac{SSE}{SST}$$

where

$$SST = \Sigma(Y - \bar{Y})^2 = \Sigma Y^2 - \frac{(\Sigma Y)^2}{n}$$

and

$$SSE = \Sigma(Y - \hat{Y})^2$$

Coefficient of Determination (Adjusted)

$$R^2(adj) = 1 - \frac{SSE/(n-k-1)}{SST/(n-1)}$$

Partial F test

H_0: $X_i, X_{i+1}, \ldots, X_j$ do not contribute

H_a: at least one of them contributes

$$F = \frac{(R_c^2 - R_r^2)/v_1}{(1 - R_c^2)/v_2}$$

where (1) R_c^2 is the R^2 including the variables in H_0 (the complete model), (2) R_r^2 is the R^2 excluding

the variables in H_0 (the reduced model), (3) $v_1 =$ the number of β's in H_0, (4) $v_2 = n - 1 -$ (number of X's in the complete model), and (5) the degrees of freedom for the F statistic are v_1 and v_2.

Variance Inflation Factor for the jth Predictor Variable

$$VIF_j = \frac{1}{1 - R_j^2}$$

where R_j^2 is the coefficient of determination obtained by regressing the jth predictor variable on the remaining $k - 1$ predictor variables.

Standardized Residual

$$\text{Standardized residual} = \frac{Y_i - \hat{Y}_i}{s\sqrt{1 - h_i}}$$

where h_i is the corresponding leverage value, $s = \sqrt{MSE}$, and $MSE = SSE/(n - k - 1)$.

Cook's Distance Measure

$$D_i = \frac{(Y_i - \hat{Y}_i)^2}{(k+1)s^2}\left[\frac{h_i}{(1 - h_i)^2}\right]$$

X Review Exercises 15.61–15.76

15.61 The following information is selected from a computer printout of a multiple regression analysis:

Predictor	Coefficient	S.D.
Constant	−1.0	.396
X_1	4.8	.512
X_2	5.9	.42

Analysis of Variance

Source	df	SS	MS	F
Model	2		147.65	
Residual				
Total	19	314.80		

a. Write the multiple regression equation.

b. What percentage of the total variation in Y is explained by the model?

c. Does the model with X_1 and X_2 contribute to the prediction of Y? Use a .05 significance level.

d. Does X_1 contribute to this model given that X_2 is in the model? Use a .05 significance level.

e. Does X_2 contribute to this model given that X_1 is in the model? Use a .05 significance level.

15.62 A company has opened several outdoor ice-skating rinks and would like to know what factors affect the attendance at the rinks. The manager believes that the following variables affect attendance:

$$X_1 = \text{temperature (forecasted high)}$$

$$X_2 = \text{wind speed (forecasted high)}$$

$$X_3 = 1 \text{ if weekend and 0 otherwise}$$

$$X_4 = X_1 X_2$$

The following least squares model was found from 30 days of data:

$$\hat{Y} = 250 + 4.8X_1 - 30X_2 + 1.3X_3 + 35X_4$$

a. What is the predicted attendance on a weekend if the forecasted high temperature is 28° F and the forecasted high wind speed is 12 miles per hour?

b. If the coefficient of determination for the model is .67, test that the overall model contributes to predicting the attendance at the ice-skating rinks. Use a .05 significance level. What is the value of the adjusted R^2?

c. If the standard deviation of the estimate of the coefficient of X_2 is 2.01, does the variable wind speed contribute to predicting the variation in attendance, assuming that the variables X_1, X_3, and X_4 are in the model? Use a .05 significance level.

15.63 A manager used two predictor variables to forecast the number of videos rented weekly at her store. The regression equation is $\hat{Y} = 97.86 - 1.48X_1 + .3756X_2$. The following output was obtained. Fill in the missing entries in the output and interpret the output. Use a significance level of 5%.

Regression Statistics

Multiple R	
R square	
Adjusted R Square	0.81
Standard Error	
Observations	11

ANOVA

	df	SS	MS
Regression	2		10027.88
Residual		3597.14	
Total	10	23652.91	

	Coefficients	Standard Error	t Stat
Intercept	97.86	16.92	
$X1$	−1.48		−6.07
$X2$	0.38	0.28	

15.64 A real-estate agent wanted to explore the feasibility of using multiple regression analysis in appraising the value of single-family homes within a certain community. The following variables were used:

$$Y = \text{selling price of a house (in dollars)}$$

$$X_1 = \text{total living area (in square feet)}$$

$$X_2 = \begin{cases} 1 & \text{if in neighborhood 1} \\ 0 & \text{if not} \end{cases}$$

$$X_3 = \begin{cases} 1 & \text{if in neighborhood 2} \\ 0 & \text{if not} \end{cases}$$

$$X_4 = \begin{cases} 1 & \text{if lot size is larger than the typical house lot} \\ 0 & \text{if not} \end{cases}$$

The data are as follows:

Y	X_1	X_2	X_3	X_4	Y	X_1	X_2	X_3	X_4
63,000	2,020	1	0	1	31,350	640	0	1	0
36,000	980	1	0	0	49,400	1,910	0	0	1
44,000	1,230	0	0	1	31,000	900	1	0	0
37,000	980	0	1	0	56,000	1,890	1	0	0
28,000	640	0	1	0	63,500	1,900	0	0	1
28,000	720	0	1	0	49,000	2,080	1	0	1
56,000	2,400	1	0	1	63,000	1,900	0	0	1
28,600	670	0	1	0					

Using a computerized statistical package, find the following:
  a. The least squares equation
  b. The 95% confidence interval for the coefficient of total living area
  c. The 95% prediction interval for selling price given that $X_1 = 1,800$, $X_2 = 1$, $X_3 = 0$, and $X_4 = 0$
  d. The overall F test for the model and the resulting conclusion using a 5% significance level.

15.65 To predict the asking price of a used Chevrolet Camaro, the following data were collected on the car's age, condition, and mileage and on whether the seller is an individual or a dealer.

Asking Price (Y)	Age (in Years) (X_1)	Mileage (in Thousands) (X_2)	Condition (Excellent, Average, Poor) (X_3)	(X_4)	Dealer or Individual (X_5)
3,000	9	70	1	0	0
2,700	9	99	0	1	0
2,995	8	120	0	1	0
5,500	7	56	1	0	1
3,988	7	50	0	1	0
3,900	7	83	0	1	0
2,800	7	106	0	1	0
6,800	6	70	0	0	1
6,295	6	66	1	0	1
3,700	6	60	0	1	0
7,450	5	55	1	0	1
6,800	5	67	0	1	0
6,795	5	62	1	0	0
6,476	5	60	0	1	0
6,450	5	55	0	1	0
4,800	5	75	0	1	0
9,695	4	44	1	0	1
9,675	4	37	0	0	1
9,595	4	44	1	0	0
8,500	4	55	1	0	0
7,995	4	46	0	1	0
6,995	4	56	0	1	0
6,450	4	65	0	1	0
14,350	3	29	0	0	1
11,965	3	23	0	1	1
11,850	3	27	0	0	1
11,000	3	31	1	0	1
7,600	3	45	0	1	0
19,888	2	18	0	0	1
16,000	2	19	0	0	1
17,650	1	9	0	0	1

The dummy variable X_3 is equal to 1 if the car is in average condition, 0 if not. The variable X_4 is equal to 1 if the car is in poor condition, 0 if not. The dummy variable X_5 is equal to 1 if the seller is a dealer and is equal to 0 if the seller is an individual. Use a computerized statistical package to answer the following questions.

a. Find the least squares equation.

b. Does the overall model contribute significantly to predicting the asking price of a used Chevrolet Camaro? Use a .01 significance level.

c. Find a 95% prediction interval for the asking price of a five-year-old Camaro in average condition with 70,000 miles, sold by an individual.

d. Calculate the correlation matrix of all the variables. Would you suspect any multicollinearity problems by observing the correlations in this matrix?

e. Do a forward regression analysis using a significance level of .10.

f. Examine the residuals. Do you detect the presence of any outliers or influential observations?

15.66 The owner of a photographic laboratory would like to explore the relationship between her weekly profits (Y) and

X_1 = number of rolls of film sold

X_2 = number of enlargements given out free for advertising purposes

X_3 = number of prints

X_4 = number of reprints

Several weeks were selected randomly, and the following data were collected.

Y	X_1	X_2	X_3	X_4	Y	X_1	X_2	X_3	X_4
350	50	15	130	50	358	62	17	125	35
414	61	18	150	39	392	55	19	150	36
385	71	12	125	45	415	59	24	157	44
429	86	21	141	36	380	63	28	140	38
415	90	22	133	40					

Use a computerized statistical package.

a. Find the least squares prediction equation.

b. Test the null hypothesis that X_4 does not contribute to predicting the variation in Y given that X_1, X_2, and X_3 are already in the model. Use a .05 significance level.

c. Find the 90% confidence interval for the mean value of Y given $X_1 = 85$, $X_2 = 20$, $X_3 = 135$, and $X_4 = 37$.

d. Find the coefficient of determination for the complete model and interpret its value.

e. Examine the residuals. Do you detect any outliers or influential observations?

15.67 When an additional independent variable is added to a regression model, the coefficient of determination can never decrease. Use the following data with the model (a) predicting Y using X_1, (b) predicting Y using X_1 and X_2, and (c) predicting Y using X_1, X_2, and X_3. Record the values of SSE, SST, R^2, R^2 (adj), and MSE. Comment on how these values change each time that a new independent variable is added to the model.

Y	X_1	X_2	X_3
2	4	1	35
3	10	6	15
4	20	11	40
5	22	18	10
6	25	25	45
12	30	31	5

15.68 An operations manager uses five independent variables to predict the productivity of a plant. Suppose that for 26 days the manager collects data and uses these 26 observations to fit a regression equation. Assume that the regression sum of squares is 95.6 and that the error sum of squares is 159.0.

a. Construct an ANOVA table. Does the overall model contribute to predicting the productivity of the plant? Use a 5% significance level.

b. Compute the R^2 and interpret its value. What is the value of the adjusted R^2?

15.69 The vice president of operations at an airline company collects performance ratings of each of its supervisors in charge of maintenance of aircraft. Data are collected on the number of hours per month spent studying new maintenance procedures (X_1), their education level (X_2), and the number of years that they have been on the job (X_3). Using 25 supervisors in the field, the operations vice president used a statistical package to obtain an error sum of squares of 43.4005 using all three independent variables to predict the ratings of each supervisor. When only X_1 was used, an error sum of squares of 56.685 was obtained. Assume that the total sum of squares was 70.26. Do the variables X_2 and X_3 contribute to the prediction of supervisor performance ratings? Use a 5% significance level.

15.70 To understand how two seemingly unrelated variables can be used to construct a regression equation in which the independent variable is a significant predictor, consider the following. Randomly generate 30 observations for 50 normally distributed random variables having a mean and standard deviation of 0 and 1. Using a statistical computer package, find the correlation matrix for the 50 variables. (In Excel, click on **Tools ➤ Data Analysis ➤ Correlation**. In SPSS, click on **Analysis ➤ Correlate ➤ Bivariate**. In MINITAB click on **Stat ➤ Basic Statistics > Correlation**.) Pick the two variables with the highest correlation and run a regression analysis with one of the variables as the dependent variable (Y) and the other as the predictor variable (X). What is the p-value for the F test using this regression equation? Note that all of the random variables are statistically independent and none of the variables should be good predictors of any of the others. However, by chance, a supposed good predictor of another random variable may appear. What precautions would you recommend to someone who is using the stepwise selection procedure with one variable being regressed on 50 variables?

15.71 [DATA SET EX15-71] *Variable description:*

Company: Name of mid-size US banking company

ROE3yr: Return on Equity by a banking company for the past three years

EPS_GR3yr: Earnings per share growth rate for a banking company for the past three years

Banking companies must adapt to changes in the economy to stay competitive. Many banks monitor the companies to which they make major loans, constantly evaluating cash flow and collateral values. That is, if a bank has an early warning system in place, it can cut its losses to maintain profitability. The ROE (return on equity) represents how well a bank can balance profitability, asset management, and financial leverage.

a. What is the prediction equation for predicting ROE3yr using EPS_GR3yr and the square of EPS_GR3yr? Does the F test indicate that the model contributes to the prediction of ROE3yr? Use a 5% significance level.

b. Do the t tests for the individual predictors (EPS_GR3yr and the square of this term) indicate that each of them contribute to the prediction of ROE3yr? Do you suspect that multicollinearity is present? What are the values of the VIF for the independent variables?

c. Remove the observation that you consider to be most influential. Repeat part a with this observation removed. Did you realize that removing an influential observation could change the conclusion when testing that a model adequately predicts its dependent variable?

(Source: "Mid-Size U.S. Banking Companies Fiscal 1998–2000," *U.S. Banker*, June 2001, p. 46.)

15.72 [DATA SET EX15-72] *Variable description:*

SecurityFirm: Name of stock brokerage firm

BattingAverage: A firm's total awards divided by the number of employed analysts

Stock-PickingAwards: Number of awards for picking stocks that outperformed the market

Earnings-ForecastingAwards: Number of awards for being the most accurate firm in forecasting the earnings of certain stocks

Twenty stock brokerage firms were selected, and each firm's batting average, number of stock-picking awards, and earnings-forecasting awards were recorded. The batting average is a score obtained by dividing the firm's total number of awards for many different categories by the number of analysts used by that firm.

a. Develop a complete second order model to predict BattingAverage using Stock-PickingAwards and Earnings-ForecastingAwards. That is, form second-order terms involving quadratic terms and the interaction term and include these in the regression model. At the 5% significance level, is there sufficient evidence to say that the model contributes to the prediction of a firm's batting average?

b. Interpret the R^2 and the R^2 (adj) for this model.

c. Form a model called the reduced model by using only Stock-PickingAwards and Earnings-ForecastingAwards in the model. What is the coefficient of determination for this model?

d. Using the reduced model in part c and the complete model in part a, test that the second order terms contribute to the prediction of a firm's batting average. Use a 5% significance level.

(Source: "Firm by Firm: Tally of Awards Ranks 82 Research Houses," *The Wall Street Journal*, June 26, 2001, p. R16.)

15.73 [DATA SET EX15-73] *Variable description:*

State: Name of State

MedianIncome: Median household income

HousingCostsExceed30%: Percentage of mortgage-paying homeowners whose housing costs exceed 30% of income

EightRoomsOrMore: Percentage of homes with 8 or more rooms

Thirty states are randomly selected and the median household income (Y), percentage of mortgage-paying homeowners whose housing costs exceed 30% of income (X_1), and percentage of homes with eight or more rooms (X_2) are recorded.

a. Test that the regression model using X_1 and X_2 contributes to the prediction of Y. Use the p-value to base your conclusion.

b. Predict the median household income for a state that has 18% of its mortgage-paying homeowners with housing costs exceeding 30% of their income, and 16% of the homes with eight or more rooms.

c. What are the VIF values for the independent variables? Is multicollinearity a problem?

d. Plot the residuals versus X_1. Also, plot the residuals versus X_2. Would you say that the plots appear to be random?

(Source: "Snapshot of U.S. Commuting, Income, Housing," *USA Today*, August 6, 2001, p. 2A.)

15.74 [DATA SET EX15-74] *Variable description:*

Company_Country: Company name and its location

AnnualRevenue: Current yearly revenue in millions of dollars

RevPriorYear: Yearly revenue in millions of dollars during the prior year

ExpandingAgg: An indicator variable that is equal to 1 if the company is expanding aggressively at the international level and 0 if not

A sample of 25 international companies that are heavily invested in the United States are listed with their current and prior years' annual revenue in millions of dollars. An indicator variable is used to denote if the company is expanding aggressively worldwide.

a. Form an interaction term with RevPriorYear and ExpandingAgg by multiplying these two variables. Test that the variables RevPriorYear, ExpandingAgg, and the interaction term contribute to the prediction of current yearly revenue. Use the p-value as a basis for your conclusion.

b. Find a 95% prediction interval for a company's current yearly revenue, given that its prior year's revenue was $18,000 million and the company was expanding aggressively worldwide. Interpret this interval.

c. Which observations would you classify as being influential? Why?

(Source: "The International 500," *Forbes*, July 23, 2001, p. 136.)

15.75 [DATA SET EX15-75] *Variable description:*

MonthlyPay: Monthly payment for a leased truck

StickerPrice: Sticker price of truck

OwnPickUp3: 1 if the customer leased a pickup within the past three years, and 0 if not

OwnPickUpGT3: 1 if the customer leased a pickup more than three years ago, and 0 if not

Owning a pickup truck through a lease arrangement has become popular with many pickup drivers. In the late 1990s, Dodge upscaled its pickups to the Quad Cab model. Spruced up with CD players, keyless entry, and automatic transmissions, pickups have taken a larger part of the market share of automotive sales. Suppose that a lease manager wished to determine if there is a relationship between the monthly payment for a leased pickup and the variables StickerPrice, OwnPickUp3, and OwnPickUpGT3. The manager believes that the monthly price that a customer is willing to negotiate may be influenced by whether they have previously leased a pickup. A random sample of 14 pickup lease agreement customers was selected. The data on StickerPrice is in units of thousands of dollars.

a. Interpret the coefficients in the regression model. Do the independent variables contribute to the prediction of monthly payment at the 5% significance level?

b. Are there any outliers or influential observations?

c. Eliminate the most influential observation and run the regression analysis again. Interpret the coefficients of this model. Do the independent variables contribute to the prediction of monthly payment at the 5% significance level?

Summary Output

Regression Statistics

Multiple R	0.941890346
R Square	0.887157423
Adjusted R Square	0.85330465
Standard Error	49.38638683
Observations	14

ANOVA

	df	SS	MS	F	Significance F
Regression	3	191753.0163	63917.6721	26.206344	4.71408E-05
Residual	10	24390.15204	2439.0152		
Total	13	216143.1683			

	Coefficients	Standard Error	t Stat	P-value	Lower 95%	Upper 95%
Intercept	-163.2625997	73.02360287	-2.23575109	0.0493587	-325.9693545	-0.5558449
StickerPrice	19.62576855	2.248387679	8.72881876	5.444E-06	14.61604774	24.635489
OwnPickUp3	195.1025757	39.94847761	4.88385509	0.0006383	106.0918053	284.11335
OwnPickUpGT3	58.46083195	35.48437318	1.64750922	0.1304729	-20.60329225	137.52496

Residual Output

Observation	Predicted MonthlyPay	Residuals	Standardized Residuals	Leverages	Cook's D
1	619.389091809	-28.621291809	-0.727684509	0.365724850	0.07633136
2	420.430193362	-31.767233362	-0.724867602	0.212542904	0.03545496
3	454.532635973	13.202044027	0.293552447	0.170729079	0.00443529
4	419.206252579	24.842107421	0.551135309	0.166998292	0.01522378
5	573.511188067	-46.139028067	-1.085381224	0.259103119	0.10299579
6	154.258377128	-67.738377128	-2.084713368	0.567125139	1.42347303
7	354.857690068	51.391509932	1.299455556	0.358723408	0.23614415
8	378.408612331	-51.761172331	-1.294325468	0.344297700	0.21991477
9	325.002563530	55.742556470	1.280231389	0.222711370	0.11740241
10	426.317923928	81.320116072	1.852194357	0.209670198	0.22753146
11	589.950438981	2.572961019	0.062694445	0.309452155	0.00044035
12	537.377337601	0.369662399	0.009687948	0.403057587	0.00001584
13	491.082960149	-1.634280149	-0.037060104	0.202693628	0.00008729
14	432.205654493	-1.779574493	-0.040468680	0.207170572	0.00010698

(Source: "Drive Buys," *The Wall Street Journal*, May 8, 1998, p. W4.)

15.76 [DATA SET EX15-76] *Variable description:*

AppraisedVal: Appraised value of home

LotSize: Size of the lot on which the home is built

HouseSize: Square footage of the house

HouseAge: Age of the house

A real-estate broker is interested in predicting the appraised value of homes in a certain subdivision. The broker selected a random sample of 20 homes. The variable AppraisedVal is recorded in units of thousands of dollars, LotSize and HouseSize are recorded in square feet, and HouseAge is recorded in years. The correlations of LotSize, HouseSize, and HouseAge with AppraisedVal are presented below.

a. Which variable would you place in a model using the forward selection procedure?

b. Construct a regression equation with the variable selected in part a. Does this independent variable contribute to the prediction of AppraisedVal at a 5% significance level?

c. Add another independent variable to the model in part b. Which variable would a forward selection procedure pick? Does this added variable contribute to the prediction of AppraisedVal at a 5% significance level?

d. Should the third variable be added to the model using a 5% significance level?

e. Find the VIFs for the independent variables that you think should be included in the model and comment on whether a multicollinearity problem exists.

Correlation of AppraisedVal and LotSize	0.01499
Correlation of AppraisedVal and HouseSize	0.91204
Correlation of AppraisedVal and HouseAge	0.57869

Computer Exercises Using the Databases

Exercise 1—Appendix F

From the database, randomly select 50 observations. Regress the variable HPAYRENT (house payment or apartment/house rent) on the prediction variables INCOME1 (primary income), INCOME2 (secondary income), and FAMLSIZE (size of family). Find the coefficient of determination for the complete model. Find a 90% confidence interval on the mean value of HPAYRENT for families having a principal income of $45,000, a secondary income of $22,000, and a family size equal to three.

Exercise 2—Appendix F

Using the data from the previous problem along with dummy variables representing the LOCATION of the residences, do both a forward regression analysis and a backward regression analysis with a significance level of .10. Compare the two resulting models.

Exercise 3—Appendix G

From the database, randomly select 50 observations. Consider a multiple regression model, where the dependent variable is SALES and predictor variables are COSTSALE (sales cost), EMPLOYEE (number of employees), NETINC (net income), ASSETS, and TOTAL. Using these predictor variables, what percentage of the variation in the SALES values has been explained? Construct a histogram of the residuals. Do the regression assumptions appear to be satisfied?

Exercise 4—Appendix G

Using the data from the previous exercise, perform both a forward regression analysis and a backward regression analysis, with a significance level of .10. Compare the resulting models.

Insights from Statistics in Action

Getting Framed Right Before Your Eyes: Evaluating the Price You Will Pay

The Statistics in Action introductory case study mentioned that *Consumer Reports* surveyed 64,000 consumers to evaluate variables such as service, quality, satisfaction, and speed in delivering a product. *Consumer Reports* lists the median price that consumers paid for a pair of glasses at each of 19 optical stores. Service, quality, satisfaction, and speed in manufacturing the glasses is measured on a five-point scale by consumers. Multiple regression analysis can be used to determine which of these consumer-provided variables differentiate the price of eyewear at the various optical stores. Use the data provided in StatInActChap15.xls to answer the following questions. Lower values for the consumer variables indicate a better rating.

1. From your own experience, which predictor variables—service, quality, satisfaction, and speed—do you believe would be the best predictors of price? Which predictor variable do you believe would make the least contribution to the prediction of price?

2. Conduct a multiple regression analysis using all four predictor variables. Does the overall model contribute to the prediction of price? Use the *p*-value as the basis for your conclusion.

3. Which predictor variables are significant at the 5% level? Find the regression equation removing those independent variables that are not significant at the 5% level.

4. What is the coefficient of determination for the model in question 2? Compare this to the coefficient of determination in question 3, with the nonsignificant variables removed. Is there much of a change in the coefficient of determination? Would you have expected the coefficient of determination to change much?

5. Find a 95% confidence interval for the mean value of the price of eyewear for optical stores in which quality and satisfaction were rated 3 and 2. Interpret this interval.

Sources: "Glasses That Change with Your Prescription," *Business Week*, March 12, 2001, p. 97; and "Clear Choices," *Consumer Reports*, June 2001, pp. 10–15.

Appendix SPSS®

Chapter 15 Appendix: Data Analysis with SPSS

Multiple Linear Regression

The SPSS procedure to carry out a multiple linear regression analysis will be illustrated using the real-estate data from Section 15.1, as illustrated below. The instructions and computer output contained in the SPSS appendix for Chapter 14 (simple linear regression) also apply to multiple linear regression. To begin, click on **Analyze ➤ Regression ➤ Linear**. Move the footage variable into the **Dependent** box and the income, famsize, and yrseduc variables into the **Independent(s)** box.

	footage	income	famsize	yrseduc
1	16	32	2	4
2	17	36	2	8
3	26	55	3	7
4	24	47	4	0
5	22	38	4	2
6	21	60	3	10
7	32	66	6	8
8	18	44	3	8
9	30	70	5	2
10	20	50	3	6

The predicted values and a check of the residuals can be obtained by clicking on **Save**. To obtain:

1. the predicted *Y* values, click on **Predicted Values ➤ Unstandardized.**

2. the standardized residuals, click on **Residuals ➤ Studentized.** *Note:* SPSS refers to the standardized residuals defined in equation 15.20 as studentized residuals, rather than standardized residuals.

3. the Cook's distance measures, click on **Distances ➤ Cook's.**

4. the sample leverages, click on **Distances ➤ Leverage values.**

As was noted in the Chapter 14 appendix, the leverage values computed by SPSS do not agree with the values computed using the KPK Excel macros and MINITAB. To obtain leverage values that agree with the values computed by these two packages, the value of $1/n$ (equal to .1 in this illustration) must be added to the leverage values computed by SPSS. If this column is named leverage, the columns shown below will appear in the data window. The predicted Y values are in the pre_1 column, the studentized residuals are in the sre_1 column, the Cook's distance measures are in the coo_1 column, and the sample leverages are in the lev_1 column. The adjusted leverage values (obtained by adding .1 to the lev_1 column) are in the far right column.

	footage	income	famsize	yrseduc	pre_1	sre_1	coo_1	lev_1	leverage
1	16	32	2	4	15.88596	.06915	.00063	.24350	.34350
2	17	36	2	8	16.01039	.59187	.04221	.22524	.32524
3	26	55	3	7	22.19496	2.12944	.33735	.12933	.22933
4	24	47	4	0	24.12143	-.07754	.00104	.30806	.40806
5	22	38	4	2	22.05099	-.03390	.00024	.35395	.45395
6	21	60	3	10	22.67604	-1.08824	.22106	.32747	.42747
7	32	66	6	8	31.17917	.97598	1.15672	.72928	.82928
8	18	44	3	8	19.89952	-1.05499	.07736	.11753	.21753
9	30	70	5	2	30.59320	-.47515	.09358	.52379	.62379
10	20	50	3	6	21.38834	-.73630	.02240	.04185	.14185

Building Quadratic and Interaction Terms

Quadratic and interaction terms can be constructed in SPSS using **Transform ➤ Compute**. For example, to include the quadratic term for income, that is, $(\text{income})^2$, enter the information in the **Target Variable** and **Numeric Expression** boxes as shown below.

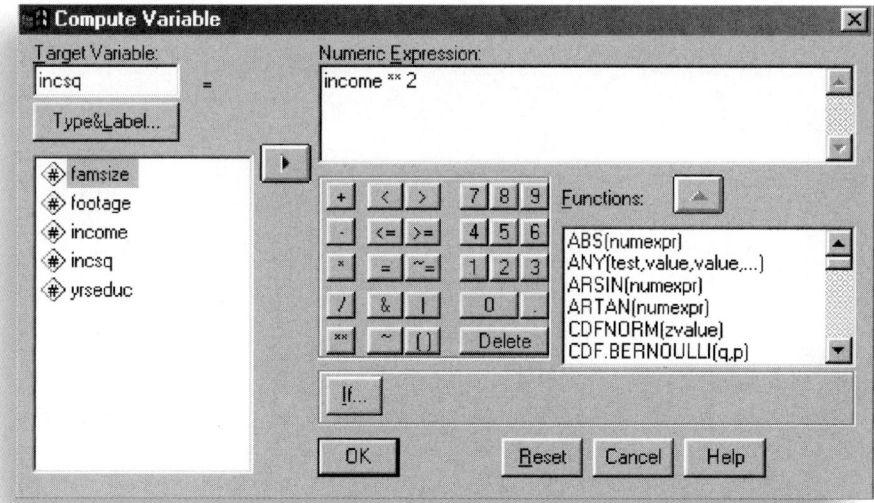

To construct an interaction term for income and family size, enter "incxfam" in the **Target Variable** box and "income*famsize" in the **Numeric Expression** box. The resulting columns are shown in the following data window.

	footage	income	famsize	yrseduc	incsq	incxfam
1	16	32	2	4	1024	64
2	17	36	2	8	1296	72
3	26	55	3	7	3025	165
4	24	47	4	0	2209	188
5	22	38	4	2	1444	152
6	21	60	3	10	3600	180
7	32	66	6	8	4356	396
8	18	44	3	8	1936	132
9	30	70	5	2	4900	350
10	20	50	3	6	2500	150

Stepwise Procedures

Forward, backward, and stepwise regression models can be obtained by clicking on **Analyze ➤ Regression ➤ Linear.** Move the footage variable into the **Dependent** box and the income, famsize, and yrseduc variables into the **Independent(s)** box.

Forward Regression. In the window below, select "Forward" in the **Method** box. By clicking on **Options,** the significance level of the F statistics can be set. In the **Linear Regression: Options** window, increasing the significance level in the **Entry** box makes it easier for variables to enter the model. Setting the **Entry** significance level at .10 and the **Removal** level at .15, the program will select variables income and famsize and will exclude variable yrseduc. *Note:* The **Removal** significance level must always be greater than the **Entry** significance level although the **Removal** value is not used in the forward selection procedure.

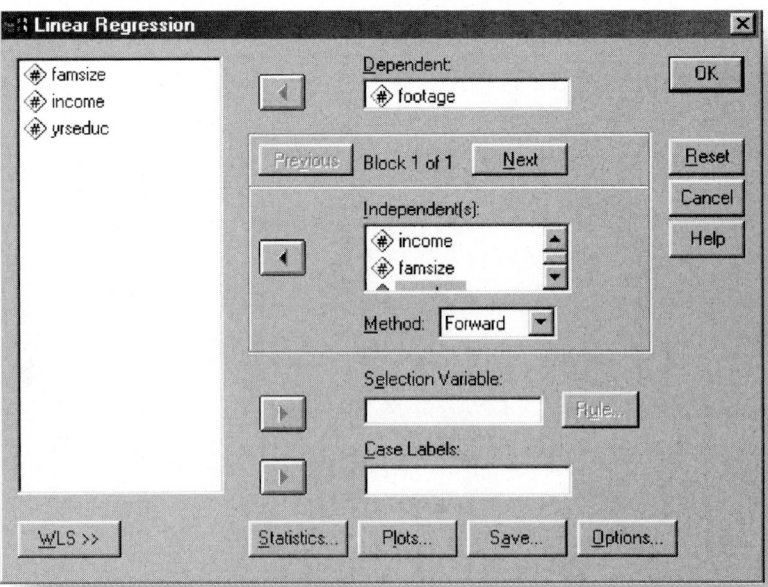

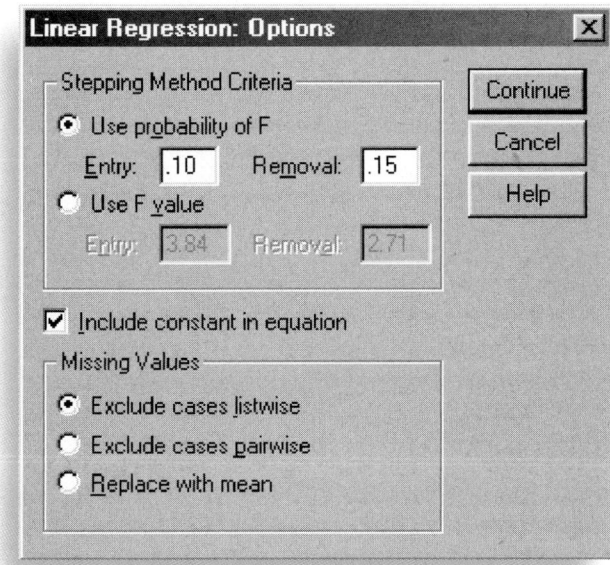

Backward Regression. In the **Linear Regression** window, select **Backward** in the **Method** box. By clicking on **Options,** the significance level of the *F* statistics can be set. Setting the **Entry** significance level at .10 (this value is not used) and the **Removal** level at .15, the program will once again select variables income and famsize and will exclude variable yrseduc.

Stepwise Regression. The most commonly used method of model selection is stepwise variable selection. This procedure is a combination of forward selection and backward elimination. Select Stepwise in the **Method** box, click on **Options,** and set the significance levels in the **Entry** box and the **Removal** box (.10 and .15, respectively, for this illustration). The variables selected using the stepwise procedure agree with the forward and backward results; namely, income and famsize are included in the model and variable yrseduc is excluded.

Note. The other option in the previous **Linear Regression: Options** screen is to specify values of the *F* statistic by clicking on **Use F value.** Enter the *F* values for entering and removing a variable into/from the model in the two boxes.

On the CD . . .
Chapter 15 Appendix: Data Analysis with MINITAB

chapter

16

Time Series Analysis and Index Numbers X

Statistics in Action
Forecasting Underlying Economic Trends: Oh CPI, Why Did You Lie?

The Consumer Price Index (CPI) is arguably the world's most quoted economic index. It has a profound ripple effect in economic decision making. A large leap in the CPI raises the specter of the Federal Reserve taking action to check inflation. This index affects pay-raise decisions, Social Security benefit decisions, standard deductions as determined by the Internal Revenue Service, stipends for food stamps, and rates on bank loans. The CPI frequently is called a cost-of-living index, but it is not a complete cost-of-living measure. The index reflects changes in the prices of goods and services commonly purchased in the marketplace.

The CPI is determined by the Bureau of Labor Statistics through an extensive survey of approximately 40,000 consumers. Information on consumer buying habits is collected on purchases in the following areas: food, housing, apparel, transportation, medical care, recreation, education, and communication. Economists often criticize the use of the CPI as not being an accurate index because it is sometimes temporarily jolted by changes due to spikes in oil prices or rapid changes in one sector of the economy. For example, real estate in certain "hot areas" of the country might make the index look higher than it would be without the housing component. Some economists refer to the *core CPI,* which removes the more volatile sectors of the economy from the computation. However, economists realize that even their modified indexes are still far from perfect and give misleading results.

Cyclical companies are firms whose earnings are strongly tied to the business cycle. These companies use the CPI and other economic indicators to forecast their earnings and make business decisions with regard to hiring or laying off employees. Examples of cyclical companies include General Motors, International Paper, and Caterpillar. Many economic indexes, including the CPI, are adjusted to remove the effect of seasonal influences. Seasonal influences are those that occur at the same time and in about the same magnitude every year. These indexes may also be affected by cycles in the economy. Examples of such cycles are presidential cycles, global changes in demand, and changes in demographics. Economists often use indexes that are seasonally adjusted or that have the effect of certain cycles removed. Policy makers and economic analysts need good current measures of the underlying economic trends to forecast patterns in the economy. An incorrect economic decision by a major corporation could result in overwhelming losses or in lost opportunities.

This chapter examines data in the form of a time series—that is, a variable, such as the CPI, recorded across time. When you have completed this chapter, you will be able to

- Describe and measure seasonal, trend, and cyclical components of variables such as the CPI.
- Make simple forecasts considering the trend and seasonal components.
- Compare the change in the price or value of certain items between any two time periods using an index number.

A Look Back/Introduction

The previous two chapters introduced you to a method of predicting the value of a dependent variable using the technique of linear regression. You determined a set of one or more predictor (independent) variables (X_1, X_2, . . .) that could be used to model the behavior of the dependent variable, Y.

When the dependent variable is measured over *time*, there is another method of describing the behavior of this variable—*time series analysis*. For example, consider the following data, where Y is the amount of electrical power consumed in Pine Bluff over a 10-year period:

Year	Power Consumption (Million kwh)
1992	95
1993	145
1994	174
1995	200
1996	224
1997	245
1998	263
1999	275
2000	283
2001	288

This is an example of a (very short) time series. Typically, a time series covers many more periods, especially when measured for each month, week, or even day. To describe the behavior of the variable Y, we examine the past data and, rather than searching for a number of predictor variables, we try to capture the patterns that exist in the Y observations over a period of time. In other words, we assume that *time-related patterns can serve as predictors*. In this illustration, one pattern is clear—the power consumption values increase from one year to the next.

The process of using the patterns contained in the past data to predict future values is referred to as **forecasting**. Forecasting using time series data has both advantages and disadvantages. The primary advantage of using time series analysis is that often you can describe your variable of interest, Y, by using only a sample of past observations. Inherent to this type of forecasting procedure is the assumption that past patterns will continue into the future. The disadvantage of time series forecasting is that the past observations often contain patterns that are difficult to extract and, as a result, the models can become very complex.

In this chapter, we will concentrate on methods of *describing* a time series by isolating its various *components* (for example, sales in December are always much higher than the yearly average). In the next chapter, methods of forecasting are discussed. We should note at this point that in general, there is no single best forecasting technique. Instead, the forecaster should attempt to match the forecasting technique to patterns observed in the time series data. Consequently, this chapter and the next chapter are highly intertwined, since by describing the nature of the time series (Chapter 16), you will have a better idea as to which forecasting technique to employ (Chapter 17).

COMPONENTS OF A TIME SERIES 16.1

A **time series** represents a variable observed across time. The time increment can be years, quarters, months, or even days. The values of the time series can be presented in a table or illustrated using a scatter diagram. Usually, the points in the graph are connected by straight lines, making it easier to detect any existing patterns; such a graph is called a *line graph*.

The time series for the power-consumption data is shown in Figure 16.1. As we noted, the power-consumption values increase steadily from one year to the next. This long-term movement in the time series is called a *trend*. These values exhibit a definite increasing trend (or growth). Trend is only one of several components that describe the behavior of any time series. The components of a time series are

- Trend (*TR*)
- Seasonal variation (*S*)
- Cyclical variation (*C*)
- Irregular activity (*I*)

The purpose of time series analysis is to describe a particular data set by estimating the various components that make up this time series. We examine each of these components individually, although time series data usually contain a mixture of all four. This section will *not* attempt to measure these components, but rather will introduce you to the nature of each component. The remainder of this chapter demonstrates methods of capturing and measuring these individual components.

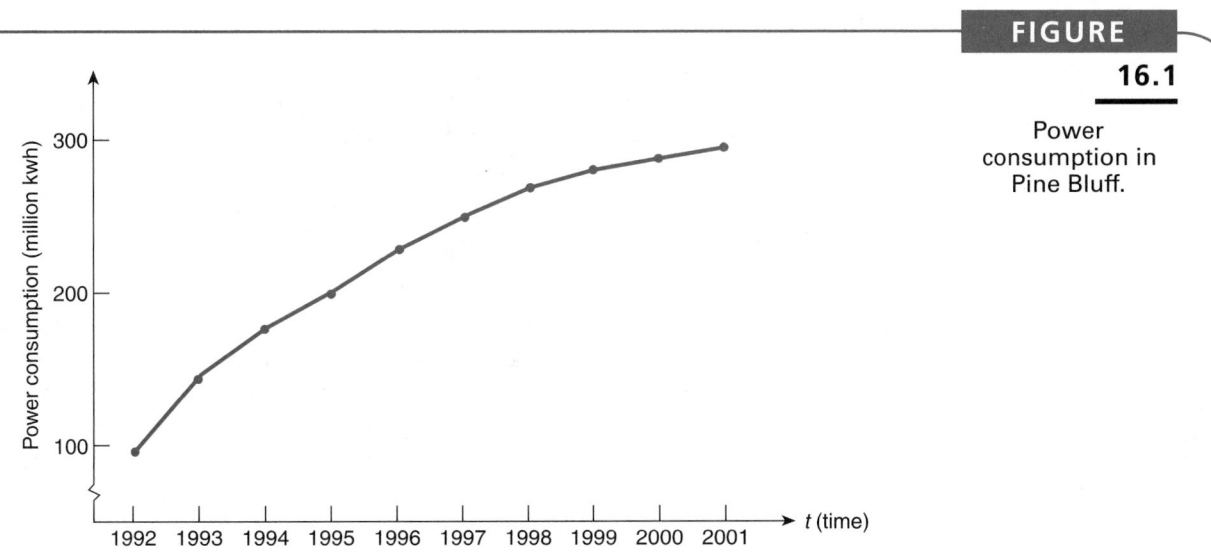

FIGURE

16.1

Power consumption in Pine Bluff.

Trend (TR)

The **trend** is a steady increase or decrease in the time series. If a particular time series is neither increasing nor decreasing over its range of time, it contains *no trend*. The trend reflects any long-term growth or decline in the observations. For example, a trend may be due to inflation, increases in the population, increases in personal income, market growth or decline, or changes in technology. Each of these factors could have a long-term effect on the variable of interest and would be reflected in the trend in the corresponding time series.

This long-term growth or decay pattern can take a variety of shapes. If the rate of change in Y from one time period to the next is relatively constant, the trend is a **linear trend:**

$$TR = b_0 + b_1 t$$

(for some b_0 and b_1), where the predictor variable is time t.

When the time series appears to be slowing down or accelerating as time increases, then a nonlinear trend may be present. It may be a **quadratic trend**

$$TR = b_0 + b_1 t + b_2 t^2$$

or a **decaying trend**

$$TR = b_0 + b_1 \left(\frac{1}{t} \right) \qquad \text{or} \qquad TR = b_0 + b_1 e^{-t}$$

These trend equations can be derived from the linear regression equations developed in Chapter 14 (for linear or decaying trend) and Chapter 15 (for quadratic trend). The linear trend equation is an application of *simple* linear regression, whereas the quadratic trend uses a *multiple* regression equation using two predictors, t and t^2. Simple linear regression techniques also can be used to derive b_0 and b_1 for the decaying trend equations, where values of t are replaced by the values of $1/t$ or e^{-t} in the data input.

The number of employees from 1994 to 2001 at Video-Comp, an expanding microcomputer-software firm, are recorded in the following table and illustrated in Figure 16.2.

Year	Number of Employees (Thousands)
1994	1.1
1995	2.4
1996	4.6
1997	5.4
1998	5.9
1999	8.0
2000	9.7
2001	11.2

The underlying long-term growth trend in this time series appears to be nearly *linear*, as represented by the trend line in Figure 16.2. To determine the equation of this line, we use the technique of simple linear regression, where X = the predictor variable = time and Y = the number of employees. We can estimate the existing trend using

$$\hat{y}_t = b_0 + b_1 t$$

where t represents the time variable and y_t is the value of Y at time period t. Here b_0 and b_1 are the least squares regression coefficients for a straight line predictor. The procedure of deriving these least squares estimates is developed later in the chapter. Figure 16.3 shows an *increasing* linear trend (y_t increases over time) and a decreasing linear trend (y_t decreases over time).

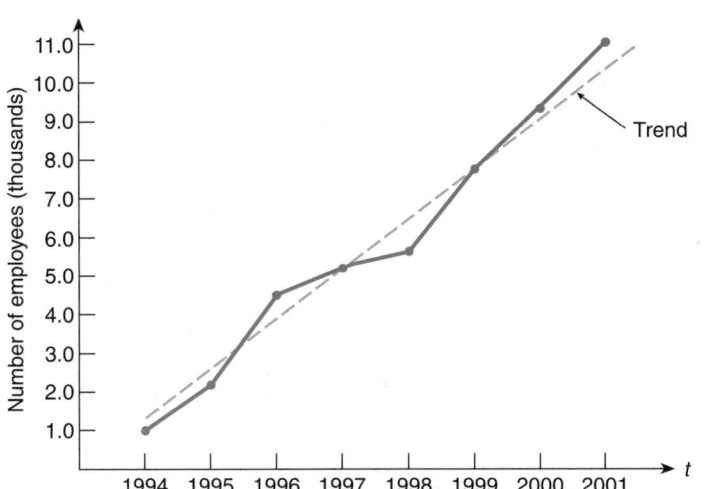

FIGURE

16.2

Number of employees at Video-Comp (an example of linear trend).

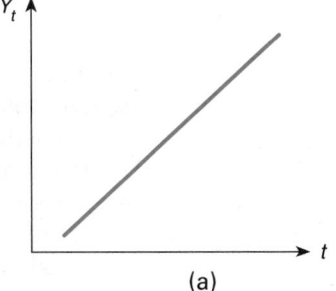

(a)

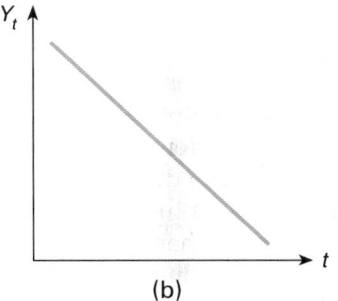

(b)

FIGURE

16.3

(a) Increasing linear trend: $TR = b_0 + b_1 t$ ($b_1 > 0$).
(b) Decreasing linear trend: $TR = b_0 + b_1 t$ ($b_1 < 0$).

What type of trend exists in the power-consumption data (Figure 16.1)?

EXAMPLE

16.1

Although this time series increases steadily, *it increases at a decreasing rate;* it starts off with large increases from one time period to the next, but these increments gradually become smaller. When the growth is linear, the values increase at a nearly constant rate. Figure 16.1 is an illustration of *quadratic trend,* where the time series randomly fluctuates about a quadratic (or curvilinear) level over time. This trend is captured by the equation

Solution

$$\hat{y}_t = b_0 + b_1 t + b_2 t^2$$

To derive these estimates, we use the multiple linear regression approach discussed in Chapter 15 (curvilinear models). Section 16.2 demonstrates this technique.

The four types of quadratic trend are summarized in Figure 16.4.

Seasonality (*S*)

Seasonal variation, or **seasonality,** refers to periodic increases or decreases that occur *within a calendar year* in a time series. They are very predictable because they occur every year. When a time series consists of annual data (as in Figure 16.1),

FIGURE

16.4

Quadratic trend.
(a) *Y* increases at a decreasing rate.
(b) *Y* decreases at an increasing rate.
(c) *Y* decreases at a decreasing rate.
(d) *Y* increases at an increasing rate.

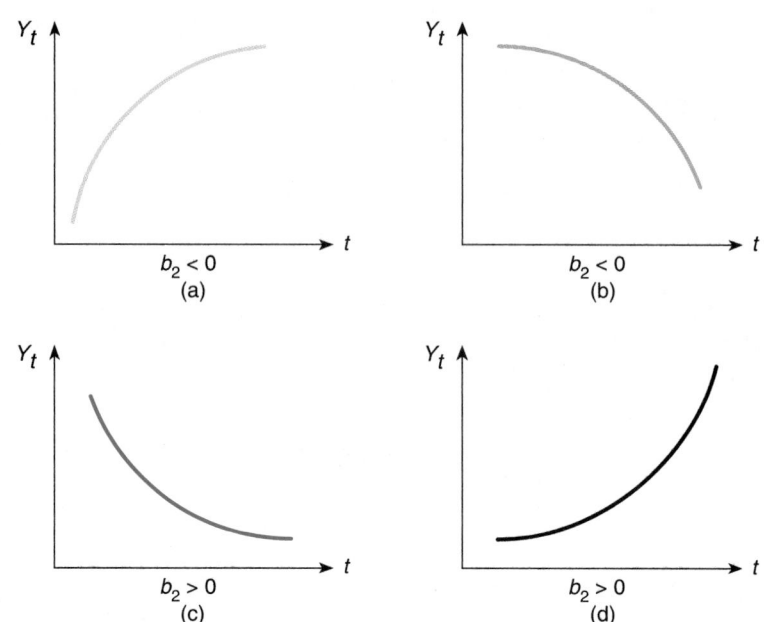

you cannot see what is going on within each year. Data reported in annual increments therefore cannot be used to examine seasonality. Seasonality may or may not exist; annual increment data are not in a form that will show whether it does.

When time series data are quarterly or monthly, seasonal variation may be evident. For example, if the power-consumption data were available for each month over these 10 years, then the resulting time series would contain 12 · 10 = 120 observations. A plot of monthly data for the last 3 years (36 observations) is shown in Figure 16.5. The seasonal effects here consist of the following characteristics:

- Extremely high power consumption during the hot summer months (July and August)
- Very high consumption during the coldest part of the winter (December and January)
- Gradually declining consumption during the spring, reaching a low level in April and then increasing until July
- Gradually declining power consumption during the fall, but beginning to increase in November

The key is that these movements in the time series follow the same pattern each year and so probably are due to seasonality. An analysis of seasonal variation is often a crucial step in planning sales and production. Just because your sales drop from one month to the next does not necessarily mean that it is time to panic. If a review of past observations indicates that sales *always* drop between these two months, then quite likely there is no cause for concern. On the production side, if sales always are extremely high in December, then you will need to increase production in the months prior to December so that you will have the necessary inventory level for this peak month. Measurement of this seasonal component is discussed later.

As mentioned earlier, a time series often contains the effect of trend and seasonality (as well as cyclical and irregular activity). The sales of Wildcat sailboats, illustrated in Figure 16.6, contain a strong linear trend as well as definite seasonal variation. In particular, the highest sales occur in the summer months of each year.

As manager of Wildcat Enterprises, would you be concerned that the sales of these boats in December 2001 were lower than those in July 2001? There may or may not be a problem; this seasonal pattern exists in Figure 16.6 despite an overall growth. More data would be required to determine whether the December

FIGURE
16.5

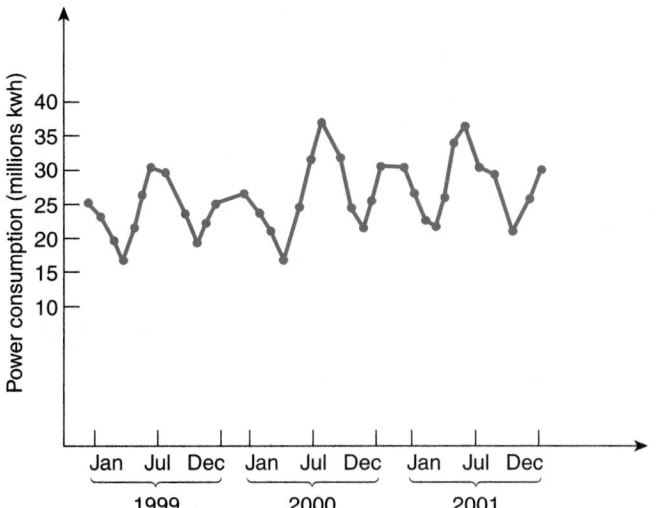

Illustration of seasonal variation. These are monthly observations; compare with annual data in Figure 16.1.

FIGURE
16.6

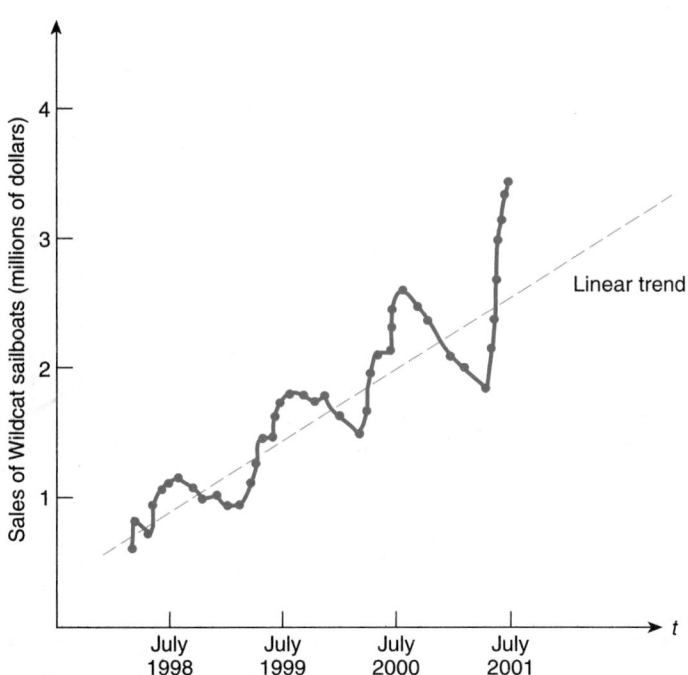

A time series containing trend and seasonal variation.

sales were lower than expected for that month. What would you think if sales in July 2002 were lower than those in July 2001? This event should definitely concern you. This is a year-to-year comparison, and seasonal variation or not, we would expect the sales for July 2002 to be larger than for July 2001 if the long-term growth trend in Figure 16.6 is still present. Lower sales in July 2002 would indicate a possible leveling off or a drop in boat sales in 2002.

Cyclical Variation (C)

Cyclical variation describes a gradual cyclical movement about the trend; it is generally attributable to business and economic conditions. The length of a cycle is the *period* of that cycle. The period of a cycle can be measured from one *peak* to

FIGURE

16.7

The cycle can be measured from P_1 to P_2, from V_1 to V_2, or from Z_1 to Z_2.

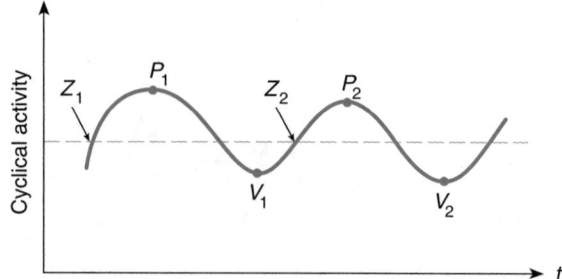

FIGURE

16.8

Annual taxes paid by Lindale Textiles (illustration of cyclical activity; Example 16.2).

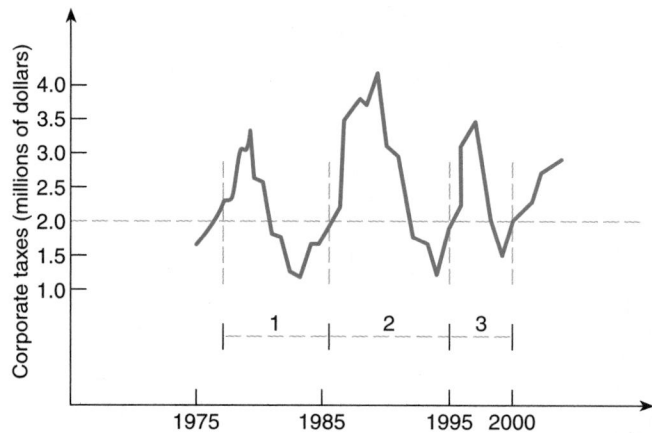

the next, one *trough* (valley) to the next, or from the time value at which the cycle crosses the horizontal line (where no cyclic activity exists) to the value where it completes the cycle and returns to this point. Figure 16.7 shows that the cycle length can be measured from P_1 to P_2, from V_1 to V_2, or from Z_1 to Z_2. In the illustrations to follow, we use the Z_1 to Z_2 approach.

In business applications, cycles typically are long-term movements, with periods ranging from 2 to 10 years. The primary difference between the cyclical and seasonal factors is the period length. Seasonal effects take place *within* one year, whereas the period for cyclical activity is usually *more than* one year.

Cyclical activity need not follow a definite, recurrent pattern. The cycles generally represent conditions within the economy, where a peak occurs at the height of an expansion (prosperity) period and is generally followed by a period of contraction in economic activity. The low point (trough) of each cycle usually takes place at the low point of an economic recession or depression. This low point is then followed by a gradual increase during the recovery period.

The annual corporate taxes paid by Lindale Textiles (a clothing manufacturer) over a 25-year period are shown in Figure 16.8. How many cycles do you observe?

Solution   The year 1977 began a cycle lasting approximately eight years. There are three cycles contained within the time series, which ends in the midst of an up cycle. Notice that the cycle lengths are not the same.

Irregular Activity (*I*)

Irregular activity consists of what is left over after accounting for the effect of any trend, seasonality, or cyclical activity. These values should consist of noise, much like the error term in the linear regression models discussed in the previous chapters. *The irregular activity should contain no observable or predictable pattern.* An extremely large irregular component can be caused by a measurement error in the variable. Such an outlier should always be checked to ensure its accuracy.

The irregular component (1) measures the random movement in your time series and (2) represents the effect introduced by unpredictable rare events, such as earthquakes, oil embargoes, or strikes.

If a noticeable jump in the resulting irregular components (when plotted across time) can be attributed to a particular rare event, you may wish to eliminate such data from the time series. You can then examine the remaining data to measure more accurately the other time series components.

Combining the Components

The time series components can be combined in various ways to describe the behavior of a particular time series. One method is to describe the time series variable, y_t, as a *sum* of these four components

$$y_t = TR_t + S_t + C_t + I_t$$

This is called the **additive structure.** The implication here is that any seasonal effects are additive from one year to the next. For example, if the seasonal effect of December for a time series representing sales is an increase of 250 units over the average yearly sales, then this same increase will occur each year regardless of the sales volume. Whether the average yearly sales are 1,000 units or 10,000 units, December should show a sales volume of approximately 1,250 (the first case) or 10,250 (the latter case).

Better success has been achieved by describing a time series using the **multiplicative structure,** where

$$y_t = TR_t \cdot S_t \cdot C_t \cdot I_t$$

Here, the seasonal effect increases or decreases according to the underlying trend and cyclical effect. Using the previous illustration, the difference between the December sales and the yearly average will be *higher* for the latter case (where the yearly average is 10,000 units). For example, for the first case, the December sales might be 1,250 (a 25% increase over the yearly average) and, for the latter situation, it might be 12,500 (also a 25% increase). This result follows from the implication in the multiplicative structure that as the sales increase from one year to the next, the changes in volume due to seasonality also increase. For our illustration, this shift was 250 units for the first case and 2,500 units for the second case.

X Exercises 16.1–16.6

Applying the New Concepts

16.1 Assume that a new company believes that its future sales will best be described by a multiplicative structure with respect to trend, seasonality, cyclical variation, and irregular activity.

  a. Describe how seasonality affects sales over time if the trend is increasing.

  b. Describe how cyclical variation affects sales over time if the trend is increasing.

16.2 The following data set shows the number of manufactured mobile homes (in thousands) since 1996. With low interest rates for most of the 1990s, mobile homes have had tough competition from the traditional home market. Plot the number of mobile homes versus time and describe the trend.

Year	1996	1997	1998	1999	2000	2001
Mobile Homes Manufactured	370	360	355	345	252	220

(Source: "Sliding Shipments," *Los Angeles Times*, June 11, 2001, p. L1.)

16.3 Construction in the housing industry usually appears to peak in the middle of the summer and to bottom out around January. If the number of new housing starts are the same for the month of March and the month of July in a particular year, of what concern would these figures be to housing construction companies? Would they be pleased, worried, or indifferent? Why?

16.4 The end-of-year inventory levels, in dollars, of West Coast Distributing are given in the following table. Estimate the period of the cyclical component by graphing the data.

Year	Inventory	Year	Inventory
1989	80	1996	80
1990	75	1997	83
1991	71	1998	80
1992	73	1999	77
1993	82	2000	79
1994	76	2001	84
1995	78		

16.5 To which of the four components of a time series would each of the following influences on housing starts contribute?
  a. Presidential election year
  b. Start of the school year in September
  c. Long-term growth of the housing industry
  d. Shortage of lumber because of a strike

16.6 Describe in words both the trend and the seasonal components for the following sales figures (in thousands of dollars). (*Hint:* Draw a graph for each.)

Month	2000	2002	Month	2000	2002
Jan	1.2	2.2	July	2.9	3.8
Feb	1.4	2.4	Aug	3.2	4.0
Mar	1.3	2.3	Sept	2.5	3.5
Apr	1.5	2.4	Oct	2.4	3.0
May	1.5	2.5	Nov	2.3	2.8
June	2.3	3.5	Dec	2.1	2.5

16.2   MEASURING TREND: NO SEASONALITY

Suppose that you have a time series containing trend and cyclical activity but no seasonality. For example, the employment data in Figure 16.2 are annual and so contain no seasonality. The same is true for the annual power-consumption data in Figure 16.1. When data are collected on a yearly basis, we are not concerned with any seasonality in the data; we need data from quarterly or shorter intervals to identify any seasonality. Yearly data may have trend (*TR*), cyclical activity (*C*), or irregular activity (*I*). If we observe a strong linear trend (as in Figure 16.2) or a quadratic trend (Figure 16.4), we can estimate it using the least squares technique developed in Chapters 14 and 15. We use simple linear regression for linear trends and multiple linear regression for quadratic trends.

Linear Trend

We begin by *coding* the variable to make the calculations (or computer input) easier.

We can find an equation for the trend line in Figure 16.2 passing through the eight observations in the time series. The least squares trend line through these eight values is sketched in Figure 16.9. The equation of the trend line is

$$\hat{y}_t = TR_t = b_0 + b_1 t$$

where t represents the time variable. For this equation, TR_t represents the trend component of the sample observation at time period t and is simply a new name for the trend effect that this equation allows us to estimate.

We could use $t = 1994, 1995, \ldots$ to represent time, but a much simpler method is to code the data, as illustrated in Figure 16.9. By using $t = 1, 2, \ldots ,$ the estimate, $\hat{y}_t$, is not affected and the calculations are easier. You are able to code the predictor variable, t, because the sample values are equally spaced—they are all one year apart. As we saw in Chapter 14, this equal spacing does not occur in

FIGURE

16.9

Least squares
trend line using
coded time data
(compare with
Figure 16.2):
$\hat{y}_t = b_0 + b_1 t$.

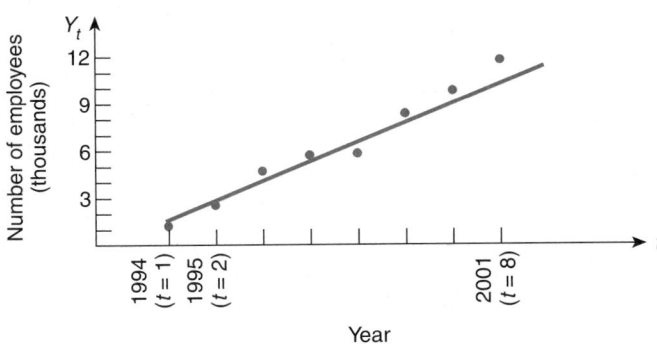

all simple regression applications. Continuing the scheme in Figure 16.9, $t = 9$ represents the year 2002, and the estimated number of employees for 2002 (using trend only) is

$$\hat{y}_9 = b_0 + b_1(9)$$

To derive the "best" line through the time series data, we use the least squares estimates discussed in Chapter 14; the independent variable here is time, t.

t	y_t	
1	1.1	$(= y_1)$
2	2.4	$(= y_2)$
3	4.6	$\vdots$
4	5.4	
5	5.9	
6	8.0	
7	9.7	
8	11.2	

The necessary calculations are

$$\sum y_t = 1.1 + 2.4 + \cdots + 11.2 = 48.3$$

$$\sum t y_t = (1)(1.1) + (2)(2.4) + \cdots + (8)(11.2) = 276.3$$

In Chapter 14, when we regressed the variable Y on a single variable X, the estimate for the slope of the least squares line (from equation 14.11) was given by

$$b_1 = \frac{\text{SCP}_{XY}}{\text{SS}_X} = \frac{\sum xy - (\sum x)(\sum y)/n}{\sum x^2 - (\sum x)^2/n}$$

where n was the number of sample observations. To determine a linear trend line for a time series, this equation becomes

$$b_1 = \frac{\sum t y_t - (\sum t)(\sum y_t)/T}{\sum t^2 - (\sum t)^2/T}$$

where $T =$ the number of observations in the time series.

The sample estimate of the intercept is

$$b_0 = \bar{y} - b_1 \bar{x} = \bar{y}_t - b_1 \bar{t}$$

where $\bar{y}_t = (y_1 + y_2 + \cdots + y_T)/T$.

Because the time variable, t, *always* is 1, 2, . . . , T, there is an easier way to calculate $\sum t$, $\sum t^2$, $\bar{t}$, b_0, and b_1.

$$\sum t = 1 + 2 + \cdots + T$$

$$= \frac{T(T+1)}{2}$$

16.1

$$\sum t^2 = 1 + 4 + \cdots + T^2$$

$$= \frac{T(T+1)(2T+1)}{6}$$

16.2

$$\bar{t} = \frac{\sum t}{T} = \frac{T+1}{2}$$

16.3

$$b_1 = \frac{12B - 6(T+1)A}{T(T^2-1)}$$

16.4

$$b_0 = \frac{A}{T} - b_1\left(\frac{T+1}{2}\right)$$

16.5

where $A = \sum y_t$ and $B = \sum ty_t$

We use these equations to derive the least squares line in Figure 16.9. By the previous results, $A = 48.3$ and $B = 276.3$. So we can now calculate

$$b_1 = \frac{12B - 6(T+1)A}{T(T^2-1)}$$

$$= \frac{12(276.3) - 6(9)(48.3)}{8(64-1)} = \frac{707.4}{504} = 1.4036$$

and

$$b_0 = \frac{A}{T} - b_1\left(\frac{T+1}{2}\right)$$

$$= \frac{48.3}{8} - (1.4036)\left(\frac{9}{2}\right) = 6.0375 - 6.3162 = -.279$$

The trend line for this time series is

$$\hat{y}_t = -.279 + 1.404t$$

We conclude that the number of employees appears to increase at the rate of 1,404 per year, on the average.

The trend line is derived using the same least squares procedure discussed in Chapter 14—you can use the computer instructions contained in the simple linear regression illustrations. A computer solution using Excel is shown in Figure 16.10. Enter the values 1 though 8 in column A and the time series values in column B.* To obtain the linear trend equation, click on **Tools ➤ Data Analysis ➤ Regression.** Enter "B1:B8" as the **Input Y Range,** "A1:A8" as the **Input X Range,** and "C1" as the **Output Range.** The regression coefficients in cells D17 and D18 agree with the previously derived trend equation.

Figure 16.10 contains the t statistic; you may be tempted to use it to determine whether time is a significant predictor of $Y =$ number of employees. However, to use this statistic, you must assume that the errors about the trend line are completely *independent* of one another and contain *no observable pattern.* Do not forget that there may well be considerable cyclical activity about the trend line, and this cyclical activity will be contained in the residuals of the regression analysis. Thus there probably will be a cyclical pattern to these residuals, so the assumption of

---

*You can generate 1, 2, . . . , 8 in column A by typing "1" in cell A1 and "2" in cell A2, highlighting these two cells, and dragging them through cell A8. This technique will be especially useful for very long time series.

FIGURE

16.10

Excel solution of
least squares trend
line.

	A	B	C	D	E	F	G	H
1	1	1.1	SUMMARY OUTPUT					
2	2	2.4						
3	3	4.6	Regression Statistics					
4	4	5.4	Multiple R	0.992				
5	5	5.9	R Square	0.985				
6	6	8.0	Adjusted R Square	0.982				
7	7	9.7	Standard Error	0.462				
8	8	11.2	Observations	8				
9								
10			ANOVA					
11				df	SS	MS	F	Significance F
12			Regression	1	82.741	82.741	388.388	1.10669E-06
13			Residual	6	1.278	0.213		
14			Total	7	84.019			
15								
16				Coefficients	Standard Error	t Stat	P-value	
17			Intercept	-0.279	0.360	-0.775	0.468	
18			X Variable 1	1.404	0.071	19.708	1.10669E-06	
19								

complete independence is not met. The errors are therefore *autocorrelated* and any test of hypothesis is invalid.

This situation poses no serious problems at this point, however, because *our intent is simply to describe the time series by measuring the various components, and not to perform a statistical test of hypothesis.* If, however, the residuals about the trend line appear to be extremely large, it suggests that a linear trend component is not appropriate.

Quadratic Trend

The nature of a quadratic trend is illustrated in Figure 16.4. This type of trend is common for a time series that increases or decreases rapidly and then gradually levels off over the observed values. We discussed a similar situation in Chapter 15, where a quadratic model of the form

$$\hat{Y} = b_0 + b_1 X + b_2 X^2$$

was used to capture a curvilinear relationship between two variables. We use exactly the same technique to describe a quadratic trend; now X is replaced by time, t.

The power-consumption time series in Figure 16.1 indicates that as time increases, the amount of power consumption (y_t) also increases, but at a decreasing rate. More specifically, the increase for 1997 to 1998 is 18; for 1998 to 1999 is 12 ($12 < 18$); for 1999 to 2000 is 8 ($8 < 12$); and for 2000 to 2001 is 5 ($5 < 8$).

When you observe a series where the *changes* from one year to the next are not (approximately) constant but seem to be either increasing or decreasing with time, these changes indicate a quadratic trend. The equation of this curvilinear (quadratic) trend is

$$\hat{y}_t = b_0 + b_1 t + b_2 t^2$$

To derive the least squares estimates b_0, b_1, and b_2, we use the multiple linear regression procedure of Chapter 15.

What would be the input to a computer program (such as Excel, SPSS, or MINITAB) for the power-consumption data? For the regression program,

FIGURE

16.11

Excel solution for
quadratic trend
(power
consumption
data).

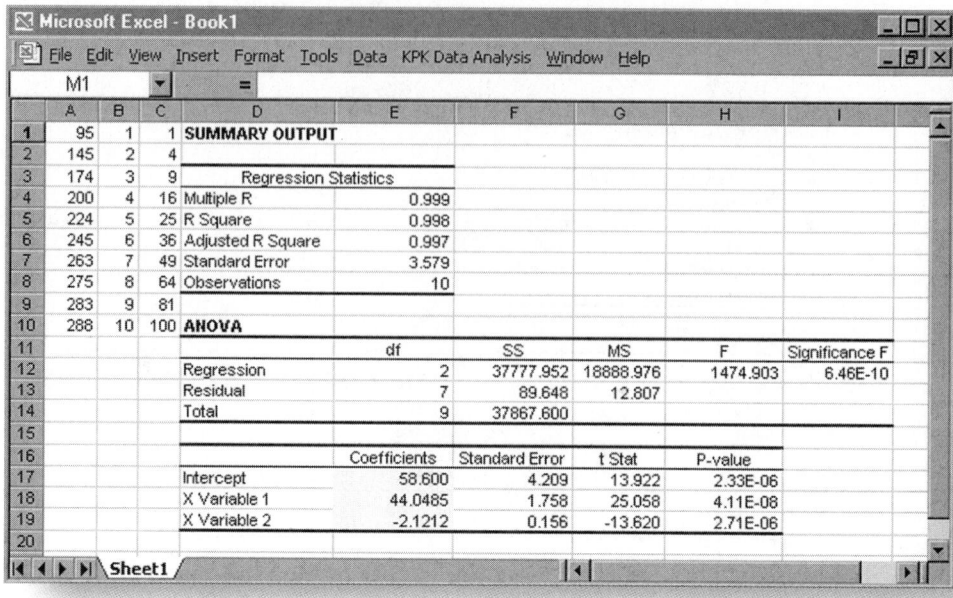

you have two predictor variables, $X_1 = t$ and $X_2 = t^2$. The resulting data configuration is

y_t	t	t^2	
95	1	1	(for 1992)
145	2	4	(for 1993)
174	3	9	(for 1994)
200	4	16	$\vdots$
224	5	25	
245	6	36	
263	7	49	
275	8	64	
283	9	81	(for 2000)
288	10	100	(for 2001)

Figure 16.11 contains the Excel solution for the quadratic trend equation. To obtain this equation, click on **Tools ➤ Data Analysis ➤ Regression.** You should enter the time series values in column A (as in Figure 16.11) and the values 1 though 10 in column B. To obtain column C, enter "=B1*B1" in cell C1 and drag this cell through cell C10. Enter "A1:A10" as the **Input Y Range,** "B1:C10" as the **Input X Range,** and "D1" as the **Output Range.** The regression coefficients in cells E17:E19 provide the quadratic trend equation

$$y_t = 58.6 + 44.0485t - 2.1212t^2$$

To illustrate the use of this equation, the actual value for the second time period is $y_2 = 145$ and the predicted value is

$$\hat{y}_2 = 58.6 + 44.0485(2) - 2.1212(2)^2 = 138.21$$

A First Look at Forecasting: Extending the Trend

Whenever a time series contains very little seasonality (such as *annual* data, which have *no* seasonality) and a strong trend, an easy method of providing future forecasts is to project the observed growth pattern, as measured by the trend equation, into the future. For example, if a city's tax revenues have increased steadily by approximately $15,000 per year over the past 10 years, it seems reasonable to expect that this pattern will continue, at least for a short time. (Of course, assuming that such a growth will continue indefinitely is a hazardous gamble, at best!)

The process of extending a trend equation is called *forecasting,* or *extrapolation.* The following examples illustrate that extending a straight-line trend equation can provide useful estimates of future values. A quadratic trend equation is, however, useful only *within* the range of the sample data, that is, for *interpolation.*

This method of forecasting is but one of many possible ways of predicting the future time series values by capturing patterns present in the past observations. Chapter 17 examines other methods of using the past observations to forecast future values.

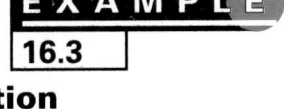
EXAMPLE 16.3

Using the trend line from Figure 16.9, estimate the number of employees in 2002.

Solution

$t = 9$ corresponds to the year 2002, so the *forecast* for this year is

$$\hat{y}_9 = -.279 + 1.404(9) = 12.357$$

that is, 12,357 employees.

As mentioned earlier, the basic assumption when using the trend line to determine a forecast is that this same pattern *will continue* into the future. This may or may not be true. Very often a time series will increase at a more or less constant rate and then begin to level off. One example is the sales of an innovative product. Such a time series will grow from one year to the next as people think that they just have to have this product, but eventually a saturation point is reached and the sales grow at a much smaller rate. If the historical data used to determine the trend line are collected during the growth stage, then you will stop short of and miss the "slowing down" of the time series, severely overestimating the sales. This problem is not a flaw in the technique; any time series model makes predictions by capturing the pattern(s) in the past observations and extending this pattern beyond the last year of the data. It does, however, place a great deal of responsibility on the person who uses the data to predict beyond the data range. If you do not know what underlying factors are driving the trend, serious errors can result.

Very often, a nonlinear growth rate can be described accurately by including a quadratic term in the trend equation. However, using such an equation to forecast *future* values is not a reliable procedure, as the following example demonstrates.

EXAMPLE 16.4

Using the trend equation from Figure 16.11

$$\hat{y}_t = TR_t = 58.6 + 44.0485t - 2.1212t^2$$

what is your forecast for the power consumption during 2002? during 2003? Use only the trend equation.

Solution

The year 2002 corresponds to $t = 11$ (the last year of your data is $t = 10$ for 2001). Your forecast for 2002 is

$$\hat{y}_{11} = 58.6 + 44.0485(11) - 2.1212(11)^2 = 286.46$$

that is, 2,864,600 kilowatt-hours. For the year 2003, your forecast is

$$\hat{y}_{12} = 58.6 + 44.0485(12) - 2.1212(12)^2 = 281.72$$

773

FIGURE
16.12

FIGURE

16.12

Illustration of how quadratic trend equations will reverse direction. The quadratic trend equation is $y_t = b_0 + b_1t + b_2t^2$, where (a) $b_2 < 0$ and (b) $b_2 > 0$.

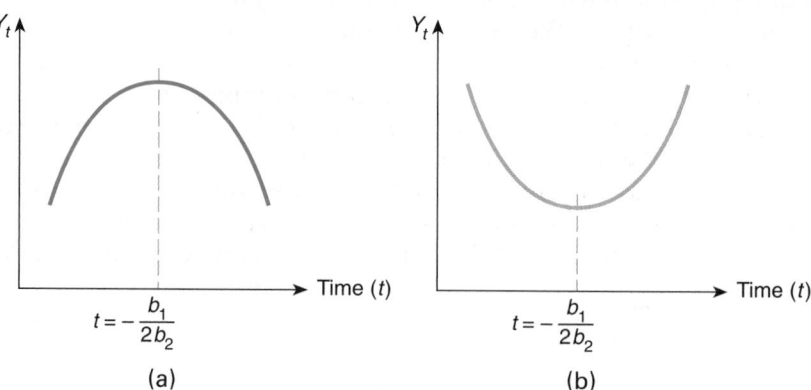

(a)   (b)

The sermon we delivered about projecting a trend line beyond the range of the data applies to a quadratic trend as well: by forecasting with such an equation, you assume that this quadratic (curved) pattern observed in the time series observations will continue.

In addition, there is another danger when forecasting with a quadratic trend equation. Every such equation looks like Figure 16.12a or b. In other words, the curve reaches a peak or trough at $t = -b_1/(2b_2)$ and then reverses direction. This change in direction is generally not seen in the sample data and produces trend estimates that are contrary to the pattern seen in the sample data. For example, rather than producing trend estimates that "slow down" with increasing time, the estimates after a certain point [namely, after $t = -b_1/(2b_2)$] will reverse direction.

The forecasts for power consumption (Example 16.4) for 2002 and 2003 provide a good illustration of this problem. Notice that the predicted value for 2002 is less than the actual value for 2001, despite a steadily increasing pattern in the time series data. Even worse, the year 2003 estimate is less than that for 2002. These values imply that the trend equation is decreasing during the years after 2001. We see that the trend equation forecasts appear to be poor estimates—we have no reason to suspect a downturn in the amount of power consumption in these future years. The trend is appropriately described by the quadratic curve, but only within the range of the data. This curve will peak at $t = -44.0485/2(-2.1212) = 10.38$ (between 2001 and 2002) and then begin to decline. Because we have no reason to believe that the demand for electrical power will decrease, the quadratic equation is no longer appropriate outside the range of the sample data.

To describe the trend *within* the years of your time series data, the quadratic trend equation may work well. However, remember that, as a *forecasting procedure, it is very dangerous; do not use it for this purpose.*

This section has demonstrated how you can derive linear or quadratic trend equations by using linear regression techniques. Extending such a trend equation into the future is a method of statistical forecasting, a subject that is discussed at length in Chapter 17.

X Exercises 16.7–16.16

Understanding the Mechanics

16.7 The following table displays annual observations from 1996 to 2001.

Year	Time (t)	y_t	ty_t
1996	1	30	
1997	2	120	
1998	3	180	
1999	4	220	
2000	5	280	
2001	6	320	
	$\Sigma t =$	$\Sigma y_t =$	$\Sigma ty_t =$

a. Complete the table.
b. Determine the least squares line.
c. What is the predicted value for the year 2002?

16.8 Using the following statistics, fit a linear trend line for time periods $t = 1, 2, \ldots, 10$.

$$\Sigma y_t = 1300, \; \Sigma t y_t = 7484$$

Applying the New Concepts

16.9 Explain why a prediction equation with a quadratic trend may be dangerous to use in forecasting even though a quadratic trend fits the historic data very well.

16.10 The amount of money deposited into savings accounts at a local bank has grown steadily over the years, as the following data indicate (deposits are the amount of money in savings accounts at the end of the year, in units of $100,000):

Year	Deposits	Year	Deposits
1994	2.1	1998	10.3
1995	4.2	1999	13.3
1996	6.4	2000	14.9
1997	8.5	2001	16.7

a. Does it appear that a quadratic trend exists in the data?
b. Calculate the equation you would use to describe the trend.

16.11 An insurance company would like to find the trend line for the amount of insurance sold annually (in millions of dollars) across time. The variable time is represented by t and is equal to $1, 2, \ldots, 8$ for the past eight years. The following statistics were collected:

$$\Sigma t y_t = 394.5 \qquad \Sigma y_t = 29.4$$

Find the trend line for these time series data.

16.12 Due to rising competition from overseas, an electronics firm has been losing its share of the market. The following data show the percent of the market that the firm has captured for the past seven years.

Year	Share of Market
1995	4.7
1996	4.3
1997	3.9
1998	3.8
1999	3.6
2000	3.0
2001	2.9

a. Does the trend appear to be linear?
b. Find the equation to estimate the trend for the time series data.
c. What would be your estimate of the electronics firm's share of the market in 2002?

16.13 Mexicans are sprinting into a wireless stampede to thwart the high cost and limited access of traditional land lines. The number of wireless lines in Mexico exceeds 14 million, surpassing the 12.3 million land lines. The following data show the number of wireless lines (in millions) from 1990 to 2000 in Mexico.

Year	1990	1991	1992	1993	1994	1995
Wireless Lines	6.1	6.2	7.1	8.5	9.2	9.3

Year	1996	1997	1998	1999	2000
Wireless Lines	9.0	9.1	10.8	11.2	12.3

a. Find the trend line for the number of wireless lines.
b. What is your estimate of the number of wireless lines for 2001?

(Source: "Talking on Air," *Dallas Morning News*, June 23, 2001, p. 1E.)

16.14 The U.S. lodging industry has experienced tremendous growth during the last decade thanks to a robust economy and relatively inexpensive air fares. The following table illustrates the industry's pretax profits in billions of dollars from 1994 to 2001.

Year	1994	1995	1996	1997	1998	1999	2000	2001
Pretax Profits	5.5	8.5	12.5	17.0	20.9	22.0	23.5	22.0

a. Estimate a linear and a quadratic trend for these data. Which do you think is a better fit?
b. What is your estimate of the percentage of pretax profits for 2002?

(Source: "Hoteliers Ponder Rate Discounts," *Hotel and Motel Management*, July 2001, p. 1.)

Using the Computer

16.15 **[DATA SET EX16-15]** *Variable description:*

Year: Year from 1981 to 2000

PC_Shipments: Number of personal computer shipments in millions worldwide

The first personal computer (PC) was introduced in 1981 by IBM. Since then, there have been many players in this fast-growing market. The number of PC shipments in 1981 was 2 million. That compares to 138 million in 2000.

a. Plot the number of shipments versus time. Do you think that a linear trend or a quadratic trend is a better fit?
b. Estimate the number of PC shipments in 2001 using an appropriate trend equation.

(Source: "Worldwide PC Shipments," *USA Today*, August 8, 2001, p. 3B.)

16.16 **[DATA SET EX16-16]** *Variable description:*

Year: Year from 1976 to 2001

Bonus: Annual bonus in thousands of dollars

A new vice president of a local bank is interested in examining the annual bonuses paid to her predecessors. She also realizes that stockholders of the bank are concerned about exorbitant bonuses. Do you believe that a linear or quadratic trend is present? What are the estimates of the expected annual bonuses for 2002 and 2003?

16.3   MEASURING CYCLICAL ACTIVITY: NO SEASONALITY

Practically every time series in a business setting contains a certain amount of cyclical activity. Cyclical activity is a gradual movement about the trend. It is generally due to economic or other long-term conditions. The overall U.S. economy tends to fluctuate through "good times" and "bad times," producing (rather unpredictable) upward and downward variation about the long-term growth or decline in a time series.

One way of describing the cyclical activity component is to represent it as a fraction of the trend. This procedure provides accurate measures of the cyclical activity provided the time series contains *little irregular activity*. Assuming that each time series observation is the *product* of its components, then

$$y_t = TR_t \cdot C_t \cdot I_t$$

because we are dealing with data containing no seasonality.

If we represent a small irregular activity component as i_t (rather than I_t), then a time series containing little irregular variation (noise) can be written as

$$y_t = TR_t \cdot C_t \cdot i_t$$

The cyclical components are then obtained by dividing each observation, y_t, by its corresponding estimate using trend only, $\hat{y}_t$.

$$\text{ratio of data to trend} = \frac{y_t}{\hat{y}_t} = \frac{\cancel{TR_t} \cdot C_t \cdot i_t}{\cancel{TR_t}} = C_t \cdot i_t$$

where y_t = actual time series observation at time period t and $\hat{y}_t = TR_t$ = the estimate of y_t using trend only. Notice that the resulting ratios still contain some irregular activity. (A method of reducing the irregular activity within these values is illustrated in Section 16.6.)

An estimate of the cyclical components can be obtained by ignoring the irregular activity components in these ratios and defining

$$C_t \cong \frac{y_t}{\hat{y}_t} \qquad \text{16.6}$$

Assuming that we are dealing with data containing no seasonality (such as annual data), equation 16.6 provides a convenient method of determining the cycles present in the data. If $C_t > 1$, the actual y_t is larger than that predicted by trend alone. Consequently, this value is somewhere in a cycle *above* the trend line. A similar argument indicates a cycle below the trend line whenever $C_t < 1$ (Figure 16.13).

FIGURE 16.13

A complete cycle within a time series.

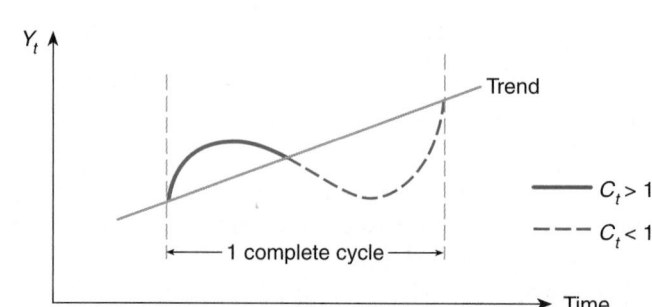

EXAMPLE
16.5

For the data in Figure 16.9, we determined a least squares trend line for the number of employees (y_t) over an eight-year period at Video-Comp. We observed a linear trend with the corresponding equation

$$\hat{y}_t = -.279 + 1.404t$$

where $t = 1$ represents 1994, $t = 2$ is for 1995, and so on. Determine and graph the cyclical activity over this period.

Solution

We can obtain Table 16.1 by using the preceding trend line. Here $\hat{y}_1 = -.279 + 1.404(1) = 1.125$, $\hat{y}_2 = -.279 + 1.404(2) = 2.529$, and so on.

To examine the cyclical activity, we can describe each component as a percentage of the trend. For example, in Table 16.1, during the first time period, the actual number of employees is 97.8% of the trend value: C_1 is .978. An illustration of the trend and cyclical activity is shown in Figure 16.14. The cycles fluctuate about the trend line. Between the years $t = 2$ (1995) and $t = 3$ (1996), $y_t = \hat{y}_t$ and a cycle begins. This cycle is completed somewhere between $t = 6$ (1999) and $t = 7$ (2000), where, once again, $y_t = \hat{y}_t$. As discussed earlier, you can also measure cycles from peak to peak or from trough to trough.

The summary of the cyclical variation (components) over the eight years is contained in Table 16.1 and Figure 16.15. The four-year cycle we described is more evident in this graph. The graph clearly indicates the beginning of the cycle, where $C_t = 1$. The cycle's peak occurs at $t = 3$ (1996), the trough is at $t = 5$ (1998), and the cycle is finally complete when C_t is again equal to 1, toward the end of 1999.

TABLE

16.1

Trend and cyclical activity (Example 16.5).

t	y_t	$\hat{y}_t$	
1	1.1	1.125	.978
2	2.4	2.529	.949
3	4.6	3.933	1.169
4	5.4	5.337	1.012
5	5.9	6.741	.875
6	8.0	8.145	.982
7	9.7	9.549	1.016
8	11.2	10.953	1.022

The third column is the trend component, and the fourth column is the cyclical component as a fraction of the trend.

FIGURE

16.14

Cyclical activity about a trend line (Example 16.5).

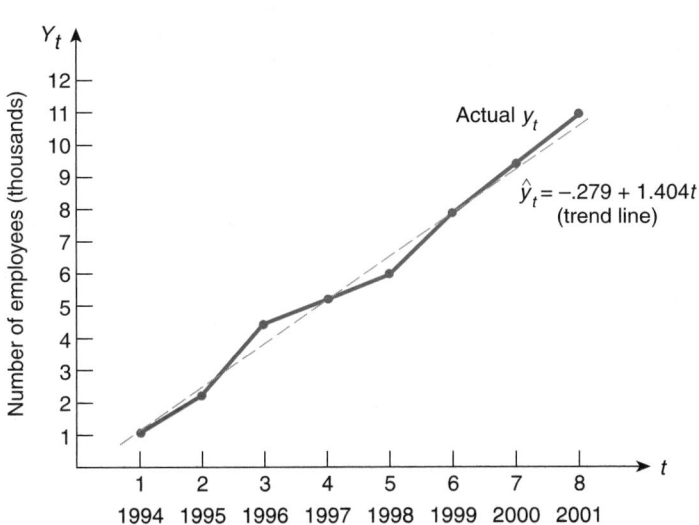

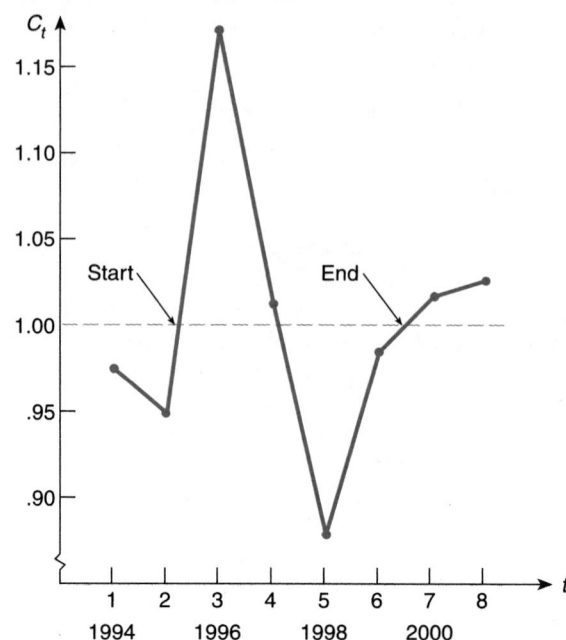

FIGURE

16.15

Cyclical components (Example 16.5).

In summary, cyclical variation represents an upward or downward movement about the overall growth or decline (that is, the trend) in the time series data. Such cycles typically last more than one year. For annual data, these components can be estimated by dividing each observation (y_t) by its corresponding estimate using the trend equation ($\hat{y}_t$).

X Exercises 16.17–16.26

Understanding the Mechanics

16.17 The following time series data are presented with the predicted values using the trend line. Find the cyclical components.

t	y_t	$\hat{y}_t$
1	1.0	1.493
2	2.0	2.752
3	5.0	4.012
4	5.5	5.271
5	6.0	6.530
6	8.0	7.790
7	10.0	9.049
8	11.0	10.309
9	11.3	11.568
10	11.8	12.827

16.18 Estimate the length of the cycle for each of the following three time series.

a. t	C_t	b. t	C_t	c. t	C_t
1	1.0	1	.3	1	3.1
2	.9	2	.7	2	2.2
3	1.7	3	1.3	3	1.2
4	.8	4	2.0	4	.9

a. t	C_t	b. t	C_t	c. t	C_t
5	1.5	5	1.5	5	.6
6	.9	6	.8	6	.3
7	1.4	7	.4	7	.7
8	.8	8	.9	8	.9
9	1.6	9	1.2	9	1.3
10	.7	10	2.4	10	1.8
		11	1.6	11	4.0
		12	.8	12	2.5
		13	.5	13	1.0
				14	.6

Applying the New Concepts

16.19 A food-store chain has the following record for yearly sales volume (in hundreds of thousands of dollars) for the past 9 years.

Year	Sales Volume	Year	Sales Volume
1993	7	1998	17
1994	15	1999	12
1995	10	2000	8
1996	5	2001	17
1997	11		

a. Find the trend line.
b. Find the cyclical components.
c. Estimate the period of the cycle.

16.20 Residential Construction of America has been growing over the long term. Because the construction company is sensitive to cyclical variations in the economy, the level of employment for the company changes from year to year, as can be seen by the following data:

Year	Full-Time Employees (in Hundreds)	Year	Full-Time Employees (in Hundreds)
1989	2.4	1996	11.7
1990	9.2	1997	17.3
1991	11.1	1998	23.1
1992	8.5	1999	28.7
1993	10.5	2000	29.3
1994	6.8	2001	25.2
1995	5.4		

a. Find the trend line.
b. Find the cyclical components.
c. Estimate the period of the cycle.

16.21 Few objects convey wealth and power like a private airplane and many companies are presently using them. Casket salesmen for Hillenbrand Industries, Inc., use them to escort funeral directors when visiting showrooms. Lumber buyers for Home Depot, Inc., based in Atlanta, fly on private airplanes to purchase inventory at out-of-the-way mills. Corning, Inc.'s technicians use them to shuttle between the company's headquarters in upstate New York and its optical-fiber plant in Wilmington, North Carolina. The following data illustrate the number of U.S. companies from 1988 to 1998 that operate turbine-powered aircraft in units of thousands.

Year	Number of U.S. Companies Operating Turbine-Powered Aircraft
1988	7.1
1989	6.7
1990	6.6
1991	6.5
1992	6.6
1993	6.7
1994	6.8
1995	7.8
1996	7.4
1997	7.5
1998	8.0

a. Find the trend line.
b. Determine the cyclical activity.
c. Does the period of the cycle appear to be longer or shorter than five years?

(Source: "Not Just for Highfliers, Corporate Planes Take Off," *The Wall Street Journal*, January 8, 1999, p. B1.)

16.22 For the data in Exercise 16.12, estimate the cyclical components.

16.23 A production manager is interested in the competitiveness of his company in manufacturing air conditioning compressors for automobiles. Data are collected over a 10-year period, and the compressor cost per unit compressor is recorded. Determine the cyclical components

for each year. Do you believe that the length of the cycle is longer than three years?

Year	Dollar Cost per Unit Compressor	Year	Dollar Cost per Unit Compressor
1992	100.4	1997	104.3
1993	103.6	1998	107.8
1994	105.2	1999	101.6
1995	102.3	2000	98.4
1996	99.8	2001	103.1

16.24 The United States is very important as a market for other countries. Since 1991, U.S. imports as a percentage of the rest of the world's gross domestic product (GDP) has increased. The following table illustrated the growth in U.S. imports from 1985 to 2000.

a. Estimate the trend line. How would you interpret the slope of this line?
b. Estimate the cyclical components and approximate the period of the cycle.

Year	Imports as a Percentage of World GDP	Year	Imports as a Percentage of World GDP
1985	2.5	1993	3.3
1986	1.9	1994	3.5
1987	2.2	1995	4.0
1988	2.4	1996	3.6
1989	2.6	1997	4.0
1990	3.2	1998	4.5
1991	2.8	1999	4.8
1992	3.1	2000	6.0

(Source: "Magnet," *The Wall Street Journal*, July 17, 2001, p. 1A.)

Using the Computer

16.25 **[DATA SET EX16-25]** *Variable description:*

Year: Year, 1985 through 2001

Applicants: Number of applicants for the supervisory positions

The manager of a paper plant needs to hire new supervisors every year because of growth in the company, turnover in the company, and promotions within the company. The manager decided to collect data from 1985 through 2001 to determine the cyclical activity. Determine the length of the cycles for this data set.

16.26 **[DATA SET EX16-26]** *Variable description:*

Year: Year from 1984 to 2000

NewVehicleSales: U.S. new vehicle sales in millions

Sales of new vehicles have undergone several downturns. During the Arab oil embargo of 1973, during the OPEC price increase in the early 1980s, and during the Gulf War in 1991, sales of new vehicles were very slow.

a. Estimate the trend equation for the sales of new vehicles from 1984 to 2000.
b. Estimate the approximate period of the cycle for sales of new vehicles between 1984 and 2000.

(Source: "Auto Sales During National Crises," *USA Today*, September 20, 2001, p. 2B.)

16.4   TYPES OF SEASONAL VARIATION

Seasonality causes another type of variation about the trend in a time series. Seasonality generally is present when the data are quarterly or monthly. It can also occur for weekly or even daily data. For example, recurrent daily effects can be expected to occur in the check-processing volume in a bank. *Seasonality* is any recurrent, constant source of variation caused by events at the particular time of year rather than by any long-term influence (as in cyclical activity). For example, one would expect to sell more snowmobiles in January than in July. In a sense, the seasonal variation appears as a cycle within a year; we do not refer to this as cyclical variation, however, due to its recurrent nature.

We will discuss two types of seasonal variation: additive and multiplicative.

Additive Seasonal Variation

One encounters **additive seasonal variation** when the amount of the variation due to seasonality *does not depend on the level y_t*. This type of seasonal variation is illustrated in Figure 16.16, which shows the sales of snowmobiles over a three-year period at the Outdoor Shop. Notice that the amount of variation for each of the winter quarters remains the same (100 units), even as the unit sales increase over the three years. For an actual application, we assume an additive effect of seasonality if these increments are of nearly the same magnitude over the observed time series.

Assume that the sales data for Jetski snowmobiles from sales area 1 were recorded quarterly over the five-year period from 1997 through 2001. The following trend line was derived:

$$TR_t = \hat{y}_t = 100 + 20t$$

The seasonal indexes for a seasonal time series represent the incremental effect of the seasons alone, apart from any trend or cyclical activity. For the Jetski data in sales area 1, these indexes were found to be

$$S_1 = +60 \text{ (winter quarter)} \qquad S_3 = -40 \text{ (summer quarter)}$$
$$S_2 = +30 \text{ (spring quarter)} \qquad S_4 = -20 \text{ (fall quarter)}$$

FIGURE

16.16

Snowmobile sales at the Outdoor Shop (additive seasonal variation).

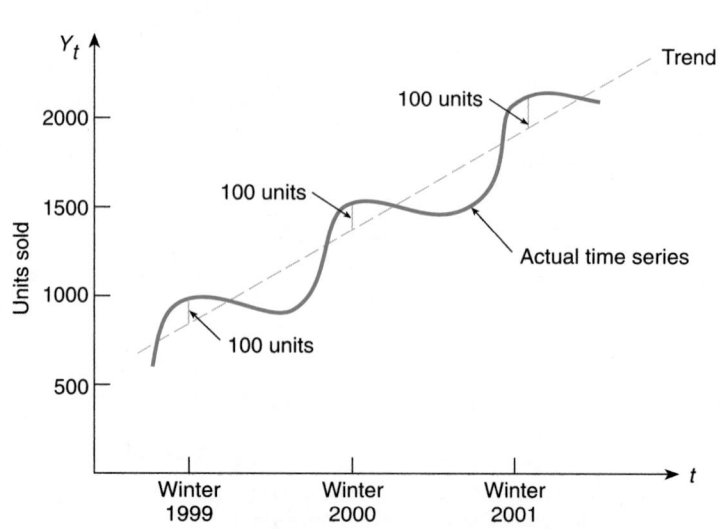

In a time series decomposition (where we actually derive these seasonal indexes), additive seasonal variation assumes that the seasonal index for, say, the winter quarter is the *same* for each year. Using the additive model, this implies that the store will sell 60 more Jetski units in the winter quarter than would be predicted by trend alone during any year. This implies that $S_1 = S_5 = S_9 = \cdots = +60$.

To estimate y_t using only the trend and seasonality, we *add* the two corresponding components.

t (Time)	$TR_t + S_t$ (Sales Estimate)
1 (winter 1997)	$[100 + 20(1)] + 60 = 180$
2 (spring 1997)	$[100 + 20(2)] + 30 = 170$
3 (summer 1997)	$[100 + 20(3)] - 40 = 120$
4 (autumn 1997)	$[100 + 20(4)] - 20 = 160$
5 (winter 1998)	$[100 + 20(5)] + 60 = 260$
6 (spring 1998)	$[100 + 20(6)] + 30 = 250$
7 (summer 1998)	$[100 + 20(7)] - 40 = 200$
8 (autumn 1998)	$[100 + 20(8)] - 20 = 240$
$\vdots$	$\vdots$

A graph of the estimated sales is shown in Figure 16.17. Notice that as the overall level of sales increases, the deviation from the trend line (due to seasonality) remains the same. If the past observations in the time series indicate that higher levels of sales produce wider seasonal fluctuations, this is an indication of multiplicative seasonal variation.

Multiplicative Seasonal Variation

Figure 16.6 shows **multiplicative seasonal variation** in the time series for the sale of Wildcat sailboats. Notice that in each successive year, the difference between the actual value and the trend value for July is larger. In multiplicative seasonal variation, the seasonal fluctuation is *proportional* to the trend level for each observation. Figure 16.18 is a general illustration of multiplicative seasonability; it shows the sales of heat pumps over a three-year period at Handy Home Center.

Considering only the effects of trend and seasonality, an estimate for a time series observation is given by

$$\text{estimate of } y_t = TR_t \cdot S_t$$

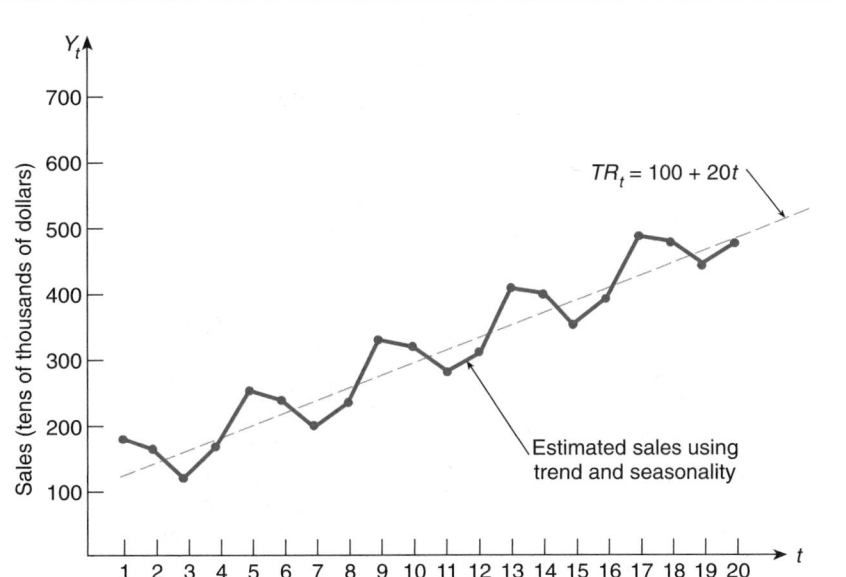

FIGURE

16.17

Jetski sales from sales area 1 (additive seasonal variation).

FIGURE

16.18

Heat-pump sales at Handy Home Center (an illustration of multiplicative seasonal variation).

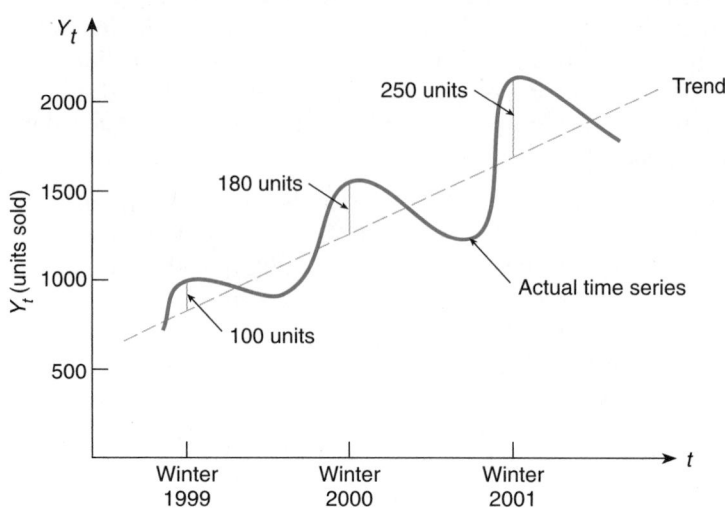

As in additive seasonal variation, the seasonal indexes, S_t, remain constant from one year to the next. When dealing with quarterly data, this means that $S_1 = S_5 = S_9 = \cdots$, $S_2 = S_6 = S_{10} = \cdots$, and so on. The next section discusses a method for determining these indexes for the case of multiplicative seasonality.

16.6

Suppose that the sales of Jetski snowmobiles from sales area 2 contain multiplicative seasonal effects with trend = $TR_t = 100 + 20t$ (as before) and these seasonal indexes:

$$S_1 = 1.4 \text{ (winter quarter)}$$

$$S_2 = 1.2 \text{ (spring quarter)}$$

$$S_3 = 0.6 \text{ (summer quarter)}$$

$$S_4 = 0.8 \text{ (autumn quarter)}$$

Determine the estimated sales using the trend and seasonal components.

Solution   The calculations for the first two years are

t (Time)	$TR_t \cdot S_t$ (Estimate)
1 (winter 1997)	$[100 + 20(1)](1.4) = 168$
2 (spring 1997)	$[100 + 20(2)](1.2) = 168$
3 (summer 1997)	$[100 + 20(3)](.6) = 96$
4 (autumn 1997)	$[100 + 20(4)](.8) = 144$
5 (winter 1998)	$[100 + 20(5)](1.4) = 280$
6 (spring 1998)	$[100 + 20(6)](1.2) = 264$
7 (summer 1998)	$[100 + 20(7)](.6) = 144$
8 (autumn 1998)	$[100 + 20(8)](.8) = 208$
$\vdots$	$\vdots$

A graph of the estimated sales over a five-year period is shown in Figure 16.19. Notice that seasonal patterns do exist, but (unlike additive variation) these fluctuations increase as the sales level rises. For a time series representing sales, this type of variation seems to make sense. If the volume of sales doubles, it is reasonable to expect a larger effect due to seasonality than occurred previously.

Remember that in practice, few time series exhibit exact additive or multiplicative seasonal effects. However, you can classify a great many time series as essentially belonging to one or the other of these two classes.

FIGURE

16.19

Jetski sales from
sales area 2
(multiplicative
seasonal
variation).

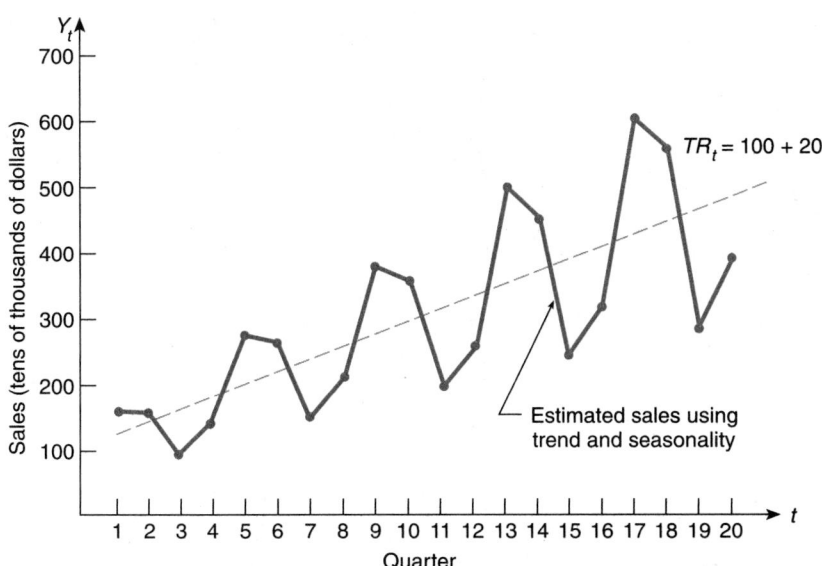

In the discussion to follow, we assume that any seasonality in the time series is *multiplicative*. Most analysts (including those in the U.S. Census Bureau) have had better success describing time series in this manner. The decomposition method to be discussed assumes that each observation is the *product* of its various components. So, the *component structure* is assumed to be

$$y_t = TR_t \cdot S_t \cdot C_t \cdot I_t$$

16.7

where the components representing seasonality, trend, cyclical variation, and noise are multiplied by one another.*

Four-Step Procedure (Multiplicative Components)

Based on the multiplicative component structure in equation 16.7, the following four-step procedure can be used to decompose a time series containing the effects of all four components.

Step 1. *Determine a seasonal index, S_t, for each time period.* For quarterly data, this involves determining four such indexes, S_1, S_2, S_3, and S_4. When the time series contains monthly observations, 12 seasonal indexes (S_1 through S_{12}) must be calculated, one for each month.

Step 2. *Deseasonalize the data.* This step is often referred to as *adjusting for seasonality;* the seasonal component is eliminated. Because we are using a multiplicative structure, we divide each observation by its corresponding seasonal index. So

$$\text{deseasonalized observation} = d_t = \frac{y_t}{S_t}$$

where

$$S_t = \begin{cases} S_1, S_2, S_3, \text{ or } S_4 & \text{(quarterly data)} \\ S_1, S_2, \ldots, \text{ or } S_{12} & \text{(monthly data)} \end{cases}$$

---

*Similar methods for determining the components of a time series containing additive seasonality also exist. Chapter 17 contains a brief discussion of this topic. For a fuller discussion of such techniques, see B. L. Bowerman and R. T. O'Connell, *Forecasting and Time Series: An Applied Approach,* 3d ed., Pacific Grove, California: Brooks/Cole, 2000.

Because $y_t = TR_t \cdot S_t \cdot C_t \cdot I_t,$

$$d_t = \frac{y_t}{S_t} = \frac{TR_t \cdot \cancel{S_t} \cdot C_t \cdot I_t}{\cancel{S_t}} = TR_t \cdot C_t \cdot I_t$$

Step 3. *Determine the trend component, TR_t.* The trend is estimated by passing a least squares line through the *deseasonalized* data. The technique is identical to that discussed in Section 16.2 (which assumed no seasonality), except that we use the d_t values rather than the original time series. This process is illustrated in the next section.

Step 4. *Determine the cyclical component, C_t.* You obtain C_t by first dividing each deseasonalized observation, d_t, by the corresponding trend value from step 3. So the cyclical estimates are derived by first calculating (for each time period)

$$\frac{d_t}{\hat{d}_t} = \frac{d_t}{TR_t} = \frac{\cancel{TR_t} \cdot C_t \cdot I_t}{\cancel{TR_t}} = C_t \cdot I_t$$

Notice that the resulting series contains cycles and irregular activity (but no trend or seasonality). A method for reducing the irregular component in these ratios is discussed in Section 16.6. The resulting values are the cyclical components, C_t.

We do not use the cyclical components to attempt to forecast future values of the time series because their behavior (and period) generally cannot be predicted. The cyclical components can be used in forecasting if one is willing to assume a particular phase in the business cycle. If one assumes, for example, that the cycle is in the midst of an upturn, a value of C_t (such as $C_t = 1.2$) can be assigned to this particular time period. In the discussion to follow, the cyclical components are obtained strictly as a means of *describing* the cyclical activity within a recorded time series.

X Exercises 16.27–16.34

Understanding the Mechanics

16.27 Assuming additive seasonal variation, find the estimate of y_t for $t = 1, 2, 3, 4$. These time periods represent four quarters.

$$TR_t = 21 + 4.5t$$

$$S_1 = 12 \qquad S_3 = -8$$

$$S_2 = 6 \qquad S_4 = -4$$

16.28 Assuming multiplicative seasonal variation, find the estimates of y_t for $t = 1, 2, 3, 4$. These time periods represent four quarters.

$$TR_t = 100 - 3t$$

$$S_1 = .82 \qquad S_3 = 1.30$$

$$S_2 = .64 \qquad S_4 = 1.24$$

Applying the New Concepts

16.29 For a six-year period (1996 to 2001) quarterly sales data (in thousands) were used to arrive at the following trend line and seasonal indexes.

$$TR_t = 35 + 2.3t \qquad \text{for } t = 1, 2, \ldots, 24$$

$$S_1 = -8.7 \qquad S_3 = 8.4$$

$$S_2 = 2.5 \qquad S_4 = 3.1$$

Estimate the sales figures for the four quarters in 2000 using an additive equation containing only the trend and seasonality components.

16.30 Advanced Digital Components has experienced rapid growth during the past several years. The quarterly data for the past four years give the following trend line and seasonal indexes. Sales units are in tens of thousands.

$$TR_t = 0.85 + 0.8t \qquad \text{for } t = 1, 2, \ldots, 16$$

$$S_1 = 0.82 \qquad S_3 = 1.20$$

$$S_2 = 1.36 \qquad S_4 = 0.62$$

Estimate the sales figures for the four quarters in the most recent year using a multiplicative equation containing only the trend and seasonality components.

16.31 Monthly data from the years 1997 through 2001 were used to find the following trend line and seasonal indexes:

$$TR_t = 1.3 + 0.5t \qquad \text{for } t = 1, 2, \ldots, 60$$

$S_1 = 0.5$	$S_4 = 1.3$	$S_7 = 2.4$	$S_{10} = 0.2$
$S_2 = 0.8$	$S_5 = 1.1$	$S_8 = 3.1$	$S_{11} = 0.2$
$S_3 = 0.6$	$S_6 = 1.4$	$S_9 = 0.3$	$S_{12} = 0.1$

Assuming a multiplicative model containing only the trend and seasonality components, estimate the data for the 12 months of 2000.

16.32 The manager of a local utility company is interested in estimating the deseasonalized quarterly usage of electric power consumption by the average household. Using deseasonalized data, the manager wants to see if a clear pattern exists. Average electrical usage is collected quarterly from 1999 through 2001 in units of millions of kilowatt hours. Assume that the data are subject to additive seasonal variation and that the seasonal indexes are $S_1 = 12.4$, $S_2 = -5.8$, $S_3 = 7.2$, and $S_4 = -6.8$. Deseasonalize the data and determine if any patterns are revealed in these seasonally adjusted values.

Year	Quarter	Electrical Usage
1999	1	62
	2	46
	3	61
	4	49
2000	1	66
	2	52
	3	67
	4	55
2001	1	76
	2	60
	3	75
	4	63

Using the Computer

16.33 [DATA SET EX16-33] *Variable description:*

Year: Year from 1992 to 2000

Quarter: Quarter denoted by 1, 2, 3, or 4.

FDI_Japan: Foreign direct investment (in billions of dollars) in Japan

Japan's gross domestic product has shown little growth in recent years. However, a bright spot in its economy is that foreign direct investment (FDI) in the country has been soaring during this time period. This increase shows that investors have faith that Japan's economy will rebound. Assume that the seasonal indexes are $S_1 = 1.0$, $S_2 = 1.18$, $S_3 = .90$, and $S_4 = .92$. If FDI in Japan is subject to multiplicative seasonal variation, what are the deseasonalized FDI figures per quarter from 1992 to 2000?

(Source: "Japanese Economy Is Showing Fresh Signs of Weakness," *The Wall Street Journal*, June 8, 2001, p. A13.)

16.34 [DATA SET EX16-34] *Variable description:*

Year_Quarter: Year and quarter from the first quarter of 1996 to the fourth quarter of 2000

HourlyComp: Percentage increase in hourly compensation

During the expanding economy and low unemployment rate from 1996 to 2000, the percentage increase in hourly compensation rose. Assuming additive seasonality, calculate the deseasonalized hourly compensation, given the following seasonal indexes: $S_1 = .2$, $S_2 = .3$, $S_3 = -3$, and $S_4 = -.2$.

(Source: "Fed's Meyer Warns to Inflation, Joblessness," *The Wall Street Journal*, June 7, 2001, p. A2.)

16.5

MEASURING SEASONALITY

Seasonality often is present in time series data collected over months or quarters. This effect is observed when, for example, some months are always higher than the average for the year. For example, if the recorded values of the time series indicate that July sales are 25% higher than the average for the year, the July index should be 1.25 using the multiplicative structure.

To conduct a time series analysis for a particular time series, we derive a seasonal index for each period during the year (4 for quarterly data, 12 for monthly data). We begin by developing a new series that contains *no seasonality*. This new series is obtained from the original time series and consists of the *centered moving averages*. Using the information calculated from the centered moving averages, we proceed through the four steps outlined in Section 16.4. This section describes how to calculate the centered moving averages and describes the first two steps (determining the seasonal indexes and deseasonalizing the data) in more detail. Example 16.9 then illustrates how the four-step procedure can be applied.

Centered Moving Averages

The **centered moving averages** provide an excellent way of isolating the seasonal components from the original time series. In addition to containing no seasonality, the centered moving averages are *smoother* (contain less irregular activity) than the original time series. Consequently, the moving averages give you a clearer picture of any existing trend within a time series containing significant seasonality and irregular activity. Other methods of smoothing a time series will be discussed in Chapter 17.

To illustrate the calculation of a moving average, consider a time series containing quarterly observations, as shown in Table 16.2.* Here,

$$(1) = \text{sum of } y_1 \text{ through } y_4$$
$$= 85 + 41 + 92 + 45 = 263$$
$$(2) = \text{sum of } y_2 \text{ through } y_5$$
$$= 41 + 92 + 45 + 90 = 268$$
$$(3) = \text{sum of } y_3 \text{ through } y_6$$
$$= 92 + 45 + 90 + 43 = 270$$

and so on.

Because each total contains four observations (one from each quarter), any quarterly seasonal effects have been removed. Consequently, there is no seasonality in the moving totals 263, 268, 270, and so on, in Table 16.2.

The first moving total in Table 16.2 is equal to $y_1 + y_2 + y_3 + y_4$. If we were to position this total in the center of these values, it would lie between $t = 2$ and $t = 3$, at $t = 2.5$. The second moving total is equal to $y_2 + y_3 + y_4 + y_5$; again, we position this total in the center between $t = 3$ and $t = 4$, at $t = 3.5$.

We then add the first two moving totals. Notice that four values went into each of these totals, so that a total of *eight* values makes up this sum. The sum of the first two moving totals is $263 + 268 = 531$. The average for the eight months in the first two moving totals is $531/8 = 66.38$. This is a *centered moving average*. The position of this centered moving average is midway between $t = 2.5$ and $t = 3.5$, at $t = 3$. We therefore conclude that 66.38 is the centered moving average corresponding to $t = 3$.

TABLE

16.2

Time series with quarterly observations.

Time	Quarter	t	y_t	Moving Totals
1990	1	1	85	(1) 263
	2	2	41	(2) 268
	3	3	92	(3) 270
	4	4	45	and so on
1991	1	5	90	
	2	6	43	
	3	7	95	
	4	8	47	
1992	1	9	92	
	⋮	⋮	⋮	

---

*An example using monthly data is given in Section 16.6.

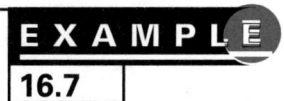

Continue the procedure using Table 16.2 and determine the centered moving average for (1) $t = 4$ and (2) $t = 5$.

EXAMPLE 16.7

Solution 1

Here we obtain

$$268 = y_2 + y_3 + y_4 + y_5$$

(positioned at $t = 3.5$) and

$$270 = y_3 + y_4 + y_5 + y_6$$

(positioned at $t = 4.5$). So the average of the eight numbers making up $268 + 270 = 538$ would be positioned midway between 3.5 and 4.5, at $t = 4$. Consequently, the centered moving average for $t = 4$ is

$$\frac{268 + 270}{8} = 67.25$$

Solution 2

Proceeding as before,

$$270 = y_3 + y_4 + y_5 + y_6$$

(positioned at $t = 4.5$) and

$$273 = y_4 + y_5 + y_6 + y_7$$

(positioned at $t = 5.5$). Therefore, the centered moving average for $t = 5$ is

$$\frac{270 + 273}{8} = 67.88$$

Assume quarterly sales data at Video-Comp were recorded over a four-year period. We now want to determine the centered moving averages for these data, shown in Table 16.3. There appears to be a definite seasonal effect within this time series; the highest sales occur in the fourth quarter of each year. Table 16.4 shows the centered moving averages for these data. The *first moving total* is

$$139 = y_1 + y_2 + y_3 + y_4$$
$$= 20 + 12 + 47 + 60$$

Its actual location is $t = 2.5$; it is positioned between $t = 2$ and $t = 3$. Similarly, the next moving total is centered at $t = 3.5$ and so appears between $t = 3$ and $t = 4$ in the table. This total is

$$159 = y_2 + y_3 + y_4 + y_5$$
$$= 12 + 47 + 60 + 40$$

Each moving total is centered midway between the values making up this total. For example, the last moving total, 369, is centered between $t = 14$ and $t = 15$, at $t = 14.5$. Here,

$$369 = y_{13} + y_{14} + y_{15} + y_{16}$$
$$= 75 + 70 + 101 + 123$$

The centered moving average at time t is the average of the moving total immediately preceding this time value and the total immediately following it. This means that, for $t = 3$,

$$37.25 = \frac{139 + 159}{8}$$

TABLE

16.3

Sales data for
Video-Comp
(millions of
dollars).

Year	Quarter 1	Quarter 2	Quarter 3	Quarter 4
1998	20	12	47	60
1999	40	32	65	76
2000	56	50	85	100
2001	75	70	101	123

TABLE

16.4

Moving averages
for Video-Comp
sales data.

Year	Quarter	t	y_t	Moving Total	Centered Moving Average	Ratio to Moving Average
1998	1	1	20	—	—	—
	2	2	12		—	—
				139		
	3	3	47		37.25	1.26
				159		
	4	4	60		42.25	1.42
				179		
1999	1	5	40		47.00	.85
				197		
	2	6	32		51.25	.62
				213		
	3	7	65		55.25	1.18
				229		
	4	8	76		59.50	1.28
				247		
2000	1	9	56		64.25	.87
				267		
	2	10	50		69.75	.72
				291		
	3	11	85		75.13	1.13
				310		
	4	12	100		80.00	1.25
				330		
2001	1	13	75		84.50	.89
				346		
	2	14	70		89.38	.78
				369		
	3	15	101		—	—
	4	16	123		—	—

For $t = 4$,

$$42.25 = \frac{159 + 179}{8}$$

and so on. Consequently, for $t = 3$, $y_3 = 47$ and the centered moving average is 37.25.

This procedure produces 12 centered moving averages; we are unable to compute this value for $t = 1, 2, 15$, or 16. Notice that the first two of these values of t are for quarters 1 and 2, whereas the remaining two correspond to quarters 3 and 4. In general, if our time series contains T observations, we can derive $T - 4$ centered moving averages using quarterly data or $T - 12$ averages for monthly data.

The moving totals and centered moving averages are formed by summing over the four quarters (seasons), so there is no seasonality present in these values. Furthermore, the irregular component has been reduced because averages always contain less random variation (noise) than do the individual values making up these averages. Representing this reduced irregular activity component as i_t (rather than I_t), we can represent a centered moving average at time t as

centered moving average at time $t = TR_t \cdot C_t \cdot i_t$

Because of this averaging procedure, the moving averages contain much less irregular activity and so are much "smoother" than the original time series. This

FIGURE

16.20

Smoothing a time series using moving averages (Video-Comp sales data).

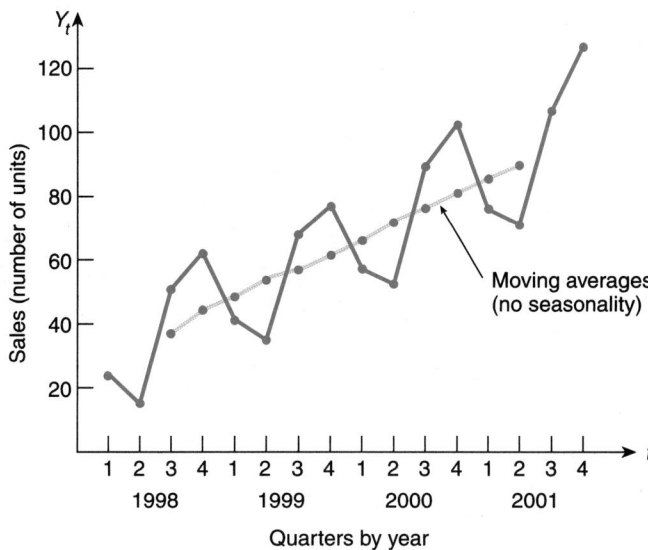

procedure thus is referred to as *smoothing* the time series to get a clearer picture of any existing trend as well as of its shape (straight line or curve).

The centered moving averages in Table 16.4 show a steadily increasing trend. Because the differences between any two adjacent moving averages are nearly the same, this trend is very *linear*. The trend is more apparent in Figure 16.20, which contains the original data with the moving averages.

To determine the four quarterly seasonal indexes, the first step is to divide each observation, y_t, by its corresponding centered moving average; the result is shown in the last column in the table.

for $t = 3$:   ratio = $47/37.25 = 1.26$ (belongs to quarter 3, 1998)

for $t = 4$:   ratio = $60/42.25 = 1.42$ (belongs to quarter 4, 1998)

⋮

for $t = 14$:   ratio = $70/89.38 = .78$ (belongs to quarter 2, 2001)

When we divide y_t by its corresponding centered moving average, we obtain

$$\text{ratio} = \frac{y_t}{\text{centered moving average}} = \frac{\mathcal{TR}_t \cdot S_t \cdot \mathcal{C}_t \cdot I_t}{\mathcal{TR}_t \cdot \mathcal{C}_t \cdot i_t}$$
$$= S_t \cdot I_t$$

Consequently, these ratios contain the seasonal effects as well as the irregular activity (noise) components. The following discussion illustrates how you can reduce the effect of the irregular activity factor by combining these ratios into a set of four seasonal indexes, one for each quarter.

Computing a Seasonal Index

The purpose of a **seasonal index** is to indicate how the time series value for each quarter (or month) compares with the average for the year. The following discussion will assume that we are dealing with a time series containing quarterly data. In the next section, we illustrate this procedure using monthly data.

We begin by collecting the ratios to moving average, placing each of them in its respective quarter. In Table 16.4, we see that 1.26 belongs to quarter 3, 1.42 to quarter 4, .85 to quarter 1, and so on. Table 16.5 is the result. Notice that there are three ratios for each quarter. In general, you always will obtain (total number of years − 1) ratios under each quarter (or month). The time series in this example

TABLE

16.5

Ratios for each quarter.

	Quarter 1	Quarter 2	Quarter 3	Quarter 4
	—	—	1.26	1.42
	.85	.62	1.18	1.28
	.87	.72	1.13	1.25
	.89	.78	—	—
Total	2.61	2.12	3.57	3.95
Average	0.870	0.707	1.190	1.317

contains four years; therefore, it has three ratios. To obtain a "typical" ratio for each quarter, you have several options, including

1. Determining an average of these ratios

2. Finding the median of these values

3. Eliminating the largest and smallest ratio within each quarter and computing a mean of the remaining ratios; this is called a *trimmed mean.*

We will follow the first procedure and calculate a mean ratio for each quarter, as illustrated in Table 16.5. When the time series contains five or more years of data, a trimmed mean offers you protection against an outlier ratio dominating the index for this quarter. Using the median ratios also helps guard against this type of situation.

A Final Adjustment

The last step in computing the seasonal indexes is to make sure that the four computed ratio averages *sum to 4* (or 12, for monthly indexes). This is accomplished by (1) adding the four averages computed in the table (call this SUM) and (2) multiplying each average by 4/SUM. The modified average obtained in this process is the seasonal index for that quarter.

16.8

Using Table 16.5, determine the four seasonal indexes.

Solution   First,

$$SUM = .870 + .707 + 1.190 + 1.317 = 4.084$$

This means that we need to multiply each of the four averages in Table 16.5 by 4/4.084 = .9794.

Quarter	Seasonal Index
1	(0.870)(.9794) = 0.852
2	(0.707)(.9794) = 0.692
3	(1.190)(.9794) = 1.166
4	(1.317)(.9794) = 1.290
	4.0

The indexes for quarters 1 and 2 are below 1.0, so the sales during these quarters typically are below the yearly average. On the other hand, quarters 3 and 4 have seasonal indexes of 1.166 and 1.290, so the sales for these quarters are higher than the average for the year.

This procedure for determining seasonal effects works well, provided the ratios in Table 16.5 are reasonably *stable*. In Example 16.8, all the ratios for quarter 2 are small (near .7) and all the ratios for quarter 4 are large (near 1.3). If strong seasonality is present, such will be the case.

Seasonal indexes can be updated as you obtain an additional year's observations on the variable of interest. You have the option of deleting the most distant year's observations prior to recalculating these values. This procedure leads to seasonal indexes that change slowly over the years.

Thus, the procedure for calculating seasonal indexes based on a determination of centered moving averages is as follows:

1. Derive the *moving* totals by summing the observations for 4 (quarterly data) or 12 (monthly data) consecutive time periods.

2. Average and center the totals by finding the *centered moving averages*.

3. Divide each observation by its corresponding centered moving average.

4. Place the ratios from step 3 in a table headed by the 4 quarters or 12 months.

5. For each column in this table, determine the mean of these ratios; these are the unadjusted seasonal indexes.

6. Make a final adjustment to guarantee that the final seasonal indexes sum to 4 (quarterly data) or 12 (monthly data); these adjusted means are the seasonal indexes.

Deseasonalizing the Data

To remove the seasonality from the data, we **deseasonalize** the time series. The resulting series contains no seasonal effects and consists of the trend, cyclical activity, and, of course, irregular activity. We write deseasonalized data as d_t.

$$d_t = \frac{y_t}{\text{corresponding seasonal index}}$$
$$= \frac{TR_t \cdot S_t \cdot C_t \cdot I_t}{S_t} = TR_t \cdot C_t \cdot I_t$$

The deseasonalized sales values from Table 16.3 are contained in Table 16.6. These values contain trend, cyclical effects, and irregular activity. Notice how the trend is much more apparent in the deseasonalized values than in the original time series.

In Table 16.6, we obtained deseasonalized values for all 16 of the original observations, including the two quarters on each end. We can use the "new" deseasonalized series to determine the **trend** and **cyclical components** of the original time series. This will be illustrated in the next section, where we apply the four-step procedure: (1) computing seasonal indexes, (2) deseasonalizing the data, (3) computing the trend components from the deseasonalized time series (d_t), and finally (4) calculating the cyclical activity.

Comments

Monthly values in the *Wall Street Journal* and other business publications are often stated as "seasonally adjusted." This simply means these values have been deseasonalized to reflect "real" changes in the variable. For example, the number of unemployed workers always increases in May because college students are looking for summer or long-term employment. To determine if there has actually been an increase in the unemployment rate, a deseasonalized (seasonally adjusted) value is generally quoted in the article or news release.

TABLE

16.6

Deseasonalized sales.

Year	t	y_t	Seasonal Index (S_t)	Deseasonalized Values
1998	1	20	.852	23.47
	2	12	.692	17.34
	3	47	1.166	40.31
	4	60	1.290	46.51
1999	5	40	.852	46.95
	6	32	.692	46.24
	7	65	1.166	55.75
	8	76	1.290	58.91
2000	9	56	.852	65.73
	10	50	.692	72.25
	11	85	1.166	72.90
	12	100	1.290	77.52
2001	13	75	.852	88.03
	14	70	.692	101.16
	15	101	1.166	86.62
	16	123	1.290	95.35

X Exercises 16.35–16.44

Understanding the Mechanics

16.35 Complete the following table.

Year	Quarter	t	y_t	Moving Total	Centered Moving Average	Ratio to Moving Average
2000	1	1	10	—		
	2	2	6	69		
	3	3	23	79		
	4	4	30	88		
2001	1	5	20	95		
	2	6	15	101		
	3	7	30	—		
	4	8	36			

16.36 Find the deseasonalized values for the following monthly time series data.

Year	t	y_t	Seasonal Index (S_t)
2001	1	20	1.12
	2	19	.98
	3	17	.96
	4	16	.93
	5	15	.92
	6	11	.90
	7	18	1.05
	8	19	1.06
	9	20	1.07
	10	22	1.05
	11	19	.96
	12	18	1.00

Applying the New Concepts

16.37 Explain why a moving average is a smoothing technique.

16.38 The following table presents the ratio to moving average figures for sales at Zano Systems, a supplier of photocopy machines. Find the seasonal indexes.

Year	Quarter 1	Quarter 2	Quarter 3	Quarter 4
1996			.88	.87
1997	1.14	1.25	.83	.86
1998	1.19	1.22	.94	.88
1999	1.23	1.35	.90	.72
2000	1.16	1.32	.94	.81
2001	1.10	1.21		

16.39 The following table presents the ratio to moving average figures for the cost of a bushel of grapefruit in a certain county in Florida. Find the seasonal indexes.

Year	Jan	Feb	Mar	Apr	May	June
1997						
1998	.90	.87	.95	.93	1.00	1.04
1999	.87	.84	.81	.88	1.01	1.02
2000	.81	.75	.82	.89	1.05	1.04
2001	.87	.81	.77	.98	1.01	1.06

Year	July	Aug	Sept	Oct	Nov	Dec
1997	1.06	1.10	1.12	1.02	1.03	.99
1998	1.08	1.14	1.15	1.06	1.04	.97
1999	1.01	1.15	1.07	1.03	1.00	.90
2000	1.10	1.21	1.18	1.10	1.07	.97
2001						

16.40 The sale of grass sod is a seasonal business. Green Garden Supplies does most of its business in May, June, July, and August. The following table presents their monthly sales (in thousands of dollars). Find the seasonal indexes. For what month is the seasonal index the largest?

Year	Jan	Feb	Mar	Apr	May	June
1997	.1	.1	1.2	2.2	4.1	4.5
1998	.1	.2	1.4	2.0	4.0	4.2
1999	.1	.2	1.3	2.2	4.3	4.4
2000	.1	.3	1.4	2.3	4.4	4.6
2001	.1	.3	1.5	2.3	4.6	4.8

Year	July	Aug	Sept	Oct	Nov	Dec
1997	5.5	5.3	3.5	1.1	.2	.1
1998	5.3	5.0	3.2	1.0	.1	.1
1999	5.6	5.3	3.5	1.1	.2	.1
2000	5.8	5.5	3.7	1.3	.3	.1
2001	6.0	5.6	3.7	1.4	.4	.1

16.41 The following table represents the ratio to moving average figures for the number of people below the poverty level in a certain county. Find the seasonal indexes.

Year	Quarter 1	Quarter 2	Quarter 3	Quarter 4
1997			.84	.83
1998	1.12	1.29	.91	.89
1999	1.17	1.24	.92	.90
2000	1.15	1.30	.92	.88
2001	1.13	1.26		

16.42 The amount of beverage sold at Chesapeake Restaurant varies according to the time of the year. The manager would like to know which quarter is most affected by seasonal variation. Business at Chesapeake Restaurant has steadily increased over the past four years. What advice can you give the manager? The following data are in units of thousands of dollars.

Year	Quarter	Beverage Sales
1998	1	22
	2	21
	3	26
	4	27
1999	1	25
	2	24
	3	29
	4	30

Year	Quarter	Beverage Sales
2000	1	29
	2	28
	3	35
	4	37
2001	1	34
	2	33
	3	40
	4	42

Using the Computer

16.43 [DATA SET EX16-43] *Variable description:*

Year: Year from 1998 to 2001

Month: One through twelve for the months of the year

JoblessFemale: Percentage of unemployed females who are married and in the civilian labor force

Unemployment among married females is typically higher than unemployment among married males. From 1998 to 2001, the strong economy has produced a much tighter job market and, therefore, the difference in the unemployment rates of married males and females has narrowed. Find the seasonal indexes for the percentage of unemployed females who are married and in the civilian labor force.

16.44 [DATA SET EX16-44] *Variable description:*

Year: Year from 1995 to 2000

Quarter: Quarter denoted by 1, 2, 3, or 4

TechIPO: Technology initial public offerings in the U.S.

Buying shares the first time they are offered to the public has considerable natural appeal, especially in a bull market. Technology initial public offerings (IPOs) soared during 1999 but fell dramatically at the end of 2000. Suppose that a mutual fund manager is interested in the seasonal indexes for technology IPOs. Using quarterly data from 1995 to 2000, compute the seasonal indexes for these data and interpret their values.

(Source: "The Coming-Out Party," *The Wall Street Journal*, October 15, 2001, p. R22.)

16.6

A TIME SERIES CONTAINING SEASONALITY, TREND, AND CYCLES

During the summer of 2001, the owner of an import/export company decided to investigate the past behavior of U.S. retail trade figures for the years 1997 through 2000. He collected the data in Table 16.7 using monthly figures released by the U.S. Department of Commerce. He suspected that these data would indicate high retail trade during December (due to holiday sales) with much lower activity during January and possibly February. For the remaining months, he had no idea

TABLE

16.7

Total U.S. retail trade (excluding motor vehicle and parts dealers) (billions of dollars).

	1997	1998	1999	2000
Jan	134.738	139.935	146.613	158.691
Feb	130.255	135.538	145.121	164.725
Mar	148.497	151.118	165.736	183.875
Apr	145.703	155.820	166.011	178.776
May	156.603	162.797	173.496	190.753
Jun	150.915	159.701	171.286	187.868
Jul	153.200	161.541	172.364	182.891
Aug	156.782	162.369	174.788	191.647
Sep	149.407	155.747	169.809	183.229
Oct	157.523	164.528	174.740	186.550
Nov	161.925	169.914	185.347	198.706
Dec	203.117	215.590	238.452	243.255

Source: U.S. Department of Commerce, Bureau of the Census, *Current Business Report*. These reports are only available electronically using Internet address **http://www.census.gov**.

whether seasonal effects would be present. He also suspected there would be a steadily increasing trend due to inflation and population growth.

The four-step procedure for decomposing (a gruesome term, we'll admit) a time series into the seasonal, trend, and cyclical components was introduced in Section 16.4. We demonstrate this method of describing a time series by using the monthly retail trade data in Example 16.9.

Microsoft ® Excel Application Use DATA16-9

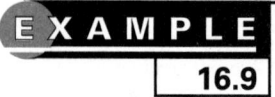

A Time Series Decomposition Using Excel

The U.S. monthly retail data for 1997 to 2000 are contained in Table 16.7 and in data set DATA 16-9. Perform a time series decomposition of these data, and discuss the results.

Solution  Begin by entering the 48 observations into column A. Click on **KPK Data Analysis ➤ Time Series Analysis ➤ Decomposition.** Select 12 as the number of time periods per year, and enter "A1:A48" in the **Input Range** box, "B1" in the **Output Range** box, and "1997" in the **First Year** box. Also, click on "A Single Column" since the data are stored in a single column (column A). The resulting output will be contained in five sheets, labeled **Components, Cyclical, Trend, Seasonal,** and **Plots.**

Step 1. *Determine the seasonal indexes.* The first step is to determine the moving totals and centered moving averages for the 48 observations in Table 16.7. This portion of the output is in the sheet labeled **Seasonal** and will be identical to the results contained in Table 16.8. Notice that when using monthly data, there is no monthly average for $t = 1$ through $t = 6$ (January through June 1997) and for $t = 43$ through 48 (July through December 2000). The first moving total is

$$1{,}848.665 = y_1 + y_2 + \cdots + y_{12}$$

$$= 134.738 + 130.255 + \cdots + 203.117$$

TABLE

16.8

Moving averages and ratios to moving average for U.S. monthly retail trade data. This output is contained in the Excel sheet labeled **Seasonal**.

Year	Month	t (1)	y_t (2)	Moving total (3)	Centered Moving Average (4)	Ratio to Moving Average (5)
1997	Jan	1	134.738			
	Feb	2	130.255			
	Mar	3	148.497			
	Apr	4	145.703			
	May	5	156.603			
	Jun	6	150.915	1848.665		
	Jul	7	153.200	1853.862	154.272	0.993
	Aug	8	156.782	1859.145	154.709	1.013
	Sep	9	149.407	1861.766	155.038	0.964
	Oct	10	157.523	1871.883	155.569	1.013
	Nov	11	161.925	1878.077	156.248	1.036
	Dec	12	203.117	1886.863	156.872	1.295
	⋮					
2000	Jan	37	158.691	2190.715	182.121	0.871
	Feb	38	164.725	2207.574	183.262	0.899
	Mar	39	183.875	2220.994	184.524	0.996
	Apr	40	178.776	2232.804	185.575	0.963
	May	41	190.753	2246.163	186.624	1.022
	Jun	42	187.868	2250.966	187.380	1.003
	Jul	43	182.891			
	Aug	44	191.647			
	Sep	45	183.229			
	Oct	46	186.550			
	Nov	47	198.706			
	Dec	48	243.255			

This value is positioned midway between $t = 1$ and $t = 12$, that is, at $t = 6.5$ (between $t = 6$ and $t = 7$). The next moving total is

$$1{,}853.862 = y_2 + y_3 + \cdots + y_{13}$$
$$= 130.255 + 148.497 + \cdots + 139.935$$

which is centered at $t = 7.5$ (between $t = 7$ and $t = 8$). So the first *centered moving average* is positioned midway between $t = 6.5$ and $t = 7.5$, at $t = 7$. This is

$$154.272 = \frac{1{,}848.665 + 1{,}853.862}{24}$$

Notice that we divide by 24, because 24 observations went into the sum of these two moving totals.

The final centered moving average is

$$187.380 = \frac{2{,}246.163 + 2{,}250.966}{24}$$

and corresponds to $t = 42$.

The Excel output and Table 16.8 also contain each ratio to moving average (column 2 divided by column 4). To illustrate:

$$0.993 = \frac{153.200}{154.272} \qquad 1.013 = \frac{156.782}{154.709}$$

TABLE

16.9

Summary of ratios. This output is in the Excel sheet labeled **Seasonal**.

	Jan	Feb	Mar	Apr	May	Jun	Jul	Aug	Sep	Oct	Nov	Dec
						Month (Period)						
1997							0.993	1.013	0.964	1.013	1.036	1.295
1998	0.888	0.857	0.952	0.979	1.018	0.994	1.000	1.001	0.954	1.002	1.029	1.299
1999	0.878	0.864	0.981	0.976	1.014	0.992	0.990	0.996	0.959	0.980	1.032	1.317
2000	0.871	0.899	0.996	0.963	1.022	1.003						
Average	0.879	0.873	0.977	0.973	1.018	0.996	0.994	1.004	0.959	0.998	1.033	1.304

and so on. These ratios are summarized in the top portion of the **Seasonal** Excel spreadsheet (under **Summary of Ratios**) and in Table 16.9, both of which also contain the average of the three values for each time period.

The final step is to adjust each of these averages in Table 16.9 so they sum to 12 (because there are 12 time periods per year). Here,

$$\text{SUM} = .879 + .873 + \cdots + 1.304 = 12.008$$

and so

$$S_1 = \text{seasonal index for January}$$

$$= .879 \left(\frac{12}{12.008} \right) = .879$$

$$S_2 = \text{seasonal index for February}$$

$$= .873 \left(\frac{12}{12.008} \right) = .873$$

$$\vdots$$

$$S_{12} = \text{seasonal index for December}$$

$$= 1.304 \left(\frac{12}{12.008} \right) = 1.303$$

The final collection of seasonal indexes is

Month	Seasonal Index	Month	Seasonal Index
Jan.	.879	July	.994
Feb.	.873	Aug.	1.003
Mar.	.976	Sept.	.958
Apr.	.972	Oct.	.997
May	1.018	Nov.	1.032
June	.995	Dec.	1.303

The sum of these seasonal indexes ($S_1 + S_2 + \cdots + S_{12}$) is 12.000. Due to rounding, this sum might not be exactly 12 on occasion, and this is perfectly acceptable.

We observe (1) a large seasonal index for December ($S_{12} = 1.303$), indicating large retail trade for this month, (2) low indexes for January and February, and (3) very little seasonality for any of the remaining months.

Step 2. *Deseasonalize the data.* We obtain the deseasonalized values (which contain no seasonality) by dividing each observation by its corresponding seasonal index. These values are contained in the Excel spreadsheet labeled **Trend** (under the column labeled D(t)) and are partially shown in Table 16.10. The trend is more apparent now because the deseasonalized values tend to increase over time.

Step 3. *Determine the trend components.* A common method for estimating trend (and the one we use) is to construct a least squares trend line (or curve)

TABLE

16.10

Year	Month	t	y_t	S_t	
1997	Jan	1	134.738	0.879	153.349
	Feb	2	130.255	0.873	149.238
	Mar	3	148.497	0.976	152.165
	Apr	4	145.703	0.972	149.871
	May	5	156.603	1.018	153.899
	Jun	6	150.915	0.995	151.602
	Jul	7	153.200	0.994	154.164
	Aug	8	156.782	1.003	156.320
	Sep	9	149.407	0.958	155.877
	Oct	10	157.523	0.997	157.919
	Nov	11	161.925	1.032	156.916
	Dec	12	203.117	1.303	155.905
	$\vdots$				
2000	Jan	37	158.691	0.879	180.611
	Feb	38	164.725	0.873	188.731
	Mar	39	183.875	0.976	188.416
	Apr	40	178.776	0.972	183.890
	May	41	190.753	1.018	187.459
	Jun	42	187.868	0.995	188.724
	Jul	43	182.891	0.994	184.042
	Aug	44	191.647	1.003	191.083
	Sep	45	183.229	0.958	191.163
	Oct	46	186.550	0.997	187.019
	Nov	47	198.706	1.032	192.559
	Dec	48	243.255	1.303	186.713

Deseasonalized monthly retail trade values. This output is in the Excel sheet labeled **Trend.**

through the deseasonalized data. From the moving averages in the Excel output (under the column **Centered Average** in the sheet labeled **Seasonal**), also shown in Table 16.8, it appears that a straight line trend equation will be appropriate; these values tend to increase at a fairly steady rate.

The calculations for the trend line are identical to those discussed in Section 16.2, using the d_i values in place of the original observations, y_i. A summary of these calculations is given in Table 16.11. The least squares line through the deseasonalized data is contained at the top of the Excel sheet labeled **Trend** and is given by

$$TR_t = \hat{d}_t = b_0 + b_1 t$$

where

$$b_1 = \frac{12B - 6(T + 1)A}{T(T^2 - 1)}$$

where now

$$A = \Sigma d_t = 8{,}108.741 \text{ and } B = \Sigma t d_t = 207{,}269.736$$

$$= \frac{12(207{,}269.736) - 6(49)(8{,}108.741)}{48(2{,}304 - 1)} = \frac{103{,}266.978}{110{,}544} = .93417$$

and

$$b_0 = \frac{A}{T} - b_1 \left(\frac{T + 1}{2} \right)$$

$$= \frac{8{,}108.741}{48} - (.93417)\frac{49}{2} = 168.932 - 22.887 = 146.045$$

TABLE

16.11

Calculations for trend line (U.S. monthly retail trade data).

t	d_t	$t \cdot d_t$
1	153.349	153.349
2	149.238	298.476
3	152.165	456.495
4	149.871	599.484
⋮	⋮	⋮
45	191.163	8602.335
46	187.019	8602.874
47	192.559	9050.273
48	186.713	8962.224
	8,108.741	207,269.736

FIGURE

16.21

Deseasonalized data and trend line (monthly U.S. retail trade).

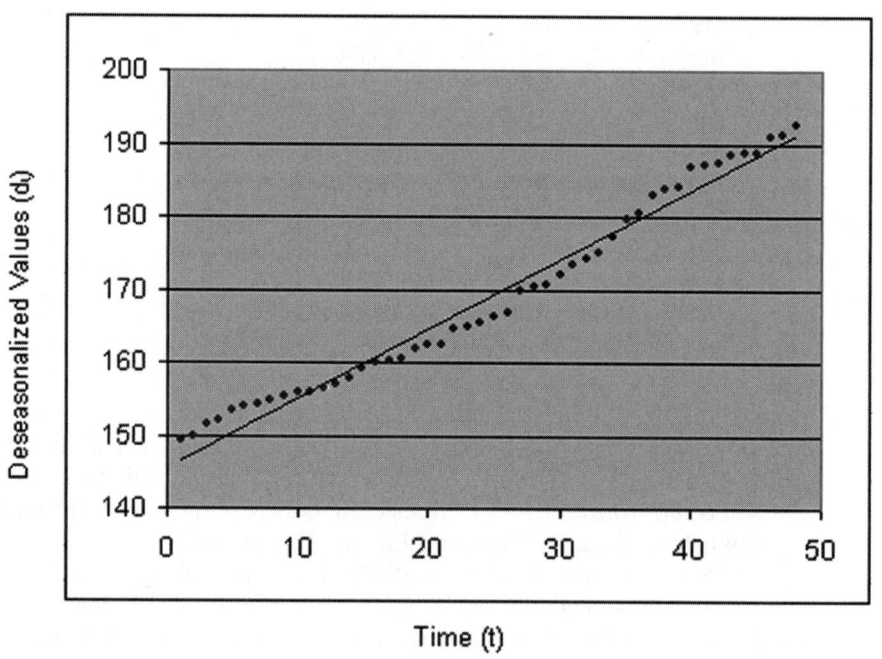

Time (t)

Consequently, the equation of the trend equation is given by

$$TR_t = \hat{d}_t = 146.045 + .934t$$

This equation agrees with the Excel result and implies that, apart from seasonal fluctuations, the U.S. retail trade is increasing at an average rate of \$934 million each month. A graph of the deseasonalized data and corresponding trend line is shown in Figure 16.21.

Step 4. *Determine the cyclical activity.* We begin by following the procedure outlined in Section 16.3. We divide each deseasonalized observation by the corresponding trend value:

$$\frac{d_t}{TR_t} = \frac{d_t}{\hat{d}_t} = \frac{\cancel{TR_t} \cdot C_t \cdot I_t}{\cancel{TR_t}} = C_t \cdot I_t$$

t	d_t	$\hat{d}_t$		Three-Month Moving Average (C_t)
1	153.349	$146.045 + .934 = 146.979$	1.0433	—
2	149.238	$146.045 + .934 = 147.913$	1.0090	1.025
3	152.165	$146.045 + .934 = 148.847$	1.0223	1.011
4	149.871	$146.045 + .934 = 149.782$	1.0006	1.015
5	153.899	$146.045 + .934 = 150.716$	1.0211	1.007
6	151.602	$146.045 + .934 = 151.650$	0.9997	1.010
⋮	⋮	⋮	⋮	⋮

TABLE 16.12

Calculating the cyclical components for the U.S. monthly retail trade data.

The resulting values contain cyclical effects as well as an irregular activity component. One method of reducing the irregular effect is to compute a series of *three-period* moving averages on the $C_t \cdot I_t$ values. This procedure greatly reduces the irregular activity effect, and the moving averages provide a much better estimate of the cyclical components. The choice of a three-period moving average is somewhat arbitrary; however, when we use an odd number of terms, the moving averages need not be centered.

A partial solution, using the first six rows of the Excel output under the column **Ratio** in the sheet labeled **Seasonal,** is shown in Table 16.12. We see that the cyclical component for $t = 2$ is C_2, where

$$C_2 = \frac{1.0433 + 1.0090 + 1.0223}{3} = 1.025$$

and the cyclical component for $t = 3$ is

$$C_3 = \frac{1.0090 + 1.0223 + 1.0006}{3} = 1.011$$

Similarly,

$$C_4 = \frac{1.0223 + 1.0006 + 1.0211}{3} = 1.015$$

and

$$C_5 = \frac{1.0006 + 1.0211 + 0.9997}{3} = 1.007$$

The complete set of smoothed cyclical values is contained in the Excel sheet labeled **Cyclical** (under the column titled **C(t)**). These components are partially reproduced in Table 16.13 (far right column) and plotted in Figure 16.22. Observe the start of a cycle beginning at the end of 1997 and ending toward the end of 2000. The data end in the midst of downward cycle with a cyclical component less than 1. In previous editions of this textbook, the cyclical components for the U.S. retail trade data ranged from .97 to 1.03 (1980–1983), .97 to 1.01 (1984–1987), .98 to 1.02 (1987–1990), .97 to 1.04 (1989–1992) and .99 to 1.01 (1994–1997).

Once the steps in the previous sections have been completed, the various components can be combined for any specified value of t.

TABLE

16.13

Cyclical components (monthly U.S. retail trade data). This output is in the Excel sheet labeled **Cyclical**.

Year	Month	d_t	$\hat{d}_t(TR_t)$		Three-Month Moving Average (C_t)
1997	Jan	153.349	146.979	1.0433	—
	Feb	149.238	147.913	1.0090	1.025
	Mar	152.165	148.847	1.0223	1.011
	Apr	149.871	149.782	1.0006	1.015
	May	153.899	150.716	1.0211	1.007
	Jun	151.602	151.650	0.9997	1.010
	Jul	154.164	152.584	1.0104	1.009
	Aug	156.320	153.518	1.0183	1.013
	Sep	155.877	154.452	1.0092	1.015
	Oct	157.919	155.387	1.0163	1.010
	Nov	156.916	156.321	1.0038	1.004
	Dec	155.905	157.255	0.9914	1.001
	⋮				
2000	Jan	180.611	180.609	1.0000	1.019
	Feb	188.731	181.543	1.0396	1.024
	Mar	188.416	182.478	1.0325	1.025
	Apr	183.890	183.412	1.0026	1.017
	May	187.459	184.346	1.0169	1.013
	Jun	188.724	185.280	1.0186	1.008
	Jul	184.042	186.214	0.9883	1.009
	Aug	191.083	187.148	1.0210	1.009
	Sep	191.163	188.083	1.0164	1.009
	Oct	187.019	189.017	0.9894	1.007
	Nov	192.559	189.951	1.0137	0.994
	Dec	186.713	190.885	0.9781	—

FIGURE

16.22

Plot of cyclical activity (monthly U.S. retail trade data).

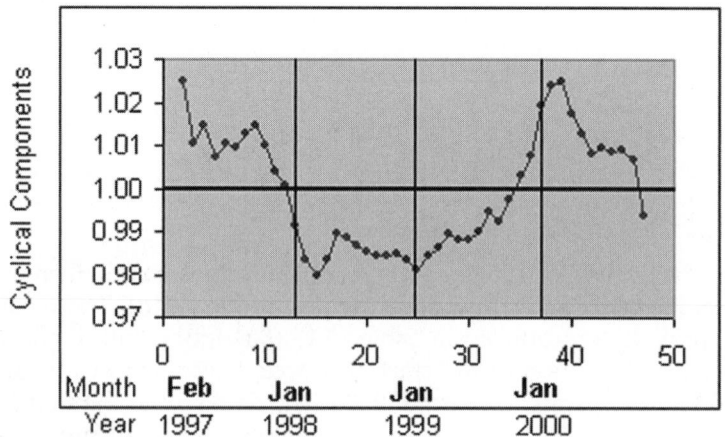

EXAMPLE

16.10

Determine the four components for (1) September 1997 and (2) March 2000.

Solution 1   The value of t for September 1997 is $t = 9$. The seasonal index for September is $S_9 = .958$. The trend component (second column of numbers in Table 16.13) is

TABLE

16.14

Time series
components for
U.S. retail trade
data. This output is
in the Excel sheet
labeled
Components.

Year	Month	y_t	TR_t	S_t	C_t	I_t
1997	Jan	134.738	146.979	0.879	—	—
	Feb	130.255	147.913	0.873	1.025	0.984
	Mar	148.497	148.847	0.976	1.011	1.012
	Apr	145.703	149.782	0.972	1.015	0.986
	May	156.603	150.716	1.018	1.007	1.014
	Jun	150.915	151.650	0.995	1.010	0.989
	Jul	153.200	152.584	0.994	1.009	1.001
	Aug	156.782	153.518	1.003	1.013	1.006
	Sep	149.407	154.452	0.958	1.015	0.995
	Oct	157.523	155.387	0.997	1.010	1.006
	Nov	161.925	156.321	1.032	1.004	1.000
	Dec	203.117	157.255	1.303	1.001	0.991
	⋮					
2000	Jan	158.691	180.609	0.879	1.019	0.981
	Feb	164.725	181.543	0.873	1.024	1.015
	Mar	183.875	182.478	0.976	1.025	1.007
	Apr	178.776	183.412	0.972	1.017	0.986
	May	190.753	184.346	1.018	1.013	1.004
	Jun	187.868	185.280	0.995	1.008	1.011
	Jul	182.891	186.214	0.994	1.009	0.979
	Aug	191.647	187.148	1.003	1.009	1.012
	Sep	183.229	188.083	0.958	1.009	1.007
	Oct	186.550	189.017	0.997	1.007	0.983
	Nov	198.706	189.951	1.032	0.994	1.020
	Dec	243.255	190.885	1.303	—	—

$TR_9 = 154.452$. The cyclical component (far right column of Table 16.13) is 1.015. Therefore,

$$S_9 \cdot TR_9 \cdot C_9 = (.958)(154.452)(1.015) = 150.184$$

The actual observation for September 1997 is $y_9 = 149.407$. Since $y_9 = S_9 \cdot TR_9 \cdot C_9 \cdot I_9$,

$$I_9 = \frac{y_9}{S_9 \cdot TR_9 \cdot C_9} = \frac{149.407}{150.184} = .995$$

and the final decomposition is

$$y_9 = 149.407 = S_9 \cdot TR_9 \cdot C_9 \cdot I_9 = (.958)(154.452)(1.015)(.995)$$

For $t = 39$ (March 2000), we have S_{39} = seasonal index for March = $S_3 = .976$. Also, **Solution 2**
$TR_{39} = 182.478$ and $C_{39} = 1.025$, from Table 16.3. Consequently,

$$I_{39} = \frac{y_{39}}{S_{39} \cdot TR_{39} \cdot C_{39}} = \frac{183.875}{182.551} = 1.007$$

The combined decomposition for this observation is

$$y_{39} = 183.875 = S_{39} \cdot TR_{39} \cdot C_{39} \cdot I_{39} = (.976)(182.478)(1.025)(1.007)$$

The components for all but the first and last observations are contained in the Excel spreadsheet labeled **Components** under the heading **Time Series Components.** The same components are partially shown in Table 16.14.

Summary of Time Series Decomposition

The time series decomposition procedure allows you to examine the presence of the following:

- Trend (a long-term growth or decline)
- Seasonality (a within-year recurrent pattern)
- Cyclical activity (upward or downward variation about the trend)

The remaining component (what is left after removing the effect of these three factors) is irregular activity. Having determined these four components, you are able to describe a particular time series by carefully examining and plotting the calculated components.

A summary of the components for the U.S. retail trade time series is contained in Table 16.14. The irregular activity components (I_t) are determined by continuing the procedure in Example 16.10. Graphs of these components are shown in Figure 16.23. These four graphs will be on the Excel sheet labeled **Plots** when using **KPK Data Analysis ➤ Time Series Analysis ➤ Decomposition.** Notice that the graph of the irregular activity components contains no obvious pattern, as we would expect. By combining the various graphs of the time series components into a single set of graphs (Figure 16.23), we can tell at a glance what is the nature of the series. The conclusions we can reach from this figure include the following.

1. There is a strong linear trend that increases over the four-year period.

2. There is a strong retail trade peak each December, followed by weak trading in January and February.

3. There is a clear cycle between the end of 1997 and the end of 2000. Retail trade for 2000 ends in the midst of a downward cycle.

Other methods of time series analysis are discussed in Chapter 17, where we examine time series forecasting.

FIGURE 16.23

Excel plots of monthly U.S. retail trade data using **KPK Data Analysis ➤ Time Series Analysis ➤ Decomposition.**

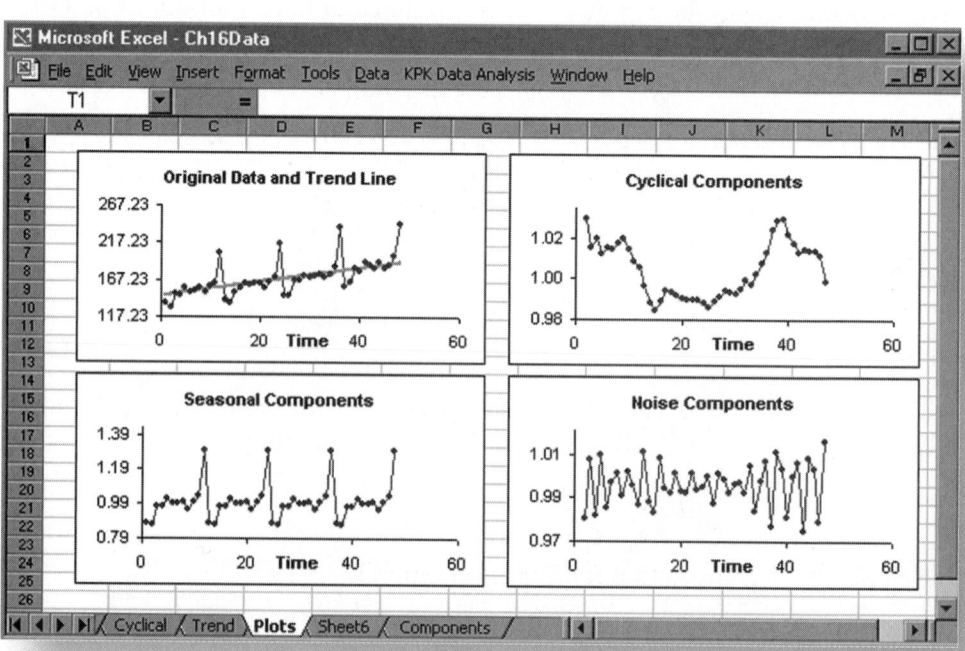

X Exercises 16.45–16.52

Understanding the Mechanics

16.45 For the month of January 2001, a researcher finds that the seasonal index is 1.2, the trend value is 100, and the cyclical component is .90. What is the irregular component if the actual observation for January 2001 is 110?

16.46 Given the following ratio to moving averages, determine the seasonal indexes.

Year	Month	Ratio to Moving Average	Year	Month	Ratio to Moving Average
1998	July	1.046	2000	Jan	.856
	Aug	1.057		Feb	.826
	Sept	.993		Mar	.969
	Oct	1.015		Apr	.952
	Nov	.996		May	1.021
	Dec	1.217		June	1.011
1999	Jan	.851		July	1.019
	Feb	.858		Aug	1.071
	Mar	.978		Sept	1.005
	Apr	.968		Oct	1.088
	May	1.010		Nov	1.026
	June	1.011		Dec	1.218
	July	1.020	2001	Jan	.881
	Aug	1.051		Feb	.843
	Sept	1.195		Mar	.982
	Oct	1.012		Apr	.956
	Nov	1.038		May	1.012
	Dec	1.252		June	1.003

Applying the New Concepts

16.47 The gross domestic product (GDP) is defined as the output of goods and services produced by labor and property located in the United States. GDP is the broadest measure of the health of the U.S. economy. The following table illustrates the deseasonalized percentage quarterly change in GDP from 1997 to 2000 and the value of the trend component for each quarter. Determine the cyclical components for the four quarters of 1999 using a multiplicative model.

Year	Quarter	Deseasonalized GDP Increase	Trend Component
1997	1	4.763	5.185
	2	7.247	5.047
	3	4.376	4.909
	4	2.113	4.771
1998	1	6.603	4.633
	2	2.825	4.495
	3	4.376	4.357
	4	5.056	4.219
1999	1	3.464	4.081
	2	2.088	3.943
	3	4.91	3.805
	4	6.264	3.667

Year	Quarter	Deseasonalized GDP Increase	Trend Component
2000	1	2.381	3.529
	2	7.001	3.391
	3	1.494	3.253
	4	1.434	3.115

(Source: "U.S. Economy Slows," *USA Today*, July 30, 2001, p. 1B.)

16.48 The amount of monthly business that an automotive repair shop receives can be described by the following trend line and seasonal indexes for the time periods January 1998 ($t = 1$) to the present. Sales are in units of thousands of dollars.

$$TR_t = 12 + .5t$$

$$S_1 = .90, S_2 = .84, S_3 = 1.00, S_4 = 1.00, S_5 = 1.02,$$

$$S_6 = 1.04, S_7 = 1.00, S_8 = 1.00, S_9 = 1.00, S_{10} = .99,$$

$$S_{11} = 1.00, S_{12} = 1.21$$

Assume that no cyclical component is present ($C_t = 1.0$). Given the following set of actual sales for the first six months of 2001, calculate the irregular activity component for the first six months of 2001.

		2001				
	Jan	Feb	Mar	Apr	May	Jun
Sales	10.6	10.5	12.0	12.5	12.9	12.8

Using the Computer

16.49 [DATA SET EX16-49] *Variable description:*

Year: Years from 1998 through 2001

Months: Months are numbered from 1 through 12

Membership: The monthly membership

The membership of a local spa fluctuates seasonally. The manager of the spa is interested in knowing what the trend line is for the spa's membership. The membership data are recorded monthly. Estimate the trend line and use it to predict the deseasonalized membership for January 2002.

16.50 [DATA SET EX16-50] *Variable description:*

Quarter_Year: Quarter and from the first quarter of 1995 to the fourth quarter of 2000

DPI_Saved: Percentage of disposable personal income saved

The low personal savings rate of Americans has been a catalyst of the growing economy. Many Americans have higher net worth because of their assets, which include financial investments, and thus feel that this justifies a low savings rate. Indeed, since 1987, Americans' net worth (assets minus debts) has roughly doubled to about $35 trillion.

a. Compute the seasonal indexes for DPI_Saved.

b. What is the cyclical component for the first quarter of 2000?

c. What is the trend line for the data?

(Source: "Personal Saving Rate," *The Wall Street Journal,* July 31, 2001, p. 1A.)

16.51 [DATA SET EX16-51] *Variable description:*

Year: Years from 1996 through 2001

Quarter: Quarters are numbered from 1 through 4

LoanApp: Number of loan applications

The manager of a branch bank is having difficulty in staffing. A good measure of banking business is the number of loan applications received quarterly. Quarterly data are collected from 1996 through 2001. Plot the origi-nal data and the trend line. Also plot the noise compo-nents over time and determine if any pattern is apparent in this plot.

16.52 [DATA SET EX16-52] *Variable description:*

Year: Years from 1997 through 2001

Quarter: Quarters are numbered from 1 through 4

Enroll: Enrollment in a retirement education seminar

A stock brokerage firm offers a free retirement seminar on a quarterly basis. Since many of the participants in the seminar will invest in financial products offered by the firm, the manager of the brokerage firm wishes to deter-mine the trend and seasonal components of the enroll-ment. Plot the trend line using the deseasonalized data. Also construct a plot of the seasonal components.

16.7 INDEX NUMBERS

How many times have you heard a remark such as, "Fifteen years ago we could have bought that house for $70,000. Now it's worth $180,000." Or "My weekly grocery bill used to be $25. Today, it's almost $100." Many people like to talk about the prices back in the "good old days," but were goods and services actually less expensive in those days?

Perhaps a particular item consumed a greater proportion of the typical con-sumer's consumable income (purchasing power) in years past. To compare effec-tively the change in the price or value of a certain item (or group of items) between any two time periods, we use an index number. An **index number** (or index) mea-sures the change in a particular item (typically a product or service) or a collection of items between two time periods.

The average hourly wages for production employees at Kessler Toy Company in 1985, 1990, 1995, and 2000 are shown in Table 16.15. Suppose we wish to com-pare the average wages for 1990, 1995, and 2000 with those for 1985. By comput-ing a ratio for each pair of wages (expressed as a *percentage* of the 1985 wage), we obtain the following set of index numbers:

$$\text{index number for 1990:} \quad \left(\frac{8.50}{7.05}\right) \cdot 100 = 120.6$$

$$\text{index number for 1995:} \quad \left(\frac{10.90}{7.05}\right) \cdot 100 = 154.6$$

$$\text{index number for 2000:} \quad \left(\frac{12.50}{7.05}\right) \cdot 100 = 177.3$$

When calculating an index number, we follow standard practice—round to the nearest tenth (as in Table 16.15) and omit the percent sign. For this application, all wages were compared to those in 1985, the *base year.* The index number for the base year is always 100.

When each index number uses the same base year, the resulting set of values is an **index time series.** An index time series is a set of index numbers determined from the same base year. The purpose of such a time series is to measure the yearly values in *constant* units (dollars, people, and so on). Because these values define a

TABLE

16.15

Average hourly wage of production employees at Kessler Toy Company.

	1985	1990	1995	2000
Wage	$ 7.05	$ 8.50	$ 10.90	$ 12.50
Index (base = 1980)	100	120.6	154.6	177.3

TABLE

16.16

Prices of four items in 1990 and 2000.

Item	1990	2000
Eggs	.75 (doz.)	1.35 (doz.)
Chicken	.95 (lb)	1.79 (lb)
Cheese	.89 (lb)	1.85 (lb)
Auto battery	$31.00 (each)	$55.00 (each)

time series, they can be analyzed and decomposed by using the methods described previously. Our purpose in this section is simply to describe how to *construct* a time series of this type.

Price Indexes

Index numbers are derived for a variety of products (goods or services) as well as locations. For example, you may wish to compare the relative costs of consumer items in Los Angeles and Minneapolis if you are considering a move. Such information is readily available or can be determined from a number of business publications or government reports. The Department of Labor and the Bureau of Labor Statistics release reports (many of them monthly) on the price and quantity of many consumer items and agricultural commodities. Often these are recorded for specific U.S. cities, providing geographical comparisons.

We focus our attention on comparison of *prices* from one year to the next; such comparisons are **price indexes.** The most popular of these indexes is the Consumer Price Index (CPI), which combines a large number (thousands) of prices for consumer goods (such as food and housing) and family services (such as health care and recreation) into a single index. It is often called the cost-of-living index.

A price index that includes more than one item is an **aggregate price index.** We examine two methods of calculating an aggregate price index.

Say we wish to measure the change in the prices of several items from 1990 to 2000, using a single price index. Table 16.16 shows four items; 1990 is the base year. Let P_0 denote the price for a particular item in the base year (1990) and P_1 represent this price during the reference year (2000). So

$$\Sigma P_0 = \text{sum of sampled prices for 1990}$$
$$= .75 + .95 + .89 + 31 = \$33.59$$

and

$$\Sigma P_1 = \text{sum of sampled prices for 2000}$$
$$= 1.35 + 1.79 + 1.85 + 55 = \$59.99$$

The ratio of these sums represents the **simple aggregate price index** for this application.

$$\text{simple aggregate price index} = \left(\frac{\sum P_1}{\sum P_0}\right) \cdot 100$$

16.8

For our example,

$$\text{index} = \left(\frac{59.99}{33.59}\right) \cdot 100 = 178.6$$

It might be tempting to conclude that, based on the prices of these four items, all prices increased by 78.6% between 1990 and 2000. Two problems arise here. The first is whether these sampled items are *representative* of the population of all price changes over this eight-year period. This is not a new problem—the same concern arose when we first introduced statistical sampling.

The second problem is that this index does not take into account the amounts of these items that are typically purchased by consumers. A significant change in the price for any single item will have a dramatic effect on the simple aggregate index, regardless of the demand for this product. The increase of $24 in the price of an automobile battery dominated the computed value of the aggregate price index; however, a typical consumer will spend much more annually on chicken than on car batteries. *The simple aggregate price index assumes that equal amounts of each item are purchased.*

For this reason, the next step is to include a measure of the quantity (Q) of each item in the price index. (We discuss methods of selecting the item quantities later.) The resulting index is known as a **weighted aggregate price index.**

$$\text{weighted aggregate price index} = \left(\frac{\sum P_1 Q}{\sum P_0 Q}\right) \cdot 100$$

16.9

EXAMPLE 16.11

Assume that a representative family each year purchases 1 automobile battery and each month consumes 6 dozen eggs, 15 pounds of chicken, and 8 pounds of cheese. Using 1990 as the base year and equation 16.9, determine the weighted aggregate price index for 2000. Use the data in Table 16.16.

Solution

The choice of time units on the quantities, Q, is arbitrary, but it is essential that we be consistent across all items. Converting the family purchases to annual units, we have $6 \cdot 12 = 72$ dozen eggs, $15 \cdot 12 = 180$ pounds of chicken, $8 \cdot 12 = 96$ pounds of cheese, and 1 car battery (Table 16.17).

The weighted aggregate price index for 2000 (using 1990 as the base year) is

$$\text{index} = \left(\frac{\sum P_1 Q}{\sum P_0 Q}\right) \cdot 100 = \left(\frac{652}{341.44}\right) \cdot 100 = 191.0$$

In this index, the increase of 91% between 1990 and 2000 is not as severely affected by the price change for the car battery as was the simple aggregate price index, which ignored annual demand for each item. All widely used business price indexes are based on some variation of the weighted aggregate price index in equation 16.9.

TABLE

16.17

Calculated aggregate price index.

Item	1990			2000		
	P_0	Q	P_0Q	P_1	Q	P_1Q
Eggs	.75	72	$ 54.00	1.35	72	$ 97.20
Chicken	.95	180	171.00	1.79	180	322.20
Cheese	.89	96	85.44	1.85	96	177.60
Auto battery	31.00	1	31.00	55.00	1	55.00
			$\sum P_0Q = 341.44$			$\sum P_1Q = 652.00$

Selection of the Quantity, Q. Because the weights in a weighted aggregate price index usually reflect the quantities consumed, a problem arises when these quantities cannot be assumed to remain constant over the time span of the index. In Example 16.11, the same quantities, Q, were applied to both time periods, so we are assuming an equal demand for the two years.

We have two options here: (1) Use the quantities for the base year (1990, here) and (2) use the quantities for the reference year (2000, here). The first method is the **Laspeyres index;** the second is the **Paasche index.**

$$\text{Laspeyres index} = \left(\frac{\sum P_1Q_0}{\sum P_0Q_0} \right) \cdot 100$$

16.10

where Q_0 represents a base-year quantity.

$$\text{Paasche index} = \left(\frac{\sum P_1Q_1}{\sum P_0Q_1} \right) \cdot 100$$

16.11

where Q_1 represents a reference-year quantity.

Each of these indexes has strengths and weaknesses. The main advantage of the Laspeyres index is that the same base-year quantities apply to all future reference years. This greatly simplifies updating of this index, particularly given that most aggregate business indexes contain a large number of items. Its main disadvantage is that it tends to give more weight to those items that show a dramatic price increase. When a particular commodity's price increases sharply, it is typically accompanied by a decrease in the demand (measured by Q) for this item, or perhaps another item may be substituted by the consumer. The Laspeyres index fails to adjust for this situation. The advantages of this index outweigh its disadvantages, however, and it is more popular than the Paasche index.

The complexity of updating the reference-year quantities for the Paasche index make it difficult (and often impossible) to apply. Furthermore, because it reflects *both* price and quantity changes, we cannot use it to reflect price changes between two time periods. Its obvious advantage is that it uses current-year quantities, which provide a more realistic and up-to-date estimate of total expense.

We have seen that there is no completely reliable and accurate method of describing aggregate price changes. All such indexes include inaccuracies introduced by using a sample of items in the index as well as by the quantities to be used for weighting. Nevertheless, we treat such an index like any other sample estimate: We use the index as an estimate of relative price changes and realize that it is subject to a certain amount of error.

Comments

1. The most widely used Laspeyres index is the Consumer Price Index (CPI), which is based on thousands of items, ranging from the price of housing to medical expenditures. The CPI is used as a measure of inflation and the cost of living in the United States. It is published monthly and is utilized by the federal government (and some private companies), which bases payment (or salary) adjustments on increases or decreases in the CPI. For example, Social Security payments and retirement benefits for federal civil service employees are tied to this index.

2. The CPI can be used to *deflate* a time series, providing a better comparison of dollar amounts across time. A value is deflated by *dividing* the actual dollar amount for this time period by the corresponding value of the CPI and then multiplying by 100. For example, if your current hourly wage is $18 and the CPI for this year is 150, then the deflated amount is $(18/150)(100) = \$12$. Consequently, the $12 amount can be compared to the hourly wage for the base year (or any other deflated wage value) to determine if there has been a change in "real" wages. This technique can also be applied to the Gross National Product (GNP) to detect real changes in the total value of goods and services.

☒ Exercises 16.53–16.62

Understanding the Mechanics

16.53 The following data are the selling prices of a particular chemical.

Year	1992	1994	1996	1998	2001
Price	24	28	34	44	50

a. Construct an index time series for the years 1990, 1992, 1996, 1998, and 2001 using 1992 as the base year.
b. Repeat part a using 1994 as the base year.

16.54 Consider the following prices and quantities of four items.

	1996		2000	
	P_0	Q_0	P_1	Q_1
Item 1	1.50	60	3.00	50
Item 2	2.00	100	2.25	90
Item 3	1.70	80	2.00	100
Item 4	4.00	20	3.50	50

a. Construct the Laspeyres index.
b. Construct the Paasche index.

Applying the New Concepts

16.55 A typical family in Jackson, Mississippi, had the following weekly buying patterns in 1996 and 2001 (prices are in dollars). Use 1996 as the base year.

Item	1996 Unit Price	1996 Quantity	2001 Unit Price	2001 Quantity
Meat	1.03	2	1.25	2
Milk	.97	3	1.19	2
Fish	.98	2	1.05	3
Oranges	.65	3	.75	4
Bread	.40	1	.62	2

a. Find the simple aggregate price index.
b. Construct the Laspeyres index.
c. Construct the Paasche index.

16.56 Explain the meaning, including the advantages and disadvantages, of the Paasche and Laspeyres weighted indexes. Comment on whether the indexes can be used as a representation of buying pattern.

16.57 The following table reflects the typical family's buying habits per 6 months on repairs for the family car. Use 1995 as the base year.

Item	1995 Price	1995 Quantity	2001 Price	2001 Quantity
Lube job	3.50	2	5.00	1
Oil change	9.50	3	13.00	2
Tune-up	29.95	1	39.95	1
New tires	35.95	2	49.00	2

a. Find the simple aggregate price index.
b. Construct the Laspeyres index.
c. Construct the Paasche index.

16.58 A conglomerate is considering buying one or more of three companies. The closing prices of the stocks of these three companies for the years 1993 to 2001 are:

Year	Better Foods	Friendly Insurance	Chock Full of Computer Chips
1993	13.500	20.125	39.25
1994	13.750	20.250	35.50
1995	14.250	20.500	31.75
1996	15.125	21.750	34.25
1997	15.500	21.500	37.75
1998	16.000	21.750	39.75
1999	16.125	22.500	40.00
2000	16.250	23.750	39.50
2001	16.750	23.500	42.25

Find an appropriate index to measure the change in the price of these three stocks for the years 1996, 1997, 1999, and 2001 using 1993 as the base year.

16.59 Suppose that, for a certain basket of goods, the Paasche index for 2001 is 115 and the Laspeyres index is

97. Assuming that the base year is 1995, interpret the meaning of the value of the two indexes.

16.60 The number of housing starts for four counties for the years 1999, 2000, and 2001 is:

County	1999	2000	2001
Brooks	1304	1505	1580
Litton	1264	1759	1987
Riverbed	1135	1443	1565
Tannon	1401	1605	1615

a. Compare the housing starts for Litton county for the years 2000 and 2001 using 1999 as the base year.

b. Compare the aggregate of housing starts for the years 2000 and 2001 for the four counties using 1999 as the base year.

16.61 Resource-based industries are an important component of the Canadian economy. The following table illustrates the quantity (consumption in thousands of kilograms) and selling price (in Canadian dollars) of three minerals commonly mined in Canada.

	Quantity		Price	
Mineral	1995	1999	1995	1999
Zinc	131	143	1.65	1.92
Copper	190	265	3.16	3.20
Nickel	21	22	14.04	10.29

a. Calculate the Laspeyres index for 1999 using 1995 as the base year.

b. Calculate the Paasche index for 1999 using 1995 as the base year.

c. Compare the two indexes.

16.62 Indexes are often confusing to investors. For example, the Dow Jones Industrial Average (DJIA) is a price-weighted index incorporating a multiplier that changes over time. In Dec. 1997, the multiplier could be interpreted to mean that a gain in the DJIA of 3.93 would result from a gain of one dollar in any one of the 30 companies that make up the DJIA. But the price-weighted DJIA also means that higher-priced stocks have a bigger impact than lower-priced stocks. Say that hypothetically an investor had bought equal dollar amounts of each Dow stock at the close of the market one day. The next day, if the Dow's 15 highest-priced stocks had each declined 5% and the 15 lowest-priced stocks each gained 5%, the DJIA would have declined 197 points or 1.5% for the day. How would the investor have fared? Does this explain how the DJIA can be confusing for investors who may not understand how a price-weighted index works?

(Source: "The Numbers Game," *Stages: The Fidelity Investments Magazine of Personal Finance,* Winter 1998, p. 21.)

 # Summary

A variable recorded over time is a **time series.** You obtain a sample of values for this variable by recording its past observations. The process of using the patterns of past data to predict future values is called **forecasting.** Because a sample of past observations is not a random one, it is extremely difficult (if not impossible) to obtain any tests of hypothesis or confidence intervals. Consequently, we resort to describing the past observations by deriving the components of the time series. This process is called **time series decomposition.** The components of a time series are (1) **trend** (a long-term growth or decline in the observations—either **linear, quadratic,** or **decaying,** (2) **seasonality** (within-year recurrent fluctuations), (3) **cyclical activity** (upward and downward movements of various lengths about the trend), and (4) **irregular activity** (what remains after the other three components have been removed).

We described methods of estimating these components for a time series. We first specify how we believe the components interact with one another, thus describing the time series variable, y_t. The **additive structure** assumes that each observation is the *sum* of its components. In particular, this structure implies that seasonal fluctuations during a particular year are not affected by the base volume for that year. In the **multiplicative structure,** each value of y_t is the *product* of the four components. In this framework, the seasonal fluctuation for a specific month (or quarter) is more apt to be a constant *percentage* of the base volume for that year; for example, sales in December might be 35% higher than the average (base) sales for that particular year. The multiplicative structure was assumed for practically all of the illustrations in this chapter and is used more commonly in practice. The Bureau of the Census uses a variation of this procedure for their time series decomposition analyses.

There are two types of seasonal variation: **additive seasonal variation,** in which the amount of variation due to seasonality does not depend on the level y_t, and **multiplicative seasonal variation,** in which the variation is proportional to the trend level for each observation.

Seasonality can be isolated from an original time series using **centered moving averages.** We described a four-step procedure for deriving time series components for a particular time series, based on the multiplicative structure: (1) determine a **seasonal index** for each month or quarter (monthly or quarterly data); (2) **deseasonalize** the data by dividing each observation by its corresponding seasonal index; (3) determine the **trend components** by deriving a least squares line or quadratic curve through the deseasonalized values; and (4) determine the **cyclical components** by, for each time period, dividing each deseasonalized value by its estimate using the trend equation and smoothing these values by computing three-period moving averages.

An **index time series,** often used by business analysts, is a time-related sequence of **index numbers** in which each value is a measure of the change in a particular item (or group of items) from one year to the next. **Price indexes** are used to compare prices over time.

An **aggregate price index** is used to compare the relative price of a set of items for any year to the price during the base year. The index for the base year always is 100. The prices for the items can be averaged **(simple aggregate price index)** or weighted by the corresponding quantity of each item **(weighted aggregate price index).** Methods of selecting these quantities include using base-year quantities (the **Laspeyres index**) or using the reference-year quantities (the **Paasche index**). The most popular Laspeyres index in practice is the Consumer Price Index (CPI).

Further Reading

Bowerman, B. L., and R. T. O'Connell, *Forecasting and Time Series: An Applied Approach,* 3rd ed., Pacific Grove, Calif.: Brooks/Cole, 2000

Brockwell, P. J., and R. A. Davis, *Introduction to Time Series and Forecasting,* New York: Springer-Verlag, 1996

Makridakis, S., S. C. Wheelwright, and R. J. Hyndman, *Forecasting: Methods and Applications,* 3rd ed., New York: Wiley, 1997

Yaffee, R. A., and M. McGee, *An Introduction to Time Series Analysis and Forecasting: With Applications of SAS and SPSS,* Burlington, Mass.: Academic Press, 2000

 # Summary of Formulas

Linear Trend Line

$$\hat{y}_t = b_0 + b_1 t$$

where

$$t = 1, 2, \ldots, T$$

$$b_1 = \frac{\sum t y_t - (\sum t)(\sum y_t)/T}{\sum t^2 - (\sum t)^2/T}$$

$$b_0 = \bar{y}_t - b_1 \bar{t}$$

Shortcut:

$$\sum t = 1 + 2 + \cdots + T$$

$$= \frac{T(T+1)}{2}$$

$$\sum t^2 = 1 + 4 + \cdots + T^2$$

$$= \frac{T(T+1)(2T+1)}{6}$$

$$\bar{t} = \frac{\sum t}{T} = \frac{T+1}{2}$$

Deseasonalized Value of y_t

$$d_t = \frac{y_t}{\text{corresponding seasonal index}}$$

Simple Aggregate Price Index

$$\left(\frac{\sum P_1}{\sum P_0}\right) \cdot 100$$

Weighted Aggregate Price Index

$$\left(\frac{\sum P_1 Q}{\sum P_0 Q}\right) \cdot 100$$

Laspeyres Index

$$\left(\frac{\sum P_1 Q_0}{\sum P_0 Q_0}\right) \cdot 100$$

where Q_0 represents a base-year quantity.

Paasche Index

$$\left(\frac{\sum P_1 Q_1}{\sum P_0 Q_1}\right) \cdot 100$$

where Q_1 represents a reference-year quantity.

16.63 Each of the following influences on the variation in profits of a national chain of department stores would contribute to which of the four components of a time series?

a. The long-term growth of the economy
b. The resignation of top managers in the company
c. Annual demand in spring and summer for garden equipment
d. The closing of several other department stores

16.64 A manufacturer of tractors has built a record number of tractors for every year for the past seven years. Given in thousands, the figures show the number of tractors built from 1995 to 2001.

Year	Tractors Built
1995	10.75
1996	11.78
1997	12.59
1998	13.4
1999	14.3
2000	15.7
2001	16.8

Find the least squares prediction equation that you would use to forecast the trend. What would you estimate the number of tractors built in 2001 to be?

16.65 Luz Chemicals, which manufactures a special-purpose baking soda, is interested in estimating the equation of the trend line for their monthly sales data (in tons) for the year 2001.

Month	Baking Soda Sales	Month	Baking Soda Sales
Jan.	28	July	34
Feb.	33	Aug.	34
Mar.	39	Sept.	35
Apr.	33	Oct.	36
May	38	Nov.	31
June	31	Dec.	37

a. Without considering the seasonality present in the monthly sales, estimate the trend line equation.
b. Using the equation obtained in part a, estimate the sales (in tons) for the month of February 2002.

16.66 Telemex, a supplier of telephone systems, has experienced moderate to rapid growth over a 12-year period. The data show the annual sales figures (in tens of thousands of dollars).

Year	Sales	Year	Sales
1990	3.1	1996	18.8
1991	6.3	1997	18.4
1992	10.5	1998	20.0
1993	10.2	1999	21.3
1994	11.5	2000	29.0
1995	14.7	2001	28.3

a. Find the trend line.
b. Find the cyclical components.
c. Graph the data and estimate the period of the cycle.

16.67 U.S. households have adopted the Internet at a slightly slower pace than what was observed for television. Perhaps this is partly due to the Internet being an active pursuit and television watching being a passive pursuit. The following data display the percent of households that have adopted the Internet from 1992 to 2001. Find the least squares trend line and compute the cyclical components of the percent of households that have adopted the Internet.

Year	Households with Internet	Year	Households with Internet
1992	1	1997	25
1993	5	1998	35
1994	8	1999	46
1995	13	2000	54
1996	24	2001	59

(Source: "Adoption Rate of Internet by Consumers Is Slowing," *The Wall Street Journal*, July 16, 2001, p. B8.)

16.68 Suppose that for the month of January 2001, the marketing department of a firm finds that the seasonal index is 1.20, the trend line value is $17,000 in sales, and the cyclical component is .79. What is the irregular component if the actual sales figure for January 2001 is $16,500?

16.69 In Chinese cities, a small but growing middle class of first-time home and car buyers is powering the country's growth. China experienced rapid growth during the early 1990s and now is seeing more moderate growth in its economy. The following data illustrate the year-to-year percentage change in its gross domestic product (GDP) from 1990 to 2001.

a. Plot these data. Would you suggest using a linear or quadratic trend line to fit the data?

b. Determine the cyclical components.

Year	China's GDP Change	Year	China's GDP Change
1990	4.0	1996	9.7
1991	9.0	1997	9.0
1992	14.0	1998	8.0
1993	13.5	1999	7.0
1994	12.5	2000	8.0
1995	10.5	2001	7.9

(Source: "China Says GDP Growth Slowed," *The Wall Street Journal*, July 18, 2001, p. 14A.)

16.70 The following table lists the number of building permits per month for nonresidential construction during the four-year period 1998 through 2001 in Parkins, Nebraska.

Year	Jan	Feb	Mar	Apr	May	June	July	Aug	Sept	Oct	Nov	Dec
1998	21	22	23	24	25	28	29	30	27	26	20	20
1999	21	24	23	25	26	25	29	32	32	27	20	18
2000	17	18	21	24	22	28	29	30	27	26	22	20
2001	17	21	23	23	24	29	31	22	28	22	21	29

a. Determine the seasonal indexes.
b. Determine the cyclical components for 1998 using a three-month moving average.
c. Determine the irregular component for July of 1998.

16.71 The average monthly utility bill for residents of the small community of Ridgecrest for the years 1998 through 2001 is:

Year	Jan	Feb	Mar	Apr	May	June	July	Aug	Sept	Oct	Nov	Dec
1998	190	180	179	130	135	145	148	153	145	153	170	185
1999	197	193	185	150	151	159	163	165	160	159	180	185
2000	215	205	193	175	171	179	185	184	180	180	173	190
2001	235	225	205	180	182	190	195	198	188	185	195	201

a. Determine the seasonal indexes.
b. Determine the trend.
c. Determine the cyclical components for 1999 using a three-period moving average.
d. Determine the irregular components for June and July 1999.

16.72 The weekly buying pattern of a typical family in a suburb of Atlanta, Georgia, for 1995 and 2001 follows.

Item	1995 Unit Price	1995 Quantity	2001 Unit Price	2001 Quantity
Chicken	2.40	1	2.75	2
Milk	1.02	3	1.19	2
Bread	.39	2	.45	2
Ground beef	1.59	3	1.89	2
Tomatoes	.39	2	.78	2

Using 1995 as the base year,
   a. Find the simple aggregate price index.
   b. Calculate the Laspeyres index.
   c. Calculate the Paasche index.
   d. Compare the indexes in parts b and c.

16.73 An operations manager has ordered four types of chemicals over the past five years. The price and quantity purchased by the manager in 1998 and 2002 are as follows.

Chemical	1998 Unit Price	1998 Quantity	2002 Unit Price	2002 Quantity
Citric Acid	10.70	50	11.80	52
Manganese Sulphate	25.75	25	29.6	23
Sodium Bichromate	4.25	110	4.30	150
Sodium Chlorite	7.50	75	8.10	100

   a. Using 1998 as the base year, find the Laspeyres index.
   b. Using 1998 as the base year, find the Paasche index.

16.74 **[DATA SET EX16-74]** *Variable description:*

Year_Quarter: Year and quarter from the first quarter of 1990 to the fourth quarter of 2000

Productivity: Percentage growth rate in productivity

High-growth periods are usually associated with a wave of innovations such as electricity or the motor vehicle. The advances in the Internet have increased the productivity of the U.S. economy in recent years. The growth rate in productivity has ranged from slightly less than 1% to slightly more than 3% during the past decade.
   a. Use the trend line and the seasonal components to forecast productivity for the four quarters of 2001.
   b. During what time period does the noise component show high variability?

(Source: "Fed's Meyer Warns of Inflation, Joblessness," *The Wall Street Journal*, June 7, 2001, p. A2.)

16.75 **[DATA SET EX16-75]** *Variable description:*

Year_Month: Year and month from April 1998 to March 2001

ElecConsump: California's monthly electricity consumption (in millions of MWh)

Rolling blackouts became common throughout parts of California during the years 2000 and 2001. Wholesale electricity prices have risen dramatically over the past couple of years. Energy experts would like to better predict surges in electricity consumption to better meet the needs of consumers. Find and interpret the seasonal indices.

(Source: "Price Shock," *The Wall Street Journal*, June 14, 2001, p. A22.)

16.76 **[DATA SET EX16-76]** *Variable description:*

Year_Quarter: Year and quarter from 1996 to 2000

Patients: Number of people undergoing laser eye surgery

The number of people who have had laser eye surgery has grown from approximately 60,000 per quarter in 1996 to approximately one million per quarter in 2000. The Food and Drug Administration (FDA) is closely monitoring complaints as more people rush to have this surgery. The FDA claims that approximately 5% of the patients experience complications, some of which cannot be corrected. The FDA is monitoring the growth in this business and is concerned that too many people are not fully aware of the risks.
   a. What are the four components of this time series for the first quarter of the year 2000?
   b. Estimate the number of patients for the first quarter of 2001 using the trend and seasonal components.

(Source: "Promise of Clear Vision Brings Misery to Some," *USA Today*, June 28, p. 1A.)

16.77 **[DATA SET EX16-77]** *Variable description:*

Year_Month: Year and month from January 1999 to December 2001

GasPrice: Average U.S. gas price

Americans use more than 115 billion gallons of gasoline and diesel fuel each year. The price of gasoline is one of the more volatile components of the economy, with seemingly no rhyme or reason as to why changes occur so dramatically. Within a couple of months, the price of gas can change by 30 cents.

    a. Plot the average U.S. gas price from January 1999 to December 2001 and describe the plot.

    b. Compute the seasonal components and interpret them.

    c. What are the cyclical and irregular components for the year 2000?

(Source: "Average U.S. Gasoline Price," *USA Today,* July 27, 2001, p. 2B.)

16.78 **[DATA SET EX16-78]** *Variable description:*

Time: Monthly data over 25 months, numbered 1 through 25

Y1: Data collected from sales of Business A

Y2: Data collected from sales of Business B

The data on sales from Business A and Business B were collected to determine if sales exhibited additive variation or multiplicative variation. Plots of these data are presented below. What type of variation do these plots exhibit? Draw a trend line for each time series. Estimate the length of the cycle.

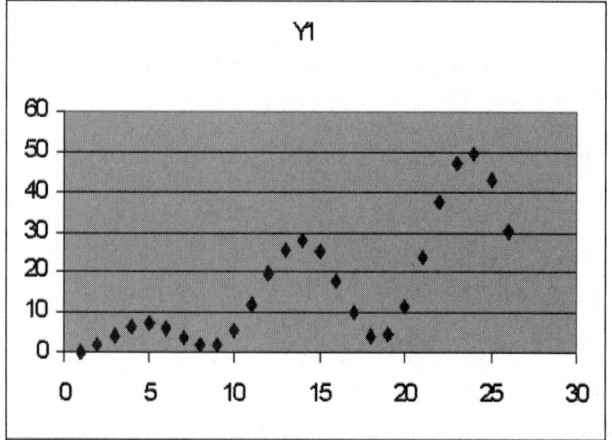

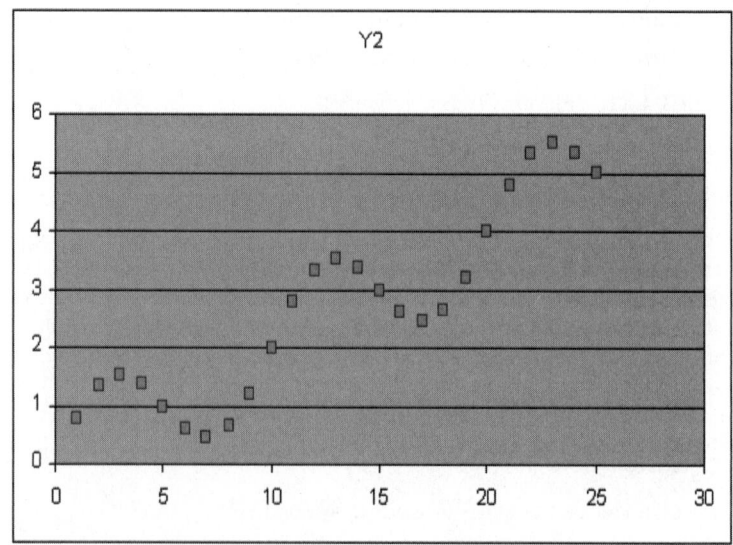

16.79 **[DATA SET EX16-79]** *Variable description:*

Time: Time periods numbered 1 through 20

Observ: Observation at specified time period

Examining a plot of the residuals versus the time variable may be helpful in developing an improved model to predict the observed values. If the least squares model of Observ regressed on Time is the appropriate model, the following plot of the residuals versus Time ideally should exhibit no pattern.

a. An estimate of eight periods was obtained for the length of the cycle that appears in the plot. Does this estimate appear reasonable to you? Would you say that the pattern approximately resembles the graph made by a sine function?

b. Examine the ANOVA table presented for the model with Observ regressed on Time. What conclusion can you draw from this ANOVA table?

c. To obtain an improved model for predicting Observ, the variable Time is replaced by the variable $\sin((2*3.14/8)*\text{Time})$, where the 8 represents the cycle length. This new variable is labeled TimeTransformed. Examine the ANOVA table presented for the model with Observ regressed on the transformed values of Time. What conclusion can you draw?

d. If you think that a different cycle length should be used, rerun the analysis using the transformed time variable with your proposed cycle length.

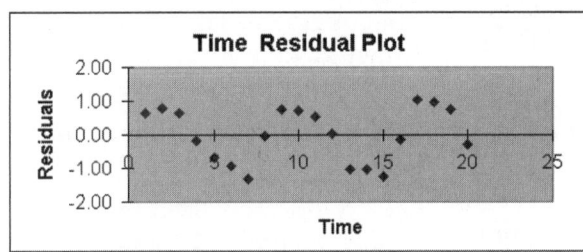

Summary Output

Regression Statistics

Multiple R	0.028134805
R Square	0.000791567
Adjusted R Square	−0.05472001
Standard Error	0.823218329
Observations	20

ANOVA

	df	SS	MS	F	Significance F
Regression	1	0.0096635	0.009663496	0.014259	0.9062707
Residual	18	12.1983915	0.677688417		
Total	19	12.208055			

	Coefficients	Standard Error	t Stat	P-value	Lower 95%	Upper 95%
Intercept	10.11152632	0.38241081	26.44152853	7.42E-16	9.3081104	10.91494
Time	−0.00381203	0.03192304	−0.11941314	0.906271	−0.0708799	0.063256

Summary Output Using Transformed Time Variable

Regression Statistics

Multiple R	0.965682296
R Square	0.932542296
Adjusted R Square	0.928794646
Standard Error	0.213896049
Observations	20

ANOVA

	df	SS	MS	F	Significance F
Regression	1	11.38452765	11.38452765	248.833869	5.5356E-12
Residual	18	0.823527355	0.04575152		
Total	19	12.208055			

	Coefficients	Standard Error	t Stat	P-value	Lower 95%	Upper 95%
Intercept	9.940516317	0.048544047	204.7731274	9.1458E-32	9.83852898	10.042504
TimeTransformed	1.082725903	0.068637867	15.77446888	5.5356E-12	0.93852298	1.2269288

Insights from Statistics in Action

Forecasting Underlying Economic Trends: Oh CPI, Why Did You Lie?

The Statistics in Action introductory case study mentioned that companies use the CPI and other economic indicators to forecast their earnings and make business decisions with regard to the future direction of the company. There are several economic indexes, such as the Producer Price Index (PPI) for measuring inflation during the production process and the Employment Cost Index (ECI) for measuring inflation in the labor market. However, the CPI is the index that gets most of the attention when determining inflation experienced by consumers in their day-to-day living expenses. Future values for economic indexes are important in negotiating government budgets, setting wage guidelines, and determining benefits.

To interpret fluctuations in the economic indexes such as the CPI, the trend, seasonal, and cyclical components of these indexes are analyzed. Economists often rely on the trend component to gain insight into the direction that inflation is headed. Eleven years of monthly data on the CPI are listed in StatInActChap16.xls. These figures have not been adjusted for seasonality or cyclical activity in the data.

1. Plot the CPI index from 1991 to 2001 in a time series graph. Relying on your own judgment and not a statistical procedure, comment on the trend of the index and the existence of seasonality.

2. Assuming that the seasonality is multiplicative in nature, determine the seasonal indexes, deseasonalize the data, determine the trend components, determine the cyclical activity, and compute the noise (irregular) components.

3. For what years is there more variability in the noise components of the CPI?

4. Find deseasonalized forecasts of the CPI for the four months of 2002 using only the trend equation. Use the seasonal indexes to adjust the deseasonalized forecasts.

5. How far into the future do you think that a researcher could predict with this model and still obtain accurate forecasts? What type of economic events do you think could make the forecasts invalid for predicting the CPI?

Sources: "Measuring Core Inflation," *Monthly Labor Review,* 124, issue 7, July 2001, p. 58; "Inflation and Prices," *Economic Trends,* March 2001, p. 2.

Appendix SPSS®

Chapter 16 Appendix: Data Analysis with SPSS

Time Series Decomposition*

The time series decomposition procedure used by SPSS will be illustrated using the U.S. monthly retail data discussed in Section 16.6. Enter the data in the first column and name this variable "data." Click on **Data ➤ Define Dates ➤ Years, months.** Enter 1997 in the **Year** box and click on **OK.** This will create three additional columns, as shown below.

---

*This procedure is not available on the SPSS student version; it is only available on the full SPSS package.

	data	year_	month_	date_
1	134.738	1997	1	JAN 1997
2	130.255	1997	2	FEB 1997
3	148.497	1997	3	MAR 1997
4	145.703	1997	4	APR 1997
5	156.603	1997	5	MAY 1997
6	150.915	1997	6	JUN 1997
7	153.200	1997	7	JUL 1997
8	156.782	1997	8	AUG 1997
9	149.407	1997	9	SEP 1997
10	157.523	1997	10	OCT 1997
11	161.925	1997	11	NOV 1997
12	203.117	1997	12	DEC 1997
13	139.935	1998	1	JAN 1998
14	135.538	1998	2	FEB 1998
15	151.118	1998	3	MAR 1998
16	155.820	1998	4	APR 1998
17	162.797	1998	5	MAY 1998
18	159.701	1998	6	JUN 1998
19	161.541	1998	7	JUL 1998
20	162.369	1998	8	AUG 1998
21	155.747	1998	9	SEP 1998
22	164.528	1998	10	OCT 1998

◄ ► \ **Data View** ∕ Variable View ∕

Click on **Analyze ➤ Time Series ➤ Seasonal Decomposition.** Move the data variable into the **Variable(s)** box and click on **OK.** The following output will appear in the display pane. SPSS calculates the seasonal indexes in a slightly different manner. Consequently, the values differ slightly from those calculated in Example 16.9, although they are quite similar.

Period	Seasonal Index (* 100)
1	87.825
2	86.462
3	98.138
4	97.622
5	101.789
6	99.470
7	99.090
8	100.102
9	96.070
10	100.184
11	103.351
12	129.897

The following new variables are being created:

Name	Label
ERR_1	Error for V1 from SEASON, MOD_1 MUL EQU 12
SAS_1	Seas adj ser for V1 from SEASON, MOD_1 MUL EQU 12
SAF_1	Seas factors for V1 from SEASON, MOD_1 MUL EQU 12
STC_1	Trend-cycle for V1 from SEASON, MOD_1 MUL EQU 12

Four additional columns are created in the data window as a result of this procedure, as shown below. The irregular/noise components (I_t) are contained in the err_1 column. The seasonal components (S_t) are in the saf_1 column. The deseasonalized values (y_t/S_t) are in the sas_1 column. SPSS does not separate out the trend and cyclical components. Rather, column stc_1 contains the $TR_t \times C_t$ components. Consequently, each y_t value is the product of the corresponding values in the stc_1, saf_1, and err_1 columns: for example, the first value (134.738) is equal to (152.3181) (.87825) (1.00722).

	data	year_	month_	date_	err_1	sas_1	saf_1	stc_1
1	134.738	1997	1	JAN 1997	1.00722	153.4172	.87825	152.3181
2	130.255	1997	2	FEB 1997	.99246	150.6492	.86462	151.7936
3	148.497	1997	3	MAR 1997	1.00060	151.3144	.98138	151.2238
4	145.703	1997	4	APR 1997	.98737	149.2527	.97622	151.1617
5	156.603	1997	5	MAY 1997	1.01113	153.8502	1.01789	152.1572
6	150.915	1997	6	JUN 1997	.99094	151.7187	.99470	153.1051
7	153.200	1997	7	JUL 1997	1.00115	154.6075	.99090	154.4303
8	156.782	1997	8	AUG 1997	1.00752	156.6217	1.00102	155.4522
9	149.407	1997	9	SEP 1997	.99582	155.5190	.96070	156.1721
10	157.523	1997	10	OCT 1997	1.00427	157.2330	1.00184	156.5641
11	161.925	1997	11	NOV 1997	.99858	156.6752	1.03351	156.8980
12	203.117	1997	12	DEC 1997	.99449	156.3683	1.29897	157.2352
13	139.935	1998	1	JAN 1998	1.01349	159.3347	.87825	157.2133
14	135.538	1998	2	FEB 1998	.99854	156.7594	.86462	156.9891
15	151.118	1998	3	MAR 1998	.98012	153.9851	.98138	157.1085
16	155.820	1998	4	APR 1998	1.00881	159.6162	.97622	158.2222
17	162.797	1998	5	MAY 1998	1.00158	159.9353	1.01789	159.6835
18	159.701	1998	6	JUN 1998	.99694	160.5515	.99470	161.0438
19	161.541	1998	7	JUL 1998	1.00727	163.0252	.99090	161.8487
20	162.369	1998	8	AUG 1998	.99874	162.2030	1.00102	162.4081
21	155.747	1998	9	SEP 1998	.99483	162.1184	.96070	162.9602
22	164.528	1998	10	OCT 1998	1.00280	164.2251	1.00184	163.7662

◄ ► \ Data View ⟨ Variable View /   ◄

On the CD . . .
Chapter 16 Appendix: Data Analysis with MINITAB

Quantitative Business Forecasting $\boxed{X}$

Statistics in Action
Going Postal with Forecasting Techniques:
Determining Which Methods Receive the Stamp of Approval

The United States Postal Service (USPS) is the most visible and ubiquitous federal institution in America. It receives no taxpayer subsidy. With nearly 900,000 employees and an annual revenue of $66 billion, the USPS employs more people than General Motors and Ford combined, and its total income exceeds that of Microsoft, McDonald's, and Coca-Cola combined. The USPS is a hybrid of a government agency and a regulated business; its most profitable product is first-class mail.

Despite the fact that the USPS has a monopoly on delivering letters to mailboxes, the long-run success of the USPS is related to how well its management is able to forecast future revenue and develop strategies for containing costs. Currently, its management is forecasting slowing growth in its revenue for the next few years. This forecast has motivated the USPS to form a business alliance with FedEx. By buying space on FedEx's airplanes, the Postal Service expects to save about $1 billion in air transportation costs and more than double the market reach of its Express Mail next-day and Priority two-day services.

With more than 650 aircraft, FedEx is one of the largest airlines in the world. The management at FedEx used a forecasting model to project increases in the number of employees needed to support this contract. This model estimated that 500 pilots and 1,000 mechanics and ground-crew members would have to be hired to meet FedEx's obligation to ensure on-time performance. With these additional employees, FedEx is able to pro-

vide about 3.5 million pounds of airlift capacity every day for postal materials—the equivalent of 30 wide-body DC-10 aircraft.

Postmaster General William J. Henderson said, "These agreements will leverage two great networks—the extensive reliability of FedEx planes and the coast-to-coast retail presence of the Postal Service."

Over the life of the agreement, FedEx has the option of placing thousands of drop boxes at post offices nationwide. Depending on the number of boxes eventually installed, FedEx will pay the Postal Service between $126 million and $232 million. FedEx's management will use forecasting models to assess economic and business conditions to make timely decisions in installing these boxes.

Good judgment and intuition may give a manager a rough idea of what will happen in the future. Forecasting models allow managers to use numbers such as projected cost and revenue to make critical decisions, rather than relying on their feelings. Managers have learned that the ability to accurately anticipate customers' needs can have a significant impact on their profits. When you have completed this chapter, you will be able to

- Discuss several forecasting procedures for making predictions of future events, such as the projected next-year revenue for USPS.
- Determine if the error terms of a multiple regression model are not independent when time series data are used.
- Evaluate the performance of several forecasting methods by using measures of forecasting accuracy.

A Look Back/Introduction

We have introduced you to several methods of capturing the behavior of a dependent variable, Y. The first procedure was linear regression, which used a set of predictor (independent) variables to explain the observed values of the dependent variable. In simple linear regression, a single predictor is used. When we had two or more predictor variables, we used a multiple linear regression model to attempt to account for the variation in the observed values of the dependent variable. These calculations were considerably more complex, and a computer solution was used to estimate the linear relationship between the dependent variable (Y) and the predictor variables ($X_1, X_2, \ldots$).

The success or failure of this technique lies in your ability to arrive at a set of predictor variables that can accurately predict past (and future) values of the dependent variable. Suppose your model fails to fit adequately the observed values of Y, with a resulting large sum of squares for error (SSE) and a low value of R^2 (coefficient of determination). Do these results imply that multiple linear regression is not a reliable method of prediction for this situation? This could be the case, but it is just as likely that you omitted one or more key variables that would have significantly improved your prediction accuracy.

The time series decomposition technique, presented in the previous chapter, uses a different approach. This procedure attempts to explain each observed value by means of its various components. These components include trend (long-term growth or decline in the time series), seasonality (predictable variation within each year), and cyclical activity (generally due to unpredictable swings in the national or international economy).

The key distinction between these two procedures is that the time series approach does not search for explanatory (predictor) variables. Rather, it seeks to capture the past behavior of the time series by analyzing its various components. More complex time series techniques (which were not discussed) use past observations to predict the value for the future. You can use a time series approach to forecast future values by "extending" the pattern into the future. For example, if your company sales have been increasing approximately 150,000 units each year over the past six years, a reasonable forecast for next year would be a sales volume of 150,000 more than the present year's value.

Statistical forecasting is, in one sense, an extension of the prediction of a dependent variable. However, we now enter a more uncertain world—that of extrapolation. In previous chapters, we warned you of the dangers of this procedure, because outside the range of your data, the predicted values become less reliable. We can only hope that tomorrow's world will be similar to today's and that patterns observed over the past will continue. This uncertainty makes forecasting fascinating.

We live in an uncertain world, and a reasonably accurate forecast can be extremely valuable for a marketing or production strategy.

This chapter introduces many (certainly not all) methods of using quantitative techniques for predicting future values of the variable of interest. We demonstrate how to forecast future values by using the past observations (the time series approach) as well as by using the multiple linear regression method. By applying the proper forecast method, you often can make the future considerably less uncertain.

METHODS OF FORECASTING

17.1

Forecasting procedures come in a variety of shapes and colors. You can arrive at a sales forecast by simply assembling a panel of experts and arriving at a collective "guess" or by constructing a highly complex statistical model that attempts to predict the future using past data. In the broadest sense, forecasting methods can be classified as **qualitative** (the panel of experts procedure) or **quantitative** (the statistical forecasting procedure). Quantitative forecasting can be carried out using two different approaches, namely, *regression* models (with several predictor variables) or **time series** models, which utilize past observations of the dependent variable to arrive at forecasted values.

Qualitative Forecasting

There are many instances when a qualitative approach to forecasting is appropriate. When no past data are available, it is impossible to construct a quantitative model to predict future values. This situation can occur when you intend to introduce a new product and no past sales data exist. Furthermore, when you introduce this product, it becomes a guessing game as to what the response will be from competitors in the field. Will they respond to your entry into the market? When will they respond? Will they lower their price to increase the demand for their product? Will they attempt to "copy" your product, and how soon can this be accomplished? Such questions do require expert opinion.

One popular method of qualitative forecasting is the **Delphi method.** With this procedure, you assemble individuals from the sales force and the market research staff and ask them to supply their predictions based on their knowledge of the area. This can be accomplished through a questionnaire or any other written set of specific questions. After this step, members of the team are informed as to the responses of the entire group and asked to reevaluate their opinions based on this new information. In this way, members of the team may be able to arrive at a *best-educated* prediction of competitor response to their market entry. Of course, it is also entirely possible that no collective agreement will be reached after several rounds of this process.

We do not pursue qualitative forecasting methods in this chapter. The interested reader is referred to the text by Bowerman and O'Connell (see the Further Reading section at the end of the chapter) for additional qualitative procedures. The remainder of the chapter focuses on the use of quantitative forecasting techniques.

Quantitative Forecasting

With a quantitative forecasting procedure, you predict future behavior of a dependent variable using information from previous time periods. This can be accomplished in one of two ways: using a *regression* model or using a *time series* model.

FIGURE

17.1

Sales for Clayton Corporation.

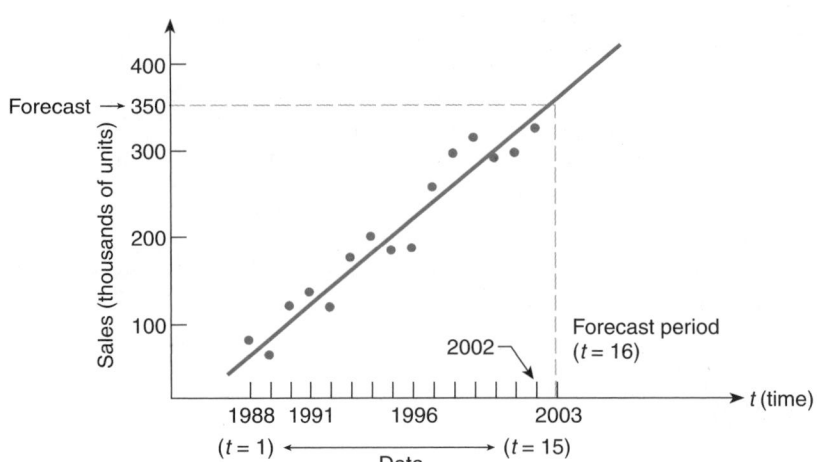

Regression Models. The multiple regression approach consists of using regression models where variation of the dependent variable is explained using several independent (predictor) variables. One main advantage of this approach is that you can measure the effect of changes in one or more of the predictor variables. Furthermore, this type of model is generally easily understood by those individuals responsible for making the final forecast decision, since it is clear which variables are assumed to have an effect on the value of the dependent variable. A drawback of this type of model as a forecasting instrument is that to predict future values of the dependent variable, it is necessary to predict future values of the predictor variables, which, in many instances, may be as uncertain as future values of the dependent variable. This forecasting procedure is discussed in Section 17.9 on the CD that accompanies this textbook.

Time Series Models. A time series forecast is made by capturing the patterns that exist in the past observations and extending them into the future. Consider the annual data reflecting the sales of the Clayton Corporation between 1988 and 2002, shown in Figure 17.1. The data reflect a strong linear trend, as shown by the line passing through the points. To estimate the sales for the year 2003, one simple method would be to extend this line to 2003, as illustrated in Figure 17.1. By graphically extending this line and observing the estimated value, we obtain

$$\hat{y}_{16} = \text{forecast for the year 2003} \cong 350$$

that is, 350,000 units. This procedure, along with methods of dealing with trend and seasonality, is discussed later in the chapter.

At first glance, it might appear that time series forecasting is easier to apply than are multiple regression models. After all, there is no need to search for a reliable set of predictor variables. It is true that time series predictors can be simple and straightforward, as is the so-called naive forecast discussed in the next section. *Frequently, however, extracting the complex and interrelated structure of an observed time series requires sophisticated and complex prediction equations.*

As in Chapter 16, we do not put any statistical bounds (such as a 95% confidence interval) on the predicted values. Rather, we suggest alternative methods of forecasting and demonstrate a way of determining the "best" forecasting procedure for a particular set of data. Of course, all forecasts are subject to error and are based on the assumption that the past historical patterns (such as the straight line in Figure 17.1) continue into the future.

In Sections 17.2 through 17.7, we examine several time series models and methods of evaluating the predictive ability of each procedure when applied to a particular set of time series data.

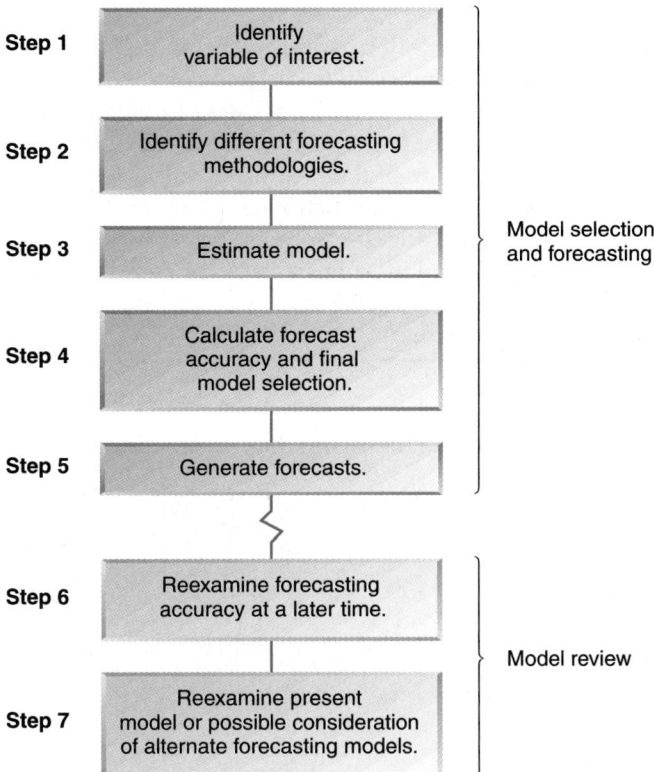

FIGURE
17.2

A step-by-step procedure for forecasting with time series data.

The procedure for selecting a forecasting model is summarized in Figure 17.2. Steps 1 through 5 are the model selection and forecasting stage. Steps 6 and 7 are the model review phase, during which you reevaluate your forecasting procedure. This step allows you to update your model using the latest observations or to consider changing your forecasting model by returning to step 2. Any forecasting technique should be reviewed; you must reexamine the forecast errors (that is, the difference between the forecasted values and the previous observations).

Remember that any quantitative forecasting technique can never replace the forecast of an individual (or team of people) who uses his or her expertise and knowledge of unpredictable future events (such as strikes, wars, or market shifts) to make forecasts. Rather, the quantitative forecast is one tool the forecaster uses. A forecast is an excellent baseline that can be modified by informed judgment.

17.2   THE NAÏVE FORECAST

Simply put, the naïve forecast procedure states that the estimate of Y for tomorrow is the actual value from today. In general,

$$\hat{y}_{t+1} = y_t \qquad t = 1, 2, 3, \ldots \qquad 17.1$$

or any time period, t.

Once again, the "hat" notation is used to denote an estimate. Equation 17.1 reads: "y hat for time period $t + 1$ is y for time t." Here, $\hat{y}_{t+1}$ presents the *forecast* for time period $t + 1$.

This method of forecasting often works well for data that are recorded for smaller time intervals (such as daily or weekly) and contain no apparent upward or downward trend among the observed values. Data of this type are not apt to shift direction suddenly from one day to the next, and the naive forecast can provide a simple, yet fairly reliable, estimate of the next day's value. On more than one occasion, this predictor has outperformed much more complex forecasting equations—particularly when applied to a difficult-to-predict time series, such as an individual stock market price. It provides an inexpensive, easy method of forecasting.

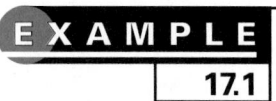

The weekly closing price for a share of Keller Toy Company stock was recorded over a 12-week period. Using the following data, determine a forecast for week 13.

Week	Price	Week	Price	Week	Price
1	60	5	64½	9	63¼
2	62¼	6	62	10	62½
3	61¾	7	63½	11	61
4	63	8	64	12	61½

Solution   The observed value for the last time period is $y_{12} = 61\frac{1}{2}$, so your forecast for the next time period is

$$\hat{y}_{13} = y_{12} = 61\frac{1}{2}$$

Notice that we are careful to distinguish between a *forecast*, such as $\hat{y}_{13}$, and an *observed* value, such as y_{12}.

One method of checking to see whether a particular forecasting technique is appropriate for your time series involves applying this procedure to each period of the observed data. For example, in Example 17.1, what would we have predicted for the fifth week using the naive forecasting equation 17.1? In other words, suppose we are at the end of the fourth week and need a forecast for $t = 5$. Using the naive predictor,

$$\hat{y}_5 = y_4 = 63$$

The actual value turned out to be $y_5 = 64\frac{1}{2}$, providing a *residual* of 1½:

$$\text{residual} = y_5 - \hat{y}_5 = 64\frac{1}{2} - 63 = 1\frac{1}{2}$$

The time series forecasting tools provided in the KPK Data Analysis Excel add-ins will allow you to carry out all of the forecasting procedures discussed in this chapter. By clicking on **KPK Data Analysis ➤ Time Series Analysis ➤ Forecasting,** you will see the screen in Figure 17.3. Using this input form will be illustrated in the following example.

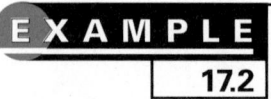

Apply the naive forecasting procedure to the 12 time periods in Example 17.1 and determine the residual for each week.

Solution   The procedure cannot be applied during the first time period ($t = 1$) because $\hat{y}_1 = y_0$ where y_0 is the closing price for the week preceding the observations in the table. If this value is available, then the forecast value for $t = 1$ can be determined; it is equal to this value. Otherwise, the forecast for this time period is left blank.

FIGURE

17.3

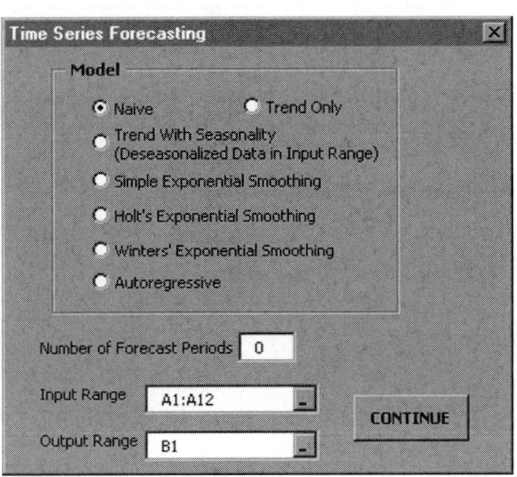

Excel input screen using **KPK Data Analysis ➤ Time Series Analysis ➤ Forecasting** using the naïve forecast procedure (Examples 17.1 and 17.2).

FIGURE

17.4

Residuals for naïve forecasts using Excel.

	A	B	C	D	E	F	G	H	I
1	60	**Naive Model**							
2	62.25	**t**	**Y(t)**	**Yhat**	**Residual**				
3	61.75	1	60.						
4	63	2	62.25	60.00	2.25				
5	64.5	3	61.75	62.25	-0.50				
6	62	4	63.	61.75	1.25				
7	63.5	5	64.5	63.00	1.50				
8	64	6	62.	64.50	-2.50				
9	63.25	7	63.5	62.00	1.50				
10	62.5	8	64.	63.50	0.50				
11	61	9	63.25	64.00	-0.75				
12	61.5	10	62.5	63.25	-0.75				
13		11	61.	62.50	-1.50				
14		12	61.5	61.00	0.50				
15									

To obtain a solution using Excel, begin by entering the 12 stock prices in column A as seen in Figure 17.4. Next, click on **KPK Data Analysis ➤ Time Series Analysis ➤ Forecasting** and enter "A1:A12" as the **Input Range** and "B1" as the **Output Range.** For this example, enter "0" in the **Number of Forecast Periods** box. By clicking on **Continue,** you will obtain the output in Figure 17.4, which contains the 11 values of $\hat{y}_t$ (in the **Yhat** column) and the 11 residuals.

When we first introduced the concept of a residual (or error) in the chapters dealing with linear regression, we stressed that small residuals were desirable. When the residuals were near zero for regression applications, this meant that the model did a good job of *fitting* the sample observations.

The same idea applies to evaluating the effectiveness of a forecasting procedure. Small residuals indicate that this particular forecast technique would have done a good job of predicting the past values of this time series. A method of combining these residuals into a single measure (much like the SSE in linear regression) will be introduced in a later section.

Exercises 17.1–17.5

Applying the New Concepts

17.1 Explain how time series analysis and multiple regression analysis differ. What is a drawback to using multiple regression in forecasting?

17.2 Explain the Delphi method of forecasting. Is this technique considered to be a qualitative or quantitative approach to forecasting?

17.3 The number of securities fraud cases seeking class-action status in the United States is presented below. Use the naïve model to obtain forecasts for the time periods between 1992 and 2000. Which time period would you say the naïve model predicted well?

Year	1991	1992	1993	1994	1995
Fraud Cases	180	201	183	225	191

Year	1996	1997	1998	1999	2000
Fraud Cases	110	185	240	203	204

(Source: "Increased Action," *The Wall Street Journal*, August 29, 2001, p. C1.)

17.4 China experienced strong economic growth during the 1990s. The following data illustrate the year-to-year percentage change in its gross domestic product (GDP) from 1990 to 2001. Use a naïve model to forecast China's GDP change for the years 1991 to 2001. What is the largest residual using the naïve model?

Year	China's GDP Change	Year	China's GDP Change
1990	4.0	1996	9.7
1991	9.0	1997	9.0
1992	14.0	1998	8.0
1993	13.5	1999	7.0
1994	12.5	2000	8.0
1995	10.5	2001	7.9

(Source: "China Says GDP Growth Slowed," *The Wall Street Journal*, July 18, 2001, p. 14A.)

17.5 What are the advantages and disadvantages of using a naïve model for forecasting? For what type of data do you think a naïve model would be fairly reliable for forecasting?

17.3   PROJECTING THE LEAST SQUARES TREND EQUATION

A Time Series Containing Trend

For data containing a strong linear or curvilinear trend, one method of predicting future values of the time series is to extend the trend line (or curve) into the forecast periods. This method was illustrated in Figure 17.1, where the data from 1988 to 2002 demonstrated a very strong linear growth over those 15 years.

Suppose that a simple linear regression analysis is performed on these data, using the 15 sales values as the dependent variable and $t = 1, 2, \ldots, 15$ as the predictor variable (as discussed in Chapter 16). The resulting least squares line, shown in Figure 17.1, turns out to be

$$\hat{y}_t = 32 + 20t$$

The estimated forecast for the year 2003 in the earlier discussion was $\hat{y}_{16} = 350$. This value was determined simply by extending the least squares line into this time period and "eyeballing" the estimate for 2003. The actual forecast is

$$\hat{y}_{16} = 32 + 20(16) = 352$$

So, our estimate of sales for the year 2003 is 352,000 units, based on the linear trend equation.

Referring to Figure 17.3, you could also have obtained this trend equation by clicking on the **Trend Only** button after entering the 15 sales values in column A.

A Time Series Containing Trend and Seasonality

The previous procedure can be adapted to situations in which the time series contains significant trend *and* seasonality. Such a situation can occur when the data are monthly or quarterly, with seasonal fluctuations about a linear or curvilinear trend.

FIGURE

17.5

Quarterly sales at
Video-Comp.

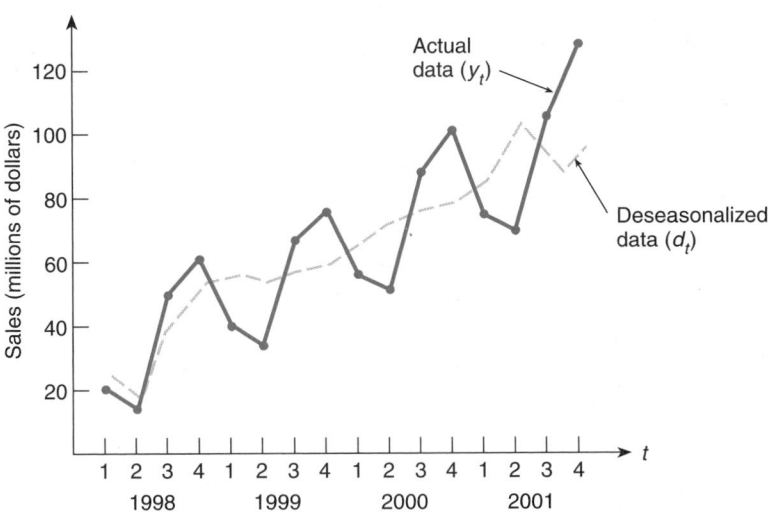

The quarterly sales for Video-Comp over a four-year period (1998–2001) were contained in Table 16.3 on page 788 and illustrated in Figure 17.5. The deseasonalized sales figures (often called *seasonally adjusted* sales) were summarized in Table 16.6 on page 000 and also graphed in Figure 17.5. Notice that the extreme seasonal fluctuations of the original time series were removed when these values were divided by the appropriate seasonal index. The indexes for this application were derived in Example 16.8, and they indicated low sales for the first two quarters, above-average sales for the third quarter, and extremely high sales during the fourth (holiday) quarter. The corresponding indexes were

$$S_1 = .852 \qquad S_3 = 1.166$$
$$S_2 = .692 \qquad S_4 = 1.290$$

To forecast future values when using seasonal data, you once again determine the least squares line (or curve), except that now you use the *deseasonalized data* (say, d_t) as your dependent variable. Once you have calculated the trend forecast, you obtain your final forecast by multiplying this deseasonalized estimate by the corresponding seasonal index. So the procedure for extending trend and seasonal components is:

1. Calculate the deseasonalized (seasonally adjusted) data from the original time series $(y_1, y_2, \ldots , y_T)$. Call these values $d_1, d_2, \ldots , d_T$.

2. Construct a least squares line through the deseasonalized data, where $(t = 1, 2, \ldots , T)$.

$$\hat{d}_t = b_0 + b_1 t$$

3. Calculate the forecast for time period $T + 1$ using

$$\hat{y}_{T+1} = (\hat{d}_{T+1}) \cdot (\text{seasonal index for } t = T + 1)$$
$$= [b_0 + b_1(T + 1)] \cdot (\text{seasonal index for } t = T + 1)$$

**EXAMPLE
17.3**

Using the Video-Comp data, what would be your forecast for the first-quarter sales for 2002? second-quarter sales?

Solution

The trend line through the deseasonalized data is contained in Figure 17.7 and illustrated in Figure 17.6. To obtain this solution, enter the 16 deseasonalized values in column A and click on **KPK Data Analysis ➤ Time Series Analysis ➤**

FIGURE

17.6

Trend line through deseasonalized data (quarterly sales, Video-Comp).

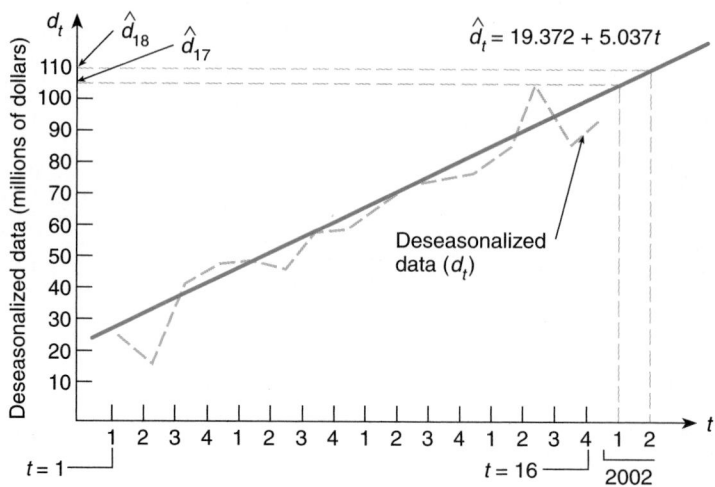

FIGURE

17.7

Excel solution for deseasonalized trend line and forecasting two periods ahead.

	A	B	C	D	E	F	G	H	I
1	23.47	Linear Trend with Seasonality Model is Y(t) = 19.372 + 5.037t							
2	17.34	t	Y(t)	Yhat	Residual		Seasonal Factors		
3	40.31	1	23.47	24.409	-0.939		0.852		
4	46.51	2	17.34	29.446	-12.106		0.692		
5	46.95	3	40.31	34.484	5.826		1.166		
6	46.24	4	46.51	39.521	6.989		1.290		
7	55.75	5	46.95	44.559	2.391				
8	58.91	6	46.24	49.596	-3.356				
9	65.73	7	55.75	54.634	1.116				
10	72.25	8	58.91	59.671	-0.761				
11	72.90	9	65.73	64.709	1.021				
12	77.52	10	72.25	69.746	2.504				
13	88.03	11	72.9	74.784	-1.884				
14	101.16	12	77.52	79.821	-2.301				
15	86.62	13	88.03	84.859	3.171				
16	95.35	14	101.16	89.896	11.264				
17		15	86.62	94.934	-8.314				
18		16	95.35	99.971	-4.621				
19									
20		Forecasts							
21		17	89.467						
22		18	76.152						

Forecasting. Select the **Trend with Seasonality** option and enter "2" as the **Number of Forecast Periods**, select "4" as the **Number of Periods per Year**, enter "A1:A16" as the **Input Range**, and "B1" as the **Output Range**. After clicking on **Continue**, select **Linear** in the **Trend** frame and enter the four seasonal indexes (.852, .692, 1.166, 1.290) by repeatedly entering a value and then clicking on the **Next Period** button. The resulting output is shown in Figure 17.7. The least squares trend line is

$$\hat{d}_t = 19.372 + 5.037t$$

This equation tells us that, apart from seasonal variation, the sales at Video-Comp are increasing by approximately $5 million each quarter. Using this equation and Figure 17.6, your deseasonalized forecast for the first quarter of 2002 (time period 17) is

$$\hat{d}_{17} = 19.372 + 5.037(17)$$

$$= 105.00$$

Now, the sales for the first quarter of each year are lower than the yearly average, as reflected in the seasonal index of $S_1 = .852$ (from Example 16.8). Consequently, your actual forecast for this time period is contained in cell C21 (Figure 17.7) and is equal to

$$\hat{y}_{17} = \hat{d}_{17} \cdot (\text{seasonal index for quarter 1})$$

$$= 105.00 \cdot .852$$

$$= 89.5 \ (\text{million dollars})$$

This procedure can be used to forecast any future time period. For the second quarter of 2002, the estimated sales will be

$$\hat{y}_{18} = \hat{d}_{18} \cdot (\text{seasonal index for quarter 2})$$

$$= [19.372 + 5.037(18)] \cdot .692$$

$$= (110.04)(.692) = 76.2 \ (\text{million dollars})$$

Do these estimates seem reasonable? Look at the observed (1998–2001) and forecast (2002) values for the first and second quarters:

Year	First-Quarter Sales	Second-Quarter Sales
1998	20	12
1999	40	32
2000	56	50
2001	75	70
2002	89.5	76.2

The forecast for the first quarter of 2002 seems to be about what we would expect, based on the past first-quarter sales. The predicted sales value for the second quarter of 2002 seems to be on the low side, with an increase of only 6.2 from the second quarter of 2001. Remember, however, that this forecasting technique contains the effect of *all* the quarters observed over the four years. By examining the past sales during the second quarter only, we are ignoring the remaining quarters, and perhaps an explanation for this seemingly low forecast lies in these values.

It is possible that this forecasting procedure is not a good one for the application in Example 17.3—there may be a better way to obtain a forecast for this situation. We show you several ways to forecast a time series and then determine which of these does the best job for a particular set of observed values. *No one procedure always performs well for all applications.*

X Exercises 17.6–17.10

Understanding the Mechanics

17.6 Several sets of quarterly data have been gathered over a 3-year period from 1999 to 2001. Find the forecasts for the four quarters of 2002 for each of the following models. Assume $t = 1, 2, \ldots$

  a. $\hat{d}_t = 5.2 + .8t$, $S_1 = .81$, $S_2 = .93$, $S_3 = 1.19$, $S_4 = 1.07$
  b. $\hat{d}_t = 10.5 + 5t$, $S_1 = .66$, $S_2 = 1.08$, $S_3 = 1.19$, $S_4 = 1.07$
  c. $\hat{d}_t = 50 - 2t$, $S_1 = 1.10$, $S_2 = 1.16$, $S_3 = .90$, $S_4 = .84$

Applying the New Concepts

17.7 For what type of data do you think the least squares trend line would be more reliable than the naïve forecast procedure? For what type of data do you think that the naïve forecast procedure would be more reliable than the least squares trend line?

17.8 The Learning Company sells educational material to households online. The company usually receives many online requests during the third and fourth quarters, which have seasonal indexes of 1.6 and 1.7, respectively. The quarterly number of online requests (deseasonalized) resulting in sales are presented below. Find the least squares trend line for the deseasonalized data and find the forecast for the number of online requests resulting in sales during the third and fourth quarters of 2002.

Year	Quarter 1	Quarter 2	Quarter 3	Quarter 4
1997	69	56	60	57
1998	68	65	68	71
1999	75	72	69	74
2000	72	79	80	81
2001	78	85	88	90

Using the Computer

17.9 **[DATA SET 17-9]** *Variable description:*

Year: Year starting in 1998 through 2001

Month: Numbered from 1 through 12 for the twelve months of the year

HousePermits: Number of new housing permits issued to build houses (deseasonalized)

A real estate developer is interested in forecasting the number of new housing permits issued for the first three months of 2002. She knows that the seasonal indexes for those three months are .7, .6, and 1.1. Monthly deseasonalized data have been collected from 1998 through 2001. Find the least squares trend line for the deseasonalized data and find the forecasts that the developer needs.

17.10 **[DATA SET 17-10]** *Variable description:*

Year: Year starting in 1996 and ending in 1999

Quarter: Numbered from 1 to 4 for each of the four quarters of the year

PretaxProf: Deseasonalized pretax profit per quarter

The German software company, SAP, benefited from the year-2000 computer problem. In addition, the company is the biggest maker of enterprise-resource-planning software, known as ERP. The company's programs automate manufacturing, human resources, and other nuts-and-bolts functions to give companies insight into the profitability of their internal operations according to "European Software Highflier SAP Comes Back to Earth" (*The Wall Street Journal*, Jan. 6, 1999, p. B8). Like most high-tech companies, the profits depend on cycles in the economy. Assume that deseasonalized pretax profit (converted into U.S. dollars from German marks) is collected from 1996 through 1999. If the quarterly indexes are .7, 1.0, .8, and 1.5, respectively, for quarters 1 through 4, what is the forecast of pretax profit for the four quarters of the year 2000?

17.4

SIMPLE EXPONENTIAL SMOOTHING

In Chapter 16, we introduced the concept of smoothing a time series by computing a set of centered *moving averages*. The moving averages were used to derive the various seasonal indexes, but they also provided a "new" time series with considerably less random variation (irregular activity) and no seasonality. Because the moving average series was much smoother, it provided a clearer picture of any existing trend or cyclical activity.

Another method of smoothing a time series, which also serves as a forecasting procedure, is **exponential smoothing.** Unlike moving averages, this technique uses all the preceding observations to determine a smoothed value for a particular time period. The method described in this section is called **simple** (or single) **exponential smoothing** and works well for a time series containing *no trend* (Figure 17.8). A time series (such as the one in this figure) is said to be **stationary** if the data exhibit no trend and the variance about the mean ($\bar{y}_t$) remains constant over time. *Simple exponential smoothing generally will track the original time series well, provided this series is stationary.* We extend the simple exponential smoothing procedure to a series containing trend and seasonality in later sections.

The simplest way to determine a smoothed value for time period t using exponential smoothing is to find a weighted sum of the actual observation for this time period, y_t, and the previous smoothed value, S_{t-1}.

$$S_t = \text{smoothed value for time period, } t$$
$$= Ay_t + (1 - A)S_{t-1} \qquad t = 2, 3, 4, \ldots \qquad 17.2$$

where A is any number between 0 and 1.

The value of A is the **smoothing constant.** Small values of A produce smoothed values giving less weight to the corresponding observation, y_t. You should use such values (say, $A < .1$) for a volatile time series containing considerable irregular activity (noise). In this way, you give more weight to the previous smoothed value, S_{t-1}, rather than to the original observation, y_t. You can use larger values of A for a more stable time series.

The smoothing procedure used here begins by setting the first smoothed value, S_1, equal to the first observation, y_1. So,

$$S_1 = y_1$$

Then,

$$S_2 = Ay_2 + (1 - A)S_1$$
$$= Ay_2 + (1 - A)y_1$$
$$S_3 = Ay_3 + (1 - A)S_2$$
$$S_4 = Ay_4 + (1 - A)S_3$$

and so on.

The average attendance (y_t, in thousands) for major events held at the Jefferson County Civic Center for the past 13 years is contained in Table 17.1. We determine the exponentially smoothed values using three smoothing constants, $A = .1$, $A = .5$, and $A = .9$.

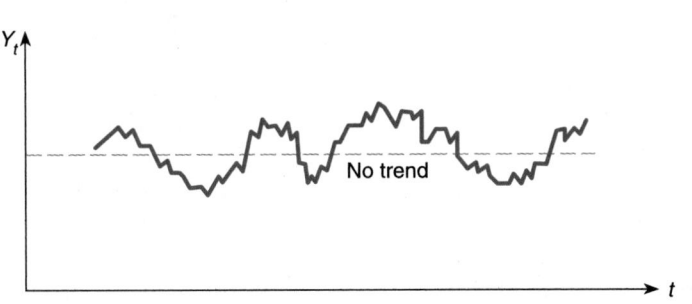

FIGURE 17.8

Illustration of a stationary time series.

TABLE 17.1

Actual and smoothed values for attendance at Jefferson Civic Center.

Year	t	y_t	$S_t (A = .1)$	$S_t (A = .5)$	$S_t (A = .9)$
1989	1	5.0	5.0	5.0	5.0
1990	2	8.0	5.3	6.5	7.7
1991	3	2.1	4.98	4.3	2.66
1992	4	7.1	5.19	5.7	6.66
1993	5	4.8	5.15	5.25	4.99
1994	6	2.0	4.84	3.62	2.30
1995	7	7.8	5.13	5.71	7.25
1996	8	5.0	5.12	5.36	5.23
1997	9	14.1	6.02	9.73	13.21
1998	10	13.0	6.72	11.36	13.02
1999	11	13.5	7.39	12.43	13.45
2000	12	14.2	8.07	13.32	14.12
2001	13	14.0	8.67	13.66	14.01

FIGURE

17.9

Smoothed values for attendance data (Table 17.1).

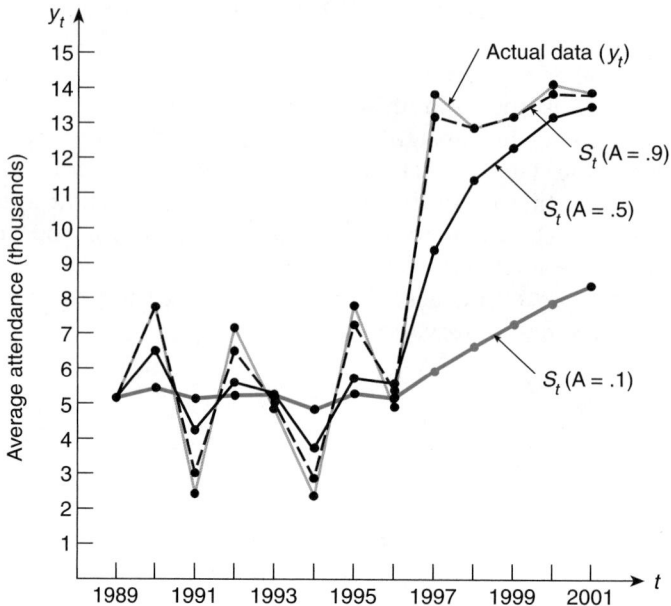

The actual time series and the three smoothed series are shown in Table 17.1 and Figure 17.9. For $A = .1$,

$$S_1 = y_1 = 5.0$$

$$S_2 = (.1)y_2 + (.9)S_1$$

$$= (.1)(8.0) + (.9)(5.0) = 5.3$$

$$S_3 = (.1)y_3 + (.9)S_2$$

$$= (.1)(2.1) + (.9)(5.3) = 4.98$$

and so on.

Notice that the average attendance, y_t, had a significant jump in 1997, when (it turns out) the facility was completely refurnished, providing better seating and more accessible snack booths. With the small value of $A = .1$, the smoothed values did not "track" the original series very well after this point. In general, when you use exponential smoothing with a small smoothing constant, the resulting series will be slow to detect any turning points or shifts in the observed values. However, such values of A provide considerable smoothing, as is evident from the values between the years 1989 and 1996.

The large value of $A = .9$ provides much better tracking (see Figure 17.9) but not much smoothing. Larger smoothing constants are more useful for a time series that does not contain a great deal of random fluctuation. Using $A = .5$ offers a compromise between these two extreme smoothing constants. Later we discuss methods of comparing the tracking ability of different values of A, in an effort to determine the best smoothing constant for a particular series.

To see why this procedure is called *exponential smoothing*, we look at how each smoothed value is obtained. First, $S_1 = y_1$. Then,

$$S_2 = Ay_2 + (1 - A)S_1$$

$$= Ay_2 + (1 - A)y_1$$

$$S_3 = Ay_3 + (1 - A)S_2$$

$$= Ay_3 + (1 - A)[Ay_2 + (1 - A)y_1]$$

$$= Ay_3 + A(1 - A)y_2 + (1 - A)^2 y_1$$

$$S_4 = Ay_4 + (1 - A)S_3$$
$$= Ay_4 + (1 - A)[Ay_3 + A(1 - A)y_2 + (1 - A)^2 y_1]$$
$$= Ay_4 + A(1 - A)y_3 + A(1 - A)^2 y_2 + (1 - A)^3 y_1$$

In general,

$$S_t = Ay_t + A(1 - A)y_{t-1} + A(1 - A)^2 y_{t-2} + \cdots + A(1 - A)^{t-2} y_2 + (1 - A)^{t-1} y_1$$

For example, if $A = .5$, then

$$S_t = .5y_t + .25y_{t-1} + .125y_{t-2} + .062y_{t-3} + \cdots$$

Therefore, each smoothed value is actually a weighted sum of *all the previous observations*. Because the more recent observations have the largest weight, they have a larger effect on the smoothed value. Notice that the weights on the observations are decreasing exponentially. Except for observation y_1, the weight given to a particular observation is some constant (namely, $1 - A$) *times* the weight given to the preceding observation. That is why this procedure is called exponential smoothing.

Forecasting Using Simple Exponential Smoothing

The naïve forecasting procedure introduced earlier predicts the time series value for tomorrow using the actual value for today. In other words, $\hat{y}_{t+1} = y_t$. The exponential smoothing process is similar, except now the forecast for tomorrow is the smoothed value from today. In general,

$$\hat{y}_{t+1} = S_t \qquad t = 1, 2, 3, \ldots$$

For the special case where $A = 1$, we have

$$\hat{y}_{t+1} = S_t = 1y_t + (1 - 1)S_{t-1} = y_t$$

and the exponential smoothing forecast is the same as that provided by the naive predictor. Because A is considerably less than 1 in practice, the smoothed forecast makes use of all the past observations, rather than only the most recent measurement.

EXAMPLE 17.4

Using simple exponential smoothing with $A = .1$, what are the predicted values and residuals for the attendance data in Table 17.1?

Solution

Suppose the year is 1989 ($t = 1$) and you want a forecast for 1990 ($t = 2$). You need the smoothed value for 1989: $\hat{y}_2 = S_1 = 5.0$. Next, the year is 1990, and you need a forecast for 1991. Here, $\hat{y}_3 = S_2 = 5.3$ (from Table 17.1).

To obtain an Excel solution, enter the 13 time series values in column A. Click on **KPK Data Analysis ➤ Time Series Analysis Forecasting** and select **Simple Exponential Smoothing**. Enter "0" as the **Number of Forecast Periods,** "A1:A13" as the **Input Range,** and "B1" as the **Output Range.** After clicking on **Continue,** select **Smoothing Constant(s) Will be Provided** and enter ".1" as the smoothing constant (A). You will obtain the output in Figure 17.10 after clicking on **Continue.**

How well does this forecasting procedure perform here? We cannot use Figure 17.9 to compare the $\hat{y}$'s and the y's because, for each time period t, we have plotted y_t and S_t. The predicted value at t, however, is $\hat{y}_t = S_{t-1}$, not S_t. So we need to shift the smoothed values in Figure 17.9 one period to the right. This is shown in Figure 17.11, which contains a plot of the values in Figure 17.10 for $A = .1$.

As we might expect from Figure 17.11, the residuals using this method are quite large from 1997 on because this value of A produces smoothed values that

FIGURE

17.10

Forecasts and residuals using Excel and KPK Data Analysis to do simple exponential smoothing on attendance data ($A = .1$).

	A	B	C	D	E	F	G	H	I
1	5.0	Simple Exponential Smoothing ($A = .1$)							
2	8.0	t	Y(t)	SM(t)	Yhat	Residual			
3	2.1	1	5.0	5.000					
4	7.1	2	8.0	5.300	5.000	3.000			
5	4.8	3	2.1	4.980	5.300	-3.200			
6	2.0	4	7.1	5.192	4.980	2.120			
7	7.8	5	4.8	5.153	5.192	-0.392			
8	5.0	6	2.0	4.838	5.153	-3.153			
9	14.1	7	7.8	5.134	4.838	2.962			
10	13.0	8	5.0	5.120	5.134	-0.134			
11	13.5	9	14.1	6.018	5.120	8.980			
12	14.2	10	13.0	6.717	6.018	6.982			
13	14.0	11	13.5	7.395	6.717	6.783			
14		12	14.2	8.075	7.395	6.805			
15		13	14.0	8.668	8.075	5.925			
16									

FIGURE

17.11

Predicted versus actual values for attendance data (Table 17.1).

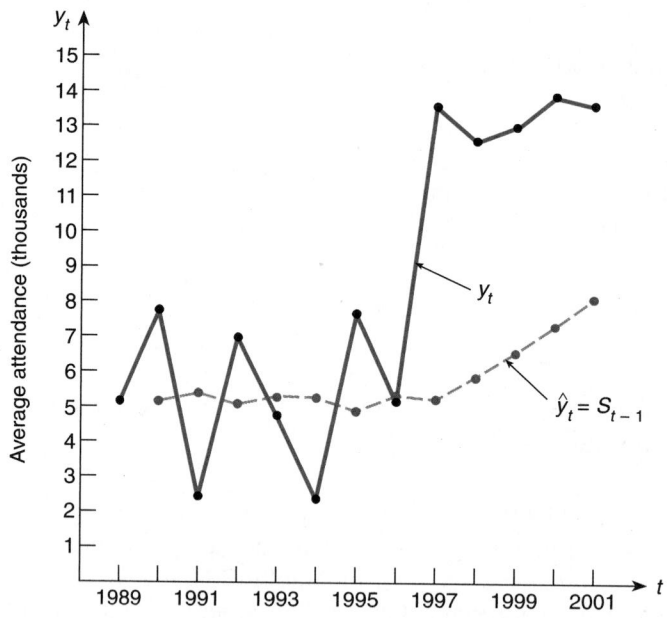

fail to adapt to the shift that occurred in 1997. This series was not a good one for simple exponential smoothing because of this sudden shift. However, between the years 1989 and 1996 (a relatively stationary set of observations), the smoothed time series contains much less noise using $A = .1$ and gives a clear indication of the lack of any trend.

Simple exponential smoothing is a popular method of forecasting, particularly when there are hundreds or perhaps thousands of forecasts to be updated for each time period. Such is the case for many inventory-control systems, which are used to predict future demand levels for each item in inventory by means of a computerized forecasting procedure. Simple exponential smoothing often is used for such situations because each forecast, $\hat{y}_{t-1}$, requires only two values: the current observation, y_t, and the previous smoothed value, S_{t-1}. There is no need to store all the previous observations. *Computationally, this procedure is very simple and requires less computer time than do more sophisticated forecasting techniques.*

X Exercises 17.11–17.15

Understanding the Mechanics

17.11 Calculate the smoothed values for the following time series data. Use simple exponential smoothing with the smoothing constant equal to .1 and also with the smoothing constant equal to .3.

Year	t	y_t	S_t $(A = .1)$	S_t $(A = .3)$
1987	1	2	2	2
1988	2	3		
1989	3	2		
1990	4	5		
1991	5	8		
1992	6	7		
1993	7	5		
1994	8	8		
1995	9	10		
1996	10	9		
1997	11	8		
1998	12	10		
1999	13	7		
2000	14	9		
2001	15	7		

Applying the New Concepts

17.12 Direct TV offers its customers 225 channels via its satellite TV system and the option of paying per movie viewed with up to 55 movie choices per day. The number of customers subscribing to Direct TV has grown slowly over the past two years.

Year	Month	Direct TV Customers in Millions
2000	July	8.3
	August	9.0
	September	8.5
	October	8.8
	November	8.9
	December	9.0
2001	January	9.8
	February	10.1
	March	9.6
	April	10.3
	May	10.0
	June	10.1

a. Using simple exponential smoothing with $A = .1$, find the residual for April, May, and June of 2001.

b. Repeat part a with $A = .3$ and compare the residuals for April, May, and June 2001.

(Source: "Satellite TV Leaders," *USA Today*, August 7, 2001, p. 3B.)

17.13 During the 12-month period from June 2000 to May 2001, the U.S. unemployment rate fluctuated around the 4.0% figure. This rate was among the lowest unemployment rates that the United States has experienced in the past 50 years. Using simple exponential smoothing with $A = .25$, predict the unemployment rate for June and July 2001.

Month	Jun	Jul	Aug	Sep	Oct	Nov
Year	2000	2000	2000	2000	2000	2000
Unemployment Rate	4.0	4.0	4.2	3.9	3.8	4.0

Month	Dec	Jan	Feb	Mar	Apr	May
Year	2000	2001	2001	2001	2001	2001
Unemployment Rate	4.0	4.2	4.2	4.3	4.6	4.4

(Source: "Job Picture Still Weak," *Dallas Morning News*, June 2, 2001, p. 1F.)

Using the Computer

17.14 **[DATA SET 17-14]** *Variable description:*

Year: 1985 to 2001

ProductivityIndex: An index to measure the overall productivity of a paper plant

The plant manager has developed a productivity index measuring plant productivity for plants that manufacture paper products. This measure has been recorded yearly and fluctuates with the demand for paper products and the number of employees hired. Use simple exponential smoothing with $A = .15$, to forecast the productivity index for the year 2002.

17.15 **[DATA SET EX17-15]** *Variable description:*

Year: Year from 1986 to 2001

RefinanceNum: Number of home loans refinanced

The trend in interest rates over the past decade has been generally downward. So as mortgage interest rates dip, homeowners consider refinancing home loans. Suppose that the manager of First State Bank in Denton, Texas, is interested in forecasting the number of homeowners refinancing their home mortgage for a better interest rate. Using simple exponential smoothing with $A = .2$, predict the number of homeowners refinancing at First State Bank in the years 2000 and 2001 and comment on the accuracy.

17.5

EXPONENTIAL SMOOTHING FOR A TIME SERIES CONTAINING TREND

The simple exponential smoothing technique discussed in the previous section always will lag behind a time series that contains a steadily increasing or decreasing trend. A procedure known as *Holt's two-parameter linear exponential smoothing* allows you to estimate separately the smoothed value of the time series as well as the average trend gain at each point in time. The resulting smoothed values track the past time series observations more accurately. We refer to this procedure as **linear exponential smoothing.** There are two equations for this method. The first, for smoothing the observations, is

$$S_t = Ay_t + (1 - A)(S_{t-1} + b_{t-1}) \qquad t = 2, 3, 4, \ldots \qquad \text{17.4}$$

The second, for smoothing the trend, is

$$b_t = B(S_t - S_{t-1}) + (1 - B)b_{t-1} \qquad t = 2, 3, 4, \ldots \qquad \text{17.5}$$

where (1) S_t is the smoothed value for time period t, (2) b_t is the smoothed *trend* estimate for this time period, and (3) A and B are smoothing constants between 0 and 1.

Smoothing the Observations (Equation 17.4)

Equation 17.4 is similar to the equation used for simple exponential smoothing, except that S_{t-1} is replaced by $(S_{t-1} + b_{t-1})$ to include the effect of the trend. The smoothing constant for this equation is $0 < A < 1$; typically, $A \leq .3$.

Smoothing the Trend (Equation 17.5)

Equation 17.5 is a new addition to the smoothing process and represents the smoothed trend. It uses a separate smoothing constant, B, to smooth the trend values. This constant also is generally less than or equal to .3. This smoothed trend estimate is updated by using a weighted sum of (1) the difference between the last two smoothed values (an estimate of the current "trend") and (2) the previous smoothed trend estimate. Such a procedure significantly reduces any randomness (irregular activity) in the trend values across time.

Forecasting Using Linear Exponential Smoothing

Linear exponential forecasting uses both the smoothed observations and the smoothed trend estimates. The forecast for time period $t + 1$ is the current smoothed value plus the current smoothed trend value.

$$\hat{y}_{t+1} = S_t + b_t \qquad t = 1, 2, 3, \ldots \qquad \text{17.6}$$

We also can use this procedure to forecast any number of time periods into the future, say, m periods. Here,

$$\hat{y}_{t+m} = S_t + mb_t \qquad t = 1, 2, 3, \ldots \qquad \text{17.7}$$

TABLE

17.2

Year	t	Actual Observation (y_t)	Smoothed Observation (S_t)	Smoothed Trend (b_t)	Forecast ($\hat{y}_t$)	Residual ($y_t - \hat{y}_t$)
1980	1	y_1	$S_1 = y_1$	b_1	—	—
1981	2	y_2	S_2	b_2	$\hat{y}_2$	$y_2 - \hat{y}_2$
1982	3	y_3	S_3	b_3	$\hat{y}_3$	$y_3 - \hat{y}_3$
1983	4	y_4	S_4	b_4	$\hat{y}_4$	$y_4 - \hat{y}_4$
⋮						

Summary for linear exponential smoothing.

The forecast using equation 17.6 is the *one-step ahead forecast*, and the value from equation 17.7 is the *m-step ahead forecast*.

Summarizing the Results

To summarize the necessary calculations for linear exponential smoothing, you can use the format in Table 17.2. The initial year for this time series is 1980. As we did for simple exponential smoothing, we continue to set the first smoothed value, S_1, equal to the first observation, y_1. A new problem arises here: the initial estimate of the trend, b_1. We examine two procedures for estimating this value.

Procedure 1. Let $b_1 = 0$. Provided you have a large number of years in your observed time series, this procedure provides an adequate initial estimate for the trend. The smoothed trend value soon "catches up" with the actual trend of the series.

Procedure 2. You can obtain a more accurate estimate of b_1 by using the first five (or so) time periods to estimate the initial trend. A least squares line is constructed through these five observations (exactly as discussed in Chapter 16), with the resulting equation $\hat{y}_t = a + bt$. The value of b provides an initial trend estimate.

We demonstrate this technique in Example 17.5, which uses both procedures to obtain the initial trend estimate, b_1.

EXAMPLE

17.5

The time series in the following table contains the city taxes (in thousands of dollars) collected in Jackson City over the past 20 quarters. Using procedures 1 and 2 to calculate an initial trend estimate, obtain the smoothed values, S_t, for each time period. Also, determine the predicted values, $\hat{y}_t$, using smoothing constants $A = .1$ and $B = .3$.

Year	Quarter	Taxes Collected	Year	Quarter	Taxes Collected
1997	1	76	2000	1	403
	2	93		2	282
	3	108		3	288
	4	128		4	387
1998	1	196	2001	1	484
	2	175		2	384
	3	141		3	330
	4	236		4	497
1999	1	256			
	2	190			
	3	227			
	4	299			

TABLE 17.3

Solution to Example 17.5 using linear exponential smoothing ($A = .1$, $B = .3$).

t	y_t	S_t	b_t	$\hat{y}_t$	$y_t - \hat{y}_t$
1	76.0	76.000	0.000		
2	93.0	77.700	0.510	76.000	17.000
3	108.0	81.189	1.404	78.210	29.790
4	128.0	87.133	2.766	82.593	45.407
5	196.0	100.509	5.949	89.899	106.101
6	175.0	113.313	8.005	106.458	68.542
7	141.0	123.286	8.596	121.318	19.682
8	236.0	142.293	11.719	131.882	104.118
9	256.0	164.211	14.779	154.013	101.987
10	190.0	180.091	15.109	178.990	11.010
11	227.0	198.380	16.063	195.200	31.800
12	299.0	222.899	18.600	214.443	84.557
13	403.0	257.649	23.445	241.499	161.501
14	282.0	281.184	23.472	281.094	0.906
15	288.0	302.991	22.972	304.656	−16.656
16	387.0	332.067	24.803	325.963	61.037
17	484.0	369.583	28.617	356.870	127.130
18	384.0	396.781	28.191	398.201	−14.201
19	330.0	415.475	25.342	424.972	−94.972
20	497.0	446.435	27.028	440.817	56.183

Solution   A summary of the results using procedure 1 (setting $b_1 = 0$) is shown in Table 17.3. To illustrate the necessary calculations here, consider $t = 10$.

1. $y_{10} = 190$

2. $S_{10} = .1y_{10} + .9(S_9 + b_9) = .1(190) + .9(164.211 + 14.779) = 180.091$

3. $b_{10} = .3(S_{10} - S_9) + .7(b_9) = .3(180.091 - 164.211) + .7(14.779) = 15.109$

4. $\hat{y}_{10} = S_9 + b_9$ (from equation 17.6) $= 164.211 + 14.779 = 178.990$

5. Residual for $t = 10$ is $y_{10} - \hat{y}_{10} = 190 - 178.990 = 11.010$

The KPK Data Analysis tool pack allows you to perform linear exponential smoothing within Excel using either procedure 1 or procedure 2. To obtain a procedure 2 solution, begin by entering the 20 city tax values in column A and clicking on **KPK Data Analysis ➤ Time Series Analysis ➤ Forecasting.** Select **Holt's Exponential Smoothing** and enter "0" as the **Number of Forecast Periods,** "A1:A20" as the **Input Range,** and "B1" as the **Output Range.** After clicking on **Continue,** select **Procedure 2** in the next screen and click on **OK.** In the next screen, select **Smoothing Constant(s) Will Be Provided** and enter ".1" as smoothing constant A and ".3" as smoothing constant B. After clicking on **Continue,** you will obtain the output in Figure 17.12. The columns in the Excel output correspond to those in Table 17.3 where the column labeled **Yhat** corresponds to the $\hat{y}_t$ column and the **Residual** column contains the $y_t - \hat{y}_t$ values.

The values of y_t and $\hat{y}_t$ (the predicted value for that time period) are shown in Figure 17.13. For this particular example, procedure 2, which used the first 5 quarters to obtain the initial trend estimate, estimated (and smoothed) the past values more accurately. The value of b_1 (in cell E3) is 27.5.

FIGURE

17.12

Excel solution to Example 17.5 using KPK Data Analysis (linear exponential smoothing with procedure 2, $A = .1$, $B = .3$).

	A	B	C	D	E	F	G	H	I	J
1	76	Holt's Exponential Smoothing (A = .1, B = .3)								
2	93	t	Y(t)	S(t)	B(t)	Yhat	Residual			
3	108	1	76	76.000	27.500					
4	128	2	93	102.450	27.185	103.500	-10.500			
5	196	3	108	127.472	26.536	129.635	-21.635			
6	175	4	128	151.407	25.756	154.007	-26.007			
7	141	5	196	179.046	26.321	177.162	18.838			
8	236	6	175	202.330	25.410	205.367	-30.367			
9	256	7	141	219.066	22.808	227.740	-86.740			
10	190	8	236	241.286	22.631	241.874	-5.874			
11	227	9	256	263.126	22.394	263.918	-7.918			
12	299	10	190	275.968	19.528	285.520	-95.520			
13	403	11	227	288.647	17.473	295.496	-68.496			
14	282	12	299	305.408	17.260	306.120	-7.120			
15	288	13	403	330.701	19.670	322.668	80.332			
16	387	14	282	343.534	17.619	350.371	-68.371			
17	484	15	288	353.837	15.424	361.152	-73.152			
18	384	16	387	371.035	15.956	369.261	17.739			
19	330	17	484	396.692	18.866	386.991	97.009			
20	497	18	384	412.403	17.920	415.559	-31.559			
21		19	330	420.290	14.910	430.323	-100.323			
22		20	497	441.380	16.764	435.200	61.800			

FIGURE

17.13

Predicted values using linear exponential smoothing ($A = .1$, $B = .3$).

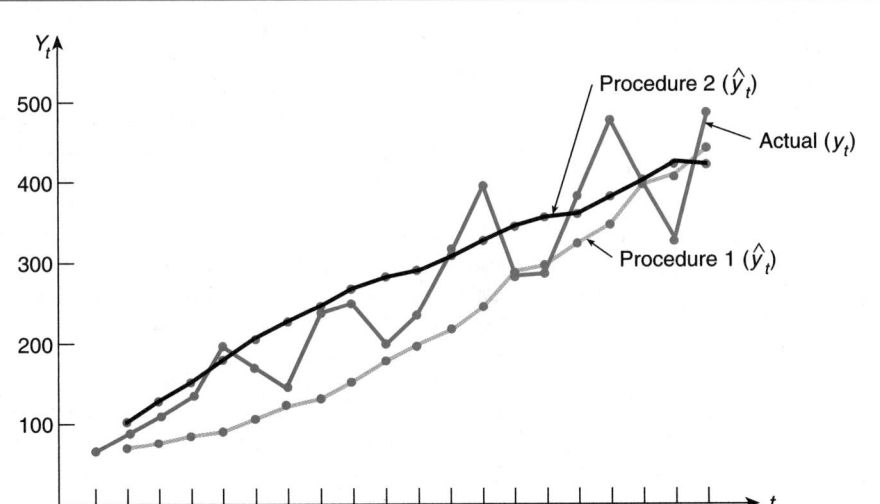

X Exercises 17.16–17.20

Understanding the Mechanics

17.16 The following values were found from a time series data set. Use Holt's two-parameter linear exponential smoothing technique to answer parts a and b.

$$Y_{10} = 12.0 \qquad S_8 = 11.0$$
$$S_9 = 11.5 \qquad b_8 = .5$$

a. Find the smoothed value at time $t = 10$ with $A = .1$ and $B = .2$.

b. Find the smoothed value at time $t = 10$ with $A = .25$ and $B = .10$.

Applying the New Concepts

17.17 The United States has encouraged Japan to increase its imports since the early 1980s. Japan has had a trade surplus since 1980. In recent years, Japan has been passing laws to open its economy to more imports. Forecast the 2002 value of Japan's imports using Holt's two-parameter linear exponential smoothing technique, estimating the slope using the first five years of data. Let $A = .3$ and $B = .1$.

Year	Value of Japan's Imports (in Billions of Dollars)
1992	230
1993	215
1994	220
1995	255
1996	305
1997	320
1998	295
1999	280
2000	320
2001	380

(Source: "Tokyo's Trade Surplus Is a Given. Isn't It?" *The Wall Street Journal*, July 17, 2001, p. 12A.)

17.18. The United States is very important as a market for other countries. Since 1991, imports into the United States as a percentage of the rest of the world's gross domestic product (GDP) has increased. The following table illustrates the growth in U.S. imports from 1985 to 2000. Forecast the 2001 imports of the United States as a percentage of World GDP using Holt's two-parameter linear exponential smoothing technique with an initial estimate of zero for the slope. Let $A = .25$ and $B = .3$.

Year	Imports as a Percentage of World GDP	Year	Imports as a Percentage of World GDP
1985	2.5	1993	3.3
1986	1.9	1994	3.5
1987	2.2	1995	4.0
1988	2.4	1996	3.6
1989	2.6	1997	4.0
1990	3.2	1998	4.5
1991	2.8	1999	4.8
1992	3.1	2000	6.0

(Source: "Magnet," *The Wall Street Journal*, July 17, 2001, p. 1A.)

Using the Computer

17.19 [DATA SET EX17-19] *Variable description:*

Year: Year from 1982 to 2001

LaborForce: Number of employees in the nonagricultural sector of St. Charles county

Value of Smoothing constant A: .5

Value of Smoothing constant B: .3

St. Charles County has a large agricultural population. However, as farming becomes more modernized, fewer employees have been needed in this sector of the population. Manufacturing and service facilities have gradually increased the number of employees in the nonagricultural industry. Using linear exponential smoothing with zero as the initial value estimate of the slope, forecast the number of employees in this sector of the economy for St. Charles County for the year 2002. Do a what-if analysis by using the data from 1991 to 2001. How sensitive is the value of the forecast to this change?

17.20 [DATA SET EX17-20] *Variable description:*

Year: Year from 1999 to 2001

Month: Month of the year

GasPrice: Average price for gasoline in the United States

Value of smoothing constant A: .25

Value of smoothing constant B: .15

The average price of gasoline rose to $1.72 in May 2001. It is the highest actual price ever for gasoline. However, this price still falls short of March 1981, when the average price, after adjusting for inflation, was $2.76. The average price for gasoline is recorded monthly for the years 1999, 2000, and 2001.

a. Using zero as an initial estimate of the slope, find the predicted value of the average price of gasoline for January 2002.

b. Using the least squares estimate from the first five years for the slope, repeat part a. Compare the predicted value from part a to the predicted value using this procedure.

(Source: "Pressure on Gas Policy Weakens," *USA Today*, July 27, 2001, p. 2B.)

17.6 EXPONENTIAL SMOOTHING METHOD FOR TREND AND SEASONALITY

As discussed earlier, seasonality is present in a time series whenever certain months or quarters are consistently higher or lower than the yearly average. In such cases, an extension of Holt's method, **Winters' linear and seasonal exponential smoothing,** offers additional flexibility. This three-parameter technique (that is, there are three smoothing constants) not only smooths the past observation and trend estimates (as does linear exponential smoothing) but also provides smoothed seasonality factors for each time period.

The smoothing equations for Winters' method are, for smoothing the observations,

$$S_t = A\left(\frac{y_t}{F_{t-L}}\right) + (1 - A)(S_{t-1} + b_{t-1})$$
$$t = L + 1, \ L + 2, \ L + 3, \ \ldots$$

17.8

for smoothing the seasonality factors,

$$F_t = B\left(\frac{y_t}{S_t}\right) + (1 - B)F_{t-L}$$
$$t = L + 1, \ L + 2, \ L + 3, \ \ldots$$

17.9

and for smoothing the trend estimates,

$$b_t = C(S_t - S_{t-1}) + (1 - C)b_{t-1}$$
$$t = L + 1, \ L + 2, \ L + 3, \ \ldots$$

17.10

Here, (1) S_t is the smoothed observation for time period t; (2) F_t is the smoothed seasonality factor for this time period; (3) b_t is the smoothed estimate of trend; (4) L is the number of periods per year ($L = 4$ for quarterly data and $L = 12$ for monthly data); and (5) A, B, and C are the three smoothing constants.

Equations 17.8 and 17.10 are similar to the corresponding equations from the linear exponential smoothing procedure, except that S_t now consists of deseasonalized smoothed values. These values are obtained by dividing each observation, y_t, by the smoothed seasonal factor from one year before that observation, F_{t-L}.

Forecasting Using Linear and Seasonal Exponential Smoothing

The procedure for forecasting using Winters' exponential smoothing method is similar to that used for Holt's. Here, the forecast for a particular quarter (month) includes the effect of all three smoothing equations. The forecast for m periods ahead is

$$\hat{y}_{t+m} = (S_t + mb_t) \cdot F_{t+m-L}$$

17.11

The term $(S_t + mb_t)$ represents the smoothed *deseasonalized* estimate and includes the smoothed trend effect. The seasonality is included in the final estimate by multiplying by the smoothed seasonality factor for the quarter (or month) one year previous to the forecast time period, namely, F_{t+m-L}. This procedure is much like that used in Section 17.3, where the deseasonalized estimate was multiplied by the corresponding seasonal index to arrive at the final forecast.

When using this procedure on the past observations, you would, for example, determine $\hat{y}_{10}$ by assuming observations, $y_1, y_2, \ldots, y_9$ are available. You would do a one-step ahead forecast ($m = 1$) using the smoothed seasonal value from the previous year; that is, $F_{10-4} = F_6$, assuming quarterly data. As a result,

$$\hat{y}_{10} = [S_9 + (1)b_9] \cdot F_6$$

Similarly,

$$\hat{y}_{11} = [S_{10} + (1)b_{10}] \cdot F_7$$

$$\hat{y}_{12} = [S_{11} + (1)b_{11}] \cdot F_8$$

and so on.

Forecasting *beyond* the range of your observations (extrapolating) is illustrated in Example 17.7.

When dealing with quarterly data, your first set of predicted values will be

$$\hat{y}_5 = [S_4 + (1)b_4] \cdot F_1$$

$$\hat{y}_6 = [S_5 + (1)b_5] \cdot F_2$$

$$\hat{y}_7 = [S_6 + (1)b_6] \cdot F_3$$

and so on. If the time series consists of monthly observations ($L = 12$), then you begin your predicted values with

$$\hat{y}_{13} = [S_{12} + (1)b_{12}] \cdot F_1$$

$$\hat{y}_{14} = [S_{13} + (1)b_{13}] \cdot F_2$$

$$\hat{y}_{15} = [S_{14} + (1)b_{14}] \cdot F_3$$

and so on.

Summarizing the Results

A method of summarizing the necessary calculations is shown in Table 17.4. Suppose that the original year of the observed time series is 1997, with quarterly observations. Initial estimates must be supplied for (1) the seasonal factors for each quarter of 1996, (2) the trend estimate for quarter 4, 1996, and (3) the smoothed value corresponding to quarter 4, 1996.

Once again, we will examine two procedures for this situation—one is quick and easy, and the other is more accurate but requires additional calculations. Procedure 1 is used in Table 17.4. Both procedures are demonstrated in Example 17.6. These are not the only procedures—can you think of one or two others?

Procedure 1

1. Set the initial seasonal factors equal to 1.

2. Set the initial trend estimate (b_0) equal to 0.

TABLE

17.4

Summary of linear and seasonal exponential smoothing (using procedure 1).

Year	Qtr.	t	Actual Observations (y_t)	Smoothed Observations (S_t)	Smoothed Seasonal Factors (F_t)	Smoothed Trend (b_t)	Forecast $(\hat{y}_t)$	Residual $(y_t - \hat{y}_t)$
1996	1				(1) 1.0			
(year 0)	2				1.0			
	3			(3)	1.0	(2)		
	4			$S_0 = y_4$	1.0	$b_0 = 0$		
1997	1	1	y_1	S_1	F_1	b_1	$\hat{y}_1 = S_0$	$y_1 - \hat{y}_1$
(year 1)	2	2	y_2	S_2	F_2	b_2	$\hat{y}_2 = S_0$	$y_2 - \hat{y}_2$
	3	3	y_3	S_3	F_3	b_3	$\hat{y}_3 = S_0$	$y_3 - \hat{y}_3$
	4	4	y_4	S_4	F_4	b_4	$\hat{y}_4 = S_0$	$y_4 - \hat{y}_4$
1998	1	5	y_5	S_5	F_5	b_5	$\hat{y}_5$	$y_5 - \hat{y}_5$
(year 2)	2	6	y_6	S_6	F_6	b_6	$\hat{y}_6$	$y_6 - \hat{y}_6$
	⋮							

3. Set the initial smoothed value for quarter 4, 1996 (S_0), equal to the actual value for quarter 4, 1997 (y_4). This value is also the *forecast value* ($\hat{y}_t$) for each of the four quarters in 1997.

Procedure 2

1. Use the first two years of data to determine the seasonal indexes. These are the four values for F_t in 1996. Actually, any number of years of data can be used here.

2. Deseasonalize the data for the first two years (or any number of years), and calculate the least squares line through these deseasonalized values, d_t. Call this line $\hat{d}_t = a + bt$. The initial trend estimate (b_0) is b.

3. The initial smoothed value for quarter 4, 1996, is $S_0 = [a + b(0)] \cdot$ (seasonal index for quarter 4 in step 1) $= a \cdot$ (seasonal index), where a is the intercept of the least squares line in step 2. Also, S_0 is the *forecast value* ($\hat{y}_t$) for each of the 4 quarters in 1997.

EXAMPLE 17.6

The quarterly taxes from Jackson City in Example 17.5 indicated significant seasonality. In particular, the first-quarter taxes appeared to be considerably larger than those for the yearly average. Using the linear and seasonal exponential smoothing procedures, determine the smoothed value, S_t, and predicted value, $\hat{y}_t$, for each time period. Use smoothing constants $A = .1$, $B = .3$, and $C = .2$.

Solution

The computed results using procedure 1 are summarized in Table 17.5, where $b_0 = 0$, $S_0 = y_4$, and the initial seasonal factors are each 1.

TABLE 17.5

Solution using linear and seasonal exponential smoothing, procedure 1 ($A = .1$, $B = .3$, $C = .2$).

	t	y_t	S_t	F_t	b_t	$\hat{y}_t$	$y_t - \hat{y}_t$
				1.0			
				1.0			
				1.0			
			128	1.0	0.0		
1997	1	76.0	122.800	0.886	−1.040	128.000	−52.000
	2	93.0	118.884	0.935	−1.615	128.000	−35.000
	3	108.0	116.342	0.978	−1.801	128.000	−20.000
	4	128.0	115.887	1.031	−1.531	128.000	0.000
1998	5	196.0	125.050	1.090	0.608	101.281	94.719
	6	175.0	131.815	1.053	1.839	117.450	57.550
	7	141.0	134.699	0.999	2.048	130.779	10.221
	8	236.0	145.954	1.207	3.889	141.034	94.966
1999	9	256.0	158.342	1.248	5.589	163.356	92.644
	10	190.0	165.589	1.081	5.921	172.547	17.453
	11	227.0	177.082	1.084	7.035	171.334	55.666
	12	299.0	190.477	1.316	8.307	222.235	76.765
2000	13	403.0	211.193	1.446	10.789	248.112	154.888
	14	282.0	225.870	1.131	11.567	239.967	42.033
	15	288.0	240.265	1.118	12.132	257.347	30.653
	16	387.0	256.568	1.374	12.966	332.116	54.884
2001	17	484.0	276.049	1.538	14.269	389.793	94.207
	18	384.0	295.231	1.182	15.252	328.427	55.573
	19	330.0	308.943	1.103	14.944	347.212	−17.212
	20	497.0	327.681	1.417	15.703	444.893	52.107

The KPK Data Analysis tool pack allows you to perform linear and seasonal exponential smoothing within Excel using either procedure 1 or procedure 2. To obtain a procedure 2 solution, begin by entering the 20 city tax values in column A and clicking on **KPK Data Analysis ➤ Time Series Analysis ➤ Forecasting.** Select **Winters' Exponential Smoothing** and enter "0" as the **Number of Forecast Periods.** Select 4 as the number of periods per year, and enter "A1:A20" as the **Input Range** and "B1" as the **Output Range.** After clicking on **Continue,** select **Procedure 2** in the next screen and click on **OK.** In the next screen, select **Smoothing Constant(s) Will Be Provided** and enter ".1" as smoothing constant A, ".3" as smoothing constant B, and ".2" as smoothing constant C. After clicking on **Continue,** you will obtain the output in Figure 17.14. The columns in the Excel output correspond to those in Table 17.5 where the column labeled **Yhat** contains the $\hat{y}_t$ values and the **Residual** column corresponds to the $y_t - \hat{y}_t$ column. Finally, for column D to contain the years (1997, . . . , 2001), select column D in your output (it should be black), click on **Insert ➤ Columns,** and enter the years in cells D3, D7, D11, D15, and D19.

With procedure 2, the first two years were used to obtain the initial seasonal factors by finding the four seasonal indexes as described in Chapter 16. These values (contained in cells C4:C7) are

$$\text{quarter } 1 = 1.23 \qquad \text{quarter } 3 = .91$$
$$\text{quarter } 2 = 0.98 \qquad \text{quarter } 4 = .88$$

Next, the data from the first two years were deseasonalized by dividing by the corresponding seasonal index to obtain the deseasonalized values, d_t. A least squares line through these eight values using the simple linear regression procedure from Chapter 16 produced:

$$\hat{d}_t = 43.8 + 23.1t$$

FIGURE

17.14

Excel solution to Example 17.6 using KPK Data Analysis (linear and seasonal exponential smoothing with procedure 2, $A = .1$, $B = .3$, $C = .2$).

	A	B	C	D	E	F	G	H	I	J	K
1	76	Initial Estimates			\multicolumn{7}{}{Winters' Exponential Smoothing (A = .1, B = .3, C = .2)}
2	93	Smoothed (S(0))	38.5		t	Y(t)	S(t)	F(t)	B(t)	Yhat	Residual
3	108	Slope (B(0))	23.1	1997	1	76.	61.619	1.231	23.104	38.500	37.500
4	128	Seasonal Factor 1	1.23		2	93.	85.740	1.011	23.307	38.500	54.500
5	196	Seasonal Factor 2	0.98		3	108.	110.011	0.932	23.500	38.500	69.500
6	175	Seasonal Factor 3	0.91		4	128.	134.705	0.901	23.739	38.500	89.500
7	141	Seasonal Factor 4	0.88	1998	5	196.	158.521	1.233	23.754	195.047	0.953
8	236				6	175.	181.351	0.997	23.569	184.354	-9.354
9	256				7	141.	199.565	0.864	22.498	190.887	-49.887
10	190				8	236.	226.048	0.944	23.295	200.094	35.906
11	227			1999	9	256.	245.177	1.176	22.462	307.350	-51.350
12	299				10	190.	259.923	0.918	20.919	266.964	-76.964
13	403				11	227.	279.031	0.849	20.557	242.654	-15.654
14	282				12	299.	301.304	0.958	20.900	282.797	16.203
15	288			2000	13	403.	324.249	1.196	21.309	378.940	24.060
16	387				14	282.	341.737	0.890	20.545	317.059	-35.059
17	484				15	288.	359.981	0.834	20.085	307.532	-19.532
18	384				16	387.	382.436	0.975	20.559	364.283	22.717
19	330			2001	17	484.	403.159	1.197	20.592	482.031	1.969
20	497				18	384.	424.530	0.894	20.747	377.065	6.935
21					19	330.	440.307	0.809	19.753	371.461	-41.461
22					20	497.	465.054	1.003	20.752	448.335	48.665

The value of 23.1 became the initial slope estimate, b_0. Finally, the initial smoothed value for quarter 4, 1996, is

$$S_0 = (43.8)(\text{initial seasonal index for quarter 4})$$
$$= (43.8)(.88) = 38.5$$

Also, $S_0 = 38.5$ becomes the forecast value ($\hat{y}_t$) for each of the quarters in 1997.

The calculations required here can be illustrated using Table 17.5 and $t = 10$ for procedure 1.

1. $y_{10} = 190$

2. $S_{10} = .1\left(\dfrac{y_{10}}{F_{10-4}}\right) + .9(S_9 + b_9)$

$= .1\left(\dfrac{y_{10}}{F_6}\right) + .9(S_9 + b_9)$

$= .1\left(\dfrac{190}{1.053}\right) + .9(158.342 + 5.589) = 165.589$

3. $F_{10} = .3\left(\dfrac{y_{10}}{S_{10}}\right) + .7F_6$

$= .3\left(\dfrac{190}{165.589}\right) + .7(1.053) = 1.081$

4. $b_{10} = .2(S_{10} - S_9) + .8b_9$
$= .2(165.589 - 158.342) + .8(5.589) = 5.921$

5. $\hat{y}_{10} = [S_9 + (1)(b_9)]F_6$ (from equation 17.11)
$= (158.342 + 5.589)]1.053$ (computer-stored value is 1.05256)
$= 172.547$

6. Residual for $t = 10$ is: $y_{10} - \hat{y}_{10} = 190 - 172.547 = 17.453$

A graphical illustration of the actual observations, y_t, and the predicted value for each time period, $\hat{y}_t$, is shown in Figure 17.15. Once again, the more complex procedure 2 performed better than did procedure 1; for the last 10 quarters, procedure 2 tracked the actual time series extremely well.

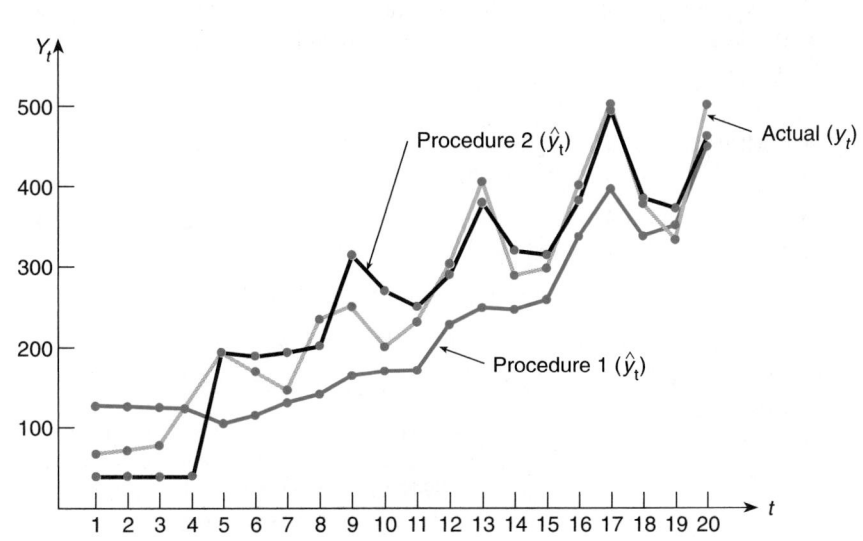

FIGURE

17.15

Forecasted values using linear and seasonal exponential smoothing ($A = .1$, $B = .3$, $C = .2$).

Exercises 17.21–17.26

Understanding the Mechanics

17.21 The following values were used in the analysis of a time series data set with Winters' linear and seasonal smoothing technique.

$$b_8 = .8 \qquad F_{10} = .9$$
$$S_9 = 16 \qquad F_6 = .8$$
$$S_8 = 14 \qquad Y_{10} = 16$$
$$S_7 = 13 \qquad L = 4$$

   a. Find the smoothed observation for time $t = 10$ with $A = .2$, $B = .1$, and $C = .1$.

   b. Find the smoothed observation for time $t = 10$ with $A = .1$, $B = .3$, and $C = .3$.

Applying the New Concepts

17.22 Ektronics manufactures electronic testing and measuring instruments. The company has managed to capture a large share of the market over the past four years. Sales of its equipment (in ten thousands) are recorded monthly for 1998–2001.

Year	Jan	Feb	Mar	Apr	May	June
1998	1.0	1.1	1.2	1.7	1.9	2.3
1999	1.7	1.4	1.5	1.7	2.4	2.7
2000	1.9	2.0	2.1	2.3	3.1	3.5
2001	2.9	2.8	2.7	3.4	3.7	4.1

Year	Jul	Aug	Sep	Oct	Nov	Dec
1998	2.7	3.1	2.5	2.3	2.0	1.9
1999	3.3	3.9	3.4	3.0	2.6	2.0
2000	4.1	4.7	4.3	3.4	2.9	2.8
2001	4.6	5.0	4.7	4.0	3.7	3.6

Use Winters' linear and seasonal smoothing technique to find the smoothed values for the first four months of 2001. Let $A = .2$, $B = .1$, and $C = .1$. Using procedure 1, set the initial estimates of the seasonal factors to 1.0 and let $b_0 = 0$.

17.23 The earnings per share of Mecta Mining, a large producer of silver, are as follows:

Year	Quarter 1	Quarter 2	Quarter 3	Quarter 4
1998	.25	.20	.27	.30
1999	.26	.24	.34	.37
2000	.30	.27	.38	.45
2001	.36	.32	.47	.50

Using the linear and seasonal exponential smoothing procedure, determine the predicted value for each quarter of 2002. Use procedure 2 and the first two years of data to obtain b_0, S_0, and the four initial seasonal factors (F). Let $A = .3$, $B = .2$, and $C = .1$.

Using the Computer

17.24 **[DATA SET EX17-24]** *Variable description:*

Year: Year from 1996 to 2000

Quarter: 1st, 2nd, 3rd, or 4th quarter

Productivity: Percentage growth in productivity

In the late 1990s, annual growth in productivity, that is, the growth in output per hour worked, roughly doubled to about 3% from the prior years. Higher productivity enables businesses to pay workers more without having to raise prices on goods and services. Determine the predicted values for the first quarter of 2001 by using Winters' linear and seasonal smoothing technique with procedure 2 so that b_0, S_0, and the first four initial seasonal factors are estimated with the first two years of data. Let $A = .2$, $B = .3$, and $C = .05$.

17.25 **[DATA SET EX17-25]** *Variable description:*

Year: Year from 1996 through 2001

Quarter: Quarter represented by 1 through 4

Membership: Membership at the Fitness and Health Center

Value of smoothing constant A: .1

Value of smoothing constant B: .2

Value of smoothing constant C: .2

The membership at the Fitness and Health Center has increased over the past six years (1996–2001). The manager of the center is interested in knowing the forecasted membership for the first quarter of the year 2002. The information is important in deciding whether to open a new center. Find this forecast using Winters' linear and seasonal smoothing technique with procedure 1, setting the initial estimates of the seasonal factors to 1.0 and let $b_0 = 0$.

17.26 **[DATA SET EX17-26]** *Variable description:*

Year: Year from 1994 through 2001

Quarter: Quarter represented by 1 through 4

PriceSqFt: Average price per square foot to build a new home in Calgary, Canada

Value of smoothing constant A: .1

Value of smoothing constant B: .15

Value of smoothing constant C: .15

The average price per square foot to build a new home in Calgary, Canada, has fluctuated over the years. Quarterly data from 1994 to 2001 were collected. Find the forecasted values for the four quarters of the year 2002. This information is important to builders who are deciding on the number of new homes to build in the area. Use procedure 2 and the first two years of data to obtain b_0, S_0, and the four initial seasonal factors.

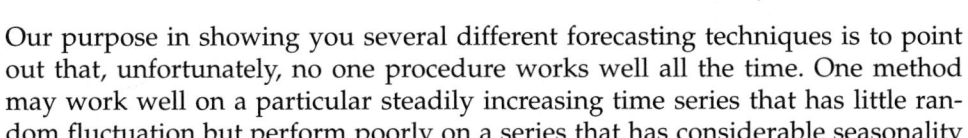

CHOOSING THE APPROPRIATE FORECASTING PROCEDURE

Our purpose in showing you several different forecasting techniques is to point out that, unfortunately, no one procedure works well all the time. One method may work well on a particular steadily increasing time series that has little random fluctuation but perform poorly on a series that has considerable seasonality or random fluctuation.

As you gain more experience in time series applications, you will be better able to choose an appropriate forecasting technique. One factor to consider is the length of your forecast. We classify the forecast periods as follows:

* *Short-term forecast:* one to three months
* *Medium-range forecast:* greater than three months but less than two years
* *Long-range forecast:* two years or more

The exponential smoothing procedures are excellent for *short-term* forecasts, whereas the component decomposition method (in Section 17.3) is useful in medium- and long-range forecasting. The latter also is a popular procedure for many short-term applications, including inventory control and production planning.

Comparing the Predicted and Observed Values

One method of deciding whether a certain forecast technique is appropriate in a particular situation is to determine how well the procedure "fits" the observed time series. You accomplish this by pretending that, in each time period, the next observation is unknown and letting the forecasting procedure "predict" the next value (the $\hat{y}_t$ values in the previous examples). Next, you compare the predicted ($\hat{y}_t$) values with the observed values (y_t).

The three most popular methods of comparing the predicted and observed values use measures involving the residuals. These measures are the mean absolute deviation, the predictive mean squared error, and the mean absolute percentage error.

The **mean absolute deviation (MAD)** is the average of the absolute values of each residual. Let

$$e_t = \text{residual at time } t$$

$$= y_t - \hat{y}_t$$

The mean absolute deviation is defined as

$$\text{MAD} = \frac{\sum |e_t|}{n}$$

17.12

where n is the number of *predicted* values obtained from the past data. For example, when using linear exponential smoothing on 20 data values, you obtain 19 predicted values because $\hat{y}_1$ is unavailable, so n is 19 and not 20.

The **predictive mean squared error (MSE)** is similar to the MAD, except we find the average of the *squared* residuals.

$$\text{(predictive) MSE} = \frac{\sum e_t^2}{n}$$

17.13

where, again, n is the number of predicted values.*

The **mean absolute percentage error (MAPE)** considers the *relative* error of each forecast. The relative error at time period t is defined as e_t/y_t. The mean absolute percentage error is defined to be

$$MAPE = \frac{\sum \left| \frac{e_t}{y_t} \right|}{n}$$

17.14

where n is the number of predicted values.

If, during a particular time period, the actual value is $y_t = 50$ and the forecast value is $\hat{y}_t = 60$, the absolute percentage error is

$$\left| \frac{50 - 60}{50} \right| = .2$$

So, the error at this time period is 20% of the actual value. Consequently, for a particular time series, the MAPE is the sum of the absolute percentage error for each predicted value divided by the number of predicted values.

The MSE severely penalizes large residuals because it *squares* each value. Consequently, you use the MSE for situations in which you prefer several small residuals to one large value and wish to be warned if there is one larger residual. The primary advantage of using the MAPE is that it can be used to compare the predictive ability of a certain forecasting technique on two different time series. By using relative error, rather than actual error, the effect of the magnitude of the time series observations has been removed from the predictive measure.

To illustrate these measures, consider Table 17.6. For forecasting method 1, there are no large residuals, whereas method 2 results in one large residual. So the MSE is smaller for method 1, but the MAD is smaller for method 2. When using any of these measures, the *smaller* the value, the *more accurate* your forecast procedure.

TABLE 17.6

Comparison of the mean absolute deviation (MAD), the mean squared error (MSE), and the mean absolute percentage error (MAPE).

Forecast	y_t	$\hat{y}_t$	$e_t = y_t - \hat{y}_t$	$\|e_t\|$	e_t^2	
Method 1	36	32	4	4	16	.111
	42	46	−4	4	16	.095
	45	49	−4	4	16	.089
				12	48	.295

MAD = 12/3 = 4.0
MSE = 48/3 = 16.0
MAPE = .295/3 = .098

Method 2	36	34	2	2	4	.056
	42	40	2	2	4	.048
	45	52	−7	7	49	.156
				11	57	.260

MAD = 11/3 = 3.67
MSE = 57/3 = 19.0
MAPE = .260/3 = .087

*The MSE that we compute as a measure of how well a forecasting procedure fits the observed data is not the same as the MSE computed in a normal ANOVA table. The ANOVA MSE is equal to SSE/(degrees of freedom for residual). In contrast, the predictive MSE is not used in any test of hypothesis and is merely the average of the squared deviations.

There is no consensus among statisticians as to which measure is preferable. Instead, it depends on the results of having large forecast residuals. If a large error is disastrous (such as in predicting the inventory level of an expensive product), then using the MSE is preferable. On the other hand, if you can afford to overlook a single severe miss, provided the general tracking is close, then the MAD serves better. When comparing the predictive accuracy of two different time series, the MAPE is the appropriate measure.

When using the KPK Data Analysis tools within Excel, the resulting spreadsheet will contain the corresponding MSE, MAD, and MAPE. To avoid any possible confusion, these values were not shown in the previous Excel solutions (Figures 17.4, 17.7, 17.10, 17.12, and 17.14). If you use Excel on the previous examples, you will see these three measures at the bottom of your spreadsheet.

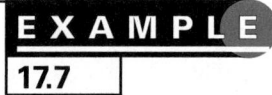

EXAMPLE 17.7

We used two types of exponential smoothing to smooth (and predict) the city taxes collected in Jackson City over the past five years. Data from the past 20 quarters are contained in the table in Example 17.5, in which we used linear exponential smoothing (with smoothing constants $A = .1$ and $B = .3$) to reduce randomness within the observations and trend values. The results are summarized in Table 17.3 and Figure 17.12, using the two procedures for providing initial estimates.

Example 17.6 examined the same data using linear and seasonal exponential smoothing, with smoothing constants $A = .1$, $B = .3$, and $C = .2$. A much better fit was obtained using the more sophisticated method of providing initial smoothed estimates (procedure 2). These results were summarized in Tables 17.5 and Figure 17.14 and are presented graphically in Figure 17.15.

Determine the predictive MSE for each of these four methods. Using the appropriate procedure, determine the forecasted tax revenue for each quarter of 2002.

Solution

1. *Linear exponential smoothing (procedure 1).* The residuals from this forecasting procedure are contained in Table 17.3. The computed predictive mean squared error is

$$\text{MSE} = \frac{(17.000)^2 + (29.790)^2 + \cdots + (56.183)^2}{19} = 5{,}670.08$$

2. *Linear exponential smoothing (procedure 2).* Based on Figures 17.12 and 17.13, we would expect a much smaller predictive MSE here. There are no surprises, because

$$\text{MSE} = \frac{(-10.500)^2 + (-21.635)^2 + \cdots + (61.800)^2}{19} = 3{,}426.50$$

3. *Linear and seasonal exponential smoothing (procedure 1).* These residuals are listed in Table 17.5, with a corresponding predictive mean squared error of

$$\text{MSE} = \frac{(-52.000)^2 + (-35.000)^2 + \cdots + (52.107)^2}{20} = 4{,}414.91$$

(Note that we divide by 20 here because 20 predicted values are available using this procedure.)

Warning: It is not valid to conclude, based on the large MSE value, that this forecasting method is less appropriate than linear exponential smoothing. Remember that we are at the mercy of the particular values of the smoothing constants, *A, B,* and *C*. Perhaps a different set of constants would have resulted in a significantly smaller MSE. Finding the best set of constants for any one application involves finding the set of values for *A, B,* and *C* that *minimize* the resulting predictive MSE. This (not insignificant) computational burden is one of the drawbacks of using Holt's and Winters' exponential smoothing techniques.

4. *Linear and seasonal exponential smoothing (procedure 2).* In Figures 17.14 and 17.15, we observed excellent agreement between the actual time series, y_t, and the predicted series, $\hat{y}_t$, using the smoothed estimates. A very small predictive MSE value would be expected here, and such is the case:

$$\text{MSE} = \frac{(37.500)^2 + (54.500)^2 + \cdots + (48.665)^2}{20} = 1{,}849.80$$

We conclude that the best choice of these four alternatives is the linear and seasonal exponential smoothing method using procedure 2 to derive the original estimates.

5. *Forecasted tax revenue.* Using equation 17.11 and the results in Figure 17.14, the forecasts for 2002 would be as follows. For the first quarter (one step ahead): $t = 20$, $L = 4$, $m = 1$, and

$$\hat{y}_{21} = [S_{20} + (1)b_{20}] \cdot F_{17}$$
$$= [464.654 + (1)(20.752)](1.197) = 581$$

For the second quarter (two steps ahead): $t = 20$, $L = 4$, $m = 2$, and

$$\hat{y}_{22} = [S_{20} + (2)b_{20}] \cdot F_{18}$$
$$= [464.654 + (2)(20.752)] \cdot (.894) = 453$$

For the third quarter (three steps ahead): $t = 20$, $L = 4$, $m = 3$, and

$$\hat{y}_{23} = [S_{20} + (3)b_{20}] \cdot F_{19}$$
$$= [464.654 + (3)(20.752)](.809) = 426$$

For the fourth quarter (four steps ahead): $t = 20$, $L = 4$, $m = 4$, and

$$\hat{y}_{24} = [S_{20} + (4)b_{20}] \cdot F_{20}$$
$$= [464.654 + (4)(20.752)] \cdot (1.003) = 549$$

Selecting the Smoothing Constants

As mentioned earlier, the computed MSE (or MAD or MAPE) value for any exponential smoothing procedure is determined not only by the procedure itself but also by the value of the necessary smoothing constants. In Example 17.6, the smoothing constants were $A = .1$, $B = .3$, and $C = .2$, with a corresponding MSE value of 1,849.80, using procedure 2. By changing these constants, you might improve the fit (lower the MSE), or you might obtain a less desirable solution (a larger MSE).

To illustrate this point, using Example 17.6 and procedure 2, for

$A = .1$, $B = .4$, $C = .3$: $\text{MSE} = 1{,}767.94$ (an improvement)

$A = .2$, $B = .2$, $C = .2$: $\text{MSE} = 2{,}145.64$

To arrive at the smallest possible predictive MSE, you must examine a variety of values, compute the MSE for each combination, and select the set of values that provides the smallest MSE. For example, if you consider all nonzero values of A, B, and C between 0 and 1, in increments of .05, you will need $(1/.05)^3 = 20^3 = 8{,}000$ different passes through the procedure to determine the corresponding 8,000 MSE values. The set of A, B, and C values that provides the smallest MSE is the one you should use in forecasting future values of the time series.

When using the KPK Data Analysis tools within Excel, you will have the option of specifying the smoothing constants or letting Excel determine the optimal smoothing constants. If you elect to use the latter procedure, you will be asked whether you want the smoothing constants that provide the minimum

MAD, minimum MSE, or minimum MAPE. This Excel routine falls under the category of *automated forecasting procedures.* By selecting this option, Excel will determine the optimal smoothing constants by searching in increments of .05. For Example 17.6 using linear and seasonal exponential smoothing (Winters' method) and procedure 2, the optimal smoothing constants are $A = .1$, $B = .6$, and $C = 0$. The smoothing constant for the trend values (B) is rather large for this illustration; however, this set of smoothing constants does provide a minimum MSE of 1,682.06. A final word here: By utilizing optimal smoothing constants, you can drastically simplify the calculations necessary to fit a model to your time series. On the negative side, however, such a "black box" procedure implies that you sacrifice some control and knowledge of the fitting process.

Determining and using optimal smoothing constants does take away one main advantage of exponential smoothing—namely, the computational simplicity of this procedure in calculating and updating smoothed estimates. If you are using this method to perform a small number of forecasts, then this poses no problem. On the other hand, if the technique is being used to forecast future demand levels continuously for thousands of inventory items, then this added complexity is a cause for concern. You will have to consider complexity versus cost on an individual application basis.

You can increase the computational burden (but also improve the accuracy) even more by using different values of the smoothing constant(s) at different times in the analysis of a time series. Such techniques are computer controlled. The constant(s) are changed automatically to adapt the process to shifts in the structure of the time series, using *adaptive control procedures.*

We showed you several forecasting procedures and methods for comparing the predictive accuracy of these techniques. Our purpose is to give you an arsenal of methodologies that will allow you to apply each procedure to a particular time series and then summarize and compare the resulting residuals. In this way, you can determine the most accurate procedure for a particular time series and use this method to arrive at a forecast.

Another forecasting model, the autoregressive model, is described in section 17.8 on the CD that accompanies this textbook. With this procedure, we again use the past observations to predict future values but in a slightly different way: we use the past values as variables in a regression equation.

X Exercises 17.27–17.34

Understanding the Mechanics

17.27 Consider the following data and their forecasts.

Year	Actual	Forecast
1992	10	—
1993	11	10
1994	14	12
1995	18	15
1996	22	17
1997	20	19
1998	19	21
1999	24	23
2000	26	24
2001	40	28

a. Compute the MAD, MAPE, and MSE for these forecasts.

b. Eliminate the data for year 2001. Then recompute the MAD, MAPE, and MSE.

c. Compare the MAD, MAPE, and MSE values in parts a and b.

17.28 The following monthly data were collected. Using the naive model, find the MAD, MAPE, and predictive MSE.

Year	Jan	Feb	Mar	Apr	May	Jun
1998	1	2	2	3	3	4
1999	3	4	4	5	4	6
2000	5	6	7	7	7	6
2001	7	8	8	10	9	11

Year	Jul	Aug	Sep	Oct	Nov	Dec
1998	5	5	6	5	5	4
1999	7	8	10	9	9	8
2000	7	8	9	12	11	10
2001	12	14	14	12	13	11

17.29 Two forecasting procedures produce the following sets of forecast errors:

Year	Month	Procedure 1	Procedure 2
2000	Jan	+5	+1
	Feb	+7	−2
	Mar	+6	+3
	Apr	+2	−1
	May	−1	+2
	June	−2	0
	July	−3	+1
	Aug	+2	+1
	Sept	+4	0
	Oct	+7	−1
	Nov	+6	+2
	Dec	+1	+1
2001	Jan	−3	−3
	Feb	−5	+1
	Mar	−4	0
	Apr	+3	−2
	May	+2	−19
	June	−1	−20

Compute the MAD and predictive MSE for each forecasting procedure. Comment on the adequacy of the forecasting procedure.

Applying the New Concepts

17.30 The following data represent the number of single-family housing starts in a certain sector of the state of California. The units are in 10,000s.

Year	Quarter 1	Quarter 2	Quarter 3	Quarter 4
1998	.6	.8	1.4	.8
1999	.9	1.1	1.7	1.3
2000	1.2	1.4	2.1	1.6
2001	1.4	1.7	2.6	1.9

a. Using the simple exponential procedure with $A = .3$, find the predicted number of housing starts for each time period, omitting the first time period. Find the predictive MSE and MAD.

b. Use Holt's two-parameter linear exponential smoothing technique to obtain a forecast for each time period, omitting the first time period. Let $A = .3$ and $B = .2$. Use the least squares estimate of the slope from the first five periods for the initial value of the slope. Find the predictive MSE and MAD.

c. Compare the forecasts obtained in parts a and b.

17.31 An investor who invested $10,000 into the T. Krow long-term-growth mutual fund would have realized a gain of 93% after five years. The following table shows the value of the $10,000 investment over this period of time.

Year	Quarter 1	Quarter 2	Quarter 3	Quarter 4
1997	10,031	9,638	12,591	12,480
1998	12,691	11,745	13,721	13,980
1999	13,043	12,680	15,376	15,860
2000	14,932	14,280	17,035	17,210
2001	16,830	15,923	18,671	19,300

a. Use Winters' linear and seasonal smoothing technique to find the forecasted value of the original $10,000 invested for each of the quarters of 1999, 2000, and 2001. Let $A = .2$, $B = .1$, and $C = .1$. Using procedure 1 and Winters' technique, set the initial estimates of the seasonal factors to 1.0 and $b_0 = 0$. Find the predictive MSE.

b. Redo part a with $A = .1$, $B = .2$, and $C = .2$. Find the predictive MSE.

c. Compare the forecasts from parts a and b using the predictive MSEs.

17.32 Explain how the MAD, MAPE, and the predictive MSE differ in what they measure. Why should the sum of the forecast errors divided by the number of forecasts not be used to compare two forecasting procedures?

Using the Computer

17.33 [DATA SET EX17-33] *Variable description:*

Year: Year from 1995 through 2001

Quarter: Quarter represented by 1 through 4

AirTripCost: Cost in dollars for a round trip ticket between Seattle and Albuquerque

Value of smoothing constant A: .22

Value of smoothing constant B: .12

Value of smoothing constant C: .10

The cost of a round-trip airline ticket on Sunset Airlines is recorded for each quarter over the years 1995 through 2001. Use Winters' technique to find smoothed values for each of the quarters of 2000 and 2001. This information is important to companies planning their travel budget for the upcoming year. Use procedure 2 and the first two years of data to obtain b_0, S_0, and the four initial seasonal factors. Find the MAPE using this procedure and determine the quarterly forecast of the airfares for the year 2002.

17.34 [DATA SET EX17-34] *Variable description:*

Year: Year from 1994 through 2001

Quarter: Quarter represented by 1 through 4

SubNewsletter: Number of subscriptions to stock market newsletter

Value of smoothing constant A: .25

Value of smoothing constant B: .22

Value of smoothing constant C: .25

The number of subscribers to a stock market investment newsletter has fluctuated over the years. Data on the number of subscriptions for each quarter of the years 1994 through 2001 are collected. The editor of the newsletter will use this information to decide on the future price of the newsletter. For the given smoothing constants, find the predictive MSE using Winters' linear and seasonal exponential smoothing technique. Use Winters' technique with procedure 1, setting the initial estimates of the seasonal factors to 1.0 and let $b_0 = 0$ to find smoothed values for each of the quarters of 2000 and 2001. Change the values of A, B, and C to .10, .05, and .05, respectively. Compare the predictive MSEs for the two sets of smoothing constants.

On the CD . . .

Section 17.8: Autoregressive Forecasting Techniques
Exercises 17.35–17.43
Section 17.9: The Other Side of Forecasting: Linear Regression
Using Time Series Data
Exercises 17.44–17.55
Section 17.10: The Problem of Autocorrelation: The Durbin-
Watson Statistic
Exercises 17.56–17.62

 # Summary

In this chapter, we have looked briefly at several popular **forecasting** techniques. To cover all aspects of time series forecasting would fill an entire textbook. It is a fascinating side of statistics because anyone having a reliable "crystal ball" technique for predicting the future definitely is one step ahead of the game. We hope that this chapter has whetted your appetite to pursue further reading in this area.

Forecasting methods can be divided into two broad categories: qualitative procedures and quantitative techniques. When arriving at a **qualitative** forecast, expert opinion is used to arrive at a best-educated estimate of future behavior. One such method is the **Delphi method,** which requires input from a team of experts. Each team member is then informed as to the responses from all other members and asked to reevaluate his or her opinion in light of this information. This process is continued for several rounds until each member of the team feels confident in his or her final decision.

Quantitative forecasting, the main emphasis of this chapter, dealt with two (sometimes overlapping) sets of procedures: time series techniques and multiple linear regression on time series data. **Time series procedures** attempt to capture the past behavior of the time series and use this information to predict future values. No external predictors are considered; only the past observations are used to describe and predict the future value of the time series variable. Time series methods include (1) the **naïve forecast procedure** where the forecast for the next time period is the observed value for the present period, (2) **projecting the least squares trend line,** which extracts and extends the trend and seasonal components, (3) **exponential smoothing,** which reduces randomness and forecasts future values by using the **smoothed** values, and (4) **autoregressive** forecasting, which predicts future values by using a linear combination of past values.

There are various exponential smoothing procedures; the proper one to use depends on the nature of the time series. **Simple exponential smoothing** works best when the time series contains neither trend nor seasonality. **Linear exponential smoothing** is better for a time series that does contain trend but has no seasonality, and **Winters' linear and seasonal exponential smoothing** should be used for a time series that has both components.

Exponential Smoothing

Type	Structure of Time Series	
	Contains Trend	Contains Seasonality
Simple exponential smoothing	NO	NO
Linear exponential smoothing	YES	NO
Linear and seasonal exponential smoothing	YES	YES

Many factors determine the strengths of any forecasting procedure, including the (1) time horizon of the forecast, (2) **stationarity** of the data, and (3) presence of trend, seasonality, or cyclical activity. To measure the forecast accuracy of a particular method, you can calculate the **predictive mean squared error (MSE),** the **mean absolute deviation (MAD),** or the **mean absolute percentage error (MAPE).** The MSE is found by squaring each of the residuals obtained by applying this technique to the past observations and then deriving the average of these squared residuals. This measure is very sensitive to one or two very large residuals. The MAD is calculated by averaging the absolute values of the residuals and is less sensitive to a single large residual. The MAPE uses the *relative* error of each forecast value to arrive at a measure of prediction accuracy. It is useful for comparing the accuracy of a particular forecasting technique on two different time series, since the effect of the magnitude of the observations has been removed.

The advantage of the time series methods is that there is no need to search for external predictors to explain the behavior of the dependent variable. One disadvantage is that the patterns within the observed values can be extremely complex and difficult to determine. Such methods often are hard to "sell" to managers, who may not be able to understand the technique.

Further Reading

Bowerman, B. L., and R. T. O'Connell, *Time Series and Forecasting: An Applied Approach*, 3rd ed., Pacific Grove, Calif.: Brooks/Cole, 2000

Brockwell, P. J., and R. A. Davis, *Introduction to Time Series and Forecasting*, New York: Springer-Verlag, 1996

Hanke, J., A. Reitsch, and D. W. Wichern, *Business Forecasting*, 7th ed., Upper Saddle River, NJ: Prentice Hall, 2001

Makridakis, S., S. C. Wheelwright, and R. J. Hyndman, *Forecasting: Methods and Applications*, 3rd ed., New York: Wiley, 1997

Mendenhall, W., and T. Sincich, *A Second Course in Statistics: Regression Analysis*, 5th ed., Upper Saddle River, NJ: Prentice-Hall, 1996

Yaffee, R. A., and M. M. McGee, *An Introduction to Time Series Analysis and Forecasting: With Applications to SAS and SPSS*, Burlington, Mass.: Academic Press, 2000

 # Summary of Formulas

Forecasting Models

1. Naïve:

$$\hat{y}_{t+1} = y_t$$

2. Using seasonality and trend:

$$\hat{y}_{t+1} = [b_0 + b_1(t+1)]$$
$$\cdot \text{(seasonal index for period } t+1)$$

3. Simple exponential smoothing:

$$\hat{y}_{t+1} = S_t$$

where

$$S_t = Ay_t + (1-A)S_{t-1}$$
$$0 < A < 1.$$

4. Using Holt's method (exponential smoothing for a time series containing trend):

$$\hat{y}_{t+1} = S_t + b_t$$

where

$$S_t = Ay_t + (1-A)(S_{t-1} + b_{t-1})$$
$$b_t = B(S_t - S_{t-1}) + (1-B)b_{t-1}$$
$$0 < A < 1, \quad 0 < B < 1$$

5. Using Winters' method (exponential smoothing for a time series containing trend and seasonality):

$$\hat{y}_{t+m} = (S_t + mb_t) \cdot F_{t+m-L}$$

where

m = number of periods ahead to be forecast

$L = 4$ for quarterly data, 12 for monthly data

$$S_t = A\left(\frac{y_t}{F_{t-L}}\right) + (1-A)(S_{t-1} + b_{t-1})$$

$$F_t = B\left(\frac{y_t}{S_t}\right) + (1-B)F_{t-L}$$

$$b_t = C(S_t - S_{t-1}) + (1-C)b_{t-1}$$

$$0 < A < 1, \qquad 0 < B < 1, \qquad 0 < C < 1$$

6. Using a pth-order autoregressive model:

$$\hat{y}_{t+1} = b_0 + b_1y_t + b_2y_{t-1} + \cdots + b_py_{t-p+1}$$

Measurements of Forecast Error

$$\text{MAD} = \frac{\sum|e_t|}{n}$$

$$\text{(predictive) MSE} = \frac{\sum e_t^2}{n}$$

$$\text{MAPE} = \frac{\sum\left|\dfrac{e_t}{y_t}\right|}{n}$$

Review Exercises 17.63–17.77

17.63 A set of monthly data has been gathered over three years from January 1999 to December 2001. From these data, the seasonal indexes for the 12 months are found to be

$S_1 = 0.75$ $S_2 = 0.85$ $S_3 = 0.95$ $S_4 = 0.99$ $S_5 = 0.90$ $S_6 = 1.01$

$S_7 = 1.20$ $S_8 = 1.10$ $S_9 = 1.15$ $S_{10} = 1.05$ $S_{11} = 1.11$ $S_{12} = 0.94$

The least squares line through the deseasonalized data is found to be

$$\hat{d}_t = 2.73 + 0.62t$$

for the 36 monthly periods. Find the forecast for monthly periods 37, 38, 39, 40, and 41.

17.64 The median price of existing homes generally moves with business cycles. During the period from June 2000 to May 2001, the economy slowed and there were no major upward shifts in the median price of a home, despite low interest rates. The following data illustrate the values of the median home price in units of thousands from June 2000 to May 2001.

Month and Year	Median Home Price
June 2000	140
July 2000	144
August 2000	144
September 2000	142
October 2000	139
November 2000	140
December 2000	140
January 2001	138
February 2001	139
March 2001	144
April 2001	144
May 2001	145

a. Using simple exponential smoothing with $A = .1$, find the residuals for April 2001 and May 2001.
b. Repeat part a with $A = .3$ and compare the residuals for April 2001 and May 2001.

(Source: "Sales of Existing Homes Slide, but Prices Jump," *The Wall Street Journal*, July 26, 2001, p. A2.)

17.65 The number of employees at Computeron has fluctuated over the past nine years. The following table lists the number of employees on the payroll at Computeron at the end of each year for the years 1993 to 2001. The company would like you to forecast employment in 2002 by using the linear exponential smoothing technique.

Year	Employees	Year	Employees
1993	1030	1998	1075
1994	1020	1999	1130
1995	1941	2000	1135
1996	1050	2001	1175
1997	1062		

a. Using the initial estimate of the slope to be zero with $A = .2$ and $B = .2$, determine the predicted value for the employment at the end of 2002.
b. Using the least squares estimate for the slope from the first three years of data, redo part a.
c. Compare the predicted values in parts a and b.

17.66 Two forecasting procedures were used to forecast the 12 quarters from 1999 to 2001. The forecast errors for each quarter are given on the next page. Compute the predictive MSE and MAD for each forecasting procedure. Interpret the results.

Year	Quarter	Procedure 1 Forecast Error	Procedure 2 Forecast Error
1999	1	−1.0	.7
	2	.5	−.5
	3	−2.1	−.2
	4	2.5	.9
2000	1	.9	.1
	2	2.1	.2
	3	−1.3	−.3
	4	1.6	.9
2001	1	2.7	11.2
	2	−1.9	−.1
	3	2.4	.2
	4	−1.2	−.2

17.67 The amount of money spent on research and development by Energy Today in finding economical uses of alternative fuels is given over a four-year period. Units are in $10,000.

Year	Quarter 1	Quarter 2	Quarter 3	Quarter 4
1998	4.2	4.5	4.8	4.0
1999	4.3	4.7	5.6	4.4
2000	4.6	4.9	5.7	4.5
2001	4.7	5.0	5.8	4.7

Use Holt's two-parameter linear exponential smoothing technique to obtain a forecast for each of the quarters except for the first time period. Let $A = .3$ and $B = .2$. Use the least squares estimate of the trend from the first five periods for the initial value of the slope. Calculate the predictive MSE.

17.68 In Holt's two-parameter linear exponential smoothing technique, why do you think the values of A and B are typically less than or equal to .3? Holt's two-parameter linear exponential smoothing technique would be equivalent to what procedure if A were equal to 1?

17.69 National Finance Company provides short-term loans to consumers to finance household goods. The amount of interest received quarterly is given in units of $10,000.

Year	Quarter 1	Quarter 2	Quarter 3	Quarter 4
1997	20	31	39	42
1998	28	35	43	45
1999	31	38	45	49
2000	35	40	43	52
2001	38	44	48	56

Determine the multiple regression equation that takes into account trend and seasonality.

17.70 An independent gas station allows its customers to buy gasoline on credit. The amount of credit on the books for the 20 quarters of the years 1997 through 2001 follows. Find the multiple regression equation that takes into account trend and seasonality. The figures in the table are in units of $10,000.

Year	Quarter 1	Quarter 2	Quarter 3	Quarter 4
1997	2.3	2.7	3.4	3.0
1998	2.4	3.0	3.6	3.2
1999	2.6	3.1	3.8	3.4
2000	3.0	3.3	4.0	3.2
2001	3.2	3.4	4.4	3.5

17.71 Using Holt's two-parameter linear exponential technique, find the smoothed value at time $t = 12$, where the observed value at $t = 12$ is 13.6 and the observed value at $t = 11$ is 12.1. Also let $S_{11} = 7.4$, $S_{10} = 10.4$, $b_{11} = 0.6$, $A = 1$, and $B = .2$.

17.72 [DATA SET EX17-72] *Variable description:*

Year: Year from 1980 to 2001

OpCap: The percentage of operating capacity used by factories

The percentage of operating capacity used by factories represents a productivity measure that economists use as a leading indicator of economic growth. Rarely do factories operate above 85% of their capacity. These figures fluctuate, depending on the outlook for the economy.

    a. Use Holt's two-parameter linear exponential smoothing technique with procedure 1 to obtain a forecast for each year. Let $A = .25$ and $B = .1$. What is the predictive MSE?

    b. Do a what-if analysis by changing A to be .1 and B to be .25 in part a. How do the results of the forecast compare to those in part a?

(Source: "Industrial Production Falls for Ninth Straight Month," *The Wall Street Journal,* July 18, 2001, p. A2.)

17.73 [DATA SET EX17-73] *Variable description:*

Year: Year from 1970 to 2001

MinWage: Minimum wage adjusted for inflation

After adjusting for inflation, the real value of the minimum wage has actually decreased over the past few years. This is in contrast to the 1970s, in which the real value of the minimum wage generally increased.

    a. Determine whether the minimum wage data from 1970 to 2000 are stationary. If the data are not stationary, determine the first differences. Would you say that the differences are stationary?

    b. Using simple regression analysis, find the regression equation for predicting MinWage using the variable Year. What is the value of the Durbin-Watson statistic? Test for positive autocorrelation of the error terms using a 5% significance level.

(Source: "A Bumpy Road for Those at the Bottom," *The Wall Street Journal,* July 19, 2001, p. A10.)

17.74 [DATA SET EX17-74] *Variable description:*

Year_Month: Year and month from September 1998 to August 2001

IPOs: Number of Initial Public Offerings in the United States

An initial public offering (IPO) is the sale of a publicly tradable stock that has previously been owned privately. Since purchases of IPOs are considered to be riskier than stock purchases for more established firms, financial analysts recommend that an IPO be bought during an economic expansion if the company has growing earnings, good products, and an offering price that when divided by earnings is less than two times the company's earnings growth rate. During economic expansions, the number of IPOs tends to increase, and during recessions, the number of IPOs tends to decrease. Use Winters' linear and seasonal smoothing technique to find the smoothed values for August 2001. Let $A = .3$, $B = .3$, and $C = .1$. Use the first two years of data to determine the seasonal indexes, trend estimate, and S_0.

(Source: "There She Is, Your Ideal," *Newsweek,* August 2001, p. 60.)

17.75 [DATA SET EX17-75] *Variable description:*

Year: Year from 1980 to 1999

China_CDE: Yearly carbon dioxide emissions in million metric tons for China

US_CDE: Yearly carbon dioxide emissions in million metric tons for the United States

Only a few years ago, environmental studies forecasted that China would emerge as the world's leading source of carbon dioxide by year 2020. However, China has adopted an energy planning strategy to make more efficient use of fuels such as coal. Data for yearly carbon dioxide emissions from China and the United States are recorded.

    a. Find the predictive MSE using the following autoregressive equation with the variable China_CDE for the years 1980 to 1999: $\hat{y}_t = b_0 + b_1 y_{t-1} + b_2 y_{t-2}$

    b. Repeat part a with the variable US_CDE.

857

c. Compare the coefficients for the autoregressive equations in parts a and b. For which country would you say an autoregressive equation with two lagged variables is a better predictor?

(Source: "China Said to Reduce Carbon Dioxide Emissions," *New York Times,* June 15, 2001, p. 6A.)

17.76 [DATA SET EX17-76] *Variable description:*

Time: Quarterly time periods numbered 1 through 20

NetProf: Quarterly net profit for school supply store

X_1: Dummy variable equal to 1 to indicate the first quarter

X_2: Dummy variable equal to 1 to indicate the second quarter

X_3: Dummy variable equal to 1 to indicate the third quarter

The manager of a school supply store kept track of the store's quarterly net profit, measured in thousands of dollars, for the five years since the store's opening. As the store's business grew, the manager noticed that profits were magnified according to seasonal effect. Therefore, by multiplying the Time variable by the dummy variables, the manager created new variables: TimeX1, TimeX2, and TimeX3. These variables are used to include the effects of interaction between the time variable and the dummy variables representing the quarter.

a. From the computer printout, would you say that the interaction terms are useful in explaining quarterly net profit?

b. What is the predictive MSE for the model using all of the independent variables, including the interaction terms? Use the computer to run a regression analysis for the model using all the independent variables but excluding the interaction terms, and find the predictive MSE. Compare these two predictive MSEs.

Summary Output

Regression Statistics

Multiple R	0.9970122
R Square	0.9940333
Adjusted R Square	0.9905528
Standard Error	1.1999653
Observations	20

ANOVA

	df	SS	MS	F	Significance F
Regression	7	2878.6505	411.235786	285.5969	2.22086E-12
Residual	12	17.279	1.43991667		
Total	19	2895.9295			

	Coefficients	Standard Error	t Stat	P-value	Lower 95%	Upper 95%
Intercept	−0.1	1.2585342	−0.0794575	0.937978	−2.842110415	2.6421104
Time	0.545	0.09486558	5.74497065	9.24E-05	0.33830565	0.7516943
X1	0.1275	1.61271494	0.07905923	0.938289	−3.386303943	3.6413039
X2	−0.71	1.66488425	−0.4264561	0.677326	−4.337471113	2.9174711
X3	0.3	1.72070585	0.17434706	0.8645	−3.449095933	4.0490959
TimeX1	−0.2925	0.13416019	−2.1802294	0.049873	−0.584809952	−0.00019
TimeX2	0.58	0.13416019	4.32318985	0.000991	0.287690048	0.87231
TimeX3	1.855	0.13416019	13.8267537	9.83E-90	1.562690048	2.14731

17.77 The manager of the school supply store in Exercise 17.76 decided to investigate another regression model, involving four independent variables. The independent variables contain quarterly net profit lagged by one through four periods and are labeled as NetProfLag1, NetProfLag2, NetProfLag3, and NetProfLag4.

a. From the computer printout, which lagged variables are useful in explaining quarterly net profit?

b. Compare the predictive MSE for this model with that found in Exercise 17.76 part b.

Summary Output

Regression Statistics

Multiple R	0.97892864
R Square	0.95830129
Adjusted R Square	0.94313812
Standard Error	3.07675185
Observations	16

ANOVA

	df	SS	MS	F	Significance F
Regression	4	2393.07895	598.269738	63.1992749	1.6143E-07
Residual	11	104.130421	9.46640194		
Total	15	2497.20938			

	Coefficients	Standard Error	t Stat	P-value	Lower 95%	Upper 95%
Intercept	5.11893227	1.74265482	2.93743329	0.01350962	1.28337294	8.9544916
NetProfLag1	−0.0614597	0.07275105	−0.8447948	0.41622153	−0.2215838	0.0986644
NetProfLag2	−0.1286208	0.08929934	−1.4403333	0.1776229	−0.3251674	0.0679258
NetProfLag3	-0.0339803	0.09040588	−0.3758637	0.71416607	−0.2329624	0.1650018
NetProfLag4	1.17197573	0.08949793	13.0950045	4.718E-08	0.97499203	1.3689594

Insights from Statistics in Action

Going Postal with Forecasting Techniques: Determining Which Methods Receive the Stamp of Approval

The Statistics in Action introductory case study mentioned that forecasting models allow managers to use numbers such as projected cost and revenue (rather than feelings) to make critical decisions. The USPS must be able to accurately forecast its future revenue because it receives no taxpayer subsidy and hence must decide how fast to boost prices and how to manage costs. Twenty-two years of annual revenue data for the USPS are listed in StatIn ActChap17.xls. For each of the following questions, use the first 19 observations as past values and forecast the values for years 1999, 2000, and 2001. Since the true values of these three years are given in the data set, a comparison can be made on the accuracy of the forecasting procedures used in answering the following questions.

1. Using simple exponential smoothing with a smoothing constant of .2, find the predictive MSE for the first 19 observations. What are the predicted values for 1999, 2000, and 2001?

2. Using Holt's two-parameter linear exponential technique with both smoothing constants equal to .2 and with zero as the initial estimate of the slope, find the predictive MSE for the first 19 observations. What are the predicted values for 1999, 2000, and 2001?

3. Repeat part 2 using the least squares estimate from the first five years as the initial slope estimate.

4. Using an autoregressive model with only one lagged independent variable that has a lag of one time period, find the predictive MSE for the first 19 observations. What are the predicted values for 1999, 2000, and 2001? Repeat using two lagged independent variables—one having a lag of one time period and the other having a lag of two time periods.

5. Compare the results from the techniques used in answering questions 1, 2, 3, and 4. Which technique would you recommend to the management of the USPS for making future decisions? Why?

Sources: "The Ugly Hybrid Behind the Mailbox," *The Wall Street Journal*, December 13, 2001, p. 1A. "Postal Service and FedEx Form Business Alliance," *Direct Marketing*, March 2001, p. 18.

Appendix SPSS®

Chapter 17 Appendix: Data Analysis with SPSS

Forecasting Using Trend

For data containing a strong linear or quadratic trend, a simple trend equation often provides an excellent method of coming up with short-term forecasts. The SPSS procedure for obtaining such a prediction equation will be illustrated using the Coca-Cola annual gross revenue data discussed in Example 17.8. Enter the years 1986–2000 in the first column and the revenue data in the second column.

	year	revenue
1	1986	8669
2	1987	7658
3	1988	8338
4	1989	8966
5	1990	10261
6	1991	11599
7	1992	13119
8	1993	14030
9	1994	16264
10	1995	18127
11	1996	18673
12	1997	18868
13	1998	18813
14	1999	19805
15	2000	20458

Click on **Analyze ➤ Regression ➤ Curve Estimation.** Fill in the **Curve Estimation** dialog box as shown below. Note that **Time** will be the predictor variable and is checked in the **Independent** frame. After clicking on **OK,** the output immediately following this dialog box will appear in the display pane. The addition of the quadratic term into the model did not produce a significant increase in R^2 (from 95.5% using the linear model to 95.6% using the quadratic model) so the forecasts will be made using the linear trend equation, $\hat{y}_t = 5991.06 + 1031.52t$.

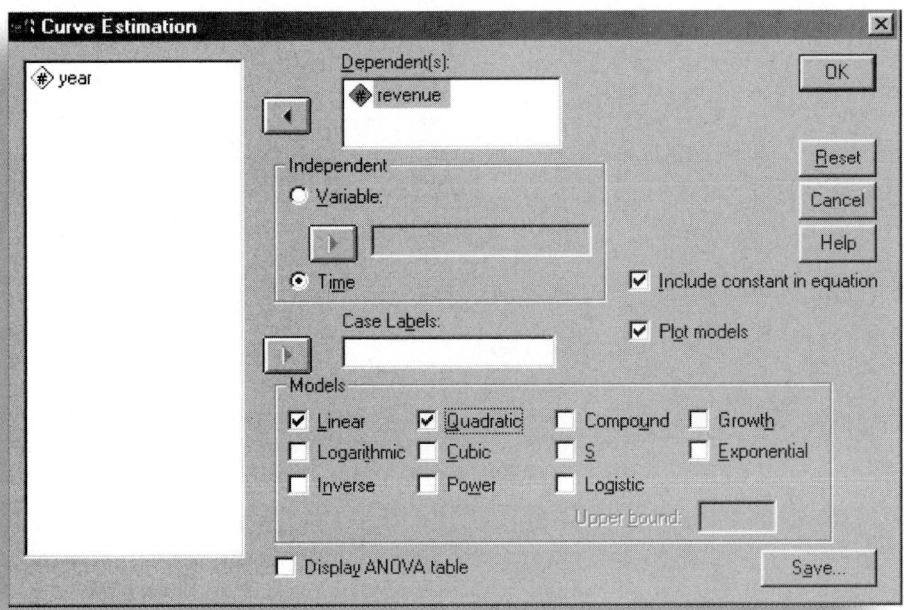

Curve Fit

MODEL: MOD_3.

Independent: Time

Dependent	Mth	Rsq	d.f.	F	Sigf	b0	b1	b2
REVENUE	LIN	.955	13	276.50	.000	5991.06	1031.52	
REVENUE	QUA	.956	12	131.30	.000	5558.17	1184.30	−9.5490

Obtaining a Forecast

To obtain the forecast for the year 2001, click on **Analyze ➤ Regression ➤ Curve Estimation.** Fill in the **Curve Estimation** dialog box as before, but omit **Quadratic** in the **Models** frame. Click on **Save** and fill in the dialog box as shown next.

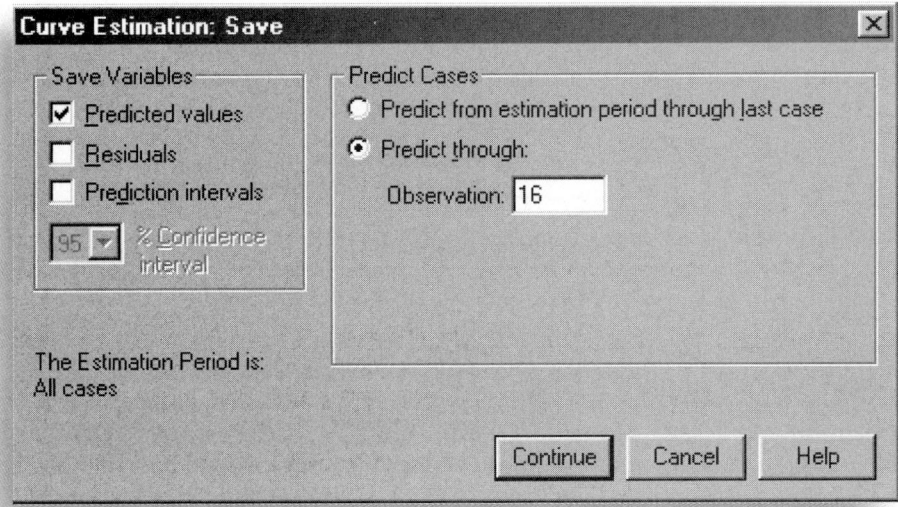

The resulting output will appear in the data window. The forecasts for each year are in the fit_1 column and the forecast for the year 2001 is seen to be 22,495.

	year	revenue	fit_1
1	1986	8669	7022.575
2	1987	7658	8054.093
3	1988	8338	9085.611
4	1989	8966	10117.13
5	1990	10261	11148.65
6	1991	11599	12180.16
7	1992	13119	13211.68
8	1993	14030	14243.20
9	1994	16264	15274.72
10	1995	18127	16306.24
11	1996	18673	17337.75
12	1997	18868	18369.27
13	1998	18813	19400.79
14	1999	19805	20432.31
15	2000	20458	21463.83
16	.	.	22495.34

Comparing the Predicted and Observed Values

To compare the predicted and observed values, click on **Transform ➤ Compute.** To calculate the MAD value, enter "mad" in the **Target Variable** box and "abs(revenue - fit_1)" in the **Numeric Expression** box. Next, click on **Analyze ➤ Descriptive Statistics ➤ Descriptive.** Move the mad variable into the **Variable(s)** box and click on **Options.** Click on the box alongside **Mean** (uncheck all the others) and click on **OK.** The following result appears in the display pane. The computed MAD value is seen to be 838.7, which agrees with the result contained in Table 17.8 using this model. To compute the MSE value, replace "abs(revenue - fit_1)" with "(revenue - fit_1)**2" in the previous **Numeric Expression** box and to compute the MAPE value use "abs((revenue - fit_1)/revenue)" in this box.

Descriptive Statistics

	N	Mean
MAD	15	838.7262
Valid N (listwise)	15	

Exponential Smoothing: Simple and Holt's Method

The SPSS procedures to carry out simple exponential smoothing (section 17.4) and Holt's linear exponential smoothing (section 17.5) are nearly identical. Holt's procedure will be illustrated using the city tax data in Example 17.5. Enter these 20 values in the first column and name this variable "taxes". Click on **Analyze ➤ Time Series ➤ Exponential Smoothing.** Move the variable labeled taxes into the **Variables** box, click on **Holt** and on **Parameters.** To duplicate the results using procedure 1 (as defined in section 17.5), fill in the boxes as shown below. Note that SPSS refers to the first smoothing constant (A) as alpha (set equal to .1) and the smoothing constant in the trend equation (B) as gamma (set equal to .3). Note also that SPSS is able to carry out a grid search to determine the optimal smoothing constants. After clicking on **Continue** and **OK,** two additional columns, fit_1 and err_1, will appear in the display pane. The residuals in the err_1 column agree with those in Table 17.3.

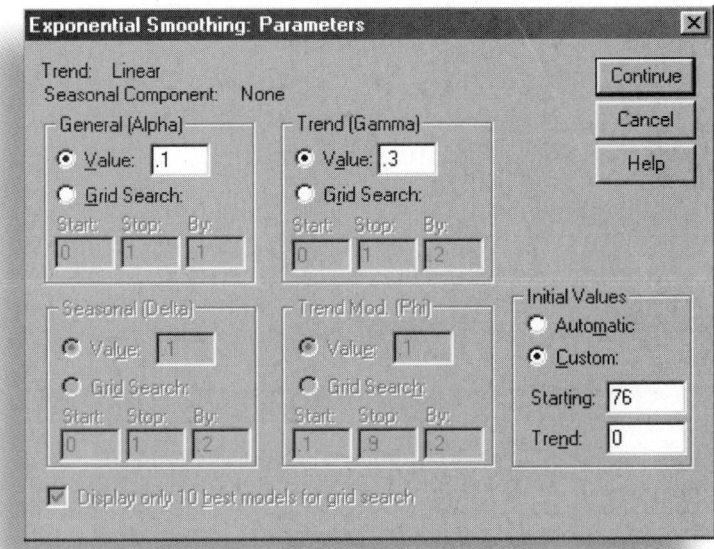

	taxes	fit_1	err_1
1	76	76.00000	.00000
2	93	76.00000	17.00000
3	108	78.21000	29.79000
4	128	82.59270	45.40730
5	196	89.89935	106.1007
6	175	106.4584	68.54165
7	141	121.3177	19.68229
8	236	131.8816	104.1184
9	256	154.0126	101.9874
10	190	178.9902	11.00979
11	227	195.2003	31.79969
12	299	214.4434	84.55661
13	403	241.4989	161.5011
14	282	281.0938	.90617
15	288	304.6565	-16.6565
16	387	325.9632	61.03683
17	484	356.8703	127.1297
18	384	398.2006	-14.2006
19	330	424.9719	-94.9719
20	497	440.8168	56.18317
21			
22			

Data View / Variable View

Comments

In the preceding **Exponential Smoothing: Parameters** dialog box, one option is to click on **Automatic** in the **Initial Values** frame to let SPSS determine the initial values for S_0 and b_0. The values calculated by SPSS are

Simple exponential smoothing: $S_0 = \bar{y}$ (average of the T values in the time series)

Holt's linear exponential smoothing: $b_0 = (y_T - y_1)/(T - 1)$ and $S_0 = y_1 - (\frac{1}{2})b_0$

Using the Residuals

The residuals in the err_1 column can be used to compute the MAD, MSE, and MAPE values. To compute the MSE, the portion of the SPSS output shown below allows for an easy calculation of this value since the predictive MSE = SSE/$(n-1)$ = 10,7731.5/19 = 5,670.1. Notice that SSE value is divided by $n-1$ (= 19, here) since the err_1 value of zero in the first row should be ignored.

The SSE is:	Alpha	Gamma	SSE
	.1000000	.3000000	107731.47715

Exponential Smoothing: Winters' Method

Winters' linear and seasonal exponential smoothing procedure will be illustrated using the city tax data in Example 17.5. Enter these 20 values in the first column and name this variable taxes. Click on **Data > Define Dates.** Select **Years, quarters** from the **Cases Are** list. Enter "1997" in the **Year** box inside the **First Case Is** frame. This creates an additional three columns in the data window, as shown below.

	taxes	year_	quarter_	date_
1	76	1997	1	Q1 1997
2	93	1997	2	Q2 1997
3	108	1997	3	Q3 1997
4	128	1997	4	Q4 1997
5	196	1998	1	Q1 1998
6	175	1998	2	Q2 1998
7	141	1998	3	Q3 1998
8	236	1998	4	Q4 1998
9	256	1999	1	Q1 1999
10	190	1999	2	Q2 1999
11	227	1999	3	Q3 1999
12	299	1999	4	Q4 1999
13	403	2000	1	Q1 2000
14	282	2000	2	Q2 2000
15	288	2000	3	Q3 2000
16	387	2000	4	Q4 2000
17	484	2001	1	Q1 2001
18	384	2001	2	Q2 2001
19	330	2001	3	Q3 2001
20	497	2001	4	Q4 2001
21				
22				

Data View / Variable View

The Winters' procedure used by SPSS will not duplicate either of the two procedures described in Section 17.6 for setting the initial seasonal factors, trend estimate, and smoothed value. The SPSS calculations for Winters' method will be illustrated by letting SPSS select the initial values and the optimal smoothing constants will be determined using a grid search procedure. Click on **Analyze ➤ Time Series ➤ Exponential Smoothing.** Move the variable labeled taxes into the **Variables** box, click on **Winters** and on **Parameters.** Specify the grid search (using increments of .1 for all three smoothing constants) as shown in the dialog box below. Click on **Continue** and **OK.**

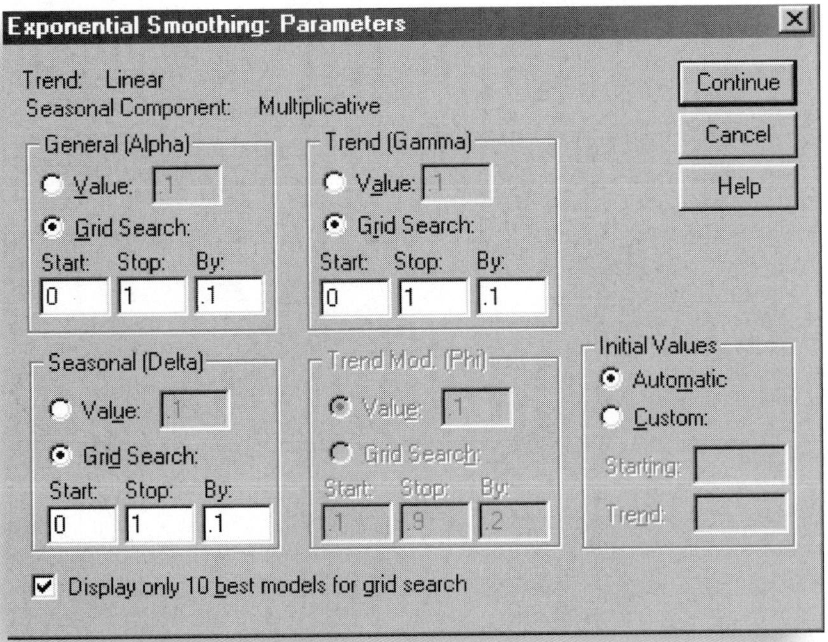

According to the following output, the optimal smoothing constants are (A = .1, B = 0, C = 0) and the minimum SSE value is 7,670.56. Note that SPSS refers to A as alpha, B as gamma, and C as delta.

Initial values:	Series	Trend
	60.93750	20.15625

DFE = 15.

The 10 smallest SSE's are:	Alpha	Gamma	Delta	SSEE
	.1000000	.0000000	.0000000	7670.56295
	.1000000	.1000000	.0000000	7918.29495
	.2000000	.0000000	.0000000	7959.95841
	.1000000	.2000000	.0000000	8300.14336
	.1000000	.0000000	.1000000	8325.92753
	.0000000	.0000000	.1000000	8377.93704
	.0000000	.1000000	.1000000	8377.93704
	.0000000	.2000000	.1000000	8377.93704
	.0000000	.3000000	.1000000	8377.93704
	.0000000	.4000000	.1000000	8377.93704

The initial trend estimate (b_0) is 20.15625. For quarterly data, SPSS calculates this value using (average of y values for the final year) minus (average of y values for the first year) divided by [4 × (number of years in the time series – 1)]. For the city tax data used here, this would be

$$\frac{423.75 - 101.25}{(4)(4)} = 20.15625$$

For monthly data, the denominator becomes [(12 × (number of years in the time series – 1)]. The initial time smoothed value (S_0) is set equal to

(average of y values for the first year) – $2b_0$ = 101.25 – (2)(20.15625) = 60.9375

For monthly data, $2b_0$ should be replaced by $6b_0$.

As a result of this procedure, the data window will contain two additional columns; the fitted values (fit_1) and the residuals (err_1), as shown below.

	taxes	year_	quarter_	date_	fit_1	err_1
1	76	1997	1	Q1 1997	100.0928	-24.0928
2	93	1997	2	Q2 1997	89.32983	3.67017
3	108	1997	3	Q3 1997	99.15935	8.84065
4	128	1997	4	Q4 1997	146.5647	-18.5647
5	196	1998	1	Q1 1998	196.8146	-.81457
6	175	1998	2	Q2 1998	161.5225	13.47752
7	141	1998	3	Q3 1998	166.4490	-25.4490
8	236	1998	4	Q4 1998	226.7555	9.24449
9	256	1999	1	Q1 1999	295.3979	-39.3979
10	190	1999	2	Q2 1999	230.5632	-40.5632
11	227	1999	3	Q3 1999	224.9688	2.03123
12	299	1999	4	Q4 1999	303.6903	-4.69030
13	403	2000	1	Q1 2000	385.1528	17.84718
14	282	2000	2	Q2 2000	300.1537	-18.1537
15	288	2000	3	Q3 2000	291.0244	-3.02443
16	387	2000	4	Q4 2000	386.0025	.99752
17	484	2001	1	Q1 2001	483.6284	.37165
18	384	2001	2	Q2 2001	370.6542	13.34579
19	330	2001	3	Q3 2001	358.7529	-28.7529
20	497	2001	4	Q4 2001	467.8193	29.18075
21						
22						

Data View / Variable View

The residuals in the err_1 column can be used to compute the MAD, MSE, and MAPE measures of fit. For this illustration, the MSE is easily calculated, since the SSE using the optimal smoothing constants was previously determined to be 7,670.56. Consequently, the predictive MSD = SSE/n = 7,670.56/20 = 383.53. Notice that the SSE values is divided by n (= 20, here) because 20 fitted values were determined.

Autocorrelations

The quarterly sales data for Video-Comp from Example 17.11 will be used for this illustration. Enter these 16 values in the first column and name this variable "sales." To construct a plot of the sample autocorrelations, click on **Graphs ➤ Time Series ➤ Autocorrelations.** Move the sales variable into the **Variables** box and click on **OK.**

The following output will appear in the display pane. As discussed in Example 17.11, there is clear evidence of seasonality in the data.

Autocorrelations: SALES

Lag	Auto-Corr.	Stand. Err.
1	.541	.228
2	.105	.220
3	.280	.212
4	.473	.204
5	.122	.195
6	−.232	.186
7	−.087	.177
8	.063	.167
9	−.176	.156
10	−.422	.144
11	−.279	.132
12	−.121	.118
13	−.234	.102
14	−.343	.083

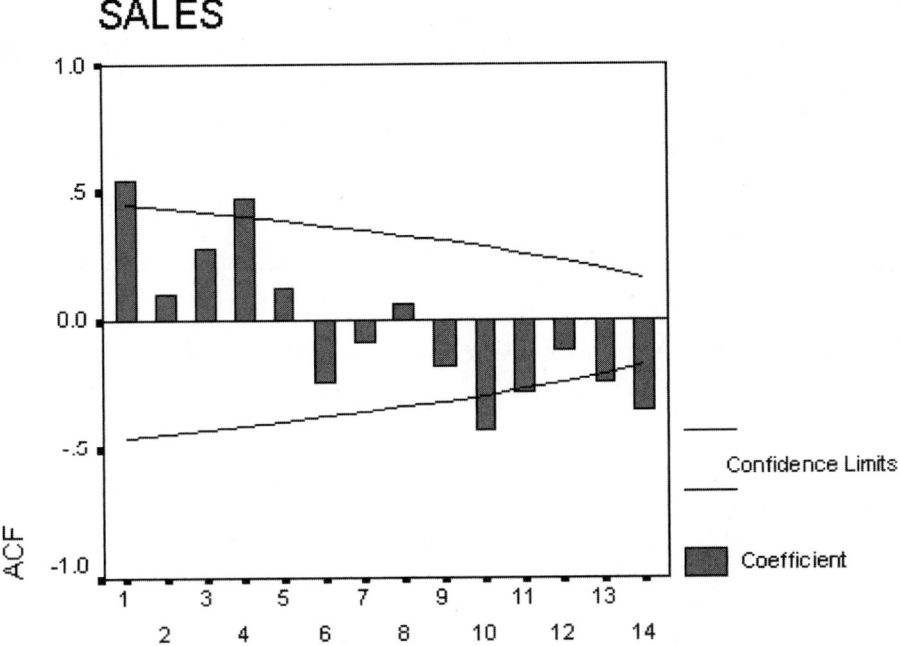

Using the First Differences

As mentioned in Section 17.8, stationarity can often be achieved by using the first differences when seasonality is present in the original time series values. Using the sales data in Example 17.11, to obtain a plot of the autocorrelations for the first differences, click on **Graphs > Time Series > Autocorrelations.** Move the sales variable into the **Variables** box, click on the box alongside **Difference** in the **Transform** frame, and click on **OK.**. The following graph will appear as part of the output in the display pane.

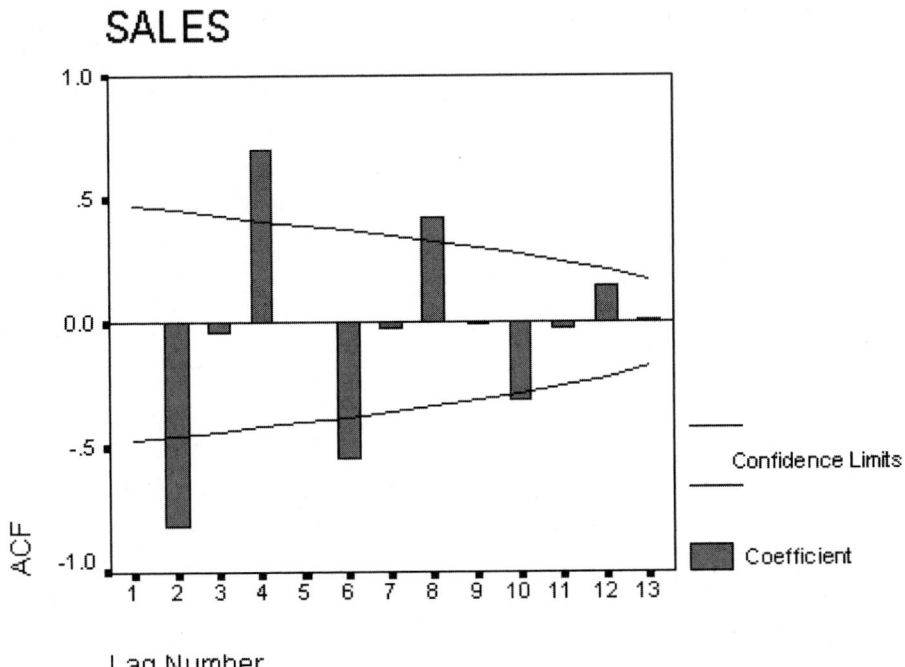

Creating a Lagged Variable

To create a lagged variable, click on **Transform ➤ Compute.** To lag the sales data in Example 17.11 by, say, two periods, **enter** "lagsale2" in the **Target Variable** box and "lag(sales,2)" in the **Numeric Expression** box. The lagged values will appear in the lagsale2 column within the data window.

On the CD . . .
Chapter 17 Appendix: Data Analysis with MINITAB

Nonparametric Statistics $\boxed{X}$

Statistics in Action
Putting Service Back into Customer Service: Assessing Survey Data to Get Blue Oval Certified

Delighting customers is good business because it is profitable. One of Ford's strategies for raising its bottom line is to delight more customers by rolling out its Blue Oval program. The Blue Oval plan uses customer surveys on a dealer's operating practices and service quality, as well as its physical appearance, to certify a dealership as having achieved a high level of customer satisfaction. To get certified and bear the prestigious blue thumbprint symbol, a dealership must pass a certification process. The blue thumbprint is a reminder that each customer is unique.

How seriously do dealerships take this certification? John Luciano, general manager of Town & Country Ford in Madison, Tennessee, says, "My whole life depends on my scores right now. I've had my scores blown up at Kinko's and posted where customers can see how well I'm treating people." Dealers that are Blue Oval certified get an average rebate of 1.25% of a vehicle's invoice price from Ford on every new vehicle they sell. Dealerships are certified annually when their customer surveys indicate more than 50% of the respondents are "completely satisfied" with their sales or service experience. Dealers know that customers must think of Ford as standing for 100% guaranteed satisfaction, not "Fix or Repair Daily."

Ford, the No. 2 automaker in the United States, is the top manufacturer of *light-duty trucks,* which include pickups, sport-utility vehicles and minivans. However, its market share of cars is declining. In fact, Honda and Toyota now

own the mid-size sedan segment, while BMW, Audi, Mercedes-Benz, and Lexus are dividing up the luxury sedan segment, territory formerly held by Cadillac and Lincoln. One of the most important consumers of trucks is affluent baby boomers. When this segment of the population reaches 55 and does not need the room or utility of a truck, what will they buy? Ford must be ready in case there is a shift in the demand for trucks. Customers who are satisfied with their truck or SUV might be prime Ford customers when they are ready to switch to a comfortable car in their golden years.

Customer surveys can help identify differences in consumer behavior, which is known to be fickle. Analysis of these surveys can assist dealers in focusing on what customers value in a car-buying or leasing experience. Customers may expect additional services such as making appointments over the Internet or quickly getting a rental car when their vehicle is being serviced. The Blue Oval program tells dealers that it is not enough to sell vehicles to customers just because their families have always bought Fords. They have to learn to delight these customers with their deal-ership experience. Nonparametric statistics can be important to interpreting survey data to assist automotive dealers in identifying strategies to delight customers. When you have completed this chapter, you will be able to

- Use nonparametric statistical procedures with data, such as ranking customer preferences or competitors, that are clearly not normally distributed and may not comply with the assumptions of standard statistical analyses such as analysis of variance or *t* tests.
- Determine if a sequence of observations is randomly generated.
- Discuss an alternative to simple regression analysis that is much less sensitive to outliers in your data.

A Look Back/Introduction

In the previous chapters, we introduced a large assortment of tests of hypothesis. These tests generally were concerned with such quantities as the mean and the variance of a population. A mean, variance, or proportion is referred to as a *parameter* in statistics, and so these tests are called *parametric tests* of hypothesis. The common underlying assumption in testing a parameter from a continuous population is that this population has a *normal* distribution. Any time you use a *t* statistic, you assume a normal population distribution. When you test more than two means using the ANOVA procedure, you also assume that the shape of the populations is normal.

What can you do if you have reason to believe that the populations under study are not normally distributed? For example, suppose that data collected previously from these populations have been extremely skewed (not symmetric). One option when dealing with means or proportions is to collect large samples. In such a situation, the Central Limit Theorem assures us that the distribution of the sample estimators is approximately normal *regardless* of the population distribution. The other alternative, particularly for small or moderate sample sizes, is to use a **nonparametric statistical procedure technique** that deals with cases in which the assumptions of normality are not true.

Many of the nonparametric statistical tests try to answer the same sorts of questions as do those tests discussed previously. With these tests, however, the assumptions can be relaxed considerably. In earlier chapters, means and medians were referred to as *measures of central tendency*. A nonparametric test concerning such a measure does not assume an underlying normal population—unlike its parametric counterpart. Consequently, nonparametric methods are used for situations that violate the assumptions of the parametric procedures.

A common method for practically all nonparametric techniques is the use of **ranks**. Given a set of data, we obtain a set of ranks by replacing each data value by its relative *position*. To illustrate this idea, consider the following eight observations:

$$10.8, 6.4, 11.7, 5.3, 9.5, 2.5, 15.1, 10.4$$

Arranged in order, these are

Position	1	2	3	4	5	6	7	8
Value	2.5	5.3	6.4	9.5	10.4	10.8	11.7	15.1

We say that the rank of the value 2.5 is 1, the rank of the value 5.3 is 2, and so forth. Replacing each value by its rank and maintaining the original order produces

$$6, 3, 7, 2, 4, 1, 8, 5$$

Most nonparametric procedures use these eight *ranks* rather than the original data values. *By using ranks, we are able to relax the assumptions regarding the underlying populations and develop tests that apply to a wider variety of situations.*

You often will encounter an application in which a numeric measurement is extremely difficult to obtain, but a rank value is not. One example is a consumer taste test; each participant finds it much easier to rank several different brands of soft drinks than to assign a numeric value to each one. The data for analysis consist of the rank assigned to each brand.

Such data are said to be *ordinal* because only the relative position of each value has any meaning (see Chapter 1). This form of data is "weaker" than the *interval* form, for which not only the positions but also the *differences* between data values are meaningful. In this text, we have dealt mostly with interval or ratio data. Data consisting of temperatures, for example, are interval data; the difference between 60° F and 70° F is the same as the difference between 65° F and 75° F (10° F). When dealing with ranks, this is not the case; there is no reason to assume that the difference between ranks 1 and 3 is the same as that between ranks 3 and 5.

In Chapter 13 we introduced one nonparametric procedure that used the chi-square statistic to test for goodness-of-fit or independence between two classifications. In this chapter, we examine other popular nonparametric methods used in a business setting. These tests of hypothesis by no means constitute all the nonparametric techniques used in practice, but they should provide you with a basis for knowing how and when to apply such a method to a particular set of sample data.

18.1 A TEST FOR RANDOMNESS: THE RUNS TEST

The concept of *randomness* is a crucial assumption behind a great many statistical procedures. In the earlier chapters, all samples were assumed to be random. The reliability of any statistical test—even if run on a high-powered computer—is suspect if the sample was not obtained in a random manner. Similarly, the t and F tests in linear regression contain the assumption that the resulting sample residuals are *independent*, with no observable pattern. This assumption implies that the *signs* of these errors should be random.

Examining Sequences

When you examine a sequence of observations or residuals, one method of detecting a lack of randomness is to observe the number of runs contained in the sequence. For a sequence containing two possible values (*A* and *B*, + and −, and so on), a **run** consists of a string of identical values.

Suppose we flip a coin 10 times, where each flip results in a head (H) or a tail (T). Consider the following three outcomes, each containing five heads and five tails.

Sequence 1	H	H	H	H	H	T	T	T	T	T
Sequence 2	H	T	H	T	H	T	H	T	H	T
Sequence 3	T	H	H	H	T	H	T	H	T	T

Only sequence 3 exhibits a random pattern. To see why, we will examine each sequence.

Sequence 1. These 10 observations contain only two runs:

$$\underbrace{\text{H H H H H}}_{\text{Run 1}} \quad \underbrace{\text{T T T T T}}_{\text{Run 2}}$$

The small number of runs is unlikely if this sequence was generated in a random manner.

Sequence 2. At first glance, this pattern may appear to be random, but there are an excessive number of runs (10):

$$\underbrace{\text{H T H T H T H T H T}}_{\substack{\text{Run 1} \qquad \qquad \text{Run 10}}}$$

Once again, the process that generated this sequence is unlikely to be random because of the large number of runs.

Sequence 3. This sequence seems to be a compromise between the first two, exhibiting neither too few runs nor too many.

$$\underline{\text{T H H H T H T H T T}}$$
$$\text{Run 1} \qquad\qquad \text{Run 7}$$

It appears that the sequence was generated in a random manner.

In this section, we use the runs test statistical procedure to test for randomness using the number of observed runs.

The Runs Test (Small Samples)

Consider a sequence of n observations, containing n_1 symbols of the first type (H, in our example) and n_2 symbols of the second type (T). So, $n = n_1 + n_2$. Let

$$R = \text{number of runs within these } n \text{ observations}$$

The situation we consider here is for small samples, where $n_1 \leq 20$ and $n_2 \leq 20$. We will demonstrate that this particular nonparametric technique is indeed distribution free; that is, it makes no assumptions about the population of H's and T's.

For the coin-tossing illustration, there are $n_1 = 5$ H's and $n_2 = 5$ T's. How many such arrangements (permutations) of these 10 symbols are there?* There are 252, partially listed in Table 18.1. This value in general can be found using

> **number of arrangements** $= A = \dfrac{n!}{n_1! \, n_2!}$ 18.1

where $n = n_1 + n_2$. For this illustration,

$$A = \frac{10!}{5!5!} = \frac{(10)(9)(8)(7)(6)}{(5)(4)(3)(2)} = 252$$

Each of these 252 arrangements is equally likely to occur, *providing* the process generating this sequence is *random,* so each has probability $1/252 = .004$.

A tally of all 252 arrangements would reveal the distribution of runs described in Table 18.2. Using the far-right column of Table 18.2, we can say, for example, that $P(R \leq 4) = .167$, since 16.7% of the arrangements had four or fewer runs. This probability is obtained *without* assuming any probability distribution for the underlying population (process) that generated a sequence of $n_1 = 5$ values of H and $n_2 = 5$ values of T. This is the beauty of nonparametric methods.

---

*The formula for the number of permutations given in Chapter 4 does not apply here because the 10 objects (symbols) are not all different (distinct).

TABLE

18.1

Partial list of the 252 arrangements for $n_1 = 5$ and $n_2 = 5$.

Arrangement Number	Arrangement	Number of Runs	
1	H H H H H T T T T T	2	← sequence 1
2	H H H H T H T T T T	4	
3	H H H H T T H T T T	4	
4	H H H H T T T H T T	4	
5	H H H H T T T T H T	4	
⋮			
130	T H H H H T T T H T	5	
131	T H H H H T T T T H	4	
132	T H H H T H H T T T	5	
133	T H H H T H T H T T	7	← sequence 3
134	T H H H T H T T H T	7	
⋮			
248	T T T T H H H H T H	4	
249	T T T T H H H T H H	4	
250	T T T T H H T H H H	4	
251	T T T T H T H H H H	4	
252	T T T T T H H H H H	2	

TABLE

18.2

Distribution of runs for $n_1 = 5$ and $n_2 = 5$.

Number of Runs (R)	Number of Times R Occurred	Relative Frequency	Cumulative Relative Frequency
2	2	.008	.008
3	8	.032	.040
4	32	.127	.167
5	48	.190	.357
6	72	.286	.643
7	48	.190	.833
8	32	.127	.960
9	8	.032	.992
10	2	.008	1.000
	252	1.000	

The hypotheses under investigation here are

H_0: the sequence was generated in a random manner

H_a: the sequence was not generated in a random manner

As mentioned earlier, we reject H_0 whenever the number of runs is too small (say, whenever $R \leq k_1$) or too large (say, whenever $R \geq k_2$).

For a significance level of $\alpha = .05$, what we need is the *largest* value of k_1 such that

$$P(R \leq k_1) \leq \frac{\alpha}{2} = .025$$

and the *smallest* value of k_2 such that

$$P(R \geq k_2) \leq \frac{\alpha}{2} = .025$$

For the case of $n_1 = 5$ and $n_2 = 5$, what are k_1 and k_2? Referring to Table 18.2, we see that for $k_1 = 2$ and $k_1 = 3$ we have $P(R \leq 2) = .008$ and $P(R \leq 3) = .040$.

Consequently, $k_1 = 2$. Also from Table 18.2,

$$P(R \geq 9) = 1 - P(R \leq 8)$$
$$= 1 - .960 = .040$$

and

$$P(R \geq 10) = 1 - P(R \leq 9)$$
$$= 1 - .992 = .008$$

and so $k_2 = 10$. Thus we reject H_0 if $R \leq 2$ or $R \geq 10$.

Table A.15 contains values of k_1 and k_2 for values of n_1 and $n_2 \leq 20$. A portion of this table is shown in Table 18.3. For each pair of numbers, the top number is k_1 and the bottom number is k_2. For the case of $n_1 = 5$ and $n_2 = 5$ (boxed in Table 18.3), we see that $k_1 = 2$ and $k_2 = 10$, as before.

We can summarize this testing procedure as follows:

Hypotheses

H_0: the sequence was generated in a random manner

H_a: the sequence was not generated in a random manner

Test Statistic (for Small Samples). R, where R denotes the number of runs in the sequence.

Procedure

Reject H_0 if $R \leq k_1$ or $R \geq k_2$

where k_1 and k_2 are the top and bottom values, respectively, in Table A.15. This table assumes $\alpha = .05$.

EXAMPLE 18.1

Using a significance level of .05, determine which of the three sequences of H's and T's in the earlier discussion were generated in a random manner.

Solution Using Table 18.3 (or Table A.15), we previously determined that $k_1 = 2$ and $k_2 = 10$, and so we reject H_0 if $R \leq 2$ or $R \geq 10$. The results are:

For sequence 1: $R = 2$, so reject H_0

For sequence 2: $R = 10$, so reject H_0

For sequence 3: $R = 7$, so fail to reject H_0

For the first two sequences we conclude that these arrangements were not the result of a random process. For the third sequence, we have no reason to suspect the presence of a nonrandom process.

The Runs Test (Large Samples)

For large samples ($n_1 > 20$ or $n_2 > 20$), the approximate distribution for R if the generating process is random will be *normal* with mean

$$\mu_R = 1 + \frac{2n_1 n_2}{n_1 + n_2} \qquad \text{18.2}$$

and standard deviation

$$\sigma_R = \sqrt{\frac{2n_1 n_2 (2n_1 n_2 - n_1 - n_2)}{(n_1 + n_2)^2 (n_1 + n_2 - 1)}} \qquad \text{18.3}$$

TABLE

18.3

A portion of Table A.15 for the runs test. For each pair of numbers, the top value is k_1 and the bottom value is k_2. This table assumes $\alpha = .05$.

	The Larger of n_1 and n_2					
The Smaller of n_1 and n_2	5	6	7	8	9	10
2						
3		2	2	2	2	2
		8	8	8	8	8
4	2	2	2	3	3	3
	9	9	10	10	10	10
5	2	3	3	3	3	3
	10	10	11	11	12	12
6		3	3	3	4	4
		11	12	12	13	13
7			3	4	4	5
			13	13	14	14
8				4	5	5
				14	14	15
9					5	5
					15	16
10						6
						16

By standardizing R in the usual way, we obtain the following summary.

Hypotheses

H_0: pattern was generated in a random manner

H_a: pattern was not generated in a random manner

Test Statistic (for Large Samples)

$$Z = \frac{R - \mu_R}{\sigma_R}$$

18.4

where (1) R denotes the number of runs in the data sequence, and (2) μ_R and σ_R are the mean and standard deviation of this random variable, defined in equations 18.2 and 18.3.

The testing procedure using the standard normal random variable is the same as in previous tests using Z. For the randomness test, a nonrandom pattern is indicated by a Z value in the right tail (too many runs) or in the left tail (too few runs).

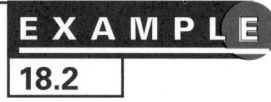

EXAMPLE

18.2

The president of Northside National Bank requested the savings-account balances for 45 randomly selected accounts of nonmarried customers. When she examined the data, she began to question the randomness of the procedure used to select the accounts. Letting M denote the account of a male and F the account of a female, the following sequence was obtained, listed in the order in which they were selected for the supposedly random sample.

M M F F F F F M F F M M M M M M F F F F M M F

M M F F M F F F F F M M M M M F F F F M M M

Based upon this sequence, would you conclude that this sample consists of 45 randomly selected males and females? Use $\alpha = .05$.

Solution   This sequence contains $R = 15$ runs. Also,

$$n_1 = \text{number of males} = 22$$

$$n_2 = \text{number of females} = 23$$

For these values of n_1 and n_2, the mean number of runs if H_0 is true is

$$\mu_R = 1 + \frac{(2)(22)(23)}{45} = 23.49$$

This implies that, on the average, whenever $n_1 = 22$ and $n_2 = 23$, you will obtain 23.49 runs.

The sample contains only 15 runs, so it could be that this sequence exhibits a nonrandom pattern, due to insufficient runs. However, this depends heavily on the standard deviation of R; therefore, to complete the analysis, we next find

$$\sigma_R = \sqrt{\frac{(2)(22)(23)[(2)(22)(23) - 45]}{(45)^2(44)}} = \sqrt{10.9832} = 3.314$$

To determine whether $R = 15$ is sufficiently small to reject the random sequence hypothesis, we calculate the test statistic.

$$Z^* = \frac{15 - 23.49}{3.314} = -2.56$$

The test procedure here (using $\alpha = .05$) is to

$$\text{reject } H_0 \text{ if } |Z| > 1.96$$

The computed Z value does have an absolute value larger than 1.96, and so we reject H_0. There is evidence that the male–female sequence is nonrandom, indicating a lack of randomness in the sampling procedure used in selecting the individual accounts from the bank records.

The standard statistical tool package within Excel does not perform any of the nonparametric tests within this chapter. However, the Excel macros within the KPK Data Analysis add-ins do provide all of these tests, including the runs test. To obtain the solution for Example 18.2, click on **KPK Data Analysis ➤ Nonparametric Procedures**. Select **Runs Test** and in the **Runs Test Using** box, click on **Series Values.*** Enter "A1:A45" in the **Input Range** box and "B1" in the **Output Range** box. The resulting output in Figure 18.1 is identical to the previous solution. Since the *p*-value of .010 is less than the significance level of .05, once again the decision is to reject H_0 and conclude that the male–female sequence was generated in a nonrandom manner.

We encounter another application of the runs test when we examine the residuals from a linear regression analysis. A key assumption when using linear regression is that the errors are *independent*. Consequently, we should observe a random pattern in the sample residuals. If the observations in our data set are recorded across time (say, 24 consecutive months), this often results in residuals that are *not* independent. In this case, we would say that the errors are correlated—more precisely, that they are *autocorrelated*, since they are correlated with each other. In Chapter 17, we computed the Durbin–Watson (DW) statistic to measure the degree of autocorrelation.

The DW statistic assumes that the errors follow a normal distribution, as do all the tests of hypothesis when using a linear regression model. The nonparametric runs test also can be used to examine the residuals, by recording the *sign* (+ or −) of each residual and counting the number of runs. This test is valid regardless of the distribution of the errors and can be used for any model that assumes the errors are uncorrelated.

---

*The **Series Signs** option for the runs test will be illustrated in the next example.

FIGURE
18.1

Excel runs test
using **KPK Data
Analysis ➤
Nonparametric
Procedures**
(Example 18.2).

	A	B	C	D	E	F	G	H
1	M	Runs test						
2	M	Number of Runs	15					
3	F	Mean	23.489					
4	F	Std. Dev.	3.314					
5	F	Z Value	-2.561					
6	F	2-Tailed p-value	0.010					
7	F							
8	M							
9	F							
10	F							

Microsoft® Excel Application Use DATA18-3

An Excel Runs Test

EXAMPLE
18.3

A financial analyst with Case Automated Equipment is examining the company's quarterly sales for the past 10 years. She suspects there is a strong trend and cyclical component in the seasonally adjusted (deseasonalized) sales figures due to steadily increasing sales and cyclical movement in the general U.S. economy.* The seasonally adjusted quarterly sales figures are contained in column B in data set DATA18-3. Using the runs test, and a significance level of $\alpha = .05$, determine if there is cyclical activity present when regressing the seasonally adjusted sales values against time. The time variable ($t = 1, 2, \ldots, 40$) is contained in column A.

Solution

Begin by opening DATA 18-3. There should be labels in the first row (**Time** and **Sales**), providing a total of 41 rows. To carry out the regression analysis, click on **KPK Data Analysis ➤ Regression.** Enter "B1:B41" as the **Y Range,** "A1:A41" as the (contiguous) **X Range,** and "C1" as the **Output Range.** Be sure to click on the box alongside **Residuals** inside the **Data** frame and on the **Residual Plots** box inside the **Plots** frame. The resulting output is shown in Figures 18.2 and 18.3. The residuals (partially shown) are contained in cells E25:E64.

If cyclical activity is present in the residuals, we would expect to see too *few* runs, since a positive (negative) residual is likely to be preceded and followed by a positive (negative) residual. Since neighboring residuals are likely to have the same sign if the residuals contain cyclical activity, this implies that the residuals will be *positively* autocorrelated. The resulting hypotheses under investigation are

H_0: no autocorrelation exists

H_a: positive autocorrelation exists

To carry out the runs test using Excel, click on **KPK Data Analysis ➤ Nonparametric Procedures.** Select **Runs Test** and click on **Series Signs** in the **Runs Test Using** box and enter "E25:E64" in the **Input Range** box and "F1" in the **Output Range** box. The resulting output is contained in cells F1:G6 in Figure 18.2. An examination of the residuals reveals $n_1 = 21$ negative residuals and $n_2 = 19$ positive residuals. The first residual value in this example is negative, and as a result, n_1 is a count of the negative residuals, and n_2 represents the number of positive residuals.

---

*A procedure for deseasonalizing time series data was discussed in Section 16.5.

FIGURE

18.2

Excel regression solution and runs test for Example 18.3 using KPK Data Analysis.

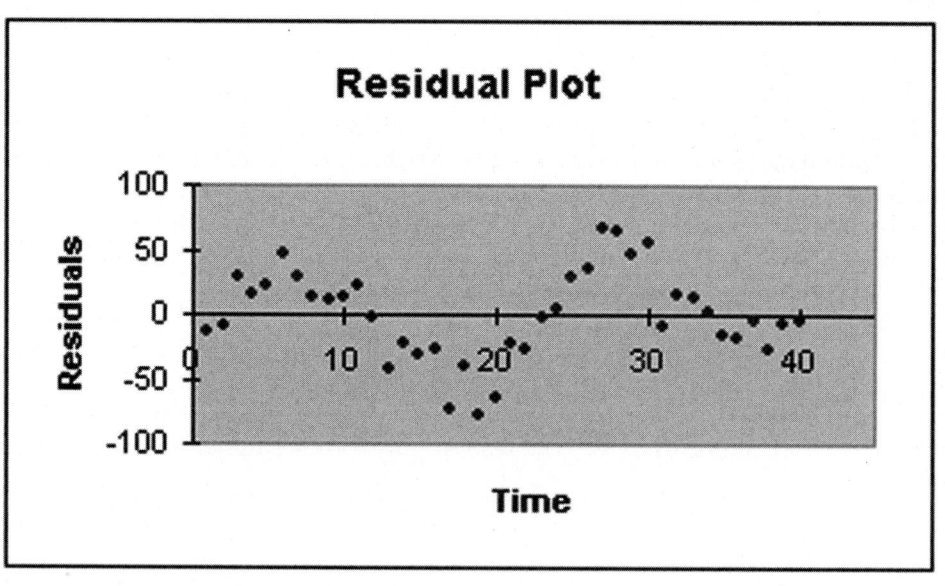

FIGURE

18.3

Excel residual plot using KPK Data Analysis (Example 18.3).

According to the output, $\mu_R = 1 + [(2)(21)(19)/40] = 20.95$. The output also contains

$$\sigma_R = \sqrt{\frac{(2)(21)(19)[(2)(21)(19) - 21 - 19]}{(40)^2(39)}} = 3.113$$

and the value of the test statistic (Z^*), where

$$Z^* = \frac{7 - 20.95}{3.113} = -4.48$$

Under H_a, we expect a small number of runs; that is, this is a *left-tailed* test. Since $\alpha = .05$, we

$$\text{reject } H_0 \text{ if } Z < -1.645$$

Because $-4.48 < -1.645$, we reject H_0 and conclude that there are too few runs in this sequence of residuals. This supports the hunch of the financial analyst that the seasonally adjusted sales figures contain cyclical activity. This can be seen in the scatter diagram of the residuals versus time in Figure 18.3. This residual plot was generated using the previous KPK Data Analysis regression procedure.

Comments

1. When you perform a one-tailed runs test, you should divide the two-tailed Excel p-value by 2 and then compare it to the level of significance (α) to make a decision. In the previous example, the resulting p-value is $.00001/2 \approx .000005$ (extremely small).

2. For a one-tailed test, be sure that the sign of the Z value is compatible with your one-tailed alternative hypothesis; that is, it should be positive when testing H_a: too many runs, and negative when testing H_a: too few runs.

X Exercises 18.1–18.10

Understanding the Mechanics

18.1 Using a significance level of 5%, determine if each of the two sequences of 0's and 1's is generated in a random manner.
  a. 1 0 1 0 0 1 0 1 0 1
  b. 1 0 0 1 0 1 1 0 1 1

18.2 A sequence contains high and low numbers. Let n_1 and n_2 equal the number of high and low numbers, respectively, in a sequence. Let R equal the number of runs. Would you conclude that the following sequences were generated in a random manner? Use a 5% significance level.
  a. $n_1 = 23$, $n_2 = 24$, $R = 15$
  b. $n_1 = 35$, $n_2 = 30$, $R = 21$
  c. $n_1 = 50$, $n_2 = 50$, $R = 35$

18.3 At the 10% significance level, can you conclude that the even and odd numbers presented here are randomly generated?

2 4 5 1 3 7 9 2 1 9 2 4 6 8 2 4 1 3 5 1 4 2 7 4 8 7 9 2 1 9
7 3 5 2 4 4 8 6 9 1 9 7 4 8 2

Applying the New Concepts

18.4 Ozark County Bank is taking applications for the position of loan officer. The following sequence lists the order in which either a male (M) or a female (F) applied for the position. Is there evidence to indicate that the sequence is not randomly generated? Use a 5% significance level.

M M M F M M F M M F M F F M M F M M M F F F F
M M F F F

18.5 After a television debate between two political candidates, a telephone line is open to viewers wishing to express their opinions on whether the Democratic (D) or the Republican (R) candidate won the debate. The following sequence represents 19 opinions of viewers in the order in which they telephoned. Using a runs test and a significance level of 5%, does the sequence indicate a nonrandom order?

R R D D R D D R R R D D R D R D D D

18.6 Conduct a runs test on the following sequence of 3's and 4's to see if there is evidence that the sequence is not randomly generated. Use a 5% significance level.

3 3 3 4 4 3 4 3 4 3 3 3 3 4 4 3 4 4 3 3 3 3 3 4 3

18.7 A certain computer program generates a sequence of random digits. Test whether there is any evidence that the following sequence of numbers is nonrandom, by considering the sequence of odd and even numbers. Use a 5% significance level.

9 8 5 3 1 1 2 2 7 4 4 3 7 3 8 1 6 5 8 4 7 9 1

18.8 For years, magazines have been the preferred way for pharmaceutical companies to advertise drugs. Conventional wisdom on Madison Avenue is that magazines often are a better way to target specific audiences with complicated messages. With magazines, companies can reach audiences they want without paying for the audience that is not being targeted. The following table lists annual advertising expenditure (in millions of dollars) by the top 10 prescription drug advertisers for the years from 1987 to 1998.

  a. Fit a regression equation through the data using year as the independent variable.

b. Find the 12 residuals using the regression equation in part a.

c. Use a runs test to determine if the sequence of positive and negative residuals in part b appear to be randomly generated over time. Use a 5% significance level.

Year	Advertising Expenditure	Year	Advertising Expenditure
1987	160.8	1993	160.8
1988	145.3	1994	170.4
1989	152.8	1995	193.5
1990	160.3	1996	285.1
1991	166.5	1997	403.6
1992	174.5	1998	360.7

(Source: "TV Gets Most Drug-Ad Spending, but Magazines Have Equal Impact," *The Wall Street Journal*, January 14, 1999, p. B8.)

Using the Computer

18.9 **[DATA SET EX18-9]** *Variable description*:

Response: A participant's response to a survey question

A survey is used to assess workers' satisfaction and productivity. Each response is coded as 1, 2, 3, or 4. As a way of determining if a participant's responses were randomly generated, a runs test is used by determining the runs above and below 2.5. For the data in Response, is there evidence to indicate that the sequence of 40 questions is not randomly generated? Use a 5% significance level.

18.10 **[DATA SET EX18-10]** *Variable description:*

Time: Time period numbered 1 through 40

RetailIndex: Retail sales index for county in southern California

A marketing analyst is examining the retail sales index for a county in southern California over a 10-year period. The retail sales index values (RetailIndex) are deseasonalized figures recorded each quarter, hence making 40 time periods available for analysis. Using the runs test, determine if there is cyclical activity present in the residuals when regressing the seasonally adjusted retail sales index against time. Use a 5% significance level.

18.2 NONPARAMETRIC TESTS OF CENTRAL TENDENCY: TWO POPULATIONS

Chapter 3 introduced you to measures of central tendency. The more commonly used measures are the mean and median, which attempt to identify the middle of a set of sample data. In Chapter 9, we introduced two populations, where the question of interest was whether the two means were the same (a two-tailed test) or whether one mean exceeded the other (a one-tailed test). A two-population test is illustrated in Figure 18.4, where the variable of interest is height.

The main assumption in Figure 18.4 is that the two populations are normally distributed. When you sample from these populations, if both sample sizes (n_1 and n_2) are *large,* you can remove this assumption. However, there is a need for a nonparametric technique for this two-population situation when (1) you have small samples and you suspect that one or both populations do not follow a normal distribution or (2) your data are such that only the relative ranks are available within each sample, such as in a consumer taste test (in other words, you are dealing with *ordinal data). The t tests from Chapter 9 assumed that the measurement scale of the data was at least interval, so these tests are inappropriate for data consisting of ranks.*

When dealing with samples from two populations in Chapter 9, we also looked at two situations:

1. The two samples are *independent.* In Figure 18.4, this would mean that a sample of n_1 female heights is obtained independently of the n_2 male heights. There is no reason to match up the first male height with the first female height, the second male height with the second female height, and so on in the two samples.

2. The two samples are *dependent,* or *paired.* This might occur in Figure 18.5 if the question were, are husbands taller than wives? The data then consist of n_1 wives and $n_2 = n_1$ husbands.

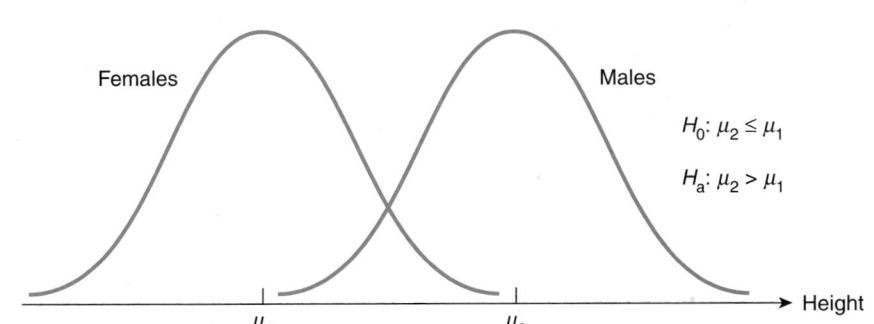

Data

Sample 1   Sample 2
(women)   (men)

| X | | X | —— Couple 1 |

| X | | X | —— Couple 2 |

| X | | X | —— Couple 3 (etc.) |

This portion of the chapter discusses the nonparametric counterparts to these two parametric tests of hypothesis. The assumptions behind the application of these methods are considerably weaker than those for the t tests in Chapter 9. These nonparametric techniques, named after the people responsible for their development, are the Mann–Whitney U test—a nonparametric procedure for situation 1 (two independent samples)—and the Wilcoxon signed rank test—a nonparametric procedure for situation 2 (two paired samples).

The parametric tests in Chapter 9 were concerned with population means. If two populations have different means, we say that these populations differ in **location.** This implies that population 1 is shifted to the left or right of population 2. When defining the corresponding nonparametric test, the hypotheses will be stated in terms of differing location rather than differing means.

The Mann–Whitney U Test for Independent Samples

The **Mann–Whitney U test** is named after H. B. Mann and R. Whitney, who developed this test in the 1940s. The purpose of this procedure is to provide a test for differing location that does not require the assumption of normal populations. The test is an alternative to the t tests from Chapter 9, which are based on this assumption.

The two-tailed hypotheses for the Mann–Whitney test can be written

H_0: the two populations have identical probability distributions

H_a: the two populations differ in location

To use the Mann–Whitney nonparametric technique, we begin by combining (pooling) the two samples into one large sample and then determining the rank of each observation in the pooled sample. Next, let

T_1 = sum of the ranks of the observations from the first sample in this pooled sample

T_2 = sum of the ranks of the observations from the second sample

The procedure is (if $n_1 = n_2$)

reject H_0 if T_1 is "significantly different" from T_2

To illustrate this technique, consider the following pooled sample, where the pooled observations have been arranged in order from smallest to largest. Here A represents a value from population A and B is a value from population B.

Value	A	A	A	A	A	B	B	B	B	B
Rank	1	2	3	4	5	6	7	8	9	10

For this pooled sample, we have

$n_1 = 5$

T_1 = sum of the ranks of the five A observations in the pooled sample

$= 1 + 2 + 3 + 4 + 5 = 15$

$n_2 = 5$

T_2 = sum of the ranks of the B observations

$= 6 + 7 + 8 + 9 + 10 = 40$

Now consider another pooled sample:

Value	A	B	B	A	B	A	A	A	B	B
Rank	1	2	3	4	5	6	7	8	9	10

For this situation, the values are $T_1 = 1 + 4 + 6 + 7 + 8 = 26$ and $T_2 = 2 + 3 + 5 + 9 + 10 = 29$.

In the first pooled sample, there is clear evidence that the second population is shifted to the right of the first population, as indicated by the large difference between $T_1 = 15$ and $T_2 = 40$. This difference is also evident when you examine this pooled sample because the values from population A are all less than those from population B. From a parametric view, this implies that $\mu_B > \mu_A$. The Mann–Whitney procedure will result in rejecting H_0: the two populations have identical probability distributions in favor of H_a: the two populations differ in location (or H_a: population A is shifted to the left of population B, had we used a one-tailed test). For the second set of 10 pooled observations, there is no indication of a difference in population location; the A and B values are fairly well mixed in the combined sample, as evidenced by the values of $T_1 = 26$ and $T_2 = 29$, which are nearly equal. The Mann–Whitney test will lead to a failure to reject the null hypothesis.

Mann–Whitney Test for Small Samples. For this test of hypothesis, small samples are defined as both $n_1 \leq 10$ and $n_2 \leq 10$. Regardless of the sample sizes, the procedure begins by finding T_1 and T_2 as described previously and then letting

$$U_1 = n_1 n_2 + \frac{n_1(n_1 + 1)}{2} - T_1 \qquad \text{18.5}$$

and

$$U_2 = n_1 n_2 + \frac{n_2(n_2 + 1)}{2} - T_2 \qquad \text{18.6}$$

The Mann–Whitney test is summarized as follows.

THE MANN–WHITNEY TEST FOR SMALL SAMPLES

Null hypothesis:

H_0: the two populations have identical probability distributions

Assumptions:

1. Random samples are obtained from each population.
2. The two samples are independent of one another—respective observations are not paired.
3. The sample data are at least ordinal.
4. If the two populations differ, they differ only in location—that is, the two populations have the same variation and shape.

Procedure:

1. Assume that $n_1 \leq n_2$ (if this is not the case, reverse your populations, so that n_1 is the smaller sample size).
2. Determine U_1 and U_2 from equations 18.5 and 18.6.
3. Use the value from Table A.10 to test H_0 versus H_a, where, once again, small p-values lead to rejecting H_0.

Two-Sided Test

H_a: the two populations differ in location

Reject H_0 if Table A.10 value for U is less than $\alpha/2$, where $U =$ minimum of U_1 and U_2.

One-Sided Test

H_a: population 1 is shifted to the right of population 2

Reject H_0 if Table A.10 value for U is less than α, where $U = U_1$.

H_a: population 1 is shifted to the left of population 2

Reject H_0 if Table A.10 value for U is less than α, where $U = U_2$.

EXAMPLE 18.4

Turner Electronics manufactures the outside casing for a new line of fax machines. They are considering two suppliers, Vendor A and Vendor B. Of concern to Turner is the durability of these casings, and they have designed a test that measures their breaking strength. A weight is dropped from a 2-inch height onto the casing, and the test determines at what maximum weight the casing cracks or becomes otherwise unusable. A random sample of eight casings from Vendor A and nine from Vendor B were subjected to the test, with the following results.

Maximum Weight in Pounds

Vendor A	92.9	78.4	70.0	75.6	110.0	83.1	75.4	98.5	
Vendor B	82.8	102.8	97.0	88.7	107.0	97.2	68.9	76.3	87.3

The quality engineers at Turner have no reason to believe the weight amounts are normally distributed, so they elect to use the Mann–Whitney procedure to determine if there is a difference between the casing strengths from the two vendors. Using $\alpha = .05$, is there a difference between the two suppliers?

Solution

The hypotheses are

H_0: the two populations have identical probability distributions

H_a: the two populations differ in location

The pooled sample (ordered) here is

68.9, 70.0, 75.4, 75.6, 76.3, 78.4, 82.8, 83.1, 87.3, 88.7, 92.9, 97.0, 97.2, 98.5, 102.8, 107.0, 110.0

Next we indicate from which sample each value in the pooled sample came.

Rank	Vendor A Sample	Vendor B Sample	Ranks for Vendor A Sample	Ranks for Vendor B Sample
1		68.9		1
2	70.0		2	
3	75.4		3	
4	75.6		4	
5		76.3		5
6	78.4		6	
7		82.8		7
8	83.1		8	
9		87.3		9
10		88.7		10
11	92.9		11	
12		97.0		12
13		97.2		13
14	98.5		14	
15		102.8		15
16		107.0		16
17	110.0		17	
			$T_1 = 65$	$T_2 = 88$

Using equations 18.5 and 18.6,

$$U_1 = (8)(9) + \frac{(8)(9)}{2} - 65 = 43$$

$$U_2 = (8)(9) + \frac{(9)(10)}{2} - 88 = 29$$

Because this is a two-sided alternative, we let U = the minimum of 29 and 43, so $U = 29$.

For $n_1 = 8$, $n_2 = 9$, and $U = 29$, the value in Table A.10 is .2707. Because this value is greater than $\alpha/2 = .025$, we fail to reject H_0. Based on these data, there is insufficient evidence to indicate a difference in the casing strength for the two vendors.

The p-value for this test is $(2)(.2707) = .5414$, which is extremely large. For a one-sided test, the p-value would be obtained by finding the value from Table A.10, *not* by doubling it.

Ties. When the pooled sample contains two or more identical observations, each is assigned a rank equal to the *average* of the ranks of the tied observations. For example, if there are two observations tied for sixth and seventh place, each is assigned a rank of 6.5. The rank of the next largest sample value is 8. We illustrate this procedure in the next section. Because of ties, the Mann–Whitney U statistic may not be a counting number (integer). If for example, $U = 42.5$,* then you should always round this value *up* to the next integer (43, here) when consulting Table A.10.

Mann–Whitney Test for Large Samples. Whenever n_1 or n_2 is greater than 10, a large-sample approximation can be used for the distribution of the Mann–Whitney U statistic. For this case, we can use either U_1 or U_2 in the test statistic for both one-sided *and* two-sided tests. The following discussion uses U_2.

In the event that the two populations have identical probability distributions (that is, H_0 is true), the U_2 statistic is approximately *normally* distributed with mean

---

*The value to the right of the decimal point will always be .5 if U is not an integer.

$$\mu_{U_2} = \frac{n_1 n_2}{2}$$

and standard deviation

$$\sigma_{U_2} = \sqrt{\frac{n_1 n_2 (n_1 + n_2 + 1)}{12}}$$

The rejection region for the various alternative hypotheses are defined in the accompanying box.

The corresponding test statistic here is

$$Z = \frac{U_2 - \mu_{U_2}}{\sigma_{U_2}}$$

THE MANN–WHITNEY TEST FOR LARGE SAMPLES

Null hypothesis

H_0 : the two populations have identical probability distributions

Assumptions: Same as for small samples.

Procedure: Determine

$$U_2 = n_1 n_2 + \frac{n_2 (n_2 + 1)}{2} - T_2$$

where T_2 = sum of the ranks for the second sample in the pooled sample.

Two-Sided Test

H_a: the two populations differ in location

Reject H_0 if $|Z| > Z_{\alpha/2}$ where (1) Z is defined in equation 18.9 and (2) $Z_{\alpha/2}$ is the value from Table A.4 having a right-tail area of $\alpha/2$.

One-Sided test

H_a: population 1 is shifted to the right of population 2

Reject H_0 if $Z > Z_\alpha$.

H_a: population 1 is shifted to the left of population 2

Reject H_0 if $Z < -Z_\alpha$.

EXAMPLE 18.5

Food World operates two supermarkets in a large metropolitan area. One of their services to customers is to cash personal checks at no charge. The owner of Food World is concerned that one of the stores (store A), situated in a low-income neighborhood, may have a greater number of checks returned due to insufficient funds in the customers' checking accounts than does store B, which is located in a higher-income area. Data were collected for 12 randomly selected six-month periods from store A; the data consisted of the number of returned checks over this period. Similar data were collected for 15 randomly selected six-month periods for store B.

| Store A | 42 | 65 | 38 | 55 | 71 | 60 | 47 | 59 | 68 | 57 | 76 | 42 | | | |
| Store B | 22 | 17 | 35 | 19 | 8 | 24 | 42 | 14 | 28 | 17 | 10 | 15 | 20 | 45 | 50 |

TABLE

18.4

Pooled sample for
Example 18.5.

Rank	Store A Sample	Store B Sample	Ranks for Store A	Ranks for Store B
1		8		1
2		10		2
3		14		3
4		15		4
5		17		5.5
6		17		5.5
7		19		7
8		20		8
9		22		9
10		24		10
11		28		11
12		35		12
13	38		13	
14	42		15	
15		42		15
16	42		15	
17		45		17
18	47		18	
19		50		19
20	55		20	
21	57		21	
22	59		22	
23	60		23	
24	65		24	
25	68		25	
26	71		26	
27	76		27	
			$T_1 = 249$	$T_2 = 129$

The pooled sample and corresponding ranks are summarized in Table 18.4.
Notice that there are two values of 17, which are tied for fifth and sixth place. Consequently, each is given a rank of $(5 + 6)/2 = 5.5$. Similarly, there is a three-way tie
for fourteenth, fifteenth, and sixteenth place, so a rank of $(14 + 15 + 16)/3 = 15$ is
given to each.

Using $\alpha = .05$, is there sufficient evidence to indicate that store A has a larger
number of returned checks than does store B?

Solution   The hypotheses for this situation are

H_0: the two populations have identical probability distributions

H_a: population A is shifted to the right of population B

The test procedure is to

reject H_0 if $Z > 1.645$

where $1.645 = Z_{.05}$ is obtained from Table A.4. From Table 18.4, we find that

$T_2 =$ sum of ranks for store B

$= 1 + 2 + 3 + 4 + 5.5 + 5.5 + \cdots + 15 + 17 + 19 = 129$

and so

$$U_2 = (12)(15) + \frac{(15)(16)}{2} - 129 = 171$$

FIGURE

18.6

Excel solution to
Example 18.5
using the
Mann–Whitney
test within KPK
Data Analysis ➤
Nonparametric
Procedures.

		Microsoft Excel - Book1					
		File Edit View Insert Format Tools Data KPK Data Analysis Window Help					
		J1 =					
	A	B	C	D	E	F	G
1	42	22	Mann-Whitney Test				
2	65	17	Test Statistic	171.0			
3	38	35	1-Tailed p-value	.0000			
4	55	19	Mean	90			
5	71	8	Std. Dev.	20.4939			
6	60	24	Z Value	3.9524			
7	47	42	Group	Sum of Ranks	Average Rank		
8	59	14	1	249.0	20.75		
9	68	28	2	129.0	8.60		
10	57	17					

Sheet1 / Sheet2 / Sheet3 /

Also, the mean and standard deviation of the U_2 statistic are

$$\mu_{U_2} = \frac{(12)(15)}{2} = 90$$

and

$$\sigma_{U_2} = \sqrt{\frac{(12)(15)(28)}{12}} = 20.49$$

The value of the resulting test statistic is

$$Z = \frac{U_2 - \mu_{U_2}}{\sigma_{U_2}} = \frac{171 - 90}{20.49} = 3.95$$

This exceeds 1.645, and so we reject H_0 and conclude that store A does in fact have a larger volume of returned checks than store B.

An Excel solution for Example 18.5 is contained in Figure 18.6. To obtain this solution, click on **KPK Data Analysis ➤ Nonparametric Procedures.** Select **Comparing Two Groups** and click on **Mann–Whitney Test** and then on **OK.** In the next form, enter "A1:A12" as the **Input Range** for sample 1 and "B1:B15" for sample 2. Enter "C1" as the **Output Range** and select **Population 1 is shifted to the right of population 2** as the alternative hypothesis.

The Excel analysis uses the values in Table A.10 to determine p-values if both n_1 and n_2 are less than or equal to 10. If either sample size is more than 10, the p-value is determined using the value of the large-sample Z statistic. For this example, both n_1 and n_2 exceed 10, so the p-value is computed as the area to the right of $Z^* = 3.95$. In Figure 18.6, this very small p-value (zero to four decimal places) again supports the alternative hypothesis and leads to the conclusion that store A has a larger volume of returned checks than store B.

Wilcoxon Signed Rank Test for Paired Samples

When your sample data consist of *paired* observations from two populations, the Mann–Whitney procedure from the previous section does not apply because it assumes *independent* samples. By *paired observations,* we mean that respective observations from each sample are matched with one another. Examples of paired observations include husband-wife, brother-sister, and before-after combinations.

A method of testing population means under this type of sampling procedure was introduced in Chapter 9, where we used a t test on the sample differences.

TABLE

18.5

Sales (thousands of dollars) for 10 cities.

City	Sales Before	Sales After
Denver	61	63
Boston	50	57
Salt Lake City	18	34
Seattle	56	48
Miami	29	44
Dallas	25	38
Atlanta	34	28
Baltimore	48	68
Topeka	37	57
Minneapolis	14	26

However, as in all *t* tests, a key assumption using this method of testing two means is that the differences are *normally distributed. When small samples from suspected nonnormal populations are used, a nonparametric technique is required.* The **Wilcoxon signed rank test** is used for such situations.

The Wilcoxon test begins like its parametric counterpart, the paired-sample *t* test, by subtracting the data pairs and using the differences to perform the test. As in the paired-sample *t* test, the hypotheses are written in terms of the location of the probability distribution for the population differences.

There are four steps involved in applying the Wilcoxon test:

1. Determine the difference for each sample pair.

2. Arrange the *absolute value* of these differences in order, assigning a rank to each.

3. Let T_+ = sum of the ranks having a positive value and T_- = sum of the ranks for the negative values.

4. T_+, T_-, or T = the minimum of T_+ and T_- is used to define a test of H_0 versus H_a.

To demonstrate the test, suppose we are interested in determining the effects of a vigorous six-month advertising campaign. Sales figures are collected before and after the campaign from 10 different cities. The results are shown in Table 18.5. We determine the paired differences and rank the corresponding absolute values in order. Ties are handled as before by assigning a rank equal to the average of the tied positions. Also, if a pair of observations has a difference equal to zero, then this pair is *deleted* from the sample, and *n* is reduced by 1. Other methods exist for handling zero differences, but this procedure is the simplest, and it works well provided there are not many zero differences.

According to Table 18.6, the negative differences are −6 and −8. Their corresponding ranks are 2 and 4. Therefore,

$$T_- = 2 + 4 = 6$$

A rule that can simplify the calculations here and serve as a check for arithmetic is that

$$T_+ + T_- = \frac{n(n+1)}{2}$$

where *n* = the number of sample pairs. In our example, *n* = 10, so

$$T_+ + T_- = \frac{(10)(11)}{2} = 55$$

which means that $T_+ = 55 - T_- = 55 - 6 = 49$.

TABLE

18.6

Sales After	Sales Before	Difference (After – Before)	|Difference|	Rank
63	61	2	2	1
57	50	7	7	3
34	18	16	16	8
48	56	–8	8	4 (–)
44	29	15	15	7
38	25	13	13	6
28	34	–6	6	2 (–)
68	48	20	20	9.5
57	37	20	20	9.5
26	14	12	12	5

Illustration of Wilcoxon signed rank procedure (Example 18.6).

The Wilcoxon Signed Rank Test for Small Samples (Paired). Once T_+ and T_- have been obtained, you can use the Wilcoxon signed rank test for testing hypotheses about the location of the population differences.

THE WILCOXON SIGNED RANK TEST FOR SMALL SAMPLES (PAIRED)

Null hypothesis:

H_0: the population differences are centered at 0

Assumptions:

1. Each data pair is randomly selected.
2. The absolute values of the differences can be ranked.

Procedure:

1. Determine the n differences using each sample pair, where each difference is defined to be sample 1 – sample 2.
2. Assign a rank to the absolute value of each difference; define T_+ = sum of the ranks of the positive values and T_- = sum of the ranks of the negative values.

Table A.11 is used to define the rejection region for the following tests.

Two-Sided Test	One-Sided Test	
H_a: the population differences are not centered at 0	H_a: the population differences are centered at a value > 0	H_a: the population differences are centered at a value < 0
Using the two-sided value from Table A.11, reject H_0 if $T \le$ table value, where T = minimum of T_+ and T_-.	Using the one-sided value from Table A.11, reject H_0 if $T_- \le$ table value.	Using the one-sided value from Table A.11, reject H_0 if $T_+ \le$ table value.

Table 18.5 contains the sales results from 10 cities before and after the six-month advertising campaign. Using $\alpha = .05$, are we able to conclude that there was a significant increase in sales after the advertising campaign?

EXAMPLE

18.6

Solution   The hypotheses here can be stated as (A = after, B = before)

$$H_0: \text{the population differences are centered at 0}$$

$$H_a: \text{the population differences are centered at a value} > 0$$

We refer to the "after" population as population 1 and the "before" population as population 2 to correspond to the difference column in Table 18.6 [our procedure assumes that each difference is sample 1 (A) – sample 2 (B)].

The values of T_+ and T_- also are derived from Table 18.6, where

$$T_- = 6 \quad \text{and} \quad T_+ = 49$$

The one-sided value in Table A.11 corresponding to $n = 10$ and $\alpha = .05$ is 11. Consequently, the test is to

$$\text{reject } H_0 \text{ if } T_- \le 11$$

Because the value of T_- is smaller than 11, we reject H_0 and conclude that there is sufficient evidence of a sales increase after the advertising campaign.

The Wilcoxon Signed Rank Test for Large Samples (Paired).   For samples consisting of $n > 15$ pairs, a large-sample approximation to the Wilcoxon test statistic can be used. An advantage to using this procedure is that p-values are much easier to determine. (A p-value is once again a measure of the strength of your conclusion.)

When using the large-sample procedure, we can define a test using either T_+ or T_-. The following hypothesis tests use T_+, the sum of the ranks for the positive differences. If the population differences are centered at zero (that is, H_0 is true), then T_+ is approximately a normal random variable with mean

$$\mu_{T_+} = \frac{n(n+1)}{4} \tag{18.10}$$

and standard deviation

$$\sigma_{T_+} = \sqrt{\frac{n(n+1)(2n+1)}{24}} \tag{18.11}$$

The corresponding test statistic is

$$Z = \frac{T_+ - \mu_{T_+}}{\sigma_{T_+}} \tag{18.12}$$

The one- and two-sided large-sample procedures are summarized in the accompanying box.

THE WILCOXON SIGNED RANK TEST FOR LARGE SAMPLES (PAIRED)

Null hypothesis:

H_0: the population differences are centered at 0

Assumptions: Same as for small samples

Procedure: (1) and (2) are the same as for small samples. Each paired difference is defined to be sample 1 – sample 2.

Two-Sided Test	One-Sided Test	
H_a: the population differences are not centered at 0	H_a: the population differences are centered at a value > 0	H_a: the population differences are centered at a value < 0
Reject H_0 if $\lvert Z \rvert > Z_{\alpha/2}$, where Z is defined in equation 18.12 and $Z_{\alpha/2}$ is the value from Table A.4 having a right-tail area of $\alpha/2$.	Reject H_0 if $Z > Z_\alpha$.	Reject H_0 if $Z < -Z_\alpha$.

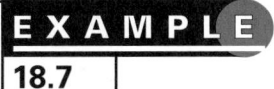

EXAMPLE 18.7

The paper produced by Glendale Container Corporation has historically contained 2% hardwood in the paper pulp. A quality engineer at Glendale believed that a 10% hardwood concentration would improve the tensile strength of the paper. Management has decided to adopt the 10% concentration, despite the slightly higher cost, if in fact the tensile strength can be demonstrated to be larger at the 10% level. An experiment is performed in which the plant runs two batches of paper a day, one at 2% concentration and one at 10% concentration. A section of paper from each of the two batches is cut, dried, and tested. The following tensile strength data were obtained:

Day	2%	10%	Day	2%	10%
1	125	119	11	113	148
2	133	120	12	131	116
3	132	139	13	128	107
4	116	148	14	119	142
5	130	148	15	112	106
6	135	109	16	111	142
7	119	137	17	128	112
8	112	116	18	135	145
9	122	122	19	106	131
10	137	131	20	118	146

Use the Wilcoxon signed rank test to determine whether the quality engineer's belief—that the tensile strength is larger for the 10% hardwood concentration—is correct. Let $\alpha = .05$.

Solution

If we let the 2% population be population 1, then the correct hypotheses are

H_0: the population differences are centered at 0

H_a: the population differences are centered at a value < 0

The alternative hypothesis agrees with Table 18.7, in which each difference is calculated using the 2% value (sample 1) minus the 10% value (sample 2). Because the values for day 9 are the same, the difference is zero, so this sample is removed from the analysis, leaving $n = 19$ pairs in the sample.

Based on a significance level of $\alpha = .05$, the proper test is to

reject H_0 if $Z < -1.645$

For a value of $n = 19$, the mean of T_+ (assuming H_0 is true) is

$$\mu_{T_+} = \frac{(19)(20)}{4} = 95$$

TABLE

18.7

Paired samples for Example 18.7.

| Hardwood Concentration | | Difference | Rank of | | | |
2%	10%	(2%–10%)	Absolute Value		+ Ranks*	– Ranks
125	119	6	3		3*	
133	120	13	7		7	
132	139	–7	5	(–)		5
116	148	–32	18	(–)		18
130	148	–18	10.5	(–)		10.5†
135	109	26	15		15	
119	137	–18	10.5	(–)		10.5†
112	116	–4	1	(–)		1
122	122	0	—		removed, so use $n = 19$ pairs	
137	131	6	3		3*	
113	148	–35	19	(–)		19
131	116	15	8		8	
128	107	21	12		12	
119	142	–23	13	(–)		13
112	106	6	3		3*	
111	142	–31	17	(–)		17
128	112	16	9		9	
135	145	–10	6	(–)		6
106	131	–25	14	(–)		14
118	146	–28	16	(–)		16
					$T_+ = 60$	$T_- = 130$

*Three-way tie; assigned rank = (2 + 3 + 4)/3 = 3.
†Two-way tie; assigned rank = (10 + 11)/2 = 10.5.

with a standard deviation of

$$\sigma_{T_+} = \sqrt{\frac{(19)(20)(39)}{24}} = 24.85$$

Table 18.7 informs us that $T_+ = 60$, and so the value of the test statistic here is

$$Z^* = \frac{60 - 95}{24.85} = -1.41$$

This value is not less than –1.645, so there is insufficient evidence to conclude that the 10% concentration produces a larger tensile strength. Glendale Container should continue to use the less expensive 2% hardwood concentration.

The p-value for this test is obtained in the usual manner by finding, in this case, the area under a standard normal curve to the left of the calculated test statistic of $Z^* = -1.41$. According to Figure 18.7 and Table A.4, the p-value is .0793. Using our rule-of-thumb procedure from before, this p-value is neither large (>.1) nor small (<.01), but it *is* greater than $\alpha = .05$, which leads us to fail to reject H_0.

An Excel solution for Example 18.7 is contained in Figure 18.8. To obtain this solution, click on **KPK Data Analysis ➤ Nonparametric Procedures**. Select **Comparing Two Groups** and click on **Wilcoxon Test** and then on **OK**. In the next form, enter "A1:B20" as the **Input Range**, enter "C1" as the **Output Range**, and select **Differences (Pop. 1 – Pop. 2) center is < 0** as the alternative hypothesis. In Figure 18.8, the p-value using the large-sample Z statistic is .0795. This is slightly more accurate than the p-value illustrated in Figure 18.7, since a more accurate value of the Z statistic was used.

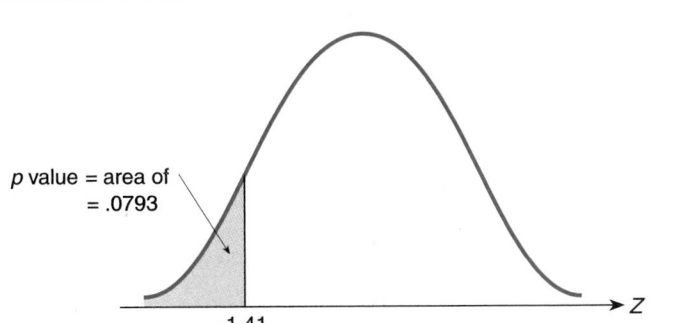

FIGURE

18.7

p-value for
Example 18.7.

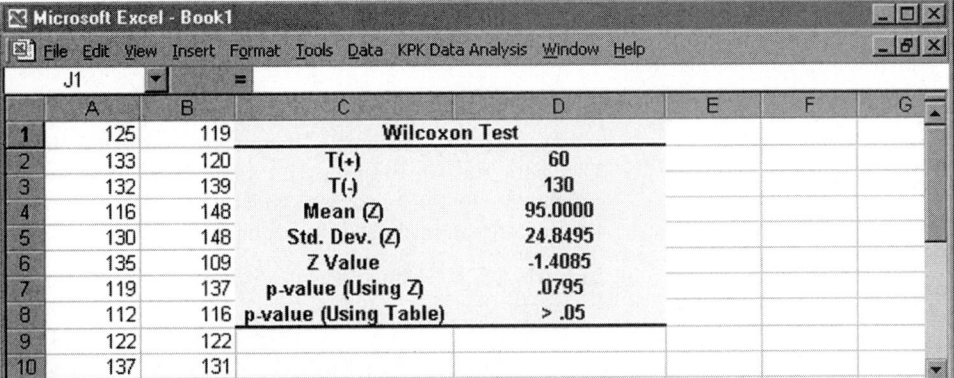

FIGURE

18.8

Excel solution to
Example 18.7
using the Wilcoxon
test within **KPK
Data Analysis ➤
Nonparametric
Procedures.**

Using Table A.11, $\alpha = .05$, and $n = 19$ (remember: there was one tie), the null hypothesis will be rejected if $T_+ \leq 54$. Since $60 > 54$, we fail to reject H_0 as before, and we also can say that the corresponding *p*-value is greater than .05. For $n \leq 50$, the KPK Data Analysis Wilcoxon test will provide a *p*-value using Table A.11. For this example, Excel will output **p-value (Using Table)** and **> .05.** This *p*-value and the large-sample *p*-value (.0795) both exceed .05, leading to the conclusion that there is insufficient evidence to indicate that the 10% concentration produces a larger tensile strength than the 2% concentration.

X   Exercises 18.11–18.35

Understanding the Mechanics

18.11 Data were collected from 10 randomly selected observations of population A and from 15 randomly selected observations of population B. The Mann–Whitney statistic can be used to test whether population A is shifted to the right of population B. The sum of the ranks for the observations from population A is 196. The sum of the ranks for the observations from population B is 129. Using a significance level of .05, is there sufficient evidence to indicate that population A is shifted to the right of population B?

18.12 Random samples of sizes 13 and 15 were drawn from populations 1 and 2, respectively. Using a significance level of .10, determine if the two populations differ in location.

Sample from Population 1			Sample from Population 2		
24	18	8	17	6	30
14	12	12	31	13	26
9	28	33	27	20	20
12	25		21	27	33
36	15		34	16	18

18.13 Ten pairs of observations from two populations were randomly selected. The sum of ranks of the positive differences (T_+) and the sum of the ranks of the negative differences (T_-) were found to be 50 and 5, respectively. Can you conclude that the population differences are centered at a value greater than 0? Use a .05 significance level.

18.14 A paired-difference experiment yielded a value of 280 for the sum of the ranks of the positive differences of 30 observations. Using a 5% significance level, is there evidence to suggest that the population difference is not centered at zero?

Applying the New Concepts

18.15 An engineer is proposing a new manufacturing process to increase the tensile strength of a certain wire. Eleven samples of wire manufactured under the proposed process are collected, and 14 samples are collected from wire manufactured under the existing process. Using the following data and a 10% significance level, test the hypothesis that there is greater tensile strength in the proposed technique.

Proposed Technique (PSI)	Existing Technique (PSI)	Proposed Technique (PSI)	Existing Technique (PSI)
1.4	1.2	2.2	1.8
2.1	1.6	2.0	1.7
1.8	1.7	1.9	2.0
1.7	1.7	2.0	1.8
1.6	2.0		1.9
1.9	1.3		1.6
1.4	1.4		2.1

18.16 The head lawyer of the Brown and Smith firm would like to know whether there is a difference in the number of errors made by the two secretaries employed in the firm. Five randomly selected documents are given to secretary A to type, and five are given to secretary B. The number of errors per document is shown in the following table. Using a 5% level of significance, test the hypothesis that there is no difference in the number of errors made by each secretary.

Secretary A	Secretary B
3	2
5	0
4	4
2	3
0	1

18.17 Nationally, the average price for a gallon of unleaded gasoline was $1.476 at the end of September 2001, compared to a high of $1.72 in the spring of 2001. In Texas the average gasoline price was $1.61. Suppose that the price of gasoline was recorded at 10 randomly selected gas stations in Dallas, Texas, in the spring and was also recorded at 10 randomly selected gas stations in Waco, Texas. Using the following data and a 5% significance level, can you conclude that the price of gasoline differs in these two locations.

Dallas	1.62 1.71 1.55 1.68 1.70 1.59 1.57 1.63 1.61 1.60
Waco	1.57 1.64 1.58 1.66 1.61 1.60 1.58 1.61 1.60 1.59

(Source: "As Autumn Breaks, Gas Prices Set to Fall. $1 a Gallon Possible for Some Markets, Analyst Predicts," *Dallas Morning News*, September 29, 2001, p. 1A.)

18.18 Two samples of light bulbs are taken from the brands Everglo and Britelite. The following table gives the life of bulbs for the collected samples. At the 1% level, is there sufficient evidence to indicate that Britelite bulbs last longer than do Everglo bulbs?

Everglo (Hours)	Britelite (Hours)	Everglo (Hours)	Britelite (Hours)
1134	1405	1107	1290
1255	1251	1095	1210
1313	1106	1401	1198
1012	1384	1109	1203
1265	1193	1150	1295
1375	1208		1102
1102	1110		1185

18.19 An economist wishes to compare the percentage increase in personal income for two suburbs of Chicago. Using the data in the following table, test at the 5% significance level the hypothesis that there is no difference in the percentage increase in personal income.

Suburb A (%)	Suburb B (%)	Suburb A (%)	Suburb B (%)
5.2	2.6	1.3	11.3
3.1	9.7	8.4	8.1
10.6	1.2	9.1	4.2
11.4	1.4	11.3	1.6
1.2	5.0	12.1	2.7
0.0	9.8	9.8	7.9

18.20 A supermarket manager was curious as to which of the two vending machines located at opposite ends of the store was used more during peak hours. During the peak hours on 12 randomly selected days, the number of users was counted for machine A. During the peak hours on another randomly selected 12 days, the number of users was counted for machine B. From the data on the following page, test at the 5% level of significance the hypothesis that there is no difference in the use of the two vending machines.

Vending Machine A	Vending Machine B	Vending Machine A	Vending Machine B
10	9	13	9
12	11	19	8
13	14	11	12
11	10	10	13
10	13	15	14
15	14	12	11

18.21 The number of reported injuries by employers appears to be declining. Experts at the Ninth Annual Business Insurance Workers Compensation and Disability Management Conference in Coronado, California, stated that the frequency of reported injuries fell by 18% in the past few years. Suppose that the National Council on Compensation Insurance conducted a study at two similar sized manufacturing plants over six quarters in which two safety programs were implemented: Safety Program A consisted of educating managers and employees on safety and health. Safety Program B consisted of making safety and health information available to those who were interested. Information on the number of reported injuries each quarter is presented below. Is there evidence that a difference exists in the number of reported injuries for the two safety programs? Use a 5% significance level.

	2002 Q1	2002 Q2	2002 Q3	2002 Q4	2003 Q1	2003 Q2
Safety Program A	3	2	1	6	5	2
Safety Program B	5	2	3	7	6	3

(Source: "Experts View Shift in Claims Frequency," *Business Insurance* 35, no. 45, November 5, 2001, p. 48.)

18.22 The number of defective electronic components in lots of two different processes are:

Process 1	Process 2	Process 1	Process 2
10	13	16	19
15	19	15	5
13	14	12	19
25	18	11	20
18	20	17	15

a. Use a *t* test, assuming equal population variances, to test that the two processes differ in location with respect to the number of defective terms. Use a .05 significance level.

b. Use the Mann–Whitney test to perform part a.

c. Which test is preferable for this type of data?

18.23 What assumption needs to be made about the sample data used in the Wilcoxon signed rank test? What assumption needs to be made about the distribution of the populations?

18.24 From 12 paired observations, it is found that by ranking the magnitude of the differences of the observations in each pair, T_+ (the sum of the ranks of the positive differences) is 27. Using a .05 significance level, can it be concluded that there is a difference in the location of the two populations?

18.25 A psychologist conducts a seminar to increase a person's self-esteem. A before-and-after test that measures each person's self-esteem is given to nine individuals. Using the following scores and a 5% significance level, is there evidence to conclude that the scores after the seminar are greater than the scores before the seminar?

Before	After	Before	After
70	74	55	58
72	88	43	41
75	71	51	63
61	62	84	80
82	89		

18.26 An insurance company believes that employees who have a college degree when hired progress faster in the company than those who do not. Pairs of employees are randomly selected; each pair consists of two people hired at the same time, one person with a college degree and the other without a college degree. The percentage increase in pay for these employees after three years is shown here. At the 10% level of significance, can you conclude that employees who have a college degree when hired progress faster than those who do not?

Without College Degree (%)	With College Degree (%)	Without College Degree (%)	With College Degree (%)
10	13	12	13
9	10	9	8
8	6	18	16
13	13	9	12
14	18	15	17
7	10	10	9
12	11	11	13
11	15	10	9
16	20		

18.27 Seven randomly selected faculty members were asked to evaluate two research project proposals on a scale from 0 to 10, with a higher score indicating a more acceptable proposal. The scores follow. Using a 5% significance level, can you conclude that the proposal for research project 2 is more acceptable than the proposal for research project 1?

Research Project 1	Research Project 2
5	7
3	5
6	9
7	6
8	9
4	6
7	10

18.28 The increase or decrease in help-wanted advertisements is an indicator of economic expansion or contraction, respectively. A sample of newspapers across the New Mexico, Texas, and Oklahoma region was selected to obtain a reading on the direction of the economy in that region. The number of help-wanted ads in November 1997 and November 1998 was recorded as an index, with 1989 being the base year. Test that the number of help-wanted ads in November 1998 have declined for the region. Use a 5% significance level.

Location of Newspaper	Help-wanted Index Nov. 1997	Help-wanted Index Nov. 1998
Albuquerque	150	145
Amarillo	132	121
Austin	210	205
Dallas	141	132
El Paso	185	180
Ft. Worth	155	164
Houston	111	95
Oklahoma	152	163
San Antonio	205	205
Tulsa	203	190

(Source: "Tracking Texas: The Help-Wanted Index," *The Wall Street Journal*, January 6, 1999, p. T1.)

18.29 The manager of a calculator-assembly plant wanted to know whether machine operators with little experience produced more defective calculators than did the experienced machine operators. The number of defective calculators produced by 20 randomly selected experienced machine operators in one week was recorded. Then, these 20 experienced operators were replaced by inexperienced machine operators and the number of defective calculators produced at these positions was recorded for one week. If the operators at each position can be considered to be a pair, use the Wilcoxon test to test that the experienced operators produced fewer defective calculators. Use a 5% significance level.

Experienced Employees	Inexperienced Employees	Experienced Employees	Inexperienced Employees
10	14	13	19
13	14	18	21
15	12	19	18
18	25	10	13
14	13	19	26
10	15	25	26
30	21	15	17
14	18	21	20
22	23	20	28
15	13	12	19

Using the Computer

18.30 **[DATA SET EX18-30]** *Variable description:*

CEO: Chief executive officers numbered from 1 to 10

Bonus2000: Bonus in thousands of dollars received by CEOs in 2000

Bonus2001: Bonus in thousands of dollars received by CEOs in 2001

A *Washington Post* survey of the 100 largest publicly traded companies in the D.C. area showed that the average salary of chief executives was $405,900 in 2000, up 13% from 1999. However, the average bonus increased 22.4% to $200,087. In 2001, the average bonus was believed to have not increased. Using a 5% significance level, is there evidence to suggest that the differences in bonuses for 2000 and 2001 are not centered at zero?

(Source: "How Washington's Corporate Elite Stack Up," *The Washington Post,* July 16, 2001, p. E01.)

18.31 **[DATA SET EX18-31]** *Variable description:*

Person: Number representing the person responding

BeforeDemo: Rating before viewing demonstration on paying bills online

AfterDemo: Rating after viewing demonstration on paying bills online

Josephine Muzzuca, a research analyst at Gallup's Toronto office, said that a Gallup poll of Canadian adults revealed that almost 40% of the adult population would be more likely to use e-billing if their privacy could be assured. Suppose she believes that bank customers would be more willing to pay online if they were given a demon-

stration at a bank that explains what happens to the information they provide. To test this belief, she randomly samples 24 individuals who are scheduled to attend a demonstration. She asks that they respond on a scale from 1 to 10 on how comfortable they feel about paying bills online (with 10 representing a completely comfortable feeling about paying online). From each participant, she collected a rating on this scale before and after the demonstration. At the 1% significance level, do the data support the belief that the ratings after viewing the demonstration are higher than those before viewing the demonstration?

(Source: "Gallup Poll Reveals Privacy Biggest Problem for E-billing," *Computer Dealer News,* 17, no. 3, p. 12.)

18.32 **[DATA SET EX18-32]** *Variable description:*

GasMileageReg: Gas mileage of a Jeep Cherokee with regular unleaded gasoline

GasMileageSup: Gas mileage of a Jeep Cherokee with supreme unleaded gasoline

A researcher working for Consumer Issues must determine if there is a difference in gas mileage of a Jeep Cherokee when regular unleaded gasoline is used and when supreme unleaded gasoline is used. A random sample of 100 1999 Jeep Cherokees was used in the study. Fifty of the jeeps were tested with regular unleaded gasoline and the other half with supreme unleaded gasoline. Each Jeep was driven by a randomly selected owner of a Jeep Cherokee. Using the variables GasMileageReg and GasMileageSup, interpret the results of a nonparametric test to determine if a difference exists at the 5% significance level. Explain how the practical significance of the results may differ from the statistical significance of the results for this problem.

18.33 **[DATA SET EX18-33]** *Variable description:*

StressA: Stress measurement for Tube A

StressB: Stress measurement for Tube B

A quality engineer is interested in determining if the stress level for Tube A is less than the stress level for Tube B. Forty-five measurements of each tube were randomly selected, and a stress test revealed each tube's stress measurement. Do the data indicate that the stress level for Tube A is less than the stress level for Tube B? Use a 1% significance level.

18.34 **[DATA SET EX18-34]** *Variable description:*

Design1: Sales using conservative style

Design2: Sales using flashy style

The management at Lion Foods is interested in placing its breakfast cereal in two different packaging designs. The first design (Design1) has a conservative style. The second design (Design2) has a flashy style. Management decides to place the products with both designs at opposite ends of the breakfast section in 25 different supermarkets. Can you conclude that there is a difference in sales (number of boxes sold) for the two designs? Use a 5% significance level.

18.35 [DATA SET EX18-35] *Variable description:*

Employee: Number indicating the employee, numbered from 1 to 35

SatisfactionBef: Job satisfaction score before promotion

SatisfactionAft: Job satisfaction score after promotion

An industrial psychologist believes that an employee's level of satisfaction with his/her job changes as the employee gets promoted. Thirty-five employees were randomly selected. A year before each employee received a promotion, a job satisfaction score was recorded. Then a year after the employee was promoted, a job satisfaction score was recorded.

a. Do the data indicate a difference in job satisfaction scores before and after promotion? Use a 5% significance level.

b. Using the paired t test, how would you answer part a?

c. Why do you believe that the results in parts a and b differ?

18.3

COMPARING MORE THAN TWO POPULATIONS: THE KRUSKAL–WALLIS TEST AND THE FRIEDMAN TEST

The Kruskal–Wallis Test

When comparing the means of more than two populations, a popular technique is the ANOVA procedure discussed in Chapter 11. One of the assumptions behind this technique is that you are dealing with normally distributed populations; the F test used in the ANOVA table is invalid unless all of the populations are nearly normally distributed with equal variances.

The nonparametric counterpart to the one-way ANOVA method is the **Kruskal–Wallis test.** It is named after W. H. Kruskal and W. A. Wallis, who published their results in 1952. This test, like many other nonparametric procedures, is relatively new, unlike most of the parametric hypothesis tests, which were developed much earlier. *The assumption of normal populations is not necessary for the Kruskal–Wallis test, making it an ideal technique for samples exhibiting a nonsymmetric (skewed) pattern.* It is also less sensitive than the ANOVA procedure to the assumption of equal variances. This test also is useful when the data consist of rankings (ordinal data) within each sample.

The assumption of normal populations becomes quite critical when dealing with small samples. As we've seen in many of the earlier tests of hypothesis, this assumption can be relaxed when larger samples are used, due to the Central Limit Theorem. However, many experiments of a business nature dealing with product comparisons result in the destruction of the product being tested. Consequently, small samples are often a necessity for such experiments, and nonparametric techniques are widely used to analyze the resulting data.

The Kruskal–Wallis test is actually an extension of the Mann–Whitney U test discussed earlier for *two* independent samples. Both procedures require that the sample values have a measurement scale that is at least ordinal (that is, each sample can be ranked from smallest to largest).

The hypotheses for this situation are similar to the Mann–Whitney hypotheses in that they are stated in terms of differing population locations. The Kruskal–Wallis hypotheses are

H_0: the k populations have identical probability distributions

H_a: at least two of the populations differ in location

Procedure. You first obtain random samples of size $n_1, n_2, \ldots, n_k$ from each of the k populations. The total sample size is $n = n_1 + n_2 + \cdots + n_k$. As with the Mann–Whitney procedure, you next pool the samples and arrange them in order, assigning a rank to each. For ties, you assign the average rank to the tied positions.

Let T_i = the total of the ranks from the ith sample. The Kruskal–Wallis test statistic (KW) is

$$KW = \frac{12}{n(n+1)} \sum_{i=1}^{k} \frac{T_i^2}{n_i} - 3(n+1)$$

18.13

The distribution of the KW statistic approximately follows a chi-square distribution with $k-1$ df. This approximation is good even if the sample sizes are small. To test H_0 versus H_a, the procedure is to

reject H_0 if KW is "large"

that is, if KW is in the right tail of the chi-square curve. This right-tail critical value is obtained from Table A.6, using a significance level = α and df = $k-1$.

THE KRUSKAL–WALLIS TEST

Hypotheses:

H_0: the k populations have identical probability distributions

H_a: at least two of the populations differ in location

Assumptions:

1. Random samples are obtained from each of the k populations.
2. The individual samples are obtained independently.
3. Values within each sample can be ranked.
4. If any two populations differ, they differ only in location—that is, all k populations have the same variation and shape.

Procedure: The individual samples are pooled and then ranked from smallest to largest. Letting T_i = the sum of the ranks of the ith sample, the KW statistic is determined using equation 18.13. The null hypothesis, H_0, is rejected if

$$KW > \chi^2_{\alpha,df}$$

where $\chi^2_{\alpha,df}$ is the value from Table A.6 corresponding to df = $k-1$, with a right-tail area = α.

EXAMPLE 18.8

Drexton Industries has a number of different brands of copying machines at their main facility. A critical factor in the attractiveness of each brand is the amount of time in which a machine is not working and is waiting for repair (downtime). Management requested a study to be made on four different brands of machines to determine whether there is a difference in the amount of downtime for these brands. Data were collected by finding the total downtime per month for 20 randomly selected months. In this way, the downtimes for five randomly selected months were obtained for each of the four brands of machine. These results are shown in Table 18.8.

Do these data indicate a difference in the amount of downtime for the four brands? Use $\alpha = .05$.

Solution There are $k = 4$ populations here, so we need the $\chi^2_{.05,3}$ value from Table A.6. Based on this value, the testing procedure is to

reject H_0 if $KW > \chi^2_{.05,3} = 7.81$

TABLE

18.8

Amount of downtime for copying machines (Example 18.8).

Brand 1	Rank	Brand 2	Rank	Brand 3	Rank	Brand 4	Rank
28	12	5	1	10	3	45	18
41	17	16	6	8	2	30	13
34	15	20	8	18	7	49	19
52	20	24	9	14	4	32	14
25	10	15	5	26	11	36	16
	$T_1 = 74$		$T_2 = 29$		$T_3 = 27$		$T_4 = 80$

FIGURE

18.9

p-value for *KW* statistic; χ^2 curve with 3 df (Example 18.8).

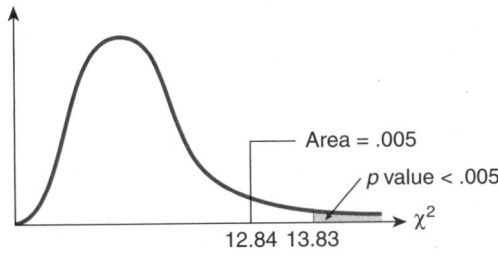

Area = .005

p value < .005

χ^2

12.84 13.83

From Table 18.8, we are able to compute the value of the *KW* statistic using the ranks of the observations in the pooled sample:

$$KW = \frac{12}{(20)(21)}\left[\frac{74^2}{5} + \frac{29^2}{5} + \frac{27^2}{5} + \frac{80^2}{5}\right] - 3(21) = 13.83$$

As a check of your calculations, make sure the ranks sum to $n(n+1)/2$. For this example, n = total number of observations = 20, and so the total of the ranks should be $(20)(21)/2 = 210$; here, $74 + 29 + 27 + 80 = 210$.

The calculated *KW* value exceeds 7.81, and so our conclusion is that there is a difference in downtime among the four brands. From the small values of T_2 and T_3, it appears that these two brands have much less downtime and are superior in this respect to brands 1 and 4.

Finally, the *p*-value here is less than .005, indicating a very strong conclusion. In other words, these data indicate a clear difference in location for the four brands. This *p*-value is illustrated in Figure 18.9.

To obtain the Excel solution for Example 18.8, click on **KPK Data Analysis ➤ Nonparametric Procedures.** Select **Comparing More Than Two Groups** and click on **Kruskal–Wallis Test** and then on **OK.** In Figure 18.10, the four samples were placed in the first four columns. *Note:* In general, these columns must be contiguous (adjacent). To carry out the test, enter "A1" as the **Upper left corner of sample data,** "E1" as the **Output Range,** and "4" as the **Number of Groups.** After clicking on **OK,** enter "5" as the **Number of Values** in each of the four samples, and then click on **OK** again. From Figure 18.10, the actual *p*-value is .0031 < .05, and so this output supports the conclusion that there is a difference in downtime for the four brands.

FIGURE
18.10

Excel solution to
Example 18.8
using the Kruskal–
Wallis test within
**KPK Data Analysis
➤ Nonparametric
Procedures.**

The Friedman Test

The topic of comparing more than two population means using dependent samples was introduced in Chapter 11, where we examined the randomized block design. Such a design consists of a single factor of interest with k levels, with the sample data organized into blocks. For this situation, the samples are not independently obtained, but data within the same block may be gathered from the same city or person or at the same point in time.

The key assumption behind the use of the randomized block design is that the variable being measured (the *dependent* variable) is normally distributed within each factor level/block combination. There are two situations for a blocked design where the use of the parametric randomized block technique is inappropriate, requiring the use of a nonparametric procedure:

1. You have no evidence to support the assumption of normality.

or

2. The sample data are ordinal (that is, consist of rankings).

When confronted with either of these two situations, the nonparametric **Friedman test** provides a correct method of testing for differences in location for the k factor-level populations. The corresponding hypotheses are

H_0: the k populations have identical probability distributions

H_a: at least two of the populations differ in location

Procedure. The k observations *within each block* are rank ordered, using the usual procedure of assigning the average of the tied positions in the event of ties within a block. Of course, this step is omitted if ordinal data are obtained initially, such as asking 50 people to rank order four particular products (or brands) according to a specified set of criteria. For this illustration, you would have $b = 50$ blocks and $k = 4$ populations defined by the four products. In addition, to remove potential bias introduced by fatigue, familiarity, and so on, the order in which the four brands are evaluated should be *randomly* determined for each person.

Define T_i = the total of the ranks for the ith population. The test statistic for the Friedman test is defined as

$$FR = \frac{12}{bk(k+1)} \sum_{i=1}^{k} T_i^2 - 3b(k+1)$$

18.14

where b = number of blocks and k = number of factor levels (populations).

The distribution of the FR statistic approximately follows a chi-square distribution with $k - 1$ df. This approximation works well provided the number of blocks (b) or the number of factor levels (k) exceeds five. Like the Kruskal–Wallis test procedure, the Friedman test procedure is to reject H_0 if FR lies in the right-tail of the chi-square curve; that is,

$$\text{reject } H_0 \text{ if FR} > \chi^2_{\alpha,df}$$

where $\chi^2_{\alpha,df}$ is the value from Table A.6 corresponding to df = $k - 1$ and right-tail area = α. This procedure is summarized in the accompanying box.

THE FRIEDMAN TEST

Hypotheses:

H_0: the k populations have identical probability distributions

H_a: at least two of the populations differ in location

Assumptions:

1. The factor levels are applied in a random manner within each block.
2. The number of blocks (b) or the number of factor levels (k) exceeds five.
3. Values within each block can be ranked.

Procedure: Values are ranked within each block. Letting T_i = sum of the ranks within the ith factor level, the FR statistic is calculated using equation 18.14. The null hypothesis is rejected if

$$\text{FR} > \chi^2_{\alpha,df}$$

where $\chi^2_{\alpha,df}$ is the chi-square value (Table A.6) with df = $k - 1$ and right-tail area = α.

EXAMPLE 18.9

In a study of the perceived attractiveness of new car warranties, a newspaper writer sent the warranties of three competing brands of automobiles (Starfire, RX1000, and Bullet) to 10 different editors of automotive magazines. At first, it was decided to have each editor assign a score from 0 (worst) to 100 (best) for each of the three warranties and use a randomized block analysis. Here the 10 editors would represent the $b = 10$ blocks, and the factor of interest would be brand of automobile, consisting of $k = 3$ levels. However, after much discussion, it became clear that each editor had his or her own set of criteria for judging a warranty, not to mention different weights for each of these various criteria.

Consequently, it was decided simply to ask each editor to rank the three warranties, rather than determine a score for each one. The warranties were assigned in a random manner for each editor. The results are summarized in Table 18.9. Use the Friedman test and a significance level of .10 to determine if there is a difference in the perceived quality of the three warranties.

Solution

The computed value of the Friedman statistic is

$$\text{FR} = \frac{12}{(10)(3)(4)}[22^2 + 14^2 + 24^2] - 3(10)(4) = 125.6 - 120 = 5.6$$

Referring to the chi-square table (A.6), using $k - 1 = 2$ df and right-tail area = .10, the test procedure is to

$$\text{reject } H_0 \text{ if FR} > 4.6052$$

TABLE

18.9

Results of new-car warranty ranking (Example 18.9).

Starfire	RX1000	Bullet
3	2	1
2	1	3
3	1	2
2	1	3
3	2	1
2	1	3
1	2	3
2	1	3
3	1	2
1	2	3
$T_1 = 22$	$T_2 = 14$	$T_3 = 24$

FIGURE

18.11

Excel solution to Example 18.9 using the Friedman test within **KPK Data Analysis ➤ Nonparametric Procedures.**

Since $5.6 > 4.6052$, we reject H_0 and conclude that there *is* a difference in the perceived quality of the three warranties. The apparent reason for this result is the fact that the RX1000 warranty was ranked first or second by all 10 editors and far outranked the warranties for the Starfire and the Bullet.

An Excel solution for Example 18.9 is shown in Figure 18.11. Select **Comparing More Than Two Groups** and click on **Friedman Test** and then on **OK.** To carry out the test, enter "A1" as the **Upper left corner** of **sample data,** "D1" as the **Output Range,** "3" as the **Number of factor levels,** and "10" as the **Number of blocks.** Be sure to select **Each row is a block** (this is the default selection) since the rows constitute the blocks. From Figure 18.11, the computed chi-square value is once again equal to 5.6, and the corresponding *p*-value is .0608. This *p*-value indicates a fairly weak result, but one that is statistically significant at a level of $\alpha = .10$. As in the previous solution, the conclusion here is that there is a difference in the perceived quality of the three warranties.

⊠ Exercises 18.36–18.54

Understanding the Mechanics

18.36 Samples of size 5 are randomly selected from four populations. A Kruskal–Wallis test is used to test if at least two of the populations differ in location. The sums of the ranks for samples 1, 2, 3, and 4 are 69, 34, 32, and 75, respectively. Do these data indicate a difference in the locations of at least two populations? Use a significance level of .05.

18.37 Use the Kruskal–Wallis statistic on the following data to determine if at least two populations differ in location. Use a .10 significance level.

Sample from Population 1	Sample from Population 2	Sample from Population 3
3.9	1.7	4.6
2.6	2.1	2.3
2.5	2.3	2.1
3.8	3.4	3.8
2.2	1.8	1.5
4.4	3.1	3.1
2.0	2.9	2.3
1.9	2.8	2.6

18.38 A randomized block design is used to analyze data from a single factor with three levels and with the sample data organized into 10 blocks. The totals of the ranks of the sample from populations 1, 2, and 3 are $T_1 = 20$, $T_2 = 14$, and $T_3 = 26$, respectively. Determine if there is a difference in location for at least two of the populations. Use the Friedman test with a .05 significance level.

18.39 The data presented here are collected using a randomized block design. Conduct a Friedman test to determine if at least two of the populations differ in location. Use a .10 significance level.

Block	A	B	C
1	15	28	31
2	10	11	15
3	5	9	3
4	10	3	8
5	39	41	50
6	16	13	18
7	27	23	25
8	2	2	9
9	1	6	12

Applying the New Concepts

18.40 Four machines are used to package 16-ounce bags of puffed wheat. Each machine is designed to package the bags so that the average bag has 16 ounces of cereal in it. From the data, in which samples of eight bags were randomly selected from each machine, is there an indication that the amount of puffed wheat packaged is not the same for all four machines? Use a .05 significance level.

Machine 1	Machine 2	Machine 3	Machine 4
15.9	16.1	15.8	16.4
15.8	16.3	15.9	16.5
16.0	16.0	16.0	16.0
15.7	15.9	16.1	16.1
16.1	16.4	16.0	16.4
16.2	15.8	16.4	16.3
15.6	16.2	16.1	16.1
15.8	16.1	15.7	16.4

18.41 Thirty new employees were selected to test two training programs. Ten of them (group A) were randomly selected for a self-paced training program. Another 10 (group B) were randomly selected for a classroom training program. The remaining 10 employees (group C) were not given any training. After the completion of the experiment, the manager evaluated the 30 employees on their productivity over a two-week span. The following ranks were given by the manager, with the highest rankings being given to those who were not productive.

Program A	Program B	Program C
6	5	1
22	21	10
25	15	11
26	4	13
20	8	2
30	12	3
16	18	7
23	24	14
28	27	17
9	29	19

From the data, is there a difference in the productivity of the three groups? Use a .05 significance level.

18.42 Mark Hulbert, editor of *Hulbert Financial Digest*, concedes that the type of market letter you want to follow during a bull market is one that recommends taking certain risks. But he is quick to point out that those gains can quickly evaporate during a down market if an investor continues to take such risks. That is why certain conservative investment styles can perform as well as high-risk ones over a long cycle. The following table shows a sample of newsletters that can be categorized as endorsing either high, average, or low risks. Each newsletter's performance is measured over an 11-year period ending January 1, 1999. Do the data provide sufficient evidence that the returns from these categories of stock market newsletters differ? Use a 5% significance level.

Newsletter	Performance in Percentage	Category of Risk
Addison-Report	8.4	Low
BI Research	11.6	High
Big Picture	7.1	High
Bob Brinker's Market Timer	8.8	Average
Cabot Market Letter	6.2	High

Newsletter	Performance in Percentage	Category of Risk
Chartist	15.0	High
Dow Theory Forecasts	9.5	Average
Equities Special Situations	4.2	High
Fabian Investment Resource	10.6	Low
Fidelity Monitor	15.1	Average
Fund Advice.com	10.1	Low
Fundline	14.8	Average
Granville Market Letter	−16.6	High
Growth Stock Outlook	6.8	Low
Insiders	13.2	High
Investment Quality Trends	13.6	Low
Investment Reporter	11.3	High
LaLoggie's Special Situation Investor	5.2	Average
Margo's Small Stocks	5.4	High
Market Logic	6.9	Average
Medical Technology Stock Letter	1.3	High
Mutual Fund Forecaster	10.1	Average
Mutual Fund Investing	7.6	Low
Mutual Fund Strategists	7.7	Average
No-Load Fund X	11.5	Average
Professional Tape Reader	1.1	Low
Systems and Forecasts	12.2	Low

(Source: "The Forbes/Hulbert Investment Letter Survey," *Forbes,* January 25, 1999, pp. 112–13.)

18.43 The management of a company that markets Soft and Fresh Detergent would like to increase sales of detergent by including a free drinking glass in the box, including a coupon worth 50 cents toward the next purchase, or using a colorful see-through plastic container for the detergent. Thirty stores in different cities were randomly selected to market the detergent in one of the three ways (10 stores for each way). The number of boxes sold in these stores over a one-month period follows. Do the data indicate a difference in the number of boxes sold for each of the marketing strategies? Use a 5% significance level.

Free Glass	Coupon	See-Through Plastic Container
350	320	374
310	315	371
250	300	332
380	315	361
290	390	356
270	311	349
340	318	331
310	330	322
290	340	368
375	314	351

18.44 The number of hours it takes three workers to complete a task is given in the following table. The task is assigned to each worker four times. Do the data indicate a significant difference in the time it takes each worker to complete the task? Use a significance level of .05.

Worker 1	Worker 2	Worker 3
3.1	3.4	3.5
3.4	3.3	3.2
3.0	3.4	3.3
3.1	3.2	3.1

18.45 The number of cars passing each of three different intersections in Crossroads City between 5:00 P.M. and 5:30 P.M. is given in the following table for randomly selected days. Fifteen days were randomly selected, and then the amount of traffic was recorded for 5 of the 15 days at each intersection. Test the null hypothesis that there is no difference in the amount of traffic at each intersection between 5:00 P.M. and 5:30 P.M. Use a 10% significance level.

Intersection 1	Intersection 2	Intersection 3
440	480	433
420	392	406
530	386	427
401	456	338
454	427	397

18.46 A manager believes that the higher-salaried employees in a certain company are more satisfied with their jobs than are the lower-salaried employees. A sample of 10 employees from each of the salary levels indicated by the following table was taken. Is there a significant difference in the satisfaction level, measured on a scale of 1 to 10 (10 being a perfectly satisfied employee), for the three groups? Use a significance level of 5%.

$25,000 to $40,000	$40,000 to $60,000	Over $60,000
4	7	8
3	8	7
7	6	6
6	7	7
5	9	5
9	3	9
1	4	10
8	9	3
7	6	8
6	7	7

18.47 The yields on short-term, tax-exempt mutual funds have tended to fluctuate less than intermediate and long-term bond funds. A money manager is interested in whether the annualized compounded percentage given in short-term tax-exempt mutual funds differs over the one-year period, the three-year period, and the five-year period ending on January 1, 1999. Do the following data (measured in percentage annualized returns) indicate a difference in the performance of short-term, tax-exempt mutual funds over these three periods of time? Use a 5% significance level.

Short-Term, Tax-Exempt Mutual Fund	1-Year Performance	3-Year Performance	5-Year Performance
CMA Tax-Exempt	2.98	3.22	3.18
Smith Barney Muni MM	2.94	3.12	3.15
Vanguard Muni: Tax-Exempt	3.34	3.54	3.59
Fidelity Muni MM	3.13	3.36	3.52
Schwab: Muni MM	2.92	3.07	3.09
Paine Weber RMA Tax-Free	2.93	3.08	3.10
Fidelity Spartan Muni MM	3.26	3.12	3.52
Strong Muni MM	3.54	3.69	3.80
Active Assets Tax-Free	2.95	3.13	3.14
Centennial Tax-Free	2.95	3.13	3.14

(Source: "Fund Performance Derby," *The Wall Street Journal,* January 22, 1999, p. C21.)

18.48 In Exercise 11.7, can you conclude that there is a significant difference in the monthly sales of the three salespeople, using the Kruskal–Wallis test statistic? Use a 5% significance level. When would you prefer the Kruskal–Wallis test to the usual ANOVA procedure?

18.49 The vice president of quality assurance at an airline company is interested in whether its three quality engineers are usually in agreement on the ratings they give to different airplane seating designs. Seven different designs are chosen at random and the quality engineers are asked to rate the comfort to the passengers on a scale from 1 to 10, with 10 representing the highest level of comfort possible. Do the given data indicate a difference in the ratings of the three quality engineers? Use a 10% significance level.

Design	Quality Engineer 1	Quality Engineer 2	Quality Engineer 3
1	5	7	8
2	4	3	5
3	6	5	4
4	9	7	8
5	5	7	4
6	8	7	6
7	9	6	8

18.50 The manager at a manufacturing plant is interested in whether there is a significant difference in the number of times four machines need to be readjusted after going out of control. Eight months are randomly selected, and the number of times the machines are readjusted per month is recorded. Do the data support the conclusion that some machines need more adjusting than others? Use a 5% significance level.

Month	Machine 1	Machine 2	Machine 3	Machine 4
1	5	6	3	6
2	4	3	7	5
3	4	5	6	3
4	5	3	4	7
5	4	4	5	6
6	10	11	9	11
7	15	18	13	16
8	3	4	5	4

Using the Computer

18.51 **[DATA SET EX18-51]** *Variable description:*

Supplier1Rating: Rating by supervisor on the quality of parts supplied by supplier 1

Supplier2Rating: Rating by supervisor on the quality of parts supplied by supplier 2

Supplier3Rating: Rating by supervisor on the quality of parts supplied by supplier 3

The vice president of an industrial firm wished to determine if the supervisors in the firm's manufacturing plant perceived a difference in the quality of parts provided by three suppliers. Sixty supervisors were randomly selected to participate in the study, and twenty of the supervisors were assigned to rate a particular supplier. The supervi-

sors responded with a number between 1 and 7, where 1 represented the "highest quality" and 7 represented the "lowest quality." What conclusion can you draw from the standard, one-way ANOVA and from the Kruskal–Wallis test? Use a 5% significance level.

18.52 **[DATA SET EX18-52]** *Variable description:*

NonExporter: Knowledge level of international trade regulations and barriers by companies that do not export

MarginalExporter: Knowledge level of international trade regulations and barriers by companies that do some exporting

ActiveExporter: Knowledge level of international trade regulations and barriers by companies that export most of their products

International marketing researchers conducted a study to determine if there is a difference in the knowledge level of companies that were classified as doing no exporting, some exporting, or high levels of exporting. A scale from 1 to 10 was used to measure the degree of perceived knowledge of international trade. Thirty companies were selected for NonExporter and MarginalExporter, while 25 companies were selected for ActiveExporter. Using an appropriate nonparametric test, what conclusion can you draw? Use a 1% significance level.

18.53 **[DATA SET EX18-53]** *Variable description:*

StoreNum: A number from 1 through 20 to indicate the convenience store

Quarter1Sales: Sales during quarter 1

Quarter2Sales: Sales during quarter 2

Quarter3Sales: Sales during quarter 3

Quarter4Sales: Sales during quarter 4

The president of a chain of convenience stores is interested in determining if a difference exists in the sales of its stores over the four quarters of last year. A random sample of 20 convenience stores was selected. Can the president conclude from this sample that a difference exists in the quarterly sales of the convenience stores? Use a 5% significance level.

18.54 **[DATA SET EX18-54]** *Variable description:*

EngineerNum: A number from 1 through 30 indicating a particular engineer

Task1Time: Completion time for task 1

Task2Time: Completion time for task 2

Task3Time: Completion time for task 3

Task4Time: Completion time for task 4

A manager is interested in the time required for mechanical engineers to complete four types of tasks. Thirty mechanical engineers are randomly selected. Each engineer completes the four tasks and the times are recorded. Compare the results using a randomized block design and using the Friedman test. What conclusions can you make? Base your decisions on the *p*-value.

On the CD . . .
Section 18.4: A Measure of Association: Spearman Rank
  Correlation
Section 18.5: An Alternative to the Least Squares Regression Line:
  A Nonparametric Approach
Exercises 18.55–18.74

Summary

A key step in applying any statistical technique correctly is to make sure that it is appropriate for the type of data that is involved. For example, performing a *t* test using a small sample containing *ordinal* data (such as a set of consumer rankings) is never correct. For situations in which your data are ordinal or from populations that you suspect are non-normally distributed, a **nonparametric technique** is often preferable. This chapter has introduced some (certainly not all) of the more popular nonparametric procedures.

The **runs test** examines a sequence containing an arrangement of two symbols (M or F, yes or no, + or –, and so on) to determine whether the sequence was generated in a random manner. We defined tests for both small samples (using Table A.15) and large samples (using a test statistic having an approximate normal distribution and Table A.4).

The **Mann–Whitney *U* test** is a nonparametric procedure for determining whether two populations differ in location using two independent samples. Unlike its counterpart, the *t* test, this test does not require that the populations be normally distributed. By combining (pooling) the samples and finding the ranks of the combined sample, you can calculate a value of the test statistic. This method can be applied both to small samples (using Table A.10) and to large samples (using an approximate normal distribution and Table A.4).

The **Wilcoxon signed rank test** is a nonparametric procedure used for determining whether the population of differences is centered at zero when dealing with two dependent (paired) samples. The Wilcoxon technique determines the differences of the paired observations and then calculates a value of the test statistic using the ranks of these differences. Both small samples (using Table A.11) and large samples (using an approximate normal distribution and Table A.4) can be tested.

The **Kruskal–Wallis test** is an extension of the Mann–Whitney test. It is used to test whether two or more populations differ in location when using independent samples. As in the Mann–Whitney procedure, the samples are pooled and then ranked from smallest to largest. The resulting ranks are then used to define a test statistic. This statistic has an approximate chi-square distribution (tabulated in Table A.6), even for fairly small sample sizes.

A nonparametric alternative to the randomized block technique (discussed in Chapter 11) is the **Friedman test.** The Friedman test does not require normal populations with equal variances, unlike the randomized block procedure. Values are ranked within each block and then summed for the various populations under consideration. The Friedman test statistic is calculated using these sums and has an approximate chi-square distribution.

These tests are summarized in Figure 18.18.

FIGURE 18.18

Summary of nonparametric tests of central tendency.

Nonparametric Tests of Central Tendency

Independent Samples — Dependent Samples

Two Populations: Mann-Whitney U Test

More Than Two Populations: Kruskal-Wallis Test

Two Populations: Wilcoxon Signed Rank Test

More Than Two Populations: Friedman Test

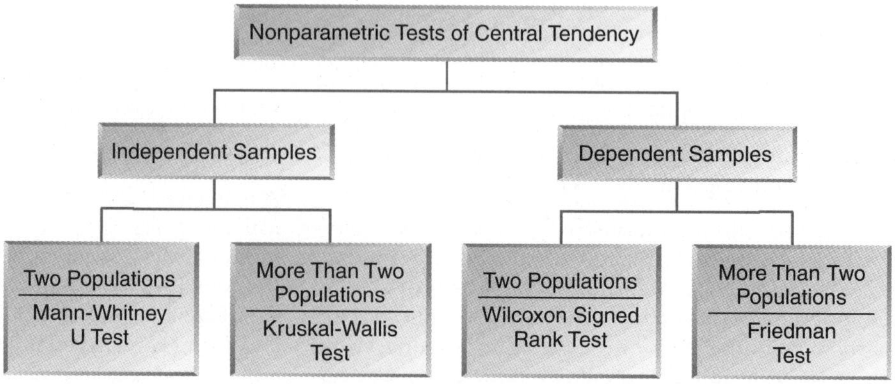

Summary of Formulas

Runs Test (Large Sample, R = Number of Runs)

$$\mu_R = 1 + \frac{2n_1 n_2}{n_1 + n_2}$$

$$\sigma_R = \sqrt{\frac{2n_1 n_2 (2n_1 n_2 - n_1 - n_2)}{(n_1 + n_2)^2 (n_1 + n_2 - 1)}}$$

Test statistic (large samples):

$$Z = \frac{R - \mu_R}{\sigma_R}$$

Mann–Whitney U Test

$$U_1 = n_1 n_2 + \frac{n_1 (n_1 + 1)}{2} - T_1$$

$$U_2 = n_1 n_2 + \frac{n_2 (n_2 + 1)}{2} - T_2$$

$$\mu_{U_2} = \frac{n_1 n_2}{2}$$

$$\sigma_{U_2} = \sqrt{\frac{n_1 n_2 (n_1 + n_2 + 1)}{12}}$$

Test statistic (large samples):

$$Z = \frac{U_2 - \mu_{U_2}}{\sigma_{U_2}}$$

Wilcoxon Signed Rank Test

$$\mu_{T_+} = \frac{n(n + 1)}{4}$$

$$\sigma_{T_+} = \sqrt{\frac{n(n + 1)(2n + 1)}{24}}$$

Test statistic (large samples):

$$Z = \frac{T_+ - \mu_{T_+}}{\sigma_{T_+}}$$

Kruskal–Wallis Test

Test statistic:

$$KW = \frac{12}{n(n + 1)} \sum_{i=1}^{k} \frac{T_i^2}{n_i} - 3(n + 1)$$

Friedman Test

Test statistic:

$$FR = \frac{12}{bk(k + 1)} \sum_{i=1}^{k} T_i^2 - 3b(k + 1)$$

X Review Exercises 18.75–18.96

18.75 Consider the following sequence of regression residuals. Using the runs test on positive and negative residuals, is there evidence to indicate that the residuals are not in random order? Use a 10% significance level.

    −.1 .2   .6 −.7   .8 .1 .2 .4 −.9 −.5 −.4 −.1 .2   .3   .1 −.2 −.3 −.6 .2 .7
     .1 .8 −.3 −.1 −.4 .2 .1 .2   .3 −.9   .1   .1 .5 −.2 −.3 −.1 −.4 −.1 .3 .1

18.76 A radio station requests that people telephone the station to express their opinion on the new property tax the city is levying. An F represents a person telephoning in who is for the tax, and an A represents one against it. Test whether the following sequence of people telephoning the radio station is nonrandomly generated. Use a 5% significance level.

FAFAAAFAAFAAAFFAFAFAAAFAA

18.77 The manager of a small-town savings and loan association is interested in finding out whether there is a relationship between the average monthly balance of a savings account and the age of the savings account. Fifteen accounts were selected at random. Do the data indicate a relationship at the .05 significance level?

Average Monthly Balance	Age of Account (Years)	Average Monthly Balance	Age of Account (Years)
2510	1.5	6148	3.8
3612	2.6	5134	4.7
5634	3.5	2614	1.1
3698	1.8	2581	1.9
3978	2.1	2501	0.5
6751	4.3	3986	4.2
5869	10.1	6645	4.1
		3582	2.3

18.78 What are the necessary assumption for conducting a t test using two independent samples? What is the corresponding nonparametric test for this statistical procedure? Do the assumptions for this test differ from those for the t test? How?

18.79 A statistician wants to determine whether two populations differ in location. After collecting a sample of size eight from each population, the statistician finds that the sum of the ranks of the observations in population 1 is 60. Is there evidence to indicate that there is a difference in location for the two population? Use a 5% significance level.

18.80 An economist wishes to test the belief that the cost of a basket of grocery items in Houston, Texas, differs from the cost of the same basket of grocery items in Atlanta, Georgia. Eight retail grocery stores in Atlanta and in Houston were randomly selected. Using the following data and a 10% significance level, test that there is no difference in the cost of the basket of grocery items for the two cities.

Houston	237	236	239	240	220	236	232	244
Atlanta	230	239	241	243	235	233	254	249

18.81 Politicians often refer to various polls to assess the confidence adults have that their children will enjoy a higher standard of living than themselves. Use the following data to regress the percentage who expect their children to have a higher standard of living (Y) on the independent variable time (t). Calculate the residuals. Use a runs test to determine if the sequence of positive and negative residuals appears to be randomly generated with respect to time. Use a 5% significance level.

Year	Quarter	Time Period (t)	Percentage Expecting Children to Have a Higher Standard of Living (Y)
1995	1	1	51.1
	2	2	44.2
	3	3	41.6
	4	4	40.3
1996	1	5	41.5
	2	6	42.7
	3	7	46.5
	4	8	48.7
1997	1	9	51.6
	2	10	53.8
	3	11	58.6
	4	12	60.3
1998	1	13	63.1
	2	14	62.4
	3	15	61.3
	4	16	61.7

(Source: "And Are Confident That Our Children Will Enjoy a Higher Standard of Living," *The Wall Street Journal,* December 10, 1998, p. A14.)

18.82 State wildlife and highway officials are installing more signs alerting motorists to be aware of deer during the month of November. The following data represent the number of accidents reported at 15 highway locations for a one-week period in which no deer warning signs are placed on the highway and for a one-week period in which deer warning signs are installed. Do the data indicate that the deer warning signs reduced the number of accidents? Use a 5% significance level.

Location	1	2	3	4	5	6	7	8	9	10	11	12	13	14	15
No Sign	2	2	4	3	2	8	9	4	6	3	6	4	2	6	4
Sign Present	1	3	3	0	3	1	2	3	1	3	3	2	3	1	5

18.83 A cooking contest was conducted: Two top chefs baked chicken and then asked 12 tasters to judge the quality of the cooking on a scale from 1 to 10, 10 being the highest score. Test the null hypothesis that there was no difference between the taster's judgment of the two chefs' quality of cooking at a significance level of .05.

Taster	Chef A	Chef B	Taster	Chef A	Chef B
1	8	7	7	9	9
2	6	10	8	10	7
3	5	9	9	9	10
4	10	4	10	8	6
5	5	8	11	4	9
6	3	7	12	7	3

18.84 Paint A, paint B, and paint C were painted on metallic surfaces and then subjected to high temperatures. Nine replications of the experiment were made. A measure of the cohesiveness of the paint was then taken. The following coded data represent the cohesiveness of the individual paints. Test the hypothesis that there was no difference in the cohesiveness for the three paints. Use a 10% significance level.

Paint A	Paint B	Paint C	Paint A	Paint B	Paint C
1.3	2.1	3.4	1.6	1.9	2.5
1.6	2.7	2.8	2.6	2.3	2.4
3.1	1.6	1.9	2.7	1.8	1.9
2.6	1.9	2.0	1.9	1.6	1.7
4.3	1.6	2.8			

18.85 A chemist was interested in knowing whether three different drugs used for insomnia were equally effective. Three groups of mice, with 10 mice to a group, were used. Each group of mice was given the adult-equivalent dosage of one of the three drugs. The time, in minutes, it took for the mice to fall asleep was recorded. Using the following data, test the null hypothesis that each drug is equally effective in reducing sleep latency. Use a significance level of 5%.

Drug 1	Drug 2	Drug 3	Drug 1	Drug 2	Drug 3
32	38	31	41	35	30
35	37	33	28	39	28
40	42	29	34	40	33
30	44	34	39	41	37
33	37	31	28	42	35

18.86 An automobile worker would like to know whether there is any difference in the comfort of three different cars. Three groups of five drivers were selected to judge the riding comfort of the three cars; one of the three cars was assigned to each group. The drivers rated the comfort of each car on a scale from 1 to 5, 5 being the most comfortable. Test that there is no difference in the comfort of the three cars from these data. Use a 5% significance level.

Car 1	Car 2	Car 3
2	5	4
4	3	1
4	4	2
3	3	5
5	2	4

18.87 **[DATA SET EX18-87]** *Variable description:*

Year: Years are numbered from 1985 to 2000

Imports: U.S. imports as a percentage of world gross domestic product

The United States is very important as a market for other countries. U.S. imports from 1985 to 2000 have trended upward. Compare the slope of the least squares regression line using Year to predict the variable Imports with the slope of the regression line through the medians.

(Source: "Magnet," *The Wall Street Journal,* July 17, 2001, p. 1A.)

18.88 **[DATA SET EX18-88]** *Variable description:*

Newspaper: Sales in thousands of dollars from advertising in newspapers

Mailers: Sales in thousands of dollars from using mailers to advertise

TV: Sales in thousands of dollars from advertising on TV

Radio: Sales in thousands of dollars from using the radio to advertise

A company uses four advertising methods to increase sales: newspapers, mailers, television, and radio. Four six-month periods were randomly selected and monthly sales were recorded for one of the six-month periods for each advertising method. Do the data indicate a difference in sales from the four advertising methods? Use a 10% significance level.

18.89 [DATA SET EX18-89] *Variable description:*

Client: Clients are numbered 1 to 15

AdjGross: Adjusted gross income in thousands of dollars

Charity: Percentage of adjusted gross income claimed as a charitable contribution

The manager of a firm that specializes in assisting individuals in filling out federal income tax forms wished to know if there was a positive association between the adjusted gross income of its clients and the percentage of their adjusted gross income that they were claiming as a charitable contribution. Fifteen clients were randomly sampled. Do the data from these clients indicate a positive relationship at the 5% significance level?

18.90 [DATA SET EX18-90] *Variable description:*

Company: Companies are numbered from 1 to 8

NEPA: Percent increase in cost due to NEPA

CWA: Percent increase in cost due to CWA

CAA: Percent increase in cost due to CAA

The Environmental Protection Agency (EPA) proposed that a new law be imposed on chemical companies that requires them to electronically report environmental data in a more timely fashion in accordance with three acts: National Environmental Policy Act (NEPA), the Clean Water Act (CWA), and the Clean Air Act (CAA). Suppose that an environmental analyst at the EPA randomly sampled eight chemical companies and recorded the percent increase in their cost due to each of these acts.

   a. Is there an association between the variables NEPA and CWA using a 5% significance level?

   b. Is there an association between the variables NEPA and CAA using a 5% significance level?

   c. Compare the slope of the regression equation through the medians in predicting NEPA from CWA with the slope of the regression equation through the medians in predicting NEPA from CAA.

(Source: "Industry Opposes EPA Record Keeping Proposal on Cost Basis," *Chemical Market Report* 260, no. 18, November 12, 2001, p. 9.)

18.91 [DATA SET EX18-91] *Variable description:*

Household: Households are numbered from 1 to 10

Chan22: Ranking of Channel 22 by a household

Chan29: Ranking of Channel 29 by a household

Chan32: Ranking of Channel 32 by a household

A marketing research firm is interested in whether there is a difference in viewers' preferences for three types of movie channels. Rankings of the channels from 1 to 3 by 10 selected households are recorded. A ranking of 1 indicates the most desirable channel. Do the data provide sufficient evidence to indicate that there is a difference in the preference for these channels? Use a 10% significance level.

18.92 [DATA SET EX18-92] *Variable description:*

Salesperson: Salespersons are numbered from 1 to 12

MedSoft: Number of sales of MedSoft software sold by a salesperson

PowerMed: Numbered of sales of PowerMed software sold by a salesperson

MEDEX: Number of sales of MEDEX software sold by a salesperson

Medical Software, Inc. sells three software products to health care facilities: MedSoft, PowerMed, MEDEX. The manager of Medical Software is interested in whether one type of product was sold more than another during the past six months. Twelve salespersons are randomly selected and the number of sales of each type of software is recorded. From the data, can the manager conclude that the three software products do not sell equally as well? Use a 5% significance level.

18.93 [DATA SET EX18-93] *Variable description:*

Year: Year from 1990 to 2000

NewVehicleSales: U.S. new vehicle sales in millions

Sales of new vehicles have undergone several downturns. During the Arab oil embargo of 1973, during the OPEC price increase in the early 1980s, and during the Gulf War in 1991, sales of new vehicles have been very slow.

a. Find the least squares regression equation to predict NewVehicleSales using the variable Year.

b. Find the regression line through the medians to predict NewVehicleSales using the variable Year.

c. Compare the slopes of the lines in parts a and b.

(Source: "Auto Sales During National Crises," *USA Today,* September 20, 2001, p. 2B.)

18.94 [DATA SET EX18-94] *Variable description:*

Person: A number from 1 to 20 to indicate the individual

NoAHA: Score from 1 to 25 measuring the performance of facial cream with no AHA

AHA: Score from 1 to 25 measuring the performance of facial cream with AHA.

Recently, facial products with alpha-hydroxy acids (AHAs) have become a favorite over-the-counter alternative in cosmetics and personal care. Avon Products touts its Anew line, which uses AHA, as being a set of groundbreaking age-reversal creams. Suppose a researcher wished to determine whether there was a significant difference between the performance of a leading facial cosmetic without AHA and one with AHA. Assume that 20 randomly selected women used the two products on opposite sides of their face for a two-month period. At the end of this period, a judge assigned two scores from 1 to 25 measuring the performance of each facial cosmetic (recorded as NoAHA and AHA). Do the data indicate a difference in the performance of the two products, one with AHA and one without AHA? Use the *p*-value to base your conclusion.

(Source: "New Age-defying Ingredients Enter the Cosmetics Arena," *Chemical Market Reporter,* May 14, 2001, p. 8.)

18.95 A home builder records the number of new construction permits issued by a county in Georgia. From a plot of the number of new construction permits over a 24-month period, the builder estimates a cyclical trend of eight months. The builder examines two regression equations to predict the new permits: one with time (Time) as the independent variable and the other with time and the new permits lagged by eight months (PermitsLag8) as the independent variables. Examine the computer printouts displaying the regression analysis for each equation. Explain the importance of using the runs test in examining the residuals.

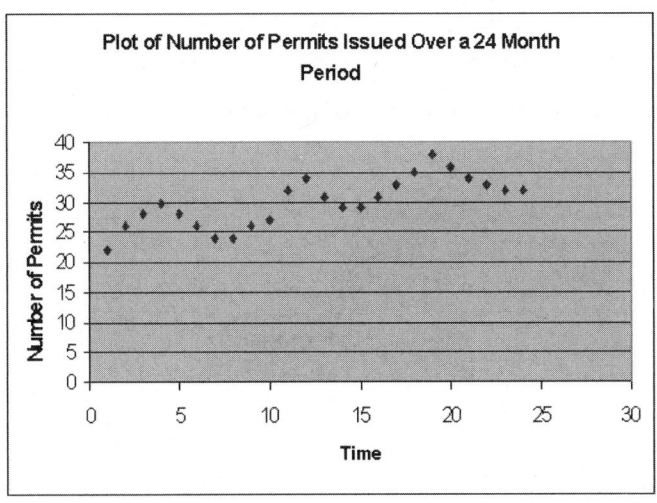

Summary Output Using Time

Regression Statistics

Multiple R	0.76703517
R Square	0.58834295
Adjusted R Square	0.56963126
Standard Error	2.70831686
Observations	24

ANOVA

	df	SS	MS	F	Significance F
Regression	1	230.6304348	230.6304	31.4425	1.22733E-05
Residual	22	161.3695652	7.33498		
Total	23	392			

	Coefficients	Standard Error	t Stat	p-value	Lower 95%	Upper 95%
Intercept	24.4021739	1.141150626	21.38383	3.3E-16	22.03556982	26.768778
Time	0.44782609	0.079863907	5.607365	1.2E-05	0.282198303	0.6134539

Runs Test for Regression Equation with Time

Number of Runs	7
Mean	13
Std. Dev.	2.395648229
Z Value	−2.50454133
2-Tailed p-value	0.012261059

Summary Output Using Time and PermitsLag8

Regression Statistics

Multiple R	0.802082959
R Square	0.643337072
Adjusted R Square	0.588465853
Standard Error	2.042109863
Observations	16

ANOVA

	df	SS	MS	F	Significance F
Regression	2	97.78723502	48.893617	11.72449	0.001229354
Residual	13	54.21276498	4.1702126		
Total	15	152			

	Coefficients	Standard Error	t Stat	p-value	Lower 95%	Upper 95%
Intercept	11.23065191	1.141150626	21.38383	3.3E-16	22.03556982	26.768778
Time	0.116328106	0.079863907	5.607365	1.2E-05	0.282198303	0.6134539
PermitsLag8	0.674718008	0.203682993	3.312588	0.005610	0.234687738	1.1147482

Runs Test for Regression Equation with Time and PermitsLag8

Number of Runs	6
Mean	8.875
Std. Dev.	1.899835519
Z Value	−1.513288898
2-Tailed p-value	0.130206339

18.96 [DATA SET EX18-96] *Variable description:*

Group1: Scores on ten test runs for product A

Group2: Scores on ten test runs for product B

Group3: Scores on ten test runs for product C

A study by *Consumer Reports* of six filtering products designed to block "objectionable" Web sites from being viewed found these filters to be generally ineffective in its test on several Web sites. Information Technology Association of America responded to the study by saying that the number of Web sites considered by *Consumer Reports* was too small and that this small sample size did not capture the diversity of approaches and methodologies used by these filters. To understand how a few outliers can affect the results of a study with a small sample size, consider three groups, each consisting of scores from test runs on evaluating one of three products. Analyze the data in Group1, Group2, and Group3 using a one-way ANOVA and using the Kruskal–Wallis test. Why do you think these two procedures give different results? Use a 10% significance level.

(Source: "Consumer Reports Criticizes Filters," *Library Journal,* March 15, 2001, p. 20.)

Insights from Statistics in Action

Putting Service Back into Customer Service: Assessing Survey Data to Get Blue Oval Certified

The Statistics in Action introductory case study mentioned that Ford dealerships must make use of customer surveys to obtain information on how satisfied customers are with their dealership experience. Surveys may contain customer rankings to denote their preferences. These types of data may not comply with the assumptions of statistical procedures such as ANOVA. Thus, nonparametric statistics can assist dealers in analyzing their survey data. Suppose that a dealership would like to compare customer preferences on four makes of trucks: Ford, Chevy, Dodge, and Nissan. Customers interested in buying a truck are asked to rank these four makes in the order that indicates their likelihood of purchase. Data from 25 customers are listed in StatInActChap 19.xls.

1. What statistical test procedure would you use for the data collected to test the belief that there is a difference in the preference of consumers for the four makes of trucks? What statistical test would you use if instead of ranks the consumers provided a rating response on a continuous scale from 1 to 100 and these data were approximately normally distributed? Would it be easier for the respondents to provide ranks of the four makes of trucks than to provide a rating response on a scale from 1 to 100?

2. Analyze the belief in question 1 using a 5% significance level. Should we be concerned with which pairs of brands are different with respect to preference, considering the outcome of this analysis?

3. Perform a Wilcoxon signed rank test for testing that differences between Ford and Chevy truck preferences are not centered at 0. Use a 5% significance level.

4. Repeat question 3 using Ford and Nissan.

5. Could the Mann–Whitney test be used instead of the Wilcoxon signed rank test in question 3? When would this test be appropriate?

Sources: "Blue Oval Standards," *Dallas Morning News,* April 30, 2001, p. 1D; and "Ford Customer Program Raising Bottom Lines," *Dallas Morning News,* April 30, 2001, p. 1D.

Computer Exercises Using the Databases

Exercise 1—Appendix F

Choose 10 observations at random from the database of households that own their home and another 10 observations at random from households that rent their home (refer to variable OWNORENT). Using the Mann–Whitney test, is there sufficient evidence to conclude that the income of the principal wage earner is significantly different for the households that own their home and for the households that rent their home? Use a 5% significance level.

Exercise 2—Appendix F

Choose 12 observations at random from the database of households that have a secondary income (INCOME2) above $25,000. Choose another 12 observations from households that have a secondary income (INCOME2) that is positive and less than $25,000. Also, choose a random sample of 12 observations from households with no secondary income. Can one conclude that there is a difference in the house payment or apartment/house rent

(HPAYRENT) for the three groups? Use the Kruskal–Wallis test with a 5% significance level.

Exercise 3—Appendix G

Randomly select 12 observations from the database of companies with an A bond rating, 12 of companies with a B bond rating, and 12 of companies with a C bond rating. Can one conclude that there is a difference in the TOTAL (long-term assets) for the three groups? Use the Kruskal–Wallis test with a 5% significance level.

Exercise 4—Appendix G

Choose 25 observations at random from the database. Is there evidence that a positive relationship exists between EMPLOYEE (the number of employees) and SALES (the amount of sales)? Use the Spearman rank correlation coefficient and test at the 1% significance level. Determine the regression line through the medians using this set of data. Interpret the slope of this line.

Appendix SPSS®

Chapter 18 Appendix: Data Analysis with SPSS

Runs Test

Using the data in Example 18.2, enter the sample values in the first column by using a value of "1" for females and "0" for males. Name this variable "gender". *Note:* SPSS will not accept nonnumeric data for the runs test. Click on **Analyze ➤ Nonparametric Tests ➤ Runs** and move the gender variable into the **Test Variable List** box. After clicking on **OK,** the following output appears in the display pane.

NPar Tests

Runs Test

	GENDER
Test Value[a]	1.00
Cases < Test Value	22
Cases >= Test Value	23
Total Cases	45
Number of Runs	15
Z	-2.411
Asymp. Sig. (2-tailed)	.016

a. Median

Note: The computed Z value of -2.411 does not agree with that found in Example 18.2. SPSS will use equation 18.4 to compute the value of Z, provided the sample size is 50 or more. For situations where $n < 50$, SPSS will (1) add .5 to the numerator of equation 18.4 if $R - \mu_R \le .5$ or (2) subtract .5 from the numerator of equation 18.4 if $R - \mu_R > .5$. For situations where $|R - \mu_R| < .5$, the Z value is set equal to zero.

Mann–Whitney Test

To illustrate the Mann–Whitney procedure, the data from Example 18.4 will be used. Enter *all* 17 data value in the first column and the vendor indicators (1 = vendor A, 2 = vendor B) in the second column. Name these variables "strength" and "vendor". To carry out the Mann–Whitney test, click on **Analyze ➤ Nonparametric Tests ➤ 2 Independent Samples.** Move the strength variable into the **Test Variable List** box and the vendor variable into the **Grouping Variable** box. Click on **Define Groups** and enter "1" in the **Group 1** box and "2" in the **Group2** box. After clicking on **OK,** the following output will appear in the display pane. The computed value of $U = 29$ agrees with that determined in Example 18.4 as does the *p*-value of .5414.

Ranks

	VENDOR	N	Mean Rank	Sum of Ranks
STRENGTH	1	8	8.13	65.00
	2	9	9.78	88.00
	Total	17		

Test Statistics[b]

	STRENGTH
Mann-Whitney U	29.000
Wilcoxon W	65.000
Z	-.674
Asymp. Sig. (2-tailed)	.501
Exact Sig. [2*(1-tailed Sig.)]	.5414[a]

a. Not corrected for ties.

b. Grouping Variable: VENDOR

Wilcoxon Signed Rank Test

To illustrate the Wilcoxon procedure, the data from Example 18.7 will be used. Enter the 2% concentration values in the first column and the 10% concentration values in the second column. Name these variables "perc2" and "perc10". To carry out the Wilcoxon test, click on **Analyze ➤ Nonparametric Tests ➤ 2 Related Samples.** Click on "perc2" to set it as Variable 1 in the **Current Selections** frame and click on "perc10" to set it as Variable 2. Click on the pointer button to set these variables in the **Test Pair(s) List** box. After clicking on **OK,** the following output will appear in the display pane. *Note:* SPSS use a correction for ties when calculating the standard deviation in equation 18.11. For this illustration, the calculated value of the test statistic ($Z = -1.41$) does agree to two decimal places with the value determined in Example 18.7.

Ranks

		N	Mean Rank	Sum of Ranks
PERC2 - PERC10	Negative Ranks	11[a]	11.82	130.00
	Positive Ranks	8[b]	7.50	60.00
	Ties	1[c]		
	Total	20		

a. PERC2 < PERC10

b. PERC2 > PERC10

c. PERC10 = PERC2

Test Statistics[b]

	PERC2 - PERC10
Z	-1.409[a]
Asymp. Sig. (2-tailed)	.159

a. Based on positive ranks.

b. Wilcoxon Signed Ranks Test

Kruskal–Wallis Test

To illustrate the Kruskal–Wallis procedure, the data from Example 18.8 will be used. Enter *all* 20 data values in the first column and the brand indicators (1 = Brand 1, . . . , 4 = Brand 4) in the second column. Name these variables "downtime" and "brand". To carry out the Kruskal–Wallis test, click on **Analyze ➤ Nonparametric Tests ➤ K Independent Samples.** Move the downtime variable into the **Test Variable List** box and the brand variable into the **Grouping Variable** box. Click on **Define Range** and enter "1" in the **Minimum** box and "4" in the **Maximum** box. After clicking on **OK,** the following output will appear in the display pane. The computed chi-square value of 13.83 agrees with that found in Example 18.8.

Ranks

	BRAND	N	Mean Rank
DOWNTIME	1	5	14.80
	2	5	5.80
	3	5	5.40
	4	5	16.00
	Total	20	

Test Statistics[a,b]

	DOWNTIME
Chi-Square	13.834
df	3
Asymp. Sig.	.003

a. Kruskal Wallis Test

b. Grouping Variable: BRAND

Friedman Test

To illustrate the Friedman procedure, the data from Example 18.9 will be used. Enter the Starfire values in the first column, the RX1000 values in the second column, and the Bullet values in the third column. Name these variables "starfire", "rx1000" and "bullet". To carry out the Friedman test, click on **Analyze ➤ Non-parametric Tests ➤ K Related Samples.** Click on each of the three variables to move them to the **Test Variables** box. After clicking on **OK,** the following output will appear in the display pane. The computed chi-square value of 5.6 and corresponding *p*-value of .061 agree with that found in Example 18.9.

Ranks

	Mean Rank
STARFIRE	2.20
RX1000	1.40
BULLET	2.40

Test Statistics[a]

N	10
Chi-Square	5.600
df	2
Asymp. Sig.	.061

a. Friedman Test

On the CD . . .

Chapter 18 Appendix: Data Analysis with MINITAB

Appendixes

APPENDIX A TABLES

TABLE A.1 Binomial probabilities $[{}_nC_x p^x(1-p)^{n-x}]$.

n	x	0.01	0.05	0.10	0.20	0.30	0.40	P 0.50	0.60	0.70	0.80	0.90	0.95	0.99	x
2	0	.980	.902	.810	.640	.490	.360	.250	.160	.090	.040	.010	.003	.000	0
	1	.020	.095	.180	.320	.420	.480	.500	.480	.420	.320	.180	.095	.020	1
	2	.000	.003	.010	.040	.090	.160	.250	.360	.490	.640	.810	.902	.980	2
3	0	.970	.857	.729	.512	.343	.216	.125	.064	.027	.008	.001	.000	.000	0
	1	.029	.135	.243	.384	.441	.432	.375	.288	.189	.096	.027	.007	.000	1
	2	.000	.007	.027	.096	.189	.288	.375	.432	.441	.384	.243	.135	.029	2
	3	.000	.000	.001	.008	.027	.064	.125	.216	.343	.512	.729	.857	.970	3
4	0	.961	.815	.656	.410	.240	.130	.063	.026	.008	.002	.000	.000	.000	0
	1	.039	.171	.292	.410	.412	.346	.250	.154	.076	.026	.004	.000	.000	1
	2	.001	.014	.049	.154	.265	.346	.375	.346	.265	.154	.049	.014	.001	2
	3	.000	.000	.004	.026	.076	.154	.250	.346	.412	.410	.292	.171	.039	3
	4	.000	.000	.000	.002	.008	.026	.063	.130	.240	.410	.656	.815	.961	4
5	0	.951	.774	.590	.328	.168	.078	.031	.010	.002	.000	.000	.000	.000	0
	1	.048	.204	.328	.410	.360	.259	.156	.077	.028	.006	.000	.000	.000	1
	2	.001	.021	.073	.205	.309	.346	.312	.230	.132	.051	.008	.001	.000	2
	3	.000	.001	.008	.051	.132	.230	.312	.346	.309	.205	.073	.021	.001	3
	4	.000	.000	.000	.006	.028	.077	.156	.259	.360	.410	.328	.204	.048	4
	5	.000	.000	.000	.000	.002	.010	.031	.078	.168	.328	.590	.774	.951	5
6	0	.941	.735	.531	.262	.118	.047	.016	.004	.001	.000	.000	.000	.000	0
	1	.057	.232	.354	.393	.303	.187	.094	.037	.010	.002	.000	.000	.000	1
	2	.001	.031	.098	.246	.324	.311	.234	.138	.060	.015	.001	.000	.000	2
	3	.000	.002	.015	.082	.185	.276	.313	.276	.185	.082	.015	.002	.000	3
	4	.000	.000	.001	.015	.060	.138	.234	.311	.324	.246	.098	.031	.001	4
	5	.000	.000	.000	.002	.010	.037	.094	.187	.303	.393	.354	.232	.057	5
	6	.000	.000	.000	.000	.001	.004	.016	.047	.118	.262	.531	.735	.941	6
7	0	.932	.698	.478	.210	.082	.028	.008	.002	.000	.000	.000	.000	.000	0
	1	.066	.257	.372	.367	.247	.131	.055	.017	.004	.000	.000	.000	.000	1
	2	.002	.041	.124	.275	.318	.261	.164	.077	.025	.004	.000	.000	.000	2
	3	.000	.004	.023	.115	.227	.290	.273	.194	.097	.029	.003	.000	.000	3
	4	.000	.000	.003	.029	.097	.194	.273	.290	.227	.115	.023	.004	.000	4
	5	.000	.000	.000	.004	.025	.077	.164	.261	.318	.275	.124	.041	.002	5
	6	.000	.000	.000	.000	.004	.017	.055	.131	.247	.367	.372	.257	.066	6
	7	.000	.000	.000	.000	.000	.002	.008	.028	.082	.210	.478	.698	.932	7
8	0	.923	.663	.430	.168	.058	.017	.004	.001	.000	.000	.000	.000	.000	0
	1	.075	.279	.383	.336	.198	.090	.031	.008	.001	.000	.000	.000	.000	1
	2	.003	.051	.149	.294	.296	.209	.109	.041	.010	.001	.000	.000	.000	2
	3	.000	.005	.033	.147	.254	.279	.219	.124	.047	.009	.000	.000	.000	3
	4	.000	.000	.005	.046	.136	.232	.273	.232	.136	.046	.005	.000	.000	4
	5	.000	.000	.000	.009	.047	.124	.219	.279	.254	.147	.033	.005	.000	5
	6	.000	.000	.000	.001	.010	.041	.109	.209	.296	.294	.149	.051	.003	6
	7	.000	.000	.000	.000	.001	.008	.031	.090	.198	.336	.383	.279	.075	7
	8	.000	.000	.000	.000	.000	.001	.004	.017	.058	.168	.430	.663	.923	8
9	0	.914	.630	.387	.134	.040	.010	.002	.000	.000	.000	.000	.000	.000	0
	1	.083	.299	.387	.302	.156	.060	.018	.004	.000	.000	.000	.000	.000	1
	2	.003	.063	.172	.302	.267	.161	.070	.021	.004	.000	.000	.000	.000	2
	3	.000	.008	.045	.176	.267	.251	.164	.074	.021	.003	.000	.000	.000	3
	4	.000	.001	.007	.066	.172	.251	.246	.167	.074	.017	.001	.000	.000	4
	5	.000	.000	.001	.017	.074	.167	.246	.251	.172	.066	.007	.001	.000	5
	6	.000	.000	.000	.003	.021	.074	.164	.251	.267	.176	.045	.008	.000	6
	7	.000	.000	.000	.000	.004	.021	.070	.161	.267	.302	.172	.063	.003	7
	8	.000	.000	.000	.000	.000	.004	.018	.060	.156	.302	.387	.299	.083	8
	9	.000	.000	.000	.000	.000	.000	.002	.010	.040	.134	.387	.630	.914	9
10	0	.904	.599	.349	.107	.028	.006	.001	.000	.000	.000	.000	.000	.000	0
	1	.091	.315	.387	.268	.121	.040	.010	.002	.000	.000	.000	.000	.000	1
	2	.004	.075	.194	.302	.233	.121	.044	.011	.001	.000	.000	.000	.000	2
	3	.000	.010	.057	.201	.267	.215	.117	.042	.009	.001	.000	.000	.000	3
	4	.000	.001	.011	.088	.200	.251	.205	.111	.037	.006	.000	.000	.000	4
	5	.000	.000	.001	.026	.103	.201	.246	.201	.103	.026	.001	.000	.000	5
	6	.000	.000	.000	.006	.037	.111	.205	.251	.200	.088	.011	.001	.000	6
	7	.000	.000	.000	.001	.009	.042	.117	.215	.267	.201	.057	.010	.000	7
	8	.000	.000	.000	.000	.001	.011	.044	.121	.233	.302	.194	.075	.004	8
	9	.000	.000	.000	.000	.000	.002	.010	.040	.121	.268	.387	.315	.091	9
	10	.000	.000	.000	.000	.000	.000	.001	.006	.028	.107	.349	.599	.904	10

TABLE A.1 Binomial probabilities $[_nC_x p^x (1 - p)^{n-x}]$ (continued).

								P							
n	x	0.01	0.05	0.10	0.20	0.30	0.40	0.50	0.60	0.70	0.80	0.90	0.95	0.99	x
11	0	.895	.569	.314	.086	.020	.004	.000	.000	.000	.000	.000	.000	.000	0
	1	.099	.329	.384	.236	.093	.027	.005	.001	.000	.000	.000	.000	.000	1
	2	.005	.087	.213	.295	.200	.089	.027	.005	.001	.000	.000	.000	.000	2
	3	.000	.014	.071	.221	.257	.177	.081	.023	.004	.000	.000	.000	.000	3
	4	.000	.001	.016	.111	.220	.236	.161	.070	.017	.002	.000	.000	.000	4
	5	.000	.000	.002	.039	.132	.221	.226	.147	.057	.010	.000	.000	.000	5
	6	.000	.000	.000	.010	.057	.147	.226	.221	.132	.039	.002	.000	.000	6
	7	.000	.000	.000	.002	.017	.070	.161	.236	.220	.111	.016	.001	.000	7
	8	.000	.000	.000	.000	.004	.023	.081	.177	.257	.221	.071	.014	.000	8
	9	.000	.000	.000	.000	.001	.005	.027	.089	.200	.295	.213	.087	.005	9
	10	.000	.000	.000	.000	.000	.001	.005	.027	.093	.236	.384	.329	.099	10
	11	.000	.000	.000	.000	.000	.000	.000	.004	.020	.086	.314	.569	.895	11
12	0	.886	.540	.282	.069	.014	.002	.000	.000	.000	.000	.000	.000	.000	0
	1	.107	.341	.377	.206	.071	.017	.003	.000	.000	.000	.000	.000	.000	1
	2	.006	.099	.230	.283	.168	.064	.016	.002	.000	.000	.000	.000	.000	2
	3	.000	.017	.085	.236	.240	.142	.054	.012	.001	.000	.000	.000	.000	3
	4	.000	.002	.021	.133	.231	.213	.121	.042	.008	.001	.000	.000	.000	4
	5	.000	.000	.004	.053	.158	.227	.193	.101	.029	.003	.000	.000	.000	5
	6	.000	.000	.000	.016	.079	.177	.226	.177	.079	.016	.000	.000	.000	6
	7	.000	.000	.000	.003	.029	.101	.193	.227	.158	.053	.004	.000	.000	7
	8	.000	.000	.000	.001	.008	.042	.121	.213	.231	.133	.021	.002	.000	8
	9	.000	.000	.000	.000	.001	.012	.054	.142	.240	.236	.085	.017	.000	9
	10	.000	.000	.000	.000	.000	.002	.016	.064	.168	.283	.230	.099	.006	10
	11	.000	.000	.000	.000	.000	.000	.003	.017	.071	.206	.377	.341	.107	11
	12	.000	.000	.000	.000	.000	.000	.000	.002	.014	.069	.282	.540	.886	12
13	0	.878	.513	.254	.055	.010	.001	.000	.000	.000	.000	.000	.000	.000	0
	1	.115	.351	.367	.179	.054	.011	.002	.000	.000	.000	.000	.000	.000	1
	2	.007	.111	.245	.268	.139	.045	.010	.001	.000	.000	.000	.000	.000	2
	3	.000	.021	.100	.246	.218	.111	.035	.006	.001	.000	.000	.000	.000	3
	4	.000	.003	.028	.154	.234	.184	.087	.024	.003	.000	.000	.000	.000	4
	5	.000	.000	.006	.069	.180	.221	.157	.066	.014	.001	.000	.000	.000	5
	6	.000	.000	.001	.023	.103	.197	.209	.131	.044	.006	.000	.000	.000	6
	7	.000	.000	.000	.006	.044	.131	.209	.197	.103	.023	.001	.000	.000	7
	8	.000	.000	.000	.001	.014	.066	.157	.221	.180	.069	.006	.000	.000	8
	9	.000	.000	.000	.000	.003	.024	.087	.184	.234	.154	.028	.003	.000	9
	10	.000	.000	.000	.000	.001	.006	.035	.111	.218	.246	.100	.021	.000	10
	11	.000	.000	.000	.000	.000	.001	.010	.045	.139	.268	.245	.111	.007	11
	12	.000	.000	.000	.000	.000	.000	.002	.011	.054	.179	.367	.351	.115	12
	13	.000	.000	.000	.000	.000	.000	.000	.001	.010	.055	.254	.513	.878	13
14	0	.869	.488	.229	.044	.007	.001	.000	.000	.000	.000	.000	.000	.000	0
	1	.123	.359	.356	.154	.041	.007	.001	.000	.000	.000	.000	.000	.000	1
	2	.008	.123	.257	.250	.113	.032	.006	.001	.000	.000	.000	.000	.000	2
	3	.000	.026	.114	.250	.194	.085	.022	.003	.000	.000	.000	.000	.000	3
	4	.000	.004	.035	.172	.229	.155	.061	.014	.001	.000	.000	.000	.000	4
	5	.000	.000	.008	.086	.196	.207	.122	.041	.007	.000	.000	.000	.000	5
	6	.000	.000	.001	.032	.126	.207	.183	.092	.023	.002	.000	.000	.000	6
	7	.000	.000	.000	.009	.062	.157	.209	.157	.062	.009	.000	.000	.000	7
	8	.000	.000	.000	.002	.023	.092	.183	.207	.126	.032	.001	.000	.000	8
	9	.000	.000	.000	.000	.007	.041	.122	.207	.196	.086	.008	.000	.000	9
	10	.000	.000	.000	.000	.001	.014	.061	.155	.229	.172	.035	.004	.000	10
	11	.000	.000	.000	.000	.000	.003	.022	.085	.194	.250	.114	.026	.000	11
	12	.000	.000	.000	.000	.000	.001	.006	.032	.113	.250	.257	.123	.008	12
	13	.000	.000	.000	.000	.000	.000	.001	.007	.041	.154	.356	.359	.123	13
	14	.000	.000	.000	.000	.000	.000	.000	.001	.007	.044	.229	.488	.869	14
15	0	.860	.463	.206	.035	.005	.000	.000	.000	.000	.000	.000	.000	.000	0
	1	.130	.366	.343	.132	.031	.005	.000	.000	.000	.000	.000	.000	.000	1
	2	.009	.135	.267	.231	.092	.022	.003	.000	.000	.000	.000	.000	.000	2
	3	.000	.031	.129	.250	.170	.063	.014	.002	.000	.000	.000	.000	.000	3
	4	.000	.005	.043	.188	.219	.127	.042	.007	.001	.000	.000	.000	.000	4
	5	.000	.001	.010	.103	.206	.186	.092	.024	.003	.000	.000	.000	.000	5
	6	.000	.000	.002	.043	.147	.207	.153	.061	.012	.001	.000	.000	.000	6
	7	.000	.000	.000	.014	.081	.177	.196	.118	.035	.003	.000	.000	.000	7
	8	.000	.000	.000	.003	.035	.118	.196	.177	.081	.014	.000	.000	.000	8
	9	.000	.000	.000	.001	.012	.061	.153	.207	.147	.043	.002	.000	.000	9
	10	.000	.000	.000	.000	.003	.024	.092	.186	.206	.103	.010	.001	.000	10
	11	.000	.000	.000	.000	.001	.007	.042	.127	.219	.188	.043	.005	.000	11
	12	.000	.000	.000	.000	.000	.002	.014	.063	.170	.250	.129	.031	.000	12
	13	.000	.000	.000	.000	.000	.000	.003	.022	.092	.231	.267	.135	.009	13
	14	.000	.000	.000	.000	.000	.000	.000	.005	.031	.132	.343	.366	.130	14
	15	.000	.000	.000	.000	.000	.000	.000	.000	.005	.035	.206	.463	.860	15

TABLE A.1 Binomial probabilities [$_nC_xp^x(1-p)^{n-x}$] (continued).

								P								
n	x	0.01	0.05	0.10	0.20	0.30	0.40	0.50	0.60	0.70	0.80	0.90	0.95	0.99	x
16	0	.851	.440	.185	.028	.003	.000	.000	.000	.000	.000	.000	.000	.000	0
	1	.138	.371	.329	.113	.023	.003	.000	.000	.000	.000	.000	.000	.000	1
	2	.010	.146	.275	.211	.073	.015	.002	.000	.000	.000	.000	.000	.000	2
	3	.000	.036	.142	.246	.146	.047	.009	.001	.000	.000	.000	.000	.000	3
	4	.000	.006	.051	.200	.204	.101	.028	.004	.000	.000	.000	.000	.000	4
	5	.000	.001	.014	.120	.210	.162	.067	.014	.001	.000	.000	.000	.000	5
	6	.000	.000	.003	.055	.165	.198	.122	.039	.006	.000	.000	.000	.000	6
	7	.000	.000	.000	.020	.101	.189	.175	.084	.019	.001	.000	.000	.000	7
	8	.000	.000	.000	.006	.049	.142	.196	.142	.049	.006	.000	.000	.000	8
	9	.000	.000	.000	.001	.019	.084	.175	.189	.101	.020	.000	.000	.000	9
	10	.000	.000	.000	.000	.006	.039	.122	.198	.165	.055	.003	.000	.000	10
	11	.000	.000	.000	.000	.001	.014	.067	.162	.210	.120	.014	.001	.000	11
	12	.000	.000	.000	.000	.000	.004	.028	.101	.204	.200	.051	.006	.000	12
	13	.000	.000	.000	.000	.000	.001	.009	.047	.146	.246	.142	.036	.000	13
	14	.000	.000	.000	.000	.000	.000	.002	.015	.073	.211	.275	.146	.010	14
	15	.000	.000	.000	.000	.000	.000	.000	.003	.023	.113	.329	.371	.138	15
	16	.000	.000	.000	.000	.000	.000	.000	.000	.003	.028	.185	.440	.851	16
17	0	.843	.418	.167	.023	.002	.000	.000	.000	.000	.000	.000	.000	.000	0
	1	.145	.374	.315	.096	.017	.002	.000	.000	.000	.000	.000	.000	.000	1
	2	.012	.158	.280	.191	.058	.010	.001	.000	.000	.000	.000	.000	.000	2
	3	.001	.041	.156	.239	.125	.034	.005	.000	.000	.000	.000	.000	.000	3
	4	.000	.008	.060	.209	.187	.080	.018	.002	.000	.000	.000	.000	.000	4
	5	.000	.001	.017	.136	.208	.138	.047	.008	.001	.000	.000	.000	.000	5
	6	.000	.000	.004	.068	.178	.184	.094	.024	.003	.000	.000	.000	.000	6
	7	.000	.000	.001	.027	.120	.193	.148	.057	.009	.000	.000	.000	.000	7
	8	.000	.000	.000	.008	.064	.161	.185	.107	.028	.002	.000	.000	.000	8
	9	.000	.000	.000	.002	.028	.107	.185	.161	.064	.008	.000	.000	.000	9
	10	.000	.000	.000	.000	.009	.057	.148	.193	.120	.027	.001	.000	.000	10
	11	.000	.000	.000	.000	.003	.024	.094	.184	.178	.068	.004	.000	.000	11
	12	.000	.000	.000	.000	.001	.008	.047	.138	.208	.136	.017	.001	.000	12
	13	.000	.000	.000	.000	.000	.002	.018	.080	.187	.209	.060	.008	.000	13
	14	.000	.000	.000	.000	.000	.000	.005	.034	.125	.239	.156	.041	.001	14
	15	.000	.000	.000	.000	.000	.000	.001	.010	.058	.191	.280	.158	.012	15
	16	.000	.000	.000	.000	.000	.000	.000	.002	.017	.096	.315	.374	.145	16
	17	.000	.000	.000	.000	.000	.000	.000	.000	.002	.023	.167	.418	.843	17
18	0	.835	.397	.150	.018	.002	.000	.000	.000	.000	.000	.000	.000	.000	0
	1	.152	.376	.300	.081	.013	.001	.000	.000	.000	.000	.000	.000	.000	1
	2	.013	.168	.284	.172	.046	.007	.001	.000	.000	.000	.000	.000	.000	2
	3	.001	.047	.168	.230	.105	.025	.003	.000	.000	.000	.000	.000	.000	3
	4	.000	.009	.070	.215	.168	.061	.012	.001	.000	.000	.000	.000	.000	4
	5	.000	.001	.022	.151	.202	.115	.033	.004	.000	.000	.000	.000	.000	5
	6	.000	.000	.005	.082	.187	.166	.071	.015	.001	.000	.000	.000	.000	6
	7	.000	.000	.001	.035	.138	.189	.121	.037	.005	.000	.000	.000	.000	7
	8	.000	.000	.000	.012	.081	.173	.167	.077	.015	.001	.000	.000	.000	8
	9	.000	.000	.000	.003	.039	.128	.185	.128	.039	.003	.000	.000	.000	9
	10	.000	.000	.000	.001	.015	.077	.167	.173	.081	.012	.000	.000	.000	10
	11	.000	.000	.000	.000	.005	.037	.121	.189	.138	.035	.001	.000	.000	11
	12	.000	.000	.000	.000	.001	.015	.071	.166	.187	.082	.005	.000	.000	12
	13	.000	.000	.000	.000	.000	.004	.033	.115	.202	.151	.022	.001	.000	13
	14	.000	.000	.000	.000	.000	.001	.012	.061	.168	.215	.070	.009	.000	14
	15	.000	.000	.000	.000	.000	.000	.003	.025	.105	.230	.168	.047	.001	15
	16	.000	.000	.000	.000	.000	.000	.001	.007	.046	.172	.284	.168	.013	16
	17	.000	.000	.000	.000	.000	.000	.000	.001	.013	.081	.300	.376	.152	17
	18	.000	.000	.000	.000	.000	.000	.000	.000	.002	.018	.150	.397	.835	18
19	0	.826	.377	.135	.014	.001	.000	.000	.000	.000	.000	.000	.000	.000	0
	1	.159	.377	.285	.068	.009	.001	.000	.000	.000	.000	.000	.000	.000	1
	2	.014	.179	.285	.154	.036	.005	.000	.000	.000	.000	.000	.000	.000	2
	3	.001	.053	.180	.218	.087	.017	.002	.000	.000	.000	.000	.000	.000	3
	4	.000	.011	.080	.218	.149	.047	.007	.001	.000	.000	.000	.000	.000	4
	5	.000	.002	.027	.164	.192	.093	.022	.002	.000	.000	.000	.000	.000	5
	6	.000	.000	.007	.095	.192	.145	.052	.008	.001	.000	.000	.000	.000	6
	7	.000	.000	.001	.044	.153	.180	.096	.024	.002	.000	.000	.000	.000	7
	8	.000	.000	.000	.017	.098	.180	.144	.053	.008	.000	.000	.000	.000	8
	9	.000	.000	.000	.005	.051	.146	.176	.098	.022	.001	.000	.000	.000	9
	10	.000	.000	.000	.001	.022	.098	.176	.146	.051	.005	.000	.000	.000	10
	11	.000	.000	.000	.000	.008	.053	.144	.180	.098	.017	.000	.000	.000	11
	12	.000	.000	.000	.000	.002	.024	.096	.180	.153	.044	.001	.000	.000	12
	13	.000	.000	.000	.000	.001	.008	.052	.145	.192	.095	.007	.000	.000	13
	14	.000	.000	.000	.000	.000	.002	.022	.093	.192	.164	.027	.002	.000	14

TABLE A.1 Binomial probabilities $[_nC_xp^x(1-p)^{n-x}]$ (continued).

								P								
n	x	0.01	0.05	0.10	0.20	0.30	0.40	0.50	0.60	0.70	0.80	0.90	0.95	0.99	x
	15	.000	.000	.000	.000	.000	.001	.007	.047	.149	.218	.080	.011	.000	15
	16	.000	.000	.000	.000	.000	.000	.002	.017	.087	.218	.180	.053	.001	16
	17	.000	.000	.000	.000	.000	.000	.000	.005	.036	.154	.285	.179	.014	17
	18	.000	.000	.000	.000	.000	.000	.000	.001	.009	.068	.285	.377	.159	18
	19	.000	.000	.000	.000	.000	.000	.000	.000	.001	.014	.135	.377	.826	19
20	0	.818	.358	.122	.012	.001	.000	.000	.000	.000	.000	.000	.000	.000	0
	1	.165	.377	.270	.058	.007	.000	.000	.000	.000	.000	.000	.000	.000	1
	2	.016	.189	.285	.137	.028	.003	.000	.000	.000	.000	.000	.000	.000	2
	3	.001	.060	.190	.205	.072	.012	.001	.000	.000	.000	.000	.000	.000	3
	4	.000	.013	.090	.218	.130	.035	.005	.000	.000	.000	.000	.000	.000	4
	5	.000	.002	.032	.175	.179	.075	.015	.001	.000	.000	.000	.000	.000	5
	6	.000	.000	.009	.109	.192	.124	.037	.005	.000	.000	.000	.000	.000	6
	7	.000	.000	.002	.055	.164	.166	.074	.015	.001	.000	.000	.000	.000	7
	8	.000	.000	.000	.022	.114	.180	.120	.035	.004	.000	.000	.000	.000	8
	9	.000	.000	.000	.007	.065	.160	.160	.071	.012	.000	.000	.000	.000	9
	10	.000	.000	.000	.002	.031	.117	.176	.117	.031	.002	.000	.000	.000	10
	11	.000	.000	.000	.000	.012	.071	.160	.160	.065	.007	.000	.000	.000	11
	12	.000	.000	.000	.000	.004	.035	.120	.180	.114	.022	.000	.000	.000	12
	13	.000	.000	.000	.000	.001	.015	.074	.166	.164	.055	.002	.000	.000	13
	14	.000	.000	.000	.000	.000	.005	.037	.124	.192	.109	.009	.000	.000	14
	15	.000	.000	.000	.000	.000	.001	.015	.075	.179	.175	.032	.002	.000	15
	16	.000	.000	.000	.000	.000	.000	.005	.035	.130	.218	.090	.013	.000	16
	17	.000	.000	.000	.000	.000	.000	.001	.012	.072	.205	.190	.060	.001	17
	18	.000	.000	.000	.000	.000	.000	.000	.003	.028	.137	.285	.189	.016	18
	19	.000	.000	.000	.000	.000	.000	.000	.000	.007	.058	.270	.377	.165	19
	20	.000	.000	.000	.000	.000	.000	.000	.000	.001	.012	.122	.358	.818	20

TABLE A.2   Cumulative Binomial Probabilities.

n	x	0.01	0.05	0.10	0.20	0.30	0.40	0.50	0.60	0.70	0.80	0.90	0.95	0.99	x
2	0	0.980	0.903	0.810	0.640	0.490	0.360	0.250	0.160	0.090	0.040	0.010	0.003	0.000	0
	1	1.000	0.998	0.990	0.960	0.910	0.840	0.750	0.640	0.510	0.360	0.190	0.098	0.020	1
	2	1.000	1.000	1.000	1.000	1.000	1.000	1.000	1.000	1.000	1.000	1.000	1.000	1.000	2
3	0	0.970	0.857	0.729	0.512	0.343	0.216	0.125	0.064	0.027	0.008	0.001	0.000	0.000	0
	1	1.000	0.993	0.972	0.896	0.784	0.648	0.500	0.352	0.216	0.104	0.028	0.007	0.000	1
	2	1.000	1.000	0.999	0.992	0.973	0.936	0.875	0.784	0.657	0.488	0.271	0.143	0.030	2
		1.000	1.000	1.000	1.000	1.000	1.000	1.000	1.000	1.000	1.000	1.000	1.000	1.000	3
4	0	0.961	0.815	0.656	0.410	0.240	0.130	0.063	0.026	0.008	0.002	0.000	0.000	0.000	0
	1	0.999	0.986	0.948	0.819	0.652	0.475	0.313	0.179	0.084	0.027	0.004	0.000	0.000	1
	2	1.000	1.000	0.996	0.973	0.916	0.821	0.688	0.525	0.348	0.181	0.052	0.014	0.001	2
	3	1.000	1.000	1.000	0.998	0.992	0.974	0.938	0.870	0.760	0.590	0.344	0.185	0.039	3
	4	1.000	1.000	1.000	1.000	1.000	1.000	1.000	1.000	1.000	1.000	1.000	1.000	1.000	4
5	0	0.951	0.774	0.590	0.328	0.168	0.078	0.031	0.010	0.002	0.000	0.000	0.000	0.000	0
	1	0.999	0.977	0.919	0.737	0.528	0.337	0.187	0.087	0.031	0.007	0.000	0.000	0.000	1
	2	1.000	0.999	0.991	0.942	0.837	0.683	0.500	0.317	0.163	0.058	0.009	0.001	0.000	2
	3	1.000	1.000	1.000	0.993	0.969	0.913	0.812	0.663	0.472	0.263	0.081	0.023	0.001	3
	4	1.000	1.000	1.000	1.000	0.998	0.990	0.969	0.922	0.832	0.672	0.410	0.226	0.049	4
	5	1.000	1.000	1.000	1.000	1.000	1.000	1.000	1.000	1.000	1.000	1.000	1.000	1.000	5
6	0	0.941	0.735	0.531	0.262	0.118	0.047	0.016	0.004	0.001	0.000	0.000	0.000	0.000	0
	1	0.999	0.967	0.886	0.655	0.420	0.233	0.109	0.041	0.011	0.002	0.000	0.000	0.000	1
	2	1.000	0.998	0.984	0.901	0.744	0.544	0.344	0.179	0.070	0.017	0.001	0.000	0.000	2
	3	1.000	1.000	0.999	0.983	0.930	0.821	0.656	0.456	0.256	0.099	0.016	0.002	0.000	3
	4	1.000	1.000	1.000	0.998	0.989	0.959	0.891	0.767	0.580	0.345	0.114	0.033	0.001	4
	5	1.000	1.000	1.000	1.000	0.999	0.996	0.984	0.953	0.882	0.738	0.469	0.265	0.059	5
	6	1.000	1.000	1.000	1.000	1.000	1.000	1.000	1.000	1.000	1.000	1.000	1.000	1.000	6
7	0	0.932	0.698	0.478	0.210	0.082	0.028	0.008	0.002	0.000	0.000	0.000	0.000	0.000	0
	1	0.998	0.956	0.850	0.577	0.329	0.159	0.063	0.019	0.004	0.000	0.000	0.000	0.000	1
	2	1.000	0.996	0.974	0.852	0.647	0.420	0.227	0.096	0.029	0.005	0.000	0.000	0.000	2
	3	1.000	1.000	0.997	0.967	0.874	0.710	0.500	0.290	0.126	0.033	0.003	0.000	0.000	3
	4	1.000	1.000	1.000	0.995	0.971	0.904	0.773	0.580	0.353	0.148	0.026	0.004	0.000	4
	5	1.000	1.000	1.000	1.000	0.996	0.981	0.938	0.841	0.671	0.423	0.150	0.044	0.002	5
	6	1.000	1.000	1.000	1.000	1.000	0.998	0.992	0.972	0.918	0.790	0.522	0.302	0.068	6
	7	1.000	1.000	1.000	1.000	1.000	1.000	1.000	1.000	1.000	1.000	1.000	1.000	1.000	7
8	0	0.923	0.663	0.430	0.168	0.058	0.017	0.004	0.001	0.000	0.000	0.000	0.000	0.000	0
	1	0.997	0.943	0.813	0.503	0.255	0.106	0.035	0.009	0.001	0.000	0.000	0.000	0.000	1
	2	1.000	0.994	0.962	0.797	0.552	0.315	0.145	0.050	0.011	0.001	0.000	0.000	0.000	2
	3	1.000	1.000	0.995	0.944	0.806	0.594	0.363	0.174	0.058	0.010	0.000	0.000	0.000	3
	4	1.000	1.000	1.000	0.990	0.942	0.826	0.637	0.406	0.194	0.056	0.005	0.000	0.000	4
	5	1.000	1.000	1.000	0.999	0.989	0.950	.0855	0.685	0.448	0.203	0.038	0.006	0.000	5
	6	1.000	1.000	1.000	1.000	0.999	0.991	0.965	0.894	0.745	0.497	0.187	0.057	0.003	6
	7	1.000	1.000	1.000	1.000	1.000	0.999	0.996	0.983	0.942	0.832	0.570	0.337	0.077	7
	8	1.000	1.000	1.000	1.000	1.000	1.000	1.000	1.000	1.000	1.000	1.000	1.000	1.000	8
9	0	0.914	0.630	0.387	0.134	0.040	0.010	0.002	0.000	0.000	0.000	0.000	0.000	0.000	0
	1	0.997	0.929	0.775	0.436	0.196	0.071	0.020	0.004	0.000	0.000	0.000	0.000	0.000	1
	2	1.000	0.992	0.947	0.738	0.463	0.232	0.090	0.025	0.004	0.000	0.000	0.000	0.000	2
	3	1.000	0.999	0.992	0.914	0.730	0.483	0.254	0.099	0.025	0.003	0.000	0.000	0.000	3
	4	1.000	1.000	0.999	0.980	0.901	0.733	0.500	0.267	0.099	0.020	0.001	0.000	0.000	4
	5	1.000	1.000	1.000	0.997	0.975	0.901	0.746	0.517	0.270	0.086	0.008	0.001	0.000	5
	6	1.000	1.000	1.000	1.000	0.996	0.975	0.910	0.768	0.537	0.262	0.053	0.008	0.000	6
	7	1.000	1.000	1.000	1.000	1.000	0.996	0.980	0.929	0.804	0.564	0.225	0.071	0.003	7
	8	1.000	1.000	1.000	1.000	1.000	1.000	0.998	0.990	0.960	0.866	0.613	0.370	0.086	8
	9	1.000	1.000	1.000	1.000	1.000	1.000	1.000	1.000	1.000	1.000	1.000	1.000	1.000	9
10	0	0.904	0.599	0.349	0.107	0.028	0.006	0.001	0.000	0.000	0.000	0.000	0.000	0.000	0
	1	0.996	0.914	0.736	0.376	0.149	0.046	0.011	0.002	0.000	0.000	0.000	0.000	0.000	1
	2	1.000	0.988	0.930	0.678	0.383	0.167	0.055	0.012	0.002	0.000	0.000	0.000	0.000	2
	3	1.000	0.999	0.987	0.879	0.650	0.382	0.172	0.055	0.011	0.001	0.000	0.000	0.000	3
	4	1.000	1.000	0.998	0.967	0.850	0.633	0.377	0.166	0.047	0.006	0.000	0.000	0.000	4
	5	1.000	1.000	1.000	0.994	0.953	0.834	0.623	0.367	0.150	0.033	0.002	0.000	0.000	5
	6	1.000	1.000	1.000	0.999	0.989	0.945	0.828	0.618	0.350	0.121	0.013	0.001	0.000	6
	7	1.000	1.000	1.000	1.000	0.998	0.988	0.945	0.833	0.617	0.322	0.070	0.012	0.000	7
	8	1.000	1.000	1.000	1.000	1.000	0.998	0.989	0.954	0.851	0.624	0.264	0.086	0.004	8
	9	1.000	1.000	1.000	1.000	1.000	1.000	0.999	0.994	0.972	0.893	0.651	0.401	0.096	9
	10	1.000	1.000	1.000	1.000	1.000	1.000	1.000	1.000	1.000	1.000	1.000	1.000	1.000	10
11	0	0.895	0.569	0.314	0.086	0.020	0.004	0.000	0.000	0.000	0.000	0.000	0.000	0.000	0
	1	0.995	0.898	0.697	0.322	0.113	0.030	0.006	0.001	0.000	0.000	0.000	0.000	0.000	1
	2	1.000	0.985	0.910	0.617	0.313	0.119	0.033	0.006	0.001	0.000	0.000	0.000	0.000	2

TABLE A.2 Cumulative Binomial Probabilities (continued).

n	x	0.01	0.05	0.10	0.20	0.30	0.40	0.50	0.60	0.70	0.80	0.90	0.95	0.99	x
	3	1.000	0.998	0.981	0.839	0.570	0.296	0.113	0.029	0.004	0.000	0.000	0.000	0.000	3
	4	1.000	1.000	0.997	0.950	0.790	0.533	0.274	0.099	0.022	0.002	0.000	0.000	0.000	4
	5	1.000	1.000	1.000	0.988	0.922	0.753	0.500	0.247	0.078	0.012	0.000	0.000	0.000	5
	6	1.000	1.000	1.000	0.998	0.978	0.901	0.726	0.467	0.210	0.050	0.003	0.000	0.000	6
	7	1.000	1.000	1.000	1.000	0.996	0.971	0.887	0.704	0.430	0.161	0.019	0.002	0.000	7
	8	1.000	1.000	1.000	1.000	0.999	0.994	0.967	0.881	0.687	0.383	0.090	0.015	0.000	8
	9	1.000	1.000	1.000	1.000	1.000	0.999	0.994	0.970	0.887	0.678	0.303	0.102	0.005	9
	10	1.000	1.000	1.000	1.000	1.000	1.000	1.000	0.996	0.980	0.914	0.686	0.431	0.105	10
	11	1.000	1.000	1.000	1.000	1.000	1.000	1.000	1.000	1.000	1.000	1.000	1.000	1.000	11
12	0	0.886	0.540	0.282	0.069	0.014	0.002	0.000	0.000	0.000	0.000	0.000	0.000	0.000	0
	1	0.994	0.882	0.659	0.275	0.085	0.020	0.003	0.000	0.000	0.000	0.000	0.000	0.000	1
	2	1.000	0.980	0.889	0.558	0.253	0.083	0.019	0.003	0.000	0.000	0.000	0.000	0.000	2
	3	1.000	0.998	0.974	0.795	0.493	0.225	0.073	0.015	0.002	0.000	0.000	0.000	0.000	3
	4	1.000	1.000	0.996	0.927	0.724	0.438	0.194	0.057	0.009	0.001	0.000	0.000	0.000	4
	5	1.000	1.000	0.999	0.981	0.882	0.665	0.387	0.158	0.039	0.004	0.000	0.000	0.000	5
	6	1.000	1.000	1.000	0.996	0.961	0.842	0.613	0.335	0.118	0.019	0.001	0.000	0.000	6
	7	1.000	1.000	1.000	0.999	0.991	0.943	0.806	0.562	0.276	0.073	0.004	0.000	0.000	7
	8	1.000	1.000	1.000	1.000	0.998	0.985	0.927	0.775	0.507	0.205	0.026	0.002	0.000	8
	9	1.000	1.000	1.000	1.000	1.000	0.997	0.981	0.917	0.747	0.442	0.111	0.020	0.000	9
	10	1.000	1.000	1.000	1.000	1.000	1.000	0.997	0.980	0.915	0.725	0.341	0.118	0.006	10
	11	1.000	1.000	1.000	1.000	1.000	1.000	1.000	0.998	0.986	0.931	0.718	0.460	0.114	11
	12	1.000	1.000	1.000	1.000	1.000	1.000	1.000	1.000	1.000	1.000	1.000	1.000	1.000	12
13	0	0.878	0.513	0.254	0.055	0.010	0.001	0.000	0.000	0.000	0.000	0.000	0.000	0.000	0
	1	0.993	0.865	0.621	0.234	0.064	0.013	0.002	0.000	0.000	0.000	0.000	0.000	0.000	1
	2	1.000	0.975	0.866	0.502	0.202	0.058	0.011	0.001	0.000	0.000	0.000	0.000	0.000	2
	3	1.000	0.997	0.966	0.747	0.421	0.169	0.046	0.008	0.001	0.000	0.000	0.000	0.000	3
	4	1.000	1.000	0.994	0.901	0.654	0.353	0.133	0.032	0.004	0.000	0.000	0.000	0.000	4
	5	1.000	1.000	0.999	0.970	0.835	0.574	0.291	0.098	0.018	0.001	0.000	0.000	0.000	5
	6	1.000	1.000	1.000	0.993	0.938	0.771	0.500	0.229	0.062	0.007	0.000	0.000	0.000	6
	7	1.000	1.000	1.000	0.999	0.982	0.902	0.709	0.426	0.165	0.030	0.001	0.000	0.000	7
	8	1.000	1.000	1.000	1.000	0.996	0.968	0.867	0.647	0.346	0.099	0.006	0.000	0.000	8
	9	1.000	1.000	1.000	1.000	0.999	0.992	0.954	0.831	0.579	0.253	0.034	0.003	0.000	9
	10	1.000	1.000	1.000	1.000	1.000	0.999	0.989	0.942	0.798	0.498	0.134	0.025	0.000	10
	11	1.000	1.000	1.000	1.000	1.000	1.000	0.998	0.987	0.936	0.766	0.379	0.135	0.007	11
	12	1.000	1.000	1.000	1.000	1.000	1.000	1.000	0.999	0.990	0.945	0.746	0.487	0.122	12
	13	1.000	1.000	1.000	1.000	1.000	1.000	1.000	1.000	1.000	1.000	1.000	1.000	1.000	13
14	0	0.869	0.488	0.229	0.044	0.007	0.001	0.000	0.000	0.000	0.000	0.000	0.000	0.000	0
	1	0.992	0.847	0.585	0.198	0.047	0.008	0.001	0.000	0.000	0.000	0.000	0.000	0.000	1
	2	1.000	0.970	0.842	0.448	0.161	0.040	0.006	0.001	0.000	0.000	0.000	0.000	0.000	2
	3	1.000	0.996	0.956	0.698	0.355	0.124	0.029	0.004	0.000	0.000	0.000	0.000	0.000	3
	4	1.000	1.000	0.991	0.870	0.584	0.279	0.090	0.018	0.002	0.000	0.000	0.000	0.000	4
	5	1.000	1.000	0.999	0.956	0.781	0.486	0.212	0.058	0.008	0.000	0.000	0.000	0.000	5
	6	1.000	1.000	1.000	0.988	0.907	0.692	0.395	0.150	0.031	0.002	0.000	0.000	0.000	6
	7	1.000	1.000	1.000	0.998	0.969	0.850	0.605	0.308	0.093	0.012	0.000	0.000	0.000	7
	8	1.000	1.000	1.000	1.000	0.992	0.942	0.788	0.514	0.219	0.044	0.001	0.000	0.000	8
	9	1.000	1.000	1.000	1.000	0.998	0.982	0.910	0.721	0.416	0.130	0.009	0.000	0.000	9
	10	1.000	1.000	1.000	1.000	1.000	0.996	0.971	0.876	0.645	0.302	0.044	0.004	0.000	10
	11	1.000	1.000	1.000	1.000	1.000	0.999	0.994	0.960	0.839	0.552	0.158	0.030	0.000	11
	12	1.000	1.000	1.000	1.000	1.000	1.000	0.999	0.992	0.953	0.802	0.415	0.153	0.008	12
	13	1.000	1.000	1.000	1.000	1.000	1.000	1.000	0.999	0.993	0.956	0.771	0.512	0.131	13
	14	1.000	1.000	1.000	1.000	1.000	1.000	1.000	1.000	1.000	1.000	1.000	1.000	1.000	14
15	0	0.860	0.463	0.206	0.035	0.005	0.000	0.000	0.000	0.000	0.000	0.000	0.000	0.000	0
	1	0.990	0.829	0.549	0.167	0.035	0.005	0.000	0.000	0.000	0.000	0.000	0.000	0.000	1
	2	1.000	0.964	0.816	0.398	0.127	0.027	0.004	0.000	0.000	0.000	0.000	0.000	0.000	2
	3	1.000	0.995	0.944	0.648	0.297	0.091	0.018	0.002	0.000	0.000	0.000	0.000	0.000	3
	4	1.000	0.999	0.987	0.836	0.515	0.217	0.059	0.009	0.001	0.000	0.000	0.000	0.000	4
	5	1.000	1.000	0.998	0.939	0.722	0.403	0.151	0.034	0.004	0.000	0.000	0.000	0.000	5
	6	1.000	1.000	1.000	0.982	0.869	0.610	0.304	0.095	0.015	0.001	0.000	0.000	0.000	6
	7	1.000	1.000	1.000	0.996	0.950	0.787	0.500	0.213	0.050	0.004	0.000	0.000	0.000	7
	8	1.000	1.000	1.000	0.999	0.985	0.905	0.696	0.390	0.131	0.018	0.000	0.000	0.000	8
	9	1.000	1.000	1.000	1.000	0.996	0.966	0.849	0.597	0.278	0.061	0.002	0.000	0.000	9
	10	1.000	1.000	1.000	1.000	0.999	0.991	0.941	0.783	0.485	0.164	0.013	0.001	0.000	10
	11	1.000	1.000	1.000	1.000	1.000	0.998	0.982	0.909	0.703	0.352	0.056	0.005	0.000	11
	12	1.000	1.000	1.000	1.000	1.000	1.000	0.996	0.973	0.873	0.602	0.184	0.036	0.000	12
	13	1.000	1.000	1.000	1.000	1.000	1.000	1.000	0.995	0.965	0.833	0.451	0.171	0.010	13
	14	1.000	1.000	1.000	1.000	1.000	1.000	1.000	1.000	0.995	0.965	0.794	0.537	0.140	14
	15	1.000	1.000	1.000	1.000	1.000	1.000	1.000	1.000	1.000	1.000	1.000	1.000	1.000	15

TABLE A.2   Cumulative Binomial Probabilities (continued).

n	x	0.01	0.05	0.10	0.20	0.30	0.40	0.50	0.60	0.70	0.80	0.90	0.95	0.99	x
16	0	0.851	0.440	0.185	0.028	0.003	0.000	0.000	0.000	0.000	0.000	0.000	0.000	0.000	0
	1	0.989	0.811	0.515	0.141	0.026	0.003	0.000	0.000	0.000	0.000	0.000	0.000	0.000	1
	2	0.999	0.957	0.789	0.352	0.099	0.018	0.002	0.000	0.000	0.000	0.000	0.000	0.000	2
	3	1.000	0.993	0.932	0.598	0.246	0.065	0.011	0.001	0.000	0.000	0.000	0.000	0.000	3
	4	1.000	0.999	0.983	0.798	0.450	0.167	0.038	0.005	0.000	0.000	0.000	0.000	0.000	4
	5	1.000	1.000	0.997	0.918	0.660	0.329	0.105	0.019	0.002	0.000	0.000	0.000	0.000	5
	6	1.000	1.000	0.999	0.973	0.825	0.527	0.227	0.058	0.007	0.000	0.000	0.000	0.000	6
	7	1.000	1.000	1.000	0.993	0.926	0.716	0.402	0.142	0.026	0.001	0.000	0.000	0.000	7
	8	1.000	1.000	1.000	0.999	0.974	0.858	0.598	0.284	0.074	0.007	0.000	0.000	0.000	8
	9	1.000	1.000	1.000	1.000	0.993	0.942	0.773	0.473	0.175	0.027	0.001	0.000	0.000	9
	10	1.000	1.000	1.000	1.000	0.998	0.981	0.895	0.671	0.340	0.082	0.003	0.000	0.000	10
	11	1.000	1.000	1.000	1.000	1.000	0.995	0.962	0.833	0.550	0.202	0.017	0.001	0.000	11
	12	1.000	1.000	1.000	1.000	1.000	0.999	0.989	0.935	0.754	0.402	0.068	0.007	0.000	12
	13	1.000	1.000	1.000	1.000	1.000	1.000	0.998	0.982	0.901	0.648	0.211	0.043	0.001	13
	14	1.000	1.000	1.000	1.000	1.000	1.000	1.000	0.997	0.974	0.859	0.485	0.189	0.011	14
	15	1.000	1.000	1.000	1.000	1.000	1.000	1.000	1.000	0.997	0.972	0.815	0.560	0.149	15
	16	1.000	1.000	1.000	1.000	1.000	1.000	1.000	1.000	1.000	1.000	1.000	1.000	1.000	16
17	0	0.843	0.418	0.167	0.023	0.002	0.000	0.000	0.000	0.000	0.000	0.000	0.000	0.000	0
	1	0.988	0.792	0.482	0.118	0.019	0.002	0.000	0.000	0.000	0.000	0.000	0.000	0.000	1
	2	0.999	0.950	0.762	0.310	0.077	0.012	0.001	0.000	0.000	0.000	0.000	0.000	0.000	2
	3	1.000	0.991	0.917	0.549	0.202	0.046	0.006	0.000	0.000	0.000	0.000	0.000	0.000	3
	4	1.000	0.999	0.978	0.758	0.389	0.126	0.025	0.003	0.000	0.000	0.000	0.000	0.000	4
	5	1.000	1.000	0.995	0.894	0.597	0.264	0.072	0.011	0.001	0.000	0.000	0.000	0.000	5
	6	1.000	1.000	0.999	0.962	0.775	0.448	0.166	0.035	0.003	0.000	0.000	0.000	0.000	6
	7	1.000	1.000	1.000	0.989	0.895	0.641	0.315	0.092	0.013	0.000	0.000	0.000	0.000	7
	8	1.000	1.000	1.000	0.997	0.960	0.801	0.500	0.199	0.040	0.003	0.000	0.000	0.000	8
	9	1.000	1.000	1.000	1.000	0.987	0.908	0.685	0.359	0.105	0.011	0.000	0.000	0.000	9
	10	1.000	1.000	1.000	1.000	0.997	0.965	0.834	0.552	0.225	0.038	0.001	0.000	0.000	10
	11	1.000	1.000	1.000	1.000	0.999	0.989	0.928	0.736	0.403	0.106	0.005	0.000	0.000	11
	12	1.000	1.000	1.000	1.000	1.000	0.997	0.975	0.874	0.611	0.242	0.022	0.001	0.000	12
	13	1.000	1.000	1.000	1.000	1.000	1.000	0.994	0.954	0.798	0.451	0.083	0.009	0.000	13
	14	1.000	1.000	1.000	1.000	1.000	1.000	0.999	0.988	0.923	0.690	0.238	0.050	0.001	14
	15	1.000	1.000	1.000	1.000	1.000	1.000	1.000	0.998	0.981	0.882	0.518	0.208	0.012	15
	16	1.000	1.000	1.000	1.000	1.000	1.000	1.000	1.000	0.998	0.977	0.833	0.582	0.157	16
	17	1.000	1.000	1.000	1.000	1.000	1.000	1.000	1.000	1.000	1.000	1.000	1.000	1.000	17
18	0	0.835	0.397	0.150	0.018	0.002	0.000	0.000	0.000	0.000	0.000	0.000	0.000	0.000	0
	1	0.986	0.774	0.450	0.099	0.014	0.001	0.000	0.000	0.000	0.000	0.000	0.000	0.000	1
	2	0.999	0.942	0.734	0.271	0.060	0.008	0.001	0.000	0.000	0.000	0.000	0.000	0.000	2
	3	1.000	0.989	0.902	0.501	0.165	0.033	0.004	0.000	0.000	0.000	0.000	0.000	0.000	3
	4	1.000	0.998	0.972	0.716	0.333	0.094	0.015	0.001	0.000	0.000	0.000	0.000	0.000	4
	5	1.000	1.000	0.994	0.867	0.534	0.209	0.048	0.006	0.000	0.000	0.000	0.000	0.000	5
	6	1.000	1.000	0.999	0.949	0.722	0.374	0.119	0.020	0.001	0.000	0.000	0.000	0.000	6
	7	1.000	1.000	1.000	0.984	0.859	0.563	0.240	0.058	0.006	0.000	0.000	0.000	0.000	7
	8	1.000	1.000	1.000	0.996	0.940	0.737	0.407	0.135	0.021	0.001	0.000	0.000	0.000	8
	9	1.000	1.000	1.000	0.999	0.979	0.865	0.593	0.263	0.060	0.004	0.000	0.000	0.000	9
	10	1.000	1.000	1.000	1.000	0.994	0.942	0.760	0.437	0.141	0.016	0.000	0.000	0.000	10
	11	1.000	1.000	1.000	1.000	0.999	0.980	0.881	0.626	0.278	0.051	0.001	0.000	0.000	11
	12	1.000	1.000	1.000	1.000	1.000	0.994	0.952	0.791	0.466	0.133	0.006	0.000	0.000	12
	13	1.000	1.000	1.000	1.000	1.000	0.999	0.985	0.906	0.667	0.284	0.028	0.002	0.000	13
	14	1.000	1.000	1.000	1.000	1.000	1.000	0.996	0.967	0.835	0.499	0.098	0.011	0.000	14
	15	1.000	1.000	1.000	1.000	1.000	1.000	0.999	0.992	0.940	0.729	0.266	0.058	0.001	15
	16	1.000	1.000	1.000	1.000	1.000	1.000	1.000	0.999	0.986	0.901	0.550	0.226	0.014	16
	17	1.000	1.000	1.000	1.000	1.000	1.000	1.000	1.000	0.998	0.982	0.850	0.603	0.165	17
	18	1.000	1.000	1.000	1.000	1.000	1.000	1.000	1.000	1.000	1.000	1.000	1.000	1.000	18
19	0	0.826	0.377	0.135	0.014	0.001	0.000	0.000	0.000	0.000	0.000	0.000	0.000	0.000	0
	1	0.985	0.755	0.420	0.083	0.010	0.001	0.000	0.000	0.000	0.000	0.000	0.000	0.000	1
	2	0.999	0.933	0.705	0.237	0.046	0.005	0.000	0.000	0.000	0.000	0.000	0.000	0.000	2
	3	1.000	0.987	0.885	0.455	0.133	0.023	0.002	0.000	0.000	0.000	0.000	0.000	0.000	3
	4	1.000	0.998	0.965	0.673	0.282	0.070	0.010	0.001	0.000	0.000	0.000	0.000	0.000	4
	5	1.000	1.000	0.991	0.837	0.474	0.163	0.032	0.003	0.000	0.000	0.000	0.000	0.000	5
	6	1.000	1.000	0.998	0.932	0.666	0.308	0.084	0.012	0.001	0.000	0.000	0.000	0.000	6
	7	1.000	1.000	1.000	0.977	0.818	0.488	0.180	0.035	0.003	0.000	0.000	0.000	0.000	7
	8	1.000	1.000	1.000	0.993	0.916	0.667	0.324	0.088	0.011	0.000	0.000	0.000	0.000	8
	9	1.000	1.000	1.000	0.998	0.967	0.814	0.500	0.186	0.033	0.002	0.000	0.000	0.000	9
	10	1.000	1.000	1.000	1.000	0.989	0.912	0.676	0.333	0.084	0.007	0.000	0.000	0.000	10
	11	1.000	1.000	1.000	1.000	0.997	0.965	0.820	0.512	0.182	0.023	0.000	0.000	0.000	11
	12	1.000	1.000	1.000	1.000	0.999	0.988	0.916	0.692	0.334	0.068	0.002	0.000	0.000	12
	13	1.000	1.000	1.000	1.000	1.000	0.997	0.968	0.837	0.526	0.163	0.009	0.000	0.000	13
	14	1.000	1.000	1.000	1.000	1.000	0.999	0.990	0.930	0.718	0.327	0.035	0.002	0.000	14

TABLE A.2   Cumulative Binomial Probabilities (continued).

								P								
n	x	0.01	0.05	0.10	0.20	0.30	0.40	0.50	0.60	0.70	0.80	0.90	0.95	0.99	x
	15	1.000	1.000	1.000	1.000	1.000	1.000	0.998	0.977	0.867	0.545	0.115	0.013	0.000	15
	16	1.000	1.000	1.000	1.000	1.000	1.000	1.000	0.995	0.954	0.763	0.295	0.067	0.001	16
	17	1.000	1.000	1.000	1.000	1.000	1.000	1.000	0.999	0.990	0.917	0.580	0.245	0.015	17
	18	1.000	1.000	1.000	1.000	1.000	1.000	1.000	1.000	0.999	0.986	0.865	0.623	0.174	18
	19	1.000	1.000	1.000	1.000	1.000	1.000	1.000	1.000	1.000	1.000	1.000	1.000	1.000	19
20	0	0.818	0.358	0.122	0.012	0.001	0.000	0.000	0.000	0.000	0.000	0.000	0.000	0.000	0
	1	0.983	0.736	0.392	0.069	0.008	0.001	0.000	0.000	0.000	0.000	0.000	0.000	0.000	1
	2	0.999	0.925	0.677	0.206	0.035	0.004	0.000	0.000	0.000	0.000	0.000	0.000	0.000	2
	3	1.000	0.984	0.867	0.411	0.107	0.016	0.001	0.000	0.000	0.000	0.000	0.000	0.000	3
	4	1.000	0.997	0.957	0.630	0.238	0.051	0.006	0.000	0.000	0.000	0.000	0.000	0.000	4
	5	1.000	1.000	0.989	0.804	0.416	0.126	0.021	0.002	0.000	0.000	0.000	0.000	0.000	5
	6	1.000	1.000	0.998	0.913	0.608	0.250	0.058	0.006	0.000	0.000	0.000	0.000	0.000	6
	7	1.000	1.000	1.000	0.968	0.772	0.416	0.132	0.021	0.001	0.000	0.000	0.000	0.000	7
	8	1.000	1.000	1.000	0.990	0.887	0.596	0.252	0.057	0.005	0.000	0.000	0.000	0.000	8
	9	1.000	1.000	1.000	0.997	0.952	0.755	0.412	0.128	0.017	0.001	0.000	0.000	0.000	9
	10	1.000	1.000	1.000	0.999	0.983	0.872	0.588	0.245	0.048	0.003	0.000	0.000	0.000	10
	11	1.000	1.000	1.000	1.000	0.995	0.943	0.748	0.404	0.113	0.010	0.000	0.000	0.000	11
	12	1.000	1.000	1.000	1.000	0.999	0.979	0.868	0.584	0.228	0.032	0.000	0.000	0.000	12
	13	1.000	1.000	1.000	1.000	1.000	0.994	0.942	0.750	0.392	0.087	0.002	0.000	0.000	13
	14	1.000	1.000	1.000	1.000	1.000	0.998	0.979	0.874	0.584	0.196	0.011	0.000	0.000	14
	15	1.000	1.000	1.000	1.000	1.000	1.000	0.994	0.949	0.762	0.370	0.043	0.003	0.000	15
	16	1.000	1.000	1.000	1.000	1.000	1.000	0.999	0.984	0.893	0.589	0.133	0.016	0.000	16
	17	1.000	1.000	1.000	1.000	1.000	1.000	1.000	0.996	0.965	0.794	0.323	0.075	0.001	17
	18	1.000	1.000	1.000	1.000	1.000	1.000	1.000	0.999	0.992	0.931	0.608	0.264	0.017	18
	19	1.000	1.000	1.000	1.000	1.000	1.000	1.000	1.000	0.999	0.988	0.878	0.642	0.182	19
	20	1.000	1.000	1.000	1.000	1.000	1.000	1.000	1.000	1.000	1.000	1.000	1.000	1.000	20

TABLE A.3

Poisson Probabilities $\left[\dfrac{e^{-\mu}\mu^{x}}{x!}\right]$.

x	0.005	0.01	0.02	0.03	0.04	0.05	0.06	0.07	0.08	0.09
0	0.9950	0.9900	0.9802	0.9704	0.9608	0.9512	0.9418	0.9324	0.9231	0.9139
1	0.0050	0.0099	0.0196	0.0291	0.0384	0.0476	0.0565	0.0653	0.0738	0.0823
2	0.0000	0.0000	0.0002	0.0004	0.0008	0.0012	0.0017	0.0023	0.0030	0.0037
3	0.0000	0.0000	0.0000	0.0000	0.0000	0.0000	0.0000	0.0001	0.0001	0.0001

x	0.1	0.2	0.3	0.4	0.5	0.6	0.7	0.8	0.9	1.0
0	0.9048	0.8187	0.7408	0.6703	0.6065	0.5488	0.4966	0.4493	0.4066	0.3679
1	0.0905	0.1637	0.2222	0.2681	0.3033	0.3293	0.3476	0.3595	0.3659	0.3679
2	0.0045	0.0164	0.0333	0.0536	0.0758	0.0988	0.1217	0.1438	0.1647	0.1839
3	0.0002	0.0011	0.0033	0.0072	0.0126	0.0198	0.0284	0.0383	0.0494	0.0613
4	0.0000	0.0001	0.0003	0.0007	0.0016	0.0030	0.0050	0.0077	0.0111	0.0153
5	0.0000	0.0000	0.0000	0.0001	0.0002	0.0004	0.0007	0.0012	0.0020	0.0031
6	0.0000	0.0000	0.0000	0.0000	0.0000	0.0000	0.0001	0.0002	0.0003	0.0005
7	0.0000	0.0000	0.0000	0.0000	0.0000	0.0000	0.0000	0.0000	0.0000	0.0001

x	1.1	1.2	1.3	1.4	1.5	1.6	1.7	1.8	1.9	2.0
0	0.3329	0.3012	0.2725	0.2466	0.2231	0.2019	0.1827	0.1653	0.1496	0.1353
1	0.3662	0.3614	0.3543	0.3452	0.3347	0.3230	0.3106	0.2975	0.2842	0.2707
2	0.2014	0.2169	0.2303	0.2417	0.2510	0.2584	0.2640	0.2678	0.2700	0.2707
3	0.0738	0.0867	0.0998	0.1128	0.1255	0.1378	0.1496	0.1607	0.1710	0.1804
4	0.0203	0.0260	0.0324	0.0395	0.0471	0.0551	0.0636	0.0723	0.0812	0.0902
5	0.0045	0.0062	0.0084	0.0111	0.0141	0.0176	0.0216	0.0260	0.0309	0.0361
6	0.0008	0.0012	0.0018	0.0026	0.0035	0.0047	0.0061	0.0078	0.0098	0.0120
7	0.0001	0.0002	0.0003	0.0005	0.0008	0.0011	0.0015	0.0020	0.0027	0.0034
8	0.0000	0.0000	0.0001	0.0001	0.0001	0.0002	0.0003	0.0005	0.0006	0.0009
9	0.0000	0.0000	0.0000	0.0000	0.0000	0.0000	0.0001	0.0001	0.0001	0.0002

x	2.1	2.2	2.3	2.4	2.5	2.6	2.7	2.8	2.9	3.0
0	0.1225	0.1108	0.1003	0.0907	0.0821	0.0743	0.0672	0.0608	0.0550	0.0498
1	0.2572	0.2438	0.2306	0.2177	0.2052	0.1931	0.1815	0.1703	0.1596	0.1494
2	0.2700	0.2681	0.2652	0.2613	0.2565	0.2510	0.2450	0.2384	0.2314	0.2240
3	0.1890	0.1966	0.2033	0.2090	0.2138	0.2176	0.2205	0.2225	0.2237	0.2240
4	0.0992	0.1082	0.1169	0.1254	0.1336	0.1414	0.1488	0.1557	0.1622	0.1680
5	0.0417	0.0476	0.0538	0.0602	0.0668	0.0735	0.0804	0.0872	0.0940	0.1008
6	0.0146	0.0174	0.0206	0.0241	0.0278	0.0319	0.0362	0.0407	0.0455	0.0504
7	0.0044	0.0055	0.0068	0.0083	0.0099	0.0118	0.0139	0.0163	0.0188	0.0216
8	0.0011	0.0015	0.0019	0.0025	0.0031	0.0038	0.0047	0.0057	0.0068	0.0081
9	0.0003	0.0004	0.0005	0.0007	0.0009	0.0011	0.0014	0.0018	0.0022	0.0027
10	0.0001	0.0001	0.0001	0.0002	0.0002	0.0003	0.0004	0.0005	0.0006	0.0008
11	0.0000	0.0000	0.0000	0.0000	0.0000	0.0001	0.0001	0.0001	0.0002	0.0002
12	0.0000	0.0000	0.0000	0.0000	0.0000	0.0000	0.0000	0.0000	0.0000	0.0001

x	3.1	3.2	3.3	3.4	3.5	3.6	3.7	3.8	3.9	4.0
0	0.0450	0.0408	0.0369	0.0334	0.0302	0.0273	0.0247	0.0224	0.0202	0.0183
1	0.1397	0.1304	0.1217	0.1135	0.1057	0.0984	0.0915	0.0850	0.0789	0.0733
2	0.2165	0.2087	0.2008	0.1929	0.1850	0.1771	0.1692	0.1615	0.1539	0.1465
3	0.2237	0.2226	0.2209	0.2186	0.2158	0.2125	0.2087	0.2046	0.2001	0.1954
4	0.1733	0.1781	0.1823	0.1858	0.1888	0.1912	0.1931	0.1944	0.1951	0.1954
5	0.1075	0.1140	0.1203	0.1264	0.1322	0.1377	0.1429	0.1477	0.1522	0.1563
6	0.0555	0.0608	0.0662	0.0716	0.0771	0.0826	0.0881	0.0936	0.0989	0.1042
7	0.0246	0.0278	0.0312	0.0348	0.0385	0.0425	0.0466	0.0508	0.0551	0.0595
8	0.0095	0.0111	0.0129	0.0148	0.0169	0.0191	0.0215	0.0241	0.0269	0.0298
9	0.0033	0.0040	0.0047	0.0056	0.0066	0.0076	0.0089	0.0102	0.0116	0.0132
10	0.0010	0.0013	0.0016	0.0019	0.0023	0.0028	0.0033	0.0039	0.0045	0.0053
11	0.0003	0.0004	0.0005	0.0006	0.0007	0.0009	0.0011	0.0013	0.0016	0.0019
12	0.0001	0.0001	0.0001	0.0002	0.0002	0.0003	0.0003	0.004	0.0005	0.0006
13	0.0000	0.0000	0.0000	0.0000	0.0001	0.0001	0.0001	0.0001	0.0002	0.0002
14	0.0000	0.0000	0.0000	0.0000	0.0000	0.0000	0.0000	0.0000	0.0000	0.0001

x	4.1	4.2	4.3	4.4	4.5	4.6	4.7	4.8	4.9	5.0
0	0.0166	0.0150	0.0136	0.0123	0.0111	0.0101	0.0091	0.0082	0.0074	0.0067
1	0.0679	0.0630	0.0583	0.0540	0.0500	0.0462	0.0427	0.0395	0.0365	0.0337
2	0.1393	0.1323	0.1254	0.1188	0.1125	0.1063	0.1005	0.0948	0.0894	0.0842
3	0.1904	0.1852	0.1798	0.1743	0.1687	0.1631	0.1574	0.1517	0.1460	0.1404
4	0.1951	0.1944	0.1933	0.1917	0.1898	0.1875	0.1849	0.1820	0.1789	0.1755
5	0.1600	0.1633	0.1662	0.1687	0.1708	0.1725	0.1738	0.1747	0.1753	0.1755
6	0.1093	0.1143	0.1191	0.1237	0.1281	0.1323	0.1362	0.1398	0.1432	0.1462
7	0.0640	0.0686	0.0732	0.0778	0.0824	0.0869	0.0914	0.0959	0.1002	0.1044
8	0.0328	0.0360	0.0393	0.0428	0.0463	0.0500	0.0537	0.0575	0.0614	0.0653
9	0.0150	0.0168	0.0188	0.0209	0.0232	0.0255	0.0281	0.0307	0.0334	0.0363
10	0.0061	0.0071	0.0081	0.0092	0.0104	0.0118	0.0132	0.0147	0.0164	0.0181
11	0.0023	0.0027	0.0032	0.0037	0.0043	0.0049	0.0056	0.0064	0.0073	0.0082

TABLE A.3

Poisson Probabilities $\left[\dfrac{e^{-\mu}\mu^{x}}{x!}\right]_{\mu}$ (continued).

x	4.1	4.2	4.3	4.4	4.5	4.6	4.7	4.8	4.9	5.0
12	0.0008	0.0009	0.0011	0.0013	0.0016	0.0019	0.0022	0.0026	0.0030	0.0034
13	0.0002	0.0003	0.0004	0.0005	0.0006	0.0007	0.0008	0.0009	0.0011	0.0013
14	0.0001	0.0001	0.0001	0.0001	0.0002	0.0002	0.0003	0.0003	0.0004	0.0005
15	0.0000	0.0000	0.0000	0.0000	0.0001	0.0001	0.0001	0.0001	0.0001	0.0002

x	5.1	5.2	5.3	5.4	5.5	5.6	5.7	5.8	5.9	6.0
0	0.0061	0.0055	0.0050	0.0045	0.0041	0.0037	0.0033	0.0030	0.0027	0.0025
1	0.0311	0.0287	0.0265	0.0244	0.0225	0.0207	0.0191	0.0176	0.0162	0.0149
2	0.0793	0.0746	0.0701	0.0659	0.0618	0.0580	0.0544	0.0509	0.0477	0.0446
3	0.1348	0.1293	0.1239	0.1185	0.1133	0.1082	0.1033	0.0985	0.0938	0.0892
4	0.1719	0.1681	0.1641	0.1600	0.1558	0.1515	0.1472	0.1428	0.1383	0.1339
5	0.1753	0.1748	0.1740	0.1728	0.1714	0.1697	0.1678	0.1656	0.1632	0.1606
6	0.1490	0.1515	0.1537	0.1555	0.1571	0.1584	0.1594	0.1601	0.1605	0.1606
7	0.1086	0.1125	0.1163	0.1200	0.1234	0.1267	0.1298	0.1326	0.1353	0.1377
8	0.0692	0.0731	0.0771	0.0810	0.0849	0.0887	0.0925	0.0962	0.0998	0.1033
9	0.0392	0.0423	0.0454	0.0486	0.0519	0.0552	0.0586	0.0620	0.0654	0.0688
10	0.0200	0.0220	0.0241	0.0262	0.0285	0.0309	0.0334	0.0359	0.0386	0.0413
11	0.0093	0.0104	0.0116	0.0129	0.0143	0.0157	0.0173	0.0190	0.0207	0.0225
12	0.0039	0.0045	0.0051	0.0058	0.0065	0.0073	0.0082	0.0092	0.0102	0.0113
13	0.0015	0.0018	0.0021	0.0024	0.0028	0.0032	0.0036	0.0041	0.0046	0.0052
14	0.0006	0.0007	0.0008	0.0009	0.0011	0.0013	0.0015	0.0017	0.0019	0.0022
15	0.0002	0.0002	0.0003	0.0003	0.0004	0.0005	0.0006	0.0007	0.0008	0.0009
16	0.0001	0.0001	0.0001	0.0001	0.0001	0.0002	0.0002	0.0002	0.0003	0.0003
17	0.0000	0.0000	0.0000	0.0000	0.0000	0.0001	0.0001	0.0001	0.0001	0.0001

x	6.1	6.2	6.3	6.4	6.5	6.6	6.7	6.8	6.9	7.0
0	0.0022	0.0020	0.0018	0.0017	0.0015	0.0014	0.0012	0.0011	0.0010	0.0009
1	0.0137	0.0126	0.0116	0.0106	0.0098	0.0090	0.0082	0.0076	0.0070	0.0064
2	0.0417	0.0390	0.0364	0.0340	0.0318	0.0296	0.0276	0.0258	0.0240	0.0223
3	0.0848	0.0806	0.0765	0.0726	0.0688	0.0652	0.0617	0.0584	0.0552	0.0521
4	0.1294	0.1249	0.1205	0.1162	0.1118	0.1076	0.1034	0.0992	0.0952	0.0912
5	0.1579	0.1549	0.1519	0.1487	0.1454	0.1420	0.1385	0.1349	0.1314	0.1277
6	0.1605	0.1601	0.1595	0.1586	0.1575	0.1562	0.1546	0.1529	0.1511	0.1490
7	0.1399	0.1418	0.1435	0.1450	0.1462	0.1472	0.1480	0.1486	0.1489	0.1490
8	0.1066	0.1099	0.1130	0.1160	0.1188	0.1215	0.1240	0.1263	0.1284	0.1304
9	0.0723	0.0757	0.0791	0.0825	0.0858	0.0891	0.0923	0.0954	0.0985	0.1014
10	0.0441	0.0469	0.0498	0.0528	0.0558	0.0588	0.0618	0.0649	0.0679	0.0710
11	0.0244	0.0265	0.0285	0.0307	0.0330	0.0353	0.0377	0.0401	0.0426	0.0452
12	0.0124	0.0137	0.0150	0.0164	0.0179	0.0194	0.0210	0.0227	0.0245	0.0263
13	0.0058	0.0065	0.0073	0.0081	0.0089	0.0099	0.0108	0.0119	0.0130	0.0142
14	0.0025	0.0029	0.0033	0.0037	0.0041	0.0046	0.0052	0.0058	0.0064	0.0071
15	0.0010	0.0012	0.0014	0.0016	0.0018	0.0020	0.0023	0.0026	0.0029	0.0033
16	0.0004	0.0005	0.0005	0.0006	0.0007	0.0008	0.0010	0.0011	0.0013	0.0014
17	0.0001	0.0002	0.0002	0.0002	0.0003	0.0003	0.0004	0.0004	0.0005	0.0006
18	0.0000	0.0001	0.0001	0.0001	0.0001	0.0001	0.0001	0.0002	0.0002	0.0002
19	0.0000	0.0000	0.0000	0.0000	0.0000	0.0000	0.0001	0.0001	0.0001	0.0001

x	7.1	7.2	7.3	7.4	7.5	7.6	7.7	7.8	7.9	8.0
0	0.0008	0.0007	0.0007	0.0006	0.0006	0.0005	0.0005	0.0004	0.0004	0.0003
1	0.0059	0.0054	0.0049	0.0045	0.0041	0.0038	0.0035	0.0032	0.0029	0.0027
2	0.0208	0.0194	0.0180	0.0167	0.0156	0.0145	0.0134	0.0125	0.0116	0.0107
3	0.0492	0.0464	0.0438	0.0413	0.0389	0.0366	0.0345	0.0324	0.0305	0.0286
4	0.0874	0.0836	0.0799	0.0764	0.0729	0.0696	0.0663	0.0632	0.0602	0.0573
5	0.1241	0.1204	0.1167	0.1130	0.1094	0.1057	0.1021	0.0986	0.0951	0.0916
6	0.1468	0.1445	0.1420	0.1394	0.1367	0.1339	0.1311	0.1282	0.1252	0.1221
7	0.1489	0.1486	0.1481	0.1474	0.1465	0.1454	0.1442	0.1428	0.1413	0.1396
8	0.1321	0.1337	0.1351	0.1363	0.1373	0.1381	0.1388	0.1392	0.1395	0.1396
9	0.1042	0.1070	0.1096	0.1121	0.1144	0.1167	0.1187	0.1207	0.1224	0.1241
10	0.0740	0.0770	0.0800	0.0829	0.0858	0.0887	0.0914	0.0941	0.0967	0.0993
11	0.0478	0.0504	0.0531	0.0558	0.0585	0.0613	0.0640	0.0667	0.0695	0.0722
12	0.0283	0.0303	0.0323	0.0344	0.0366	0.0388	0.0411	0.0434	0.0457	0.0481
13	0.0154	0.0168	0.0181	0.0196	0.0211	0.0227	0.0243	0.0260	0.0278	0.0296
14	0.0078	0.0086	0.0095	0.0104	0.0113	0.0123	0.0134	0.0145	0.0157	0.0169
15	0.0037	0.0041	0.0046	0.0051	0.0057	0.0062	0.0069	0.0075	0.0083	0.0090
16	0.0016	0.0019	0.0021	0.0024	0.0026	0.0030	0.0033	0.0037	0.0041	0.0045
17	0.0007	0.0008	0.0009	0.0010	0.0012	0.0013	0.0015	0.0017	0.0019	0.0021
18	0.0003	0.0003	0.0004	0.0004	0.0005	0.0006	0.0006	0.0007	0.0008	0.0009
19	0.0001	0.0001	0.0001	0.0002	0.0002	0.0002	0.0003	0.0003	0.0003	0.0004
20	0.0000	0.0000	0.0001	0.0001	0.0001	0.0001	0.0001	0.0001	0.0001	0.0002
21	0.0000	0.0000	0.0000	0.0000	0.0000	0.0000	0.0000	0.0000	0.0001	0.0001

TABLE A.3

Poisson Probabilities $\left[\dfrac{e^{-\mu}\mu^x}{x!}\right]$ (continued).

μ

x	8.1	8.2	8.3	8.4	8.5	8.6	8.7	8.8	8.9	9.0
0	0.0003	0.0003	0.0002	0.0002	0.0002	0.0002	0.0002	0.0002	0.0001	0.0001
1	0.0025	0.0023	0.0021	0.0019	0.0017	0.0016	0.0014	0.0013	0.0012	0.0011
2	0.0100	0.0092	0.0086	0.0079	0.0074	0.0068	0.0063	0.0058	0.0054	0.0050
3	0.0269	0.0252	0.0237	0.0222	0.0208	0.0195	0.0183	0.0171	0.0160	0.0150
4	0.0544	0.0517	0.0491	0.0466	0.0443	0.0420	0.0398	0.0377	0.0357	0.0337
5	0.0882	0.0849	0.0816	0.0784	0.0752	0.0722	0.0692	0.0663	0.0635	0.0607
6	0.1191	0.1160	0.1128	0.1097	0.1066	0.1034	0.1003	0.0972	0.0941	0.0911
7	0.1378	0.1358	0.1338	0.1317	0.1294	0.1271	0.1247	0.1222	0.1197	0.1171
8	0.1395	0.1392	0.1388	0.1382	0.1375	0.1366	0.1356	0.1344	0.1332	0.1318
9	0.1256	0.1269	0.1280	0.1290	0.1299	0.1306	0.1311	0.1315	0.1317	0.1318
10	0.1017	0.1040	0.1063	0.1084	0.1104	0.1123	0.1140	0.1157	0.1172	0.1186
11	0.0749	0.0776	0.0802	0.0828	0.0853	0.0878	0.0902	0.0925	0.0948	0.0970
12	0.0505	0.0530	0.0555	0.0579	0.0604	0.0629	0.0654	0.0679	0.0703	0.0728
13	0.0315	0.0334	0.0354	0.0374	0.0395	0.0416	0.0438	0.0459	0.0481	0.0504
14	0.0182	0.0196	0.0210	0.0225	0.0240	0.0256	0.0272	0.0289	0.0306	0.0324
15	0.0098	0.0107	0.0116	0.0126	0.0136	0.0147	0.0158	0.0169	0.0182	0.0194
16	0.0050	0.0055	0.0060	0.0066	0.0072	0.0079	0.0086	0.0093	0.0101	0.0109
17	0.0024	0.0026	0.0029	0.0033	0.0036	0.0040	0.0044	0.0048	0.0053	0.0058
18	0.0011	0.0012	0.0014	0.0015	0.0017	0.0019	0.0021	0.0024	0.0026	0.0029
19	0.0005	0.0005	0.0006	0.0007	0.0008	0.0009	0.0010	0.0011	0.0012	0.0014
20	0.0002	0.0002	0.0002	0.0003	0.0003	0.0004	0.0004	0.0005	0.0005	0.0006
21	0.0001	0.0001	0.0001	0.0001	0.0001	0.0002	0.0002	0.0002	0.0002	0.0003
22	0.0000	0.0000	0.0000	0.0000	0.0001	0.0001	0.0001	0.0001	0.0001	0.0001

x	9.1	9.2	9.3	9.4	9.5	9.6	9.7	9.8	9.9	10.0
0	0.0001	0.0001	0.0001	0.0001	0.0001	0.0001	0.0001	0.0001	0.0001	0.0000
1	0.0010	0.0009	0.0009	0.0008	0.0007	0.0007	0.0006	0.0005	0.0005	0.0005
2	0.0046	0.0043	0.0040	0.0037	0.0034	0.0031	0.0029	0.0027	0.0025	0.0023
3	0.0140	0.0131	0.0123	0.0115	0.0107	0.0100	0.0093	0.0087	0.0081	0.0076
4	0.0319	0.0302	0.0285	0.0269	0.0254	0.0240	0.0226	0.0213	0.0201	0.0189
5	0.0581	0.0555	0.0530	0.0506	0.0483	0.0460	0.0439	0.0418	0.0398	0.0378
6	0.0881	0.0851	0.0822	0.0793	0.0764	0.0736	0.0709	0.0682	0.0656	0.0631
7	0.1145	0.1118	0.1091	0.1064	0.1037	0.1010	0.0982	0.0955	0.0928	0.0901
8	0.1302	0.1286	0.1269	0.1251	0.1232	0.1212	0.1191	0.1170	0.1148	0.1126
9	0.1317	0.1315	0.1311	0.1306	0.1300	0.1293	0.1284	0.1274	0.1263	0.1251
10	0.1198	0.1210	0.1219	0.1228	0.1235	0.1241	0.1245	0.1249	0.1250	0.1251
11	0.0991	0.1012	0.1031	0.1049	0.1067	0.1083	0.1098	0.1112	0.1125	0.1137
12	0.0752	0.0776	0.0799	0.0822	0.0844	0.0866	0.0888	0.0908	0.0928	0.0948
13	0.0526	0.0549	0.0572	0.0594	0.0617	0.0640	0.0662	0.0685	0.0707	0.0729
14	0.0342	0.0361	0.0380	0.0399	0.0419	0.0439	0.0459	0.0479	0.0500	0.0521
15	0.0208	0.0221	0.0235	0.0250	0.0265	0.0281	0.0297	0.0313	0.0330	0.0347
16	0.0118	0.0127	0.0137	0.0147	0.0157	0.0168	0.0180	0.0192	0.0204	0.0217
17	0.0063	0.0069	0.0075	0.0081	0.0088	0.0095	0.0103	0.0111	0.0119	0.0128
18	0.0032	0.0035	0.0039	0.0042	0.0046	0.0051	0.0055	0.0060	0.0065	0.0071
19	0.0015	0.0017	0.0019	0.0021	0.0023	0.0026	0.0028	0.0031	0.0034	0.0037
20	0.0007	0.0008	0.0009	0.0010	0.0011	0.0012	0.0014	0.0015	0.0017	0.0019
21	0.0003	0.0003	0.0004	0.0004	0.0005	0.0006	0.0006	0.0007	0.0008	0.0009
22	0.0001	0.0001	0.0002	0.0002	0.0002	0.0002	0.0003	0.0003	0.0004	0.0004
23	0.0000	0.0001	0.0001	0.0001	0.0001	0.0001	0.0001	0.0001	0.0002	0.0002
24	0.0000	0.0000	0.0000	0.0000	0.0000	0.0000	0.0000	0.0001	0.0001	0.0001

TABLE A.4

Areas of the standard normal distribution. The entries in this table are the probabilities that a standard normal random variable is between 0 and z (the shaded area).

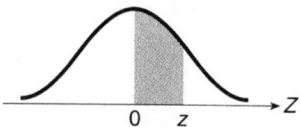

Second Decimal Place in z

z	0.00	0.01	0.02	0.03	0.04	0.05	0.06	0.07	0.08	0.09
0.0	0.0000	0.0040	0.0080	0.0120	0.0160	0.0199	0.0239	0.0279	0.0319	0.0359
0.1	0.0398	0.0438	0.0478	0.0517	0.0557	0.0596	0.0636	0.0675	0.0714	0.0753
0.2	0.0793	0.0832	0.0871	0.0910	0.0948	0.0987	0.1026	0.1064	0.1103	0.1141
0.3	0.1179	0.1217	0.1255	0.1293	0.1331	0.1368	0.1406	0.1443	0.1480	0.1517
0.4	0.1554	0.1591	0.1628	0.1664	0.1700	0.1736	0.1772	0.1808	0.1844	0.1879
0.5	0.1915	0.1950	0.1985	0.2019	0.2054	0.2088	0.2123	0.2157	0.2190	0.2224
0.6	0.2257	0.2291	0.2324	0.2357	0.2389	0.2422	0.2454	0.2486	0.2517	0.2549
0.7	0.2580	0.2611	0.2642	0.2673	0.2704	0.2734	0.2764	0.2794	0.2823	0.2852
0.8	0.2881	0.2910	0.2939	0.2967	0.2995	0.3023	0.3051	0.3078	0.3106	0.3133
0.9	0.3159	0.3186	0.3212	0.3238	0.3264	0.3289	0.3315	0.3340	0.3365	0.3389
1.0	0.3413	0.3438	0.3461	0.3485	0.3508	0.3531	0.3554	0.3577	0.3599	0.3621
1.1	0.3643	0.3665	0.3686	0.3708	0.3729	0.3749	0.3770	0.3790	0.3810	0.3830
1.2	0.3849	0.3869	0.3888	0.3907	0.3925	0.3944	0.3962	0.3980	0.3997	0.4015
1.3	0.4032	0.4049	0.4066	0.4082	0.4099	0.4115	0.4131	0.4147	0.4162	0.4177
1.4	0.4192	0.4207	0.4222	0.4236	0.4251	0.4265	0.4279	0.4292	0.4306	0.4319
1.5	0.4332	0.4345	0.4357	0.4370	0.4382	0.4394	0.4406	0.4418	0.4429	0.4441
1.6	0.4452	0.4463	0.4474	0.4484	0.4495	0.4505	0.4515	0.4525	0.4535	0.4545
1.7	0.4554	0.4564	0.4573	0.4582	0.4591	0.4599	0.4608	0.4616	0.4625	0.4633
1.8	0.4641	0.4649	0.4656	0.4664	0.4671	0.4678	0.4686	0.4693	0.4699	0.4706
1.9	0.4713	0.4719	0.4726	0.4732	0.4738	0.4744	0.4750	0.4756	0.4761	0.4767
2.0	0.4772	0.4778	0.4783	0.4788	0.4793	0.4798	0.4803	0.4808	0.4812	0.4817
2.1	0.4821	0.4826	0.4830	0.4834	0.4838	0.4842	0.4846	0.4850	0.4854	0.4857
2.2	0.4861	0.4864	0.4868	0.4871	0.4875	0.4878	0.4881	0.4884	0.4887	0.4890
2.3	0.4893	0.4896	0.4898	0.4901	0.4904	0.4906	0.4909	0.4911	0.4913	0.4916
2.4	0.4918	0.4920	0.4922	0.4925	0.4927	0.4929	0.4931	0.4932	0.4934	0.4936
2.5	0.4938	0.4940	0.4941	0.4943	0.4945	0.4946	0.4948	0.4949	0.4951	0.4952
2.6	0.4953	0.4955	0.4956	0.4957	0.4959	0.4960	0.4961	0.4962	0.4963	0.4964
2.7	0.4965	0.4966	0.4967	0.4968	0.4969	0.4970	0.4971	0.4972	0.4973	0.4974
2.8	0.4974	0.4975	0.4976	0.4977	0.4977	0.4978	0.4979	0.4979	0.4980	0.4981
2.9	0.4981	0.4982	0.4982	0.4983	0.4984	0.4984	0.4985	0.4985	0.4986	0.4986
3.0	0.4987	0.4987	0.4987	0.4988	0.4988	0.4989	0.4989	0.4989	0.4990	0.4990
3.1	0.4990	0.4991	0.4991	0.4991	0.4992	0.4992	0.4992	0.4992	0.4993	0.4993
3.2	0.4993	0.4993	0.4994	0.4994	0.4994	0.4994	0.4994	0.4995	0.4995	0.4995
3.3	0.4995	0.4995	0.4995	0.4996	0.4996	0.4996	0.4996	0.4996	0.4996	0.4997
3.4	0.4997	0.4997	0.4997	0.4997	0.4997	0.4997	0.4997	0.4997	0.4997	0.4998
3.5	0.4998									
4.0	0.49997									
4.5	0.499997									
5.0	0.4999997									

TABLE A.5 Critical values of *t*.

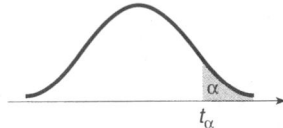

Degrees of Freedom	$t_{.100}$	$t_{.050}$	$t_{.025}$	$t_{.010}$	$t_{.005}$
1	3.078	6.314	12.706	31.821	63.657
2	1.886	2.920	4.303	6.965	9.925
3	1.638	2.353	3.182	4.541	5.841
4	1.533	2.132	2.776	3.747	4.604
5	1.476	2.015	2.571	3.365	4.032
6	1.440	1.943	2.447	3.143	3.707
7	1.415	1.895	2.365	2.998	3.499
8	1.397	1.860	2.306	2.896	3.355
9	1.383	1.833	2.262	2.821	3.250
10	1.372	1.812	2.228	2.764	3.169
11	1.363	1.796	2.201	2.718	3.106
12	1.356	1.782	2.179	2.681	3.055
13	1.350	1.771	2.160	2.650	3.012
14	1.345	1.761	2.145	2.624	2.977
15	1.341	1.753	2.131	2.602	2.947
16	1.337	1.746	2.120	2.583	2.921
17	1.333	1.740	2.110	2.567	2.898
18	1.330	1.734	2.101	2.552	2.878
19	1.328	1.729	2.093	2.539	2.861
20	1.325	1.725	2.086	2.528	2.845
21	1.323	1.721	2.080	2.518	2.831
22	1.321	1.717	2.074	2.508	2.819
23	1.319	1.714	2.069	2.500	2.807
24	1.318	1.711	2.064	2.492	2.797
25	1.316	1.708	2.060	2.485	2.787
26	1.315	1.706	2.056	2.479	2.779
27	1.314	1.703	2.052	2.473	2.771
28	1.313	1.701	2.048	2.467	2.763
29	1.311	1.699	2.045	2.462	2.756
30	1.310	1.697	2.042	2.457	2.750
35	1.306	1.690	2.030	2.438	2.724
40	1.303	1.684	2.021	2.423	2.704
50	1.299	1.676	2.009	2.403	2.678
60	1.296	1.671	2.000	2.390	2.660
120	1.289	1.658	1.980	2.358	2.617
∞	1.282	1.645	1.960	2.326	2.576

TABLE A.6 Critical values of χ^2.

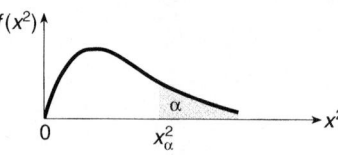

Degrees of Freedom	$\chi^2_{.995}$	$\chi^2_{.990}$	$\chi^2_{.975}$	$\chi^2_{.950}$	$\chi^2_{.900}$
1	0.0000	0.0002	0.0010	0.0039	0.0158
2	0.0100	0.0201	0.0506	0.1026	0.2107
3	0.0717	0.1148	0.2158	0.3518	0.5844
4	0.2070	0.2971	0.4844	0.7107	1.0636
5	0.4117	0.5543	0.8312	1.1455	1.6103
6	0.6757	0.8721	1.2373	1.6354	2.2041
7	0.9893	1.2390	1.6899	2.1673	2.8331
8	1.3444	1.6465	2.1797	2.7326	3.4895
9	1.7349	2.0879	2.7004	3.3251	4.1682
10	2.1559	2.5582	3.2470	3.9403	4.8652
11	2.6032	3.0535	3.8157	4.5748	5.5778
12	3.0738	3.5706	4.4038	5.2260	6.3038
13	3.5650	4.1069	5.0088	5.8919	7.0415
14	4.0747	4.6604	5.6287	6.5706	7.7895
15	4.6009	5.2293	6.2621	7.2609	8.5468
16	5.1422	5.8122	6.9077	7.9616	9.3122
17	5.6972	6.4078	7.5642	8.6718	10.0852
18	6.2648	7.0149	8.2307	9.3905	10.8649
19	6.8440	7.6327	8.9065	10.1170	11.6509
20	7.4338	8.2604	9.5908	10.8508	12.4426
21	8.0337	8.8972	10.2829	11.5913	13.2396
22	8.6427	9.5425	10.9823	12.3380	14.0415
23	9.2604	10.1957	11.6886	13.0905	14.8480
24	9.8862	10.8564	12.4012	13.8484	15.6587
25	10.5197	11.5240	13.1197	14.6114	16.4734
26	11.1602	12.1981	13.8439	15.3792	17.2919
27	11.8076	12.8785	14.5734	16.1514	18.1139
28	12.4613	13.5647	15.3079	16.9279	18.9392
29	13.1211	14.2565	16.0471	17.7084	19.7677
30	13.7867	14.9535	16.7908	18.4927	20.5992
40	20.7065	22.1643	24.4330	26.5093	29.0505
50	27.9907	29.7067	32.3574	34.7643	37.6886
60	35.5345	37.4849	40.4817	43.1880	46.4589
70	43.2752	45.4417	48.7576	51.7393	55.3289
80	51.1719	53.5401	57.1532	60.3915	64.2778
90	59.1963	61.7541	65.6466	69.1260	73.2911
100	67.3276	70.0649	74.2219	77.9295	82.3581

TABLE A.6 Critical values of χ^2 (continued).

Degrees of Freedom	$\chi^2_{.100}$	$\chi^2_{.0.50}$	$\chi^2_{.025}$	$\chi^2_{.010}$	$\chi^2_{.005}$
1	2.7055	3.8415	5.0239	6.6349	7.8794
2	4.6052	5.9915	7.3778	9.2103	10.5966
3	6.2514	7.8147	9.3484	11.3449	12.8382
4	7.7794	9.4877	11.1433	13.2767	14.8603
5	9.2364	11.0705	12.8325	15.0863	16.7496
6	10.6446	12.5916	14.4494	16.8119	18.5476
7	12.0170	14.0671	16.0128	18.4753	20.2777
8	13.3616	15.5073	17.5345	20.0902	21.9550
9	14.6837	16.9190	19.0228	21.6660	23.5894
10	15.9872	18.3070	20.4832	23.2093	25.1882
11	17.2750	19.6751	21.9200	24.7250	26.7568
12	18.5493	21.0261	23.3367	26.2170	28.2995
13	19.8119	22.3620	24.7356	27.6882	29.8195
14	21.0641	23.6848	26.1189	29.1412	31.3193
15	22.3071	24.9958	27.4884	30.5779	32.8013
16	23.5418	26.2962	28.8454	31.9999	34.2672
17	24.7690	27.5871	30.1910	33.4087	35.7185
18	25.9894	28.8693	31.5264	34.8053	37.1565
19	27.2036	30.1435	32.8523	36.1909	38.5823
20	28.4120	31.4104	34.1696	37.5662	39.9968
21	29.6151	32.6706	35.4789	38.9322	41.4011
22	30.8133	33.9244	36.7807	40.2894	42.7957
23	32.0069	35.1725	38.0756	41.6384	44.1813
24	33.1962	36.4150	39.3641	42.9798	45.5585
25	34.3816	37.6525	40.6465	44.3141	46.9279
26	35.5632	38.8851	41.9232	45.6417	48.2899
27	36.7412	40.1133	43.1945	46.9629	49.6449
28	37.9159	41.3371	44.4608	48.2782	50.9934
29	39.0875	42.5570	45.7223	49.5879	52.3356
30	40.2560	43.7730	46.9792	50.8922	53.6720
40	51.8051	55.7585	59.3417	63.6907	66.7660
50	63.1671	67.5048	71.4202	76.1539	79.4900
60	74.3970	79.0819	83.2977	88.3794	91.9517
70	85.5270	90.5312	95.0232	100.4252	104.2149
80	96.5782	101.8795	106.6286	112.3288	116.3211
90	107.5650	113.1453	118.1359	124.1163	128.2989
100	118.4980	124.3421	129.5612	135.8067	140.1695

TABLE A.7a

Percentage points of the F distribution. $\alpha = .10$.

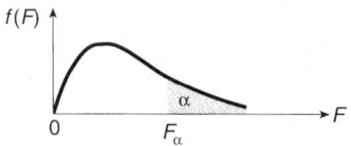

Numerator Degrees of Freedom

v_2	1	2	3	4	5	6	7	8	9
1	39.86	49.50	53.59	55.83	57.24	58.20	58.91	59.44	59.86
2	8.53	9.00	9.16	9.24	9.29	9.33	9.35	9.37	9.38
3	5.54	5.46	5.39	5.34	5.31	5.28	5.27	5.25	5.24
4	4.54	4.32	4.19	4.11	4.05	4.01	3.98	3.95	3.94
5	4.06	3.78	3.62	3.52	3.45	3.40	3.37	3.34	3.32
6	3.78	3.46	3.29	3.18	3.11	3.05	3.01	2.98	2.96
7	3.59	3.26	3.07	2.96	2.88	2.83	2.78	2.75	2.72
8	3.46	3.11	2.92	2.81	2.73	2.67	2.62	2.59	2.56
9	3.36	3.01	2.81	2.69	2.61	2.55	2.51	2.47	2.44
10	3.29	2.92	2.73	2.61	2.52	2.46	2.41	2.38	2.35
11	3.23	2.86	2.66	2.54	2.45	2.39	2.34	2.30	2.27
12	3.18	2.81	2.61	2.48	2.39	2.33	2.28	2.24	2.21
13	3.14	2.76	2.56	2.43	2.35	2.28	2.23	2.20	2.16
14	3.10	2.73	2.52	2.39	2.31	2.24	2.19	2.15	2.12
15	3.07	2.70	2.49	2.36	2.27	2.21	2.16	2.12	2.09
16	3.05	2.67	2.46	2.33	2.24	2.18	2.13	2.09	2.06
17	3.03	2.64	2.44	2.31	2.22	2.15	2.10	2.06	2.03
18	3.01	2.62	2.42	2.29	2.20	2.13	2.08	2.04	2.00
19	2.99	2.61	2.40	2.27	2.18	2.11	2.06	2.02	1.98
20	2.97	2.59	2.38	2.25	2.16	2.09	2.04	2.00	1.96
21	2.96	2.57	2.36	2.23	2.14	2.08	2.02	1.98	1.95
22	2.95	2.56	2.35	2.22	2.13	2.06	2.01	1.97	1.93
23	2.94	2.55	2.34	2.21	2.11	2.05	1.99	1.95	1.92
24	2.93	2.54	2.33	2.19	2.10	2.04	1.98	1.94	1.91
25	2.92	2.53	2.32	2.18	2.09	2.02	1.97	1.93	1.89
26	2.91	2.52	2.31	2.17	2.08	2.01	1.96	1.92	1.88
27	2.90	2.51	2.30	2.17	2.07	2.00	1.95	1.91	1.87
28	2.89	2.50	2.29	2.16	2.06	2.00	1.94	1.90	1.87
29	2.89	2.50	2.28	2.15	2.06	1.99	1.93	1.89	1.86
30	2.88	2.49	2.28	2.14	2.05	1.98	1.93	1.88	1.85
40	2.84	2.44	2.23	2.09	2.00	1.93	1.87	1.83	1.79
60	2.79	2.39	2.18	2.04	1.95	1.87	1.82	1.77	1.74
120	2.75	2.35	2.13	1.99	1.90	1.82	1.77	1.72	1.68
∞	2.71	2.30	2.08	1.94	1.85	1.77	1.72	1.67	1.63

Denominator Degrees of Freedom

TABLE A.7a

Percentage points of the F distribution. α = .10 (continued).

Numerator Degrees of Freedom

v_2 \ v_1	10	12	15	20	24	30	40	60	120	∞
1	60.19	60.71	61.22	61.74	62.00	62.26	62.53	62.79	63.06	63.33
2	9.39	9.41	9.42	9.44	9.45	9.46	9.47	9.47	9.48	9.49
3	5.23	5.22	5.20	5.18	5.18	5.17	5.16	5.15	5.14	5.13
4	3.92	3.90	3.87	3.84	3.83	3.82	3.80	3.79	3.78	3.76
5	3.30	3.27	3.24	3.21	3.19	3.17	3.16	3.14	3.12	3.10
6	2.94	2.90	2.87	2.84	2.82	2.80	2.78	2.76	2.74	2.72
7	2.70	2.67	2.63	2.59	2.58	2.56	2.54	2.51	2.49	2.47
8	2.54	2.50	2.46	2.42	2.40	2.38	2.36	2.34	2.32	2.29
9	2.42	2.38	2.34	2.30	2.28	2.25	2.23	2.21	2.18	2.16
10	2.32	2.28	2.24	2.20	2.18	2.16	2.13	2.11	2.08	2.06
11	2.25	2.21	2.17	2.12	2.10	2.08	2.05	2.03	2.00	1.97
12	2.19	2.15	2.10	2.06	2.04	2.01	1.99	1.96	1.93	1.90
13	2.14	2.10	2.05	2.01	1.98	1.96	1.93	1.90	1.88	1.85
14	2.10	2.05	2.01	1.96	1.94	1.91	1.89	1.86	1.83	1.80
15	2.06	2.02	1.97	1.92	1.90	1.87	1.85	1.82	1.79	1.76
16	2.03	1.99	1.94	1.89	1.87	1.84	1.81	1.78	1.75	1.72
17	2.00	1.96	1.91	1.86	1.84	1.81	1.78	1.75	1.72	1.69
18	1.98	1.93	1.89	1.84	1.81	1.78	1.75	1.72	1.69	1.66
19	1.96	1.91	1.86	1.81	1.79	1.76	1.73	1.70	1.67	1.63
20	1.94	1.89	1.84	1.79	1.77	1.74	1.71	1.68	1.64	1.61
21	1.92	1.87	1.83	1.78	1.75	1.72	1.69	1.66	1.62	1.59
22	1.90	1.86	1.81	1.76	1.73	1.70	1.67	1.64	1.60	1.57
23	1.89	1.84	1.80	1.74	1.72	1.69	1.66	1.62	1.59	1.55
24	1.88	1.83	1.78	1.73	1.70	1.67	1.64	1.61	1.57	1.53
25	1.87	1.82	1.77	1.72	1.69	1.66	1.63	1.59	1.56	1.52
26	1.86	1.81	1.76	1.71	1.68	1.65	1.61	1.58	1.54	1.50
27	1.85	1.80	1.75	1.70	1.67	1.64	1.60	1.57	1.53	1.49
28	1.84	1.79	1.74	1.69	1.66	1.63	1.59	1.56	1.52	1.48
29	1.83	1.78	1.73	1.68	1.65	1.62	1.58	1.55	1.51	1.47
30	1.82	1.77	1.72	1.67	1.64	1.61	1.57	1.54	1.50	1.46
40	1.76	1.71	1.66	1.61	1.57	1.54	1.51	1.47	1.42	1.38
60	1.71	1.66	1.60	1.54	1.51	1.48	1.44	1.40	1.35	1.29
120	1.65	1.60	1.55	1.48	1.45	1.41	1.37	1.32	1.26	1.19
∞	1.60	1.55	1.49	1.42	1.38	1.34	1.30	1.24	1.17	1.00

Denominator Degrees of Freedom

TABLE A.7b   Percentage points of the F distribution. α = .05.

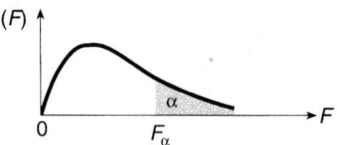

Numerator Degrees of Freedom

v_2 \ v_1	1	2	3	4	5	6	7	8	9
1	161.4	199.5	215.7	224.6	230.2	234.0	236.8	238.9	240.5
2	18.51	19.00	19.16	19.25	19.30	19.33	19.35	19.37	19.38
3	10.13	9.55	9.28	9.12	9.01	8.94	8.89	8.85	8.81
4	7.71	6.94	6.59	6.39	6.26	6.16	6.09	6.04	6.00
5	6.61	5.79	5.41	5.19	5.05	4.95	4.88	4.82	4.77
6	5.99	5.14	4.76	4.53	4.39	4.28	4.21	4.15	4.10
7	5.59	4.74	4.35	4.12	3.97	3.87	3.79	3.73	3.68
8	5.32	4.46	4.07	3.84	3.69	3.58	3.50	3.44	3.39
9	5.12	4.26	3.86	3.63	3.48	3.37	3.29	3.23	3.18
10	4.96	4.10	3.71	3.48	3.33	3.22	3.14	3.07	3.02
11	4.84	3.98	3.59	3.36	3.20	3.09	3.01	2.95	2.90
12	4.75	3.89	3.49	3.26	3.11	3.00	2.91	2.85	2.80
13	4.67	3.81	3.41	3.18	3.03	2.92	2.83	2.77	2.71
14	4.60	3.74	3.34	3.11	2.96	2.85	2.76	2.70	2.65
15	4.54	3.68	3.29	3.06	2.90	2.79	2.71	2.64	2.59
16	4.49	3.63	3.24	3.01	2.85	2.74	2.66	2.59	2.54
17	4.45	3.59	3.20	2.96	2.81	2.70	2.61	2.55	2.49
18	4.41	3.55	3.16	2.93	2.77	2.66	2.58	2.51	2.46
19	4.38	3.52	3.13	2.90	2.74	2.63	2.54	2.48	2.42
20	4.35	3.49	3.10	2.87	2.71	2.60	2.51	2.45	2.39
21	4.32	3.47	3.07	2.84	2.68	2.57	2.49	2.42	2.37
22	4.30	3.44	3.05	2.82	2.66	2.55	2.46	2.40	2.34
23	4.28	3.42	3.03	2.80	2.64	2.53	2.44	2.37	2.32
24	4.26	3.40	3.01	2.78	2.62	2.51	2.42	2.36	2.30
25	4.24	3.39	2.99	2.76	2.60	2.49	2.40	2.34	2.28
26	4.23	3.37	2.98	2.74	2.59	2.47	2.39	2.32	2.27
27	4.21	3.35	2.96	2.73	2.57	2.46	2.37	2.31	2.25
28	4.20	3.34	2.95	2.71	2.56	2.45	2.36	2.29	2.24
29	4.18	3.33	2.93	2.70	2.55	2.43	2.35	2.28	2.22
30	4.17	3.32	2.92	2.69	2.53	2.42	2.33	2.27	2.21
40	4.08	3.23	2.84	2.61	2.45	2.34	2.25	2.18	2.12
60	4.00	3.15	2.76	2.53	2.37	2.25	2.17	2.10	2.04
120	3.92	3.07	2.68	2.45	2.29	2.18	2.09	2.02	1.96
∞	3.84	3.00	2.60	2.37	2.21	2.10	2.01	1.94	1.88

Denominator Degrees of Freedom

TABLE A.7b Percentage points of the *F* distribution. $\alpha = .05$ (continued).

Numerator Degrees of Freedom

v_2 \ v_1	10	12	15	20	24	30	40	60	120	∞
1	241.9	243.9	245.9	248.0	249.1	250.1	251.1	252.2	253.3	254.3
2	19.40	19.41	19.43	19.45	19.45	19.46	19.47	19.48	19.49	19.50
3	8.79	8.74	8.70	8.66	8.64	8.62	8.59	8.57	8.55	8.53
4	5.96	5.91	5.86	5.80	5.77	5.75	5.72	5.69	5.66	5.63
5	4.74	4.68	4.62	4.56	4.53	4.50	4.46	4.43	4.40	4.37
6	4.06	4.00	3.94	3.87	3.84	3.81	3.77	3.74	3.70	3.67
7	3.64	3.57	3.51	3.44	3.41	3.38	3.34	3.30	3.27	3.23
8	3.35	3.28	3.22	3.15	3.12	3.08	3.04	3.01	2.97	2.93
9	3.14	3.07	3.01	2.94	2.90	2.86	2.83	2.79	2.75	2.71
10	2.98	2.91	2.85	2.77	2.74	2.70	2.66	2.62	2.58	2.54
11	2.85	2.79	2.72	2.65	2.61	2.57	2.53	2.49	2.45	2.40
12	2.75	2.69	2.62	2.54	2.51	2.47	2.43	2.38	2.34	2.30
13	2.67	2.60	2.53	2.46	2.42	2.38	2.34	2.30	2.25	2.21
14	2.60	2.53	2.46	2.39	2.35	2.31	2.27	2.22	2.18	2.13
15	2.54	2.48	2.40	2.33	2.29	2.25	2.20	2.16	2.11	2.07
16	2.49	2.42	2.35	2.28	2.24	2.19	2.15	2.11	2.06	2.01
17	2.45	2.38	2.31	2.23	2.19	2.15	2.10	2.06	2.01	1.96
18	2.41	2.34	2.27	2.19	2.15	2.11	2.06	2.02	1.97	1.92
19	2.38	2.31	2.23	2.16	2.11	2.07	2.03	1.98	1.93	1.88
20	2.35	2.28	2.20	2.12	2.08	2.04	1.99	1.95	1.90	1.84
21	2.32	2.25	2.18	2.10	2.05	2.01	1.96	1.92	1.87	1.81
22	2.30	2.23	2.15	2.07	2.03	1.98	1.94	1.89	1.84	1.78
23	2.27	2.20	2.13	2.05	2.01	1.96	1.91	1.86	1.81	1.76
24	2.25	2.18	2.11	2.03	1.98	1.94	1.89	1.84	1.79	1.73
25	2.24	2.16	2.09	2.01	1.96	1.92	1.87	1.82	1.77	1.71
26	2.22	2.15	2.07	1.99	1.95	1.90	1.85	1.80	1.75	1.69
27	2.20	2.13	2.06	1.97	1.93	1.88	1.84	1.79	1.73	1.67
28	2.19	2.12	2.04	1.96	1.91	1.87	1.82	1.77	1.71	1.65
29	2.18	2.10	2.03	1.94	1.90	1.85	1.81	1.75	1.70	1.64
30	2.16	2.09	2.01	1.93	1.89	1.84	1.79	1.74	1.68	1.62
40	2.08	2.00	1.92	1.84	1.79	1.74	1.69	1.64	1.58	1.51
60	1.99	1.92	1.84	1.75	1.70	1.65	1.59	1.53	1.47	1.39
120	1.91	1.83	1.75	1.66	1.61	1.55	1.50	1.43	1.35	1.25
∞	1.83	1.75	1.67	1.57	1.52	1.46	1.39	1.32	1.22	1.00

Denominator Degrees of Freedom

TABLE A.7c   Percentage points of the *F* distribution. α = .025.

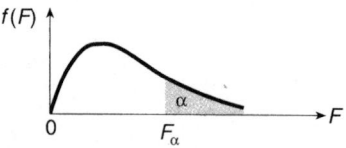

Numerator Degrees of Freedom

ν_2 \ ν_1	1	2	3	4	5	6	7	8	9
1	647.8	799.5	864.2	899.6	921.8	937.1	948.2	956.6	963.3
2	38.51	39.00	39.17	39.25	39.30	39.33	39.36	39.37	39.39
3	17.44	16.04	15.44	15.10	14.88	14.73	14.62	14.54	14.47
4	12.22	10.65	9.98	9.60	9.36	9.20	9.07	8.98	8.90
5	10.01	8.43	7.76	7.39	7.15	6.98	6.85	6.76	6.68
6	8.81	7.26	6.60	6.23	5.99	5.82	5.70	5.60	5.52
7	8.07	6.54	5.89	5.52	5.29	5.12	4.99	4.90	4.82
8	7.57	6.06	5.42	5.05	4.82	4.65	4.53	4.43	4.36
9	7.21	5.71	5.08	4.72	4.48	4.32	4.20	4.10	4.03
10	6.94	5.46	4.83	4.47	4.24	4.07	3.95	3.85	3.78
11	6.72	5.26	4.63	4.28	4.04	3.88	3.76	3.66	3.59
12	6.55	5.10	4.47	4.12	3.89	3.73	3.61	3.51	3.44
13	6.41	4.97	4.35	4.00	3.77	3.60	3.48	3.39	3.31
14	6.30	4.86	4.24	3.89	3.66	3.50	3.38	3.29	3.21
15	6.20	4.77	4.15	3.80	3.58	3.41	3.29	3.20	3.12
16	6.12	4.69	4.08	3.73	3.50	3.34	3.22	3.12	3.05
17	6.04	4.62	4.01	3.66	3.44	3.28	3.16	3.06	2.98
18	5.98	4.56	3.95	3.61	3.38	3.22	3.10	3.01	2.93
19	5.92	4.51	3.90	3.56	3.33	3.17	3.05	2.96	2.88
20	5.87	4.46	3.86	3.51	3.29	3.13	3.01	2.91	2.84
21	5.83	4.42	3.82	3.48	3.25	3.09	2.97	2.87	2.80
22	5.79	4.38	3.78	3.44	3.22	3.05	2.93	2.84	2.76
23	5.75	4.35	3.75	3.41	3.18	3.02	2.90	2.81	2.73
24	5.72	4.32	3.72	3.38	3.15	2.99	2.87	2.78	2.70
25	5.69	4.29	3.69	3.35	3.13	2.97	2.85	2.75	2.68
26	5.66	4.27	3.67	3.33	3.10	2.94	2.82	2.73	2.65
27	5.63	4.24	3.65	3.31	3.08	2.92	2.80	2.71	2.63
28	5.61	4.22	3.63	3.29	3.06	2.90	2.78	2.69	2.61
29	5.59	4.20	3.61	3.27	3.04	2.88	2.76	2.67	2.59
30	5.57	4.18	3.59	3.25	3.03	2.87	2.75	2.65	2.57
40	5.42	4.05	3.46	3.13	2.90	2.74	2.62	2.53	2.45
60	5.29	3.93	3.34	3.01	2.79	2.63	2.51	2.41	2.33
120	5.15	3.80	3.23	2.89	2.67	2.52	2.39	2.30	2.22
∞	5.02	3.69	3.12	2.79	2.57	2.41	2.29	2.19	2.11

Denominator Degrees of Freedom

TABLE A.7c — Percentage points of the *F* distribution. $\alpha = .025$ (continued).

Numerator Degrees of Freedom

v_2 \ v_1	10	12	15	20	24	30	40	60	120	∞
1	968.6	976.7	984.9	993.1	997.3	1001	1006	1010	1014	1018
2	37.40	39.41	39.43	39.45	39.46	39.46	39.47	39.48	39.49	39.50
3	14.42	14.34	14.25	14.17	14.12	14.08	14.04	13.99	13.95	13.90
4	8.84	8.75	8.66	8.56	8.51	8.46	8.41	8.36	8.31	8.26
5	6.62	6.52	6.43	6.33	6.28	6.23	6.18	6.12	6.07	6.02
6	5.46	5.37	5.27	5.17	5.12	5.07	5.01	4.96	4.90	4.85
7	4.76	4.67	4.57	4.47	4.41	4.36	4.31	4.25	4.20	4.14
8	4.30	4.20	4.10	4.00	3.95	3.89	3.84	3.78	3.73	3.67
9	3.96	3.87	3.77	3.67	3.61	3.56	3.51	3.45	3.39	3.33
10	3.72	3.62	3.52	3.42	3.37	3.31	3.26	3.20	3.14	3.08
11	3.53	3.43	3.33	3.23	3.17	3.12	3.06	3.00	2.94	2.88
12	3.37	3.28	3.18	3.07	3.02	2.96	2.91	2.85	2.79	2.73
13	3.25	3.15	3.05	2.95	2.89	2.84	2.78	2.72	2.66	2.60
14	3.15	3.05	2.95	2.84	2.79	2.73	2.67	2.61	2.55	2.49
15	3.06	2.96	2.86	2.76	2.70	2.64	2.59	2.52	2.46	2.40
16	2.99	2.89	2.79	2.68	2.63	2.57	2.51	2.45	2.38	2.32
17	2.92	2.82	2.72	2.62	2.56	2.50	2.44	2.38	2.32	2.25
18	2.87	2.77	2.67	2.56	2.50	2.44	2.38	2.32	2.26	2.19
19	2.82	2.72	2.62	2.51	2.45	2.39	2.33	2.27	2.20	2.13
20	2.77	2.68	2.57	2.46	2.41	2.35	2.29	2.22	2.16	2.09
21	2.73	2.64	2.53	2.42	2.37	2.31	2.25	2.18	2.11	2.04
22	2.70	2.60	2.50	2.39	2.33	2.27	2.21	2.14	2.08	2.00
23	2.67	2.57	2.47	2.36	2.30	2.24	2.18	2.11	2.04	1.97
24	2.64	2.54	2.44	2.33	2.27	2.21	2.15	2.08	2.01	1.94
25	2.61	2.51	2.41	2.30	2.24	2.18	2.12	2.05	1.98	1.91
26	2.59	2.49	2.39	2.28	2.22	2.16	2.09	2.03	1.95	1.88
27	2.57	2.47	2.36	2.25	2.19	2.13	2.07	2.00	1.93	1.85
28	2.55	2.45	2.34	2.23	2.17	2.11	2.05	1.98	1.91	1.83
29	2.53	2.43	2.32	2.21	2.15	2.09	2.03	1.96	1.89	1.81
30	2.51	2.41	2.31	2.20	2.14	2.07	2.01	1.94	1.87	1.79
40	2.39	2.29	2.18	2.07	2.01	1.94	1.88	1.80	1.72	1.64
60	2.27	2.17	2.06	1.94	1.88	1.82	1.74	1.67	1.58	1.48
120	2.16	2.05	1.94	1.82	1.76	1.69	1.61	1.53	1.43	1.31
∞	2.05	1.94	1.83	1.71	1.64	1.57	1.48	1.39	1.27	1.00

Denominator Degrees of Freedom (row labels v_2)

TABLE A.7d

Percentage points of the F distribution. $\alpha = .01$.

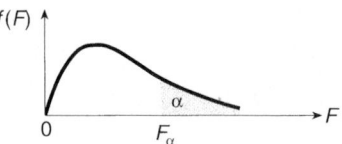

Numerator Degrees of Freedom

v_2 \ v_1	1	2	3	4	5	6	7	8	9
1	4052	4999	5404	5624	5764	5859	5928	5981	6022
2	98.50	99.00	99.16	99.25	99.30	99.33	99.36	99.38	99.39
3	34.12	30.82	29.46	28.71	28.24	27.91	27.67	27.49	27.34
4	21.20	18.00	16.69	15.98	15.52	15.21	14.98	14.80	14.66
5	16.26	13.27	12.06	11.39	10.97	10.67	10.46	10.29	10.16
6	13.75	10.92	9.78	9.15	8.75	8.47	8.26	8.10	7.98
7	12.25	9.55	8.45	7.85	7.46	7.19	6.99	6.84	6.72
8	11.26	8.65	7.59	7.01	6.63	6.37	6.18	6.03	5.91
9	10.56	8.02	6.99	6.42	6.06	5.80	5.61	5.47	5.35
10	10.04	7.56	6.55	5.99	5.64	5.39	5.20	5.06	4.94
11	9.65	7.21	6.22	5.67	5.32	5.07	4.89	4.74	4.63
12	9.33	6.93	5.95	5.41	5.06	4.82	4.64	4.50	4.39
13	9.07	6.70	5.74	5.21	4.86	4.62	4.44	4.30	4.19
14	8.86	6.51	5.56	5.04	4.69	4.46	4.28	4.14	4.03
15	8.68	6.36	5.42	4.89	4.56	4.32	4.14	4.00	3.89
16	8.53	6.23	5.29	4.77	4.44	4.20	4.03	3.89	3.78
17	8.40	6.11	5.19	4.67	4.34	4.10	3.93	3.79	3.68
18	8.29	6.01	5.09	4.58	4.25	4.01	3.84	3.71	3.60
19	8.18	5.93	5.01	4.50	4.17	3.94	3.77	3.63	3.52
20	8.10	5.85	4.94	4.43	4.10	3.87	3.70	3.56	3.46
21	8.02	5.78	4.87	4.37	4.04	3.81	3.64	3.51	3.40
22	7.95	5.72	4.82	4.31	3.99	3.76	3.59	3.45	3.35
23	7.88	5.66	4.76	4.26	3.94	3.71	3.54	3.41	3.30
24	7.82	5.61	4.72	4.22	3.90	3.67	3.50	3.36	3.26
25	7.77	5.57	4.68	4.18	3.85	3.63	3.46	3.32	3.22
26	7.72	5.53	4.64	4.14	3.82	3.59	3.42	3.29	3.18
27	7.68	5.49	4.60	4.11	3.78	3.56	3.39	3.26	3.15
28	7.64	5.45	4.57	4.07	3.75	3.53	3.36	3.23	3.12
29	7.60	5.42	4.54	4.04	3.73	3.50	3.33	3.20	3.09
30	7.56	5.39	4.51	4.02	3.70	3.47	3.30	3.17	3.07
40	7.31	5.18	4.31	3.83	3.51	3.29	3.12	2.99	2.89
60	7.08	4.98	4.13	3.65	3.34	3.12	2.95	2.82	2.72
120	6.85	4.79	3.95	3.48	3.17	2.96	2.79	2.66	2.56
∞	6.63	4.61	3.78	3.32	3.02	2.80	2.64	2.51	2.41

Denominator Degrees of Freedom

TABLE A.7d Percentage points of the *F* distribution. $\alpha = .01$ (continued).

Numerator Degrees of Freedom

v_2 \ v_1	10	12	15	20	24	30	40	60	120	∞
1	6056.	6107.	6157.	6209.	6234.	6260.	6286.	6313.	6340.	6366.
2	99.40	99.42	99.43	99.45	99.46	99.47	99.48	99.48	99.49	99.50
3	27.23	27.05	26.87	26.69	26.60	26.50	26.41	26.32	26.22	26.13
4	14.55	14.37	14.20	14.02	13.93	13.84	13.75	13.65	13.56	13.46
5	10.05	9.89	9.72	9.55	9.47	9.38	9.29	9.20	9.11	9.02
6	7.87	7.72	7.56	7.40	7.31	7.23	7.14	7.06	6.97	6.88
7	6.62	6.47	6.31	6.16	6.07	5.99	5.91	5.82	5.74	5.65
8	5.81	5.67	5.52	5.36	5.28	5.20	5.12	5.03	4.95	4.86
9	5.26	5.11	4.96	4.81	4.73	4.65	4.57	4.48	4.40	4.31
10	4.85	4.71	4.56	4.41	4.33	4.25	4.17	4.08	4.00	3.91
11	4.54	4.40	4.25	4.10	4.02	3.94	3.86	3.78	3.69	3.60
12	4.30	4.16	4.01	3.86	3.78	3.70	3.62	3.54	3.45	3.36
13	4.10	3.96	3.82	3.66	3.59	3.51	3.43	3.34	3.25	3.17
14	3.94	3.80	3.66	3.51	3.43	3.35	3.27	3.18	3.09	3.00
15	3.80	3.67	3.52	3.37	3.29	3.21	3.13	3.05	2.96	2.87
16	3.69	3.55	3.41	3.26	3.18	3.10	3.02	2.93	2.84	2.75
17	3.59	3.46	3.31	3.16	3.08	3.00	2.92	2.83	2.75	2.65
18	3.51	3.37	3.23	3.08	3.00	2.92	2.84	2.75	2.66	2.57
19	3.43	3.30	3.15	3.00	2.92	2.84	2.76	2.67	2.58	2.49
20	3.37	3.23	3.09	2.94	2.86	2.78	2.69	2.61	2.52	2.42
21	3.31	3.17	3.03	2.88	2.80	2.72	2.64	2.55	2.46	2.36
22	3.26	3.12	2.98	2.83	2.75	2.67	2.58	2.50	2.40	2.31
23	3.21	3.07	2.93	2.78	2.70	2.62	2.54	2.45	2.35	2.26
24	3.17	3.03	2.89	2.74	2.66	2.58	2.49	2.40	2.31	2.21
25	3.13	2.99	2.85	2.70	2.62	2.54	2.45	2.36	2.27	2.17
26	3.09	2.96	2.81	2.66	2.58	2.50	2.42	2.33	2.23	2.13
27	3.06	2.93	2.78	2.63	2.55	2.47	2.38	2.29	2.20	2.10
28	3.03	2.90	2.75	2.60	2.52	2.44	2.35	2.26	2.17	2.06
29	3.00	2.87	2.73	2.57	2.49	2.41	2.33	2.23	2.14	2.03
30	2.98	2.84	2.70	2.55	2.47	2.39	2.30	2.21	2.11	2.01
40	2.80	2.66	2.52	2.37	2.29	2.20	2.11	2.02	1.92	1.80
60	2.63	2.50	2.35	2.20	2.12	2.03	1.94	1.84	1.73	1.60
120	2.47	2.34	2.19	2.03	1.95	1.86	1.76	1.66	1.53	1.38
∞	2.32	2.18	2.04	1.88	1.79	1.70	1.59	1.47	1.32	1.00

Denominator Degrees of Freedom

TABLE A.8   Confidence interval for a population proportion, small sample.

n = 5

	α = .05		α = .10	
	P_L	P_U	P_L	P_U
x = 1	0.005	0.716	0.010	0.657
2	0.053	0.853	0.076	0.811
3	0.147	0.947	0.189	0.924
4	0.284	0.995	0.343	0.990

n = 6

	α = .05		α = .10	
	P_L	P_U	P_L	P_U
x = 1	0.004	0.641	0.009	0.582
2	0.043	0.777	0.063	0.729
3	0.118	0.882	0.153	0.847
4	0.223	0.957	0.271	0.937
5	0.359	0.996	0.418	0.991

n = 7

	α = .05		α = .10	
	P_L	P_U	P_L	P_U
x = 1	0.004	0.579	0.007	0.521
2	0.037	0.710	0.053	0.659
3	0.099	0.816	0.129	0.775
4	0.184	0.901	0.225	0.871
5	0.290	0.963	0.341	0.947
6	0.421	0.996	0.479	0.993

n = 8

	α = .05		α = .10	
	P_L	P_U	P_L	P_U
x = 1	0.003	0.527	0.006	0.471
2	0.032	0.651	0.046	0.600
3	0.085	0.755	0.111	0.711
4	0.157	0.843	0.193	0.807
5	0.245	0.915	0.289	0.889
6	0.349	0.968	0.400	0.954
7	0.473	0.997	0.529	0.994

n = 9

	α = .05		α = .10	
	P_L	P_U	P_L	P_U
x = 1	0.003	0.482	0.006	0.429
2	0.028	0.600	0.041	0.550
3	0.075	0.701	0.098	0.655
4	0.137	0.788	0.169	0.749
5	0.212	0.863	0.251	0.831
6	0.299	0.925	0.345	0.902
7	0.400	0.972	0.450	0.959
8	0.518	0.997	0.571	0.994

n = 10

	α = .05		α = .10	
	P_L	P_U	P_L	P_U
x = 1	0.003	0.445	0.005	0.394
2	0.025	0.556	0.037	0.507
3	0.067	0.652	0.087	0.607
4	0.122	0.738	0.150	0.696
5	0.187	0.813	0.222	0.778
6	0.262	0.878	0.304	0.850
7	0.348	0.933	0.393	0.913
8	0.444	0.975	0.493	0.963
9	0.555	0.997	0.606	0.995

n = 11

	α = .05		α = .10	
	P_L	P_U	P_L	P_U
x = 1	0.002	0.413	0.005	0.364
2	0.023	0.518	0.033	0.470
3	0.060	0.610	0.079	0.564
4	0.109	0.692	0.135	0.650
5	0.167	0.766	0.200	0.729
6	0.234	0.833	0.271	0.800
7	0.308	0.891	0.350	0.865

n = 11

	α = .05		α = .10	
	P_L	P_U	P_L	P_U
8	0.390	0.940	0.436	0.921
9	0.482	0.977	0.530	0.967
10	0.587	0.998	0.636	0.995

n = 12

	α = .05		α = .10	
	P_L	P_U	P_L	P_U
x = 1	0.002	0.385	0.004	0.339
2	0.021	0.484	0.030	0.438
3	0.055	0.572	0.072	0.527
4	0.099	0.651	0.123	0.609
5	0.152	0.723	0.181	0.685
6	0.211	0.789	0.245	0.755
7	0.277	0.848	0.315	0.819
8	0.349	0.901	0.391	0.877
9	0.428	0.945	0.473	0.928
10	0.516	0.979	0.562	0.970
11	0.615	0.998	0.661	0.996

n = 13

	α = .05		α = .10	
	P_L	P_U	P_L	P_U
x = 1	0.002	0.360	0.004	0.316
2	0.019	0.454	0.028	0.410
3	0.050	0.538	0.066	0.495
4	0.091	0.614	0.113	0.573
5	0.139	0.684	0.166	0.645
6	0.192	0.749	0.224	0.713
7	0.251	0.808	0.287	0.776
8	0.316	0.861	0.355	0.834
9	0.386	0.909	0.427	0.887
10	0.462	0.950	0.505	0.934
11	0.546	0.981	0.590	0.972
12	0.640	0.998	0.684	0.996

n = 14

	α = .05		α = .10	
	P_L	P_U	P_L	P_U
x = 1	0.002	0.339	0.004	0.297
2	0.018	0.428	0.026	0.385
3	0.047	0.508	0.061	0.466
4	0.084	0.581	0.104	0.540
5	0.128	0.649	0.153	0.610
6	0.177	0.711	0.206	0.675
7	0.230	0.770	0.264	0.736
8	0.289	0.823	0.325	0.794
9	0.351	0.872	0.390	0.847
10	0.419	0.916	0.460	0.896
11	0.492	0.953	0.534	0.939
12	0.572	0.982	0.615	0.974
13	0.661	0.998	0.703	0.996

n = 15

	α = .05		α = .10	
	P_L	P_U	P_L	P_U
x = 1	0.002	0.319	0.003	0.279
2	0.017	0.405	0.024	0.363
3	0.043	0.481	0.057	0.440
4	0.078	0.551	0.097	0.511
5	0.118	0.616	0.142	0.577
6	0.163	0.677	0.191	0.640
7	0.213	0.734	0.244	0.700
8	0.266	0.787	0.300	0.756
9	0.323	0.837	0.360	0.809
10	0.384	0.882	0.423	0.858
11	0.449	0.922	0.489	0.903
12	0.519	0.957	0.560	0.943
13	0.595	0.983	0.637	0.976
14	0.681	0.998	0.721	0.997

TABLE A.8 Confidence interval for a population proportion, small sample (continued).

n = 16	α = .05		α = .10	
	P_L	P_U	P_L	P_U
x = 1	0.002	0.302	0.003	0.264
2	0.016	0.383	0.023	0.344
3	0.040	0.456	0.053	0.417
4	0.073	0.524	0.090	0.484
5	0.110	0.587	0.132	0.548
6	0.152	0.646	0.178	0.609
7	0.198	0.701	0.227	0.667
8	0.247	0.753	0.279	0.721
9	0.299	0.802	0.333	0.773
10	0.354	0.848	0.391	0.822
11	0.413	0.890	0.452	0.868
12	0.476	0.927	0.516	0.910
13	0.544	0.960	0.583	0.947
14	0.617	0.984	0.656	0.977
15	0.698	0.998	0.736	0.997

n = 17	α = .05		α = .10	
	P_L	P_U	P_L	P_U
x = 1	0.001	0.287	0.003	0.250
2	0.015	0.364	0.021	0.326
3	0.038	0.434	0.050	0.396
4	0.068	0.499	0.085	0.461
5	0.103	0.560	0.124	0.522
6	0.142	0.617	0.166	0.580
7	0.184	0.671	0.212	0.636
8	0.230	0.722	0.260	0.689
9	0.278	0.770	0.311	0.740
10	0.329	0.816	0.364	0.788
11	0.383	0.858	0.420	0.834
12	0.440	0.897	0.478	0.876
13	0.501	0.932	0.539	0.915
14	0.566	0.962	0.604	0.950
15	0.636	0.985	0.674	0.979
16	0.713	0.999	0.750	0.997

n = 18	α = .05		α = .10	
	P_L	P_U	P_L	P_U
x = 1	0.001	0.273	0.003	0.238
2	0.014	0.347	0.020	0.310
3	0.036	0.414	0.047	0.377
4	0.064	0.476	0.080	0.439
5	0.097	0.535	0.116	0.498
6	0.133	0.590	0.156	0.554
7	0.173	0.643	0.199	0.608
8	0.215	0.692	0.244	0.659
9	0.260	0.740	0.291	0.709
10	0.308	0.785	0.341	0.756
11	0.357	0.827	0.392	0.801
12	0.410	0.867	0.446	0.844
13	0.465	0.903	0.502	0.884
14	0.524	0.936	0.561	0.920
15	0.586	0.964	0.623	0.953
16	0.653	0.986	0.690	0.980
17	0.727	0.999	0.762	0.997

n = 19	α = .05		α = .10	
	P_L	P_U	P_L	P_U
x = 1	0.001	0.260	0.003	0.226
2	0.013	0.331	0.019	0.296
3	0.034	0.396	0.044	0.359
4	0.061	0.456	0.075	0.419
5	0.091	0.512	0.110	0.476
6	0.126	0.565	0.147	0.530
7	0.163	0.616	0.188	0.582
8	0.203	0.665	0.230	0.632
9	0.244	0.711	0.274	0.680
10	0.289	0.756	0.320	0.726
11	0.335	0.797	0.368	0.770
12	0.384	0.837	0.418	0.812
13	0.435	0.874	0.470	0.853
14	0.488	0.909	0.524	0.890
15	0.544	0.939	0.581	0.925
16	0.604	0.966	0.641	0.956
17	0.669	0.987	0.704	0.981
18	0.740	0.999	0.774	0.997

n = 20	α = .05		α = .10	
	P_L	P_U	P_L	P_U
x = 1	0.001	0.249	0.003	0.216
2	0.012	0.317	0.018	0.283
3	0.032	0.379	0.042	0.344
4	0.057	0.437	0.071	0.401
5	0.087	0.491	0.104	0.456
6	0.119	0.543	0.140	0.508
7	0.154	0.592	0.177	0.558
8	0.191	0.639	0.217	0.606
9	0.231	0.685	0.259	0.653
10	0.272	0.728	0.302	0.698
11	0.315	0.769	0.347	0.741
12	0.361	0.809	0.394	0.783
13	0.408	0.846	0.442	0.823
14	0.457	0.881	0.492	0.860
15	0.509	0.913	0.544	0.896
16	0.563	0.943	0.599	0.929
17	0.621	0.968	0.656	0.958
18	0.683	0.988	0.717	0.982
19	0.751	0.999	0.784	0.997

TABLE A.9a Critical values for the Durbin–Watson DW statistic. $\alpha = .05$.

n	k = 1 d_L	k = 1 d_U	k = 2 d_L	k = 2 d_U	k = 3 d_L	k = 3 d_U	k = 4 d_L	k = 4 d_U	k = 5 d_L	k = 5 d_U
15	1.08	1.36	0.95	1.54	0.82	1.75	0.69	1.97	0.56	2.21
16	1.10	1.37	0.98	1.54	0.86	1.73	0.74	1.93	0.62	2.15
17	1.13	1.38	1.02	1.54	0.90	1.71	0.78	1.90	0.67	2.10
18	1.16	1.39	1.05	1.53	0.93	1.69	0.82	1.87	0.71	2.06
19	1.18	1.40	1.08	1.53	0.97	1.68	0.86	1.85	0.75	2.02
20	1.20	1.41	1.10	1.54	1.00	1.68	0.90	1.83	0.79	1.99
21	1.22	1.42	1.13	1.54	1.03	1.67	0.93	1.81	0.83	1.96
22	1.24	1.43	1.15	1.54	1.05	1.66	0.96	1.80	0.86	1.94
23	1.26	1.44	1.17	1.54	1.08	1.66	0.99	1.79	0.90	1.92
24	1.27	1.45	1.19	1.55	1.10	1.66	1.01	1.78	0.93	1.90
25	1.29	1.45	1.21	1.55	1.12	1.66	1.04	1.77	0.95	1.89
26	1.30	1.46	1.22	1.55	1.14	1.65	1.06	1.76	0.98	1.88
27	1.32	1.47	1.24	1.56	1.16	1.65	1.08	1.76	1.01	1.86
28	1.33	1.48	1.26	1.56	1.18	1.65	1.10	1.75	1.03	1.85
29	1.34	1.48	1.27	1.56	1.20	1.65	1.12	1.74	1.05	1.84
30	1.35	1.49	1.28	1.57	1.21	1.65	1.14	1.74	1.07	1.83
31	1.36	1.50	1.30	1.57	1.23	1.65	1.16	1.74	1.09	1.83
32	1.37	1.50	1.31	1.57	1.24	1.65	1.18	1.73	1.11	1.82
33	1.38	1.51	1.32	1.58	1.26	1.65	1.19	1.73	1.13	1.81
34	1.39	1.51	1.33	1.58	1.27	1.65	1.21	1.73	1.15	1.81
35	1.40	1.52	1.34	1.58	1.28	1.65	1.22	1.73	1.16	1.80
36	1.41	1.52	1.35	1.59	1.29	1.65	1.24	1.73	1.18	1.80
37	1.42	1.53	1.36	1.59	1.31	1.66	1.25	1.72	1.19	1.80
38	1.43	1.54	1.37	1.59	1.32	1.66	1.26	1.72	1.21	1.79
39	1.43	1.54	1.38	1.60	1.33	1.66	1.27	1.72	1.22	1.79
40	1.44	1.54	1.39	1.60	1.34	1.66	1.29	1.72	1.23	1.79
45	1.48	1.57	1.43	1.62	1.38	1.67	1.34	1.72	1.29	1.78
50	1.50	1.59	1.46	1.63	1.42	1.67	1.38	1.72	1.34	1.77
55	1.53	1.60	1.49	1.64	1.45	1.68	1.41	1.72	1.38	1.77
60	1.55	1.62	1.51	1.65	1.48	1.69	1.44	1.73	1.41	1.77
65	1.57	1.63	1.54	1.66	1.50	1.70	1.47	1.73	1.44	1.77
70	1.58	1.64	1.55	1.67	1.52	1.70	1.49	1.74	1.46	1.77
75	1.60	1.65	1.57	1.68	1.54	1.71	1.51	1.74	1.49	1.77
80	1.61	1.66	1.59	1.69	1.56	1.72	1.53	1.74	1.51	1.77
85	1.62	1.67	1.60	1.70	1.57	1.72	1.55	1.75	1.52	1.77
90	1.63	1.68	1.61	1.70	1.59	1.73	1.57	1.75	1.54	1.78
95	1.64	1.69	1.62	1.71	1.60	1.73	1.58	1.75	1.56	1.78
100	1.65	1.69	1.63	1.72	1.61	1.74	1.59	1.76	1.57	1.78

TABLE A.9b Critical values for the Durbin–Watson DW statistic. $\alpha = .01$.

n	k = 1 d_L	d_U	k = 2 d_L	d_U	k = 3 d_L	d_U	k = 4 d_L	d_U	k = 5 d_L	d_U
15	0.81	1.07	0.70	1.25	0.59	1.46	0.49	1.70	0.39	1.96
16	0.84	1.09	0.74	1.25	0.63	1.44	0.53	1.66	0.44	1.90
17	0.87	1.10	0.77	1.25	0.67	1.43	0.57	1.63	0.48	1.85
18	0.90	1.12	0.80	1.26	0.71	1.42	0.61	1.60	0.52	1.80
19	0.93	1.13	0.83	1.26	0.74	1.41	0.65	1.58	0.56	1.77
20	0.95	1.15	0.86	1.27	0.77	1.41	0.68	1.57	0.60	1.74
21	0.97	1.16	0.89	1.27	0.80	1.41	0.72	1.55	0.63	1.71
22	1.00	1.17	0.91	1.28	0.83	1.40	0.75	1.54	0.66	1.69
23	1.02	1.19	0.94	1.29	0.86	1.40	0.77	1.53	0.70	1.67
24	1.04	1.20	0.96	1.30	0.88	1.41	0.80	1.53	0.72	1.66
25	1.05	1.21	0.98	1.30	0.90	1.41	0.83	1.52	0.75	1.65
26	1.07	1.22	1.00	1.31	0.93	1.41	0.85	1.52	0.78	1.64
27	1.09	1.23	1.02	1.32	0.95	1.41	0.88	1.51	0.81	1.63
28	1.10	1.24	1.04	1.32	0.97	1.41	0.90	1.51	0.83	1.62
29	1.12	1.25	1.05	1.33	0.99	1.42	0.92	1.51	0.85	1.61
30	1.13	1.26	1.07	1.34	1.01	1.42	0.94	1.51	0.88	1.61
31	1.15	1.27	1.08	1.34	1.02	1.42	0.96	1.51	0.90	1.60
32	1.16	1.28	1.10	1.35	1.04	1.43	0.98	1.51	0.92	1.60
33	1.17	1.29	1.11	1.36	1.05	1.43	1.00	1.51	0.94	1.59
34	1.18	1.30	1.13	1.36	1.07	1.43	1.01	1.51	0.95	1.59
35	1.19	1.31	1.14	1.37	1.08	1.44	1.03	1.51	0.97	1.59
36	1.21	1.32	1.15	1.38	1.10	1.44	1.04	1.51	0.99	1.59
37	1.22	1.32	1.16	1.38	1.11	1.45	1.06	1.51	1.00	1.59
38	1.23	1.33	1.18	1.39	1.12	1.45	1.07	1.52	1.02	1.58
39	1.24	1.34	1.19	1.39	1.14	1.45	1.09	1.52	1.03	1.58
40	1.25	1.34	1.20	1.40	1.15	1.46	1.10	1.52	1.05	1.58
45	1.29	1.38	1.24	1.42	1.20	1.48	1.16	1.53	1.11	1.58
50	1.32	1.40	1.28	1.45	1.24	1.49	1.20	1.54	1.16	1.59
55	1.36	1.43	1.32	1.47	1.28	1.51	1.25	1.55	1.21	1.59
60	1.38	1.45	1.35	1.48	1.32	1.52	1.28	1.56	1.25	1.60
65	1.41	1.47	1.38	1.50	1.35	1.53	1.31	1.57	1.28	1.61
70	1.43	1.49	1.40	1.52	1.37	1.55	1.34	1.58	1.31	1.61
75	1.45	1.50	1.42	1.53	1.39	1.56	1.37	1.59	1.34	1.62
80	1.47	1.52	1.44	1.54	1.42	1.57	1.39	1.60	1.36	1.62
85	1.48	1.53	1.46	1.55	1.43	1.58	1.41	1.60	1.39	1.63
90	1.50	1.54	1.47	1.56	1.45	1.59	1.43	1.61	1.41	1.64
95	1.51	1.55	1.49	1.57	1.47	1.60	1.45	1.62	1.42	1.64
100	1.52	1.56	1.50	1.58	1.48	1.60	1.46	1.63	1.44	1.65

TABLE A.10 Distribution function for the Mann–Whitney U statistic.* This table contains the value of $P(U \leq U_0)$, where $n_1 \leq n_2$.

$n_2 = 3$ U_0	1	2	3
0	.25	.10	.05
1	.50	.20	.10
2		.40	.20
3		.60	.35
4			.50

$n_2 = 4$ U_0	1	2	3	4
0	.2000	.0667	.0286	.0143
1	.4000	.1333	.0571	.0286
2	.6000	.2667	.1143	.0571
3		.4000	.2000	.1000
4		.6000	.3143	.1714
5			.4286	.2429
6			.5714	.3429
7				.4429
8				.5571

$n_2 = 5$ U_0	1	2	3	4	5
0	.1667	.0476	.0179	.0079	.0040
1	.3333	.0952	.0357	.0159	.0079
2	.5000	.1905	.0714	.0317	.0159
3		.2857	.1250	.0556	.0278
4		.4286	.1964	.0952	.0476
5		.5714	.2857	.1429	.0754
6			.3929	.2063	.1111
7			.5000	.2778	.1548
8				.3651	.2103
9				.4524	.2738
10				.5476	.3452
11					.4206
12					.5000

*Computed by M. Pagano, Dept. of Statistics, University of Florida. Reprinted by permission from *Statistics for Management and Economics*, 5th ed., by William Mendenhall and James E. Reinmuth. Copyright © 1986 by PWS-KENT Publishers, Boston.

TABLE A.10 Distribution function for the Mann–Whitney *U* statistic (continued).

$n_2 = 6$ U_0	1	2	3	n_1 4	5	6
0	.1429	.0357	.0119	.0048	.0022	.0011
1	.2857	.0714	.0238	.0095	.0043	.0022
2	.4286	.1429	.0476	.0190	.0087	.0043
3	.5714	.2143	.0833	.0333	.0152	.0076
4		.3214	.1310	.0571	.0260	.0130
5		.4286	.1905	.0857	.0411	.0206
6		.5714	.2738	.1286	.0628	.0325
7			.3571	.1762	.0887	.0465
8			.4524	.2381	.1234	.0660
9			.5476	.3048	.1645	.0898
10				.3810	.2143	.1201
11				.4571	.2684	.1548
12				.5429	.3312	.1970
13					.3961	.2424
14					.4654	.2944
15					.5346	.3496
16						.4091
17						.4686
18						.5314

$n_2 = 7$ U_0	1	2	3	n_1 4	5	6	7
0	.1250	.0278	.0083	.0030	.0013	.0006	.0003
1	.2500	.0556	.0167	.0061	.0025	.0012	.0006
2	.3750	.1111	.0333	.0121	.0051	.0023	.0012
3	.5000	.1667	.0583	.0212	.0088	.0041	.0020
4		.2500	.0917	.0364	.0152	.0070	.0035
5		.3333	.1333	.0545	.0240	.0111	.0055
6		.4444	.1917	.0818	.0366	.0175	.0087
7		.5556	.2583	.1152	.0530	.0256	.0131
8			.3333	.1576	.0745	.0367	.0189
9			.4167	.2061	.1010	.0507	.0265
10			.5000	.2636	.1338	.0688	.0364
11				.3242	.1717	.0903	.0487
12				.3939	.2159	.1171	.0641
13				.4636	.2652	.1474	.0825
14				.5364	.3194	.1830	.1043
15					.3775	.2226	.1297
16					.4381	.2669	.1588
17					.5000	.3141	.1914
18						.3654	.2279
19						.4178	.2675
20						.4726	.3100
21						.5274	.3552
22							.4024
23							.4508
24							.5000

TABLE A.10   Distribution function for the Mann–Whitney U statistic (continued).

$n_2 = 8$ U_0	1	2	3	4	n_1 5	6	7	8
0	.1111	.0222	.0061	.0020	.0008	.0003	.0002	.0001
1	.2222	.0444	.0121	.0040	.0016	.0007	.0003	.0002
2	.3333	.0889	.0242	.0081	.0031	.0013	.0006	.0003
3	.4444	.1333	.0424	.0141	.0054	.0023	.0011	.0005
4	.5556	.2000	.0667	.0242	.0093	.0040	.0019	.0009
5		.2667	.0970	.0364	.0148	.0063	.0030	.0015
6		.3556	.1394	.0545	.0225	.0100	.0047	.0023
7		.4444	.1879	.0768	.0326	.0147	.0070	.0035
8		.5556	.2485	.1071	.0466	.0213	.0103	.0052
9			.3152	.1414	.0637	.0296	.0145	.0074
10			.3879	.1838	.0855	.0406	.0200	.0103
11			.4606	.2303	.1111	.0539	.0270	.0141
12			.5394	.2848	.1422	.0709	.0361	.0190
13				.3414	.1772	.0906	.0469	.0249
14				.4040	.2176	.1142	.0603	.0325
15				.4667	.2618	.1412	.0760	.0415
16				.5333	.3108	.1725	.0946	.0524
17					.3621	.2068	.1159	.0652
18					.4165	.2454	.1405	.0803
19					.4716	.2864	.1678	.0974
20					.5284	.3310	.1984	.1172
21						.3773	.2317	.1393
22						.4259	.2679	.1641
23						.4749	.3063	.1911
24						.5251	.3472	.2209
25							.3894	.2527
26							.4333	.2869
27							.4775	.3227
28							.5225	.3605
29								.3992
30								.4392
31								.4796
32								.5204

TABLE A.10 Distribution function for the Mann–Whitney U statistic (continued).

$n_2 = 9$	U_0	1	2	3	4	5	6	7	8	9
	0	.1000	.0182	.0045	.0014	.0005	.0002	.0001	.0000	.0000
	1	.2000	.0364	.0091	.0028	.0010	.0004	.0002	.0001	.0000
	2	.3000	.0727	.0182	.0056	.0020	.0008	.0003	.0002	.0001
	3	.4000	.1091	.0318	.0098	.0035	.0014	.0006	.0003	.0001
	4	.5000	.1636	.0500	.0168	.0060	.0024	.0010	.0005	.0002
	5		.2182	.0727	.0252	.0095	.0038	.0017	.0008	.0004
	6		.2909	.1045	.0378	.0145	.0060	.0026	.0012	.0006
	7		.3636	.1409	.0531	.0210	.0088	.0039	.0019	.0009
	8		.4545	.1864	.0741	.0300	.0128	.0058	.0028	.0014
	9		.5455	.2409	.0993	.0415	.0180	.0082	.0039	.0020
	10			.3000	.1301	.0559	.0248	.0115	.0056	.0028
	11			.3636	.1650	.0734	.0332	.0156	.0076	.0039
	12			.4318	.2070	.0949	.0440	.0209	.0103	.0053
	13			.5000	.2517	.1199	.0567	.0274	.0137	.0071
	14				.3021	.1489	.0723	.0356	.0180	.0094
	15				.3552	.1818	.0905	.0454	.0232	.0122
	16				.4126	.2188	.1119	.0571	.0296	.0157
	17				.4699	.2592	.1361	.0708	.0372	.0200
	18				.5301	.3032	.1638	.0869	.0464	.0252
	19					.3497	.1942	.1052	.0570	.0313
	20					.3986	.2280	.1261	.0694	.0385
	21					.4491	.2643	.1496	.0836	.0470
	22					.5000	.3035	.1755	.0998	.0567
	23						.3445	.2039	.1179	.0680
	24						.3878	.2349	.1383	.0807
	25						.4320	.2680	.1606	.0951
	26						.4773	.3032	.1852	.1112
	27						.5227	.3403	.2117	.1290
	28							.3788	.2404	.1487
	29							.4185	.2707	.1701
	30							.4591	.3029	.1933
	31							.5000	.3365	.2181
	32								.3715	.2447
	33								.4074	.2729
	34								.4442	.3024
	35								.4813	.3332
	36								.5187	.3652
	37									.3981
	38									.4317
	39									.4657
	40									.5000

TABLE A.10　Distribution function for the Mann–Whitney U statistic (continued).

$n_2 = 10$ U_0	1	2	3	4	5	6	7	8	9	10
0	.0909	.0152	.0035	.0010	.0003	.0001	.0001	.0000	.0000	.0000
1	.1818	.0303	.0070	.0020	.0007	.0002	.0001	.0000	.0000	.0000
2	.2727	.0606	.0140	.0040	.0013	.0005	.0002	.0001	.0000	.0000
3	.3636	.0909	.0245	.0070	.0023	.0009	.0004	.0002	.0001	.0000
4	.4545	.1364	.0385	.0120	.0040	.0015	.0006	.0003	.0001	.0001
5	.5455	.1818	.0559	.0180	.0063	.0024	.0010	.0004	.0002	.0001
6		.2424	.0804	.0270	.0097	.0037	.0015	.0007	.0003	.0002
7		.3030	.1084	.0380	.0140	.0055	.0023	.0010	.0005	.0002
8		.3788	.1434	.0529	.0200	.0080	.0034	.0015	.0007	.0004
9		.4545	.1853	.0709	.0276	.0112	.0048	.0022	.0011	.0005
10		.5455	.2343	.0939	.0376	.0156	.0068	.0031	.0015	.0008
11			.2867	.1199	.0496	.0210	.0093	.0043	.0021	.0010
12			.3462	.1518	.0646	.0280	.0125	.0058	.0028	.0014
13			.4056	.1868	.0823	.0363	.0165	.0078	.0038	.0019
14			.4685	.2268	.1032	.0467	.0215	.0103	.0051	.0026
15			.5315	.2697	.1272	.0589	.0277	.0133	.0066	.0034
16				.3177	.1548	.0736	.0351	.0171	.0086	.0045
17				.3666	.1855	.0903	.0439	.0217	.0110	.0057
18				.4196	.2198	.1099	.0544	.0273	.0140	.0073
19				.4725	.2567	.1317	.0665	.0338	.0175	.0093
20				.5275	.2970	.1566	.0806	.0416	.0217	.0116
21					.3393	.1838	.0966	.0506	.0267	.0144
22					.3839	.2139	.1148	.0610	.0326	.0177
23					.4296	.2461	.1349	.0729	.0394	.0216
24					.4765	.2811	.1574	.0864	.0474	.0262
25					.5235	.3177	.1819	.1015	.0564	.0315
26						.3564	.2087	.1185	.0667	.0376
27						.3962	.2374	.1371	.0782	.0446
28						.4374	.2681	.1577	.0912	.0526
29						.4789	.3004	.1800	.1055	.0615
30						.5211	.3345	.2041	.1214	.0716
31							.3698	.2299	.1388	.0827
32							.4063	.2574	.1577	.0952
33							.4434	.2863	.1781	.1088
34							.4811	.3167	.2001	.1237
35							.5189	.3482	.2235	.1399
36								.3809	.2483	.1575
37								.4143	.2745	.1763
38								.4484	.3019	.1965
39								.4827	.3304	.2179
40								.5173	.3598	.2406
41									.3901	.2644
42									.4211	.2894
43									.4524	.3153
44									.4841	.3421
45									.5159	.3697
46										.3980
47										.4267
48										.4559
49										.4853
50										.5147

TABLE A.11 Critical values of the Wilcoxon signed rank test ($n = 5, \ldots, 50$).

1-sided	2-sided	n = 5	n = 6	n = 7	n = 8	n = 9	n = 10
$\alpha = .05$	$\alpha = .10$	1	2	4	6	8	11
$\alpha = .025$	$\alpha = .05$		1	2	4	6	8
$\alpha = .01$	$\alpha = .02$			0	2	3	5
$\alpha = .005$	$\alpha = .01$				0	2	3

1-sided	2-sided	n = 11	n = 12	n = 13	n = 14	n = 15	n = 16
$\alpha = .05$	$\alpha = .10$	14	17	21	26	30	36
$\alpha = .025$	$\alpha = .05$	11	14	17	21	25	30
$\alpha = .01$	$\alpha = .02$	7	10	13	16	20	24
$\alpha = .005$	$\alpha = .01$	5	7	10	13	16	19

1-sided	2-sided	n = 17	n = 18	n = 19	n = 20	n = 21	n = 22
$\alpha = .05$	$\alpha = .10$	41	47	54	60	68	75
$\alpha = .025$	$\alpha = .05$	35	40	46	52	59	66
$\alpha = .01$	$\alpha = .02$	28	33	38	43	49	56
$\alpha = .005$	$\alpha = .01$	23	28	32	37	43	49

1-sided	2-sided	n = 23	n = 24	n = 25	n = 26	n = 27	n = 28
$\alpha = .05$	$\alpha = .10$	83	92	101	110	120	130
$\alpha = .025$	$\alpha = .05$	73	81	90	98	107	117
$\alpha = .01$	$\alpha = .02$	62	69	77	85	93	102
$\alpha = .005$	$\alpha = .01$	55	61	68	76	84	92

1-sided	2-sided	n = 29	n = 30	n = 31	n = 32	n = 33	n = 34
$\alpha = .05$	$\alpha = .10$	141	152	163	175	188	201
$\alpha = .025$	$\alpha = .05$	127	137	148	159	171	183
$\alpha = .01$	$\alpha = .02$	111	120	130	141	151	162
$\alpha = .005$	$\alpha = .01$	100	109	118	128	138	149

1-sided	2-sided	n = 35	n = 36	n = 37	n = 38	n = 39	
$\alpha = .05$	$\alpha = .10$	214	228	242	256	271	
$\alpha = .025$	$\alpha = .05$	195	208	222	235	250	
$\alpha = .01$	$\alpha = .02$	174	186	198	211	224	
$\alpha = .005$	$\alpha = .01$	160	171	183	195	208	

1-sided	2-sided	n = 40	n = 41	n = 42	n = 43	n = 44	n = 45
$\alpha = .05$	$\alpha = .10$	287	303	319	336	353	371
$\alpha = .025$	$\alpha = .05$	264	279	295	311	327	344
$\alpha = .01$	$\alpha = .02$	238	252	267	281	297	313
$\alpha = .005$	$\alpha = .01$	221	234	248	262	277	292

1-sided	2-sided	n = 46	n = 47	n = 48	n = 49	n = 50	
$\alpha = .05$	$\alpha = .10$	389	408	427	446	466	
$\alpha = .025$	$\alpha = .05$	361	379	397	415	434	
$\alpha = .01$	$\alpha = .02$	329	345	362	380	398	
$\alpha = .005$	$\alpha = .01$	307	323	339	356	373	

From F. Wilcoxon and R. A. Wilcox, "Some Rapid Approximate Statistical Procedures," 1964.
Reproduced with the permission of the American Cyanamid Company.

TABLE A.12 Critical values of Spearman rank correlation coefficient.

n	$\alpha = .05$	$\alpha = .025$	$\alpha = .01$	$\alpha = .005$
5	0.900	—-	—-	—-
6	0.829	0.886	0.943	—-
7	0.714	0.786	0.893	0.929
8	0.643	0.738	0.833	0.881
9	0.600	0.700	0.783	0.833
10	0.564	0.648	0.745	0.794
11	0.536	0.618	0.709	0.755
12	0.503	0.587	0.678	0.727
13	0.484	0.560	0.648	0.703
14	0.464	0.538	0.626	0.679
15	0.446	0.521	0.603	0.654
16	0.429	0.503	0.582	0.635
17	0.414	0.488	0.566	0.618
18	0.401	0.472	0.550	0.600
19	0.391	0.460	0.535	0.584
20	0.380	0.447	0.522	0.570
21	0.370	0.436	0.509	0.556
22	0.361	0.425	0.497	0.544
23	0.353	0.416	0.486	0.532
24	0.344	0.407	0.476	0.521
25	0.337	0.398	0.466	0.511
26	0.331	0.390	0.457	0.501
27	0.324	0.383	0.449	0.492
28	0.318	0.375	0.441	0.483
29	0.312	0.368	0.433	0.475
30	0.306	0.362	0.425	0.467

TABLE A.13 Random numbers.

88063	44081	27881	20544	54802	94639	76854	08398	51702	01598
97134	65739	04746	97065	35420	11206	72065	43239	62670	08375
36244	31702	66102	42639	53502	82134	09415	81969	37728	75870
91689	09130	20873	49007	95041	31004	35656	62244	62441	11385
41288	02012	24127	21345	75277	89793	53265	71356	21314	34577
63516	49383	68914	38532	58384	10128	62540	16107	93726	49215
82732	26444	67803	32565	02947	79515	31445	62602	49872	27358
88826	44598	62872	77533	52909	54647	80973	83450	50614	45247
85845	50745	59071	30938	82293	91795	79500	72431	36250	24702
81962	18010	28301	08045	04820	58021	45419	59091	47131	91852
20925	86600	58118	18213	27456	36737	53704	93994	73968	80982
15890	10913	16143	20549	12496	31578	87560	37472	14588	38826
36397	72038	28498	45390	83358	37635	74391	19008	91707	33743
65899	06950	00168	00727	82686	26766	44413	91278	39649	68256
39269	07965	98347	26525	63332	10402	63187	39690	11339	08063
83362	99342	50805	04433	43332	92542	98113	12849	86996	76640
39390	18062	17416	16456	16449	54778	55603	78809	09485	89428
97530	45542	83500	28817	27104	63801	23383	42753	43032	94181
81978	54406	65359	96444	42113	23037	08327	24646	71222	94835
85477	97009	79077	94130	09651	16584	14164	11611	55532	10722
03985	47735	04522	58934	55356	07990	20019	19304	65752	01094
12475	65300	68183	47018	45860	92648	38939	74709	72206	60777
81662	51907	61426	38284	70375	15384	78270	23960	05675	16345
94927	33317	17494	94257	69578	67299	57754	45289	39370	35507
34615	29080	73593	45342	81274	19475	13480	80661	61140	86594
30956	50995	01179	66379	66031	27190	45696	45572	02263	39991
58826	78534	01391	66155	52601	61227	32224	02049	51770	00372
99451	70949	28689	47783	06971	73576	97788	90528	80959	57716
31300	27179	80497	88234	36068	75020	60424	76015	48957	37930
68903	09205	36468	55577	06251	14517	50707	91842	18807	79463
42957	69832	96868	41532	92322	26151	04219	52847	30634	44289
06387	06880	13353	69805	54913	27691	26540	06137	73601	06223
93334	66789	50514	47098	67237	61763	60246	54799	53920	75893
73579	17045	13607	96624	42021	93639	73967	22031	47191	18507
44261	15095	57971	85433	34271	92635	00432	32010	10135	55776
29495	39804	97907	46383	66311	49068	90353	55061	72038	00102
39865	56395	78208	06690	60139	51739	02493	17062	98792	43370
79355	68728	31453	90733	17669	80089	35979	56803	22015	10778
33454	13035	35641	11854	56659	54363	96475	55393	87872	58495
33207	29692	69522	74428	18074	10731	88763	74818	93818	86960

| TABLE A.14 | Critical values of Hartley's H-statistic, $\alpha = .05$. n = number of observations in each sample; k = number of samples. |

	k										
n	**2**	**3**	**4**	**5**	**6**	**7**	**8**	**9**	**10**	**11**	**12**
3	39.0	87.5	142	202	266	333	403	475	550	626	704
4	15.4	27.8	39.2	50.7	62.0	72.9	83.5	93.9	104	114	124
5	9.60	15.5	20.6	25.2	29.5	33.6	37.5	41.1	44.6	48.0	51.4
6	7.15	10.8	13.7	16.3	18.7	20.8	22.9	24.7	26.5	28.2	29.9
7	5.82	8.38	10.4	12.1	13.7	15.0	16.3	17.5	18.6	19.7	20.7
8	4.99	6.94	8.44	9.70	10.8	11.8	12.7	13.5	14.3	15.1	15.8
9	4.43	6.00	7.18	8.12	9.03	9.78	10.5	11.1	11.7	12.2	12.7
10	4.03	5.34	6.31	7.11	7.80	8.41	8.95	9.45	9.91	10.3	10.7
11	3.72	4.85	5.67	6.34	6.92	7.42	7.87	8.28	8.66	9.01	9.34
13	3.28	4.16	4.79	5.30	5.72	6.09	6.42	6.72	7.00	7.25	7.48
16	2.86	3.54	4.01	4.37	4.68	4.95	5.19	5.40	5.59	5.77	5.93
21	2.46	2.95	3.29	3.54	3.76	3.94	4.10	4.24	4.37	4.49	4.59
31	2.07	2.40	2.61	2.78	2.91	3.02	3.12	3.21	3.29	3.36	3.39
61	1.67	1.85	1.96	2.04	2.11	2.17	2.22	2.26	2.30	2.33	2.36
∞	1.00	1.00	1.00	1.00	1.00	1.00	1.00	1.00	1.00	1.00	1.00

TABLE A.15

Critical values for the number of runs R, in samples of size (n_1, n_2). The null hypothesis is rejected if $R \leq k_1$ or $R \geq k_2$, where for each n_1 and n_2 the top value is k_1 and the bottom value is k_2. This table assumes a significance level of $\alpha = .05$.

THE SMALLER OF n_1 AND n_2	THE LARGER OF n_1 AND n_2															
	5	6	7	8	9	10	11	12	13	14	15	16	17	18	19	20
2								2	2	2	2	2	2	2	2	2
								6	6	6	6	6	6	6	6	6
3		2	2	2	2	2	2	2	2	2	3	3	3	3	3	3
		8	8	8	8	8	8	8	8	8	8	8	8	8	8	8
4	2	2	2	3	3	3	3	3	3	3	3	4	4	4	4	4
	9	9	10	10	10	10	10	10	10	10	10	10	10	10	10	10
5	2	3	3	3	3	3	4	4	4	4	4	4	4	5	5	5
	10	10	11	11	12	12	12	12	12	12	12	12	12	12	12	12
6		3	3	3	4	4	4	4	5	5	5	5	5	5	6	6
		11	12	12	13	13	13	13	14	14	14	14	14	14	14	14
7			3	4	4	5	5	5	5	5	6	6	6	6	6	6
			13	13	14	14	14	14	15	15	15	16	16	16	16	16
8				4	5	5	5	6	6	6	6	6	7	7	7	7
				14	14	15	15	16	16	16	16	17	17	17	17	17
9					5	5	6	6	6	7	7	7	7	8	8	8
					15	16	16	16	17	17	18	18	18	18	18	18
10						6	6	7	7	7	7	8	8	8	8	9
						16	17	17	18	18	18	19	19	19	20	20
11							7	7	7	8	8	8	9	9	9	9
							17	18	19	19	19	20	20	20	21	21
12								7	8	8	8	9	9	9	10	10
								19	19	20	20	21	21	21	22	22
13									8	9	9	9	10	10	10	10
									20	20	21	21	22	22	23	23
14										9	9	10	10	10	11	11
										21	22	22	23	23	23	24
15											10	10	11	11	11	12
											22	23	23	24	24	25
16												11	11	11	12	12
												23	24	25	25	25
17													11	12	12	13
													25	25	26	26
18														12	13	13
														26	26	27
19															13	13
															27	27
20																14
																28

TABLE A.16

Critical values of the studentized range (Q) distribution. The values listed in the table are the critical values of Q for $\alpha = .05$ and $\alpha = .01$, as a function of degrees of freedom for MS(error) and k (the number of means).

df for MS(ERROR) (v)	α	\multicolumn{10}{c}{k (NUMBER OF MEANS)}									
		2	3	4	5	6	7	8	9	10	11
5	.05	3.64	4.60	5.22	5.67	6.03	6.33	6.58	6.80	6.99	7.17
	.01	5.70	6.98	7.80	8.42	8.91	9.32	9.67	9.97	10.24	10.48
6	.05	3.46	4.34	4.90	5.30	5.63	5.90	6.12	6.32	6.49	6.65
	.01	5.24	6.33	7.03	7.56	7.97	8.32	8.61	8.87	9.10	9.30
7	.05	3.34	4.16	4.68	5.06	5.36	5.61	5.82	6.00	6.16	6.30
	.01	4.95	5.92	6.54	7.01	7.37	7.68	7.94	8.17	8.37	8.55
8	.05	3.26	4.04	4.53	4.89	5.17	5.40	5.60	5.77	5.92	6.05
	.01	4.75	5.64	6.20	6.62	6.96	7.24	7.47	7.68	7.86	8.03
9	.05	3.20	3.95	4.41	4.76	5.02	5.24	5.43	5.59	5.74	5.87
	.01	4.60	5.43	5.96	6.35	6.66	6.91	7.13	7.33	7.49	7.65
10	.05	3.15	3.88	4.33	4.65	4.91	5.12	5.30	5.46	5.60	5.72
	.01	4.48	5.27	5.77	6.14	6.43	6.67	6.87	7.05	7.21	7.36
11	.05	3.11	3.82	4.26	4.57	4.82	5.03	5.20	5.35	5.49	5.61
	.01	4.39	5.15	5.62	5.97	6.25	6.48	6.67	6.84	6.99	7.13
12	.05	3.08	3.77	4.20	4.51	4.75	4.95	5.12	5.27	5.39	5.51
	.01	4.32	5.05	5.50	5.84	6.10	6.32	6.51	6.67	6.81	6.94
13	.05	3.06	3.73	4.15	4.45	4.69	4.88	5.05	5.19	5.32	5.43
	.01	4.26	4.96	5.40	5.73	5.98	6.19	6.37	6.53	6.67	6.79
14	.05	3.03	3.70	4.11	4.41	4.64	4.83	4.99	5.13	5.25	5.36
	.01	4.21	4.89	5.32	5.63	5.88	6.08	6.26	6.41	6.54	6.66
15	.05	3.01	3.67	4.08	4.37	4.59	4.78	4.94	5.08	5.20	5.31
	.01	4.17	4.84	5.25	5.56	5.80	5.99	6.16	6.31	6.44	6.55
16	.05	3.00	3.65	4.05	4.33	4.56	4.74	4.90	5.03	5.15	5.26
	.01	4.13	4.79	5.19	5.49	5.72	5.92	6.08	6.22	6.35	6.46
17	.05	2.98	3.63	4.02	4.30	4.52	4.70	4.86	4.99	5.11	5.21
	.01	4.10	4.74	5.14	5.43	5.66	5.85	6.01	6.15	6.27	6.38
18	.05	2.97	3.61	4.00	4.28	4.49	4.67	4.82	4.96	5.07	5.17
	.01	4.07	4.70	5.09	5.38	5.60	5.79	5.94	6.08	6.20	6.31
19	.05	2.96	3.59	3.98	4.25	4.47	4.65	4.79	4.92	5.04	5.14
	.01	4.05	4.67	5.05	5.33	5.55	5.73	5.89	6.02	6.14	6.25
20	.05	2.95	3.58	3.96	4.23	4.45	4.62	4.77	4.90	5.01	5.11
	.01	4.02	4.64	5.02	5.29	5.51	5.69	5.84	5.97	6.09	6.19
24	.05	2.92	3.53	3.90	4.17	4.37	4.54	4.68	4.81	4.92	5.01
	.01	3.96	4.55	4.91	5.17	5.37	5.54	5.69	5.81	5.92	6.02
30	.05	2.89	3.49	3.85	4.10	4.30	4.46	4.60	4.72	4.82	4.92
	.01	3.89	4.45	4.80	5.05	5.24	5.40	5.54	5.65	5.76	5.85
40	.05	2.86	3.44	3.79	4.04	4.23	4.39	4.52	4.63	4.73	4.82
	.01	3.82	4.37	4.70	4.93	5.11	5.26	5.39	5.50	5.60	5.69
60	.05	2.83	3.40	3.74	3.98	4.16	4.31	4.44	4.55	4.65	4.73
	.01	3.76	4.28	4.59	4.82	4.99	5.13	5.25	5.36	5.45	5.53
120	.05	2.80	3.36	3.68	3.92	4.10	4.24	4.36	4.47	4.56	4.64
	.01	3.70	4.20	4.50	4.71	4.87	5.01	5.12	5.21	5.30	5.37
∞	.05	2.77	3.31	3.63	3.86	4.03	4.17	4.29	4.39	4.47	4.55
	.01	3.64	4.12	4.40	4.60	4.76	4.88	4.99	5.08	5.16	5.23

TABLE A.17 Quantiles of the Kendall Test Statistic.

n	$V_{.90}$	$V_{.95}$	$V_{.975}$	$V_{.990}$	$V_{.995}$
4	4	4	6	6	6
5	6	6	8	8	10
6	7	9	11	11	13
7	9	11	13	15	17
8	10	14	16	18	20
9	12	16	18	22	24
10	15	19	21	25	27
11	17	21	25	29	31
12	18	24	28	34	36
13	22	26	32	38	42
14	23	31	35	41	45
15	27	33	39	47	51
16	28	36	44	50	56
17	32	40	48	56	62
18	35	43	51	61	67
19	37	47	55	65	73
20	40	50	60	70	78
21	42	54	64	76	84
22	45	59	69	81	89
23	49	63	73	87	97
24	52	66	78	92	102
25	56	70	84	98	108
26	59	75	89	105	115
27	61	79	93	111	123
28	66	84	98	116	128
29	68	88	104	124	136
30	73	93	109	129	143
31	75	97	115	135	149
32	80	102	120	142	158
33	84	106	126	150	164
34	87	111	131	155	173
35	91	115	137	163	179
36	94	120	144	170	188
37	98	126	150	176	196
38	103	131	155	183	203
39	107	137	161	191	211
40	110	142	168	198	220
41	114	146	174	206	228
42	119	151	181	213	235
43	123	157	187	221	245
44	128	162	194	228	252
45	132	168	200	236	262
46	135	173	207	245	271
47	141	179	213	253	279
48	144	186	220	260	288
49	150	190	228	268	296
50	153	197	233	277	305
51	159	203	241	285	315
52	162	208	248	294	324
53	168	214	256	302	334
54	173	221	263	311	343
55	177	227	269	319	353
56	182	232	276	328	362
57	186	240	284	336	372
58	191	245	291	345	381
59	197	251	299	355	391
60	202	258	306	364	402

From W. J. Conover, *Practical Nonparametric Statistics*, 2/e, Table A-12. © 1980, John Wiley & Sons, New York. This material is used by permission of John Wiley & Sons, Inc.

APPENDIX B ANSWERS TO ODD-NUMBERED EXERCISES

Chapter 1

1.1 The following populations are examples of populations that would be of interest to a business manager: **a.** Consumers of a certain product. **b.** Employees of a company. **c.** All electrical components manufactured by a factory. A business manager would prefer to sample from a population rather than take a census because of the cost and time involved.

1.3 Inferential statistics

1.5 a. Quantitative, ratio **b.** Qualitative, ordinal **c.** Qualitative, nominal **d.** Quantitative, interval **e.** Qualitative, ordinal

1.7 Telephone interviews conducted during a class project would be primary data.

1.9 a. Primary **b.** Secondary **c.** Primary. **d.** Secondary

1.11 a. To use Table A.13, do the following:

1. Start at an arbitrary position.
2. Select twenty five-digit numbers by reading either across or down the table.
3. For each five-digit number selected, place a decimal between the second and third digits and round to the nearest integer. If any numbers are over 70, then continue to select random numbers until twenty numbers have been selected.

1.13 Give five categories of income and ask the respondent to which category does he/she belong.

1.15 Some comments motivating a person to fill out the questionnaire should be included. A closing statement may thank respondents for their time.

1.17 a. This is a leading question. **b.** Ask the question about the "Nightly Business Report" after the respondent lists their favorite television programs. **c.** It is not clear whether "large" refers to population or area.

1.19 a. Population consists of all individuals with a high net worth. **b.** Ask the general questions first and then ask the specific questions. **c.** The individual may not base his/her decision on whether the economy is slowing down.

1.21 a. The firms that buy computer chips from the company. **b.** A table of random numbers can be used. Also Excel, SPSS, or MINITAB can be used to generate random numbers. **c.** Satisfaction by firms that buy from the company. **d.** The average of the responses can be used as the statistic to estimate the parameter in part (c).

1.23 a. The population is customers using America Online. **b.** A random sample could be selected by numbering all accounts and then randomly selecting a subset. **c.** Selecting customers by using a random sample would provide a more representative sample.

1.25 a. Represents a sample of employees at General Motors if randomly selected from the population of all employees at General Motors. **b.** Sample **c.** Sample **d.** Population of all possible ways of choosing two cards from a deck of 52 cards. **e.** Sample

1.27 1. Ratio – Quantitative, 2. Ratio – Quantitative, 3. Nominal – Qualitative, 4. Ordinal – Qualitative, 5. Ordinal – Qualitative, 6. Ratio – Quantitative

1.29 a. Computer buyers who have purchased Apple's new product. **b.** A random sample can be selected from warranties on file. **c.** Demographics: 1. What is your age? 2. Your highest level of education is high school, college, or graduate school? 3. How many children in your household?

Questions on satisfaction: 1. On a scale from 1 to 10 (perfect), how would you rate your satisfaction with your new TiBook? 2. Do you consider the TiBook to be attractively priced? 3. What feature do you like the most about the TiBook?

d. A discount on future purchases could be offered.

e. For those purchasers that did not respond to the survey, the company might try to contact them by telephone or perhaps further entice their participation by offering frequent flyer miles.

Chapter 2

2.1 a. 1,000

b.

Lower Class Limit	Upper Class Limit
0	1000
1000	2000
2000	3000
3000	4000
4000	5000
5000	6000
6000	7000
7000	8000

c. $1200/8062 = .1488$
$1500/8062 = .1861$
$2500/8062 = .3101$
$2300/8062 = .2853$
$500/8062 = .0620$
$50/8062 = .0062$
$10/8062 = .0012$
$2/8062 = .0002$

2.3 a. $(224,000 - 111,000)/5 = 22,600$. Use a class width of 25,000.

Class Number	Class
1	110,000 and under 135,000
2	135,000 and under 160,000
3	160,000 and under 185,000
4	185,000 and under 210,000
5	210,000 and under 235,000

b. $(224,000 - 111,000)/6 = 18,833$. Use a class width of 20,000.

Class Number	Class
1	110,000 and under 130,000
2	130,000 and under 150,000
3	150,000 and under 170,000
4	170,000 and under 190,000
5	190,000 and under 210,000
6	210,000 and under 230,000

c. $(224,000 - 111,000)/12 = 9,416.7$. Use a class width of 10,000.

Class Number	Class
1	110,000 and under 120,000
2	120,000 and under 130,000
3	130,000 and under 140,000
4	140,000 and under 150,000
5	150,000 and under 160,000
6	160,000 and under 170,000
7	170,000 and under 180,000
8	180,000 and under 190,000
9	190,000 and under 200,000
10	200,000 and under 210,000
11	210,000 and under 220,000
12	220,000 and under 230,000

2.5 a. Frequency distributions are easier to examine than the raw data.

b.

Weekly Earnings	Frequency	Relative Frequency
$ 0 and under $211	1462	.2183
$211 and under $334	1295	.1934
$334 and under $493	1354	.2022
$493 and under $730	1297	.1937
$730 and higher	1288	.1924

c. .1937 + .1924 = .3861

2.7 a. PE

Frequency Distribution Table

Class	Class Limits	Frequency
1	15 and under 20	5
2	20 and under 25	4
3	25 and under 30	6
4	30 and under 35	2
5	35 and under 40	3
6	40 and under 45	4
7	45 and under 50	2
8	50 and under 55	1
9	55 and under 60	1

b. **Frequency Distribution Table**

Class	Class Limits	Frequency
1	15 and under 22	7
2	22 and under 29	6
3	29 and under 36	5
4	36 and under 43	5
5	43 and under 50	3
6	50 and under 57	2

c. By showing a histogram, it is hoped that the person viewing the histogram will quickly understand the shape of the data distribution.

2.9 c.

Class Number	Frequency	Cumulative Frequency	Relative Frequency	Cumulative Relative Frequency
1	15	15	.375	.375
2	10	25	.25	.625
3	8	33	.20	.825
4	5	38	.125	.95
5	2	40	.05	1.00
	40			

2.11 b. CW = .5; Number of classes = 7; Class intervals are 1 and under 1.5, . . . , 4 and under 4.5.

2.13 Number of Times Used WWW

Frequency Distribution Table

Class	Class Limits	Frequency
1	0 and under 4	3
2	4 and under 8	6
3	8 and under 12	8
4	12 and under 16	9
5	16 and under 20	6
6	20 and under 24	3
7	24 and under 28	1

2.15 The most commonly quoted price is 99.

2.17 a. Class intervals are 15–24, . . . , 95–104; Cumulative relative frequencies are .03, .20, .33, .46, .56, .69, .82, .92, .99.

2.19 a. Number of Users

Frequency Distribution Table

Class	Class Limits	Frequency
1	0 and under 6	4
2	6 and under 12	6
3	12 and under 18	3
4	18 and under 24	1
5	24 and under 30	0
6	30 and under 36	1

2.21 a. The distribution has two peaks. The smaller peak is at 76.25 and the larger peak is at 86.25.

Class Limits	Relative Freq	Cum Rel Freq
75 and under 77.5	.13	.13
77.5 and under 80	.09	.22
80 and under 82.5	.09	.30
82.5 and under 85	.13	.43
85 and under 87.5	.30	.73
87.5 and under 90	.17	.91
90 and under 92.5	.09	1.00

b. If "acceptable" is defined as the top 50%, this value would be any loudspeaker with a score of more than 85 (approximately).

2.23 Class intervals are 4–8, . . . , 24–28. Cumulative frequencies are 6, 12, 16, 18, 20.

2.25

a.
Class Limits	Relative Freq
15 and under 17	.10
17 and under 19	.48
19 and under 21	24
21 and under 23	.14
23 and under 25	.05

b.
Class Limits	Relative Freq
15 and under 17	.08
17 and under 19	.46
19 and under 21	.27
21 and under 23	.14
23 and under 25	.05

2.31 c. The percentages for all the companies increase considerably when the two top companies are omitted.

2.33 a. Most of the loans are being borrowed by Mexico, China, Brazil and Indonesia. **b.** Bar charts and pie charts do not order the categories and do not have a cumulative scale.

2.37 a. The four largest bars show that Phillips, RCA, Sanyo, and Sony are the four largest companies in consumer electronics.

2.39 a. Pie charts show that recruiting online for directors will increase while recruiting for managers and team leaders will decrease.

2.41 a. Very few investors prefer 100% bonds and 0% stocks. Also, the mixture of 0% bonds and 100% stocks is the least preferred out of the remaining investment mixes. **b.** As the salary level increases, the number of investors in the salary category decreases. **c.** When the investors with at least 80K are omitted, clear preferences are 70% bonds and 30% stocks and 50% bonds and 50% stocks.

2.43 The three-dimensional pie chart makes BEA appear to have a more impressive share of the market although the percentages are the same as in the two-dimensional pie chart.

2.51 a. There are no outliers. **b.** The distribution is uniformly shaped from 20 to under 30. The interval 15 and under 20 and the interval 30 and under 35 only have a single observation. The interval from 10 and under 15 is close to the frequency of the values from 20 and under 30.

2.55 a. The stem-and-leaf diagram and the histogram show similar shapes.

2.57 b. Ford, General Motors, and DaimlerChrylser make up approximately 67% of the market. Note that General Motors and Ford make up more than half of the market and that the top six automakers make up over 90% of the market.

2.59 Both histograms are similar in that they start off high and then the relative frequency decreases as the values for the class intervals increase.

2.61 a. The histogram is approximately bell-shaped. **b.** Approximately twenty percent of the states have a math proficiency value of 30 or more.

Chapter 3

3.1 a. mean = 19.2; median = 12; midrange = 26. **b.** mean = 4.8; median = 3 ; midrange = 6.5

3.3 a. 1, 2, 7, 8, 9 **b.** 1, 3, 10, 18, 19

3.5 No, the median does not have to change by the same amount that the mean changes.

3.7 Mean = 55.77/14 = 3.98
Median = (.5 + .68)/2 = .59
If 26.30 is omitted, the value of the mean will change more than if any other values were omitted. After omitting 26.30, the mean is 29.47/13 = 2.267. The median is .5.

3.9 a. mean = 80.15; median = 79.95; midrange = 78. **b.** mean = 81.85; median = 82.6; midrange = 80.5.

3.11 a. mean = 50,345,266.5; median = 31,314,038.5; midrange = 80,421,913.5. **b.** mean = 32,811,477.5; median = 26,613,436; midrange = 59,783,055.5. **c.** The new mean and median would be equal to the mean and median of the raw data multiplied by 120. **d.** The mean is 6,041,431,980. The median is 3,757,684,620.

3.13 a. Range = 8; $\bar{x} = 30/5 = 6$; $s = 3.16$; CV = 52.7%. **b.** Range = 80; $\bar{x} = 300/5 = 60$; $s = 31.62$; CV = 52.7%. **c.** Range = .08; $\bar{x} = .3/5 = .06$; $s = .0316$; CV = 52.7%.

3.15 a. $\bar{x} = 1650/16 = 103.125$. **b.** Approximate standard deviation is Range/4 = (200 − 40)/ 4 = 40. **c.** $s = 51.377$. **d.** CV = 49.8%.

3.17 $\sum (x - \bar{x})^2 = \sum x^2 - 2(\sum x)^2/n + (\sum x)^2/n = \sum x^2 - (\sum x)^2/n.$

3.19 a. An approximation to the standard deviation is $(948 - 84.9)/4 \doteq 216.$ **b.** $\bar{x} = 493.85$; $s = 346.7912$. **d.** $\bar{x} = 482.56$; $s = 275.2681$.

3.21 a. Mean is 85.2, standard deviation is 47.6, coefficient of variation is 100(47.6/85.2) = 55.87%, and the variance is 2266.182. **b.** The mean should change by dividing its value by 60. The standard deviation should change by dividing its value by 60. The variance should change by dividing its value by 3600. **c.** Mean is 1.42, standard deviation is .793, and the variance is .6295.

3.23 Median is 1.5, Mean is 10/10 = 1 and $s^2 = (20 - (10)^2/10)/9 = 1.111$; $s = 1.054$; $Sk = 3(\bar{x} - Md)/s = 3(1 - 1.5)/1.054 = -1.423$

3.25 a. −2 **b.** 3 **c.** 55 **d.** 37.5

3.27 a. 73.5 **b.** 105.5 **c.** 75 = 25th percentile; 103 = 75th percentile. **d.** $\bar{x} = 90.6333$; median = 87.5; $s = 19.71781$; $Sk = 0.47673.$ **e.** The data are slightly skewed to the right.

3.29 a. 3.0496 **b.** −1.443; −.4591; .1967; .52466; 1.18049. **c.** 1

3.31 a. The mean and standard deviation are 60.0 and 23.40, respectively; CV = 39.0%. **b.** CV = 27.2%. **d.** Sk = .64. **e.** $Q_3 = 830$, $Q_1 = 520$, IQR = 310. The IQR should not be affected by a single outlier.

3.33 b. The mean, median, and standard deviation are 971.4, 457.5, and 1149.799. Pearson's coefficient of skewness = 1.34. **c.** The mean, median, and standard deviation are 626.029, 388.0, and 550.013. Pearson's coefficient of skewness = 1.30.

3.35 a. 80 to 120 **b.** 100 ± 3(20)

3.37 a. $\bar{x} = 44.8$; $s = 10.5283$. **b.** 44.8 ± 2(10.5283). **c.** 44.8 ± 3(10.5283). **d.** Yes.

3.39 $\bar{x} = 50.5$; $s = 9.7512$; $n = 30$; $\bar{x} \pm s = 40.749$ to 60.2512, 90% of the data values fall in this interval; $\bar{x} \pm 2s = 30.997$ to 70.002, 93.33% of the data values fall in this interval; $\bar{x} \pm 3s = 21.246$ to 79.753, 93.33% of data values fall in this interval.

3.41 $\bar{x} \pm 2s = 90.633 \pm 2(19.71781)$; 96.667% of the data actually lie within this interval.

3.43 a. The bounds are −1099.06 and 5821.06. **b.** The bounds are −1769.408 and 7675.408. **e.** The bounds using one standard deviation are 592 and 5314 for the 1998 data. Two observations are outside of these bounds.

3.45 a. The following interval contains at least 75% of the data. $\bar{x} - 2s$ to $\bar{x} + 2s$; 18335.76 − 2(2268.515) to 18335.76 + 2(2268.515); $13,798.73 to $22,872.79. The following interval contains at least 89% of the data. $\bar{x} - 3s$ to $\bar{x} + 3s$; 18,335.76 − 3(2268.515) to 18335.76 + 3(2268.515); $11,530.22 to $25,141.31
b. 196 observations (98%) of the data lie within 2 standard deviations of the mean. The minimum number expected by Chebyshev's inequality is 150. 199 observations (99.5%) of the data lie within 2 standard deviations of the mean. The minimum number expected by Chebyshev's inequality is 178.

3.47 a. $\bar{x} \doteq 30$ **b.** $s^2 \doteq 204.0816$ **c.** $s \doteq 14.2857$

3.49 a. $\bar{x} \doteq 164.0909$ **b.** $s \doteq 38.7801$

3.51 a. $\bar{x} \doteq 19.8$ **b.** $s \doteq 5.8353$

3.55 a. The first, second, and third quartiles are 20, 24.5, and 32. **b.** The largest and smallest values are 70 and 12. **c.** The box plot shows that observation 70 is an extreme value and that the median is closer to the first quartile than to the third quartile (the data are skewed right).

3.57 b. The distribution of the data is skewed to the right. The observation 12.5 is a mild outlier.

3.59 The data are skewed left. No outliers were detected.

3.61 a. Mean, median, and midrange are 976.857, 856, 949.5. **b.** .9923 **c.** −.457 (Chevrolet), 1.30 (Suzuki)

3.63 a. 6.268 to 8.204 **b.** Interquartile range is .7. There is no change in the interquartile range when 8.0 is omitted.

3.65 a. $Q_1 = 2.7$; $Q_3 = 4.1$; IQR = 1.4; $s = 1.1757$. **b.** $Q_1 = 2.7$; $Q_3 = 3.8$; IQR = 1.1; $s = .8206$.

3.67 a. The mean and standard deviation for the Legg Mason Value fund are 24.267 and 18.738, respectively. The mean and standard deviation for the Fidelity Aggressive fund are 28.55 and 36.452, respectively. **b.** Sharpe ratio for the Legg Mason Value fund: 1.081. Sharpe ratio for the Fidelity Aggressive fund: .674.

3.69 a. The data are approximately bell-shaped. **b.** Sk = .32. **c.** By the empirical rule, approximately 68% of the values should fall between −1.155 and 1.655.

3.71 $45 to $105

3.73 The supervisor should accept the shipment.

3.75 a. The values of .60 and .84 are extreme outliers. **b.** The mean, median, and standard deviation are .249, .20, and .158, respectively. **c.** The coefficient of skewness = .930. **d.** The values of .60 and .84 are outliers.

3.77 b. The data appear to have come from a bell-shaped distribution. **c.** $\bar{x} = 50.2167$, $s = 15.913$, and $Sk = .04$

3.79 a. (1.00716) raised to the 20th power is equal to 1.000357. The geometric mean is equal to this value minus one, or .000357, which is practically 0%. **b.** The mean is .031 or 3.1% and the median is .065 or 6.5%. However, these figures give a misleading average rate of return since the actual return would be closer to 0%.

Chapter 4

4.1 a. P(B) = 1.25 cannot be a probability. **b.** The sum of the probabilities do not sum to one. **c.** The sum of the probabilities cannot be greater than one.

4.3 a. .10 **b.** .25 **c.** .60 **d.** .70

4.5 A and B are mutually exclusive.

4.7 a .2667 **b.** .5867

4.9 a. .541 **b.** .015 **c.** .5 **d.** .949 **e.** 0

4.11 a. .7 **b.** .2 **c.** .9 **d.** .5

4.13 a. .209 **b.** .524 **c.** .139 **d.** The events are not independent. **e.** .594 **f.** .367

4.15 a. .875 **b.** .35 **c.** .917 **d.** If the events of no tuition reimbursement and at least 3 months of leave had a frequency value of 0 in the table, then these two events would be mutually exclusive.

4.17 b. .1 **c.** .3 **d.** .6667

4.19 a. .8 **b.** .857 **c.** .1 **d.** .333

4.21 a. .5 **b.** .8 **c.** 0 **d.** .5 **e.** 0 **f.** .2857 **g.** .375

4.23 A and B are independent.

4.25 a. .24 **b.** .76 **c.** .36

4.27 .5926

4.29 a. .54 **b.** 0.86 **c.** 0.675

4.31 .90

4.33 b. .722 **c.** .917 **d.** .625 **e.** .423

4.35 a. Try different numbers of people to see how large a group of people is necessary for the relative frequency to be at least .5 (approximately).

4.37 a. .34 **b.** .25

4.39 E_1 = drug user; B = test is positive; P(B) = .1044; $P(E_1 \mid B)$ = .9569

4.41 .048

4.43 a. .0395 **b.** .405

4.45 a. The events A, B, and C are mutually exclusive. **b.** No, since (.2)(.3)(.5) ≠ .06.

4.47 a. P(A) = .5; P(B) = .5; P(C) = .5. **b.** P(A and B) = .25; P(A and C) = .25; P(B and C) = .25. **c.** P(A and B and C) = 0. **d.** A and B, A and C, and B and C are pairwise independent. But A, B, and C are not mutually independent.

4.49 a. .0029 **b.** .0304

4.51 a. P(Project A is successful) = .671; P(Project B is successful) = .678.

4.53 a. 45 **b.** 3,628,800 **c.** 5040

4.55 56

4.57 3003

4.59 380

4.61 20,000

4.63 16

4.65 15

4.69 .0222

4.71 0.0222

4.73 a. .12 **b.** .58 **c.** .3 **d.** 0 **e.** 0 **f.** 1 **g.** .012 **h.** .8

4.75 a. 0.091 **b.** 0.125 **c.** 0.273

4.77 a. .143 **b.** .143 **c.** .2857 **d.** 1.0

4.79 a. .1237 **b.** .4571 **c.** .3781 **d.** Age and the frequency of viewing internet advertising are not independent.

4.81 a. .34 **b.** .2941

4.83 a. 0.8 **b.** 0.2

4.85 a. .80 **b.** .24

4.87 a. Therefore, these two events are not independent. **b.** .42

4.89 a. .40 **b.** .355

4.91 .8712

Chapter 5

5.1 a. P(Circuit board needs to be returned to factory) = 2/8 = .25 **b.** P(Circuit board is in good working condition) = 3/8 = .375

5.3 b. P(X > 1) = .75 **c.** P(X = 1 or X = 3) = .75

5.5 12 outcomes, each with probability 1/12.

5.7 a. N = no refund (owes); R = refund; Possible pairs: RR, RN, NR. **b.** X = 2 for RR; X = 1 for RN; X = 1 for NR. **c.** P(X = 1) = 2/3; P(X = 2) = 1/3.

5.9 a. Valid **b.** Not valid **c.** Valid **d.** Not valid **e.** Not valid

5.11 Yes

5.13 Yes

5.15 Yes, this function is a probability mass function since all probability values are between 0 and 1 and they sum to 1.0.

5.17 P(X = x) = 1/3 for x = 2, 4, 6

5.19 b. The sum = 7 has a probability of 6/36 = .1667. **c.** The probability that the sum of dice will be between 5 and 8 should be approximately 20/36 = .556.

5.21 a. μ = 33.33; σ = 9.428. **b.** μ = 17.909; σ = 7.704.

5.23 μ = 3; σ^2 = 3.

5.25 a. μ = −.01; σ = .9327. **b.** μ = 1.99; σ = .9327.

5.27 c. The mean is 2.5 and standard deviation is 1.118

5.29 a. P(X = 2) = .044 **b.** P(X > 2) = .945 **c.** P(X ≤ 2) = .055 **d.** P(X < 2) = .011 **e.** P(X ≥ 2) = .989

5.31 .3647

5.33 .506

5.35 a. .382782 **b.** .22057 **c.** mean for part (a) is 3.0, mean for part (b) is 3.7

5.37 a. .001 **b.** 3 **c.** σ = 1.55 **d.** .982

5.39 .7636

5.41 a. n = 100 and p = .5 P(X ≥ 50) = .5398 **b.** n = 100 and p = .7 P(X ≥ 50) = 1.000 **c.** n = 100 and p = .662 P(X ≥ 50) = .9997 **d.** Expected number of families that are owners from New York is 50, from Indiana is 70, and from across the USA is 66.2. **e.** Standard deviation for the number of families that are owners from New York is 5, from Indiana is 4.58, and from across the USA is 4.73.

5.43 a. P(X = 8) = .1396 **b.** P(X < 8) = .4529 **c.** P(X ≤ 8) = .5925 **d.** P(X > 8) = .4075 **e.** P(8 ≤ X ≤ 10) = .3630

5.45 0.6353

5.47 a. P(X = 2) = .3 **b.** Using n = 5, P(X = 2) = .417. Using n = 6, P(X = 2) = .5. Using n = 7, P(X = 2) = .525.

5.49 a. P(X ≥ 8) = .7797 **b.** P(X ≤ 12) = .7916 **c.** The mean is 10 and the standard deviation is sqrt(10) = 3.16. **d.** The conditions for a Poisson distribution can be justified.

5.51 a. .5831 **b.** .0487

5.53 a. .9004 **b.** 2.83

5.55 a. .1992 **b.** 1.732

5.57 Only b is a property of a discrete probability distribution.

5.59 a. X can be equal to 1, 3, 4, 5, or 7. **b.** P(X = 1) = P(X = 3) = P(X = 5) = P(X = 7) = 1/6 and P(X = 4) = 2/6. **c.** μ = 4 **d.** σ^2 = 3.332

5.61 This is not a likely occurrence.

5.63 .623

5.65 b. The mean is 2.68; the standard deviation is 2.328.

5.67 P(X = 2) = 0.3739

5.69 a. .224 **b.** 1.73

5.71 Consider this expression to be a hypergeometric with N = 500, n = 10, k = 200, and x = 3. Since n/N is less than .05, the binomial distribution (using p = .4) provides a good approximation.

5.73 .5

5.75 a. $P(X \le 250) = .2477$ **b.** For $p = .28$, $P(X \le 250) = .0180$. For $p = .30$, $P(X \le 250) = .0003$. For $p = .32$, $P(X \le 250)$ is approximately 0. **c.** For $p = .24$, $P(X \le 250) = .7823$. For $p = .22$, $P(X \le 250) = .9892$. For $p = .20$, $P(X \le 250) = .9999$.

Chapter 6

6.3 a. .4772 **b.** .1102 **c.** .8591

6.5 a. 0.8907 **b.** 0.8907 **c.** 0.8907 **d.** 0.475 **e.** .3344

6.7 a. 1.03 **b.** 1.03 **c.** −1.76 **d.** 2.0 **e.** −2.0

6.9 a. $P(Z > 2) = .0228$ **b.** $P(Z > 3.4) = .0003$ **c.** $P(Z < −1.8) = .0359$ **d.** $P(Z < −3.8) = .000007$

6.11 a. .1587 **b.** 0.0228 **c.** .3830

6.13 0.0808

6.15 82.5

6.17 a. $P(X > 3) = .1841$ **b.** $P(X > 3) = .2266$ **c.** $P(X > 3) = .2810$

6.19 a. $P(X < 2000) = .8413$ **b.** $P(X < 1200) = .0013$.

6.21 a. 10 **b.** 2

6.23 a. The refund damage value of $117.51 yields a probability less than .01.

6.25 The histogram of data with a standard deviation of 5 shows that the data are more dispersed than a histogram of data with a standard deviation of 1 or 3.

6.27 b. .7019 **c.** .4639

6.29 .9612

6.31 a. $P(X \le 8) = .5793$ **b.** $P(X \le 2) = .015$

6.33 One can conclude that if the proportion of times that the generated binomially distributed values lie within the interval 2 to 5 is much different from 68%, then the normal distribution should not be used to approximate the binomial distribution for this particular n and p.

6.35 a. $\mu = 62.5$; $\sigma = 4.33$; Probability is .58. **b.** 66.94

6.37 a. 0.524 **b.** 23.15 **c.** 1.819

6.39 .51

6.41 0.2997

6.43 Let X be an exponentially distributed random variable with $\mu = 200$. $P(X > 200) = .368$

6.45 a. The uniform distribution most closely approximates the distribution of BotErr and TopErr. **b.** The approximate shape of TotalErr is normal.

6.47 a. $P(X < x) = .50$ implies that $x = $ mean $= \$150$. **b.** $X = \$171$. **c.** $X = \$171$.

6.49 .6700

6.51 60% of the time, the price of the yen to the dollar will be between 125.8 and 134.2.

6.53 87.12

6.55 Probability is .344; $\sigma = 30$

6.57 58.89%

6.59 0.0668

6.61 .4168

6.63 a. The mean is $65 and the standard deviation is 8.66. **b.** $71 **c.** The mean is $125 and the standard deviation is $14.43. **d.** $135.

6.65 50%

6.67 a. .223 **b.** .0228

6.69 $\sigma^2 = 43.03$

6.71 $\sigma = 12.158$

6.73 a. .3935 **b.** .8647

Chapter 7

7.1 a. .8413 **b.** .1359

7.3 a. The Central Limit Theorem tells us that the distribution of the sample mean is approximately normally distributed with a mean of 4 and a standard deviation of $1/\sqrt{50}$. **b.** If the sample size were increased to 100, the approximation of the normal distribution would be much closer for the distribution of $\bar{X}$. The mean would be 4 and the standard deviation would be $1/\sqrt{100}$.

7.5 .0022

7.7 a. .6826 **b.** .7888

7.9 a. .9115 **b.** .8729 **c.** .8599

7.11 0.7960

7.13 0.0823

7.15 0.0038

7.17 a. With the fpc, $P(\bar{X} < 80) = .2578$ Without the fpc, $P(\bar{X} < 80) = .2643$ **b.** With the fpc, $P(\bar{X} < 80) = .1736$ Without the fpc, $P(\bar{X} < 80) = .1867$ **c.** With the fpc, $P(\bar{X} < 80) = .0792$ Without the fpc, $P(\bar{X} < 80) = .1038$ **d.** With the fpc, $P(\bar{X} < 80) = .0107$ Without the fpc, $P(\bar{X} < 80) = .0367$

7.19 38.04 to 41.96

7.21 a. 169.183 to 180.817 **b.** 168.069 to 181.931 **c.** 165.891 to 184.109

7.25 a. 5.18 to 6.82 **b.** 5.42 to 6.41 **c.** 5.59 to 6.41

7.27 38.62 to 45.98

7.29 a. 30.715 to 37.145 **b.** 29.495 to 38.365

7.31 a. −1.325 **b.** 1.325 **c.** −1.725

7.33 a. 46.134 to 53.866 **b.** 45.32 to 54.68 **c.** 43.603 to 56.397

7.35 a. 62.24 to 73.76 **b.** 63.21 to 72.79

7.37 302.37 to 317.63

7.39 9.79 to 12.11

7.41 a. 2.600 to 2.728 **b.** 2.480 to 2.707

7.43 a. 68 **b.** 31 **c.** 271

7.45 16

7.47 6.1033

7.49 22

7.51 103

7.53 For a confidence level of 90%, a sample size of 271 is needed, whereas with a confidence level of 99%, a sample size of 664 is needed.

7.55 Answers will vary due to the random nature of the bootstrap method.

7.57 Answers will vary due to the random nature of the bootstrap method.

7.61 Answers will vary due to the random nature of the bootstrap method.

7.63 Answers will vary due to the random nature of the bootstrap method.

7.65 14.286 to 17.628

7.67 4.47 to 5.61

7.69 2.54 to 4.25

7.71 a. .1587 **b.** .0008

7.73 a. The point estimate of the average weight is 50. **b.** The sample standard deviation is .2.

7.79 3.46 to 4.42

7.81 97

7.83 9.56 to 10.792

7.85 **a.** 5.208 to 5.448 **b.** 5.224 to 5.428

7.87 **a.** 2.563 to 3.127 **b.** 2.568 to 3.122

Chapter 8

8.1 **a.** H_0: The containers are filled to 24 ounces; H_a: The containers are filled to an amount different from 24 ounces.

8.3 **a.** True **b.** True **c.** True **d.** False

8.5 $Z^* = 4.65$; reject H_0.

8.7 **b.** $Z^* = 2.17$; fail to reject H_0. **c.** $Z^* = 3.06$; reject H_0.

8.9 Since the 95% confidence interval does not contain 2.0, reject H_0.

8.11 **a.** 408.615 to 451.385 **b.** $Z^* = -5.38$; reject H_0.

8.13 **a.** .5912 **b.** 1.0

8.15 **a.** The histogram appears to have a bell-shaped appearance. **b.** $Z^* = -1.059$; fail to reject H_0. **c.** 130.515 to 155.818.

8.17 **a.** H_0: $\mu \geq \mu_0$; H_a: $\mu < \mu_0$. **b.** H_0: $\mu \geq 30$; H_a: $\mu < 30$. **c.** H_0: $\mu = 15$; H_a: $\mu \neq 15$.

8.19 **a.** $Z^* = 2$; reject H_0. **b.** $Z^* = 0$; fail to reject H_0.

8.21 $Z^* = 1.67$; reject H_0.

8.23 .7642

8.25 **a.** $Z^* = 2.34$; reject H_0.

8.27 **a.** fail to reject H_0 **b.** reject H_0 **c.** fail to reject H_0 **d.** reject H_0

8.29 **a.** .0114 **b.** .0057 **c.** .0614 **d.** .0307

8.31 **a.** p-value = .0524 **b.** fail to reject H_0.

8.33 $Z^* = -1.29$; p-value = .0985; fail to reject H_0.

8.35 **a.** p-value = .21; fail to reject H_0.

8.37 **a.** $t^* = .968$; fail to reject H_0. **b.** $t^* = .968$; fail to reject H_0. **c.** $t^* = -4.6$; reject H_0. **d.** $t^* = -1.4$; fail to reject H_0.

8.39 $t^* = -1.3$; fail to reject H_0.

8.41 $t^* = 2.67$; reject H_0.

8.43 $t^* = 3.2$; reject H_0.

8.45 **a.** p-value = .094

8.47 **a.** $\chi^{2*} < 3.9403$ or $\chi^{2*} > 18.3070$. **b.** $\chi^{2*} < 16.7908$ or $\chi^{2*} > 46.9792$. **c.** $\chi^{2*} < .9893$ or $\chi^{2*} > 20.2777$. **d.** $\chi^{2*} < 57.1532$ or $\chi^{2*} > 106.6286$.

8.49 **a.** 5.6355 to 24.237 **b.** 2.374 to 4.923 **c.** $\chi^{2*} = 4.4352$; reject H_0.

8.51 **a.** 1.31 to 2.48 **b.** $\chi^{2*} = 4.5$; reject H_0.

8.53 $\chi^{2*} = 21.39$; p-value > .10; fail to reject H_0.

8.55 **a.** The histograms show that the ratings for channel 5 are spread over a wide range. **b.** At the 1% significance level, there is evidence that Channel 8's ratings exceed 10. This conclusion is not supported by the data for Channel 5 and Channel 11. **c.** At the 1% significance level, the data support that the standard deviation for the ratings of Channel 5 exceed .7. The data do not support this conclusion for Channel 8 and Channel 11.

8.57 Only b and d can be acceptable alternative hypotheses.

8.59 **a.** True **b.** True **c.** True **d.** False **e.** True

8.61 **a.** .2274 **b.** .1279 **c.** .9830

8.63 $Z^* = -3.5$; p-value is .0004; reject H_0.

8.65 **a.** $Z^* = 1.95$; fail to reject H_0. **b.** $t^* = 1.95$; fail to reject H_0.

8.67 **a.** 4087.84 to 4912.16 **b.** Since the 99% confidence interval does not contain the hypothesized value of 4000, reject H_0.

8.69 $t^* = -1.068$; fail to reject H_0.

8.71 **a.** $t^* = 1.72$; fail to reject H_0.

8.73 $\chi^{2*} = 14.37$; fail to reject H_0.

8.75 $\chi^{2*} = 27.22$; fail to reject H_0.

8.77 **a.** 5.969 to 6.885 **b.** 5.881 to 6.973 **c.** 5.709 to 7.145

8.79 **a.** $t^* = 2.025$; reject H_0.

8.81 As the degrees of freedom increase the shape of the chi-square distribution becomes more symmetrical in appearance.

Chapter 9

9.1 **a.** Dependent samples **b.** Independent samples **c.** Independent samples

9.3 **a.** Dependent samples **b.** The samples are independent.

9.5 The sample of men and the sample of women are dependent.

9.7 **a.** The marketing analyst can have each person rate both brands of sausage. **b.** The marketing analyst can have each person rate only one of the brands of sausage.

9.9 **a.** −10.80 to −1.20 **b.** $Z^* = -2.06$; reject H_0.

9.11 $n_1 = 104$ $n_2 = 208$

9.13 −4.849 to −2.951

9.15 $Z^* = 3.70$; reject H_0.

9.17 $n_1 = 74$, $n_2 = 137$

9.19 $Z^* = 1.47$; p-value = .1416; fail to reject H_0.

9.21 $Z^* = -2.66$; reject H_0.

9.23 **b.** $Z^* = -1.52$; reject H_0.

9.25 **a.** $s_p = 1.711$ **b.** −3.132 to −.868 **c.** −3.3982 to −.8018

9.27 $t'^* = .4595$; fail to reject H_0.

9.29 $t^* = 0.4595$; fail to reject H_0.

9.31 −48.364 to −1.636

9.33 df = 18; $t^* = .618$; fail to reject H_0.

9.37 **a.** $F_{.025,19,14} \doteq F_{.025,20,14} = 2.84$; $F_{.975,19,14} \doteq 1/F_{.025,15,19} = .3816$. **b.** $F_{.90,4,14} \doteq 1/F_{.10,15,4} = .258$. **c.** $F_{.01,18,10} \doteq F_{.01,20,10} = 4.41$.

9.39 **a.** $F^* = 6.46$; reject H_0.

9.41 $F^* = .156$; reject H_0.

9.43 **a.** $F^* = .501$; reject H_0.

9.45 **a.** $F^* = 1.37$; fail to reject H_0. **b.** The results in part (a) remain the same when 5 points are subtracted from each grade.

9.47 **a.** $t^* = 3.02$; reject H_0. **b.** $.005 < p$-value < .01

9.49 **a.** .668 to 3.53 **b.** $t_D^* = 2.689$; reject H_0.

9.51 $t^* = 4.46$; reject H_0.

9.53 **a.** Fail to reject H_0.

9.55 **a.** $t^* = -1.89$; fail to reject H_0. **b.** $t^* = -1.89$; fail to reject H_0.

9.57 **a.** $Z^* = -.197$; p-value = .8414. **b.** df = 44; $t^* = 1.59$; $.05 < p$-value < .10. **c.** $Z^* = 0.063$; p-value = .4761.

9.59 $t^* = 3.8443$; reject H_0.

9.61 **a.** 10.35 to 17.25 **b.** $Z^* = -.90$; fail to reject H_0. **c.** The confidence interval in part b cannot be used to test the hypothesis in part a since the hypothesis in part a is a one-tail hypothesis.

9.63 **a.** 2.55 to 6.28 **b.** 1.91 to 4.71

9.65 $F^* = 2.56$; fail to reject H_0.

9.67 $t^* = 3.90$; reject H_0.

9.69 **a.** Yes, the p-value = .07939 is less than .10. **b.** $t^* = 1.159$; fail to reject H_0.

9.71 **a.** $t_D^* = 1.928$; reject H_0. **b.** A 95% confidence interval for $\mu_d = \mu_1 - \mu_2$ is 1.956 to 3.511. A 99% confidence interval for $\mu_d = \mu_1 - \mu_2$ is 1.685 to 3.781.

Chapter 10

10.1 a. .213 to .734 **b.** .315 to .769 **c.** .318 to .682 **d.** .36 to .64

10.3. a. $n = 94$ **b.** $n = 370$ **c.** $n = 1026$

10.5 95% confidence interval is .465 to .903; 90% confidence interval is .502 to .884

10.7 a. $n = 357$ **b.** $n = 424$

10.9 a. $n = 3613$ **b.** $n = 1474$

10.11 2019

10.13 a. .270 to .380 **b.** $n = 1486$

10.15 a. .468 to .632 **b.** .421 to .679

10.17 a. $Z^* = -1.212$; p-value = .2262. **b.** $Z^* = -1.212$ from part (a); p-value = .1131. **c.** $Z^* = .90$; p-value = .184; fail to reject H_0.

10.19 Since $.5 < p_L = .502$, reject H_0.

10.21 n must be greater than or equal to 167.

10.23 a. $Z^* = -2.649$; reject H_0.

10.25 $n = 363$

10.27 $Z^* = .207$; fail to reject H_0.

10.29 $Z^* = .20$; fail to reject H_0.

10.31 a. $-.1872$ to .0372 **b.** $Z^* = -1.15$ **c.** p-value = .2502

10.35 $n_1 = 1791$ and $n_2 = 1719$

10.37 $Z^* = -.91$; p-value = .3628; fail to reject H_0.

10.39 a. $Z^* = .795$; fail to reject H_0. **b.** $\bar{p} = .05$ **c.** $Z^* = .7947$

10.41 a. fail to reject H_0 **b.** .003 to .226

10.43 a. Since $.5 > p_L = .360$, fail to reject H_0. **b.** (.323, .837) **c.** $n = 152$

10.45 $n = 1119$

10.47 $Z^* = 1.3488$; reject H_0

10.49 a. Estimate of Microsoft's share of the market for handheld operating systems = .23. **b.** Margin of error = .13. **c.** $n = 42$.

10.53 p-value = .3557; fail to reject H_0.

10.55 $Z^* = -.512$: fail to reject H_0.

10.57 a. .0222 to .1278 **b.** $n_1 = 480$; $n_2 = 406$

10.59 a. $n_1 = 1247$ and $n_2 = 1220$. **b.** $n_1 = 2136$ and $n_2 = 2136$.

10.61 a. $n_1 = 442$ and $n_2 = 300$. **b.** $n_1 = 312$ and $n_2 = 212$. **c.** The requirements for the validity of the confidence interval are satisfied.

10.63 d. We would expect $(.90)(40) = 36$ intervals to contain $p = .5$. In the graph, there are 34 intervals that contain $p = .5$.

Chapter 11

11.1 a. $t^* = 1.782$ **b.** SST = 28.5; SS(factor) = 8.1; SSE = 20.4; $F^* = 3.18$ **c.** MSE = $2.55 = s_p^2$ **d.** $t^2 = (1.782)^2 = 3.18$ and $F = 3.18$. Yes, $t^2 = F$.

11.3 a.

ANOVA				
Source	df	SS	MS	F
Factor	3	252.908	84.30	22.48
Error	15	56.25	3.75	
Total	18	309.158		

b. reject H_0 **c.** 9.81 to 13.19; 18.15 to 21.85 **d.** -11.00 to -6.00 **e.** $H^* = 2.83$; fail to reject H_0 **f.** No

11.5 a.

ANOVA				
Source	df	SS	MS	F
Factor	2	54.1111	27.0556	12.82
Error	15	31.6667	2.1111	
Total	17	85.7778		

b. p-value < .01 **e.** $D = 2.18$; conclude that $\mu_1 \neq \mu_3$ and $\mu_2 \neq \mu_3$.

11.7 a.

ANOVA				
Source	df	SS	MS	F
Factor	2	74026.1	37013.05	8.7670
Error	21	88659.2	4221.8667	
Total	23	162685.3		

b. p-value < .01 **c.** $D = 82.2414$; conclude that $\mu_J \neq \mu_R$ and $\mu_J \neq \mu_T$.

11.9 Since $F^* = 2.11$, fail to reject H_0.

11.11 a. Dallas and Arlington differ and Fort Worth and Arlington differ at the 5% significance level.

11.13 a.

ANOVA				
Source	df	SS	MS	F
Factor	2	12	6	.715
Error	72	604	8.39	
Total	74	616		

Fail to reject H_0 **b.** No

11.15 a. Since the p-value = .1113 > .05, fail to reject H_0. **b.** Since the Hartley value = 2.966 < Critical Value = 5.34, fail to reject H_0.

11.17 a. Closing techniques 2 and 3 appear to be significantly different. **b.** Yes, p-value is .0029. **c.** Techniques 2 and 3 differ. **e.** The ANOVA table remains the same. **f.** The sums of squares are multiplied by 100 but the value of the F statistic remains the same.

11.19 a. Completely randomized design, randomized block design, and two-way factorial design. **b.** Randomized block design. **d.** One dependent variable. **e.** 4 treatments are being considered. 24 observations are made. **f.** 24 treatments are being considered. The minimum number of total observations is 48.

11.21 a. Use a completely randomized design. **b.** Use a randomized block design. **c.** Randomize the order of the restaurants evaluated.

11.23 b. Since $F^* = 4.63$, reject H_0.

11.25 b. Since $F^* = 103.941 > F_{.05,3,9} = 3.86$, reject H_0. **c.** Since $F^* = 230.294 > F_{.05,3,9} = 3.86$, reject H_0. **d.** D = 1.515

11.27 a.

ANOVA				
Source	df	SS	MS	F
Factor	2	20.333	10.167	17.931
Blocks	5	112.5	22.5	39.682
Error	10	5.667	0.567	
Total	17	138.5		

b. Reject H_0 **d.** There is a significant block effect at $\alpha = .01$.

11.31

ANOVA				
Source	df	SS	MS	F
Factor	3	130	43.333	4.73
Blocks	4	280	70	7.63
Error	12	110	9.1667	
Total	19	520		

11.33 b.

ANOVA				
Source	df	SS	MS	F
Factor	2	25.87	12.93	4.97
Blocks	9	50.80	5.64	2.17
Error	18	46.80	2.60	
Total	29	123.47		

Reject H_0 **c.** Baltimore Sun and St. Louis Post-Dispatch differ.

11.35 a. Since $F^* = 2.063 < F_{.10,2,14} = 2.73$, fail to reject H_0. **b.** Since $F^* = 29.415 > F_{.10,7,14} = 2.19$, reject H_0. **c.** -2.194 to $-.156$

11.37 a. $F^* = .85$; fail to reject H_0. **b.** $F^* = 2.71$; reject H_0. **c.** No

11.39 a.

ANOVA				
Source	df	SS	MS	F
Keyboard Type (A)	2	242.67	121.335	68.242
Software Type (B)	2	8.22	4.11	2.312
Interaction	4	11.11	2.778	1.562
Error	18	32	1.778	
Total	26	294		

11.41

ANOVA				
Source	df	SS	MS	F
CV	1	11718.06	11718.06	6.91
DT	1	19010.02	19010.02	11.22
CV×DT	1	632.52	632.52	.37
Error	396	671215.97	1694.99	
Total	399	702576.57		

Conclusion for testing CV and DT: Reject H_0
Conclusion for testing CV×DT: Fail to reject H_0

11.43 a.

ANOVA				
Source	df	SS	MS	F
Exp Level	1	40.64	40.64	14.51
Speed Level	3	40.17	13.39	4.78
Interaction	3	11.67	3.89	1.39
Error	56	156.88	2.80	
Total	63	249.36		

Conclusion for Exp Level and Speed Level: Reject H_0
Conclusion for Interaction: Fail to reject H_0
b. (Experience Level 1, Speed C) differs from (Experience Level 2, Speed A), (Experience Level 2, Speed B), (Experience Level 1, Speed A), and (Experience Level 2, Speed C). (Experience Level 1, Speed D) differs from (Experience Level 2, Speed A) and (Experience Level 2, Speed B). **c.** The conclusions are the same for part (a). (Experience Level 2, Speed A) differs from (Experience Level 1, Speed C) for part (b).

11.45 a.

ANOVA				
Source	df	SS	MS	F
Factor	5	.688	.1376	2.31
Error	18	1.070	.0594	
Total	23	1.758		

Fail to reject H_0. **b.** $H^* = 3.25$; fail to reject H_0.

11.47 a.

ANOVA				
Source	df	SS	MS	F
Factor	2	1591	795	4.55
Error	12	2098	175	
Total	14	3689		

b. $.025 < p$-value $< .05$ **c.** 37.6 ± 12.89 **d.** 11.6 ± 25.35
e. $D = 22.30$; $\bar{x}_3 - \bar{x}_1 = 25.2 > D$.

11.49 a.

ANOVA				
Source	df	SS	MS	F
Manager Level	2	780.8	390.4	5.93
Sex	1	122.7	122.7	1.86
Interaction	2	84.8	42.4	.64
Error	12	790.0	65.8	
Total	17	1778.3		

11.51 $F^* = 18.1$

11.53 a. $F^* = 43.353$; reject H_0. **b.** $D = 15.24$.

11.55 b. Since $F^* = 2.038 < F_{.10, 2, 27} = 2.51$, fail to reject H_0.

11.57 $H = 2.67$; fail to reject H_0.

11.59 a. 9 **b.** 15 **c.** Increase the sample size.

11.61 a.

ANOVA				
Source	df	SS	MS	F
Type	1	88.20	88.20	.43
Cost	1	88.20	88.20	.43
Interaction	1	135.20	135.20	.66
Error	16	3269.60	204.35	
Total	19	3581.20		

Fail to reject H_0 for all tests. **b.** No **c.** The value of the F statistics do not change.

11.65 a. Because the lines are not parallel there appears to be an interaction effect.

b.

ANOVA				
Source	df	SS	MS	F
Experience	3	614.79	204.93	29.45
Help System	2	2.33	1.17	.17
Interaction	6	136.33	22.72	3.27
Error	12	83.50	6.96	
Total	23	836.96		

Test for interaction: Reject H_0.

Chapter 12

12.3 a. quality characteristic **b.** control chart **c.** process

12.7 Roughly half of the MNBQA point total (450 out of 1000) comes from Category 7: Business Results.

12.11 Flowchart should have several decision nodes such as "Is the bank's interest rate competitive?" and "Do the applicants qualify for the amount of the loan?"

12.13 A Pareto chart can be used to display the results.

12.15 Main branches might consist of 1. Waiting to be seated, 2. Ordering the meal, 3. Enjoying the meal, and 4. Filing complaints or compliments. Secondary branches can be attached to these main branches.

12.21 $\bar{X}$ Chart: UCL = 449.49; CL = 427.05; LCL = 404.61. R Chart: UCL = 82.23; CL = 38.90; LCL = 0.

12.23 a. UCL = 2.45; CL = 1.32; LCL = 0.18.

12.25 a. UCL = .0219; CL = .01175; LCL = .0016. **b.** Observations appear to decrease and then increase.

12.27 For Northern: UCL = 1454.2; CL = 848.47; LCL = 242.7. For Southern: UCL = 1551.123; CL = 757.633; LCL = −35.857.

12.29 For $\bar{X}$ chart: UCL = 24.84; CL = 19.71; LCL = 14.58. For R chart: UCL = 16.07; CL = 7.04; LCL = 0.

12.31 For $\bar{X}$ chart: UCL = 10.86; CL = 10.01; LCL = 9.16. For R chart: UCL = 2.14; CL = .83; LCL = 0.

12.35 UCL = .115; CL = .05; LCL = 0

12.37 a. $\bar{p} = .307$; UCL = .58; CL = .307; LCL = .03. **b.** No

12.39 UCL = 6.822; CL = 2.286; LCL = 0

12.41 For the c chart: UCL = 11.29; CL = 4.75; LCL = 0.

12.43 a. For the c chart; UCL = 13.578; CL = 6.143; LCL = 0. **b.** No, since two plotted values exceed the UCL.

12.47 Process A: $C_p = 0.78$ (inadequate); Process B: $C_p = 1.13$ (adequate); Process C: $C_p = 2.16$ (good); Process D: $C_p = 1.11$ (adequate).

12.51 a. $s' = 7.28$; $C_{pm} = 0.97$. **b.** $s' = 6.20$; $C_{pm} = 1.14$. **c.** C_{pm} converges to C_p.

12.53 a. Process A **b.** For process A, $C_{pk} = 1.08$; for process B, $C_{pk} = 1.22$. **c.** Process B, since it is more capable.

12.55 a. $C_p = 1.41$ **b.** $C_{pk} = 1.38$

12.63 Since the variation about the target value is expected to be larger than the usual variance, C_p is usually larger than C_{pm}.

12.65 The process is considered out of control because the first six points are increasing and also the sixth observation is above 84.

12.67 a. Scatter diagram **b.** Flowchart **c.** Control chart **d.** Pareto chart **e.** Cause-and-effect diagram

12.69 UCL = 86.66, CL = 82.475, LCL = 78.286 for the X-bar chart; UCL = 13.123, CL = 5.750, LCL = 0 for the R chart.

12.71 a. c chart **b.** UCL = 6.14; CL = 1.95; LCL = 0. **c.** In control.

12.73 a. The $\bar{X}$ chart contains patterns 2, 5, and 6. **b.** The R chart gives out-of-control signals.

Chapter 13

13.1 $\chi^{2*} = 7.8$, fail to reject H_0.

13.3 $\chi^{2*} = 2.92$; fail to reject H_0.

13.5 $\chi^{2*} = .8125$; fail to reject H_0.

13.7 $\chi^{2*} = 14.65$, reject H_0.

13.9 $\chi^2_{.10,3} = 6.2514$; fail to reject H_0.

13.11 $\chi^{2*} = .4184$; fail to reject H_0.

13.13 $\chi^{2*} = 2.24$; fail to reject H_0.

13.15 d. $\chi^{2*} = 128.45$ (pool $X = 0,1$ and $X \geq 6$); reject H_0. **e.** $\chi^{2*} = 2.57$ (pool $X \geq 4$); fail to reject H_0.

13.17 $\chi^{2*} = 15.3383$; reject H_0.

13.19 b. No cells should be pooled. **c.** $\chi^{2*} = 28.94$. **d.** Reject H_0.

13.21 a. $\chi^{2*} = 6.004$; fail to reject H_0. **b.** p-value $> .10$.

13.23 a. $\chi^{2*} = 2.32$, fail to reject H_0. **b.** $\chi^{2*} = 10.10$, reject H_0.

13.25 a. $\chi^{2*} = 71.154$; reject H_0. **b.** $\chi^{2*} = .076$; fail to reject H_0.

13.27 $\chi^{2*} = 7.692$; fail to reject H_0.

13.29 $\chi^{2*} = 6.35$, fail to reject H_0.

13.31 $\chi^{2*} = .351$; fail to reject H_0.

13.33 $\chi^{2*} = 2.0749$; fail to reject H_0.

13.35 $\chi^{2*} = 4.6969$; fail to reject H_0.

13.37 a. $\chi^{2*} = 15.3203$; fail to reject H_0. p-value is slightly greater than .05.

13.39 $\chi^{2*} = 13.29$, reject H_0.

13.41 $\chi^{2*} = 15.9$; reject H_0.

13.43 $\chi^{2*} = 25.61$, reject H_0.

13.45 a. $\bar{x} = 28.35$; $s = 19.96$. **b.** $\chi^{2*} = 36.8822$; reject H_0. **c.** p-value $< .005$ **d.** Conclusion does not change if the significance level is .05 or .01.

13.47 $\chi^{2*} = 2.9915$; fail to reject H_0. **b.** p-value $> .10$.

13.49 $\chi^{2*} = 9.24$, reject H_0.

13.51 b. $\chi^{2*} = 10.88$; reject H_0. **c.** $\chi^{2*} = .586$; fail to reject H_0.

Chapter 14

14.1 a. $\sum x = 24$; $\sum y = 53$; $\sum xy = 333$; $\sum x^2 = 154$; $\sum y^2 = 729$. **b.** $b_1 = 2.0258$; $b_0 = 0.876$. **c.** $r = 0.9759$.

14.3 b. $b_1 = .954$ $b_0 = -10.5$

14.7 b. $\hat{Y} = 11.278 + .0803X$ **c.** $r = .688$

14.9 b. $r = .601$ **c.** $b_1 = 1.395$ $b_0 = .835$

14.11 When the magnitude of the correlation and the sample size is large, it should be relatively easy to draw the least squares line.

14.13 a. $s = 1.4376$ **b.** 16 residuals (80%) fall within $2s$ of the mean of the residuals.

14.15 a. $\hat{Y} = -3.8889 + 5.8199X$ **b.** slope is 5.8199; intercept is -3.8889. **c.** $s^2 = 25.906$

14.17 $s = 2.6624$; all the sample residuals are within two standard deviations of the mean.

14.19 a. $b_1 = .532$ $b_0 = .164$ **b.** $r = .9999$

14.21 a. $\hat{Y} = .7195 + .75097X$ **b.** Yes, although there is a slight left skew.

14.23 a. $t^* = 1.875$; fail to reject H_0. **b.** -1.578 to 7.578

14.25 $t^* = 27.1601$; reject H_0.

14.27 a. $t^* = -1.54$; fail to reject H_0.

14.29 a. $-.375$ to $-.035$ **b.** Since 0 is not in the 99% confidence interval, reject H_0.

14.31 a. r^2 with Experience is .12. r^2 with TimeToSell is .66. **b.** For TimeToSell, regression model is $\hat{Y} = 265.16 + 99.27X$; $t^* = 11.9$, yes. **c.** $t^* = 11.9$, reject H_0

14.33 a. $H_0: \rho \geq 0$ vs. $H_a: \rho < 0$ **b.** $r = -.981$ **c.** coefficient of determination $= .962$ **d.** $t^* = -10.06$; reject H_0.

14.35 $r^2 = .97$, $t^* = 17.45$, reject H_0.

14.37 b. $t^* = -.4450$; fail to reject H_0.

14.39 $t^* = -10.88$; reject H_0.

14.41 a. $.95$, $t^* = 20.73$, reject H_0 **b.** $t^* = 20.73$, reject H_0 **c.** $.95$

14.43 a. $b_1 = 2.433$ $b_0 = -32.041$ **b.** -24.987 to 9.573 **c.** -34.5538 to 19.1398 **e.** The fifth observation is considered influential.

14.45 95% confidence interval for the mean of Y at $X = 35$: 18.465 to 27.325; 95% prediction interval for the value of Y at $X = 35$: 11.249 to 34.540

14.47 25.45 to 36.61; Observation 4 is an outlier and an influential observation.

14.49 20782.6 to 30739.7

14.51 7.2049 to 8.4543; $s_{\hat{y}} = 0.9897$.

14.53 No. The value of $X = 15$ is probably not in the range of incomes for executives in Chicago.

14.55 a. $\hat{Y} = -1.58 + .035X$ **b.** The largest Cook's D is .25. **c.** There are no patterns, but there are three large standardized residuals and one large leverage value.

14.57 b. Observation 15 is the most influential with a Cook's D of .32. **c.** With observation 15, the r^2 is .964. Omitting observation 15, the r^2 is .975.

14.59 a. $b_1 = .009317$ $b_0 = .1146$ **b.** $t^* = 13.45$; reject H_0. **c.** .00772 to .01091 **d.** 95% prediction interval for the value of Y at $X = 110$: 1.003 to 1.276

14.63 a. $\hat{Y} = 35.606 - .368X$ **b.** $s^2 = 90.878$

14.65 b. $b_1 = 1.1674$; $b_0 = -0.8711$; $t^* = 10.2493$; reject H_0 (i.e., a significant positive relationship exists). **c.** 0.8396 to 1.4952 **d.** $r^2 = 0.8536$ **e.** 4.032 to 10.569

14.67 a. $t^* = 19.0454$; reject H_0. **b.** 2.028 to 2.455

14.69 b. $b_1 = 1.087$ $b_0 = -775.381$ **c.** The regression equation appears to predict well for observations 5, 6, 9, and 10, as these observations have very small standardized residuals. **d.** Observation 20 is considered influential since Cook's D is greater than .8.

14.71 a. Total and Campbell, Total and Pet, Total and Private, and Campbell and Pet. **b.** Since the null hypothesis that the correlation between Campbell and Private is zero cannot be rejected, Campbell would not be a good predictor of Private. **c.** Campbell **d.** .7499 to 1.1201

14.73 b. $b_1 = 6507.678$ $b_0 = .785$ **c.** $b_1 = .901$ $b_0 = .351.646$

Chapter 15

15.1 a. 16 **b.** 30

15.3 $\hat{\sigma}_e = 3.4565$

15.5 a. $\hat{Y} = 0.0090 + 1.1102X_1 + 0.13855X_2$ **b.** SSE $= 4.7289$

15.7 a. $\hat{Y} = -878.386 + 42.019X_1 + 46.505X_1$. **b.** If SSE $= 0$, then the prediction equation would be a perfect predictor.

15.9 a. $F^* = 116.25$; reject H_0. **b.** $t^* = 9.615$; reject H_0. **c.** $t^* = 19.05$; reject H_0.

15.11 a. $t^* = 3.1509$; reject H_0. **b.** $t^* = -2.205$; reject H_0.

15.13 We are 95% confident that the regression coefficient for Horsepower is between $-.172$ to -024. We are 95% confident that the regression coefficient for Engine Size is between -1.207 to 6.870.

15.15

ANOVA TABLE

Source	df	SS	MS	F
Regression	2	1165.66	582.83	30.17
Residual	7	135.24	19.32	
Total	9	1300.90		

15.17 $F^* = 4$; fail to reject H_0.

15.19 a. $F^* = 182.5$, reject H_0; $t^* = 15.25$, reject H_0 for MinutesTalked; $t^* = 15.87$, reject H_0 for MonthlyCharge

15.21 $R^2 = .896$; $R^2(\text{adj}) = .844$.

15.23 $F^* = 14.056$; reject H_0.

15.25 $F^* = 2.718$; fail to reject H_0.

15.27 For PP, $t^* = -2.16$ and for QI, $t^* = -1.414$. Since $t_{.025,241} \doteq 1.96$, PP contributes to the prediction of TT. SSR = 35.769, SSE = 206.9, $F^* = 20.83$. Since $F_{.05,2,241} \doteq 3.00$; reject H_0.

15.29 a. $\hat{Y} = 58.02 + 3.79X_1$, $R^2 = .0997$. **b.** $\hat{Y} = -11.62 + 4.60X_1 + 9.14X_2 + 2.53X_3$; $R^2 = .982$; partial $F = 514.7$; reject H_0.

15.31 X_1 and X_2 are highly correlated. X_4 and X_5 are highly correlated.

15.33 a. Yes, the overall F statistic is significant, but the individual t statistics yield a conclusion of fail to reject H_0. **b.** VIF = $1/(1 - (.9908)^2) = 54.6$. **c.** No.

15.35 $\hat{Y} = 43.532 + 1.824X_2 - 892X_3$.

15.37 $F^* = 34.51$, reject H_0. **b.** No **c.** 17.7

15.39 a. 36 **b.** 39 **c.** 32 **d.** $F^* = 4$; reject H_0.

15.41 The final model is $\hat{Y} = 24.126 + 2.152X_1 - 2.120X_2$.

15.43 a. X_3 **b.** X_3

15.47 Assumption of equal variances for the error terms appears to have been violated.

15.49 a. 8.984 to 20.816 **b.** 4.895 to 24.905

15.53 a. $t^* = 14.8$ and $t^* = 8.5$ for AdRev and SubscriberRev, respectively. Reject H_0. **b.** 237.47 to 405.93 **c.** Observation 1 is influential. $R^2 = .977$ with observation 1 and $R^2 = .998$ without observation 1.

15.55 a. $\hat{Y} = 18.1 - 5X_1$ **b.** $\hat{Y} = 10.1 + 5X_1$ **c.** No, the prediction lines are not parallel.

15.57 p-value for interaction term is .0130, reject H_0. Without the interaction term, $R^2 = .9688$. With the interaction term, $R^2 = .9837$. Partial $F = 9.10$.

15.59 b. Observations 46 and 47 appear to be the most influential with standardized residuals of 3.75 and 4.43 and Cook's D values of .4 and .6, respectively.

15.61 a. $\hat{Y} = -1.0 + 4.8X_1 + 5.9X_2$

b.

ANOVA TABLE

Source	df	SS	MS	F
Model	2	295.3	147.65	128.4
Residual	17	19.5	1.15	
Total	19	314.8		

$R^2 = .938$ **c.** $F^* = 128.4$; reject H_0. **d.** $t^* = 9.375$; reject H_0. **e.** $t^* = 14.05$; reject H_0.

15.63 There is not sufficient evidence to conclude that X_2 contributes to the model.

15.65 a. $\hat{Y} = 17357 - 1132X_1 - 33.2X_2 - 2556X_3 - 3275X_4 + 776X_5$

b.

ANOVA TABLE

Source	df	SS	MS	F
Regression	5	516005120	103201024	43.29
Error	25	59597456	2383898	
Total	30	575602432		

c. 5192 to 8437 **e.** A forward regression procedure would select the following model at the .10 significance level: $\hat{Y} = 14510 - 1581X_1 + 2841X_5$. **f.** Observation 29 appears to be an outlier since the standardized residual is equal to 3.255.

15.67 a. SSE decreases and R-square increases while SST remains unchanged.

15.69 a. $F^* = 3.21$; the data do not indicate that X_2 and X_3 contribute to the prediction of performance ratings.

15.71 a. $F^* = 4.999$; reject H_0. **b.** VIFs are both equal to 34.758.

15.73 b. $\hat{Y} = 34,976$ **c.** Both VIFs are equal to 1.220.

15.75 a. StickerPrice and OwnPickUp3 contribute to the prediction of MonthlyPay. **b.** Observation 6 is influential. **c.** R^2 decreases from .887 to .829 and all three predictors are significant.

Chapter 16

16.1 The amplitudes of the seasonal and cyclical effects become more dramatic after a long period of time.

16.5 a. Cyclical variation **b.** Seasonal variation **c.** Trend **d.** Irregular activity

16.7 b. $b_0 = -5.33$; $b_1 = 56.286$ **c.** 388.667

16.11 $\hat{y}_t = -24.418 + 6.2429t$

16.13 a. $b_0 = 5.540$ $b_1 = .574$ **b.** 12.428

16.15 a. A quadratic trend would provide a better fit than a linear trend. **b.** 139.95 million

16.19 c. Approximately 4 years.

16.21 a. $b_0 = 6.360$, $b_1 = .117$ **c.** The cycle appears to be longer than 5 years.

16.23 a. Cyclical components: .976, 1.01, 1.02, .996, .97, 1.02, 1.05, .99, .96, 1.01 **b.** The length of the cycle is slightly more than 3 years.

16.25 a. Cyclical components: .96, .99, 1.06, 1.01, .94, 1.01, 1.09, .98, .92, .99, 1.12, .99, .90, 1.01, 1.13, .99, .93 **b.** The length of the cycles are 3 years, 5 years, and 3 years.

16.27 At times 1, 2, 3, and 4, $\hat{y}_t$ is 37.5, 36, 26.5, and 35.

16.29 1st quarter: 65.4; 2nd quarter: 78.9; 3rd quarter: 87.1; 4th quarter: 84.1.

16.31 For times 37 through 48, predicted data values are: 9.9, 16.24, 12.48, 27.69, 23.98, 31.22, 54.72, 72.23, 7.14, 4.86, 4.96, 2.53.

16.33 Deseasonalized FDI figures can be obtained by dividing FDI by the appropriate seasonal index. For 2000, figures are 26.00, 26.02, 26.00, and 25.98.

16.35 Centered moving averages are 18.5, 20.875, 22.875, 24.50. Ratio to moving average: 1.24, 1.44, .87, .61.

16.39 Seasonal indexes are .8710, .8256, .8458, .9291, 1.0276, 1.0503, 1.0730, 1.1614, 1.1411, 1.0629, 1.0452, .9670.

16.41 Seasonal indexes are 1.0913, 1.2155, .8573, .8358.

16.43 Seasonal indexes are .889, 1.081, 1.009, .965, 1.053, 1.001, .945, 1.077, 1.043, 1.000, .976, .961.

16.45 $I_t = 1.0185$

16.47 .859, .890, 1.176, 1.224

16.49 Trend line through the deseasonalized data is TR(t) = 458.655 + 6.853t, TR(49) = 794.45

16.53 a. Index numbers are: 100, 116.67, 141.67, 183.33, 208.33. **b.** Index numbers are: 85.71, 100.00, 121.43, 157.14, 178.57

16.55 a. 120.6 **b.** 119.0 **c.** 118.7

16.57 a. 135.6 **b.** 136.11 **c.** 135.9

16.61 a. Laspeyres index = 96.78 **b.** Paasche Index = 97.59

16.63 a. Trend **b.** Irregular **c.** Seasonal **d.** Irregular

16.65 a. $\hat{y}_t = 32.697 + .213t$ for $t = 1, 2, 3, \ldots$ **b.** $\hat{y}_{14} = 32.697 + .213(14) = 35.68$.

16.67 $b_0 = -10.40$ $b_1 = 6.80$

16.69 $\hat{y}_t = 6.139 + 1.745t - 0.149t^2$ is the trend component.

16.71 a. Seasonal indexes are 1.20, 1.15, 1.07, .92, .91, .95, .96, .96, .92, .93, .99, 1.05. **b.** $\hat{d}_t = 151.806 + 1.094t$ **c.** Cyclical components are 1.02, 1.01, 1.00, .99, .97, .98, .98, .99, .98, 1.00, 1.00, 1.01. **d.** June, irregular = 1.00; July, irregular = 1.00.

16.73 a. Laspeyres index = 109.13 **b.** Paasche Index = 108.41

16.75 Seasonal indexes are .919, .983, 1.052, 1.120, 1.151, 1.041, 1.010, .924, .988, .960, .884, .967

16.77 Seasonal indexes are .935, .963, 1.006, .997, 1.035, 1.089, 1.027, .990, 1.000, 1.009, .980, .967

Chapter 17

17.3 The naïve model predicted the value for 2000 very well since the residual is relatively small.

17.9 $\hat{y}_t = 44.113 + .723t$ **b.** Forecasts for the first three months of 2002: 55.688, 48.166, 89.101

17.11 $S_t(A = .1)$: 2, 2.1, 2.09, 2.381, 2.9429, 3.3486, 3.5137, 3.9623, 4.5661, 5.0095, 5.3085, 5.7777, 5.8999, 6.2099, 6.2890; $S_t(A = .3)$: 2, 2.3, 2.21, 3.047, 4.5329, 5.2730, 5.1911, 6.0338, 7.2236, 7.7566, 7.8296, 8.4807, 8.0365, 8.3255, 7.9278.

17.13 The forecasted values for June and July of 2001 are 4.286 and 4.286.

17.15 The forecasted values for 2000 and 2001 are 140.7 and 142.5, respectively.

17.17 The forecast for the year 2002 is 371.105.

17.19 Using all of the data, the forecast for the year 2002 is 81053. Using the data from 1991 to 2001, the forecast for the year 2002 is 81186.

17.21 a. 17.536 **b.** 17.444

17.23 Initial seasonal factors are .95, .83, 1.07, and 1.16. Least squares line is .2287 + .0109t. Forecasts for each quarter are .404, .361, .491, .538.

17.25 Forecast for the first quarter of 2002 is 313.37.

17.27 a. MAPE = .1335; MSE = 21.4. **b.** MAD = 2.125; MAPE = .1127; MSE = 6.12.

17.29 Procedure 1: MAD = 3.556; MSE = 16.556. Procedure 2: MAD = 3.333; MSE = 44.556.

17.31 a. MSE = 2,295,837 **b.** MSE = 2,713,905

17.33 MAPE = 4.894; Forecasts for the four quarters of the year 2002 are 417.134, 406.891, 462.702, and 462.320.

17.35 Predictive MSE = 7.712

17.37 a. $r_1 = 0.693$; $r_2 = 0.108$; $r_3 = -0.355$; $r_4 = -0.428$. **b.** One possible model is $\hat{y}_t = b_0 + b_1 y_{t-1} = 11.542 + 0.7105 y_{t-1}$

17.39 $r_1 = .504$; $r_2 = .024$; $r_3 = .299$; $r_4 = .489$; $r_5 = .061$; $r_6 = -.275$; $r_7 = -.070$; $r_8 = .093$; $r_9 = -.176$; $r_{10} = -.407$; $r_{11} = -.256$; $r_{12} = -.129$. The data do not appear to be stationary.

17.41 The series of second differences appears to be stationary with two period seasonal spikes.

17.43 Predictive MSE's for 1st order and 2nd order autoregressive models are 2.698 and 2.653, respectively.

17.45 $\hat{y}_t = 5.96 - .47t - .43Q1 - .30Q2 - .10Q3$; MSE = SSE/12 = .237

17.47 $\hat{y}_t = .275 + .013t - .0735Q_1 - .1215Q_2 - .027Q_3$; $R^2 = .954$

17.49 $\hat{y}_t = 3.96 + 1.04t$; predictive MSE = 7.30; $\hat{y}_t = 5.122 + .996t - 3.562Q_1 - 2.341Q_2 + 3.379Q_3$; predictive MSE = .386

17.51 a. $\hat{y}_t = 108.52 + .0031X_t$ **b.** $\hat{y}_t = 74.454 + 0.252X_{t-1}$ **c.** R^2 for part (a) is 0.0 (approx.); R^2 for part (b) is .957.

17.53 $\hat{y}_t = 28.156 - .233$MedianPersonalIncome − .279MedianPersonalIncomeLagged

17.55 $R^2 = .0069$ when SalesMonthly is regressed on AdvExpend. $R^2 = .100$ when SalesMonthly is regressed on AdvExpendLag.

17.57 DW = 0 implies severe positive autocorrelation. DW = 2 implies no autocorrelation is present. DW = 4 implies severe negative autocorrelation.

17.59 DW = 2.66; fail to reject H_0.

17.61 DW = 0.56; This low value of DW indicates possible positive autocorrelation.

17.63 $\hat{y}_{37} = 19.25$; $\hat{y}_{38} = 22.35$; $\hat{y}_{39} = 25.56$; $\hat{y}_{40} = 27.25$; $\hat{y}_{41} = 25.34$

17.65 a. 2313.35 **b.** 1135.78

17.67 MSE = .32

17.69 Let $Q_1 = 1$ for quarter 1, $Q_2 = 1$ for quarter 2, $Q_3 = 1$ for quarter 3. The regression equation is $\hat{y}_t = 39.275 - 16.019Q_1 - 9.613Q_2 - 4.406Q_3 + 0.79375t$

17.71 8.56

17.73 DW = .43; reject H_0.

17.75 a. $\hat{y}_t = 119.511 + 1.378y_{t-1} - .548y_{t-2}$; Predictive MSE = 1185.583 **b.** $\hat{y}_t = 44.130 + 1.387y_{t-1} - .412y_{t-2}$; Predictive MSE = 540.904

17.77 a. NetProfLag4 is useful in explaining quarterly net profit. **b.** Predictive MSE = 6.508.

Chapter 18

18.1 a. R = 9; fail to reject H_0. **b.** R = 7; fail to reject H_0.

18.3 $Z^* = -2.56$; reject H_0.

18.5 R = 10; fail to reject H_0.

18.7 R = 13; fail to reject H_0.

18.9 R = 12, p-value = .00615; reject H_0.

18.11 $Z^* > 1.645$; reject H_0.

18.13 $T_+ = 50$; $T_- = 5$; reject H_0.

18.15 $Z^* = 1.09$; fail to reject H_0.

18.17 U = 38; fail to reject H_0.

18.19 $Z^* = .953$; fail to reject H_0.

18.21 T = Min(15, 0) = 0; reject H_0.

18.25 $T_+ = 12$; $T_- = 33$; fail to reject H_0.

18.27 $T_+ = 1.5$; $T_- = 26.5$; reject H_0.

18.29 $Z^* = -2.13$; reject H_0.

18.31 $T_+ = 24.5$; reject H_0.

18.33 $Z^* = -6.3145$; reject H_0.

18.35 a. $Z^* = -2.0638$; p-value = .0390; reject H_0. **b.** $t^* = -1.75$; p-value = .0886; fail to reject H_0.

18.37 KW = .485; fail to reject H_0.

18.39 FR = 4.17; fail to reject H_0.

18.41 KW = 7.649; reject H_0.

18.43 KW = 6.83; reject H_0.

18.45 KW = 2.105; fail to reject H_0.

18.47 FR = 16.20; reject H_0.

18.49 FR = 2; fail to reject H_0.

18.51 p-value for the one-way ANOVA is .061; fail to reject H_0. p-value for the Kruskal-Wallis test is .0487; reject H_0.

18.53 Computed Chi-square for Friedman test is 4.02; p-value = .2593; fail to reject H_0.

18.55 $r_s = -.794$; reject H_0.

18.57 $r_s = -.330$; fail to reject H_0.

18.59 $r_s = -.944$; reject H_0.

18.61 $r_s = .948$; reject H_0.

18.63 b. Pearson product moment correlation = .739; Spearman rank correlation = .735.

18.65 $r_s = .964$; reject H_0.

18.67 Intercept = 2.2857 and slope = 1.4048.

18.69 Intercept = $-.500$ and slope = 2.80.

18.71 Intercept = 102,268.78 and slope = 1.0380.

18.73 Intercept = 62, slope = -5.00.

18.75 $Z^* = -2.20$; reject H_0.

18.77 $r_s = .84$; reject H_0.

18.79 $U_1 = 40$, $U_2 = 24$, $U = 24$; fail to reject H_0.

18.81 $R = 4$; p-value = .01255; reject H_0.

18.83 $T = 27.5$; fail to reject H_0.

18.85 KW = 13.36; reject H_0.

18.87 Least squares line: $\hat{Y} = -416.2 + .211X$; Regression line through the medians: $\hat{Y} = -395.25 + .200X$

18.89 $r_s = .893$; reject H_0.

18.91 FR = 3.2; fail to reject H_0.

18.93 a. $\hat{Y} = -701.3 + .359$ Year **b.** $\hat{y} = -607.8 + .3125$ Year

Chapter 19

19.1 Under state S_1, action A_1 is the best. Under state S_2, action A_1 or A_2 is the best. Under state S_3, action A_2 or A_3 is the best. Under state S_4, action A_3 is the best.

19.3

Action	5	6	7	8	9	10	11	12	13
				States of Nature					
7	-20	5	30	30	30	30	30	30	30
8	-30	-5	20	45	45	45	45	45	45
9	-40	-15	10	35	60	60	60	60	60
10	-50	-25	0	25	50	75	75	75	75
11	-60	-35	-10	15	40	65	90	90	90
12	-70	-45	-20	5	30	55	80	105	105
13	-80	-55	-30	-5	20	45	70	95	120

19.5

Action	$S_1(100)$	$S_2(125)$	$S_3(150)$
	States of Nature		
A_1	90	90	90
A_2	62.5	112.5	112.5
A_3	35	85	135

19.7 a. No, because under S_2 there is no 0. **b.** No, because there is a negative value in the table.

19.9 The minimax decision is A_2. The maximax decision is A_3.

19.11 Expected Payoffs: 6.4, 31, 54; Risks: 138.24, 369.00, 1044

19.13

Action	S_1	S_2	S_3
	States of Nature		
A_1	150	60	10
A_2	100	20	0
A_3	50	0	35
A_4	0	40	160

a. The minimax decision is A_3. **b.** The decision is A_3 based on the maximum expected payoff. **c.** Risk $(A_1) = 0$; Risk $(A_2) = 169$; Risk $(A_3) = 1642.1875$; Risk $(A_4) = 9850$.

19.15 The maximum expected payoff is for A_3.

19.17 EVPI = 155.5

19.19 Payoff Table:

Action	1500	2000	2500
	States of Nature		
1500	750	750	750
2000	600	1000	1000
2500	450	850	1250

$110 is the maximum amount that the manager would be willing to pay for perfect information.

19.21 The maximum expected payoff decision is given by A_3; EVPI = 9,150.

19.23 EVPI = 22.75; A_1 is inadmissible.

19.25 a. A_2 is the decision based on the maximum expected payoff. **b.** A_2 is the decision based on the maximum expected utility.

19.27 The decision is A_2 or A_3 based on the maximum expected utility of the payoff.

19.29 a. The decision is A_2 based on the maximum expected utility of the payoff. **b.** The manager is a risk avoider.

19.31

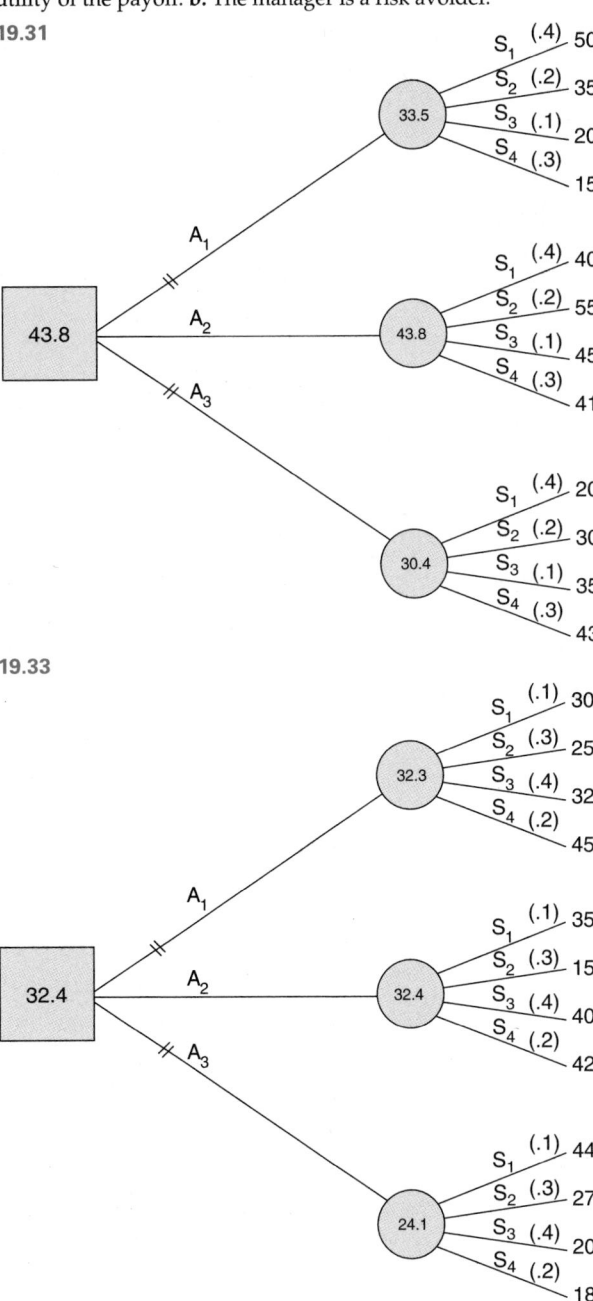

19.33

19.35

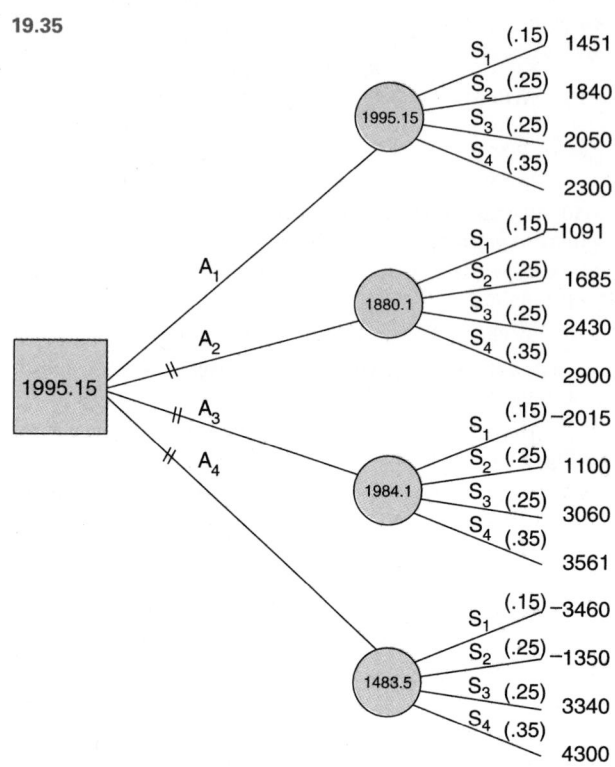

19.37 $P(A_1 | B) = .111$; $P(A_2 | B) = .111$; $P(A_3 | B) = .222$; $P(A_4 | B) = .185$; $P(A_5 | B) = .370$.

19.39 $P(\text{Life}) = .0734$; $P(\text{Shawna} | \text{Life}) = .3597$

19.41 $P(B) = .26$; $P(S_1 | B) = .2308$; $P(S_2 | B) = .2308$; $P(S_3 | B) = .4615$; $P(S_4 | B) = .0769$. Maximum expected utility of 33.23 occurs for A_2.

19.43 EVPI = 3000; yes.

19.45 a. Net expected gain of hiring the consultant is 3.428. **b.** 22.85%

19.47 b. Minimax decision is action A_3. **c.** The maximax decision is A_3, since the largest payoff is 120 under S_4.

19.49 The change of probabilities will not affect the minimax decision. Using the expected payoffs, action A_4 is the optimal action for sets 1, 2, and 4, and action A_1 is optimal for sets 3 and 5.

19.51 One example is the following: For $0 \leq p \leq 1000$, $U(p) = .05p$, and for $1000 < p \leq 2000$, $120 - .13p + .00006p^2$.

19.53 EVSI = 600, EVPI = 6000, Efficiency = 10%.

19.55 The maximum payoff with the consultant is 1157.08. The maximum payoff without the consultant is 1105 using A_3. Since $1157.08 - 1105 = 52.08$, which is less than 350, it is not worthwhile to use the consultant's service.

19.57 a. Risk taker **b.** Risk neutral **c.** Risk avoider

19.59 $P(\text{Male}) = .4875$; $P(\text{own car} | \text{Male}) = .733$

index